DOCUMENTS
RELATING TO THE
COLONIAL HISTORY
OF THE
STATE OF NEW JERSEY,

FIRST SERIES - VOLUME XXXIII

CALENDAR OF NEW JERSEY WILLS,

VOLUME IV 1761-1770

A. Van Doren Honeyman

HERITAGE BOOKS
2008

HERITAGE BOOKS
AN IMPRINT OF HERITAGE BOOKS, INC.

Books, CDs, and more—Worldwide

For our listing of thousands of titles see our website
at
www.HeritageBooks.com

Published 2008 by
HERITAGE BOOKS, INC.
Publishing Division
100 Railroad Ave. #104
Westminster, Maryland 21157

Copyright © 1928 A. Van Doren Honeyman

Other books by the author:

Documents Relating to the Colonial History of the State of New Jersey, Calendar of New Jersey Wills, Volume V: 1771-1780
Documents Relating to the Colonial History of the State of New Jersey, Calendar of New Jersey Wills, Volume III, 1751-1760
The van Doorn Family (Van Doorn, Van Dorn, Van Doren, Etc.) in Holland and America, 1088-1908
CD: *Joannes Nevius and His Descendants*
CD: *The van Doorn Family (Van Doorn, Van Dorn, Van Doren, Etc.) in Holland and America, 1088-1908*

All rights reserved. No part of this book may be reproduced or transmitted in any form or by any means, electronic or mechanical, including photocopying, recording or by any information storage and retrieval system without written permission from the author, except for the inclusion of brief quotations in a review.

International Standard Book Numbers
Paperbound: 978-1-58549-034-9
Clothbound: 978-0-7884-7061-5

Introductory Note

This, the fourth volume of Abstracts of Wills of New Jersey, includes wills, administrations and guardianships appearing on the records in Trenton as filed or recorded from Jan. 1, 1761, to December 31, 1770, a period of ten years. The abstracts were made by Dr. Joseph H. Satterthwaite, of Trenton and the Index under superintendence of the Editor.

First dates in boldface type are often prior to 1760, and indicate when the will to which the date refers was executed (not probated). The name so printed is according to the signature to the will, however it may differ in the text that follows.

All proper names of persons and places are believed to be printed as in the originals. This early period was one, however, when names were spelled so indifferently that the reader may have to consider various ways of spelling in order to discover certain of the surnames.

The Index does not repeat the surnames of those whose wills, etc., are abstracted, except in the instances where alternative spellings, in parentheses, are so extremely divergent from the alphabetical arrangement that they may not be otherwise discovered. But neither first nor alternative spellings can always be considered to be correct spellings, according to modern usages.

This publication is made possible by Legislative appropriation.

THE EDITOR

Calendar of New Jersey Wills

NOTE.—The books cited as Libers 1, 2, 3, etc., are of West Jersey wills. Those cited as Libers A, B, C, etc., are of East Jersey wills. Where matters beside recorded wills, such as inventories, accounts, etc., are noted, the originals may be found in the proper envelopes (arranged by counties), reference to which is made in the volumes (three volumes) entitled "Index to Wills," published by the Secretary of State in 1912 and 1913, which should always be consulted in case originals are to be referred to. Where the chief matter is not of record in books, the envelope numbers are given herewith, although in Bergen, Essex, Middlesex and Monmouth counties, the original papers are bound instead of being in envelopes. All original matters herein abstracted are to be found in the Secretary of State's office at Trenton. All proper names are believed to be spelled as in the originals.

1765, Nov. 29. Aalse, Jurrie, of Acquecnock, Essex Co.; will of. Wife, Marritje, use of real and personal, while my widow. My son, Garret Van Rype, five shillings. Sons—Garret Van Rype and Johannis Van Rype, all my lands. Son, Dirk Van Rype, £100. Daughter, Marragrietje, £110. Executors—son Garret Van Rype, and friend David Marinas. Witnesses—John Bonin, John Van Vegten, John Bagley. Proved June 13, 1766.　　　　　　　　　　　　Lib. I, p. 8.

1768, Jan. 14. Aaron, Simon, of Essex Co. Int. Adm'r—Enoch Moore, principal creditor, (of said Simon Aaron, a free negro), of said Co. Fellowbondsman—Joseph DeCamp, of Middlesex Co. Witness—John Mackay.
　　1768, Jan. 26. Inventory, £26.19.4, made by Samuel Shotwell and Edward Moore.　　　　　　　　　　　　　　　　　　Lib. I, p. 208.

1767, Mar. 14. Aaronson, Aaron, of Waterford Twsp., Gloucester Co.; will of. Daughter, Kezia Parr, and Rebecca Nicholson, plantation where I live. Wife, Rebecca, £20 yearly, and said daughters to provide for her. Daughter, Mary Woolman, £200. Grandchildren—Samuel, John Aaronson, Sarah, and Ashur Woolman, £100 each, and my daughter Mary to have the use of it till Samuel is 21. Grandson, John Aaronson Woolman, my watch. Granddaughter, Sarah Woolman, case of drawers. To my daughter, Rebecca, a negro, and £10. To daughters, Mary, Kezia, and Rebecca, the rest, except my walnut table I give to granddaughter, Sarah Woolman. Executors my daughters, Kezia and Rebecca. Witnesses—Isaac Horner, John Shivers, Jr., Samuel Clements. Proved April 23, 1767. Lib. 13, p. 109.

1757, Nov. 22. Abbott, James, of Amwell, Hunterdon Co., yeoman; will of. Wife, Cathrine, 1-3 of movable estate, while my widow. Son, James, and my youngest son, William, my lands upon which I dwell; and they are to pay to my son, Benjamin, £50, and £50 yearly, till £150 are paid. To son, Joseph Abbot, £30. To Martha Skyort, £15, when she is 18; but if she die, then her legacy to be divided between Ellen Robins' children when they come of age. My daughter, Cathrine, rest of movable estate. If any of my daughter Ellen's children, by her former husband, die before they come of age, their part shall be divided among the other two. To my son Job's child, named Job, £10 when he is 21. Executors—Jacob Birdsall and Thomas Whitson, Jr. Witnesses—Thomas Sutton, Samuel Bean, Henry Whitson. Proved May 14, 1765.

1765, May 1. Inventory, £24.1.3, made by William Hunt and Richard Reed.

1765, May 13. Renunciation by Thomas Whitson, of Bucks Co., Penna., who declines to act as an executor.

1768, May 4. Account by Jacob Birdsall, sole executor.

Lib. 12, p. 214; Lib. 13, p. 438.

1759, Aug. 6. Abbott, Samuel, Elsinboro Twsp., Salem Co.; will of. Son, William, place where I live, together with a certain right of land of 85 acres. Daughter, Rebeckah Abbott, the plantation that I bought of Thomas Goodwin. Wife, Hannah, given movables, and ½ the profits of both plantations. Executors—wife, Hannah, and son, William. Witnesses—Joshua Thompson, Henry Stubbines, Mary Thompson.

1760, July 7. Codicil. I also appoint my daughter, Rebeckah Abbot, an executrix. Witnesses—John Thompson, John Garrel, Mary Thompson. Proved June 3, 1761.

1760, Dec. 27. Inventory, £1106.11.1, by Joshua Thompson and Charles Fogg. Lib. 11, p. 9.

1762, May 21. Abit, Edith, of Gloucester Co. Int. Adm'r—Burroughs Abit. Fellowbondsman—Jacob Spicer; both of Greenwich Township, said Co., yeoman. Edith Abit was the late wife of said Burroughs. Lib. 11, p. 225.

1766, April 29. Abit (Abbitt), Joseph, of Amwell, Hunterdon Co. Int. Adm'r—William Abit. Fellowbondsman—Daniel Kelsey; both of said place.

1766, April 29. Inventory, £147.7.1, by George Corwine and Samuel Corwine. "A legacy left him by his father, James Abit, £30."

Lib. 12, p. 422.

1765, Aug. 10. Abraham, James, of Freehold, Monmouth Co.; will of. Real and personal estate to be sold. Son, George, my pew in Topanamus church, and ½ my pew in Spotshood church. Son, James, my other pew in Topanamus church, and ½ my pew in Spotshood church. Son, John, ten shillings. To my daughters, Elizabeth's, three children, £150 when 21. To daughter, Mary, wife of John Combs, Sr., £150; daughter, Sarah, wife of John Combs, Jr., £150; daughters, Ann, Pheby and Jeane, £150 each; daughters, Hannah and Margaret, £150. Rest of my estate to sons George, James and John, daughter Mary, wife of John Combs, Sr., and daughter Sarah, wife of John Combs, Jr., and to daughters Ann, Pheby and Jeane, and the children of my daughters Hannah and Margaret. Executors—son, James, John Combs, Sr., and Nicholas Everson. Witnesses—Alexander Scoby, Thomas Smith, Andrew Maid. Proved Oct. 10, 1765.

1765, Sept. 30. Inventory, £698.13.1, made by John Perrine, and ——— ———(?). Bonds, notes, and debts, due from many people, as mentioned in said Inventory. Lib. H, p. 563; File No. 3505-3520 M.

1756, Aug. 3. Abraham, Samuel, of Perth Amboy, Middlesex Co.; will of. I give all my estate to my brothers and sisters. Executors —James, Abraham, Jr., and John Combs. Witnesses—William Dayton, Peter Perine, James Smith. Proved June 20, 1761.
Goods were sold by vandue to Charles Abraham, George Abraham, John Abraham, and James Abraham. Lib. G, p. 453.

1762, April 22. Abrahams, Abraham, guardian. Whereas Abraham Abrahams, brother-in-law of Jacob Louzada, son and heir of Moses Louzada, late of Middlesex Co., merchant, by his petiton stated that the said Moses Louzada died intestate in 1755, leaving Hannah, his widow, and several children, and that Hannah took out letters of administration, and that Moses had estate in Somerset and Middlesex counties, which descended to the said Jacob Louzada as being the eldest son and heir, and that Jacob for several years has been a lunatic, and that he may be appointed guardian of the said Jacob while he is of unsound mind; therefore the said Abraham Abrahams, of New York, Robert Sproull, and David Gosling, of Perth Amboy, go on a bond, wherein said Abraham Abrahams is made guardian as aforesaid.
1764, Feb. 24. Revocation. Whereas Abraham Abrahams, brother-in-law of Jacob Louzada, son and heir at law of Moses Louzada, was appointed guardian of said Jacob, which letters were granted without inquisition taken, and not in due manner, and Jacob, who is now of age, has applied that the letters may be made void, and that he may take possession of his own property, therefore the letters are made void. Lib. H, pp. 134, 332.

1762, April 16. Ackerman, Abraham, of New Barbadoes, Bergen Co.; will of. Son, Hendrick, and daughter, Rachel, dwelling house where I live. Son, John, Dutch bible, for his birthright. Daughter, Altye, £60, and daughter, Rachel, £16 at day of marriage. To my children, Altye, John, Abraham, Hendrick and Rachel, each a silver spoon; also Hendrickye, the daughter of my son Abraham, to have one. Real estate to my five children equally. My wife to command whole estate for one year. Executors—friend, Abraham Lowrance Ackerman and Guillian Berthoff. Witnesses—John Earle, Morris Earle and Willam Provoost. Proved Aug. 3, 1762. Lib. H, p. 295.
1762, July 16. Inventory, £101.18.8, made by Reynier V. Giesen, Esq., and Jacob Zabreskie. File No. 760 B.

1757, Aug. 20. Ackerman, Cornelius, of Bergen Co.; will of. Wife to have possession of estate while my widow. The £40 which I have paid towards buying the land of Abraham Ackerman shall be due to my wife from Peter and Lowrence, by order of father. If my wife marry again, the things given her by her father and mother is to be hers, but the things that are mine to go to my daughter Elizabeth. Executors—my wife and brother-in-law, John Zabriskie. Witnesses—Guillian Bertholf, John Hoppe and E. Ackerman. Proved Jan. 27, 1767, Lenah Ackerman sworn as Executrix. Lib. I, p. 91.

1760, May 13. Ackerman, David, Sr., of Paramus, Bergen Co.; will of. Oldest son, Abraham, my Bible. Son, Garret, the farm I live on, and he is to give his mother ½ he raises. Wife, Margaret. Rest of my children, Abram, David, Lowrance, Jannetie Ackerman, Alis Vanvoorhis, Altie Ackerman, and Alis Vanblerkum my moveable

estate. Executors—son, David, and son in law, Jacobus Vanvoorhis. Witnesses—William Cairns, Cornelia Cairns and Don Cairns. Proved Nov. 25, 1760. Probate granted to Jacobus Vanvoorhis, (the other Ex'r, David Ackerman, being dead). Also proved Sept. 30, 1761.
1760, Aug. 18. Inventory, £107.6.9, made by Johannis Ackerman and Wm. Cairns. Lib. H, p. 59.

1767, Feb. 5. Ackerman, David, of Bergen Co. Int. Adm'x—Nelletje Ackerman, the widow. Fellowbondsman—Jacobus Ackerman, of said Co. Witness—Morris Earle.
1767, Feb. 5. Inventory, £21.2.0, made by Abraham Ackerman, and Guilliam Bertholf. Lib. I, p. 151.

1757, Dec. 12. Ackerman, Gerret, of Saddle River, in Bergen Co.; yeoman; will of. Son, Abram, 100 acres on east side of Saddle River, and woodland in northwest corner of old plantation. Son, Albert, farm where I live. Daughters, Thellitie, Staltie, Lena and Lizabeth, £100 each. Wife, Jannitie, my whole estate. Executors—sons Abram and Albert.
1758, Apr. 1. Codicil. Witnesses—William Hoppe, Roelef Westervelt and Treyntie Westervelt. Proved Sept. 6, 1762. Lib. H, p. 280.

1759, Aug. 1. Ackerman, Johannis, of Paremis, Bergen Co.; yeoman; will of. Wife, Elizabeth, use of estate while my widow. Son, Abraham, devised land, and he is to pay £30, to the rest of the children. Son, William, land on north side of the brook, and he is to pay to my other sons. Son David, the land between Abraham and William's. Sons—Johannis, Gerrit and Petrus also given land. Son, Cornelius, £40. Daughter, Aaltje, £5. Executors—Abraham Lawrence Ackerman, and Abraham Abrahamse Ackerman. Witnesses—Jacob Banta, Lena Banta, and Robert Livesey. Proved July 4, 1760, by Robert Livesey. Probate July 4, 1760, to Abraham Lawrense Ackerman and Abraham Abrahamse Ackerman. Also proved Aug. 19, 1761, by Jacob Banta and Lena Banta. (For inventory see preceding volume of Wills (Vol. III, p. 6), the will not there appearing).
Lib. H, p. 52; File, No. 495 B.

1765, June 15. Ackland, Philip, of Great Egg Harbor, Gloucester Co. Int. Adm'x—Elizabeth Ackland. Fellowbondsman—Christopher Lucas; both of said place.
1765, June 8. Inventory, £8.1.7, made by Christopher Lucas and Benjamin Brush. Lib. 12, p. 119.

1769, Feb. 4. Acritt, James, of Pilesgrove Twsp., Salem Co., yeoman; will of. Son, James, the plantation on which he lives, of 340 acres, and, after his death, to my two grandsons, James and Joseph Eacritt, sons of said James. James to have the part his father lives on, and Joseph that where Butler lives on. The 300 acres where I live to my son John; but, if he will not live on it, then it is to be rented, and the rent paid to his two sons, Isaac and the next son, when they are 21. To my friend, Jacob Richman, my cane. The 100 acres at Sepack's Neck to be sold, and money given to daughter Mary, and my grand daughters, daughters of James and John. Executor—Jacob Richman. Witnesses—John Read, Samuel Read, John Combs. Proved April 17, 1769. Lib. 13, p. 539.

CALENDAR OF WILLS—1761-1770   9

1767, April 15, Adair, Alexander, of Bethlehem Twsp., Hunterdon Co.; will of. My goods to be sold. To William Miller, my sister's son, 18 pence. To William Hankeson, £1. To Rev. John Hanno, £1 To John Miller, my sister's son, the rest of my estate. Executor—Samuel Polen. Superintendent—Rev. John Hanno. Witnesses—Joseph Osmun, William Hankinson, Susanna Hankinson. Proved June 6, 1767.
1767, May 21. Inventory, £50.6.10, made by, Francis McShane and William Hankinson.
1769, Oct. 12. Account made by Samuel Poling, the executor.
Lib. 13, p. 196; Lib. 14, p. 126.

1754, March 6. Adams, David, of Great Egg Harbor, Gloucester Co.; will of. Sons, Jonas and David, my homestead where I live. Out lands and cedar swamps to be sold. Executors—my wife, Cathrine, and Robert Morss. Witnesses—Japhet Leeds, Nicholas Sooy, Joseph Addams, Jr. Proved March 24, 1763.
1763, Feb. 5. Inventory, £23.17.6. made by Nehemiah Leeds, and Nicholas Sooy.
1772, Jan. 25. Account by Robert Morss, as executor.
Lib. 11, p. 311.

1767, Sept. 11. Adams, Matthew, of Hunterdon Co.; will of. Son, John, £10. Wife, Lydia, household goods. If my wife chooses, she may keep the place for 12 years, for which she shall keep my mother, and bring up all the children with the profits of the place. If my wife do not keep the place, then my executors are to dispose of it, and put the money to interest, and keep my mother and children there with; and at the end of 12 years, all of my estate, with the portion left to me and my wife by her father, John Chambers, deceased, to be divided in seven parts, and given to my wife Lydia, daughter Elenor, and sons, John, James, Benjamin, Elijah, and David, each one part. Executors—my wife, and my friends, John McDowel and John King. Witnesses—James Graham, Alexander McEowen, Andrew Rynor. Proved March 16, 1768.   Lib. 12, p. 515.

1762, Feb. 11. Adams, William, of Alloways Creek, Salem Co.; will of. Son, William, my plantation in Penns Neck, which formerly belonged to Hugh McAdams, and contains 105 acres; also 40 acres of woodland, which I purchased of Jeremiah Baker. Son, Seth, 150 acres, which Seth's grandfather, Edward Hancock, purchased, and was formerly Malakey Davis's, and joins to Reneir Vanhist and William Hancock, and after Seth's death, one-half of the 150 acres to my son David; but if he dies then to Job Adams; but if he dies then to my daughter Sarah Adams; but if she die, then to my son William. Son William to have the other half, and he is to have the care of my son Seth as long as he shall live. Son, David, to have the plantation where I live, that I bought of Benjamin Alling, in Alloways Creek Neck, of 100 acres. Rest of my estate to my son, Job Adams, and to Sarah Adams. Executors—friend, Edward Hancock, and my son, William. Witnesses—John Dickinson, Peter Amble, Roger Sherron. Proved March 13, 1769.
1769, Feb. 18. Probate to both Executors.
1769, March 13. Isaac Mulford, of Lower Alloways Creek Twp., Salem Co., weaver; and John Vanculin, of same place, yeoman; declared that they went to the house of William Adams to set up

with him in his last sickness, about the 11th or 12th of February last; and William called his children, and said to them that it was his will that the two children which he had by his last wife, viz., Ezra and Hannah, should have £25 each, and that his son, David, must pay it.
1769, March 13. Inventory £326.5.8, made by Thomas Sayre and John Stewart. Lib. 14, p. 106; Lib. 14, p. 152.

1766, Nov. 24. Addams, Joseph, of Gloucester Co.; will of. Wife, Sarah, to have bed, negro Stephen, cows and horses. Daughters, Rebecca, Mary and Jane Addams, 3 cows each, when 18. Wife is pregnant; the child to be provided for. Son, John, to be bound out, and to have the land that James Murfy lives on. Part of plantation to be sold, and the rest to go to son Joseph. Executors—my wife, and friend, Nehemiah Leeds. Witnesses—Peter Romine, Japhet Leeds, Elizabeth Lawrence, Nicholas Sooy. Proved Feb. 10, 1769.
1769, Jan. 25. Inventory, £78.8.6, of goods of Joseph Addams, of Great Egg Harbor Twsp., Gloucester Co., made by Nicholas Sooy and Peter Covenover. Lib. 14, p. 80.

1763, Dec. 27. Addis, John, of New Brunswick, Middlesex Co.; will of. To my wife, Mary, and my daughter, Mary, all my real and personal estate. Executors—my said wife, and my father in law, Gysbert Van Sickle. Witnesses—Lucas Voorhees, David Gano, Harman Schunamon. Proved March 3, 1764. Lib. H, p. 408.

1761, Feb. 3. Addoms, John, of Wantage, Sussex Co., husbandman; will of. Daughter, Deborah Addoms, a bed. Daughter, Caterine Addoms, a bed. Son, John Addoms, the land called the New Intent. Sons, Evi and Silvanus, the place I live on. Son, Robert, £50. Their mother to live in the house while she is my widow. Son, Uriah, a mare. Mentions "the four girls." Grandson, John Macklucke, a mare. Executors—sons, John and Silvanus. Witnesses—Joseph Crowell, Jeremiah Washburn. Proved Nov. 19, 1762.
1763, Jan. 7. Inventory, £202.10.9, made by Andrew Wilson, and Samuel Crowell. Lib. 11, p. 292.

1762, Nov. 19. Addoms, John, Jr., of Wantage, Sussex Co., yeoman. Int. Adm'x—Sarah Addoms (widow.) Fellowbondsman—Silvanus Addoms, yeoman; both of said place.
1762, April 27. Inventory, £183.6.2, made by Samuel Crowell and Andrew Willson. "Land called New Intent, of 70 acres."
Lib. 11, p. 288.

1761, July 30. Alberson, Jacob, of Gloucester, Gloucester Co., yeoman. Int. Adm'x—Patience Alberson, widow. Fellowbondsman—Joseph Harrison, both of said Co. Witnesses—Sarah Howell and John Ladd.
1761, July 16. Inventory, £669.0.1, made by Michael Fisher and Joseph Harrison.
1763, April 7. Account made by Patience Albertson, as Adm'x.
Lib. 10, p. 435.

1766, Nov. 8. Albertson, Enoch, of Gloucester Twsp. and Co.; will of. Son, Isaac, £100. Daughter, Rebecca, £20. Wife, Elizabeth, rest. Land to be sold. Executors—my wife and my brother, Isaac

Albertson. Witnesses—James Boggs, Archibald Ingram. Proved Dec. 1, 1766.
1766, Nov. 22. Inventory, £224.15.9, made by Gabriel Daves and Josiah Albertson. Lib. 16, p. 148.

1762, Feb. 24. Albertson, Ephraim, Jr., of Gloucester Co., Ward. Eldest son, and heir of Ephraim Albertson, of Town and Co. of Gloucester, yeoman, who left lands by will to said son; and the son made choice of his friend, Aaron Albertson, of Newton, to be his Guardian. Witness—Sarah Howell.
1762, Feb. 24. Guardian, Aaron Albertson, of Newton Twsp., Gloucester Co., yeoman. Fellowbondsman—William Harrison, Jr., and John Griffith, both of Town and Co., yeoman. Witnesses—William Harrison and Sarah Howell. Lib. 11, p. 89.

1768, July 20. Albertson, Sarah, of Gloucester Co., Ward. Daughter of William Albertson of said Co. Guardian—Samuel Clement, Esq. Fellowbondsman—Ebenezer Hopkins, both of said Co. Witness—James Talman. Lib. 13, p. 437.

1767, May 23. Alexander, David, of Salem Co. Int. Adm'x—Catharine Alexander, widow. Fellowbondsmen—John Mecum and Giles Lambson, yeomen; all of Penns Neck, said Co.
1767, May 8. Inventory, £99.14.4, made by Allen Congelton and Giles Lambson. Lib. 13, p. 189.

1762, April 1. Alexander, William, of Newton, Gloucester Co. Int. Adm'r—Reuben Eastlack, yeoman. Fellowbondsman—Jacob Borrough, yeoman; both of said Township.
1762, March 30. Inventory, £164.13.9, made by Isaac Mickle and Jacob Borrough. File 783 H.

1760, Aug. 20. Alford, John, of Charles Town, Middlesex Co., Mass.; will of. I give £10 to the following widows, viz., Widow Wakefield in Boston, my wife; her cousin, Sarah Bradick, and my next neighbor, Widow Williams. Wife, Margaret, to have all my place, except the gold watch which I give to my sister, Joana Alford. Wife to have £700 and to live in my house. My brother, Benjamin Alford, £10. Sister, Joanna Alford, £500. Nephews, John Alford Tyng and James Tyng, £50. Nephew, Jonathan Tyng. As much as possible is to be collected, out of the estate of their father, Eleazer Tyng, Esq. To my nephew, the Rev. Edward Winslow, at Stratford, in Conn., for his daughter Margaret Alford Winslow, my neices, Margaret Pollard, Hannah Winslow, Mary Winslow, and my nephew. Thomas Alford Winslow, £10 each, as well as that due me from their father, Joshua Winslow. Nephew, John Winslow, niece, Elizabeth Loring, £50; and to my niece Sarah Vrylant, £50, and to John Loring, £20. My real and personal in New Jersey, Conn., Mass., or Island of Kitts, to be used to the best purposes that can be. Executors—Edmund Trowbridge, of Cambridge, and Richard Cary, of Charles Town. Witnesses—Joseph Lamson, William Lambson, John Lamson. Proved Oct. 27, 1761.
On the same date John Winslow and Sarah, his wife; Sampson Stoddard, of Chelmsford, and Margant his wife; John Alford Tyng and James Tyng, both of Dunstable; Elizabeth Loung, widow, and Sarah Vreling, spinster, both of Boston, did all object to the probate

of said will, as, among other reasons, the testator was old and not of sound mind; after which an agreement was made between the parties concerned. Lib. 11, p. 427.

1761, May 23. Allan, William, of Bedminster Twsp., Somerset Co., yeoman; will of. Oldest son, John, the £48 that he owes me. Son, William, if he returns alive from sea, £50. Sons, Robert and Joseph, the house I live in, and the mill and land whereon they stand, and my 92 acres joining the mill lot. Daughter, Rachel, a cow. Daughter, Hannah, a cow. Daughter, Margaret, a cow. My youngest daughter, Elizabeth, to live with Robert and Joseph, till she is 18, when she is to have £25. Wife, Sufiah, while my widow, the front room in the house I live in, and the bed I lie on, and to have meat, drink, fire, candle and washing. Executors—son Robert, and my friends, John Barkley, of Bedminster, and Aaron Boylan, of Baskingridge. Witnesses—Jeremiah Bright, John Barkley, John Smith. Proved July 6, 1761. Lib. H, p. 2.

1769, Jan. 9. Allback, Morris, of Roxbury, Morris Co.; will of. Wife, Annah, beds. Son, John William, Bible. Son, Philip, books. Wife to take choice of goods and rest to be sold and money given to wife, and two children, John William, Philip and Elizabeth. Executors—my wife and Philip Ike. Witnesses—Augustine Reid, Coonrod Rerick, Tetrick Stroble. Proved March 22, 1769. Lib. K, p. 78.

1754, March 22. Allen, David, of Manasquan, in town of Shrewsbury, Monmouth Co., yeoman; will of. Wife, Catharine, £150, and some goods. Daughter, Mercy, wife of Thomas Jeffery, the plantation they live on, near Manasquan Bridge, except the west half of the meadow, which is given to my only son, and, after her death to her sons. Son, Samuel, the rest of my estate, and he is to allow my brother, Joseph Allen, to board with him; but if my brother should become unable to pay his board, then my son is to keep him in a good manner. Executors—son, Samuel, and my son-in-law, Thomas Jeffery. Witnesses—Joseph Lawrence, Ananiah Gifford, Jr., Anthony Woodward, Jr., Jacob Dennis. Proved April 18, 1760, and also April 13, 1761.

1760, March 5. Inventory, made by James Irons, David Johnston and Samuel Osborn. Lib. G, p. 425.

1762, June 22. Allen, Ephraim, of Shrewsbury, Monmouth Co., Ward. Son of Joseph Allen, of said place, yeoman, deceased. Makes choice of his friend, Joseph Potter, yeoman, as his guardian, till full age.

1763, June 22. Guardian—Joseph Potter, of said Co. Fellowbondsman—Arent Schuyler, of City of Burlington. File No. 2885 M.

1764, June 22. Allen, Jacob, of Morristown, Morris Co. Int. Adm'r —Henry Allen, a relative. Fellowbondsman—Israel Ward; both of said town. Witness—John Mackay.

1764, June 22. Renunciation, by Elizabeth Allen, the widow, in favor of Henry Allen. Witnesses—Israel Ward and Ezekiel Cheever.

1764, June 23. Inventory, made by David Ward and Laurince Willson.

1764, Sept. 21. Account made by Adm'r. Lib. H, p. 349.

CALENDAR OF WILLS—1761-1770   13

1759, June 12. Allen, James, of Northampton Twsp., Burlington Co., yeoman; will of. Son, John, land near Mt. Holly, that I bought of Richard Prickett, of 28 acres, when 21. Son, James, farm where I live. Executors—son, James, and kinsman, William Woolston. Witnesses—Joseph Stokes, Jacob Prickitt, Jr., and Gab. Blond.
1760, Dec. 7. Codicil. Brother, Robert Allen, clothing. Granddaughter, Dorothy Allin, gold ring. Grandson, Samuel Allin, £5. To Saboelah, the daughter of Frances Alkinton, a bed. To Samuel Allin, son of George, dec'd, a calf. Witnesses—Joseph Stokes and Thomas Parkinson. Proved Sept. 19, 1761. Lib. 10, p. 367.
1761, Sept. 18. Inventory, £192.14.5, made by James Dobbin and Robert Sherred.

1767, Nov. 16. Allen, Job, of Pequanack Twsp., Morris Co. Int. Adm'r—Jacob Ford, Jr. Fellowbondsman—Thomas Kinney; both of said place. Witness—Joseph Ball.
1767, Nov. 10. Renunciation by Christian Allen in favor of Jacob Ford, Jr. Witness—John Walton, Jr. Lib. I, p. 208.

1762, April 12. Allen, John, of Hanover, Morris Co., weaver; will of, Real and personal to be sold, and money divided between my wife, Sarah, and my son, Daniel. If David decease in his nonage, then his ½ to be given to my wife's children. Executors—Jonathan Ford and Benjamin Halsey. Witnesses—David Ogden, Eunis Ford, Ezekiel Cheever. Proved May 20, 1762. Lib. H, p. 126.

1761, May 22. Allen, Joseph, of Shrewsbury, Monmouth Co., yeoman; will of. Wife, Sarah, use of the plantation which joins the Whale Pond Brook. Eldest son, John, farm where I live, which was left him by his grandfather Allen; also the land I bought of Daniel Williams. Sons, Ephraim Allen and William Jackson Allen, the land that joins Whale Pond Brook, after wife's death. Youngest daughter, Sarah, £20. Daughters, Mary, Lydig and Sarah Allen, £40 each. Mary's to be paid when 18, and the two youngest when 14. To my mother, Hance, £30. Executors—friends, Stephen Cook and Joseph Jackson. Witnesses—Job Cook, Edward Patterson Cook, Stephen Woolley. Proved June 6, 1761. Lib. H, p. 128.

1761, Oct. 2. Allen, Joseph, of Shrewsbury, Monmouth Co., cordwainer; will of. Wife, Hannah, £20. My wife and my sons, Ebenezer, John and Daniel, to have an equal share. Daughters, Margaret and Johanna, £20 each less than the sons. Sons to be put to trades. Executors—Richard Lawrence and Samuel Scott. Witnesses—Edmond Lafetra, James Lafetra, James Hill. Proved Nov. 19, 1761.
1761, Nov. 19. Inventory, made by George Allen and Edmond Lafetra. Lib. H, p. 43.

1765, Nov. 16. Allen, Joseph, of Greenwich Township, Gloucester Co., yeoman; will of. Brother Benjamin Allen, my lands, when he is 21, except my Landing place. To Thomas West, a Landing on Manto Creek, to extend from my wharf to Thomas West's wharf. If Benjamin die before 21, then the lands to be sold, and money divided among my sisters, Abigail Allen, Rebecca Lodge, Patience Allen, Elizabeth Allen and Deborah Allen, and my mother, Patience Allen. Executor—friend, Jacob Spicer. Witnesses—Israel West, Benjamin Hooton, William Scull. Proved May 6, 1769. Lib. 14, p. 183.

1764, April 25. Allen, Judah, of Shrewsbury, Monmouth Co., ward. Son of Ralph Allen, of said place, deceased; who makes choice of Benjamin Brookfield as his Guardian.
1764, April 25. Guardian—Benjamin Brookfield. Fellowbondsman —Nathaniel Higgins; both of Elizabeth Town, Essex Co. Witnesses —Elias Woodruff and Robert Ogden. File Nos. 2985-2988 M.

1766, Dec. 22. Allen, Thomas, of Upper Penns Neck, Salem Co., yeoman; will of. Wife, Cathrine, the household goods, and the 50 acres of land in her charge, that belongs to her son, Daniel. Son, Thomas, to have part of that 100 acres which I bought last; and John to have that part above the road; but Margaret Murphy is to have the use of the house for 2 years. Sons, Jeremiah and Richard, £5 each. Rest of money to my daughters, Elizabeth, Mary, and Ledona. Executor—son, Richard. Witnesses—John Smith, Andrew Linmier, Robert Howard. Proved Feb. 1, 1768.
1768, Feb. 1. Renunciation, by Richard Allen.
1768, Feb. 1. Adm'r—Abel Harris. Fellowbondsman—Robert Howard and John Smith, yeomen; all of Penns Neck, Salem.
1768, Jan. 29. Inventory, £59.2.6, made by Robert Howard and Richard Allen. Lib. 13, p. 386.

1756, Nov. 17. Allen, William, of Bethlehem [Hunterdon Co.]; will of. My estate to be sold and the proceeds to be given to my wife, in order to bring up my children. Executors—son, William Allin, and my friend, Charles Hoff, Jr. Witnesses—John Cowan, Martha Erwine and Thomas Allen. (No proof of will.) Recorded 1765.
File Nos. 7715-7716 C.

1764, Aug. 28. Alling, John, of Elizabeth Town Boro, Essex Co.; will of. Wife, Abirgirl, ⅓ the moveables, and use of ⅓ the lands. Sons, Daniel, and Joseph, the plantation where I live, which I purchased of Matthias Alling, formerly belonging to Josiah Brodwill, lying in Turkey, at the head of land of John Clark, when they are 21. Daughters, Hannah Hicks, Phebe Meker, Unis Boyd and Abirgirl, rest of moveables. Executors—kindmen, Isaac Woodruff and Amos Potter, and Stephen Meeker. Witnesses—John Ogden, John Ogden, Jr., Ezekiel Ogden. Proved Dec. 12, 1764. Lib. I, p. 302.

1765, Jan. 30. Allinson, Elizabeth, of City and County of Burlington; will of. Son, Samuel Allinson, all my estate, he paying out to each of my three sons, Peter, Joseph and Jacob Allinson, £50; also to pay to my granddaughters, Elizabeth and Mary Allinson, daughters of my deceased son Thomas Allinson, £25; also to pay to Mary Holmes, £5. Daughters-in-law, Elinor Allinson and Mary Clothier, wearing apparel. Son, Jacob, is absent, and not known whether living or dead. Executors—my brother, Thomas Scattergood and son, Samuel Allinson. Witnesses—John Hoskins, Mary Holmes, John Hoskins. Proved Sept. 12, 1768. Lib. 13, p. 429.

1761, May 2. Allison, John, of Burlington Co. Int. Adm'r—Joseph Allison, of said Co. Fellowbondsman—John Allison, of same place. Adm. 342.

1766, June 3. Allison, Richard, of Hopewell, Hunterdon Co., sadler; will of. Son, Burgiss, my books. Wife, Ruth, rest of personal and

real estate, to enable her to bring up my two children; that is to say, till my son, Burgiss Hall, comes to the age of 21, and then I give to said son, Burgiss Hall, 1-3 of my estate, and the other 2-3 to remain for my wife, till my daughter, Anna, is 18, and then I give to Anna, ½ of the said 2-3, and the other ½ to my wife. Executors—my son, Burgiss Hall, and my friends, Safety McGee and John Butler, Jr., both of Bordentown. Witnesses—Samuel Mullady, Stephen Burrowes, Josiah Ellis. Proved June 17, 1766.
Lib. 12, p. 389.

1768, March 9. Allman, Solomon, of Lower Penns Neck, Salem Co. Int. Adm'x—Jane Allman, widow. Fellowbondsmen—Matthias Lambson and Hance Lambson, yeomen; all of said place.
1768, March 9. Inventory, £393.0.6, made by Andrew Sinnickson and William Stretch.
Lib. 13, p. 334.

1768, Aug. 17. Anderson, Benjamin, of Hopewell, Hunterdon Co.; will of. Eldest son, Joseph Anderson, 20 shillings. Daughter, Hannah Johnson, £80 and some goods. Rest of real and personal to my four sons, Joseph, Joshua, Elijah and Benjamin. Executors—my four sons, and my son in law, Abraham Johnson. Witnesses—John Houghton, Sarah Houghton, Azariah Hunt. Proved May 4, 1769.
1769, April 11. Inventory, £147.7.11, made by Azariah Hunt and John Houghton.
Lib. 14, p. 149.

1765, Dec. 6. Anderson, Cornelius, of Hopewell, Hunterdon Co., yeoman; will of. Wife, Coterin, £15 every year, beds, cows, etc. Son, Cornelius, £10, to be paid to him five years after my death, with ⅓ the profits of the plantation. Son, Thomas, rest of my estate. Executors—said Thomas Anderson and Daniel Drake. Witnesses—Joseph Bonham, John Smith, Timothy Smith. Proved Aug. 19, 1768.
1768, Aug. 12. Inventory, £424.8.0, made by John Hart and Timothy Smith.
1778, Jan. 5. Account, by Daniel Drake, the Executor.
Lib. 12, p. 511; Lib. 18, p. 689.

1766, Sept. 24. Anderson, James, of Somerset Co. Int. Adm'rs—John Anderson and Kenneth Anderson, father and brother of said James. Fellowbondsman—Joseph Newton; all of Freehold, Monmouth Co.
1766, Oct. 3. Inventory, £267.0.7, made by Peter Perrine, Edmund Leslie, James Hude, William Laird, Jacob Wikoff, Thomas Cook, Philip Stockton, and Robert Embly.
Lib. I, p. 5.

1761, June 17. Anderson, John, Esq., of Greenwich Twsp., Sussex Co.; will of. Son, James, £20, as he is the oldest son. The rest of my children to have £20, except my daughter, Mary, she appearing, shall have an equal share with the other children; if she does not appear, then to her daughter, Margaret Briggs, when she is 18. Wife, Rachel, the rest of my estate. Executors—my wife, and my son John. Witnesses—Robert McMurtrie, John McClenachan, John Drum. Proved July 3, 1761.
1761, June 29. Inventory, £116.19.3, made by William Launder and Jonathan Pettit.
Lib. 10, p. 475.

1762, Sept. 9. Anderson, John, of Bridgewater, Somerset Co., merchant; will of. Personal and real estate to be sold. Wife, Martha, £40. To the Presbyterian Congregation at Bound Brook, £5. To my daughters, Mary, Martha and Hannah, who are married, £20 each. To my daughters, Margaret, Priscilla, Elizabeth and Sarah, £25 each, when they are 21. Executors—wife, and my friend, Samuel Kemble. Witnesses—Hendrick Fisher, Jr., Jacob Harris, Elias V. Court. Proved Jan. 3, 1766.

1765, Dec. 6. Inventory, £447.16.4, made by John Miller and Michael Field.   Lib. H, p. 584.

1767, Jan. 29. Anderson, John, of Sussex Co. Int. Adm'r—Israel Swayze. Fellowbondsman—Samuel Lundy; both of said Co. Witnesses—Ephraim Darby and Thomas Anderson.

1767, Jan. 16. Inventory, £14.17.7, made by John Read and Samuel Lundy.

1768, April 4. Account made by Adm'r.

Lib. 12, p. 467; Lib. 12, p. 521.

1762, March 11. Anderson, Joseph, of Alloways Creek, Salem Co., yeoman; will of. My estate to be divided between Simon Anderson and Thomas Anderson, when they are 21. Executor—uncle, George Warner. Witnesses—John Kille, Isaac Anderson, Francis Dunham. Proved May 31, 1762.

1762, April 16. Inventory, £26.8.6, made by Samuel Sims, and John Kille.   Lib. 11, p. 190.

1765, April 9. Anderson, Nathaniel, of Newark, Essex Co. Int. Adm'r—Timothy Anderson, (alias Andress), the eldest son. Fellowbondsman—Joseph Riggs; both of said place.

1766, March 28. Inventory, £14.12.2, made by John Ogden and Samuel Huntington. Signed by Timothy Andress, Adm'r.

1767, May 21. Account made by Timothy Andress, Adm'r, on estate of Nathaniel Andress.   Lib. H, p. 423.

1765, June 7. Anderson, Rachel, of Phillipsburg, Sussex Co.; will of; being the widow of John Anderson, Esq., late of Greenwich Twsp. All real and personal to be sold; moneys to be put to interest for the benefit of my son, Bartholomew, who is an idiot. The said interest is to be paid to my son John, who is to provide for my son Bartholomew. What may be left, after the death and burial of Bartholomew, to be given to my surviving daughters. To my sons, James Anderson and John Anderson, one shilling each. Executors—Alexander White and David Hays, both of Greenwich, yeomen. Witnesses—Jonathan Pettit, Garshom Barns, Mary Shearman. Proved Aug. 29, 1766.

1766, June 19. Renunciation, by David Hays and Alexander White. Witnesses—Daniel Harker, Elizabeth White and Thomas Hays.

1765, Aug. 29. Adm'r, with will annexed. Daniel Harker. Fellowbandsman—Valtin Vougt.

1770, Oct. 24. Account made by Daniel Harker, Adm'r with will annexed. Includes house and lot in Phillipsburg, £7. Deborah McCarty and Mary Shearman paid for nursing. Paid for board, etc., of Bartholomew Anderson, for four years, and for his nursing and funeral expenses.   Lib. 12, p. 456; Lib. 15, p. 66.

1768, July 7. Anderson, Thomas, of Hopewell, Hunterdon Co. Int. Adm'x—Penelope Anderson. Fellowbondsman—John Jewell, of Amwell, said Co. Witnesses—Margaret Kirkpatrick and Wm. Kirkpatrick.
1768, July 6. Inventory, £176.17.3, made by, John Hart and Daniel Drake.
1774, June 3. Account by, Ralph Hart and Penelope Hart, late Penelope Anderson. Includes three hats for his children, 13 shillings, one of whom is son Andrew Pamela, Amos, and Reubin. also schooling three children, Lib. 13, p. 440; Lib. 15, p. 517.

1764, Dec. 1. Andrews, Benajah, of Philadelphia; will of. Brothers, Edward and Peter Andrews, my apparel. My wife, and children, Benjamin and Esther Andrews, to be supported till they are of age; then real and personal estate to be divided equally. Mentions brother, Peter, and sister, Elizabeth Andrews. Executors—my wife, Ann, father-in-law, Benjamin Kendall, and my friend, Owen Jones, of Philadelphia. Witnesses—Isaac Moss, Edward Andrews, Elizabeth Parker. Proved Jan. 17, 1765. Lib. 12, p. 54.

1763, March 11. Andrews, Edward, of Middletown, Monmouth Co. Int. Adm'r—George Fitz Randolph. Fellowbondsman—James Brooks; both of Middlesex Co.
1763, March 9. Renunciation by Alice Andrews, the widow, who leaves it to the creditors. Lib. H, p. 221.

1761, Jan. 4. Andrews, Hannah, of Gloucester Co. Int. Adm'r—Benajah Andrews. Fellowbondsman—Thomas Webster; both of said Co.
1760, Dec. 2. Inventory, £28.2.1, made by William Wood and Lawrence Webster. Lib. 10, p. 171

1763, June 8. Andrews, Mordicai, of Little Egg Harbor, Burlington Co.; will of. Land on Pohateung Creek, of 929 acres, to be sold. Sons, Jacob and Isaac, my plantation. My wife, Mary, household goods. Daughter, Prudence, bed. Daughter, Elizabeth, bed. Daughter, Sarah, bed. Grandson, Joseph Andrews, £10 when 21. Daughter, Kesiah Shrouds, £10. Remainder to wife, Mary. Executors—wife and my cousin, Isaac Andrews, and my son, Jacob. Witnesses—Hananiah Gaunt, Daniel Shrouds, John Gauntt. Proved Aug. 3, 1763.
Lib. 11, p. 384.

1763, June 25. Andrews, Peter, of Little Egg Harbor, Burlington Co., Int. Adm'x—Hannah Andrews, of said place. Bondsman—Joseph Mapes, of Great Egg Harbor, in Gloucester Co. Witness—Samuel Allinson. Lib. 11, p. 413.
1763, Feb. 22. Inventory, £141.10.6, made by Joseph Parker and Annaniah Gaunt.
1766, May 21. Account by Hannah Andrews, Adm'x.

1763, Oct. 13. Andrews, Phebe, of Salem Town, Salem Co., widow. Int. Adm'r—Thomas Norris, shipwright. Fellowbondsmen—Lewis Owen, joiner, and Thomas Goodwin, yeoman; all of said place. Witness—Joseph Kay. Lib. 12, p. 176.

1763, March 7. Andrews, Samuel, of Little Egg Harbor, Burlington Co.; will of. Daughter, Esther Lippincott, £500. Wife, Elizabeth, the rest while my widow, and, after her death, the plantation to be sold, and money given, to my daughter, Esther Lippincot ¼ part; daughter, Hannah Mathis, ¼; daughter, Mary Parsal, ¼; and to my grandchildren, Jere Andrews, Mary and Sarah Andrews, the children of my son Peter, deceased, ¼. To Mary Gifford a bed. Executors—sons-in-law, Joseph Lippincott and John Persell. Witnesses—Joseph Parker, Sr., Peter Parker, Joseph Parker, Jr. Proved May 24, 1763.
Lib. 11, p. 324.

1763, April 25. Inventory, £254.14.0, made by Joseph Parker and Peter Parker.

1760, Aug. 29. Androvet, John, of Staten Island, Richmond Co., New York, boatman; will of. Wife, Leah Androvet, use of real and personal. My daughter, Mary Androvet, being the youngest one, that part of plantation next the water, which will be along Peter Androvet's line, and Joseph Soper. Daughters, Elenor and Leah, rest of plantation, which would be along the land of Israel Dusosways. I give to Elinor Woglom and Leah Tappin a meadow at Freshkill, called Long Neck, of 7 acres, and meadow at Woodbridge, called Sunken Marsh, of 7 acres. Executors—my wife, and daughter, Mary Androvet. Witnesses—Rebecca Androvet, Catherine Androvet, Laughlen Fallon. Proved Sept. 10, 1765.

Also, at the same time, probate was granted to Leah Androvet and Mary Tappen, late Mary Androvet.
Lib. H, p. 602.

1770, Oct. 1. Angevine, John, of Burlington Co. Int. Adm'r—Darling Conroe, of said Co. Fellowbondsman—John West. Witness—Samuel Coles, Jr.

1770, Sept. 24. Inventory, £44.2.2, made by James Cattell and Samuel Coles, Jr.
Lib. 15, p. 71.

1768, Oct. 25. Antill, Edward, of Piscataway, Middlesex Co., but now of Shrewsbury, Monmouth Co.; will of. Wife, Anne, £1000, in trust for the benefit of my children. Daughters, Sarah and Isabella, provided for while single. Son, Edward, has been educated, and he to have 1-6 part of remainder. Daughter, Mary, wife of Richard Cochran, son John, son Lewis, each to have 1-6 part. Daughters, Sarah and Isabella, to have 2-6 parts applied to their benefit. Executrix—my wife. Witnesses—Mary Boggs, James Boggs, V. Pearse Ashfield.

1770, July 14. Codicil. I appoint son, Lewis, as executor, with my wife. Witnesses—John Webster, Jacob Boice, Randolph Drake. Proved Aug. 21, 1770.
Lib. K, p. 237.

1762, Jan. 27. Antram, Hannah, of Burlington Co., ward. Daughter of Isaac Antram of Springfield deceased. Guardian—Thomas Conarroe of Northampton Twp. said Co. Bondsman—Zachariah Antram of City of Burlington.
Lib. 11, p. 205.

1768, June 14. Antram, Hannah, of Burlington Co. (late Hannah D'Cow). Int. Adm'r—David Antram. Fellowbondsman—William Taylor; both of Springfield, said Co.

1768, Aug. 18. Inventory, £280.17.7, made by Benjamin Gibbs and Nathan Folwell.
Lib. 13, p. 435.

CALENDAR OF WILLS—1761-1770   19

1770, Nov. 16. Appelget, Thomas, of South Amboy, Middlesex Co., farmer; will of. Wife, Sarah, £200. Eldest son, Gabriel, 20 acres of land, which I bought of John Thorp, lying in Monmouth Co. Second son, Ezekiel, that house where he dwells, near Cranberry Brook, and 110 acres adjoining. Youngest son, Anthony, this house and plantation of about 200 acres; also 20 acres on north side of Cranberry Brook, that joins Benjamin Appelget's land. Rest of lands to be sold. Daughter, Sarah Appelget, £100. Granddaughter, Rachel Appelget, the daughter of said Sarah, £20. Wife, Sarah, to have the rest. Executor—son, Anthony. Witnesses—Thomas Morford, Thomas Cox, Nathaniel Fitz Randolph. Proved Dec. 3, 1770. Lib. K, p. 259.

1765, Oct. 1. Applegate, Jacob, of Middletown, Monmouth Co.; will of. Wife, Catteam, the use of half my lands, while my widow. Son, Sylvester, my land up to the headline. Son, Ebenezer, all my lands in Middletown. I give to Hannay, Soloman and Rebecor Tilton all my lands the sotherd line of the creek, where John Tillton lives; but they are to pay to Cattrin Hart £30 a piece. Daughter, Cattrin Hart, 3 cows. Executors—Peter Tillton in West Jersey, and Nathan Tillton in Middletown. Witnesses—Chrineyonce Van Mater, William Thompson. Proved May 11, 1768.
1768, May 9. Inventory, £290.13.5, made by Benjamin Johnson and James Mott, Jr.
1774, Jan. 19. Account made by executors. Money was paid to Levy Hart, Keziah West, Catherine Applegate, and others.
Lib. I, p. 284.

1766, Dec. 9. Applegate, John, of Monmouth Co. Int. Adm'r—Levi Hart, principal creditor. Fellowbondsman—Jonas Solomon; both of said Co.   Lib. I. p. 8.

1766, Dec. 11. Appleton, Joseph, of Nottingham, Burlington Co., Int. Adm'r—Josiah Appleton. Bondsmen—Josiah Appleton, Jr., and Benjamin Yard; all of Trenton, in Hunterdon Co. Witness—John Allen.   File No. 7887 C.

1765, Oct. 31. Arbin, Philip, of Sussex Co. Int. Adm'r—Nathaniel Pettit. Fellowbondsman—Amos Pettit; both of Newton, said Co. Witnesses—Hezekiah Dunn and Ephraim Darby.   Lib. 12, p. 423.

1758, Nov. 2. Aressmith, Edmon, of Somerset Co., farmer; will of. Wife, Mary, my real and personal, while my widow, and she to live on the plantation with my children, and, when sold, to be divided among my children, viz., Antje (wife of Cornelius Sedan), Mary, Joseph, Thomas, John, Edmon, Benjamin, and Nicholas. Executors—my wife and my friend John Brokaw. Witnesses—Isaac Brokaw, Abraham Hoff, Neltje Hoff. Proved June 1, 1761.
1759, Jan. 29. Inventory, £68.9.5, made by Jacobes Messeler and Bergon Hoff.   Lib. G, p. 439.

1756, Dec. 29. Arnold, Henry, of New York City, mariner; will of. Wife, Sarah, all personal; but if she be "ensient," then the child or children to have a share. Executors—my wife, and my friend Thomas Duncan, of said City, merchant. Witnesses—Rebeker Shourt, Jane Dekey, James Emott.
1764, Sept. 4. Codicil. On the 2nd of June, 1764, I bought a farm of Isaac Romyn, lying in Duchess Co., New York; also a farm in

Shrewsbury, New Jersey, in 3 different parcels; which lands are to be sold. To my nephew, Henry Arnold, son of my brother John, £500; and to my sister, Susannah March's children, £500; and to my sister-in-law, Hilah Dekay, £500. Rest I give to my wife, Sarah. Executors—my wife, and my friend James Sacket. Witnesses—Mary Ludlow, Margaut Parks, Cary Ludlow. Proved Oct. 3, 1764.

Lib. H, p. 458.

1767, March 14. Aronson, Aaron, of Waterford Twsp, Gloucester Co.; will of. Daughters, Kezia Parr and Rebecca Nickleson, plantation on which I live. Wife, Rebecca, £20 yearly, and to be supported by said daughters. Daughter, Mary Woolman, £200. To my 4 grandchildren, Samuel, John Aronson, Sarah, and Asher Woolman, £100 each. To said grandson, John Aronson Woolman, my watch. To granddaughter, Sarah Woolman, desk. Executors—daughters, Kezia and Rebecca. Witnesses—Isaac Hornor, John Shivers, Jr., Samuel Clement. Proved April 23, 1767.

1767, April 23. Inventory, £927.3.5, made by Henry Wood and Samuel Burrough.

1769, June 24. Account by Joseph Burroughs, surviving executor (in right of his wife, late Kesiah Parr) of the will of Aaron Aronson. "Legacy to Abner Woolman's children, £400." Lib. 13, p. 109.

1769, Aug. 5. Ashfield, Lewis Morris, of Monmouth Co.; will of. In order that my son and heir-at-law, Redford Ashfield, have all my real and personal estate, I give it to him with the provision that he pay the following legacies: to daughter, Mary Ashfield, £1,000, when she is 19; to my daughter, Euphemia Ashfield, £1,000, when 19; to my daughters, Lydia and Elizabeth, £1,000 each, when 19; to my daughter, Catherine, £1,000 when 19; to my godson, James Horne, £500 immediately after my death; "to my natural daughter, Helena, now at nurse at" Mrs. Trafford's in Shrewsbury, £500; and to Mrs. Mary Mount, £300, immediately after my death, making in the whole, £6,300. Executor—son Redford. Witnesses—Nicholas Van Brunt, Hendrick Voorhees, Cornelius Hageman. Proved Aug. 22, 1770.

1770, Aug. 20. Renunciation, by Redford Ashfield. Witnesses—Thomas G. Stelle, and Samuel Finley. Also renunciation, by Mary Ashfield and Euphemia Ashfield, daughters of Lewis Morris Ashefield, "being now to the age of 17." Witnesses—Thomas G. Stelle and Samuel Finley.

1770, Aug. 22. Adm'r—Vincent Pierce Ashefield, brother of the Honorable Lewis Morris Ashfield. Fellowbondsmen—Michael Kearny and John Wardell, Esq., of Shrewsbury, said Co. Witnesses—Nicholas Van Brunt and Henry Wardell. Lib. K, p. 232.

1762, May 10. Asson, Thomas, of New Hanover, Burlington Co. Int. Adm'rs—Pinset Asson and William Clevinger. Fellowbondsman—Isaac Ivins Jr; all of said place. Witness—Samuel Allinson.

1762, May 8. Inventory, £48.14.0, made by Jacob Andrews, and Isaac Ivins Jr.

1762, Oct. 4. Account by Pinset Asson and William Clevinger, Adm'rs. Lib. 11, p. 225.

1761, June 1. Atkinson, Hope, of Springfield Township, Burlington Co., widow; will of. Daughter, Hannah Atkinson, goods. Son, Michael Atkinson, is under age and a cripple, and to have lands. Execu-

tor—daughter, Hannah Atkinson. Witnesses—John Lavenner, Francis Shinn, Samuel Harris. Proved June 22, 1761. Lib. 10, p. 217.
1761, June 20. Inventory, £179.5.1½, made by George Briggs and Samuel Harris.

1764, Sept. 26. Atkinson, Hope, of Northampton Twsp, Burlington Co., ward. Daughter of William Atkinson, of same place. Bond of Vincent Leeds, yeoman, of said place, as Guardian. Bondsman—Daniel Ellis, Esq., of Burlington. Witness—Joseph Read, Surrogate. Lib. 12, p. 21.

1765, April 20. Atkinson, John, of Springfield, Burlington Co., yeoman; will of. Wife, Susannah, my plantation of 50 acres, while my widow. Son, Moses, the said plantation, when wife's term expires. Son, Samuel, £20. Son, James, £100. Daughter, Hannah Coppothite, £30. Daughters, Abigail Eldridge, Elizabeth Fenton and Patience Conrow, £30 each. Grandson, John Coppothite £2. Executors—two oldest sons, Samuel and James. Witnesses—John Woolman, Sarah Woolman, Hannah Ridgway. Proved Feb. 1, 1769.
1769, Jan. 24. Inventory, £164.11.2, made by Thomas Butcher and Samuel Shinn. Lib. 14, p. 44.

1766, June 19. Atkinson, Jonathan, of Springfield Twsp., Burlington Co.; petition of, making choice of Samuel Wright, of New Hanover Twsp., said Co. as his Guardian, till he is of full age. Said Jonathan is son of Jonathan Atkinson of Springfield Twsp. File No. 7889 C.

1767, May 27. Atkinson, William, of Springfield, Burlington Co., yeoman; will of. Son, William, the farm where I live, when he is 21, and he to pay to my daughter, Hannah, £25, and to his mother, £10 yearly. Son, Adin, the land joining Edward Gaskill, when 21. Daughter, Hannah, £25 when 18. Wife, the right of her dower, and use of lands till sons come 21. Executors—my wife and brother, John Atkinson. Witnesses—Aaron Atkinson, Thomas Fenimore, Shadlock Pancoast. Proved Nov. 14, 1767.
1767, Nov. 21. Inventory, £204.5.6, made by John Fenimore and Shadlock Pancoast. Lib. 13, p. 250.

1763, Jan. 15. Austin, Amos, of Evesham, Burlington Co., yeoman; will of. Eldest son, Caleb, 5 shillings. Eldest daughter, Vesti Rodgers, 5 shillings. Daughter, Mary Summers, 5 shillings. Son, Seth, 5 shillings. Daughter, Patience Austin, 5 shillings. Daughter, Esther, 5 shillings. Youngest son, Amos, goods. Executors—friends Francis Austin and Thomas Shinn. Witnesses—Daniel Earnest, Esther Nailor, Thomas Parkinson. Proved Dec. 15, 1770.
1770, Dec. 3. Inventory, £142.1.2, made by Jacob Prickit and Isaac Evans. Lib. 15, p. 96.

1764, Feb. 20. Austin, Moses, of Newton, Sussex Co., yeoman. Int. Adm'rs—Susannah Austin and Moses Ayers. Fellowbondsman—Ephraim Darby; all of said place.
1764, Feb. 17. Inventory, £267.14.6, made by Michael Ayers, and Philip Hoffman. Lib. 12, p. 1.

1762, March 30. Austin, William, of Evesham in Burlington Co.; will of. My part of the saw mill, in tenure of Benjamin Thomas, to be sold. Son, Jacob, 130 acres of my plantation I lately lived on, in

Evesham, and now in tenure of Daniel Earnest. Son, Francis, 70 acres of the east end. Daughter, Ann, £10, when 21. Daughter, Hannah, £10, when 21. Children, Tamer, Ann, Francis, Hannah, to be supported. Wife, Hannah, 75 acres of land. Executors—wife Hannah, and my friend Francis Austin. Witnesses—John Tanner, Robert Bishop, Thomas Parkinson. Proved July 23, 1762. Lib. 11, p. 172.
1762, July 22. Inventory, £155.6.4, made by Benjamin Haines and Robert Bishop.
1775, June 1. Account of Francis Austin and Hannah Austin, Executors. Lib. 15, p. 533.

1763, July 25. Axford, Jonathan, of Waterford Twsp., Gloucester Co., yeoman; will of. To James Axford (son of my eldest brother, Charles Axford), five shillings. "To Charles Day, Charles Axford (son of my said eldest brother Charles Axford), and my brother John Axford's four sons, to wit, the eldest son named Samuel (to ye best of my memory), the other three, John, Jonathan and Abraham Axford, all the residue. Executors—said Charles Axford (son of my eldest brother, Charles) and Samuel Clement, Jr., of Haddenfield. Witnesses—Isaac Matlack, John Gill, Henry Crawford. Proved Sept. 15, 1763.
1763, Sept. 9. Inventory, £286.1.0, made by John Gill and Isaac Kay. Lib. 11, p. 408.

1769, Aug. 17. Ayars, Burgan, of Pilesgrove, Salem Co., yeoman. Int. Adm'x—Susanna Ayars, widow. Fellowbondsmen—Henry Paullin and George Gauger, yeomen; all of said place.
1769, July 4. Inventory, £185.16.7, made by John Mayhew and Jacob Richman. Lib. 14, p. 112.

1761, June 5. Ayars, Isaac, of Cumberland Co. Int. Adm'x—Jane Ayars. Fellowbondsman—Jonathan Davis; both of Stow Creek, said Co. Witnesses—Azel Peirson and Abigail Ewing.
1761, June 5. Inventory, £260.18.3, made by Jonathan Davis and Azel Peirson. Lib. 10, p. 438.

1766, June 3. Ayars, Isaac, of Salem Co. Int. Adm'x—Jane Ayars, widow. Fellowbondsman—Nathan Ayars, yeoman; both of New Pilesgrove, said Co.
1766, June 2. Inventory, £5.8.0, made by Nathan Ayars and John Kelley. Lib. 12, u. 318.

1762, Nov. —. Ayars, Nathan, of Stow Creek, Cumberland Co., carpenter; will of. My wife, Elizabeth, my plantation where I live, while my widow, and then to my son, Nathan. To sons, Micajah, Elijah and Azariah, 500 acres in Salem Co. Executors—my wife and Jonathan Ayars. Witnesses—Joseph Ayars, Jonathan Davis, Isaac Ayars, Jr. Likewise, my daughter, Ruth, is to have £40, and daughter Phebe, £10. Proved March 13, 1769.
1769, March 7. Inventory, £217.4.3, made by Elnathan Davis, and Hugh Dunn. Lib. 13, p. 503.

1770, Aug. 29. Ayars, Stephen, of Upper Penns Neck, Salem Co., yeoman; will of. Wife, Hester, all she had when I married her. Eldest son, Surrage, to be put to a trade. Daughter, Liddey, to be bound to a tayloress. Son, Caleb, to be put to a trade. My younger daughter, Elizabeth, shall be in care of my wife till she is 18. Children to have estate when of age. Executors—my wife and friend, Isaac Summers. Witnesses—Christopher Graff, Poltis Risnar and John Gill. Proved Sept. 24, 1770.

1770, Sept. 7. Inventory, £321, made by Thomas Pedrick and Christopher Graff.

1775, May 23. Account by Esther Guest, late Esther Ayars, Executrix. Lib. 15, pp. 239, 534.

1767, March 28. Ayers, Martin, of Elizabeth Borough, Essex Co. Int. Adm'r—James Carpenter, yeoman, brother-in-law of said Martin Ayres. Fellowbondsman—Samuel Woodruff; both of said place. Witnesses—Daniel Wade and Samuel Woodruff, 4th.

1767, March 28. Renunciation of Hannah Ayers, the widow of said Martin, in favor of her brother, James Carpenter. Witness—Sarah Potter.

1767, March 30. Inventory, £205.3.2, made by John Ogden and John Lum. Lib. I, p. 131.

1770, Oct. 5. Bacon, Daniel, of Stow Creek, Cumberland Co. Int. Adm'r—Benjamin Green. Fellowbondsman—Clark Smith; both of Lower Alloways Creek, Salem Co., yeomen. Lib. 15, p. 74.

1763, Feb. 1. Bacon, Isaac, of Greenwich Twsp., Cumberland Co., yeoman; will of. Wife, Sarah, one third of moveables. Son, Abel, rest of personal and real, when 21; he to be kept at school till 15, and then to be bound as clerk to George Trenchard, Esq., till he is 20. If Abel die before 20, then I give to my nephew, John Shephard, £100. Executor—brother, Obediah Robbins, Esq. Witnesses—Nathaniel Bacon, John Ware, Maskell Ewing. Proved March 25, 1763.

1763, March 10. Inventory, £661.11.7, made by Philip Dennis and Charles Davis. Lib. 11, p. 403.

1764, Jan. 16. Bacon, Jeremiah, of Greenwich, Cumberland Co. Int. Adm'x—Hannah Bacon, widow. Fellowbondsmen—David Shepherd and Seth Bowen, yeomen; all of said place. Witness—Phebe Ewing.

1764, Jan. 12. Inventory, £177.18.11, made by David Shepherd and Seth Bowen. Lib. 11, p. 495.

1768, Jan. 16. Bacon, Jeremiah, of Stow Creek Twsp., Cumberland Co.; will of. Plantation where I live to be sold. Wife, Rachel, £100. Son, Shepherd, £150. Four daughters—Sarah, Elizabeth, Hannah, and Liddea, £100. Executors—my brother in law, John Ewing, and my wife. Witnesses—John Shepherd, Reuben Dare, Ozwell Sutton. Proved Feb. 12, 1768.

1768, Feb. 4. Inventory, £185.13.11, made by Annanias Sayre, and John Shepherd. Lib. 13, p. 323.

1769, Jan. 21. Bacon, Margaret, of Greenwich Twsp., Cumberland Co.; will of. Son, Joseph Bacon, £10. Son, Richard Bacon, £7 and ¼ acre of land. Son, Jesse Bacon, £10. Daughter, Deborah Bacon, 4 acres of land, and 3 acres in the Barrons above Greenwich. Daughters, Esther, Margaret, Prudence and Elizabeth, the rest of my lands. Executors—son, Joseph Bacon. Witnesses—Prudence Dennis, Sarah Dennis, Philip Dennis. Proved March 21, 1769.

1769, March 20. Inventory, £110.8.9, made by Benjamin Tyler and Philip Dennis. Lib. 14, p. 18.

1764, Jan. 17. Bacon, Mary, of Greenwich, Cumberland Co., widow; will of. Youngest son, Nathan, £10. Eldest daughter, Rachel Robbins, 20 shillings. Daughter, Anne Ware, 20 shillings. Granddaughter, Mary Sayres, £8. Eldest son, Jacob Bacon, rest of estate. Executor—son, Jacob. Witnesses—William Bacon, Tabitha Bacon, Rachel Hodges. Proved April 20, 1764.
1764, April 16. Inventory, £162.5.6, made by Jonathan Walling and Elnathan Ware. Lib. 12, p. 6.

1770, Feb. 9. Bacon, Thomas, of Pilesgrove Twsp., Salem Co., yeoman; will of. Daughter, Mary Hutchason, my homestead, and the house and land over Oldmans Creek, of 357 acres, but if she should marry again, then she shall have it no longer; and she is to have the cedar swamp in Gloucester Co., while she is in the same condition; after her death or marriage my grandsons, Thomas Hutchason and John Hutchason, to have the same. If Thomas Hutchason should come back and live with his wife again, who is my daughter, then care to be used that he have no control of said property that is left to my daughter Mary. I give to Jeremiah Bacon, living in Penna., by some said to be my son, 5 shillings. My friend, Samuel Hogate, is to see that my daughter's husband does not spend her portion. Executors—my daughter, Mary Hutchinson, and my grandson, Thomas Hutchinson. Witnesses—John Hutchinson, Samuel Shivers, Jacob Richman. Proved April 23, 1770.
1770, Feb. 21. Inventory, £167,15.1, made by Jacob Spicer and Samuel Shivers. Lib. 14, p. 259.

——. —— ——. Bailey, Nathaniel, of Monmouth Co.; will of. Wife, Hannah, all my estate, and she to pay my debts by the assistance of my oldest son, Nathaniel, and youngest son, John. I give to my said sons all my carpenter tools. Executors—my wife and said sons. Witnesses—Daniel Stevenson, Isaac Mires. Proved Oct. 17, 1768.
1768, Oct. 27. Inventory, £140.4.4, made by John Walling and Joseph Dorsett, Sr. Lib. K, p. 18.

1768, Nov. 3. Baily, Hannah, of Monmouth Co. Int. Adm'r—Joseph Baily. Fellowbondsman—Nathaniel Baily and Joseph Dorsett, Sr., all of said Co. Witnesses—John Taylor and William Taylor. Lib. I, p. 364.

1763, July 17. Bainbridge, Edmund, the elder, of Maidenhead, Hunterdon Co.; will of. I desire my grave to be beside those of my children, and I order a tomb to be erected, and, at the death of my wife, I order one for her. Wife, Abigail, £15 yearly, and she to board with my son Absalom. Son, John, £100. Son, Peter, £100. Son, Edmund, £100. Daughter, Abigail, £50. Granddaughters, Sarah, and Catharine Hall. Daughter, Sarah, £60. Grand children—Francis, Sarah and Catharine Hall. To my grandsons, Edmund, the son of John; Edmund, the son of Peter, and Edmund, the son of Edmund, £10 each. Son, Absalom, rest of goods, and my lands, when 21; but, if he die, then his share to go to my children—John, Peter, Edmund, Abigail and Sarah. Executors—my wife and son, Absalom. Witnesses—Joseph Higbee, Abraham Hunt, Joseph Reed, Jr. Proved April 16, 1770. Lib. 14, p. 293.

1760, July 16. Bainbridge, John, Sr., of Hopewell, Hunterdon Co., yeoman; will of. Wife, Mary, ⅓ the profits of the plantation where I live, including both sides the creek, and also, various goods, and stock on farm. Eldest son, John, £5. Second son, Theophilus, all my land and plantation whereon I live, on both sides of the creek, and any otherways possessed, except 110 acres, as hereafter described; he paying to my son John, as above, and other legacies. Third son, Edmund, the said 110 acres, which is on the west side of Jacobs Creek, and now in possession of my eldest son, John. Fourth son, William, £40. To my three eldest daughters, Hannah, Mary and Rebeckah, rest of moveable estate. Fourth daughter, Sarah, £30, when 18. Fifth daughter, Abigail, £50. Executors—wife, Mary, and my two sons, Theophilus, and Edmund. Witnesses—Rebeckah Burrowes, Martha Ellis, Josiah Ellis.

1761, May 9. Codicil. My son, Edmund, is dead, so my son, William, to have the land on the west side of Jacobs Creek, and the rest of said 110 acres I give to son Theophilus. Witnesses—Rebecca Burrowes, Josiah Ellis, Martha Ellis. Proved March 5, 1765.
Lib. 12, p. 146.

1764, June 13. Baird, Alexander, of Somerset Co. Int. Adm'r— William Baird. Fellowbondsman—Lucas Voorhees; both of said Co.

1764, July 2. Inventory, £117.2.6, made by Adriaen Bennet and Henry Crusee. Lib. 12, p. 16.

1763, Sept. 25. Baird, Margaret, of Tewksbury, Hunterdon Co.; widow of William Baird; will of. Grandson, George O'Harrah, 10 shillings, when 21. Grandson, James O'Harah, £20. My daughter, Margaret Jennings, rest of personal and real. Executors—Isaiah Jennings and Margaret Jennings. Witnesses—Richard Porter, John Welsh, George Williams. Proved Jan. 2, 1764.

1763, Dec. 15. Inventory, £300.14.0, made by, Richard Porter and Andrew Schandler. Lib. 11, p. 522.

1765, Feb. 17. Baird, Richard, of Readings town, Hunterdon Co.; will of. Wife, Elizabeth, as many household goods as she may want. Rest of personal and real estate to be sold and the money divided between my wife, and my two sons, William and John, and my daughter, Elizabeth, to have ½ as much. Sons are not 12 years of age. Executors—my wife and my father-in-law, John Ross. Witnesses—Richard Porter, Peter Covenhoven, William Porter. Proved March 20, 1765.

1765, March 9. Inventory, £394.10.6, made by Aaron Lane and Peter Couvenhoven.

1768, June 24. Account, by John Rose, executor.
Lib. 12, p. 136; Lib. 13, p. 440.

1754, March 5. Baker, Daniel, of New Brunswick, Middlesex Co., yeoman; will of. My eldest daughter, Ann Chapman, £15. My youngest daughter, Agnis Tomson, £15. Real estate to be sold, and ½ the money to be given to the children of my daughter, Ann Chapman, and the other ½ to the children of my daughter, Agnis Tomson. Executors—son-in-law, John Tomson, and friend, Jonathan Combs. Witnessses—Simon Van Dike, Peter Gulick, John Van Dike (son of Simon). Proved April 6, 1764. Lib. H, p. 417.

1764, Nov. 22. Baker, Daniel, of Middlesex Co. Int. Adm'x—Susannah Baker, the widow, of said Co. Fellowbondsman—Thomas Baker, of Essex Co. Lib. H, p. 375.

1762, April 18. Baker, Joseph, of Bridgetown, Burlington Co.; will of. Wife, Rachel, one half of the profits of house and lot where I live, and the other ½ to my daughter, Hannah. Son, John, the personal estate. Witnesses—George Kemble, Nathan Albertson, Jm Mulock.
1762, April 18. Codicil. Executors to be my wife, Rachel, and her father, Thomas Kimble. Witnesses—same as above.
1762, July 5. Adm'x—Rachel Baker. Lib. 11, p. 226.

1762, July 5. Baker, Joseph, of Northampton, Burlington Co. Int. Adm'x—Rachel Baker. Fellowbondsman—Samuel Kemble; both of said place. Witness—Samuel Allinson.
1762, May 17. Inventory, £97.17.9, made by Henry Knight and Daniel Jones, Jr.
1767, Sept. 2. Account, made by Rachel Jewell, late Rachel Baker, Adm'x. Lib. 11, p. 226.

1766, June 7. Baker, Thomas, of Greenwich, Gloucester Co., husbandman. Int. Adm'r—Adam Sharp. Fellowbondsman—Isaiah Davenport; both of said place. Witness—Sarah Howell.
1765, Dec. 26. Inventory, £20.5.10½, made by Isaiah Davenport and —— ——? Lib. 12, p. 381.

1764, May 12. Baldwin, Aaron, of Newark, Essex Co.; will of. Wife, Dorcas, real and personal while my widow. All my lands to my sons, when the younger comes to age. Eldest son's part to remain in hands of his mother till his brothers are of age; then they to take it and care for him, as long as they shall live. To each of my eldest daughters, £16. Executors—my wife, Dorcas, and Elijah Baldwin. Witnesses—Lewis Nichols, John Crane, Obadiah Bruen. Proved May 23, 1764.
1764, June 7. Inventory, £130.5.0, made by John Crane and Nehemiah Baldwin. Lib. H, p. 440.

1763, June 3. Baldwin, Elihu, of Mendham, Morris Co. Int. Adm'r—John Cary, of said place, carpenter. Fellowbondsman—Jephthah Byram, of Newton, Sussex Co., yeoman. Witness—William Hyndman. Lib. 11, p. 475.

———, —— ——. Baldwin, Elijah, of Newark, Essex Co.; will of. Wife, Elizabeth, £100. Sons, Nathaniel and Elias, my house and home lot. To my other sons, Cornelius, Luther, Zachaes and Jonathan, and the child of which my wife is pregnant, if a son, all my other lands, but, if it be a girl, then to Cornelius, Luther, Zachaus, and Jonathan, and they to pay to her £100. Daughters, Phebe, and Hannah, £100 each. (Hannah not yet 18). Wife to have use of all estate till the children are of age. Executors—my wife, Elizabeth, my brother, Ebenezer Baldwin, and my sons, Nathaniel and Elias. Witnesses—Isaac Baldwin, Samuel Curry, William Burnet. Proved June 4, 1766. Lib. I, p. 12.

1770, Aug. 26. Baldwin, Joseph, of Hopewell, Hunterdon Co., yeoman; will of. Wife, Elizabeth, to be provided for by son Nathaniel. To son, Nathaniel, rest of personal and real, and he is to provide for his two sisters, Elizabeth and Jemima, till they are 18, and then give my daughter, Elizabeth, £50, and Jemima like sum. Executors—my wife and son, Nathaniel. Witnesses—William Bainbridge, Foster Burrowes, Josiah Ellis. Proved Oct. 15, 1770. Lib. 14, p. 336.

1765, Nov. 28. Baldwin, Nehemiah, of Newark, Essex Co.; will of. Wife, Mary, use of real and personal, until my son Joel is 21, and then ⅓ of the same. Son, Isaac, £30, when 21. Sons, Samuel, £230, who is to be sent to college. To sons, Isaac, Joel, Jesse and Caleb, all my lands. Daughter, Eunice Baldwin, £80. Daughters, Mary, Sarah and Phebe, £60 when 18. After my wife's death the remainder to my children, Isaac, Joel, Samuel, Jesse, Caleb, Hannah, Eunice, Mary, Sarah and Phebe. Executors—my wife, my brother Stephen Baldwin, Elijah Baldwin, Thomas Brown and Ebenezer Baldwin. Witnesses—Joseph Riggs, William Burnet, David Ogden. Proved Dec. 27, 1765.
1767. —— ——. Inventory, £238.8.7½, made by Stephen Baldwin, Ebenezer Baldwin and Thomas Brown.
1769, Oct. 5. Account made by Executors. Paid Unice Brown, her legacy, whose husband is Daniel Brown. (She being a daughter of testator.) Lib. I, p. 10.

1764, March 17. Baldwin, Samuel, of Morristown, Morris Co.; will of. Wife, Elizabeth, £40. Also £40, to my son Samuel. Boyce Prudden, my son-in-law, £8. Remainder to my wife, son and daughter. Executors—Silas Halsey, of Morristown, and Nehemiah Baldwin, of Newark. Witnesses—Ezekiel Cheever, Jonas Goble, Susannah Hayes. Proved April 23, 1764. Lib. H, p. 431.

1764, July 16. Baldwine, Jonas, of Woodbridge, Middlesex Co., doctor; will of. Moveables and lands to be sold. Wife, Mary, to have all, except, £70 which I give to children of my father-in-law, Nathaniel Fitz Randolph, viz., Robert, Thomas, Nathaniel, Catrine, Margaret, Elizabeth and Edward. Executors—wife, Mary, Eseck Fitz Randolph, and Joseph Shotwell. Witnesses—Cowperthwaite Copland, Mary Bunn, John Lovce. Proved July 30, 1764. Lib. H, p. 451.

1767, Aug. 3. Baley, Thomas, of Borough of Elizabeth, Essex Co.; will of. Wife, Phebe Baley, her thirds and the wench, Dinah, till son, Thomas, is of age. Son, John, negro boy, Zeb. To sons, John, Thaddeus, Squire, Samuel and Thomas, all my lands. Daughters, Mary and Esther, each £10. Daughters, Phebe, Deborah and Nancy, each £40. Executors—Isaac Woodruff and Jonathan J. Dayton, who are to pay the children when they come of age. Witnesses—Nathaniel Sturgis, Samuel Durand, Stephen Bedford. Proved Oct. 1, 1768.
Lib. K, p. 34.

1764, Sept. 18. Ball, Ezra, of Knowlton, Sussex Co., yeoman. Int. Adm'r—Isaiah Ball, Fellowbondsman—William Rush; both of said place, yeomen.
1764, Sept. 17. Inventory, £6.12.10, made by William Rush and Richard Manning. Isaiah Ball and Zopher Ball are surviving partners of Ezra Ball, deceased. Lib. 12, p. 233.

1768, April 18. Ball, John, Jr., of Hanover Twsp., Morris Co., will of. Wife, Bettey, the use of my house and home lot, given to me by deed from my father, and other lands. Son, Ephraim, horse and saddle. Daughter, Jemime, £20. Sons, Ephraim and Moses, 6 acres which I bought of Henry Burnet. Son, John, my home lot. Daughters, Abigail and Luce, £20 each when 18. Executors—wife, Bettey, and brother, Samuel Ball. Witnesses—John Ball, Enoch Beach, William Broadwell. Proved Jan. 19, 1769. Lib. K, p. 61.

1770, March 8. Ball, John, of Elizabeth Town, Essex Co., painter; will of. To my wife, £10 and use of real and personal, while my widow. Children, William, John and Mary Ball, to have the use of the remainder for their keep and schooling, as my executors think propr, and, when they are 21, are to have the principal. Executors —my wife, Tamer, and Edward Thomas. Witnesses—Broughton Reynolds, Stephen Potter, Enoch Scudder. Proved April 10, 1770.
Lib. K, p. 201.

1763, March 18. Ball, Samuel, of Newark, Essex Co., yeoman. Int. Adm'x—Sarah Ball, the widow. Fellowbondsmen—Eleazer Baldwin and Phinehas Baldwin; all of Newark.
1763, June 21. Inventory, £295.17.8, made by Nathaniel Farrand and Caleb Wheler. Lib H, p. 356.

1761, Feb. 16. Ballard, Joseph, of Burlington Co. Int. Adm'r— William Imlay, of Bordentown, said Co., merchant. Fellowbondsman—William Potts, of said Co.
1761, Feb. 17. Inventory, £12.2.3, made by John Butler, Jr., and Samuel Farnsworth. Lib. 10, p. 173.

1761, May 4. Ballingr, Joshua, of Evesham, Burlington Co., yeoman; will of. Daughter, Charity, her own mother's bed, and £10. Daughter, Martha, her mother's chest, when 18, and £15. Wife, Naomi, household goods. Son, Thomas, land; and his younger brothers, Zacheus and Enoch, £100 each, when 21. Executors—my wife and friend, Josiah Prickett. Witnesses—Abraham Leeds, Agnes Hewlings, Enoch Roberts. Proved June 22, 1761. Lib. 10, p. 208.
1761, June 15. Inventory, £417.0.11, made by James Cattell and Isaac Evens.

1763, Feb. 25. Ballinger, Thomas, of Evesham, Burlington Co., ward. Son of Joshua Ballinger of said place. Bond of Francis Dudly, of said Co., husbandman, as Guardian. Fellowbondsman— Daniel Ellis, of City and Co. of Burlington. Witness—Samuel Allinson. Lib. 11, p. 279.

1770, April 14. Balts, Jacob, of Cape May Co. Int. Adm'r—Reuben Ludlam. Fellowbondsman—Silvanus Tounsend; both of same Co. Witnesses—Eli Eldridge and John Phillips.
1770, April 24. Inventory, £171.4.10, made by Silvanus Tounsend and Eli Eldredge..
1771, account by Adm'r. Includes "expenses on said estate by Henry Linn, one of the heirs to said estate, for trouble in proving heirship, Power of Att'y," etc. Lib. 15, p. 72; Lib. 14, p. 409.

1761, March 19. Bancraft, David, of Cape May Co., blacksmith; will of. Wife, Abigail, ⅓ of moveable estate, and ⅓ of land during life. Eldest son, David, my house and land when 21, he to pay to his brother, Samuel, £10. Rest of moveable estate to be turned into money and put to interest for use of my son Samuel Bancraft and Margaret Bancraft, and they to have principal, the son when 21 and daughter when 18. Son, David, my shop and tools, but my brother, Ephraim, to have the use of them till David is 21, and Ephraim to pay 40 shillings each year to my widow, Abigail, and to take my son David at age of 16 years and teach him the smith trade. "Whereas I have left an account against my father's estate, and I give them 10 years before it is paid." Executors—brother-in-law, Richard Stiles, and my wife, Agigail. Witnesses—Aaron Eldredge, Mary Simpkins, Frances Taylor. Proved June 25, 1761.

1761, April 25. Inventory, £83.3.3, made by John Eldredge and Isaac Newton.   Iib. 11, p. 76.

1768, April 11. Bancraft, John, of Cape May Co. Int. Adm'x—Phebe Bancraft, relict of said John. Fellowbondsmen—John Eldredge and John Newton; both of said Co., Gentlemen. Witnesses—Nathan Church and Seth Whilldin.

1768, April 6. Inventory, £107.6.8, made by John Eldredge and John Newton.   Lib. 13, p. 332.

1759, July 4. Bancraft, Samuel, of Cape May Co.; will of. Wife, Margrate, use of ⅓ my land while my widow. Son, David, the land that is on the east side of the Kings road. Sons, David and Ephraim, the rest of lands. Daughter, Sarah Buck, 5 shillings. Daughter, Phebe Bancraft, 5 shillings. Daughter, Elizabeth Reeves, £10. Daughter, Johannah Bancraft, £10. Grandson, John Newton, 5 shillings. Executors—my wife and son Ephraim. Witnesses—Benjamin Laughton, Elizabeth Stillwell, John Leek. Proved June 25, 1761.

1760, Nov. 9. Inventory, £55.10.0, made by Isaac Newton and John Eldredge.   Lib. 11, p. 69.

1761, June 25. Bancraft, Thomas, of Cape May Co. Int. Adm'r—John Bancraft. Fellowbondsman—John Eldredge; both of said Co. Witnesses—Elizabeth Stillwell and Elijah Hughes.

1761, June 25. Inventory, £69.9.3, made by John Eldredge and Isaac Newton.   Lib. 11, p. 73.

1760, June 6. Banta, Jacob, of Paramus, Bergen Co.; will of. My moveable estate and 25 acrs, and two places in the church, to be sold. Farm to be rented till my oldest son is of age. Wife, Lena. Oldest son, John, one shilling, and when he is of age, the farm to be sold, and money equally to sons John and Wiert, they to provide for their mother. Executors—wife, Lenna, and my brothers, David Banta and Hendrick Banta. Witnesses—David Ackerman, Albert Ackerman and Williams Cairns.

1762, Sept. 15. Codicil. Son, Hendrick, to be an equal sharer with my sons John and Weirt. Witnesses—David Ackerman, Albert Ackerman and William Cairns. Proved Feb. 4, 1764.   Lib. H, p. 402.

1767, April 14. Banta, Jacob, of Bergen Co. Int. Adm'r—Derrick Banta, the eldest son. Fellowbondsman—Reynier Van Giesen; both of said Co. Witness—John Mackay.

1767, April 22. Inventory, £62.7.9, made by Davyd Banta and Yoosse Zabrisk.   Lib. I, p. 107.

1764, Sept. 5. Barbar, Matthias, of Hardwick, Sussex Co., innkeeper. Int. Adm'x—Jane Barbar, widow. Fellowbondsman—John Todd, yeoman; both of said Co.
1764, Aug. 21. Inventory, £150.4.0, made by Jeremiah Hendershot and John Todd. Lib. 12, p. 285.

1765, July 26. Barber, Hannah, of Pilesgrove, Salem Co. Int. Adm'r—George Lawrence, of Penns Neck, said Co., yeoman. Fellowbonrsmen—Jechonias Wood, tanner, and John Loyd, cordwainer; both of Pilesgrove.
1765, July 18. Inventory, £53.3.0, made by Jechonias Wood and John Loyd. Lib. 12, p. 227.

1765, May 25. Barber, Jacob, of Pilesgrove, Salem Co., carpenter. Int. Adm'x—Rebecca Barber, widow. Fellowbondsmen—Peter Keen and Isaac Barber, yeomen; all of said place.
1765, May 15. Inventory, £86.19.7, made by Peter Keen and Isaac Barber. Lib. 12, p. 227.

1770, April 21. Barberie, John, of City of Perth Amboy, Middlesex Co.; will of. Real estate to be sold. I have given to my daughter, Susanna Johnston, wife of John Johnston, Jr., £110, and each of my children are to have a like sum when 21. Wife, Gertruyde, rest of my estate, for the benefit of my children, namely, Catherine, Susanna, Peter, John, Andrew, Frances, Oliver, Lambert and Gertruyde. who are to have the rest after wife's death. Executors—wife, Gertruyde, my daughter, Catherine; sons, Peter and John, as they come of age, and John Smyth. Witnesses—Ravaud Kearny, Stephen Johnston, John Thomson. Proved Sept. 22, 1770.
1785, Feb. 17. Adm's—Bowes Reed, and James Throckmorten. Fellowbondsman—John Lawrence. The said Adm's were appointed to execute the purposes of the wills of John and Gertrude Barberie, according to an Act of the Legislature. Witnesses—Thomas Adams and Lambert Barberie. Lib. K, p. 242.

1769, Dec. 11. Bard, Peter, of Mount Holly in Burlington Co. Int. Samuel Bard renounced, as he was in poor health, and desired that Dr. John Bard, or his son, Samuel Bard, and Daniel Ellis, of Burlington, may be made Adm'rs. Witnesses—Henry Paxson and John De Normandie.
1769, Dec. 14. Bond of Daniel Ellis as Adm'r. Fellowbondsman—James Sterling, of said Burlington, merchant. Lib. 14, p. 124.

1769, Nov. 27. Bard, Samuel, of Burlington Co.; will of. The brick house in Mount Holly, and the land joining the Iron Works, and all other real I bought of my father, and my personal estate, to be sold; and wife, Mary, to have proceeds. Executors—father, Peter Bard, and friend, Zachariah Rossell. Witnesses—Sarah Treadwell, Jonathan Odell, Sarah Bard. Proved Dec. 20, 1769. Lib. 14, p. 135.
1769, Dec. 28. Inventory, £270.2.9, made by John Clark and Daniel Jones, Jr.

1762, Jan. 13. Bardan, John, of New Barbadoes, Bergen Co.; will of. Son, John, my Dutch Bible for his birthright. Daughters, Eva and Sarah, land on west side of road. Sons, Isaac and Hendrick, rest of real. Children, John, Isaac, Hendrick, Sarah and Eva my timber.

Executors—son, John and son-in-law, Poulus VanDer Beek. Witnesses—Isaac Vanderbeek, Jacob Zabriskie and Guilliam Bertholf.
Proved 2 July, 1762. Lib. H, p. 287.

1749, June 23. Barkalow, William, of Upper Freehold, Monmouth Co.; will of. Wife, Annitie, the whole estate, while my widow. To my 3 children, my whole estate, only I give my eldest son, Aurt, £10 more. Executors—my wife, and my brothers, John Hance, and William Williamson. Witnesses—Lefferd Lefferson, Lucas Drvedt, William Dunterfield. Proved April 29, 1767.
1766, Sept. 11. Renunciation, made by Aeltie Barkalow and William Williamson, stating that William Barkalow made his will when he had but 3 children, but, recovering his health, lived till the 8th of August last, and had other 5 children, and as he died unexpectedly and made no other will; and we being made executors in said will, do refuse to execute the same, to the wronging of the other 5 children, and the three that were then living, being willing to come to a just division with the other five, we do refuse to act, and I, Aeltie Barkalow, desire my sons, Arthur Barkalow and Derick Barkalow, and my brother-in-law, Peter Forman, to be Administrators.
1766, Sept. 11. Renunciation, made by John Hance.
1766, Sept. 15. Inventory £826.0.6, of some cattle at Wadeing River, in Burlington Co.
1766, Sept. 23. Inventory, £739.0.6, made by Robert Rhea and James Lawrence.
1767, April 14. Adm's—Arthur Barkalow, Derick Barcalow and Peter Forman; all of said Co. Fellowbondsman—James Lawrence.
Lib. 12, p. 469.

1765, Jan. 24. Barker, Richard, of Stow Creek, Cumberland Co., cooper; will of. Wife, Ruth, ⅛ the personal estate, and the rest divided in 7 parts, and eldest son, John, to have two parts; son, Samuel, one part; son, William, one part; son, Isaac, one part; daughter, Mary Barker, one part, and son, Richard, one part. (William, Isaac and Richard, under 21, and Mary not 18). Executors—wife, and son, John. Witnesses—Samuel Wood, Wade Barker, Ann Garison. Proved Feb. 19, 1765.
1765, Feb. 19. Inventory, £745.4.7, made by Reuben Jarman and Daniel Maskell. Lib. 12, p. 82.

1724, Jan. 9. Barker, Samuel, of Barlbrough, Co. of Darby, England, Gent; will of. Niece, Mary Bullus, who lives with me, all my houses and lands in Co. of Darby, during her life. Grandson, Samuel Boulsbey, to have said lands, after her death, as also my lands in West New Jersey. Mentions grandsons and granddaughter, Boulbies; granddaughter, Elizabeth Boden, Martha Boulby, the mother of said Samuel Boulsby; three daughters of my son-in-law, Thomas Boulsbey; my grandson, Jordan Boldsby; daughter, Martha Boulsbey, and Thomas Boulsbey, her husband; daughter-in-law, Mary Parker. Executor—said Mary Bullus. Witnesses—Jer. Ludlam, William Mackon, George Marshall, and Samuel Bullus. Proved Jan. 8, 1729.
Examined at Barlbrough by John Tantum, and Daniel Bacon, "who declare the above to be a true copy, this Feb. 4, 1729." Examined with the original, this June 25, 1761. Lib. 10, p. 303.

1770, March 19. Barker, William, of Greenwich, Cumberland Co. Int. Adm'x—Hannah Barker, widow. Fellowbondsman—John Barker, of Hopewell, said Co., yeoman.
1771, Feb. 15. Inventory, £89.0.0, made by Thomas Maskell and Reuben Jerman. Lib. 15, p. 7.

1763, Oct. 5. Barklow, William, of Somerset Co. Ward. Son of Farrington Barklow, of said Co., deceased, who makes choice of John Vandyke as his Guardian.
1763, Oct. 5. Guardian—John Van Dike, of Somerset Co., yeoman. Fellowbondsman—Daniel Barcolow, of Middlesex Co., yeoman.
Lib. 11, p. 442.

1760, March 27. Barns, Abraham, of Cumberland Co.; will of. Wife, Prisylah, to have 100 acres where Jonathan Barns lives, in a tract taken up by a right surveyed by Jacob Richman, and 40 acres of marsh below Ebenezer Wescut, while she lives; and if the child that she is going to have be a girl, then I give to my two daughters, my lands; if it be a son, then I give him ⅔. Executors—Enoch Bowen and my wife, Prisylah. Witnesses—Joseph Haines, James Harris, Hannah Filer. Proved April 25, 1765.
1765, May 1. Inventory, £152.12.8, made by Enos Seeley and Joseph Datan. Lib. 12, p. 165.

1766, June 5. Barns, David and Samuel, of Cumberland Co. Wards. Petition of Phebe Hays, late widow of David Barns, late of Fairfield, Cumberland Co., deceased, and mother of Samuel and David Barns, stated that these children had lands granted to them by deed from their grandfather, Samuel Barns, since the death of their father, and that her sons made choice of her brother Jonathan Bowen, as their Guardian, till 14.
1766, May 5. Guardian—Jonathan Bowen, of Hopewell, said Co. Fellowbondsmen—Seth Bowen, of Greenwich, said Co.; shipwright.
Lib. 12, p. 328.

1765, Jan. 3. Barratt, Abigail, of Hopewell, Cumberland Co. Int. Adm'rs—James Barratt, and Caleb Barratt, both of Hopewell, yeomen. Witnesses—Phebe Ewing and Maskell Ewing.
1765, Jan. 9. Inventory, £107.2.6½, made by Jonathan Ayars and Samuel Harris. Lib. 12, p. 103.

1762, Jan 22. Barratt, Gwin, of Salem Twsp., Salem Co., spinster; will of. Sister, Elizabeth Mulford, all my real and personal, except what is hereafter excepted, and she must take care of my sister, Rachel Barratt, during her life; but, if she do not, then my brother, George Colson, or any other surviving brother, or sister, shall have the said estate, and keep said Rachel Barratt. My brother, George Colson, is to take care of my nephew, Enoch Barratt, and, when he is 15 years of age, to put him to learn a trade. Executors—brother-in-law, Stephen Mulford, and my brother, George Colson, that is to say, that Stephen Mulford is to be one of my executors so long as my sister, Elizabeth (his wife), shall live. Witnesses—Thomas Goodwin, Robert Wilson. Proved May 5, 1762. Lib. 11, p. 188.

1768, Feb. 22. Bartholomew, Daniel, of Amwell Twsp., Hunterdon Co. Int. Adm'rs—John Bartholomew, yeoman. Fellowbondsman—

CALENDAR OF WILLS—1761-1770   33

John Hanna, clerk, both of Bethlehem Twsp., said Co. Witness—Margaret Kirkpatrick.
1768, Feb. 24. Inventory, £113.17.9, made by Garret Lake and Thomas Lake.
1769, Feb. 17. Account made by Johan Bartholomew, the Adm'r. "Paid James Yeomans Kelly, for schooling the children, £1." "Goods and cash, which Elizabeth Bartholomew had to her use" (the widow).
Lib. 13, p. 335; Lib. 13, p. 494.

1768, Oct. 11. Bartow, Daniel, of Middlesex Co. Int. Adm's—Isaac Harris, principal creditor. Fellowbondsman—John Pearsall; both of said Co.
1768, Oct. 10. Renunciation, made by Unis Bartow, the widow, in favor of Doctor Isaac Harris.
1768, Oct. 11. Inventory, £41.17.9, made by Daniel Drake and James Lennox.
Lib. I, p. 336.

1769, Feb. 15. Bartrom, John, of Bergen Co., blacksmith; will of. Wife, Agnes, use of real and personal. Eldest son, Joseph, the old place at Wimbeamis. Daughter, Ann, £20, when 21. Son, Antoney, house, shop and stoves. Executors—wife, Agnis, and my brother-in-law, Joost Beam. Witnesses—James Miller, Dedrick Tise and James Board.
1769, May 3. Agnis Bartram renounced in presence of Coenraet Beam and Abram Beam. Proved April 29, 1769.
Lib. K, p. 97.

1763, Jan. 29. Bartron, David, of Readington, Hunterdon Co. Int. Adm'r—John Bartron.
Lib. 11, p. 339.

1761, Dec. 31. Bassett, Stephen, of Essex Co., merchant; will of. Wife, Ann, use of real and personal, and at her death, or marriage, to be divided among my children, Ann, Mary, Susannah and Eleanor. Daughters, Susannah and Eleanor, when they come of age, or are married, to have £60 each for their outset. Executors—my friend, Peter Simmons, sadler, and my wife, Ann. Witnesses—Petrus Poulusse, Robert Drummond, Jr., David Marinus. Proved May 2, 1763.
Lib. H, p. 388.

1769, Jan. 6. Bassett, William, of Pilesgrove Twsp., Salem Co., yeoman; will of. Personal and real estate to be sold. Wife, Phebe, £150, and the profits of my estate, and to bring up my children. Daughters, Mary Bassett and Abigail Bassett, the remainder when 18. Mentioned sister, Elizabeth Davis's four sons, Elisha, Isaac, John and Thomas Davis. Executrix—my wife. Witnesses—Reese Kindell, George Colson, William Colson. Proved Feb. 25, 1769.
1769, Feb. 22. Inventory, £225.8.6, made by Lamuel Lippincott and Jacob Davis.
Lib. 13, p. 498.

1767, Aug. 28. Bassett, Zebedee, of Salem Co. Int. Adm'x—Rachel Bassett, widow. Fellowbondsmen—Daniel Bassett and Adam Rudderford, yeomen; all of Pilesgrove, Salem Co.
1767, Aug. 15. Inventory, £204.2.2, made by Joseph Champneys and Peter Keen.
Lib. 13, p. 190.

1766, Nov. 8. Bastedo, John, of Middlesex Co. Int. Adm's—Robert Armstrong and Catharine Armstrong, late Catharine Bastedo,

3

widow of said John Bastedo. Fellowbondsman—Hugh Armstrong; all of said Co. Lib. I, p. 7.
1766, Oct. 27. Inventory, £118.1.8, made by George Wetherill and Daniel South.
1766, Dec. 23. Inventory, £58.10.0, made by Daniel South, and Samuel Okeson.
Account (not dated) made by Adm'rs.

1768, July 23. Bastedo, Joseph, of Middlesex Co., blacksmith; will of. Brother, Thomas Bastedo, all real and personal, and he to pay to my brother John, after my mother's death, £30, and to my sister, Hannah Bastedo, £30, and to brother, William, £30, and to my sister, Anne, £30, and to my brother, George, £30. Executors—friends, George Garretson and Joakim Gulick, son of Samuel. Witnesses—Samuel Grom, Joglem Gulyck, Samuel Smith. Proved Nov. 28, 1768.
Lib. K, p. 6.

1767, March 25. Bastick, Henry, late of Philadelphia. Int. Bond of John Bastick, of Philadelphia, carpenter, as Adm'r. Bondsman—John Shaw, of same place, inn keeper. Witness—Joseph Read.
Lib. 13, p. 102.

1765, Jan. 29. Bate, Elizabeth, of Gloucester Twsp. and Co., widow; will of. Daughter, Mary Harker, my plantation in said Twsp., whereon I make my home with Thomas Bishop, till her son, Joseph Bate Harker, is 21, when he shall have the same; and my daughter, Mary Harker, shall pay to her sisters, Martha Hunt and Abigail Grinaway, £5 each. Granddaughter Mary Clark, my bed. Grandson, Samuel Flanningim, £8. Son, George Flaningin, the rest. Executor —my son George. If my grandson, Joseph Bate Harker, should die before 21, then the said lands shall descend to his brother, John Harker. Witnesses—Laban Langstaff, Tatum Williams, Joseph Garwood. Proved Jan. 22, 1768.
1768, Jan. 22. Adm'r—Jonathan Aborn, with the will annexed. Inventory, £11.19.0. Lib. 12, p. 494.

1769, Feb. 28. Bateman, Moses, of Fairfield, Cumberland Co. Int. Adm'rs—Nehemiah Bateman and Thomas Joslin; both of said Co., yeomen.
1769, Feb. 10. Inventory, £65.0.3, made by Silas Newcomb and John Bateman.
1770, March 24. Account by both Adm'rs. "Cash received from the Sheriff, on the sale of land, £45.6.9." Lib. 13, p. 497; Lib. 15, p. 13.

1763, April 14. Bateman, Thomas, of Cumberland Co. Ward. Son of Thomas Bateman, of Fairfield, in said Co. Guardian—John Bateman, of Fairfield Twsp., said Co. Fellowbondsman—John Bereman, of Stow Creek, said Co.; both yeomen. Witnesses—Abigail Ewing and Phebe Ewing. Lib. 11, p. 410.

1760, March 6. Bates, John, of Hanover, Morris Co.; will of. All my lands and effects to be laid out for the maintenance of my mother, Abigail Bates, during her life. David Bates, the son of William Bates, my lands and effects. Executor—brother, Joseph Kitchel. Witnesses—Abraham Kitchel, Moses Kitchel, John Acken. Proved Oct. 12, 1761. Lib. H, p. 71.

CALENDAR OF WILLS—1761-1770   35

1766, March 27. Bates, John, of Deptford Twsp., Gloucester Co., yeoman; will of. Wife, Sarah, my personal estate. Son, Daniel, plantation which I had of my father on one of the branches of Great Mantoes Creek, in this Twsp., but he is to support my father, Daniel Bates, in such a manner as I have agreed to do; but my wife is to support him till my son comes of age. Rest of real to be sold, and ⅓ the money to be given to my wife, and the rest to my other children, namely, Joseph, Joshua, John, Aaron, Elizabeth and Sarah. Executors—my wife, and my friend, Joshua Evans. Witnesses—Allan Sharp, Bartholomew Stiles, S. Blackwood. Proved April 15, 1767.
1767, March 18. Inventory, £301.17.3, made by Joshua Stokes and Allan Sharp.   Lib. 13, p. 123.

1765, Sept. 6. Bates, Thomas, of Hanover, Morris Co.; will of. My wife to have household goods and her maintenance out of the estate. Son, Daniel Bates, £30. Daughter, Sarah Bates, £10. Rest to children, Daniel Bates, Sarah Bates, Hannah Bates, Rachel Bates, Eunis Bates, and Mary Bates. Land to be sold. Executors—Nehemiah Baldwin and Joseph Kitchel. Witnesses—Joseph Foster, Grace Ford, Moses Kitchel. Proved Dec. 3, 1766.   Lib. I, p. 180.

1767, Dec. 8. Bates, William, of Fequanack, Morris Co.; will of. Wife, Rebecca, a third of my estate, and the rest to my two daughters, Cathrine and Rhoda. Executors—my wife, and my friend, John Huntington, cooper. Witnesses—Ephraim Goble, Stephen Beach. Proved Sept. 3, 1770.
1770, Feb. 17. Renunciation by Rebecca Bates. Witnesses—Ephraim Goble and Stephen Beach.   Lib. K, p. 278

1766, Sept. 14. Batten, Francis, of Greenwich, Gloucester Co., yeoman; will of. Wife, Ann, £20, and the ⅓ part of my real estate. Son, Thomas Batten, land which I bought of John Allford. Son, Francis, 50 acres which my brother, John, used to have. Son, Edward, land I bought of Elias Boys. Son, Abner, the meadow by Joseph Shute, on Raccoon Creek. Son, Richard, land that was bought of John Allford. To Benjamin Cheesman, the son of Benjamin Cheesman, 4 acres on Raccoon Creek. To Elizabeth, four acres and 5 shillings. To Hannah Boys, 5 shillings. To Mary Rumford, 5 shillings. To Ann Horner, £4, to be left with her mother to buy a set of drawers. To Zillah Gill, £5, to be left in her mother's hands. To my daughter, Sarah Batten, £20. To my daughter, Deborah Batten, £20. To sons Edward and Abner, rest of moveable estate. Executors—my wife, and my son, Thomas. Witnesses—Josiah Fowler, Simon Kam, William Guest, Sr. Proved July 17, 1767.
1767, June 27. Inventory, £1030.14.11, made by William Guest and Jacob Spicer.   Lib. 13, p. 127.

1762, Nov. 21. Baynton, Benjamin, of Burlington, gentleman; will of. Cousin, Elizabeth Stapleford, £50. Friend, Thomas Polegreen, £5. Cousin, Jane Dirkinderin, of Philadelphia, shopkeeper, £10. Aunt Ann Wheeler my house and chaise. Niece, Mary Baynton, eldest daughter of my brother, John Baynton, gold watch. Niece, Esther Baynton, gold ring. Nephew, Benjamin Baynton, Jr., silver watch. Aunt Anna Wheeler, all real and personal that was devised to me by my mother, Mary Baynton. The personal and real devised to me by my father, Peter Baynton, I give to my brother, John Baynton. Executors—Aunt Ann Wheeler and my brother, John Baynton. Witnesses—Stephen Woolley, Lindsay Coats, John Barnes, Jr. Proved Aug. 13, 1763. Lib. 11, p. 375.

1768, June 4. Beach, Abner, of Hanover, Morris Co.; will of. Wife, Sarah, my lands and goods. Son, Joseph, 5 shillings. Executors—my wife, and my son Isaac. Witnesses—Samuel Parritt, Isaac Sergeant, John Cobb. Proved Dec. 8, 1768. Lib. K, p. 60.

1768, Oct. 22. Beach, Ephraim, of Hanover, Morris Co. Int. Adm'rs —John Cobb and Benjamin Howell; both of said place.
1768, Oct. 22. Renunciation by Deborah Beach, widow of Ephraim, in favor of John Cobb and Benjamin Howell. Witness—Samuel Beach. Lib. I, p. 363.

1765, Feb. 15. Beach, Joseph, of Mendham, Morris Co.; will of. The land I bought of Mr. Byram's executors, and that land lying before John Cory's door, of 10 acres, and the field joining Samuel Day, to be sold. Wife, Eunice, ⅓ of the moveable estate, and use of ⅓ the lands; and the use of all lands till the children are old enough to put out. Son, Abner, rest of lands. Children, Mary, Eunice, Rachel, Joseph, Nathaniel, Hannah, Elias, Mathias, Samuel and Sary, £10 each. Executors—brother, Elisha Beach, and friends, John Cory and David Thompson. Witnesses—Isaac Rabbit, Samuel Hudson, William Hudson. Proved March 13, 1765. Lib. H, p. 499.

1765, Feb. 26. Beakes, David, of Freehold, Monmouth Co., cordwainer. Int. Adm'r—Edmund Beakes, Jr. Fellowbondsman—John Wetherill; both of said place.
1765, Feb. 22. Inventory, £29.11.11, made by Thomas Miller and John Wetherill. Lib. 12, p. 61.

1761, Feb. 27. Beakes, William, of Upper Freehold, Monmouth Co., joiner; will of. Wife, Anne, £140, and use of 2 acres, and to live in the house with my son, David, which house and land my son, David, is to have after his mother is done with it; and if David leave no heirs, then it shall go to my son, Edmund. In order that my wife may bring up my 2 grandsons, viz., William and John, I give her £20 more. To my daughter, Elizabeth Thomas, £45, after the sale of my plantation. Daughter, Anne Beakes, £45. Grandsons, William and John Morford, £10 each, when they are 21. Plantation to be sold, which place was surveyed by my brother, Edmund Beakes. Son, David, to have the said lot. Rest of my estate to my sons, David, Edmund, Stephen, Abraham and Samuel. As my son, David, is subject to fits, I order his share to be put to interest, and the interest paid to such person as shall have the care of him. Executors —my wife, Anne, and my son, Edmund. Witnesses—William Lawrie, Jesse Woodward, Edmund Beakes. Proved Aug. 8, 1761.
1761, June 23. Inventory, £268.2.4, made by John Steward and Thomas Miller. Lib. 11, p. 63.

1766, Aug. 2. Beaty, James, of Lebanon, Hunterdon Co.; will of, Wife, Jane, the fourth of my personal and real. Children to have schooling. Children, Isabel Beaty, Alexander Beaty, Mary Beaty, Samuel Beaty, James Beaty, Esther Beaty, Jane Beaty, and such

child or children as my wife is or shall be pregnant with at the time of my decease, to have rest of estate. Executors—friends, James Martin and Alexander Rea. Witnesses—George Beaty, Robert Beaty, William Rea. Proved Feb. 16, 1767.
1766, Nov. 13. Inventory, £234.6.0, made by Thomas Hunter and Thomas Likens. Lib. 13, p. 209.

1763, June 15. Beck, John Casselton, of Essex Co. Ward. Son of John Beck, of Elizabeth Borough, said Co. Guardian—Elias Woodruff. Fellowbondsman—William Barnet; both of said Borough.
Lib. H, p. 246.

1768, Oct. 28. Bedell, Daniel, of Morristown, Morris Co. Int. Adm'r—Mathias Clark. Fellowbondsman—Abraham Rutan; both of said place.
1768, Oct. 27. Renunciation, by Agness Bedell, the widow; in favor of Mathias Clark, the highest creditor. Witness—Benjamin Bedell.
1768, Oct. 29. Inventory, made by Isaac Clark and Thomas Orsborn. Lib. I, p.363.

1761, Oct. 11. Bedell, Jacob, Sr., of Essex Co.; will of. Sons, John and Jacob, the plantation on which they live. Son, Benjamin, plantation where I live. Wife, Martha, and my sons, Daniel, Joseph and Michael, and my daughter, Martha Lains, my moveable estate. Executors—my sons, Absolom and John Bedell. Witnesses—Jonathan Elmer, Elnathan Cory, Daniel Cox. Proved Dec. 23, 1763. Lib. H, p. 326.

1768, July 11. Bedell, Jacob, of Morris Co. Int. Adm'r—Benjamin Bedell, of Essex Co. Fellowbondsman—Kennedy Vance, of Morris Co.
1768, July 13. Inventory, made by Stephen Clark and William Calwall. Lib. I, p. 302.

1768, Jan. 9. Bedell, John, of Elizabeth Town, Essex Co. Int. Adm'r—Benjamin Bedell. Fellowbondsman—Jonas Vallentine; both of Elizabeth Borough, yeomen. Witnesses—John Richards and Robert Ogden.
1768, Jan. 8. Renunciation of Hannah Bedell, the widow of John Bedell, in favor of Benjamin Bedell. Witnesses—Obadiah Valentine and William Gray. John Parson, largest creditor and the widow make choice that Benjamin Bedell, brother of the deceased, should administer.
1768, Jan. 12. Inventory, £16.5.3, made by Jeremiah Ludlam and Jonah Vallentine.
1768, Jan. 12. Account made by Adm'r.
"The land sold per the Sheriff, £72."
Files 2569-2570G; 2573-2576G; 3691-3694G.

1758, June 28. Bedent, John, of Fairfield, Cumberland Co.; will of. Daughters, Elizabeth Hildidge, Mary Robbins, Rebecka Blizard and Naomi Blizard, 10 shillings each. Daughter, Keziah Dean, a cow. Grandson, Moses Barrott, 5 shillings. Grandson, Samuel Shepherd, 5 shillings. Wife, Abigail, rest of estate. Executors—my wife and son-in-law, John Robins. Witnesses—Anne Lore, Sarah Ogden, John Ogden, Jonadab Shepherd, William Paullin, David Shepherd. Proved Aug. 18, 1761. Lib. 11, p. 170.

1760, Feb. 13. Bedlow, Susannah, of Shrewsbury, Monmouth Co.; will of. Eldest daughter, Mary, £50. House and lot to be sold, and money put to interest and divided between my daughters, Mary and Susannah, both of whom are married. To Josiah Holmes a silver tankard for the good will I bear him. Executor—said Josiah Holmes. Witnesses—Samuel Scott, James Hill, James Grover. Proved Oct. 28, 1763. Lib. I, p. 160.

1767, Oct. 8. Bee, Amos, of Gloucester Co. Ward. Son of Ephraim Bee, of Greenwich, said Co. Guardian—Jonathan Ayars. Fellowbondsman—Isaac Ayars; both of Cumberland Co. File No. 329 F.

1767, Aug. 31. Bee, Ephraim, of Greenwich, Gloucester Co., yeoman; will of. Son, Ephraim Bee, plantation where I live, and he is to find my widow, sufficient meat, drink, washing, lodging and apparel, while she is my widow. Son, Amos, 100 acres in Alloways Twsp., Salem Co. Son, Amos, to have £60 when he is 21. Daughter, Sophia Bee, £20, when she is of age. Son, Asa, £20 if he stays with his brother, Ephraim, till he is 21. Daughter, Elizabeth, 5 shillings. Daughter, Ann, £3, after Adam Sharp, her husband, pays a bond of £37, and a note of £7.10.0. Executors—my friend, Jonathan Hairs, of Cumberland Co., and my son, Ephraim. Witnesses—Amy Scott, Thomas Clark, Anthony Rush. Proved Sept. 16, 1767.
1767, Sept. 15. Inventory, £330.5.2¾, made by Thomas Clark and Joseph Bivins.
1770, Nov. 8. Account by Ephraim Bee, acting Executor.
Lib. 13, p. 135; Lib. 15, p. 64.

1767, Oct. 8. Bee, Ephraim. Ward. Guardian—Jonathan Ayars.
Lib. 13, p. 280.

1768, Jan. 9. Beedle, John. Int. Adm'r—Benjamin Beedle.
Lib. I, p. 208.

1769, Dec. 21. Beekman, Henry, of Raritan, Somerset Co., yeoman; will of. To nephews and nieces, the children of my late brother, Martin Beekman, deceased, all my real and personal estate; that is to say, to Elizabeth, Henry, Samuel, Anne and John. Executors —nephews, Henry and Samuel Beekman. Witnesses—John Baptist Dumont, Francis Brasier, Mary Dumont. Proved Jan. 15, 1770.
Lib. K, p. 148.

1762, Sept. 29. Bell, James, of Trenton, Hunterdon Co., carpenter; will of. Wife, Elizabeth, house I live in. To James Davis, £8 when of age. To James Bell Meshat, lot I bought of Squire Lewis. Executors—my wife, Alexander Chambers and John Chambers. Witnesses—Josiah Appleton, Robert Quigley, Benjamin Yard. Proved Oct. 6, 1762. Lib. 11, p. 351.

1765, Sept. 28. Bellis, Peter, of Sussex Co.; will of. Wife, Cristeen, my plantation where I live, the mills and stock, as long as she lives; but she may sell if she likes, when all is to be divided between my wife and children; except a lot of land on Paulins Kiln, joining lands of Philip Bellis, Lar Kikendal and James Brown, which lot I give to my three sons, Philip, Peter and William. John Frees is to live on the place where he now lives for 7 years. Son,

Philip, to have £50 out of the place where he formerly lived. Executors—my wife, Christian, and my son, Philip. Witnesses—Anthony Stutte, James Hanna, Richard Lanen. Proved Feb. 7, 1767.
1767, Feb. 7. Inventory, £208.17.0, made by Richard Lannen and John Green. Lib. 12, p. 464.

1761, March 7. Belliss, Adam, Sr., of Amwell Twsp., Hunterdon Co.; will of. Wife, Catherine Bellows, £200, after the expiration of 10 years. Eldest son, William Bellows, £15 more than the rest of children. Second son, Peter, £10 more than rest; and all my children to have their shares when grown up. My place to be sold after 10 years. Wife given household goods. Executors—my brother, Han William Bellows, and my wife, Catherine. Witnesses—Cornelius Williamson, Johannes Young, Mark Blair. Proved April 6, 1761.
1761, April 4. Inventory, £271.1.2, made by John Young and Cornelius Williamson. Lib. 10, p. 553.

1767, June 13. Benners, Christian, of Salem Co. Int. Adm'x—Maudlin Benners, of Mannington, widow. Fellowbondsmen—Andrew Road, of Alloways Creek, said Co., yeoman, and Matthias Miller, of Deerfield, Cumberland Co., yeoman.
1767, June 3. Inventory, £245.13.0 made by Richard Sparks and Adam Kiger. Lib. 13, p. 191.

1761, Oct. 30. Bennet, John, of Somerset Co., blacksmith. Int. Adm'r—Jaques Voorheese. Fellowbondsman—Hendrick Fisher; both of said Co.
1761, Oct. 19. Inventory, £10.1.6, made at Millstone, by Jan Kroesen, John Van Derveer and Corneles Van Hengeler.
1761, Oct. 27. Renunciation, by Geertie Bennet, the widow, in favor of Jaques Voorhees. Witness—Peter Schenck.
1761, Oct. 30. Account by Adm'r. Lib. H, p. 35.

1764, July 8.. Bennet, Mary, of Bridgetown in Twsp. of Northampton, Burlington Co., midwife; will of. Son, William Bennet, 5 shillings. Daughter, Mary Bennet, rest of real and personal. Executrix—my daughter, Mary Bennet. Witnesses—Daniel Jones, Jr., James McElhago, Aaron Smith. Proved Nov. 21, 1766.
Inventory, £112.16.6, made by Aaron Smith and Daniel Jones, Jr. Lib. 13, p. 49.

1766, April 23. Bennet, Richard, of Springfield, Burlington Co.; will of. My friend, William Stockton, to pay my debts out of money he has in trust; and the rest, except £52 that belongs to my sister, Mary Purkins, to be given to said Stockton's son, Richard. To brother, Joseph Bennet, and to Mary Purkins, Abiah Bennet (my sisters) living in New England, a mortgage of £210. Witnesses—Robert Foster, Peter Fenimore, Thomas Rozel. Proved Oct. 27, 1766.
1766, Oct. 27. Inventory, £414.19.11, made by David Stockton and Thomas Rozel. Lib. 13, p. 3.

1764, Aug. 27. Bennett, Ezekiel, of Alloways Creek, Salem Co. Int. Adm'x—Rachel Bennett, of said place, widow. Fellowbondsmen—Samuel Scudder, cordwainer, and John Pagett, yeoman; both of said place.

1764, Aug. 13. Inventory, £109.11.9, made by Thomas Sayre and John Pagett.
1768, March 10. Account, by Rachel Bennett.
Lib. 12, p. 177; Lib. 13, p. 333.

1764, April 7. Bensen, Gerret, of Hackinsack, Bergen Co., yeoman; will of. Wife, Eva, real and personal till son John is 21, then to have her living. My mother, Elizabeth Bensen, to be maintained. Mentions brothers and sisters, and daughters Elizabeth, Marytje and Jannetje. Wife now pregnant. Executors—brother, John Bensen and brother-in-law, John Bourdan. Witnesses—Johannis Bougart, Derick Lozeyr and Robert Livesey. Proved May 6, 1765.
1765, May 6. Inventory, £190.5.0, made by Johannis Bougart and Derick Lozeyr.
Lib. H, p. 574.

1767, May 28. Bergen, Frederick, of Somerset Co., yeoman; will of. Wife, Gerretie, use of real and personal. Son, Hendrick, cows. Son, Jacob, £5 for his birthright. Son, Hendrick, the plantation. Son, Jacob, £75. Daughter, Gerretje Bergen, now the wife of John Vandyck, Jr., £75. Daughter, Elsie Bergen, now the wife of Koenraet Ten Eyck, Jr., £75. Executors—my wife, Gerretje, my son Jacob, and son Hendrick. Witnesses—Peter Peterson, Cornelius Peterson, Paul Miller. Proved Nov. 22, 1762.
Lib. K, p. 103.

1768, April 25. Berkinshire, Thomas, of Burlington Co. Int. Bond of William Calvert as Adm'r. Fellowbondsman—Zachariah Rossell; both of said Co. Witness—Samuel Bard.
Lib. 13, p. 433.

1749, June 12. Berry, John, of Bergen Co., yeoman; will of. Sons, John, Samuel, Phillip, William and Abraham, my lands. Sons, John and Samuel, the land I bought of my grandfather Berry. Wife to have goods and to live in the place. Daughter, Mary, £25. Witnesses—Thomas Richarson, Gerret Van Voorst and George Vreland. Proved Nov. 19, 1767.
1767, Nov. 19. John Berry and Samuel Berry, of New Barbadoes, appointed Adm'rs with will annexed.
1767, Nov. 26. Inventory, £644.3.0, made by John Vreeland and Hendrick Kip.
Lib. I, p. 275.

1763, Jan. 29. Bertron, David, of Reading Town, Hunterdon Co. Int. Adm'r—John Bartron. Fellowbondsman—Edward Wilmot; both of said place.
1763, Jan. 28. Inventory, £29.5.8, made by Edward Wilmot and Isaac Dumott.
Lib. 11, p. 339.

1763, Aug. 4. Bevens, Evan, of Morris Co. Int. Adm'x—Hannah Bevens, the widow. Fellowbondsman—David Linn; both of said Co.
1763, Aug. 2. Inventory, £64.15.0, made by Wyllys Pierson and Stephen Mahurin.
Lib. H, p. 324.

1764, Oct. 27. Bevin, Philip, of Amwell Twsp., Hunterdon Co., yeoman; will of. Wife, Elizabeth, some personal estate and live stock. Rest of personal estate to be sold, and money put to interest, and interset, with rent of farm and other lots, I give to my wife, and she to maintain our young son, Philip; and he is to have the real when 21. Executors—friends, George Reading, Johantiel Risler, Tunis Kase,

and John Shriner. Witnesses—Daniel Robins, Isaac Robins, Mary Blair. Proved April 22, 1765.
1765, Jan. 28. Inventory, £111.12.6, made by Philip Calvin and Francis Passon.
1769, March 11. Account, by George Reading and Hontel Resler, Executors. Lib. 12, p. 139; Lib. 13, p. 493.

1761, Aug. 28. Bickerdike, Gideon, of Trenton, Hunterdon Co.; will of. Wife, Hannah, the goods she brought with her. She is to have all that shall remain after debts are paid; after her death to be divided between my sister, Mary, and her two daughters, Lydia and Ruth; and my reason is, because Stacy was taken care of by his father, and my sister, Jael, and her children, are also well provided for. To my cousin, Lydia Blakey, ½ dozen teaspoons. To cousins, Joshua and William Blakey, 3 silver spoons each. Cousin, Stacy Beaks, gold buttons. Cousin, Lydia Beakes, silver buckles. Cousin, Ruth Beakes, silver buckles and silver spoons, marked "J. D. G. B. D. C." Executrix—Esther Bickerdike. Witnessed, 14 of Feb., 1762, by Stacy Potts, Nathan Wright, Hannah Wright. Proved Feb. 26, 1762.
1762, Feb. 23. Inventory, £507.19.0¾, made by William Cleayton and Edmond Beakes.
1768, Oct. 14. Account by Esther Hoskins, late Esther Bickerdike. Twenty-two acres of land was sold to Stacy Potts for £184.5.3; lot of land was sold to Stacy Beakes for £33. Paid Hannah Bickerdike her dower, £100. Lib. 11, p. 140; Lib. 12, p. 522.

1769, Jan. 14. Bickerdike, Hannah, of Chesterfield Twsp., Burlington Co.; will of. Widow of Gideon Bickerdike. Granddaughter, Elizabeth Playtor, wife of George Playtor, a meadow in said Twsp., which I reserve for myself from the plantation which I sold to William Nutt, and, after her death, to go to her son, Watson. Granddaughter, Elizabeth Playtor, my right in land in Nottingham Twsp., and, after her death, to her son Watson. Granddaughter, Anne Welldon, my plantation in Chesterfield Twsp., which I bought of William Nutt, but if she dies without heirs, then it is to go to my grandson, Nathan Wright, and if they both die, then it is to be sold and divided among the rest of my grandchildren. Granddaughter, Hannah Welldon, £20, when 18. To my three youngest grandchildren, Catharine Wright, Rebecca Wright and Nathan Wright, £20 each, when of age. Executors—my cousin, Marmaduke Watson, and my granddaughter, Ann Welldon. Witnesses—William Nutt, George Apelgate, John Watkinson. Proved April 15, 1769.
Lib. 13, p. 514.
1769, April 12. Inventory, £446.19.2, made by Joseph Thorn and Stacy Fenton.

1766, Aug. 27. Bigger, Martha, of Bethlehem Twsp., Hunterdon Co.; will of. Son, Thomas Flemen, £5. Son, Andrew Flemen, £5. Son, William Flemen, £5. Son, Joseph Biggerd, £10. To Robert Riggerd, son of Joseph, £10. To James Riggerd, my son, £10. To James and Martha Riggerd, both the children of Robert Riggerd, £10. To my five daughters-in-law, my apparel, but Elizabeth Riggerd to have her choice of gown; the other for Mary Flemen (wife of Thomas Flemen), Tely Flemen (wife of William), Ann Riggerd (wife of Joseph Reggerd), Ann Riggerd (widow of Robert); the apparel to be

to them. Son, Andrew Flemen, 5 yards of "worst." Rest to my sons, Joseph Reggerd, James Riggerd and John Rigerd (son of James Rigger). Executors—son, James Riggird, and Francis McShane. Witnesses—Thomas Little, Catrein Littel, Jane Littel. Proved Nov. 1, 1766. [Spellings as in will, but "Bigger" proper surname].
1766, Sept. 4. Inventory, £82.13.0, made by Joseph Gorden, and Robart Little. Lib. 12, p. 408.

1766, Oct. 10. Biggers, Robert, of Bethlehem, Hunterdon Co. Int. Adm'x—Ann Biggers. Fellowbondsman—Joseph Gordon; both of said place.
1766, Aug. 7. Inventory, £116.3.3, made by Francis McShane and Joseph Gordon. Lib. 12, p. 422.

1763, Jan. 28. Biggs, Daniel, of Hopewell, Cumberland Co. Int. Adm'r—William Biggs. Fellowbondsman—John Burgin; both yeomen and of Hopewell Twsp., said Co.
1763, Jan. 27. Inventory, £195.3.10, made by Jacob Moore and John Burgin. Lib. 11, p. 305.

1763, Sept. 13. Biles, George, of Hunterdon Co. Int. Adm'rs—Thomas Biles and William Biles, Jr. Fellowbondsmen—Benjamin Biles and William Cleayton; all of said Co.
1763, Sept. 12. Inventory, £168.4.6, made by William Cleayton and Benjamin Biles. Lib. 11, p. 459.

1765, Sept. 23. Billopp, Sarah, of Perth Amboy, Middlesex Co.; will of. Widow of Thomas Billopp. Eldest son, Christopher Billopp, £100. Rest of my estate to my seven children, namely, Mary (widow of Richard Nickleson), Elizabeth, Rachel, Thomas, Sarah, Catharine and Jasper. Executors—my sons, Christopher and Thomas. Witnesses—John Berrien, Samuel Sarjant, Francis Goelet. Proved Sept. 7, 1770.
1771, May. Inventory, £2141.8.10, filed by Christopher Billopp.
Lib. K, p. 235.

1766, Aug. 25. Bills, Gershom, of Shrewsbury, Monmouth Co.; will of. All my lands to be sold, except ¼ of an acre at burying yard. After debts are paid, rest to my wife, Margaret, and children, Hannah Jackson, Daniel Bills, Rebecah Bills, Rachel Bills, Sarah Bills, Solvanes Bills, Solvester Bills, Thomas Bills and Elizabeth Bills. Those young children, which I have by my wife Margaret to be brought up on their own legacy. Executors—my friends, William Jackson, Jr., and Thomas Tilton, and my son, Daniel. Witnesses—William Pearce, Thomas Tilton, David Curtis, Jr. Proved Sept. 27, 1766.
1766, Sept. 1. Inventory made by David Johnson and Benjamin Jackson. Lib. I, p. 97.

1769, Jan. 5. Bills, William, of Shrewsbury, Monmouth Co. Ward. Son of Nathaniel Bills of said place; makes choice of Thomas Davis as his Guardian till he is 21.
1769, Jan. 5. Guardian—Thomas Davis, of Philadelphia. Fellowbondsman—John Lawrence, of City of Burlington. Witness—Joseph Read. Lib. 12, p. 523.

CALENDAR OF WILLS—1761-1770   43

1761, Feb. 27, Binge, William, of Maidenhead, Hunterdon Co., farmer; will of. Eldest son, William, all my now dwelling plantation, except what is excepted, joining land that did belong to John Johnson, deceased, Capt. John Price and John Hoff, and contains 200 acres. Youngest son, Jacob, £100. Wife, Hannah, use of negro girl Dinah, and, after my wife's death, to my daughter, Elizabeth Binge. Wife is otherwise provided for. Son, Jacob, to be put to a trade. Executors—my wife, and my son, William. Witnesses—Nathaniel Randolph, Rebekah Randolph, Samuel Randolph. Proved Feb. 18, 1767.
1767, Feb. 17. Inventory, £1066.3.6, made by John Johnson and Nathaniel Randolph.
1768, April 8. Account by William Binge, the Executor.
Lib. 13, p. 213.

1763, Feb. 18. Bird, Abigail and Margaret, of Elizabeth Town, Essex Co. Wards. Children of John Bird of said place, aged 10 and 8 years. Guardian—Samuel Wood. Fellowbondsman—Ephraim Terrill; both of said Co. Witness—John Smyth.
1763, Feb. 17. Petition of Abraham Clark, Jr., Thomas Clark, William P. Smith, Robert Ogden and Samuel Woodruff; inhabitants of Elizabeth Town, who recommend Samuel Wood, uncle of the children, as a proper person to act as Guardian. Their father, John Bird, had land in right of his wife, who is deceased since her husband, and they both died intestate.
Lib. H, p. 221.

1769, Aug. 12. Birkham, John, of Burlington, inn holder; will of. Wife, Dinah and my two daughters, to have all, share and share alike; the daughters when 18. Executor—Daniel Ellis, Esq., of Burlington. Witnesses—John Shaw, Thamson Neall, William Shaw. Proved Sept. 6, 1769.
Lib. 14, p. 74.
1769, Aug. 22. Inventory, £155.18.11, made by Isaac Heulings and John Carty.

1770, July 25. Bishop, Jeremiah, of Cumberland Co. Int. Adm'x —Anna Bishop, widow. Fellowbondsmen—Benjamin Lupton and Nathaniel Harris; all of Hopewell Twsp., said Co.
1770, July 2. Inventory, £62.7.6, made by Benjamin Lupton and Nathaniel Harris.
Lib. 15, p. 69.

1760, Dec. 15. Bishop, John, of Northampton, in Burlington Co., yeoman; will of. Wife, Rebecca, and my three daughters, Ruth, Anne and Sarah, my personal estate. Wife, Rebecca, use of plantation till my son, William, is 21. Son, William, my plantation where I dwell, which was given me by my father Thomas Bishop, and he is to pay to my youngest son, John, £100. Executors—wife, Rebecca, and my son, William. Witnesses—Caleb Ogborn, Joseph Burr, Jr., John Burr, Jr. Proved Feb. 19, 1761.
Lib. 10, p. 364.
1761, Feb. 5. Inventory, £560.16.0½, made by Thomas Moore and Joseph Burr, Jr.

1763, Dec. 6. Bishop, John, of Northampton in Burlington Co., Ward. Bond of John Hatkinson and wife, Elizabeth, as guardians of said John Bishop, son of Benjamin Bishop of same place.
Lib. 11, p. 455.

1758, March 2. Bishop, Vincent, of Burlington Co. Ward. Son and heir of Joshua Bishop. Bond of Martha Stiles as Guardian. Fellowbondsmen—John Briggs and Edward Stiles, all of said Co. Witness—Samuel Bard. Lib. 13, p. 315.

1759, Dec. 28. Bishop, Vincent, of Burlington Co. Ward. Son of Joshua Bishop, of same place; makes choice of John Briggs for his Guardian; who is appointed. Bondsman—Job Briggs; all of said Co. Lib. 14, p. 125.

1761, April 8. Bishop, William, of Greenwich Twsp., Sussex Co.; will of. Plantation to be sold and the money given to my wife and children, Joseph, William, David and John. Executors—brothers-in-law, David Henry and John Henry. Witnesses—Samuel Vanhook, Sarah Henry, Philip Chapman. Proved May 5, 1761.
1761, April 23. Inventory, £335.17.6, made by Alexander White and David Hays.
1766, Nov. 19. Account by both Executors. Lib. 11, p. 61.

1763, Dec. 6. Bispham, John, of Northampton, Burlington Co. Ward. Guardians—John Hatkinson and Elizabeth his wife. (The said John Bispham being the son of Benjamin). Witness—Charles Read. Lib. 11, p. 455.

1770, March 1. Bispham, Thomas, of Philadelphia, tavern keeper; will of. All real and personal in New Jersey to be sold, and the money to be given to my wife, Sarah, and my five children, Joseph, Benjamin, Thomas, Hinchman and Elizabeth, when they are of age. Executors—brother-in-law, John Hinchman, of Gloucester Co., N. J., my wife, Sarah, and my brother, John Bispham. Witnesses—John Hatkinson, Samuel Clement, Paul Isaac Voto. Proved at Philadelphia, Aug. 3, 1770. Proved in N. J. Aug. 7, 1770. Lib. 15, p. 42.

1760, June 21. Black, Sarah, of Chesterfield Twsp., Burlington Co.; will of. Son, Samuel, £10. Son Edward, £12. Daughter, Mary Pope, £10. Daughter, Ann Wright, £10. Grandsons, Ezra Black, John Black, William Black, Joseph Pope, Nathaniel Pope, John Pope, Thomas Wright, Abner Wright, Amos Wright and John Black (son of Thomas), £8 each. Grandson, Edward Black (son of William), £62. Grandson, John Black (son of Edward), £8. Granddaughters, Hannah and Sarah Gaunt, £18 each. Granddaughter, Achsah Black, £6. Granddaughters, Ann Black and Ann Wright, £6 each. Granddaughter, Elizabeth Wright, bed. Son-in-law, Samuel Gaunt, and my daughter-in-laws, Mary Black of Springfield, Mary Black of Mansfield, and Amy Potts, 5 shillings each. To Chesterfield Monthly Meeting, £5. Daughters, Mary Pope and Ann Wright, my apparel. Executors—son-in-law and daughter, Amos Wright and Ann Wright, his wife, and, if they die, then their son, Abner Wright. Witnesses—Edward Rockhill and Elizabeth Rockhill. Proved Sept. 27, 1769. Lib. 14, p. 189.
1769, Aug. 8. Inventory, £454.6.1, made by Edward Rockhill and Ezra Black.

1764, March 25. Blackford, Nathaniel, of Piscataway, Middlesex Co.; will of. Wife, Mary, use of my plantation to bring up my children. Sons, John, Benjamin and Nathaniel, my farm, when they are 21.

My daughter, Desia Blackford, £100. Daughter, Sophia, £100. I give to my daughters the pewter that did belong to my first wife. Executors—my wife, and my brother, John Blackford. Witnesses—John Smith, Stephen Bunels, Daniel Barto. Proved April 12, 1764.
1764, April 11. Inventory, £252.19.11, made by Jacob Boice and John Hepburn. Lib H, p. 337.

1749, April 5. Blacklidg, Philip, of Elizabeth Town, Essex Co.; will of. Daughter, Ann, 5 shillings. To son, Zachariah, son Phillip, daughter Cathrine, daughter Elenah, son Benjamin, son Jacob, each 5 shillings. To wife, Willempe, all my lands and goods. Executrix—my wife. Witnesses—Mathias Miller, Samuel Man, John Ross. Proved July 11, 1761. Lib. H, p. 24.

1764, June 28. Blackwood, Alexander, of Deptford, Gloucester Co., fuller. Int.. Adm'r—Samuel Blackwood. Fellowbondsman—Joseph Tatem; both of said Co., yeomen. Witness—Sarah Howell.
Lib. 12, p. 15.

1761, April 3. Blackwood, John, of Gloucester Co. Int. Adm'rs—Margaret Blackwood and Samuel Blackwood. Fellowbondsmen—John Hider and Samuel Mifflin; all of said Co. Witness—James Clark. Lib. 10, p. 160.

1761, Jan. 2. Blain, William, of New Brunswick, Middlesex Co. Int. Adm'r—Barney Lowrey, of New York City, who is son-in-law of said William Blain. Fellowbondsman—Abraham Cocever, of New Brunswick.' Witnesses—Ann Hude and James Hude, Jr.
Lib. G, p. 458.

1699, May 12. Blaine, John, of Wapping, in the Parish of Stepney, als. Stebonheath, in Co. of Middlesex (England), merchant; will of. Wife, Margaret Blaine, all the rent that is due to me from the two houses in Black Fryars, London, and for the farm at Hornsey, in said Co., lately occupied by Thomas Buddock, and for my moiety of the 3 messuages in Aldgate in London, which I bought of William Waddis, and now in tenure of Samuel Maine, draper, Zachariah Limcox, hosier, and Humphrey Cock, milliner. After my wife's death, the lands shall go to such persons as my late father-in-law, Thomas Farley, by his will did appoint; but the three messuages in London I give to my five children, Thomas Blaine, Margaret Blaine, Elizabeth (now the wife of Robert Barclay), Farley Blaine, and Mary Blaine. To son, Thomas, the ⅛ part of the ship "Susan," of which he is Master; and I give him all my lands in East New Jersey. To daughter, Margaret Blaine, £800. Daughter, Farley Blaine, £800. Daughter, Mary Blaine, £800. Grandson, John Blaine, son of my said son, £50. To my granddaughter, Margaret Barclay, daughter of my daughter Elizabeth, £50. To my brother, James Blaine, and my friend, Roger Newham, a 5 guinea piece of gold to each of them. To Joseph Caydle and William Saunders, £10, to be given to the poor belonging to the meeting at Ratcliffe, called Quakers. My brothers, James and Benjamin, are to give £5 to the poor of the neighborhood. The rest to be given to my children when they are of age. Executors—my wife, my brother, James, and my friend, Roger Newham. Witnesses—Benjamin Blaine, Mary Cudlip, Thomas Butler.

Whereas since making the above will, my daughter Margaret has, by my consent, married Abraham Coleman, therefore I make the £800 bequest void. This is made as my codicil, this 4th of Nov., 1699, and signed before William Ruddock and Thomas Butler. Proved Jan. 16, 1768, and exemplification thereof is herein given out of the Registry of the Prerogative Court of Canterbury; the which will having before been proved on 3rd of Jan., 1699, and letters were granted to Margaret Blaine, James Blaine and Roger Newham, as Executors. Lib. I, p. 317.

1766, July 9. Blair, Alexander, of the Landing, Middlesex Co., yeoman; will of. All real and personal estate to my wife, Jannikje. Executors—my wife, and my friend, Michael Field. Witnesses—Barnabus Lagrange, Daniel Bray, Andres Ten Eick. Proved March 30, 1768. Lib. I, p. 230.

1768, March 30. Blake, Israel, of Mannington Precinct, Salem Co., innholder; will of. My brother, Garret Black, one shilling. Sister, Sarah Black, one shilling. Wife, Elizabeth, rest of my estate. Executrix—my wife. Witnesses—William Barrat, Charles Hamilton, Anna Hamilton. Proved June 13, 1768.

1768, May 11. Inventory made by Thomas Bullock and William Barrat. Lib. 12, p. 539.

1770, Jan. 9. Blauw, Cornelius, of Bergen Co. Int. Adm'rs—Mary Blauw (the widow), Johannes Demarest and Daniel Isaac Browne. Fellowbondsman—Lawrence Ackerman; all of Bergen Co. Witness—Matthias McDermott. Lib. K, p. 143.

1755, Sept. 22. Blinkerhoff, Cornelius, of Gemonepa, Bergen Co., yeoman; will of. Wife, Eegje, use of real and personal while my widow. Son, Hendrick, the choice of the two plantations, one at Gemonepa and Pemberpog and Bergen, the other at the "Engles Neborhood." Son, Hartman, the other plantation. Daughter, Marita, the bond given by her former husband, Helmig Vanhoute. To the children of my daughter, Clasie, £200. To Eegje, wife of Abram Sicelse, £200. To daughter, Geesie Blinkerhoff, $200. Moveables to daughter, Clasie, the wife of Gerret Croese. Witnesses—Claes Vreelandt, Gerrit Vreelandt and Reynier V. Giese.

1757, Nov. 9. Codicil. Witnesses—Claes Vreland. Proved Oct. 23, 1770.

1770, Oct. 25. Bond of Hendrick Blinkerhoff and Hartman Blinkerhoff as Adm'rs with will annexed. Claes Vreelandt, fellowbondsman; all of Bergen Town in Bergen Co. Lib. K, p. 318.

1764, Sept. 7. Blond, Gabriel, of Burlington, Burlington Co.; will of. Brother, Alexander, at Boston, £10. Sister, Philipa, £10. Sister, Mary Anne, £10. To my housekeeper, the widow Elizabeth Duffle, household goods, and the use of the house I bought of James Maxwell in said City. If there is no news of my son James Alexander in five years, then, after the death of Elizabeth, the house is to be for Mathew Dawson, youngest son of Elizabeth Duffle, but, if he die under 21, then the house is to be for the Library Company of Burlington. Executor—friend, Abraham Hertlings. Witnesses—Samuel Allinson, Joseph Read, William Terrill. Proved Nov. 24, 1766.
Lib. 13, p. 16.

1763, Oct. 20. Bloodgood, Francis, of South Amboy Twsp., Middlesex Co.; will of. My lands in the South ward of Perth Amboy, and in Woodbridge Twsp., to be sold. Wife, Judah, interest of £200. The money from the sale of lands to be given to my four sons and two daughters, viz., William, John, Abraham, Francis, Martha and Mary. To all my children I give all my rights to land in Marineck Township, Westchester Co., New York, in the East Neck of Richbell's Patent. Executors—my friends, William Morgan and Daniel Morgan. Witnesses—Thomas Warne, Joshua Warne, Obadiah Herbert. Proved July 30, 1766.

1766, Aug. 28. Inventory, £209.9.0, made by James Morgan and John Herbert.

1767, May 12. Renunciation by William Morgan. Witnesses—Thomas Ellison and Anna Morgan.

1767, May 23. Judith Bloodgood, and John Bloodgood, one of the sons of Francis Bloodgood deceased, Adm's of the estate of Francis Bloodgood, which yet remains unadministered by Daniel Morgan, late Executor of said Francis Bloodgood, now also deceased. Fellowbondsmen—William Lorton and William Bloodgood.

1767, Aug. 31. Account of Daniel Morgan deceased, late Executor of Francis Bloodgood, and now the account of James Morgan, Executor of Daniel Morgan, for so much of the goods of Francis Bloodgood as came to the hands of Daniel Morgan.

Lib. H, p. 633; Lib. I, p. 108.

1767, April 22. Bloomfield, William, of Middlesex Co. Ward. Benjamin Bloomfield, the father of said William, states that his son has been a lunatic for some time, and is not able to provide for himself or family, and he must be confined with chains, and, your petitioner being old, is not able to provide for, nor take care of himself, therefore asks that a Letter of Guardianship be granted to my son, Ezekiel Bloomfield, to take charge of my son, William.

We, the subscribers, living in Woodbridge, and near neighbors to Benjamin Bloomfield, an aged, infirm person, can assure that the representation of his son's case is true. [Signed by] Moses Bloomfield, Jonathan Bloomfield, Joseph Bloomfield and Nathaniel Heard.

1767, April 23. Guardian—Ezekiel Bloomfield. Fellowbondsman—George Herriot; both of Woodbridge. Lib. 12, p. 478.

1762, March 8. Board, Elizabeth, relict of Cornelius Board, of Bergen Co.; will of. Son, Joseph Board, land near Kingwood, which I had by deed from Jonathan Davis and Joseph Bartram, dated May 6, 1754, and also another tract near said place, which I had by deed from my son, James Board, Jan. 10, 1755. Daughters, Susanna Sutherland, Sarah Ervin and Martha Board, to have my personal estate. Executors—sons, David Board and Joseph Board. Witnesses—Marey Slot, Jeane Brown and James Board. Proved Nov. 7, 1762.

Lib. H, p. 347.

1769, June 14. Bodine, Abraham, of Somerset Co., yeoman; will of. Wife, Mary, use of real and personal, till my youngest son, Cornelius, is 21. Son, Cornelius, all real. Eldest son, John, £50 when 21. Daughters, Mary, Jane, and Sarah, each £25, when married. To all my children, John, Cornelius, Judith, Mary, Catrine, Jane and Sarah, moveables. Executors—Peter Van Nest and John Van Nest, both sons of Peter Van Nest, deceased, of North Branch of Raritan.

Witnesses—Jacob V: Nor Strand, Aurie Lane, William Lane. Proved July 3, 1769.
1769, July 1. Inventory, £153.17.0, made by Peter Dumont, Abraham Ten Eick and Aurie Lane. Lib. K, p. 112.

1769, Dec. 29. Bodine, Frederick, of Bridgewater Twsp., Somerset Co.; will of. Wife, Elsie, to have real and personal, while my widow. Sons, Isaac, John and Gysbert, plantation I live on. Daughters, Sarah (wife of John Vannest), Mary (wife of Simon Cole), Elizabeth Bodine, Elsie Bodine, and Catherine Bodine, £25 each. Executors—friends, Jacob Bogert and Peter Vannest, and my wife, Elsie. Witnesses—Harmen Lane, Agnes Arrison, John Mets. Proved at Bedminster, Oct. 29, 1770. Lib. L, p. 46.

1770, Sept. 19. Bodine, John, of Somerset Co. Int. Adm'rs—William Van Doren and Jacobus Van Voorhees. Fellowbondsman—Hendrick Sedam; all of said Co.
1770, Sept. 19. Inventory, £94.0.4, made by Rinere Van Nest and Hendrick Sedam.
1772, Feb. 3. Account, by Adm'rs. Lib. K, p. 245.

1760, Aug. 8. Boice, Cornelius, of Piscataway, Middlesex Co., farmer; will of. Son, Cornelius, 40 shillings. Rest of personal and real to my wife, Lydia, to maintain the rest of the family that remain with her, while she is my widow. Daughter, Lydia Fontine, widow, household goods, at wife's death. To son, Cornelius, ½ of my plantation, and to my son, Dennis Vandine Boyce, the other half. Executors—my wife, my brother-in-law, Derick Fulkerson, and cousin, John Boice. Witnesses—Reune Runyon, John Webster, Jeremiah Hemsted. Proved May 28, 1761.
1761, June 2. Inventory, £406.13.1, made by Randolph Drake and Leonard Boice. Lib. G, p. 436.

1759, May 4. Bolmer, John, of Somerset Co.; will of. Brother, Robert, the house and four acres that join to his lot, after my mother's death; and he to pay £8 to brother, Abraham. Rest of land to my brothers, Alabartes, Abraham and Robert. Sisters, Ann, Rosanna, Magdalen, Elizabeth, and Jane, £5 each. Executors—David Sutton, and my brother, Abraham. Witnesses—Isaac Van Tyle, Mary Van Tyle, Abraham Van Tuyl. Proved Jan. 4, 1764.
1764, Nov. 30. Inventory, £16.4.6, made by Jabez Smith and Audery Montony.
1768, Nov. 19. Account by David Sutton, as Executor.
Lib. H, p. 404.

1769, May 26. Bolts, Jacob, of Burlington Co. Int. Adm'r—Joseph Ellis, of Town and Co. of Gloucester. Fellowbondsman—John Cox, of Moorestown, Burlington Co. Witness—Robert Burchan.
Lib. 14, p. 63.

1762, Feb. 8. Bond, Stephen, of Elizabeth Town, Essex Co. Ward. One of the children of Robert Bond of said place, and over 14 years of age. Guardian—Nathaniel Bond. Fellowbondsman—Moses Price; both of said town, yeomen. Lib. H, p. 76.

CALENDAR OF WILLS—1761-1770   49

1757, Dec. 10. Bonham, Zedekiah, of Piscataway, Middlesex Co.; will of. Wife, Anna Bonham, ⅓ my personal estate and the goods she brought with her. She is to bring up my children, Zerujah and Katrin, that God has blessed us with. Daughters, Sarah Randolph, Zerujah Bonham, and Katrin Bonham, to have the personal. Daughter, Zerujah, 100 acres. Daughter, Katrin, 100 acres. But if they die, then my grandson, Zedekiah Fitz Randolph, the son of Malachi Fitz Randolph and Sarah Fitz Randolph, shall have the lands. Executors—my wife, Anna, and Jeremiah Dunn. Witnesses—James Martin, Benjamin Martin, Peter Martin, Jr. Proved Jan. 21, 1761.
1761, Jan. 18. Inventory £52.5.2, made by Richard Merrell and Az. Dunham.   .Lib. G, p. 354.

1768, Jan. 28. Bonnel, Abraham, of Kingwood Twsp., Hunterdon Co., innholder; will of. Son, Abraham, £5, and the same amount to my other three sons, Isaac, Jacob and John. Son, John, to have a tract of land in Gloucester Co., at Great Egg Harbor, of 100 acres. Rest of real and personal I give to my wife, Mary. Executors—my wife, and my son, Isaac. Witnesses—Isaac Leet, Lazarus Adams. Proved April 1, 1768.
1768, March 31. Inventory, £217.2.1, made by Daniel Lake and Tunis Aike.   Lib. 12, p. 520.

1761, Jan. 23. Bonnel, Joseph, of Borough of Elizabeth, Essex Co., yeoman; will of. Wife, Phebe, movable estate, and £35. Brother, Synesey, apparel. Land to be sold. Father, Joseph Bonnel, rest of cash from sale of land. Executors—my wife, my father, Joseph Bonnel, and Moses Baldwin. Witnesses—Samuel Walter, Jacamiah Smith, Obadiah Smith. Proved Nov. 24, 1761.   Lib. H, p. 72.

1761, Nov. 3. Bonnel, Joseph, of Elizabeth Town, Essex Co.; will of. Wife, Sarah, all my goods and also hogs, corn, etc. Daughter, Keziah Bonnel, £25, when 18. Son, John, to be supported, and, after his death, all lands to be sold and money given to my two sons, Sinecy Bonnel and Doctor Wats Bonnel. Executors—friends, Timothy Whitehead and Caleb Brown, and my wife, Sarah. Witnesses—Moses Baldwin, Phebe Potter, Phebe Baldwin. Proved Dec. 5, 1761.
1762, Jan. 9 Inventory, £354.19.7, made by Amos Day and Samuel Thompson. Land sold to Richard Townley, £44.17.6, and to John Shipman, £140.11.0. Paid by Ex's of Joseph Bonnel, Jr., £60.17.7.
                                                                            Lib H, p. 86.

1760, April 3. Bonnel, Sarah, of Borough of Elizabeth, Essex Co.; will of, being the wife of Benjamin Bonnel. Gives £15 to the daughters of my deceased sister, Elizabeth More; also £15 to the daughters of my deceased sister, Mary Wade. To my sister, Hannah Crammer, my Bible. My apparel to be given to my sister, Hannah Crammer, the eldest daughter of my deceased sister, Moor, and the eldest daughter of my deceased sister, Wade. My niece, Phebe Potter, daughter of my brother, Noadiah, deceased, one spoon. Nephew, Samuel Potter, son of my brother Daniel, one spoon, and also to my nephew, Amos Potter. To Sarah Potter, daughter of my nephew, Nathaniel Potter, gold ring. Husband, Benjamin Bonnel, a cow. Lands to be sold. I give 20 shillings to the children of my brother Joseph Potter; and also to the children of my other brethren and

4

sisters, namely, "Daniel Potter's children, Hannah Crammer's, Samuel Potter's (deceased), Elizabeth Moor's (deceased), Noadiah Potter's (deceased), and Mary Wade's (deceased), each family part and part alike." Executors—friends, Amos Potter and Noadiah Potter. Witnesses—John Darbe, John Searing, Job Mulford. Proved Jan. 19, 1761. Lib. G, p. 353.

1765, Feb. 22. Bonney, Perez, of Woodbridge, Middlesex Co. Int. Adm'r—James Bonney, the eldest brother. Fellowbondsman—John Pain; both of said place.
1765, March 29. Inventory, £15.18.6 (carpenter's tools, etc.), made by David Edgar and John Rawlison.
1765, April 9. Account by James Bonney, the Executor.
Lib. H, p. 394.

1758, Sept. 27. Boof, Hendrick, of New Brunswick, Middlesex Co.; will of. My wife, Barbara Margreta Boof, all real and personal estate. Executrix—my wife. Witnesses—Jacob Heyer, Thomas Longfield, William Ouke. Proved Jan. 23, 1769.
1769, Jan. 30. Probate granted to Barbara Margreta Gibb, late Barbara Margreta Boof. Lib. K, p. 53.

1769, July 28. Boosy John, of Elizabeth Town, Essex Co. Ward. Son of Abraham Boosy, of said place, deceased. Guardian—Nehemiah Wade. Lib. K, p. 118.

1770, Nov. 5. Booth, Isabel, of Stow Creek, Cumberland Co., spinster; will of. To William Hunt my right in a lot I bought of Benjamin Tylor, when 21. To James Booth Hunt, £43, when 21. To John Hunt, £43, when 21. To John Neeley, £10, when 21. To William Neeley, £43, when 21. To William McClong, 5 shillings, and to Esther McMonagle, also £5. Executors—friends, Joseph Neeley and William McMonagle. Witnesses—Josiah Miller, Mark Bacon, Thomas Ewing. Proved Nov. 24, 1770.
1770, Nov. 24. Inventory, £180.6.8, made by Thomas Ewing and Maskell Ewing.
1772, May 19. Account by William McMonigill and Joseph Neely, the Executors. Lib. 15, p. 61; Lib. 14, p. 423.

1766, March 28. Borden, Benjamin, of Burlington Co., yeoman; will of. My father, Jonathan Borden, all my estate, and at his death, if anything be left, then to my half brothers, Jonathan Borden and Thomas Borden. Executors—Aaron Wills and Jonah Woolman. Witnesses—James Robinson, John Smith. Proved April 18, 1766.
1766, May 15. Inventory, £58.18.11, made by Abraham Kille and John Hunt.
1770, Oct. 20. Account of Jonah Woolman and Aaron Wills, Adm'rs of Benjamin Borden of Willinborough, Burlington Co.
Lib. 13, p. 34; Lib. 15, p. 64.

1769, Dec. 9. Borden, Benjamin, of Shrewsbury, Monmouth Co. Int. Adm'r—Thomas Borden. Fellowbondsman—John Corlies; both of said place. Witnesses—Samuel Hunt and Isabella Hunt.
1769, Dec. 11. Inventory, £172.9.11, made by John Hartshorne and Morris Dehaert.
1772, May 18. Account by Adm'r. Lib. K, p. 142.

CALENDAR OF WILLS—1761-1770   51

1769, Feb. 12. Borden, Jonathan, of Upper Penns Neck, Salem Co., yeoman; will of. My wife, Martha, all real and personal, till children are of age. Son, Joseph, plantation where I live, of 155 acres when he is of age; but he is to pay £15 to my eldest daughter, Hannah, and £15 to my daughter, Mary. Son, Samuel, the plantation on Salem Creek, of 69 acres. Son, Jonathan, land I bought of Jacob Sly, of 48 acres. Executrix—my wife. Witnesses—Robert Howard, Martin Katz, Casper Gauger. Proved Oct. 11, 1769.
1769, July 26. Inventory, £172.10.4, made by Robert Howard and William Robinson.   Lib. 14, p. 100.

1763, July 16. Borden, Joseph, of Bordentown, Burlington Co., yeoman; will of. My daughter, Rebecca Brown, land I bought of William Freek of Bucks Co., Pa., and, at her death, to be sold, and money divided among her children. Daughter, Hannah Lawrence, house and land where I live. Grandson, Pernal Clayton, land where Timothy Bunting and Rachel Taylor now live. My grandchildren, Ann Beven and Mary How, £150 each. Grandson, Joseph Clayton, £175. Daughter, Elizabeth, house in Crosswicks, and, at her death, to her son Joseph, and her daughter Ann, and her son John. Daughter, Ann Potts, land. Daughter Amy Potts, house where David Thomas lives, and house where Daniel Price lives, and a lot that fronts Tallman Smith. Daughters, Hannah Lawrence, Ann Potts and Amy Potts, the plantation in Chesterfield. Son, Joseph, land I bought of Widow Allen, in Mansfield. Joseph Brown is husband of the said Rebecca Brown. The agreement between me and my present wife shall be performed. Executors—sons-in-law, John Lawrence and William Potts, and daughter, Ann Potts. Witnesses—John Taylor, John Watts and Timothy Bunting. Proved Oct. 7, 1765. Lib. 12, p. 192.
1765, Oct. 4. Inventory, £2902.17.6½, made by Thomas Watson and Abel Middleton.

1757, Nov. 18. Borden, Safty, of Bordentown, Burlington Co., yeoman; will of. My wife, Martha, use of house and lot, also personal estate while my widow. To two of my wife's children, Richard Walton and Martha Stevenson £70. My grandson, Safty Meghee, one acre of land joining Thomas Gridges; also £50 after his grandmother's death, and he is to take care of his aunt Hannah Borden. Grandson, James Meghee, a lot. My brother, Joseph Borden, £6 and 10 shillings, it being due him from my son, Richard. Granddaughter, Cathrine Britten, and my son, Richard Borden's, children, the remainder, after their grandmother's death. Executors—cousin, Joseph Borden, Jr., and my friend, William Pott. Witnesses—James Jolly, Ruth Allison, Richard Allison. Proved Sept. 10, 1761.   Lib. 11, p. 199.
1761, Aug. 13. Inventory, £258.10.9, made by Richard Allison and William Imlay.

1763, May 10. Borradaill, Marjery, of Burlington Co.; will of Widow of Arthur Borradaill. My four youngest children, viz., William, John, Sarah and Ruth, £5 each. Daughter, Hannah Elton, 5 shillings. Daughters, Rebecah Shute, Elizabeth Brown, Esther Venable and Mary Venable the rest. My daughter, Ruth, to be put with Joshua Bispham to be brought up till she is 18. Executor—son-in-law, Samuel Shute. Witnesses—Joshua Bispham, John Cox. Proved Dec. 3, 1763.   Lib. 11, p. 433.
1763, Dec. 3. Inventory, £132.5.8, made by John Lippincott and John Cox.

1763, Nov. 19. Borton, Jacob, of Evesham in Burlington Co. Int. Adm'r—Abraham Borton. Fellowbondsmen—Benjamin Haines and Thomas Brooks; all of said Co. Lib. 11, p. 424.
  1763, Nov. 15. Inventory, £135.7.3, made by Thomas Brooks and Benjamin Haines.
  1764, Account of Abraham Borton as Adm'r.

1761, June 28. Borton, Obadiah, of Evesham Twsp., Burlington Co.; will of. Son, Benjamin, to have 20 acres of my land, and son, Job, 20 acres, and my two sons, Samuel and John, the rest. Daughters, Jane and Phebe, £20 each. Wife, Mary, profits of my farm till sons are 21. Executors—wife, Mary, and my friends, William Foster and Benjamin Haines. Witnesses—Isaac Evens, James Cattell, Abraham Borton.
  1761, July 6. Codicil. Witnesses—Edward Darnell, William Borton, Abigail Borton. Proved July 28, 1761. Lib. 10, p. 301.
  1761, July 22. Inventory, £337.5.8, made by John Woolman and James Cattell.
  1764, Aug. 4. Account of Executors.

1760, Oct. 28. Borton, William, of Evesham, Burlington Co.; will of. Son, William, 188 acres of my plantation; also my meadow joining my brother, Obadiah, and he to pay to my wife £7 yearly. Son, Caleb, 290 acres when 21. Daughter, Sarah Borton, £40 when 18. Son, Joshua, part of plantation I bought of Freedom Lippincott; also 11 acres I bought of Andrew Conaro. Son, Josiah, the last ½ of said plantation. Daughter, Hannah Borton, £40. My wife, Abigail, the profits of my lands. Executors—my wife and my friend, Isaac Evens. Witnesses—Obadiah Borton, Sarah Woolman, John Woolman. Proved June 3, 1763. Lib. 11, p. 317.
  1763, June 6. Inventory, £472.1.8, made by Benjamin Moore and Benjamin Haines.

1763, May 9. Bouttenhouse, Daniel, of Morris Co. Int. Adm'r—John Carl, largest creditor. Fellowbondsman—Peter Layton; both of said Co. Witness—Sarah Nuttman.
  1763, May 7. Renunciation by, Saphira Bouttenhouse, his widow. Witness—Peter Layton.
  1763, May 11. Inventory, £44.0.10, made by Daniel Cooper and Peter Layton.
  1765, Dec. 31. Account by Adm'r. File No. 179N.

1770, Sept. 15. Bower, David, of Fairfield Township, Cumberland Co.; will of. Wife, Tamsen, goods. Brother, John, a salt marsh, of which he possesses one-half. Daughter, Hanna, £5, and she to be bound out as a tayloress, and is to teach my daughter, Tamson, the trade, who is also to have £5. My two youngest sons, David and Eli, £10 each. Son, Ebenezer, all my land, when 21. Executors—my wife, Tamson, and brother-in-law, Levi Stratton. Witnesses—Samuel Wescot, Jeremiah Harris and William Ramsay. Proved Oct. 11, 1770.
  1770, Sept. 28. Inventory, £222.15.4, made by Joseph Ogden and Theo. Elmer.
  1774, Nov. 25. Account, by both Executors. "Expense of the widow, in supporting two children, the eldest not three years old, for 4 years, £50." Lib. 15, p. 89.

CALENDAR OF WILLS—1761-1770 53

1767, June 13. Bower, Ebenezer, of Fairfield, Cumberland Co., yeoman; will of. Son, John, 10 shillings. Daughter, Hannah Preston, like sum. Wife, Priscilla, her dower and a mare and saddle. Son, David, plantation where I live. Executor—son, David. Witnesses—David Hustod, Jr., Joseph Norbury, John Husman. Proved Feb. 28, 1769.
1767, Dec. 4. Inventory, £157.8.3, made by Thomas Harris and Joseph Dayton. Lib. 14, p. 35.

1769, Sept. 17. Bower, Priscilla, of Fairfield, Cumberland Co.; will of. Son, David Bower, 6 shillings. Son, John Bower, 6 shillings. Grandson, Burrhus Brooks, 6 shillings. Granddaughter, Lucy Brooks, 6 sheep. Daughter, Hannah Preston, the rest of estate. Executor—Isaac Preston. Witnesses—Theodosia Anderson, Abigail Harris, John Westcott. Proved Nov. 27, 1769.
1769, Nov. 27. Inventory, £50.8.9, made by David Wescote and Levi Preston. Lib. 14, p. 133.

1766, July 30. Bowland, James, of Salem Co., mariner. Int. Adm'r —Jonathan Roberts. Fellowbondsmen—Andrew Peterson and William Philpot, Jr.; all of Mannington, said Co. Lib. 12, p. 316.

1761, Feb. 13. Bowman, Providence. Int. Inventory, £169.16.3; "this is the whole legacy, of Providence Bowman, wife of John Bowman, given her by the will of her father." Inventory, £47.1.0; "this is the whole legacy, given to her by her mother." (See, for Adm'r, "N. J. Archives," Vol. 32, p. 37). File No 3401 L.

1761, Jan. 13. Bowne Obadiah, of Middletown, Monmouth Co., yeoman; will of. Wife, Catharine, to be maintained out of my estate. Daughter, Mary Ann, £10. Son, James, £2 and my gun. Son, Gershom, £2 and a gun, and he to be taught to write and cypher. Son, Phillip, £2 and the gun, formerly belonging to my father. Daughter, Mitilday, to be put out to learn a trade. Daughter, Ann, £30, when she is 21. Son, Samuel, £2 and a gun. Son, Obediah, rest of my personal, and real estate. Executors—friend, John Van Brackle, and son, Obediah. Witnesses—Edward Andrews, William Bowne, Andrew Brannan. Proved March 23, 1761. Lib. G, p. 402.

1764, March 14. Bowne, Obadiah, of Metawon, in Middletown, Monmouth Co.; will of. Wife to have the use of my estate, to support my seven children till the sons are 21 and the daughters 18, when both real and personal are to be sold; and then my wife to have £160, and the rest I give to my 7 children, John, Obadiah, Andrew, Philip, Fredrick, Anna and Catharine. Executors—Samuel Forman, Augustine Reid, my wife, Ann, and son, John, when old enough. Witnesses—Nathan Smith, Richard Hartshorne, John Bowne. Proved June 15, 1764. Lib. H, p. 444.

1765, July 30. Bowne, Thomas, of Middletown, Monmouth Co., mariner. Int. Adm'r—Samuel Reid, of Freehold, said Co. Fellowbondsmen—Thomas Kearney and James Kearney, both of Middletown.
1765, July 19. Renunciation, by Helena Bowne, the widow of said Thomas, in favor of Samuel Reid. Witnesses—Mary Reid and Mary Vanmater. Lib. H, p. 505.

1767, April 10. Boyes, John, of Woolwich, Gloucester Co. Int. Adm'x—Martha Boyes, widow. Fellowbondsman—Robert Russell, yeoman; both of said place. Witness—Hannah Ladd.
    1767, April 2. Inventory, £188.16.9½, made by William Key and Thomas Roberts.
    1768, Dec. 10. Account by Martha Bryan, late Martha Boys.
    Lib. 13, p. 132.

1767, Aug. 28. Boys, Nathan, of Woolwich Twsp., Gloucester Co.; will of. Wife, Susannah, use of all estate while my widow. Son, Elias, the rest of my lands, after 60 acres are taken off of the southwest end, of which I give 30 acres to my son, Abraham, and 30 to son, Nathan. Daughter, Catherine Reynolds, £6. Grandson, Robert Boys, son of John Boys, deceased, £1. Executors—my wife and my son, Elias Boys. Witnesses—John Fouracres, Josiah Fowler, Elizabeth Fouracres. Proved April 11, 1769. Lib. 14, p. 21.

1766, April 8. Brackney, Frances, of Chester Twsp. Burlington Co., widow; will of. My son, Mathias Brackney, 5 shillings. My son, John Brackney, 5 shillings. Daughter, Elizabeth Wallen, 5 shillings. Daughter, Hannah Nordike, 5 shillings. Son, Joseph Brackney, the residue. Executor—said son, Joseph. Witnesses—William Wallace and John Cox. Proved Aug. 23, 1766. Lib. 12, p. 299.
    1766, Aug. 19. Inventory, £116.11.10, made by Richard Borden and James Borden, Jr.

1762, July 21. Bradberry, Richard, of Acquacknong, Essex Co. Int. Adm'x—Elizabeth Bradbury, the widow. Fellowbondsman—Hendrick Van Giesen; both of said place. Witness—Francis Van Dyk.
    1762, Sept. 8. Inventory, £1331.7.½, made by Isaac Lyon and Thomas Longworth.
    1762. Account made by Elizabeth Bradberry. Lib. H, p. 172.

1766, Sept. 23. Braddock, Robert, of Evesham, Burlington Co., yeoman; will of. My wife, the personal estate and use of plantation, and she to educate my 4 sons, John, Daniel, Barzila and Robert, till they are 15. Son, Reuben, the plantation where he lives, and he shall pay my youngest sons, £5 each. To John Braddock a lot at lower corner of the meeting house. To Robert Braddock a lot of 30 acres. To Barzilla Braddock 120 acres. To Daniel Braddock rest of my homestead. Sons, Ruben, Reaboam, John, Daniel, Barzillai and Robert, my cedar swamp in Gloucester Co. Daughter, Barsheba Hutton, 20 shillings. Daughter, Rachel Crispan, a like sum. Son, Rehoboam, to have a deed for the plantation I bought of Isaac Stratton. Executors—wife, Frances, and friend, Joseph Willcox. Witnesses—John Brannin, Thomas Parkinson, Abraham Smith. Proved June 27, 1767.
    1767, June 13. Inventory, £323.14.1½, made by Jacob Prickit and Daniel Stratton. Lib. 13, p. 86.
    1774, May 11. Account of Joseph Willcox, Adm'r of Robert Braddock. Lib. 15, p. 516.

1763, May 6. Bradway, Jonathan, of Salem Co., farmer; will of. Son, Jonathan Bradway, the plantation I bought of Samuel Moore, where my son now lives; also a piece of marsh at the New Crossway, he paying to my son, Nathan, £10, and paying to his mother, Susannah Bradway, £4 a year. Son, William, my plantation, and he to pay to his mother £8 a year, and to his sister, Sarah Bradway, £15, and to his brother, Nathan, £10. My daughter, Rachel Hancock, £5. Son, Edward, £5. Rest of my moveable estate to my wife, Susannah, my daughter, Sarah Bradway, and my son, Nathan Bradway. Executors—sons, Edward and Nathan. Witnesses—John Stretch, Jonathan Stretch, Samuel Stretch. Proved April 13, 1765.

1765, April 13. Inventory, £280.2.0, made by John Stewart and Bradway Keasbey. Lib. 12, p. 172.

1764, July 5. Brady, Barnabas, of Essex Co. Int. Adm'r—Nehemiah Wade, one of the largest creditors. Fellowbondsman—George Ross; both of Borough of Elizabeth. Witness—Robert Ogden.

1765, Aug. 27. Inventory, £12.11.10, made by Robert Wade and William Clark. Lib. H, p. 372; File No. 92 S.

1765, Oct. 2. Branin, Michael, of Burlington Co. Int. Admr's—Elizabeth Branin and Joem Branin, of said Co. Bondsman—John Antrim, of same place. Lib. 12, p. 187.

1765, Oct. 22. Inventory, £533.7.2, made by Thomas Shinn and Robert Bishop.

1770, June 9. Brannon, Luke, of Montague, Sussex Co. Int. Adm'r—Anthony Van Etten. Fellowbondsman—Isaac Meddagh; both of said place. Witnesses—Mary Anderson and Thomas Anderson.

1770, June 6. Inventory, £21.8.3, made by Isaac Vantuyl and Isaac Meddagh.

1772, Jan. 9. Account, byAdm'r. Lib. 14, p. 421; Lib. 15, p. 69.

1761, Sept. 9. Brasier, James, of Salem, Salem Co. Int. Adm'r—Abel Harris. Fellowbondsman—William Philpot, Jr.; both of Penns Neck, Salem Co.

1761, Aug. 31. Inventory, £12.14.0, made by Francis Philpot and William Philpot. Lib. 11, p. 37.

1766, July 17. Brass, Henry, of Piscataway Twsp., Middlesex Co., yeoman; will of. All real and personal to be sold. Brother, Luke, and his son, Henry, ⅝ of my estate. Sister, Geertje Codmus, ¼ of my estate. Sister, Elizabeth Hopper, the rest. Executor—friend, Francis Brasier, of Raritan Landing. Witnesses—Henry Beekman, John Cowman, Charles Smock. Proved Aug. 19, 1766. Lib. I, p. 52.

1766, July 8. Bray, Elizabeth, of Middletown, Monmouth Co.; will of. Son, John Bray, a mare and household goods. Daughter, Elizabeth Leuquear, goods. Son James' wife, a petticoat. Son, Samuel Bray, goods. Son, James Bray, goods, and to his daughter Elizabeth, plates, etc. Grandson, Samuel Smalley, £3 and goods; and to William Smalley goods. My granddaughter, Hannah Leuquear, a saddle. Executors—son, John Bray, and Andrew Bowne, Jr. Witnesses—Thomas Worthington, George Reid. Proved April 2, 1768.
Lib. K, p. 20.

1764, Jan. 27. Bray, John, of Middletown, Monmouth Co., yeoman; will of. Wife, Elizabeth, use of my land. My oldest son, John, has already had a plantation given to him, of 300 acres. I have given to son, James, 300 acres. Second son, Samuel, place where I live; and he to pay to my sons, John and James, and my daughter Elizabeth, £100. The land that I had intended to give to daughter, Susannah, of 200 acres, to be sold, and the money to be paid to Susannah's children, viz., Samuel Bray Smalley, John Smalley and William Smalley, and her three daughters, Surviah, Elizabeth and Prudence. There is an action in law now between me and John Smalley, the father of my daughter, Susannah's children, which is to be paid for out of the money given to said children. To grandson, John Smalley, I give land at Middletown Point, that joins John Brakel. Daughter, Elizabeth, the land that is left that I bought of Samuel Bickley, at Delaware River, and joins land that was my brother, James Bray's. Executors—sons, John and Samuel. Witnesses—Thomas Loyd, Isaac Vandorn, Benjamin Thorp, William Lawrence, Samuel Holmes. Proved March 6, 1765.

1765, March 4. Inventory, £552.5.0, made by Richard Crawford, James Mott and William Bowne. Lib. H, p. 489.

1758, Aug. 21. Brayman, Benjamin, of New Hanover, Burlington Co.; will of. My son, Samuel, my lands. Wife, Elizabeth, the profits of the lands, to bring up my children. Executor—friend, William Stockton. Witnesses—John Middleton, Henry Clarke, Elizabeth Parker. Proved Sept. 18, 1762. Lib. 11, p. 231.

1762, Sept. 9. Inventory, £41.0.6, made by Jonathan Hough and Samuel Wright.

1764, Oct. 18. Brayman, Thomas, of Greenwich, Gloucester Co.; will of. Wife, Elizabeth, profits of my lands, to bring up my youngest children. Son, Isaac, plantation where I live, of 50 acres, and ½ of my meadow at Mantua Creek. Son, Ezekiel, rest of lands. Daughter, Sarah, 20 shillings. Daughter, Elizabeth, £10. Executors—my wife, and my friend, Thomas Clark. Witnesses—Adam Sharp, John Bright, Stogdel Sharp. Proved Dec. 10, 1764.

1764, Oct. 30. Inventory, £131.5.6, made by John Bright and Alexander Randall. Lib. 12, p. 287.

1765, July 25. Braziel, Christopher, of Amwell Twsp., Hunterdon Co. Int. Adm'x—Jane Brazeil, widow of Christopher. Fellowbondsmen—Jacob Van Noorstrand, of Somerset Co., and Aurie Lane, of same. Witness—Thomas Atkinson.

1765, July 25. Inventory, £176.18.11, made by Thomas Atkinson and Peter Wyckof. Lib. 12, p. 283.

1768, Aug. 22. Brewer, Adam, of Squancome, Shrewsbury Twsp., Monmouth Co.; will of. Son, William, all that meadow located in Marshes Bogg, and all my Proprietors Rights. Wife, Mary, all the rights that she may obtain by the death of former husband, John Curlis, deceased; also the use of ½ my land, except one acre where the mill stands. Son, George, ½ my land on east side of the brook, and ½ the grist mill, and, after death of the wife, the land she uses. Son, Elazerus, the land west of the brook, except one acre, which I reserve for the use of a burying-yard, where the burying-yard now is; also ½ of the mill, and, after the death of Elazerus, I give to Adam Brewer, his son, all the said land. Daughter, Magdilene Brewer, £100 when 21. Rest of moveable estate to son, William, and his six sisters, Hannah, Elizabeth, Rachel, Mary, Margaret and Deborah. Executors—son-in-law, James Lefetra, and my wife, Mary. Witnesses—John Burnett, Thomas North, John Morris, Jr. Proved March 15, 1769.

CALENDAR OF WILLS—1761-1770   57

1769, March 10. Inventory, £667.4.2, made by Aaron Robins, James Davis and Thomas North. Lib. K, p. 79.

1769, Jan. 4. Brewer, Derrick, of Somerset Co. Int. Adm'r—John Dunn, of said Co. Fellowbondsman—Edward Higgins, of Middlesex Co.
1769, Dec. 15. Account by Adm'r. Balance due the estate, 11 shillings and 11 pence. File No. 365 R.

1768, Nov. 16. Brewster, Francis, of Greenwich, Cumberland Co., shop keeper; will of. Youngest son, Gilbert, £150, when 21. Son, Joseph, part of the homestead. Son, Samuel, rest of land. Daughters, Hannah, Ruth and Anne, £100 each, when they are 21. Sons, Ebenezer, and Benjamin, £50 each. Son, Daniel, £25 and Bible. Wife, Rebecca, rest of personal estate, and she to be Guardian of my children, except Hannah, and she to have Thomas Ewing as her Guardian. (Some of the children are by a first wife). Executors—wife, Rebecca, and my friend, Thomas Ewing. Witnesses—Isaac Watson, Abigail Peck, Uriah Bacon. Proved Dec. 2, 1768.
1768, Dec. 7. Inventory, £1351,10.4½, made by Thomas Maskell and Maskell Ewing. Lib. 13, p. 489.

1759, March 6. Brian, Jacob, of Reckless Town, in Twsp. of Chesterfield, Burlington Co.; will of. Wife, Mary, all real and personal but she to pay 20 pistoles to my friend, Samuel Peart. Executor—wife, Mary. Witnesses—Elizabeth Forman, Anne Reckless, Joseph Peace.
1759, April 11. Republished. Witnesses—Hannah Woodward, Neal McGrachy, Anne Reckless.
1763, Aug. 25. Republished. Witnesses—Francis Giffing, Abraham Heulings, John Shaw. Proved Jan. 9, 1768. Lib. 13, p. 293.
1767, Dec. 15. Inventory, £260.8.11, made by John Hutchin and Job Lippincott.

1765, June 5. Brian, Marmaduke, of Gloucester Co.; will of. Land to be sold, and all moveable goods, except household goods, and money divided among my wife and two children, and, if they die under age, then that share to my said wife, Mary, to whom I give the household goods. Executors—my wife, and my friend, Samuel Duemineer. Witnesses—Cornelius Thomas, John Maffett, Thomas E. Marsh. Proved July 23, 1765.
1765, July 16. Inventory, £77.7.9, made by John Maffet and George Flaningham. Lib. 12, p. 157.

1767, May 25. Brian, Mary, of Northampton, Burlington Co., widow of Abraham; will of. Son, Uriah Briant, 20 shillings. Daughter, Rebecca Brian, my apparel. Rest of personal and real to son, Thomas Brian, and daughter, Rebecca. Executors—said son and daughter, Thomas and Rebecca. Witnesses—Samuel Clark, Aquila Shinn, Henry Paxson. Proved July 6, 1767. Lib. 13, p. 85.
1767, July 3. Inventory, £192.2.10, made by Henry Paxson and Thomas Fenimore.

1767, May 15. Briant, Thomas, of Greenwich, Gloucester Co., yeoman; will of. To wife, 60 acres, and rest of lands to be sold. Son, William, one yoke of oxen. Executors—my wife, Martha, and James

Hinchman. Witnesses—James Simpson, George Cook, Drusilla Garnor. Proved July 24, 1767.
1767, July 25. Renunciation by James Hinchman. Witnesses—Barnerd Coofman, and Joseph Hinchman.
1767, June 4. Inventory made by John Driver and Mathew Tomlins, Jr. Lib. 13, p. 113.

1769, June 6. Brick, Hannah, of Cumberland Co. Ward. Daughter of Joseph Brick, of Stoe Creek, said Co., dec'd. Guardian—Ephraim Lloyd, of Penns Neck, Salem Co. Fellowbondsman—Ephraim Brick, of Stoe Creek. Lib. 13, p. 529.

1763, March 29. Brick, Joseph, of Stow Creek Precinct, Cumberland Co., yeoman; will of. Wife, Elizabeth. ⅓ of real and personal. Daughter, Sarah, 10 shillings. Son, Joseph, plantation where I live, and the house we call the Read House, and the old house; also my grist and saw mill; and he to pay to my son, William, £30, when 21. Son, Ephraim, house and plantation bought of Leonard Gibbon and Nicholes, of 177 acres Son, William, 200 acres. Daughter, Elizabeth, £20. Daughter, Hannah, £30 when 18. Son, John, my land east of Salem road, and, when he is 14, he shall be bound out to a trade. To my 4th daughter, Rachel, £30. Executors—my wife, and son, Joseph. Witnesses—Joshua Brick, James Glasspell, David Long. Proved April 27, 1763.
1763, April 11. Inventory, £357.0.8, made by Jonathan Ayars and Daniel Bowen.
1769, Aug. 28. Account of Jacob Brown and Elizabeth his wife, late Elizabeth Brick, surviving Executrix of Joseph Brick, late of Stow Creek. Lib. 11, p. 400; Lib. 14, p. 122.

1763, Nov. 28. Brick, Joseph, of Stow Creek, Cumberland Co. Int. Adm'x—Elizabeth Brick. Fellowbondsman—Seley Mills; both of Stow Creek Twsp. Witness—Bartholomew Hunt.
1763, Nov. 18. Inventory, £162.8.3., made by Bartholomew Hunt and Seley Mills. Lib. 11, p. 475.

1766, Oct. 30. Brick, William, of Cumberland Co.; will of. Brother, Ephraim Brick, £20. Sister, Hannah Brick, £40, when 18. Second brother, John Brick, £100, when 21. Youngest sister, Rachel, £40. Executor—my father-in-law, Jacob Brown. Witnesses—Evan Butler, Robert Armstrong. Proved Oct. 12, 1767.
1767, Nov. 4. Inventory, £153.8.6½, made by John Simkins and Daniel Brewster.
1771, Feb. 19. Account made by Jacob Brown. "The deceased carried a pocket book to sea with him." Lib. 13, p. 280; Lib. 15, p. 102.

1764, June 22. Bridge, David, of Morris Co. Int. Adm'r—Israel Ward. Fellowbondsman—Henry Allen; both of said Co.
1762, Oct. 18. Renunciation, by Chloe Bridge, the widow, in favor of Israel Ward. Witness—Daniel Cogswell.
1764, Sept. 20. Inventory, £8.12.1, made by Joseph Day and David Ward. Lib. H, p. 349.

1762, June 26. Briggs, Francis, of Northampton, Burlington Co., yeoman; will of. Son, David, my land in Salem Co. in Alloways Creek Precinct, on Hill Neck branch, of 141 acres. Son, John, the

rest of my lands in Salem Co., and he to pay to my son, Abel, £50, when 21. Son, Job, my plantation where I dwell, and he to pay to my son, Abel, £100. My wife, ⅓ of moveable estate. Daughters, Mary and Sarah, rest of moveable estate. Wife, Rachel, profits of my plantation. Executors—wife, Rachel, and my son, Job. Witnesses—Henry Taylor, Isaiah Peters, Joseph Goldy. Proved June 11, 1763. Lib. 11, p. 322.
1763, June 9. Inventory, £584.3.8, made by Amariah Foster and Burbridge Brock.
1767, May 6. Account by Executors.

1760, Aug. 22. Briggs, George, of Northampton Twsp., Burlington Co.; Will of. Son, Levi, plantation where I live. Son, George, land where Christian Eseld lives, and my land in Salem Co. Wife, Sarah, use of said land where Christian Eseld lives. Two oldest daughters, Theodocia King and Sarah Budd, and four youngest daughters, Ann, Hannah, Elizabeth and Rebeckah, rest of the personals. Daughter, Ann Vinicomb. Executors—friends, Thomas Budd and John Goldy, and my son, Levi. Witnesses—Samuel Jones, Thomas Edmon, Christian Elsellow. Proved Aug. 17, 1761.
1761, Aug. 14. Inventory, £505.4.7, made by James Dobbin and Amariah Foster. Lib. 10, p. 297.

1765, July 29. Briggs, Hannah, of Northampton, Burlington Co. Ward. Daughter of George Briggs of said place. Bond of Vincent Leeds, of Northampton Twsp., gent., as Guardian. Bondsman—Samuel Jones, of said Co. Lib. 12, p. 127

1766, Dec. 26. Briggs, Levi, of Northampton Twsp., Burlington Co. Int. Adm'r—John Goldy of New Hanover Twsp. Fellowbondsman—Joshua Norcross, of same place, blacksmith. Ann Briggs, the widow, renounced in presence of Job Rogers. Lib. 12, p. 385.
1767, Jan. 9. Inventory, £128.9.5, made by Thomas Reynolds and Edward Pancoast.

1765, Feb. 4. Briggs, Mary, of Northampton in Burlington Co., spinster; will of. My mother, Rachel Briggs to have all, but, when she dies or marries, then my brother, Abel Briggs, to have ⅓, and the rest to go to my brothers, David Briggs, Job Briggs and John Briggs. Executrix—my mother. Witnesses—Burbidge Brock, Samuel Jones, Joseph Goldy. Proved Feb. 18, 1765.
Lib. 12, p. 56.
1765, Feb. 16. Inventory, £25.11.6, made by Thomas Budd and John Goldy.

1765, Feb. 18. Briggs, Sarah, of Northampton in Burlington Co., Int. Adm'x—Rachel Briggs, the mother of said Sarah, of same place. Fellowbondsman—Thomas Budd, of said place. Witness—Samuel Jones. Lib. 12, p. 57.
1765, Feb. 16. Inventory, £14.11.6, made by Thomas Budd and John Goldy.
1767, May 6. Account by Rachel Briggs, the Adm'x.

1761, Jan. 22. Bright, John, Sr., of Greenwich Twsp., Gloucester Co., yeoman; will of. Daughter, Elizabeth, 5 shillings. Daughter, Ami, a bed, cow. Son, James, a mare. Wife, Mary, my lands, and

rest of moveables, while my widow. Son, James, to have lands after wife's death. Executors—my wife and son James. Witnesses—Danial Bennett, David Paul, Benjamin Braman. Proved May 1, 1762.
1762, April 24. Inventory, £125.6.6, made by Andrew Long and Francis Eastlake. Lib. 11, p. 123.

1769, Aug. 14. Brink, Peter, of Montague, Sussex Co. Int. Adm'r —Henry William Cortrecht, Fellowbondsman—Abraham Vanaken; both of said place. Witness—David Frazer.
1769, June 21. Renunciation, by Alida Brinck, widow of said Peter, in favor of John Cortrecht and Henrick William Cortrecht. Witnesses—William Ennes and Abraham Vanaken.
1769, June 21. Inventory, £28.14.9, made by Abraham Van Aken and William Ennes.
1770, Aug. 20. Account, by Adm'r. Lib. 15, p. 5; Lib. 15, p. 65.

1761, Dec. 8. Brink, Thomas, of Walpack Twsp., Sussex Co., yeoman; will of. Wife, Anne, ⅓ of my whole estate, and at her death the whole to be given to my 11 children, viz., Nicholas, James, Eve, Hendrika, Rachel, Cathrine, Sarah, John, Thomas, Yanatie, and Franzintie. Executors—Emanuel Gonsales, of Upper Smithfield, Northampton Co., Penna., and my wife. Witnesses—Thomas Hesom, James Bartron, Joseph Chestnore. Proved June 25, 1763.
1762, July 7. Inventory, £64.3.0, made by Thomas Hesom, and John Westbrook. Lib. 11, p. 466.

1765, April 7. Britten, Nicholas, of Borough of Elizabeth, Essex Co.; will of. Wife, Kiziah, £100. Executor to sell a tract of land on west side of Robinson's Branch, which I bought of Jacob Baker, and which is bounded by Ebenezer Cutter, Henry Frazee, heirs of Othaniel Campbell; also ¼ part of land I purchased of Nathaniel Hubbell, in company with Thomas Clark, Esq., dec'd, Ephraim Terrill and Abraham Clark, Jr., and being the land whereon I now live; together with my part of the fulling mills, lately erected, and being in the bounds of Elizabeth Town. Children, John Britain, Daniel Britain and Pheby Terrill Britain, to have the rest, after debts are paid, when they are 21. Executors—friend, Jonathan Bishop, and my brother-in-law, Abraham Terrill. Witnesses—William Hetfield, Abraham Terrill, Joseph DeCamp. Proved July 17, 1766.
1766, April 11. Inventory, £88.11.6, made by Benjamin Marsh and John Parker. Lib. H, p. 629.

1758, Aug. 30. Brock, John, of Chester, Burlington Co., yeoman; will of. My dwelling, grist mill and land to my sons, Uriah and John Brock, when of full age. If my wife is with child, it is to have its share. Wife, Mercy, to have rent of mill till my sons are of age. Executors—my wife and brother-in-law, John Hillier. Witnesses—William Fenimore, William Seed, Samuel Atkinson. Proved March 30, 1761.
1761, March 30. Inventory, £210.16.11½, made by Andrew Andreson and Abraham Hewlings. Lib. 10, p. 333; File No. 6931-6936 C.

1761, May 25. Brock, Oddy, of Northampton, Burlington Co.; will of. To grandson, Uriah Brock (eldest son of my son, John), £1, when 21. My present wife, Martha, household goods. Granddaughter, Frances Brock, a pan. Rest to my children, Burbag Brock, Thomas Brock, and daughter, Millisent, wife of Samuel Sheldon. Ex-

ecutor—friend, John Fenimore. Witnesses—Samuel Farrington, Edward Andrews, Joseph Farrington. Proved June 2, 1761.
Lib. 10, p. 340.
1762, Jan. 15. Inventory, £130.3.6½, made by Nathaniel Wilkinson and James Childs.

1765, May 22. Brockholls, Henry, of Pompton, Bergen Co.; will of. Wife, Mary, £1,000, and all the goods that belonged to her at our marriage. Henry Brockholst Philipse, the son of Frederick Philipse, £100. Harry Brockholst Livingston, son of William Livingston, £100. Beverly Robinson, Jr., son of Beverly Robinson, £100. Of rest of real and personal I give ½ to the children of my sister, Johanna Philipse, widow of Colonel Frederick Philipse; that is to say, to my nephews, the said Frederick Philipse and Philip Philipse, and my nieces, Susannah, wife of said Beverly Robinson, and Mary, wife of Roger Morris, Esq., and the other ½ to children of my sister, Susanna French, deceased, who are now living, and the children of Mary Brown, deceased, who was also a daughter of my sister, Susannah French, in the following manner, viz., ¼ to Anne, wife of David Van Horne, Susanna, wife of William Livingston, and Elizabeth, wife of David Clarkson; and ¼ to Anne and Sarah Brown, daughters of my niece Mary Brown. Land to be sold. Executors—Frederick Philipse, Beverly Robinson, William Livingston and David Clarkson. Witnesses—Casprus Schuyler, Castina Schuyler, Elizabeth Post and Martinus Post. Proved June 12, 1766. Lib. H, p. 607.

1764, Nov. 24. Brooks, Timothy, of Hopewell, Cumberland Co.; mariner. Int. Adm'x—Abigail Brooks. Fellowbondsman—Seth Bowen; both of said Co. Witness—Samuel Fithian.
1764, Nov. 23. Inventory, £184.6.0, made by Seth Bowen and Samuel Fithian. Lib. 12, p. 103.

1764, March 30. Brown, Abraham, of Chesterfield, Burlington Co.; will of. Sister-in-law, Jane Richardson, table, etc. Nephew, Joseph Brown, land in Chesterfield, where Joseph Steward, wheelwright, now lives, of 32 acres, which I bought of Joseph Borden. To my son and heir, Joseph Brown, the farm where I live, of 170 acres, which I bought of William Chapman, and the rest of estate, and, if he die under age, then to go to my nephew, the said Joseph Brown. Executors—my kinsman, Joseph Steward, Sr., blacksmith, of Hanover, and said nephew, Joseph Brown. Witnesses—Joseph Willits, Michael Burows, William Chapman. Proved May 8, 1764. Lib. 11, p. 513.
1764, May 8. Inventory, £46.19.3, made by John Bullock and William Chapman.

1764, March 24. Brown, Ebenezer, of Evesham, Burlington Co. Int. Adm'r—Benjamin Thomas, of Evesham. Fellowbondsman—Caleb Brown, of Gloucester Co. Witness—Joseph Read. Lib. 1, p. 537.
1764, Sept. 18. Inventory, £4.18.6, made by Robert Bishop and Lawrence Webster.

1764, Sept. 24. Brown, Ebenezer, of Haddonfield, Gloucester Co. Int. Adm'x—Elizabeth Brown. Fellowbondsman—Samuel Brown; both of said place. Witnesses—Jacob Clement, Hugh Creighton, Samuel Allinson.
1764, Aug. 27. Inventory, £49.6.7, made by John Gill and Samuel Clement, Jr. Lib. 12, p. 27.

1760, May 2. Brown, James, of Tewksbury, Hunterdon Co., yeoman; will of. Wife, Margaret, £100, and my moveable estate. Sons, James, Robert, Joseph and Solomon, 5 shillings each. Executors—Samuel Barkley, John Todd and David Carlisle. Witnesses—Abraham Willet, Samuel Craig, William Leslie. Proved May 25, 1764.
　　1764, June 7. Inventory, £197.0.2, made by William Ker and John Henry.　　　　　　　　　　　　　　　　　　　　　　　　　Lib. H, p. 441.

1761, Oct. 14. Brown, James, of Woodbridge, Middlesex Co.; will of. Eldest son, George Brown, the land which I bought of John Codington; also near 20 acres, lying at the head of William Stone's place, which I bought of the Executors of Edward Crowell; also a salt marsh of 8 or ·9 acres, which I bought of James Clarkson, at Papiack Neck, with ¾ of an acre adjoining, near the oyster bed. Son, Thomas, salt marsh which I bought of Marion Gilchrist; also the land I bought of Robert Pressmill; also a marsh on the Sunken Marsh; also ½ of the upland in Papiack Neck, not yet given away. My granddaughters, Cathrine and Margaret Brown, daughters of my son John Brown, the land lying between William Stone and James Smith, which I bought of Edward Crowell, deceased, when they are 18. To son, John, rest of my land. Daughter, Agnes Moores, £60. Daughter, Christian Cutter, £50. Daughter, Ursilla Black, £100. Daughter, Anipell Jaquish, £100. Granddaughter, Easther Cutter, £20, when 18. My wife, Agness, £70, and otherwise provided for. Executors—sons, Thomas and John. Witnesses—Ananias Luvis, Joseph Brown, David Edgar.　　　　　　　　　　　　　　　Proved Nov. 12, 1761.
　　1761, Nov. 14. Inventory made by George Brown and Jonathan Kinsey.　　　　　　　　　　　　　　　　　　　　　　　　　Lib. H, p. 44.

1765, Dec. 11. Brown, James, of Providence, Rhode Island; will of. Son, George, £500. Daughter, Ann Brown, wife of Daniel Brown, one right in my lands at Otter Creek, and £200. Daughter, Hope, wife of Archibald Campbell, one right in my lands at Otter Creek, and £200. Granddaughters, Ann and Lucy Perkins, daughters of daughter Mary Perkins, one right in my lands at Otter Creek and £100, when they come of age. Daughter, Elizabeth, the wife of Joseph Tillinghast, one right in my lands at Otter Creek and £200. Daughter, Hermione Brown, one right in my lands at Otter Creek, and £300, and to have an outfit. Grandson, James Noyce Brown, the son of my son George, my right in the Susquehanna Purchase, and one right in my lands at Otter Creek. Daughter-in-law, Mary Brown, widow of my son James Noyce Brown, all that can be recovered of her deceased husband's estate, and what may be due from my attorney, Capt. Richard Hide, of Norwich, and from Capt. James Carr, on account of what I paid to Esquire Backees of Norwich for an execution obtained against me for my son James, being bound for Carr's appearance at suit of John Read. My real estate in Perth Amboy in the Jerseys to be sold. My plate and watch I give to my four daughters. Son, George, the rest of real. Executors—Nicholas Tillinghast, of Providence, and my brother, Clark Brown, of Newport. Witnesses—George Jackson, William Pearce, William Wheaton. Proved at Providence, Dec. 21, 1765, and recorded in Council Book No. 5, page 406; James Angell, Clerk of the Council.　　　Vol. D3, p. 73, of Deeds.

1768, Aug. 4. Brown, Job, of Newark, Essex Co., cooper; will of. Wife, Phebe, ⅓ of my moveable estate, and ⅓ the use of my lands. Sons, Joseph and Job, all my lands, they paying to my son, Eleazar,

CALENDAR OF WILLS—1761-1770   63

£60, but Eleazer to have a meadow. One lot of land to be sold, and money given to daughters, Phebe, Hannah, Mary and Abigail. Executors—my kinsman, Joseph Riggs, Esq., and my son, Joseph. Witnesses—Elihu Ward, Samuel Freeman, Bethuel Peirson. Proved Oct. 15, 1768. Lib. I, p. 354.

1761, May 6. Brown, John, Jr., of Newark, Essex Co.; will of. Wife, Sarah, my house and 10 acres, and she to take care of my son, Stephen. Son, Ezekiel, ½ the rest of lands. Sons, Jonathan and Caleb, the other half. Daughter, Mary, £40 and a negro. If son, Stephen, outlives his mother, then he is to be taken care of by my three sons as they come of age. Executors—my wife and my brother, David Brown. Witnesses—Obadiah Bruen, Sylvanus Howell. Proved July 15, 1761.

1761, July 27. Inventory, £145.12.0, made by Nathaniel Johnson and Obadiah Bruen. Lib. H, p. 70.

1765, March 25. Brown, Margaret, of Hunterdon Co.; will of. Widow of James Brown. Daughter, Martha, £50. Daughter, Mary, £50. Son, Samuel Barkley, £20. Son, Robert Barkley, 5 shillings. To Walter Barkley, 5 shillings. Daughters, Martha and Mary, the rest. Executors—David Carlile, John Tod and Samuel Barkley. Witnesses—John Henry, James King, John King. Proved Oct. 16, 1769.

1769, Oct. 21. Inventory, £141.6.7, made by William Ker and Thomas Adams. Lib. 14, p. 147.

1764, Nov. 29. Brown, Martha, of Mansfield Twsp., Burlington Co.; will of. The widow of Zebulon Brown. Son, Samuel Brown, 10 shillings. Son, Jonathan Brown, spoon. Daughter, Leah Ellis, saddle. Daughter, Alice Garwood, 20 shillings, and her husband, Samuel Garwood, to have no demand on it. Daughter, Martha Tuley goods. To son Zebulon's son, Jonathan, a gun. To Jonathan's wife, Hannah, a looking glass. To Jonathan Brown's daughter, Mary Brown, a gown. Executors—friend, Arent Schyler, and my daughter, Leah. Witnesses—Joseph Folwell, Ephraim Betts, John Watkinson. Proved Jan. 1, 1765.

1764, Dec. 27. Inventory, £51.18.9, made by Philip White and William Wilson. Lib. 12, p. 37.

1765, Sept. 12. Brown, Phinehas, of Essex Co. Ward. Eldest son of Stephen Brown, of Newark, deceased, who died intestate, leaving real and personal estate, and leaving two sons, and two daughters. Phinehas, who is 15 years of age, makes petition and prays that his uncle, Joel Brown, of Newark, may be made his Guardian. Petition dated July 23, 1765. Joel Brown appointed Guardian, with Caleb Brown on his bond. File No. 3451-3454 G.

1763, June 17. Brown, Samuel, of Bernards Town, Somerset Co., yeoman; will of. To the Society of Presbyterians in Baskingridge, £200. Wife, Mary, £200, and the profits of my lands, except the land I bought of Benjamin Lewis, which is to be sold. Brother, Isaah Brown, Bible. Brothers, Aaron, Benoni and James, £25 each. My half-brother, Henry Haines, £12. My half-sister, Rebecca Haines, as she was called before her marriage, £12. My adopted daughter, Mary Woods, now the wife of William Cross, £60. After my wife's death all lands to be sold, and money given to brother, Isaah Brown, brother Aaron Brown, brother Benoni Brown and brother James Brown. To John Derry, £25, the day he is free. Rest to my brother, Henry Haines, and my sister, Rebecca. Executors—friends, John Ayers, and John Roy. Witnesses—Stirling, Stephen Ogden, Thomas Talmage. Proved Dec. 22, 1763.

1764, March 12. Inventory, £855.15.11, made by John Lyon and John Ayers. (Plantation bought of Benjamin Lewis was sold for £333).

1772, Jan. 22. Account by both Executors. Lib. H, p. 321.

1765, Jan. 19. Brown, Samuel, of Mansfield Twsp., Burlington Co., yeoman; will of. Son, Asa, a part of my land, when 21. Son, John, also a part, when 21. Son, Abraham, the rest of my plantation where I live, when 21. Wife, Ann, household goods, and also use of meadow which my mother had, while my widow. Son, Joseph, £30. Son, Clayton, £25. Esther English, £5. Executors—brother-in-law, Michael Buffin, and my wife. Witnesses—Ephraim Betts, Margaret English, John Watkinson. Proved March 14, 1765. Lib. 12, p. 66.

1765, March 11. Inventory, £188.12.9, made by William Wilson and Abner Woolman.

1764, June 4. Brown, Stephen, of Elizabeth Borough, Essex Co.; will of. Grandson, Henry Brown, son of my son Benjamin Brown, deceased, the house in which my son lived, and the land belonging to it. Son, Caleb, the house he lives in. Son, Joel, the house I live in, and land to go with the same. Grandson, William Brown, son of my son Stephen, a meadow lot. Wife, Prudence, ⅓ of my house and land, while my widow. Daughters, Temperance Meeker, Abigail Riggs and Unis Thompson, 40 shillings each. Remainder to my children, Caleb, Joel, Temperance, Abigail and Unis, my granddaughter, Turah, and my grandchildren, the children of my son Stephen Brown, deceased. Executors—sons, Caleb and Joel. Witnesses—Josiah Crane, William Man, John Ogden. Proved April 10, 1767.
Lib. I, p. 145.

1760, May 20. Brown, Thomas, of Hopewell Twsp., Cumberland Co., yeoman; will of. Wife, Bathniphleath, all she possessed before marriage, and also £10. My Executors to defend a suit, commenced against me by Jonathan Burden. Daughter, Mary, to learn the trade of "tayloris." Sons, John and David, and daughters, Mary, Phebe, Elizabeth and Mabell Brown, who are not of age. Son, Daniel, 40 acres of the upper end of my land. Son, Thomas, rest of lands, when 21. Executors—friends, Jonathan Holmes and Samuel Fithian. Witnesses—Noah Miller, Abijah Holmes, John Coffyson. Proved Feb. 25, 1761.

1760, Dec. 8. Inventory, £437.5.1, made by Benjamin Holme and Obadiah Robins. Lib. 10, p. 183.

1762, July 31. Brown, Thomas, of Roxbury, Morris Co. Int. Adm'x—Pheby Brown, widow. Fellowbondsman—Thomas Brown; both of said place. Witness—John Van Tuyl.

1762, June 29. Inventory £50.2.5, made by John Van Tuyl and Thomas Kelsey.

1764, April 5. Account by Adm'x. Lib. 11, p. 287.

CALENDAR OF WILLS—1761-1770   65

1767, April 27. Brown, Thomas, of Trenton, Hunterdon Co. Int. Adm'r—John Phillips, of Middlesex Co. Fellowbondsman—Joseph Phillips, of Hunterdon Co. Witness—John Allen.
1767, Feb. 13. Inventory, £18.18.0, made by Stephen Laning and Jonathan Furman.
1767, May 11. Sale of goods by vendue, £16.7.4.
1769, Jan. 31. Account made by Administrator.   Lib. 13, p. 207.

1762, April 8. Brown, William, of Mendham, Morris Co.; will of. Wife, Jane, ⅓ the goods. Land on east side of plantation where I live to be sold. The rest of plantation and the money to remain in hands of wife, to bring up my children; the money to be given to my boys and girls, when they come of age. Executors—wife, Jane, and Job Loure. Witnesses—Jabesh Bears, Gilburd Ludlum, Jacomiah (Jeremiah) Forgeson. Proved April 15, 1762.
1762, June 16. Inventory, £979.4.7, made by William Hulburd, and Robert Adams.   Lib. H, p. 136.

1762, July 17. Brown, William, of Trenton, Hunterdon Co. Int. Adm'r—James Cumine, (Cumming), barber. Fellowbondsman—William Pidgeon, Attorney-at-law; both of said place. Witness—Isaac DeCow.   Lib. 11, p. 516.

1761, April 4. Brown, Zebulon, of Burlington, in Burlington Co.; will of. Son, Jonathan, the part of my plantation that is rented, when 21. My wife, Bathsheba, must rent a small house and move to it. Executors—my wife and my friend, Peter Harvey. Witnesses—Leah Ellis, Martha Mott, Rednap Howell. Proved April 17, 1761.
1761, April 16. Renunciation by Bathsheba Brown, the widow, in presence of Martha Mott.   Lib. 10, p. 353.
1761, April 16. Inventory, £54.17.10, made by Job Ridgway and William Folwell.
1771, Nov. 18. Account of Peter Ellis, Ex'r of Peter Harvey, who was Ex'r of Zebulon Brown.

1764, Aug. 23. Browne, John, of Newark, Essex Co.; will of. Son, David, land joining on Moses Baldwin and John Brown, deceased; also land on Elizabeth River. Daughters, Mary, Sibel and Elizabeth, the moveable estate in my house. Son, Moses, 5 shillings. "To Enoch of the children of my beloved son John, deceased, 5 shillings." Son, Zebedee, 20 shillings. Executors—my son, David, and friend, Obadiah Bruen. Witnesses—Obadiah Bruen, James Keen, Timothy Pierson. Proved April 25, 1769.   Lib. K, p. 81.

1757, April 21. Bryan, Peter, of Gloucester Co., school master; will of. To John Erwin, of Greenwich, in said Co., farmer, all personal estate. Executor—said John Erwin. Witnesses—Patrick McCannon, Alexander Randall, Hannah Rose. Proved Feb. 10, 1761.
1761, Feb. 9. Inventory, £12.16.9, made by Isaac Lord and Nixon Chattin.   Lib. 10, p. 398.

1760, July 10. Bryant, Ebenezer, of Borough of Elizabeth, Essex Co., attorney-at-law; will of. All my property to be in hands of William Peartree Smith, my executor, in trust; he to sell all real, if he thinks best, and money to be paid to my wife, Elizabeth. To Presbyterian Church in Elizabeth Town, £50. To the College of New Jersey, £50. Brother, Joshua Bryant, owes me £30, which debt is can-

5

celled. Executor—my brother-in-law, William Peartree Smith. Witnesses—Andrew Whitehead, William Bryant, Elizabeth Bryant. Proved Feb. 5, 1761.

1761, June 12. Inventory, £535.19.11, made by Stephen Crane and Joseph Woodruff, Jr. Lib. G, p. 450.

1765, July 19. Brynbery, Christian, of Penns Neck, Salem Co. Ward. Son of Peter Brynbery, of said place, blacksmith, dec'd, who, being heir-at-law of his father, makes choice of Francis Miles as his Guardian.

1765, July 19. Guardian—Francis Miles. Fellowbondsman—John Mecum; both of Penns Neck, yeomen. Lib. 12, p. 178.

1768, May 27. Buck, Joseph, of Cape May Co.; will of. Lands and effects to be sold. Wife, Lydia ⅓; rest to my four children, Judath, Theody (daughters), and Swain and Lamuel (sons). Executors—wife, Lydia, and Levi Eldredge. Witnesses—Daniel Mulford, Elizabeth Reeves, Nathaniel Foster. Proved July 5, 1768.

1768, June 30. Inventory, £146.14.4, made by James Whilldin and Henry Hand. Lib. 13, p. 527.

1764, Oct. 15. Budd, Catherine, of New Hanover, Burlington Co., widow; will of. Son, Joseph Budd, a bond which I have against him. Son, Henry Budd, negro Doras, when 21. Son, Daniel Budd, £15, when 21. Granddaughters, Autis and Catherine Reynolds, £15 each, when 18. Son, William Budd, my servant girl's time, named Catherine Jonson; also the residue. Executor—son, William. Witnesses—John Goldy, Joseph Goldy. Proved Nov. 17, 1764. Lib. 12, p. 30.

1764, Nov. 5. Inventory, £278.8.8, made by John Goldy and Burbridge Brock.

1761, May 25. Budd, Margaret, of Northampton Twsp., Burlington Co., widow; will of. To my only surviving daughter, Mary Budd, all my clothing; but, if she die, then to my granddaughter, Elizabeth Ross, wife of Alexander Ross. Granddaughter Rebeckah Jolly, £5. Grandchildren, Mary Hopewell, Deborah Budd, Margaret Cowgill and Margaret Budd, £5 each. Executor—said Alexander Ross. Witnesses—Colin Campbell, Elizabeth Elton, Mary Campbell. Proved May 12, 1762.

1762, May 10. Inventory, £144.16.9, made by Henry Paxson and Thomas Shinn. Lib. 11, p. 209.

1766, July 23. Budd, Samuel, Sr., of New Hanover Twsp., Burlington Co., yeoman; will of. Wife, Sarah, bed and case of drawers. Rest of personal estate to be sold, and then wife to have £50, and the rest of money to daughters, Lydea, Theodocia and Hannah, my brother, John Budd's, daughter, Sarah Budd, and my cousin, William Budd, Sr.'s, children. Executors—friends, Solomon Shinn, and cousin, Thomas Budd, Sr. Witnesses—John Mullen, Edward Pancoast, Joseph Goldy. Proved Dec. 19, 1769.

1769, Dec. 1. Renunciation of Thomas Budd.

1769, Dec. 18. Renunciation of Solomon Shinn in presence of Joshua Norcross.

1769, Dec. 19. Bond of Sarah Budd as Adm'x. with will annexed. Fellowbondsman—Joshua Norcross, of Northampton Twsp., Burlington Co. Witness—James Williams. Lib. 14, p. 139.

1769, Sept. 22. Inventory, £132.7.9, made by Joseph Budd and Burbage Brock.

1770, Aug. 23. Budd, William, Sr., of New Hanover Twsp., Burlington Co., yeoman; Will of. Wife, Susannah, £200. Son, Samuel, plantation I purchased of Joseph Shinn, except 7 acres I had surveyed off; also 20 acres on the road to New Mills; but he is to pay to my son, Levi £100, when Levi is 21. Son, Eli, part of tract where I dwell. Son, Jonathan, rest of my plantation, and the above said 7 acres, and he to pay to my son, George, £100. Son, Jonathan, to have ½ the cedar swamp I bought of my brother, David Budd, and he to provide for his mother. Daughter, Mary, wife of Thomas Platt, £13. Daughters, Elizabeth, Rachel and Rebecca, £50 each, when 18. Executors—sons, Samuel, Jonathan and Eli. Witnesses—Thomas Budd, Joseph Lamb, Joseph Goldy. Proved Sept. 15, 1770.
1770, Sept. 14. Inventory, £835.10.9½, made by Thomas Budd and Joseph Lamb. Lib. 14, p. 313; File No. 8633 C.

1759, Dec. 22. Bullus, Francis, of Attercliffe, Parish of Sheffield, Co. of York, gentleman; will of. Nephew, Samuel Bullus, son of my late brother John Bullus, deceased, all my lands, but he to pay £4 a year to my mother, Louldae Brierly, given to her by the will of Mary Ludlam, my late aunt. But 2,000 acres in New Jersey I give to William Bousor, of Attercliffe, yeoman, and John Turner, of Sheffield, mercer. If the said Samuel Bullus die without issue, then the lands to go to my sisters, Hannah Dickinson and Elizabeth Woodcock. The said William Bousor and John Turner, are to act as Trustees only for the said Samuel Bullus. To my housekeeper, Susanna Jackson, £50. Rest to sisters, Hannah, the wife of John Dickinson, and Elizabeth Woodcock. Executors—said two sisters. Witnesses —John Emerson, Benjamin Hoole, William Bamforth. Proved Feb. 1, 1760, and probate granted to Hannah, the wife of John Dickinson, of Sheffield, Co. of York, cutler, and Elizabeth, the wife of Richard Woodcock, of Barnsley, said Co., sailor; all of which was extracted 11th of May, 1765, by John Clough, proctor. Lib. 12, p. 182.

1761, Aug. 24. Burcham, John, Sr., of Frederick Co., Virginia. Int. Adm'r—John Burcham, Jr., of said place, farmer. Fellowbondsman—Samuel Davis, of Amwell, Hunterdon Co.
1761, July 2. Inventory, £141.1.7, of goods which are in this Province, made by Thomas Ruckman. Lib. 10, p. 603.

1762, Oct. 7. Burdge, Benjamin, of Monmouth Co. Ward. Aged 15 years, and the son of David Burdge, of said Co., deceased. Guardian—Patience Burdge, widow. Fellowbondsman—Uriah Burdge; both of said Co. Lib. H, p. 189.

1763, Feb. 2. Burdsall, Stephen, of Monmouth Co.; will of. To sons, Stephen, Richard and Joseph, my lands, when they come of age. Wife, Deliverance, ⅓ of my lands and saw mill, while my widow. Daughter, Mary Burdsall, £10. Daughters, Sarah Burdsall, Elizabeth Burdsall and Phebe Burdsall, each £10. Executors—my wife and son, Stephen. Witnesses—Timothy Ridgway, Gervas Pharo, John Gifford. Proved Oct. 25, 1764. Lib. H, p. 491.

1766, June 14. Burk, Alexander, of Salem Co. Int. Adm'r—John Mason. Fellowbondsmen—William Goodwin and William Hancock, Jr., of Elsinboro, said Co., yeomen.
    1766, June 11. Inventory, £36.2.4, made by William Goodwin and William Hancock.   Lib. 12, p. 317.

1766, Nov. 5. Burnet, David, of Hanover, Morris Co.; will of. Wife, Abigail, use of all my real and personal estate, till my son, Daniel, is 21, and also use of the land given to son Ichabud. Son, Daniel, my home lot and 5 acres over the road. Son, Ichabud, 12 acres on Bottle Hill, lying between Jeremiah Genung and Josiah Miller. Daughter, Hannah Burnet, £15, when 18. Daughter, Rhode Burnet, £15, when 18. Daughter, Mary Burnet, £15. Executors—wife, Abigail, and friends, David Bruen and Thomas Genung. Witnesses—Thomas Bonnel, Stephen Ward, Stephen Howell. Proved Jan. 1, 1767.
                                                                    Lib. I, p. 181.

1763, June 2. Burnet, John, of Perth Amboy, Middlesex Co. Int. Adm'r—William Burnet, only brother of said John. Fellowbondsman —John Smyth; both of said place.   Lib. I, p. 207.

1767, March 17. Burr, Joseph, of Northampton, Burlington Co.; will of. Sons, Henry and Joseph, my plantation where I live. My wife to enjoy profits from said land. Son, Henry, must pay to my son William £60, and to my wife Jane £200. Daughters, Mary Ridgway, Ann Deacon, Jane Ridgway and Rebecca Burr. Son, Robert, 3 tracts of land at Richland, Bucks Co., Pa., that I bought of John Haines, Abraham Griffith and John Parrot; also 5 acres that I bought of Job Lancaster. Son, William, the land I bought of Job Lancaster, except the said 5 acres. Executrix—wife, Jane. Overseers, George Deacon and Solomon Ridgway. Witnesses—Daniel Ellis, John Antram, John Norcross. Proved June 1, 1767.   Lib. 13, p. 74.

1768, July 20. Burroughs, Rebecca, of Gloucester Co. Int. Late Rebecca Nicholson. Adm'r—Isaac Burroughs. Fellowbondsman— Samuel Burroughs; both of said Co.
    1769, Jan. 16. Inventory, £68.15.10, made by Samuel Harrison and Samuel Clement. "Due on bonds from John Githens, Simon Ellis, Jr., Benjamin Thackery, and Mary Zane."   Lib. 13, p. 436.

1758, Jan. 4. Burrowes, Thomas, of Hopewell, Hunterdon Co., yeoman; will of. Advanced in years. Wife, Mercy, ⅓ my moveable estate, except what is reserved to my grandaughter, Mercy Burrowes. Wife may have ⅓ the profits of my lands. Granddaughter, Mercy Burrowes, ⅓ my moveable estate, which I have given to my wife. My 3 granddaughters, Rachel, Rebekah and Charity, daughters of my eldest son Thomas, £5 each. Sons, Edward, and Eden, each £15. I have given a bond to my wife's son, Gersham Moore, which my son Stephen is to pay. Son, Stephen, plantation where I live. Son, John, 20 shillings. Grandaughter, Hannah Brinsley, daughter of Zebulon and Charity Stout, £5. My daughter, Hannah, £15. Personal estate given to, sons, Edward and Eden, and daughters, Charity and Hannah. Executors—sons, Stephen and Edward, and my friend Jonathan Smith, son of Andrew Smith. Witnesses—Jeremiah Woolsey, John Carpenter, Josiah Ellis.

1761, Nov. 26. Codicil. To Mercy Burrowes above named, now the wife of Henry Mershon, £5. To grandchildren, daughters of my dau. Hannah, £10, namely, Charity Disborrough, Rachel Disborrough, and Mercy Disborrough, grandson, Foster Burrows. Witnesses—John Carpenter, David Stout, John Guild. Proved Dec. 15, 1764.
1764, Dec. 12. Inventory, £152.12.7, made by Benjamin Moore and Andrew Muirheid.
1765, June 10. Account made by the Executors. Lib. 12, p. 150.

1768, Jan. 23. Burtis, John, of Upper Freehold, Monmouth Co.; will of. Wife, Susannah, £50 and some goods. Rest of personal and real to be sold, and money given to my daughters, Elizabeth and Ann, when 21; (said daughters are not yet 14). Executors—my uncles, Joseph Bullock and Thomas Thorn. Witnesses—William Burtis, George Bullock, Thomas Lewis Woodward. Proved Feb. 18, 1768.
1768, Feb. 11. Inventory, £160.8.6, made by John Leonard and David Wright. Lib. 13, p. 317.

1768, March 5. Burton, Ann, of Burlington Co. Int. Adm'r—Isaiah Robins. Fellowbondsman—Joseph Clayton; both of said Co.
1768, Feb. 29. Inventory, £13.16.4, made by Joseph Clayton and Joseph Scholey. Lib. 13, p. 434.
1769, April 29. Account made by Adm'r. Lib. 13, p. 434.

1763, April 4. Burwell, John, of Monmouth Co. Int. Adm'r—Joseph Burwell, eldest son of said John. Fellowbondsman—John Burwell, of Morris Co.
1763, April 3. Renunciation by, Agnes Burwell, the widow; in favor of her son, Joseph.
1763, April 15. Inventory, made by John Mitchell and Charles Marsh. Lib. H, p. 227.

1762, Aug. 30. Butcher, Richard, Jr., of Stow Creek, Salem Co. Int. Adm'r—Job Butcher. Fellowbondsman—Aaron Butcher; both of said place, yeomen.
1762, Sept. 3. Inventory, £554.5.2, made by John Wheaton and Thomas Sayre. Lib. 11, p. 250.

1769, March 5. Butler, John, Sr., of Greenwich, Cumberland Co., yeoman; will of. Son, John, the plantation in Bacon's Neck, and he to support his mother, Priscilla, my wife. After John's death I give the plantation to his son, Amos; but, if Amos die before he comes of age, then I give it to his brother, John; and, if John die before he become of age, then it is to be sold, and the money divided among the surviving children of my son, John. If my son, John, should die before his present wife, Elizabeth, then she shall have ½ the profits of said plantation, and the remaining part I give to my three grandchildren, Lydia Butler, Mary Butler and Rachel Butler. Executor—my son, John Butler. Witnesses—William Fithian, John Fiddis and Joseph Norbury. Proved March 24, 1769. Lib. 14, p. 13.

1770, April 14. Butler, John, of Mansfield, Burlington Co. Int. Adm'r—Samuel Allen, of Nottingham, said Co. Fellowbondsman—Nathan Robbins, of Upper Freehold, Monmouth Co. Lib. 15, p. 8.

1766, Jan. 11. Buzby, John, of Newton Township, Gloucester Co., yeoman; will of. Wife, Sarah, the part of the plantation where I dwell, which I bought of my sister-in-law, Kezia Ellis, which was caused to be divided by a Writ of Partition; also ⅓ of the swamp, which was devised to me by my father, and which I purchased of my brother, Samuel Buzby; and the same shall be divided off by Isaac Mickle and Samuel Clement, and they are to give a certificate, which is to be recorded in the Secretary's office. Son, John, the rest of my plantation and the other ⅔ of the swamp. Daughter, Precilla Buzby, £400, when she is 18. Sister, Hannah's son, John Haines, £50, when 21. Said sister has other children. Speaks of brother, Jabez. If my daughter die, then ½ of her share is to go to Rachel Wickward, and the other ½ to my cousin, Jane Taylor's children. Mentions uncle, Thomas Buzby, and cousin, Joseph Buzby. Executors—my wife and my friends, Isaac Mickle and Samuel Clement. Witnesses—Aaron Oakford, Grace Evens, William Evens. Proved Aug. 8, 1766. Lib. 12, p. 369.

1762, Sept. 9. Byram, Ebenezer, of Mendham, Morris Co.; will of. Lands may be sold. Eldest son, Edward, to have as much as his younger brothers, and £100 more. Sons, Ebenezer, Napthali, and Joseph, to have double to what my daughters will have. Wife to be equal with my younger sons, and to have the profits of the whole estate till the children are all of age. Daughters, Huldah, Abigail, Anna, Mary and Phebe, to have an equal half part with my younger sons; except that Huldah have £70 less than what she has already had. My wife is supposed to be pregnant, and that child is to have its share. Executors—my wife, Abigail, my son, Edward, my brother, Jeptha Byram, and Isaac Babbit. Witnesses—Asa Cooke, David Thompson, Samuel Hudson. Proved Sept. 27, 1762.

1763, March 10. Inventory, £4,130.9.5, made by Joseph Beach and Daniel Cary. Lib. H, p. 289.

1760, May 20. Byrnes, Richard, of Middlesex Co.; will of. I am about to travel. To my friend, James Abraham, Jr., some clothing, and he is to go to William Preston's and get 3 shirts, etc. He is to have the prizes in the lotteries. Executor—said James Abraham, Jr. Witnesses—Arthur Edmonds, John Nevill, William Thomson. Proved Feb. 19, 1761.

1761, May 10. Inventory of the goods of "Richard Burns," made by John Combs and William Jolley. Lib. G, p. 362.

1763, June 27. Cadmus, Hartman, of Slotterdam, Bergen Co., yeoman; will of. Wife, Maragrietje, all goods she brought, and she to live with my son, Dirk. Son, Dirk, all lands. My daughter, Marritje, goods, and £130. Executors—brother, Abraham Cadmus, and my friend, John Cadmus, both of Slotterdam. Witnesses—David Marinus, Johannis Van Hoorn and Isaac Cadmus. Proved Aug. 14, 1764.

1764, Aug. 14. Bond of Cornelius Post (son in law of Hartman Cadmus) of Slotterdam, as Adm'r, with will annexed; Abraham Cadmus and John Cadmus renounced. Lib. H, p. 377.

1763, Sept. 23. Calvin, Daniel, of Town and Co. of Gloucester. Int. Adm'r—Lawrence Shanow. Fellowbondsman—Joseph Ellis; both of said place. Witness—Samuel Allinson. Lib. 11, p. 440.

CALENDAR OF WILLS—1761-1770   71

1761, Dec. 14. Cambell, Jonathan, of Woodbridge, Middlesex Co.; will of. Wife, Mary, all my real and personal, except 5 shillings, which I give to my cousin, Jessy Cambell (son of my brother David Cambell). Executors—my wife, and David Kint. Witnesses—Daniel Donham, Catharine Donham, Mary Wright. Proved May 25, 1767.
Lib. I, p. 111.

1769, Aug. 30. Camp, John, of Essex Co. Int. Adm'x—Sarah Camp, his widow. Lib, K, p. 121.

1766, Aug. 15. Campbell, Rev. Colin, of City and Co. of Burlington. Int. Adm'x—Mary Campbell, the widow. Fellowbondsmen—Abraham Hewlings, of Burlington, and Peter Bard, of Mount Holly, said Co., merchants.
1766, Aug. 26. Inventory, £3,050.6.6, made by Daniel Ellis and Isaac Hewlings.
1773, March 15. Mary Campbell sworn, and said that the inventory was perfect. Lib. 12, p. 295.

1764, Dec. 31. Campbell, John, of Somerset Co. Int. Adm'r—Archibald Campbell, the eldest son. Fellowbondsman—Greear Brown; both of said Co.
1764, Dec. 28. Renunciation, by Margrit Campbell, the widow, in favor of her son, Archibald Campbell.
1765, March 6. Inventory, £78.13.6, made by Michael Schooley and Thomas Irwin. Lib. H, p. 376.

1768, Jan. 8. Campion, Richard, of City and Co. of Burlington. Int. Adm'rs—Sarah Campion (widow), and John Campion, of Northampton, said Co., carpenter. Witness—William Heulings.
1768, Jan. 7. Inventory, £86.2.6, made by Thomas Rodman and William Heulings. Lib. 13, p. 311.

1768, Oct. 8. Camron, John, of Greenwich Twsp., Gloucester Co., shipwright; will of. My real and personal to be divided equally among my wife, Mary, and our four children, namely, George, John, Rebecca and Abraham, when children are of full age. Executors—wife, and my friend, Jacob Spicer. Witnesses—David Brown, Jonathan Chew, Daniel Bennett. Proved Jan. 14, 1769.
1769, Jan. 10. Inventory, £354.8.0, made by John Brown and David Brown. Lib. 14, p. 33.

1761, Feb. 10. Capherdy, Peter, of Chesterfield, Burlington Co. Int. Adm'r—Richard Martin. Fellowbondsman—Joseph Wright; both of Arneys Town, said Co. Lib. 10, p. 173.

1769, May 29. Carl, Jacob, of Morris Co.; will of. Wife, Rebecca, use of ⅓ my lands hereafter given to my son, Jonas. Eldest son, Uriah Carl, £100, after taking out what I paid on bond to Joseph Carl, of Staten Island; and to Uriah's eldest daughter, Mary. Son, John, land where he lives; also the land in the Great Swamp. Son, Jonas, land where I live. Daughter, Sarah Baird, £50. Executors—sons, John and Jonas, and friend Peter Layton. Witnesses—Daniel Cooper, Jr., Elias Runyon, Mercy More. Proved Dec. 4, 1769. Lib. K, p. 177.

1769, Jan. 16. Carle, John, of Hopewell, Cumberland Co. Int. Adm'rs—Catherine Carle and Samuel Carle, both of said place, widow and yeoman, and Hugh Dunn, of Stow Creek, said Co., yeoman.
1769, Jan. 6. Inventory, £98.8.11, made by Hugh Dunn and Benjamin Dunn. Lib. 13, p. 498.

1765, Oct. 31. Carman, James, of City of Perth Amboy, Middlesex Co. Int. Adm'x—Mary Carman, widow of James. Fellowbondsman—Thomas Lyall; both of said City. Witness—John Terrill.
Lib. H, p. 540.

1763, April 19. Carman, Joseph, of Greenwich, Gloucester Co., carpenter. Int. Adm'r—Jacob Spicer. Fellowbondsman—Azariah Shinn; both of said place. Witness—Sarah Howell.
1763, April 28. Inventory, £80.7.0, made by George Flannigan and Samuel Shivers. Lib. 11, p. 313.

1768, Feb. 14. Carman, Richard, of Woodbridge Twsp., Middlesex Co., farmer; will of. My grandson, Stephen Carman, £5, by virtue of his being my heir-at-law. Son, Richard, all my lands. Daughter, Abigail, wife of Hugh Dunn, £350. Daughter, Kezia, £150, and the right to reside with Richard, and to have her living from the land during the time she is a widow. Rest of estate to grandchildren, Stephen Carman, Samuel Carman, Abigail Bloodgood, Mary Carman, Richard Carman, Phineas Carman, and Sarah and Margaret Dunn. Executors—son, Richard, and my daughter, Kezia. Witnesses—Moses Morris, Margaret Carman, Reuben Evens. Proved Jan. 21, 1769. Probate granted to Richard Carman and Kezia Loofborrow.
1769, Jan. 23. Inventory, £1,182.12.11, made by James Rowland and Reuben Evins; both of Woodbridge. Lib. K, p. 51.

1769, May 30. Carman, Richard, of Woodbridge, Middlesex Co. Int. Adm'r—James Rowland. Fellowbondsman—Stephen Carman; both of said Co.
1769, May 30. Renunciation, by Kezia Martin, sister, and Stephen Carman, nephew of Richard Carman, Jr.
1769, May 31. Inventory, £525.5.3, made by Isaac Tappen and Reuben Evens. Lib. K, p. 93.

1767, Nov. 20. Carman, Stephen, of Middlesex Co. Int. Adm'rs—Isabel Carman, the widow and Richard Carman, Jr., brother of Stephen. Fellowbondsman—Jeremiah Dunn; all of said Co.
1767, Sept. 5. Inventory, £143.9.2, made by James Rowland and Jacob Shotwell. Lib. I, p. 175.

1761, Feb. 5. Carr, John, of Hunterdon Co. Int. Adm'r—Charles Stewart. Fellowbondsman—John Hackett; both of said Co.
Lib. 10, p. 172.

1766, July 30. Carrle, John, of Acquacknung, Essex Co. Int. Adm'r—Jacob Carrle, brother of said John. Fellowbondsman—James Gray; both of said place. Witness—Michael Vreeland. Lib. I, p. 7.

1769, Feb. 17. Carrol, George. Int. Adm'r—John Jerolman.
Lib. I, p. 364.

CALENDAR OF WILLS—1761-1770   73

1761, Dec. 22. Carson, David, of Salem Co., shallopman. Int. Adm'r—Doctor John Budd. Fellowbondsman—Augustine Moore; both of Salem, said Co.   Lib. 11, p. 36.

1759, Oct. 29. Carter, John, Sr., of Deptford, Gloucester Co.; will of. Eldest son, John, all my plantation, except 6 acres. Son, Daniel, the said 6 acres, to be taken off the upper part. (Daniel is not 21.) Rest of my goods to my children and grandchildren, that is, my deceased son, Samuel (left 3 children), son Jeremiah, daughter Martha Taylor, Sarah Cattell, and daughter, Joana Carter. Executor—son, John. Witnesses—Michael Fisher, Charles Fisher, John Fisher. Proved April 1, 1762.
1762, Jan. 8. Inventory, £19..8.9, made by Thomas Nightingale and George Flaningam.   Lib. 11, p. 121.

1770, Sept. 6. Carter, Luke, of Hanover, Morris Co., yeoman; will of. Wife, Hannah, her choice of room, after mother's; all the goods she brought, and £300. Wife supposed to be pregnant, and that child is provided for. My brothers, George and Thomas, given legacies. Executors—my wife, my brother-in-law, Josiah Miller, and my brother, George Carter. Witnesses—Thomas Genung, Theophilus Miller, Ezekiel Cheever. Proved Sept. 27, 1770.   Lib. K, p. 277.

1770, Oct. 18. Carter, Nicholas, of Hanover, Morris Co., yeoman; will of. Children—Jonathan, Anna, Experience, Hannah, Abraham, Nehemiah, Moses, Nicholas, David, Comfort and Kezia, each 5 shillings. Wife, Susanna, use of rest of personal and real estate, and, after her death, to my son Reuben, or when he is 21; but if he die, then to go to his sisters, Comfort and Kezia. Executors—my wife and son, Nehemiah. Witnesses—Joseph Foster, Thomas Genung, Ezekiel Cheever. Proved Nov. 22, 1770.   Lib. K, p. 298.

1770, Dec. 26. Carter, William, of Trenton, Hunterdon Co. Int. Adm'rs—Daniel Clark and William Chambers; both of said place.
1770, Dec. 26. Inventory, £8.18.0, made by John Chambers and Benjamin Clark.   Lib. 15, p. 75.

1762, July 22. Case, Ichabod, of Roxbury, Morris Co.; will of. My wife to have this house and land while my widow, and afterwards to go to my son William. Of the bond I hold against Justus King and Richard Sweazay, for £50, I give my said son £10, and £10 to my daughter, Abigail, and £10 to my daughter, Hannah, and £10 to my daughter, Kezia, and the other £10 to my grandson, Joseph Case, when he is 21. Executors—wife, Hannah, and Constant King. Witnesses—Isaiah Younglove, Barnabus Curtice. Proved Sept. 28, 1762.
    Lib. H, p. 292.

1765, Feb. 9. Castner, Johannis, of Bridgewater, Somerset Co.; will of. Wife, Margaret, to be maintained during her life, and after her death, the residence to be given to my children; and my youngest son, Coonrod, shall have £10 more than his brothers, and my daughter Anne to have 30 shillings more than her sisters. My sons are John, Daniel, Jacob, Peter, Michael, Coonrod; and my daughters are Kathrine, Anne, Ursula. Executors—sons, John and Daniel. Witnesses—John Appleman, Johan Georg Mayer, Lucas Tiepple. Proved May 20, 1765.

1765, April 26. Inventory, £95, made by Lucas Dibbel and John Appleman.　Lib. H, p. 510.

1760, June 5. Catterling, Francis, of Morristown, Morris Co., yeoman; will of. My eldest son, Francis, 10 shillings. About Oct. 31, 1751, I bought of Joseph Prudden and Jonathan Osborn the land I live on, which I give to my wife, Phebe, while my widow; after which I give it to my five sons, Isaac, James, Joseph, Benjamin and Jacob. After my wife's death, I give the household goods to my daughters, Phebe and Susannah. Daughter, Mary, £3. Daughter, Martha, £3. Executrix—my wife, Phebe. Witnesses—Peter Kemble. Hannah Osborn, Mary Solegard. Proved Dec. 27, 1768. Lib. K, p. 32.

1763, Oct. 10. Catterling, Jacob, of Morristown, Morris Co. Int. Adm'r—Thomas Kinney. Fellowbondsman—Jacob Ford, Jr.; both of said place. Witness—Thomas Moseley.　File No. 180 N.

1765, April 10. Chamberlain, William, of Shrewsbury, Monmouth Co.; will of. Son, Samuel, after the death of my wife, Jane, all my goods; but, if he die before my wife, then to my son, Thomas. Samuel to have the land I bought of David Knott. Son, James, 5 shillings. Sons, John and Thomas, each 5 shillings. Executor—son, Samuel. Witnesses—Amos Willis, John Holmes, Mary Bennet. Proved July 30, 1770.

1770, June 20. Inventory, £128.9.0, made by Thomas Potter, and John Holmes.　Lib. K, p. 231.

1763, May 28. Chambers, John, of Bernards Town, Somerset Co., yeoman; will of. Wife, Eleanor, an equal part of personal and real, with my children. Eldest son, Robert's son, John, £1. Son, David, £1. Daughter, Martha, equal part of residue, and daughter, Lydia, an equal part, as also daughter, Elizabeth, and also Mary. Grandson, David Ayers, an equal part. Granddaughter, Phebe. Executors—my wife and Robert Adams. Witnesses—John Bescherer, Elizabeth Patterson, Andrew Patterson. Proved April 24, 1767.
Lib. I, p. 122.

1764, Jan. 20. Chambers, John, Esq., of New York City; will of. To be buried in Trinity Church-yard. To Augustus Van Courtlandt, whom I brought up, ½ of my law books, and the other ½ I give to John Jay, son of Peter Jay, my brother-in-law. Wife, Ann Chambers, my land in Orange Co., called Cheescocks, which I bought of Elizabeth Denn, dec.; also my lands which I got from her father, Col. Jacobus Van Courtlandt, dec'd, after her death. I give the house where I live, with the water lot, to Augustus Van Courtlandt, and the house I bought of Col. Fredrick Philipse and the children of John Bruger; also I give him the house where he lives, and I give to him and his sister, Eve White, and to Ann White, daughter of said Eve, all lands in Montgomery Ward, New York City. To James Van Courtlandt, Augustus Van Courtlandt and Fredrick Van Courtlandt, three brothers, the rest of lands. Wife, Ann, my moveables and negros. To Col. Vincent Matthews, £300. To John Bartow, of Westchester, who lived with me, £50. To Lambert Moore, £50. Executors —my wife, and, after her death, my brother-in-law, Peter Jay, my nephew, John Livingston, of New York, merchants, and my nephews, James Van Courtlandt, and Augustus Van Courtlandt. Witnesses— Richard Nicholls, John Kelly, Benjamin Helme. Proved Aug. 15, 1764.　Lib. H, p. 353.

1761, Jan. 10. Chambless, Jacob, of Alloways Creek Twsp., Salem Co., carpenter; will of. Oldest son, James Chamless, 5 shillings. Wife, Sarah, all my lands. Executrix—my wife, Sarah. Witnesses—Philip Tyler, James Finley, John Hillman. Proved April 25, 1761.
1761, April 7. Inventory, £39.6.0, made by Richard Moore and Philip Tyler. Lib. 11, p. 15.

1767, Jan. 15. Chamless, Nathaniel, of Alloways Creek, Salem Co., yeoman; will of. Wife, Susanna, £700. Grandson, Chamless Hart, a house and lot in Salem, formerly belonging to Thomas Thompson. Daughter, Hannah Hart, £50. Daughter, Rebecca Wharton, £150. Granddaughter, Sarah Hancok, £80. Cousin, James Chamless, £20. To my daughters, Hannah Hart and Rebecca Wharton, and my two granddaughters, Susannah Test and Sarah Hancock, rest of personal estate. Executors—sons-in-law, John Hart and John Wharton. Witnesses—Elijah Bowen, Samuel Hancock, Thomas Sayre. Proved April 15, 1767.
1767, March 19. Inventory, £4,549.1.6, made by William Oakford and Thomas Sayre. Lib. 13, p. 177.

1765, Aug. 14. Champion, John, of Great Egg Harbor, Gloucester Co., inn holder; will of. My wife, ⅝ of my moveables to be in the care of my son, Joseph, as trustee. Sons, Joseph, and John, each 10 shillings. Son, Nathaniel, my plantation, and rest of moveable estate. Executor—son, Nathaniel. Witnesses—Harmen Rosekrans, John Little, John Baly. Proved Sept. 20, 1766.
1765, Nov. 26. Inventory, made by John Little, and Philip Scull.
Lib. 12, p. 375.

1766, Dec. 1. Champion, Thomas, of Haddonfield, Gloucester Co., "taylor." Int. Adm'x—Deborah Champion, widow of Thomas. Fellowbondsman—John Barton, of Waterford Twsp., said Co., yeoman. Witness—Jacob Clement.
1766, Nov. 25. Inventory, £830.17.3¼ made by, Jacob Clement and Josiah Shivers.
1773, Nov. 2. Account by Deborah Champion. Lib. 12, p. 382.

1764, Feb. 2. Chandler, Amer, of Shrewsbury, Monmouth Co., brick layer; will of. Wife, Dorothy, all real and personal while my widow. Sons, Pontias and Asahel, house and land, after wife's death. Daughter, Leady, now wife of Edward Paterson Cook, and daughter, Rebecka, now wife of William Mount, and daughter, Elizabeth, and my sons Benjamin, George, John and Thomas, and daughter Dorathy, at age of 21, to each 5 shillings. Executors—wife and son, Pontius. Witnesses—Job Cook, Asher West, Thomas White. Proved May 12, 1764.
1764, June 23. Inventory, made by Asher West and Job Cook.
Lib. H, p. 439.

1766, Feb. 8. Chandler, John, of Alloways Creek, Salem Co., yeoman; will of. Son, Joseph Chandler, the several tracts of land which I purchased of Francis Dunam, Isaac Anderson and Charles Fogg. To my wife the goods she brought at time of our marriage, and £15 yearly, and the profits of my plantation that I bought of Benjamin Allen. Daughter, Easter Decker, £5. Daughter, Rebecca Smith, £5. Daughter, Mary Laing, £5. Daughter, Abigail Chandler, £5. To my son-in-law, Clarck Smith, the farm I bought of Benjamin Allen; that is, if he pays the above legacies; and also pays all the debts of Josiah Chandler, deceased. Executor—friend, George Warner. Trustee—friend, Charles Fogg. Witnesses—Page Perry, Isaac Anderson, Mary Anderson. Proved March 24, 1766. Lib. 12, p. 314.

1765, Oct. 20. Chandler, Josiah, of Alloways Creek, Salem Co.; will of. My eldest brother, John Chandler, my lands. Brother, Joseph, the tract his father, John Chandler, purchased of Frances Dunham and Isaac Anderson. Sisters, Esther Dikers, Rebeckah Smith, Mary Savage and Abigail Chandler, each £10. Executor—brother, John. Overseers—William Bradway and John Stewart. Witnesses—Thomas Thompson, Job Ware, Sarah Groff. Proved Jan. 10, 1767.

1767, Jan. 10. George Warner, of said Alloways Creek, yeoman, appointed Adm'r with the will annexed. Fellowbondsmen—Charles Fogg, of Alloways Creek, yeoman, and Roger Sherron, of Town of Salem, inn keeper. (The Executor died before probate of the will).
Lib. 13, p. 187.

1762, Sept. 4. Chandler, Moses, of Essex Co.; will of. Wife, Mary, house and land where I live, while my widow, and, after that, to my oldest daughter, Marian. Wife to bring up and educate our two children. Daughter, Phebe, my house and land, formerly purchased by uncle, John Chandler, of John Donnington, and joins the lot of Thomas Ross, containing 6¼ acres, when Phebe is 21. If both my children die under age, then the house and lot where I live I give to my brother, John Chandler, and my wife, Mary, equally. Executors—my wife, Mary, Caleb Crane, and Benjamin Spinning. Witnesses—John Blanchard, John Chetwood, Ellit Cresey. Proved Sept. 10, 1764.

1762, Sept. 21. Inventory, £65, made by William Ross and Ebenezer Spinning. Witnesses—Caleb Crane, Mary Brant, Benjamin Spining.
Lib. I, p. 135.

1770, Nov. 22. Chandler, Stephen, of Woodbridge Twsp., Middlesex Co. Int. Adm'r—Samuel Barron. Fellowbondsman—Jonathan Clawson; both of said place.

1770, Nov. 21. Renunciation, by Susanna Chandler, the widow.

1771, Jan. 10. Inventory, £39.9.8, made by Jonathan Frazee and Daniel Dunham. Also account made by Adm'r. Lib. K, p. 255.

1760, Aug. 29. Chattin, Abraham, of Deptford Twsp., Gloucester Co., yeoman; will of. Son, John, 5 shillings. Son, Nixon, 5 shillings; also same amount to son, Abraham, and son, James. Son Francis, £10, and same amount to son Josiah. Daughter, Mary Zane, 5 shillings. Daughter, Sarah Robson, £5. Wife, Phebe, the rest of personal estate, and house and lot in Woodbury during her life. Son, Josiah, all my lands. Executrix—my wife Phebe. Witnesses—James Brown, John Snowden, James Hinchman. Proved Jan. 20, 1761.
Lib. 10, p. 399.

1765, Feb. 4. Chattin, Phebe, of Deptford, Gloucester Co. Int. Adm'r—Joshua Ward. Fellowbondsman—Joseph Ward; both of said place, yeomen. Witness—Jehu Ward.

1765, Feb. 13. Inventory, £148.13.0, made by Joseph Ward and Habakuk Ward. Lib. 12, p. 47.

CALENDAR OF WILLS—1761-1770   77

1764, March 1. Cheesman, William, of Waterford Twsp., Gloucester Co., yeoman; will of. Wife, Sarah, the goods which she desires to keep, and my house and lot, which I purchased of Henry Jones, of Moorestown, during her life, and, after her death, said house and lot I give to my neice, Margaret Cheesman, daughter of my brother, Peter Cheesman, when she is 21. My neice, Parthenia Jolly, daughter of my sister, Deborah, £50 when 18. Niece, Abigail Thorn, daughter of John Thorn, deceased, £20 when 18, but, if she die, then to her brother, John Thorn. Remainder to sister Margaret Smallwood, Thomas Cheesman, son of my brother, Peter Cheesman, William Cheesman, son of my brother, Thomas, and William Jones, son of my sister, Naomi. Executors—nephew, Jeremiah Jones and my friend, Samuel Blackwood. Witnesses—Mary Brien, Abigail Blackwood, Mary Blackwood, Joseph Blackwood. Proved Jan. 30, 1766.
  1765, Dec. 3. Renunciation, by Samuel Blackwood, of Deptford Twsp., said Co. Witnesses—John Cox and John Brick.
  1765, Dec. 3. Inventory, £652.7.10, made by John Cox and John Brick.
  1770, Aug. 9. Account by Jeremiah Jones, as Executor.
                                      Lib. 12, p. 377; Lib. 15, p. 46.

1759, Aug. 13. Chester, Samuel, of Greenwich Twsp., Gloucester Co.; will of. Wife, Amey, all real and personal, and the real may be sold. Executors—my wife, Amey, and friend, Thomas Denny. Witnesses—John Boys, Laurance Strang, William Sweeten. Proved March 2, 1764.
  1764, Jan. 27. Inventory, £34.17.2, made by Thomas Roberts and Mathew Gill.   Lib. 11, p. 519.

1763, March 16. Chester, Thomas, of Greenwich, Gloucester Co. Int. Adm'r—Samuel Chester. Fellowbondsman—Thomas Roberts; both of said place. Witness—Sarah Howell.
  1763, March 16. Renunciation of Catherine Chester, widow of said Thomas Chester, in favor of her brother-in-law, Samuel Chester. Witness—Thomas James.
  1763, March 15. Inventory, £92.14.5, made by Mathew Gill and Thomas Roberts.
  1764, July 24. Adm'x, de bonis non—Amy Chester, a widow. Fellowbondsman—Nathan Boys, yeoman; both of Greenwich. Witness —Sarah Howell.
  1764, Dec. 24. Account of Amy Chester, administratrix de bonis non, of the estate of Thomas Chester left unadministered by Samuel Chester, deceased, administrator of said Thomas.
                                      Lib. 11, p. 313; Lib. 12, p. 15.

1764, May 11. Chesterman, Benjamin, of Monmouth Co. Int. Adm'x—Hannah Chesterman, the widow. Fellowbondsman—William Crawford; both of said place.   Lib. H, p. 334.

1762, June 28. Chew, John, of Town and County of Gloucester, yeoman. Int. Adm'x—Elizabeth Chew, widow. Fellowbondsman— Joseph Hugg, yeoman; both of said place. Witness—Hannah Kaighin.
  1762, May 28. Inventory, £57.13.10, made by Joseph Hugg and Joseph Ellis.
  1763, Dec. 20. Account made by Adm'x.   Lib. 11, p. 277.

1761, March 31. Chidester, Mable, of Roxbury, Morris Co. Int. Adm'r—Samuel Chidester. Fellowbondsman—Moses Thomkens; both of said place, yeomen. Witness—John Van Tuyl.
1761, March 27. Inventory, £45.2.9, made by John Van Tuyl and David Sutton. Lib. 10, p. 464.

1770, April 6. Christeen, John, of Bergen Co. Int. Adm'rs—Stephen Bourdett, Jr., Abraham Montanye and John Day; all of said Co. Fellowbondsman—Thomas Moore. Witness—John Zabrisky.
1768, Sept. 30. Inventory, £283.4.9, made by Stephen Bourdett, Abraham Montonye and John Day. Lib. K, p. 256.

1768, March 20. Christopher, Barnt, of Hopewell, Hunterdon Co.: will of. Eldest son, Barnt, one half of my plantation, and he to pay to my second son, John, £100 in three years after my wife gives her consent to dividing the land into two parts. Wife, Catherine, to have use of plantation, till my youngest son Daniel is 21. My third son, Jesse, the other ½ of the plantation, he paying to his brother, Daniel, £100. Daniel to be sent to school till he is 16. Daughters, Catherine, Anne and Elizabeth, rest of personal estate. Executors—my wife, Catherine, and my son, Barnt. Witnesses—Nathan Moore, James Hunt, Reuben Armitage. Proved June 20, 1768.
1768, May 8. Inventory, £103.10.6, made by Nathan Moore and Reuben Armitage. Lib. 12, p. 517.

1749, April 13. Christy, James, of Schraelingburg, Bergen Co.; will of. Wife, Magdeleen. Eldest son, John. Children—Jacomyn, wife of David Van Orden, Antie Stage, John Christy, Lea Van Orden, Mary, wife of Fil, David Christy, Elisabet ———, William Christy, Rachel ———, Daniel Christy, Sarah Christy, and Magdeleen Christy. Son, William all my land. Executors—wife and sons John and William. Witnesses—David Jacobus Demarest, Jacobes Demarest and David Demarest, Sr. Proved, May 24, 1768.
1768, May 23. Inventory, £9-4-0, made by David Van Orden and Johannes Westervelt. Lib. I, p. 328.

1761, April 7. Church, Silas, of Fairfield, Cumberland Co., weaver; will of. To my wife, Martha, profits of all real and moveables, but, if she marry, then my brother-in-law Benjamin Stites to take my estate in his hands as Trustee, and take care of my children. Son, Joseph, plantation where I live, he giving his brother, Christopher, privilege of getting hay, and wintering 20 head of cattle while he lives. Son, Christopher, my lands at Cape May. Daughters, Deborah Church and Alice Church, ⅖ of the rest of my estate. Executors—my wife, Martha, and father, Joseph Page. Witnesses—Stephen Clark, Edmond Shaw, David Shepherd. Proved April 22, 1761.
1761, April 17. Inventory, £144.17.2, made by David Shepherd and Stephen Clerk. Lib. 11, p. 169.

1765, Feb. 4. Clap, George, of Hanover, Burlington Co., yeoman; will of. Son-in-law, Job Shinn, and my son, John Clap, the house and lot where I live, when John is 21. Wife, Rebeccah, the use of said house and the rest of estate, and to provide for the children, and, after her death, to my daughter, Tacy Clap. Executors—my wife and her brother, William Shinn. Witnesses—William Clap, Abigail Shinn, Samuel Atkinson. Proved Feb. 13, 1765.

1765, Feb. 12. Inventory, £67.0.11½, made by Francis Shinn and William Budd. Sr. Lib. 12, p. 43.

1765, Oct. 21. Clark, Abraham, of Elizabeth Town, Essex Co. Int. Adm'r—Benjamin Marsh. Fellowbondsmen—Andrew Craig and Abraham Marsh; all of said place. Witness—John Terrill.
1765, Oct. 19. Renunciation by Sarah Clark, the widow, in favor of Benjamin Marsh. Witness—Abraham Clark. Lib. H, p. 540.

1763, Nov. 7. Clark, Benjamin and Phebe, of Salem Co. Wards. Petition of John Jarman, showing that, by the request of his sister, Esther Peirson, late of Stow Creek Twsp., Cumberland Co., deceased; he had left in his care Benjamin Clark and Phebe Clark, son and daughter of the said sister, Esther Peirson, by her former husband, Samuel Clark, being now orphan children and under the age of 14. So as to see that no injustice should be done them in regard to the estate left them by their father, said Samuel Clark, then and now in the hands of Azel Peirson, late husband of said Esther Peirson, who refuses to deliver up the same, or to account therefor by a legal settlement: Therefore the said Jarman prays to be appointed Guardian.
1763, Nov. 8. Guardian—John Jarman, of Salem Co. Fellowbondsman—John Lawrence, of Burlington. Witnesses—William Heulings and John Hutchin. Lib. 11, p. 476.

1755, July 2. Clark, Charles, of Deerfield, Cumberland Co., yeoman; will of. Wife, Mary, benefit of my plantation, while my widow. Son, Samuel, my lands, but, if he die under age, then to my two brothers, Daniel Clark and Benjamin Clark. Executors—my wife, and my son, Daniel. Witnesses—Benjamin Garrison, Samuel Hannah, Robert Dair, Jr. Proved Dec. 1, 1761.
1761, Dec. 1. Inventory, £320.6.8, made by Samuel Hannah and Nathan Leek. Lib. 11, p. 164.

1761, Dec. 11. Clark, Charles, of Cumberland Co. Ward. Eldest son of Samuel Clark, of Deerfield, said Co., who died intestate, leaving lands. Guardians—Azel Peirson, of Stow Creek, and Reuben Jarman, of Hopewell; both of said Co. Fellowbondsman—John Jarman, of Piles Grove, Salem Co., yeoman. Witness—George Peirson.
Lib. 10, p. 439.

1769, April 17. Clark, Cornelius. Int. Adm'rs—Elizabeth Clark and William Ray. Inventory, £293.4.6. Lib. 13, p. 531.

1761, April 29. Clark, David, of Morristown, Morris Co. Int. Adm'r—Benjamin Hathaway, yeoman. Fellowbondsman—James Frost, blacksmith; both of said Co. Witness—Samuel Heard.
1761, April 24. Renunciation by Sarah Clark, widow of said David, in favor of Benjamin Hathaway. Witness—Henry Primrose.
Lib. H, p. 13.

1763, Dec. 26. Clark, Edward, of Upper Penns Neck, Salem Co., yeoman; will of. Wife, Mary, all my real and personal estate. Executrix—my wife. Witnesses—Robert Howard, Hananiah Clark, Mary Howard. Proved Feb. 17, 1764.
1764, Feb. 4. Inventory, £27.13.0, made by William Summerall and Adam Clark. Lib. 11, p. 486.

1767, Aug. 1. Clark, Elizabeth, of Elizabeth Town, Essex Co.; will of. Widow; late Elizabeth Radley. Son, William Radley, ½ the house and land where I live, which is to join the land late his brother's, John Radly, and, after William's death, to his child or children. The other ½ to my son, Ichabud Radly. Son, Henry Radly, a lot in Elizabeth Town, when he is 21. My woodland near John Little I give to my son John, son William, son Ichabud and son Henry. Daughter, Elizabeth, wife of Daniel Sale, a silver tea pot. Daughter, Maryan, wife of Barnaby Shute, various goods, and, at her death, to her children. Daughters, Elizabeth Sale, Maryan Shute and Sarah, the wife of Silas Halsey, the remainder. Executors—friend, Doctor William Barnett, my son-in-law, Daniel Sale, and my son, Henry Radley. Witnesses—Ellit Cresey, James Howard, Nathan Woodruff. Proved Sept. 8, 1767. Lib. I, p. 199.

1765, Oct. 31. Clark, Ezekiel, of Essex Co. Ward. Son of Abraham Clark, of said Co. Guardian—William Barnet. Fellowbondsman—Benjamin Marsh; both of Elizabeth Town, said Co. Witness —John Mackay. Lib. H, p. 541.

1765, Sept. 10. Clark, Thomas, of Borough of Elizabeth, Essex Co.; will of. Wife, Elizabeth, the bed she brought me, and £50, and goods to the amount of £50, and, by a joynture, I have settled a messuage and tenement upon her, during her life. Grandson, Aaron Clarke, the lands I bought from Andrew Hampton. Grandson, Thomas Clarke, land I bought from William Winans, and my son, Abraham Clarke, may cut fire wood there from. Executor—son, Abraham. Witnesses—Jonathan Hampton, Christopher Manlove, Lydia Gastelowe. Proved Oct. 1, 1765. Lib. H, p. 572.

1768, June 8. Clarke, John, of New Windsor, Middlesex Co. Int. Adm'rs—William Clarke, of Upper Freehold, Monmouth Co., and Thomas Clarke, of New Windsor. Fellowbondsman—James Clark, Jr., of New Windsor.
1768, June 8. Inventory, £367.5.2, made by James Worth and James Clark, Jr. Lib. 13, p. 408.

1766, May 23. Clarkson, John, of Kingwood, Hunterdon Co., Docter of physick. Int. Adm'r—Daniel Cahill, of said place. Fellowbondsman—George Alexander, of Amwell.
1766, May 16. Inventory, £27.0.6, made by Henry Coate and John Tomson.
1767, Sept. 3. Account by Adm'r. Lib. 12, p. 421.

1761, Jan. 17. Clawson, Thomas, of Piscataway Twsp., Middlesex Co.; will of. I bought a certain estate, known by the name of Mercer's Mills, lately belonging to Doctor William Mercer, and there is £2,000 yet due to Mercer, and I wish my wife, Anne, and my sons, Brant Clawson and Josiah Clawson, to remain on the place for five years, and to make payments; at the end of said time it may be sold, with my other personal and real, and £50 given to my wife, Ann, and £50 to my daughter, Ann Dunn, and £50 to my daughter, Mary, and £50 to my daughter, Elizabeth, and £50 to my daughter, Hannah, and £50 to my daughter, Sarah. Sons, William, Richard, John, Josias and Brant, the residue, when they are of age. Executors—my son, William Clawson, and Peter Cubert. Witnesses—Thomas Mackfarson, John Campbell, William Haddon. Proved Feb. 5, 1761.

1761, Feb. 2. Inventory, £2,246.17.1, made by Tobias Van Norden and Elias V. Court. Lib. G, p. 360.

1768, Dec. 15. Cleavenger, William, of Monmouth Co. Int. Adm'x —Mercy Cleavenger. Fellowbondsman—Pinset Asson; both of said Co.
1768, Dec. 15. Inventory, £202.18.1, made by Isaac Ivins and Amos Wright.
1769, Nov. 13. Account by Mercy Cleavenger, Adm'x.
Lib. 12, p. 526; Lib. 14, p. 127.

1765, Aug. 2. Clement, Samuel, of Newton, Township, Gloucester Co., yeoman; will of. Wife, Ruth, £100, and £15 yearly. Son, Jacob, plantation where he lives, and 5 acres of my meadow; also the cedar swamp I bought of Samuel Sharp. Son, Samuel, all my plantation where I live (except as excepted) that I bought of Samuel Boggs; and 50 acres of meadow that joins Timber Creek, and he to pay to my granddaughters, Mary Harrison and Rebecca Harrison, £10 each, when they are 18. Son, Joseph, 350 acres where he lives, and a cedar swamp, on the main branch of Great Egg Harbor River. Son, Abel, the rest of the plantation, mentioned as bequeathed to son Joseph, when Abel is 21. My daughters, Abigail Blackwood, Rebecca Clement and Rachel Clement, £75 each. Son, Thomas, land that was formerly called the Saw Mill Tract, which I bought of Elizabeth Hutchinson, when he is 21. Daughter, Abigail Blackwood, one acre in Haddonfield. Daughter, Rebecca, is single. My brethren, Jacob Clement, and John Hinchman, to divide lands. My son, Samuel, is to educate my sons Abel, and Thomas, for which he is to have the land in Gloucestertown, which was left to me by my grandmother, Sarah Bull. Executors—son, Samuel, and my son, Joseph, to be assisted by my brethren, John Hinchman, and Jacob Clement. Witnesses—William Griscom, Thomas Redman, Jr., John Langdale. Proved Oct. 23, 1765. Lib. 12, p. 197.

1768, Oct. 3. Clover, Paul, of Hunterdon Co. Ward. Son of Peter Clover, of Lebanon, said Co., dec'd. Makes choice of John Anderson, Esq., and Christopher Voght, both of Lebanon, as his Guardians.
1768, Oct. 3. Guardians—John Anderson, Esq., and Christopher Voght. Fellowbondsman—Coonrod Pickel, of said place. Witness— Jacob Mattison. Lib. 12, p. 523.

1767, Sept. 3. Clover, Peter, of Kingwood, Hunterdon Co. Int. Adm'x—Catherine Clover. Fellowbondsman—Christopher Vought; both of Lebanon, said Co.
1766, Dec. 15. Inventory, £307.2.10, made by Christopher Vought and James Martin.
1768, Nov. 15. Account by Catharine Clover. Includes "for 2 years boarding three small children." Lib. 12, p. 522; Lib. 13, p. 199.

1768, Oct. 3. Clover, Sarah, Philips and Isaac, of Hunterdon Co. Wards. Daughter and sons of Peter Clover, of Lebanon, said Co., who, with their mother, Catherine Clover, make choice of John Anderson, Esq., and Christopher Voght, both of Lebanon, as their Guardians.

1768, Oct. 3. Guardians—John Anderson, Esq., and Christopher Voght. Fellowbondsmen—Coonrod Pickel and Catharine Clover. Witness—Jacob Mattison.
1768, Oct. 3. Renunciation of Catharine Clover, widow of Peter Clover, in favor of John Anderson, Esq., and Christopher Voght, to be guardians of above infants. Lib. 12, p. 523.

1767, Feb. 15. Cobb, Paul, of Cumberland Co.; will of. Son, William Cobb, the home place and the old meadow and "cripple." Son, Joshua, the new meadow, and 100 acres. The guns and hoes to be divided between William, Joshua, Calop and Paul, and they must have trades and £10. Daughter, Theodoa, a cow. Wife to have cattle, sheep and moveables. Witnesses—Job Glassling, John Cobb, Philip Grace. Proved July 16, 1767. Administration with the will annexed was granted to Priscilla Cobb. Lib. 13, p. 246.

1761, April 22. Cobb, William, of Morris River, Cumberland Co. Int. Adm'rs—John Cobb and Paul Cobb. Fellowbondsman—Hezekiah Lore; all of said place. Witness—Abraham Jones.
1761, April 15. Inventory, £145.12.6, made by Hezekiah Lore and Abraham Jones. Lib. 10, p. 179.

1767, Jan. 5. Cock, Jacob, of Western Precinct, Somerset Co.; will of. Land joining Henry Cock may be sold, if needed to pay debts. Wife, Catherine, to have the rent of place, and care of children till they are old enough to put to trades. Son, Edward, £5. Son, John, ½ my land, and the other half to the said Edward. Daughter, Mary Cock, £25. Executors—Edward Hall, Henry Cock, Cornelius Low (son of Albert), and my wife. Witnesses—William Low, Abraham Parsell, Henry More. Proved Aug. 19, 1768.
1768, Sept. 23. Inventory, £59.4.0, made by Abraham Low and Martynus Hogelant. Mentions brother, Jacob. Lib. I, p. 315.

1770, Oct. 14. Coddington, Jonathan, of Woodbridge, Middlesex Co., yeoman; will of. "Being very sick with the smallpox." Brother, Enoch, 50 acres and the salt marsh, and he to allow my mother, Sarah Coddington, her right of dower. Rest of real and personal to my sisters, they allowing my mother her right of dower. Sisters are named as Abigail Coddington, Keziah Coddington and Phebe Coddington. Executors—my uncle, Moses Conger, and friend, John Doobs. Witnesses—James Mulford, William Rose, George Brown. Proved Nov. 23, 1770. Lib. K, p. 257.

1766, Aug. 4. Codington, Daniel, of Middlesex Co. Int. Adm'x—Sarah Codington. Fellowbondsman—Jacob Fitz Randolph; both of said Co. File No. 4293 L.

1768, April 21. Codington, John, of Middlesex Co. Ward. Son of John Codington. Guardian—John Noe. Fellowbondsman—William Edgar; both of said Co. Witnesses—Thomas Skinner, Jr., and James Kelly. Lib. I, p. 302.

1761, May 4. Coe, Joseph, of Middlesex Co. Int. Adm'r—Joseph Coe, the only son. Fellowbondsman—Peter Dickerson, of Morris Co.
1761, Sept. 19. Inventory, £608.12.11, made by Solomon Munson and John Brookfield. Lib. G, p. 373.

CALENDAR OF WILLS—1761-1770   83

1762, May 12. Coeman, Johannes, of Second River, Essex Co., yeoman; will of. Son, Hendrick Coeman, land on which I live. Son, John, land at Stonehouse Plains, except the house and house lot, which house and lot I give to my daughter, Lea, now the wife of Geape Spier. Daughters, Annatie, Arryantie, Margrietie, Marytie and Lea, £140 and 10 shillings, to be divided as follows: to Annatie, 10 shillings; to Aryantie, £35; to Margrietie, £35; to Marytie, £35; and to Lea, £35. Executors—said Hendrick and Abram Van Ripe, the husband of my daughter, Margrietie. Witnesses—Casparus Van Wienckel, William Dow, Peter Codmus. Proved Aug. 2, 1762.
Lib. H, p. 293.

[No date]. Coffin, Stephen, of Alloways Creek Neck, Salem Co.; will of. My wife, Sarah Coffin, and my children may live on the plantation till my time is out. Personal estate to my wife and my children, Sarah Coffin, Cynde Coffin, Rane Coffin, Mary Coffin (my daughters), and Thomas Coffin, my son. Executors—Seth Bowen and Efrem Shepherd. Witnesses—Thomas Bent, Elizabeth Denn. Proved Oct. 13, 1767.
1767, Oct. 12. Inventory, £209.3.0, made by John Ware and Isaac Mulford.
Lib. 13, p. 276.

1770, March 29. Cohoon, John, of Greenwich, Sussex Co. Ward. Only son of Walter Cohoon, of said place, deceased; and having lands devised to him by his father, he makes choice of Andries Young as his Guardian.
1770, March 29. Guardian—Andres Young. Fellowbondsman—Daniel Piper; both of said Co. Witnesses—Mary Anderson and Thomas Anderson.
Lib. 15, p. 1.

1761, April 1. Cohoon, Walter, of Greenwich Twsp., Sussex Co., yeoman; will of. To my wife, £100, and she to live on the plantation. Son, John Cohoon, plantation, when he is 21. Daughter, Margret Cohoon, £100, for her lifetime, or her husband's lifetime. Daughter, Elizabeth Cohoon, £100. Daughter, Jannet, £100, if she shall come into our town. Daughter, Catren Cohoon, £100, when she is 18. Daughter, Martahe (Martha?) Cohoon, £100, when 18. Daughter, Ester Cohoon, £100, when 18. Grandson, Walter Young, a mare and £10, and he to be under the care of my wife. Executors—Alexander White and my wife, Mary. Witnesses—Alexander White, Mary Cohoon, Margrat White. Proved May 5, 1761.
1761, April 11. Inventory, £880.11.1, made by John Sharp and David Hays.
1764, May 17. Account, both Executors.   Lib. 11, p. 54.

1762, March 2. Cole, Benjamin, of Reading Twsp., Hunterdon Co.; will of. Wife, Gertry, £5 yearly. Real and personal to be sold. Children, Sarah, Ezekiel, and Arriantia; a room is to be reserved for my mother as long as she lives. Executors—brother, Ezekiel Cole, and my friend, George Reading. Witnesses—Abrahm Short, David Cole, Edward Wilmot. Proved April10, 1762.
1762, April 2. Inventory, £145.9.2, made by Abraham Shurts and David Cole.
1770, May 21. Account by Executors. Rent of farm, £63. Sales of farm, £1450. Money received from Peter Kinney, David Cole, Hendrick Lewis, Amos Sweesy, Mary Lewis, Isaiah Cole and Ezekiel

Cole, £10.1.5, the deceased's ¼ part of £100, remaining of his father's estate, after the debts are paid. Cash paid George Reading, one of the executors of estate of Tunis Cole, on a bond, £26.2.4. Paid Ledna Graff. Legacies paid: Sarah Cole, Isaiah Cole. Cash paid John Cole and Thomas Cole, on account of their quit claim to the estate, £6. Cash paid Rebecca Coxe, on account of overplus land, £106.13.4. Lib. 11, p. 135; Lib. 15, p. 66.

1756, Oct. 9. Cole, David, of Macachkemeek, Sussex Co., wheelwright; will of. Son, Josias Cole, a rifle. Children, Josias Cole, Jacob Cole, Benjamin Cole, Samuel Cole, Cathrynje Cole, Margritje Cole, Sarah Cole, and Syffya Cole, all real and personal, after death of my wife, Lenora. Executors—son, Josias and my father-in-law, Jacob Westvael. Witnesses—Jacobus Davenport, Ijaaje Cool, William Ennes. Proved April 2, 1761. Lib. 10, p. 477.

1765, Sept. 23. Cole, Thomas, of Readington, Hunterdon Co. Int. Adm'r—Ezekiel Cole. Fellowbondsman—David Cole; both of said place.
1765, Sept. 21. Inventory, £219.11.0, made by Nicholas Egbert and Benjamin Allegar.
1773, Aug. 14. Account by Ezekiel Cole, Adm'r. "Goods were left with the widow, to enable her, in part, to bring up her children."
Lib. 12, p. 226.

1768, June 11. Coleman, John, of Morris River, Cumberland Co. Int. Adm'r—Jacob Coleman. Fellowbondsman—Cornelius Clark; both of said place.
1768, Feb. 16. Inventory, £49.10.6, made by Cornelius Clark, and Jonas Hoffman.
1768, Feb 18. Renunciation by Rebecca Coleman, (widow of John Coleman) in favor of their son, Jacob Coleman. Lib. 13, p. 441.

1763, Aug. 16. Coleman, Joshua, of Walpack, Sussex Co.; will of. Late of Goshon, New York. Wife, Sarah, ⅓ my real and personal; to my eldest son, Joshua, who at present behaves not well, I give but £5, but, if he soon behaves, he may have equal with the rest of the children. Children—Joel, Samuel, Timothy, Isral, Jared, Sarah, Dorothy and Lydea. Executors—my wife, Sarah, David Marain and Samuel Coleman. Witnesses—Isaac Van Neste, Timothy Hollister, Ephraim Herriott. Proved Oct. 15, 1763.
1763, Sept. 13. Inventory, £106.18.1, made by Isaac Van Kampen and Isaac Van Nest. Lib. 11, p. 461.

1769, Feb. 2. Coles, Jane, of City and Co. of Burlington; will of. To St. Mary's Church of Burlington, £5. Daughter, Grace Coles, the residue. Executrix—said Grace. Witnesses—James Talman, Daniel Ellis, Isa. Pearson Rodman. Proved May 8, 1769. Lib. 14, p. 49.

1754, July 12. Coles, Samuel, of Waterford Township, Gloucester Co., yeoman; will of. My mother, ⅓ of my estate. Brothers, Joseph, and Benjamin Matlack, £5 each. Sisters—Rebeckah, and Abigail Matlack, £5 each. Uncle Kindle Coles, £50. Aunt, Jane Coles, £50. Cousin, Thomas Coles, £50. Cousins, Samuel Coles and Joseph Coles, £10 each. Cousins—Mary, and Martha Coles, £20 each. Cousin, Mary Brown, £20. Cousins, Hannah, Barshaba, and Mary Coles, £5 each. Uncle, Henry Wood, £50. Cousin, Samuel Hugg, £10. Cousin, John Hinchman, £5. My plantation in Greenwich Twsp., Gloucester Co., I give to my executors. Executors—my friends, Kindle Coles, Samuel Hugg, John Hinchman, who are to pay my debts, and, if there be any overplus, to divide it among my aunt Rachel Robarts' children, and my aunt Mary Tonkins' children, and my aunt Susannah Bud's children, and my uncle Samuel Cole's children. Witnesses— Jacob Clement, William Hinchman, James Clement. Proved July 23, 1764.

1764, July 16. Inventory, £236.4.10, "of Samuel Coles, son of Joseph Coles," made by Jacob Clement and Samuel Spicer.

1770, Feb. 7. Account of Kendell Coles and John Hinchman, surviving executors of Samuel Coles, Jr. Lib. 12, p. 10; Lib. 15, p. 13.

1761, Jan. 14. Collings, William, of Greenwich, Cumberland Co., saddletree maker; will of. Wife, Elizabeth, all my estate, except the legacies hereafter mentioned; but, if she outlive my mother, or leave an heir, then my estate to go to her; otherwise to return to the estate. My sister, Elizabeth Street, £5. Humphrey Fithian, and Phebe, his wife, (my wife's uncle and aunt), £5. My brother, Richard Collins, 5 shillings. Executors—Thomas Campbell, of Philadelphia, merchant, my sister, Elizabeth Street, and my wife. Witnesses —Daniel Wheeten, Hannah Mulford, Maskell Ewing. Proved Nov. 5, 1762.

1762, Nov. 5. Inventory, £12.5.0, made by Francis Brewster and Hugh Stathem. Lib. 11, p. 308.

1761, May 30. Collins, Francis, of Evesham, Burlington Co., yeoman; will of. Friend Charity Garwood, £60. Son, Joshua, Bible. Son, John, a chest that did belong to the estate of Daniel Morgan. Son, Job, a chest. Daughter, Prissilla, clothing that did belong to her mother. Rest of my estate to be sold. My children, Joshua, John, Job and Prissilla Collins, the rest, when of age, except £15, which I give my brother John Collins. My son-in-law, Ephraim Haines, £15. To each of daughters-in-law, Hannah Sleeper, Mary Enoch and Hope Haines, £15. Sister's, Susannah Garwood's children. Executors—my brother, John Collins, and friend, Enoch Roberts. Witnesses—John Cox, Daniel Lippincott. Proved June 12. 1761.
Lib. 10, p. 355.

1761, June 10. Inventory, £843.13.11, made by Micajah Wills and Daniel Lippencott.

1769, March 3. Account by Enoch Roberts, surviving Executor.
Lib. 13, p. 495.

1760, May 23. Collins, John, Sr., of Evesham, Burlington Co., yeoman; will of. My daughter, Sybila Gaskill, £30, and furniture. Daughter, Susannah Garwood, furniture. Grandson, Thomas Garwood, my surveyor's book. Son, John Collins, my gun. Son, Francis Collins, £3. Son, Joseph, the legacy given to his mother by his grandfather's, Samuel Kimble's, will. Grandson, Edward Collins, son of my son Joseph, £3, when 21. Daughters, Sarah Bates, Charity Cane, Lize Hugg, Mary Budd and Prissilla Evens, £3 each. Executors— friends, Joshua Humphris and Joshua Stokes. Proved March 16, 1761. Lib. 10, p. 346.

1761, March 9. Inventory, £172.14.5, made by Joshua Ballinger and David Oliphant. Includes "To a warrant for 50 acres of land, £4.17.0."

1768, Jan. 5. Collins, John, of Waterford, Gloucester Co., farmer; will of. I order my executor to fulfill an agreement made between me and Patiance, my wife, before our marriage, dated 17 of Nov., 1766. My cousin, John Garwood, blacksmith, my desk. Cousin, Thomas Garwood, £15. To all the rest of my sister's Susannah Garwood's, children, £15 each. To Samuel Ballinger, taylor (son of Amariah Ballinger, deceased), £15. Cousin, John Moore, (son of Benjamin Moore), my clock. To my daughter, Mary, wife of Samuel Hugg, the rest of moveable estate, and also my plantation, houses, lands, saw mill, and cedar swamp; but, if she die without heirs, then I give the lands to my cousins, John and Job Collins, sons of my brother, Francis Collins, deceased. Executor—my son-in-law, Samuel Hugg. Witnesses—Enoch Roberts, Aaron Albertson, Abraham Allen. Proved Jan. 25, 1768.

1768, Jan. 18. Inventory, £838.8.3, made by Joshua Stokes and Enoch Roberts. Lib. 13, p. 297.

1761, April 16. Collins, Joseph, of Hardwick, Sussex Co.; will of. Wife, Lydda, ½ of my estate. Daughter Elizabeth, the other ½, when she is 18. "My estate is in a difficult circumstance at present." Executors—Henry Crossly, my brother, George Allen, and my wife. Witnesses—Solomon Willits, Jr., Nathan Armstrong, Henry Collins. Proved May 13, 1761.

1761, May 7. Inventory, £104.2.2, made by Nathan Armstrong and Thomas Lundy.

1764, Aug. 30. Account by Executors. Lib. 10, p. 482.

1769, Sept. 28. Colman, Ephraim, of Roxbury, Morris Co.; will of. Real and personal estate to be sold, and, of the proceeds, my wife, Susanna, to have one third, and the rest to be divided among my children, namely, Elizabeth, Susanna, Mahitable, Sarah, and Penelope, when they are of age. If my wife have another child, it is to have a share. Executors—my wife and John Carns, of Mendam, said Co. Witnesses—Moses Cooper, Benjamin Corwin, Jecamiah Rogers. Proved Nov. 3, 1769.

1769, Oct. Inventory, made by Daniel Budd and Caleb Swayze.
Lib. K, p. 219; File No. 255 N.

1768, Nov. 9. Compton, William, of Middletown, Monmouth Co. Int. Adm'x—Jane Compton. Fellowbondsmen—Richard Jaques and John Wall; all of said place. Witnesses—Zephaniah Morris, and Thomas Willett, Jr.

1768, Nov. 14. Inventory, made by William Applegate and Nathaniel Leonard.

1768, Nov. 17. List of goods, sold at vendue, to Mathias Compton, William Compton, Jane Compton and others.
Lib. I, p. 364; File No. 3471 M.

1770, Nov. 21. Conckling, John, of Hanover, Morris Co. Int. Adm'x—Abigail Concklin, his widow. Fellowbondsman—Abraham Corey; both of said Co. Witness—John Doughty.

1770, Dec. 1. Inventory, made by Thomas Genung and Thomas Bonnel. Lib. K, p. 256.

1767, Feb. 1. Condict, Peter, of Morristown, Morris Co., yeoman; will of. Wife, Phebe, my personal estate, of which she may give portions to my eight children as wisdom may direct. Son, Ebenezer, my land on the southeast side of the mountain, called the Mine Mountain, and he to pay to my sons, Joseph and Nathaniel, each £10. Son, Peter, my other lands, and he to pay to my son, Silas, £10, and to find provisions for my wife. Executors—my wife, Phebe, and my sons, Joseph and Silas. Witnesses—Benoni Hathaway, Jedediah Mills, Thaddeus Dodd. Proved Aug. 25, 1768. Lib. I, p. 334.

[No date]. **Conger, Benjamin,** of Morristown, Morris Co., yeoman; will of. Wife, Experience, ⅓ the money from the sale of personal estate, and the use of ⅓ my real, while my widow. Son, Daniel, ½ of my apparel, and 10 acres on east end of my place, during his life, and then to go to his son Jonas. Son, Daniel, use of 10 acres, known as the Dixon orchard, and, after his death, to his son Benjamin. Daughter, Abigail, £10. Daughter, Elizabeth, £10. Son, Enoch, ½ of my apparel and the rest of my real, and, after his death, to go to his sons, Benjamin and Jonas. Daughter, Lydia, £50, and, if she die unmarried, then to Sarah, and Martha Goble, daughters of Simeon and Abigail Goble, £20, and to Lydia, daughter of Benjamin and Elizabeth Goble, £15, and to Zipporah and Abigail, daughters of Daniel and Mary Conger, £15. Executors—friend, Jonathan Stiles, and my son, Enoch. Witnesses—Samuel Olliver, John Primrose, Ezekiel Cheever. Proved March 10, 1762. Lib. H, p. 146.

1767, Feb. 14. Conger, John, of Hanover Twsp., Morris Co.; will of. Wife, Sarah, £50, and the use of all real and personal for 5 years, when my lands are to be divided between my sons, Joseph and John, and they are to pay £30 to each of my sons, Stephen, Zenus, Thomas, David and James, as they come 21, and to pay my daughters, Sarah and Phebe, £15, when 21. Executors—brother, Thomas Brown, and Joseph Tuttle, Jr., and my wife. Witnesses—Samuel Ball, William Broadwell, Daniel Burnet. Proved Dec. 22, 1767. Lib. I, p. 259.

1765, Oct. 30. Connaway, Margaret, of Lower Penns Neck, Salem Co., widow. Int. Adm'rs—Daniel Taylor, of Fairfield Twsp., Cumberland Co., yeoman, and Joseph Philpot, of Lower Penns Neck, yeoman. Fellowbondsmen—John Gilljohnson and Gabriel Danielson, both of Lower Penns Neck, Salem Co., yeomen. Lib. 12, p. 304.

1768, June 22. Conner, John, of Monmouth Co.; will of. To friend, William Morton, of Shrewsbury, merchant, all my estate, after debts are paid. Executor—said William Morton. Witnesses—James Anderson, Robert Lippincott. Proved July 27, 1768.
1768, July 2. Inventory, £72.5.11, made by David Knott and John Hamton. Lib. I, p. 310.

1751, April 10. Cons, Johannes, of Lebanon, Hunterdon Co., "cupper;" will of. Wife, Mary, all estate, after debts are paid. Executrix—wife, Mary. Witnesses—Ralph Smith, Henry Smith, Huldah Smith.
1769, Feb. 6. Being called this day by testator, to attest this his last will, it being for the above, new witnesses were Philip Schuiler, Jacob Schuiler. Proved March 16, 1769. Anna Mary Kuns, the Executor, was sworn same date.
1769, March 4. Inventory, £423.4.8, made by Philip Schuiler and Christopher Kern, of the estate of John Kuns, of Twixbury, Hunterdon Co. [Name is written Cons, Cuns, Kuns, and Constant].
Lib. 14, p. 39.

1765, March 13. Cook, Obadiah, of Hanover, Morris Co. Int. Adm'r—Joel Halsey, brother-in-law to said Cook. Fellowbondsman —John Cobb; both of said place. Witness—Lewis Ogden.
Lib. H, p. 423.

1767, Sept. 21. Cooke, William, of Upper Freehold, Monmouth Co.; will of. My wife, £100. Son, Jacob, spoons, etc. Son, Job, spoons, etc. Son, William, silver buckles. Son, Joseph, 2 cows. Daughter, Margaret, a bed. Daughter, Lydia, bed. Daughter, Phebe, spoons, etc. Daughter, Hannah, spoons, etc. Daughters, Margaret, Lydia, Phebe and Hannah, £50 each, when 18. Rest of estate to my sons, Jacob, Job, William and Joseph, when 21. There is a bond due to my father-in-law, Thomas White, of £100, from me and son Jacob, which is to be paid out of Jacob's share. My wife to educate my children, Lydia, Phebe, Joseph and Hannah. Rest of personal and real to be sold. Executors—my brothers-in-law, Thomas White, Jr., and Timothy Corliss. Witnesses—John Leonard, Richard Robins, Thomas Emley. Proved Oct. 9, 1767.
1767, Oct. 7. Inventory, £1309.8.3, made by William Lawrie and John Leonard.
1783, March 20. Account by Exec'rs.
Lib. 13, p. 258; Lib. 24, p. 138.

1770, April 10. Cool, Crest, of Amwell Twsp., Hunterdon Co.; will of. Eldest son, Peter, 10 shillings. Wife, Mary, use of real and to bring up my small children. Son, Crest, to stay 2 years with his mother. Sons, Peter, William and Phillip, have had of my estate. Sons are Peter, William, Phillip, Crest and Paul, and daughters are Catherine, Mary and Elizabeth. Executors—nephews, Crest Cool and Paul Cool, Jr. Witnesses—John Deats, Jacob Mattison, Kerlach Young. Proved Aug. 27, 1770.
1770, Aug. 14. Inventory, £176.4.0, made by John Gregg and Gershom Lee.
1787, Sept. 24. Account by Christopher Cool and Paul Kuhl, on the estate of "Crist Kuhl." Lib. 14, p. 306.

1767, Dec. 18. Cool, William, of Burlington Co. Int. Adm'r—Simon Cool, of Princeton, Somerset Co. Fellowbondsman—Evan Reynolds, of Burlington Co. Witness—Bowes Reed.
1767, Dec. 18. Eve Cool, the widow of William Cool, late of Swancum in Monmouth Co., renounced. Lib. 14, p. 434.

1761, Feb. 20. Coon, Thomas, of North Precinct, Somerset Co., yeoman; will of. Wife, Catherine, moveable estate. Son, Moses Coon, use of my farm where I dwell, and 40 acres at the Swamp, during the life of my wife; and she to be maintained by him. Land to be sold after death of wife; then son, Moses, to have £100; sons, Thomas, John, Mickal, and Benjamin, each £50; son, Abraham, £50, but as he is not capable of taking care of himself, the £50 to be paid to the other sons, and they are to care for him. Granddaughter, Hannah Urmston, £50, which I give to her instead to her mother. Granddaughters, Ann and Mary Merrol, (the daughters of my daughter, Jean Merrol, the wife of Philip Merrol), £50. Daughter, Jean Merrol, £50. Executors—sons, Thomas, and Benjamin, and my friend, John Roy. Witnesses—Jacob Cosart, Thomas Urmston, Anthony Cosart. Proved March 18, 1761.
1761, March 16. Inventory, £278.19.4, made by Robert Dennes and Abraham Van Tuyl. Lib. G, p. 400.

1763, April 13. Cooper, Benjamin, Jr., of Newton, Gloucester Co., shipwright; will of. Wife, Elizabeth, personal estate, and use of house and lot where I now live, till my son, James, is 21, when he is to have it. Executors—brother, James Cooper, and my friend, Joseph Lovett; both of Philadelphia, who are hatters. Witnesses—Thomas Sach Walker, Joseph Lovett, Bradford Roberts. Proved May 7, 1764.
1764, May 3. Inventory, £242.18.11, made by John Stone and Josiah Shivers. Lib. 11, p. 515.

1764, Sept. 27. Cooper, Caleb, of Elizabeth Town, Essex Co. Ward. Son of John Cooper, of said place, deceased. He makes choice of William Cooper as his Guardian.
1764, Sept. 27. Guardian—William Cooper. Fellowbondsman—Elihu Crane; both of said Co. Lib. 12, p. 21.

1761, Jan. 14. Cooper, Ebenezer, of Monmouth Co. Int. Adm'r—James Williams, brother-in-law of said Ebenezer Cooper. Fellowbondsman—Robert Iseltine; both of Perth Amboy. Lib. G, p. 343.

1766, Oct. 20. Cooper, Elizabeth, of Burlington Co., widow; will of. Sister, Ann Pancoast, clothing. Rest of my estate to my brother's, John Curtis's children, and my brother's, Joseph Curtis's children, and my sister's, Ann Pancoast's children. Executor—kinsman, Caleb Shreve. Witnesses—Moses Ivins, William Shreve, Thomasin Pancoast. Proved Nov. 21, 1766. Lib. 13, p. 50.
1766, Nov. 22. Inventory, £214.9.4, made by Moses Ivins and William Shreve.

1764, March 16. Cooper, George, of Shrewsbury, Monmouth Co. Int. Adm'r—Philip Cooper. Fellowbondsman—David Knott; both of said place. Witnesses—Anthony Dennis and Benjamin Dennis.
1764, Feb. 10. Renunciation, by Barbery Cooper, widow of said George, in favor of Philip Cooper, son of said George. Witnesses—James Morris and James Rice.
1764, March 12. Inventory, £58.5.6, made by James Rice and James Morris.
1766, June 18. Account filed by Adm'r. Lib. H, p. 350.

1769, Feb. 22. Cooper, Hester, of Greenwich, Gloucester Co., widow. Int. Adm'r—Moses Long. Fellowbondsman—Andrew Lock; both of said place, yeomen. Witness—Benjamin Lodge.
1769, Feb. 21. Inventory, made by Benjamin Lodge and William Long. Lib. 13, p. 531.

1765, Feb. 26. Cooper, Isaac, of Newton, Gloucester Co., yeoman; will of. Wife, Hannah, profits of all my lands in said Twsp., until my sons, Joseph and Marmaduke, are 21, and I give her £600. Daughter, Lydia Noble, £5. Daughter, Hannah West, £5. Daughter, Mary West, £20, yearly. Daughter, Elizabeth Cooper, ⅓ of my plantation in Whitemarsh, Penn'a., the other ⅔ being lately conveyed to my sons-in-law, Samuel Noble and Charles West; and I give her £500. Son, Joseph, the plantation where I dwell, of 430 acres, and the land I bought of Henry Thorn, and the swamp I bought of Richard Fry, and the meadow at Clomnel, except what I will devise to son, Marmaduke. Son, Joseph, the plantation I bought of John Newby, when he is 21. Son, Marmaduke, the plantation in Newton, fronting on the Delaware River and the southwest side of Cooper's Creek, now in tenure of John Stone; also the plantation in tenure of Thomas Hepard, and a meadow at Clemnel Creek, of 154 acres; and a meadow, which I purchased of Garrat Vanneman, and ⅓ of remainder of Garrat Vanneman's plantation, which I lately bought of Thomas Clark and wife; also the land on north west of my plantation, where I live, bounded by my brother, Benjamin Cooper, and William Cooper; and the land I bought of Edward Williams; also £500, when he is 21. Son, Joseph, the rest of my estate. Trustees—son-in-law, Charles West, and my kinsman, Joseph Morgan and David Cooper. Executors—son, Joseph, and my son-in-law, Samuel Noble. Witnesses—Darius Vanneman, James Gill, Jacob Spicer. Proved Dec. 23, 1767.

1768, Jan. 1. Inventory, £6,003.13.2¼, made by Henry Wood, David Branson and Richard Weekes.

1770, March 20. Account by Charles West. Lib. 13, p. 281.

1762, March 20. Cooper, John, of Middletown, Monmouth Co., farmer; will of. To wife, £50. Oldest son, Ezekiel, my dwelling and land. Son, William, the house that formerly belonged to Ebenezer Washburn. Sons, Samuel and Benjamin, rest of lands and salt meadow. Daughters, Helen and Lydia, moveable estate. Executors—my friends, Richard, Francis and Eseck Hartshorn. Witnesses—Thomas Hartshorne, Safety Bowne, John Colhoun. Proved May 28, 1762.

1762, May 28. Inventory, £301.5.11, made by Safety Bowne and Samuel Bowne.

1765, April 24. Account filed by Eseck Hartshorne, one of the Executors. Lib. H, p. 159.

1763, Jan. 28. Cooper, Marmaduke, of Newton, Gloucester Co. Ward, Petition of Marmaduke Cooper, son of Isaac Cooper, of said place, deceased, who makes choice of Joseph Morgan and Charles West as his Guardians till 21.

1770, March 3. Account of Charles West, of Philadelphia, who was Guardian of Marmaduke Cooper, of Gloucester Co., was settled and approved. Lib. 15, p. 9; File 958 H.

1760, April 21. Corlies, Jacob, of Shrewsbury, Monmouth Co., carpenter; will of. Wife, Sarah, use of my plantation, and she to educate and bring up my two youngest children, Jacob and Sarah. Sons, Britten and Benjamin, my tools and £20. Daughter, Elizabeth, bed, etc. Daughter, Abigal Corlies, bed, etc. Son, Peter, £10, when 21. Son, George, £10, when 21. Son, Jacob, dishes. Daughter, Sarah Corlies, bed, etc., when 18. Executors—brother, Joseph Corlies, and my son, Britten. Witnesses—Joseph Potter, William Cook, Thomas Borden, Jr. Proved Jan. 8, 1768.

1768, March 10. Inventory, £764.0.2, made by Benjamin Wolcott and Joseph Potter. Lib. I, p. 210.

1762, March 27. Cornell, Cornelius, of Middlesex Co., yeoman; will of. I order 100 acres of land to be sold, and the rest divided into 3 parts when my youngest son Peter is 21, and I give ⅓ to son, Cornelius, and ⅓ to son, Roeleff, and ⅓ to son, Peter. Wife, Gerribragh, the goods I had from her at marriage. Daughters, Helena and Johanna, each £35 at days of marriage. Executors—my sons, Cornelius and Roeleff, my brothers, Jacobus and Adrian Cornell, and my friend,

Leffert Waldron. Witnesses—Simon Van Dike, Lukes Voorhees, Barnard Lagrange. Proved May 25, 1762.
1762, May 29. Inventory, made by David Devoe and Crikes Voorhees. Lib. H, p. 298.

1761, May 30. Cornell, William, of Millstone, Somerset Co., yeoman; will of. Wife, Gretye, all real and personal while my widow. Names grandson, William Cornell, son of my son Cornelius, deceased, and daughters, Jannetye, Matye, Peternelletye, Marregaretta, Syteye, and Gertye. Executors—sons-in-law, Lucus Nevius, Jacobus Nevius, Stephen Terhune, and Peter Wyckoff. Witnesses—Peter Schenk, Peter Stryker, John Stryker. Proved May 19, 1762.
1762, March 24. Inventory, made by Gerret Terhune and Rem Gerritsen. Lib. H, p. 124.

1760, Dec. 12. Corson, Peter, of Upper Precinct, Cape May Co., gentleman; will of. Son, Levy, that land by Rem Corson's, and ⅓ of 47 acres at the head of said land, and ⅙ of 41 acres joining James Hathorn. Son, Jesse, rest of my home tract, and tract lying between sons, Peter and Levi, and supposed to be 80 acres; also ½ of the land that lies back of James Godfrey, and ⅙ of the 41 acres, and ½ of that joining James Hathorn. Son, Darius, 8 shillings. Daughter, Rachel Corson, £17. Daughter, Elizabeth Corson, £17. Wife, Rachel, personal estate. Executors—wife and son, Darious. Witnesses—Joseph Corson, Jacob Corson, Peter Corson. Proved April 4, 1764.
1764, April 3. Inventory, £106.17.1, made by Joseph Corson and Daniel Townsend. Lib. 11, p. 505.

1769, Jan. 7. Corssen, John, of Hardwick Twsp., Sussex Co., yeoman; will of. Wife to have use of real and personal, and, after her death, to be divided among my children, Peter, Abraham, William, Vantuyle, and Richard, when they are 21. Son, Jacob, 40 acres, where his new house is. Son, Isaac, 5 shillings. Sons, Benjamin and John, rest of land. Executors—friends, Moses Ayres, Esq., and Samson Dildine. Witnesses—Ephraim Darby, Joseph Reeder, Rachel Reeder. Proved Feb. 27, 1770.
1770, Feb. 24. Inventory, £52.19.6, made by Daniel Harker and Michael Ayers.
1773, Sept. 17. Account, by Executors. Lib. 14, p. 540; Lib. 15, p. 36.

1769, Feb. 25. Cory, David, Sr., of Morris Co. Int. Adm'r—David Cory, the eldest son. Fellowbondsman—John Campfield; both of Hanover Twsp., said Co. Witness—Abraham Cory.
1769, March 20. Inventory, £69.3.1, made by Barnabas Carter and Thomas Genung. (The goods were in the hands of Mary Cory, his widow). Lib. K, p. 77.

1762, July 6. Cory, Elnathan, of Elizabeth Borough, Essex Co.; will of. Wife, Sarah, her dowry. Son, Ebenezer, 30 acres on south side of road, and my great Bible. Son, Daniel, my right to lands on west side of Pesaick River. Son, James, 40 acres that join Benjamin Pettit. Son, Joseph, 30 acres on line of John Crane. Son, Thomas, my house and orchard, and contains ½ of the land on north side of road, joining James Cory; and the other ½ to son, Jeremiah. Daughter, Mary, £15, when 18. Grandaughter, Sarah Cory, £15, at

18. Son, Thomas, is to pay to my son, Job, £35, and son, James, is to pay Job, £35. The rest of my estate to my children, Ebenezer, Sarah Johnson, Daniel, James, Thomas, Job, Jeremiah, Joseph and Mary. Executors—sons, James and Thomas. Witnesses—John Osborn, Jonathan Elmer, Peter Fleming. Proved Oct. 27, 1766.
Lib. I, p. 142.

1765, Oct. 29. Cory, John, of Borough of Elizabeth, Essex Co., yeoman; will of. Eldest son, John, £5, and what I have given him. Son, Jacob, the land at Turkey, which was conveyed to me by my brother, Elnathan Cory; also ⅓ my salt meadow. Son, Abner, 62 acres in the Neck; also ⅓ my salt meadow. Son, David, my plantation where I live, which was left me by my father, John Cory, deceased; also ⅓ my salt meadow. Daughter, Hannah, £20. Daughters, Phebe, Sarah and Rachel, £5 each. Wife, Martha, a bed. Sons, Jacob, Abner and David, rest of moveable estate. Land in Westfield, which I purchased of my son John, whereon he lives, containing 30 acres, to be sold. Son, John, owes me £170, which is secured to me by mortgage, and I wish my executors to recover. Executors—sons, Jacob and Abner. Witnesses—Joseph Tooker, Luteshe Clark, Abraham Clark. Proved Aug. 26, 1768. Lib. K, p. 38.

1765, Dec. 28. Cotheal, Henry, of Woodbridge, Middlesex Co.; will of. Wife, Sarah, £40 and use of house and 22½ acres where I live, and, after her death, to be sold. Daughters, Elizabeth and Charlotte, £80, when 18. If my daughters die, then to my brother William, one half; and the other half "to my brother, yoing Eddys, for oldest sons." Executors—my friends, John Dove and David Crow. Witnesses—Reuben Ayers, Selah Norton, Samual Goodin. Proved March 4, 1766. Lib. H, p. 593.

1761, April 15. Cotheal, William, of Woodbridge, Middlesex Co.; will of. Real and moveable estate to be sold. Son, William, £50. Son, Henry, £50. Daughter, Sarah Eddy, £30. Daughter, Rachel Cotheal, £50, Daughter, Margaret Freeman. £20. Sons, William, Henry, Alexander, and Isaac, the rest. (Isaac not yet 21.) Executors—Gawin Eddy and Henry Cotheal, my sons. Witnesses—Reuben Ayers, Thomas Runyon, James Clarkson. Proved April 24, 1761.
Lib. G, p. 427.

1763, Oct. 10. Cotterling, Jacob, of Elizabeth Town. Int. Adm'r—Thomas Kenney, the principal creditor. Lib. H, p. 324.

1762, Jan. 3. Cotton, Samuel, formerly of Philadelphia, gent. Int. Adm'r—James Childs, of Philadelphia merchant. Fellowbondsman—Darling Conarroe, of Chester, Burlington Co., farmer. Witness—Samuel Allinson. Lib. 11, p. 242.

1760, Jan. 23. Couck, George, of Roxbury, Morris Co.; will of. Wife, Ann, ⅓ my estate. Son, George Coke, 6 shillings. The rest of my estate to my son and daughters, when they are 21. If my wife can not bring them up, my Executors are to do so. Executors—John Waldorf and Martin Waldorf. Witnesses—Anthony Waldorf, Bernard Mowry, Margaret Waldorf. Proved April 9, 1761.
1761, March 12. Inventory, £176.8.1, made by Christopher Carne and Roluff Roluffson.
1763, Jan. 22. Account, by Executors. Lib. 10, p. 468.

CALENDAR OF WILLS—1761-1770 93

1770, Sept. 14. Coursen, Jacob, of Roxbury Twsp., Morris Co. Int. Adm'r—Jabez Hayton. Fellowbondsman—Jabesh Bell; both of said Co.
1770, Sept. 13. Renunciation by Hester Corsen in favor of her father, Jabez Heaton. Witness—Joseph Caldwell.   Lib. K, p. 256.

1763, Nov. 23. Covenhoven, Albert, of Monmouth Co. Int. Adm'rs —William Covenhoven and Mary Covenhoven, the father and widow of said Albert. Fellowbondsman—David Covenhoven; all of said Co. Witnesses—John Heire, Jr., and William Lippincott, Jr.
1763, Oct. 26. Inventory, £234.11.6, made by William Wikoff and John Campbell.   Lib. H, p. 369.

1766, Aug. 11. Covenhoven, John, of Western Precinct, Somerset Co.; will of. Wife to have use of all real and personal till eldest son, David, is 21, and then a division is to be made between my two sons, David and John. Executors—Peter Vorhease, James Nephew and Peter Vorheas, son of Hendrick. Witnesses—Pieter Nevius, Gizebert Lane, Aaron Sutphen. Proved May 14, 1767.
1767, May 15. Inventory, £1,129.1.4, made by Gizebert Lane, Aurt Sutphen and Pieter Nevius.   Lib. I, p. 110.

1765, Oct. 8. Covenhoven, Mathias, of Middletown, Monmouth Co.; will of. Wife, Williampe, the bed which she brought when I married her, and £21 per annum. Son, William, and my youngest son, Matthias, all my lands (Matthias not of age). Rest of personal estate to my sons, Jacob and Peter, and my daughters, Sarah, Jannetie, Williampe and Anna, when they are of age. Executors—Daniel, son of John Hendrickson, dec'd (my sister's son), and Cornelius Covenhoven, son of William Covenhoven, dec'd. Witnesses—Cornelius Luyster, Joseph Golden and Richard Stillwell. Proved April 23, 1766.
1765, Oct. 25. Inventory, £1,254.5.0, made by Joseph Golden and Richard Crawford.   Lib. I, p. 324.

1764, Nov. 16. Covenhoven, William, of Penns Neck, Middlesex Co., yeoman; will of. Eldest son, John Covenhoven, £5. Wife, Cristion, the legacy that is due to her from her father, Cornelius Lane, deceased, and also £100. Lands to be sold. Son, John, £40. Money from sale of land to my children, John, Cornelius, William, Peter, Hermanus, Gilbert, Jacob, Dominicus, Mary (wife of Jacob Schenck) and Jacoba Covenhoven. Executors—son, John Covenhoven, and son-in-law, Jacob Schenck. Witnesses—John Covenhoven, John Cox, Tho. Atkin, Joseph Skelton. Proved April 10, 1765.
1765, March 19. Inventory, £288.5.3, made by Joseph Skelton and Joseph Olden.   Lib. H, p. 506.

1761, June 15. Covert, Francis, of Freehold, Monmouth Co. Int. Adm'x—Sarah Covert, widow of said Francis. Fellowbondsman— George Reed; both of said Co.
1761, June 25. Inventory, £80.13.7, made by Richard Crawford and Aaron Brewer.   Lib. G, p. 442.

1767, May 9. Cowell, Christian, of Amwell Twsp., Hunterdon Co., yeoman; will of. To wife, ⅛ part of moveable estate, and interest of £100. Son, Chris, £5. Grandchild, John Yeoger, £25. Children, Mortice Cowl, Coonrade Cowl, John Cowl, Modlean Rockefellow,

Surviah Cowl, and the issue of my daughter, Ann Sarah Counting, one part of the remainder. The interest of the share of my daughter, Ann Sarah, to be paid to her during her life. Lands to be sold. Executors—son, Mortice, and Richard Rounsevell, Jr. Witnesses—Samuel Kitchen, Thomas Lake, William Rockfallar. Proved May 23, 1767.

1767, May 16. Inventory, £384.10.9, made by Samuel Kitchen and Philip Petters. Lib. 13, p. 202.

1760, Nov. 29. Cowell, David, of Trenton, Hunterdon Co.; will of. To the Presbyterian Congregation of Trenton, £50. To the College of New Jersey, £50. To my aged father, 20 dollars, yearly. Nephew, David Cowell, student at Nassau Hall, 20 dollars yearly for 3 years. Sister, Anna Fisher, £50. Sister, Martha Blake, £50. Margaret, wife of Richard Fisher (late the widow of my brother, Joseph), £10; and a like amount to each of the children which she had by my brother, viz., Samuel Cowell and Olive Haws. Brother, Ebenezer Cowell, of New England, the rest. Executor—said Ebenezer Cowell, Witnesses—Samuel Tucker, Jr., Arthur Howell, Benjamin Yard, George Davis. Proved Jan. 24, 1761.

1761, Feb. 10. Inventory, £965.4.11, made by Joseph Yard and Moore Furman. Lib. 10, p. 589.

1763, April 27. Cowens, George. Int. Adm'r—John Souter, of New Castle Co., Penna. Fellowbondsman—Michael Cowens, of same place. Witness—Jasper Smith. Amount of estate, £91.6.6½. Lib. 11, p. 302.

1765, Jan. 9, Cowgill, Isaac, of Chesterfield Twsp., Burlington Co.; will of. Wife, Rachel, profits of several tracts of land, and, after her death, said lands to go to my sons, George and Isaac. Son, John, £50. Daughter, Rachel Hall, £50. Granddaughter, Lydia Cowgill (daughter of John and Jemime Cowgill), £20 when 18; and to granddaughter, Rachel Cowgill (her sister), £15 when 18. Executors—my wife, Joseph Curtis and Aaron Watson. Witnesses—George Playton, John Taylor, Samuel Shourds, medius. Proved Dec. 31, 1766.

1766, Dec. 30. Renunciation of Aaron Watson.

1766, Dec. 23. Inventory, £563.9.4, made by Joseph Richards and Joshua Foster. Lib. 13, p. 41.

1770, March 29. Cowperthwaite, Thomas, of Manington, Salem Co., yeoman; will of. Lands to be sold. To my wife all she brought with her. Children, Thomas, Samuel and Mark, remainder of my estate. Executors—my brothers, John, William and Hugh. Witnesses—Isack Butterworth, Elizabeth Darling. William Cowperthwaite. Proved May 8, 1770.

1771, April 5. Renunciation by John Cowperthwaite. Witnesses—Catharine Smith and Sarah Smith.

1771, March 30. Renunciation by William Cowperthwaite. Witnesses—Gabriel Allen and John Loveless.

1770, April 10. Inventory, £706.5.7, made by Mounce Keen and Elisha Bassett, Jr.

1775, Feb. 4. Account by Hugh Cowperthwaite. Names father of deceased as Thomas Cowperthwaite. Lib. 15, p. 246; Lib. 15, p. 538.

CALENDAR OF WILLS—1761-1770   95

1767, June 24. Cox, John, of Sussex Co.; will of. Wife, Mary, ⅓ of my estate. Children, Jacob Cox, Samuel Cox, Mary Cox, Dorcas Cox, Phinis Cox, Elizabeth Cox, John Cox, Marcey Cox, Benjamin Cox and William Cox, the other two-thirds. Executors—my wife and Moses Ayers. Witnesses—Ephraim Drake, Benonia Ayston, Philip Hoffman. Proved Feb. 13, 1768.
 1768, Feb. 1. Inventory, £21.15.4, made by Nathaniel Ayers and Thomas Terrill.
 1769, Feb. 16. Account by Moses Ayers, acting Executor.
Lib. 12, p. 533; Lib. 13, p. 533.

1767, Dec. 17. Cox, Joseph, of Readington, Hunterdon Co., millwright; will of. Wife, Sarah, all that she has had from her parents since she was my wife. Place where I live and moveables to be sold, and the money I give to my son, Thomas. The land in Upper Freehold, in Monmouth Co., where my father lives, to remain in his possession during his, Thomas Cox's, and my mother's, Rebecca Cox's, lives, and then to be sold and the money given to my son, Thomas, when 21. If my son die, then all to be divided between my wife, Sarah, my mother Rebacah Cox, and my 2 sisters, Deborah and Catrine Cox. Executors—my friends, John Tenbrook and John Bray, Jr. Witnesses—Samuel Williams, Peter Sutfin, Samuel Barclay. Proved March 16, 1768. Lib. 12, p. 513.

1763, Dec. 23. Cox, Newbury, of Chester Township, Burlington Co. Int. Adm'r—Richard Cox, of said Co. Fellowbondsman—Samuel Gaskill, of said place.
 1763, Dec. 23. Inventory, £57.19.11, made by John Cox and Samuel Gaskill. Lib. 11, p. 447.

1761, Jan. 17. Cox, Peter, of Bridgewater, Somerset Co. Int. Adm'x—Phebe Cox, widow of said Peter. Fellowbondsman—William Winans; both of said Co.
 1761, June 16. Inventory, made by Josiaph Colter and Peter Williamson. Lib. G, p. 344.

1768, Dec. 9. Cox, William, of Chester Twsp. in Burlington Co., yeoman; will of. Plantation to be sold. After debts are paid, ½ to my two children when of age, and ½ to wife, Sarah. Executrix—wife, Sarah. Witnesses—Andrew Anderson, Henry Jones, John Cox. Proved June 14, 1769. Lib. 14, p. 55.
 1769, Feb. 9. Inventory, £397.17.7, made by Joshua Wright and Isaac Rogers.
 1770, July 14. Account of Sarah Cox, Adm'x. Lib. 15, p. 9.

1769, March 21. Cozens, Elizabeth, of Greenwich, Gloucester Co. Int. Adm'r—Jacob Cozens, yeoman. Fellowbondsman—Joshua Cozens; both of said place. Witness—Restore Lippincott.
 1769, March 11. Inventory, £144.7.11, made by Restore Lippincott and Benjamin Lodge. Lib. 13, p. 532.

1762, Oct. 9. Cozens, Samuel, of Greenwich, Gloucester Co., yeoman; will of. Wife, Hannah, personal estate. Sons, Elijah, Jacob, Benjamin and Samuel, all my lands. Son, Elijah, my homestead where I live. Son, Jacob, a 5-acre lot on Mantees Creek. Sons, Benjamin and Samuel, a 10-acre lot in Twsp. of Deptford. Wife, Hannah,

the rents from lands, till sons are of age. Executors—my wife and friend, Solomon Lippincott. Witnesses—Samuel Parker, Daniel Cozens. Proved Dec. 31, 1762.
1762, Nov. 11. Inventory, £347.17.2½, made by Joshua Lord and William Wilkins. Lib. 11, p. 284.

1767, May 30. Cozier, John, of Egg Harbor, Gloucester Co., husbandman. Int. Adm'x—Sarah Cozier, widow. Fellowbondsman—Benjamin Ingersull, yeoman; both of said place.
1767, April 20. Inventory, £48.4.0, made by John Hickman and Benjamin Ingersoll. File 933 H.

1765, June 24. Craig, Andrew, Jr., of Essex Co. Ward. Son of James Craig. Guardian—James Clark. Fellowbondsman—Daniel Pierson; both of said Co. Lib. H, p. 480.

1763, March 5. Craig, James, of Elizabeth Borough, Essex Co., yeoman; will of. Daughters, Lydia, Hannah, Sarah and Susanna, 20 acres, to be taken in a square off of that part of my land joining Jonathan Hampton and Samuel Meeker. Sons, James, Andrew and Daniel, rest of my real estate. Wife, Phebe, ⅓ my moveable estate and the profits of ⅓ my real. Children are all young. Executors—friends, Daniel Pierson and Isaac Hendricks. Witnesses—John Doobs, Jacob Hendricks, Josiah Walcott. Proved April 27, 1763.
Lib. H, p. 233.

1766, Sept. 2. Craig, William, of Alexandria, Hunterdon Co.; will of. Names sons, James and William. Wife, Mary, to have all that money due to me in Joseph Bever's hands. Sons, Joseph, as much seed rye as he wants. Rest of my estate to son, William, and my daughter, Nancy. Executor—Andrew Puckins. Witnesses—Thomas Craig, Samuel Everitt. Proved Oct. 10, 1766.
1766, Sept. 5. Inventory, £174.12.4, made by Samuel Everitt and James McQuarlin. Lib. 12, p. 406.

1763, May 25. Craige, Andrew, of Borough of Elizabeth, Essex Co., yeoman; will of. Wife, Hannah, use of my farm for one year, except a lot hereafter left to my daughter, Lidiah Hendrix. When my grandson, Jeams Craige, is 21, then she is to have ⅓ the farm. My daughter, Lediah Hendrix, the above excepted land, which is bounded by John Crane, Jr., and Isaac Hendrix, and by land that did belong to Christopher Crane, deceased, and Jeams Crage, deceased. Grandson, Isaac Hendrix, the said land after Lidia's death. Grandson, David Littell, 12 acres of my farm. Grandson, Jeamse Crag, my dwelling house and one acre. Grandson, Andrew Crage, my salt marsh in the Raway meadows, and in partnership with John Crage, deceased. My grandson, David Littell, to be educated. Grandchildren, Lidiah, Catron, Elizabeth, Androw and Nathaniel Little, £3 each. Granddaughters, Abegal Hendrix and Ester Beedel, rest of personal. Executors—Jeams Clark and Daniel Pierson, who are to be guardians of the legatees, who are under age. Witnesses—John Crane, Jr., Thomas Coddington, John Stites. Proved Aug. 22, 1763.
1763, Aug. 3. Inventory, £270.8.11, made by the Executors. Includes, "Due from the Exr's of James Craige, dec'd, £27.6.1."
Lib. H, p. 317.

1763, Oct. 28. Craige, Phebe, of Elizabeth Borough, Essex Co.; will of. Widow of James Craig. Sister, Keziah Terrill, clothing, etc. Son, Daniel, and daughter, Susannah, rest of estate; but if both children die under age, then I give the same to my brother, Josiah Terrill, and sister, Keziah Terrill. Executor—friend, John Doobs. Witnesses—Amos Terrill, Abraham Terrill. Proved Jan. 28, 1764.
Lib. H, p. 329.

1766, June 7. Cramer, Jacob, of Little Egg Harbor Twsp., Burlington Co., yeoman; will of. Wife, Phebe, ⅔ of moveables and profits of lands, and to bring up my children, Ann, Phoebe and Sarah Cramer, and the one yet to be born. Executors—John Gaunt and Seymour Cramer. Witnesses—Lewis Darnel, Andrew Boazorth, John Leek. Proved July 28, 1766. Lib. 13, p. 12.
1766, July 21. Inventory, £103.2.10, made by Jonathan Pettit and Lewis Darnel.

1770, Sept. 25.—Crandel, Reuben, of Morris River, Cumberland Co. Int. Adm'x—Rebecca Crandel, widow. Fellowbondsman—Nebuchadnezzar Riggin, yeoman; both of said place.
1770, Sept. 8. Inventory, £32.13.0, made by Robert Peters and Nebuchadnezzer Riggin. Lib. 15, p. 73.

1761, April 8. Crane, Edmund, of Morristown, Morris Co., yeoman; will of. Wife, Abigail, her ⅓ and £150. Son, Stephen, £10. Daughter, Affia Persons, £10. Daughter, Rhoda Person, £10. Granddaughter, Abigail Squire, £50, when she is 18, but the bond that I gave to her father, Jonathan Squire, for £42, is to be reduced out of it. Son, Josiah, £60, when of age. Sons, Ezekiel and John, house and home lot. Sons, James and David, the upper lot, near Horse Hill. Executors—my wife, Abigail, and my brother-in-law, Joseph Kitchel. Witnesses—Samuel Ford, Eleazar Hatheway, William Dixon. Proved March 9, 1762. Lib. H, p. 148.

1764, Dec. 22. Crane, Isaac, of Elizabeth Town, Essex Co. Int. Adm'r—David Crane, of Connecticut Farms, the eldest son and heir, at the desire of the widow, Martha Crane. Fellowbondsman—John Potter, of Elizabeth Town. Witness—Martha Crane. Lib. H, p. 411.

1763, Feb. 25. Crane, John, of Elizabeth Town, Essex Co.; will of. Wife, Mary, my white horse. Son John, land where he lives, lying on Raway river; also land joining the above, which I bought of Andrew Craige last Spring, of 22 acres; also a piece of salt meadow in Raway meadows, near Transbee's Point, of 4 acres, and ½ which was devised to me by father, John Crane, and the ½ of the grist mill and sawmill to the same; and John is to pay to my son, Isaac, £62. Son, Isaac, to have land at Turkey, in Borough of Elizabeth, which I purchased of Elijah Davis, of 170 acres; and 17 acres joining the same, which I bought of Isaac Jones, and a meadow in Raway meadows, near Thompson Creek, of 3 acres. Son, Joseph, land at Turkey that I purchased of Zebulon Smith, of about 60 acres; also ½ of land on northwest side of Isaac Hendricks, which I bought of Ephraim Terrill and Jonathan Allen, of 82½ acres. Son, Jacob, my homestead where I live, excepting ½ of my mills; also 50 acres near Daniel Ross, Jr., which was devised to me by my father, John Crane; and the other ½ that I bought of Ephraim Terrill and Jonathan Allan. Daughter, Esther, a bed. Personal goods to be sold and money invested, and interest to be paid to daughter, Hannah Robinson, and also to daughter, Sarah, and also to daughter, Esther. Executors—brothers, Jacob Dehart and Benjamin Crane, and my nephew, John Dehart. Witnesses—Timothy Whitehead, Jr., Isaac Hendricks, Jr., John Blanchard. Proved Sept. 19, 1763.

1763, Sept. 20. Inventory, £3,997.4.11½, made by Stephen Crane and John Denman. (John Crane died Sept. 12, 1763).

Lib. H, p. 341.

1764, Sept. 15.—Crane, Jonathan, of Elizabeth Borough, Essex Co.; will of. One-third of my personal estate, in trust, for my daughter, Hannah, wife of William Terry. The real estate, which I hereafter give to my grandson, William Marsh, I give to my daughter Mary, wife of Jonathan Marsh, Jr., till my said grandson is 21; and my daughter Mary is to maintain her mother. The other ⅔ I give to my daughter, Rebeckah, wife of Joseph Acon. Grandson, William Marsh, 85 acres at the southwest end of my farm, where I live, and a small tract, on the south side of the first mountain, joining land of Andrew Hetfield, and he is to keep his grandmother, my wife. My grandson, Stephen Woodruff, the rest of the farm where I live, and he is to pay to his sister, Sarah Woodruff, £10, when 18. Executors—my brother, Stephen Crane, and John Stites. Witnesses—James Badgley, Mary Hetfield, Andrew Hetfield. Proved Nov. 15, 1766.

Lib. I, p. 137.

1769, Dec. 22. Crane, Joseph, of Newark, Essex Co.; will of. Wife, Elizabeth, all real and personal, to enable her to bring up my children, except what I give to my son, John Crane. To my son John, 20 shillings. Executors—my wife, my brother, Israel Crane, and my brother-in-law, Eliphelet Johnson. Witnesses—Josiah Crane, Asher Brown, Elias Bedford. Proved March 29, 1770. Lib. K, p. 192.

1763, June 18. Crane, Nathaniel, of Borough of Elizabeth, Essex Co. Ward. Son of Samuel Crane, of said place, dec'd. Guardian—Nathaniel Bonnel. Fellowbondsman—Elijah Woodruff; both of Elizabeth Town. Witness—John Mackay. Lib. H, p. 247.

1770, May 4. Crawford, Job, of Middletown, Monmouth Co.; will of. Sons, Joshua and George, my lands, when 21. Wife, Anne, use of the land, and money from sale of goods. Executors—brothers, William Crawford and Benjamin Morris. Witnesses—Thomas Loyd, Jr., Jacob Burnet and Richard Crawford. Proved Aug. 11, 1770.

Lib. K, p. 234.

1761, July 27. Crawford, Jonathan, of Newark, Essex Co. Int. Adm'x—Phebe Crawford, the widow, of said place. Fellowbondsman—Samuel Douglass, of Bernard Twsp., Somerset Co.

1761, July 29. Inventory, made by Isaac Lyon and Thomas Longworth.

Lib. H, p. 14.

1761, Nov. 11. Crawford, Phebe, of Newark, Essex Co. Int. Adm'r—Nathaniel Dalglish, of Morris Co. Fellowbondsman—Nehemiah Baldwin, of Newark, Essex Co. Lib. H, p. 73.

1763, March 16. Crawford, William, of Middlesex Co. Int. Adm'r —Redford Crawford (sometimes called William Redford Crawford). Fellowbondsman—Thomas Berry; both of Somerset Co. The above Redford Crawford, who is the eldest son, to administer the goods which remain left by Andrew Smyth, the late Executor of said William Crawford. (See "N. J. Archives," Vol. 32, p. 80, for will).
Lib. H, p. 320.

1770, Feb. 8. Creeger, Andries, of Lebanon Twsp., Hunterdon Co., yeoman; will of. Wife, Ann, ⅓ my personal estate. Son, William, £5. Son, John, weaving loom. Son, Peter, has had a horse, and my son, Jacob, is to have one. Daughters—Ann, Christeen and Elizabeth. Executors—sons, William and John, and my wife, Ann. Witnesses—Peter Wyckof, Abraham Couwenhoven, Johannes Roenbaug. Proved April 7, 1770.
1770, March 22. Inventory, £371.6.6, made by Peter Wyckof and Harman Cline.
Lib. 15, p. 28.

1766, April 19. Cresse, Israel, of Cape May Co. Int. Adm'x—Hannah Cresse, widow. Fellowbondsman—William Goff; both of said Co. Witness—Margaret Goff.
1766, April 18. Inventory, £73.0.1, made by John Shaw and Lewis Cresse.
Lib. 12, p. 357.

1764, July 17. Cresse, James, of Cape May Co. Int. Adm'x—Elizabeth Cresse. Fellowbondsmen—Joseph Hildreth and Joshua Hildreth; all of said Co. Witnesses—William Billings, Jr., and John Cresse.
Lib. 12, p. 333.

1766, Dec. 22. Cresse, Lewis, of Cape May Co., yeoman; will of. Son, Philip, part of lands. Son, David, part of lands. My right in the islands and marshes, lying near Five Mile Beach, I give to my 5 sons, Philip, David, Anthony, Amos and Nathan. To wife, Elizabeth, £10 over her rights. My daughter, Hannah, moveables. Son, Philip, to be Guardian of Nathan. Executors—my wife and my son, Philip. Witnesses—Abner Corson, Shamgar Hand, Jemima Hand, Martha Smith. Proved July 29, 1769.
1769, Aug. 11. Inventory, £495.14.0½, made by Thomas Smith and John Smith.
Lib. 14, p. 184.

1768, April 27. Cresse, Robert, of Cape May Co., gentleman; will of. Wife, Mary, one-half of my lands, and one-half of moveable estate while my widow. Son, Robert, a piece of land on Wills Creek, and is along land that was my brother's, John Cresse's. Daughter, Hannah Cresse, a piece of land on Wills Creek, and is along Jesse Hand's line. Daughter, Esther Cresse, also land. Son, Jonathan, the rest of lands adjoining where I live. Executors—my wife and my son, Jonathan. Witnesses—Samson Hawks, Zeruiah Hedges, Thomas Smith. Proved June 20, 1768.
1768, June 16. Inventory, £96.0.3, made by John Leonard and Thomas Smith.
Lib. 15, p. 243.

1761, Nov. 27. Cripps, Hannah, of Mount Holly, Northampton Twsp., Burlington Co. Ward. Eldest daughter of Samuel Cripps of said place. Bond of Henry Paxson as Guardian. Fellowbondsman —Joseph Imlay; both of Burlington Co., yeomen. Witness—Caleb Newbold.
Lib. 11, p. 205.

1761, Oct. 10. Cripps, Samuel, of Northampton, Burlington Co., yeoman; will of. Daughter, Grace Cripps, that part of my plantation lying next to Bridgetown, bounded by my brother, Benjamin Cripps. Daughter, Martha Cripps, also part of my plantation. Daughter, Mary Cripps, also part of my plantation. My eldest daughter, Hannah Cripps, the rest of the plantation, including the dwelling. My younger daughter, Grace Cripps, £100. Executors— friends, Henry Paxson, Esq., and John Woolman. Witnesses—Revell Elton, John Burr, Jr., Dorcas Davis. Proved Nov. 3, 1761.
1762, March 1. Renunciation of John Woolman. Lib. 11, p. 201.
1761, Nov. 2. Inventory, £1228.7.2, made by Thomas Moore and Joseph Mullen.

1766, Oct. 22. Cromey, James, of Pilesgrove, Salem Co.; will of. Nephew, James Grasbury, my plantation at Stow Creek, when he comes of age; except that my wife shall live on it during her life. The plantation where I live to be sold. My relations, Margaret Deboys, Mary Abbet, Elizabeth Grasbury, and Nancy Grasbury, 5 shillings each. Wife, Elizabeth Crummey, my personal estate. Executors—my wife, "and my little Jacob Deboys." Witnesses—Edward Wood, Thomas Wolfenden, John Vail. Proved July 5, 1768.
1768, June 28. Inventory, £227.7.0, made by William McMonigill and Samuel Sherry. Lib. 13, p. 478.

1761, Jan. 8. Crosby, John, of Willingborough, Burlington Co. Int. Adm'rs—John Crosby and Patrick Kelly. Fellowbondsman— Samuel Newton; all of said Co.
1760, Dec. 26. Inventory, £67.14.11, made by William Heulings.
Lib. 10, p. 170.

1763, Oct. 29. Cross, Benjamin, of Alloways Creek, Salem Co., blacksmith. Int. Adm'r—John Beesly. Fellowbondsman—Thomas Sayre, merchant; both of said place.
1763, June 18. Inventory, £17.1.11, made by Philip Tyler and Thomas Sayre. Lib. 11, p. 488.

1761, Feb. 27. Crow, Samuel, of Woodbridge, Middlesex Co., carpenter; will of. Wife, Elizabeth, £50, and use of house where I did formerly live near Amboy, with 30 acres. Son, David Crow, 50 acres that I bought of Levi Ayers. Sons, John and Samuel, rest of lot I bought of Levi Ayers, and the one I bought of John Cambel. Daughter, Elizabeth Crow, 10 shillings, and the same amount to daughter, Sarah Crow, and to son, James, and to son, Thomas, and to daughter, Martha Crow, and to son, Abraham. To son, David, £100. Son, James, is under 16, and Elizabeth and Sarah under 18. Executors— friend, Reziah Runyon, and my son, David. Witnesses—Stephen Chandler, James Clarkson, William Cotheal. Proved March 13, 1761.
1761, March 7. Inventory, £1,255.16.1, made by Jonathan Frazee and James Clarkson.
Account (no date), made by both Ex'rs. Lib. G, p. 397.

1764, May 31. Crowell, Samuel, of Newark, Essex Co. Int. Adm'r —Joseph Crowell. Fellowbondsman—Joseph Riggs, Jr.; both of said place.
1764, June 6. Inventory, made by Ebenezar Hedden and Joseph Riggs, Jr. Lib. H, p. 377.

1765, June 3. Crowell, Samuel, of Cape May Co.; will of. Advanced in years. Son, Josiah, lands where I live. Son, Thomas, land that I bought of Elisha Eldredge and Silas Hand. Son, Mathew, land I bought of Eleazer Crawford, at Fishing Creek, near Nathaniel Foster. Son, David, land I bought of James Hedges and Ellis Hughes. Sons to have the lands when they are 21. Wife, Phebe, what the law directs. Rest of moveable estate to my son, Seale Crowell, and 4 daughters, Mary Eldredge, Elizabeth Bancraft, Ruth Crowell and Lowes Crowell. Executors—son, Josiah Crowell, and Thomas Crowell. Witnesses—John Eldredge, John Eldredge, Jr., Elizabeth Jenkins. Proved March 14, 1768.
1768, March 19. Inventory, £184.7.6, made by John Eldredge and Ezekiel Eldredge. Lib. 13, p. 378.

1767, May 30. Crozier, John, of Gloucester Co. Int. Adm'x— Sarah Crozier. Inventory, £48.4.0. Lib. 13, p. 133.

1761, Oct. 31. Cubberly, Anne, of Windsor Twsp., Middlesex Co.; will of. Widow of Thomas Cubberly. To be buried by her husband. Son, William Cubberly, silver watch, made by Charles Clay, London, No. 1040. Daughter, Mary Cubberly, rest of personal and real. Executrix—said Mary Cubberly. Witnesses—Jonathan Hutchinson, Jonathan Pullen, Thomas Thomas. Proved Dec. 21, 1769.
1769, Dec. 19. Inventory, £283.6.5, made by William Cubberley and John Cubberley. Lib. 14, p. 237.

1761, Feb. 10. Culley, John, of Elizabeth Borough, Essex Co. Int. Adm'r—Daniel Marsh, of said Co. Fellowbondsman—Samuel Jaques, of Middlesex Co.
1761, Feb. 10. Renunciation of Hannah Culley, widow of said John, in favor of her brother, Daniel Marsh. Witness—John Marsh.
Lib. G, p. 359; File No. 3005-'8 G.

1769, Feb. 27. Cumine, James, of Trenton, Hunterdon Co.; will of. Wife, Jane, all real and personal estate during her life, and, after her death, my real to go to James Cumine, William Cumine, Samuel Cumine, and Joseph Cumine, sons of William Cumine, of Nottingham, in Chester Co., Penna. To David McCullough, and his son, James, both of Philadelphia, £10 each. To the Presbyterian Church of Trenton, £10. Executrix—my wife. Witnesses—Neill McGill, John Wright, John Wigton. Proved July 17, 1770. Lib. 14, p. 277.

1764, Jan. 26. Cumming, Robert, of Freehold, Monmouth Co.; will of. Son, Lawrence, £100. Daughter, Mary McWhorter, £100. Of the rest of my personal and real, I give ½ to my wife, Mary, and the other ½ to my children by her, viz., Catheren, Ann, Margaret and John. Executors—Rev. William Tennant, Doctor Nathaniel Scudder and my wife. Witnesses—Samuel Finley, Samuel Blair, Richard Stockton. Proved May 23, 1769. Lib. K, p. 131.

1769, Dec. 16. Cundict, Peter, of Newark, Essex Co., yeoman; will of. Wife, Eunie, a tract of land that was her father's, Joseph Smith, lying on east side of road that leads to John Smith's; also the rents of my lands, except what I hereafter mention. To my mother, two cows. Sisters—Mary Parsonate, Sarah Harrison and Susanna Ward, £15 each. Cousin, Elizabeth Williams, £10. If my children die, then I give ½ to my brother, Timothy Cundict, and the other ½ to my three sisters. Executors—my wife, Eunie, my uncle, Isaac Cundict, and my brother-in-law, John Dod. Witnesses—Jared Harrison, Joseph Harrison, Lydia Harrison. Proved March 7, 1770. Letters were granted to Eunice Cundict, Isaac Cundict and John Dod, same date. Lib. K, p. 191.

1760, Dec. 18. Curtis, John, of Manasquan, Shrewsbury Twsp., Monmouth Co., farmer; will of. Eldest son, David, ⅓ of my rights on Manasquan Beach. Daughter, Sarah, 5 shillings. Son, John, 5 shillings. Daughter, Rebeckah, 5 shillings. Son, Peter, a gun. Daughter, Rachel, a bed. Rest of personal and real to be sold, and ⅓ part I give to my wife, Mary, and the rest to my 4 children, Jonathan, Meribah, Thomas, and Anne. Executors—my wife and my brother, David Curtis.
Witnesses—Thomas Rouze, Moses Havens, James Lawrence. Proved May 1, 1761.
1761, Oct. 30. Inventory, made by James Lawrence and Daniel Butter.
1761, May 11. Renunciation by David Curtis. Witness—Anne White. Lib. H, p. 8.

1766, May 7. Curtis, John, of Mansfield Twsp., Burlington Co., yeoman; will of. Wife, Marsey, my personal estate, and ⅓ of rents of plantation. Sons, Thomas and Jonathan, said plantation, they paying £200 to my son, John. To sons, Robert and Clem, £150 each. Daughters, Grace Shreeve and Elizabeth Curtis, £15 each. Executors—wife, Marsey, and my son, Jonathan, and friend, Caleb Shreeve. Witnesses—Joseph Rockhill, Grace Hancock, Thomas Folkes. Proved Aug. 4, 1766. Lib. 13, p. 9.

1765, Jan. 26. Curtis, Joseph, of Mansfield Twsp., Burlington Co., miller; will of. All real and personal to be sold, and proceeds divided among my widow and children. Executors—my wife, Ann, and her brother, Marmaduke Watson. Witnesses—Isaac Cowgill, Jr., Samuel Harris, Adin Pancoast. Proved March 4, 1765.
Lib. 12, p. 62.
1765, Feb. 18. Inventory, £744.11.11, made by Joseph English and Samuel Farnsworth.

1766, Dec. 9. Cutler, James, of Newton Township, Gloucester Co., blacksmith; will of. My goods to be sold. Brother, Thomas Cutler, 5 shillings. Remainder to my brother, Thomas, and my sister, Elenor. Executor—Daniel Smith. Witnesses—Thomas Gethings, Thomas Redman. Proved Dec. 18, 1766.
1766, Dec. 10. Renunciation by Daniel Smith. Witness—Jacob Seares.
1766, Dec. 17. Renunciation, by Thomas Cutler, elder brother, and residuary legatee, in favor of Robert Friend Price. Witness—Samuel Blackwood.
1766, Dec. 18. Adm'r—Robert Friend Price, with will annexed. Fellowbondsmen—Samuel Blackwood, of Gloucester Co., and Samuel Allinson, of City of Burlington. Witness—Benjamin Thackray.
1766, Dec. 22. Inventory, £226.12.9, made by Edward Gibbs and John Gill. Lib. 12, p. 360.

1769, Nov. 18. Cutter, Ephraim, of Woodbridge, Middlesex Co.; will of. Real and personal to be sold. Wife, Susannah, and my children, John, Samuel, Mercy Cutter, Agness Cutter, and Mary Cutter, the rest after debts are paid; that is, when children are of age. Executor—George Brown. Witnesses—Andrew Bloomfield, Thomas Bloomfield, Thomas Bloomfield, Jr. (Will signed by both Ephraim Cutter and wife Susannah Cutter). Proved Jan. 24, 1770. Lib. K, p. 143.

1767, April 24. Cutter, Joseph, of Woodbridge, Middlesex Co.; will of. Wife, Ann, £120. Eldest son, Campyon Cutter, that part of my plantation that my father gave me, and ½ of the salt meadow, he paying to his brother, Joseph, £100. Son, Joseph, rest of my land which my father gave me, and what I bought, and the other half of the meadow. Daughter, Joanna, £100, when she is 18. Also £100 to the child my wife is big with, if it be a daughter. My wife to live on the farm. Executors—wife, Ann, and my brother-in-law, Francis Campyon. Witnesses—David Evens, Isaac Tappen, Nathaniel Fitz Randolph. Proved June 17, 1767. Lib. I, p. 126.

1763, May 25. Cutter, Richard, of Woodbridge, Middlesex Co. Ward. Petition of Abraham Clark, Jr., of Borough of Elizabeth, and others, of Woodbridge, stating that Samuel Cutter, of Woodbridge, and his wife, are both dead, and left one son, named Richard Cutter, under 10 years of age, who is possessed of real and personal estate, and part of personal is in the possession of said Abraham Clark, Adm'r of estate of Eliphalet Frazee, dec'd, grandfather of said child, and Executor to Thomas Scudder, dec'd, who was Executor of the mother of said child, and the said child has resided with and been under the care of its uncle, Ephraim Cutter, of Woodbridge; therefore they pray that the said Ephraim Cutter may be appointed Guardian. Signed by, Abraham Clark, Jr., Richard Cutter, and William Cutter.

1763, May 30. Guardian—Ephraim Cutter. Fellowbondsman—Robert Lee; both of said Co. Lib. H, p. 245.

1768, June 1. Cutter, Richard, of Woodbridge, Middlesex Co. Int. Adm'r—William Cutter, brother of Richard, of said place.

1768, June 1. Renunciation by Charity Cutter, the widow, in favor of William Cutter. Witness—Moses Bloodgood. Lib. I, p. 302.

1770, Aug. 24. Cuyler, Henry, of New York, merchant; will of. I give my sugar house and the land belonging to the same, with my dwelling house, to my sons, Henry Cuyler and Barend R. Cuyler; but they are to pay to my wife £360 yearly. Wife to have use of goods during life, and then to be divided among my six children. Propriety rights in East Jersey, to my sons, Henry and Barend R., and John Smyth of Perth Amboy, and to sell my shares for the benefit of my 6 children. Executors—sons, Henry and Barend R. Cuyler, and said John Smyth. Witnesses—George Ludlow, William W. Ludlow, William Ludlow. Proved Oct. 12, 1770.

1785, April 10. Whereas James Parker, of New Brunswick, by an Act of the Legislature, was appointed trustee to execute the purposes of the wills of Henry Cuyler, the elder, and Henry Cuyler, the younger, deceased.

1787, Sept. 20. Bowes Reed, of Burlington, was appointed trustee for the above purposes. Lib. K, p. 247.

1768, May 11. Cuylinger, Philip, of Reading town, Hunterdon Co. Int. Adm'rs—Isaac Demott, of said place, and Abraham Bertron, of Tewksbury, said Co. Witness—Edward Wilmot.
  1768, May 11. Inventory, £72.7.2, made by Joseph Hankerson and Edward Wilmot.
  1785, Jan. 20. Account by Abraham Bertron, surviving Adm'r.
Lib. 13, p. 439; Lib. 27, p. 117.

1767, June 16. Dalbo, Peter, Jr., of Woolwich Township, Gloucester Co., waterman. Int. Request of Peter Dalbo, Sr., that letters of administration on the estate of his son, Peter Dalbo, Jr., may be granted to his (eldest) son, Gabriel Dalbo, to whom I have given Letters of Attorney, I being of great age. (Signed), Peter Dalbo, by mark. Witnesses—Thomas James, John Scott, William Cooper.
  1767, June 13. Citation to Jonas Dalbo, of Twsp. of Woolwich. Whereas Peter Dalbo, of said Twsp., by his petition hath represented that you, the said Jonas Dalbo, have in an irregular manner obtained Letters of Administration, on the estate of his son, Peter Dalbo, Jr., without putting in sufficient security, to the prejudice of him, the said Peter Dalbo, who is legally intitled to the estate, and he desires that you be cited to show cause why said Letters should not be repealed. Therefore you are to appear on Tuesday, the 23 of instant June, and show cause, etc.
  1767, June 24. Adm'r—Gabriel Dalbo, of Greenwich, yeoman. Fellowbondsman—John Scott, of Woolwich, yeoman; both of said Co.
  1767, March 19. Inventory, £140.14.1, made by George Vanleer and Daniel Adams.
  1769, July 17. Account of Gabriel Dalbo, Adm'r.
Lib. 13, p. 132; File No. 934 H.

1768, Jan. 8. Dalbow, John, of Upper Penns Neck, Salem Co., yeoman; will of. Sons, William and Samuel Dalbo, all my lands when they come of age. Son, Andrew, £50. Daughter, Susannah Dalbo, £10 when she is of age. Wife, Eals, the ⅓ of my moveable estate. Executors—my wife and brother, Charles Dalbow. Witnesses—Gabriel Dalbow, Margret Sparks, Samuel Linch. Proved Feb. 18, 1768. (Probate to Alice Dalbo and Charles Dalbow).
  1768, Feb. 1. Inventory, £150.5.8, made by John Helms and Samuel Linch. Lib. 13, p. 384.

1764, Aug. 8. Daniel, William, of Alloways Creek Precinct, Salem Co.; will of. Wife, Rebecca Daniel, ⅓ of my estate; and the other ⅔ I give to my eight children, Joseph, Thomas, Sarah, William, John, Joel, Edmond and James, when they are 21. My brother, James Daniel, is to have the bringing up of my son, John. Executors—my wife and my son John. Assistant—Benjamin Tyler. Witnesses—Edward Keasbey, Thomas Sayre, David Long. Proved Sept. 28, 1764.
  1764, Sept. 13. Inventory, £314.2.7, made by Edward Keasbey and Thomas Sayre. Lib. 12, p. 85.

1764, Jan. 14. Daniels, Jonathan, of Woodbridge, Middlesex Co.; will of. Wife, Mary, moveable estate and use of my house and lands. Son, William, 10 shillings. Son, Benajah, 14 shillings. Son, Jonathan, 14 shillings. Daughter, Johannah Woods, £20. Daughter, Eunes Bartow, £20. Daughter, Lois Tharp, £20. Daughter, Thankful Daniels, £20. Grandson, Isaac Childs, £10. Grandson, Henry

CALENDAR OF WILLS—1761-1770   105

Childs, £10. Granddaughter, Hannah Childs, a bed. Executors—son, Benajah, and friend, Timothy Frazee. Witnesses—David Stuard, Jr., John Stuard, James Clarkson. Proved Nov. 21, 1764.   Lib. H, p. 469.

1770, Dec. 7. Daniels, Uriah, of Essex Co. Int. Adm'r—Recompence Stanbury.
1771, Jan. 28. Inventory, £32.1.10, made by William Derby and Isaac Clark.   Lib. K, p. 257.

1770, Dec. 21. Darby, Elias, of Essex Co. Int. Adm'r—William Darby, brother of said Elias.
1770, Dec. 24. Inventory, £138.15.8, made by Recompence Stanbery and Isaac Clark.   Lib. K, p. 256.

1768, Dec. 16. Dare, Benoni, of Greenwich Township, Cumberland Co.; will of. Wife, ⅓ of personal estate. Grandsons, Benoni, and Elkanah, 114 acres, according to my son Elkanah's will. I also give them 6 acres of marsh, but, if my daughter-in-law, now wife of Michael Lea, should bring any account against my estate, then the said marsh and 14 acres to be sold to pay said account. Grandsons, Annes and John, 50 acres as it is divided by their father's will. Son, William Dare, 40 acres where he lives, formerly assigned to him. Rest of my lands in Stow Creek Twsp. not above given, to my son, Abiel Dare. Son, Reuben, plantation I live on, he paying £100 to my son James, and £10 to my grandson Benjamin Dare, when 21. Granddaughter, Prudence Hall, and grandson, David Long, 5 shillings each. Daughters, Elaner, Elizabeth and Rachel, rest of moveable estate. Friend, Ananias Sayre, to be Trustee for grandsons, Benoni and Elkanah Dare. Executors—son, Reuben, and my wife, Clemens. Witnesses—Isaac Grace, John Gray, Ephraim Sheppard. Proved Aug. 14, 1770.
1770, Aug. 13. Inventory, £263.10.9, made by Thomas Maskell and Mark Sheppard.   Lib. 14, p. 317.

1770, Sept. 2. Daten, Joseph, of Fairfield, Cumberland Co.; will of. Wife, Prudence, ⅓ my personal, and use of plantation where I live; also £20 to bring up my son, Leonard, to the age of 14. Son, Joseph, the plantation where he lives that was my father's, on the east side of the highway, and woodland adjoining, which I bought of John Barns, and a salt marsh, which was my father's, on Stow Creek; also the swamp in Buckshutem. Sons, Eli and Henry, the plantation where I live. (Henry is under 21.) Son, Leonard, lot of woodland at White Marsh; also salt marsh below William Meeks, when he is 21. Daughter, Mary Daten, £40. Daughter, Anne Dayton, £40, when she is 18. Executor—Theophilus Elmer. Witnesses—Sarah Harris, Isaac Harris, John Burk. Proved Dec. 14, 1770.
1770, Dec. 11. Inventory, £427.18.1, made by Joseph Ogden and David Wescote.
1775, April 13. Account by Executor.
    Lib. 14, p. 328; Lib. 15, p. 532.

1766, Feb. 24.—Daton, Jonah, of Pilesgrove Twsp., Salem Co., yeoman; will of. Daughters, Zerviah and Phebe Daton, all my estate, when they are 21. Legacy to John Powell, my apprentice. Executor —friend, Ephraim Fithian. Witnesses—Fithian Stratton, Jonathan Stratton, Isaac Harris. Proved April 14, 1767.

1766, March 11. Inventory, £94.3.8, made by Ezekiel Foster and William Russel. Lib. 13, p. 181.

1770, Feb. 6. Datten, David, of Fairfield, Cumberland Co.; will of. My lands to be sold, except my homestead. Wife, Ann Daton, moveables. Son, David, my homestead. Daughters, Hannah Datten and Ruth Datten, rest of estate, when 18. Executor—friend, Silas Newcomb. Witnesses—Joseph Daten, Jr., Ephraim Datten and George Ferebe. Proved Feb. 28, 1770.
1770, Feb. 13. Inventory, £314.7.10, made by Theophilus Elmer and Joseph Dayten.
1772, July 13. Account by Executor. Lib. 14, p. 437; Lib. 15, p. 22.

1768, Feb. 6. Davenport, Humphrey, of New Foundland, Bergen Co.; will of. Wife, Elizabeth all real and personal while my widow. Son, Jacob, grist mill and saw mill. Sons, Cornelius and John, land where I live. Son, Nathaniel, £20. Son, Peter, £29. Daughters, Ann Mary and Catharine, goods. Executors—son, Jacob, John Pailaman and my wife. Witnesses—Peter Snier, Philip Price and George Betay. Proved Oct. 25, 1768. Lib. I, p. 360.

1766, May 28. Davenport, Isaac, of Greenwich, Gloucester Co., waterman. Int. Adm'r—Isaiah Davenport, clock maker. Fellowbondsman—George Vanleer, yeoman; both of said place. Witness—Samuel Vanleer.
1766, Feb. 15. Inventory, £62.5.6, made by George Vanleer and Jacob Fislar. Lib. 12, p. 380.

1758, Jan. 3. Davis, Daniel, of Deerfield, Cumberland Co., yeoman; will of. Wife, Deborah, part of the moveables and use of some land. Sons, Bradway and Uriah, all my lands. Daughter, Mary Brooks, 5 shillings. Daughter, Patience Miller, also 5. Son, Amon, £5. Daughter, Hannah, a bed. Rest of my moveable estate to my three youngest children, and the three youngest children of my wife, namely, Joseph Davis, Hannah Davis and Arthur Davis, and unto David Lummis, Henry Lummis and Edward Lummis, as they come of age. My daughter, Hannah, is to live with my wife till she is 15. Son, Amon, is to learn trade of carpenter with Jeremiah Miller till he is 15. Executors—my wife and my son, Bradway. Witnesses—Nathan Leek, Henry Seely, Samuel Hannah, John Keen. Proved Feb. 14, 1763.
1763, Feb. 8. Inventory, £190.11.1, made by Jeremiah Foster and Samuel Leek.
1764, March 2. Account by both Executors. Lib. 11, p. 306.

1760, Sept. 10. Davis, Elizabeth, of Pilesgrove, Salem Co.; will of. Daughter, Abigail, pewter platter. Daughter, Rachel, platter and other goods. Daughter, Ellen, a bed. Sary, the wife of John Roberson, a chest of drawers. To my three younger granddaughters, Rebecka, Mary and Amre, one pound, 10 shillings each. William Basset my cane. Susanah Morgan, my "tea tacling." To Sary Smith, a wench; and, if said Sary Smith should die before her mother, she is to go to Rachel, and then to Susanna, at the death of her mother. Rest of my estate to my two daughters, Abigail and Rachel. Executors—daughters, Abigail and Rachel. Witnesses—Jacob Elwell, David Elwell, Joel Elwell. Proved Feb. 16, 1762.

1761, Dec. 11. Inventory, £62.13.1, made by Edward Draper and Samuel Lippincott. Lib. 11, p. 34.
1762, March 16. Adm'r—Elisha Bassett, of Pilesgrove, yeoman. Fellowbondsman—Jacob Elwell, yeoman, of said place. Witness—David Bush, Jr. "Whereas, Elizabeth Davis appointed Abigail Bassett and Rachel Morgan as Executors, and Abigail refused to act, and Rachel died before probate, therefore the said Elisha Bassett was appointed Adm'r with the will annexed."

1762, Feb. 22. Davis, John, of Borough of Elizabeth, Somerset (?) Co.; will of. Wife, Keziah, use of the lands to bring up my children, but, if she marry, the lands to be sold and the money divided among my children. Executors—my friends, Henry Davis and William Line. Witnesses—Edward Drake, Jacob Davis, Joseph Jones. Proved March 3, 1764.
1764, March 6. Inventory, made by Samuel Yamans and Joseph Vail.
1767, Feb. 3. Account, by both Executors. Amount of Inventory, £40.15.6. Land sold for £28.11.3. Lib. H, p. 410.

1763, March 1. Davis, John, of Pilesgrove, Salem Co., sadler; will of. Son, John, all my lands, when he is 21; but my wife to have the use of the land till he is 21. Wife to have the moveable estate. Executors—my wife and my cousin, David Davis. Witnesses—Benjamin Test, Thomas Graves, David Davis. Proved April 25, 1763.
1763, April 5. Inventory, £179.9.6, made by Isaac Barber and Benjamin Test.
1765, March 16. Account by Executor. Lib. 11, p. 396.

1768, Jan. 23. Davis, John, of Elizabeth Borough, Essex Co., blacksmith; will of. Wife, Suzanah, my homestead of 70 acres where I live. Daughter, Suzanah Frasey, 10 acres. Daughter, Sarah Scuder, 10 acres. Daughter, Elizabeth Rous, 10 acres. Grandson, Jacob Davis, 52 acres of that farm I bought of Hial Pamely. Grandson, John Davis, a meadow. Son, Zachariah, rest of estate. Executors—wife, and son Zachariah, and my son-in-law, John Scuder. Witnesses—Joseph Acken, John Hinds, John Stiles. Proved March 3, 1768.
1768, March 7. Inventory made by Daniel Perrine and David Miller. Lib. I, p. 306.

1764, Aug. 15, Davis, Jonathan, of Cohansey, Cumberland Co., minister; will of. Wife, Esther, ½ my moveable estate and profits of ½ my plantation. Eldest son, Jarman, plantation I bought of Eliakim Earl, of one hundred acres, and a meadow in Alloways Creek Precinct, in Salem Co. Son, Elnathan, plantation where he lives, of 50 acres; also my home plantation, where I live, he paying to my youngest daughter, Naomi Davis, £50 when she is 18. Eldest daughter, Edith Dunn, and her husband, Benjamin Dunn, £100. Plantation leased to Jeremiah Robbins to be sold. Executors—my wife, Esther, and my youngest son, Elnathan. Witnesses—Samuel Davis, Jeremiah Robbins, Sarah Robins. Proved Feb. 21, 1769.
1769, Feb. 15. Inventory, £671.16.4, made by Jonathan Ayars and Hugh Dunn.
1770, Jan. 19. Adm'r—Elnathan Davis, of Hopewell, Cumberland Co., surveyor. Fellowbondsman—Jonathan Ayars, of Stow Creek, said Co. It appears that, after debts and legacies were paid, there

remained a residue of £240.8.10, of which Elnathan Davis, acting Executor, prays administration.
1770, Jan. 24. Account of Elnathan Davis, acting Executor.
Lib. 14, p. 60; Lib. 15, pp. 4, 14.

1768, July 10. Davis, Nathaniel, of Elizabeth Town, Essex Co. Int. Adm'r—Samuel Woodruff, principal creditor of said Davis. Fellowbondsman—Robert Ogden, Jr., of Elizabeth Borough. Witnesses—Robert Ogden and Elizabeth Williams. Lib. I, p. 336.

1766, July 10. Davis, Rebecca, of Trenton, Hunterdon Co. Int. Adm'r—Alexander Chambers. Fellowbondsman—Benjamin Yard; both of said place. Witness—Thomas Sutton.
1766, July 12. Inventory, £35.16.8, made by Edmund Beakes and Conrad Kotts.
1767, Sept. 12. Account by Adm'r. Lib. 12, p. 386.

1761, March 4. Davis, Samuel, of Hunterdon Co. Int. Adm'r—Richard Stockton, Esq., of Princeton, Somerset Co. Fellowbondsman—Theophilus Severns, of Trenton. Witness—Mary Severns. (The above Rev. Samuel Davis was President of the College of New Jersey). Lib. 10, p. 462.

1769, March 13. Davis, Samuel, of Gloucester Co. Int. Adm'rs—Ann Davis, and Owen Davis. Fellowbondsman—John Wallace; all of said Co.
1769, Feb. 28. Inventory, £200, made by John Wallace and Joseph Morgan. Lib. 13, p. 496; File No. 8529 C.

1762, Sept. 17. Davis, Simon, of Greenwich, Sussex Co., yeoman. Int. Adm'x—Sarah Davis, of Oxford, said Co., widow. Fellowbondsman—James Hayes, of said place, yeoman.
1762, Sept. 16. Inventory, £90.1.3, made by James Hayes and John Vanata. Lib. 11, p. 288.

1768, Nov. 27. Davis, Susannah, of Westfield, Borough of Elizabeth, Essex Co. widow; will of. Daughter, Elizabeth Ross, a bed. Granddaughter, Annar Davis, a bed. Grandson, John Davis, a cow. Grandson, Abraham Davis, a cow. Daughters, Sarah Scudder and Elizabeth Ross, and granddaughters, Susannah Frazee and Mary Frazee, the rest of my estate, each daughter to have ⅓, and the grand daughters the other ⅓. Executors—my sons-in-law, John Scudder and Isaac Frazee. Witnesses—Samuel Yamans, Jacob Marss, Sarah Tucker. Proved April 7, 1769.
1769, April 8. Inventory, made by William Miller and William Peirson. Lib. K, p. 76.

1763, May 17. Davis, William, of New Hanover Twsp., Burlington Co., yeoman; will of. Wife, Ann, provided for on the farm. Son, Joseph, bed and horse. Son, William, a horse, and all that his grandfather left him; also my great Bible. Daughter, Ann Davis rest of personal. Son, Joseph, that part of my plantation whereon I dwell, that was my father's, he paying to my son, Howell, £100, after Joseph is 21, and paying to his mother £6 yearly. Son, William, the rest of plantation, he paying to my grandson, William Davis, £5 when 21. Executors—wife, Anne, and sons, Joseph and William. Witnesses—Samuel Rogers, David Lippincott, Joseph Goldy.

CALENDAR OF WILLS—1761-1770   109

1763, Aug. 6. Codicil. My son Howell also to be an Ex'r. Witnesses—James Davies, Isaac Pitman, Joseph Goldy. Proved Aug. 22, 1763.   Lib. 11, p. 377.
1763, Aug. 19. Inventory, £499.17.3½, made by Thomas Budd and John Goldy.
1767, April 7. Account of Ann Davis and Howell Davis, Ex'rs of William Davis.

1764, March 14. Davis, William, of Gloucester Co.; will of. My wife the best bed. Son, William, my pocket book. Daughter, Elizabeth, looking glass. Rest to my wife and children. Executors— my brother, Gabriel Davis, and brother, Joel Clark. Children not of age. Witnesses—Thomas Brian, William Goforth, Jacob Ware. Proved March 23, 1764.
1764, March 26. Inventory, £391, made by Jacob Clement, farmer, and Joal Hillman.
1765, March 23. Account by Executors.   Lib. 11, p. 517.

1758, June 21. Davison, Andrew, of Freehold, Monmouth Co., yeoman; will of. My wife, Catherine, all my estate, while my widow. Daughters, Margret and Susannah, a negro girl, when wife is done with her. My three sons, William, John and James, all my lands. Daughters, Margaret Davison, and Susannah Davison, £30 each. Boys and girls to have schooling. Executors—my wife, my brother George, and friend William Rue. Witnesses—Joseph Newton, James Abraham, Jr., John Truax. Proved Sept. 20, 1766.
1766, Sept. 19. Inventory, made by, John Truax, William Hankinson, and William Laird.   Lib. I, p. 30.

1765, Oct. 29. Davison, George, of Somerset Co., yeoman; will of. Wife, Rozanah, ⅓ of the profits of my land. Sons, William and Peter Davison, all my lands. My four daughters are single, and now live with me, and they are, Sarah, Mary, Anne and Jemima, and each is to have £20. My six daughters are, Margaret, Providence, Sarah, Mary, Anne and Jemima, and each to have £20. Executors—friends, Richard Runyon, and my son, William. Witnesses—John Collyer, Jonathan Sutton, Jacob Lewis. Proved Aug. 4, 1767.   Lib. I, p. 157.

1766, Oct. 1. Day, Charles, of Waterford Township, Gloucester Co. Int. Adm'x—Leaticia Day. Fellowbondsman—Isaac Albertson; both of said Co. Witness—Henry Wood.
1765, Oct. 9. Inventory, £188.10.9, made by Henry Wood and John Shivers.   Lib. 12, p. 187.

1763, Feb. 9. Day, Silas, of Morristown, Morris Co., cooper; will of. Wife, Phebe, use of all my estate while my widow, and, after her death or marriage, one-half to be at her disposal, and other half to my brethren, Ezekiel, David, Jeduthun, Robert, Samuel, Abraham, Jared and Jehiel; except I give to Silas Condict's daughter, Elizabeth Phebe, as much as either of my brothers. Land I bought of Silas Condict to be sold. Executor—Silas Condict. Witnesses—Daniel Carmichael, John Hatheway, Benony Hathaway. Proved April 7, 1763.
1763, April 20. Inventory, £310.15.7, made by Joseph Condict and Abraham Casterline.   Lib. H, p. 385.

1760, Oct. 16. Dean, John, of Trenton, Hunterdon Co., yeoman; will of. Son, Stephen Dean, plantation whereon I live. Son, John, £30. Son, Jacob, six shillings. Daughter, Martha Green, 2 cattle. Daughter, Elizabeth Lane, one cow. Daughters, Martha Green and Hannah James, rest of cattle. Executor—son, Stephen. Witnesses—Richard Laning, Gershom Mott, James Dean. Proved Feb. 4, 1761.
 1761, Feb. 12. Inventory, £100.1.6½, made by Richard Laning and John Mott. Lib. 10, p. 548.

1763, May 26. Deboogh, Lawrence, of Upper Freehold Twsp., Monmouth Co.; will of. Lands to be sold. Wife, Deborah Deboogh, £100. Children, Mary, William, John, and James, personal estate when they are 21. Executors—wife, Deborah, and my brother-in-law, Joseph Robins. Witnesses—Abraham Anderson, Francis Mount, John Lawrence. Proved June 15, 1763.
 1763, June 6. Inventory, £76.13.1, made by John Laming and William Compton. Lib. 11, p. 330.

1763, Nov. 8. DeCamp, Garret, of Somerset Co. Int. Adm'x—Susannah DeCamp, the widow. Fellowbondsman—Christopher Haydon (Haddon); both of said Co. Witness—John Mackay.
Lib. H, p. 304.

1764, Feb. 9. Decamp, John, of Essex Co.; will of. Son, Aaron, £5. To the heirs of son John, deceased, ¼ of my estate, except the legacies given to others; and his oldest son, Lawrence, is to have £— more than the rest. Daughters, Sarah Oughtletree, another ¼. To the heirs of my daughter, Mary Vannauman, dec'd, one other ¼. Daughter, Dinah Powers, to her heirs, she being deceased, another ¼. To the Society of Turky, £3. Land to be sold. Executors—William Parrot, yeoman, and Recompence Stanbary, shopkeeper, and Jacob Bedell, yeoman. Witnesses—Jonathan Mulford, Abraham Rutan, William Coles. Proved May 28, 1766. Lib. H, p. 610.

1760, Aug. 29. Decker, Anderis, of Montague, Sussex Co., cordwainer; will of. Son, Andreas, 4 sides of leather, because he is the eldest son now alive. Sons, Andreas, Christopher, Casparus Feryenmoet Decker, Johannis Decker, Petrus Decker, Jacob Decker, and Phillipus Decker, all my real estate. Daughters, Ledia Weller (wife of Johannis Weller), Gretie Westvael (widow of Cornelis Westvael), Sarah Decker, Dievertie Decker and Elizabeth Decker, to each £10. Wife, Dievertie, shall be master of all my estate while she is my widow. Executors—my sons, Andreas Decker, Casparus Feryenmoet Decker, and Jacob Decker. Witnesses—Jacobus Hornbeek. Petrus Hooghteeling, William Ennes. Proved June 8, 1763.
 1763, June 24. Inventory, £86.4.6, made by Abraham Shimer and William Ennes. Lib. 11, p. 462.

1764, April 24. Decker, Hendrick, of Wantage, Sussex Co., yeoman. Int. Adm'r—Joseph Barton, of said place, yeoman. Fellowbondsman—Amos Pettit, of Newton, said Co., yeoman. Witness—Cornelius Fryer.
 1764, April 10. Renunciation by Hannah Decker, saying she is old and "not able to go down," and her sons do decline to do it. Asks for Joseph Barton to be made Adm'r, as he is one of the creditors. Witness—John Crowell. Lib. 11, p. 538.

CALENDAR OF WILLS—1761-1770   III

1762, Aug. 23. Decker, Jacobus, of Wantage, Sussex Co. Int. Adm'x—Ellinor Decker, of said place, widow. Fellowbondsmen—Peter Decker and John Crowell; both of said place, yeomen.
1762, July 3. Inventory, £108.13.0, made by Peteres Decker and Henderick Huykendal.   Lib. 11, p. 289.

1763, July 18. DeCow, Isaac, of Mansfield Twsp., Burlington Co., yeoman; will of. My friends, the children of John Scholly late of Chesterfield, weaver, deceased, £26 among them, the same to be paid to John Thompson, he giving security to pay the same as above. To Mary, the wife of Samuel Satterthwaite, Jr., £5. Daughter, Hannah Decow, ½ of my personal estate, and priviledge of my "Logg" house, where Adam Pettit lately removed from, while she is single, and she is to have ⅓ the rents till my son, Isaac, is 16. Son, Isaac, rest of real and personal. Executors—Eber Decow (my brother), and William White (my brother-in-law). Witnesses—John Decow, John Robinson, Mary Aronson. Proved May 3, 1765.   Lib. 12, p. 108.
1765, April 10. Inventory, £300.10.10, made by David Rockhill and John Newbold.
1767, Aug. 14. Account of Eber DeCow and William White as Ex'rs of Isaac DeCow.

1761, Oct. 17. Dehart, Matthias, of Essex Co. Int. Adm'rs—Matthias Dehart and Jacob Dehart, both of Elizabeth Town, said Co. Witness—Elizabeth Hetfield.
1761, Oct. 16. Renunciation of Baltas Dehart and Samuel Dehart, brothers of Matthias Dehart, in favor of Doctor Matthias Dehart. Witness—John Chetwood.
1761, Oct. 26. Inventory, £2112.9.5½, made by Jonathan Thompson and Thomas Price.   Lib. H, p. 35.

1766, April 28. DeHart, Matthias, of Elizabeth Town, Essex Co.; will of. Wife, Catharine, ⅓ of real and personal estate. Children, William, Cyrus, Jacob, Maurity, Johannah Margaret, and Abigail Ametia Christina DeHart, the remainder. Executors—my wife, and my brother, John DeHart. Witnesses—George Emott, Christopher Manlove, James Gaithwaite. Proved Aug. 21, 1766.
1766, Sept. 9. Inventory, made by, George Mitchell and William ———.   Lib. I, p. 148.

1770, July 18. Delatush, Henry, of Mansfield, Burlington Co., shopkeeper; will of. All real and personal to be sold, except the burying-ground where my daughter, Rebecca, is buried, situate in Mansfield at a place called Black Horse, which lot I reserve for the use of my family's burial ground forever. The money from said sales to be divided among my wife, Rebecca, son, Henry, and children of my son, John, namely, Rebecca, Hannah and Eleanor. Executor—my son, Henry. Witnesses—Elijah Field, Eliakim Higgins, Joseph Imlay. Proved Oct. 29, 1770.
1770, Oct. 24. Inventory, £925.5.8½, made by Joseph Gibbs and Joseph Imlay.   Lib. 15, p. 57.

1766, June 11. Delatush, John, of Mansfield Twsp., Burlington Co., blacksmith. Int. Adm'rs—Elizabeth Delatush and Henry Delatush, Jr. Fellowbondsman—Henry Delatush, Sr.; all of said Co. Witness—Thomas Folke.   Lib. 12, p. 291.

1766, April 22. Inventory, £318.13.5, made by Thomas Folkes and Joseph English.

1763, April 1. Demaree, Pieter, of Bergen Co.; will of. Eldest son, Peter, his part of the woodland and ½ of cleared land where he lives. Son, Jacobus, 2 acres where he lives. Sons, John, Jacobus, David and Samuel, rest of real estate. My five sons shall pay to my daughters and grandchildren £100, viz., to Mary, 1/12, Treyntie 1/12, Sarah 1/12, Leya 1/12, Margaret 1/12, Ledeya 1/12, Mary 1/12, Anna 1/12, Madlentie 1/12. To children of Hester 1/12; to children of Jackmintye 1/12, and to children of Elizabeth 1/12. Daughter, Madlena my easy chair. Wife, Mary use of whole estate while my widow. Executors —my wife, Mary, my friend, Lorance Van Buskirck, Esq., and my friend, George Blinckerhof. Witnesses—David Brower, Jacob Brower and Jan Brower. Proved Oct. 2, 1763. Lib. H, p. 312.

1742, June 23. Demarest, David, of Hackinsack, Bergen Co.; will of. Wife, Maatie, use of whole estate. Son, Samuel, broad axe. Sons, Christian and Jacob, my land, except that part I gave to daughter, Elizabeth, where she lives. Second son, Joast, has had £50. Daughter, Mary, wife of Thomas Eckeson, £7. Daughter, Elizabeth, wife of William Camel, the deed for her house lot. Daughter, Mary, £30. Daughter, Sarah Demarest, £30. Daughter, Rachel Demarest, £30. Youngest dau., Annatie Demarest, £30. The bonds of my brother-in-law, Jacobus Pike, and cousin, David Demarest, to be paid. Executor—wife, Maatie. Witnesses—Andres V. Boskerk, David Demarest and Simon Demarest. Proved Feb. 13, 1761.
1761, Feb. 10. Bond of Christian Demarest, of Hackinsack, as Adm'r, with will annexed. (The wife, Martie, had lately died. The eldest son, Samuel, refused to act as Adm'r). Lib. G, p. 374.

1763, Dec. 18. Demarest, David, of Hackensack, Bergen Co., yeoman; will of. Wife, Catrina, to manage the plantation where I live while my widow. My eldest son, Nicolais, the mare I gave him when he was first "mared," and the land he now has, so as to make 25 acres; he paying to my daughter, Elizabet, £11, and to my daughter, Grietee, £11, and my daughter, Lidea, £11. My sons, Petrius, Daved, Gilyaem and Jacobes, each 25 acres out of the land called the Gore. Sons, Samuel and Gerret, plantation where I live, except 25 acres to Nicholaes. Wife, Catrina, £100, which I had from her father, Van houte. Daughter, Sara, £25. Daughter Trynte, £50. Daughter, Marya, £50. Executors—wife, Catrina, my eldest son, Nicolaes, my son David, and my cousin, Johannes Demarest. Witnesses—Jacobus Blinkerhof, Isaac Boogert and Jan Eckeson.
1767, March 28. Codicil. To children of Sara, £5 each. Witness— Johannis Demarest. Proved Feb. 24, 1768. Lib. I, p. 246.
1768, Feb. 25. Inventory, £657-2-6, made by David Demarest and Reynir Quackenbos.

1761, Oct. 15. Demarest, Samuel, of Hackensack, Bergen Co. yeoman; will of. Wife, Lea, use of real and personal while my widow. Son, Samuel, the Dutch Bible. Land to be sold when youngest child comes 21, and money divided among my children, Samuel, Daniel, Cornelius, David, Petrus, Jacobus and Rebecca Demarest. Executors— brother, David Samuelse Demarest, and my brother-in-law, Daniel Demarest. Witnesses—John Bensen, Benjamin Westervelt and Robert Livesey. Proved April 6, 1762. Lib. H, p. 154.

1761, Dec. 12. Inventory, £290-5-0, made by Johannis Demarest and John Bensen.

1754, May 6. Demarest, Simon, of Hackinsack in Bergen Co., yeoman; will of. Wife, Vroutie, use of real and personal while widow. Eldest son, Samuel, 28 shillings. Son, Cornelius, land at Rindageamak, which I had of David Ackerman. Youngest son, Jacob, land where my improvements are, on which I live. Son, Daniel, my loom. Four sons, Daniel, John, David and Petres, land I bought of Nicholas Ackerman, at Ridageamack. Son, Daniel, being lame, is to have a negro boy to do his work. Daughter, Catelentie, wife of Sibe Banta, £60, and daughter, Maria, wife of Nicholas Ackerman, £60, and eldest son, Samuel, £60 from the sale of personal estate, but, if it is not sufficient, then must be made up by my sons, Cornelius, Daniel, John, David, Petres and Jacob. Executors—wife, Vroutie, and my two eldest sons, Samuel and Cornelius. Witnesses—Theodore Valleau, William Campbell and Albert Zabriskie. Proved April 8, 1761.
Lib. G, p. 423.

1763, Dec. 19. Dennelsbeck, Frederick, of Pilesgrove Twsp., Salem Co.; will of. Son, John Dennelsbeck, my plantation, which I had by deed from William Conkelin, for 222½ acres, out of which there is to be reserved 3 acres of swamp, called Gravelly Pond, for son Frederick. Son, John, is to have ½ the cedar swamp, which 1 bought from Ephraim Seirs. Should my son Frederick marry a woman that has no Dutch blood, or part Dutch, he shall have only 5 shillings; otherwise I give him my homestead plantation, that 1 bought of Alexandet King, of 2,000 acres; also a lot above the Beaver Dam, and the other ½ of Cedar swamp I bought of Ephraim Seers, and the 3 acres of swamp already mentioned. Executors—sons John and Frederick, and friend, Michael Miller. Witnesses—Frederick Garrison, John Garrison, Jacob Richman. Proved Dec. 9. 1766. Lib. 12, p. 308.

1767, Sept. 29. Dennis, Joseph, Sr., of Sussex Co.; will of. Sons, Joseph and Ezekiel, all real and personal estate, and they are to pay the following legacies: To son, Nathaniel, £130; son, John, £2. Executors—sons, Joseph and Ezekiel. Witnesses—Hugh Hagerty, Joseph Barton, Patrick Haggerty. Proved April 7, 1770.
Lib. 15, p. 34.

1760, Nov. 8. Dennis, Phillip, of Shrewsbury, Monmouth Co., yeoman; will of. To wife, Rachel, £80. Sons, John and Joseph, my lands, when Joseph is 21. Eldest daughter, Zilpha, £100; youngest daughter, Sarah, £100, when 18 and 16 years of age. Executors—friends, Webley Edwards and Cornelius Lane, son of Cornelius. Witnesses—Henry Green, George Smith, Stephen Woolley, Anthony Dennis. Proved Jan. 10, 1761.
1760, Dec. 30. Inventory, £357.17.10, made by Job. Cook and Henry Green. Lib. H, p. 14.

1767, May 1. Dennis, Philip, of Greenwich Twsp. Cumberland Co.; will of. Wife, Lucy, a case of drawers that was left to her by her father; also her share of personal estate. Son, Philip, my plantation where I live, except what I give to my son, Jonathan. Son, Jonathan, the northeast corner of said plantation. Wife and two daughters, Prudence and Elizabeth Dennis, rest of personal. Daughter, Grace Bowen, £20. Daughter, Rachel Smith, £5. Executors—wife, and son, Philip. Witnesses—Ebenezer Miller, Mark Reeve, John Sheppard. Proved May 28, 1768.

1768, May 25. Inventory, £295.19.10, made by Charles Davis and Mark Sheppard. Lib. 13, p. 414.

1763, Dec. 2. Denniston, John, of New Brunswick, Middlesex Co.; will of. Son, Arthur, is to support his mother, my wife, Mary. To daughter, Hannah Blane, £7. Daughter, Jane, wife of Samuel Branson, £50. Son, Arthur, the rest. Executors—my son, Arthur and Andrew McDowell. Witnesses—John Lyle, John Lyle, Jr., Andrew Brown. Proved June 13, 1764. Lib. H, p. 444.

[Not dated]. Denny, John, of Woolwich Township, Gloucester Co., yeoman; will of. Wife, Sarah, 2 beds and 2 cows. Rest of moveable estate and plantation to be sold, and the money to be equally divided between my wife, Sarah, and all my children, Priscilla Denny, Thomas Denny, Miles Denny, Sarah Denny, William Denny and John Denny. Brother-in-law, William Matson, shall have my son, William, until he be bound to a trade. Executors—my wife, Sarah, and my brother, Thomas Denny. Witnesses—John Derickson, Moses Hoffman, Elizabeth Hoffman. Proved Oct. 8, 1768.

1768, Sept. 27. Inventory, £237.8.3, made by John Derickson and Mathew Gill. Lib. 13, p. 485.

1766, Aug. 25.—Denton, Samuel, of Middlesex Co. Int. Adm'r—John Denton, brother and principal creditor, of Somerset Co. Fellowbondsman—Anthony Denton, of Middlesex Co.

1766, Aug. 23. Renunciation by Sarah Denton, South Ward of New Brunswick.

1766, Aug. 14. Inventory of goods of Samuel Denton, cooper, made by John Sutphen and Albert Terhune. Lib. H, p. 641.

1765, Aug. 27. Depue, John, of Wantage, Sussex Co. Int. Adm'x—Rachel Depue, widow of said John. Fellowbondsmen—John Depue, of Walpack, and Joseph Barton, of Newton; all of said Co. Witness—Hezekiah Smith.

1765, Aug. 27. Inventory, £283.11.6, made by George Kimble and Joseph Barton. Lib. 12, p. 225.

1766, May 15. Devooer, Hendrick, of Reading Twsp., Hunterdon Co.; will of. Wife, Catherine, use of real and personal during her life, and, after her death, all to be sold and divided among my children, except my oldest son, Henry, who is to have 10 shillings above the rest. If my sons, Henry, Daniel, John and James, and my daughters, Elizabeth, Rachel, Catherine, Sarah, Leah, Anne and Margaret, should die without issue, then their share to go to the rest. Children are to be put to school. Executors—friend, Benjamin Allegar, and John Emans. Witnesses—John Cole, Isack Demott, Edward Wilmot. Proved July 5, 1766.

1766, July 4. Inventory, £238.1.5½, made by Edward Wilmot and Isack Demott. Lib. 12, p. 402.

1761, May 22. DeWitt, Luke, of Monmouth Co. Int. Adm'r—Luke DeWitt. Fellowbondsman—Peter Imlay; both of said Co.

1761, May 16. Inventory, £420.16.7, made by John Polhemus and Peter Imlay. Lib. 10, p. 175.

CALENDAR OF WILLS—1761-1770   115

1761, Aug. 4. Dey, Deyrck, of New York City; will of. Son, Tunis Dey, all my real and personal estate in New Jersey. Daughter, Jane, wife of John Varck, two lots Nos. 33 and 37, and £1,000. Daughter, Ann Dey, lots Nos. 34 and 38, and £1,000, and an outset when she is married, like her sister. Daughter, Mary Dey, lots Nos. 35 and 36, and £1,000, and an outset. Executors—my said four children. Witnesses—Christofel Van Bomel, Gerrit Van Bomel, Lawrence Wessells. Proved Oct. 27, 1764. Lib. H, p. 380.
1765, Feb. 7. Received out of the office, the will of Derick Dey. (Signed) David Shaw, Mary Shaw.

1769, Nov. 7. Diament, Lois, of Fairfield Twsp., Cumberland Co.; will of. Son, Hedges Diament, £20, one horse and 2 sheep. To my 3 sons, and 2 daughters, viz., Jonathan, James and Nathaniel and Lois Bennit and Sarah Swing, each 5 shillings. Daughters, Dorcas Diament, Elizabeth Diament and Rhoda Diament, and my son, Hedges, rest of estate. Tombstone to be put to grave of my deceased husband. Executors—daughters, Dorcas Diament and Elizabeth Diament. Witnesses—Ambrose Whitacar, Ruth Whitacar, Elkanah Powell. Proved Dec. 31, 1770.
1770, Dec. 29. Inventory, £96.9.4, made by Daniel Bateman and Jeremiah Nixon. Lib. 14, p. 311.

1766, April 23. Diament, Nathaniel, of Fairfield, Cumberland Co.; will of. Wife, Lowis, ⅓ the personal estate, and the use of ⅓ my lands and marsh, on Jones' island. Son, Jonathan, ⅓ my land on said island, except the piece called Island of Marsh, which contains 30 acres; also the house which my son, James, now possesses. Son, James, ⅓ of the land on said Island, (except that piece of marsh before excepted). Son, Nathaniel, the other ⅓ of said Island. Son, Hedgis, that piece of salt marsh on the said island, of 30 acres, which has been excepted; also the land at Bear Swamp, of 190 acres. Daughter, Lowis Bennit, £5. Daughter, Sarah Swing, £5. Daughter, Darcos Diament, £40. Daughter, Elizabeth, £40. Daughter, Ruth Powell, £5. Daughter, Roda Diament, £40. Sons, Jonathan, Nathaniel, and Hedgis, my husbandry utensils. Executors—sons, Jonathan and James. Witnesses—Theophilus Elmer, Jeremiah Nixon, Jr., Theodosia Anderson.
1766, April 23. Codicil. If those my daughters, that are not married, viz., Darcos, Elizabeth and Rhoda, to whom I have given £40, be married, and have any of my estate, then they are to have only £5 each. Witnesses—Theophilus Elmer, Jeremiah Nixson, Jr., Theodosia Anderson. Proved May 14, 1767.
1767, April 28. Inventory, £256.15.6, made by David Wescote and Ephraim Harris. Lib. 13, p. 164.

1763, Dec. 29. Dickason, William, of Alloways Creek, Salem Co. Ward. Petition by Margaret Rea, wife of John Rea, of said place, stating that she has a son, named William Dickason, being of the age of 7 years and 8 months, by her late husband, Mark Dickason, of said place, deceased; and she prays that John Holme may be made Guardian, till the child is 14.
1763, Dec. 29. Guradian—John Holme, Esq. Fellowbondsman—John Dickeson, both of said place. Lib. 11, p. 448.

1763, April 27. Dickeson, William, of Alloways Creek Precinct, Salem Co., yeoman; will of. Wife, Abigail, £30, and the goods she brought with her. Son, William, 130 acres of the northeast end of my land where I live, that joins Jacob Davis, and the land formerly belonging to Thomas Stonebanks. Son, James, the rest of said plantation. Son, John, 5 shillings. To the 3 daughters, of my daughter Sarah, deceased, viz., Mary Ann, Catherine and Elizabeth Lee, £5 each. To my four daughters, Ann Moore, Judith Hamilton, Mary Thompson and Margaret Craig, the rest of personal estate. Executors—son, James, and my son-in-law, William Craig. Witnesses—John Holme, George Dickinson, George White. Proved April 2, 1764.

1764, Jan. 30. Inventory, £425.3.4, made by John Holme and William Oakford. Lib. 12, p. 87.

1770, Sept. 8. Dickeson, William, of Salem Co. Ward. Son of Mark Dickinson, of said place, having lands devised to him by his father, makes choice of John Holme, Esq., as his Guardian.

1770, Sept. 8. Guardian—John Holme, Esq. Fellowbondsman—John Dickeson, of Upper Alloways Creek, Salem Co. Lib. 14, p. 404.

1761, Oct. 28. Dickey, Deborah, of Salem Co. Int. Adm'r—Robert Kitt, of Manington, said Co. Fellowbondsmen—William Barrat, of said place, and William Cattell, of Penns Neck, said Co.

1761, Oct. 28. Inventory, £14.15.0, made by William Barratt and William Cattell. Lib. 11. p. 35.

1764, March 27. Dickinson, Joseph, of Pilesgrove Twsp., Salem Co., yeoman; will of. Wife, Jane, ½ my moveable estate, and ⅓ the profits of the land. To Joseph Dickinson, son of George Dickinson, ⅔ the plantation where I live, and ½ my moveable estate, when he is 21. If Joseph should die without heirs, then his brother, George, is to have his share. To said George, son of George Dickinson, ⅔ of the land I bought of Simon Warner, and, if he die, then to go to my brother George's son, Jacob. Executors—my wife and Joseph Dickinson. Witnesses—James Bond, Patrick Gray, John Richman. Proved May 5, 1764.

1764, April 19. Inventory, £374.5.0, made by John Holme and John Richman. Lib. 12, p. 95.

1761, June 27. Dickinson, Nathaniel, of Manington, Salem Co. Int. Adm'x—Sarah Dickinson, widow. Fellowbondsmen—John Thompson and William Harvey, yeomen; all of said place.

1761, May 29. Inventory, £66.13.4, made by Nathaniel Hall and William Harvey. Lib. 10, p. 435.

1760, Oct. 30. Dike, Sarah, of Freehold, Monmouth Co.; will of. To the four children of James English, Sr., Jonathan, John, Margaret and Elizabeth, the money there is after the debts are paid. To Elizabeth English the house and furniture therein. To Margaret and Elizabeth English some goods. Executors—Joseph Ker and Robert McGallard. Witnesses—William Cole, David English, Bryan Gollohar. Proved May 10, 1765.

1765, May 7. Inventory, £118.17.2, made by James Bradshaw, David English and William Cole. Lib. H, p. 503.

1769, Oct. 16. Dildine, Herman, of Lebanon Twsp., Hunterdon Co.; will of. Oldest son, Henry, £55. Son, Daniel, live stock, etc. Daughter, Jane Savage's, 2 children, Jane and Mary Ann, £40. To Jane, the

daughter of my daughter Eve, a colt. To the children of my daughter, Sarah, £40 when the youngest is of age. To the children of my son, Herman, £40 when of age. To daughters, Elizabeth, Rachel, and Catherine, £40 each. Daughter, Ann, £40. Wife, Yanakico, use of all estate. Son, Henry, apparel. If my son Herman should be alive and come and make any demand, then I give him £40. Executors—son, Daniel, and my loving Christopher Wooff. Witnesses—James Best, William Best, Edward Wilmot. Proved Oct. 27, 1769.
1769, Oct. 26. Inventory, £185.15.10, made by Edward Wilmot and John Speeder (Spader). Lib. 14, p. 144.

1760, June 17. Dildine, Uriah, of Hardwick, Sussex Co.; will of. To my wife all my moveable estate, and, at her death, to my six daughters. I have helped pay for land for son Sampson, so I give to his eldest son, Uriah, 5 shillings. I have also helped pay for my son, Uriah's, land. Executors—Harman Lane and Cornelius Low, Jr. Witnesses—John Marlatt, John Van Sickle, Jr., Steintie Van Sickle. Proved April 30, 1761.
1761, April 2. Inventory, £116.12.6, made by Nathan Armstrong, and Allen Nixon. Lib. 10, p. 478.

1769, Nov. 2. Dilts, Peter, of Amwell, Hunterdon Co., yeoman; will of. Wife, Mary, £300, and otherwise provided for. Lands to be sold and the money divided among my children, John, Harman, John Bodine, George Sharpenstine, and children of my son, Peter (being one son, and 2 daughters). Executors—son-in-law, John Bodine, and Henry Dilts. Witnesses—Peter Houshel, John Duckworth, John Opdyck. Proved Jan. 24, 1770.
1770, Jan. 24. Renunciation by Henry Dilts.
1770, Jan. 20. Inventory, £65.8.2, made by William Hoogland and John Opdycke.
1787, May 10. Account by John Bodine, acting Executor. (Plantation (360 acres) sold for £558. Legacies were paid to George Sharpenstine, John Diltz, Harmon Diltz and D. Howell; also to J. Smith and Peter Barrick, two of the legatees of Peter Dilts, Jr., deceased.
Lib. 15, p. 38.

1765, May 21. Dilshaver, John, of Stow Creek, Cumberland Co. Ward. Son of Michael Tilsaver, of said place, yeoman. Guardian—Samuel Hannah, of Deerfield, said Co., yeoman. Fellowbondsman—Benjamin Garrison, of same place, yeoman. Witnesses—Daniel Clark and Maskell Ewing. The said John Tilsilver is over 14 years of age and made choice of his Guardian. (See also Tilsilver). Lib. 12, p. 170.

1765, Feb. 28. Dingman, Adam, of Walpack Twsp., Sussex Co., Gent., will of. Wife, Mary, her support, while she is my widow. Jacob, my first born, the best horse. Sons, Jacob, Adam, Jacobus, Samuel, Peteress, to have my lands. Daughters, Marytie and Eve, £50 each. Executors, my brother, Andries Dingman, of Upper Smithfield, Northampton Co., Penna., and Abraham Van Campen, Esq. of Walpack Twsp. Witnesses—Nicholas Emins, Joseph Chestnor, ———? Proved Aug. 27, 1765.
1765, April 6. Inventory, £419.2.8, made by Nicholas Emins and Johannes Westbrook.
1768, June 24. Account, by Andries Dingman, surviving Executor.
Lib. 12, p. 216; Lib. 12, p. 521.

1769, April 1. Disosway, Israel, of Staten Island. Int. Adm'r—Cornelius Disosway, brother of said Israel, of said place. Fellowbondsman—Nathaniel Fitz Randolph, of Woodbridge, Middlesex Co.
Lib. K, p. 76.

1766, Dec. 30. Dod, Daniel, of Newark, Essex Co., yeoman; will of. Wife, Sarah, enough to make her comfortable. Daughters—Eunice Baldwin and Sarah Freeman, £5 each. Sons, Thomas and Amos, salt meadow. Son, Isaac, £15. Son, Joseph, £5. Son, Caleb, £15. My Indian purchase-right over the mountain, and at Whepennung, to my sons, Thomas, Daniel, Joseph and Amos. Son, Amos, my dwelling house, and rest of lands. Executors—sons, Daniel and Amos. Witnesses—John Peirson, John Dod, Jr., Samuel Billington. Proved Feb. 27, 1767.
Lib. I, p. 184.

1768, June 25. Dod, John, of Newark, Essex Co.; will of. Wife, Jemima, what the law provides. Daughter, Jemima, £15 and my loom, when 18. Daughter, Elizabeth, £20 when 18. Sons Adonijah and Nekoda, my land over the mountain, at a place called the Great Swamp; that is, 70 acres to Adonijah, and 30 acres to Nekoda. Sons, Abel, Matthew and James, my dwelling and land about it, viz., to Abel, ¼ part, and the rest equally to the other two sons. If the purchase right over the mountain be decided and lost, then Adonijah and Nekoda shall have their part in my house land. Executors—my brother-in-law, Amos Harrison, Esq., and my son, Adonijah. Witnesses—Daniel Cundict, Benjamin Williams, Jr., John Dod, Jr. Proved Oct. 18, 1768.
Lib. I, p. 352.

1761, March 11. Dorsett, James, of Monmouth Co.; will of. Wife, Ann, the use of my plantation, along with my two sons, Joseph and James. Son, Andrew, £50, and ⅓ of my salt meadows at Canaskunk. Sons, James and Joseph, my land where I dwell, which land is to be sold after death of my wife. Daughters, Elizabeth and Mary Dorsett, household goods. Sons, Joseph and James, the rest of my salt meadows. Title to be given to Elias Bayley, to whom I have sold land. The land formerly belonging to my brother, Samuel, to be sold. Executors—my wife, son Joseph Dorsett, and John Williams, Sr., of Freehold. Witnesses—Richard Herbert, John Dorsett, Rachel Pearse. Proved June 14, 1762.
Lib. H, p. 130.

1766, Sept. 20. Dorsett, John, of Middletown, Monmouth Co. Int. Adm'r—Lewis Forman, one of the creditors. Fellowbondsman—Thomas Hunn; both of said Co. Witness—Elijah Dunham.
1766, Sept. 15. Renunciation, by Catherine Dorsett, widow of said John, in favor of Lewis Forman. Witness—John Bowne.
Lib. H, p. 642.

1767, March 18. Doty, John, of Mendham, Morris Co., yeoman. Int. Adm'r—Nathaniel Doty, Jr., the eldest brother. Fellowbondsman—Jacob Doty; both of said place.
Lib. I, p. 208.

1768, Sept. 3. Doty, Joseph, of Borough of Elizabeth, Essex Co.; will of. Wife, Sarah, my homestead where I live. Son, George, 5 shillings. My two sons, Anthony and John, 5 shillings each. Oldest daughter, Elizabeth, wife of Jeremiah Ludlow, deceased, 5 shillings; and like sum to youngest daughter, Sarah, wife of William Carl.

CALENDAR OF WILLS—1761-1770   119

To my said 3 sons, all of New Brittan, all my lands. Executors—wife, Sarah, and son, John. Witnesses—Phebe Hedger, Uriah Hedgers, Jr., William Willcocks. Proved Oct. 14, 1768.
Lib. K, p. 48.

1763, Oct. 29. Doud, Cornelius, of Trenton, Hunterdon Co. Int. Adm'r—Aaron Doud, of Sussex Co. Fellowbondsman—James Cunine, of Hunterdon Co. Witness—Micajah How.   Lib. 11, p. 459.

1765, Nov. 21. Dougherty, Edward, of Penns Neck, Salem Co.; will of. Son, James, plantation where I live, when he is 21; but, if he die under age, then it is to go to my three daughters, Rebecca, Catherine and Elizabeth Doughertys. My wife is to have ⅓ my moveable estate, and the other ⅔ to my daughters, Rebecca and Elizabeth. Daughter, Catherine Dougherty, my little plantation, where Susannah Scott now lives, which contains 23 acres. Wife, Elizabeth, is to have ⅓ the profits of the land. Executors—my friends, Andrew Standley and Allen Congleton. Witnesses—Joseph Corbet, William Cartey, William Stretch. Proved Dec. 21, 1765.
1765, Dec. 19. Inventory, £425.0.9, made by Henry Sparks and Thomas Thackra.   Lib. 12, p. 301.

1766, Feb. 5. Doughty, Edward, of Great Egg Harbor, Gloucester Co., carpenter; will of. Wife, Margaret, ⅓ house and plantation where I dwell, and ⅓ my grist mill; also live stock and household goods; and, after wife's death, the goods to be divided among my three daughters, Mary Lee, Margaret Risley and Rebecca Risley. Son, Edward, Jr., my plantation and all my lands, except 200 acres and my mill on Absecon beach, and, after his death, to his son Edward. Son, Robert, 4 acres where his house and mill stand, and also my grist mill; also the ½ of my sawmill; and the other ½ of saw mill I give to my son Edward. Son, Thomas, and my son, Abner, the land that was formerly Isaac Adams'. Son, Jonathan, the plantation where he dwells. Son, John, 100 acres joining John Engersol's land; also 50 acres on Clames Branch, and 50 acres on Absecon Creek. Executor—son, Edward. Witnesses—Richard Risley, Debrow Cordrey, Rebecca Risley. Proved March 28, 1770 by Deborah Cordery.
1770, March 23. Inventory, £64.1.0, made by Amos Ireland and John Steelman.   Lib. 14, p. 263.

1762, Dec. 9. Douglass, John, of Burlington Co. Int. Adm'r—Thomas Douglass. Fellowbondsman—Jacob Lawrence; both of said Co.   Lib. 11, p. 240; File No. 7261 C.

1768, June 21. Douglass, Thomas, of Chesterfield, Burlington Co. Int. Adm'r—Phineas Bunting, of said place. Fellowbondsman——John Robins, of Allen Town, Monmouth Co.
1768, June 10. Inventory, £334.0.5, made by William Miller and George Middleton.
1768, June 21. Renunciation by Elizabeth Douglass, the widow.
Lib. 13, p. 434.

1765, April 30. Dowd, Aaron, of Trenton, Hunterdon Co., attorney-at-law; will of. Formerly of Newton in Sussex Co. Executors are to buy headstones, of marble, for Cornelius Dowd, Hannah Dowd and myself, and have the names cut thereon. To Ann Dowd, the widow of my father, Cornelius Dowd, £15. To the Presbyterian Church in Newtown and Hardwick, £10, towards building a meeting house on Charles Pettit's land in Hardwick, Sussex Co. To the managers, for building a schoolhouse, near Amos Pettit's in Newtown, £5. To Sarah, the wife of Joseph Yard, £30, for gratitude for the tender care she hath taken of me in my illness. To Benjamin Cooper, the books I hold with him in partnership. Friend, Joseph Phillips, my riding chair and mare. To Elizabeth and Ann Pettit, who are daughters of Amos Pettit, £20 each, when they are 18. My messuage in Trenton, containing 13 acres, which I hold by 2 deeds (one from Trustees of Robert Smith, dated 22 of April, 1758, and the other from Thomas Tindall and Mary his wife, dated 3 of Nov., 1761), I give to Wanell Cottnam (son of Abraham Cottnam), but, if he die before he is 21, then I give the same to George Cottnam, who is also a son of said Abraham. Land which I hold by deed from Cornelius and Ann Dowd I give to Joseph Phillips, Jr. I desire my apprentice, Isaac Lafoliot, to be bound to a person who will give him a trade and education. Executors—Abraham Cottnam, Esq., and Joseph Phillips. Witnesses—Arch'd William Yard, Isaac Allen, Robert Dodd. Proved June 22, 1765. Lib. 12, p. 144.

1768, March 9. Downy, John, of City of New Brunswick, Middlesex Co.; will of. To wife, Ann, £200. Son, John, £200. Daughter, Elizabeth, £200. Executrix—wife, Ann. Witnesses—Joseph Vickers, Jacob Wiser, William Oake. Proved May 16, 1768. Lib. I. p. 269.

1770, July 28. Dragstrum, Herman, of Woolwich, Gloucester Co., waterman. Int. Adm'r—Isaac Justison, yeoman. Fellowbondsman —Thomas Denny, Esq.; both of said place. Witnesses—Gideon Dennis and John Ladd.
1770, July 9. Inventory, £60.1.6, made by Andrew Vanneman and Thomas Denny.
1770, July 9. Renunciation by his widow, Elizabeth Dragstrum, in favor of her brother, Isaac Justes. Lib. 15, p. 47.

1759, July 28. Drake, Abraham, of Roxbury Twsp., Morris Co.; will of. Grandsons, Abraham and Jacob, the sons of my son Abraham, all my lands and grist mill; and they are to pay to my eldest son, Nathaniel, 20 shillings, and to my son, Jacob, 10 shillings, and to my son, Elisha, £40. Executors—my said grandsons. Witnesses —William Boyd, Thomas Throckmorton, John Van Tuyl. Proved May 6, 1763. Lib. 11, p. 456.

1763, June 22. Drake, Benjamin, of Hopewell Twsp., Hunterdon Co.; will of. "Being aged." Wife, Hannah, all the goods she brought when I married her; also £50. Daughter, Rebecca, £40. Son, Zachariah, £40. Daughter, Hannah, £40. Grandson, William Drake, the son of William Drake, £5. To Isaac Eaton, minister of Baptist Church of Hopewell, £2. Son, Edmond, my plantation where I live. Executors—my sons, Edmond and Zachariah Drake. Witnesses— John Lamburt, Daniel Gano, John Drake. Proved Aug. 30, 1763.
1763, Sept. 20. Inventory, £231.19.11, made by Reuben Armitage and William Bryant. Lib. 11, p. 422.

CALENDAR OF WILLS—1761-1770   121

1767, Jan. 15. Drake, Edmond, of Hopewell, Hunterdon Co.; will of. My Executors are to sell my estate at public sale and to pay the legacies ordered by my father's will that remain unpaid; and my father's apparel is to be divided between my three brothers, Thomas, Nathan and Daniel. Son, Nicholas, my apparel. Daughter, Catherine, £10. Daughter, Elizabeth, my bed. Executors—friends, Ephraim Runyan and John Drake. Witnesses—Jacob Stout, Azariah Hunt. Proved Feb. 3, 1767.
1767, Feb. 2. Inventory, £287.11.7, made by Reuben Armitage and Azariah Hunt. Lib. 13, p. 216.

1765. March 13. Drake, Nathaniel, Sr., of Roxbury, Morris Co. Int. Adm'rs—Nathaniel Drake, Jr., and Samuel Drake, sons of Nathaniel Drake, Sr. Fellowbondsman—Jabesh Bell; all of said place.
Lib. H, p. 423.

1759, Feb. 21. Drake, Patience, of Piscataway, Middlesex Co., widow; will of. Grandson, Ephraim Drake, son of Ephraim Drake, deceased, 4 shillings. Daughter, Rachel Runyon, set of curtains. Daughters, Martha Joans, Rachel Runyon and Elizabeth Burges, my apparel, sheets, etc. Grandson, Joseph Drake, son of Joseph, deceased, Bible. Grandson, Reuben Drake, son of said Joseph, silver headed cane. Grandson, Ephraim Drake, son of said Joseph, books. Grandson, Embly Drake, son of said Joseph, books. Grandson, Hezekiah Dunham, son of Hez: Dunham, deceased, 40 shillings. Grand children, Patience and Francis Drake, daughter and son of Henry Drake, deceased, £10 and 10 shillings, which my son Henry borrowed of me. Grandchildren, the sons and daughters of my 3 sons, deceased, to wit, James, Henry and Joseph Drake, the rest of estate. Executors—friends, Benjamin Stelle and Phinehas Dunn. Witnesses —Henry Sharp, Denah Furgerson, Joseph Davis. Proved April 7, 1762. Lib. H, p. 96.

1763, Jan. 18. Draper, Edward, of Pilesgrove, Salem Co., weaver. Int. Adm'r—Isaac Barber, of said place, yeoman. Fellowbondsmen —Daniel Bassett, yeoman, and Jechonias Wood, tanner; both of said place.
1763, Jan. 6. Inventory, £295.11.10, made by Thomas Barber and Daniel Bassett. Lib. 11, p. 371.

1764, March 5. Dreen, John, of Hanover Twsp., Morris Co. Int. Adm'r—John Cobb, who was approved by the creditors. Fellowbondsmen—Jacob Allerton and Joseph Kitchel; all of said place. Witness—Oliver Spencer.
1764, Oct. 2. Inventory, made by Joseph Bond and Reuben Riggs.
Lib. H, p.356.

1767, April 20. Driller, William, of Sussex Co. Int. Adm'x— Mary Driller. Fellowbondsmen—John Green and Martin Shipley, all of Oxford, said Co. Witness—James Hanna.
1767, April 20. Inventory, £131.1.6, made by Richard Lannen and John Green.
1770, May 24. Account by Adm'x.   Lib. 12, p. 466; Lib. 15, p. 65.

1768, July 15. Drummond, Evan, of Middlesex Co. Int. Adm'r—John Mackay. Fellowbondsman—John Johnston; both of Perth Amboy, said Co. This Adm'n is for the goods which remain unadministered by Andrew Johnston and Andrew Hay, Executors of Evan Drummond, who are now also deceased. Witness—John Thomson.
File No. 4507 L. (See Lib. C, p. 139).

1768, Nov. 24. Drummond, Thomas, of Somerset Co. Int. Adm'r—Daniel Irwin. Fellowbondsman—Allan Cameron; both of said Co.
1768, Nov. 24. Inventory, £39.12.3, "of estate of Thomas Drummond of Bernardstown, laborer," made by William Davison and Allan Cameron.
1771, June 1. Account made at Baskingridge, by Adm'r.
Lib. I, p. 363.

1770, Feb. 6. Dubois, Garret, of Pitts Grove, Salem Co., bricklayer. Int. Adm'rs—Lurany Dubois, widow, and David Dubois, blacksmith. Fellowbondsmen—Jacob Dubois, blacksmith, and Samuel Elwell, merchant; all of said place. (See Israel Dubois).
1770, Jan. 30. Inventory, £217.17.9, made by John Mayhew and Jacob Elwell. File No. 1161 Q.

1770, Feb. 6. Dubois, Israel, of Salem. Int. Adm'rs—Lurany Dubois and David Dubois. Inventory, £217.17.9. (See Garret Dubois).
Lib. 15, p. 6.

1768, Sept. 7. Dubois, Jacob, of Pilesgrove, Salem Co.; will of. Sons, John and Benjamin, the place where I live, when the youngest is 21. Wife to have ½ my real and personal estate to help her bring up the children. Son, Solomon, £30. Son, Josiah, £30. Daughter, Mary, £30. Wife now pregnant, and that child to have £15. Excutors—my wife, Mary, and my brother, Peter. Witnesses—Cornelius Dubois, John Gray, John Nelson. Proved Oct. 13, 1768.
1768, Oct. 10. Inventory, £358.13.0, made by Mathew Nieukirk and Jacob Dubois. Lib. 13, p. 479.

1768, Dec. 10. Duffield, Adam, of Hopewell, Cumberland Co. Int. Adm'r—John Gray, of Piles Grove, Salem Co., doctor. Fellowbondsman—Daniel Stretch, of Stow Creek, Cumberland Co., yeoman.
1768, Nov. 28. Inventory, £30.3.4, made by Daniel Stretch and Jacob Paullin. Lib. 13, p. 477.

1762, Dec. 8. Duglass, John, of Chesterfield, Burlington Co. Inventory £68.8.11. made by Jacob Lawrence and Abel Middleton. (See Lib. 11, p. 240). File No. 7261 C.

1769, Aug. 23. Dumont, Rynear, of Somerset Co. Int. Adm'x—Hannah Dumont, widow of said Rynear. Fellowbondsman—Samuel Blewer; both of said Co. Witness—Thomas Andrews.
1769, Aug. 24. Inventory, £183.14.3, made by John Vroom and John Ten Eick. Lib. K. p. 121.

1767, Sept. 21. Duncan, Mary, of Somerset Co. Int. Adm'r—John Carey, of said Co. Fellowbondsman—John Skinner, of Middlesex Co. The said John Carey is principal creditor. Lib. I, p. 152.

1761, April 7. Dunlap, Elizabeth, of Pilesgrove, Salem Co., widow; will of. Grandson, John Wetherington, £10 when 21. To grandchildren, David Wetherington and his sisters, Hannah, Rachel and

Sarah Wetherington, rest of my personal estate. Executor—my friend, Thomas Barber. Witnesses—Benjamin Johnson, Hannah Barber, Edward Draper. Proved May 1, 1761.
1761, April 20. Inventory, £440.8.11, made by Elisha Bassett and Edward Draper. Lib. 11, p. 13.

1767, Nov. 2. Dunlap, John, of Pilesgrove, Salem Co. Int. Adm'x —Jane Dunlap, widow. Fellowbondsmeh—David Dubois and James Dunlap, yeomen; all of said place.
1767, Oct. 29. Inventory, £428.12.0, made by Jacob Elwell and Jacob Davis. Lib. 13, p. 279.

1770, Jan. 22. Dunn, Hezekiah, of Newton, Sussex Co. Int. Adm'rs —Hezekiah Dunn and Ephraim Darby. Fellowbondsman—William Landon; all of said place. Witness—David Frazer. Lib. 15, p. 2.

1762, Feb. 1. Dunn, John, of Penns Neck, Salem Co., yeoman. Int. Adm'x—Catherine Dunn, of said place, widow. Fellowbondsmen— John Mecum, of said place, yeoman, and Andrew Murdock, of Town of Salem, shopkeeper.
1766, Oct. 18. Account by David Alexander and Catherine, his wife, late Catherine Dunn, Adm'x of John Dunn. "Paid Sarah Dunn for dower £48.1.0." Lib. 12, p. 304.

1760, Feb. 13. Dunn, Phineas, of Piscataway, Middlesex Co., yeoman; will of. Wife, Elizabeth, £50, to enable her to maintain the child she goes with. Wife is to have her support from the estate. Son, Jeremiah, my homestead where I live, and the land I bought of Jonathan Dunham, deceased, and the lot I bought of Joseph Mitchel, and the salt meadow which I bought of Jeremiah Drake, deceased. Son, Reuben, lot I bought of my brother, Benjamin Dunn, and the lot I bought of Daniel Dunham, adjoining thereto, and a salt meadow I bought of Joseph Hull, and one I bought of Boyley Arnold. Eldest daughter, Rachel Moore, the interest of £50, for her disobedient and barbarous carriage to me, her tender parent, and I will her no more. Daughter, Sarah, £50 when 18. Son, Jephtha, £250 when 18. Daughter, Sarah, to be put to live with my relatives, John and Anna Skillman. To my kinsman, Peter Sutten, £8. The unborn child is provided for. Executors—my friend, Nehemiah Dunham, and my brother, Benjamin Dunn. Witnesses—Masheck Hull, William Manning, Joseph Davis. Proved Sept. 4, 1761. Lib. H, p. 30.

1766, April 22. Dunn, Sarah, of Salem, Salem Co., widow; will of. Daughter, Sarah Prockler, 5 shillings. Daughter, Ameay Murdock, the house and lot where I live, and, after her death, to my grandson, John Murdock; but if he die before he is of age, then to my granddaughter, Hester Murdock. Executor—friend, Edward Keasbey. Witnesses—Samuel Sims, Thomas Vaughan, Nathaniel Holmes. Proved May 21, 1768.
1768, May 21. Inventory, £108.19.0, made by Samuel Sims and John Craven. Lib. 13, p. 395.

1767, Dec. 18. Dunn, William, of Somerset Co. Int. Adm'r—John Dunn, the principal creditor and father-in-law, of said Co. Fellowbondsman—Edward Higgins, of Middlesex Co.

1767, Dec. 21. Inventory, £13.6.7, made by Jacob Bergen and Peter Berrien.
1767, Dec. 18. Account by Adm'r. Lib. I, p. 208.

1767, Jan. 24. Duseberry, George, of Newton, Sussex Co.; will of. Wife, Cattorn, ⅛ of my estate, and all she brought with her when I married her. Son, John, a horse and cow. Rest to be divided between my daughters. Executors—wife, Cattorn, Peter Corcelius and Japheth Byron, Esq. Witnesses—John Hockabary, Peter Space, Japheth Byram. Proved Nov. 26, 1767.
1767, Feb. 23. Inventory, £57.3.10, made by John Snuke and Johannis Conave. (See George Teireberger). Lib. 12, p. 532.

1761, June 1. Dye, James, of South Ward of Perth Amboy, Middlesex Co., yeoman; will of. My plantation to be sold. Of my estate, my wife, Sarah, is to have 2 parts, my sons, James, Andrew, David, John and Benjamin, each 2 parts, and my daughters, Mercy, Rachel, Anne and Sarah, each 1 part, when of age. Executors—wife, Sarah, my brother, Vinson Dye, and my friend, John Tomson. Witnesses—Stephen Warne, George Job, Stephen Warne, Jr.
1763, Dec. 13. Codicil. The money which is due me by virtue of the will of my father, John Dye, to be collected. Witnesses—same as in will. Proved April 6, 1764.
1764, April 17. Inventory, made by Vincent Dye and John Tomson. Lib. H, p. 427.

1769, Feb. 4. Eacritt, James, of Pilesgrove Township, Salem Co., yeoman; will of. The plantation that my son, James, lives on, of 340 acres, to be for him during his life, and then to go to my two grandsons, James Eacritt and Joseph Eacritt, sons of said son James. The plantation I live on, of 300 acres, to my son, John; in case he has a mind to live on it, he may during his life, but, if he will not live on it, it is to be rented, and the rent paid to his two sons, Isaac, and the next son, when they are 21; and after my son, John's, death, I give the said lands to my 2 grandsons, Isaac and his next eldest brother, sons of said John. To my friend, Jacob Richman, my cane and silver buckles. The remainder of my estate to be divided as follows: To my daughter, Mary, an equal part with all my granddaughters, of my sons James and John. Executor—friend, Jacob Richman. Witnesses—John Read, Samuel Read, John Coombs. Proved April 17, 1769.
1769, April 14. Inventory, £137.13.4, made by John Mayhew and Thomas Sparks. Lib. 13, p. 539.

1765, July 15. Eagles, Alexander, of Newark, Essex Co., trader; will of. To my old mother, Margaret Eagles, £20. Sister, Margaret Nevens, £30. Sister, Easter Slit, in Ireland, £30. The five children of my sister, Mary, late wife of John Craig, £30. My brother, William Eagles, and brother, Thomas Eagles' 2 sons, viz., Thomas and Alexander, ½ of the residue. Executors—my brother, Thomas, and David Burnit. Witnesses—David Burnet, Thomas Eagles, Robert Boyd. Proved July 29, 1765. Lib. H, p. 545.

1766, Oct. 21. Eastlack, Reuben, of Waterford Twsp., Gloucester Co., yeoman; will of. My mother, Ann Alexander, £24. Sister, Hannah Eastlack, £5. Wife, Ann Eastlack, rest of my estate. Execu-

CALENDAR OF WILLS—1761-1770 125

tors—my wife, and my friend, Isaac Mickle. Witnesses—Joseph Armstrong, Elizabeth Rabley, Richard Weekes. Proved Dec. 11, 1766.
1766, Nov. 13. Inventory, £231.14.0, made by Richard Weekes and Owen Davis. Lib. 12, p. 361.

1769, May 25. Eatton, Joanna, of Shrewsbury, Monmouth Co., widow; will of. Daughter, Margaret Berrien, furniture. Daughter, Joanna Spencer's, daughters, all the rest. My negro man may be free, by paying my daughter, Sarah Tole, 40 shillings a year. Executors —daughters, Sarah Tole, and Joanna Spencer. Witnesses—Stephen Wardell, Jeremiah Bonham, Joseph Leonard. Proved Jan. 15, 1770.
1770, Jan. 2. Inventory, £621.11.9, made by Jeremiah Bonham and Joseph Allen. Lib. K, p. 163.

1756, March 30. Eatton, Joseph, of Shrewsbury, Monmouth Co., surgeon; will of. Wife, Lucy, the improvement of half of my lands. Sons, John and Thomas, lands, and they are to be educated at the directions of my brother, Thomas Eatton. Executor—my brother, Thomas Eatton. Witnesses—John Allen, Jr., John Lippincott, Jr., Mary Lippincott. Proved May 6, 1761.
1761, June 1. Whereas Joseph Eaton, in his will, appointed his brother, Thomas Eaton, to be his executor, and the said Thomas is removed out of the Province, into the Government of Georgia, now Lucy Eaton, the widow of Joseph, is appointed Adm'x with the will annexed. Fellowbondsman—Joseph Leonard, of said place.
1761, May 8. Inventory £584.19.0, made by Josiah Holmes and Jeremiah Bonham. Lib. G, p. 445.

1766, June 28. Eayre, Ner, of Evesham, Burlington Co., carpenter. Int. Adm'r—Isaac Haines, of Northampton, said Co. Fellowbondsman—Lawrence Webster, of Evesham.
1766, June 19. Renunciation, by Grace Eayre, widow of Nerr Eayre. Witnesses—William Rogers and Thomas Haines.
1766, Feb. 21. Inventory, £135.19.8, made by Benjamin More and Lawrence Webster. Lib. 12, p. 294.

1765, May 3. Eayre, Richard, of Northampton, Burlington Co., fuller, will of. Wife, Hannah, to enjoy the whole of estate, except that part ordered to be sold. Son, Asa, my fulling mill, lot belonging to dwelling, and lot between the races, when 21. Son, Thomas, house and lot where Robert Powell lives, and lot of 35 acres, between lands of my brother, Thomas, and John Eayres, when 21. Son, Richard, land on south side of creek. Daughter, Mary Eayre £100 when 21. Executors—wife, Hannah, and my brother, Habbakuk Eayre. Witnesses—Robert Powell, William Calvert, Thomas Eayre. Proved June 13, 1765.
1765, June 10. Inventory, £233.13.3, made by Robert Powell and Solomon Haines. Lib. 12, p. 116.
1771, Feb. 4. Account of Hannah Eayre and Habakkuk Eayre, Ex'rs. Lib. 15, p. 101.

1761, Jan. 20. Eayre, Thomas, of Evesham, Burlington Co., yeoman; will of. Eldest son, Habbakkuk, 10 shillings. Son, Thomas, house, grist and saw mill on Ancokus creek. Son, Richard, a house and fulling mill. Son, Thomas, pine land. Sons, Richard and John, land at the Bear swamp. Son, Joseph, £500. Daughter, Sarah Burr, wife of Henry Burr, 10 shillings. Daughter, Hannah Eayre, £200. Execu-

tors—sons, Habbakkuk and Thomas. Witnesses—Jacob Wigmore, John Burr, Jr., Stephen Sarish. Proved Feb. 11, 1761. Lib. 10, p. 348.
1761, Jan. 10. Inventory, £1051.5.6, made by Joseph Mullen and Solomon Haines.

1765, Oct. 24. Eayre, Thomas, of Eayres Town, in Northampton, Burlington Co., yeoman; will of. Wife, Kitura, various goods and £30; also to be paid £30 yearly by my son, Hoza. Daughter, Rebeccah Eayre, 90 acres when 21. Son, Hoza, my house, mill and saw mill, called Eayre's Mills, and 10 acres which I bought of my brother, Richard Eayre, dec'd. Son, Levi, several tracts. Youngest son, Thomas, lands. Residue of estate to my wife and all my children. My children are Habbakkuk, Richard, dec'd, John and Joseph. Executors—my brother, Habbakkuk Eayre, and brother-in-law, John Moore. Witnesses—Robert Powell, Ner Eayre, John Burr, Jr.
1765, Oct. 24. Codicil. Witnesses—John Burr, Jr., Ner Eayre.
1770, Feb. 28. Codicil. Younger daughter, Hannah Eayre, land I bought of John Fisher. I also make my brother, John Eayre, one of the executors. Witnesses—Henry Burr, John Wills, John Burr. Proved March 24, 1770.
1770, March 22. Inventory, £668.3.3. made by Hezekiah Jones and Abraham Borton. Lib. 14, p. 285.
1770, May 22. Account of Habakkuk Eayre, John Eayre and John Moore, Ex'rs of Thomas Eayre, Jr., who was Ex'r of his father, Thomas Eayre. "Legacy paid to Joseph Eayre and to Sarah Eayre." Later accounts Jan. 16, 1772. File 9135 C. (See Lib. 10, p. 348).

1762, May 15. Eazler, Christopher, of Monmouth Co. Int. Adm'r—Hendrick Goegletts. Fellowbondsman—John Taylor; both of Middletown, said Co.
1762, June 3. Inventory, made by John Dorsett and Joseph Dorsett. Lib. H, p. 103.

1763, Jan. 18. Edgar, Alexander, of Woodbridge, Middlesex Co.; will of. Wife, Mary Edgar, cows, negros, goods, etc. Son, Thomas, house where I live, and 100 acres to be taken off the lower end, and 10 acres of woodland off of that place joining Joseph Freeman, and he is to pay £200 to my son, William. To son, James, the rest of my home place, and 5 acres of woodland adjoining Joseph Freeman, and he is to pay £50 to my son, William. Son, David, the place that formerly belonged to Thomas Pike, which I bought of Samuel Crower, and the rest of that lot by Joseph Freeman. Son, William, £450 when he is 21. Daughter, Sarah, £100 when 18. Daughter, Jannet, £150 when 18. Daughter, Mary, £150 when 18. That 11 acres of land which I bought of James Kelly, Jr., to be sold. Executors—wife, Mary, and my brothers, David Edgar and William Smith. Witnesses—Moses Bloomfield, Jonathan Bloomfield, Jonathan Alston. Proved Aug. 22, 1763. Lib. H, p. 283.

1759, May 5. Edsall, James, of Bergen Co., weaver; will of. Eldest brother, John, a mourning ring. Mother, Mary Banks, interest of the bond of Anttebee Earle, and, at her death, equally to my brothers and sisters, viz., John Edsall, Elizabeth Earle, Mary Wendell, Catrian Edsall, Anne Edsall, Hana Edsall and Samuel Edsall. Executors—uncle, John Edsall, and Hartman Brinkerhoff. Witnesses—Jacob Banta, Calasa Brinkerhoff and James McKinley. Proved Dec. 7, 1764. Lib. H, p. 504.

1766, Sept. 15. Edwards, James, of Cape May Co., gentleman; will of. Daughter, Mary Mulford, ⅓ my plantation, on northeast side, and ⅓ my back land, and same never to be sold, but to descend from heir to heir forever. Daughter Elizabeth Edwards, ⅓ my plantaion, to the southwest of Mary Mulford's, and ⅓ my back land, and never to be sold but to descend from heir to heir forever. Daughter, Rachel Crowell, ⅓ my plantation, to the southwest of Elizabeth Edwards', and ⅓ my back lands, and never to be sold, but to descend from heir to heir forever. My daughter, Rachel Crowell, may live in the "leento" for the space of 10 years. My daughter, Mary Mulford, is to pay to my granddaughter, Sarah Hand, £10, when she is 21. Daughter, Rachel Crowell, is to pay her £15, and daughter, Elizabeth Edwards, to pay her, £25. Executors—my daughter, Mary Mulford, my son-in-law, Ezekiel Mulford, my daughter, Rachel Crowell, my son-in-law, Jacob Crowell. Witnesses—Abner Corson, Lewis Cresse, Anthony Cresse.
1766, Sept. 18. Codicil. I appoint Henry Hand, of the Lower Precinct, as Guardian of my daughter, Elizabeth Edwards.
1766, Oct. 31. Codicil. My son-in-law, Jacob Crowell, is to be Guardian of my daughter, Elizabeth. I now make my son-in-law, Jacob Crowell, Executor, instead of Mary Mulford, Ezekiel Mulford and Rachel Crowell. Proved Nov. 24, 1767.
1766, Dec. 29. Inventory, £85.5.1, made by John Eldredge and Lewis Cresse. Lib. 13, p. 361.

1764, April 6. Edwards, John, of Haines Neck, Salem Co., yeoman; will of. Wife, Mary, use of all my lands to bring up the children; but, if she marry, then my sons, Daniel and John, to have the said land. Son, Brandriff Edwards, £3 when 21. Son, Joseph, £5. To rest of my children the remainder of my personal estate. Executors —son, Daniel, and Francis Miles. Witnesses—Michael Pedrick, Hannah Maines, William Stretch. Proved Sept. 29, 1764.
1764, May 8. Inventory, £303.16.10, made by Michael Pedrick and John Procter. Lib. 12, p. 98.

1769, Oct. 16. Egberts, Isaac, of New Brunswick, Middlesex Co.; will of. Wife, Catharine, silver teaspoons, bed, etc., and use of all real and personal till my youngest child is 14, or her marriage, when estate is to be divided between my wife and daughters, Barbara, Francyntje and Femmetje, son Thomas, daughters Susanna and Maria, son Jacobus, and daughter Fannetje. Executors—my wife and friends, Thomas Van Dyck and John Schuurman. Witnesses— William Ouke, John Van Buren, Andrew Norwood. Proved Dec. 25, 1769. Lib. K, p. 168.

1764, June 2. Egborson, Lawrence, of Elizabeth Town, Essex Co. Int. Adm'r—Lawrence Egborson (Egbertson) yeoman. Fellowbondsman—Samuel Tyler, clothier; both of said place. Witness—Uzal Woodruff.
1764, June 1. Renunciation of Christian Egborson, widow of Lawrence Egborson, in favor of her son, Lawrence Egbertson. Witnesses—Samuel Tyler, and Isaac Gillam. Lib. H, p. 357.

1767, June 15. Eggman, Christopher, of Waterford Twsp., Gloucester Co., yeoman. Int. Adm'x—Deborah Eggman, widow. Fellowbondsman—John Wallace, of said place.
1767, June 11. Inventory, £44.4.6, made by John Stone, and John Wallace. Lib. 13, p. 104.

1762, June 18. Eglington, Timothy, Greenwich, Gloucester Co. Account by John Eglington, the Adm'r. (See "N. J. Archives," Vol. 32, p. 103). File No. 703 H.

1763, Jan. 31, Eldredge, Thomas, of Cape May Co. Int. Adm'x—Glory Eldredge (who signs her name "Glory Aner Eldredge") Fellowbondsman—Eli Eldredge; both of said Co. Witnesses—Jacob Hand and Zebulon Swain.
 1763, Jan. 31. Inventory, £228.14.7½, made by Providence Ludlam and Zebulon Swain. Lib. 11, p. 414.

1765, June 17. Eldredge, William, of Cape May Co.; will of. My wife, use of ⅓ my lands, with the house I live in, and at her death to my sons, John and Eli. Wife, Esther, ⅓ of moveable estate. Daughter, Esther Garison, £20. Daughter, Hannah Morris, £20. Grandson, Elihu Eldredge £10 when 21. Grandson, Daniel Eldredge, £8 when 21. Granddaughter, Mary Eldredge, 20 shillings when 18. Grandson, Thomas Eldredge, £8 when 21. Executors—sons, Jehu and Eli. Witnesses—Daniel Hildreth, Joshua Hildreth, Jr., Mary Peterson. Proved Jan. 16, 1769.
 1769, Jan. 25. Inventory, £110.12.1½, made by Zebulon Swain and Philip Godfrey. Lib. 14, p. 175.

1764, Oct. 9. Eldridge, Jonathan, of Springfield, Burlington Co., yeoman; will of. Wife, Abigail, household goods, and my Executors are to build a house, 18 by 22 feet, one story high, on that part of my plantation called Chestnut Island, for her while my widow, and to pay to her £10 yearly; and I also give her £50. My nephew, Samuel Brain, £40 when 21 and 3 yearly payments thereafter. To niece, Charity, the wife of Milentus Woolston, £6. Son, John, ⅓ of the plantation where I live, when 21, and a third of the rest of my lands. Son, David, one other third of said lands. Son, Daniel, one other third, on conditions as follows: that my sons, John, David and Daniel, my sons Noah and Job, my daughter, Mary, and the child therewith my wife is pregnant, an equal share of the whole estate. Executors—my brother, Obadiah Eldridge and Jabez Eldridge. Witnesses—John Zelley, Cornelius Morford, Daniel Jones, Jr. Proved Nov. 3, 1764. Lib. 12, p. 28.
 1764, Oct. 17. Inventory, £1,452.5.1, made by Thomas Butcher and John Zelley.

1761, April 12, Eldridge, Obadiah, of Springfield, Burlington Co., yeoman; will of. Son, Reuben, £20. Sons, Ezekiel, Obadiah and Jonathan, 5 shillings each. Daughter, Ame (Amy) McClutch, £5. My clothing to my 5 sons. My plantation in Springfield that joins James Langstaff to my daughter, Sarah Harris, the wife of John Harris, and at her death to my son, Jabez. Executrix—daughter, Sarah Harris. Witnesses—Abel Thomas, Sarah Woolman, John Woolman. Proved May 24, 1762. Lib. 11, p. 208.
 1762, May 15. Inventory, £121.10.7½, made by Lot Ridgway and Richard Collins.

1767, Nov. 4. Ellett, Sarah, of Salem Co. Int. Adm'r—Charles Ellett, of Mannington, said Co. Fellowbondsmen—Edmund Wetherby, of Mannington, and Daniel Wetherby, of Penns Neck, said Co.
Lib. 13, p. 279.

CALDENDAR OF WILLS—1761-1770   129

1756, Dec. 10. Ellis, Francis, of Mansfield, Burlington Co.; will of. Son, John, the plantation where I live, and he to pay to his brother, Aaron, £50. Son, Aaron, a cedar swamp. Daughter, Elizabeth, the wife of Joseph English, one shilling. Son, Peter, £25 when 21. Son, Job, £20 when 21. Son, Barzillai, £25 when 21. Daughter, Sarah, £20 when 18. Wife, Leah, £50, and "diet off the farm." Executors—sons, Aaron and John. Witnesses—John Fenimore, Jr., John Ditchfield, John Fenimore. Proved March 9, 1761.   Lib. 10, p. 153.

1763, Oct. 29. Ellis, Mary, of Gloucester Co. Ward. Daughter of Jonathan Ellis, deceased, of said Co., who makes choice of Thomas Reading as her guardian.
1763, Oct. 29. Guardian—Thomas Reading, of Amwell, Hunterdon Co. Fellowbondsman—Joseph Hollinshead, of City of Burlington. Witness—Jacob Hollinshead.   Lib. 11, p. 419.

1761, June 13. Ellison, John, of Burlington Co., Int. Adm'r—Joseph Ellison. Fellowbondsmen—John Ellison and James Ellison; all of Mansfield Twsp., said Co.   Lib. 10, p. 176.
1761, April 29. Inventory, £320.17.9, made by George Folwell and William Folwell.

1767, Aug. 20. Ellison, Samuel, of South Ward of Perth Amboy, Middlesex Co.; will of. Wife, Jane, goods with which to keep house. The land joining David Provost, in South Amboy, the salt meadow in Cheesequakes meadow, and the bog at the "burnt fly," to be sold, the money to be put to interest, and, at the end of 13 years, to be divided between my 2 sons, Seth and Samuel; during which time my wife is to live on my place. Wife to have the rent of the place where William Stevenson lives, and, after 13 years, to be sold, and the money divided between my daughters, Margaret, Martha, Sarah and Mary; also the infant my wife is pregnant with. Executors—my sister's husband, Obadiah Buckalew, and my cousin, James Morgan; both of South Amboy. Witnesses—John Green, Joseph Ellison, Obadiah Herbert. Proved Aug. 31, 1767.
1767, Sept. 2. Inventory, £451.10.10, made by Samuel Ker, Samuel Warne, Joshua Warne.
1767, Sept. 7. List of goods sold, to Joseph Ellison, Seth Ellison, Jr., Jane Ellison widow, and others, to the amount of £376.7.3.
1768, Nov. 7. Account filed. Payments to Abraham Tappen, at Staten Island; to Cathern Ker, midwife, and to others. Lib. I, p. 154.

1770, March 20. Ellison, Seth, of South Ward of Perth Amboy, Middlesex Co.; will of. Eldest son, Thomas, all my lands in Hempstead, Long Island. Daughter, Sarah Lamberson, that part of my plantation lying to the west of Cornelius Lamberson's house, and is part of the plantation I live on. To said Sarah, and my son Joseph, land on west side of the brook. Daughter, Martha Buckalew, the land in Middletown Twsp., Monmouth Co. Son, Joseph, the ½ of the plantation I live on (except what is given to daughter Sarah), and the other ½ to my grandsons, Seth and Samuel (sons of my son Samuel, deceased). My wife, Martha, to live in this house, and my son, Joseph, to provide for his mother. Executors—son, Joseph, and my nephew, William Morgan. Witnesses—John Davison, Daniel Morrell, Obadiah Herbert. Proved May 24, 1770.   Lib. K, p. 206.

9

1766, Sept. 10. Ellison, Thomas, of Shrewsbury, Monmouth Co., yeoman; will of. My wife, Margaret, £5, besides the sum that was agreed upon between us before marriage. Daughter, Annar Allen's, eldest son, Samuel Allen, 5 shillings. Granddaughters, Elizabeth Ellison and Mary Ellison, £5 each; but, if they die, then it is to go to my 3 daughters, Rebekah, Hannah and Elizabeth. Daughter, Elizabeth Morris, £30. Daughter, Rebekah Ellison, £40. Daughter, Hannah, £40. Lands to be sold. Sons, Amos, Lewis and Thomas, rest of estate. Executors—friend, William Morton, and my son, Lewis. Witnesses—William Brewer, Robert Morris, Garret Longstreet. Proved Dec. 1, 1770.
1770, Nov. 24. Inventory, made by Garret Longstreet, Samuel Osborn, William Jackson, Jr.   Lib. K, p. 291.

1770, April 9. Elmer, Abigail, of Fairfield, Cumberland Co.; widow of Daniel Elmer, Esq.; will of. Daughter, Abigail Ray, widow of James Ray, £10. Son, Daniel Elmer, £1. Sons, Jonathan and Timothy, £5 each. Son, Ebenezer, £1. Daughter, Deborah, wife of Lot Fithian, £1. Daughter, Victarina, £5. Daughter, Violetta Elmer, £20 (not 14). Son, Ebenezer Elmer, all my land, he paying to my daughter, Violetta Elmer, £50, as directed in my husband's will, when she is 18. Executors—sons, Daniel Elmer and Jonathan Elmer. Witnesses—Joseph Wescot, Ephraim Harris, William Ramsay. Proved Oct. 11, 1770.
1770, July 11. Inventory, £47.14.10, made by David Wescote and Ephraim Harris.   Lib. 14, p. 325.

1761, April 9. Elmer, Daniel, of Fairfield, Cumberland Co.; will of. My executors to pay James Ray, on his removing from the plantation where he lives, all sums he has expended towards the building of the house where he lives. My wife, Abigail, ⅓ my personal estate, and use of ½ the land on south side of Cedar Creek, in Fairfield. Son, Daniel, ½ my land near Flying Point aforesaid, of about 500 acres, he paying to my 2 sons, Jonathan and Timothy, £25 each, when 21. Son, Daniel ½ my salt meadow on Jones' Island. Son, Ebenezer, ½ the land near Flying Point, he paying to my daughter, Violetta Elmer, £50, when she is 18. Daughter, Abigail Ray, £10; also to her and to her husband, James Ray, the use of the place where they live till Aug. 1, 1762. Daughter, Deborah Elmer, £40, when 18. Daughter, Victorina Elmer, £40, when 18. Daughter, Violetta Elmer, 20 shillings when 18. Executors—wife, Abigail, and my son, Daniel. Witnesses—Jonathan Lorance, Henry Peirson, Hannah Peirson. Proved June 26, 1761.
1761, May 20. Inventory, £691.2.2, made by Thomas Harris and Jonathan Lorance.   Lib. 11, p. 152.

1770, April 6. Elston, Elizabeth, of Middlesex Co. Ward. Daughter of Spencer Elston, of said Co., deceased, who makes choice of John Elston as her Guardian.
1770, April 6. Guardian—John Elston. Fellowbondsman—Thomas P. Force; both of Woodbridge, said Co.   Lib. K, p. 191.

1762, Oct. 1. Elstone, Benjamin, of Woodbridge, Middlseex Co. Int. Adm'r—Jonathan Bishop, a creditor. Fellowbondsman—Samuel Jaques; both of said place. Witness—John Smyth.
                      Lib. H, p. 189.

1764, May 11. Elton, Revell, Esq., of Northampton, Burlington Co.; will of. Wife, Ann, all personal estate, and profits of plantation now in tenure of son, Revell, during her life. Son, Robert, and my two daughters, Elizabeth, the wife of William Lindal, and Hannah, the widow of John Deacon, Jr., 5 shillings each. Son, Thomas, a cedar swamp of 3 acres, and ½ of my landing, known as Gerrish's Landing. Son, Revell, my plantation, after the death of my wife. Executor—son, Revell. Assistant—Henry Paxson, Esq. Witnesses—Peter Bard, John Clark, Daniel Jones, Jr. Proved Feb. 28, 1765. Lib. 12, p. 70.

1765, June 15. Elver, Anthony, of Cape May Co. Int. Adm'r—Silas Goff, gent. Fellowbondsman—William Goff; both of said Co. Witness—John Shaw.
1765, March 5. Inventory, £20.7.9, made by John Shaw and William Goff. Lib. 12, p. 249.

1763, May 18. Elwell, Mary, of Penns Neck, Salem Co., widow. Int. Adm'r—Hance Jaquat. Fellowbondsmen—Joseph Jaquat and John Hickman; all of Lower Penns Neck, said Co.
1763, Feb. 4. Inventory, £52.11.5, made by John Hickman and Hugh Davis. Lib. 11, p. 372.

1761, Feb. 16. Ely, Jacob, of Greenwich, Sussex Co., tailor; will of. To my sister's children, John Hunt, Joshua Hunt and Sarah Hunt, £10 each. Rest of my estate to my brother, Isaac Ely's children, and to my brother, Thomas Ely's children, and to my sister, Sarah Hunt's children, and to my sister, Elizabeth Powner's children. Excutors—my friends, William Bishop and Jonathan Robins. Witnesses—Christopher Folkenberg, Christian Sharpenstine. Proved April 2, 1761.
1761, March 7. Inventory, £564.18.11, made by Christyon Sharpenstine and William Robins. Lib. 10, p. 569.

1767, July 25. Ely, John, of Trenton, Hunterdon Co.; will of. Brother, Stephen Ely, 20 shillings. Brother, George Ely, a like amount. Daughter, Elizabeth Ely, £200 when 21. Wife, Sarah Ely, rest of my estate. Executrix—my wife, Sarah. Witnesses—Samuel John Wells, Robert Singer, David Brearley, Jr. Proved Sept. 19, 1767. Lib. 13, p. 248.

1763, Nov. 10. Ely, William, of Trenton, Hunterdon Co.; will of. Son, John Ely, £5. Wife, Jemima, may live in my house near Peter Hankerson's. Son, Stephen, house where I live, and the lot where James Mathis and Richard Burden now live, which joins it, as also that of Joseph DeCow. Son, George, the land I bought of David and Mahlon Wright, on the Maidenhead road. The land which I bought of Benjamin Biles, on the Hopewell road, joining Elizabeth Biles and Andrew Reed, to be sold. My four youngest children to have schooling. Daughter, Rebecca, is under 8. Son, George, to be put to a trade. My six daughters are, Jemima, Elizabeth, Mary, Frances, ———, Rebecca. Three daughters have married, and three are single. The estate which came by my mother, by the name of Venebel, if got, to be divided between my sons, George and Stephen. Executors—friends, Nathan Beakes of Trenton, and Moore Furman of Philadelphia. Witnesses—Obadiah Howell, John Rickey, Daniel Laning. Proved April 19, 1770.

1769, Sept. 1. Renunciation, by Nathan Beakes. Witness—Hannah Beakes.

1769, Sept. 1. Renunciation, by Moore Furman. Witness—John White.

1770, April 19. Adm'r with will annexed—George Rozell, of Maidenhead, Hunterdon Co. Fellowbondsman—John Rozell, of Nottingham, Burlington Co. Lib. 14, p. 240.

1761, April 4. Emley, Elisha, of Kingwood Twsp., Hunterdon Co., yeoman; will of. Real and personal to be sold, except my riding horse and saddle, which I give to my wife, Anne. To Ziba Osmun, my apparel. The money to be divided between my wife and children "that now is, or that may be born," supposing my wife to be pregnant; when children are of age they are to have their share. Executors—my wife, Anne, my father-in-law, Thomas Atkinson, and my brother, John Emley. Witnesses—Ralph Hunt, Solomon Mott, Samuel Kester. Proved May 4, 1761.

1761, April 25. Inventory, £969.19.5, made by John Mullinner and John Grandin. Lib. 11, p. 43.

1758, Sept. 7. Emley, John, of Kingwood Twsp., Hunterdon Co., yeoman; will of. Son, Elisha, 7 acres of land on the south side of his plantation, for which he has a deed given by me, being part of that land I purchased of my son, William's, estate and of William Cheesman. Son, John, the rest of that tract in the Great Swamp, on the south side of Cornelius Quick and John Biles. Son, Robert, the land in Sussex Co., near the Great Meadows, and north of Samuel Green, of 310 acres. Daughter, Mary Emley, £25. Daughter, Elizabeth Mott, £5. Daughter, Rebecca Emley, £25. Daughter, Ann Emley, £25, when she is 18. Granddaughter, Sarah Emley, the daughter of my eldest son and heir, William, deceased, 10 shillings, when she is 18. Plantation where I live, and other lands, to be sold, and the money given to my children, John, Robert, Mary, Rebecca and Ann Emley, Sarah Watson and Elizabeth Mott. Executors—sons, Elisha, John and Robert. Witnesses—Samuel Large, Jacob Large, Thomas Barton, Robert Gordon, William Myers, Samuel Kesster. Proved May 4, 1761.

1761, April 24. Inventory, £1,466.5.6, made by John Mullinner and John Grandin. Lib. 10, p. 544.

1768, July 11. Emmons, Benjamin, of Middlesex Co.; will of. Son, Isaac, £5. Son, Henry, and my daughter, Rebecca, the rest of estate, both real and personal. Executors—son, Henry, and my son-in-law, Jocham Gulick. Witnesses—Thomas Badcock, John Van Buran, Jacob Van Dike. Proved April 19, 1770.

1770, April 18. Inventory, made by, Thomas Badcock and Bartholomew Feurt. Lib. K, p. 200.

1761, Aug. 3. Endecott, John, of Twsp. and Co. of Gloucester. Int. Adm'x—Ruth Endecott. Fellowbondsman—John Hillman, yeoman; both of said Co.

1760, Oct. 3. Inventory, £127.9.3, made by John Hillman and Ezekiel Harker. Lib. 10, p. 372.

CALENDAR OF WILLS—1761-1770   133

1767, May 28. Endicott, Ruth, of Twsp. and Co. of Gloucester; widow. Int. Adm'r—Jacob Matlock, yeoman. Fellowbondsman—Richard Price, yeoman, both of said place.   File No. 3523 H.

1761, Oct. 5. English, David, of Upper Freehold, Monmouth Co. Int. Adm'rs—William Woodward and Robert English. Fellowbondsman—John Wetherill; all of said Co.
1761, Oct. 3. Renunciation by Anne English, widow of said David, in favor of William Woodward and Robert English. Witness—Ragat Hull.
1761, Sept. 23. Inventory, £376.8.3, made by Robert Newell and John Wetherill.
1771, May 22. Account by Adm'rs. Money paid to Robert English, Elisha Lawrence, Margaret Newell, Elizabeth Imlay, David English, Ann English; also for the maintenance of Mary English, daughter of the deceased, for 6 years, the other children being provided for by their grandfather.   Lib. 10, p. 390; Lib. 15, p. 100.

1762, July 20. English, David, Jr., of Freehold, Monmouth Co., trader; will of. My shop goods are to be sold. Son, David, my house and lot where I live, and that tract of land over the road, which I bought of William Covenover, and that tract I bought of Joseph Kerr; but if my wife have a son within 9 months after my decease, then it shall have the tract I bought of Joseph Kerr, and 3 acres over the road against Robert English's and Moses Davis' houses. Wife, Jane, £200. Daughters, Jane and Margret, £200 each. Wife to enjoy the land until son, David, comes of age. John Smith to serve his time out with my wife. Executors—wife, Jane, James Robinson and Robert English. Witnesses—Robert English, John English, Jonathan English. Proved Oct. 22, 1762.   Lib. H, p. 193.

1761, April 6. English, James, of Mansfield Twsp., Burlington Co.; will of. Sons, Joseph and Abraham, plantation where I live; the said plantation joins that of my late father, William English. Son, William, my grist mill. Son, Jacob, £25. Daughters, Sarah English, Hannah English, Elizabeth English and Mary English, £10 each. Widow to have personal estate and profits of lands to educate my young children. Executors—wife, Mary, and my brother-in-law, Jacob Hays. Witnesses—Arent Schuyler, Thomas English, Rednap Howell. Proved May 6, 1761. (Short codicil attached, with no date).
Lib. 10, p. 324.

1766, June 26. English, James, Jr., of Upper Freehold, Monmouth Co., miller. Int. Adm'x—Catharine English, widow of James. Fellowbondsman—Robert Hutchinson, yeoman; both of said place. Witness—Isaac Price.
1766, April 20. Inventory, £1277.3.7, made by Isaac Price and Thomas Lawrie.
1771, June 24. Account by Adm'x. Lib. 12, p. 294; Lib. 14, p. 407.

1766, Dec. 24. English, Robert, of Upper Freehold, Monmouth Co., wheelwright; will of. Son, Robert, all real where I live, and the part where son David lived, and he to pay to my grandchildren the legacies mentioned. He is to have where David lived, till my grandson, David English, is 23. Grandson, Robert Parent, £40. Grandson, Samuel Parent, £40. Grandson, William English, £250.

Grandson, David English, £250. Granddaughter, Mary English, £80. Executor—my son, Robert; and, to assist him, I appoint my friend, Peter Emley, son of William, and Peter Talman, son of Benjamin. Witnesses—John Hendrickson, David Scott, William Reynolds. Proved Feb. 25, 1767.   Lib. 12, p. 473.

1768, Feb. 20. English, Robert, of Freehold, Monmouth Co., blacksmith; will of. Wife, Jane, all the goods she brought with her; and she is otherwise provided for. Son, Robert, the lot I live on, and my other lands, when he is of age. Friend, Stephen Pangburn, £8. Executors—my wife, and my friend, Mathew Rue. Witnesses—Robert McGallird, Moses Davis, William Rue. Proved May 9, 1768.
  1769, May 3. Inventory, £248.0.4, made by William Covenhoven and Robert McGalliard.   Lib. I, p. 244.

1762, Feb. 3. English, Thomas, Jr., of Mansfield Twsp., Burlington Co. Ward. Son of the late Abraham English of said place. Guardian—Thomas English, of said township. Fellowbondsman—Moses English, of same place, yeoman. Witness—Samuel Allinson.
  Letter (with no date) by the said Ward, who wishes to have the above appointed Guardian removed, as his property is going to destruction—the mill, bridges, dam, corn in the mill—and all for want of care.   Lib. 11, p. 204.

1761, Jan. 27. English, William, of Mansfield Twsp., Burlington Co., yeoman; will of. Son, James, the land he lives on that I bought of Robert Stacy in said township, and land I bought of Thomas Potts, except 22 acres; also ½ the grist-mill. Grandson, Thomas English, the farm I live on, and ½ the grist-mill; but, if he die, then to my daughter, Ann Ellison, and the 2 children she had by Thomas Addas. Son-in-law, James Ellison, 3 acres. Son, James English, to pay to his brother-in-law, Jacob Hays, £26. Margaret Homes shall be set free after my decease, and I give her a bed and cow. Rest of household goods to be divided between my daughter, Anne Ellison, and Margaret Homes. Executors—my friends, James English and James Ellison. Witnesses—Thomas Biddle, Joseph Garwood, Samuel English. Proved April 9, 1761.   Lib. 10, p. 362.
  1761, April 13. Inventory, £44.7.6, made by George Folwell and Edward Boulton.
  1762, June 3. Account of James Ellison, surviving Executor.

1761, Jan. 23. Enockson, Gabriel, of Gloucester Co. Int. Adm'r—James Halton. Fellowbondsman—Thomas Denny; both of Greenwich Twsp., said Co., yeomen.
  1761, Feb. 2. Inventory, £24.9.3, made by John Denny and Thomas Denny.   Lib. 10, p. 292.

1764, March 14. Ent, Valentine, of Amwell, Hunterdon Co., tanner; will of. Wife, Susanah, ⅓ the moveable estate, and £100 out of real. To each of my sons £100, when 21. To each of my daughters £50, when 18. Executors—my wife, Susanah Ent, and my brothers, Peter More and Daniel More. Witnesses—Jane Huff, Catherin Opdycke, Samuel Opdycke, John Opdycke. Proved Aug. 25, 1770.
  1770, Aug. 25. Renunciation, by Danial Moor.
  1770, Aug. 23. Inventory, £587.5.6, made by John Opdyck and Richard Green. (Testator died, July 25, 1770).   Lib. 14, p. 344.

1748, Dec. 26. Enyard, John, of Woodbridge, Middlesex Co.; will of. Son, Silas, 5 shillings. Son, John, a like amount. Daughter, Annah Congar, a stear. Wife, Mary Inyard, use of lands, till youngest sons are 21. Daughters, Rachel Nortwak, Alche Inyard and Elsie Inyard, moveables. To my wife's daughter, Elizabeth Darlin, a gum table. Sons, David and Benjamin, my lands when they are of age. Executors—wife, Mary, and my friend, William McDaniel. Witnesses—Robert Thornell, Jean Thornell, James Clarkson. Proved May 19, 1763.
    1763, May 18. Renunciation by Mary Enyard.
    1763, June 7. Inventory, £43.13.5, made by David Crow and James Rowland.
    [No date]. Account by William McDaniel, the Executor.
    Lib. H, p. 262.

1762, Nov. 21, Erickson, Mickel, of Freehold, Monmouth Co.; will of. Wife, Martha, £50, and the household goods, except a pewter platter that belongs to my daughter, Deborah Wright, and one that belongs to my daughter, Susannah Erickson. Daughter, Deborah Wright, £10. Daughter, Susannah Erickson, £15. To Huldah Catchion, £10. Sons, Michael and John, my lands. Executors—James English, Sr., and Jonathan Ray Gordon. Witnesses—William Cole, Robert McConnell, Bryan Gollohar. Proved Dec. 16, 1762.
    1762, Dec. 13. Inventory, £261.6.8, made by Robert English and William Cowenhoven.   Lib. H, p. 211.

1769, Jan. 24. Ernest, John, of New York City, merchant; will of. Son, Anthony Ernest, my watch and gold seal. Wife, Sarah, use of goods and negros, till my youngest child is 21, and then goods and slaves to be sold and the money divided between my wife and my children then living. Real estate to be sold and the interest of the money to be applied to keep my family; and, when the youngest child is 21, the principal to be given to my wife and 5 children, Anthony, Mathew, Sarah, John and Anna Maria. Executors—wife, Sarah, my father-in-law, Anthony Ten Eyck, and William Bayard, of New York City, gentleman. Witnesses—Theodorus Van Wyck, Thomas Ellison, Jr., Nicholas Quackinbosh. Proved in New York Feb. 13, 1769, by Thomas Ellison, Jr., and Nicholas Quackinbosh, both of New York, and proved in New Jersey on the same date.
    Lib. K, p. 82.

1764, Jan. 20. Erwine, James, of Bethlehem, Hunterdon Co. Int. Adm'x—Jane McKnight. Fellowbondsmen—James McKnight and William Johnson; all of said Co.
    1761, April 1. Inventory, £47.15.6, made by John Bassett and James McKnight.   Lib. 11, p. 526.

1768, Oct. 24. Eskill, John, of Mendom (Mendham), Morris Co., yeoman; will of. Lands to be sold and money given to my wife, Mary, and my sons, John, Davias and Noah, and my daughters, Elizabeth and Hannah; to said children when of age. Executors—wife, Mary, David Estell and Silas Condict. Witnesses—Samuel Willis, William Estill, Isaac Morris. Proved Nov. 21, 1768.   Lib. K, p. 9.

1761, Nov. 30. Estaugh, Elizabeth, of Haddonfield, Newton Twsp., Gloucester Co., widow; will of. My kinswoman, Sarah Hopkins, relict of my kinsman, Ebenezer Hopkins, the use of my upper house and lot, which I purchased of the Executor of Samuel Mickle, now in the "tenor" of Thomas Edgerton, and at her death to be sold and divided among her children by my kinsman Ebenezer Hopkins; and the other part of said house and lot, now in "tenor" of Rachel Lippincott and son, ——— Smith, I give to Ann Hopkins, youngest daughter of my said kinswoman, as well as £300 when she is 18; but if she die, then the house to be sold, and proceeds to go to her brothers, viz., Haddon and Ebenezer Hopkins. The said Sarah Hopkins to have the use of the house where I live, or where she lives. My kinsman, John Estaugh Hopkins, being one of the children of my relations aforesaid, my plantation called New Haddonfield, in said Twsp., including 125 acres purchased of Joseph Collins, except some lots hereafter mentioned; also ⅛ part of a Proprietory of land, which my father, John Haddon, purchased of Richard Mathews, and he is to allow his mother, the said Sarah Hopkins, corn for her use. My kinswoman, Elizabeth Estaugh Hopkins, one of the children aforesaid, £500. Haddon Hopkins, another child, my house and lot in Haddonfield, next to Isaac Andrews; also my plantation, called Little Stebbing, purchased of Jonathan Belton, Lucy Hubbs and Robert Montgomery, of 157 acres; also ½ of Willis' Propriety, which my father purchased of Thomas Willis, when he is 21. My kinsman, Ebenezer Hopkins, another child of above, house and lot, next to his brother Haddon; and the other ½ of Willis' Propriety, when 21. Sarah Hopkins, another child of the above, house and lot in Haddonfield, in "tenor" of Elizabeth Craig, and joining the house in "tenor" of Ann Banks, and £300 when 18. Mary Hopkins, another child of above, house and lot in "tenor" of widow Cooper, and £300 when 18. If any of the children run out in marriage, contrary to the rules of our Society, then they shall not have the above mentioned sums. My kinswoman, Mary Stephens, relict of Robert Stephens, late of Newton, that lot in Philadelphia which my husband, John Estaugh, purchased of her former husband, Joseph Kaighin, and, at her death, to her son, Joseph Kaighin; I also give her my house and lot in Haddonfield, now in tenure of Ann Banks. I give to her 2 sons, John and Joseph Kaighin (by her former husband Joseph Kaighin) ⅙ of a Propriety which was purchased of Richard Mathews; and also to their 3 children, Joseph, James and Elizabeth Kaighin, £50 each. Hannah Estaugh (relict of James Estaugh, late of Philadelphia) and her 3 children, Joseph, David and Grace, £50 each. My kinsman, John Gill, 1-16 part of Propriety purchased by my father, John Haddon, of the Ex'rs of Richard Moss; also the meadow that joins his father, John Gill, deceased, and John Estaugh. My kinswoman, Mary Thorn, £100, and, after her death, to her grandchildren by her son John Gill, and her daughter, Hannah Redman, deceased. To my relations and friends, viz., Thomas Redman and his 3 children by his former wife, Hannah, the daughter of John Gill and Mary his wife, viz., Thomas, John and Mary, each £20; and to Isaac Andrews, Daniel Stanten, of Philadelphia, and Abigail Fisher, daughter of William Cooper of Philadelphia, and Elizabeth Craig, to each £10; and to Rachel Lippincott, Mary Sharp, Ann Gant, Mary Garwood, to each £5. My kinswoman, Sarah Hopkins, and her 4 daughters, my household goods, etc. I give all my interest and right in the Pennsylvania Land Company, or Partnership, in London, ' let the same extend to 156 shares," to be equally divided between them (their said mother) and her children, viz., John Estaugh Hopkins, Haddon, Ebenezer, Elizabeth

CALENDAR OF WILLS—1761-1770   137

Estaugh Hopkins, Sarah, Mary and Ann. Executors—friend, William Mickle, Sr., and my kinsman, John Gill. Overseers—friends, James and David Cooper. Witnesses—Samuel Clement, Jr., Beulah Clement, Thomas Cummings. Proved April 21, 1762.
1762, April 13. Inventory, £7,855.2.6½, made by Samuel Clement and Isaac Andrews.
1766, Nov. 14. Account by Executors. Ann Hopkins' legacy paid to James Whital, her Guardian. Mary Hopkins' legacy paid to James Whital, her Guardian. Ebenezer Hopkins' legacy paid to John Estaugh Hopkins, his Guardian. Rachel Lippincott's legacy. Abigail Fisher's legacy paid her husband. Mary Thorne's legacy paid her husband.   Lib. 11, p. 113.

1753, May 28. Eveland, David, of Amwell Twsp., Hunterdon Co.; will of. Personal and real to be sold and money put tn interest, and the income given to my wife, Mary, while she is my widow, and, after her death, money to go to my children, John, Peter, Frederick, Margreta, Magdelane, Catherine and Mary. Executors—friends, Adam Teach, Henry Graff and John Anderson. Witnesses—George Reading, John Edmonds, John George Bender. Proved Nov. 9, 1761.
1761, Oct. 26. Inventory, £66.14.11, made by John Young and Jacob Wolaver.   Lib. 11, p. 147.

1766, June 3. Eveland, John, of Newton, Sussex Co. Int. Adm'r—Frederick Eveland, Jr. Fellowbondsman—Uriah Addoms; both of said Co. Witness—Hannah Pettit.
1765, Nov. 5. Inventory, £145.3.1, made by Uriah Addoms and John Westbrook.   Lib. 12, p. 434.

1768, Nov. 7. Evens, Jacob, of Elsinboro, Salem Co.; will of. Wife, Mary, £120, and pork, beef, etc., for her use and her 6 children. Rest to all my seven children. Executors—my wife and Joshua Strach. Witnesses—William Goodwin, Aaron Evens, Rebekah Evens. Proved Oct. 31, 1769.   Lib. 15, p. 262.

1766, March 27. Evens, Nathan, of Evesham, Burlington Co.; will of. Wife, Syllania, my personal estate and the use of real estate, till my eldest son is 21. Sons, Jacob, Joseph and Nathan, 40 acres of land, each; and Jacob's is to join my brother, Jacob, and Joseph is to join Elizabeth Troth, dec'd. Son, Isaac, the rest of my lands, and he is to pay to my three daughters, Susanna, Elizabeth and Sarah, £20 each. Executors—my brother, Isaac Evens, Enoch Evens and Joseph Roberts. Witnesses—Joseph Heulings, Samuel Heulings, Elizabeth Andrews. Proved March 17, 1769.
1769, March 8. Inventory, £241.16.2, made by Joshua Lippincott and Micajah Wills.   Lib. 14, p. 41.

1759, April 3. Evens, William, of Evesham Tws'p, Burlington Co., yeoman; will of. Wife, Sarah, ⅓ my moveable estate, and the other ⅔ to my daughters, Hannah, Esther, Mary, Rebeckah, Deborah and Sarah Evens, when they are 18. Son, Enoch, my lands, when 21. Executors—my brothers, John Roberts and Isaac Evens. Witnesses—Abram Allen, John Champion, Daniel Lippencott.
1761, May 23. Codicil. I now have another son, named William, who is to have £100 when 21. Witnesses—Jm's Mulock, Catherine French, William Foster. Proved June 22, 1761.   Lib. 10, p. 212.

1761, June 18. Inventory, £404.7.6, made by Jacob Prickit and James Cattell.
1763, Dec. 6. Account by Executors.

1764, June 21. Everingham, Joseph, of Burlington Co. Int. Bond of Mary Everingham (his widow) as Adm'x. Fellowbondsman—Joseph Ivins, of said Co. Witness—Joseph Read. Lib. 11, p. 538.
1764, June 21. Inventory, £19.10.0, made by John Richardson, Jr., and Joseph Ivins.
1765, June 22. Account by Adm'x.
1767, July 27. Another account entered at the request of John Watson, who has married the widow.

1760, June 12. Everitt, Benjamin, of Maidenhead, Hunterdon Co.; will of. Wife, Phebe Everitt, all my estate. Executors—my wife and Moore Furman. If it should happen that I should not die, and should not return to my family in the space of 12 months after date hereof, in that case my wife and Moore Furman are to sell enough of my goods to pay my debts. Witnesses—Elijah Hunt, Abraham Hunt. Proved March 10, 1761.
1761, Feb. 26. Inventory, £561.1.8, made by James Clarke, and Robert Guthrey. Lib. 10, p. 545.

1764, Oct. 15.—Everitt, Francis, of Woodbridge, Middlesex Co. Int. Adm'x—Sarah Everitt, widow of said Francis. Fellowbondsman—George Brown; both of said place. Lib. H, p. 370.

1756, May 29. Everitt, John, of Bethlehem, Hunterdon Co.; will of. Wife, Hannah, furniture, live stock, negro called Dorcas, etc. Eldest son, Moses, £3. Son, Joseph, £25. Son, Benjamin, £10. Son, John, £10. To Abel Everitt, £2, and the rest to be divided between my four daughters, namely, Sarah, Elizabeth, Mary and Hannah. Executors —my wife, Joseph Reeder and James Warford. Witnesses—Reuben Armitage, Cornelius Polhemus, Gershom Palmer. Proved July 12, 1761.
1761, June 20. Inventory, £298.2.1, made by Daniel Lake and Melakiah Bonham.
1768, June 17. Account by James Warford, Executor. Money paid for attendance on the widow, in her illness, £30; to John Mitchell, John Lake and Cornelius Hoff, legatees; to Moses Everitt, son of the deceased, and to Joseph Everitt, Benjamin Everitt, John Everitt and Abel Everitt, 3, 25, 10, 10, and 2 pounds, respectively.
Lib. 11, p. 465; Lib. 13, p. 439.

1765, May 21. Evins, William, of Hopewell Twsp., Hunterdon Co.; will of. Wife, Rachel, all estate, in order to assist her in bringing up our only daughter. Executors—my wife and my friend, Daniel Drake. Witnesses—John Stilwell, Daniel Hart. Proved May 25, 1765.
1765, May 25. Inventory, £100.2.0, made by Cornelius Anderson and Daniel Hart. Lib. 12, p. 208.

1768, Oct. 25. Ewan, Absalom, of Burlington Co.; will of. Son, David, £10. Wife, Rachel, £3 and 10 shillings, in order to help bring up my son, Levi, who is to be bound at age of 14 to a good master. Son, Absalom, my house and lands, he paying said annuity to widow. My daughters the residue. Executors—son, David, and my son-in-

law, John Lame. Witnesses—Joseph Lippincott, Mary Lippincott, John Antram, Joseph Arney. Proved Nov. 15, 1768. Lib. 12, p. 535.
1768, Nov. 14. Inventory, £42.6.5, made by Joseph Lippincott and John Burr.

1762, May 22. Ewan, Ambrose, of Northampton, Burlington Co. Int. Adm'r—Burbage Brock. Fellowbondsman—Joshua Norcross; both of said place. Witness—Samuel Allinson. Lib. 11, p. 225.
1762, May 21. Inventory, £16, made by Zachariah Rossell and Thomas Reynolds.
1763, May 18. Account of Adm'r. Includes "Taking children to burial, 10 shillings".

1761, Jan. 11. Eyre, George, of City of Burlington; will of. Son, Emanuel, my brick house where my sister lives, and ¼ my lands where I live. Daughter, Sarah Eyre, to have use of part of said house. Son, John, my wooden house, and ¼ my lands. Son, Samuel, the brick house where I live. Son, Benjamin George Eyre, lands when 21. Daughters, Sarah, Mary, Martha and Ann, money from sale of lands. My son, Samuel, is to be guardian of my son, Benjamin. Wife to have money from sale of land. Executors—sons, Samuel, Emanuel, Jehu and Benjamin George Eyre. Witnesses—Stephen Harris, Paul Bradshaw, Frederick Taylor. Proved Jan. 21, 1761. Lib. 10, p. 150.
1761, Feb. 9. Inventory, £125.4.9, made by William Smith and Levi Murrel.

1764, Dec. 10. Fagan, James, of Newtown, Sussex Co., laborer. Int. Adm'x—Anne Fagan, widow. Fellowbondsman—John Woolverton, yeoman; both of said Co. Witness—George Space.
1764, Dec. 10. Inventory, £40.5.0, made by George Space and John Woolverton. Lib. 12, p. 232.

1762, Feb. 11. Falconbury, Christopher, of Twsp. of Greenwich, Sussex Co., yeoman; will of. Wife to have the moveable estate and to have a living on the plantation, and, at her death, I give to daughter, Margaret Falconbury, Godfry Melicks and wife, Crastful Melick and Margret Melick, the two children of Godfry Melick, all my plantation; that is, my daughter, Marget, shall have all the plantation, and the said children shall have £100 each. John Sharp is to have £100, and his son that was named for me £100. Christian Sharp is to have £50. To the Dutch Meeting House, that is to be built, £50. Executors—Godfrey Melick and Christian Sharp. Witnesses—John Sharps, Alexander White, Wilhelm Woolwever. Proved May 7, 1762.
1762, March 1. Inventory, £405.6.2, made by Alexander White and Joseph Beavers.
1778, May 26. Account, by Christian Sharps, Executor. Boarding the widow charged for, for over ten years.
Lib. 11, p. 296; Lib. 16, p. 524.

1764, Oct. 29. Fancher, Richard, of Roxbury, Morris Co.; will of. Son, William, 100 acres which I bought of John Alin, it being the place where I dwell. Son, Benjamin, 114 acres, where he lives, which I bought of William Garner. Son, David, 5 shillings. Son, Richard, 5 shillings. Daughters, Martha Bell, 5 shillings. Daughter, Amy Fancher, 5 shillings. Wife, Martha, the rest of my moveable estate. Executors—my wife and my friend, William Griffin. Witnesses—William Hopkins, Jr., Abigail Pen, Rachel Harker. Proved Nov. 12, 1764. Lib. H, p. 525.

1764, Feb. 27. Farnsworth, Amariah, Ward. Guardian—John Lovell, Amariah Farnsworth being son of Nathaniel Farnsworth, of Bordentown, deceased (but only for so much as may be due to said infant from the estate of John Lovell, deceased). Fellowbondsman —Samuel Farnsworth. Lib. 11, p. 480.

1764, Feb. 27. Farnsworth, Rachel, Ward. Guardian—John Lovell. Rachel Farnsworth being daughter of Nathaniel Farnsworth of Bordentown, deceased, (but only for so much as may be due to said infant from the estate of John Lovell, deceased). Fellowbondsman —Samuel Farnsworth. Lib. 11, p. 480.

1760, Dec. 3. Faron, Peter, of Burlington City and Co.; will of. Niece, Elizabeth Henry and husband, John Henry, my two lots in Second St., said City, with the house thereon, and they are to maintain my sister, Elizabeth, the mother of said Elizabeth Henry. Plantation where I live to be sold. Niece, Abigail Bishop, £25. Housekeeper, Marget Younger, £25. Sarah Crispin, £25. My wife's grandson, Joseph Marriott, £10. Nephew, Samuel Smith, £12. Other to nephew, Thomas Wetherill, Christopher Wetherill and Samuel Wetherill. Other nieces, Mary Crispin, Elizabeth Johnson and Ann Moore. Executors—Thomas Wetherill and friend, John Woolman. Witnesses —John Smith, Abel Thomas, Josiah Haines. Proved Jan. 3, 1763.
Lib. 11, p. 269.
1762, Dec. 27. Inventory, £216.14.10, made by Edward Cathrall and John Smith.

1764, March 12. Farrand, Daniel, of Newark, Essex Co. Int. Adm'x—Margaret Farrand, the widow. Fellowbondsman—John Low, Esq.; both of said place. Lib. H, p. 422.

1762, June 28. Farrill, Cornelius, of Bethlehem, Hunterdon Co. Int. Adm'rs—Mary Farrill, of said place, and Charles Hoff, of Kingwood, said Co. Witness—Gabriel Hoff.
1762, June 29. Inventory, £36.3.6, made by Thomas Littell and Constantine O'Neill. Lib. 11, p. 337.

1767, Aug. 26. Farrol, John, of Elizabeth Town, Essex Co., laborer. Int. Adm'r—William Barker, weaver. Fellowbondsman—John Trotter, yeoman; both of said place. Lib. I, p. 208.

1754, Dec. 13. Fawcet, Grace, of Greenwich Twsp., Gloucester Co.; will of. Widow of John Fawcet. Son, Walter Fawcet, Bible, bed, etc., and he to pay to his son, Nathan Fawcet, £10, when he is 21, and to pay to his other children £6 each. To my eldest daughter, Estherter Holmes, £40. To Mary Kay, wife of William Kay, and to Anna Silver, wife of Aaron Silver, each a Bible. I give to all my grandchildren a Bible. Rebecca Pedrick, daughter of Thomas and Rebecca Pedrick, £5. Nathan Pedrick, son of Thomas and Rebecca Pedrick, £5, when 20. To my youngest daughter the rest of my estate. Executor—my said youngest daughter, Lydia Fawcet. Witnesses—Andrew Tate, Thomas Wilkins, Thomas Wilkins, Jr. Proved March 30, 1761. Lib. 10, p. 373.

CALENDAR OF WILLS—1761-1770   141

1769, Feb. 4. Fenell, Patrick, of Sussex Co.; will of. Wife, Sebina, all my estate, both personal and real. Executrix—my wife, Sabina. Witnesses—Martin Delany, William Miller. Proved Feb. 20, 1769.   Lib. 13, p. 553.

1762, Jan. 29. Fenton, Samuel, of Chesterfield, Burlington Co., yeoman; will of. Wife, to have goods. Son, Thomas, plantation where I live, and at his death to his eldest son, but, if he have none, then to all my daughters. Wife to have £10 yearly. Son, Stacy, lot 1 bought of William Miller, and lot I bought of Exr's of Samuel Large. Son, Samuel, land near Bordentown. Daughter, Elizabeth Fenton, a cow. Rest of personal to be sold, and money given to my wife, and daughters, Sarah, Mary and Martha Fenton. Executors—son, Thomas, and my friend, Thomas Miller. Witnesses—Samuel Wheatcraft, Edward Wheatcraft, John Oliver. Proved Sept. 28, 1767.
   Lib. 13, p. 92.
   1767, Sept. 10. Inventory, £99.2.7, made by Benjamin Field and William Quicksall.

1761, July 15. Ferguson, Duncan, of Greenwich, Gloucester Co. Int. Adm'r—Charles Boyle, of said place, ditcher. Fellowbondsman—James Ward, of Deptford, said Co., yeoman. Witnesses——John Ladd and Hannah Ladd.   Lib. 10, p. 290.

1764, Sept. 24. Ferguson, John, of City of Burlington. Int. Adm'x—Martha Ferguson, relict of said John. Fellowbondsman—Daniel Ellis, Esq.; both of said City.   Lib. 12, p. 21.

1761, July 15. Ferrymon, Duncan, of Greenwich, Gloucester Co. Int. Adm'r—Charles Boyle.   Lib. 10, p. 290.

1770, Dec. 10. Finley, Robert, of Salem Co. Int. Adm'x—Magdalene Patterson, of Pilesgrove, widow. Fellowbondsmen—Bateman Lloyd, of Salem, gent., and Archibald Hamilton, of Mannington; all of said Co.   Lib. 14, p. 412.

1766, June 25. Finley, Samuel, of Somerset Co.; will of. President of College of Princeton. Daughter, Rebecca Breese, a negro girl, Peg. Rest of real and personal to be sold, except the annuity that shall arise from the Corporation of the Widows' Fund; and ⅓ of that annuity I give to my wife, Ann; and I also give her ⅓ of the rest of my estate. The remaining ⅔ from the Fund and the estate I give to my children, Joseph, Susannah, Samuel, John, Ebenezer and Edward, when they come of age. Executors—my wife, Ann, and my son-in-law, Samuel Breese, of Newark, and friend, Richard Stockton, of Princeton. Witnesses—James Thomson, Samuel Blair, Daniel Roberdeau. Proved July 22, 1766.   Lib. 12, p. 438.

1765, Jan. 9. Finn, Solomon, of Bergen Co. Int. Adm'x—Elizabeth Finn, widow. Fellowbondsman—John Bardon; both of said Co. Witness—Lewis Ogden.   Lib. H, p. 423.

1763, Sept. 30. Fish, John, of Deptford Township, Gloucester Co., farmer; will of. Wife, best bed and chest. Son, Casper, hat. Son, John, gun. Executors—said two sons. Witnesses—Moses Cox, Elizabeth Rambo, John Rambo. Proved Aug. 1, 1764.

1763, Oct. 5. Inventory, £52.16.8, made by John Rambo and Benjamin Lodge.
1765, Jan. 11. Account by John Fish, acting Executor.
Lib. 12, p. 14.

1769, Feb. 7. Fish, William, of Hunterdon Co. Int. Adm'r—Isaac Herin. Fellowbondsman—Noah Hunt; both of said place.
1769, March 16. Inventory, £200.12.8, made by Azariah Hunt and Noah Hunt. Includes "a legacy given in his father's will, £20."
Lib. 13, p. 498.

1761, July 27. Fisher, Martin, of Lebanon Twsp., Hunterdon Co., yeoman; will of. Son, Jacob, 20 shillings and the Dutch Bible. Wife, Margaret, my personal estate and rents of real. Son, Coonrade, is to live with my wife. Children, Jacob, Philip, Margaret, Ann, Mary and Elizabeth, the rest. Executors—friends, Harmanus Kline, Sr., and Abram Wrunkle. Witnesses—Peter Hemry, John Forrester, Cornelius Flamisfelt. Proved Feb. 27, 1763.
1768, March 12. Renunciation by Adam Wrunkle. Witness—John Bray.
1768, Jan. 16. Inventory, £322.19.0, made by Jacob Hummer and Peter Hemmery.
1779, June 2. Account by Harmon Kline. Lib. 13, p. 447.

1769, April 24. Fisher, Peter, of Saddle River Precinct, Bergen Co.; will of. Eldest son, John, 20 shillings. Grandson, Peter, son of Isaac Fisher, dec'd, ½ of my lands. Grandson, Isaac, son of Isaac Fisher, dec'd, other ½. Daughter, Leah, £30. Granddaughter, Elizabeth Fisher, daughter of Isaac Fisher, dec'd, ½ of rest of personal. Granddaughter, Moritey, daughter of Isaac Fisher, dec'd, other ½. Executors—friends, James Board, David Board and Philip Schuyler. Witnesses—Robert Belsire, Henry French and Abigail French. Proved May 6, 1769.
Lib. K, p. 99.

1770, Feb. 5. Fitch, James, of Kingwood Twsp., Hunterdon Co., wheelwright; will of. Eldest son, William, 5 shillings. Rest of personal and real to be used to bring up my youngest children, till the youngest son, James, is 21, at which time my wife, Rachel, shall have ⅓ of moveables and ⅓ the profits of the land. The rest of estate I give to youngest son, James; but he is to pay to my daughter, Charity, £30, and also a quilt, gown, etc., which belonged to my former wife; and also, to Anna Fitch, my younger daughter, £30. Executors—John Sherred, of Alexandria Twsp., who is a merchant; and Benjamin Jones, of Kingwood. Witnesses—Lazarus Adams, Jeremiah King, John Gulick. Proved March 31, 1770.
1770, March 26. Inventory, £215.16.6, made by Isaac Leet and John Gulick.
1794, Feb. 6. Account, by John Sherrerd, surviving Executor.
Lib. 14, p. 254.

1766, July 30. Fithian, Aaron, of Fairfield, Cumberland Co. Ward. Son of David Fithian, of said place, dec'd. Guardian—Jonathan Fithian. Fellowbondsman—Lot Fithian; both of said place. Witness—Ephraim Daton.
Lib. 12, p. 328.

1763, Dec. 15. Fithian, David, of Fairfield, Cumberland Co., cordwainer; will of. Sister, Temperance Fithian, spoons. Half brother and sister, Jeremiah Buck and Phebe Buck, £4 each, when they are of age. Brothers, Lot Fithian, Jonathan Fithian and Aaron Fithian, the rest. Executor—friend, Robert Low. Witnesses—Abigail Thomson, Levi Stratton, Martha Bennet. Proved Jan. 12, 1764.
1764, Jan. 5. Inventory, £74.16.4, made by David Westcoat and Ephraim Harris.
1765, March 1. Account by Executor. Lib. 11, p. 497.

1762, April 24. Fithian, Ephraim, of Fairfield, Cumberland Co.; will of. Brothers, Lot, Jonathan and Aaron, all my lands. Sister, Temperance Fithian, moveables, along with my brothers, David, Lot, Jonathan, and Aaron. Executors—my brothers, David and Lot. Witnesses—David Westcoat, Elizabeth Westcoat, Christian Whitaker. Proved Nov. 16, 1762.
1762, July 14. Inventory, £83.18.7, made by Robert Low and William Fithian. Lib. 11, p. 271.

1763, Sept. 12. Fithian, Humphrey, of Greenwich, Cumberland Co. Int. Adm'rs—Ephraim Fithian and Jonathan Bowen, Jr., both of said place, yeomen. Witnesses—Abigail Ewing and Maskell Ewing.
1763, Sept. 13. Inventory, £35.3.9, made by David Shepherd, and Josiah Fithian. Lib. 11, p. 474.

1766, Nov. 22. Fithian, Josiah, of Greenwich, Cumberland Co., cordwainer; will of. Wife, Ann, ⅓ the personal estate. The residue to my child, if one should be born, but, if not, or it die under age, then to my brother, Joseph, I give my real estate, and the rest to my brother, Samuel. Executors—said brothers, Samuel and Joseph Fithian. Witnesses—John Grimes, Thomas Ewing, Jr., Aaron Cresse. Proved Dec. 27, 1766.
1767, Dec. 4. Inventory, £495.5.3½, made by Jonathan Holmes and Jacob Mulford. Lib. 12, p. 325.

1765, April 4. Fithian, Lot, of Greenwich, Cumberland Co. Int. Adm'rs—Judith Fithian, widow. Fellowbondsman—Jonathan Bowen, Jr., yeoman; both of said place. Witness—Thomas Maskell.
1765, April 6. Inventory, £87.12.3, made by Samuel Fithian and Thomas Maskell. Lib. 12, p. 170.

1766, May 26. Fithian, Sarah, of Cumberland Co. Ward. Only daughter of Samuel Fithian, late of Greenwich, said Co. Guardian —Maskell Ewing, Esq. Fellowbondsman—Enoch Moore, yeoman; both of said Greenwich. Witnesses—Elnathan Ware and James Ewing. Lib. 12, p. 327.

1764, April 10. Fitzpatrick, John, of Alloways Creek Precinct, Salem Co.; will of. Son, Samuel, plantation where I live, and a tract I bought of John Mason, and another of Francis Test; and one of Jonas Scroggin and his wife, Ann, is to be divided between my four daughters, Grace, Lydia, Mary and Sarah. Executors—son, Samuel, and my son-in-law, Samuel Oakford. Witnesses—James Sims, James Young, Thomas Sayre.

1764, April 10. Codicil. To my grandchildren, Rebecca and Hannah Patrick, daughters of John Patrick, Jr., deceased, £10 each. Witnesses—same as in will. Proved April 23, 1764.
1764, April 21. Inventory, £186.6.6, made by John Durney and Thomas Sayre. Lib. 12, p. 89.

[No date]. **Fitz Randolph, Isaac**, of Kingwood Twsp., Hunterdon Co., sadler; will of. Wife, Catherine, given some moveables, and the rest to be sold, and if the money is not enough to pay debts, then the tavern lot and two acres of meadow to be sold; and money, not used, to be put to interest for benefit of wife in order to bring up my son, Jacob, and my daughters, Elizabeth Fitz Randolph and Grace Fitz Randolph. I give to my wife and children all my right to the estate of Darling Hagerman, late of Somerset Co. Executors —my wife and my father, Jacob Fitz Randolph, and my father-in-law, Charles Hoff. Witnesses—Joseph Stout, Theodosia Stout, William Garrison. Proved Oct. 31, 1768.
1768, Oct. 25. Inventory, £83.3.6, made by Benjamin Jones and Daniel Cahill. Lib. 12, p. 526.

1766, June 17. Fitzrandolph, Jonathan, of Woodbridge, Middlesex Co. Int. Adm'r—Benajah Danels, son-in-law and principal creditor. Fellowbondsman—John Pain; both of said Co. Lib. H, p. 619.

1766, Aug. 6. Fleeck, James, of Acquacknung, Essex Co. Int. Adm'rs—Archibald McVickar and Robert Robinson; both of New York City, and principal creditors. Fellowbondsman—Samuel Menish (Minnis). Witnesses—David Marinus and Samuel Iynner.
File No. 3549-3550 G.

1764, Oct. 15. Fletcher, Lydia, of Greenwich Twsp., Gloucester Co., widow. Int. Adm'r—William Snowden. Fellowbondsman—Isaac Ballinger; both of Deptford Twsp., said Co., yeoman. Witness—Sarah Howell.
1764, Oct. 15. Inventory, £84.6.6, made by James Whitall and James Hinchman.
1767, June 15. Account by Adm'r. Lib. 12, p. 37.

1762, Oct. 1. Fletcher, William, of Greenwich, Gloucester Co. Int. Adm'x—Lydia Fletcher, of said place, widow. Fellowbondsman—William Snowden, of Deptford Twsp., said Co., yeoman. Witness—Hannah Kaighn.
1762, Sept. 29. Inventory, £217.2.6, made by Nathan Lord and William Snowden. Lib. 11, p. 277.

1766, June 17. Fletcher, William, of Greenwich, Gloucester Co. Ward. Eldest son and heir of William Fletcher, of said place, yeoman. Having lands by descent from his father, he makes choice of William Snowden as his Guardian.
1766, June 17. Guardian—William Snowden. Fellowbondsman—Isaac Ballinger; both of Deptford, Gloucester Co., yeomen. Witnesses—Hannah Ladd and John Ladd. Lib. 12, p. 383.

1767, Jan. 27. Flomerfelt, Zachariah, of Bethlehem, Hunterdon Co. Int. Adm'x—Mary Flomerfelt, of said place. Fellowbondsman—John Spader, of Amwell, said Co.
1767, Jan. 26. Inventory, £101.7.10, made by Francis Lock and Thomas Lake. File No. 701 J.

1761, June 24. Flower, Dominique, of Greenwich, Cumberland Co. Int. Adm'r—John Keen, of Dearfield, said Co. Fellowbondsman—Isaac Penton, of Greenwich. Witnesses—Mary Ewing and Abigail Ewing. Lib. 10, p. 438.

1764, Jan. 16. Flower, John, of Cape May Co., yeoman. Int. Adm'r—William Flower, gent. Fellowbondsman—George Newton, gent.; both of said Co.
1763, Dec. 21. Inventory, £909.8.7, made by John Eldredge and Timothy Hand. Lib. 11, p. 504.

1769, Dec. 31. Flowers, William, of Cape May Co., yeoman; will of. Wife, Mary, ⅓ of moveable estate. Son, William, land on which I live, and a tract of 22 acres that I bought of Samuel Jones, on Delaware Bay. Daughter, Silvitha, Flowers' land on which Benjamin Ingram lives. Daughter, Judith Flowers, land where Mary Taylor lives. Daughter, Mary Flowers, land I bought of Daniel Swain, Esq. Executor—my wife. Witnesses—Samuel Eldredge, Edward Church, Jonathan Mills. Proved Jan. 20, 1770.
1770, Jan. 22. Adm'rs—Henry Hand and Downes Edmunds. Fellowbondsmen—Timothy Hand and Christopher Foster, gentlemen; all of Cape May Co. Witnesses—Zeruiah Hughes and Abigail Reeves.
1770, Jan. 20. Inventory, £372.1.11, made by Christopher Foster and Timothy Hand. Lib. 14, p. 270.

1757, April 6. Fogg, Daniel, of Alloways Creek, Salem Co., yeoman; will of. Daughter, Mary Fogg, all my real estate, and ½ personal; but, if my wife have a son, then he is to have the real, and must pay £50 to my said daughter when he is 21. If my children die before 21, then I give my brother, Samuel, all my real. My wife, ½ of my personal estate. Executors—my two brothers, Samuel Fogg and Charles Fogg. Witnesses—Mathew Morrison, Robert Walker, Francis Halter. Proved June 15, 1761.
1761, Jan. 28. Inventory, £276.15.1, made by John Holme and William Oakford. Lib. 11, p. 20.

1754, April 4. Folckerse, Johannis, of Bridgewater Twsp., Somerset Co., yeoman; will of. Wife, Elizabeth Folckerse, £600. To the Reformed Protestant Dutch Church of Raritan, £100. Lands to be sold and the money given to my brothers, Folkert, Philip, Joseph, and Dirck Folkertse; to William Van Noortwyck, son of my half sister, Folkertje, the wife of Simon Van Noortwyck; to my sister, Rebeccah, the wife of Cornelius Tunisse; and to my sister, Annatie, widow of Dirck Hoogelandt. If I die before Margaret Stevens, "of whom I have in lease the farm," whereon I live, which is dated 1st of May, 1731, my Executors to let out the same as long as the lease continues, and, with the money, discharge the requirements in said lease. Executors—Peter Van Nest, son of Joris Van Nest, and Samuel Staats Coejemans. Witnesses—William Crooke, Mickeal Hegeman, Abraham Lott, Jr. Proved June 22, 1761.
1761, June 29. Inventory, £555.15.10, made by John Van Middlesworth, Abraham Vanneste and Jacob Van Noorstrand.
Lib. G, p. 456.

1756, May 1. Folk, Christian, of Somerset Co.; will of. My wife, the house where I live and the goods, and, after her death, to sons, Henderick and Philip, and daughter, Barbary. Executrix—wife, Anna Danitia Folk. Witnesses—Hendrick Van Arsdalen, Isaac Van Arsdalen, Isaac Amerman. Proved May 10, 1768. Lib. K, p. 2.

1763, March 28. Folwell, William, of Mansfield Twsp., Burlington Co., yeoman; will of. Wife, Elizabeth, ½ my moveable estate. The other ½ to daughter, Hope, except my large Bible to go to my son, Joseph. Son, John, gold buttons. Son, Joseph, plantation I bought of Benjamin Swain. Son, John, plantation that I live on. Executors—son, Joseph, and my brother, Edward Rockhill Witnesses—William Wilson, Mary Woolman, Joseph Talman. Proved May 3, 1763. Lib. 11, p. 303.
1763, April 29. Inventory, £455.0.5, made by John Folwell and Joseph English.

1764, Jan. 18. Fontine, Abraham, of Somerset Co. Int. Adm'x—Elizabeth Fontine, of said place; his widow. Fellowbondsman—John Schurman, of Middlesex Co. Lib. H, p. 324.

1762, May 28. Fontyn, Johannes, of Somerset Co.; will of. Wife, Agness Fontine, £200. To Agnes Yorks, the daughter of Peter Yorks, the interest of £100, till she is 18. To Peter Yorks, £50. To Jacob Deriemer, a loom. My brother, Jacob Fontyn, apparel and cane. Rest of personal and real to my brothers, Jacob and Abraham; my sisters, Mary Suydam and Lea Smook; and the children of my brother, Renyer, deceased, namely, Charles, Abraham, Lena and Sarah. Executors—wife, Agnes, friend, Gerrit Voorhees and said Peter Yorks. Witnesses—William Oake, John Van Bueren, Derck Van Veghten, Jr. Proved Feb. 4, 1763.
1763, Feb. 4. Inventory, £516.13.9, made by Derrik Rappaljee, and John Parcell. Lib. H, p. 368.

1757, Aug. 16. Foord, William, of Nottingham Twsp., Burlington Co., yeoman; will of. Wife, Margaret, all moveable estate and profits of my plantation, to bring up my children. Sons, William and James, said plantation at wife's death or marriage. Daughters, Elizabeth, Rebeckah, Sarah, Margaret, Anne and Lidia Foord, £5 each. Executors—my brother, John Foord, and Joseph Kille. Witnesses—Cornelius Appleton, Josiah Appleton, John Abbott. Proved Feb. 26, 1765.
1763, March 30. Joseph Killy renounced.
1763, April 4. John Foord renounced. Lib. 12, p. 78.

1762, Sept. 25. Foord, William, of Woodbridge, Middlesex Co.; will of. Lands to be sold. Son, Samuel, £200. Youngest daughter, Sarah Foord, £50, and as much goods as my other daughters had at their marriage. Granddaughter, Unice Cutter, a bed. Wife, Mary, rest of estate. Executors—my wife, my friend, David Evins, and my son, Samuel. Witnesses—Dennes Combs, Stephen Carman, Jr., David Herriot. Proved Nov. 10, 1762.
1762, Nov. 19. Inventory, £387.17.1, made by Alexander Edgar and Nathaniel Fitz Randolph. Lib. H, p. 201.
1763, April 18. Inventory, £86.5.6, made by John Abbott and Joseph Chambers. (Margaret Foord, Adm'x with will annexed, was sworn in 1765).

1770, Nov. 21. Force, James, of Newark Twsp., Essex Co.; will of. Children to be put to trade when old enough. All given to children (names not given). Executors—John Gilderslee and Walter Smith. Witnesses—Moses Clark, Isaac Force, David Clark. Proved Dec. 8, 1770. Letters granted to John Gildersleave and Walter Smith, at same time. Lib. K, p. 269.

1768, Nov. 23. Force, Timothy, of Newark Twsp., Essex Co. Int. Adm'rs—Rachael Force and Isaac Force. Fellowbondsman—Henry Earl, Jr.; all of same place. Witness—James Carter. Lib. I, p. 364.

1767, Feb. 6. Ford, John, of Morristown, Morris Co.; will of. Moveable estate to be sold, and, out of the money, my four children, Mahlon, Chilion, David and Nathan, shall be brought up. The plantation where I live, and that where Solomon Brown lives by lease, and known by name of Mallepardis, and the land in Roxbury Twsp., all are to be divided when my eldest son, Mahlon, is 21, and he shall have his choice; and Chilion, when he is 21, shall have his choice; and the same with David and Nathan, when they are 21. Executors—my father, Jacob Ford, Jacob Ford, Jr., Samuel Tuthill and Moses Tuttle. Witnesses—Jabez Campfield, Joseph Wood, Frederick King. Proved March 12, 1767. Lib. I, p. 186.

1764, Sept. 3. Fordham, Richard, of City of Burlington, ship carpenter. Int. Adm'r—William Skeels. Fellowbondsman—Samuel Allinson; both of said City. Witness—Levi Murrel. Lib. 12, p. 16.

1764, Aug. 27. Inventory, £36.6.0, made by William Smith and Levi Murrel.

1764, Oct. 19. Account by William Skeeler as Adm'r.

1766, Sept. 13. Foreman, Jonathan, of Cape May Co. Ward. Son of Jonathan Foreman. Guardian—Joshua Shaw. Fellowbondsman—George Taylor; both of Lower Precinct in said Co. Witnesses—John Tounsend, John Taylor, Marcy Taylor. Lib. 12, p. 327.

1763, Oct. 19. Foreman, Martha, of Cape May Co. Ward. Daughter of Jonathan Foreman. Guardian—John Shaw. Fellowbondsman—Lewis Cresse; both of said Co. Witnesses—Henry Young and George Norton. Lib. 11, p. 439.

1762, July 6. Forgerson, Uriah, of Wantage Twsp., Sussex Co. Int. Adm'x—Susannah Forgerson, widow of said Uriah. Fellowbondsman—Job Loree, of Mendum, Morris Co. File No. 57 S.

1768, Aug. 22. Forman, George, of Somerset Co. Int. Adm'r—Lewis Forman, of Monmouth Co., merchant, who is a brother to said George. Fellowbondsman—Richard McDonald, Esq., of Somerset Co. Lib. I, p. 336.

1759, June 20. Forman, Jonathan, Esq., of Freehold, Monmouth Co.; will of."being old." Wife, Margaret, ½ of my farm where I live and the household goods, which, after her death, are to be divided among my children and granddaughter, Eleanor Van Dorn. Son, Samuel, £10. Son, John, £10. Son, Peter, the land that joins Nicholas Stillwell and George Rhe. To the youngest children of my son, Jonathan, deceased, £20 each, when they are 21 (in all £60);

but, if the eldest brother, when he is of age, shall give to his youngest brother and two sisters a share of their father's estate, then he shall have his part of the £60, "and his equal part that I designed for their father of my brother Samuel Forman, deceased's estate, hereafter mentioned." Daughter, Mary, wife of Robert Rhe, £100. Granddaughter, Eleanor Van Dorn, furniture, cows, negro, etc. Son, David, the rest of my lands. Eldest son, Samuel, aforesaid, ⅓ of my lands in New England, which were bequeathed to me by my brother, Samuel Forman, dec'd, and the other ⅔ to my other children. My brother Samuel, in his will, left me land at Portsmouth, Rhode Island, of 62 acres, as well as to my brothers, Joseph and Ezekiel, and there was to be paid out to our three sisters, Hannah Madock, Mary Romine, and Rebecca, £50 each, but Ezekiel died before brother Samuel; therefore that bequest was void, and I, being heir-at-law to that part, was willing and did pay half of said legacies given to my three sisters; therefore my brother Joseph and myself have sold the said land, and paid the legacies to our sisters. But I am willing that brother, Ezekiel's, children, shall enjoy what was left to him, had he lived to inherit it, although it was not to his children, for at the time brother Samuel made his will brother Ezekiel had no children, therefore it is fallen to me, and I give the rest of the money to my brother, Ezekiel's, children, as follows: to Samuel (son of Ezekiel) £80; to Thomas, £70; to Aaron, £70; to Ezekiel, £70. Executors—wife, Margaret, and my sons, Samuel and Peter. Witnesses—John Van Cafe, Thomas Leonard, James Robinson, John Henderson.

1761, June 6. Codicil. To daughter, Mary, wife of Robert Rhe, a negro called Nanny. My granddaughter, Eleanor Van Dorn, is still unmarried. To son, Samuel, 16½ acres in Freetown, in New England. Witnesses—John Van Clafe, James Robinson, John Henderson. Proved Jan. 20, 1763. Lib. H, p. 215.

1768, March 16. Forman, Ursilla, of Middletown, Monmouth Co.; will of. Son, George, the bonds I have of him. Son-in-law, George Walker, bonds due to me from him. Daughters, Priscilla, Lydia and Phebe, my apparel. Son, Lewis, Bible. Rest of my estate to my sons, Lewis, Andrew and Robert, and to my daughters, Lydia and Phebe. Executors—son, Lewis. Witnesses—Samuel Ker, Peter Conrey, Thomas Hunn. Proved May 30, 1768. Lib. I, p. 241.

1761, Nov. 29. Fort, Ann, of Northampton, Burlington Co.; will of. Son, Rodger Fort, chest. Daughter, Edith, chest. Daughter, Joana Lay, £5. Granddaughters, Ann Price and Hannah Price ,beds, etc. Rest of personal and real to my two daughters, Esther Murphy and Edith Price. Executors—daughters, Esther Murphy and Edith Price, and my friend, Daniel Jones. Witnesses—Samuel Reeve, Edward Mullen, Joseph Harrington. Proved Oct. 9, 1762. Lib. 11, p. 235.

1762, Aug. 19. Inventory, £54.16.0, made by John Budd.

1763, Oct. 14. Account by Thomas Berkinshea and Esther, his wife, late Esther Murphy, as Executrix of estate of Ann Fort.

1764, May 31. Forth, Benjamin, of Maryland. Int. Adm'r—James Hines, (Hinds), of Queen Anns Co., Maryland, yeoman. Fellowbondsman—James Davis, of Gloucester Co. Witness—Robert Cooper.

1764, May 31. Inventory, £22.8.7, made by James Davis and Jacob Clement. Lib. 11, p. 522.

CALENDAR OF WILLS—1761-1770   149

1762, Oct. 13. Foster, David, of Cape May Co. Int. Adm'r—Samuel Foster. Fellowbondsman—Jonathan Smith; both of said Co. Witnesses—Tabitha Townsend and Mary Young.
1762, Oct. 26. Inventory, £121.8.0, made by John Shaw and John Smith.   Lib. 11, p. 414.

1761, March 21. Foster, John, of Burlington Co. Int. Adm'r—Edward Tonkin. Fellowbondsman—Joseph Hollinshead; both of same Co.
1761, March 21. Ann Foster, widow of said John, renounced in favor of Edward Tonkin.   Lib. 10, p. 174.
1761, Sept. 19. Amount, £19.14.1, received by Adm'r. Same day account filed.

1749, Oct. 28. Foster, Josiah, of Bridgetown, Burlington Co.; will of. Wife, Amie, real and personal during life. Daughters, Rebecca and Hannah, houses in Bridgetown, after wife's death. Son, William, farm in Evesham. Executor—son, William. Witnesses—William Jones, James Lippincott, Peter Andrews.
1753, July 5. Codicil. Witness—Joseph Barr, James Eldridge, Thomas Wilkins.
1760, Aug. 16. Codicil. Wife, Amie, given annuity. Witnesses—John Bail, Thomas Borden. Proved April 16, 1770.   Lib. 14, p. 213.

1769, Feb. 17. Foster, Nathaniel, of Cape May Co.; will of. Wife, Mary, ⅓ of my lands and ⅓ of the moveables. Son, Salathiel, the rest of lands, and he to pay to my son, Nathaniel, £22, and also pay to my daughter, Esther Hand, £2. Executor—son, Salathiel. Witnesses—Aaron Eldredge, Samuel Woodruff, Richard Wood. Proved Feb. 20, 1769.
1769, Feb. 22. Inventory, £90.11.7, made by John Eldredge and Aaron Eldredge.   Lib. 14, p. 180.

1763, June 6. Foster, Nathaniel, Jr., of Roxbury, Morris Co., blacksmith. Int. Adm'r—Nathaniel Foster, of Lebanon, Hunterdon Co., blacksmith. Fellowbondsman—Michael Welsh, of Roxbury, Morris Co., yeoman, and Thomas Silverthorn, of Mansfield Woodhouse, Sussex Co., yeoman. Witness—William Hyndman.
1763, June 6. Renunciation, by Mary Foster,[1] in favor of her father-in-law, Nathaniel Foster. Witness—Aaron Doud.
1763, June 4. Inventory, £46.12.5, made by John Likens and James Newman.
1765, May 23. Account by Adm'r.   Lib. 11, p. 457; File No. 1441 N.

1762, Dec. 17. Foster, Samuel, of Cape May Co., carpenter; will of. Wife, Elizabeth, all my estate, except a bed to my daughter, Hannah Foster. Son, Jonathan, 20 acres. Son, William, rest of lands. Daughter, Elizabeth Stites, 5 shillings. Daughter, Marjery Young, £6. Daughter, Mary Foster, £6. Daughter, Hannah Foster, £6. Grandson, Samuel Foster, £5. Executors—my wife and Jonathan Smith. Witnesses—Philip Cresse, Nathaniel Jenkins, —— Stites. Proved July 23, 1764.
1764, July 21. Inventory, £128.14.8, made by John Shaw and Daniel Smith.   Lib. 12, p. 32.

1766, March 24. Fountain, Charles, of New Brunswick, Middlesex Co.; will of. Son, Charles, 10 shillings. Son, Ephra, 5 shillings. Sons, John and Samuel, each 5 shillings. Daughter, Mary Snoterly (?), 5 shillings. Daughters, Hannah Fisher, Cathrin Blackhorn, Sarah Hays and Jemime Higbe, each 5 shillings. Rest to be divided between my wife, Sophira, my sons, Isaac, Abram and Jacob, and my daughter, Eve. Executor—friend, John Ryder. I give to my last wife's four children an equal share with my wife, when my said children are brought up. Witnesses—John Whitlock, George Rollin, Reuben Runyon. Proved May 26, 1766. Lib. H, p. 613.

1765, Oct. 7. Fowler, Thomas, of Morris River, Cumberland Co. Int. Adm'r—Joseph Savage, of Cape May Co. Fellowbondsman—Richard Lore, of Fairfield, Cumberland Co. Witness—Abigail Ewing.
1766, Feb. 22. Inventory, £16.15.0, made by John Daniels and Nathan Young.
1767, May 7. Account by Adm'r. Lib. 12, p. 249.

1765, Jan. 28. Fox, Leonard, of Shrewsbury, Monmouth Co. Int. Adm'x—Anne Fox, widow of Leonard Fox, householder, deceased. Fellowbondsman—Daniel Wainwright, yeoman; both of said place. Witnesses—Anthony Dennis and Benjamin Dennis.
1765, Feb. 2. Inventory, £18.3.0, made by Stanfel Logan and James Johnston. Lib. H, p. 619.

1762, Feb. 26. Fraser, Gelens, of Trenton, Hunterdon Co.; will of. To my friend, Ralph Jones, all my goods and bills. Executor—said Ralph Jones. Witnesses—Isaac Green, Obadiah Howell, Elijah Jones. Proved March 8, 1762. Lib. 11, p. 134.

1762, Feb. 26. Frazee, Gershom, of Borough of Elizabeth, Essex Co. Ward. Petition, stating that there is an estate belonging to Gershom Frazee, heir to Abraham Frazie, of said Borough, deceased, which estate is under a lease given by the Adm'rs, and the tenant is cutting and destroying the timber, and carrying the same to market, and the said estate is listed to be ruined; therefore we relatives of said orphan beg you to appoint a Guardian. Signed by Isaac Frazie, Sr., Isaac Frazee, Jr., Samuel Frazee, Gershom Frazee, Jacob Winans, Isaac Littell, Eljia Stits, Caleb Scudder, Moses Littell and Joseph Acken.
1762, March 1. Guardian—Moses Frazee, of Essex Co., of Gershom Frazee, aged 7 years, one of the children of Abraham Frazee, deceased. Fellowbondsmen—James Still Coberly and Gershom Frazee; both of said Co. Lib. H, p. 77.

1762, Nov. 17. Frazee, Gershom, and Jemima, of Essex Co. Wards. Children of Abraham Frazee, of said Co., deceased; aged 7 and 5 years. Guardian—Timothy Frazee, of Middlesex Co. Fellowbondsman—John Lee, of Essex Co. Lib. H, p. 202.

1769, May 8. Frazee, Gershom, of Essex Co. Ward. Son of Abrahom Frazee, of said Co., who makes choice of Joseph Bird as his Guardian.
1769, May 8. Guardian—Joseph Bird, of said Co. Fellowbondsmen—John Lee, of said Co., and Timothy Frazee, of Middlesex Co. Witness—Thomas Andrews. Lib. K, p. 89.

1761, Dec. 2. Frazee, James, of Essex Co. Ward Son of Eliphalet Frazee, of said Co. Guardian—Abraham Clark, Jr. Fellowbondsman—Robert Ogden, Esq.; both of said Co. Lib. H, p. 42.

1764, Feb. 14. Frazee, James, of Elizabeth Town, Essex Co. Ward. Petition, stating that he is under age and his guardian, Abraham Clark, Jr., requests to be released, and he makes choice of George Brown as Guardian. Letter signed by Abraham Clark, Jr., dated Feb. 11, 1764, requests release.
1764, Feb. 21. Guardian—George Brown, of Middlesex Co. (James Frazee is 16 and son of Eliphalet Frazee, deceased). Fellowbondsman—John Moore, of Middlesex Co.
Lib. H, p. 42; Files No. 3363-3368 G, and 2643-2646 G.

1767, June 29. Frazee, Samuel, of Essex Co. Int. Adm'x—Sarah Frazee. Fellowbondsman—Moses Little; both of said Co. Witness —John Terrill. Lib. I, p. 131.

(?) Feb. 2. Frazee, Stephen, of Shrewsbury Twsp., Monmouth Co., yeoman; will of. Wife, Sara, the use of this room I lie in, and this bed. My eldest son, Stephen, 5 shillings. My 2nd son, Joseph, 5 shillings. My youngest sons, Benjamin, Jonathan and David, all my land on Squan River. Lands in the mountains to be sold. Household goods to my four daughters. Executors—my wife and her brother, Joseph Allen. Witnesses—Samuel Weston, Ephraim Frazee, Henry Ross. Proved April 10, 1766.
1766, April 22. Inventory, made by David Johnston, John Jeffery and John Palmar Clarke. Lib. H, p. 612.

1765, March 8. Frazier, Thomas, of Bernards Town, Somerset Co., yeoman; will of. Wife, Hannah, use of £83 and household goods, while my widow. Daughter, Mary Frazer, £40. To Thomas Frazer, begotten on the body of Mary Parker by my son, Thomas, now deceased (as it is said), £10. Son, William, rest of my moveable and real estate, and he is to find his mother provisions. Executors— friend, John Roy, and son, William. Witnesses—David Parker, Elisha Ayers, Brice Ricky. Proved May 7, 1765. Lib. H, p. 518.

1766, Sept. 5. Freck, Barnard, of Chesterfield, Burlington Co., husbandman. Int. Adm'r—Joshua Bunting. Fellowbondsman—Aaron Bunting; both of said place. Lib. 12, p. 295.
1766, Oct. 13. Inventory, £34.12.4, made by Jacob Lawrence and Israel Bunting.
1768, May 27. Account by Adm'r. Lib. 13, p. 434.

1763, Nov. 8. Freeman, Alexander, of Woodbridge, Middlesex Co. Int. Adm'r—Isaac Freeman, Jr. Fellowbondsman—Joseph Shotwell, Jr.; both of said place.
1763, Nov. 8. Renunciation by Grace Freeman, the widow, in favor of Isaac Freeman, Jr. Witness—William Godbeer.
1763, Nov. 17. Inventory, made by Joseph Freeman and Joseph Shotwell. Lib. H, p. 304.

1763, Jan. 31. Freeman, Andrew, of Woodbridge, Middlesex Co. Ward. Son of William Freeman of said place, deceased. Age 20 years. Guardian—Joseph Smith, of Hunterdon Co. Fellowbondsman —John Smith, of Middlesex Co. Witness—John Smyth. Lib. H, p. 220.

1763, Jan. 7. Freeman, Henry, of Woodbridge Twsp., Middlesex Co.; will of. Greatgrandson, John Freeman, heir-at-law and grandson of my eldest son, John Freeman, deceased, 5 shillings. Grandson, Isaac Freeman, son of my eldest son, John Freeman, deceased, land which I bought of Edward Wilkison, deceased, and 30 acres joining the same, which I bought of Francis Walker, deceased; both being in said Twsp. Land which I bought of Joseph Insle, lying in Woodbridge, known by the name of Horse Neck, and containing 60 acres, to be sold. To the 5 daughters of my daughter, Rachel Runyon, £100. Son, Samuel, £100. Daughter, Mary Dunham, £50. Daughter, Elizabeth Runyon, £50. My granddaughter, Eliner Worth, £10. Son, Samuel, land where his son, Jonathan, lives, which I bought of William Moores; also a salt meadow that I bought of William Stone, at Craines Neck. Son, Joseph, 15 acres of salt meadow in the Raritan Meadows, near Roundabouts, which I bought of John Smyth, Scotchman. Son, Benjamin, land in Morris Co., where he lives, of 100 acres. Son, Isaac, land I bought of Samuel Martin, and 2 lots joining thereto, one of which I bought of Miles Bunn, and the other of Thomas Pike; also a salt meadow I bought of Benjamin Bloomfield. Son, Henry, my homestead, which I bought of John Smyth, Scotchman, and George Darling; also a salt meadow, joining to Samuel Barron, which I purchased of Mathew Moores, deceased. Son, James, land where he lives, of 100 acres. Executors—sons, Samuel, Joseph and Isaac, and my friend, David Evins. Witnesses—Isaac Cotheal, Benjamin Thornell, David Herriot. Proved Oct. 13, 1763.

1763, Oct. 14. Inventory, made by Reuben Evens and David Herriot. Lib. H, p. 304.

1752, June 8. Freeman, John, of Woodbridge, Middlesex Co., yeoman; will of. Eldest son, Henry, the several tracts of land which I had in that deed of sale from Obadiah Ayers, dated 28 May, 1733; also ½ of 5 acres of salt marsh in the Raritan Meadows, which I had of my father, Henry, which is described in a deed of sale to Thomas Smith from Anna Thornell. Son, Alexander, land I bought of my brother, Joseph, of 67 acres, being the place where my son now lives; also the rest of the salt marsh. Son, Isaac, land on east side of my house and on the north of the highway, of 90 acres; also the east part of the land on the south side of the road, of 9 acres. Son, James, the rest of my home place. Sons, Henry and Alexander, the land where my brother lives, called Horseneck. Wife, Martha, provided for. Eldest daughter, Sarah, the wife of John Smith, the bill of £80 which I have against her. Daughter, Mary, wife of Samuel Force, £80. Daughter, Elizabeth, £80. Daughter, Martha, £80. Daughter, Charity, £80. Wife, Martha, £80. Executors—eldest son, Henry, and my wife. Witnesses—Mary Donham, Anne Skinner, David Donham. Proved April 1, 1761.

1763, July 25. Citation to Martha Freeman, widow and executrix of John Freeman, stating that Samuel Force, father of Charity and Mary Force, granddaughters and legatees of said John Freeman, has complained that an account has not been made; now ordered to file her account.

1772. Account by Martha Freeman. Paid legacies to Mary Force and Charity White. Paid to father Freeman, £38.13.6.

Lib. G, p. 410; Lib. H, p. 264.

CALENDAR OF WILLS—1761-1770   153

1760, April 15. Freeman, Jonathan, of Woodbridge, Middlesex Co., yeoman; will of. Wife, Charety, ⅓ the moveable estate and the use of the land, which is to be sold after her marriage or death, My brothers, Joseph, Isaac, Benjamin and James, and my sisters, Elizabeth Runyon and Mary Donham, and the daughters of my sister, Rachel Runyan, and my nephew, Jonathan Freeman, and my niece, Damcras Hatfield, the rest. Executors—brother, Joseph Freeman, and my friend, Samuel Force. Witnesses—James Haydock, Thomas Latham, Joseph Shotwell. Proved Dec. 22, 1761.   Lib. H, p. 65.

1763, June 7. Freeman, Sarah, of Woodbridge, Middlesex Co. Int. Adm'x—Phebe Ayres. Fellowbondsman—John Bane; both of said place. Whereas the said Sarah Freeman died intestate, and whereas, on the 21 of Jan., 1760, letters of Adm'n on her estate were granted to Frazee Ayres, (principal creditor of Sarah Freeman), who is since deceased, leaving goods which were of the said Sarah Freeman, unadministered, now the said Phebe Ayres is appointed.
1760, Jan. 19. Inventory, £61.4.5, made by Samuel Kelly and Joseph Ayers.
1763, June 30. Account by Reuben Ayers and Phebe Ayers, executors of Frazee Ayers, Adm'r to Sarah Freeman, to all the goods that were of Sarah Freeman. Includes funeral charges of her child, £0.15.0.   Lib. H, p. 245; Lib. G, p. 123.

1764, Aug. 31. Freeman, William, of Salem Co., Schoolmaster. Int. Adm'r—John Budd, Esq. Fellowbondsmen—Joseph Burroughs, Esq., and Edward Test, merchant; all of Town of Salem.   Lib. 12, p. 73.

1761, May 29. Frelandt, Simon, of Bergen Co.; will of. Names my present wife, Rachel, and the child that is yet to be born; also my sisters and brothers, Enogh, John, Abraham, Leya, and Annaty. Executors—my wife and my brother, Enogh. Witnesses—Albert Terheun, Michel Van Wincle, Guilliam Bertholf. Proved Feb. 9, 1765.
Lib. H, p. 492.

1762, Jan. 30. Freman, Stephen, Jr., of Hanover, Morris Co., yeoman; will of. Personal and real to be sold, and the money to be for benefit of my wife, Sarah, to help her to bring up my children. Executors—wife, Sarah, and my brother-in-law, Mathew Fairchild. Witnesses—Jacob Ford, John Mitchell, Jr., Timothy Johnes. Proved March 9, 1762.   Lib. H, p. 143.

1770, May 16. French, John, of Morris Co. Int. Adm'r—Henry French. Fellowbondsman—David Sayre; both of said Co.
1770, May 17. Inventory, made by David Sayre and Kennedy Vance.
Lib. K, p. 203.

1767, Oct. 15. Fresneau, Peter, of Middletown, Monmouth Co.; will of. My estate in Albany and Orange County, and in West Chester Co., all in New York; and my right in mines, lands, etc., in Sims Berry Twsp., and in Stratford, now in possession of David Lewis, of said Stratford and Simsberry, being both in Connecticut; also my right in Monmouth Co. and Middlesex Co., in N. J., shall stand in the hands of my executors, Agness Fresneau and John Morin Scott, Esq., of New York City, whom I appoint my Executors. My personal estate to remain with my widow till my youngest child comes to age, and then to be divided among them; but my widow shall first come in for her 1/5, both of real and personal, before any of my children shall lay claim thereto. Witnesses—Hones Van Pelt, David Watson, and John Burrowes. Proved Feb. 7, 1770. Lib. K, p. 161.

1762, May 8. Frost, Ezekiel, of Roxbury Twsp., Morris Co. Int. Adm'x—Alice Frost. Fellowbondsman—William Dugles, both of said Co. Witness—Roger Flanavan. Lib. 11, p. 287.

1762, Nov. 14. Fulkersen, Derck, of Somerset Co., yeoman; will of. Wife, Casaiah (Kezia), use of real and personal estate while my widow. Eldest son, Philip, 200 acres of the rear of my lands. Youngest son, Derrick, my home place, and the rest of my lands. Should the youngest daughter marry, she is to have an outset. Daughters, Anne and Mary, £350 each. Executors—my wife, my brother-in-law, William Vanduyn, and my friend, John Vanortwyke, of Somerset Co. Witnesses—Pieter Couwenhoven, Cornelus Sebring, Elias V: Court. Proved May 30, 1763.
1763, June 13. Inventory, made by Abraham Vandorn, and Cornelus Sebring. Lib. H, p. 266.

1763, Feb. 2.. Fullerton, James, of Somerset Co. Int. Adm'r—Robert Adams, of Morris Co., to whom the widow of James desires that letters be granted. Fellowbondsman—Benjamin Lewis, of Somerset Co.
1763, Feb. 8. Inventory, £113.4.11, made by John Durham and Brice Ricky. Lib. H, p. 221.

1764, April 12. Furman, John, of Amwell, Hunterdon Co. Ward. Son of Thomas Furman, of said place, deceased. Makes petition that William Cornell, of Hopewell, said Co., may be made his Guardian.
1764, April 12. Guardian—William Cornell. Fellowbondsman—Cornell Stevenson, of Springfield, Burlington Co. Witness—Joseph Read. Lib. 11, p. 493.

1764, Sept. 16. Furnis, Martha, of Bordentown, Burlington Co., widow; will of. Son, Wilton Furnis, the interest of £100 and the interest of the money arising from sales of house and lot given him by my father, Richard Wright. My son-in-law, John Taylor, and my daughter, Hannah Taylor, to have the care of my son, Milton. My daughter, Hannah Taylor, to have the rest as given to me by my father. Executors—son-in-law, John Taylor, and my daughter, Hannah Taylor. Witnesses—Thomas Bliss, Joshua Bunting and Eliz. Musgrove. Proved June 9, 1766. Lib. 13, p. 29.

1763, April 12. Gach, Thomas, of Woodbridge Township, Middlesex Co.; will of. Eldest son, John, one-half the plantation where he lives (except 10 acres at the west end that was surveyed in my own right), with 4 acres of salt meadow at the south end of my meadow below Strawberry Hill; also three and a-half acres in Raritan meadows with ½ my freehold right in the Commons. Grandson, Thomas Gach, the other ½ of said plantation, but to remain to the use of his father, John Gach, during John's life. Son, Philip, my home plantation, where I live, and the rest of the salt meadow, and land on Strawberry Hill, and the lot adjoining Jonathan Harned and John Harned, and also the said 10 acres; also ½ of my freehold right

CALENDAR OF WILLS—1761-1770 155

in the Commons of Woodbridge, when he is 21. Daughters—Mary, Elizabeth, Sarah, Martha and Anne; all the several lots on the south side of the road that leads to Amboy to be sold, and the money to be divided between them and Thomas Shotwell, son of my deceased daughter, Esther. Wife, Elizabeth, the use of the said lands. Executors—my wife and James Eddy. Witnesses—Samuel F. Parker, James Parker, Samuel Inslee. Proved March 9, 1770. Lib. K, p. 183.

1763, April 14. Gallahan, Charles, of Alloways Creek, Salem Co. Int. Adm'x—Anna Gallahan. Fellowbondsman—Robert Walker; both of said place.
1763, March 21. Inventory, £83.7.0, made by William Walker and William Oakford. Lib. 11, p. 374.

1763, Sept. 27. Gamble, William, of near Londonderry, Ireland. Ward. Said William is son of John Gamble. Guardian—Redmond Conyngham, of Philadelphia. Fellowbondsmen—Richard Stevens and Charles Coxe, both of Philadelphia. Witness—Charles Read.
Lib. 11, p. 442.

1769, Oct. 9. Gano, David, of City of New Brunswick, Middlesex Co.; will of. Wife, Catharine, use of house, store and dock, and, after her death, to be sold and the money divided among children, Mary, David, Elizabeth and Catharine. Wife to have the plantation on George's Road till my son, David, comes of age, when it is to be sold, and money divided among children and my wife. Executors—friends, John Lile, Jr., and John Schureman. Witnesses—John Dennis, Josiah Applegate, Peter Lott. Proved May 14, 1770.
1770, May 5. Inventory, £146.13.7, made by Jasper Farmer and Andrew McDowell. Lib. K, p. 202.

1763, Aug. 22. Gano, George, of Middlesex Co. Int. Adm'rs—Rachel Gano, the widow, and David Gano, brother of said George Gano; both of said place. Fellowbondsman—Henry Vankirk.
1763, July 30. Inventory, £671.3.6, made by John Lyle and John Schuurman. Lib. H, p. 270.

1768, July 15. Gansolis, Rymerick, of New York. Int. Adm'r—Peter Quick, of Sussex Co. Fellowbondsman—Jasper Smith, of Hunterdon Co. Witness—George Reading.
1768, July 15. Inventory, £105.3.8, rendered in by Peter Quick, Adm'r., of goods within New Jersey, of the estate of "Rymerick Gansalies." Lib. 13, p. 440.

1769, Feb. 26. Gardiner, James, of Woolwich, Gloucester Co.; will of. To my wife, £200, and the money from the sale of my real estate to my three sons, Joseph, Ephraim and Job, when they are 21. Sons to be put to trade when 14. Executors—Joshua Lippincott and John Test, both of said Co. Witnesses—Framton Dell, Ellenor Moon and Jacob Spicer. Proved April 27, 1769.
1784, June 1. Account of Rebecca Lippincott, Executrix of Joshua Lippincott, who was the surviving Executor of James Gardner. Includes "Cash paid Marg. Gardner, widow of James Gardner, supposed to be out of the sale of the land, £200." Lib. 14, p. 54; Lib. 26, p. 49.

1768, Feb. 25. Gardner, Richard, of Wantage, Sussex Co., yeoman; will of. Wife, Isable, and daughter, Hannah, to have all real and personal, except such as hereafter named; and, if my daughter die without issue, then her real is to go to my sister's children, the said sister being Rachel Collard. I have a bond against Elijah Collard, but his widow (my sister), who lives on that farm, is not to be disturbed while she is the widow. Richard Collard, my sister's son, is to have a tract in Walpack, of 54 acres. Executors—my wife, Isable, my son-in-law, John Forgeson, and my friend, John Herring. Witnesses—Mickel Crosman, John Cimbel, John Herring. Proved June 3, 1768.
1768, May 5. Inventory, £1151.3.8, made by Jonathan Cooley and Samuel Meeker. Lib. 12, p. 529.

1767, Oct. 28. Gardner, Sarah, of Morris Co. Int. Adm'r—Peter Kemble, principal creditor. Fellowbondsman—Stephen Conkling; both of Morristown, said Co. Witness—Chloe Bridge. Lib. I, p. 208.

1761, April 8. Garon, John, of Perth Amboy, Middlesex Co. Int. Adm'rs—Elizabeth Garon, the widow, and Ephraim Donham; both of said place.
1761, April 6. Inventory, made by Peter Lott and Daniel Morgan. Lib. G, p. 369.

1767, Sept. 17. Garrabrants, Jacob, of Aghquacknonk, Essex Co.; will of. Real and personal, to my wife, Catharine, my daughters, Maritie Garrabrants and Trintie Garrabrants, my son, Peter, and my daughter, Rykje Garrabrants, each 1/5 part. Executors—friend, Francis Post, and my wife. Witnesses—Garrabrant Garrabrants, Abraham Garrabrants, Peter Degarmo. Proved Oct. 7, 1767.
Lib. I, p. 192.

1763, July 24. Garretson, Jacob, of Cape May Co., yeoman; will of. Granddaughter, Mercy Daniels, goods when 18. Wife, Martha, rest of personal estate. Children, Rem Garrison, Garret Garrison, Rebecca Wilson and Phebe Goldin, personal at wife's death. Plantation of 320 acres of which ½ I give to Rem Garrison and ½ to Garret Garrison, but my wife to have the use of same while my widow. Wife to be Guardian of Garret. Executors—my wife and said Rem Garrison. Witnesses—Daniel Garretson, Hannah Eldredge, Jacob Spicer. Proved June 8, 1765.
1765, April 30. Inventory, £157.2.7, made by John Willets and Isaac Baner. Lib. 12, p. 128.

1765, Aug. 19. Garrison, Abraham, of Deerfield, Cumberland Co., yeoman; will of. Wife, Marcy, ⅓ the moveable estate, and the use of ⅕ the lands. (Daughter, Christian, wife of Joseph Chamlis, 5 shillings. This was crossed out). Rachel, wife of Hance Wolson, 5 shillings. Son, Isaac, 5 shillings. Sons, Joseph and Samuel, 5 shillings each. Son, Levi, lands on east side of Burlington road. Son, Abraham, also land. Rest of moveables to be sold and divided among my children, Levi Garrison, Elizabeth Foster (wife of Christofor Foster), and Abraham Garrison, who is under 21. Executors—Son, Levi, and Fithian Stratton. Witnesses—William Thorne, John Ambler, Mary Coleman. Proved Oct. 22, 1766.
1766, Oct. 16. Inventory, £72.16.9, made by John Ambler and Daniel Garrison. Lib. 12, p. 321.

1767, June 26. Garrison, Fredrick, of Pilesgrove Twsp., Salem Co. Int. Adm'rs—Jemima Garrison and Samuel Garrison. Fellowbondsman—John Read; all of said place. Witness—Carter Trenchard.
1767, June 22. Inventory, £596.10.11, made by Jacob Richman and John Mayhew. Lib. 13, p. 191.

1770, Jan. 20. Garrison, Garret, of Fairfield, Cumberland Co., yeoman; will of. Wife, Sarah, ⅓ my moveables. Son, Garret, 15 acres of marsh, and son, William, 10 acres. Son, David, ½ of my homestead, and ½ the rest of lands, and to son, Ruban, the other ½. Daughter, Sarah, 5 acres of marsh, and daughter, Phebe, 10 acres. Moveable estate to children, William, David, Phebe, Nancy, Prudence and Reuben. Executors—my wife and son, David. Witnesses—Thomas Heaton, Aaron Peterson, Ephraim Heaton. Proved Nov. 6, 1770.
1770, Oct. 29. Inventory, £38.7.0, made by John Bragg and William Pepper. Lib. 14, p. 309.

1770, Feb. 13. Garrison, Hannah, of Dearfield, Cumberland Co. Int. Adm'r—Abraham Garrison. Fellowbondsman—Dan Bowen; both of said place.
1770, Feb. 12. Inventory, £28.18.8, made by Dan Bowen and Joseph Smith. Lib. 15, p. 4.

1767, May 12. Garrison, Isaac, of Dearfield Twsp., Cumberland Co., farmer; will of. All lands and moveables to be sold. Wife, Hannah, to have ⅓ and £10 more, to help her bring up the child. Son, Isaac, £10. Daughter, Mary Covoing, 5 shillings. Daughter, Hannah Gagers, 5 shillings. Daughter, Ester Garrison, £5. Son, Abraham, £30. Daughter, Rumey Garrison, 20 shillings. Daughter, Catren Garrison, 30 shillings. Son, Bennet, £5. Son, Joseph, £5. Sons, Jeremiah, Syles and Alfeas, £5 each. Executors—my wife and Daniel Clark. Witnesses—John Stevens and Joseph Smith. Proved July 11, 1767.
1767, May 23. Inventory, £46.7.2, made by Daniel Bowen and Joseph Smith. Lib. 12, p. 486.

1765, Jan. 11. Garrison, Samuel, of Pilesgrove, Salem Co.; will of. Wife, Lydia, 1/3 of my estate. To my 3 married daughters, Phebe, Sarah and Damaris, £3 each. Three eldest sons, Stephen, Samuel and John, £10 each. Youngest son, Abraham, £10. Youngest daughters, Hannah, Rachel, Unice and Lydia, £10. Plantation to be sold. Wife to have the rest. Executors—my wife and Broadway Davis. Witnesses—Isaac Elwell, Benjamin Garrison, David Platts. Proved Feb. 1, 1765.
1765, Jan. 26. Inventory, £189.12.6, made by Benjamin Garrison and Daniel Clark.
1770, Aug. 6. Account by John Miller, Executor, in right of his wife, Lydia, late Lydia Garrison, Executrix of late Samuel Garrison. Includes "Unice Garrison, her sickness, and 3 months for doctor, and expenses of funeral, £40." Lib. 12, p. 175; Lib. 15, p. 42.

1760, Feb. 28. Garwood, Jacob, of Mansfield Twsp., Burlington Co., yeoman; will of. "Advanced in years." Son, Samuel, £50. Second son, Jacob, £100. Grandsons, the sons of my son Samuel, £10 each. Children of my daughter, Rachel Buffin, wife of John Buffin, Jr., £10 each. Child or children of my daughter, Elizabeth, wife of John Delatush, with which she is now pregnant, £10. My two daughters (now single), Lydia and Mary, £20 each, and furniture. Land to be sold and the money divided among my children, Jacob, Rachel Buffin, Elizabeth Delatush, Lydia Garwood and Mary Garwood. As my son, Jacob, may be imposed on, I appoint my Executors as his Trustees. Executors—friends, Joseph Curtis and Peter Harvey. Witnesses—Adam Pettit, Mary Buffin, Isaac DeCow, Hannah DeCow. Proved March 2, 1761. Lib. 10, p. 321.

1761, Feb. 28. Inventory, £173.18.10, made by George Folwell and Joseph English.

1772, Nov. 12. Account of Peter Ellis, Ex'r of Peter Harvey and Anne Ivins, late Anne Curtis, Ex'x of her husband, Joseph Curtis, which Peter Harvey and Joseph Curtis were Ex'rs of Jacob Garwood. "Lands sold for £637.10.0." Lib. 14, p. 501.

1763, Sept. 10. Garwood, William, of Evesham, Burlington Co., yeoman; will of. Wife, Jane, £150. Son, Joseph, my lands. Daughter, Jane Prickett, £50. Daughter, Sarah Bishop, £50. Daughter, Rebekah Garwood, £100. Executors—son, Joseph, and 'my friend, Francis Austin. Witnesses—Thomas Shinn, David Fisher, Thomas Parkinson. Proved May 21, 1767. Lib. 13, p. 70.

1767, May 19. Inventory, £250.19.6, made by Daniel Stratton and Robert Bishop.

1761, Sept. 15. Gaskill, Josiah, of Northampton, Burlington Co.; will of. Son, Jacob, 5 shillings. Son, Josiah, 5 shillings. Wife, Mary, eatables. Son, Joseph, 20 acres of my plantation. My grandson, Aaron Gaskill, son of Jacob, 4 acres. Daughter, Thamer Ewan, cow, etc. Wife, the use of plantation while my widow. Grandson, David Ewan, my plantation. Greatgrandson, Benajah King, son of Robert King, £5. Greatgrandson, Jonathan Gaskill, the son of my grandson, Joshua Gaskill, £5. Executors—wife, Mary, and friend, Joseph Lippincott. Witnesses—James Budd, Jacob Powell, John Woolman, Proved Oct. 13, 1761. Lib. 11, p. 211.

1761, Oct. 12. Inventory, £109.9.6, made by John Woolman and James Budd.

1765, July 1. Gaskill, Meribah, of Burlington Co. Ward. Daughter of Samuel Gaskill. Guardian—Thomas Conarroe, of Northampton Twsp., said Co., yeoman. Fellowbondsman—Daniel Jones, Jr., of Mount Holly, said Co., innkeeper. Witness—John Read.
Lib. 12, p. 127.

1769, Feb. 6. Gass, Peter, of Sussex Co.; will of. Son, Peter, horses, cow and plow, to make him equal with my eldest son, George. Youngest daughter, Barbary, a cow and wheel, to make her equal with my other daughters. Wife, Cattern, the rest of my estate, and, after her death, to be divided among all my children. Executors—Peter Clickener and George Rasor. Witnesses—John Snuke, Johannis Knoffe, Japheth Byram. Proved March 2, 1769.

1769, Feb. 28. Inventory, £122.6.8, made by Coonrod Gontryman, and Peter Corcelius.

1771, May 25. Account by Peter Cleckner, and George Razor, Executors of Peter Coss. Catherine Cass, Peter Coss and Barbery Cass, were paid their legacies. Lib. 13, p. 552; Lib. 15, p. 104.

CALENDAR OF WILLS—1761-1770   159

1765, April 17. Gerreson, Gerret H., of Achquechnonk, Essex Co.; will of. Debts to be paid by sons, Hendrick and Peter. Son, Hendrick, the large Bible; also that land I bought of Gerret Post. Son, Peter, land on which I live. Son, Peter, to have a suit of clothes, the same as Hendrick had when he married. To the children of my daughter, Margret, dec'd., £125 each, both being under age. Executors—my friend, Michael Vreland, and my two sons. Witnesses— Michael Vreelandt, Poulis Poulison, Jr., David Marinus. Proved Feb. 24, 1766.   Lib. I, p. 257.

1745-6, Feb. 4. Gerritson, Wilhelmus, of Somerset Co., yeoman; will of. Real and personal estate to be sold and the money put to interest for the benefit of my wife and children. Wife, Mary, to have the use of the money till the youngest child is 12 years old. Eldest son, John, my Bible. Sons, John and Samuel, my clothing. Children, John, Eyda, Anna and Samuel, rest. Executors—my brothers, Rem Gerritsen and John Gerritsen. Witnesses—Samuel Gerritsen, Petrus Wyckof, Derrick Kroesen. Proved March 22, 1755.
1768, March 8. Citation, issued to Rem Garritsen, surviving Executor of will of Wilhelmus Garritsen, on complaint of Samuel Garritsen, one of the sons of said deceased, that the said Rem should appear on the 12 of April next and make his account.
Lib. F, p. 255; Lib. I, p. 214.

1767, Dec. 28. Gibbon, Leonard, of Cumberland Co.; will of. Wife, Mary, some moveable estate and rents of real, to bring up my children. Son, Mason, my plantation, called the Mill place; also the place where John Mulford lives. Wife to take care of son, Mason, till he is 10 years old; then my Executor shall put him to learning. Daughter, Rebecka Gibbons, that tract above the mill pond. Daughter, Martha Gibbons, plantation where Ananias Sayre, Jr., lives. Executors—my brother, John Gibbons, and Doctor Samuel Ward. Witnesses—Ananias Sayre, Jr., Samuel Fithian, Dan Simkins. Proved Jan. 27, 1768.
1768, Jan. 29. Inventory, £542.10.0, made by Ananias Sayre, Jr., and Dan Simkins.   Lib. 13, p. 319.

1768, July 21. Gibbs, Elizabeth, of Mansfield Twsp., Burlington Co., widow; will of. Sons, Richard Gibbs and Francis Gibbs, £50 each. My two daughters, Elizabeth Gibbs and Mary Gibbs, residue. Executors—said two daughters. Witnesses—Sarah Atkinson, Samuel Black, Proved Oct. 19, 1768.
1768, Oct. 12. Inventory, £162.5.5, made by Samuel Black and Benjamin Gibbs.   Lib. 13, p. 462.

1766, July 19. Giberson, Hannah, of Monmouth Co., widow; will of. To my son, John's, son Guisbert, £1. The rest of my estate I give to my daughters, Elizabeth, Easther, Helanor, Elydia and Mary, and to my granddaughters, Meribah (the daughter of my daughter Meribah), Elizabeth, (the daughter of my daughter Hannah). Said Meribah is single and under age; also Elizabeth is single. Executors—Moses Laird and Samuel Forman. Witnesses—Gisbert Giberson, John Everingham, James Gaston. Proved Jan. 3, 1767.
Lib. 12, p. 467.

1767, Dec. 2. Gibson, Luke, of Deptford, Gloucester Co., yeoman. Int. Adm'rs—James Cooper and Joshua Lord; yeomen. Fellowbondsman—Joseph Gibson, yeoman; all of said place. Witness—Samuel Mickle.
1767, Dec. 5. Inventory, £223.6.3, made by Richard Clarke and Benjamin Heritage. Lib. 13, p. 278.

1762, Sept. 1. Giddes, John, of Somerset Co., yeoman; will of. Wife, Prudence, the use of my estate till my oldest son, John, is 21. Sons, John, Jeremiah and Asher, my lands; and they shall maintain my daughter, Rachel. Executors—my wife and friend, Robert Carliel. Witnesses—Joseph Brown, Robert Dennes, Abraham Van Tuyl. Proved Oct. 19, 1762.
1762, Oct. 16. Inventory, £261.7.1, made by Joseph Brown and Abraham Van Tuyl. Lib. H, p. 191.

1762, Aug. 23. Giffin, David, of Perth Amboy, Middlesex Co. Int. Adm'r—John Griggs, principal creditor. Fellowbondsman—Peter McClean; both of said place.
1762, June 28. Renunciation by George Giffing on his father's estate, in favor of John Griggs.
1762, Aug. 18. Inventory, made by Robert King and Alexander Campbell. Goods were retained by Mary Harriot for board.
Lib. H, p. 178.

1762, April 14. Gifford, Archer, of New Germantown, Hunterdon Co. Int. Adm'x—Catherine Gifford, widow of said Archer. Fellowbondsmen—John Mehelm and John Welsh. Lib. H, p. 78.

1767, Dec. 29. Gifford, Samuel, of Shrewsbury, Monmouth Co.; will of. To James Gifford, the eldest son of my brother, Josiah, 5 shillings. Wife, Hannah, rest of my real and personal. Executrix—my wife, Hannah. Witnesses—Thomas Van Norte, Catherine Van Norte, Azariah Hunt. Proved Jan. 30, 1769.
1769, Jan. 23. Inventory, £81.5.0, made by Thomas Van Norte and Azariah Hunt. Lib. K, p. 54.

1764, Dec. 24. Gill, Thomas, of Chester, Burlington Co., yeoman; will of. Wife, Mary, £50 and the goods she brought when I married her. Daughter, Hannah Gill, spoons marked "H. G.," also £20. Son, Thomas, ½ of my lands where I live, when 21. Other ½ of land to be sold. Executors—friends, Samuel Stokes and John Lippincott. Witnesses—James Borden, William Wallace, John Cox. Proved Jan. 20, 1765.
1765, Jan. 18. Inventory, £192.4.11, made by John Cox and Job Haines. Lib. 12, p. 45.
1770, July 2. Account by Samuel Stokes and John Lippincott, Ex'rs. "Plantation sold to William Wallace, £719." Lib. 15, p. 11.

1769, May 26. Gilliland, David, of New Brunswick, Middlesex Co.; will of. Eldest son, James, 10 shillings. Son, John, a like amount. Daughters, Mary Loyel, Catherine Lucar, Margaret Denton, Elinor and Elizabeth, each 10 shillings. Son, David, 80 acres of my plantation, and to my youngest son, Mathew, the rest of my plantation where I live. Wife, Elizabeth, the use of said plantation while she lives. Executors—my wife, and son, David. Witnesses—John Wetherill, Jr., Isaac Snedeker, John McCormick. Proved June 13, 1769. Lib. K, p. 111.

CALENDAR OF WILLS—1761-1770   161

1770, July 11. Gilljohnson, Errick, of Lower Penns Neck, Salem Co., yeoman. Int. Adm'r—William Gilljohnson. Fellowbondsmen—Sinnick Sinnickson and John Park; all of said place, yeomen.
1770, Feb. 24. Inventory, £56.15.0, made by Sinnick Sinnickson and John Park.   Lib. 15, p. 7.

1770, July 11. Gilljohnson, Errick, of Lower Penns Neck, Salem Co., yeoman; will of. Lands to be sold. To Michael Butler, £20. John Park, £15. Rest to John Park, Jean Mecum, and Ann Lambson. Catharine Allman to have a share. Executor—David Edmiston. Witnesses—Anne Peterson, Margaret Pennington, Ann Peterson, Jr. Proved July 31, 1770.
1770, July 30. Inventory, £211.15.5, made by Andrew Sinnickson and Sinnick Sinnickson. Account against the Township for £9.
    Lib. 15, p. 59.

1761, March 22. Gilljohnson, Henry, of Penns Neck, Salem Co.; will of. Wife, Cathrine Gilljohnson, her dowry of my lands. Son, Ereck, £80. Son, William Gilljohnson, my lands, when he is 21. Daughter, Ann Jenkens, £3. Executor—son, Ereck Gilljohnson. Witnesses—Michel Butler, Martin Gilljohnson, John Poog. Proved March 11, 1763.
1763, March 11. Inventory, £94.11.0, made by Andrew Sinnickson and Thomas Thackra.   Lib. 11, p. 398.

1767, Sept. 26. Gilljohnson, John, of Lower Penns Neck, Salem Co., yeoman; will of. Lands to be sold. Wife, Isabella Gilljohnson, to have moveables. The money to be given to my four daughters, except my daughter, now Ann Philpot, is to have £20 less than the rest. Daughter, Catharine, a bed. Daughter, Rebecca, a table. Daughter, Margaret, a cupboard. Executors—Sinnick Sinnickson, of Lower Penns Neck. Witnesses—Francis Philpot, Samuel Elwell, David Edmiston. Proved Dec. 4, 1767.
1767, Nov. 28. Inventory, £148.9.3, made by Andrew Standly and David Edmiston.   Lib. 14, p. 96.

1764, March 14. Gilman, Abraham, of Stow Creek, Cumberland Co. Int. Adm'x—Rachel Gilman, widow, of said place. Fellowbondsman—John Soullard, of Deerfield, said Co., yeoman. Witness—David Long.
1764, March 13. Inventory, £133.19.9, made by David Long and John Soullard.   Lib. 12, p. 6.

1765, July 18. Ginnet, Margaret, of Mount Holly, Burlington Co. Int. Adm'r—George Hunsinger. Fellowbondsman—Joseph Butterworth; both of Mount Holly. Witness—Robert Burchan.
1765, July 17. Inventory, £17.10.6, made by Stacy Budd and Joseph Butterworth.   Lib. 12, p. 126.
1766, July 17. Account by Adm'r.

1770, Sept. 25. Glan, Gabriel, of Fairfield, Cumberland Co. Int. Adm'r—John Robbins. Fellowbondsman—David Shepherd, yeoman; both of said place.
1770, Sept. 18. Inventory, £309.7.2, made by David Shepherd and William Dalles.
1774, June 18. Account made by John Robbens. Includes payment to "Gabriel Glan, £64.14.10."   Lib. 15, p. 74.

11

1762, April 14. Glover, Uriah, of Roxbury, Morris Co.; will of. Wife, Martha, ½ of my furniture. Son, John, 5 shillings. Daughters, Rebecca Hull and Martha Hull, like sum of 5 shillings. Son, Charles, £20 when 21. Daughter, Deborah, rest of goods. Son, Uriah Glover, all my lands. Executors—my wife and son, Uriah. Witnesses—Obadiah Seward, Frederick King, Constant King. Proved Nov. 20, 1769. Lib. K, p. 216.

1762, Aug. 18. Godly, William, of Mansfield Woodhouse, Sussex Co., yeoman; will of. Real and personal to be sold. I order £400 used to bring up my younger children. Wife, Mary, 1/3 the remainder. Children—Ann, Rebecca, Edward, Achsah, Mary, William, John and Joseph, the other two-thirds. Executors—my wife and Joseph King, Sr., of Amwell. Witnesses—Nathaniel Skiner, Robert Laning, Richard Shackleton. Proved Nov. 16, 1762. Lib. 11, p. 366.

1767, Sept. 4. Goelet, Francis, of Perth Amboy, Middlesex Co. Int. Adm'x—Elizabeth Goelet, the widow. Fellowbondsman—Samuel Sarjant; both of said place. Witness—John Berrien.
1767, Sept. 12. Inventory, £137.12.7, made by Jonathan Deare and John Griggs. Lib. I, p. 152.

1761, July 12. Goff, Jeremiah, of Morrices River, Cumberland Co.; will of. "Being old." Wife, Asenath Goff, furniture. Son, Joseph, plantation where I live. Sons—Joseph Jeremiah Goff, Nathan Goff and John Goff, land I bought of Nicholas Cruesen, of 318 acres. Eldest son, Joseph, to pay the debt I owe said Cruesen. Daughters, Mary Goff and Hannah Goff, rest of moveables. Executors—wife and son, Joseph. Witnesses—John Davis, Samuel Heaton, Levi Heaton. Proved Aug. 25, 1761.
1761, Aug. 17. Inventory, £113.13.6, made by John Bragg, and John Terry. Lib. 11, p. 162.

1754, April 11. Goff, John, of Upper Precinct, Cape May Co.; yeoman; will of. Wife, Mary, ⅓ of moveable estate. Sons, David, and John, my lands in Cape May Co. Sons, William and Thomas, my lands in Cumberland Co. Executor—wife, Mary, while my widow, but, if she marry, then son, David. Witnesses—Joseph Savage, Clement Daniels, Deborah Daniels. Proved Feb. 11, 1761.
1761, Feb. 17. Inventory, £27.8.7, made by Levi Crandal and William Robinson. Lib. 10, p. 164.

1768, May 31. Goff, Margaret, of Cape May Co. Int. Adm'r—John Cresse. Fellowbondsman—John Smith; both of said Co. Witness—Elihu Smith.
1768, May 31. Inventory, £46.19.2, made by John Smith and Elihu Smith. Lib. 13, p. 442.

1765, March 12. Goff, Silas, of Cape May Co., weaver; will of. Wife, Rachel, one half of my estate while my widow. Daughters, Hannah and Phebe, my lands and cedar swamp. Executors—my wife and my father, William Goff. Witnesses—William Goff, Mary Norton, John Cresse. Proved Feb. 21, 1767, by John Cresse, the other two witnesses being dead.
1767, Jan. 9. Inventory, £134.6.1½, made by Lewis Cresse and John Smith. Lib. 13, p. 137.

1765, Dec. 15. Goff, William, of Cape May Co., yeoman; will of. Wife, Margaret, 1/3 of my moveables, and the other 2/3 to my daughters, Mary, Hanahah, Prissiller and Rhoda. Son, Silus, plantation where he lives. Son, William, plantation where I live, one acre excepted. Daughter, Hannah, Cresse, one acre whereon her "fraim" now stands, during her widowhood. Son, William, a bond. Executors—wife, Margaret, and sons, Silus and William Goof. Witnesses—Daniel Hildreth, Benjamin Stites, Lydia Foster.
1765, Dec. 16. Codicil. Witnesses—John Leonard, Lydia Foster, Mathas Foster, Anne Leonard. Proved Jan. 18, 1766.
1766, April 18. Inventory, £113.3.8, made by John Shaw and Lewis Cresse. Lib. 12, p. 344.

1763, April 27. Gogen, Edmond, of Morris River, Cumberland Co. Int. Adm'r—Joseph Savage, of Cape May Co. Fellowbondsman—Levi Crandal, of Morris River. Witness—Thomas Ewing.
1763, April 26. Inventory, £18.5.9, made by Levi Crandal and Joseph Lord. File No. 28 F.

1765, March 13. Goldin, John, of Morris River Twsp., Cumberland Co.; will of. Wife, Rebecca, moveable estate, except things given to son, Samuely. Wife, 2/3 of my land. Daughter, Sary Garrison, 5 shillings, and the like sum to my daughter, Mary Smith, and to Judeth Goldin, Hannah Goldin, Rebecca Goldin, Catherine Goldin, Rachel Goldin, and Jean Goldin, my children, each 5 shillings. Executors—friend, John Mackey, and my wife. Witnesses—John Willets and James Goldin. Proved Dec. 20, 1766.
1766, Dec. 22. Inventory, £161.11.4, made by Joseph Champion and Andrew Godfrey. Lib. 12, p. 353.

1761, Nov. 3. Goldsmith, William, of Suffolk Co., New York. Int. Adm'r—Joseph Goldsmith, of said place, brother to said William. Fellowbondsman—Job Camp, of Essex Co. Lib. H, p. 36.

1769, Feb. 16. Gomez, Isaac, of New York, merchant; will of. Wife, Deborah Gomez, an annuity of £150, and the use of the house and lot on Queen's Street, said City, where I dwell, and all my plate and the slaves she wants. After the death of my wife I give to my daughter, Ester Gomez, £600, and ½ my plate. To the Ruler of the Jewish Synagogue in this City, £15. Rest of my personal and real to my son, Mattathias. Executor—son, Mattathias. Witnesses—John Dunlap, Jonathan Morrell, Moses Smith. Proved Oct. 23, 1770. Lib. K, p. 330.

1770, July 16. Goold, James, of Essex Co., joiner; will of. Sons, Samuel and John Goold, all my land, when John comes of age. Granddaughter, Cate Arvey, 2 cows and household goods. Executors—Bethuel Pierson and Benjamin Baldwin. Witnesses—Bethuel Pierson, Jonas Whittemore. Proved Aug. 5, 1770. Lib. K, p. 230.

1768, Sept. 16. Gordon, John, Jr., of Freehold, Monmouth Co. Int. Adm'r—David Gordon, his father. Fellowbondsman—John Longstreet, Jr.; both of said place. Witness—Henry Waddell.
File No. 3449 M.

1765, Oct. 24. Gorman, Thomas, of Trenton, Hunterdon Co. Int. Adm'r—William Tucker. Fellowbondsman—John Chambers; both of said place.
1765, Oct. 30. Inventory, £10.19.5, made by Charles Oxford and Thomas Barnes. Lib. 12, p. 245.

1765, Aug. 2. Gould, John, of Acquacnonck Twsp., Essex Co., farmer; will of. Son, John, the improvement lying in Horseneck purchase. Son, Joseph, 1/3 my homestead, and 1/3 the land in the English purchase, and also his house. Son, Stephen, 1/3 the homestead, and 1/3 of land in English purchase. Son, Samuel, 1/3 the homestead, and 1/3 the land in English purchase. Those sons are to maintain my wife, Abigail. Daughter, Sarah Ryker, her oldest son, £8, and to her second son, £9, and to Sarah Ryker, £8. Elizabeth Brower to have a cow. Executors—sons, John and Joseph, and my brother, Thomas Gould. Witnesses—Sarah Gould, Joseph Cory, Jemima Day. Proved May 30, 1766. Lib. I, p. 54.

1765, Sept. 9. Goulden, Joseph, of Dearfield Twsp., Cumberland Co.; will of. Eldest son, John, my saw mill. Son, Joseph, my grist mill. Son, Samuel, 80 acres, when 21. Daughters, Sarah Golder, and Abilal (Abigail) Golder, £3. Executors—sons, John and Joseph. Witnesses—Daniel Moore, Mark Bowen, James Loper, Jr. Proved Oct. 23, 1765.
1765, Oct. 18. Inventory, £155.18.3¼, made by James Loper and Mark Bowen. Lib. 12, p. 243.

1769, Sept. 19. Graham, George, of Maidenhead, Hunterdon Co.; will of. Wife, Mary, £60 of lands, and, after death of wife, my niece, Lydia Noble, shall have £60. Son, William, now in England, my watch. My three children, now living in Co. of Cumberland, England, viz., William, John and Jane Collins, £100. Nephew, Jacob Noble, my apparel. Daughter, Frances, the daughter of Ruth Touson, rest of my real and personal. Executors—my wife, Mary, and my daughter, Frances, and my friend Ralph Hunt. Witnesses—John Johnson, Azariah Hunt, William McCoy. Proved Oct. 28, 1769.
Lib. 14, p. 130.

1761, Nov. 1. Graham, Mary, of Bedminster, Somerset Co.; will of. Granddaughter, Mary Jones, wife of Jonathan Jones, £5. Granddaughter, Mary McEowen, £10. Granddaughter, Mary Hannah, wife of Rev. John Hannah, £5. Grandson, Stephen McCrea, son of Rev. James McCrea, £10. Granddaughter, Mary Graham, daughter of William Graham, £10. Daughter, Sarah Henry, wife of Daniel Henry, goods. Rest to son, William Graham, son, James Graham, and daughter, Sarah Henry. Executors—my children, William and James Graham, and Sarah Henry. Witnesses—Garret Voorhees, Ezekiel Akeley, Andrew Porter. Proved June 8, 1763. Lib. H, p. 255.

1760, Nov. 15. Graisbury, James, of Newton Twsp., Gloucester Co.; will of. Sons, James, Joseph and Benjamen, all my real estate in Newton. Daughter, Mary Franklin, £100. Daughter, Ann Warner, £100. Wife, Mary, remainder. Executors—sons, James, and Joseph. Witnesses—Joseph Thackray, Stephen Thackray. Proved Dec. 30, 1762.
1762, Dec. 24. Inventory, £470.12.0¾, made by John Branson and David Branson. Lib. 11, p. 282.

1762, July 8. Grant, John, of Bernards Town, Somerset Co., yeoman; will of. Wife, Eleanor, £50 that were left her by her father, 2 cows and household goods, and ⅓ the profits of my plantation while my widow. The north end of my plantation, next to Aaron Boylon, I give to my son, David. Son, George, my house and ⅓ the land. Son, John, the other third. Daughter, Martha, £50. Daughter, Christial, £50. Daughter, Elenor, £50. Daughter, Margrete, £50, when she is 17. Daughter, Mary, £50, when 17. Son, John, is not yet 21. Executors—wife, Elenor, and my brothers-in-law, Peter Williamson and Francis Coarsort. Witnesses—Jonathan Ayers, Nathaniel Ayers, James Kilpatrick, John Roy. Proved Aug. 12, 1762.

1762, Aug. 19. Inventory, £418.0.6, made by Peter Williamson and Francis Cossaart, Executors; and Nathaniel Ayers and William Annin, appraisers. Lib. H, p. 173.

1756, March 2. Gray, Jacob, of Amwell Twsp., Hunterdon Co.; will of. Eldest son, Isaac, £10. Wife, Ann, use of all real and personal estate to bring up my children. Sons, Isaac, and Aurt, all my lands. Daughter, Elizabeth, £50. Daughter, Susannah, £50. Daughter, Ann, £50. Daughter, Mary, £50. Executors—my wife, Ann; son, Isaac, and my friend, Cornelius Weigheoff. Witnesses—Hugh Hunter, Sarah Mattison, Jacob Mattison. Proved Jan. 13, 1764.

1763, Dec. 7. Inventory, £524.7.2, made by Thomas Atkinson and Gershom Lee. Lib. 11, p. 523.

1763, Dec. 30. Green, Ephraim, of Somerset Co. Int. Adm'rs— Gershom Conger and Mary, his wife, late Mary Green, widow of Ephraim Green, they being of Middlesex Co. Fellowbondsman— James Conger, of Somerset Co. Lib. H, p. 323.

1769, Sept. 6. Green, Henry, of Shrewsbury, Monmouth Co.; will of. Son, Henry, farm on west side of Whale Pond, bounded by the sea, William Jackson, Richard Jeffery and the Whale Pond. Son, William, £150. Sons, John and Jeams, plantation where I live. Daughter, Sarah, wife of Joseph Cook, £20. Daughter, Rachel, wife of Vincent White, £20. Daughters, Rebecca and Elizabeth, £25 each. Daughters, Mary, wife of William Perce, and Charity, wife of Thomas White, only one shilling each, by reason of their husband's misbehavior. To Rebecca Leaqusie, £20. Wife, Rebecca, all estate while my widow. Executors—my wife and four sons. Witnesses—Cornelius Lane, Gideon Tallman, Lewis Jeffery. Proved Jan. 5, 1770.

1769, Dec. 12. Inventory, made by Job Cook and Cornelius Lane. Lib. K, p. 159.

1763, March 1. Green, Joseph, of Evesham, Burlington Co., weaver. Int. Adm'x—Sarah Green. Fellowbondsmen—Charles French and Nathan Haines; all of said Co.

1763, Feb. 24. Inventory, £78.16.9, made by Charles French and Nathan Haines. Lib. 11, p. 269.

1766, Sept. 16. Green, Robert, of Greenwich Twsp., Sussex Co.; will of. Wife, Eve, my whole estate till my son John is 21; then he to have ½ the plantation, and my wife the other half. Wife is pregnant, and that child is provided for. The plantation on Scotts Hill to be rented. Daughter, Elizabeth Green, £40 when 18. Daughter, Mary Green, £40. Daughter, Jean Green, £40 when 18. Daugh-

ter, Lyda Green, £45 when 18. When Lydia comes of age the plantation on the hill to be sold. Executrix—wife, Eve. Witnesses—Alexander White, John Maxwell, Andres Yong. Proved Nov. 26, 1766.
1766, Oct. 9. Inventory, £258.1.6, made by John Maxwell and Alexander White. Lib. 12, p. 431.

1763, March 17. Griffing, William, Jr., of Roxbury, Morris Co.; will of. Sons, John and Gabriel, all my lands where I live bought by my father of Benjamin Maning and John Throckmorton, and 10 acres on the mountain that I bought of Ephraim Hopkins. Daughter, Sarah Griffing, £20. Children all under age, and, if they die, then ½ the lands to be my wife's, and the other half to go to my five brothers, Zodok, Robard, Ebenezer, Jasper and Francis. Wife, Hannah, rest of moveable estate. Executors—father, William Griffing, and Aaron Starke. Witnesses—Jabesh Haton, William Dugles, Jr., Zophar Carns. Proved May 2, 1764.
1764, May 8. Inventory, made by Aaron Starke and William Baird.
Lib. H, p. 435.

1762, March 23. Griggs, Benjamin, of Somerset Co., yeoman; will of. Son, Daniel, £200. Grandson, Benjamin Griggs, son of John Griggs, deceased, £25. Children, Samuel, Barrent, Benjamin, Daniel, Reuben, and daughters Martha Vanderbeek (wife of Rem Vanderbeeck), Jane Bennitt (wife of Aron Bennitt), and Elianer Sutfin (wife of John Sutfin), rest of my estate. Wife to be supported. Executors—my sons, Samuel and Daniel, and son-in-law Rem Vanderbeck. Witnesses—Nicholas Veghte, Francis Feurt, Isaac Wilkins. Proved Feb. 23, 1768. Lib. I, p. 214.

1768, Jan. 20. Griggs, Benjamin, of Somerset Co. Int. Adm'r—Daniel Griggs, one of the sons and principal creditor.
1768, Jan. 18. Inventory, £261.7.0, made by Andrew Gordon and John Feavel. Lib. I, p. 208.

1761, Nov. 17. Griggs, Daniel, of Amwell Twsp., Hunterdon Co.; will of. Brothers, John, Jocham and Samuel, all my real estate left me by my father, and they to pay to my sisters, Catherine, Mary and Margaret, the legacies that my father ordered. Executors—brothers, John, Jocham and Samuel. Witnesses—Peter Peterson, Jacob Mattison, John Young. Proved Sept. 27, 1762. Lib. 11, p. 341.

1765, Jan. 31. Griggs, Reuben, of Somerset Co., physician; will of. Brother, Barrent Griggs, £150, to be deducted from the bonds he gave me for the place he now lives on in Sower Land. I discharge my brother, Daniel, from the debts due me for my doctoring. Rest of personal and real to be sold, except my apparel, and divided in six parts. To my brother, John's children, one part. To my brother, Samuel, one part. To brother, Barrent, one part. Brother, Daniel, one part. Brother, Benjamin's, children, one part. Sister, Jane's, children, one part. Sister, Martha, one part. To the children of my sister, Eleanor, which she has by Theodorus Monfort, late deceased, and the children which she has by John Sutfin, one part. [Make 7 parts]. My apparel I give to Benjamin Griggs, James Griggs, Daniel Griggs, John Griggs and William Griggs, sons of my brother, John. Executors—my brother, Samuel Griggs, and my brothers-in-law, John Sutfin and Rem VanderBeek. Witnesses—Cornelius Simonson,

Samuel Smith, Jan Seymesen. Before signing, I give to Adrian Bennet's 2 daughters, Margaret and Barbary, £8 each, above what I have already given them. Proved March 18, 1765.
1773, June 1. Account by Executors. Includes "Land sold at Kingston, £175.13.4." Lib. H, p. 500.

1758, March 8. Griggs, Thomas, of Bordentown, Burlington Co., "laybour;" will of. My half brother, Gersham Wollin, 20 shillings. Niece, Edeth Updike, £20, when 18. Wife, Ann, my house in Bordentown and the residue. Executors—my wife and my friend, Edward Williams. Witnesses—John Thompson, Robert Ashton, Samuel Farnsworth. Proved May 23, 1763.
1763, May 20. Inventory, £387.17.5, made by Samuel Shourds and John Browne. Lib. 11, p. 329.

1757, Aug. 19. Groom, Peter, Sr., of Windsor, Middlesex Co., yeoman; will of. Son, Peter, £5. Daughter, Sarah Nawley, £10. William Updick, £30, for 10 acres of land I bought of him; and I give said 10 acres to my son, Thomas; also the meadow on south side of Sanpink, above the Cross Ditch, of 4 acres, which joins Thomas Tindal; also 30 acres of upland on south side of Sanpink. Son, Moses, my house and plantation, where I live. Wife, Elizabeth, my moveable estate, and the profits of my plantation, till son, Moses, is 21. If Rachel Garrison live with my wife till she is 18, she is to have a cow. If Thomas Edgment, who lives with me, inclines to live with my family, then he is to have a decent funeral. Executors—son, Peter, and Moses Groom. Witnesses—Joseph Skelton, William Updike, Dominicus Covenhoven. Proved March 4, 1768.
1768, Feb. 23. Inventory, £20.19.6, made by Dominicus Covenhoven and William Updike. Lib. 13, p. 315.

1750, April 13. Guisbertson, Guisbert, of Monmouth Co., yeoman; will of. Wife, Hannah, use of all my lands, a house in Allentown, and 3 lots near the same town; and, after her death, all to be sold, and £50 given to each of my son, John's, children, and the rest to be given to my own daughters. To Guisbert Guisbertson, the son and heir of my eldest son and heir, John, deceased, 5 shillings. To Guisbert Guisbertson and William Guisbertson, (my sons), the plantation where I live. Moveable estate to be sold and money divided between my daughters, Elizabeth, Esther, Hannah, Meribah, Helena, Lydia and Mary Guisbertson; but Elizabeth and Esther shall have £20 less than the others. Executors—wife, Hannah; son, Guisbert Guisbertson, and my brother-in-law, Samuel Parent. Witnesses—Daniel Williams, John Cox, William Lawrence. Proved May 19, 1766.
1766, May 9. Inventory, £1,147.13.0, made by David Gordon, Samuel Forman, Jr., and Moses Laird. Lib. 12, p. 443.

1768, Oct. 12. Hackenburger, Herbert, of Lebanon, Hunterdon Co., yeoman; will of. My wife, ⅓ of my estate. Son, John, 5 shillings. My wife, Margaret, has hers forever. Children—John, Peter. Foost, Henry, Christopher, Harman, Eve Anney, Elsse, Margret, Anna Elizabeth, Elizabeth, Catren and Mary, the rest. Executor—son, Peter. Witnesses—Nicholas Linnenberger, William Albach, Herbert Rodenbah. Proved June 13, 1769.
1769, June 8. Inventory, £75.10.3, made by Nicholas Linnenberger, and Johannes Brodenbach.
1771, Feb. 16. Account by Executor. Lib. 14, p. 58; Lib. 15, p. 103.

1766, Oct. 25. Hackett, John, of Sussex Co. Int. Adm'rs—Elizabeth Hackett, Archibald Stewart, Joseph Reed, Jr. Fellowbondsmen—Thomas Reading and Thomas Lowrey. Witness—John Sherrerd. Lib. 13, p. 199.

1767, Aug. 6. Hackett, Samuel, of Hunterdon Co. Ward. Son and heir of John Hackett, late of Sussex Co., who makes petition, as also Elizabeth Hackett, his mother, and John Reading, her father, that George Reading may be made Guardian.
1767, Aug. 6. Guardian—George Reading, of Mansfield Woodhouse Twsp., Sussex Co. Fellowbondsmen—Charles Stewart, of Kingwood, Hunterdon Co., yeoman, and Isaac De Cow, of Trenton. (The above Elizabeth Hackett, the mother, is now about to leave the Province).
Lib. 14, p. 125.

1769, Oct. 26. Hackett, Samuel, of Hunterdon Co. Ward. Petition of George Reading, stating that his sister, Elizabeth Hackett, lately arriving from Europe, and having been Guardian of her son, Samuel Hackett, during her absence, now desires that she may be made his Guardian.
1769, Oct. 27. Guardian—Elizabeth Hackett. Fellowbondsmen—Joseph Reading and Samuel Tucker, all of said Co. Lib. 14, p. 125.

1761, July 5. Hackney, Elizabeth, of Chester Twsp., Burlington Co.; will of. To my sister, Rebeckah Matlack's (deceased) four daughters, viz., Mary, Susannah, Elizabeth and Rebeckah, £10 each and my apparel, when 18. Cousin, Jeremiah Ozban, £20, when 21. My brother, Thomas Hackney's, eldest son, viz., William, £5, when 21. Brother, Joseph Hackney's, eldest son, viz., Joshua, £5, when 21. My cousin, Susannah Dudley, £5, when 18. Brother, Joseph Hackney, my Bible. Brothers, Thomas and Joseph Hackney, residue. Executor—brother, Joseph. Witnesses—Noah Haines, Hannah Turner, Jonas Cattell. Proved June 11, 1762.
1762, May 28. Inventory, £175.19.6, made by Darling Conaroe and Richard Borden. Lib. 11, p. 197.

1762, April 16. Haff, Lawrence, of Kingwood Twsp., Hunterdon Co.; will of. Son, Lawrence Haff, Jr., 5 shillings. Wife, Martha, rest of the estate, during her life, and then to go to John Haff, Cornelius Haff, Abraham Haff, Richard Haff, Coneactia Jones, and my son, Lawrence Haff's, children, and my daughter, Margaret Palmer's, children. Executors—my wife, Martha, Cornelius Haff and Benjamin Jones. My son, Peter Haff's child, shall have an equal share of my estate. Witnesses—John Emley, Rebeckah Stevenson, Jane Stevenson. Proved Nov. 4, 1762.
1762, Aug. 26. Inventory, £322.8.0, made by John Emley and Samuel Baker.
1769, Feb. 17. Account by Benjamin Jones, surviving and acting Executor of the estate of Lawrence Hoff. Includes paying John Hoff, for keeping Martha Hoff, the widow, in her illness, for 4 years and 7 months at 15 s. per week £178.8.0. Lib. 11, p. 359; Lib. 13, p. 494.

1754, Aug. 8. Hageman, Adrian, of Somerset Co.; will of. Wife, Mary, £30 yearly. I have provided for all my sons, except Simon and Benjamin, by giving them a deed for lands; so now I give to sons, Simon and Benjamin, the plantation where I live, of 350 acres. My personal estate I give to all my children, Hendrick, John, Adrian, Joseph, Simon, Jacobus and Benjamin; and my daughters, viz., Geertje, married to John Manley; Mary, married to Adrian Hegeman, and Cathrine, married to Samuel Waldron.
Some of my sons, and sons-in-law gave me bonds, viz., John Hegeman, 6 of Aug., 1744, for £350; Adrian Hegeman, 15 of May, 1749, for £132; Joseph Hegeman, 12 of March, 1754, for £97; Simon Hegeman, 1754, for £400; Jacobus Hegeman, 20 of May, 1754, for £300; John Manley, 15 of May, 1749, for £12; Adrian Hegeman, my son-in-law, 1754, for 68; Benjamin Hegeman, 1754, for £400. Executors— sons, Hendrick, John, and Simon. Witnesses—William Ouke, Henry Bicker, Abraham Heyer. Proved July 27, 1762.
1762, June 22. Inventory, £440.9.2, made by Cornelus De Hart, Peter Sedam, and Andrew Brown. Lib. H, p. 165.

1765, June 22. Hager, John, of Roxberry, Morris Co. Int. Adm'r —Lawrence Hager. Fellowbondsman—John Piser; both of said place. Lib. 12, p. 225.

1768, Feb. 19. Haines, Anthony, of Salem Co. Int. Adm'rs—Jemima Haines, widow, of Mannington, and Hugh Haines, yeoman, of said place. Fellowbondsmen—David Allen, of Mannington, yeoman, and Jacob Hollinshead, of Town of Salem, watch maker.
1768, Feb. 20. Inventory, £74.15.4, made by David Allen and John Johnson. Lib. 13, p. 334

1767, Aug. 18. Haines, Daniel, of Springfield, Burlington Co., yeoman; will of. Son, Moses, 5 shillings. Son, Thomas, 5 shillings. Son, Joseph, plantation where I dwell; and he is to pay to my son, Simeon, £50, and to my daughter, Priscilla Antram, £6, and to my daughter, Mary Brian, or to her children, 20 shillings, for 7 years. My daughter, Elizabeth Pancost, 5 shillings, she having had hers. Executor—son, Joseph. Witnesses—Jacob Merrit, John Woolman, Thomasin Merrit. Proved Oct. 7, 1767.
1767, Sept. 28. Inventory, £35.14.3, made by John Fenimore and William Ridgway. Lib. 13, p. 99.
1770, Oct. 25. Account by Executors. Lib. 15, p. 64.

1765, Dec. 26. Haines, Edmund, of Evesham, Burlington Co.; will of. Brother, Simeon, to have negro, Phillip. Wife, Elizabeth, personal estate, and use of real while my widow, to help bring up my children. Daughters, Sarah and Hannah, my lands. Brother, Isaiah. Executors—my wife and my brother-in-law, Joseph Warrington. Witnesses—Hannah French, Elizabeth French, Isaac Evens. Proved Feb. 21, 1766.
1766, Feb. 14. Inventory, £672.8.10, made by Isaac Evans and John Cox. Lib. 12, p. 288.

1766, Aug. 26. Haines, Grace, of Evesham, Burlington Co., widow of Abram Haines; will of. Son, Isaac Haines, £50, and daughter, Grace, £10, when she is 18. Son, Simeon, £30, if he lives six months after my death. Son, Isaiah Haines, £50. Daughter, Agness Hackney, my apparel, and to her daughter, Grace, a bed when 18. Granddaughter, Grace, the daughter of my son Joshua, dec'd, and Mary Haines, daughter of Joshua, dec'd, a Bible. To son, Abram's, daughter, Catherine, and to son, Benjamin's daughter, Mary, each a Bible. Granddaughter, Mary Sharp, £7 when 18. Grandson, Thomas Haines, a Bible. Son, Simeon, his bed. Executors—sons, Benjamin and Noah. Witnesses—Isaac Evens, Martha West, Samuel Evens. Proved Nov. 7, 1769.

1769, July 31. Inventory, £889.11.4, made by William Foster and Isaac Evans. Lib. 14, p. 142; 8535 C.

1768, Feb. 11. Haines, Joseph, of Salem Co. Int. Adm'rs—Ann Haines, of Mannington, widow; and John Barnes, of Pilesgrove, yeoman. Fellowbondsmen—Richard Haines, of Pilesgrove, yeoman, and Jacob Hollinshead, of Town of Salem, watchmaker.

1768, Feb. 15. Inventory, £365.15.11, made by William Harvey and Ephraim Haines. Lib. 13, p. 333.

1770, June 6. Haines, Margaret, of Northampton Twsp., Burlington Co., widow. Int. Adm'r—Isaac Haines, yeoman. Fellowbondsman—Silvanus Zelley, yeoman; both of said place.

1770, June 10. Inventory, £248.5.¾, made by John Ridgway and Thomas Cooper. Lib. 15, p. 48.

1762, Aug. 27. Haines, Thomas, of Chesterfield Twsp., Burlington Co., yeoman; will of. Sons, Joseph and Thomas Haines, 10 shillings each. Wife, the plantation where I dwell, while my widow. Son, Josiah, said plantation. Daughters, Charity and Rebeckah, £5 each. Executors—my wife, Rebeckah, and my son, Josiah. Witnesses—James Newell, William Ireton, John Newbold. Proved May 2, 1767.

1767, May 11. Inventory, £192.3.3, made by Samuel Taylor and John Newbold. Lib. 13, p. 60.

1765, Dec. 1. Haines, Thomas, of Newton Twsp., Gloucester Co., yeoman; will of. Personal and real estate to be sold, and money to go to my wife, Hannah, to bring up my children. Sons to be put out to trade. Wife, Hannah, is to pay to my son, John, £5 when he is 21. Executors—my wife, and my brother-in-law, Aaron Oakford. Witnesses—John Buzby, William Evens, Gerardus Clarkson. Proved Jan. 29, 1766.

1766, Jan. 21. Inventory, £209.2.0, made by Isaac Mickle and Benjamin Thackray. Lib. 12, p. 285.

1763, June 25. Hall, Benjamin, of Shrewsbury, Monmouth Co. Int. Adm'r—Benjamin Rogers. Fellowbondsman—Samuel Allen; both of Manasquan, in town of Shrewsbury, said Co., yeomen. Witnesses—William Curlies and Robert Ledson.

1763, Nov. 11. Inventory, made by David Johnston and William Brewer. Lib. H, p. 494.

1768, Oct. 29. Hall, Clement, of Elsinboro, Salem Co., yeoman; will of. I give 10 acres of marsh, which my father, William Hall, purchased of William Smith, and lying in Mannington, unto my mother, Elizabeth Hall. I give a part of the lot, whereon Aaron Silver lives, in Salem, joining William Hall's lot, unto Benjamin Acton, son of John Acton. A lot joining to the above unto Sarah Acton wife of Joseph Acton, of Manington, and a lot to Mary Smith, wife of Joseph Smith, of Salem. Rest of lands to be sold, and money given to my children, viz., Prudence, Clement, Sarah, John, Joseph and Morris Hall. Executors—wife, Margaret, and John Mason. Witnesses—Samuel Maines, Thomas Ambler, Grant Gibbon. Proved March 10, 1769. Probate to both Executors Feb. 9, 1769.   Lib. 14, p. 102.

1764, Jan. 25. Hall, Francis, of Burlington Co.; will of. Son, John, a bed. Son, George, a desk. Son, Abel, a chest. Son, Abner, my gun when 21. Son, Joseph, a desk. Daughter, Esther Earl, 5 shillings. Daughter, Sarah Hall, 5 shillings. Daughter, Ann Hall, 5 shillings. Wife, Naomi, rest of personal estate. Executor—my wife. Witnesses—Thomas Middleton, Joseph Steward, George Middleton. Proved Nov. 28, 1764.   Lib. 12, p. 34.

1761, March 25. Hall, John, of Lebanon, Hunterdon Co. Int. Adm'rs —Catharine Hall, of said place, and Richard Hall, of Elizabeth Town, Essex Co. Fellowbondsman—Cornelius Bodine, of Lebanon, Hunterdon Co.   Lib. 10, p. 461.

1768, May 24. Hall, Mable, of Mansfield Twsp., Burlington Co.; will of. Granddaughter, Mary Shoemaker, the daughter of my son, Isaac Shoemaker, silver shoe buckles. Granddaughter, Mable Shoemaker, spoons. Granddaughter, Susanna Shoemaker, the daughter of my son, Benjamin Shoemaker, a bonnet. Cousin, Mary Archer, a teapot. Cousin, Elizabeth Shreve, sidesaddle. Mentions Pheby Kindal, daughter of my sister, Rachel. To Sarah Archer, pillow cases. To Rachel Kindal, pillow cases. To four of my granddaughters, viz., Mary Shoemaker, Mable Shoemaker, Susanna Shoemaker and the youngest daughter of my son, Benjamin Shoemaker, apparel. My house to be sold, and the money to go to my sons, Isaac Shoemaker and Benjamin Shoemaker, and they are to pay to my son, Jacob Shoemaker, £6, and to son, Amos Shoemaker £6. Executors—sons, Isaac and Benjamin Shoemaker. Witnesses—Abner Woolman, Joseph Archer, William Kearns. Proved June 13, 1768.
1768, May 28. Inventory, £16.11.1, made by William White and Joseph Archer.   Lib. 13, p. 424.

1769, Dec. 25. Hall, Thomas, of Bloomingdale, Morris Co. Int. Adm'x—Hannah Hall. Fellowbondsman—Jesse Fairchild, of Charlotte Enburgh. Witness—Abraham Ogden.   File No. 893 B.
1770, Jan. 17. Inventory, £44.14.9, made by Jesse Fairchild and Peter Francisco.   Lib. K, p. 256.

1752, May 20. Hall, William, of Mannington, Salem Co.; will of. Son, Clement Hall, the land in Salem, except 6 acres, which I give to his brother, Edward Hall, and his part to join to his cousin, John Hall. The lands that join to town of Salem I give to sons, Clement and Edward. Son, Nathaniel, plantation I live on, after my wife's death. Daughter, Susannah, and Sarah Acton, £50 each. Wife, Elizabeth, all my "negers." Rest to wife, and my daughters, Elizabeth Hall and Mary Hall. Sons, Clement and Nathan, rest of lands. Executors— my wife and sons, Clement and Nathaniel. Witnesses—Elizabeth Hall, Mary Hall, Adam Cook. Proved Jan. 15, 1761.
1760, July 1. Inventory, £609.2.9, made by Isaac Sharp and Preston Carpenter.   Lib. 10, p. 502.

1761, Nov. 26. Halter, Casper, of Alloways Creek, Salem Co. Int. Adm'r—Richard Wistar. Fellowbondsman—Bartholomew Hyatt, Jr.; both of said Co.
1761, July 23. Inventory, £33.19.6, made by Joseph Thompson and Benjamin Thompson. Lib. 11, p. 37.

1761, June 23. Halter, Francis, of Alloways Creek, Salem Co., doctor of physick. Int. Adm'x—Margaret Halter, widow. Fellowbondsman—William Oakford, yeoman; both of said place.
1761, June 16. Inventory, £109.12.9, made by John Holme and William Oakford. Lib. 10, p. 434.

1767, April 30. Halter, John Martin, of Alloways Creek Twsp., Salem Co., glass blower; will of. My wife to have £50, and what she brought with her. My only son, Peter Halter, £100, and to be coequal with his sisters. I have given £25 to my oldest daughter, Margaret, which is to be allowed in her share. The rest to all my children, who are, son Peter, Margaret, Catharine, and Mary Ann. Executors—son, Peter, and my brother-in-law, Philip Souther. Witnesses—Philip Wentzell, Andrew Roth, William McKasson. Proved Oct. 23, 1767. Lib. 13, p. 266.

1764, Jan. 7. Hambleton, Stephen, of Morristown, Morris Co. Int. Adm'rs—Benjamin Fowler and Joseph Osborn, yeomen; both of said Co. Said Adm'rs are two of the largest creditors. Witness—Jacob Hamton.
1764, Jan. 11. Inventory, £23.6.10, made by Samuel Frost and Joseph Lacy.
1764, Nov. 19. Account by Benjamin Fowler, Adm'r. Lib. H, p. 375.

1769, Sept. 14. Hamilton, Charles, of Alloways Creek, Salem Co.; will of. Wife, Anne, all my real and personal estate, except my apparel, which I give to my brother, John Hamilton. Executrix—my wife, Anne. Witnesses—John Smith, Thomas Test, William Pyfrow. Proved Nov. 17, 1769.
1769, Nov. 9. Inventory, £177.18.6, made by Thomas Test and William Willis. Lib. 14, p. 104.

1762, Oct. 4. Hamilton, Hannah, of Cape May Co. Int. Adm'r—William Simkins. Fellowbondsman—Ephraim Kent; both of said Co. Witnesses—Jacob Richardson and Daniel Cresse.
1762, March 6. Inventory, £28.15.5, of Hannah Hamilton, widow, made by Ephraim Kent and Ephraim Bancroft. File No. 231 E.

1766, Oct. 14. Hamilton, John, of Middlesex Co. Int. Adm'r—William Sickals. Fellowbondsman—Newel Ferman; both of Somerset Co.
1766, Oct. 14. Renunciation, by Sarah Hamilton in favor of William Sekels, the largest creditor.
1766, Oct. 18. Inventory of estate of John Hamilton, of Windsor Twsp., carpenter, made by Chris Doughty, John Sickels, Ephraim Maning, John Rozel and Joseph Olden. Lib. I, p. 6.

1766, Oct. 9. Hamilton, Nathaniel, of Deptford, Gloucester Co., doctor. Int. Adm'r—Hugh Tomb, of Phila., doctor. Fellowbondsman—William Hugg, of town and Co. of Gloucester, yeoman. Witnesses—Hannah Ladd and John Ladd. Lib. 12, p. 360.

1761, March 13. Hammell, John, of Mansfield, Burlington Co., farmer; will of. Son, Laban, and daughters, Catherine and Deborah, each a bed. Son, John, to sell the rest of goods and plantation, and the moneys to be divided among my children, viz., John, James, Catharine, Elizabeth, Mary, Rachel, William, Deborah and Laban. Laban, Catharine and Deborah are not married. Witnesses—Nathan Wright, Rebekah Wright, Joseph Curtis.
    1765, Oct. 29. Codicil. To son, William, only 5 shillings. Witnesses—Amos Miller, James Pearson, Peter Tallman. Proved Nov. 28, 1770.
    1770, Nov. 27. Inventory, £62.0.9, made by John Folwell and Peter Tallman. Lib. 14, p. 333.
    1772, March 21. Account by John Hammell, the son and Ex'r of John Hammell, dec'd. Lib. 14, p. 418.

1768, Nov. 7. Hammell, William, of Burlington Co. Int. Adm'r—Peter Harvey, of Mansfield Twsp., said Co. Fellowbondsman—William Potts, of same place. Witness—Robert Burchan. The widow, Elizabeth Hammell, renounced.
    1768, Oct. 29, Inventory, £180.6.6, made by Thomas Biddle and William Potts. Lib. 12, p. 525.

1761, July 17. Hammitt, Daniel, of Greenwich, Gloucester Co. Int. Adm'r—Samuel Hammitt, of said place, husbandman. Fellowbondsman—Mathias Matson, of Deptford, yeoman. Witnesses—John Ladd and Hannah Ladd. Lib. 10, p. 437.

1764, Nov. 17. Hampton, Jacob, of Borough of Elizabeth, Essex Co.; will of. Wife, Mary, use of house and land, until my youngest son is 10 years of age. The salt meadow I bought of Ebenezer Sayre to be sold, to support and school my children. When my youngest son is 10, my wife is then to have ½ of the personal estate, and my daughters, to wit., Sarah, Mary and Anna Hampton, to have the other ½. Sons, Jacob, Abraham and Andrew, my lands when the youngest is 21. Executors—my brother, Abner Hampton, and friend, Jeams Haydock. Witnesses—John Elston, Cowperthwaite Copland, Samuel Elston, Jr. Proved Jan. 15, 1765. Lib. H, p. 481.

1766, July 31. Hampton, William, Jr., of Waterford, Gloucester Co., husbandman. Int. Adm'r—Peter Breach. Fellowbondsman—John Eastlack; both of Newton, said Co., yeomen. Witnesses—Hannah Ladd and John Ladd.
    1766, July 29. Inventory, £55.7.5, made by John Gill and David Branson. Lib. 12, p. 381.

1756, May 13. Hance, Isaac, of Shrewsbury, Monmouth Co., yeoman; will of. Wife, Mary, all the goods she brought with her at our marriage, and is otherwise provided for. My eldest son, Timothy, land where he lives, at Rumsom, joining the plantation that I bought of Seth Allen. The land on north side of Kettle Creek I give to my three sons, Timothy, John and Jacob. The land where I live at Rumsom to my two youngest sons, John and Jacob. Executors—my three sons, Timothy, John and Jacob, being all the children I have. Witnesses—Jacob Dennis, William Hulet, Benjamin Wolcott. Proved Sept. 11, 1764. Lib. H, p. 453.

1765, June 3. Hance, John, of Shrewsbury, Monmouth Co., yeoman; will of. Wife, Catharine, use of real and personal estate till my youngest son, John, be 14 years of age, if she remain my widow; and, after that, till my eldest son, Waples, be 21, at which time he may take my homestead where I live, on Rumson Neck, in his possession, which I give to him, he providing for his mother, and he is to pay to his brother, John £500, and to his sister, Rachel, £50. The rest of my lands in the Jerseys, Maryland, or Pennsylvania, I give to son, John. Executors—my wife, and my two brothers, Timothy and Jacob Hance. Witnesses—Joseph Parker, Benjamin Dennis, John Gamage. Proved Oct. 28, 1769.

1769, Sept. 6. Inventory, made by Richard Lawrence and John Brinley. Lib. K, p. 171.

1760, Nov. 21. Hancock, William, of Salem Co.; will of. To my wife the use of the plantation while she lives. Son, William, the said place, after my wife's death; he paying to my grandson, William Alrich, £100 when 21. I also give to son, William, plantation where he lives in Elsinboro; also the plantation in Penns Neck. Grandsons, William and Thomas, sons of my son, Thomas, the plantation in Elsinboro, called Anne's Grove. To the three daughters of my son, Thomas, the meadow on the River shore, which I bought of Joseph Kingston. To each of my daughter, Sarah's, children, £70, when 18. Of the rest of my personal estate I give ⅓ to my wife, and ⅓ to my daughter, Lydia, wife of Samuel Alrich, and ⅓ my executors are to put at interest, for my daughter, Rebecca, the wife of Vesser Alrich, and pay them the income during the life of Rebecca, and, if she outlive her husband, then the securities are to be turned over to her. Executors—son, William, and my son-in-law, Samuel Alrich. Witnesses—Abraham Hewlings, John Carty, Samuel Blackwood. Proved Dec. 28, 1762. Lib. 11, p. 273.

1762, Aug. 26. Hand, Abigail, of Cape May Co. Int. Adm'r—Lewis Cresse. Fellowbondsman—John Shaw; both of said Co. Witness—George Norton.

1762, Aug. 27. Inventory, £17.9.9, made by John Shaw and Elijah Hand.

1769, Aug. 7. Account of Lewis Cresse and Abigail Hand, executors of Gideon Hand. "David Hand, as a legacy, £106.12.3¾." (See under Gideon Hand, Lib. 11, p. 226). Lib. 11, p. 224; Lib. 15, p. 10.

1760, Dec. 12. Hand, Abraham, of Cape May Co.; will of. Wife, Esther, all real and personal. If I have no child, then my estate to fall to my cousin, Jesse Hand. Executors—my wife and my cousin, Jesse Hand. Witnesses—Silvanus Townsend, Jr., Jacob Smith, Levi Eldredge. Proved April 3, 1761.

1761, Jan. 16. Inventory, £104.5.5, made by John Leonard and Silvanus Townsend. Lib. 11, p. 74.

1765, May 25. Hand, Anne, of Cape May Co. Int. Adm'r—Shamgar Hand, or his heirs. Fellowbondsman—Lewis Cresse, gentleman; both of said Co. Witnesses—John Shaw and George Norton.

1765, April 26. Inventory, £138.8.11½, made by John Shaw and Lewis Cresse.

1771, Account by Shamgar Hand, Adm'r.
Lib. 12, p. 249; Lib. 14, p. 410.

CALENDAR OF WILLS—1761-1770   175

1767, Aug. 27. Hand, Cornelius, of Cape May Co. Int. Adm'x—Deborah Hand, the widow. Fellowbondsman—Jeremiah Ludlam; both of said Co. Witnesses—Benjamin Stites and Eli Eldredge.
1767, Aug. 27. Inventory, £530.9.8, made by Eli Eldredge and Benjamin Stites.
1770, April 30. Account by Jonathan Jenkins, who married Deborah Hand, the widow of Cornelius Hand.
Lib. 13, p. 146; Lib. 15, p. 15.

1768, June 2. Hand, Daniel, of Cape May Co., yeoman; will of. Wife, Judah, one-third my lands, and one-third of moveable estate, during her life. Son, John, the west part of homestead. Son, Eli, the next part. Son, Daniel, the east part. To my three sons, my right on Five Mile beach. Daughter, Judah, to have moveables, when 18. Executors—wife, Judah, and Aaron Eldredge. Witnesses—Daniel Crowell, Hannah Crowell, Mercy Hughes. Proved Aug. 6, 1768.
1768, Aug. 5. Inventory, £213.13.3, made by Richard Stites and Daniel Crowell.   Lib. 13, p. 470.

1760, Oct. 2. Hand, Eleazar, of Cape May Co.; will of. Wife, Jerusha, all lands while my widow. Eldest son, Ellis, land where I live. Youngest son, James, lands on Fishing Creek. Daughters, Elizabeth and Johanah, my moveable estate. Executors—wife, Jerusha, and brother, Henry Hand. Youngest children, Johanah and James, are to have learning. My brother, Timothy, to take the oldest boy and keep him till 21. Oldest girl to live with her uncle Henry, till 18. Witnesses—Ebenezer Johnson, Hance Woolson, Elizabeth Hand. Proved March 26, 1761.
1761, Jan. 2. Inventory, £153.2.4, made by John Eldredge and Ebenezer Johnson.   Lib. 10, p. 166.

1768, March 8. Hand, Elihu, of Cape May Co. Int. Adm'rs—Lydia Hand, spinster, and Silas Hand. Fellowbondsman—Isaac Matthews; all of said Co. Witnesses—Zeruiah Hughes and Henry Hand.
1768, Feb. 29. Inventory, £82.16.7, made by Cornelius Schellenger and Henry Hand.   Lib. 13, p. 332.

1762, Feb. 5. Hand, Gideon, of Cape May Co.; will of. Wife, Abigail, £100, and use of lands while my widow to bring up my children. Son, Absulam, and the child my wife is big with, all my lands. Executors—wife, Abigail, and Lewis Cresse. Witnesses—Silas Goff, Thomas Smith, Richard Swain. Proved June 14, 1762.
1762, June 10. Inventory, £360.9.11, made by John Shaw and Elijah Hand.
1769, Aug. 7. Account of Lewis Cresse, Adm'r of Abigail Hand, relict of Gideon Hand. (See under Abigail Hand).
Lib. 11, p. 226; Lib. 15, p. 10.

1765, May 20. Hand, Isaiah, of Cape May Co. Int. Adm'x—Susannah Hand, widow of said Isaiah. Fellowbondsman—Daniel Crowell, of said Co. Witnesses—Henry Young and Henry Hand.
1765, May 16. Inventory, £290.15.0, made by Henry Hand and Daniel Crowell.   Lib. 12, p. 128.

1760, Aug. 5. Hand, Jeremiah, of Middle Parish, Cape May Co., yeoman; will of. Wife, Deborah, ½ of my moveable estate, and ½ the plantation, while my widow. Daughter, Experience Edmonds, wife of Downs Edmonds, lands adjoining James Miller, in the Lower Parish. Daughters, Jane, and Judith, £100 each, when 21. Son, Jesse, the rest of real estate. Executor—son, Jesse. Witnesses—John Leonard, Abraham Hand, Jonathan Hildreth, Joseph Norbury. Proved April 3, 1761.

1762, Jan. 29. Inventory, £331.17.6, made by Jacob Spicer and James Godfrey. Lib. 11, p. 78.

1767, June 27. Hand, Jeremiah, of Cape May Co. Int. Adm'x—Martha Hand, the widow. Fellowbondsman—Daniel Swain, Esq., of said Co. Witnesses—John Eldredge and Zerulah Hughes.

1767, June 23. Inventory, £224.19.6, made by John Eldredge and Daniel Swain.

1771, Account by Martha Hand. Lib. 13, p. 146; Lib. 14, p. 410.

1770, Aug. 8. Hand, Ludlam, of Cape May Co. Int. Adm'r—Jesse Hand. Fellowbondsman—Nathaniel Hand; both of said Co. Witnesses—Benjamin Stites and Jonathan Leaming.

1770, Aug. 2. Inventory, £229.12.11, made by Benjamin Stites and Nathaniel Hand.

1779, Account by Adm'r. Lib. 15, p. 70; 22, p. 360.

1761, Jan. 31. Hand, Nathan, of Cape May Co. Ward. Son of Nathan Hand, Sr. Guardian—Elijah Hand. Fellowbondsman—Jacob Spicer; both of said Co. Witnesses—Cornelius Hand and Hugh Hathorn. Lib. 11, p. 71.

1764, Dec. 17. Hand, Neri, of Cape May Co. Ward. Son of Thomas Hand, of said Co. Guardian—David Hand. Fellowbondsman—John Shaw; both of said Co. Witnesses—Henry Young and George Norton. Lib. 12, p. 128.

1766, Feb. 8. Hand, Recompence, of Cape May Co. Int. Adm'r—Jonathan Hand. Fellowbondsman—Thomas Smith, gentleman; both of said Co. Witness—John Eldredge.

1765, Jan. 2. Inventory, £312.8.9½, made by John Eldredge and Thomas Smith. Lib. 12, p. 357.

1769, March 22. Hand, Recompence, of Fairfield, Cumberland Co. Int. Adm'x—Martha Hand, of said place. Fellowbondsman—Jonathan Hand, of Middle Precinct, Cape May Co.

1769, Feb. 21. Inventory, £255.0.6, made by David Shepherd and William Dalles.

1771, March 20. Account by Martha Sheppard, late Martha Hand, Adm'x. Lib. 13, p. 530; Lib. 15, p. 103.

1760, Dec. 10. Hand, Shamgar, of Cape May Co., yeoman; will of. Son, Stephen, 100 acres of my homestead, next to James Cresse. Son, Shamgar, the rest of my homestead, and 25 acres of back land. Son, William, the rest of my back lands. My youngest son, Cornelius, may cut timber off the land. Eldest daughter, Abigail, the wife of Gideon Hand, 5 shillings. Speaks of "small children." Executors—wife, Ann, and son, Shamgar. Witnesses—Nathan Stites, Nathaniel Jenkins, Daniel Hewet. Proved March 11, 1761.

1761, March 3. Inventory, £154.5.4, made by Lewis Cresse and Joshua Hildreth.

1771. Account made by Shamgar Hand, and Anne Hand, the Executors. Lib. 10, p. 162; Lib. 14, p. 408.

1770, May 1. Hand, Silas, of Cape May Co.; will of. Wife, Mary, ⅓ my personal estate, and ⅓ of the profits of my real. Son, Silas, 200 acres, which was bought of Thomas Hand. Sons, Elisha and Jonathan, the rest of lands belonging to the plantation where I dwell, which are part of 4 tracts, and after the said 200 acres are taken off, may be esteemed 400 acres. Son, Isaiah, two tracts at Nummies, of 179 acres, and 8 acres of cedar swamp, bought of Jeremiah Ludlam. To all of my children, Elisha Hand, Silas Hand, Jonathan Hand, Patience Hand, Sarah Hand, Mary Hand, Isaiah Hand, Jane Hand and Rhoda Hand, ⅔ of my moveable estate. Children to be educated. Executor—wife, Mary, and my two sons, Elisha and Silas. Witnesses—Constantine Hughes, Elisheba Hughes, Constantine Foster. Proved May 16, 1770.

1770, May 30. Inventory, £316.11.2, made by Robert Parson and Henry Hand.

1774, March 22. Account by Mary Edmunds (late Mary Hand), Executor of Silas Hand. Lib. 14, p. 339; Lib. 15, p. 531.

1770, May 16. Hand, Silas, of Cape May Co. Ward. Son of Silas Hand of said Co. Guardian—James Whilldin, Esq. Fellowbondsman —Daniel Swain; both of said Co. Witnesses—Mary Hand and Zeruiah Hughes. Lib. 15, p. 68.

1752, Sept. 14. Hannah, Michael, of Deerfield, Cumberland Co., farmer; will of. My wife, the mare that I bought of John Bateman, and the use of ⅓ my plantation. Daughter, Meriam, £5. Daughter, Mary, £7. Daughters, Meriam, Sarah and Mary, rest of my moveable estate. Son, Samuel, all my lands. Executor—son, Samuel. Witnesses—Joseph Peek, Samuel Clark, Charles Clark. Proved Oct. 6, 1763.

1763, Sept. 23. Inventory, £119.18.2, made by Benjamin Garrison and Isaac Elwell. Lib. 11, p. 457.

1769, March 8. Hannah, Samuel, of Deerfield Township, Cumberland Co., husbandman; will of. Wife, Lida, ⅓ of my moveable estate, and use of wench called Daff, and, after death of my wife, the wench to be sold and money divided between my three youngest children, Abigail Hannah, Silas Hannah and Mary Hannah. Wife, Lidia, ⅓ of my two plantations, that is, the one where I dwell, and the one left me by my father, Michael Hannah, while my widow. Son, James, plantation where I live, and ⅓ my cedar swamp, called Green Swamp, which is in Broad Neck; also ⅓ the cedar swamp on Morris River, called Muskee; and he is to pay to my son, Silas, £20 when 21. Son, Preston, plantation which was left me by my father, and ⅓ of Green Swamp, and ⅓ of the one on Morris River. Son, Silas, plantation I bought of John Jackson, and ⅓ of swamp in Broad Neck, and ⅓ of the one on Morris River, when 21. Sons, Preston and Silas, the salt marsh lying at Isaac Preston's. Daughters, Abigail Hannah and Mary Hannah, £50 to each, when they are 18. Executors—son, James, and friend, Daniel Clark. Witnesses—

James Davis, Jr., John Dilshaver and Rachel Davis. Proved Nov. 8, 1770.
1770, Nov. 6. Inventory, £464.5.4, made by Joseph Sneathen and Samuel Ogden.
1774, June 28. Account by Daniel Clark, surviving Executor. Payments to Lydia Whitecar; Enos Seeley as Guardian for Hannah Petty; James Hanna, for keeping Mary Hanna 1½ yrs.; for Abigail's trade and clothing; Lydia Hannah, the widow; James Hannah's Executor. Lib. 15, p. 92.

1766, Nov. 23. Harcor (Harcourt), Samuel, of Pilesgrove Twsp., Salem Co., yeoman; will of. Son, Samuel, 5 shillings. Daughter, Jemima Garrison, 5 shillings. Daughter, Jedidah Hudson, 5 shillings. Daughter, Ladema Groof, 2 shillings and 6 pence. Daughter, Rachel Harcor, 5 shillings. Grandsons, Samuel Garrison, John Garrison, David Garrison, Isaac Garrison, Joseph Garrison and Frederick Garrison, £30 each, when of age. Granddaughter, Elizabeth Reed, 5 shillings. Great-granddaughter, Jemima Reed, £25 when 18. Granddaughter, Hannah Hudson £20. Grandson, Joseph Garrison, rest when of age. Executors—Jacob Richman and my grandson, Samuel Garrison. Witnesses—Rachel Rudderford, Francis Marshall, John Hunt. Proved Feb. 20, 1767.
1766, Dec. 6. Inventory, £341.17.10, made by Thomas Sparks and John Hunt. Lib. 13, p. 172.

1764, June 10, Hardin, Martin, of Amwell Twsp., Hunterdon Co., yeoman; will of. Wife, Anna, house where we live, during her life, and use of moveable estate and rents of lands. Son, Martin Hardin, all my lands at the death of my wife; but provided that he lives longer than his wife, Catharine; if he die before Catharine, then the lands shall be sold and the money divided between my surviving children, Samuel, Susannah Silverthorn, and Anna Tomson. My son, Martin, shall pay to my granddaughter, Phebe Tomson, £50, and to my granddaughter, Anna Tomson, £50. My daughter, Susannah Silverthorn, during her widowhood, shall have the use of the room where her bed stands, and shall have £3 and 10 shillings during widowhood. Executors—son, Samuel, and my son-in-law, George Tomson. Witnesses—Edmund Freeman, Moses Rettinghousen, Uriah Bonham. Proved June 1, 1765.
1765, May 30. Inventory, £273.11.9, made by Thomas Hunt and Jonathan Higgins. Lib. 12, p. 222.

1763, Jan. 28. Harker, Cornelius, of Sussex Co. Ward. Son of James Harker, of said Co., deceased, who died intestate. Said Cornelius has a right to a portion of his father's personal estate, and he makes choice of his friend, Absalom Bonham, as his Guardian.
1763, Jan. 28. Guardian—Absalom Bonham, of Kingwood, Hunterdon Co. Fellowbondsman—Malakiah Bonham, of same place. Witnesses—Thomas Hooton, Mary Severns. Lib. 11, p. 279.

1765, Feb. 2. Harker, Ezekiel, of Greenwich, Gloucester Co., yeoman. Int. Adm'x—Mary Harker, widow. Fellowbondsman—Thomas Denny; both of said place. Witnesses—Sarah Howell and John Ladd.
1765, Jan. 21. Inventory, £246.9.10, made by Ezekiel Wright and Thomas Denny. Lib. 12, p. 103.

CALENDAR OF WILLS—1761-1770   179

1764, March 22. Harker, Samuel, of Roxbury, Morris Co., minister of the Gospel; will of. Wife, Deborah, ⅓ of my estate. Then my estate is to be divided into 5 parts; and I give my son, Ahimaaz, 2 parts, and to my daughters, Rachel, Jemina, and Massa, a part. My son, Daniel, who is foolish, to be supported by my wife and my son, Ahimaaz. Executors—son, Ahimaaz, and Samuel Grandin. Witnesses—Jemima Turner, Abigal Pew, Thomas Dains. Proved May 2, 1764. Lib. H, p. 435.

1769, April 8. Harpell, Peter, of Monmouth Co. Int. Adm'rs—Christian Harpell and John Andrews. Inventory, £19.4.4.
1772, Feb. 7. Account by John Andrews.
Lib. 14, p. 436; Lib. 15, p. 8.

1770, Oct. 26. Harris, David, of Hopewell, Cumberland Co. Int. Adm'rs—Joshua Ewing and James Ewing; both of Greenwich Twsp., said Co., weavers.
1770, Oct. 26. Renunciation of Mary Harris, the widow.
1770, Oct. 29. Inventory, £109.16.9, made by Maskell Ewing and Jonathan Harris.
1772, June 1. Account by both Executors.
Lib. 14, p. 420; Lib. 15, p. 75.

1761, July 7. Harris, Jacob, of Cumberland Co. Int. Adm'rs—Rachel Harris and Daniel Harris, of Hopewell Twsp., said Co. Witnesses—Nicholas Johnson and Samuel Harris, Jr.
1761, June 19. Inventory, £202.2.11, made by Nicholas Johnson and Samuel Harris, Jr. Lib. 10, p. 437.

1767, Sept. 22. Harris Jeremiah, of Fairfield, Cumberland Co. Ward. Son of Jeremiah Harris, of said place, who by will left land to his son. Guardian—Joseph Daten. Fellowbondsman—Robert Low; both of said place, yeomen. Witness—Thomas Ewing, Jr.
Lib. 12, p. 487.

1767, Sept. 22. Harris, Reuben, of Fairfield, Cumberland Co. Ward. Son of Jeremiah Harris, of said place, deceased. Guardian—Joseph Daten. Fellowbondsman—Robert Low; both of said place, yeomen. Witness—Thomas Ewing, Jr. Lib. 12, p. 488.

1765, July 30. Harris, Samuel, of Chesterfield Twsp., Burlington Co., schoolmaster. Int. Adm'r—Samuel Black, of Mansfield Twsp., said Co. Fellowbondsman—Joseph Rockhill, of same place, yeoman.
1765, July 30. Susannah Harris, the widow, renounced in favor of Samuel Black.
1765, July 20. Inventory, £115.1.3, made by Joseph Reckless, Anthony Taylor and William Phares.
1766, March 29. Account by Adm'r. Lib. 12, p. 154; Adm. 259.

1770, July 17. Harris, Samuel, of Middlesex Co. Int. Adm'x—Hannah Harris, his widow. Fellowbondsman—William Roberts, of Morris Co.
1770, July 18. Inventory of the estate of Samuel Harris, of Piscataway, made by John Miller and John Sebring, Jr.
1771, July 16. Goods were kept by the widow.
1773, March 24. Account by Hannah Harris. Lib. K, p. 232.

1767, May 14. Harris, Zephaniah, of Mansfield, Burlington Co. Int. Adm'r—Isaac Harris, of Woolwich Twsp., Gloucester Co., yeoman. Fellowbondsman—Thomas Curtis, of Mansfield, Burlington Co., yeoman.
1767, May 30. Inventory, £15.0.0, made by Isaac Cowgill and William Nutt.
1771, Jan. 10. Account by Adm'r. Lib. 13, p. 103; Lib. 15, p. 101.

1759, April 24, Harrison, Alice, of Hanover Twsp., Burlington Co.; will of. Grandson, William Steward, £5, and to his brother, John Steward, £10, being in the hands of his father, John Steward. Son, Josiah Steward's, two sons, Joseph and Josiah, 20 shillings apiece. Granddaughter, Martha Chapman, £5. Residue to my son, John Steward, Joseph Steward, Elizabeth Reckless, Alice Fowler, Alice Feagins, Elizabeth Parent and Susannah Steward. Executor—son, John. Witnesses—Benjamin Kirby, Ann Kirby, Edmond Bower. Proved Feb. 11, 1761. Lib. 12, p. 320.

1767, May 21. Harrison, Jabez, of Newark, Essex Co.; will of. To Jabez Harrison Seayre, son of my sister, Lydia Seayre, my sword, marked "O. B." My wife, Abigail, rest of personal estate. To Jonathan Sayrs my lands. To the three sons of my sister, Abigail Johnson, dec'd, Daniel, Uzal and Eliphelet, £5 each. My sister, Eunice Conger, £10. Daughter of my sister, Eunice Lydia Johnson, £15. Executors—my wife and my friend, Jonathan Sayres. Witnesses—Benjamin Johnson, Uzal Johnson, Jr., David Ogden, 3d. Proved March 21, 1768. Lib. I, p. 263.

1761, Nov. 7. Harrison, Joseph, of Township and Co. of Gloucester; will of. To Samuel Clement, Jr., all my lands, except a cedar swamp on Great Egg Harbor River. Brother, Samuel Harrison, ¼ of said swamp (which contains 136 acres). One-fourth of said swamp is to be conveyed to William Hugg, and the rest to be sold. My daughter, Mary, a negro girl. Daughter, Rebecca, a negro boy when she is of age. Friend, John Hinchman, a gun. Sister-in-law, Abigail Clement, a negro. Sister-in-law, Rebecca Clement, a negro. To the two sisters, Abigail and Rebecca, the apparel that was my wife's. Brother-in-law, Samuel Clement, Jr., apparel. Executors—my brothers, Samuel Harrison and Samuel Clement, Jr. Witnesses—William Harrison, Jr., Samuel Hugg, Beulah Clement. Proved Dec. 21, 1761.
1761, Nov. 23. Inventory, £1,476.15.11, made by George Kemble and John Mickle. Lib. 11, p. 83.

1755, Jan. 18. .Harrison, Moses, of Newark, Essex Co.; will of. Daughter, Mary Dod, £10. My other four daughters, a tract of land on the hill west of Newark, bounded by Joseph Rogers, John Crane and David Ogden, and contains 9¼ acres, which land is to be sold and the money given to the daughters, to wit., Anna, Demaras, Abigail and Sarah, when they are of age. Son, Jonas, the rest of my lands. Executors—son, Jonas, and Jabez Harrison. Witnesses—Josiah Crane, John Cockram, Nathaniel Farrand. Proved Feb. 27, 1765. Lib. H, p. 579.

1762, Jan. 9. Harrison, Samuel, Sr., of Town and Co. of Gloucester, yeoman; will of. Son, Samuel, lot in town of Gloucester, known by the name of Long Lot, purchased of Samuel Green. Wife, Abigail, £150, bed, etc.; and the rest of personal estate to my wife and daughter, Abigail Harrison, and if daughter, Abigail, die under age, then her share to go to son, Samuel, and my daughter, Rebecca Harrison. Daughter, Ann Hugg, 5 shillings. Executors—my wife and son, Samuel. Witnesses—Joseph Ellis, William Hyland, John Griffith. Proved Oct. 18, 1762. Lib. 11, p. 252.

1770, April 20. Harrison, Thomas, of New Hanover, Burlington Co., weaver; will of. Daughters, Rachel, Sarah, Ann, Tacey and Mary, £30 each, when they are 21. Wife, Sarah, rest of personal. Son, Stephen, the plantation I bought of John Earl. Son, Thomas, rest of lands. Executors—my wife and my brother, Isaac Harrison. Witnesses—Joseph Bullock, George Bullock, Stephen Kirby. Proved June 23, 1770. Lib. 14, p. 228.
1770, June 18. Inventory, £503.18.8½, made by John Bullock and Joseph Bullock.

1761, April 19. Harrison, William, of Greenwich Twsp., Gloucester Co.; will of. Son, William, plantation where I formerly lived, and where he now lives, to him and his heirs, and, for want of such, then to my daughter, Priscilla, and, if she have no heirs, then to daughter, Hannah. Daughter, Priscilla, two lots in Gloucester. My son, William, and Thomas Ellis, to carry on the saw mill for 2 years agreeable to a contract which I made with them, which was that my son, William, and my son-in-law, Thomas Ellis, were to deliver boards in Philadelphia for my daughter, Priscilla, to have ½ the profits. Daughter, Priscilla, plantation where I live, together with the said saw mill. My malt house to be rented for 20 years. Daughter, Mary Wells, £10. Daughter, Ann Simson, £10. To each of my grandchildren, £10. Executors—daughter, Priscilla, and my friend, Simeon Ellis, of Deptford Twsp. Witnesses—John Sharp, Thomas James, Johan Christopher Blumlain. Proved Nov. 1, 1762.
Lib. 11, p. 266.

1768, Nov. 8. Harrison, William, of Monmouth Co. Int. Adm'r— Thomas Harrison, of Upper Freehold, said Co. File No. 3451 M.

1765, Sept. 30. Harshall, Christian, of Reading, Hunterdon Co., yeoman; will of. Wife, Elizabeth, £20 a year, and all the goods she brought with her at the time of our marriage; also my son-in-law, John Smith, is to provide for her. Cattle to be divided into 3 parts, and wife to have ⅓ part, and daughters, Christeen and Susanna, to have the other ⅔. Son, Anthony, who has children under 21, £12. Daughter, Susanna Shafer, some goods. My son-in-law, John Smith, will occupy my farm. The rest of the time of my boy, John Bartenheart, I give to my wife while she is my widow, and after that to the use of William Shafer. Executors—my wife, son-in-law, John Smith, and my friend, Thomas Reading. Witnesses—Daniel Reading, John Sharp, John Reading. Proved March 1, 1769.
1769, Feb. 28. Inventory, £1,705.17.11, made by Mordecai McKinney and Peter Newal.
1788, Oct. 28. Citation to John Smith, acting Executor, to settle his accounts. Thomas Pierce and Elsey, his wife, had said citation issued.
1789, Aug. 29. Account made by Johannes Smith, acting Executor.

1790, Feb. 1. Account by Auditors, which states that there was an annuity paid to the widow, 10 years, 3 months and 12 days, to Aug. 5, 1789. Lib. 13, p. 505.

1762, Nov. 9. Hart, Dennis, of Pilesgrove, Salem Co., yeoman; will of. Wife, Ann Hart, household goods, hogs, mare, cattle, and grain. Son, Zebulon Hart, livestock, tools, etc. Sons, Nehemiah, Jonathan, Samuel and John, and to my daughters, Elizabeth and Amy, each 5 shillings. Executor—son, Zebulon. Witnesses—Abraham Du Bois, James Simpson, John Tullis. Proved Nov. 19, 1762.
1762, Nov. 17. Inventory by Jacob Elwell and Jacob Du Bois.
Lib. 11, p. 374.

1704, Dec. 19. Hart, Thomas, of Enfield (England), merchant; will of. My house and land in England, New Jersey, or elsewhere, to be sold, except one town lot and one outlot in New Jersey, which I give to my cousin, Richard Ashfield, of New York. I impower Thomas Bowell, of New Jersey, and Rip Vandam, of New York, to sell the said lands in America, and remit the produce thereof to Theodore Enliston and John Freame. To the two daughters of my cousin, Richard Ashfield, deceased, £50. To cousin, Elizabeth Holmes, £10. To John Warner, of Waltham Abby, and Andrew Warner, of Waltham Cross, £10 each. To my cousin, Priscilla Freame, £50. To Priscilla Benthall, Mary Benthall and Eliz. Benthall, the three daughters of my son, Walter Benthall, £50 each. Sister, Patience Ashfield, my plate and goods. Daughter, Ann Enliston, five broad p's of gold. Sister, Patience Ashfield, £100. Rest to my sister, Patience Ashfield, and my daughter, Mary Benthall, wife of Walter Benthall. To Elizabeth Hardy, my servant, 40 shillings. Executrix —Patience Ashfield. Overseers—said John Freame and Theodore Enliston.
Exemplification given out of the Prerogative Court of Canterbury, that on 30th of Feb., 1704, at London, was found the will of Thomas Hart, of Enfield, County of Middlesex, merchant, and probate granted to Patience Ashfield. Given at London, at time of above search, 22nd of May, 1766. Lib. K, p. 56.

1763, Nov. 12, Hart, William, of Philadelphia. Int. Adm'r—John Hart, of Philadelphia. Fellowbondsman—William Hewlings, of Burlington.
1763, Nov. 15. Inventory, £10.9.3, made by Francis Ennis and Aaron Oakford; and consists of wearing apparel and sea chest.
1765, Feb. 1. Account by Adm'r. Lib. 11, p. 424.

1765, Jan. 1. Hartshorn, Samuel Wright. Ward. Son of Thomas Hartshorn and grandson of Samuel Wright, of New Hanover, in Burlington Co., both deceased. Guardian—Joseph Tantum, of said Co. Fellowbondsman—Thomas Folkes, of same. Witness—Joseph Read. Lib. 12, p. 37.

1765, May 18. Hartshorne, Catherine, of Middletown, Monmouth Co.; will of. Widow of Hugh Hartshorne. Granddaughter, Margaret White, daughter of Robert White and my daughter Margaret, deceased, 35 shillings a year to clothe her. Said granddaughter has brother, Richard, and sisters, Deborah and Frances. Grandsons, Samuel and John Van Brockle, all the money that shall be due to

me from the estate of their father, James Van Brockle, deceased. Granddaughter, Lydia Worthley, a negro. Granddaughters, Margaret and Catherine, daughters of my daughter Rebeccah by her former husband, George Right, £10 each. Daughter, Rebeccah, wife of William Nixon, my bed. Rest of my estate to daughter, Rebeccah, and my daughter, Mary, the wife of Elias Baily. Executors —kinsmen, Philip Lewis and Robert Hartshorne. Witnesses—Joseph West, Richard Lawrence, Alice Lawrence. Proved Sept. 30, 1767.
1767, Sept. 21. Inventory, made by John Wall and John Walling.
Lib. I, p. 175.

1762, Nov. 26. Hathaway, Benoni, of Morris Co. Ward, aged 19 years, and son of Benjamin Hathaway, of said Co., deceased. Makes choice of Thomas Troop, of said Co., as his Guardian, who is appointed. Fellowbondsman—Ralph Tucker, of Essex Co.
Lib. H, p. 202.

1763, July 13. Hathaway, Benoni, of Morris Co. Ward. Son of Benjamin Hathaway, of said Co., deceased. Makes choice of Samuel Roberts, of said Co., as his Guardian, who is appointed. Fellowbondsman—Eleazar Hatheway, of said Co. Lib. H, p. 258.

1762, Feb. 12. Hatheway, Benjamin, Esq., of Morristown, Morris Co.; will of. Wife, Elizabeth, ½ the yearly profits of my grist mill, and a cow, etc. Daughters, Rebecca, Thankful, Abigail and Kezia, the rest of moveable estate, except the blacksmith tools, which I give to my son, Jonathan. Son, John, land on Whippaning River, of 40 acres; also the house brother Clark lives in, and 3 acres. Son, Benoni, the other lands on the river. Son, Joseph, 40 acres with the small house on it. Son, Eliazar, also 40 acres. Son, Gershom, 50 acres, joining Joseph and Eliazar. Son, Benjamin, rest of the land on river, and the iron works at Mendham. Son, Jonathan, 50 acres where he lives, which once belonged to Thomas Allerton. Son, Clemens, also 50 acres. Son, Job, 50 acres. Samuel Baldwin may have ¼ and one half-quarter of the grist mill, he paying £25 for the ¼. Executors—Mathew Lum and Benjamin Halsey. Witnesses —Samuel Ford, Benjamin Lindsly, Timothy Johnes. Proved April 26, 1762. Lib. H, p. 117.

1766, May 30. Hathorn, James, of Cape May Co.; will of. Son, Hugh, plantation that I live on, and 10 acres of cedar swamp in the Old Bridge Neck. Daughter, Anne Godfrey, part of a tract in Cumberland Co. at Tuckaho. Grandson, James Godfrey, the said land, after the death of Anne. Daughter, Sarah Plumer, the other part of the land I gave to Anne. Grandsons, Joseph Plumer, James Plumer and Samuel Plumer, the said land, at the decease of Sarah. My wife, Cattron, one-third my land during her life. Grandchildren, Sarah Covenover and James Covenover, £50 each. Executor—son, Hugh. Witnesses—Francis Taylor, Japheth Hand, Elihugh Hand. Proved Jan. 15, 1767. Lib. 13, p. 139.
1767, Jan. 14. Inventory, £218.0.9, made by John Willets and Joseph Corson.
1767, Dec. 17. Account by the Executor.

1765, Feb. 7. Havens, George, of Shrewsbury, Monmouth Co. Int. Adm'r—William Jackson, Jr. Fellowbondsman—Benjamin Jackson,

yeoman; both of said place. Witnesses—Hannah Holmes and Sarah Shipherd.
1765, Feb. 4. Renunciation by Hannah Havens, widow of said George Havens, in favor of William Jackson, Jr. Witness—Josias Sharman.
1765, Feb. 1. Inventory by John Hamton and Benjamin Jackson.
Lib. H, p. 511.

1767, March 23. Havens, George, of Sussex Co. Int. Adm'r—William Havens, yeoman. Fellowbondsman—Japheth Byran, Esq.; both of Hardyston, said Co. Witness—John Pettit.
1767, March 17. Renunciation by Mary Havens in favor of her son, William Havens.
1767, April 3. Inventory, £54.12.9, made by Elezer Cary and Joseph Manning.
Lib. 12, p. 466.

1763, July 6. Havens, Thomas, of Wantage, Sussex Co.; will of. Wife, Sarah, £20 and ⅓ the personal estate. Son, Isaac, £37. Son, Darling, £37. Son, Joseph, £37. Daughter, Abigail, 10 shillings. Daughter, Experience, 10 shillings. Executors—my wife and son, Darling. Executors—George Havens, William Havens, Robert Willson. Proved Dec. 3, 1763.
1763, Nov. 8. Inventory, £112.6.6, made by Elijah Collard and Ephraim Martin.
Lib. 12, p. 3.

1762, Jan. 15. Haviland, Joseph, of Woodbridge, Middlesex Co. Int. Adm'x—Martha Haviland, the widow. Fellowbondsman—Francis Campion; both of said place.
1762, Jan. 23. Inventory, £9.4.0, made by David Evens and Benjamin Thornell.
1762, Sept. 3. Account by Martha Haviland.
Lib. H, p. 75.

1767, Oct. 8. Hawkins, Peter, of Fairfield, Cumberland Co.; will of. To that child my wife is pregnant with, ⅓ my moveable estate. Wife, Elizabeth, the rest of my estate. Executors—my wife and my friend, David Shepherd. Witnesses—William Paullin, Jr., Jonathan Sockwell. Proved Jan. 26, 1768.
1767, Oct. 26. Inventory, £148.19.10, made by William Paullin and Moses Bateman.
1768, June 6. Account by David Shepherd, the Ex'r.
Lib. 13, p. 322.

1770, Sept. 6. Hawkins, William, of Evesham, Burlington Co., mariner. Int. Adm'r—Thomas Shinn, Esq., of Mount Holly. Fellowbondsman—John Estell, of said Co., yeoman. Witness—Joseph Read.
1770, Sept. 5. Inventory, £59.3.1, made by George Payne and Benjamin Brush.
Lib. 15, p. 74.

1770, Aug. 20. Hawley, Andrew, of Morris Co. Int. Adm'r—The Right Honorable William Earl of Stirling; principal creditor. Fellowbondsman—John Carey, Esq., both of New Jersey.
Lib. K, p. 245.

1763, Feb. 3. Haywood, James, late of Mannahockin, Monmouth Co., but now of Mount Holly in Burlington Co.; will of. Wife,

CALENDAR OF WILLS—1761-1770

Charity, £20 yearly; also one room in my house at Mannahockin, where my son, Thomas, lives. Son, John, my plantation at Mannahockin, of 2,000 acres. Land leased to son William, I give him. Son, Thomas, land near the above. Son, George, £300. To the five children of my daughter, Ann Pangborn, which she had by her former husband, Haselton, to wit, James, Mary, William, Mercy and Ann Haselton, £10 each. My daughter, Elizabeth Fitzrandolph, wife of Benjamin, £50. Daughter, Mary Fitzrandolph, wife of Joseph, £50. Daughters, Martha Haywood and Zipporah Haywood, £70 each when 18. Executors—sons-in-law, Benjamin Fitzrandolph and Joseph Fitzrandolph, and my son, George. Witnesses—Zachariah Rossell, Thomas Reynolds, John Clark.
1763, Feb. 3. Codicil. Witnesses—John Budd, John Clark, Joseph McCully. Proved May 13, 1767. Lib. 13, p. 62.
1767, April 29. Inventory, £1,188.4.9, by Reuben Fitz Randolph
1774, March 21. Account by Exr's.

1762, June 3. Heard, Mary, of Woodbridge, Middlesex Co., widow. Int. Adm'r—John Taylor, son-in-law to said Mary Heard. Fellowbondsman—Cyrenius Van Mater; both of Middletown, Monmouth Co.
1762, May 25. Inventory, made by David Herriot and Nathaniel Fitz Randolph. Lib. H, p. 190.

1763, April 19. Heard, William, of Woodbridge, Middlesex Co.; will of. Lands to be sold. Wife, Susannah, all estate, in order that she may bring up my children. Executors—my wife and my friend, Mordecai Marsh. Witnesses—Daniel Moores, Matthew Moores, John Moores. Proved July 2, 1763. Lib. H, p. 263.

1769, Nov. 1. Heath, Richard, of Hunterdon Co. Int. Adm'r—David Heath. Fellowbondsman—Walter Cane; both of said Co. Witness—Benjamin Yard, Jr.
1769, Nov. 8. Inventory, made by Walter Cane and Abraham Larew, in presence of Nathaniel Field and William Wood.
1771, July 1. Account by David Heath, Adm'r of Richard Heath, of Amwell. Lib. 14, p. 122; Lib. 14, p. 405.

1762, Sept. 30. Heaton, John, of Hardwick, Sussex Co., yeoman. Int. Adm'r—Benjamin Heaton. Fellowbondsman—Samuel Willson; both of said place, yeomen.
1762, Sept. 23. Inventory, £29.15.6, made by Samuel Willson, Samuel Lundy and John Pettit. Lib. 11, p. 287.

1761, July 15. Heays, Jacob, of Burlington; will of. Son, William Heays, my land, and he is to pay my daughter, Mary Heays, £25 when 21, and to the child yet unborn £25. Wife, Margrat, use of land. Executor—Arent Schuyler. Witnesses—Martha Brown, Mary Schuyler, Daniel Ellis. Proved Nov. 2, 1761. Lib. 10, p. 427.
1761, Nov. 2. Inventory, £261.10.9, made by Job Ridgway and John Richardson.

1764, Sept. 16. Hebern, Mary, of Hopewell, Hunterdon Co. Int. Adm'r—Benjamin Stout. Fellowbondsman—Samuel Hunt; both of said place.
1764, Sept. 10. Inventory, £20.1.0, of "Mary Hepburn"; made by John Hart and Jacob Golden.
1765, Sept. 30. Account made by Adm'r. Lib. 12, p. 60.

1761, June 23. Hecter, Francis, of Alloways Creek, Salem Co., doctor of physick. Int. Adm'x—Margaret Hectar. Inventory, £109.12.9. Lib. 10, p. 434.

1770, March 17. Hedden, Elezar, of Essex Co.; will of. Wife, use of house where I live, and use of ⅓ of all my estate. Son, Edward, ½ of my lands. Son, Elezar, the other half. Edward to maintain the younger children till Elezar is 21, and then he shall do his ½ also. To Kaziah, £10, that being the record she has received. To Ruth, $10, which she has received. To Mary, Fighehe, Nehemiah, Phebe and Jones, £10 each when of age. Executors—Edward Hedden and Moses Baldwin. Witnesses—Elijah Hedden, John Lindsley, Samuel Camp. Proved April 30, 1770. Lib. K, p. 424.

1765, Oct. 29. Hedger, Eliakim, of Somerset Co.; will of. Being old. Wife, Margaret Hedger, the six new red chairs I bought of Stephen Trusdal, other goods, and 2 negros. Youngest son, John, land I bought of Samuel Large. Son, Samuel, land I bought of Aaron Hughs. Son, Joseph, land where the house stands, during his life, and then to his two sons, Stevenson Hedger and Thomas Hedger. Grandsons, Joseph Hedger and Samuel Hedger, sons of my son, Benjamin, deceased, also land. Daughters, Elizabeth Lewis, Sarah Hedger and Mary Stevenson, rest of moveables. Executors—Cornwell Stevenson and my sons, Samuel Hedger and John Hedger. Witnesses—Isaac Furman, Obadiah Pettit, Ann Pettit. Proved Feb. 25, 1767. Lib. 12, p. 470.

1765, Sept. 29. Hedges, James, of Cape May Co.; will of. Wife, Marey, moveable goods. Son, James, 10 shillings. Son, David, clothing. Daughter, Zeruiah Hedges, bed. Land in Lower Precinct to be sold. Son, David, ½ the money from said sale. Daughters, Margret Rodgers and Zeruiah Hedges, other ½ of money. To wife, ⅓ the residue, and to son, David, and daughters, Margaret Hedges and Zeruiah Hedges, the other ⅔. Executor—Joshua Shaw, Sr. Witnesses—Robert Parsons, Sarah Parsons, James Whilldin. Proved Nov. 11, 1765. Lib. 12, p. 334.

1766, Dec. 16. Hedges, Stephen, of Morristown, Morris Co. Int. Adm'rs—Mary Hedges, widow of Stephen, and Stephen Conkling. Fellowbondsman—Thomas Cleverly; all of said place.
1766, Dec. 19. Inventory, made by Robert Goble and Benjamin Halsey. Lib. I, p. 207.

1763, March 12. Helms, Okanes, of Greenwich Twsp., Gloucester Co.; will of. Sister, Deborah Angelo, all real and personal. Executrix—my said sister. Witnesses—William Towers, Jane Griffin, Thomas James. Proved April 4, 1763. Lib. 16, p. 149.

1760, Jan. 15. Henarie, Michael, of Reading Twsp., Hunterdon Co.; will of. To my eldest son, William's, eldest son, named Arthur, 5 shillings when he is 21. Wife, Jane, £15 yearly, to be paid by my son John; I also give her £130, now in the hands of my son David, excepting out of it, to my grandson John, son of my son Michael, £50 when he is 21. To my wife I give the interest of £30, now in the hands of 'my son-in-law, William Bishop. To sons, Michael, Daniel and David, 5 shillings each. Son, John, the land I bought

of Abraham Dellemater and the widow Bogart. Son, Nathaniel, the land I bought of Nicholas Emmons; but Nathaniel is now gone to sea, and, if he never returns, then the said land to go to my son, John. Daughters, Margaret and Sarah, the land I bought of John Rubert. My books I give to my children, Easter, Michael, Daniel, David, John, Nathaniel, Margaret and Sarah. Executors—sons, David and John, and my friend, Jacob Mattison. Witnesses—Joseph Mattison, Aaron Mattison, Jr., Hendrick Gardener. Proved Jan. 7, 1761.
1761, Jan. 5. Inventory, £712.8.0, made by Thomas Atkinson and Gershom Lee.
1767, Nov. 24. Account by Executors. (The widow is now deceased). Lib. 10, p. 540.

1766, June 9. Hendricks, Tunis, of Reading Town, Hunterdon Co., yeoman; will of. Wife, Catherine, all real and personal during her life, and, after her death, all to be divided between my three children, viz., Catherine, wife of Paul Hortong; Leanah, wife of Michael Cole, and Mary, wife of John Stires. Executors—Benjamin Allegar, Ezekiel Cole and Edward Wilmot. Witnesses—Abraham McKinney, George Searle, Peter Lisk. Proved Nov. 3, 1768.
1768, Oct. 20. Inventory, £190.12.2, made by Nicholas Egbert and George Biggs. Lib. 12, p. 540.

1755, July 4. Hendrickson, Andrew, of Greenwich Twsp., Gloucester Co.; will of. Son, David, my plantation where I live, and 10 acres of swamp on Timber Creek, but, if David die, then the plantation to go to my youngest son, Okenus. Eldest son, Jonas, land joining to Hance Urian. Son, David, to have my share of meadow, which I and my brother Henry bought, on Popopow Créek. Son, Jonas, a meadow, Wife, Elizabeth, bed. My moveable estate to all my children. Son, Okenus, to be put to trade. Executors—my brother-in-law, John Denny, and my wife. Witnesses—Peter Homan, John Reynolds, Jester Lock. Proved Dec. 29, 1760. Letters granted Jan. 2, 1761.
1760, Nov. 12. Inventory, £150.12.3, made by John Reynolds and Charles Lock. Lib. 10, p. 406.

1761, July 18. Hendrickson, Catharine, of Greenwich, Gloucester Co. Int. Adm'x—Catharine Hendrickson. Fellowbondsman—John Lock, yeoman; both of said place. Witness—Alexander Randall.
1761, June 22. Inventory, £192.11.5, made by Alexander Randall and John Lock.
1764, Feb. 25. Account by Adm'x. Lib. 10, p. 436.

1769, May 10. Hendrickson, David and Okenus, of Gloucester Co. Wards. Sons of Andrew Hendrickson, of said Co., and they make choice of Thomas Clark as Guardian.
1769, May 10. Guardian—Thomas Clark. Fellowbondsman—Jeffery Clark; both of said Co. Lib. 13, p. 539.

1761, April 20. Hendrickson, Peter, of Greenwich, Gloucester Co., yeoman; will of. Son, Andrew, my lands. Daughter, Modelen, £15 when of age. Wife, Catherine, the ⅓ of my land. Executor—John Lock. Witnesses—Daniel Bennett, Andrew Culin, John Lock. I also make my wife one of the Executors. Proved July 18, 1761.
1761, June 22. Inventory, £214.0.0, made by Alexander Randall and John Lock. Lib. 11, p. 97.

1765, Nov. 25. Hennion, Andries, of Slauterdam, Bergen Co., yeoman; will of. Wife, Elizabeth, real and personal while my widow. Son, John, is to have it if she marry. There is a farm at Praikeness, in Bergen Co., in possession of my brothers, Peter and Abraham, and the interest is to be collected from them. Executors—my wife and David Hennion, of Praikiness, and John Andries Cadmus, of Slauterdam. Witnesses—Robert Hogg, Derck Berdan and Garrat Van Wagenen. Proved April 1, 1766.
1766, March 27. Elizabeth Hennion, the widow, renounced.
Lib. H, p. 621.

1761, March 5. Henry, Jane, of Reading Township, Hunterdon Co.; will of. Widow of Michael Henry. Grandson, Arthur Henry, 5 shillings. Son-in-law, William Bishop, the rest of my estate. Executors—my son, John Henry, and my son-in-law, William Bishop. Witnesses—Nathaniel Henry, Sarah Henry. Proved Nov. 26, 1763.
1761, July 31. Inventory, £16.11.11, of goods left her by will of her husband, appraised by David Henry and Jacob Mattison.
1767, Dec. 26. Inventory, £86.13.3, made by John Stoll and Edward Wilmot.
1768, Jan. 22. Account by John Henry, Executor. Lib. 11, p. 445.

1766, Sept. 17. Henry, John, of New Brunswick, Middlesex Co., taylor; will of. Wife, Jane, ½ of my house and lot where I live, and ½ of the furniture. Son, Alexander, £20. Son, William, £7. Son, John, ½ of said house and lot, and, after wife is done with it, the other half; and he is to have rest of estate. Executors—wife, Jane, my son, John, and my friend, John Lyle. Witnesses—Paul le Boyteul, Andrew Petterson, John Grimes. Proved Dec. 10, 1766.
1766, Dec. 6. Inventory, made by John Grimes and John Lyle, Jr.
Lib. I, p. 71.

1767, March 17. Henry, Micah, of Greenwich, Sussex Co. Ward. Son of William Henry, of said place, deceased, and he makes choice of Jacob Mattison and John Henry as his Guardians.
1767, March 17. Guardians—Jacob Mattison and John Henry, both of said Co. Fellowbondsman—Thomas Lowrey, of said Co.
Lib. 13, p. 209.

1763, May 5. Henry, Nathaniel, of Hunterdon Co., farmer; will of. Brother, David Henry, all my real and personal estate, he paying to my brother, Michael Henry, £150, and to my brother, Daniel Henry, £100, and to brother, John, and my sisters, Margaret and Sarah, £20 each; and also to pay to my eldest sister's three sons, William, David and John, £50 each. Executor—brother, David. Witnesses—William Jones, Christopher Longstreet, Jacob Tidd. Proved May 17, 1763.
1763, May 16. Inventory, £138.5.2, made by David Henry.
Lib. 11, p. 539.

1761, July 13. Herbert, John, of Upper Freehold, Monmouth Co. Int. Adm'x—Elizabeth Herbert, widow of said John. Fellowbondsman—John Coward; both of said place.
1761, July 4. Inventory, £196.15.2, made by John Coward and Joseph Grover.
Lib. G, p. 445.

CALENDAR OF WILLS—1761-1770   189

1763, Aug. 17. Heritage, Benjamin, of Chester, Burlington Co., yeoman; will of. Son, Daniel, ½ of my plantation, and he is to pay to his brother, Joshua, £50 when 21. Son, Joshua, the other ½ of plantation. Sons, Daniel, Joshua, Samuel and Benjamin, my cedar swamp. Son, Samuel, £50 when 21. Son, Benjamin, £50 when 21. Wife, Keziah, use of land till Daniel is 21, as also the rest of estate. Executors—my wife and son, Daniel. Witness—Isaac Rogers, Edward French, John Cox. Proved Dec. 3, 1763.   Lib. 11, p. 435.
1763, Sept. 26. Inventory, £420.16.4, made by John Cox and Isaac Rogers.

1759, Oct. 16. Heritage, Richard, of Deptford, Gloucester Co., yeoman; will of. Son, Judah, land in said Twsp., which I bought of Joseph Knight, he paying to his mother £5 yearly. Son, Benjamin, plantation where I live, he paying to his mother £7 yearly. Wife, Sarah, bed, etc. Son, Joseph, £50. Daughter, Williams, £5. Daughter, Tabitha Pullen, 5 shillings. Daughter, Hannah Heritage, £20. Executors—sons, Judah and Benjamin. Witnesses—George Flaningam, Isaac Flaningam, Richard Clarke. Proved March 17, 1768.
Lib. 12, p. 501.

1765, April 9. Heritage, Samuel, of Burlington Co. Ward. Son of Benjamin Heritage of said Co., carpenter. Guardian—Daniel Heritage, of Moorestown, said Co., yeoman. Fellowbondsman—George Matlack, of same place. Witness, Thomas Millidge.
Lib. 12, p. 76.

1769, April 8. Herpel, Peter, of Upper Freehold, Monmouth Co. Int. Adm'rs—Christian Herpel and John Andrews. Fellowbondsman—John Kirby; all of said place.
1769, June 17. Inventory, £19.4.4, made by David Gorden and Thomas Kirby.
1772, Feb. 7. Account by John Andrews.
Lib. 14, p. 436; Lib. 15, p. 8; File No. 3555 M.

1734, July 26. Herriott, Andrew, of Woodbridge Twsp., Middlesex Co.; will of. My lands to be sold, and the money to be used to bring up my children. Wife, Mary, personal estate. Executors—my wife, and Reverend William Skinner. Witnesses—William Bloodgood, Josas Fleming, Mary Bloodgood, Ham Fleming. Proved Oct. 31, 1764.   Lib. H, p. 468.

1762, July 19. Hetfield, Isaac, of Elizabeth Borough, Essex Co., yeoman; will of. Wife, Sarah, income of ⅓ my real. Daughters, Sarah Clark and Abigail Jouet, £5 each. Son, Isaac, the pasture land, that joins my father, Price, Caleb Halstead and Matthias Hetfield, for which I gave deed; also ½ my salt meadow that I bought of widow Lambert. Son, Benjamin, my house and part of homestead. Son, Moses, 35 acres near Samuel Wood. Son, Andrew, land near the First Mountain, and part of the meadow. Daughter, Phebe, £30, when she is 21. Executors—my wife, Sarah, and my son-in-law, Abraham Clark. Witnesses—Josiah Wynants, David Man, Jacob Hetfield, Jr. Proved Dec. 26, 1762.
1762, Dec. 29. Inventory, made by Samuel Hetfield and David Man.   Lib. H, p. 264.

1765, Oct. 30. Heurtin, William, of Newark, Essex Co. Int. Adm'x—Susannah Heurtin (Huntin). Fellowbondsman — Joshua Heurtin; both of said place. Lib. H, p. 541.

1769, Aug. 2. Hewet, Thomas, Jr., of Cape May Co. Int. Adm'rs —Hannah Hewet, the widow, and Thomas Hewet, Sr., both of said Co.
1769, July. Inventory, £42.2.1, made by Benjamin Stites and Joshua Hildreth. Lib. 15, p. 5.

1761, Aug. 23. Hewit, Joseph, of Cape May Co. Int. Adm'x—Lydia Hewit. Fellowbondsman—Joshua Hildreth; both of said Co. Witnesses—Nathaniel Hand and Thomas Hewit.
1761, July 28. Inventory, £68.16.0, made by John Shaw and Lewis Cresse. Lib. 11, p. 73.

1762, Feb. 25. Hewit, Joseph, of Cape May Co., yeoman; will of. Sons, Elijah and Shamgar, my lands, and, if either die, then to fall to my son, Benaiah. Daughter, Phebe Hewit, a cow and bed. Daughter, Zeruel Hewit, a cow and bed. My wife, ⅓ personal estate, and rest to youngest son, Benaiah. My youngest [younger] children, Zeruel, Shamgar and Benaiah, to be bound out to trades. Executor— Elijah, my son. Witnesses—Nathaniel Jenkins, Nathan Shaw, Henry Hewit. Proved May 26, 1762.
1762, May 25. Inventory, £130.11.2, made by Thomas Smith and Daniel Smith. Lib. 11, p. 228.

1766, June 6. Hewit, Moses, of Greenwich, Gloucester Co. Ward. Only son and heir of Moses Hewit, of said place, yeoman, and being out of wardship, by the death of his late mother, and having lands from his father, makes choice of his friend, John Fowler, as his Guardian.
1766, June 6. Guardian—John Fowler, husbandman. Fellowbondsman—Isaac Butterworth, yeoman; both of Deptford, said Co. Witnesses—Sarah Howell and John Ladd. Lib. 12, p. 282.

1759, Dec. 16. Hews, Hannah, of Elsinboro, Salem Co., widow; will of. James Hutson to have my moveable estate. Son, John Hews, those lots which I purchased of John Chandler; also my right to lands which I hold in common with Samuel Nicholson; but John paying to each of his sisters £20; that is to say, to Mary Hutson and Martha Hews, when she is 18. Executors—friend, John Stewart, and my son, John Hews. Witnesses—Thomas Johnson, Henry Stubbines, Adam Kirk. Proved Feb. 6, 1761.
1760, Nov. 11. Renunciation, by John Stewart. Lib. 10, p. 505.

1766, Sept. 13. Hildebrand, George, of Manington, Salem Co., yeoman. Int. Adm'x—Elinor Hildebrand, widow. Fellowbondsmen— David Crawley and Isaac Hildebrand; all of said place. Witness— Elisha Bassett, Jr.
1766, Dec. 14. Inventory, £222.7.11, made by Elisha Bassett, Jr., and William Harvey. Lib. 12, p. 317.

1769, May 18. Hildreth, Daniel, of Cape May Co.; will of. Cedar swamp to be sold, and also ½ of 56 acres on the head of William Goff's land. Brother, Joseph Hildreth, the other ½ of the 56 acres.

Wife, Prissilla, the use of the other lands to bring up the children. My children, Elizabeth Hildreth and Aaron and Daniel, to have the said lands, when of age. Executors—my wife, Priscella, and my brother, Joseph. Witnesses—Francis Taylor, Ziliah Hildreth, Thomas Smith. Proved Feb. 6, 1770.

1770, Jan. 12. Inventory, £163.5.½, made by Joshua Hildreth and Thomas Smith. Lib. 15, p. 79.

1766, Aug. 1. Hildreth, James, of Cape May Co., carpenter; will of. Daughter, Phebe Hildreth, land I bought of Daniel Hildreth, when she is 20 years old. Son, James, ½ of my other lands; and son, Joseph, the other ½, when 21. Wife, Lydia, use of all estate. Executors—my wife, Lydia, and my brother, Joseph Hildreth. Witnesses—John Cresse, Daniel Hildreth, Zibiah Hildreth. Proved May 28, 1767, and letters granted to Joseph Hildreth, the surviving Executor.

1767, May 29. Inventory, £47.1.3, made by Thomas Smith and Elihu Smith. Lib. 12, p. 492.

1761, Jan. 17. Hill, Anne, of Northampton, Burlington Co., widow of Robert Hill; will of. Daughter, Anne Hill, to have all when 18. Executor—friend, Thomas Budd, farmer. Witnesses—Ann Gaskill, John Burr, Jr. Proved Jan. 27, 1761.

1761, Jan. 24. Inventory, £75.3.6, made by George Briggs and James Dobbin.

1763, March 31. Account by Ex'r. Lib. 10, p. 359.

1766, April 10. Hill, William, of Waterford Twsp., Gloucester Co., yeoman; will of. Wife, all my goods and plantation where I live, during her life. Grandson, William Carter, Jr., the plantation, when he is of age, but, if he die, then to his brother, John; and their sister, Sarah, is to have £10. William Carter, Sr., shall take care of the place till Junior comes of age. Brother, Moses Hill, 5 shillings. Executrix—my wife, Sarah. Witnesses—Abner Bennet, John Crowell, William McCarrell. Proved Oct. 2, 1766.

1766, Oct. 1. Inventory, £79.1.10, made by William McCarrell and William Carter. Lib. 12, p. 367.

1767, Oct. 2. Hillier, Abraham, of Northampton, Burlington Co.; will of. Brother, Isaac, land bought of Daniel Wills, and Isaac is to pay yearly to my mother £10. Mother, Sarah Hillier, £30 pounds. Brother, Jacob, plantation where I live. Sister, Martha Ridgway, £10. Brothers, John and Samuel, each 5 shillings. Sister, Mary Hillier, 5 shillings. Remainder to my brother, Jacob, he paying to my brother, Joseph, £100, and to sisters, Mary and Elizabeth Hillier, £75 each. Executors—brothers, Isaac and Jacob. Witnesses—Job Ellis, Asher Woolman, Abraham Oakley. Proved Oct. 27, 1767.

1767, Nov. 20. Inventory, £380.3.2, made by Aaron Wills and Asher Woolman. Lib. 13, p. 253.

1766, May 17. Hillier, Edward, of Northampton Twsp., Burlington Co.; will of. Wife, Sarah, £40. Son, John Hillier, back part of my plantation. Son, Isaac, land. Son, Abraham, the rest of my plantation. Son, Jacob, house in Mt. Holly. Son, Joseph, £100. Sons, Samuel and Joseph, land I bought of John Burr, Sr., when 21. Daughter, Martha Ridgway, £40. Daughters, Mary and Elizabeth,

£70 each, when 18. Son, Joseph, to be put to a trade when 15. Remainder to my sons, Isaac, Abraham, Jacob, John, Samuel and Joseph. Executors—sons, Isaac and Abraham. Witnesses—Uriah Woolman, George Elkinton, William Prosser. Proved June 21, 1766.
   1766, June 12. Inventory, £554.2.0, made by George Elkinton and Asher Woolman.   Lib. 13, p. 4.

   1762, Aug. 14. Hillman, Daniel, of Waterford, Gloucester Co., yeoman; will of. Real estate to be sold, and all personal, except as my wife, Abigail, shall take. Wife, Abigail, ⅓ of my estate, and the other ⅔ to my five children, one of which is yet unborn. My daughters are Sarah Hillman, Elizabeth Hillman; sons, Daniel and Samuel. Executors—my wife, Abigail, and my friend, John Gill, of Haddonfield, and he to be Guardian of the children. Witnesses—Jacob Mills, Rebecca Nicholson, Samuel Spicer. Proved Sept. 19, 1763.
   1763, Aug. 15. Inventory, £747.13.9, made by Joseph Morgan and Henry Wood.
   1767, June 5. Account by both Executors.   Lib. 11, p. 410.

   1765, Jan. 8. Hillman, Elizabeth, of Deptford, Gloucester Co., widow; will of. To my granddaughter, Sarah, my gown. To daughters-in-law, Hannah Hillman, Abigail Hillman, Mary Hillman and Drusella Hillman, the rest of clothing. Sons, John Hillman, James Hillman and Joseph Hillman, and my two grandsons, Daniel and James Hillman, sons of Daniel Hillman, deceased, the rest. Executors—son, Joseph, and John Sparks. Witnesses—John Stephens, George Wilkie, Constantine Wilkins. Proved Feb. 11, 1765.
                                                                                            Lib. 12, p. 251.

   1767, Dec. 22. Hillman, James, of Township and Co. of Gloucester, yeoman; will of. Wife, Mary, to have the plantation where I dwell till son, James, is 21. Son, James, my plantation, when 21; except ½ acre between the house and the lands of the heirs of George Marple, which my wife is to have; but, if James should die, then the plantation is to descend to my daughters, Elizabeth and Mary Hillman, when they are 21; my wife having the privilege of the 47 acres and one-half, which join lands of the late Gabriel Davis, and being the same which I purchased of John Hamton. Son, James, my cedar swamp, which I purchased of Gabriel Davis, except one acre thereof, which joins the swamp of Amos Haines, which I order my Executors to give title to Edward Gibbs. One acre of stone quarry was devised by my father to my brothers, Daniel and Joseph, which I order my executors to confirm. Executors—my wife and my friend, John Gill. Witnesses—William Hampton, Samuel Clement, John Hillman. Proved Jan. 12, 1768.
   1768, Jan. 4. Inventory, £457.12.10½, made by John Hinchman and Josiah Albertson.   Lib. 13, p. 304.

   1764, June 29. Hillman, John, of Twsp. and Co. of Gloucester, yeoman; will of. Wife, Elizabeth, ⅓ my personal estate, and ⅓ the saw mill and homestead. Son, Joab, land on south branch of Cooper's Creek, where Solomon Eldridge lives, and ⅓ the saw mill. Son, Josiah, the homestead, grist mill and ⅓ the saw mill. Son, Daniel, 100 acres that I bought of John Mickle, sheriff, of the property of Maham Southwick. Grandsons, James Hillman and Joseph

Hillman, land which I bought of Henry Woodrow, of 194 acres. Son, Josiah, ⅓ my personal estate. Sons, Joab, Joseph and Daniel, ⅓ the personal. Executor—son, Josiah. Witnesses—William Clarke, Daniel Able, Isaac Tomlinson. Proved July 18, 1764.
 1764, July 16. Inventory, £253.14.10, made by Thomas Bate and Isaac Tomlinson. Lib. 12, p. 8.

 1768, Feb. 27. Hillman, Joseph, of Gloucester Twsp. and Co., yeoman; will of. Wife, Prucilla, ¼ the money from the sales of my real and personal estate, to bring up my two children, till my son, Daniel, is of age to learn a trade. Son, Daniel, to have ¼ the money from the sales, and my daughter, Letticia Hillman, to have ¼. My brother, Daniel's, two sons, Daniel and Samuel, ¼. Executors—my wife and my friend, Jacob Jennings. Witnesses—Tatum Williams, John Hinchman, James Talman. Imprimis—I give to Ephraim Cheeseman, my apparel. Proved May 4, 1768. Letters granted to Priscilla Hillman and Jacob Jenings. Lib. 12, p. 496.

 1768, Aug. 26. Hilyard, Ann, of Waterford, Gloucester Co., widow; will of. Oldest daughter, Sarah Craddock, £5, if she come to demand it. Oldest son, Joseph Hillyard, ½ of the yearly income, "which he is to pay to me;" and the other ½ I give to my son, Abraham Hilyard, and my granddaughter, Ann Hammitt. Granddaughter, Lydia Pimm, daughter of Joseph Pimm, case of drawers. Daughter, Hannah Pimm, wife of Joseph Pimm, bed, etc. Executor—son-in-law, Joseph Pimm. Witnesses—Nathan Mills, Abraham Allen, Jacob Albertson. Proved Sept. 20, 1768.
 1768, Sept. 19. Inventory, £104.2.2, made by Joshua Lippincott and Abraham Allen. Lib. 12, p. 499.

 1768, Nov. 1. Hinchman, Jacob, of Gloucester Co., yeoman. Int. Adm'r—Joseph Ellis. Fellowbondsman—William Hugg, yeoman; both of Gloucester. Lib. 14, p. 20.

 1768, Nov. 1. Hinchman, James, of Gloucester Co., yeoman. Int. Adm'r—Joseph Ellis. Fellowbondsman—William Hugg; both of said Co., yeomen. Witness—John Ladd. Lib. 14, p. 20.

 1763, Sept. 11. Hinds, Joseph, Jr., of Elizabeth Town, Essex Co. Int. Adm'rs—Elizabeth Hinds, the widow, and Samuel Hinds. Fellowbondsman—John Davis, yeoman; all of said place. Witness—John Scudder.
 1763, Sept. 15. Inventory, £97.16.8, made by Joseph Acken and Matthias Hetfield, Jr. Lib. H, p. 324.

 1766, June 30. Hinds, Joseph, of Borough of Elizabeth, Essex Co., yeoman; will of. Son, John, land I bought of Ebenezar Sayrs, of 46 acres, and bounded by Ezra Sayre, John Cory and Benjamin Williams; also a salt meadow I bought of Jonathan Woodruff, of 4 acres and ¼, which joins Piles Creek. Son, Billy, the plantation whereon I dwell, bounded by Daniel Halsey, Elias Wynans, John Clawson, and John Paul; and a tract of about 24 acres, which I bought of Ebenezar Williams, bounded by land of Benjamin Williams, deceased, (devised to his daughter Elizabeth), and by John Crain and Caleb Crain, which I bought of Samuel Miller, Jr.; also 6 acres of salt meadow devised to me by my father. Wife, Elizabeth, my riding chair. Tract of 56 acres to be sold, and money given to my daughters, Lydia and Sarah Hinds, when age of 18. Executors—friend, John Clawson, and son-in-law, Benjamin Williams. Witnesses—Andrew Craig, Daniel Marsh, Joseph De Camp.

1769, Dec. 12. Codicil. To son, Billy, I give a tract of land which joins my homestead, and which I bought of Joseph Halsey, and on the back of the deed from said Halsey I executed a deed of gift to my son Billy, by the name of William Hinds. Witnesses—Daniel Halsey, Elias Winans, Cornelius Sayre. Proved Jan. 8, 1770.
Lib. K, p. 173.

1766, Feb. 8. Hinds, Stephen, of Borough of Elizabeth, Essex Co.; will of. Wife, Rebecca, £15. Son, Stephen, all my lands. Grandson, Benjamin Thompson, £40, his mother to enjoy the use of it during her lifetime. Grandson, Euzel Woodruff, £50, his mother to enjoy the use of it during her lifetime. Grandson, Pearsons Woodruff, £50, his mother to enjoy the use of it. Daughter, Sarah Hinds, £70. Daughter, Mary Hinds, £70. My friend, Thomas Strong, who lives on Long Island, in East Hampton, £5. Executors—son, Stephen, and my son-in-law, Jonathan Thompson, and my son-in-law, Seth Woodruff. Witnesses—Eliakim Higgins, Frederick Bonniel, Caleb Jefferys. Proved Dec. 1, 1770. Lib. K, p. 273.

1770, June 19. Hiner, William, of Alexandria Twsp., Hunterdon Co. Int. Adm'r—John Hiner. Fellowbondsman—Abraham Young; both of said place.

1770, June 19. Renunciation by Harbert Hiner, eldest son of William Hiner, dec'd.

1770, June 18. Inventory, £258.19.4¼, made by Abraham Young and Samuel Everitt.

1771, April 23. Account by Adm'r. Lib. 15, p. 73; Lib. 15, p. 103.

1763, Feb. 7. Hobbs, Elizabeth, of Hopewell Township, Hunterdon Co.; will of. To the Baptist Church of Hopewell, £6 and 5 shillings. Books are given to John Gano, at New York, Enoch Green, Jonathan Dunham in Piscataway, Benjamin Miller at Scotch Plains, Joseph Powell, and the great Bible to Sarah Gano, the wife of Daniel Gano, Sr. To Archa Hill, my bed. To Elizabeth Ege, daughter of Adam Ege, chest of drawers. Executors—Rev. Isaac Eaton and John Hart, Esq., both of Hopewell. Witnesses—John Titus, Jonathan Smith, Hezekiah Bonham. Proved Feb. 7, 1767.

1767, Jan. 12. Inventory, £382.5.0, made by Nehemiah Stout and Samuel Stout, Jr. Lib. 13, p. 211.

1758, June 30. Hobbs, John, of Hopewell, Hunterdon Co., weaver; will of. Wife, Elizabeth, all real and personal estate. Executors—Isaac Eaton, Captain David Stout, both of Hopewell, and my wife. Witnesses—Derrick Hogeland, Jr., Josiah Howell, Abigail Hogeland. Proved June 18, 1761.

1761, June 12. Inventory, £388.7.7, made by John Hart and Joseph Powell. Lib. 11, p. 47.

1755, June 2. Hoff, Charles, of Hopewell, Hunterdon Co., yeoman; will of. Wife, Angelica, ⅓ of my moveable estate, and ⅓ the profits of land. Eldest son, Charles Hoff, £10. Son, Cornelius, the plantation where I live. Son, Peter, £50. Sons, James and Gabriel,

£10 each. Daughters, Patience and Johanna, £10 each. Executors—sons, Charles and Cornelius. Witnesses—Henry Pinkerton, Jonathan Furman, Thomas Craven. Proved Feb. 9, 1764.
1764, Jan. 3. Inventory, £165.14.0, made by Henry Pinkerton and John Welling, Sr. Lib. 11, p. 528.

1769, Feb. 17. Hoff, Lawrence. Account, made by Benjamin Jones, the Executor, which was settled and approved. Lib. 13, p. 494.

1769, Nov. 29. Hoffman, David, of Cumberland Co. Ward. Son of John Hoffman, of Morris River, said Co. Guardian—Samuel Hannah, of Dearfield, yeoman. Fellowbondsman—Richard Cayford (Kayford), of Hopewell; both of said Co. Witness—James Ewing.
Lib. 14, p. 125.

1763, May 20. Hoffman, James, of Penns Neck, Salem Co. Int. Adm'r—Moses Hoffman, of Upper Penns Neck, said Co., yeoman. Fellowbondsman—Jochonias Wood, of Pilesgrove, said Co., tanner.
1763, May 2. Inventory, £57.15.8, made by Jechonias Wood and Thomas Pedrick. Lib. 11, p. 372.

1770, Jan. 3. Hoffman, Moses, of Upper Penns Neck, Salem Co., yeoman; will of. Household goods to wife, Elizabeth, and the profits of the plantation, now leased to Stephen Ayars. Son, Jeremiah, my plantation on Oldmans Creek. Son, Thomas, the other plantation on said Creek, and joins Jeremiah's lands. Son, Moses, £100 when 21. My daughter, Ellinor Batton, £100. Daughter, Deborah Battin, £100. Daughter, Mary Hoffman, £100. Executors—my wife and my brother-in-law, Thomas Denny. Witnesses—Christopher Graff, Samuel Silver, Lydia Dawson. Proved March 6, 1770.
1770, Jan. 19. Inventory, £409.18.9, made by Charles Dalbow and Samuel Linch. Lib. 14, p. 282.

1764, May 3. Hoffman, Pieter, of Amwell, Hunterdon Co.; will of. Wife, Gertrauta, and my eldest son, William, shall live in the place for 10 years, and they are to bring up the minor boys and daughters. Mentions as children, "William, Henry, and the rest." Executors—friends, Adam Poock and William Berg. Witnesses—John Sharp, Christopher Strempfel, Christopher Gobrecht. Proved April 9, 1766.
1766, April 4. Inventory, £129.13.0, made by Peter Rockfeller and John Sharp. Lib. 13, p. 225.

1766, Dec. 20. Hoffman, William, of Amwell Twsp., Hunterdon Co.; will of. Son, Johannes, £6. Wife, Anna Maria, ⅓ of my moveable estate. Son, Johannes Hoffman, and Philip Diltz, my son-in-law, jointly, to manage plantation, and give to my wife ⅓ of every thing they raise; at death of wife, all my estate shall go to my children, Johannes Hoffman, William Hoffman and Mary, the wife of Philip Diltz; but they are to pay to my stepchildren, namely, Peter Diltz, Philip Diltz, Christian Diltz, Catharine Beyer and Anna Elizabeth Snyder, £5 to each. Executor—friend, Henry Hoffman. Witnesses—Christian Cowell, John Hoppoch, Timothy Buzzard.
1767, Jan. 21. Codicil. Son, William, to have the same benefit of the house and plantation as son, Johannes, has. Witnesses—John Hoppoch, Pitter Subbery, John Hublar. Proved April 4, 1767.
1767, April 3. Inventory, £94.0.4, made by Francis Beson and John Teil Russeler. Lib. 13, p. 241.

1761, Jan. 27. Hogbin, Hezekiah, of Alloways Creek, Salem Co. Int. Adm'rs—Mary Hogbin, widow, and John Holme, yeoman. Fellowbondsman—William Oakford, yeoman; all of said place.
 1761, Jan. 26. Inventory, £122, made by Nehemiah Hogbin and William Oakford.
 1765, March 13. Account made by John Holme, surviving Adm'r.
Lib. 10, p. 441.

1763, March 23. Hogeland, Derrick, Jr., of Amwell, Hunterdon Co.; will of. Wife, Abigail, all the goods she brought to me by marriage, and she shall have all the benefit of my estate to bring up the children, till the eldest is 18 (being a female); then real and personal to be sold, and given to each child equally, viz., Abigail, Rhoda and Mary Hogeland. Executors—Obediah Howell, John Hogeland and Abigail Hogeland. Witnesses—John Sutton, Joseph Higgins, Joseph Leigh. Proved April 20, 1763.
 1763, Apri 9. Inventory, £268.2.4, made by Joseph Higgens and Joseph Leigh. Lib. 11, p. 352.

1765, Aug. 21. Hogeland, Derrick, of Amwell Twsp., Hunterdon Co.; will of. Eldest son, John, as a birth right, 10 shillings. Wife, Mary, use of plantation of 240 acres, where I live, and interest of bonds in hands of my son, John, my son, William, and my son, James. My aged mother, named Jacobe, is to be maintained. Son, Joseph, £100. Grandson, Daineal, son of Henry Hoogeland, deceased, £10 when 21. Legacies given to daughter, Sarah; sons, John, William, James and George; and my daughters, Mary and Siche; and my other sons, Abraham, Joseph, Amos; and the children of my son, Derrick, deceased, being three of them. Executors—sons, John, William and George. Witnesses—Joseph Higgens, John Shamp, John Barber. Proved Oct. 5, 1765.
 1765, Sept. 28. Inventory, £472.14.6, made by Joseph Higgens and John Jewell.
 1793, Oct. 29. Account by William Hoogland, surviving Executor. Goods were sold "after the death of widow." Lib. 12, p. 397.

1767, July 17. Hogeland, Martynis, of Windsor, Middlesex Co., yeoman; will of. My share of my grandfather, Christopher Hogeland's, estate, to be sold, it being in New York. Wife, Phebe, the lands where I dwell, during her life, and she to take care of my son, John, and my daughters, Arianche and Jane. Son, Ouke, a silver tumbler. After wife's death the place to be sold, and money given to my sons, Ouke, Martin, Christopher, John and Cornelius, and my daughters, Elinor, Jane, Idah, Phebe and Arianche. Executors—wife, Phebe, my sons, Ouke and Christopher, and my brother's son, Christopher Hogeland. Witnesses—Richard Hutchinson, Jr., William Hutchinson, Jr., Stephen Warne. Proved Feb. 10, 1768.
 1768, Feb. 9. Inventory, made by Koert Voorhies, and Cornelius Voorhies. Lib. 13, p. 308.

1761, Oct. 25. Hoking, Roger, of Pilesgrove Twsp., Salem Co., yeoman; will of. Grandson, Samuel Hockings, all my lands; and he is to pay to his four sisters, Mary Huckings, £15, Barbary Huckings, £10, Patience Huckings, £10, and to Rebecca Huckings, £10. My daughter, Hannah Barber, £20. Daughters, Elizabeth Hughes, Susan-

nah Garrison, Hulda White, and Hendrence Vert, rest of moveable estate. Executors—son-in-law, James Hughes and David Davis. Witnesses—Dorothy Davis, David Davis, Mary Huckings.
1761, Dec. 10. Codicil. My daughter-in-law, Marcy Huckings, is to have the profits of my lands mentioned in my will, for 2 years. Witnesses—same as in will. Proved March 16, 1764.
1763, Aug. 13. Inventory, £168.14.11, made by Elisha Bassett and Daniel Bassett.
1767, June 15. Account, by the Executors. Lib. 12, p. 100.

1769, July 8. Holcomb, Samuel, of Amwell Twsp., Hunterdon Co., yeoman; will of. Wife, Eleanor, £12 yearly, to be paid by sons, Richard and Thomas; and otherwise provided for. Eldest son, John, £5. Grandson, Samuel, son of my son John, £10. Son, Jacob, £5. Third son, Samuel, the house that he lives in, and 15 acres thereunto belonging, which I bought of Caleb Farley. Fourth son, George, five acres which I bought of John Smith, which is now in possession of Wm. Muirhead, and 30 acres adjoining, which is part of 100 acres I bought of Richard Smith of Burlington. Fifth son, Elijah, rest of the 100 acres. Sixth and seventh sons, Richard and Thomas, the home place where I live, and Thomas is to pay his brother, Richard, £50. Daughter, Phebe, the wife of Henry Lott, £40. Daughter, Elizabeth, $100 when she is 20. Executors—brother, Richard Holcomb, and my son, Samuel. Witnesses—Richard Hinds, William Gano, Josiah Ellis.
1769, July 16. Codicil. Same witnesses. Proved Sept. 21, 1769.
1769, Sept. 19. Inventory, £608.15.6, made by John Hogeland, and William Gano.
1773, May 25. Account by Executors.
Lib. 14, p. 201; Lib. 14, p. 514.

1764, March 13. Hollings, Israel, of Waterford, Gloucester Co. Int. Adm'r—Michael Hollings. Fellowbondsman—Walter Burk; both of said Co.
1764, March 7. Renunciation of Abraham Hullings; in which he states that Israel Hullins and his wife died intestate, and he, Abraham Hullins, of Phila. being the eldest brother of Israel, have right to act as Adm'r, but desire my brother, Michael Hullins, of Waterford Twsp., to act in my place. Witness—Walter Burk.
1764, March 9. Inventory, £163.7.8¾, made by John Shivers and Josiah Shivers.
1766, Dec. 20. Account by Michael Hullings. Lib. 11, p. 537.

1761, May 30. Hollings, Michael, of Gloucester Co. Ward. Son of Lorance Hollings, of said place. Guardian—Israel Hewlings.
Lib. 10, p. 439.

1764, Oct. 4. Hollinshead, Benjamin, of Evesham, Burlington Co., merchant. Int. Adm'x—Jerusha Hollinshead of Northampton. Fellowbondsman—David Oliphant, of Evesham. Lib. 12, p. 27.
1764, Nov. 24. Adm'r—John Hollinshead, of Chester Twsp., on estate of Benjamin Hollinshead, late of Northampton, left unadministered by Jerusha Holinshead. Fellowbondsmen—John Hillier and John Eayre, yeomen. Lib. 12, p. 36.
1776, March 19. Inventory, £497.8.1, made by John Cox and Noah Haines. Also account of John Hollinshead, Adm'r. Lib. 16, p. 498.

1759, Oct. 13. Hollinshead, Edward, of Greenwich, Gloucester Co., yeoman; will of. Wife, Susannah, £100, and furniture. Real to be sold, and money given to sons, Jacob and Ryner, when of age. Executors—brothers, Hugh Hollinshead and Joseph Hollinshead. Witnesses—John Rambo, Cornelius Dewees, Benjamin Lodge. Proved June 18, 1761.
    1761, June 15. Inventory, £471.9.7, made by Thomas Rice and Samuel Sims.
    1767, June 5. Account by both Exr's.   Lib. 11, p. 108.

1770, Nov. 23. Hollinshead, Hugh, of Chester Twsp., Burlington Co. Int. Adm'r—Hugh Hollinshead, of said Twsp. Fellowbondsmen—William Higbee and Richard Fenimore. Witness—Joseph Stokes, Jr.
    1770, Nov. 23. Renunciation by Anna Hollinshead and John Hollinshead, widow and eldest son.   Lib. 15, p. 70.
    1770, Nov. 9. Inventory, £715.16.0, made by Enoch Roberts, Richard Fenimore, William Higbee.

1761, June 18. Holloway, James, of Chesterfield Twsp., Burlington Co., yeoman; will of. Son, Benjamin, house and land where I live; he paying to daughter, Mary Holloway, £25, and to daughter, Ann Holloway, £25, and to daughter, Rebecca Holloway, £25, and to daughter, Avis Holloway, £25. My sons, Samuel, James and David, my lands, some of which are at Barnegat and undivided between my brother, George, and me. Son, Joseph, 100 acres on Mill Creek. Wife, Rebecca, use of lands till my sons are of age. Executors—my wife, Rebecca, and my friend, Michael Newbold. Witnesses—George Holloway, William Page, Samuel Harris. Proved Aug. 10, 1761.
    Lib. 10, p. 299.

1760, Feb. 19. Holloway, Malachi, of Mendham, Morris Co.; will of. Son, Elkenah, ½ of my land, which will be 38½ acres. Son, Elijah, the other ½ of my land. My wife, Elizabeth, to have a good maintenance. If both sons die, then the land is to go to my wife, and, when she dies then to Nehemiah Holloway, and my three daughters, viz., Patience, Judeth and Elizabeth. Executors—sons, Elkenah and Elijah. Witnesses—John Brown, John Brown, Jr., Elizabeth Bobet. Proved July 6, 1762.
    1762, June 22. Inventory, made by Isaac Babbit and John Brown.
    Lib. H, p. 297.

1758, Feb. 13. Holman, Francis, of Somerset Co., inn keeper; will of. Real to be sold. Son, Daniel, my gun. Son, Robert, my Bible. Wife, Catherin, £5 and an equal share with my sons, Daniel and Robert (except wife's portion, which she is to receive from her father), which I give to my three daughters, Mary, Catherin and Jean, when 18. Sons to be bound to trades, when 14. Executors—my wife and John Thomson. Witnesses—William Wooling, Daniel Hendrickson, Andrew Brown. Proved Nov. 29, 1764.
    1764, Nov. 22. Inventory, £96.17.0, made by Daniel South, and Joshua Higgins.
    1766, May 5. Account by Catherine Holman, Executrix.
    1766, July 11. Citation issued to Catherine Badcock, late Catherine Holman, to prove her account, on complaint of Robert Holman.

1767, Sept. 14. Account made by Catharine Badcock, wife of William Badcock, and late widow of Francis Holman.
Lib. H, p. 477; Lib. H, p. 625.

1767, Aug. 8. Holme, John, the elder, of Waterford Twsp., Gloucester Co., yeoman; will of. Wife, Esther, use of my plantation, and at her decease to be sold and the money to be divided between my four children, John, Lydia, Johanna and Phebe. Son, John, the land I purchased of Samuel Dennis, of 40 acres, which joins land of Isaac Kay and Amos Haines. Grandchildren, John and Thomas Lukemanear, £10 each, when 21; but, if they both die, then the £20 to go to the other children of my said daughter, Lydia. Executor—brother-in-law, Thomas Bate. Witnesses—John Matlack, Benjamin Holme, Samuel Clement. Proved Sept. 8, 1767.
1767, Aug. 29. Inventory, £55.18.9, made by John Matlack and Benjamin Hartley.
1778, Aug. 4. Account by Executor. Lib. 13, p. 116; Lib. 18, p. 688.

1762, June 20. Holmes, James, late of Upper Freehold, Monmouth Co.; will of. Debts of my brother, Samuel Holmes, deceased, to be paid. To Obadiah Holmes, Jr., son of my brother, Samuel Holmes, deceased, land in Amboy. A tract in Upper Freehold to be sold. To James Holmes, and Mary Holmes, children of my brother, Samuel, deceased, £100 each. The rest of my estate to the children of my brothers and sister, viz., children of Jonathan Holmes, Obadiah Holmes, Joseph Holmes, Samuel Holmes, deceased, John Holmes, deceased, and Mary Mott, deceased. Executors—my brother, Obadiah Holmes, brother-in-law, James Mott, and Obadiah Holmes, Jr., son of my brother, Samuel, deceased. Witnesses—John McConnell, Thomas Loyd, John Loyd. Proved Sept. 28, 1762.
1762, Dec. 30. Inventory, £5,840.6.8, made by Richard Crawford and William Crawford.
Lib. H, p. 185.

1760, June 14. Holmes, Jonathan, of Middletown, Monmouth Co., yeoman; will of. Son, Samuel, east half of my plantation. Son, John, the other half. John to allow his mother a good living. Said sons are to pay to my daughter, Deliverance, wife of Peter Bowne, £50. Daughter, Sarah, wife of John Throckmorton, £100. Granddaughter, Rebecah Holmes Tice, £20, when 18. Executors—sons, Samuel and John, and friend, Joseph Throckmorton. Witnesses—Johannis Bennet, Margaret Morris, Valentine Welch. Proved Jan. 30, 1767.
Lib. I, p. 78.

1766, Sept. 6. Holmes, Jonathan, Jr., of Freehold, Monmouth Co.; will of. Sons, William and James, all real and personal estate, and they are to pay debts and legacies. Sons, Jonathan and John, and daughter, Alice Van Brackle, 5 shillings each. Son, Samuel, £380. Daughter, Crose Horne, £60. To four grandchildren, children of my son, Joseph, £12. Son, Daniel, £150. Daughter, Catharine Schenck, £10. Executors—my sons, William, James and Samuel; also Daniel Holmes. Witnesses—Obadiah Holmes, Obadiah Holmes, Jr., Asher Holmes. Proved Nov. 2, 1768. Probate to William "Homes" as Executor, Oct. 23, 1770.
1796, Aug. 8. Adm'r—Philip Holmes. Fellowbondsmen—Jacob Tice and Nehemiah Shumway; all of Monmouth Co. Whereas, Jonathan Holmes, Jr., made his will, and appointed William Holmes and

Daniel Holmes, his Executor, and the said Executors are since dead, and have left a part of the estate unadministered upon, therefore Philip Holmes is appointed Administrator.

Lib. K, p. 264; Lib. 35, p. 520.

1763, Sept. 22. Holmes, Joseph, of Shrewsbury, Monmouth Co. Int. Adm'rs—James Mott and James Mott, Jr. Fellowbondsman—Obadiah Holmes, Jr.; all of said Co. Witness—Mary Herbert.

1763, Sept. 14. Renunciation by Sarah Holmes, the widow, in favor of her father, James Mott, and her brother, James Mott, Jr.

1763, Oct. 12. Inventory, £1,704.13.4, made by John Little and Joseph Price.

1767, Oct. 5. Account filed by Adm'rs. Includes cash received, for land, which was sold by John Taylor, Sheriff of said Co., by virtue of an execution against said land, at the suit of John Burrows and William Hendrickson, Executors of Abraham Watson, £2,613.9.4.

Lib. H, p. 292.

1762, March 23. Holmes, Margaret, of City and Co. of Burlington. Ward. Aged above 14. Daughter of Thomas Holmes, blacksmith. Guardian—Samuel Allinson, of said City. Fellowbondsman—Thomas Pryor, Jr., of same place, gent. Witnesses—Daniel Ellis and Gabriel Blond.

Lib. 11, p. 204.

1761, Nov. 26. Holmes, Mary, of Elsinboro, Salem Co., widow. Int. Adm'r—Clement Hall, yeoman, of said place. Fellowbondsmen—Robert Johnson and Joseph Burroughs, of Town of Salem.

Lib. 11, p. 36.

1766, Sept. 21. Honnold, Matthias, of Bethlehem, Hunterdon Co. Int. Adm'x—Barbara Honnold. Fellowbondsman—Cornelius Anderson; both of said place.

1766, Sept. 19. Inventory, £84.10.6, made by Cornelius Anderson and William Bate.

Lib. 12, p. 423.

1762, July 14. Honywell, Richard, of Oxford Twsp., Sussex Co., yeoman; will of. Wife to have one-third. Daughters—Martha, Elizabeth, Mary, Marget and Bathsheba, rest of chattels, when they are 18. Executors—Henry Crosley and John Reed, who are to sell the lands. Witnesses—Joseph Runnels, William Jones, John Hunnywell. Will signed by Richard Honywell and Rachel Honywell. Proved Sept. 9, 1762.

1762, Sept. 8. Inventory, £146.0.2, made by Jonathan Hopkins and George Allen.

1764, Jan. 26. Account made by both Executors. Four of the children were bound out.

Lib. 11, p. 291.

1763, Sept. 14. Hoogeland, Christopher, of Windsor, Middlesex Co., merchant. Int. Adm'rs—Jacob Hoogeland, brother of Christopher, and Peter Schenk; both of Somerset Co. Witness—John Johnston.

1763, Sept. 13. Renunciation by Susanna Hoogeland, the widow. Witnesses—Andrew Sidle and Cornelius Hegeman.

1763, Sept. 20. Inventory, £355.7.3½, made by Peter Ten Eick, Richard Major and John Ely. (Contains many names of people who gave notes and bonds.)

1763, Sept. 20. Inventory, £434.8.4½, made by same appraisers. (Includes dry goods and groceries). Account, "as now stands in his ledger," includes following as some of the names given: Robert Chambers, Altie Dorland, Richard Reed of Freehold, Elizabeth Giberson, John Davison, Sr., of Windsor, John Lemmon, fidler, John Green, tailor, Martha Brittan (daughter of Benjamin), Margret Tropt, widow, John Applegate, carter, Nicholas Britten, Jr., Benj. Britten, Jr., Johannes Ritticer, William Davison, Sr., Cranberry, Mary Hull (daughter of John), James Vaughn, Ammasiah Davison, Captain Joseph Vaughn, John Giberson, Monmouth, John Smith, Penns Neck, Henry Fisher, worsted comber, Gisabert Giberson, Sr., Sarah Brittain, William Mount (son of Mathew), Barnt Heggerman, brewer, Sarah Serjent, William Wilky, tailor, Elizabeth McConnell (wife of Samuel), William Hutchins (son of Richard), Rachel Peters, widow, Houghton Mershon, Thomas Kerns (son of Richard), Grace Gordon, Cranbury, John Job, brick maker, Rachel Hankins (daughter of Daniel), Samuel Mead, John Smith (son of Ellen), Elizal Holman (daughter of Gibert Gibertson), Joseph Cox, millwright, Daniel Hews (son of William), Peter Trout (son of John), Thomas Mount, cooper, John Smith, tavern keeper, Mary Schooley, widow, Joseph Schooley, Joseph South, shoe maker, Martha Fenton, Daniel South, Daniel Swain, and many others. Amount on ledger, £939.1.8.
Lib. H, p. 274.

1767, Jan. 28. Hoogeland, John, Esq., of Sowerland, Somerset Co.; will of. Daughter, Idah, an outset, to be as much as other daughters. Wife, Dinah, may stay on the plantation as long as my widow. Son, Jacob, a negro, etc. Daughter, Dinah, a negro. Daughter, Lenah, the negro that lives with her. Daughter, Eydah, a negro. Grandson, John Hoogeland, son of my son Jacob, £20, to be put to interest by my two sons-in-law, Johannis Van Nest and Jores Bergen, till he is 21. Son, Jacob, 1/6 part of my estate; daughter, Dinah, 1/6; daughter, Lenah, 1/6; daughter, Eydah, 1/6; grandson, James Perrine (son of my daughter, Maria), 1/6 when 21; grandchildren, Margaret and Dinah Hoogeland (children of my eldest son, Christopher, deceased), 1/6 part. Executors—son, Jacob, my sons-in-law, Johanes Van Neste and Jores Bergen, and my nephew, Christopher Hoogeland, Jr. (son of my brother, Christopher). Witnesses—Johannes Stryker, Abraham Duboys, Jacob Bergen, Jr. Proved Feb. 28, 1767. Lib. I, p. 116.

1770, Oct. 30. Hoogland, James, of Sussex Co. Int. Adm'x—Mary Hoogland. Fellowbondsmen—Samuel Carpenter and Henry Vanover; all of said Co.
1770, Oct. 26. Inventory, £81.19.8, made by Gabriel Willson, Henry Vanover and Samuel Carpenter. Lib. 15, p. 69.

1742, Aug. 20. Hooper, Sarah, of Perth Amboy, Middlesex Co., widow; will of. Daughter, Isabella Hooper, all my lots of land, which I have in New York. Rest of real and personal to my son, Robert Lettice Hooper, and my said daughter, Isabella Hooper. Executrix—said daughter. Witnesses—Rebea Legat, Elinor Williams, Philip Kearney. Proved July 10, 1765. Lib. H, p. 505.

1763, Feb. 22. Hopkins, Ann, of Gloucester Co. Ward. Petition of Sarah Hopkins, widow of Ebenezer Hopkins, late of Newton in said Co., yeoman, deceased, in behalf of Ann Hopkins, daughter of petitioner, and of said Ebenezer Hopkins; stating that Ann is under 14, and that she, Sarah, is not willing to be Guardian, and Ann, having real estate devised from Elizabeth Estaugh, late of Newton, widow, deceased; therefore she desires her friend, James Whiteall, of Deptford, to be Guardian of said Ann till she is 14. Witnesses— Hannah Ladd and John Ladd.

1763, Feb. 22. Guardian—James Whitall, yeoman. Fellowbondsman—John Estaugh Hopkins, yeoman; both of Deptford Township, Gloucester Co. Witnesses—Hannah Ladd and John Ladd.
Lib. 11, p. 278.

1762, June 12. Hopkins, Ebenezer, of Gloucester Co. Ward. Petition of said Ebenezer, who is son of Ebenezer Hopkins, of Haddonfield, said Co., yeoman, deceased; making choice of John Estaugh Hopkins (his brother) of Deptford, as his Guardian.

1762, June 12. Guardian—John Estaugh Hopkins. Fellowbondsman—John Gill, of Haddonfield. Lib. 11, p. 125.

1762, June 12. Hopkins, Haddon, of Gloucester Co. Ward. Petition of said Haddon, son of Ebenezer Hopkins, of Haddonfield, said Co., yeoman, deceased; making choice of his brother, John Estaugh Hopkins, of Deptford, as his Guardian, till 21.

1762, June 12. Guardian—John Estaugh Hopkins. Fellowbondsman—John Gill, of Haddonfield. Lib. 11, p. 125.

1768, May 24. Hopkins, Haddon, of Gloucester Co. Int. Adm'x— Hannah Hopkins. Fellowbondsman—Joshua Stokes; both of said Co.

1768, May 21. Inventory, £950.11.11½, made by Jacob Clement and Samuel Clement.

1769, June 23. Account by Hannah Hopkins. A debt was paid to Sarah Hopkins. Lib. 13, p. 435.

1768, May 24. Hopkins, Hezekiah, of Gloucester Co. Ward. Petition of Hannah Hopkins, widow of Haddon Hopkins, and mother to said Hezekiah, who is son of Haddon, stating that Hezekiah has real and personal estate that needs care, and prays that Joshua Stokes may be appointed Guardian of said Hezekiah.

1768, May 24. Guardian—Joshua Stokes. Fellowbondsman—Griffith Morgan; both of said Co. Witnesses—Elizabeth Stokes and Charles Pettit. Lib. 13, p. 436.

1763, Feb. 22. Hopkins, Mary, of Gloucester Co. Ward. Petition of Sarah Hopkins, widow of Ebenezer Hopkins, of Newton in said Co., yeoman, deceased, in behalf of Mary Hopkins, daughter of said petitioner, and of said Ebenezer, stating that she is not willing to be the Guardian of said Sarah, who has real estate by devise from Elizabeth Estaugh, late of Newton, widow, deceased; therefore she prays that her friend, James Whitall, of Deptford, yeoman, may be made Guardian of said Mary, till she is 14. Witnesses—Hannah Ladd and John Ladd.

1763, Feb. 22. Guardian—James Whitall, yeoman. Fellowbondsman—John Estaugh Hopkins, yeoman; both of Deptford Township, said Co. Witnesses—Hannah Ladd and John Ladd. Lib. 11, p. 278.

1765, July 19. Hopkins, Mary, of Newton, Gloucester Co. Ward. Daughter of Ebenezer Hopkins, of said place, yeoman, deceased; says that her aunt, Elizabeth Estaugh, gave by will certain lands which need care, and she chooses her brother, John Estaugh Hopkins, to be her Guardian, till 21.

1765, July 19. Guardian—John Estaugh Hopkins, yeoman. Fellowbondsman—Haddon Hopkins; both of said Co. Witnesses—Hannah Ladd and John Ladd. Lib. 12, p. 126.

1763, Feb. 22. Hopkins, Sarah, Jr., of Gloucester Co. Ward. Petition of said Sarah, who is one of the daughters of Ebenezer Hopkins, of Newton, said Co., deceased; stating that she has lands by devise, from her aunt Elizabeth Estaugh; therefore she makes choice of her brother John Estaugh Hopkins, of Deptford, to be her Guardian, till she is 21. Witnesses—Hannah Ladd and John Ladd.

1763, Feb. 22. Guardian—John Estaugh Hopkins, yeoman. Fellowbondsman—James Whitall, yeoman; both of Deptford Twsp., said Co. Witnesses—Hannah Ladd and John Ladd. Lib. 11, p. 279.

1765, Aug. 8. Hoppaugh, Jost, of Amwell Twsp., Hunterdon Co., yeoman; will of. Wife, Mary, articles as mentioned, and sons, John and Peter, to provide for her. She may live with John, or may remove to live with her children. To Peter Aller, of Kingwood, husband of my youngest daughter, Ann, £135. Eldest son, John, land which I bought of Peter Foxe, 24 Jan., 1749. Son, Peter, land now in his possession, which I bought of Peter Foxe, 16 Dec., 1756. Land where I live I give to said John and Peter; the same was bought of Jacob Peter Sniter. Daughter, Lenah, wife of Peter Young, £80. Daughter, Elizabeth, wife of Peter Hann, £80. Daughter Ann, wife of Peter Aller, £80. Executor—son, John. Witnesses—David Heath, Philip Dilz, Richard Rounsavell, Jr. Proved Sept. 21, 1765.

1765, Sept. 19. Inventory, £849.2.10, made by Peter Rockefeller and Richard Rounsavell, Jr.

1767, Sept. 7. Account by Executor.

Lib. 12, p. 218; Lib. 13, p. 328.

1760, Aug. 16. Hoppe, Andrees, of Hoghokus, Bergen Co.; will of. Wife, Marytie, use of real and personal while my widow. If my wife get an heir, it shall have £150. At her death (if she have no heir), then my estate to devolve into the hands of my brothers, Hendrick Hoppe, Albert Hoppe, Garrit Hoppe, John Hoppe, and my sisters, Antye Ackerman, Tryntie Sabriski, and my sister, Hendricki's, children, that is to say, John, Abraham and Hendrick, and her daughters, Aaltye, and Ragel, my said sister, Hendricki, being dead. Executors—brothers, Garrit Janse Hoppe and John Janse Hoppe. Witnesses—Abraham V. Buskirk, Benjamin Olden. Proved Nov. 13, 1760, by Benjamin Olden. Proved Aug. 4, 1761, by Abraham Buskirk.

Lib. H, p. 50.

1767, April 18. Hopper, John, of Deptford, Gloucester Co., yeoman. Int. Adm'rs—Isaac Hopper and Joshua Hopper. Fellowbondsman—Isaac Ballinger; all of said place; yeomen.

1767, April 9. Inventory, £207.10.2, made by Isaac Ballinger and Samuel Ladd. Lib. 13, p. 131.

1761, Aug. 7. Hopper, Joseph, of Mannington, Salem Co., cordwainer. Int. Adm'r—William Roberts, yeoman, of said place. Fellowbondsmen—William Harvy, yeoman, of said place, and Abel Harris, yeoman, of Penns Neck, said Co.
    1761, Aug. 1. Renunciation by Catren Hopper, widow of Joseph.
    1761, July 25. Inventory, £24.13.6, made by William Harvey and William Peterson.
    1763, Sept. 10. Account by Adm'r. Lib. 11, p. 36.

1766, July 29. Hopper, Samuel, of Greenwich Twsp., Gloucester Co.; will of. Lands and chattels to be sold. Wife, £300. Son, John, 5 shillings. Daughter, Mary Hopper, £250. Daughter, Elizabeth, £150. Executor—my friend, James Hinchman. Witnesses—Caleb Bickham, Isaac Hopper, Margret Boyle. Proved Jan. 12, 1767.
    1766, Aug. 25. Inventory, £405.6.0, made by Caleb Bickham and Nehemiah Andrews. Lib. 13, p. 114.

1761, Nov. 22. Hopple, Nicholas, of Gloucester Co. Int. Adm'x—Mary Hopple, the widow. Fellowbondsman—Ansell Long; both of Greenwich, said Co.
    1761, Nov. 21. Inventory, made by Andrew Long and Ansell Long.
    File No. 755H.

1770, Sept. 2. Horn, Simon, of Rocksbury Twsp., Morris Co., farmer; will of. To John Horn, my brother, William Horn's, eldest son, 40 shillings. My brother, Samuel, my apparel; my gun, to his eldest son, Andrew; my smooth gun to his second son, William. Youngest sister, Charity, a cow; to her daughter Ester, a mare. Remainder to my brother, Samuel's, two eldest sons, Andrew and William, and to my two sisters, Rachel and Charity. Executors—Aaron Stark and Miller Blatchly. Witnesses—William Throckmorton, Charity Hough, Daniel Jones. Proved Sept. 22, 1770.
    1770, Sept. 19. Inventory, made by William Salmon and William Throckmorton. Lib. K, p. 281.

1763, July 28. Hornor, Isaac, of New Hanover Twsp., Burlington Co.; will of. Wife, house where I live and 5 acres of plow land, and 2 acres of meadow. Son, William, house at Crosswicks Creek, he paying the legatees hereafter mentioned; otherwise the legatees, Isaac Horner and Content, (alias John) Horner, to enter the plantation if he refuse to do so. Daughter, Mary, wife of John Clevenger, £10. Sons, William and Joshua, £20 each more than the rest. Residue to my children, William Horner, Joshua Horner, Hannah (wife of James Garwood), Isaac Horner and Content (alias John) Horner; but as Hannah, wife of James Garwood, is dead, her share shall go to her children when 21. Executors—William Horner, Isaac Horner and Content (alias John) Horner. Witness—James London, John Emley, William Potter. Proved Aug. 27, 1763. Lib. 11, p. 379.
    1763, Aug. 19. Inventory, £488.9.6, made by Amos Wright and Samuel Emley.
    1773, Jan. 23. Account of William Hornor, acting Exr.
    Lib. 14, p. 514.

1770, Nov. 17. Horner, Joseph, of Burlington Co. Int. Adm'r—John Thorne. Fellowbondsman—William Wood; both of Chesterfield Twsp., said Co. Witness—Silas Parvin.

1770, Nov. 10. Renunciation of Sarah Horner, the widow, in favor of John Thorne. Witness—Lucy Taylor. Lib. 15, p. 72.
1770, Nov. 3. Inventory, £99.7.5, made by William Wood and Cleayton Newbold.
1771, May 31. Account by Adm'r. Lib. 15, p. 102.

1766, Sept. 29. Hornor, Samuel, of Princeton, Middlesex Co.; will of. Wife, Mary, £300. Daughter, Amy, £200, when 18. Daughter, Sarah, £200, when 18. Son, John, gun and watch, when 21. Sons, John, Samuel and Joseph, rest of personal and real. Executors—my wife, my brother, Joseph, and friend, Robert Stockton. Witnesses—Jonathan Baldwin, James Leonard, Josiah Furman, Jr. Proved Nov. 14, 1766.
1766, Nov. 5. Inventory, £620.19.3, made by Job Stockton and Jonathan Baldwin. Farm at Kingston, valued at £1,030; and one at Princeton, at £1,250. Lib. 12, p. 448.

1761, Dec. 4. Horsfull, John, of Upper Freehold Twsp., Monmouth Co., yeoman; will of. Wife, Ruth, £150, and the use of the land west of house till my son, Richard, is 21. To only son, Richard Horsfull, all my lands; except the house and lot that I bought of John Phineas, which I give to my daughter, Martha Horsfull, when she is 18. Daughter, Sarah, £200, when 18. Daughter, Mary, £200. Daughter, Hannah, £200. Daughter, Ruth, £200. Executors—my wife, and my brother-in-law, Michael Rogers. Witnesses—William Imlay, Robert Montgomerie, Alexander Montgomerie. Proved March 6, 1762.
1762, Jan. 27. Inventory, £2,539.15.5, made by Moses Robins and Thomas Miller. Lib. 12, p. 434.

1764, March 28. Hough, Barnett, of Amwell, Hunterdon Co. Int. Adm'r—Christian Hough. Lib. 11, p. 525.

1761, March 5. Houshell, Jacob, of Amwell, Hunterdon Co.; will of. Son, Mathias Houshell, ½ of my plantation, and £10 to be paid him by my son-in-law, Jacob Case. Son, Peter, ½ of the plantation I bought of Daniel Carrioll, and he to pay to his sister, Mary, £50, when she is 18. Son, Martin, rest of my plantation where I live, when he is 21. Son-in-law, Jacob Case, the other part of the Carrioll place. Executors—my brother, Mathias Houshal, and Peter Lefler. Witnesses—Johannes Rake, William Bellosfelt, John Ringo. Proved April 4, 1761.
1761, April 13. Inventory, £795.3.6, made by Peter Prall and Cornelius Williamson. Lib. 10, p. 563.

1761, Feb. 5. Houshell, Johannes, of Amwell Twsp., Hunterdon Co.; will of. Wife, Nelley, £10, to be paid by my sons, Peter and William, yearly; and they shall provide for their mother. Sons, Peter and William, the plantation I live on, and the house and lot I bought from Andrew Trimmer, excepting thereout the burying-ground for the use of the family forever. Son-in-law, Andrew Trimmer, £50. Granddaughter, Mary Trimmer, one cow. Daughter, Elizabeth's, children, £40, when they are of age. Executors—my brothers, Jacob and Mathias. Witnesses—Cornelius Ringo, Christian Lupp, John Ringo. Proved April 4, 1761. Lib. 10, p. 571.

1760, May 20. Housman, John, of Middlesex Co.; will of. "I am enlisted in the New Jersey Regiment." To Godfried Warner all my estate. Executor—said Godfried Warner. Witnesses—John Smith, Andrew Smith, Jonathan Skinner. Proved June 1, 1761.
Lib. G, p. 438.

1763, Dec. 7. Hovey, John, of Fairfield, Cumberland Co. Int. Adm'r —John Budd, of Salem, Salem Co., doctor. Fellowbondsman—William Dalles, of Fairfield, Cumberland Co., yeoman. Witness—Howell Powell.
1763, Nov. 16. Inventory, £743.17.11, made by William Dalles and Richard Lore.
1767, May 26. Adm'r—William Dalles, of Fairfield, Cumberland Co.; all which were unadministered in the hands of John Budd. Fellowbondsman—William Dalles, Jr., of Fairfield. Witness—Jonathan Lore.
1768, April 29. Account by William Dalles.
Lib. 11, p. 496; Lib. 11, p. 517; Lib. 13, p. 419.

1768, May 12. How, Mary, (formerly Mary Cleayton). Int. Adm'r —Micajah How, of Trenton, Hunterdon Co. Fellowbondsman—Samuel How of Burlington. Witness—Robert Burchan. Lib. 13, p. 435.

1762, June 9. Howard, Joseph, of Morris Co. Int. Adm'r—John Tuttle, of said Co. Fellowbondsman—Thomas Woodruff, of Essex Co. Witness—Moses Littell.
1762, May 29. Renunciation by Anna Hayward, widow of Joseph Howard, in favor of John Tuttle, largest creditor. Witnesses—Joseph Kitchel and Ebenezer Hayward Lib. H, p. 271.

1763, April 19. Howard, Robert, of Upper Penns Neck, Salem Co., yeoman. Int. Adm'rs—Edward Clark and John Hatton. Fellowbondsmen—William Dalbow and William Miller; all of said place, yeoman.
1763, March 11. Inventory, £116.19.3, of the goods of Robert Howard, Jr., made by William Dalbow and William Miller. Lib. 11, p. 373.

1760, Aug. 17. Howel, David, of Newark, Essex Co.; will of. Son, Sylvanus, £20. Wife, Bethia, rest of real and personal. Executrix— my wife, Bethia. Witnesses—Josiah Beach, Josiah Gilbart, Isaac Ogden, Jr. Proved Aug. 3, 1762. Lib. H, p. 172.

1768, May 4. Howell, Abraham, of Morristown, Morris Co., yeoman; will of. Brothers, Silas, Henry, Caleb, John and Samuel, and my only sister, Mary, all my estate. The real and personal to be sold. Executors—brother, Silas, and my friend, Jonathan Stiles. Witnesses —Sarah Clark, Charity Pitney, Timothy Johnes. Proved Jan. 14, 1769.
Lib. K, p. 150.

1762, Aug. 20. Howell, Arthur, of Trenton, Hunterdon Co.; will of. Son, Richard, all my lands. Daughter, Mary Coalman, £10. Daughter, Sarah Howell, £15. Daughter, Abigail Howell, £15. Grandson, Arthur Howell, 30 shillings and pistol. Wife, Hannah, the goods she brought to me, and no more. Executors—son, Richard, and friend, Obediah Howell. Witnesses—Richard Laning, Daniel Laning, Margaret Evins. Proved Dec. 9, 1762. Lib. 11, p. 502.

CALENDAR OF WILLS—1761-1770   207

1766, June 11. Howell, Benjamin, of Greenwich, Gloucester Co., shipwright. Int. Adm'x—Rebecca Howell, of said place, widow. Fellowbondsman—Thomas Robinson, of Philadelphia, merchant.
1766, March 5. Inventory, £543.14.7, made by Thomas Denny and Samuel Hewes.
1769, May 10. Account by Rebecca Howell, Adm'x.
Lib. 12, p. 381; Lib. 13, p. 534.

1770, Nov. 2. Howell, Bethia. Int. Adm'x—Mary Howell, daughter-in-law of said Bethia. Fellowbondsman—Ebenezer Ward; both of Newark, Essex Co. Witness—Mary Ogden.   Lib. K, p. 256.

1757, Aug. 27. Howell, Daniel, of Trenton, Hunterdon Co.; will of. Wife, Abigail, ⅓ my personal estate, and ½ the profits of my lands till my son, Daniel, is 21. Son, Daniel, the land west of the Maidenhead road, and he to pay to my son, Hezekiah, £30. Son. Hezekiah, 15 acres on the Scotch road. Son, John, the land east of Maidenhead road. Daughters, Phebe Howell, Unice Howell and Abigail Howell, £30 each, when 18. Executors—brothers, Hezekiah Howell and Daniel Clark. Witnesses—Stephen Rose, David James, Daniel Laning. Proved Oct. 8, 1763.
1763, Oct. 3. Inventory, £420.7.6, made by John Moore and Daniel Laning.   Lib. 11, p. 472.

1768, Aug. 27. Howell, Mica, of Morris Co.; will of. Daughter, Ann Howell, 5 shillings. Daughters, Rachel Totten and Mary Broadwell, a like amount. Daughters, Sibbah, various goods. Plantation to be sold and ½ the proceeds to my son William, and the other to my sons, John, Mica and Jonathan, when they are 21. The lot on Long Island, near Brickils, to be sold, and given to my four sons. Executors—my friends, William Parrat and Jonathan Mulford. Witnesses—John Winans, Christopher Wamsly, Thomas Osborn. Proved Dec. 4, 1768.
1768, Dec. 12. Inventory, made by William Parrot and Jonathan Mulford.   Lib. K, p. 12.

1761, March 11. Howke, Tobias, of Bernard Twsp., Somerset Co., yeoman; will of. My wife, ⅓ of my estate, while my widow. Son, Jacob, daughter, Ann, and Daniel, also my son, the other ⅔rds. The last two children are under age. Executor—friend, Philip Cox. Witnesses—Isaac Doty, John Roy, John Bowman. Proved April 6, 1761.
1761, April 3. Inventory, £249.13.9, made by Samuel Dunn and Amos Sutton.   Lib. G, p. 417.

1760, July 11. Hubbell, Nathaniel, of Lebanon, Hunterdon Co.; will of. Wife, Elizabeth Hubbell, the interest of the money that was put into the lands of Capt. Daniel Potter and Stephen Crane. Sons, Abijah, Ezekiel and Nathaniel, each 5 shillings. To my children, Lois, Asa, Esther, Mary and Susanna, rest of personal and real. Executors—son, Asa, and my friend, Philip Kearny. Witnesses—Joseph Willis, David Scudder, Andrew Bloomfield. Proved May 28, 1761.
1761, May 28. Renunciation by Philip Kearney.   Lib. H, p. 78.

1749, Feb. 2. Hude, James, Esq., of New Brunswick, Middlesex Co.; will of. Son, James, £100, when 21. Wife, Mary Hude, 1/9 part of real and personal estate. Children, James, Mary, Catherine Hude,

Anne Hude, Robert, Susannah Hude, Halenah Hude, Margaret Hude, 1/9 part each. To the child which I may get, a share. Wife to have income, to bring up children. Executors—my wife, my son, James, my brother-in-law, Simon Johnston, and my friend, Francis Costigin, and in case my wife marry then my daughter, Mary Hude. Witnesses—Philip French, William Mercer, Anthony White.

1762, Sept. 29. Codicil. My friend, Francis Costigin, is not to be an executor, but, in his stead, my daughter, Mary Hude. Son, James, my house in New Brunswick, on Burnet street. Witnesses—Henry Guest, William Harrison, Andrew Norwood. Proved March 12, 1768.

1769, March. Inventory, £4,583.7.2, made by Richard Gibb and Az. Dunham. Lib. I, p. 216.

1768, May 20. Hudnut, Nathaniel, of Hopewell Twsp., Hunterdon Co.; will of. Wife, Naomi, all my estate. Executrix—my said wife. Witnesses—John Hart, Isaac Eaton, Elce Howton. Proved Oct. 26, 1768.

1768, Aug. 15. Inventory, £42.12.0, made by John Hart and John Hunt. Lib. 13, p. 475.

1766, July 29. Hudson, Obed, of Alloways Creek, Salem Co. Ward. Only son of Isaac Hudson, of said place, who by will left lands to his son. Guardian—Constant Smith. Fellowbondsman—Enoch Moore; both of Greenwich, Cumberland Co., yeomen. Lib. 12, p. 327.

1769, Dec. 7. Huff, Joseph, of Somerset Co. Int. Adm'r—John Van Derveer. Fellowbondsman—Jacobus Van Derveer; both of said Co. Witness—William Redford Crawford.

1769, Dec. 6. Renunciation by Catharine Huff. Witnesses—Moses Craig and James Graham.

1769, Dec. 12. Inventory, £15.7.0, made by Gerret Voorhees and Stephen Hunt. Lib. K, p. 142.

1765, April 8. Hugg, Samuel, of Haddonfield, Gloucester Co., blacksmith. Int. Adm'x—Leze Hugg, of said place, widow. Fellowbondsman—Joseph Collins, of Waterford Twsp., said Co.

1765, March 25. Inventory, £1,055.16.2, made by Isaac Kay and Samuel Collins.

1768, Aug. 4. Account by Adm'x. Lib. 12, p. 75.

1769, Feb. 26. Huggens, Masey, of Pilesgrove, Salem Co., widow; will of. Daughters, Barbery, Patience, Hannah, Rebecca and Elizabeth Huggens, all my estate, as they come 18. Daughter, Mary Huggens, shall have only 5 shillings, on account of keeping her child two years, and other reasons. Son, Samuel Huggins, only 5 shillings. Son, Thomas Huggens, to be equal with my first daughters. Executor—friend, Daniel Bassett. Witnesses—Renes White, Elizabeth Bassett. Proved April 3, 1769.

1769, March 20. Inventory, made by Isaac Barber and David Davis. Lib. 14, p. 160.

1762, Aug. 19. Hughes, Elijah, of Cape May Co. Int. Adm'rs—Hannah Hughes and Elijah Hughes. Fellowbondsman—Richard Stites; all of Cape May Co. Witness—Daniel Crowell.

1762, June 29. Inventory, £238.15.0, made by Richard Stites and Daniel Crowell.

CALENDAR OF WILLS—1761-1770 209

1768, April 21. Account by Elijah Hughes and Hannah Hughes, the
Adm'rs. Lib. 11, p. 228; Lib. 13, p. 332.

1768, April 25. Hughes, Hugh, of Morris Co. Int. Adm'x—Sarah
Hughes. Fellowbondsman—Reverend John Darby; both of said Co.
Lib. I, p. 301.

1763, Jan. 15. Hughes, John, of Cape May Co., yeoman. Int.
Adm'x—Martha Hughes. Fellowbondsman—David Corson; both of
said Co. Witnesses—Mary Young and Henry Young. Lib. 11, p. 414.

1764, April 24. Hughes, John, of Cape May Co., yeoman. Int.
Adm'r—Jedidiah Hughes. Fellowbondsman—John Eldredge; both of
said Co. Witnesses—William Mathews and Phebe Young.
 1761, April 6. Inventory, £299.8.5, made by William Mathews and
John Eldredge. Lib. 11, p. 504.

1762, Dec. 30. Hull, Benjamin and Sarah, of Somerset Co. Wards.
Children of Jacob Hull, of said Co., deceased. Benjamin is aged 16
years and Sarah is 15. Guardian—Daniel Farnsworth. Fellowbondsman—John Stevenson; both of Hunterdon Co. Lib. H, p. 207.

1765, Feb. 27. Hull, Joseph, Esq., of Newton, Sussex Co.; will of.
Children, Isaac Hull, Mercy Hunt, Stille Hull, Samuel Hull, Jacob
Hull and David Hull, each £1. My wife, Phebe, to have ⅓ my personal and real estate, until my daughter, Sarah's, decease, or till
she is 18, or in case of the death of my wife. Daughter-in-law,
Abigail Carpenter, £10. Rest to daughter, Sarah. Executors—friends,
Ephraim Darby and Ephraim Martin. Witnesses—William Dunn,
Samuel Lundy, James Hyndshaw. Proved Sept. 1, 1768.
 1766, Nov. 20. Renunciation by Ephraim Martin. Lib. 13, p. 522.

1768, Feb. 1. Hull, Margaret, of Amwell, Hunterdon Co.; will of.
Daughters, Patience Williamson, Margaret Thatcher, Mary Ann
Cane and Johanna South, all real and personal estate. Sons, Moses
Hull, Gershom Hull, John Hull, and Daniel Hull, 6 shillings each.
Executor—Joseph Thatcher, Sr. Witnesses—Bartholomew Thatcher,
Martha Boyd, Thomas Sutton. Proved Jan. 26, 1769.
 1769, Jan. 29. Renunciation by Joseph Thatcher.
 1769, Jan. 26. Adm'r—Moses Hull, of Windsor Twsp., Middlesex Co.
Fellowbondsman—Joseph Thatcher, of Amwell, Hunterdon Co.
 1769, Jan. 24. Inventory, £108.4.2, made by Daniel Robins and Jonathan Higgins.
 1772, April 24. Account by Moses Hull. Paid Walter Cane, £6;
Joseph Thatcher, £6; Patience Williamson, £6; Edmund South, according to the qualifications of Jonathan Higgins, £7.4.0.
Lib. 14, p. 37; Lib. 14, p. 502.

[No date]. Hull, Samuel, of Amwell Twsp., Hunterdon Co., yeoman; will of. Wife, Margaret, living from the plantation and £10
yearly. Eldest son, Moses, ¼ of an acre in the northwest corner of
plantation, joining Peter Hart. Son, Gashim, £10. Son, John, £10.
Son, Daniel, my plantation, except the ¼ acre. Daughters, Patience
Williamson, Margaret Thatcher, Mary Anne Crane and Johanah
South, moveables. Executors—my son-in-law, William Williamson,

14

my son, Daniel, and Garret Williamson. Witnesses—Peter Hoffman, George Trout, John Ringo. Proved July 6, 1761.

1761, June 29. Inventory, £101.14.7, made by George Trout and Jonathan Higgins. Lib. 11, p. 52.

1761, May 30. Hullings, Michael, of Gloucester Co. Ward. Son of Lawrence Hullings, of said place. Makes choice of his brother, Israel Hullings, to be his Guardian, till 21.

1761, May 30. Guardian—Israel Hullings, of Waterford Twsp., said Co., tailor. Fellowbondsman—Francis Austin, of Evesham Twsp., Burlington Co., carpenter. Lib. 10, p. 439.

1766, May 3. Hummer, Harbert, of Somerset Co.; will of. Son, Jacob, land where he lives, and he to give £40 to his four sisters. Son, Tunis, land where he lives, and he to give £100 to his four sisters. Son, Adam, land where he lives, and he to give £100 to his four sisters. Son, Harbert, the place of my abode, and he to give £100 to his four sisters. My wife to live on the place, and she to have ½ of what is gained on it. To my four daughters my moveable effects. Executors—son, Harbert, and my son-in-law, Peter Young. My two daughters, Eve and Alse, are to have outfits when married. Witnesses—Adam Broach, Puness Cornell, Andrew Yeakley. Proved Oct. 2, 1766.

1766, Oct. 18. Inventory, £1,352.7.6, made by Samuel Corwine and Peter Rockerfeller. Lib. I, p. 119.

1769, April 18. Hunloke, Mary, of Elizabeth Town, Essex Co. Int. Adm'r—William Barnet. Lib. K, p. 117.

1765, March 2. Hunloke, Sarah, of Elizabeth Borough, Essex Co.; will of. Daughter, Mary Hunloke, all my estate, she paying to my grandson, Hunloke Woodruff, 20 shillings. Grandsons, William Smith, James Smith and Joseph Smith, 5 shillings each. Granddaughters, Sarah Smith and Ann Smith, 5 shillings each. Executors—daughter, Mary Hunloke, and my son-in-law, Joseph Woodruff, Jr. Witnesses—Isaac Woodruff, Jr., Ellit Crissy, William Crissy. Proved June 1, 1766. Lib. I, p. 39.

1767, Sept. 3. Hunt, Abigail, of Maidenhead Twsp., Hunterdon Co.; will of, being widow of late Samuel Hunt. Son, Ralph Hunt, my negros, stock and goods. Executor—said son, Ralph. Witnesses—Cornelius Ringo, John Phillips, Joseph Worth. Proved Jan. 5, 1770.

1770, Jan. 8. Inventory, £74.8.0, made by John Bainbridge and Joseph Phillips.

1770, May 24. Inventory, £58.15.6, made by Joseph Phillips and John Brearley, of goods found in Sussex Co. Lib. 15, p. 20.

1769, Nov. 19. Hunt, Benjamin, of Hunterdon Co. Int. Adm'r—Samuel Hunt. Fellowbondsman—John Hunt; both of Hopewell, said Co. Witness—Abraham Appleton.

1769, Oct. 16. Renunciation by Patience Hunt, widow of Benjamin Hunt, late of Amwell. Witness—Gershom Lee. Lib. 14, p. 123.

1762, Dec. 11. Hunt, Enoch, of Hopewell, Hunterdon Co. Int. Adm'r—Noah Hunt, of said place. Fellowbondsman—Theophilus Severns, of Trenton, said Co. Witness—Mary Severns.

CALENDAR OF WILLS—1761-1770 211

1763, Aug. 17. Inventory, £33.17.8, made by Edward Hunt and Nathaniel Hunt.
1763, Dec. 8. Account by Adm'r. Lib. 11, p. 336.

1762, April 2. Hunt, John, of Borough of Elizabeth, Essex Co.; will of. My executors are to take up a bond and mortgage in the hands of Mathias Williamson, and a mortgage in the hands of Andrew Craig, both of Elizabeth Town. Wife, Sarah, my dwelling house nigh Elizabeth Town Bridge, and the barn and lot on the other side of the road, while she is my widow. Daughter, Sarah, to have as much moveables, as my daughter, Mary Shackely, upon her marriage with my son-in-law, Peter Shackely. Grandson, William Hunt Shackely, watch, gold buttons, etc., which formerly belonged to my son, William, deceased. Granddaughter, Sarah Shackely, £10, at age of 20. Daughter, Mary Shackely, and daughter, Sarah Hunt, all that which was due to my son, William Hunt, dec'd, and not yet paid, and is in the hands of Capt. King, of New York. Executors—wife, Sarah, and my daughter, Sarah Hunt. Witnesses— T. B. Chandler, James Bruff, John Jones. Proved March 21, 1763.
Lib. H, p. 248.

1768, March 25. Hunt, Mansfield, of Kingwood, Hunterdon Co. Int. Adm'rs—Hannah Hunt, Joseph Hunt and William Hunt; all of said place. Witnesses—Margaret Kirkpatrick and William Kirkpatrick.
1768, March 24. Inventory, £316.14.0, made by Derick Marlatt and Thomas Mackfarson. Lib. 13, p. 335.

1770, May 8. Hunt, Martha, of Chester Twsp., Burlington Co., widow; will of. Son, Joshua Hunt, house and 10 acres in Moorestown, which was purchased (in part) with the legacy of £50 devised to him by his father, Robert Hunt, when he is 21. Daughter, Elizabeth Hunt, a bed. Daughter, Esther Hunt, sheets. Daughter, Hope Hunt, curtains. Executor—friend, Jacob Evans, of Evesham. Trustee—brother-in-law, Peter Harvey, to have care of my children. Witnesses—Abraham Swain, John Cox, Richard Brinkinshire. Proved July 10, 1770. Lib. 14, p. 272.
1770, June 27. Inventory, £94.13.4, made by John Cox and John Risdon.
1772, Jan. 8. Account by Executor. Lib. 14, p. 418.

1759, Aug. 23. Hunt, Robert, of Evesham, Burlington Co., cordwainer; will of. Wife, Martha, to bring up my younger children, and to have the chest of drawers that she brought with her, and to have a horse and cow, and my right in the plantation and tract of land whereon her mother lives, and the profits of all my lands, till my sons, John and Robert, are 21, and the uses of personal estate till my daughters and son, Joshua, are of age, and also £50. Son, John, 69 acres which were bought of Phillip Wallace, when he is 21. Son, Robert, several tracts in Evesham Twsp., of 42 acres; also house and lot in Colestown, joining the lot where I live. Daughter, Abigail Evans, £5. Daughter, Elizabeth Hunt, £40, when 18. Daughter, Esther Hunt, £40, when 18. Son, Joshua, £50, when 21. Daughter, Hope Hunt, £40, when 18. Executors—brother, Peter Harvey, Enoch Roberts, and my son, John. Witnesses—John Cox, Samuel Collins, Abraham Wilson. Proved March 29, 1764. Lib. 11, p. 488.

1764, March 10. Inventory, £403.6.10, made by John Cox and Abraham Wilson. Includes "Two apprentice lads' time, to wit, Enoch Haines, £5, and Benjamin Hopewell, £10."

1768, Jan. 23. Hunt, William, of Newton, Sussex Co. Int. Adm'x —Martha Hunt. Fellowbondsman—Amos Pettit; both of said place. Witness—Mary Gammon.

1768, Jan. 23. Inventory, £49.8.6, made by Nathaniel Pettit and Amos Pettit. Lib. 12, p. 522.

1765, Oct. 30. Huntin, William, of Newark, Essex Co. Int. Adm'x —Susannah Huntin, widow of said William. Lib. H, p. 541.

1770, March 15. Huntington, Simon, of Morristown, Morris Co.; will of. Wife, Thankful, ⅓, after debts are paid. Brother, Samuel Huntington, my sermon books. Children—Samuel Huntington, Jr., Eunice Ogden, Phebe Gard, Elizabeth Person, Sarah Winter and Simon Huntington, Jr. (son of John Huntington, my eldest son), rest of my estate; and the share of Simon is to be given to John, his father, till he is of age. Executors—wife, Thankfull, and my brother, Samuel Huntington. Witnesses—Mary Natar, Silas Haines, John Huntington. Proved Sept. 3, 1770.

1770, Aug. 27. Renunciation by Samuel Huntington. Witness— Daniel Keney. Lib. K, p. 279.

1770, Oct. 11. Huston, Alexander, of Newton, Sussex Co. Int. Adm'x—Agnes Huston. Fellowbondsmen—James Morrow and John Pettit; all of said place.

1770, Oct. 15. Inventory, £58.10.0, made by [names not given].
Lib. 15, p. 69.

1769, Dec. 2. Hutchinson, Ezekiel, of Gloucester Co. Int. Adm'r —John Brown. Fellowbondsman—Joshua Lord, both of Deptford, said Co., yeomen. Witness—Elizabeth Mickle.

1769, Nov. 18. Inventory, £157.17.0, made by John English and Thomas Clark.

1771, Dec. 17. Account by Adm'r. Lib. 14, p. 409; Lib. 15, p. 46.

1761, April 4. Hutchinson, William, of Evesham, Burlington Co., laborer. Int. Adm'r—William Rogers. Fellowbondsman—James Cattell; both of said place. Lib. 10, p. 175.

1761, April 2. Inventory, £23.16.0, made by Benjamin Haines and James Cattell.

1769, Dec. 20. Iler, George, of Mannington, Salem Co.; will of. To Abigail Carpenter, daughter of William Carpenter, of said Mannington, all my estate, when she is of age; but, if she die, then Mary Carpenter, daughter of William Carpenter, is to have said estate. Executor—the said William Carpenter. Witnesses—John Roberts, John Lindon. Proved Jan. 25, 1770. Lib. 15, p. 26.

1763, Jan. 10. Iliff, Edmund, of Gloucester Co. Int. Adm'r—Daniel Ellis. Lib. 11, p. 247.

1761, June 7. Imlay, Alice, of Upper Freehold, Monmouth Co., widow; will of. Son, Peter Imlay, all real and personal estate; and

CALENDAR OF WILLS—1761-1770   213

he to pay to my son, John Imlay, five shillings; and to my grandchild, Robert Imlay, a son of my son Peter, £10, when he is 21; but, if he die, then it is to be paid to my son, Peter's, two other children, Peggey Imlay and Gilbert Imlay. Executor—son, Peter. Witnesses—Stephen Pangburn, John Polhemus, Thomas Nowlan. Proved Aug. 17, 1761.   Lib. 11, p. 195.

1764, April 18. Imlay, Johnston, of Kingwood, Hunterdon Co. Int. Adm'rs—Izabel Imlay and John Imlay. Fellowbondsmen—John Allen and Joseph King; all of said Co. Witnesses—John Coate and J. V. Montgomerie.
1764, April 23. Inventory, £354.18.11, made by Thomas Atkinson and George Reading.   Lib. 11, p. 504.

1760, May 31. Ingersul, Elizabeth, of Great Egg Harbor Township, Gloucester Co.; will of. My eldest son, Daniel Ingersul, 1/5 of my estate. Son, Benjamin Ingersul, 1/5 of estate. Son, Joseph Ingersul, 1/5 also. Son, Ebenezer Ingersul, 1/5 also. Son, John Ingersul, 1/5. Executors—sons, Joseph and John. Witnesses—Samuel Risley, Judith Risley, John Steward. Proved March 5, 1762.
1762, March 5. Inventory, £305.13.11, made by Joseph Mapes and Samuel Risley.
1763, April 16. Account by both Executors.   Lib. 11, p. 85.

1758, Sept. 16. Inslee, Joseph, of Lower Makefield, Bucks Co., Penna., innholder; will of. My two daughters, Sarah and Ann, to have as much as my two daughters, Margaret and Elizabeth, have had. Wife, Sarah, various household goods. Lands to be sold, and ½ the money to son Joseph; and other ½ to be put to interest for benefit of my wife, and, at her death or marriage, to my four daughters, Margaret, Elizabeth, Sarah and Ann. Executors—wife and my son, Joseph. Witnesses—Robert Hellings, Thomas Yardley, T. Wood. Proved Feb. 25, 1765.   Lib. 12, p. 105.

1762, April 19. Ireland, Daniel, of Great Egg Harbor, Gloucester Co. Int. Adm'r—Daniel Ireland. Fellowbondsman—William Mapes; both of said place. Witnesses—Job Young and Phebe Young.
1762, April 12. Inventory, £109.16.5, made by James Somers and William Mapes.   Lib. 11, p. 71.

1764, April 11. Ireland, Daniel, of Great Egg Harbor, Gloucester Co.; will of. Wife, the use of my real and personal estate till my children are 21, when they are to have their shares, and the wife ½ the personal. Daughters, Ruth, Pheby and Rhody, plantation where I live and rest of personal. Executors—my brothers, Reuben and Thomas Ireland. Witnesses—Uriah Howell, Noah Smith, Thomas Ireland. Proved Feb. 17, 1768.
1767, Nov. 30. Inventory, £85.1.4, made by William Mapes and Noah Smith.
1774, April 14. Account by Mary Ireland, widow of Thomas Ireland, executrix of said Thomas Ireland, who was the acting executor of Daniel Ireland.   Lib. 13, p. 312; Lib. 15, p. 521.

1764, Oct. 25. Ireland, John, of Great Egg Harbor, Gloucester Co.; will of. My saw mill and lands to be sold. Sons, Daniel, Thomas Jonathan and James, £20 each, when they are 21. Wife, Rebeckah.

to have the use of rest. Son, John, the plantation I bought of Benjamin Betts. Daughter, Rebeckah Ireland, a bed. Executor—friend, Gideon Scull. Witnesses—Samuel Snell, Elijah Barret, Peter Tilton. Proved Jan. 2, 1765.

1764, Dec. 18. Inventory, £136.18.1, made by Return Badcock and Thomas Ireland.

1767, April 27. Account by Gideon Scull, Executor. Lib. 12, p. 40.

1768, Aug. 5. Ireland, John, of Cape May Co. Int. Adm'rs—Thomas Ludlam and William Robinson, both of said Co. Fellowbondsman—Daniel Crowell. Witnesses—Archibald Hughes and Zeruiah Hughes.

1768, Aug. 8. Inventory, £83.8.6, made by Reuben Ludlam and Nathan Youngs.

1769, Aug. 5. Account by Adm'rs. Lib. 13, p. 442; Lib. 14, p. 23.

1761, Oct. 16. Ireland, Joseph, of Egg Harbor, Gloucester Co., yeoman. Int. Adm'r—Joseph Ireland. Fellowbondsman—Edmund Cordeary; both of Great Egg Harbor, said Co., yeomen.

1761, Aug. 13. Inventory, £201.8.0, made by Amos Ireland and Edmund Cordeary. Lib. 11, p. 90.

1767, July 15. Ireland, Micajah and Israel, of Cumberland Co. Wards. Children of Jacob Ireland of said Co. Said children make choice of their brother, Annanias Ireland, to be their Guardian, in presence of William Russell and Thomas Bacon. Said Annanias Ireland, of Hopewell Twsp, said Co., carpenter, appointed Guardian, with Joseph Ayars on his bond. File No. 334 F.

1762, Dec. 3. Irons, James, of Shrewsbury, Monmouth Co. Int. Adm'rs—James Irons, the eldest son, and William Morton. Fellowbondsman—William Brewer; all of said place. Witnesses—Jacob Dennis, Jr., and Anthony Dennis. Renunciation by Thomas White and Deborah White, formerly widow of James Irons, of Squan, deceased, in favor of James Irons and William Morton. Witnesses—Rachel White and Hannah White.

1762, Oct. 29. Inventory, made by Gersham Bills, Samuel Osborn and Thomas Ellison. Lib. H, p. 203; File No. 2495 M.

1766, June 16. Irons, James, of Shrewsbury, Monmouth Co. Int. Adm'x—Ellen Irons, the widow. Fellowbondsman—Garret Longstreet, yeoman; both of said place. Witnesses—Isaac Hance and Anthony Dennis.

1766, March 15. Inventory, made by Gabriel Woodmansee and John Grant. Lib. H, p. 641.

1760, Feb. 12. Iseltine (Iselton), Matthias, of Perth Amboy. Inventory, £129.7.0, made by Robert Sproul and Nicholas Johnson.

1767, July 3. Account by Nicholas Everson, as Executor.
 Lib. G, p. 126.

(For will, see 32 N. J. Archives, p. 173).

1769, March 28. Iszard, John, of Cumberland Co.; will of. Wife, Sarah, £1 and what the law gives her. Eldest son, Mical, my lands at Morris River and Dividing creek. My younger sons, James, Gabriel and Johnis, moveables. Executors—my wife, and my son, Mich-

ael. Witnesses—John Terry, Christopher Foster, Elizabeth Foster. Proved June 7, 1769.
1769, May 2. Inventory, £144.14.8, made by John Terry and Christopher Foster. Lib. 14, p. 10.

1767, July 19. Ivins, Isaac, of Mansfield, Burlington Co., shopkeeper; will of. My wife, all the household goods that were hers when I married her, and £15 yearly. The residue to my children. Executors—son, Joseph, and my son-in-law, John Thorn. Witnesses—William Walton, Aaron Taylor, John Robinson. Proved July 11, 1768.
1768, July 11. Inventory, £4,706.0.7, made by Caleb Shreve and John Chapman. Lib. 13, p. 381.
1773, Dec. 31. Account by Executors. Cash paid the following legatees, viz., Ann Nutt, Isaac Ivins, Solomon Ivins, Lydia Folwell, William Shreve, William Ivins, Samuel Ivins, Moses Ivins, Joseph Ivins, John Thorne. Lib. 14, p. 538.

1763, Dec. 20. Jackman, Elizabeth, of Mount Holly, Burlington Co., widow; will of. Daughter, Hannah Stapler, bed and such clothing as my friend, Elizabeth Ross, shall think proper for her. Friend, Elizabeth Ross, my gold ring. Friend, Mary Hopewell, cloak. Said Elizabeth Ross to take care of my daughter, Hannah Stapler, who is incapable to care for herself, but, if my friend Elizabeth Ross do not live, then Sarah, the wife of Daniel Jones, to care for my said daughter. After the death of my daughter the amount that is left I give to my friend, Stephen Stapler, of Philadelphia, and my friends, Alexander Ross and his wife, Elizabeth Ross. Executors—said Stephen Stapler and John Clark, of Mount Holly. Witnesses—Ann Sharp, Daniel Jones, Jr., James McElhago. Proved April 19, 1764.
Lib. 11, p. 498.
1764, April 17. Inventory, £502.11.3, made by John Woolman and Daniel Jones, Jr.

1769, Oct. 6. Jackson, Joseph, of Pequannock, Morris Co. Int. Adm'r—Stephen Jackson. Fellowbondsman—Nathaniel Mitchel; both of said Co. Witness—Malcolm McCouny.
1769, Oct. 5. Renunciation, by Mary Jackson, the widow; and William Jackson, the son of said Joseph. Witnesses—Hartshorne Fitz Randolph and Nathaniel Mitchel.
1769, Oct. 4. Inventory, made by Hartshorne Fitz Randolph and Nathaniel Mitchel. Lib. K, p. 223.

1761, Feb. 15. Jackson, William, Jr., of Shrewsbury, Monmouth Co.; will of. Wife, Athaliah, £10. Daughter, Mary, a silver spoon. Wife, use of real and personal estate; and, after death or marriage, son Nathan to have the lands, and he is to pay £15 to his sister, Mary, and the like sum to his sister, Deborah. Daughters, Margaret and Lydia, £15 each. The rest to all my sons and daughters. Executors—my brother-in-law, Joseph Allen, and wife, Athaliah. Witnesses—Amos White, Thomas White, William Smith. Proved June 8, 1761.
1762, Sept. 2. Adm'rs—Josiah Holmes and Joseph Jackson, both of Shrewsbury; of all estate which is unadministered by Athaliah, his widow, the only acting Executor, now also deceased. Fellowbondsman—Joseph Potter, of said place. Lib. H, p. 186; Lib. H, p. 188.

1769, Feb. 27. Jacoaks, Mary, of Monmouth Co. Ward. Daughter of Thomas Jacoaks, of said Co., deceased, who makes choice of Thomas Davis as her Guardian.
1769, Feb. 27. Guardian—Thomas Davis, of Philadelphia. Fellowbondsman—John Lawrence, of Burlington. Lib. 13, p. 496.

1760, May 25. Jacobuse, Hendrick, of Peckmans River, Essex Co., yeoman; will of. Being aged. Wife, Egje, to have a comfortable support from all my sons. Sons, John, Jacobus, Johannis, Adrijaan, Peter, Hendrick, Derrick, and Garret, all my lands. Daughter, Aaltje, to have goods, the same as rest of daughters have had. Daughters, Jannitje, Helena, Fytje and Aaltje, £30 each. Executors —Michiel Vreeland, "Leut," and Jacob van Rype, blacksmith. Witnesses—David Marinus, John Carree, Gerret Gerretse. Proved Feb. 7, 1763. Lib. H, p. 382.

1759, Dec. 15. Jacobusse, Gerrit, of Peequanack, Bergen Co., yeoman; will of. My eldest son, Simon, 15 shillings. Son, Jacobus, land where I live of 200 acres. Eldest daughter, Jannetie Bertolf, £30. Wife, Joanna, ⅛ of the grain that grows, etc.; also personal estate, and, when she is done with it, then to my children, viz., Simon, Jacobus, Jannetie Bartolf, Rachel Francisco and Hester Van Houten. Executors—brothers-in-law, Hendrick Van Ness and Isaac Van Ness. Witnesses—George Reyerse, Thomas Jones and "Huns yinng finen B." Proved Oct. 21, 1768. Lib. I, p. 362.

1767, April 12. Jagard, James, of Deptford Township, Gloucester Co., yeoman; will of. Wife, Anne, bed and furniture. Oldest son, James, plantation where John Watson lives, being the land I bought of my father, William Jagard, dec'd. Son, Samuel, all this plantation of two tracts whereon I now dwell, being the land that I purchased at different times of Samuel Davis and Joseph Perce. Son, Thomas, that land called Smoats Meadow, lying in Timber Creek, and being the land I bought of John Perce; also the land at Wards Landing, which I purchased of Levi Perce, shoemaker; also the plantation I purchased of Christian Zimmerman, on a branch of Maurice River, now in the tenure of said Zimmerman. Daughter, Anne Jagard, the plantation I bought of Robert Down, now in tenure of John Pew, lying on a branch of Woodbury Creek, and a tract adjoining, which I bought of the devisees of Thomas Wilkins. (Said daughter not yet 18). To my three sons all my other lands. Daughter, Anne, £6, being the sum left her by my mother. Executors—my wife, Anne, and my friends, Joshua Lord and Samuel Blackwood. Witnesses—Ann Fenimore, James Hinds, Jeremiah Carter. Proved May 11, 1767.
1767, May 1. Inventory, £1,164.14.8, made by John Sparks and Randall Marshall. Lib. 14, p. 92.

1766, Dec. 24. Jagger, Jonathan, of Dearfield, Cumberland Co. Int. Adm'r—John Jagger. Fellowbondsman—Daniel Clark; both of said place, yeomen.
1766, Dec. 16. Inventory, £125.10.6, made by Ezekiel Foster and Daniel Clark. Lib. 12, p. 326.

1767, July 27. James, Joseph, of Woodstown, Salem Co. Int. Adm'x—Elizabeth James, widow, of Pilesgrove, said Co. Fellowbondsmen—John Lloyd and John Hoffman, yeomen; both of Pilesgrove.

CALENDAR OF WILLS—1761-1770   217

1767, June 1. Inventory, £111.18.0, made by Jechonias Wood and Robert Sparks. Lib. 13, p. 190.

1766, Nov. 25. Jane, Thomas, of Bergen Co. Int. Grace Jane, the widow, renounced, and desired that letters be granted to Samuel Crane and Jabez Harrison of Newark, principal creditors. Witness —Joseph Budd.
1766, Nov. 26. Bond of Samuel Crane and Jabez Harrison as Adm'rs. Witness—Lewis Ogden. File No. 704 B.

1766, Oct. 13. Janney, Richard, of New Windsor, Middlesex Co. Int. Adm'rs—Thomas Janney, of Bucks Co., Pa., and Giles Worth, of Hopewell. Fellowbondsman—Phillip Palmer, of Trenton.
1766, Oct. 14. Inventory, £102.6.0, made by John Clarke and Ezekiel Smith. Lib. 12, p. 456.

1761, Dec. 10. Jaques, David, of Middlesex Co., mariner; will of. Wife, Sarah, ⅓ of all my estate, and the use of the whole estate to bring up my children, till the youngest is 18, and the rest of estate to be divided between children, Samuel, Henry, Enos and Hannah. Executors—brother, Samuel Jaques, and Jonathan Bishop. Witnesses—Jonas Baldwin, David Stille, Edward Wilkison, Jr. Proved May 27, 1769. Lib. K, p. 93.

1764, Feb. 18. Jaques, John, of Middlesex Co. Int. Adm'rs— Samuel Jaques and Samuel Jaques, Jr. Fellowbondsman—David Jaques; all of said Co.
1764, Feb. 18. Renunciation by Rhoda Jaques, the widow.
Lib. H, p. 330.

1769, April 11. Jarman, John, of Alloways Creek, Salem Co.; will of. My wife to have the use of my home place to bring up the children. Oldest son, Malliciah, 125 acres, which I bought of Charles Clark. Son, Ezekiel, 130 acres of my home place. Son, Jonathan, the two places lying between the first mentioned two. Son, Daniel, the place on the Main Branch, where Paul Longbog died, of 100 acres. Son, Azariah, place where David Jager lives, of 100 acres. Youngest son, John, land I bought of Lewis Johnson, in Indian Neck. Daughter, Elizabeth, 12 shillings when she is 21, and £12 when 22. Daughter, Sarah, £35. Executors—wife, Mary, and my friend, Jacob Fries, Sr. Witnesses—Jonathan Jarman, George Freas, John Buck. Proved May 18, 1769.
1769, May 9. Inventory, £460.7.9, made by John Buck and Joseph Sneathing. Lib. 13, p. 535.

1765, Sept. 19. Jatt, Philip, of Essex Co. Ward. Son of John Jatt, of Elizabeth Town, said Co. Guardian—Anthony Willment, of said place.
1765, Sept. 17. Petition by Thomas B. Chandler, Rector of St. John's Church, John ——— (?), Church Warden, Matt. Hetfield, Justice of the Peace, who pray that said Wilment may be made Guardian, he being a man of good character and very proper to have charge of the lad. File No. 3523-3526 G.

1762, April 25. Jefferis, John, of Deptford Twsp., Gloucester Co., yeoman; will of. I give all my estate, (except what I give to son, Constantin) to my wife, till my sons, Francis, John, Barzilliah, Joshua and Asay, are of full age, when each is to be paid £6, and my daughter, Mary Jefferis, £6, when 18. Son, Constantin Jefferis, a meadow taken of James Whital, for a term of years. My daughter, Alice Jefferis, 6 pence. Residue to my wife, and, after her death, to children that we have had since our marriage. Executors—my wife and son, Constantin. Witnesses—James Brown, James Cooper. Proved June 20, 1762.

1762, May 4. Inventory, £320.12.4, made by James Brown and James Cooper, the appraisers, and Mary Jefferis and Constantine Jefferis, the Executors. Lib. 11, p. 120.

1761, Aug. 26. Jefferys, Caleb, Jr., of Essex Co. Int. Adm'r—Ebenezar Sturgis, husband of Mary Sturgis, late Mary Jefferys, widow of Caleb Jefferys, Jr. Lib. H, p. 13.

1760, July 29. Jenkins, Hannah, of Penns Neck, Salem Co., widow; will of. Eldest son, John Elwell, 10 shillings. Daughter-in-law, Mary Elwell, £6. Son-in-law, John Poag, one cow. Son, Isaac Elwell, 10 shillings. Son, Treviss Jenkins, clothes press. Son, Nicholas Jenkins, pair of oxen. Sons, Treviss and Nicholas Jenkins, plantation where I live. I order my apprentice, William Wright, to be free when 21. Executors—sons, Treviss and Nicholas. Witnesses—George Mellin, John Hickman, Samuel Whitehorne. Proved July 27, 1762.

1760, Dec. 23. Inventory, £115.4.2, made by Peter Brynbery and Samuel Whitehorne. Lib. 11, p. 251.

1763, July 29. Jenkins, John, of Hunterdon Co. Int. Adm'r—Judah Foulke, of Philadelphia, merchant. Fellowbondsman—Daniel Ellis, of City of Burlington. Lib. 11, p. 413.

1755, Nov. 21. Jenkins, Nathaniel, of Cape May Co., yeoman; will of. Wife, Esther, one-third of personal estate. Sons, Nathaniel and Jonathan, the lands where I live, which I bought of my father, April 12, 1737. Son, Ephraim, the land back of the above. My marsh and oyster ground I give to sons, Nathaniel, Jonathan and Ephraim. Personal estate that is left I give to my five daughters, viz., Phebe Smith, widow, Hannah Stites, wife of Thomas Stites, Mary Smith, wife of John Smith, Rhoda Jenkins and Ansis Jenkins. Executors—my daughter, Mary, and John, her husband, till Nathaniel, my son, is 17 years old, and then he is to be Executor with them till my son, Jonathan, is 17 years old, and then he is to be Executor with them till my son Ephraim is 17 years old, and then my will is that my sons, Nathaniel, Jonathan and Ephraim, shall be the Executors. Witnesses—Jonathan Stites, Jonadab Jenkins, Deborah Jenkins. Proved May 3, 1770.

1771, Aug. 5. Inventory, £21.11.6, made by Daniel Smith and Joshua Hildreth. Lib. 15, p. 185.

1764, July 24. Jennings, Jonathan, of Elizabeth, Somerset Co. (?), yeoman; will of. Wife, Mary, use of house and land I bought of Elisha Smalley and John Davis, while my widow, and she is to bring up my son, Dennis, till he is put to a trade, when 14. My old homestead,

which I purchased of my father, Joseph Jennings, to be sold; also the plantation I bought of Jonathan Shephard, near Cranbury; then debts are to be paid, and son, Dennis, to have overplus. Executors—my brother, Isaac Jennings, and Henry Davis, of Somerset Co. Witnesses—Jacob Clarke, Lovel Morris, Agnes Jennings. Proved Oct. 30, 1764.
1764, Oct. 31. Inventory, made by Joseph Allen, the 3rd, and William Line. Lib. H, p. 464.

1764, Sept. 11. Jessup, Stephen, of Deerfield, Cumberland Co.; will of. Youngest son, Daniel, this place where I live. Wife, Mary, ⅓ of the above during her life, and ⅓ the moveable estate. Eldest son, John, use of said place till Daniel is 21. Son, Isaac, £20, when 21. Eldest daughter, Sarah Jessup, £20. Daughter, Abigail Davis, £3. Executors—wife, Mary, and my son, John; and my friends, Joseph Peck and John Miller, to assist them. Witnesses—Abraham Rose, Samuel Ogden, Constant Peck. Proved Nov. 17, 1764.
1764, Nov. 1. Inventory, £163.16.4, made by Constant Peck and Benjamin Garrison. Lib. 12, p. 58.

1767, Feb. 24. Jewell, George, of Elizabeth Borough, Essex Co.; will of. Son, George, 20 acres in the Great Swamp, joining Caleb Brown. Son, Cornelas, 10 acres in said Swamp, joining land of Jonathan Meeker. Son, Samuel, all the plantation where I live. Sons, John and Samuel, meadow in Elizabeth Town Great Meadows. Grandsons, Moses Jewell and Samuel Jewell, sons of my son Moses, deceased, 8 acres in the Great Swamp. Granddaughter, Elizabeth Jewell, daughter of my son, Samuel, £5. Granddaughter, Mary Jewell, daughter of my son, Samuel, £10. Grandchildren, viz., Samuel, George, Jeams and Elihu, children of my son, Samuel, rest of moveable estate. Executor—son, Samuel. Witnesses—John Ogden, Ephraim Baker, Jr., Ephram Baker. Proved Jan. 11, 1770. Lib. K, p. 164.

1770, Jan. 1. Johnson, Benjamin, of Cape May Co., gentlemen; will of. Wife, Anna (after things mentioned below), use of lands and personal estate, and, at her death, to be to my son Daniel. Son, David, a chain, chair and spade. Daughter, Sarah Stephenson, £12. Grandson, Aaron Stephenson, gun. Executors—my sons, Daniel and David. Witnesses—Thomas Smith, Eli Eldredge, Aner Eldredge. Proved May 24, 1770.
1770, Feb. 27. Inventory, £147.16.4, made by Thomas Smith and Eli Eldredge. Lib. 15, p. 75.

1770, March 5. Johnson, Cornelius, of Kingwood, Hunterdon Co.; will of. Wife, Ann, household goods and cattle. Son, Jacobus, £200. Son, Cornelius, £200. Son, Joseph, £200, when 21. Daughter, Sarah, £40. Daughter, Elizabeth, £50. Daughter, Mary, £50. Daughter, Rachel, £40. Daughter, Ann, £70. Daughter, Winifret, £60. Daughter, Johanna, £70. Daughter, Rebecca, £70. Grandson, William, a mare, when he is 21. I desire the estate to be sold in one year. Executors—sons, Jacobus and Cornelius. Witnesses—James Stout, Jacobus Johnson, Benjamin Johnson. Proved April 27, 1770.
1786, May. Citation to Cornelius Johnson, surviving Executor, to show cause why he has not filed an account.
1786, Oct. 27. Account by Cornelius Johnson. Lib. 15, p. 55.

1770, Nov. 10. Johnson, David, of Essex Co. Int. Adm'rs—Eliphalet Johnson and Samuel Huntington. Lib. K, p. 256.

1766, Sept. 2. Johnson, Ebenezer, of Cape May Co.; will of. Wife, Amey, ⅓ the moveables, and ⅓ my lands while widow. My sister, Phebe Johnson, £6. Daughters, Jerusha, Abigail and Neomy, moveables. My son, Gideon, apparel and all my lands. Executors—my wife and son, Gideon, and Downes Edmunds. Witnesses—Mary Hand, Enos Buck, Mary Hoffman. Proved Oct. 11, 1766.
1766, Oct. 23. Inventory, £189.11.4, made by Isaac Newton and Henry Hand.
1774, April 11. Account by Downes Edmunds (surviving Ex'r).
Lib. 12, p. 354; Lib. 15, p. 531.

1741, April 14. Johnson, Eupham, of Middlesex Co., widow; will of. Advanced in years. That 300 acres, which is part of a tract of 2,118, in Bergen Co., which was devised to me by my husband, to be sold. Granddaughter, Eupham Smyth, £20. Daughter, Mary, the residue. Executors—sons, Andrew and Lewis Johnson. Witnesses—William Burnet, Thomas Skinner, Laurance Smyth.
1744, Dec. 11. Codicil. My daughter, Mary, is deceased; therefore I give to daughter, Margaret Smyth. I have not heard for several years from Scotland, but I believe I have some estate there, which I give to my sons, Andrew and Lewis, and my daughter, Margaret, and my grandson, Elisha Parker. Witnesses—Mary Lyell, John Smyth, Andrew Smyth. Proved Nov. 13, 1764. Lib. H, p. 379.

1766, Feb. 27. Johnson, Garret, of Hopewell, Hunterdon Co.; will of. Wife, Judith, £100. Son, Joseph, 5 shillings. Son, Cornelius, in consideration of a dowry left him by his grandfather, of £50, a tract in Virginia, called 200 acres, except what is hereafter excepted. Daughter, Ann Hoff, £60. Son, Rutt, south part of my land. Son, Robert, the north part. Daughter, Elizabeth Morrell, 100 acres of the 200 in Va. Son, Daniel, £100, when he is 21. Daughters, Hannah, Criston, Patience, Eve and Mary, £100, when they are 18. Executors—son, Rutt, Cornelius Hoff, and Henry Margerum. Witnesses—John Gary, Cornelius Vannoy, Henry Margerum. Proved April 2, 1766.
1766, March 26. Inventory, £356.14.7, made by John Hart and Joseph Burroughs. Lib. 12, p. 400.

1770, July 5. Johnson, Gideon, of Cape May Co. Int. Adm'x—Lydia Johnson (widow of said Gideon). Fellowbondsman—Downes Edmunds, yeoman; both of said Co. Witnesses—Abraham Woolson and Jonathan Leaming.
1770, July 4. Inventory, £109.14.1½, made by Jonathan Leaming and Abraham Woolson. Lib. 14, p. 400.

1762, Nov. 2. Johnson, Henry, of Roxbury Twsp., Morris Co.; will of. Wife, Elliner, use of the farm and moveables, till my youngest son, Zacherias, is 21. When all is sold the money is to be divided among my children, viz., Richard, Henry, John, Elliner, Zackeas, Mary Leuy, and Zacherias. The forge and saw mill to be sold as seems best. Executors—my wife, son Richard, and friend, John Van Tuyl. Witnesses—Jabesh Heaton, Jr., Timothy Skinner, Daniel Heaton, Jr. Proved March 17, 1763.
1763, March 15. Inventory, £1,110.11.4, made by John Lafever and William Boyd. Lib. 11, p. 460.

1764, May 16. Johnson, Henry, of Pilesgrove Twsp., Salem Co.; will of. Wife, Jean, what the law gives her. Son, Henry, 5 shillings. Son, John, 2 horses, and to have William Moore, till he comes of age. Sons, Samuel and William, each £30. Daughter, Jean Johnson, a cow. To Samuel Johnson's daughter, Phebe Johnson, £5. To my daughters, Hannah Johnson, Phebe Johnson, £2, when of age. Executors—sons, Samuel, and William. Witnesses—Joseph Cocks, William Garrison, Jonah Daton. Proved Dec. 25, 1764.
1764, Dec. 8. Inventory, £45.3.3, made by Isaac Stratton and Samuel Carll. Lib. 12, p. 179.

1736, Oct. 16. Johnson, Hezekiah, of Newark, Essex Co.; will of. Wife, Anna, use of ⅓ of my lands, and £30. Grandson, Samuel Johnson, a lot of 19 acres in Newark, bounded south by John Johnson, west by Two-mile creek, north by Josiah Lyon, and east by road; also 10 of woodland in bounds of Newark, bounded by Michael Tompkins, Hugh Roberts, Jonathan Tichnor, and by my own lands, being the westerly part of land I bought of John More, when Samuel is 21. Son, Mathew, ½ of my home lot, the south part thereof. Son, Joseph, the north part thereof, and my last 2 named sons, to have the rest of my lands. Daughter, Elizabeth, £4. Daughter, Phebe, £50. Daughter, Johana, £50. Daughter, Jemimah, £50. [Foregoing] to be paid to them when 18. Twelve acres may be sold, if there is need, which lie in common with Eliphelet Johnson, Nathaniel Johnson, Samuel Johnson and John Johnson, near my old sawmill, being the land I bought of Timothy Johnson. Executors—my wife, and sons, Mathew and Joseph. Witnesses—Nathaniel Anderson, Joseph Ball, Jacob Ogden. Proved Jan. 2, 1767. Lib. I, p. 255.

1761, Dec. 5. Johnson, Jeremiah, of Hanover, Morris Co. Int. Adm'rs—Hannah Johnson, widow, of said Co., and Ezekiel Johnson, of Essex Co. Fellowbondsman—Joseph Heddon, of Essex Co.
1761, Dec. 12. Inventory, made by Benjamin Coe and Zechariah Fairchild. File No. 150 N.

1756, Nov. 10. Johnson, Johannis, of Amwell, Hunterdon Co., cooper; will of. Wife, Maria, £7 yearly, while my widow. Grandson, Johannis Johnson, son of my son, Johannis, deceased, £7. Real to be sold, and the money divided among my three daughters, and the four children of my son, Johannis, dec'd, to wit., Alida, widow of Samuel Barber; Magdelena, wife of John Barber; Geertrue, wife of Caleb Faarly; and the four children of my son, Johannis, dec'd, Johannis, Sari, Susana, Cathrina. Executors—John Barber and Caleb Faarly. Witnesses—James Darompel, Peter Vandolah and James Ashton. Proved March 2, 1762.
1762, April 24. Inventory, £69.13.9, made by Abraham Deremer and William Taylor.
1775, April 13. Account, made(by John Barber and Caleb Farlee, as Executors.
1778, May 3. Account by the Executors.
1779, Oct. 5. Account by both Executors. Lib. 11, p. 142.

1768, May 30. Johnson, John, of Dearfield, Cumberland Co. Int. Adm'r—Benjamin Johnson, of Piles Grove, Salem Co. Fellowbondsman—Daniel Garrison, of said Dearfield.
1768, May 25. Inventory, £141.2.1, made by Thomas Nichols and Daniel Garrison. Lib. 13, p. 419.

1770, March 10. Johnson, John, of Manington, Salem Co. Int. Adm'x—Mary Johnson, widow. Fellowbondsmen—Christopher Smith and William Harvey, yeomen; all of said place.

1770, March 1. Inventory, £283.3.1, made by Christopher Smith and William Harvey. Lib. 15, p. 6.

1765, Jan. 7. Johnson, Joseph, of Newark, Essex Co.; will of. Wife, Mary, use of all estate, during her life. Son, James, my lot in Newark, and ⅓ my lot at Wolf Harbor, and ⅓ the salt meadow. Son, Benjamin, my homestead, where I live, ⅓ the lot at Wolf Harbor, ⅓ my salt meadow, and my land in Mill Brook Swamp, which I bought of Samuel Davice; and Benjamin is to support my son, Robert, during his life. Grandson, Jonathan Johnson, the lot I bought of Charles Woodroff, and ⅓ the lot at Wolf Harbor, and ⅓ the salt meadows. Daughter, Phebe Attwood, £100, and negro, Ann. Daughter, Experience Governeur, £100, and a wench. Executor—wife, Mary, and my son, Benjamin. Witnesses—Gabriel Ogden, Uzal Ogden Jr., John Ogden. Proved Oct. 5, 1765. Lib. H, p. 561.

1764, Nov. 12. Johnson, Nathaniel, of Newark, Essex Co.; will of. Wife, Sarah, £200, and furniture. Son, Stephen, the orchard and land, which I bought of my brother, Eliphalet Johnson. Grandson, Josiah Ward, £50, when 21. Grandson, Jacob Jamison Banks, £50, when 21. Daughter, Martha Ward, ½ the rest of personal. Daughter, Catharine Banks, the other ½. My grandson, Stephen Johnson, house and land, where he lives, which I bought of Capt. Nath. Wheeler, he allowing his mother, a room, and ⅓ the land, during her widowhood. Grandson, Nathaniel Johnson, the house and land, which I bought of Zophar Beach, of 8 acres. Grandson, Jotham Johnson, that land above Two-Mile Brook, which I bought of Col. Joseph Tuttle. Grandsons, Nathaniel and Jotham Johnson, land I bought of Deacon Tuttle, and the land I bought of Josiah Lyon, they paying my granddaughter, Mary Johnson, £60. Son, David Johnson, the homestead, and the meadow below Indian Corner. Children, David, Stephen, Martha Ward, Catharine Banks, and my grandson, Stephen Johnson, son of Thomas Johnson, dec'd, ⅔ of my claim in lands, lately belonging to my brother, Eliphalet Johnson, dec'd, and the other ⅓ I give to children of my brother, Timothy, viz., Jabez Johnson, Sarah Camp, and to the children of my brother, John Johnson, deceased, viz., Eliphalet, Uzal and David. Executors—son, David, and sons-in-law, Uzal Ward and James Banks. Witnesses—Timothy Bruene, Jr., Theophilus Pierson, Daniel Ball. Proved April 15, 1765. Lib. H, p. 549.

1766, Nov. 19. Johnson, Samuel, of Cape May Co., waterman. Int. Adm'r—Gideon Johnson, his brother. Fellowbondsman—Abraham Woolson; both of said Co.

1767, July 24. Inventory, £36.17.0, made by Benjamin Ingrum and Hance Woolson. Lib. 12, p. 358.

1761, May 5. Johnson, Thomas, of Great Egg harbor, Gloucester Co. Int. Adm'r—Joseph Johnson, of said place. Fellowbondsman—John Leek, of Little Egg Harbor, Burlington Co.

1761, March 3. Inventory, £474.6, made by William Read and Nehemiah Leeds.

1770, June 26. Account by Sarah Johnson, Executrix of Joseph Johnson, who was Adm'r of Thomas Johnson.

Lib. 10, p. 294; Lib. 15, p. 17.

1763, Oct. 8. Johnson, Thomas, of Perth Amboy, Middlesex Co., Capt. Int. Adm'rs—Reuben Potter and David Gosling. Fellowbondsman—George Johnson, all of said place.
1763, Oct. 7. Renunciation by Catharine Johnson, the widow, and Stephen Skinner, a principal creditor.
1763, Oct. 10. Inventory, made by Robert Sproul and Thomas Skinner. Lib. H, p. 291.

1765, Feb. 13. Johnson, Thomas, of Mansfield Twsp., Burlington Co., yeoman. Int. Adm'r—Peter Tallman, of same place. Fellowbondsman—John Lawrence, of Burlington.
1764, Feb. 11. Renunciation by the widow, Sallie Johnson, who makes choice of the said Peter Tallman. Lib. 12, p. 43.

1760, May 24. Johnson, William, of Borough of Elizabeth, Essex Co.; will of. Advanced in age. Wife, Susannah, use of ½ the lands, and ½ my moveables. Daughter, Elizabeth Johnson, my house and land, when 18. Sons—William Pool and Robert Pool. Executors—my wife and my friend, Benjamin Clark, 3rd. Witnesses—Peter Lyon, Johannah Lyon, Sarah Clark. Proved Jan. 19, 1763. Lib. H, p. 213.

1761, May 2. Johnston, Andrew, of Perth Amboy, Middlesex Co.; will of. Eldest son, John, that part of a tract in Perth Amboy, called Forsters Neck, on south side of Market street; also the east half of the Town lot, which joins to David Johnston, whereon his house stands; also the bank lot fronting the same. Son, Stephen, that part of Forsters Neck, which lies on the north side of Market street; also the other ½ of the Town lot, which joins northerly the lot of John Stevens, and east on the half devised to my son, John; also that bank lot, fronting David Johnston's house, which I bought of John Stevens. Rest of lands to be sold. Whereas my son-in-law, John Barberie, is entitled by gift from me to ¼ part of £1,300, which the mills at Matcheponia were sold for, I give to my daughter, Mary, my son, John, my daughters, Catherine and Elizabeth, my son, Stephen, and my grandson, William Terrill, each of them a like sum, with that of my said son-in-law, when they are of age. The rest of my estate I give to my son-in-law, John Barberie, and his wife, Gertruyd, daughter of mine; daughter, Mary; son, John; daughter, Catherine; daughter, Elizabeth; son, Stephen, and to my grandson, William Terrill (son of my daughter, Anne Terrill, deceased). Executors—said John Barberie and Gertruyd, his wife, my daughter, Mary Johnston, my son, John, my daughters, Cathrine, and Elizabeth Johnston, and, as they come of age, my son, Stephen, and my grandson, William Terrill. Assistants—friends, Robert Hunter Morris, and John Stevens. Witnesses—John Stevens, Alexander Campbell, Thomas Bartow. Proved July 7, 1762. Lib. H, p. 161.

1764, Jan. 9. Johnston, John, of Freehold, Monmouth Co. Int. Adm'rs—Hendrick Johnston, a relation, and Thomas Leonard. Fellowbondsman—Joseph Morford; all of said Co., yeomen. Witnesses—George Allen and John Lippincott, Jr. (The said Thomas Leonard is a creditor of John Johnston). Lib. H, p. 330.

1765, March 1. Johnston, Joseph, of Great Egg Harbor, Gloucester Co., husbandman; will of. Wife, Sarah, all the goods she brought with her, and £30 more, and the use of my homestead, and the use of

12 acres of salt meadow. Youngest son, David, my homestead. Son, Joseph, the land I bought of Evi Smith. Son, William, land I bought of Joseph Addoms. My daughters, to wit, Sarah Leeds, Elizabeth Cordery, Hannah Johnston, Mary Johnston and Michel Johnston, £30 each. Grandson, David Johnston, £5. Executors—my wife and my son, Joseph. Witnesses—Anne Leeds, Hannah Leeds, Josiah Leeds, Japhet Leeds. Proved June 26, 1770.

1770, June 20. Renunciation of Joseph Johnston, who refuses to act, and "throw it up to my mother-in-law, Sarah Johnston."

1770, June 6. Inventory, £514.3.10, made by Japhet Leeds and Evi Smith.

1771, May 21. Account by Sarah Johnston, as Executrix. Legacies paid to Isaac Cordery, Isaac Andrews, William Johnston, Joseph Johnston, Caleb Cramer and Daniel Johnston.

Lib. 14, p. 230; Lib. 15, p. 100.

1767, March 4. Joline, John, of Elizabeth Town, Essex Co. Int. Adm'r—Matthias Joline. Fellowbondsman—Elias Woodruff; both of said place. Witnesses—Timothy Edwards and Robert Ogden, Jr.

Lib. I, p. 131.

1764, July 31. Jolly, John, of Burlington Co. Int. Adm'r—John Woodward, of said Co., on estate "of John Jolly Son Charles Jolly of ye County of Burlington." Fellowbondsman—Joseph Borden Jr. of said Co. Inventory £86.4.5 (no date). Adm. 246.

(Also given as John Woodward, Adm'r of estate "of John Jolly, Son of George Jolly, late of the County of Burlington"). Lib. 12, p. 13.

1769, Nov. 4. Jolly, John, of South Amboy, Middlesex Co.; will of. Daughter, Mary Johnson, wife of Mathias Johnson, bed and bedding. My daughter-in-law, Elizabeth Jolly, wife of John Jolly, £10. Eldest son, John, 5 shillings. Daughter, Nancy Bissett, wife of Andrew Bissett; and my daughter, Martilla Willmouth, wife of Peter Willmouth, the rest of my estate, except the lands made over to Martilla Willmouth, by deed of gift. Executor—James Abrahams. Witnesses—Samuel Neilson, Adam Sharp, Sarah Huls. Proved Nov. 24, 1769.

1769, Nov. Inventory, £137.6.5, made by John Perrine and Robert Brown. Also a further Inventory of £145.8.11. Amounts of notes, £152.18.1.

1771, Aug. 21. Account by Executor. Lib. K, p. 145.

1762, Nov. 3. Jones, Andrew, of Fairfield, Cumberland Co. Int. Adm'rs—Hannah Jones, widow, and Joseph Ogden; both of said place. Witnesses—Ephraim Harris and Ruth Ogden.

1762, Oct. 14. Inventory, £101.13.7, made by Ephraim Harris and Theophilus Elmer.

1764, Jan. 4. Account by Adm'rs. Lib. 11, p. 278.

1761, Nov. 21. Jones, Caleb, of Borough of Elizabeth, Essex Co.; will of. Moveables to be sold. Wife, Mary, £10, and use of plantation until my oldest son, Edward, is 21. Son, Edward, my rights in undivided lands. Sons, Edward, Jacob and Caleb, my plantation. To each of my daughters, Catharine, Mary, Abigail and Tabitha, £10, when 18, or married. Executors—brothers, William and Isaac Jones. Witnesses—William Carl, Jesse Osborn, Jonathan Elmer. Proved April 1, 1762.

1762, March 8. Inventory, £93.9.7, made by William Parsons and William Parrat.
1766, Nov. 14. Account by both Executors. Lib. H, p. 101.

1761, June 24. Jones, Daniel, of Somerset Co., soldier; will of. Wife, Rachel, all real and personal estate. Executors—my wife and Nathaniel Ayers. Witnesses—John Hogg, Margaret Leferty, Bryan Leferty. Proved Oct. 7, 1761.
1761, Oct. 19. Inventory, £53.4.0, made by Bryan Leferty and Aaron Boylan. Lib. H, p. 36.
1735. On a wrapper with this date, is the following: ["Whereas Dav. Jones, of Gloucester, in County of Gloucester, cordwainer, died intestate, and hath left behind him no kin, except 2 daughters, Susanna and Alice Jones, both minors, and Jon. Whiteall as near friend, prays letters of administration"]. File 528 Q.

1768, Feb. 29. Jones, Edward, of Burlington Co. Int. Adm'r—Jabez Eldredge. Fellowbondsman—Thomas Jones; both of said Co. Witness—Zachariah Rossell. Lib. 13, p. 315.
1768, Feb. 29. Renunciation by Mary Jones, widow of Edward Jones, of Mount Holly, dec'd.
1768, Feb. 29. Inventory, £32.14.2, made by John Clark and Peter Allinson.

1763, Sept. 26. Jones, John, of Salem, Salem Co., attorney-at-law. Int. Adm'r—Samuel Reynolds, of Marcus Hook, Chester Co., Penna., miller, of the estate which is unadministered in the hands of Mary Jones. Fellowbondsman—Thomas Goodwin, of Town of Salem, malster. Lib. 11, p. 419.

1761, Jan. 12. Jones, Samuel, of Burlington. Int. Adm'r—Abraham Hewlings. Fellowbondsman—Daniel Ellis; both of said City.
Lib. 10, p. 171.
1761, Jan. 12. Renunciation by "Rachel Jones, the widow of Samuel Jones and daughter of Sarah Thomas, both late of the City of Burlington."
1761, Jan. 26. Inventory, £111.13.6, made by John Ferguson and Daniel Ellis.
1761, Aug. 4. Account by Adm'r.

1765, Oct. 31—Jones, Samuel, of Newark, Essex Co. Int. Adm'r—John Jones, the eldest son. Fellowbondsmen—Joseph Jones and Cornelius Jones; all of said place. Witness—Lewis Ogden.
Lib, I, p. 7.

1769, Feb. 25. Jones, Serviah, of Middlesex Co. Ward. Daughter of Samuel Jones, of said Co., deceased, who has a legacy bequeathed to her by her father, and also lands descended to her from her grandfather, Daniel Jones; therefore she makes choice of Mathias Brackney as her Guardian.
1769, Feb. 25. Guardian—Mathias Brackney, of Hardwick, Sussex Co. Fellowbondsman—Philip Hoffman, of Newton, said Co.
Lib. 13, p. 496.

1768, Oct. 4. Jones, Stephen, of Elizabeth Borough, Essex Co. Int. Adm'rs—William Maxfell and Isaac Crane. Fellowbondsman—William Jones; all of same place, yeomen. (The adm'rs are two of the largest creditors.) Witnesses—Mary Ogden and Robert Ogden.

1768, Sept. 26. Renunciation of Hannah Jones, widow of Stephen Jones, in favor of the principal creditors. Witness—Samuel Potter.
Lib. I, p. 364.

1766, Oct. 15. Jones, Thomas, of Stafford Twsp., Monmouth Co.; will of. Wife, Rebecca, the profits of my land till my sons come of age, when the said land is to be divided between my sons, David and John; and each son is to pay £10 to my three daughters. Executors—wife, Rebecca, and Nathan Bartlett. Witnesses—Levi Cramer, John Arnoll, Andrew Cramer. Proved Feb. 4, 1767.

1766, Nov. 8. Inventory, £179.1.0, made by Levi Cramer and Micaiah Willets. Lib. 12, p. 477.

1766, Nov. 26. Jones, Thomas, of Bergen Co. Int. Adm'rs—Samuel Crane and Jabez Harrison, both of Essex Co., principal creditors; Grace Jones, the widow, having renounced. Lib. I, p. 7.

1770, March 27. Jones, Thomas, of Kingwood Twsp., Hunterdon Co. Int. Adm'r—John McFarson (McPherson). Fellowbondsman—William Myers; both of said place.

1770, March 23. Inventory, £47.7.0, made by William Myers and John Emley. Lib. 15, p. 2.

1768, Oct. 15. Jones, William, of Elizabeth, Essex Co., weaver; will of. Wife, Martha, all the goods that she brought to me. Son, Isaac, the plantation. Son, William, £20, when he is 21. Daughters, Phebe, and Sarah, £10 each, when 18. Executor—son, Isaac. Witnesses—John Ross, James Innes and Ezekiel Sayre. Proved Dec. 10, 1768. Lib. K, p. 44.

1769, Jan. 15. Joralemon, Dirck, of Second River, Essex Co., yeoman; will of. I, Richard Joralemon, order my aunt, Margaret Stanberry, to be handsomely maintained, as long as she lives. Son, Jacobus, all real and personal, except reserving for the use of my sister, Auriantjie Wauters, the use of a room, while a widow. Executors—friends, Rynea Brown and Joseph Kingsland. Witnesses—Hendrick Brown, William Kingsland, Henry Kingsland, Henry Joralemon. Proved March 13, 1769.

1769, March 8. Inventory of Richard (Dirck) Jerolaman, made by William Dow and Henry King. Also signed, "Reynier Brown and Joseph Kingsland, the Executors." Lib. K, p. 69.

1760, May 22. Journey, Peter, of Shrewsbury, Monmouth Co.; will of. Eldest son, John, only £5, as he has not behaved himself. Daughter, Catharine Journey, £5 only, she having disobliged me. Son, James, a negro boy. Rest of personal and real to be sold and the money given to my wife, Audery, and my children, James Journey, Elizabeth Journey, Audery Journey, Joseph Journey and Ann Journey, when my youngest is of age. Executors—brother, James, and Thomas Ellison, both of Shrewsbury, and John Williams, of Freehold. Witnesses—Josiah Halstead, James Rousell, Josiah Holmes. Proved Sept. 29, 1761.

1761, Oct. 1. Inventory, made by Gersham Bills and William Morton.
1761, Oct. 13. Sold at public sale goods to the following—Audry Journee, James Journee, John Journee, Elizabeth Journee, Caleb Allen, Samuel Romine, and others.
1764, May 29. Account by Exec'rs. Lib. H, p. 405.

1762, July 30. Justeson, Justa, of Greenwich, Gloucester Co., yeoman. Int. Adm'r—Isaac Justeson, yeoman. Fellowbondsman—Thomas Denny, yeoman; both of said place. Witness—Samuel Mickle.
1762, July 26. Inventory, £131.0.8, made by Thomas Denny and Mathew Gill. Lib. 11, p. 125.

1764, Jan. 20. Justice, Peter, of Penns Neck, Salem Co.; will of. Son, Andrew, plantation where he lives, of 130 acres, and 5 of meadow, and joins Israel Longacre. Son, Peter, the plantation where I dwell, which I bought of Michael Pedrick, except 5 acres willed to my son, Andrew. Plantation on Beaver Creek, where Alpheus Burton lives, to be sold, and the money to be paid to my two daughters, Brittah Burton and Rebecca Justice, £21 to each; and the rest to my four daughters, Martha Pedrick, Brittah Burton, Christiana Boon and Rebecca Justice. To my five daughters, Martha, Brittah, Christiana, Susannah and Rebeckah, my moveable estate. Executors—my son, Peter, and Robert Pedrick. Witnesses—William Guest, George Lawrence, Thomas Guinnell. Proved April 10, 1766.
1766, April 5. Inventory, £124.7.0, made by William Guest and Mathew Gill. Lib. 12, p. 306.

1769, April 18. Kaese, William, of Amwell, Hunterdon Co.; will of. Wife, Elizabeth Kase, ⅓ my whole estate; and the rest to be divided among my children, Mary, Peter, Catharine, William, Philip, Frank, Charity, Adam, Christian, Henry and Margaret. Some of the children are married. Executors—my wife and my sons, Peter and Adam. Witnesses—Peter Wyckoff, Adam Dates, Catreen Wyckoff. Proved May 5, 1769.
1769, May 4. Inventory, £418.4.0½, made by Joseph Moore and William Young. Lib. 14, p. 172.

1770, May 3. Kaighin, John, of Newton, Gloucester Co., doctor of physic; will of. Sister, Elizabeth Donaldson, £50. Uncle, David Estaugh, £50. Aunt, Grace Estaugh, £30. To my relations, Ann Butcher, and Esther Butcher, two of the daughters of my brother, Joseph Kaighin's wife, £2 each. My brother, Joseph, my old field, and the house and lot in Haddonfield, now in tenure of Josiah Albertson, during his life, and, after his death, to the Monthly Meeting of Friends of Haddonfield. Brother, James, my mulatto boy, Primis; and my brother, James, is to have the lands in Newton, where I dwell. If my brothers die, then James' share is to go to my friends, Isaac Andrews, of Haddonfield, tanner, and Joshua Evens, of Newton township, and they, in such case, to pay to Sarah Holloway of Philadelphia, spinster, £20 yearly. To my brother, Joseph, my lot in Philadelphia, late the property of my late grandfather, John Kaighin. Executor—brother, Joseph. Witnesses—Isaac Mickle, Joseph Allen, Jr., Samuel Spicer. Proved June 5, 1770.
1770, May 19. Inventory, £992.10.3, made by Joshua Evens, and Samuel Spicer. Lib. 14, p. 299.

1756, Jan. 14. Kattz, Michael, of Penns Neck, Salem Co., weaver; will of. Wife, Ursillah Catt, the third of my personal and real estate, and, after her death, then to all my children. Son, Michael Catt, to be equal with the rest of my children, but, if he, and his wife and children should be dead, then to the rest of my children. My son, Lutes Catt, to have his share. Son, George, plantation where I live, of 35 acres. My two daughters, Christiana and Catharine Catt Sly, equal shares with my sons. Executors—my wife, Ursillah Catt, and my son, George Catt. Witnesses—August Frantz Holtz, Zachariah Jorden, William Guest. Proved Aug. 16, 1764. Christiana Kattz and George Katts, the Executors named in the above will, were sworn same date.

1764, Aug. 6. Inventory, £110.7.0, made by John Helm and Samuel Linch. Lib. 12, p. 92.

1767, May 26. Kay, Joseph, of Waterford, Gloucester Co., will of. Wife, Ann, £100. Children, Josiah Kay, Isaac Kay and Rebecah Kay, the rest. Children are young. Executors—my wife and my brother, Isaac Kay. Witnesses—Francis Kay, Whitten Cripps, Samuel Thompson. Proved Oct. 21, 1767.

1767, Aug. 5. Inventory, £729.17.6, made by John Gill and John Gruffyth. Lib. 13, p. 254.

1762, July 15. Kay, Josiah, Jr., of Waterford Twsp., Gloucester Co., yeoman; will of. To my brother, Joseph Kay's, two children, Josiah and Rebecca Kay, £5 each. To my two brothers, Joseph and Isaac Kay, the rest of my estate. My executors are to convey 8 acres of marsh, in Salem Co., to Andrew Murdock, if he pay two bonds, which I assigned over to Rebecca Leans. Executors—my brothers, Joseph and Isaac Kay. Witnesses—Josiah Kay, Joseph Parker, Samued Clement, Jr. Proved Sept. 9, 1762.

1762, Sept. 8. Inventory, £189.17.5½, made by Thomas Bate and John Burrough, Jr. Lib. 11, p. 260.

1764, Dec. 1. Keating, Robert, of Burlington, peruke maker. Int. Adm'x—Ann Keating, widow. Fellowbondsman—Isaac Heulings; both of said city. Lib. 12, p. 35.

1765, Jan. 15. Inventory, £38.12.0, made by William Smith and Abraham Hewlings.

1761, April 13. Kelly, William, of Pilesgrove, Salem Co., weaver; will of. Wife, Mary Kelly, all my personal estate in America and Ireland. Executrix—my wife. Witnesses—Robert Clark, Israel Lock, Samuel Linch, Jr. Proved Dec. 4, 1761.

1761, Oct. 30. Inventory, £33.9.10, made by Robert Clark and Israel Lock. Lib. 10, p. 432.

1770, April 13. Kelsey, Joseph, of Roxbury, Morris Co.; will of. Land and moveables to be sold. What remains, after debts are paid, is to be put to interest, and all given to my daughter, Sarah Kelsey, when she is 18. Executors—my brother, William Kelsey, and my father-in-law, William Griffing. Witnesses—Lydia Griffing, Jasper Griffing, Joshua Dickerson. Proved May 25, 1770.

1770, May 28. Inventory, £67.19.2, made by Shubel Luse and Jabesh Bell. Lib. K, p. 212.

1761, April 4. Kembell, John Peter, of Hopewell Twsp., Hunterdon Co.; will of. Wife, Mary, all my lands. Oldest son, Philip, 2 guineas, 3 pounds and 10 shillings, and so much to my son, William. To my four youngest children, the lands, at their mother's death; and to Peter, the youngest, £10; and to Christian, £8. Executor—my wife Mary. Witnesses—Samuel Hunt, Christian Lupp, Moses Baldwin. Proved July 3, 1761.
1761, Aug. 12. Inventory, £76.14.0, made by Wilson Hunt.
Lib. 11, p. 49.

1764, March 5. Kemble, Thomas, of Northampton, Burlington Co., yeoman; will of. Son-in-law, William Edgman, and Elizabeth, his wife, the northeast part of my plantation, of 22½ acres. Granddaughter, Mary Stackhouse, also land. Son-in-law, William Jewell, and Rachel, his wife, my negro Sarah. Grandson, William Murfin, land on east side of High St., Mount Holly. Wife, Mary, furniture and negros, and use of my new house where my son, Vespation, lately lived. Granddaughter, Susanna Kemble, a negro. Son, Samuel, rest of my plantation where I live, being part in Burlington and part in Northampton, and he to pay to my wife £5 yearly. Grandson, John Murfin, £25, and a negro. Daughter, Abigail Hains, 5 shillings. Son, Vespation, £5. Executors—wife, Mary, and my son, Samuel. Witnesses—Richard Cox, Robert Fenton, John Burr, Jr. Proved Oct. 1, 1766. Lib. 13, p. 45.
1766, Sept. 9. Inventory, £709.7.0, made by John Antram and Josiah Haines.

1767, March 17. Kennedy, Elizabeth, of Greenwich, Sussex Co. Ward. Late Elizabeth Henry, and daughter of William Henry, of said place, deceased, makes choice of Jacob Mattison and John Henry, as her Guardians.
1767, March 17. Guardians—John Mattison and John Henry, both of said Co. Fellowbondsman—Thomas Lowrey, of said Co.
Lib. 13, p. 209.

1763, Jan. 6. Kennedy, Thomas, of Trenton, Hunterdon Co. Int. Adm'r—Moore Furman. Fellowbondsman—Theophilus Severns, both of said place. Witnesses—Mary Severns and Robert Singer.
Lib. 11, p. 280.

1756, Sept. 30. Kenney, Jacob, of Somerset Co., yeoman; will of. Wife, Kertitie, house where I live, while my widow. Son, Jacob, £200, and what I have given him. Son, Simon, all my real estate, and he is to keep his mother. Daughter, Williampe Kessart, £10. Daughter, Gertitie Yeark, £10. Daughter, Catharine Kessart, £10. Daughters, Ann Williamson, and Dorothy Dennis, each £10. Executors—son, Simon, and my friend, Joachim Gulick. Witnesses—Thomas Fevrt, Joseph Smith, Gabriel Luff. Proved March 13, 1762.
1762, March 10. Inventory, made by Jacob Berger, Lucas Voorhees and David Nevius. Lib. H, p. 99.

1766, Feb. 27. Kenney, John, of Hanover, Morris Co.; will of. Eldest daughter, Mary Parritt, £5. Real and personal to be sold and the money divided between my other three daughters, Johanah Price, Elizabeth Kenney and Abigail Cooper. Executors—Thomas Kenney and Jacob Ford, Jr. Witnesses—Abraham Tappen, Thomas Millidge, Augustine Moore. Proved March 19, 1766. Lib. I, p. 177.

1762, Nov. 4. Kent, Thomas, of Morristown, Morris Co., yeoman; will of. Real and personal to be sold, and then my daughter, Abigail, wife of Jabesh Eaton, of Roxbury, to have one-fourth; and my daughter, Phebe, wife of Isaac Johnson, of Cohansey, £5; and the rest to my granddaughter, Mary Johnson, who lives with me, and my daughter, Mercy, wife of John Cole. Executors—Deacon Mathew Lum, and Daniel Lindsly. Witnesses—Henry Primrose, James Pitney, Timothy Johnes. Proved July 30, 1764. Lib. H, p. 450.

1761, June 19. Kent, William, of Woodbridge, Middlesex Co.; will of. Wife, Charity, all moveable estate, in order to bring up the children, and the use of my land. Son, Phinehas, my land when he is 21, but he is to pay to my daughter, Elizabeth, £15 when she is 21. If son, Phinehas, should die, then I give the land to my brother, David Evans, his son, Lewis Evans, and heirs. Executors—brother, David Evans, and friend, Nathaniel Fitz Randolph. Witnesses—Mary Stone, Rebecca Stone, Abraham Tappen. Proved July 15, 1761.
1761, July 18. Inventory, £278.15.0, made by Thomas Gach and David Kent. Lib. H, p. 4.

1764, Sept. 28. Kerkuff, Urban, of Reading Twsp., Hunterdon Co.; will of. Eldest son, John, some pewter. Wife, Catherine, my real estate and rest of personal. Executors—my wife and my friend, John Emmons. Witnesses—John Henry, Mary Henry, Jacob Mattison. Proved April 27, 1768.
1768, April 20. Inventory, £52.6.0¾, made by Jacob Mattison and John Henry. Lib. 13, p. 449.

1760, June 20. Kerlin, Peter, of Mansfield Twsp., Burlington Co., cordwainer; will of. Daughter, Susannah Kerlin, £5. Daughter, Mary Kerlin, £12. Son, Joseph, my land, he paying to his brother, John, ½ the value thereof. Executors—Thomas Smith and Solomon Ridgway. Witnesses—Henry Delatush, Thomas Richards, James Reynolds. Proved March 26, 1762.
1762, March 25. Renunciation by Solomon Ridgway.
1762, March 2. Inventory, £32.8.9, made by John Buffin and Lyndon Brown. Lib. 11, p. 215.

1763, Nov. 25. Ketchin, Joseph, of Sussex Co. Int. Adm'rs—John Garrison, Esq., and Mary Ketchin. Fellowbondsman—William Hill, of Amwell, Hunterdon Co. Lib. 11, p. 447.

1762, May 31. Keyt, John, of Elizabeth Town, Essex Co. Int. Adm'r—James Keyt, the nearest relative. Fellowbondsman—William Styles, carpenter; both of said place. Witness—Andrew Ross.
Lib. H, p. 271.

1761, July 18. Kidd, Mary, of Mannington Precinct, Salem Co., widow; will of. Daughter, Sarah Kidd, my apparel, saddle, colt, etc. Son, William Smith, his bed. Son, James Mason, his bed. Son, Joseph Kidd, a bed and cow. Rest to daughter, Sarah Kidd, William Smith and James Mason. Executor—son, James Mason. Witnesses—Christian Benner, Elizabeth Burn, William Barratt. Proved Oct. 10, 1761.
1761, Oct. 1. Inventory, £218.17.2, made by Mounce Keen, Jr., and Richard Hackett.
1763, Nov. 23. Account by Executor. Lib. 11, p. 26.

1769, May 9. Killey, David, of Shrewsbury, Monmouth Co. Int. Adm'r—James Woolley. Fellowbondsman—Edmund Williams; both of said place. Witness—John Hamersley. Lib. K, p. 91.

1767, Oct. 6. Killey, Hannah, widow of Joseph, of Nottingham Twsp., Burlington Co.; will of. Cousin, Rhoda Tilton, £100 when 18. Cousin, Lydia Tilton, £100. Sister, Elizabeth Tilton, wife of Daniel, the interest of the above legacies till her children are 18. Sister, Esther Lippincott, £100. Sister, Patience Middleton, £100, and to her daughter, Rebekah Burden, £10, and to her daughter, Guly Potter, £10. Executor—cousin, William Tilton. Witnesses—John Warner, Samuel Middleton, Edmond Bower. Proved April 2, 1770.
1770, March 27. Renunciation by William Tilton. Witnesses—Samuel Middleton, James Woolley. Lib. 14, p. 268.
1770, April 2. Adm'r—Daniel Tilton, with the will annexed. Fellowbondsman—Thomas Thorn; both of Nottingham, Burlington Co.
1770, April 2. Inventory, £514.5.1, made by Amos Middleton and Thomas Thorn.

1752, June 10. Killey, Joseph, of Upper Freehold Twsp., Monmouth Co., yeoman; will of. Wife, Hannah, £150. If my wife be with child it shall have £50. Sons, David and Samuel, my lands. Executors—my wife and my friend, John Ford. Witnesses—George Middleton, Abel Middleton, Amos Middleton. Proved March 15, 1769.
1765, Jan. 10. Renunciation by John Foord.
1765, Jan. 14. Inventory, £1,879.3.3, made by William Lawrie and Amos Middleton.
1769, March 15. Renunciation by Hannah Killey.
1769, March 15. Adm'r—David Killey. Fellowbondsman—Amos Middleton; both of Freehold, said Co. Witness—Abel Middleton.
Lib. 14, p. 31.

1764, Aug. 21. Kimble, Daniel, of Newton, Gloucester Co., yeoman; will of. To my eldest brother's son, Joseph Kimble, 5 shillings. To my sister, Sarah Antrem's, two eldest sons, Jinnens Stephenson and Joseph Stephenson, £40 each. Cousin, Daniel Handcock, £40, when 21. To Hannah Eastlack, £40. To Sarah Alexander, £10, when she is 20. The rest to my three sisters' other children, except my sister, Ellenor's, daughter, Easter. Executors—my friends, William Handcock and Joseph Antram, both of Burlington Co.
1764, Aug. 27. Richard Weekes, one of the witnesses, declared that he wrote the within will by order of the Testator, and, after he wrote it, he read it to him, who then set up in bed, in order to sign the same, but was so ill that he could not sign it, but declared the contents thereof was his will. And Isaac Mickle, one of the witnesses, and a neighbor of the Testator, declared that he approved of the contents of said will.
1764, Sept. 1. Inventory, £681.17.1, made by David Branson and Isaac Mickle. Lib. 12, p. 18.

1765, March 25. Kimpson, Samuel, of Burlington Co.; will of. Real and personal to be under the management of Aaron Watson, of Bordentown. Wife, Susannah, and my children to have benefit of whole estate till my youngest child is of age; then ⅓ to go to my wife, ⅓ to son Solomon and ⅓ to my daughter, Mary. Executors—

my wife and said Aaron Watson. Witnesses—Peter Corne and William Thomson. Proved Oct. 6, 1767.

1765, June 14. Inventory, £78.16.6, made by Thomas Lipper and Richard Lott. (The Inventory was made in South Amboy Twsp., Middlesex Co., Samuel Kimpson "being late of that place."
Lib. 13, p. 98; File 8183 C; 4421 L).

1764, June 12. Kimsey, Nathan, of Deptford, Gloucester Co. Ward. Son and devisee of Thomas Kimsey, of said place, yeoman, deceased; having lands devised to him by his father, he makes choice of his brother, Job Kimsey, to be his Guardian, till he is 21. Witness— Sarah Howell.

1764, June 12. Guardian—Job Kimsey, joiner. Fellowbondsman— John Sparks, innholder; both of said place. William Wood, the late Guardian, has deceased. Witness—Sarah Howell. Lib. 14, p. 21.

1760, April 11. King, Andrew, of Springfield, Burlington Co.; will of. Lands and personal effects to be sold, and, after debts are paid, I give the rest to my friends, David Ridgway, the son of Joseph, Sarah Fenimore and Priscilla Fenimore, the daughters of John Fenimore. Executor—friend, John Fenimore. Witnesses—James Childs, Moses Haines, Lwick Bennet. Proved Feb. 22, 1763.

1762, Jan. 14. Inventory, £4.0.1, made by Nathaniel Wilkinson and James Childs. Lib. 11, p. 261.

1758, June 5. King, John, of Borough of Elizabeth, Essex Co., yeoman; will of. Son, Jeremiah, £5, and what he has already had. Lands to be sold and the money given to my wife, Mary, and my daughters, Mary, Abigil, Ann and Rachel. (The last two under age). Son, David, is disordered in his reason, and can not provide for his own support; therefore my daughters are to provide for him. Executors— my friends, Ephraim Terril and Abraham Shotwell. Witnesses— Joseph Marsh, Thomas Latham, Joseph Shotwell. Proved Feb. 8, 1762.
Lib. H, p. 84.

1763, Dec. 12. King, John, of Mannington, Salem Co.; will of. Daughter, Ann King, a chest of drawers. My plantation, called Briget Vances, to be sold. Son, William, to be put to a trade. Son, Samuel, 5 shillings. Son, John, 5 shillings. Daughter, Gennot Cooper, 5 shillings. Daughter, Elizabeth Noles, £30. Daughter, Martha King, 5 shillings. Daughter, Ann King. £30. Son, William, rest of lands. Executors—friends, William Moore and Erasmus Kent. Witnesses— David Taylor, Abner Penton, Ezekiel Camp. Proved Feb. 22, 1764.

1764, Feb. 23. Inventory, £95.16.5, made by Daniel Smith, Jr., and Joseph Fogg. Lib. 12, p. 230.

1759, Oct. 20. King, Joseph, Sr., of Kingwood Twsp., Hunterdon Co., yeoman; will of. Son, Joseph, 5 shillings, as I have given to him much. Son, William, 5 shillings, he having had his portion. Granddaughter, Mercy Hunt, some goods, which are now in keeping of my son, William. My plantation in Kingwood, where I lately lived, to be sold. Executors—my eldest son, Joseph, and my son-in-law, Mansfield Hunt, my grandson, Joseph Hunt, my grandson, Joseph King (the son of my son William). Witnesses—John Mullinner, Thomas Coate, John Brock. Proved Jan. 2, 1762. Lib. 11, p. 343.

1761, May 25. King, Joseph, Jr., of Amwell Twsp., Hunterdon Co., yeoman; will of. Wife, Mary, a bed. Daughter, Jane King, a bed. Daughter, Hannah King, a bed. Daughter, Alice Maris, a bed. My grist mill and 10-acre lot to be sold, which is in Kingwood Twsp.; also 50 acres of land, where Joseph Pegg now lives, at the upper end of my tract, and the money to be divided between my wife and daughters. Sons, George and Nathan, rest of my lands, after death or marriage of wife. Sons, Nathan and George, are not 21. Executors—my wife, my son, George, and my son-in-law, John Stevenson. I desire my father-in-law, John Simcock, to assist them. Witnesses—William French, Thomas Coate, William Paxson. Proved Sept. 14, 1768. Lib. 13, p. 451.

1764, June 6. King, Joseph, of Kingwood, Hunterdon Co. Ward. Grandson of Joseph King, of said place, deceased. He makes choice of Robert Emley as his Guardian.
1764, June 6. Guardian—Robert Emley, of Kingwood, said Co. Fellowbondsman—Joseph Hollinshead, of City of Burlington. Witness—Joseph Read. Lib. 11, p. 521.

1763, May 27. King, Mary, of Essex Co., widow. Int. Adm'r—Jeremiah King, of Hunterdon Co. Fellowbondsman—John Wood, of Essex Co.
1763, May 28. Inventory, £91.9.2, made by William Oliver and Samuel Shotwell. Lib. H, p. 244.

1766, June 2. King, Samuel, of New Hanover, Burlington Co., miller. Int. Adm'x—Theodocia King, widow, of said place. Fellowbondsman—Thomas Budd, yeoman, of Northampton, said Co.
Lib. 12, p. 290.
1766, April 2. Inventory, £116.5.11, made by Thomas Budd and John Goldy.

1768, Oct. 12. Kingsland, Edmund, of New York City, ship carpenter; will of. Wife, Mary, all real and personal, to maintain the children, and, at her death, what remains to be given to my four children. Son, John, to have 10 shillings extra, for his birthright. Executrix—wife. Witnesses—Nathaniel Kingsland, Mark Dempsey, Richard Kingsland. Proved May 22, 1769. Lib. K, p. 94.

1763, Aug. 18. Kingsland, John, of New Barbadoes, Bergen Co., yeoman; will of. Wife to be maintained by my son, Richard, and he is to have ½ of my land where I live, and 5 acres of salt meadow near the Hackinsack River, which I gave him by deed, dated May 8, 1758. Daughter, Sarah, a cow and calf. Daughter, Nedemia, 8 acres of land, she being yet unmarried. Rest to grandson, John Kingsland, son of my eldest son, Isaac, dec'd; two grandchildren, the children of my daughter, Elizabeth, dec'd; daughter, Sarah; daughter, Hester, wife of James Butler; son, Edmund. Executors—my wife and Evert Van Zeyl. Witnesses—Teunis Joralemon, Derick Joralemon, Isaac Kingsland. Proved Aug. 10, 1768, when letters granted to Evert Van Zeyl, the surviving Executor. Lib. I, p. 330.

1770, Aug. 17. Kingsland, Nedemiah, of New Barbadoes Neck, in Bergen Co.; will of. Sister-in-law, Mary Kingsland, wife of my brother, Richard, my real estate, and, if she does not dispose of it before her death, then to her daughter, Mary Kingsland. Executors —my cousin, Charles Kingsland, the son of Isaac Kingsland, and the said Mary Kingsland. Witnesses—Abraham Kingsland, Aaron Kingsland and Charles Kingsland. Proved Oct. 23, 1770. Lib. K, p. 267.

1762, Nov. 2. Kinnan, Joseph, of Bernards Town, Somerset Co. Int. Adm's—Ruth Kinnan, the widow, of said place, Thomas Kinnan, of Morris Co., and Edward Lewis, of Somerset Co. Fellowbondsman —Gawin McCoy, of Somerset Co.
1762, Nov. 4. Inventory, £1,016.14.4, made by Thomas Riggs and John Collyer. Lib. H, p. 197.

1765, Sept. 16. Kinsey, Jonathan, of Woodbridge, Middlesex Co. Int. Adm'x—Sarah Rolph, principal creditor. Fellowbondsman— David Jaques; both of said place.
1765, Sept. 14. Renunciation by Annabell Kinsey, the widow. Witness—George Brown. Lib. H, p. 530.

1762, May 24. Kinsey, Mary, of Gloucester Co. Ward. Petition of said Mary, who is daughter of Thomas Kinsey, of Deptford, said Co., yeoman, deceased. Said Thomas, by will, made William Wood, the Guardian, who is now deceased; therefore she prays that her friend, John Wilkins, may be appointed her Guardian. Witness— Job Kinsey.
1762, May 24. Guardian—John Wilkins, yeoman. Fellowbondsman —James Whiteall, yeoman; both of Deptford Twsp., said Co. Witness—Job Kinsey. Lib. 11, p. 126.

1757, July 6. Kinsey, Thomas, of Woodbury Creek, Gloucester Co., yeoman; will of. Eldest son, Job, all my lands, except my plantation whereon Nathan Lord lives, when he is 21. Son, Nathan, plantation whereon Nathan Lord lives. Daughter, Mary Kinsey, personal estate. If my children die, my lands are to pass to my "affected" brother, John Kinsey. My cousin, William Wood, to be Guardian of all my children. Executor—my brother-in-law, John Wilkins. Witnesses—Robert Cooper, James Miller, Mary Miller. Proved Feb. 18, 1761.
1761, Feb. 18. Inventory, £259.11.5½, of the personal estate of Thomas Kimsey, "late of Deptford Twsp., Gloucester Co.," made by William Wilkins and Nixon Chattin. Lib. 10, p. 382.

1763, Oct. 5. Kip, Jacob, of Saddle River, Bergen Co., now residing in New York; will of. Wife, Geesje, goods she had of her father, Cornelius Brinkerhoff, and also £500. To Elizabeth Kip, wife of Claes Danielse Romyn, £300. To Rynier Bordan, £100, to be divided between himself and his sisters' and brothers' children. My brothers, Hendrick Kip, Peter Kip, and Isaac Kip, and the children of my sisters, deceased, namely, Anatje Van Voorhees, Catharina Ter Hune, and Elizabeth Brinckerhoff, the remainder. Executors—my friends, Hendrick Kip (Peter's son), and Claas Danielson Romyn, both of Hackensack. Witnesses—Peter Lott, William Brede and Evert Byvanck. Proved Oct. 17, 1763. Lib. H, p. 370.
1764, April 14. Inventory, £387.3.2, made by Peter Zabriskie and Reynier V. Giese, at the request of Hendrick Peterse Kipp and Class Danielse Romine.

1769, Sept. 26. Kirkpatrick, William, of Hunterdon Co. Int. Adm'x —Margaret Kirkpatrick. Fellowbondsman—Jacob Mattison; both of Amwell Twsp., said Co. Witness—Abraham Williamson.
1769, Sept. 22. Inventory, £957.17.2, of estate of "Reverend William Kirkpatrick, of Amwell Twsp.," made at his dwelling house by Jacob Mattison and Lewis Chamberlin. Lib. 14, p. 123.

1745, Sept. 8. Kitchin, James, of Amwell, Hunterdon Co., yeoman; will of. Wife, Elizabeth, to have maintainance on plantation. My oldest son, Benjamin, a horse. Sons, Benjamin, Thomas, and James, my plantation. Daughters, what can be spared. Wife may be pregnant. Executors—my wife, and son, Benjamin. My friend, John Robins, to be trustee till Benjamin is of age. Witnesses—George Baylis, Amos Thatcher, John Lewis. Proved July 28, 1761.
1761, July 27. Inventory, £235.17.6, made by Jacob Swallow and Richard Green. Lib. 11, p. 50.

1757, Oct. 29. Kitchin, Thomas, of Amwell, Hunterdon Co.; will of. Wife, Sarah, to possess my plantation of 100 acres. Daughter, Hannah, the wife of William Barns, £40, and their children, John, Samuel, Sarah and William Barns, £15 each, when of age. Daughter, Ann, wife of Vincent Robins, £40, and children, Sarah Robins, Obadiah Robins, John Robins and William Robins, £15 each, when of age. Daughter, Mercy Kitchin, £120. Executors—my wife and my friend, Andrew Pierce. Witnesses—Daniel Robins, George Trimer, Richard Rounsavell, Jr. Proved April 18, 1764.
1764, April 17. Inventory, £628.3.8, made by Jonathan Furman and Abraham Bonnel.
1770, April 27. Account by Andrew Peairs, surviving Executor. Paid to Sarah Barns, William Barns, John Peters (a legatee), Sarah Robins, Samuel Kitchin, Mary Lewis, Samuel Barns (legacy), Andrew Pierse (legacy), William Barns (legacy), Ann Robins (legacy).
Lib. 11, p. 526; Lib. 15, p. 66.

1762, June 28. Kleinehoff, Paul, of Second River, Essex Co.; will of. Son, John, £10, and the lands left me by my wife's father, John Hinds. Children, Hannah, Peter and Sarah, the rest of my estate. Wife to have the use of all estate till children are old enough to support themselves. Executors—Job Herryman, of Elizabeth Town, Thomas Tyson, of Second River, and Peter Kleinehoff, of Boheamia in Maryland. Witnesses—William Dow, Adrian Dow, William King. Proved Sept. 9, 1762. Lib. H, p. 306.

1766, Aug. 13. Knab, Frederick, of Tewksbury, Hunterdon Co. Int. Adm'r—Jacob Coffer. Fellowbondsmen—William Schuiler and Jacob Lewis; all of said Co. Lib. 12, p. 422.

1762, Sept. 9. Knap, Daniel, of Newark, Essex Co.; will of. Eldest son, James, £10. The rest of my estate to my sons, James and Thomas, when they come of age; but, if they die, then to my brothers, Jonathan and James Knap, and to the male heirs of my sisters, Martha Hodge and Mary Bister. Executors—friends, Nehemiah Baldwin and Thomas Brown. Witnesses—Jabez Campfield, Patrick Vance, Jonas Baldwin. Proved March 3, 1763.
1763, May 4. Inventory, £1,539.13.11, made by Joseph Riggs and Obadiah Bruen. Lib. H, p. 383.

1762, April 13. Knap, Rebecca, of Woodbridge, Middlesex Co.; will of. To Sarah Tomson, £12, and gown. To Mary Badger, £5, and to her mother, Sessell Badger, money to provide for her. Rest to my daughter, Elizabeth Knap, when she comes of age. Executors—friends, Daniel Crooe and David Evens. Witnesses—James Thomson, Phebe Morriss, Samuel Preston. Proved May 4, 1762.

1762, May 5. Inventory, made by Cornelius Vandehovar and James Manning. Lib. H, p. 122.

1769, April 3. Knight, William, of New Windsor, Middlesex Co. Int. Adm'x—Hannah Knight. Fellowbondsman—James Clark, Jr.; both of said place. Witness—David Brearly, Surrogate.

1769, March 18. Inventory, £74.6.6, made by Jacob Green and James Clark, Jr. Lib. 13, p. 497.

1769, Feb. 2. Knipe (Nipe), Jonathan. Int. Adm'r—Isaac Quigley.

1770, June 29. Inventory, £84.8.9, made by Isaac Arey and Abner Arey. Same date account filed by Adm'r. Lib. 14, p. 124; 15, p. 11.

1770, Feb. 17. Knott, Peter, of Shrewsbury, Monmouth Co.; will of. Son, David, the farm where I live, at Shark River, and he to pay to my wife, Jane, all that I made with her by a contract before marriage, and £8 more. Son, David, to have the mortgage I hold against Daniel Seabrook. Son, Samuel, £100, should my Executors think him reformed enough to have it. Grandson, William Lippincott, £50. Grandson, Samuel Lippincott, £50. Daughter, Rachel, wife of Peter Vandike, £250. Daughter, Abigail, wife of Gawen Drummond, £150. Daughter, Mercy, wife of Coonrod Hendrickson, £50. Daughter, Catharine, wife of James Wilson, £30. To Rebecca, wife of Remembrance Lippincott, who is my daughter, £50. Executors—sons-in-law, Gawen Drummond and Coonrod Hendrickson. Witnesses—Samuel Longstreet, Richard Lawrence, Abraham Strong. Proved March 17, 1770.

1770, March 10. Inventory, £1,713.10.10, made by Samuel Longstreet and Benjamin Jackson. Lib. K, p. 185.

1766, Nov. Koch, Henry, of Amwell Twsp., Hunterdon Co.; will of. Wife, Catherine, £12 every year. To Elizabeth Sneider, £25. To the children of my son, Barnard Koch, deceased, £50, being for their father's birthright. Grandson, Henry Koch, £50. Daughters, Margaret, and Maria, moveables. Lands to surviving children and my said son's surviving children; that is to say, my daughter, Margaret, who is espoused to Johan Christian Smith; my daughter, Maria, she is espoused to Jacobus Teats. Executors—John Garrison, Johan Kase and William Young. Witnesses—Henry Graff, William Diatz, Philip Yager. Proved May 10, 1768.

1768, May 9. Inventory, £186.13.3, made by Peter Young and Freegift Stout, Jr.

1770, May 24. Account by John Case and John Garrison, Executors of "Henry Cock." Lib. 12, p. 507; Lib. 15, p. 67.

1764, March 28. Kough, Barnet, of Amwell, Hunterdon Co. Int. Adm'x—Cristina Kough, widow of said Barnet. Fellowbondsman—Adam Deeds; both of said place. Witness—John Garrison.

CALENDAR OF WILLS—1761-1770   237

1764, March 27. Inventory, £84.13.1, made by John Case and John Garrison, Jr.
1764, May 15. Account by Christeen Kough, Adm'x.   Lib. 11, p. 525.

1762, Oct. 16. Kuykendal, Martinus, of Montague, Sussex Co., yeoman. Int. Adm'x—Cattryntie Kukendal, widow. Fellowbondsmen —Hendrick Kuykendal and Jacob Westfaul, yeomen; all of said Co.
1762, Sept. 21. Inventory, £164.13.6., made by Solomon Cuykendal and Hendrick Kuykendal.   Lib. 11, p. 289.

1754, Sept. 16. Kuyper, Hendrick, of Bergen Co., yeoman; will of. Eldest son, Henry Kuyper, the plantation in Bergen Co., called Hoseseimer, he paying £100 to his sister, Annetie, wife of Nicholas Winekoop, 3 years after his mother's death; and also paying to my daughter, Catharina's (late wife of Gerrit New Kerck's) children, £100, namely, Matthew, Henry, Catharina and Jannetie. Daughter, Geertie, wife of John Van Dalson, the house in New York, where he lives, in the West Ward, on Cortland Street; and my daughter, Jonneke, is to have the house and lot lying at the east side of the house which I gave to my daughter, Geertie. Daughter, Marretie, wife of Roelf Vanderlinde, 100 acres on the north side of the 1,000 acres at Norreshonck, in Qrange Co. Daughter, Elizabet, wife of William Siggelse, £100. My wife, Jannetie Cuper, shall keep my farm and have the rents. Executors—son, Henry, my wife, Jannetie, and my friend, Jacobus Stoutenburgh. Witnesses—Jacob Vanvoorhis, Christopher Steymets, Abraham Mesier. Proved July 27, 1764.
Lib. H, p. 449.

1765, Sept. 8. Lacey, Henry, of Morristown, Morris Co., yeoman; will of. Wife, Hannah, use of real and personal during her life. Sons, Joseph, David and Abraham, all the real, after death of wife. Daughter, Sarah, £5. Daughters, Sarah, Rebecca, Hannah, Mary and Prudence, the personal estate. Executors—sons, Joseph and David. Witnesses—James Burnet, Matthias Burnett, Ezekiel Cheever. Proved July 16, 1768.
1768, July 16. Renunciation by David Lacy.   Lib. I, p. 295.

1765, Aug. 27. Lain, Ralph, of Lebanon, Hunterdon Co. Int. Adm'x —Susannah Lain. Fellowbondsman—John Hackett; both of said Co.
1765, May 16. Inventory, made by Samuel Swackhamer and Casper Erick.   Lib. 12, p. 225.

1768, March 1. Laing, David, of Piscataway, Middlesex Co.; will of. Wife, Mary, use of lands till sons, Abraham, Isaac and Joseph are 14. I also give her £250. Son, John, plantation where I live, and ½ of the meadow which I bought of the Executors of Samuel Laing; also 2 acres of salt meadow, and 10 acres of timber land, on the northeast corner of a tract of 150 acres, which was left me by my father. Son, Jacob, the lands I bought of Amos Donham, Jacob Laing, and Alexander Thomson, and Henry and David Faurot. Son, Jacob, £100 when 21. Son, David, the said 150 acres left me by my father, except the 10 acres given to John, and 15 acres, which I will give to son, Joseph. Son, David, £100, when 21. Son, Abraham, land joining the heirs of James Martin, which belonged to my father, except 6 acres that I bought. Son, Isaac, land joining Samuel Randal and others. Son, Joseph, tract I bought of George Parker and the said 6 acres. Daughter, Elizabeth, wife of Benjamin Pound, £180. Daughter, Mary Laing, £250, when 18. Daughters, Sarah Laing and Susannah Laing, £250 each. Executors—my wife, my son, John, and my friend, John Webster. Witnesses—John Daniel, Benjamin Van Vocter, Daniel Barto. Proved April 21, 1768.

1768, April 22. Inventory, £161.9.4, made by Joseph F. Randolph and Jacob Laing. (Inventory contains many names). Lib. I, p. 277.

1761, Feb. 7. Lake, Mary, of Gloucester Co. Int. Adm'r—Abel Lee. Fellowbondsman—Edward Doughty, Jr., both of said Co.

1761, Jan. 9. "Great Egg Harbor." Inventory, £79.19,5½, made by Amos Ireland and Edward Doughty, Jr. Lib. 10. p. 172.

1755, Feb. 11. Lake, Thomas, of Amwell Twsp., Hunterdon Co.; will of. Son, Thomas, 100 acres where he lives, being the east end of land which I bought of Thomas Gordon. Son, Garrat, 100 acres on the west side. Wife, Jane, the tract where I live, while my widow. Son, John, land where I live, which I bought of Adam Aller, after wife's marriage or death. Daughter, Winefreat Hull, £15. Daughter, Sarah Bets, £15. Daughter, Cathrine Sutphin, £15. Daughter, Ann Aller, £15. Daughter, Ellen Lake, £15. Granddaughter, Jane Hull, a "wheal," and cow, when 18. Executors—sons, Garrat and John. Witnesses—William Line. Humphrey Hughes, Nichlass Zayn(?). Proved Oct. 19, 1765.

1765, Oct. 17. Inventory, £63.12.8, made by Jonathan Higgins and Richard Rounsavall. Lib. 12, p. 393.

1761, March 22. Lamb, Jacob, of Evesham, Burlington Co.; will of. Wife, Lydia, £60; also food and furniture and £20 yearly. To my daughter Margaret Antram, land in Mount Holly that I bought of Mary West. Daughters, Ann, wife of Abraham Leeds, Margaret Antram and Sarah Lamb, a cedar swamp. Daughter, Sarah Lamb, £150, when 18. Son, Jacob, £150, when 21; also rest of lands. Executors—brother, Joseph Lamb, and my friend, Joshua Ballinger. Witnesses—Margaret Haines, Isaac Evens, Thomas Haines, Jr. Proved April 8, 1761.

1761, April 3. Inventory, £2,122.13.3, made by William Evens, Isaac Evens, James Cattell. Lib. 10, p. 335.

1770, March 28. Account by Joseph Lamb, the surviving Executor. Lib. 15, p. 14.

1761, June 1. Lamberson, James, of Middlesex Co. Int. Adm'r—Simon Lamberson, brother to James. Fellowbondsman—Cornelius Lamberson; both of said Co.

1761, June 1. Renunciation by Sarah Lamberson, the widow, in favor of Simon Lamberson.

1761, June 2. Inventory, made by William Rose and Cornelius Lamberson. Lib. G, p. 387.

1763, March 19. Lambert, Gershom, of Amwell, Hunterdon Co.; will of. Wife, Sarah, my household goods and use of £200, and the privilege in the house, on my lot in Kingwood, with my father. My father to have the privilege as above said, and £200. Son, John, a colt. Farm where I live to be sold. Youngest son, Gershom, house and lot in Kingwood. To two daughters, £100 each, when 18. Eldest son, John, £10. Rest to my sons, John and Joseph. Executors—

friends, John Embley and "Cozin," Abraham Larew. Witnesses—Caleb Farlee, William Gano. Proved April 23, 1763.
1763, April 21. Renunciation by John Emley. Also by Abraham Larew. Witnesses—John Barber and Joseph Higgens.
1763, April 23. Adm'rs—Sarah Lambert and Jeremiah Lambert; both of Amwell. Fellowbondsman—Joseph Higgins, of said place.
1763, April 22. Inventory, £421.17.1, made by Joseph Higgens and John Barber.
1764, Dec. 6. Account by both Adm'rs. Includes "Paid Thomas Inyerd, for nursing smallpox." Lib. 11, p. 419.

1763, Feb. 4. Lambert, John, of Amwell, Hunterdon Co., yeoman; will of. Sons, John, Gershom and Jeremiah, plantation where I live. Wife, Mary, £80 and various goods. Four youngest daughters to have money. Executors—my brother, Gershom Lambert, and Jeremiah Lambert. Witnesses—Thomas Sutton, Samuel Furman. Proved March 29, 1763.
1763, March 21. Inventory, £199.17.7, made by Joseph Higgens and William Gano. Lib. 11, p. 310.

1764, Nov. 29. Lambert, John, of Hopewell, Hunterdon Co.; will of. Wife, Mary, bed and furniture. Rest of real and personal to be sold, except what belongs to my daughter, Anner. Wife, Mary, the ⅓ of the whole of my estate during her widowhood, and she is to bring up my two youngest children, Jeremiah and Mary, till my son, Jeremy, is fit to put to a trade. Son, Joseph, £20. Son, Daniel, to have the lot, which he now has. Rest to my children in general. Executors—sons, Daniel and Joseph. Witnesses—John Fidler, Timothy Titus, Noah Hart. Proved Jan. 3, 1765.
1764, Dec. 27. Inventory, £217.12.6, made by John Titus and Timothy Smith.
1766, June 2. Account by Executors. Lib. 12, p. 132.

1761, June 19. Lambson, Sarah, of Penns Neck, Salem Co., widow. Int. Adm'r—Solomon Alman. Fellowbondsmen—John Gilljohnson, and Sinnick Sinnickson; all of said place; yeomen.
1761, May 29. Inventory, £117.14.7, made by John Phillpott and Henry Peterson. Lib. 10, p. 437.

1761, March 11. Lander, William, Jr., of Bethlehem, Hunterdon Co. Int. Adm'r—Henry Lander. Fellowbondsman—John Parke; both of said place. Witness—Mary Smith.
1761, March 9. Inventory, £20.1.1, made by Jonathan Robins and John Parke. Includes "Book account of William Lander, Sr.," and "Money in hands of John Lander." Lib. 10, p. 460.

1760, Sept. 11. Lane, Abraham, of Middlesex Co.; will of. Wife, Hannah, £5, and some furniture. Son, Abraham, £100. Real estate to be sold. Daughters, Rebecca and Hannah, to have as much as the other daughters had at marriage. Wife to have use of estate to support children, and, after her death, the residue to my children, viz., Mary, wife of Aaron Van Sickle; Jane, wife of Samuel Osborn; Lucretia, wife of Arie Lane; Rebecca, Hannah and Abraham. Executors—wife, brother, Gysbert Lane, and Bernardus Lagrange. Witnesses—Evert Duyckinck, Henry Kip, Andres Ten Eick. Proved Oct. 3, 1761. Lib. H, p. 80.

1762, April 28. Lane, Cornelius, of Shrewsbury, Monmouth Co. Int. Adm'r—Cornelius Lane, the eldest son, of said Co. Fellowbondsman—George Reading, of Hunterdon Co.
1762, March 5. Inventory, £193.6.10, made by Ebenezer Wordel and Job Cook. Lib. H, p. 78.

1762, Sept. 9. Lane, Gisbert, of Somerset Co., yeoman; will of. Son, Arie, the south ½ of my plantation, and to son, William, the north half. Daughters, Hannah and Elizabeth, £400. Wife, Hannah, to be provided for by the sons. Executors—my wife and sons, Arie and William. Witnesses—Peter Dumont, Peter Vroom, Barnard Lagrange. Proved April 12, 1763.
1763, April 21. Inventory, £759.18.9, made by Peter Vroom, John Vroom and Peter Dumont. Lib. H, p. 227.

1762, Dec. 27. Lane, Henry, of Paramus, Bergen Co., merchant; will of. Wife, Elizabeth, ⅓ my estate. Son, William, ⅓ my estate. Daughter, Gesie Lena, ⅓ my estate. If both children die, then my estate to be to my wife, Elizabeth, and her mother, Gesie Lena Rousby. All my real in Bergen Co., and in City or Co. of New York, to be sold. Executors—my wife and William Rousby, merchant in New York. Witnesses—David Ackerman, Samuel Ackerman, Hendrick Oldis and Anne Baldwin. Proved Jan. 29, 1763. Lib. H, p. 366.

1738, Nov. 1. Lane, Jacob, of Freehold, Monmouth Co.; will of. Son, Jacob, £5. Son, Matthias, all my lands and my goods, he paying all the legacies to son, Jacob, and daughters, Helena, Jane, Arajantie, and Elizabeth. To daughter, Helena Amack, £40. Daughter, Jane Van Cleef, £40. Daughter, Arajantie Golden, £40. Daughter, Elizabeth Van Matren, £40. Executors—son, Matthias, and my brother-in-law, Derick Barkalow. Witnesses—Ann Henderson, Rachel Mitchel, John Henderson. Proved Feb. 16, 1762, by Rachel Mitchel, alias Dennis.
1762, Feb. 16. Inventory, £43.12.6, made by Isaac Sutphen, Derik Sutphen, Jr., and John Henderson. Lib. H, p. 82.
1768, March 11. **Langbog, Paul,** of Salem Co. Int. Adm'r—Jacob Freas. Inventory £100.14.6. Lib. 13, p. 335.

1763, April 29. Langevelt, Christina, of Hunterdon Co. Int. Adm'r—Boston Myers, of Bethlehem, said Co. Fellowbondsman—Nicholas Tilman, of Amwell, said Co. The said Christina Langevelt was "late Christina Lambert." Lib. 11, p. 338.

1770, Nov. 14. Langley, William, of Salem Co.; will of. My goods are to be sold, and, after debts are paid, the rest to be divided between my wife and daughter, provided that my wife, Mary, will take care of my daughter, Sarah, for one year, in sickness or health, as she is destitute of a home. Executor—Edward Roberts. Witnesses —John Gosling, Edward Roberts. Proved Nov. 24, 1770.
1770, Nov. 23. Inventory, £106.15.10, made by Charles Ellet and James Parker. Lib. 15, p. 212.

1769, June 26. Langstaff, James, of Springfield, Burlington Co., yeoman; will of. Son, George my lands and £100. Daughter, Mary Fox, £300. Daughters, Susannah Langstaff and Elizabeth Langstaff,

each a bed, and they to have the remainder. Executor—son, George. Witnesses—Jacob Merrit, John Woolman, Thomasin Merrit. Proved Oct. 17, 1769.
1769, Oct. 16. Inventory, £1,386.6.2, made by Thomas Budd and John Goldy. File No. 8539 C.

1760, Aug. 26. Langstaff, John, of Piscataway, Middlesex Co.; will of. Wife, Mary, use of all personal and real, while my widow. Grandson, John Langstaff, son of John Langstaff, deceased, lands south of Ambrose Brook, and ½ of new lots of salt meadow in Piscataway Salt meadows, the north half of the 5 acre lot, and the east end of the other lot; and, if he die without issue, then the land south of Ambrose Brook, to be divided between my son, Henry, and my three daughters, Charlotte, Mary and Martha, and two granddaughters, Sarah and Priscilla, daughters of John Langstaff, deceased. The said John Langstaff shall pay to his sister, Sarah Langstaff, £40, and to his sister, Priscilla, Langstaff, £40. Son, Henry, ½ of 2 lots of salt meadow in Piscataway, the south end of 5-acre lot, and west end of other lot. Grandsons, John and William Hopkins, sons of my daughter, Sarah Hopkins, deceased, each £5. Executors—wife, Mary, and son, Henry. Witnesses—David Conger, John Willson, Jr., John Arnold. Proved May 26, 1761. Lib. G, p. 434.

1770, March 15. Laquier, John, of Amwell Twsp., Hunterdon Co. Int. Adm'r—William Adams. Fellowbondsman—Joshua Corshon; both of said place.
1770, March 19. Inventory, £101.9.1, made by Nathaniel Hunt, and Joseph Leigh.
1770, June 24. Account by William Adams, Adm'r.
1772, Dec. 10. Samuel Stevenson appointed Adm'r to continue settlement of estate. Fellowbondsman—Thomas Stevenson.
Lib. 14, p. 407; Lib. 15, p. 3.

1762, June 26. Larew, Daniel, of Amwell, Hunterdon Co., yeoman; will of. I give my estate to my wife, Margaret Larew, and my children which are born, or likely to be born, as follows: The children to be raised and educated out of the estate till my sons are 21, and my daughters 18. Executors—my friends, William Williamson and Abraham Laroe, both of Amwell. Witnesses—Moses Larowe, David Larowe, William Williamson. Proved Aug. 11, 1762. (Testator died June 27, 1762).
1762, July 31. Inventory, £218.13.0, made by John Opdyck and Moses Larowe. Lib. 11, p. 358.

1767, Aug. 4. Large, Elizabeth, of Kingwood Twsp., Hunterdon Co.; will of. All my estate to be sold, except one case of drawers, which I give to Rebecca Kester. To my sister, Rebecca Pritt, £10. To Elizabeth Myers, daughter of William Myers, and to Elizabeth Price, daughter of my sister, Ann Price, to each £5. Sons-in-law, Jacob Large and Robert Large, the rest of my estate. Executors— said Jacob Large and Robert Large. Witnesses—John Emley, Amie Stockton, Samuel Webster. Proved Oct. 21, 1767.
1767, Aug. 31. Inventory, £108.14.0, made by Samuel Webster and John Emley.

1787, March 24. Account by Samuel Kester, surviving Executor of Robert Large, who was acting Executor of Elizabeth Large. Cash paid to Elizabeth Large, John Sherrard, Robert Large, Jr., W. Myers, Elizabeth Stevenson, Jr., John Stockton, Thompson Price, Solomon Mott, Jacob Large, Rebecca Pritt (legacy of £10), Elizabeth Bivan (legacy of £5), and others.

1790, Nov. 11. A further account of Samuel Kester. Paid Elizabeth Myers' legacy in full, by her order, in favor of William Paxton.

Lib. 13, p. 268.

1765, May 20. Large, Samuel, of Kingwood Twsp., Hunterdon Co., yeoman; will of. Eldest son, Jacob Large, 10 shillings. Son, Robert, £4. I have given to my two sons, Jacob and Robert, deeds for all my lands. Wife, Elizabeth, all the residue. Executrix—my wife. Witnesses—Mary Emley, Rebecca Pritty, Robert Emley. Proved July 26, 1765.

1765, July 6. Inventory, £220.1.7, made by James Willson and Robert Emley. Lib. 12, p. 212.

1760, April 29. Laroe, Samuel, of Romapogh in Bergen Co.; will of. Son, Jacobus, 10 acres of land for his birthright, and ⅓ of the plantation where I live. Daughter, Waybrough, ⅓ of plantation where she lives. Daughter, Mary, ⅓ of plantation where she lives. Son, Jacobus, and my daughter, Mary, each ½ of the new mill. Executors —my son, Jacobus, and my sons-in-law, John Bertolf and Jacob Kogh. Witnesses—Lambartus Laroe, Jacobus Laroe and John Myer. Proved Oct. 9, 1761. Lib. H, p. 67.

1766, Oct. 2. Lashells, Ralph, of Middlesex Co. Int. Adm'x—Anne Lashells, widow of said Ralph. Fellowbondsman—Lewis Forman, of Monmouth Co.

1766, Oct. 7. Inventory, made by Coonradt Hendricks and Lasyor Morrell. Lib. I, p. 6.

1766, March 12. Lawrence, Daniel, of Lower Precinct of Cape May Co., clerk; will of. Daughter, Nancy Lawrence, all the cloth that was her mother's. Son, Benjamin, books. Son, Daniel, 16 acres of land joining Daniel Hand on the west, Elijah Hughes on the south and southwest. Wife, Sarah; and my children, Nancy Lawrence, Benjamin Lawrence, Deborah Lawrence and Daniel Lawrence, my household goods and 2 negros. Executors—my wife and my friends, Rev. Andrew Hunter, Rev. William Ramsey, James Whilldin, Esq. and Thomas Hand. Witnesses—Henry Stevens, Mary Hughes, Elenor Whilldin, and Elijah Hughes.

1766, March 17. Codicil. Proved Dec. 8, 1766. (Sarah Lawrence qualified as Executrix, same date; and Andrew Hunter, as Executor, Nov. 12, 1772).

1766, July 23. Inventory, £455.14.10, made by John Eldredge and Henry Hand.

1775, Oct. 9. Account by Amy Hunter, Executrix to Rev. Andrew Hunter, one of the Executors of Rev. Daniel Lawrence. Includes "To keeping 4 small children for 2 years, £39.1.10."

Lib. 12, p. 338; Lib. 15, p. 547.

1762, Jan. 24. Lawrence, John, of Elizabeth Borough, Essex Co.; will of. Being aged. Wife, Susannah, use of real and personal estate. Daughters, Elizabeth Whitehead, Hannah Roberts and Ame

Black, all my land in said Borough, after my wife's death. Grandson, Samuel Lawrence, land near the Red Root in Middlesex Co., of 10 acres, which I hold by virtue of a mortgage from John Eastwood. Grandson, John Lawrence (who is now beyond the sea), my gold buttons, provided he return home within one year after the present war is ended. Granddaughter, Susannah Lawrence, bed, spoons, etc. My wife's daughter, Grace Tharp, £10. My wife's granddaughter, Sarah Tharp, £10. My grandson, Samuel Lawrence, £10. My grandson, Thomas Lawrence, £2. My granddaughter, Rachel Lawrence, £5. Rest of my personal estate to my three daughters and grandchildren by my son, William, deceased. Executors—friends, Amos Morss and Abraham Clark, Jr. Witnesses—Joseph Bird, Richard Nicholas, David Hetfield. Proved Nov. 11, 1766. Lib. I, p. 16.

1767, Jan. 16. Lawrence, John, of Chesterfield, Burlington Co., yeoman; will of. My wife, Hannah, £200. Son, Benjamin, cedar swamp in Cumberland, East New Jersey, and land in Crosswicks. Fifty acres at south end of plantation where I live to be sold. Son, Jacob, the rest of plantation. Daughters, Elizabeth Imley, Amey Harbert and Deborah Vandike, the rest. Executors—wife, Hannah, and sons, Benjamin and Jacob. Witnesses—Amos Middleton, Abel Middleton, Benjamin David. Proved April 15, 1767.
1767, April 9. Inventory, £606.0.5, made by William Miller and Abel Middleton. Lib. 13, p. 68.

1764, March 15. Lawrence, Jonathan, of Fairfield, Cumberland Co. Int. Adm'x—Abigail Lawrence. Inventory, £860.18.0. Lib. 12, p. 5.

1766, June 25. Lawrence, Jonathan, of Fairfield, Cumberland Co. Ward. Son of Jonathan Lawrence, of said place. Guardian—David Pierson. Fellowbondsman—Joseph Daten; both of said place, yeoman. Lib. 12, p. 327.

1761, July 29. Lawrence, Rachel, of Philadelphia; will of. Son, John Lawrence, land on the River Schuylkill, which I bought of my son and was purchased by him from Joseph Shute, and joins land belonging now to Joseph Galloway. Daughter, Mary Masters, some dishes. Granddaughter, Mary Masters, a stand. Granddaughter, Catherine, the daughter of my son, Thomas, my negro girl, Pegg. Granddaughter, Elizabeth, daughter of my son, John, silver can. Granddaughter, Rachel, daughter of my son, Thomas, gold watch. Son, Thomas, the rest of my estate. Executor—said son, Thomas. Witnesses—Valentine Standley, James Armitage, Richard Sewell. Proved May 11, 1768. (The will was first proved in Philadelphia and the original returned to that office from New Jersey).
Lib. 13, p. 336.

1768, Jan. 17. Lawrence, Sarah, of Cape May Co.; will of. I desire that my two youngest children, Deborah and Daniel, have all I possess. Executor—James Whillden, Esq. Witnesses—Daniel Crowell, Elenor Whillden and Henry Hand. Proved Feb. 9, 1768.
1768, Feb. 9. Inventory, £416.13.0, made by John Eldredge and Henry Hand.
1774, May 17. Account by Executor. Includes legacies paid to Ann Lawrence, Jacob Hughes and wife, and Nancy Lawrence.
Lib. 13, p. 525; Lib. 15, p. 518.

1770, Sept. 20. Lawson, William, of Town of Waterbury, Connecticut; will of. (By copy). My estate to be sold and money sent to my father in Ireland, but, if he be dead, then to my brothers and sisters. Executor—my friend, Thomas Philips, of Waterbury, Conn. Witnesses—Thomas Wiggins, William Hick, James Huston. Proved Dec. 25, 1770.

1770, Dec. 26. Inventory, £28.18.6, made by Jacob Hyer and Thomas Wiggins. Lib. K, p. 255.

1767, Jan. 30. Leadly, John, of Salem, Salem Co., gentleman. Int. Adm'r—Grant Gibbon, Esq. Fellowbondsmen—Robert Johnson, Esq., and Joseph Smith, joiner; all of said place.

1767, Jan. 26. Inventory, £44.2.10, made by Joseph Vanneman and Joseph Smith. Lib. 13, p. 189.

1759, Oct. 12. Leaming, Lydia, of Cape May Co.; will of. Widow of Aaron Leaming. I own a plantation where I formerly lived, between James Edwards and Jeremiah Leaming, and I give to my son, Jeremiah Leaming, a part of the same; and he is to pay to my son, Richard Shaw, £65, and to my daughter, Lydia Taylor, £65, and to my son, John Shaw, £65, and to my son, Joshua Shaw, £65, and to my son, Nathan Shaw, £40. Son, Aaron Leaming, the rest of lands. Son, Richard Shaw, £50. The residue to my children, Lydia Taylor, John Shaw, Joshua Shaw, Nathan Shaw, Aaron Leaming, Jeremiah Leaming and Elizabeth Leaming. Executors—sons, John Shaw and Aaron Leaming; but, if John refuse, then my son, Joshua Shaw. Witnesses—Samuel Foster, Ephraim Edwards, Lewis Cresse. Proved Oct. 8, 1762.

1762, Oct. 2. Inventory, £863.14.4½, made by Jacob Richardson and Lewis Cresse.

1773, Feb. 13. Account by Executors. Lib. 11, p. 236; Lib. 14, p. 514.

1769, April 8. Leamount, John, of Somerset Co. Int. Admr—Thomas Burgie. Fellowbondsman—John Colyer; both of said Co. Witness—Margaret Penier.

1769, April 7. Inventory, £23.4.1, made at Barnardstown, by James Morrison and John Colyer.

1770, Sept. 4. Account by Adm'r. Lib. K, p. 93; File No. 373 R.

1765, Oct. 31. Leddel, John, of Somerset Co. Ward. Son of William Leddel, of said Co., deceased. Guardian—John Carl. Fellowbondsman—Peter Layton; both of Morris Co. Lib. H, p. 541.

1759, Feb. 7. Leddel, William, of Somerset Co., surgeon; will of. Whereas my wife has a child with her, named John, which child was begotten in my absence, and while I was on my lawful affairs in the West Indies; for which reason I disown said child, and, as he may by law be intitled to estate, I give him 5 shillings only. To William, the firstborn child of Easter Nightingal, of Somerset Co., who goes by the name of William Leddel, a lot of land which I bought from Matthias Degarmo, 15 of Feb., 1751, and contains 30 acres; and the land that joins to it, which I bought from John Philipse in 1754, of 75 acres, and land I bought from Elisha Frazee, 17 of Aug. 1758, of 23 acres; also my watch, cane and fire arms. I give my personal estate to my daughter, Mary Magdalen, the said William Leddel, Sarah, the daughter and 2nd born child of the said Easter Nightingal,

Easter, the daughter and 3rd born child of said Easter Nightingal, and Elizabeth, the daughter, 4th and last born child of said Easter. But my daughter, Mary Magdalen, or the Executors of my father, Joseph Leddel, are to clear my estate of any demand on account of a certain bond given by me to my father. To my friend, Easter Nightingal, a share of the personal estate. Daughter, Mary Magdalen, the land I bought from John Hampton, 15 of Jan., 1752, of about 29 acres, and a lot I bought from Ephraim Frazee, 4th of April, 1755, of 6 acres. Executors—my friends, Edward Lewis, of Somerset Co., and Doctor Moses Bloomfield, of Woodbridge, Middlesex Co., and my friend, the said Easter Nightingal, of Somerset Co. Witnesses—Caleb Jones, Daniel Sayre, David Sayre. Proved June 22, 1761.
Lib. G, p. 454.

1765, Aug. 27. Leddel, William, of Somerset Co. Ward. Son of William Leddel, of said Co., deceased. Guardian—John Carl. Fellowbondsman—Peter Layten; both of Morris Co. Lib. H, p. 520.

1762, May 19. Lee, Mary, and others, of Essex Co. Wards. Guardian—William Edgar, of Woodbridge, Middlesex Co.; of Mary Lee, William Lee and Abraham Lee, children of Abraham Lee, of Essex Co., deceased, the said Edgar being also Executor of the will of Abraham Lee. Said children are under 14 years of age. Fellowbondsman—Robert Lee, of Middlesex Co. Witness—John Smyth.
Lib. H, p. 106.

1765, Jan. 30. Leeds, Daniel, of Great Egg Harbor, Gloucester Co., farmer; will of. To Mary Leeds, daughter of Robert Leeds, a bed. Wife, Rebecca, use of my plantation, to bring up my children. Daughters, Susanna Leeds, Dorcas Leeds, and Rachel Leeds, the plantation, and my other land. If my children die, then I give my estate to my three brothers, John, Japhet and Nehemiah. Executors—my brother, Japhet Leeds, Daniel Smith, and my wife. Witnesses—Ann Leeds, Benjamin Hoffmin and Felix Leeds. Proved March 21, 1765.
1765, March 13. Inventory, £1,348.10.2, made by Jesse Smith and Evi Smith.
1784, Sept. 18. Account by Rebecca Smith (late Rebecca Leeds) the surviving Executor. Includes "Paid Nehemiah Leeds, for his son Laban. Paid doctor's bill, nursing, and funeral expenses, of Darkes Leeds, deceased, £12.10.0. For clothing and support of the three legatees, to wit., Susannah Leeds, 6 yrs. and 7 mo., £79; Rachel Leeds, 15 yrs. and 7 mo., £187; and Darkis Leeds, 8 yrs. and 3 mo., £99." Lib. 12, p. 65; Lib. 25, p. 544.

1760, Jan. 9. Leeds, Hannah, of Northampton, Burlington Co., widow; will of. My eldest daughter, Sarah Briggs, £30. My second daughter, Mary Kenton, £35. My youngest daughter, Rebeckah Ridgway, £35. Son, Titan Leeds, 5 shillings. Son, Abraham Leeds, rest of real and personal. Executor—son, Abraham Leeds, of Evesham. Witnesses—John Murphy, Robert Fenton, Richard Liven. Proved April 1, 1761. Lib. 10, p. 341.

1764, Dec. 27. Leeds, Vincent, of Northampton Twsp., Burlington Co., yeoman; will of. To Mary Knight, alias Mary Roswell, £50. To Barbary Inger, £10. Remainder to my wife, Anna, both personal and real, to the children of my brother, Philo Leeds, viz., Samuel, Jemima Leeds, Marcy Leeds, Isajah, Joseph, Anne Leeds and Sarah Leeds, and the daughter of my brother-in-law, Nathaniel Thomas, viz., Rebeckah Thomas. As I am Guardian to Hope Atkinson, I desire my brother-in-law Thomas Budd, to take my place therein. Executors—wife, Anna, and my brother-in-law, Thomas Budd. Witnesses—Ezekiel Haines, Titan Leeds, George Bliss. Proved Dec. 24, 1767.

1767, Dec. 22. Inventory, £880.1.4½, made by Joseph Burr and John Goldy. Lib. 13, p. 262.

1769, July 20. Leferty, Bryan, of Somerset Co. Int. Adm'x—Mary Leferty, widow of said Bryan. Fellowbondsman—John Gaston, of said place, merchant. Witnesses—William Sickels and Mary Vandeventer. Lib. K, p. 143.

1763, May 1. Lefters, Peter, of Middletown, Monmouth Co., yeoman; will of. Wife, Mary, the bed standing in the east outward room of my father's dwelling house, and all the goods she had when I married her. My daughter, Mary, £5, when 18. Son, John, £25, when 21. Executors—my brother, Benjamin Lefferts, and brother-in-law, Gysbert Vanmater. Witnesses—Chrineyonce Vanmater, Jacob Vanmater, Albert Polhemas. Proved May 30, 1763.

1763, June 10. Inventory, £462.9.10, made by Benjamin Vanmater, Cyrenius Vanmater and Daniel Polhemus. Lib. H, p. 389.

1768, Dec. 6. Lefferson, Aukes, of Middletown, Monmouth Co., yeoman; will of. Grandson, Aurie Lefferson, eldest son of my deceased eldest son, Leffert, £5. Son, Benjamin, £50. Daughter, Mary, £30. Grandchildren, Mary and John, being children of my deceased son, Peter, £12. Land to be sold and money given to daughter, Abigail Vanmater, son, Benjamin, grandson, Aukes Wikoff (son of my deceased daughter Altia), daughter Mary, grandchildren, Mary and John, and the six grandchildren, children of my deceased son, Leffert. Executors—son, Benjamin, and my friends, Garret Wyckoff and Cyrenus Vanmater. Witnesses—Chrineyoncy Van Mater, Cornelius Van Mater, Tobies Polhemus. Proved April 2, 1770.

1770, March 20. Inventory, £2,402.6.5, made by Benjamin Vanmater and Richard Lawrence. Lib. K, p. 198.

1763, June 4. Lefferts, Abraham, of New York City, merchant; will of. Son, Dirck Leffertse, two houses and one stone house, in Montgomery Ward, said City, adjoining house of William Walton and Jacobus Roosevelt; also a lot on the East River; also land in Albany, and a lot in Goshen Twsp. Daughter, Elizabeth, wife of Peter Clopper, house where I live on Queen Street; and house on Maiden Lane, between houses of Jechamiah Allen and John Taylor, which, after the deaths of her and her husband, are to be for my grandchildren, Elizabeth and Catharine, the children of said Elizabeth. My grandson, Abraham, son of my son, Dirck, £100; and to Sarah, the daughter of my son, Dirck, £100. Executors—son, Dirck, and my daughter, Elizabeth Clopper. Witnesses—John Broome, Gilbert Burger, John McKesson. Proved May 16, 1768. Lib. I, p. 232.

1764, Jan. 20. Leforge, David, of Cedar Brook, in Piscataway, Middlesex Co., miller; will of. My land that belongs to me, of the plantation formerly my father's, in Piscataway, to be sold. Wife, Sarah, the furniture she brought with her. Daughter-in-law, Phebe Pearsall, £5 and a cow. Wife to have use of rest, and daughter, Phebe, to have the same, when she is 18, but, if she die, then to go to the now living children of my brothers, John and Nathaniel, and those that are now living of my sisters, Francis Blackford and Sarah Jones. Executors—my wife and my brothers, James Manning and Joseph Randolph. Witnesses—William Campbell, James Manning, Jr., John Pearsall. Proved May 9, 1764.

1764, May 8. Inventory, made by Samuel Drake and Daniel Drake.
Lib. H, p. 438.

1769, April 14. Leforge, Nicholas, of Piscataway, Middlesex Co.; will of. Wife, Syche, £50, and some goods, and the land where I live, and the other lot, while my widow; and she is to take care of my children, namely, Nicholas, Jacob, Nelly and Rachel. Executors—friends, Jacob Boice and Benjamin Runyon. Witnesses—David Leforge, Jacob Titsworth, Reune Runyon. Proved May 22, 1769.

1769, May 23. Inventory, made by Reune Runyon and David Coriell.
Lib. K, p. 106.

1763, Oct. 14. Leforge, Temperance, of Piscataway, Middlesex Co.; will of. Sister, Frances Agner, a bed. Sister, Mary Auten, chairs, etc. Rest of my estate to the said two sisters. Executors—friends, William Tietsoort and Peter Runyon. Witnesses—Hendrick Lane, William Horn, Henry Beekman. Proved Nov. 24, 1763.

1763, Nov. 24. Inventory, £108.10.6, made by Ishmael Shippey and Daniel Bray.
Lib. H, p. 339.

1763, March 21. Legg, Samuel, of New York City, house carpenter; will of. My wife, Elizabeth, all my household goods. Eldest son, Henry, £5. Youngest son, Samuel, £5. Eldest daughter, Sarah, £5. Second daughter, Elce, £5. Youngest daughter, Phebe, £5. Real to be sold, and the interest of the money is to be for the use of my wife. Executors—son, Henry, and my son-in-law, Jacob Loveberry. Witnesses—Philip Pelton, William Oglvie, John Woods. Proved Sept. 3, 1763.
Lib. H, p. 272.

1758, Aug. 31. Leonard, Anne, of Perth Amboy, Middlesex Co.; will of. Widow of Capt. Samuel Leonard. Son-in-law, John Berrien, £200. Granddaughter, Elizabeth Lawrence, £200, when she is of age; provided she continue under the care of my daughter, Rachel Sarjant, or live in such other place as my daughters, Sarah Billop, Rachel Sarjant, Elizabeth Goelet, or my Executor, think proper. Son-in-law, John Lawrence, £50. Sister, Mary Farrington, my ½ part of the house where I live, and the house where Edward Griffin lately lived, and, after her death, then to my daughters, Sarah Billop, widow of Thomas Billop, and Rachel Sarjant, wife of Samuel Sarjant; as also the 2 acres of land in Perth Amboy, east of Market Street, which formerly belonged to my father-in-law, Benjamin Griffith, and afterwards to my mother, and whereon I now live. To daughter, Elizabeth Goelet, during her life, my brick house, contiguous to the Court House, which Samuel Leonard, my late husband, bought of William Hodshon, and the new house by it, to be finished; and, after her death, the same is to go to my daughters, Sarah Billop, Rachel Sarjant, and my grandson, John Goelet. Rest of my estate to my daughters, Sarah, Rachel and Elizabeth. The share of Elizabeth Goelet is to be managed by my Executor during the life of her present husband, Francis Goelet, and, after his death, if it should please God he should die, then her share is to be given to her. Executor—my son-in-law, John Berrien. Witnesses—John Smyth, Norris Thorp, Alexander Watson. Proved June 13, 1761. Lib. H, p. 9.

1759, Nov. 4. Leonard, Henry, of Essex Co.; will of. Wife, Euphame Arrabella Leonard, ¼ of my real and personal. The rest to my sons, Robert Morris Leonard and Henry Leonard, and my daughter, Susanna Leonard. My sister, Sarah Leonard, £10. Executors—brothers, Samuel and Thomas Leonard, my brother-in-law, Samuel Cook, Courtland Skinner and my wife, Euphame Arrabella Leonard. Witnesses—William Ely, Elizabeth Stogdell. Proved Nov. 2, 1761. Lib. H, p. 39.

1761, June 1. Leonard, Joshua, of Morris Co. Int. Adm'r—Paul Leonard. Fellowbondsman—David Tuttle; both of said Co.

1761, May 29. Renunciation by Sarah Leonard, the widow, in favor of Paul Leonard. Witness—Josiah Leonard. Lib. H, p. 442.

1763, Dec. 13. Leonard, Nathaniel, of Middletown, Monmouth Co., yeoman; will of. My wife, Deliverance, £50. Son, John, 10 acres where he lives, on the place I bought of the Executors of Benjamin Cooper. Rest of personal and real to be divided between my sons, John, Nathaniel, Joseph and Thomas. Son, Nathaniel, to have my homestead, where I live, and he shall take care of his mother, and provide for his brother, Thomas, while a minor. Executors—sons, John, Nathaniel and Joseph, and my relation, Andrew Bowne (son of John). Witnesses—James Winter, Phebe Taylor, Samuel Bown. Proved Dec. 29, 1763.

1764, Jan. 4. Inventory, £399.11.9, made by John Layton, Samuel Bowne, William Bowne. Lib. H, p. 527.

1768, March 8. Leonard, Thomas, of Hunterdon Co. Int. Adm'r—Edmond Beakes. Fellowbondsman—John Everet; both of Trenton Twsp., said Co. Witness—Bowes Reed. Lib. 13, p. 438.

1768, Sept. 8. Leslie, William, of Perth Amboy, Middlesex Co. Ward. Son of George Leslie, of same place, deceased. He makes choice of Doctor John Cochran as his Guardian.

1768, Sept. 8. Guardian—John Cochran, of New Brunswick, Doctor of physick. Fellowbondsman—Stephen Skinner, Esq., of Perth Amboy; both of said Co. Witness—Isaac Browne. Lib. I, p. 336.

1766, Nov. 5. Letts, Francis, of Middlesex Co. Int. Adm'x—Catharine Letts, the widow. Fellowbondsman—William Lorton; both of said Co.

1766, Nov. 11. Inventory, made by David Gosling and John Griggs.

1766, Dec. 9. Account by Catharine Letts. Includes "Paid to the school master, 14 shillings." File No. 1447-1449 L; 4337-4338 L.

1768, Oct. 22, Levigood, Peter, of Greenwich, Cumberland Co., yeoman; will of. To Thomas Maskell, son of Daniel Maskell, my coat;

CALENDAR OF WILLS—1761-1770 249

also rest of estate. Executor—Daniel Maskell. Witnesses—Jonathan Bowen, Jr., James Ewing, Joseph Hutton. Proved Dec. 12, 1768.
1768, Oct. 26. Inventory, £50.13.7, made by Thomas Maskell and Jonathan Bowen, Jr. Lib. 13, p. 487.

1764, Nov. 27. Lewis, Elizabeth, of Hunterdon Co. Ward. Daughter of John Lewis, of Amwell, said Co. She makes choice of her friend, Samuel Thatcher, of Amwell, as her Guardian.
1764, Nov. 27. Guardian—Samuel Thatcher. Fellowbondsman—Andrew Crawford. Lib. 12, p. 36.

1764, Nov. 27. Lewis, Jacob and John, of Hunterdon Co. Ward. Sons and devisees of John Lewis, of Amwell, said Co. They make choice of their friend, Andrew Crawford, of Bethlehem, said Co., as their Guardian.
1764, Nov. 27. Guardian—Andrew Crawford. Fellowbondsman—Samuel Thatcher, of Amwell. Lib. 12, p. 36.

1761, March 9. Lewis, Sarah, of Waterford, Gloucester Co. Int. Adm'r—Christopher Eggmen (Egmond). Fellowbondsman—Bartholomew Eggmen (Edgmon); both of said Co.
1761, March 7. Inventory, £13.14.0, made by Bartholomew Eggmen and Isaac Fish. Lib. 10, p. 174.

1763, Sept. 17. Lewis, Thomas, of Bernards Town, Somerset Co.; will of. My wife to have use of that part of plantation where I live, that I bought of Edward Lewis, of 31 acres, which was first conveyed by James Alexander to Samuel Rolfe, and by him to Edward Lewis. Sons, Jacob and Zepheniah, the plantation I bought of Daniel Sutton, of 190 acres, and they are to pay the bonds which I owe to John Ayers and John Primrose. Daughters, Ann, Sarah, Mary and Rachel, my personal estate. Executor—my brother, Edward Lewis, of Bernards Town. Witnesses—Zachariah Sutton, William Doty, John Brees. Proved Oct. 5, 1763. Lib. H, p. 309.

1765, Oct. 23. Lewis, Walter, of Great Egg Harbor, Gloucester Co. Int. Adm'r—Christopher Lucas. Fellowbondsman—Richard Westcoat; both of Egg Harbor, yeomen. Witness—Thomas Clark.
1765, Oct. 22. Inventory, £26.15.6, made by John Hawkins and Richard Westcoat. Lib. 12, p. 284.

1747, Nov. 2. Leydecker, Ryck, of Hackinsack in Bergen Co., yeoman; will of. Wife, Mary, all real and personal while my widow. Sons, Gerrit Lydecker and Sam Benson Lydecker, all my fast estate. Daughters, Cornelia, Marretje, Elizabeth, Rachel and Cathrina Lydecker, £25 each. Executors—my wife, Mary, and, after her death, my brothers, Cornelius Lydecker and Abraham Lydecker, both of Hackinsack. Witnesses—Robert Livesey, Isaac Delamater, Edmund Lynott and Phillip McCarguin. Proved July 28, 1766. Lib. H, p. 635.

1761, March 1. Leyton, John, of Shrewsbury, Monmouth Co., yeoman; will of. All my debts to be paid by my four eldest sons. All real, and personal to my four sons, Safety Layton, Andrew Layton, John Layton, and William Layton, when William is 21. The said sons are to take care of my three youngest daughters, and of my daughter, Ann, till she is 18. The said four sons are to provide for their mother, and also for my son, Thomas, till he is 16, when he is to have £100. Daughter, Catharine, £15. Daughter, Hester, £30. Daughter, Hannah, £30. Daughter, Ann, £30. Executors—sons, Safety, Andrew, John and William. Witnesses—Samuel Layton, George Harrison, John Morris. Proved May 13, 1761.

1761, June 1. Inventory, £199.16.0, made by Joseph Burdge and George Rhe.   Lib. G, p. 448.

1762, April 19. Liddon, Perryman, of Gloucester Co. Ward. Petition of said Perryman Liddon, eldest son and heir of Henry Liddon, of Greenwich Twsp., yeoman, deceased, stating that he has lands by descent from his father, and prays that his friend, Samuel Liddon, may be made his Guardian, till 21. Witnesses—John Ladd and Hannah Ladd.

1762, April 19. Guardian—Samuel Liddon, yeoman. Fellowbondsman—Jacob Spicer, yeoman, both of Greenwich Twsp. Witnesses—Hannah Ladd and John Ladd.   Lib. 11, p. 127.

1762, Sept. 17. Lie, George, of Pilesgrove, Salem Co., laborer. Int. Adm'r—Hendrick Faber (Fover). Fellowbondsman—John Nelson, both of said place, yeomen.   Lib. 11, p. 372.

1755, Sept. 23. Liens, Coonrad, of Saddle River Precinct, Bergen Co., yeoman; will of. Son, Daniel, a gun. Wife, Cathren, all real and personal while my widow. The place where I live to be divided into 3 parts; one lot to go to Coonrad Liens (alias Rutan), a son that my wife had before I married her, and one lot to my son, Daniel, and the third lot to my son, Abraham. Son, Peter, ½ of two other small lots, and the other ½ to my son Henry. Son, John Liens, a maintainance from Coonrad Liens, Alice Rutan, Daniel Liens, Abraham Liens, Peter Liens and Henry Liens. Daughter, Rachel Liens, £20. Daughter, Margrete Liens, £20. Daughter, Magdalen Liens, £20. Daughter, Cathrine Liens, £20. After death or marriage of my wife, the personal estate to be divided among Coonrad Liens (alias Rutan), my sons, Daniel Liens, John Liens, Peter Liens, Abraham Liens, Henry Liens, and my daughters, Rachel Liens, Margret Liens, Magdalen Liens, Catherin Liens. Executor—son, Daniel. Witnesses—Joost Beam, Joseph Bartram and Coonrad Beam.

1763, June 2. Codicil. My three sons, Coonrad Liens, Jr., Abraham Liens and Daniel Liens, shall allow my son, Anthony Liens 10 acres (not of age). Witnesses—Robert Clark, John Liens and Abraham Liens, Sr. Proved Oct. 12, 1769.   Lib. K, p. 137.

1763, June 23. Linch, Samuel, of Penns Neck, Salem Co.; will of. Son, Samuel Linch, all my lands. Daughter, Hannah Linch, a bed, and 3 cows. Daughter, Rebecca, 20 shillings. Wife, Magdelen, to have her thirds. Rest of moveable estate to my daughters, Elizabeth, Sarah, Mary and Hannah Linch, and each to have £15. Executors—son, Samuel, and Obadiah Loyd. Witnesses—Robert Clark, James Clark, John Gray. Proved Sept. 7, 1763.

1763, Sept. 5. Inventory, £319.6.5, made by William Guest and Robert Clark.   Lib. 11, p. 450.

1779, May 3. Account of "Samuel Lynch," by John Lockhart, Adm'r. Value of goods, £238.5.5.   Lib. 22, p. 67; File No. 1289½ Q.

1762, Nov. 4. Lindsley, Aaron, of Essex Co. Ward. Son of Stephen Lindsley, of said Co., deceased. Guardian—Joseph Wood. Fellowbondsman—Isaac Winans; both of Morris Co. Lib. H, p. 198.

1762, April 7. Lindsly, Elihu, of Morris Co.; will of. Eldest son, Jabes, land on south side of Morristown road. Youngest son, Elihu, land on north side. Daughter, Sarah, a bed and £3. Daughters, Elizabeth, Kezia and Sarah, rest of personal. Executors—friends, Benjamin Lindsly and William Smith. Witnesses—Stephen Morehouse, Lawrence Willison, Moses Browne. Proved April 24, 1762.
1762, May 4. Inventory, made by Richard Minthorn and Paul Day.
Lib. H, p. 135.

1770, March 12. Lindsly, Junia, of Morristown, Morris Co., yeoman; will of. My land where I live and the tract at the Great Pond to be sold. To wife, Hannah, and to each daughter, Charity, Mary and Rachel, £50. To sons, Ephraim, Junia, Agur and Nehemiah, £100 each. Sons to be put to trades. Executors—my brother, John Lindsly, and friend, Ebenezer Condict. Witnesses—Jacob Goble, Mary Cooper, Timothy Johnes. Proved April 9, 1770. Lib. K, p. 215.

1763, Aug. 7. Linken, Nathan, of Sussex Co., yeoman; will of. Wife, Hannah, £50 and various goods. My sister, Tabitha Linken, £25. Sons, Daniel and Thomas, rest of estate, when 21. Real estate to be sold. Abigail Lenard, who has lived with me for some time, is to have something. Executors—Joseph Givin and Thomas Hoovy, both of Mendham in Morris Co. Witnesses—John Wood, Mary Youngs, Brice Ricky. Proved Aug. 26, 1763.
1763, Sept. 2. Inventory, £284.10.6, made by Robert Huie and Brice Riky. Lib. I, p. 34.

1765, Jan. 6. Linmier, Christianna, Christopher, Nicholas and Sarah, of Penns Neck, Salem Co. Wards. Children of Christopher Lynmire, of said place, deceased, having lands devised to them by their father, make choice of John Pitman as their Guardian, in case of the sons till 21. Same day John Pitman appointed Guardian. Fellowbondsman—John Helm, both of Upper Penns Neck Twsp., yeoman. Lib. 12, p. 178.

1762, March 22. Lippincott, David, of Upper Freehold, Monmouth Co.; will of. Wife, Rebecca, £60, and otherwise provided for. Son, David, £150. Son, Jonathan, plantation where I live. Daughter, Mary Parent, £30, when she is 21. Daughter, Rhoda Lippincott, £40, when 21. Sons, David and Jonathan, my cedar swamp. Grandson, Solomon Lippincott, £5. Grandson, David Parent, £4. Executors—son, Jonathan, and Daniel Saxton. Witnesses—Sarah Sexton, Marget Smart, Samuel Emley. Proved May 20, 1762.
1762, April 28. Inventory, £621.8.0, made by William Lawrie and Samuel Emley. Lib. 11, p. 179.

1764, May 17. Lippincott, Freedom, of Evesham Twsp., Burlington Co., yeoman; will of. To my daughter, Hope Jones, 5 shillings; and also the children she had by her first husband, Thomas Wallace, deceased, viz., Rebecca, Thomas, Hope and Mary, each 5 shillings; and also to the two children she has by her present husband, Henry Jones, viz., Caleb and Sarah, each 5 shillings. To my granddaughter,

Mary Basset, daughter of my daughter Mary, £10 when 18. Son, Daniel, riding creature and saddle. Remainder to my sons, Solomon, Samuel, Joshua and Daniel, and my grandson, Job Lippincott, son of my son Caleb, deceased. Executors—sons, Samuel and Daniel. Witnesses—Abraham Allen, Henry Glass, Hannah Eldridge. Proved Sept. 2, 1768.

1768, Sept. 1. Inventory, £139.17.10, made by Micajah Wills and Abraham Allen. Lib. 13, p. 420.

1768, Aug. 29. Lippincott, Jacob, of Chester Twsp., Burlington Co. Ward. Son of Jacob Lippincott, of said place; makes choice of Abraham Heulings, of said Twsp., as his Guardian, till 21. Said Heulings appointed, with Ezekiel Lippincott, of said Twsp., on his bond. Lib. 13, p. 433.

1764, Dec. 15. Lippincott, John, of Shrewsbury, Monmouth Co., blacksmith; will of. Wife, Mary, use of real and personal, while my widow, and she is to educate the children. Children, William, Jacob, Lydia, Margaret and John, all the estate, when 21. Executors—friends, Joseph Potter and Richard Lawrence. Witnesses—Richard Tole, Joseph Hulit, Andrew Stephens. Proved Jan. 17, 1765.
Lib. H, p. 565.

1760, Nov. 20. Lippincott, Obadiah, of Shrewsbury, Monmouth Co.; will of. All my lands at Kettle Creek to my four sons, which lands I bought of the Executors of Thomas Lippincott, said sons being, Jacob, Robert, Samuel and Judiah (all under age). Wife, Phebe, use of real till sons are 21. Executor—my brother, John Lippincott. Witnesses—Benjamin Wolcott, Samuel Lippincott and John Craddock. Proved Jan. 31, 1761. Lib. G, p. 390.

1768, Feb. 25. Lippincott, Remembrance, of Twsp. and Co. of Gloucester, laborer; will of. After debts are paid estate to be divided between Richard Cheesman, Uriah Cheesman, Richard Cheesman, Jr., Deborah Smallwood, Drusilla Hillman, Tamer Jones, Ephraim Cheesman, Isable Cheesman and James Rowand. Executor—friend, Richard Cheesman, Sr. Witnesses—Edward Bruin, Isaac Tomlinson. Proved Feb. 20, 1769.

1768, April 15. Inventory, £65.7.6, made by Lazarus Pine and Edward Bruin. Lib. 14, p. 51.

1763, April 15. Lippincott, William, of Shrewsbury, Monmouth Co., yeoman; will of. Advanced in years. Son, Darius, land at Squancom, in Shrewsbury, of 12 acres. I have already given to my four sons, Wilber, Samuel, Remembrance and James. Daughter, Abigail, wife of John Grandine, £20. Wife, Hannah, personal estate and, at her death, to go to my four daughters, Sarah, Increase, Phebe and Hannah. Executors—wife, Hannah, and my son-in-law, Nathan Tilton. Witnesses—Andrew Stephens, Avis Fisher, Miln Parker. Proved Feb. 11, 1765.

1765, Feb. 11. Renunciation by Hannah Lippincott, the widow, "being old and infirm." Witness—Elihu Williams.

1765, Feb. 11. Inventory, £81.2.1, made by Joseph Potter and Elihu Williams. Lib. H, p. 529; Lib. H, p. 534.

1763, Jan. 20. Littell (Little), Jacob, of Elizabeth Town, Essex Co. Int. Adm'x—Mary Little, the widow. Fellowbondsman—John Little; both of said place.
1763, Feb. 15. Inventory, £50.15.8, made by John Stites and Thomas Thompson. Lib. H, p. 272.

1767, Aug. 6. Little, Elizabeth, of Penns Neck, Salem Co. Int. Adm'r—John Redstreak, yeoman. Fellowbondsmen—William Robinson and Jacob Townsend, yeomen; all of said place.
1767, Aug. 5. Inventory, £102.17.3, made by William Robinson and Jacob Townsend. Lib. 13, p. 190.

1761, Jan. 1. Little, Robert, of Borough of Elizabeth, Essex Co., yeoman; will of. Daughter, Phebe Locker, one acre and a half of my homestead, and it is to include my house; and, at her death, I give ½ acre thereof to my grandson, Robert Little Locker, and the other acre to her other children. Son, Joseph Little, my salt meadow and, at his death, to go to his son, William. Speaks of a brother, Jonathan Little, holding a mortgage. Grandchildren, Robert Little, son to Joseph Little, and Robert Little Locker, son of my daughter, Phebe Locker, my right to the undivided lands in the Elizabeth Town purchase. If son, Joseph, bring any account against my estate, then my Executors are to charge him for keeping his daughter, Sarah, the time she lived with me; and, if my son-in-law, John Locker, bring any account against my estate, then my Executors are to rent out the land I have devised to my daughter, Phebe, his wife, long enough to discharge said debt. Granddaughter, Sarah Little, to have schooling, to the amount of £5, till 18. Household goods to be sold, and money to be given to my grandchildren, Robert Little, William Little and Sarah Little (children of Joseph Little) and Robert Little Locker, John Yeates Locker and Ann Locker (children of my daughter, Phebe Locker). Executors—friends, William Winans and John Burrows. Witnesses—Ebenezer Spining, Elihu Woodruff, John Jones. Proved July 9, 1761.
1761, May 9. Inventory, £106.19.10, made by Henry Garthwaite and Ebenezer Spining. Lib. H, p. 21.

1765, May 6. Little, Thomas, of Kingwood, Hunterdon Co.; will of. My mother to be provided for. My daughters, Jane and Martha, £30 each, when 21. Rest of my estate to my wife, Ester, and my sons, William, Andrew, John, James, Christopher and Robert; but my children are to be schooled. Sons, William and Andrew, to have the lands. Executors—John Hanna and my son, William. Witnesses—Richard Crooks, Joseph Sinclair, Elizabeth Sinclair. Proved July 29, 1765.
1765, July 1. "These are to certifie that we the mother, and now the widow of the within named Thomas Little, deceased, do hereby acknowledge the said Thomas Little's will hereunto annexed, the same being read unto us, and we fully understand, being fully content, and submiting thereto, we desire the same to be fully prosecuted to the true intent and meaning of said will, as witness our hands and seals the day and year abovesaid. Esther Little, by mark. (Seal). Witnesses. Thomas Litle, Thomas Fleming."
1765, July 8. Inventory, £470.0.11, made by John Cowan and Philip Titus. Lib. 12, p. 210.

1766, Sept. 29. Little, Thomas, of Bethlehem Twsp., Hunterdon Co.; will of. Wife, Jane, £30. Son, Joseph, £30, and the rest of Leonard Cryster's time. Son, Thomas, £30. Son, William, £30. Daughter, Elizabeth Little, £30. Daughter, Mary Foster, £5. Daughter, Jane £30. Rest to my wife and children, in general. Executors—sons, Joseph and Thomas. Witnesses—Johan Bartholomew, James Bigger, Francis McShane. Proved Nov. 17, 1766.

1766, Nov. 11. Inventory, £327.2.11, made by Francis McShane and Johan Bartholomew. Lib. 12, p. 407.

1762, Oct. 19. Little, William, of Mansfield, Burlington Co. Int. Adm'r—Peter Tallman of same place. Fellowbondsman—Samuel Allinson of Burlington.

1762, Oct. 19. Renunciation by Amey Little, the widow.
Lib. 11, p. 240.

1762, Oct. 21. Inventory, £46.14.5½, made by Peter Tallman.

1765, Jan. 7. Livermore, Isaac, of Rockaway, Morris Co. Int. Adm'r—Henry Broadwell, at the request of the principal creditors. Fellowbondsman—Noadiah Potter; both of Elizabeth Borough, Essex Co. Lib. H, p. 423.

1763, April 23. Lock, Jonas, of Greenwich Twsp., Gloucester Co.; will of. To my sister's daughter, Marcy Cox, one cow. My sister-in-law, Charles Lock's wife, a mare. Cousin, Peter Lock, son of Charles Lock, rest of moveable estate and my lands. Executor—cousin, Andrew Lock. Witnesses—Thomas Denny, William Homan, Has Urine. Proved June 10, 1765.

1765, June 10. Renunciation of Andrew Lock. Witnesses—William Homan and Mathew Gill.

1765, June 11. Administrator, with the will annexed—Charles Lock, of Greenwich Twsp., said Co., yeoman. Fellowbondsman—Mathew Gill, of same place, weaver.

1765, May 29. Inventory, £127.12.9, made by Mathew Gill and William Homan. Lib. 12, p. 168.

1761, Sept. 14. Lock, Swan, of Greenwich Twsp., Gloucester Co., yeoman. Int. Adm'x—Sarah Lock. Fellowbondsman—John Reynalds; both of said Co. Witness—Samuel Mickle.

1761, Aug. 20. Inventory, £126.10.4½, made by John Reynalds and John Wilkinson. Lib. 10, p. 434.

1762, Oct. 30. Lockhart, James, of Somerset Co. Int. Adm'x—Mary Lockhart, his widow. Fellowbondsman—Thomas Berry; both of said place. Lib. H, p. 197.

1763, June 7. Logan, John, of Morris Co. Int. Adm'r—Thomas Logan, father of said John. Fellowbondsman—Brice Rickey, of Somerset Co.

1763, July 8. Inventory, £263.13.1, made by Morgin Young and Samuel Muckelrath. Lib. H, p. 245.

1762, May 27. Long, Ansell, of Gloucester Co., yeoman; will of. Brother, David Long, to be Guardian of my three sons, Jonathan, Constantine and Uriah. Lands may be sold for the benefit of my sons.

Executors—my said brother and my cousin, Joseph Paullin. Witnesses—Andrew Long, Alexander Randall, Silas Randall. Proved June 22, 1762.
 1762, June 21. Inventory, £146.15.10, made by Abraham Long and Andrew Long.
 1770, April 18. Account of Lucy Long, Executrix of David Long (who was one of the Executors of Ansel Long), and Joseph Paullin.
Lib. 11, p. 265; Lib. 15, p. 15.

1770, Feb. 14. Long, Constantine, of Greenwich, Gloucester Co. Ward. Son of Ansel Long, of said place, who, by will, left a legacy to Constantine. Guardian—William Newcomb, of Fairfield, Cumberland Co., yeoman. Fellowbondsman—Moses Remington, of Greenwich, Cumberland Co., yeoman. Lib. 15, p. 1.

1768, Nov. 16. Long, Daniel, of Elsinboro, Salem Co., laborer. Int. Adm'x—Prudence Long, of said place, widow. Fellowbondsmen—John Firth, of said place, carpenter, and Thomas Norris, of Town of Salem, ship wright.
 1768, Dec. 6. Inventory, £90.15.10, made by John Firth and William Abbott. Lib. 13, p. 477.

1769, May 14. Long, David, of Cumberland Co.; will of. My wife, Lucy, may sell my real and moveable estate, and I give her ½ of my estate, and the other ½ to son Peter, when 21. Executrix—my wife; and uncle, Thomas Sayrs, to be assistant to her. Witnesses—Elijah Bowen, Jr., Daniel Bowen, Ruth Langlee. Proved Dec. 8, 1769.
 1769, Dec. 6. Inventory, £201.12.5, made by John Wheaton and Ephraim Mills. Lib. 14, p. 168.

1764, May 3. Long, John, of Hopewell Twsp., Cumberland Co., yeoman; will of. Brother, David Long, all personal and real estate, but he to keep and educate my son, David, till 17, and then shall put to interest £50; which my son is to have when 21; but, if he die, then the sum is to go to all my brothers and sisters. Executor—brother, David. Witnesses—George Peirson, Robert Kelsay, Hannah Mulford. Proved June 11, 1764.
 1764, June 11. Inventory, £59.7.0, made by George Peirson and Daniel Stretch.
 1765, Feb. 1. Account by Executor. Lib. 12, p. 24.

1769, Dec. 9. Long, Jonathan, of Greenwich, Gloucester Co. Ward. Son of Ansell Long, of said place, who, by will left a legacy to Jonathan. Guardian—William Newcomb, of Fairfield, Cumberland Co. Fellowbondsman—Abel Shepherd, of Greenwich, Cumberland Co., yeoman. Lib. 15, p. 4.

1766, Aug. 19. Longfield, Henry, of New Brunswick, Middlesex Co.; will of. Goods to be sold, as also my lands, but reserving the family graveyard, of ¼ acre. The money to be given to the children, Thomas, Mary, Catherine, and, in trust, for Cornelius, but, if he reform, he may have his share. Executors—James Neilson and Samuel Kemble. Witnesses—Edward Antill, Anthony White, John Cochran. Proved Sept. 15, 1770. Lib. K, p. 241.

1760, Jan. 10. Longstreet, Aron, of Shrewsbury Twsp., in Manasquan, Monmouth Co.; will of. "I am son of Derick Longstreet, and am very sick with smallpox." The lands willed to me by my father I give to my brothers, Samuel and Derrick. To Catharine, my brother Stoffle's daughter, £40. To Else, my brother Stoffel's daughter, £40, To my mother, cows and sheep. I desire my uncle, Samuel, to have a deed for ¼ part of the lands which was Hartshorn's, purchased in partnership before my father's death. Executors—my uncle, Samuel, and my brother-in-law, Peter Wycoff. Witnesses—Anne Osborn, Moses Richards, Remembrance Lippincott. Proved Oct. 3, 1761.

1762, April 10. Inventory, made by William Morton and Gersham Bills. Lib. H, p. 494.

1759, Dec. 23. Longstreet, Richard, of Shrewsbury, Monmouth Co., yeoman; will of. Wife, Alice, the profits of the plantation, upon which my house stands, which plantation my father bought of John West, and, by his will, gave to me. Eldest son (now living), Samuel, my plantation at Shark River, and 3 acres of meadow off of that place which I bought of Joseph Pearce. My two younger sons, Aury and Richard, the rest of my lands. My three eldest daughters (being married), £100 each. Daughter, Alice, £100 and an outset. My younger daughter, Anne, who is not married, £120. My three eldest daughters are named, Catharine, Moica and Mary. Granddaughters, Catharine and Alice, being daughters of my eldest son, Stoffel, £30 each, when they are 21. Executors—sons, Samuel and Aury. Witnesses—William Brewer, Michael Roberson, Thomas Bell, Mery Wilkins. Proved April 18, 1761. Probate to Samuel Longstreet, surviving executor, the son, Aury, being dead.

1761, June 10. Inventory, made by James Lawrence and Samuel Osborn. Lib. G, p. 384.

1761, July 8. Longworth, David, of Newark, Essex Co. Int. Adm'r—Isaac Longworth, heir-at-law. Fellowbondsman—Uzal Ogden; both of said place. Witness—Lewis Ogden. Lib. H, p. 14.

1765, April 13. Loofborrow, Abraham, of City of Perth Amboy, Middlesex Co. Int. Adm'r—Thomas Skinner, Jr., principal creditor. Fellowbondsman—Thomas Crowell; both of said place. Witness—John Thomson.

1765, April 13. Renunciation of Kezia Loofbourrow, the widow.
Lib. H, p. 419.

1764, May 12. Loots, Johannis, of Tieneck in Bergen Co., yeoman; will of. Cousin, Wiert Banta, £5 for his birthright. My fast lands in Tiene-fly to the heirs of Paulus Loots, dec'd. Cousins, Wiert Banta, Jacob Banta, Paulus Banta and David Banta, land in Bergen Co. in the mountains, and they shall pay to the heirs of Paulus Loots, dec'd, namely, John Hendrickse Banta and Geesje Cammegaar, £40 each; also to Jacob Andriese Westervelt £25. My sister, Tryntje Cammegaar, a maintainance while unmarried. Sister, Geesje Cammegaar, a negro. To the heirs of Paulus Loots, dec'd, namely, John Banta and Geesje Cammegaar, wood. Moveable estate to my cousins, namely, Wiert Hendrickse Banta, Jacob Banta, Paulus Banta, David Banta, and the children of their sister Lena. Executors—my cousins, Wiert Hendrickse Banta and Jacob Hendrickse Banta. Witnesses—

CALENDAR OF WILLS—1761-1770 257

Robert Livesey, Siebelj Banta and Albert H. Banta. Proved June 15, 1764. Lib. H, p. 447.
1764, June 15. Inventory, £640.7.4, made by Peter Zabriskie and Albert Banta. 788 B.

1762, Aug. 16. Loots, Paul, of Hackensack in Bergen Co., yeoman; will of. My portion of land at Tieneck shall remain in possession of my brother, John Loots. Wife, Rachel, is to remain in same right. To my sister, Geesje Cammegaar, and my cousin, John Hendrickse Banta, after the death of my brother, John Loots, all real. To the heirs of my sister, Tryntje Cammegaar, £200. To Andries Westervelt, son of Jacob Westervelt, now living with me, £24. Executors—cousins, John Hendrickse Banta and John Acker. Witnesses—Albert H. Banta, Casparus Westervelt and Robert Livesey. Proved Oct. 16, 1763. Lib. H, p. 392.
1764, Jan. 7. Inventory, £400, made by Johannis Demarest and Peter Zabriskie. 616 B.

1764, March 15. Lorance, Jonathan, of Fairfield, Cumberland Co. Int. Adm'x—Abigail Lorance. Fellowbondsmen—David Ogden and Nathaniel Ogden; all of said place. Witnesses—Joseph Ogden and James Ray.
1764, March 9. Inventory, £860.18.0, made by Joseph Ogden and James Ray. Lib. 12, p. 5.

1766, Oct. 6. Lord, Joseph, of Morris River, Cumberland Co., yeoman; will of. Son, Nathaniel Lord, 10 shillings. Daughter, Catharine Westcoate, 10 shillings. Daughter, Flowrandor Corson, 10 shillings. Wife, Mary, ⅓ the personal estate. Son, George, £40, when 21. Sons, Joseph and Absolam, and daughters, Hannah and Mary, rest of estate, when they are of age. Executors—wife, Mary, and my son, George. Overseer—friend, Abraham Jones, Esq., of Morris River. Witnesses—William McGlaughlin, Thomas Daniels, Jussta Lock. Proved Feb. 25, 1767.
1767, Feb. 20. Inventory, £184.10.1, made by Thomas Daniels and Joseph Savage. Lib. 13, p. 155.

1760, April 17. Lord, Joshua, of Deptford Twsp., Gloucester Co., yeoman; will of. My body to be buried by my son, Joshua. Son, Joshua, all my lands, and he is to allow my daughter, Elizabeth Lord, the use of the house. Son, Joshua, to have the time of my servant lad, William Carson. Grandson, Phinehas Lord, saddle and bridle. Son-in-law, Joseph Gibson, to have clothing, etc., and to his wife, who is my daughter Sarah, £5. Daughter, Eunice, wife of John Starr, £5. Daughter, Elizabeth, the residue. Executrix—daughter, Elizabeth. Witnesses—William Wilkins, Anthony Sharp, Mary Sharp. Proved Feb. 16, 1761. Lib. 10, p. 392.

1770, March 12. Lore, Hezekiah, of Morris River, Cumberland Co., farmer; will of. Wife, Deborah, ⅓ of moveable estate. Son, Jonathan, £5. Son, David, is to give to Ichabod Lore's 3 sons, £4 each, when they are 21. Son, David, my tools. My daughters, Sarah, Hannah and Rebekah, the rest of moveable estate. The salt meadow below Fortascue Island below Nantuxet Neck, to my four daughters,

17

Elizabeth, Sarah, Hannah and Rebekah. Son, David, my plantation. Executors—sons, Jonathan and David. Witnesses. William Vanhook, Annanias Shaw, John Bragg. Proved June 15, 1770.

1770, June 29. Inventory, £223.3.9, made by David Shepherd and William Newcomb. Lib. 14, p. 331.

1769, June 13. Lore, Ichabud, of Cumberland Co.; will of. Wife, Elizabeth, all moveable estate, and use of lands for 5 years, and she is to give my sons learning. Son, Dolas, plantation where I live, which was formerly in three tracts, containing 216 acres. Son, Hezekiah, plantation where Nathaniel Hewet lives, of 300 acres. Son, Lewis, 50 acres, on west side of Seder bridge and creek. Sons, Dolas, Hezekiah and Lewis, a swamp near Dividing Creek. Executors—father-in-law, William Dollas, and David Shepherd. Witnesses—Seth Lore, Phebe Lore, Gideon Heaton. Proved July 26, 1769.

1769, July 24. Inventory, £142.11.10, made by Seth Lore and Gideon Heaton. Lib. 14, p. 119.

1762, March 16. Loree, Samuel, of Mendham, Morris Co., yeoman; will of. The 30 acres where Elijah Brown lives to be sold. Wife, Sybil, rent of my plantation, till my son comes of age. Son, Samuel, rest of lands, when he is of age. Daughters, Joanna, Mary and Elizabeth, £30 each, as they are of age. Executors—friends, Jabez Bears and Benjamin Halsey. Witnesses—Henry Antell, Ezekiel Beach, Nathaniel Tingley. Proved April 15, 1762.

1762, April 19. Inventory, made by Samuel Mills and Alexander Aikman. Lib. H, p. 141.

1765, June 4. Losey, John, Sr., of Mendham Twsp., Morris Co., yeoman; will of. Wife, Jane, to have negro, Dinah, and, at wife's death, to my daughter, Elizabeth. My wife and two youngest daughters, Elizabeth Losey and Jane Losey, my household goods. Son, James Puf Losey, my lands. Son, Cornelius, £26. Son, John, £100. Son, Timothy, £30. Son, Philip, £80, when 21. Daughter, Mary Pitney, £5. Daughter, Catharine Burwell, £5. Daughter, Jane Losey, £20, when 18. Executors—friends, Isaac Southard and John Ayers. Witnesses—Nathaniel Mitchell, James Young, Richard Dell. Proved July 2, 1765. Lib. H, p. 547.

1762, July 24. Lott, Peter, Jr., of South Ward of City of Perth Amboy, Middlesex Co.; will of. My real and personal may be sold. To wife, Mary, 1/5 part of my estate. Son, Gershom, 1/5 part. Daughter, Ruth Lott, 1/5 part. Son, Danied, 1/5 part. Son, Peter, 1/5 part. Daniel and Peter to be educated. Executors—my wife and my brother, Richard Lott, and Doctor Richard Jaques. Witnesses—John Waterhouse, Robert Iselstine, Jonathan Deare. Proved July 27, 1762.

1762, Aug. 19. Inventory, £624.17.4, made by N. Everson and Robert Johnston. Lib. H, p.163.

1764, Feb. 19. Lott, Peter, Sr., of Middlesex Co., innkeeper; will of. Grandson, Gershom Lott, 5 shillings. Rest of real and personal to be divided between my wife, Catharine, and my four sons, Henry, Abram, George and Charles. Executors—my wife, Richard Lott and Timothy Smith. Above sons are not of age. Witnesses—Jonathan Rolfe, Levi Lott. Proved April 6, 1764.

1764, April 3. Inventory, £129.12.8, made by Jonathan Rolfe and Robert Brown.
1766, April 28. Account by Catharine Lott and Richard Lott.
Lib. H, p. 424.

1763, Feb. 10. Lounsberry, Jeremiah, of Pilesgrove, Salem Co., yeoman; will of. Son, Samuel, the plantation where I live; but, if he die, then to my daughter, Hannah Lounsberry. Samuel is to pay to Hannah £30. Sons, John and Jeremiah, 5 shillings each. Daughters, Pheby, Mary and Ann, 5 shillings each. Wife, Mary, to have the profits of the plantation during her life. The rest to my wife, in order to bring up Samuel and Hannah. Executors—my wife and my friend, Richard Kirby. Witnesses—Larance Holsten, Solomon Smith, Samuel Linch, Jr. Proved Feb. 26, 1763.
1763, Feb. 22. Inventory, £165.4.1, made by Larance Holsten and Samuel Linch, Jr. Lib. 11, p. 388.

1766, Oct. 2. Lounsbury, John, of Upper Penns Neck, Salem Co., yeoman; will of. Wife, Sarah, all my moveables, to bring up my children. Executrix—my wife. Witnesses—William Beetle, Robert Howard, Sarah Summerl. Proved Nov. 12, 1766.
1766, Nov. 8. Inventory, £181.5.3, made by William Beetle and Robert Howard. Lib. 12, p. 304.

1764, Dec. 7. Louzada, Aaron, of Bridgewater, Somerset Co., merchant; will of. "Being of old age." Wife, Blume Louzada, £200, and the use of the real and personal estate to bring up my children. Children to be put to trades. To Benjamin Louzada, and Abigel Lowzada, children of Moses Louzada, £50 each. Executors—my wife, and my friends, Samson Simson, of New York City, and Hendrick Fisher, of Somerset Co. Witnesses—James Coun, Josiah Stanbury, Elias V:Court. Proved Jan. 30, 1765.
1765, March 7. Inventory, £466.10.8, made by Josiah Stanbury and Elias V:Court. Lib. H, p. 486.

1762, Sept. 28. Lovell, John, of Burlington Co. Int. Adm'rs—James Wills and John Lovell, both of said Co. Fellowbondsman—Ephraim Anderson, of Hunterdon Co. Witness—Samuel Allinson.
Lib. 11, p. 231.
1762, Sept. 28. Inventory, £235.1.2, made by Ephraim Anderson and Samuel Harker.

1739, Sept. 24. Low, Albert, of Raritan, Somerset Co., yeoman; will of. Wife, Susannah, use of all real and personal while my widow. Sons, Abraham and Cornelius Low, all my estate, after wife's death, and they to pay to my daughter, Mary Pittinger, £100. Executors—my wife, and, after her death, my sons, Abraham and Cornelius Low. Witnesses—Cornelius Low, Hugh Hicks, Teunis Middagh. Proved Feb. 20, 1761. Lib. G, p. 392.

1763, March 24. Low, Cornelius, of Reading Twsp., Hunterdon Co., yeoman; will of. Son, Derick Low, to have £5. I have, by an indenture of bargain, with my sons, Derrick, Cornelius, John and Gerrit, let my lands for rents, with several reserves, also mentioned in said indenture, dated 7 of Aug., 1758, and they are to pay the said rents every year to my wife, Judick Low. After the death of my wife the said sons are to have said land. Daughters, Marytje (the wife of Abraham Bodine), Judick (the wife of Johannis Van Neste) and Antje, each to have £300. Executors—my wife and sons, Derick, and Cornelius. Witnesses—George Cock, Sarah Preston, Teunis Middagh. Proved Aug. 16, 1763.

1763, Sept. 27. Inventory, £1,276.15.4, made by John Verbrycke and Thomas Vanfleet. Lib. 11, p. 468.

1769, Aug. 23. Low, Cornelius, Jr., of New Brunswick, Middlesex Co.; will of. Wife, Catherine, my slaves and use of goods; also the use of my house, till son, James, is 21. Rest of real to be sold and money given to wife, Catherine, son, James, and daughters, Johannah Low and Maria Margaret Low, when children are of age. Executors —my wife and brothers, Isaac Low and Nicholas Low, and my brother-in-law, James Hude. Witnesses—Evert Duyckinck, William Neilson, David Ogden. Proved Nov. 30, 1769. Lib. K, p. 197.

1764, May 6. Low, Lawrence, of Reading Twsp., Hunterdon Co., yeoman; will of. Son, John, a good cow and weaver's loom. Son, Guisbert, the great Dutch Bible. Son, Henry, a mare and colt. Wife, Charity, use of rest of personal and real estate, to bring up our children in their minority. Sons, John, Henry and Guisbert, my land. Daughters, Yanaca, Elizabeth, Charity and Wynea, £400. Mother, Yanaca Low, is provided for. Executors—sons, John and Henry, and my friend, George Reading. Witnesses—Thomas Vanfleet, John Louw, Peter Van Deventer. Proved Nov. 19, 1764.

1764, Nov. 17. Inventory, £249.15.0, made by John Low and Thomas Vanfleet. Lib. 12, p. 141.

1769, Feb. 17. Low, Robert, of Fairfield, Cumberland Co. Int. Adm'r—Joseph Daton. Fellowbondsman—Theophilus Elmer; both of said Fairfield.

1769, Feb. 15. Inventory, £110.9.2, made by Thomas Harris and Theophilus Elmer.

1770, April 25. Account by Adm'r. Lib. 13, p. 496; Lib. 15, p. 12.

1762, April 21. Lowzada, Jacob, of Middlesex Co. Ward. Petition by Abraham Abrahams, stating that Moses Louzada, late of said Co., merchant, deceased, died intestate in 1750, leaving a widow and several children, and that Hannah Louzada, the widow of said Moses, took out letters of administration; that Moses had an estate in Middlesex and Somerset counties, which descended to Jacob Louzada, the eldest son and heir, and that Jacob Louzada has for several years been a lunatic; that the petitioner's wife is the daughter of said Moses Louzada, and sister of said Jacob; therefore he prays to be made Guardian of said Jacob Louzada.

1762, April 22. Guardian—Abraham Abrahams, of New York. Fellowbondsmen—Robert Sproul and David Gosling, of Perth Amboy.

1764, Feb. 24. It appearing that Letters of Guardianship were granted without inquisition, and not in due form, and Jacob Louzada, who is now of age, has applied to vacate said letters that he may take possession of the estate as heir-at-law, said letters are revoked and made void. Lib. H, p. 134; Lib. H, p. 332.

1767, Dec. 1. Loyd, John, of Pilesgrove, Salem Co.; will of. The land I bought of John Holton and his wife to be sold. Wife, Mary

Loyd, £35. My children, Hannah and Elizabeth Loyd, and sons, Nicodemous and Wood Loyd, rest of money, when they are 21. Son, Nicodemous, ½ acre joining to line of Jachonias Wood, and to son, Wood Loyd, ½ acre. Son, John, the rest of my land. Executors—my wife, Mary, Joseph Shinn and Mathew Gill. Witnesses—Patrick Graye, Alexander Ware, Jacob Tagart. Proved Jan. 26, 1768.
1768, Jan. 22. Renunciation by Joseph Shinn and Mathew Gill. Witnesses—John Gray and Bateman Lloyd.
1768, Jan. 22. Inventory, £319.3.7, made by Daniel Bassett and Obadiah Loyd. Lib. 13, p. 390.

1763, March 5. Lozer, Hillebrant, of Hackinsack, Bergen Co., blacksmith; will of. To children of my son Nicholas, dec'd, large Bible, and ⅓ of my land. Son, Peter, also ⅓, as also ⅓ to son, John. Daughters, Jannetje and Antje Lozier, shall be maintained till they are 18, and they shall have an outset as my other daughters have had. My son-in-law, Benjamin Westervelt, is obliged to me by a bond. Witnesses—John Benson and Robert Livesey. Proved Aug. 3, 1763. Lib. H, p. 315.
1763, Aug. 24. Inventory, £1,019.6.6, made by Cornelus Van Boskerk and Corneles Leydecker.
1763, Sept. 6. Bond of Peter Lozier, the eldest son, as Adm'r.

1745, April 12. Lozier, Nicolas, of Hackinsack, Bergen Co., shoemaker; will of. My brother-in-law, Jacob Derkse Banta, and my son-in-law, David Demarest, both of Hackinsack, to be the tutors of my minor children. Oldest son, Anthony, my land where he formerly lived. Son, Johannis, lot of land adjoining it. Son, Petrus, land where he formerly lived, called the Hook. Son, Lucas, and son, Derrick, to have land. Sons, Jacobus and Benjamin, that land on the plain. Sons, Jacob and Abraham, farm where I live. Wife, Antie, to be maintained. Son, Hillebrant, my smith tools. To all the children by my first wife, Traintje, viz., Anthony, Jannetje, Petrus, Johannis, Mary, Hillebrant, Antje, Lucas, Jacobus, and Benjamin, £5 each. Children, Traintje, Hester, Rachel, Derrick, Jacob, Abraham, Lea and Margrietje Lozier, each an outset. Executors—wife, Antje, brother-in-law, Jacob Derkse Banta, and son-in-law, David Demarest. Witnesses—Johannis Vanhooren, Silvester Earle, Robert Livesey. Proved April 8, 1761. Lib. G, p. 419.

1766, Sept. 27. Lozier, Peter, of Bergen Co., shoemaker; will of. Wife, Elizabeth, £50. To the children of my brother, Nicholas Lozier, deceased, meadow in Old Hackinsack. Sister, Antje Lozier, bed. Brother, John Lozier, rest of real and personal, and he is to pay to my eldest sister's daughter, Castina, £15. Executors—wife, Elizabeth, my brother, John, and my brother-in-law, Aart Couper. Witnesses—John Bensen, Hendrick Banta and Robert Livesey. Proved Nov. 3, 1767. Lib. I, p. 206.
1767, Nov. 3. Arent Cooper and Elizabeth Lozier, the widow, renounced in presence of Robert Livesey and Hendrick Banta. 599 B.

1768, March 19. Ludlam, Jeremiah, of Elizabeth Borough, Essex Co.; will of. Wife, Elizabeth, use of house and lands, till my daughter, Mary, is 14, then the house and lands are to be sold and the money given to my children, viz., Samuel, Temperance, Deborah,

Wilk, Daniel, Joseph, Mercy, Jeremiah and Mary. Daughter, Temperance, a bed that was her mother's. Daughter, Deborah, a bed that was her mother's. Sons, Wilk, Daniel, Joseph and Jeremiah, to be put to trades. Executors—brother-in-law, George Doughty, and my wife, Elizabeth. Witnesses—Jonathan Elmer, Benjamin Ball, Elizabeth Doty. Proved Aug. 1, 1768. Lib. I, p. 312.

1760, Jan. 3. Ludlam, Joseph, Sr., of Cape May Co., yeoman; will of. Grandson, Joseph Ludlam (elder son of my son, Joseph, dec'd), all my right in the beach that is called Ludlam's Beach, with the plantation whereon I dwell, and all other lands, when he is 30 years of age; and, if he live that long, forever. Carmon Smith is married to one of my relations, and I give to his wife, Lydia Smith, an ox. My son, Isaac, 5 shillings. My personal estate I give to my son, Jeremiah, and my daughters, Abigail Scull and Elizabeth Cresse, 1/6 part of my personal to each, and 1/6 part to my grandchildren (the children of my son, Anthony, dec'd), and 1/6 to my grandchildren (the children of my son, Joseph), and 1/6 to Phebe Young (the wife of Henry Young, Esq.). Executors—Providence Ludlam, Abigail Scull and Elizabeth Cresse. Witnesses—Silvanus Townsend, William Mason, Jacob Spicer. Proved Feb. 12, 1761.

1761, Feb. 12. Inventory, £267.6.4, made by Jesse Hand and Silvanus Townsend. Some tobacco and one "cain" was all owed to John Scull and his wife. Lib. 11, p. 80.

1765, Aug. 30. Account by Providence Ludlam, as one of the Executors. (Abigail Scull, being aged and infirm, could not appear).

1765, Oct. 31. Ludlam, Joseph, of Parish of Westfield, Elizabeth Borough, Essex Co., yeoman; will of. Wife, Ann, use of my land and moveable estate. Son, Cornelius, 5 shillings. Son, Matthias, a like sum. Daughter, Ann, wife of John Searing, like sum. Daughter, Susana, wife of Samuel Wood, a bed. Grandson, Abraham Ludlam, 5 shillings. Grandson, Maline Ludlam, a colt. My two grandsons above named, Matthias, son of Matthias Ludlam, and Maline, son of Matthias Ludlam, rest of land and moveables. Executors—sons, Cornelius and Matthias. Witnesses—Henry Hayes, Matthias Ludlam, Ebenezer Price. Proved July 4, 1766.

1765, Oct. 31. Inventory.

1799, Aug. 14. Whereas Cornelus Ludlam and Matthias Ludlam, the Executors, both having died, therefore Meline Ludlam was appointed Adm'r, together with Henry Ludlam, and Levi Crane on his bond; all of Essex Co. Lib. I, p. 149; Lib. 38, p. 264.

1768, Oct. 1. Ludlam, Nehemiah, of Middlesex Co., student in physick; will of. My eldest sister's son, Nehemiah Hinksman, £100. Brother-in-law, Robert Hinksman, rest of personal and real. Executor—said brother-in-law. Witnesses—Hezekiah Stites, John Phillips, William Clawson. Proved Nov. 21, 1768. Lib. K, p. 5.

1764, May 1. Ludlow, Jeremiah, of Morris Co.; will of. Son, Jeremiah Ludlow, £10. My wife, Elizabeth, use of the rest of my estate, and, after her death, to my grandchildren, viz., Samuel Ludlow; Temperance Ludlow; Deborah Ludlow; Wilkey Ludlow; Daniel Ludlow; they being children of my son, Jeremiah; and to John Ludlow, son of my son, Cornelius, when they are 21. Executor—son, Cornelius. Wit-

nesses—John Roll, John Carl, Ebenezer Beebout. Proved Aug. 27, 1764.
1764, Aug. 8. Inventory, £62.18.2, made by Jacob Carl and Richard Runyon. Lib. H, p. 452.

1770, May 21. Ludlum, Obadiah, of Elizabeth Town, Essex Co.; will of. Son, Obadiah, the rent of the plantation where I live, which place I hired of Jonathan Woodruff, Jr. Grandson, Jacob Ludlum, £50, when 21. Daughter, Sarah Ludlum, bed, etc., when 18. Executor—friend, Noah Marsh. Witnesses—John Cory, Samuel Miller, Jr., 3d, Mary Woodruff. Proved May 24, 1770. Lib. K, p. 205.

1770, March 3. Luke, William, of Windsor, Middlesex Co. Int. Adm'rs—Elizabeth Luke, widow of said William, and Robert DeBow; both of said place.
1770, Feb. 28. Inventory, £111.10.7, made by John Tindall and Joseph Cox. Lib. 15, p. 9.

1764, June 1. Lummus, Daniel, of Cumberland Co., yeoman; will of. Wife, Judith Lummus, ⅓ the profits of my land and use of goods. Son, Jonathan, 100 acres, which was bought of Executors of Henry Brooks. Son, Daniel, 50 acres, as well as other tracts, and he to pay to his sisters, Sarah and Tomson Lummus, £20 each, when they are 18. Sons, Ebenezer and Joseph, rest of lands. Daughters, Catharine and Hannah Lummus, the residue. Executors—my wife and friend, Joseph Daton. Witnesses—Benjamin Davis, David Sayers, Lydia Sayers. Proved March 17, 1769.
1769, March 3. Inventory, £46.0.7, made by Thomas Harris and Ephraim Harris.
1770, April 25. Account by Joseph Daton, Executor, of Daniel Lummus, of Fairfield, deceased. Lib. 14, p. 7; Lib. 15, p. 12.

1767, Oct. 5. Lupardus, Christianus, of Piscataway, Middlesex Co.; will of. Daughters, Antje and Lammetje, goods that were my wife's, deceased. Son, William, £600. Son, Christianus, £400. Daughter, Annatie Durie, wife of Cornelius Durie on Long Island, £200. Daughter, Antje, £200. Daughter, Lammetje, £280, as she had no outset, and the others had. Son, Rem, £50. Granddaughter, Anne Van Winkle, £50. All real and personal to be sold, except what is stated above. Executors—my eldest son, William Peter Lot, of Flat Bush, Long Island, and Cornelius Durre, of Brookland, on said Island. Witnesses—Azariah Dunham, Isaac Elbertson, William Oake.
1767, Oct. 14. Codicil. Son, Christianus, two horses, etc. Son, William, silver tankard. Witnesses—William Oake, Nathaniel Manning, Stephen Campbell. Proved March 5, 1768. Lib. I, p. 224.

1763, Jan. 3. Lupp, Christian, of Amwell Twsp., Hunterdon Co., yeoman; will of. Wife, Maria, use of land till children come of age; but, if she marry again, then she shall have 200 acres in Sussex Co. Son, Jacob, 200 acres. Son, Christin, 200 acres. Daughter, Elizabeth, 146 acres, all in said Sussex Co. My youngest daughter, Maria, shall be equal with Elizabeth, and shall have a lot that I bought of Gershom Mott. Brothers, Peter Lupp and John Lupp. My youngest daughter, Mary. Executors—Philip Kumbel, heir, and my brother, Peter Lupp, and my wife, Maria. Witnesses—Phillip Kempel, Wil-

liam Snuck, Peter Houshill, Johannes Godhart. Proved May 24, 1763. Probate granted to Peter Lupp, Maria Lupp and Phillip Kempel.
Lib. 11, p. 369.

1761, March 26. Lupton, Christopher, of Cape May Co. Int. Adm'x —Marcy Lupton. Fellowbondsman—Benjamin Ingrum; both of said Co. Witnesses—Henry Hand and John Eldredge.
1761, Jan. 28. Inventory, £97.16.0, made by Benjamin Ingrum and Henry Hand. Lib. 10, p. 163.

1766, Aug. 3. Luyster, Johannes, of Middletown, Monmouth Co.; will of. Wife, Sarah, use of all real and personal while my widow, after which all is to be divided between my brothers, Peter and Cornelius Luyster, and my loving deceased Sarah's children, except what is hereafter given. Brother, Peter, ⅓ my estate, Cornelius ⅓, and to my sister, Sarah's children, ⅓. My wife is to have the goods she brought with her. Sister, Lucreatia, £50. To Sarah Sodam, daughter of my sister, Sarah, £20. To Jane Barkelow, daughter of my sister, Ann, £20. Executors—brother, Cornelius, cousin, Cornelius Swart, and cousin, John Smock, Jr. Witnesses—Hendrick Brewer, Daniel Covenhoven, Joseph Willson. Proved Oct. 14, 1766.
1766, Oct. 20. Inventory, £416.7.8, made by John Bowne and Joseph Golden. Lib. K, p. 261.

1766, Oct. 18. Lycan, Nicholas, of Chester Twsp., Burlington Co. Int. Adm'r—Jacob Lycan, of Great Egg Harbor, Gloucester Co. Fellowbondsman—Robert Stiles, of Chester Twsp. Witness—John Shaw.
1766, Oct. 17. Inventory, £125.19.3, made by Joshua Roberts and Robert Stiles. Lib. 12, p. 385.
1766, Nov. 4. Account by Adm'r.

1764, June 23. Lyon, Abigail, of Essex Co. Int. Adm'r—Peter Lyon, son of said Abigail. Fellowbondsman—Ichabod Grammon; both of said Co. Witness—John Mackay.
1764, June 27. Inventory by Benjamin Crane and Isaac Meeker.
Lib. H, p. 349.

1763, Nov. 17. Lyon, Isaac, of Newark, Essex Co.; will of. Daughter, Abigail, £60. Daughter, Jane, £40. Granddaughter, Lucy Pierson, £30. Son, John, a negro. Son, Eliphelit, £5. Wife, Hannah, use of the homestead. Rest of real and personal to my sons, John and Mattaniah, and they are to maintain their mother. Executors—sons, John and Mattaniah. Witnesses—Elijah Bruen, Joseph Hayes, Jr., Samuel Hayes. Proved Feb. 28, 1764. Lib. H, p. 407.

1770, Dec. 14. Lyon, Justus, of Bergen Co. Int. Adm'r—Samuel Knap. Fellowbondsman—Guliaen Bertholf; both of said Co. Witness —John Zabriski. Lib. K, p. 257.

1761, Feb. 17. Lyon, Nathaniel, of Newark, Essex Co. Int. Adm'r —Jonathan Lyon, heir-at-law. Fellowbondsman—Ichabod Grummon; both of said place. Witness—Lewis Ogden.
1761, Feb. 23. Inventory, £118.9.10, made by Nathaniel Johnson and Abraham Lyon. Lib. G, p. 370.

CALENDAR OF WILLS—1761-1770   265

1770, Aug. 27. Lyon, Samuel, of Morristown, Morris Co. Int. Adm'r —Nathaniel Armstrong. Fellowbondsman—Ezra Halsey; both of said Co.
1770, Oct. 2. Inventory, made by Ezra Halsey and Henry Actell.
Lib. K, p. 268.

1769, July 31. McBride, Roger, of Princeton, Somerset Co. Int. Adm'r—Thomas Irwin, principal creditor. Fellowbondsman—Richard Paterson; both of said place. Witnesses—Mehitable Kinnan and Jonathan Sergeant.
1769, Dec. 1. Inventory, £4.10.4, made by Thomas Maxwell and Thomas Norris; both of said place.   Lib. K, p. 118.

1769, May 13. McCaslin, Patrick, of Hardyston, Sussex Co.; will of. One-half of my real and personal to my wife, and the other half to the children of my daughter, Mary Boughanan. My daughter, Nancey Leport, 5 shillings. Executor—friend, Samuel Whitehead. Witnesses —Asa Morris, Vincent Wainright, John Hill. Proved Sept. 23, 1769.
1769, Sept. 16. Inventory, £79.4.11, made by Henry Simson and Joseph Parry.   Lib. 14, p. 155.

1762, Dec. 9. McClean, Joseph, of Gloucester Co. Int. Adm'r— Samuel McClean. Fellowbondsman—Charles Day; both of said Co., yeomen.   File No. 3476 H.

1761, March 23. MacCleese, John, of Middletown, Monmouth Co. Int. Adm'x—Catherine MacCleese, the widow. Fellowbondsmen— Cornelius MacCleese, and John MacCleese; all of said place.
1761, March 28. Inventory, £35.8.7, made by John Cooper and Esek Hartshorne.   Lib. H, p. 35.

1770, July 28. McClutche, James, of Northampton, Burlington Co. Int. Adm'x—Amy McClutche, the widow. Fellowbondsman—Jabez Eldridge, of Mount Holly, said Co., yeoman.
1770, July 26. Inventory, £90.1.10, made by Joshua Norcross and Joseph Goldy.   Lib. 15, p. 47.
1770, Dec. 7. Adm'r—Hugh McClutche, of Northampton Twsp., farmer, of all goods left unadministered, by Amy McClutche, who is also deceased. Fellowbondsman—John Carman, of same place, yeoman.
1770, Dec. 7. Inventory, £71.8.4, made by Joseph Goldy and John Carman.   Lib. 15, p. 70.
1772, Nov. 16. Account by Hugh McClutche, Adm'r. Lib. 14, p. 515.

1764, Jan. 13. McClutchey, Daniel, of Nottingham Twsp., Burlington Co. Int. Adm'r—Timothy Abbott, of said place. Fellowbondsman—John Bacon, of City of Burlington. Witness—Joseph Read.
Lib. 11, p. 468.
1764, Jan. 9. Inventory, £28.11.6, by Joseph Chambers and John Abbott.
1764, Oct. 31. Account by Adm'r.

1765, Feb. 7. McCollister, Archibald, of Salem Co. Int. Adm'r— John McCollister. Fellowbondsman—John Richman; both of said Co.
1765, Feb. 5. Inventory, £40.10.6, made by Robert Clark and Obadiah Loyd.
1766, Jan. 10. Account by Adm'r.   Lib. 12, p. 174.

1769, April 25. McCollum, John, Jr., of Bernards Town, Somerset Co.; will of. Wife, Elizabeth, use of the lands till son, John, is 21, when my lands and goods are to be sold, and £50 given to my wife, £20 to son, John, and rest divided between my wife and children, John, and Margret (to be spedily paid), and Ephraim and Jacob to be paid when 21. Executors—wife, Elizabeth, my brother, Jacob, and my brother-in-law, Mathew McDowel. Witnesses—John Roy, John Mack Collum, Thomas McCollum, Hannah Urmston. Proved Aug. 17, 1769.

1769, Sept. 25. Inventory, £207.16.5, made by Eliphelet Whitaker and Thomas Morrow.

1773, May 26. Account by Elizabeth Ayers, late Elizabeth McCollum, now wife of David Ayers. Lib. K, p. 465.

1759, April 14. McCord, William, of Pilesgrove Twsp., Salem Co., yeoman; will of. Lands to be sold and money divided between Moses Hill and Ann Roberson, daughter of William Roberson. To Elizabeth Loyd, Jr., £20. To William Roberson rest of moveable estate. Fullaky Loyd to live on the land during her life. Executor—Mounce Keen, Jr. Witnesses—David Seley, Seeley Keen, James Bond.

1759, April 14. Codicil. Same witnesses. Proved June 15, 1767, by James Bond, the only surviving witness.

1767, June 15. Inventory, £47.3.9, made by James Bond and Elisha Bassett.

1771, Sept. 14. Account by Executor. Lib. 13, p. 176; Lib. 14, p. 410.

1763, June 16. MacCorpin, Anna, of Knowlton Twsp., Sussex Co., yeoman; will of. Son, Umfre, 10 shillings. All estate to be sold and the value to be given to my son, Joseph, when he is 21, which will be in 1766, in November. Executor—John Read. Witnesses—William Rush, Elizabeth Rush, Thankfull Read. Proved March 26, 1764.

1764, March 21. Inventory, £52.14.0, made by John Hunnywell and Abraham Boscherer. Lib. 12, p. 2.

1766, June 5. McCrea, James, of Bedminster, Somerset Co., minister of the Gospel; will of. Eldest son, John, £10. Wife, Cathrine, £250 and interest of £250 yearly. Daughter, Mary Hannah, the wife of Rev. John Hannah (Hanna), £80. Son, William, 5 shillings. Son, John, £100 in trust. Sons, James, Samuel and Stephen. Daughter, Jane. James to have £350; Samuel, £320; Stephen, £300; Jane, £170, when she is 21. Sons—Robert, Philip, Gilbert, and Creighton, each £250, when 21. Daughter, Cathrine, £150. The 100 acres bought of William Axtell to be sold. My estate in Bedminster Township I give to my wife, son James, and friends, John King and Robert Barclay, in trust, to sell and pay debts and legacies. Executors—wife, son James, said John King and Robert Barclay. Witnesses—John Mehelm, William Adems, Sarah Yeandall. Proved July 10, 1769.

1769, Aug. 7. Renunciation by John King and Robert Barkley. Witness—William Stewart. Lib. K, p. 151.

1767, April 21. McCrery, John, of Amwell, Hunterdon Co. Int. Adm'r—Andrew McCrery, of said place. Fellowbondsman—Samuel Stout, of Hopewell, said Co.

1767, April 9. Inventory, £79.17.0, made by John Hart and David Stout. Lib. 13, p. 207.

1760, April 10. McDowel, Ephraim, of Bedminster, Somerset Co., yeoman; will of. Sons, John, Ephraim and Mathew, all my lands and chattels; and John and Mathew are to have this place I live on. Said sons to pay the legacies I leave to my wife, Ben and Elizabeth. To wife, £50, and £10 that Mathew Adems owes me, and I allow her the room that John Hanna lived in. Daughter, Elizabeth, £60. Son, Benjamin, £30. Son, Peter, the best cow. Daughter, Mary Simonton, a cow, and Ephraim Simonton a heifer. Daughter, Peggy, £10. Executors—my wife and son, John; and I appoint William Colavel to superintend them. Witnesses—John Sloan, Henry Sloan, John Hanna. Proved Sept. 14, 1762. Lib. H, p. 182.

1762, May 8. McEowen, Daniel, Esq., of Bedminster, Somerset Co.; will of. Real and personal to be sold. Mother, Ann McEowen, £10. The rest to be given to my children, Hugh, George, Daniel, Alexander, William and Mary, when they are of age. Executors—my brother, Alexander McEowen, my brother, David Kilpatrick, and friends, John Roy and Alexander Linn. Witnesses—Peter Penier, George Bemer, John Castner, Jr. Proved June 15, 1762.
1762, June 17. Inventory, £480, of estate of "Daniel McKeown," Esq., made by Andrew Patterson and Brian Laffarty. Lib. H, p. 132.

1760, Dec. 13. McEvers, Patrick, of Perth Amboy, Middlesex Co.; will of. I order £500 to be put to interest, and the interest paid yearly to Martha Todd, the wife of Joseph Todd, of Bucks Co., Penna., and, after her death, the principal to be divided among her children; but, if Martha dies without issue, then between Catharine Bayard, James McEvers and Charles McEvers. To niece, Mary Apthorp, £50. To Miss Margaret Sarjant, £30. Rest of personal and real to James McEvers, Charles McEvers and Catharine Bayard. Executors—nephews, James McEvers, Charles McEvers and William Bayard. Witnesses—Lewis Johnston, Cortland Skinner, Stephen Skinner. Proved Oct. 26, 1767. Lib. I, p. 168.

1762, Aug. 6. McEwen, John, of New York City, blacksmith; will of. Friend, John Lowree, ropemaker, all my real and personal, and my share of the prize money which shall be taken by the Ship "Privateer," called "Royal Charlotte," James Owman, the Commander. Executor—said John Lowree. Witnesses—Zacharias Cutland, Henry Peckwell. Proved April 7, 1763. Lib. H, p. 357.

1765, May 30. McFarland, John, of Greenwich, Sussex Co.; will of. Wife, Mary, ⅓ my goods, and the rest to be sold and the money given to my son, William, my daughter Elizabeth, and the child that my wife is pregnant with. Daughters, Mary and Anne, £5 more than the rest. Executor—my brother, James McFarland. Witnesses—Thomas Craig, Philip Chapman. Proved Aug. 26, 1765.
1765, July 3. Inventory, £124.13.5, made by John Sharp and Thomas Craig. Lib. 12, p. 207.

1758, Jan. 16. McFerran, Hugh, of Freehold, Monmouth Co.; will of. Daughters, Elizabeth Tomson, Margaret McFerran, Isabel McFerran and Susannah McFerran, all the money from the sale of land and goods. Executors—friends, James English, Sr., and David English, Sr. Witnesses—Jonathan English, Robert McGallird, Bryan Gollohar. Proved March 24, 1769.

1769, March 24. Renunciation by James English. Witnesses—Peter Smith and Jonathan English.
1769, March 23. Inventory, £33.10.2, made by Joseph Ker, Robert McGalliard, Wm. Covenhoven. Lib. K, p. 70.

1761, Jan. 14. McGrah, Martin, of Manington, Salem Co., blacksmith. Int. Adm'x—Catherine McGrah, of said place, widow. Fellowbondsmen—Jonathan Woodnutt, of said place, yeoman, and William Tuft, of Town of Salem, innkeeper. Witness—Clement Hall.
1760, Dec. 29. Inventory, £319.17.7, made by Charles Ellet and Whitten Cripps. Lib. 10, p. 441.

1767, Sept. 13. McKean, Robert, of Perth Amboy, Middlesex Co., clerk; will of. A Missionary from the Society for Propagation of the Gospel in Foreign Parts at Perth Amboy. To my father, William McKean, £10. My brother-in-law, Richard Cochran, £20. Wife, Isabella, ½ of the rest. To my little nephew, Robert McKean, son of my brother Thomas, of the town and Co. of Newcastle, Delaware; my brother, Thomas, and brother, William; and my only sister, Dorothea Thompson, wife of John Thompson, the rest. Executors—brother, Thomas, and my brother-in-law, Richard Cochran. Witnesses—Gannatta Harrison, Lewis Antill, Thomas McKean. Proved Dec. 9, 1767.
1767, Oct. 19. Inventory, £264.17.0, made by Gannatta Harrison, Lewis Antill and Nathaniel Manning.
1767, Dec. 14. Inventory, £123, of the rest of the estate, made by Nathaniel Manning and James Boggs.
1771, June 21. Account by Executors. Lib. I, p. 194.

1762, Feb. 15. McKnight, William, of Freehold, Monmouth Co. Int. Adm'rs—Sarah McKnight, widow of said William, and Alexander Laird, brother-in-law of said William. Fellowbondsman—Robert James; all of said place.
1761, Nov. 5. Inventory, made by Michael Sweetman, William Laird and Michael Johnston. Lib. H, p. 76.

1770, Feb. 27. McLaughlin, William, of Morris River, Cumberland Co. Int. Adm'x—Elizabeth McLaughlin, widow. Fellowbondsman—Nebuchadnezzar Riggin, yeoman; both of said place.
1770, Feb. 20. Inventory, £59.9.6, made by Nebuchadnezzar Riggin and Hezekiah Shaw. Lib. 15, p. 6.

1761, Aug. 3. McMortry, Alexander, of Bethlehem, Hunterdon Co. Int. Adm'r—Daniel Cahill, of said place, farmer. Fellowbondsman—Abraham Cottnam, of Trenton, said Co. Witness—Anne DeCow.
Lib. 10, p. 603.

1769, April 26. McMullan, Ephraim, of Newton, Sussex Co. Int. Adm'r—James Holmes. Fellowbondsman—David Frazer; both of said Co. Lib. 13, p. 530.

1761, June 2. McMurtrie, Joseph, of Oxford Twsp., Sussex Co.; will of. Son, Abram, 20 chain of that place I live on; and to son, John, the lower ½ of 20 chain; both fronting on Delaware River and up to the Greenwich road. None of it to be sold, I being the first pur-

chaser, and have a right to will it. Mary shall build at the Springs, at the line under the little hill, and have it her lifetime; and Agnes from the white oak tree at the wagon road, which is 40 chains across. Executor—Thomas McMurtrie. Witnesses—James Stinson, Archibald Stinson, Gideon Rickey. "If Joseph and James do not come and make a demand, then give them 7s. 6d. apiece, or any other that hath by whole blood, let them have 7.6 apiece." Proved May 25, 1762.
1761, Nov. 5. Inventory, £66.8.0, made by John Lowry and Robert Huil. Lib. 11, p. 298.

1763, March 28. McNish, John, of Northampton Twsp., Burlington Co.; yeoman; will of. Refers to Alexander McBride. Executor—my friend, Alexander McBride. Witnesses—James McCulley, James McElhage, Alexander Ross. Proved June 28, 1763.
1763, June 15. Renunciation by Alexander McBride. Lib. 11, p. 335.
1763, June 28. Adm'r—James McElhage, of Northampton Twsp., with will annexed. Fellowbondsman—John Forqueher, of same place.
File No. 7513-1716.

1766, Dec. 26. McQuean, William, of Deptford Twsp., Gloucester Co., yeoman. Int. Adm'rs—John Dilkes and Elizabeth McQuean, widow. Fellowbondsman—Aaron Dilkes; all of said place. Witness —Hannah Ladd.
1766, Feb. 24. Inventory, £237.10.6, made by Thomas Nightingale and John Hillman.
1769, April 13. Samuel Allison writes, that William McQuean died intestate, leaving a wife and 2 children; that the widow and John Wilkes did administer, since which time the widow has married Samuel Leek. The children have both lived with the mother about 3 years, till her marriage; the son, John, has since then lived with John Dilks. The eldest was 8 years old, and the youngest about 6, at the father's death.
1770, May 14. Account by John Dilkes, as Adm'r.
Lib. 12, p. 380; Lib. 15, p. 16.

1764, April 19. McSurley, Felix, of Chesterfield, Burlington Co. Int. Adm'r—Tallman Smith. Fellowbondsman—Joshua Bunting; both of said Co. Witness—Samuel Allinson. Lib. 11, p. 537.
1764, April 27. Inventory, £52.9.7.
1767, June 12. Account by Adm'r, on estate of Felix McSurley, "laborer."

1766, Oct. 15. McSurley, James, of Nottingham, Burlington Co. Int. Adm'r—Hugh Newell, farmer. Fellowbondsman—William Miller, yeoman; both of said place. Lib. 12, p. 385.
1766, Oct. 2. Inventory, £22.8.0, made by William Miller and Tobias Polemus.
1768, Jan. 15. Account by Adm'r.

1769, May 27. Mackay, John, of Stow Creek, Cumberland Co. Int. Adm'r—Jonathan Bradway, of said place. Fellowbondsman—John Sheppard, of Greenwich, said Co. Lib. 13, p. 530.

1769, Oct. 4. Mackey, Mary, of Bridgewater Twsp., Somerset Co.; will of. Daughter, Mary, a bed. Daughter, Prudence, a bed. Then my real and personal to be sold and divided among my 3 youngest children, Richard Mackey, Mary and Prudence. Eldest son, John, 5 shillings. Executor—Joseph Mackey. Witnesses—William Crooke, Gershom Barns, Levi Lott. Proved May 21, 1770. Lib. K, p. 263.

1764, Aug. 29. Mackey, William, of Lebanon, Hunterdon Co. Int. Adm'x—Mary Mackey. Fellowbondsman—John Mulliner; both of said place.
1764, Aug. 27. Inventory, £142.9.8, made by John Mullinner and Peter Newal. Lib. 12, p. 16.

1770, July 28. Manners, John, of Amwell Twsp., Hunterdon Co.; will of. "Stricken in years." Wife, Rebecca Manners, use of personal and real estate all her life. Daughter, Rebecca Hill, and her husband, Joseph Hill, to have, after my wife's death, the plantation they now live on, in Kingwood, and, after their deaths, to their children, John Hill and Elizabeth Hill, and to Mary Hunt, granddaughter of said Joseph and Rebecca Hill. Daughter, Lydia Stout, £15, and the use of 70 acres she now lives on in Amwell, and, after her death, to her surviving children. My grandson, Anthony Stout, son of Lydia Stout, £10. Granddaughter, Elizabeth Stout, daughter of said Lydia, £5. Granddaughter, Rebecca, daughter of said Lydia, £5. Granddaughter, Anne, daughter of said Lydia, £5. Grandson, Daniel Exeene, son of my daughter, Elizabeth, £40. Grandson, John Manners, £20, to be paid to him by his father (my son John), when he is 21. To the Baptist Church of Hopewell, £21, to be paid by my sons, John and Joseph. Son, John, my lands. Executors—my wife and friend, Rev. David Sutton. Witnesses—Joseph Eaton, Samuel Hill, Gershom Craven. Proved Oct. 8, 1770.
1770, Oct. 8. Inventory, £14.10.7, made by David Stout and Peter Young, Jr. Lib. 14, p. 319.

1766, Dec. 26. Manning, James, of Essex Co.; will of. Eldest son, Jeremiah, 10 shillings; also a bond for £35. Son, James, negro, Zip. Son, Joseph, south part of my plantation, except a piece that is given to my son, Enoch, at the southwest corner. Son, Enoch, north part of my plantation. Son, John, the plantation at Dead River, which I bought of William Pen, and 10 acres that I bought of Paul Randolph. Daughter, Christian, the wife of Joseph Tingley, a wench. Wife, enough goods to keep house with. Sons, John and Enoch, to be put to trades. Executors—sons, Jeremiah Manning, Joseph Manning and Joseph Tingley. Witnesses—Mary Manning, John Blackford, Henry Davis. Proved March 31, 1767. Lib. I, p. 123.

1765, Oct. 18. Manning, Nathaniel, of Piscataway, Middlesex Co., yeoman; will of. Son, Thomas, 50 acres at Dismal, and a salt meadow at Great Pond, when he comes of age. Son, Nathaniel, 20 acres at the east end of the lot that I bought of my brother, Isaac Manning, and south side of Gershom Manning. Son, Benjamin, rest of lands and house where I live. Wife, Mary, ⅓ the profits of the land. Daughter, Elizabeth Hull, a negro. Daughter, Margaret, a negro; also a negro to daughter, Mary, and one to my daughter, Rachel. Daughter, Sarah, £30 when 18. The four youngest children are Margaret, Mary, Rachel and Sarah. If son, Thomas, die, his share to go to his surviving brothers, viz., Nathaniel, William and Benjamin. Executors—sons, Nathaniel, William and Benjamin. Witnesses—John Dennes, Benjamin Foster, Moses Martin. Proved Feb. 10, 1766. Lib. H, p. 589.

1759, Oct. 5. Marlott, Abraham, of Springfield Twsp., Burlington Co.; will of. My plantation where I live, with land which I bought of Stephen Gaskill, and part of Ezekiel Eldridge, to my son, Jacob. Son, Abraham, the farm where he lives. Wife, a bed and horse. Remainder to my wife and my eight children. Daughter, Sarah, to have her share when 18. Son, Isaac, cedar swamp. Executors—wife, Sarah, and son, Isaac. Witnesses—Lott Ridgway, Jonathan Hough, William Lovett Smith. Proved Sept. 7, 1761.
  1761, Sept. 2. Inventory, £846.16.10¾, made by Francis Vencombe and Lott Ridgway. Lib. 10, p. 370.
  1762, Nov. 12. Account by Sarah Meritt and Isaac Meritt, the Executors of Abraham Marriott. Each legatee's share £91.9.9; John Fort, Sr., in full of wife's share; John Brasonton, in full of wife's share; Aaron Gaskill, in full of wife's share; John Acrit (?), in full of wife's share; Henry Lishman, in full of wife's share; Abraham Merit, his share; Jacob Merrit, his share; Sarah Merrit, her share; Isaac Merrit, his share.

1766, Sept. 22. Marpole, George, of Twsp., and Co. of Gloucester, yeoman. Int. Adm'r—John Hinchman, Esq., of said Co. Fellowbondsman—John Hatkinson, of Mount Holly, Burlington Co., merchant.
  1767, Sept. 10. Inventory, £1,497.11.3½, made by Josiah Albortson and John Gill. Lib. 12, p. 384.

1764, May 11. Marsalas, Peter, of Trenton, Hunterdon Co., carpenter; will of. Son, Eden, £110 and 1/5 of my real estate, when 21. Wife, Hannah, 1/5 my real. Daughters, Rachel, Mary and Elizabeth, 1/5 my real, when 18. Executors—wife, Hannah, only during her widowhood, and Thomas Moore and Stacy Potts, both of Trenton. Witnesses—Thomas Barnes, William Lister, Mary Lancaster. Proved June 30, 1764.
  1764, July 4. Inventory, £857.13.11, made by Edmond Beakes and Charles Axford, Jr. Lib. 12, p. 17.

1765, May 28. Marsh, Charles, of Monmouth Co. Int. Adm'rs—Easter Marsh and Richard Marsh, the widow and eldest son, both of said Co. Fellowbondsman—Samuel Jaques, of Middlesex Co.
Lib. H, p. 426.

1770, Jan. 20. Marsh, David, of Hunterdon Co. Int. Adm'rs—Mary Marsh and William Coats; both of said Co. Witness—George King.
  1769, Nov. 23. Inventory, £76.11.3, made by Valentine Martin and Thomas Mackfarson. Lib. 14, p. 122.

1764, June 26. Marsh, Mephibosheth, of Borough of Elizabeth, Essex Co.; will of. The plantation that I live on; land I bought of Elias Marsh, and 2 lots of salt meadow, which father gave me by deed, I give to my 3 sons, to wit., Mephibosheth, Jacob and Cornelius, when the youngest is 21. Daughter, Comfort, £20. Daughter, Suviah, £20. Granddaughters, Jane Marsh and Jane Conger, £20 each. Grandsons, Joseph Marsh, Stephen Marsh and Jehial Marsh, £50 each, when 21. To my son's widow, Esther Marsh, the same freedom on my place, as she has had. Wife, Elizabeth, £20 a year. The overplus to be given to my children, Mephibosheth Marsh, Jacob Marsh, Cornelius Marsh, Elizabeth Conger, Comfort Marsh, Zeruiah Marsh. That given to my daughter, Elizabeth Conger, I intend for her 3 children. Executors—my said three sons. Witnesses—Jacob Shotwell, Thomas Latham, Joseph Shotwell. Proved Oct. 4, 1764.

1764, Sept. 20. Inventory, £265.2.2, made by Amos Morss and Benjamin Marsh. Lib. H, p. 460.

1767, Nov. 2. Marsh, Thomas Ellit, of Deptford, Gloucester Co., schoolmaster. Int. Adm'r—Benjamin Carpenter, weaver. Fellowbondsman—Joseph Tatem, cordwainer and innholder; both of said place.

1767, Oct. 29. Inventory, £9.10.2, made by Thomas Nightingale and Samuel Eldridge. Lib. 13, p. 437.

1763, Dec. 5. Marsh, William, of Hardyston, Sussex Co., minister. Int. Adm'r—Jacob Marsh, of said place, yeoman. Fellowbondsmen—Nathaniel Pettit and Isaac Hull, of Newton, said Co., yeomen.
Lib. 12, p. 5.

1764, Oct. 12. Marshall, James, of Middlesex Co. Int. Adm'x—Rachel Marshall, the widow. Fellowbondsman—Henry Lane, of Essex Co. Lib. H, p. 370.

1769, July 9. Marshall, John, of Penns Neck Twsp., Salem Co., blacksmith; will of. Lands in Cohansey to be sold. Wife, Elizabeth, ½ of all my estate. Rest to my children, when my son, Joseph, is 10 years of age. My tools to son, Francis. Executors—my wife and my brothers-in-law, John Sparks and Richard Sparks. Witnesses—Henry Sparks, Elizabeth Marshall, Thomas Sparks. Proved Aug. 14, 1769.

1769, July 28. Inventory, £142.5.10, made by Henry Sparks and Allen Congelton. Lib. 14, p. 207.

1770, April 11. Marshall, John, of Penns Neck, Salem Co.; will of. Wife, Mary, all real and personal during her life, and, after her death, to my stepson, Ananias Elwell, and his heirs, and, for that default, to the heirs of my uncle, Benjamin Hawly. Executors—my wife, and her son, Ananias Elwell. Witnesses—Moses Hill, John Pennington, Samuel Baker. Proved April 23, 1770.

1770, April 21. Inventory, £219.17.4, made by Hance Lambson and Samuel Baker. Lib. 14, p. 212.

1764, Jan. 21. Marshall, Thomas, of Amwell Twsp., Hunterdon Co., yeoman; will of. Wife, Catharine, live stock, household goods, etc. Nephew, Charles Marshall, my gun. To Jeromus Rapellie, £20, for the services he has done me. I give my farm to the said Charles Marshall and to Cathrine, my present wife, for the term of five years, and they are to maintain the family and my father and mother-in-law, viz., Abraham and Sarah Delamater, after which time, Charles can have the farm, he paying to my wife £15 yearly. Executors—my friends, Thomas Reading and Hugh Hicks. Witnesses—Benjamin Stout, Cornelius Low, John Cole. Proved Feb. 29, 1764.

1764, Feb. 22. Inventory, £292.5.11, made by Benjamin Stout and Bartholomew Thatcher. Lib. 11, p. 530.

CALENDAR OF WILLS—1761-1770   273

1767, Sept. 15. Marten, William, of Mendham Twsp., Morris Co., yeoman; will of. Wife, Elizabeth, use of my farm and moveable estate, which are to be sold after her death and the money divided among my nine children, William, Elijah, John, Azariah, James, Peter, Elizabeth, Rhoda and Jemihah. Executors—my wife, son, John, and friend, James McVicar. Witnesses—William Stewart, Robart Comins, Brice Rikey. Proved Oct. 29, 1767.
1767, Oct. 22. Inventory, £201.14.0, made by Asa Cooke and Brice Rikey.   Lib. I, p. 170.

1763, Jan. 31. Martin, Charity, of Woodbridge, Middlesex Co. Int. Adm'r—Samuel Jaques, of said place. Fellowbondsman—Moses Bishop, of said Co.   Lib. H, p. 220.

1761, March 5. Martin, Hugh, Esq., of Lebanon, Hunterdon Co.; will of. My personal estate to my wife and two daughters, Martha and Jane, and my children are to have their living till they are 17. My two sons, who are at college, are to be brought up out of my real estate. My sons, Alexander, James and Thomas, £20 each. If my son James choose to come home and work on the farm, then I give my said farm to my sons, James, Samuel and Robert. Executors —sons, James and Samuel. Witnesses—John Hanna, James Martin, Jr., Martha Martin.
1761, March 6. Codicil. Wife, Jean, to have the negro wench, Cate. Daughter, Martha Martin, to have wench, Bell. Son, Alexander, to have negro boy, Brom; and son, James, to have Prince. Son, Alexander, to be one of the Executors. Daughters, Martha and Jean, to have £60 each. Witnesses—James Martin, Jr., Samuel Rogers, Martha Martin. Proved May 12, 1761.
1761, May 6. Inventory, £362.4.6.   Lib. 11, p. 45.

1761, Dec. 1. Martin, James, of Lebanon, Hunterdon Co.; will of. Wife, Anne, £15 yearly, and to be provided for on the farm. Son, James, my farm, and he to pay the legacies. Son, William, £200, when 21. Daughter, Martha, £50, at marriage. Daughter, Mary, £50, at marriage. Daughter, Ann, £50, when she is of age. Daughter, Rachel, a like sum, when of age. Executors—wife, Ann, and son, James. Witnesses—John Anderson, William Rogers, Charles Stewart. Proved Dec. 31, 1761.
1761, Dec. 28. Inventory, £235.2.6, made by John Anderson and Charles Stewart.   Lib. 11, p. 144.

1766, Oct. 25. Martin, James, of Piscataway, Middlesex Co.; will of. Wife, Ruth, £150, live stock, and household goods; also profits of real estate till it is disposed of. Son, Azariah, the land I last bought of my brother, Peter, and the west part of the salt meadow that I bought of my father, when he is 21; and he is to pay to his sister, Sarah Martin, £150. Son, James, land where I live, and ½ of the land I bought of Ebenezer Daniels, and 5 acres of salt meadow I bought of Nathaniel Heard, when he is 21; and he is to pay to his sister, Ruth Martin, £140, and to his sister, Jane, £30, when she is 18. Son, Phinehas, the land at the plains, that I bought of my brother, Jacob Martin, and the other ½ of the land I bought of Ebenezer Daniels, when he is 21; and he is to pay to his sister, Jane, £70. Son, Gideon, the land at Dismall, which I bought of my father, of about

18

20 acres; also 10 acres which I had of my father; also the 30 acres I bought of my brother, Peter, and the rest of meadow I bought of Nathaniel Heard, when he is 21, he paying to his sister, Esther Martin, £150. Daughter, Sarah Martin, £150, to be paid by son, Azariah. Daughter, Ruth Martin, £140, to be paid her by my son, James. Daughter, Jane Martin, £100. The land which I bought of Samuel Mackferson, in Piscataway, and the land in Sussex Co., which I bought of Levi Hinds and Andrew Smalley, to be sold. Executors —my father-in-law, Jonathan Dunham, and my friend, Joseph Fitz Randolph, both of Piscataway, and brother-in-law, Azariah Dunham. Witnesses—John Holton, Jr., Benjamin Martin, Jacob Martin, Jr. Proved Jan. 13, 1767. Lib. I, p. 73.

1763, July 15. Martin, James, Jr., of Middlesex Co. Ward. Son of James Martin, late of South Ward of City of Perth Amboy. Guardian —Sarah Rolph. Fellowbondsman—Joseph Moore; both of Woodbridge, said Co. Witness—John Thomson. Lib. H, p. 258.

1761, March 3. Martin, John, of Greenwich, Gloucester Co., farmer; will of. "Am greatly advanced in years." Daughter, Patience Lodge, £7; and to grandson, John Lodge, £5, when of age. Daughter, Rachel Moffat, has already had hers. Granddaughter, Sarah Moffat, £5. Daughter, Sarah Martin, £25. Wife, Mary, rest of estate. Executrix —said wife, Mary. Witnesses—Michael Fisher, George Flaningam. Proved May 5, 1761.

1761, April 27. Inventory, £131.3.8¼, made by George Flaningam and Michael Fisher. Lib. 10, p. 390.

1761, May 27. Martin, John, of Essex Co. Int. Adm'r—John Smalley, of Somerset Co. Fellowbondsman—David Sayre, of Morris Co.
Lib. G, p. 381.

1768, May 4. Martin, Jonathan, of Piscataway, Middlesex Co., yeoman; will of. Of the personal estate I give ⅓ to my wife, and ⅓ to my granddaughter, Lydia Shotwell, and ⅓ for support of my son, William. My land in Windsor Twsp. to be sold (it was bought of Samuel Dunn, 29 of Dec., 1763), and the money to be put to interest, for support of son, William; and, if he die, it is to be divided between my daughter, Catharine, my granddaughter, Elizabeth Hayden (the daughter of John Sutton), my granddaughter, Prudence (the daughter of Joseph Howard). The lands I claim of the Elizabeth Town purchase, I give to my daughters, Martha, Anne, Elizabeth, Rachel, Cathrine, and Sarah. Of my lands at Rockciticus, which I purchased of Jonathan Scott and John Scott, ½ I give to my son-in-law, Daniel Dunham, ¼ to my son, Peter, and ¼ to my grandsons, John Martin and Jonathan Martin. Executors—son-in-law, Daniel Dunham and friend, Samuel Dunham. Witnesses—Jacob Martin, Jr., James Martin, Jr., Elias V. Court. Proved Aug. 17, 1768. Lib. I, p. 313.

1765, Jan. 14. Martin, Joseph, of Middlesex Co. Int. Adm'r— George Marshall. Fellowbondsman—Thomas Moore; both of Essex Co.

1765, Jan. 12. Renunciation by William Martin, eldest brother of Joseph Martin, in favor of George Marshall, for use of creditors.
Lib. H, p. 376.

CALENDAR OF WILLS—1761-1770   275

1763, Feb. 12. Martin, Merick, of Woodbridge, Middlesex Co.; will of. Real and personal to be sold and proceeds to be given to my wife, Hope, and my children, John (eldest son), Joseph, Katherina Martin, William, Benjamin, and Isaac, each 1/7 part. Executors—my brother, William Martin, and my friend, Joseph Moore. Witnesses—Francis Everitt, William Moore, George Brown. Proved March 16, 1763.
Lib. H, p. 221.

1765, Oct. 28. Martin, Rheuben, of Piscataway, Middlesex Co. Int. Adm'r—John Martin, Jr., of said place. Fellowbondsman—Samuel Dunham, of said Co.   File No. 4205 L.

1765, Oct. 28. Martin, Sarah, of Piscataway, Middlesex Co.; will of. "I am the daughter of Moses Martin." To brother, Joshua Martin, 5 shillings. Sister, Margaret Wilson, clothing. Sister, Rachel Griffith, also clothing. Cousin, Isbel Wilson, daughter of my sister, Margaret Wilson, also clothing, and likewise to cousin, Sarah Griffith, daughter of my sister, Rachel Griffith. Cousin, Sarah Griffith, goods. The salt meadow that father, Moses Martin, gave me in his will, to be sold, and money to be given to cousins, Isbel Wilson, Robert Wilson and Joshua Wilson, and their mother (my sister), Margaret Wilson, and cousins, Sarah Griffith and John Griffith, and their mother (my sister), Rachel Griffith. Cousin, Rachel Martin, daughter of my brother, Joshua Martin, silk cape, and to his other two children, Runyon and Margret Martin, money also. Executors—Moses Martin, Jr., and Isaac Ferret. Witnesses—Isaac Stelle, Jeremiah Dunn, Margaret Dunn. Proved Oct. 23, 1767.

1767, Oct. 26. Inventory, made by Joshua Martin and Henry Langstaff, Jr.   Lib. I, p. 166.

1761, Feb. 21. Martin, Thomas, of Bucks Co., Pa. Int. Adm'r— Hugh Martin, Esq., of Lebanon, Hunterdon Co. Fellowbondsman— Theophilus Severns, of Trenton. Witness—Rachel Hooton.

1761, Nov. 13. Adm'rs—David Marple and Mary Marple, late widow of Thomas Martin. Fellowbondsman—Moore Furman, of Trenton. Witness—George Douglass.

1761, Nov. 14. Inventory, £257, made by Moore Furman and Benjamin Johnson.   Lib. 10, p. 460; Lib. 11, p. 132.

1767, Oct. 6. Martin, Thomas, of Woodbridge, Middlesex Co., weaver; will of. Sons, Mulford and Thomas Martin, to be supported from the profits of my estate; which estate they are to have when old enough. Executors—Isaac Faurot, Nathaniel Martin and Samuel Ayres. Witnesses—James Ayers, Daniel Compton, Neil Campbell, John Jackson Sheridan. Proved Oct. 19, 1767.

1767, Oct. 21. Inventory, £232.5.1, made by James Manning and Henry Langstaff.

1775, June 8. Account by Executors. Land was sold as follows: To Benjamin Thornell, for £99.7.8; to Samuel Martin, for £102.1.3; salt meadow to Dugal Campbell, for £11.19.6; land to Samuel Martin, "for which no deed is yet given."   Lib. I, p. 162.

1762, March 3. Masters, Richard, of Newton, Sussex Co., yeoman. Int. Adm'r—William Masters. Fellowbondsman—George Havens; both of said place, yeomen.

1761, Oct. 7. Inventory, £63.7.4, made by Jonathan Smalley and George Havens.   Lib. 11, p. 289.

1763, May 2. Mathis, Jeremiah, of Little Egg Harbor, Burlington Co. Int. Adm'x—Hannah Mathis. Fellowbondsman—Job Mathis; both of same place. Witness—Robert Norris.
  1763, April 28. Inventory, £138.15.6, made by James Belanger and Daniel Shourds. Lib. 11, p. 302.
  1766, May 21. Account of Administratrix.

1763, Oct. 22. Mathis, Joseph, of Hopewell, Hunterdon Co. Int. Adm'r—William Mathis, of said place. Fellowbondsman—Samuel Corwine, of Amwell, said Co. Witness—Henry Matthis.
  1763, Oct. 20. Inventory, £44.2.3, made by Timothy Brush and Samuel Corwine.
  1764, Dec. 31. Account by William Mathis. Lib. 11, p. 446.

1761, May 22. Matlack, George, of Chester, Burlington Co., carpenter; will of. Son, Thomas, the house and lot which I purchased of my brother, Josiah Matlack, in Moorestown, and contains 35 acres; also a piece of meadow, fenced off from the plantation whereon I dwell, of 3 acres. Son, William, the land between that of said Thomas and mine where I live, which I bought of Arthur Bunadaill, of 45 acres. Son, George, plantation where I live, except what is reserved for a sawmill, of 100 acres. The said sawmill and one acre, I give to my three sons. Personal estate to be sold, and daughter, Mary Matlack, to have £50; and daughter, Susannah Matlack, £50, when 18; and daughter, Elizabeth Matlack, £50, when 18; and daughter Rebeckah Matlack, £50, when 18. Executors—son, Thomas, and my friend, John Lippincott. Witnesses—Thomas Morton, John Matlack, John Cox. Proved May 6, 1766.
  1766, May 5. Inventory, £449.2.3, made by Samuel Stokes and John Cox. Lib. 13, p. 35.
  1775, Jan. 23. Account by Executors.

1768, Dec. 12. Matlack, George, of Burlington Co. Ward. Son of George Matlack, of Chester Twsp., said Co. Guardian—Joseph Willcox. Fellowbondsman—Francis Dudley; both of Evesham Twsp., said Co. Witness—Robert Burchan. Lib. 12, p. 523.

1767, March 28. Matlack, Isaac, of Waterford Twsp., Gloucester Co. Int. Adm'x—Rebecca Matlack, the widow. Fellowbondsman—Thomas Bate, yeoman; both of said place. Witnesses—Samuel Shaw and Joseph Read.
  1767, Jan. 13. Inventory, £365.15.5, made by Joshua Stokes and Thomas Bate. Lib. 13, p. 102.

1767, Jan. 4. Matlack, Jeremiah, of Chester Twsp., Burlington Co., yeoman; will of. Wife, Elizabeth, £30, and to be maintained by sons. Sons, John and Jeremiah, my lands. Executors—friends, Joshua and Enoch Roberts. Witnesses—John Roberts, John Cowperthwaite, Joseph Roberts. Proved Feb. 13, 1767. Lib. 13, p. 52.
  1767, Feb. 9. Inventory, £755.15.2, made by Joshua Roberts and Enoch Roberts.

1765, Feb. 26. Matlack, John, of Waterford, Gloucester Co., yeoman; will of. To son, Isaac; son, John; daughter, Hannah Maxel, wife of John Maxel; daughter, Kezia Heritage, widow of Benjamin

CALENDAR OF WILLS—1761-1770   277

Heritage; daughter, Esther French, wife of Jonathan French; and daughter, Sarah Browning, wife of Joseph Browning, 5 shillings each. To the heirs of my son, Jacob Matlack, deceased, 5 shillings. To Samuel Lippincott, son of my daughter, Bathsheba, late wife of Ezekial Lippincott, 5 shillings. My son, Benjamin, the plantation where he lives, which was divided from the place where I now live some years ago. Son, Ephraim, plantation where I live. Daughter, Lydia Matlack, £7 and things she calls hers. Daughters, Lydia Matlack and Mary Hillman, wife of Joab Hillman, the residue. Executors—friends, Nathaniel Lippincott and his son, Caleb Lippincott. Witnesses—Joshua Stokes, William Bates, Abraham Allen. Proved March 14, 1765.

1765, March 9. Inventory, £125.9.1, made by Joshua Stokes and William Bates.   Lib. 12, p. 76.

1770, April 17. Matson, Israel, of Deptford, Gloucester Co. Int. Adm'r—James Pedrick, of Frankford, Philadelphia Co. (Penn'a), mason. Fellowbondsman—Constantine Lord, of said Deptford, yeoman. Witness—Elizabeth Mickle.

1770, April 14. Inventory, £265.17.0, made by John Jessup and Constantine Lord.   Lib. 15, p. 46.

1767, May 18. Matson, Matthias, of Gloucester Co., yeoman; will of. I order that I be buried on the plantation and nowhere else. Wife, Elizabeth, £100, and many household goods. Daughters—Hepsabey, and Mary, my two plantations; Hepsiba to have the homestead, and Mary the other place, when they are of age. My daughter, Sarah, the value of ⅓ my lands. Executors—my wife and my brother, William Matson. "Burying ground where I am to be buried to be done up with cedar boards, and nailed on posts, and it is always to be kept up by them that lives on my place afterwards." Witnesses—John Pinyard, Martha Pinyard, Jacob Richman. Proved June 3, 1767.

1767, May 28. Inventory, £191.5.9, made by John Pinyard and Caleb Lippincott.   Lib. 13, p. 118.

1765, March 26. Matthews, Samuel, of Cape May Co., gentleman; will of. Son, Samuel, plantation I bought of Amos Johnson, of 106 acres, located in Middle Precinct; and is part of that plantation that formerly belonged to Benjamin Johnson (my last wife's father) and where he lived. Son, Elijah, land where I live, located in the Middle Precinct. Daughter, Mary Matthews, £300, who will be 18 years old on 19th of June, 1774. And whereas the said Benjamin Johnson gave my daughter, Mary, £5, and her grandmother, Penelope Johnson, gave her a bed which bequests are in my hands they are to be paid, and she is to have the clothing that was her mother's. My son, Samuel, is to be the Guardian of my daughter, Mary. Executors—Samuel and Elijah, my sons. Witnesses—Jeremiah Ludlam, Mary Leaming, Aaron Leaming, Jonathan Leaming.

1765, July 2. Codicil. Proved May 25, 1768.

1768, June 8. Inventory, £741.2.0¼, made by John Townsend and James Godfrey.   Lib. 15, p. 463.

1766, Aug. 9. Matthews, William, of Cape May Co., gentleman; will of. Oldest son, John, the northwest side of my plantation where I live, of 80 acres. Son, Isaac, 100 acres where my dwelling house stands. Son, Richard, the rest of the land. I own ¼ of certain islands, in Middle Precinct, on the northwest side of Five Mile Beach, in partnership with Richard Shaw and Lewis Cresse; and I give my part to my son, Thomas. My sons, John and Isaac, are to support and care for my unfortunate daughter, Martha, for four years after my decease, and after that time to be supported by John, Isaac and Richard to the end of her life. My wife, Bathia, the best bed and ⅓ my moveable estate. The remainder to my daughters, Lydia, Elizabeth, Elishaba and Bathia Matthews, and to my granddaughters, Jane and Esther Edwards. Executors—my wife and my son, Isaac. Witnesses—Ephraim Edwards, Aaron Leaming, James Edwards, Samuel Matthews. Proved March 19, 1767.

1767, March 24. Inventory, £133.12.4, made by John Eldredge and Samuel Matthews. Lib. 13, p. 141.

1762, Feb. 2. Mattison, Aaron, of Freehold, Monmouth Co., yeoman; will of. Daughter, Mary Hugan, £50. Wife, Elizabeth, ½ the profits of my farm and use of moveable estate, and, after her marriage or death, to be sold, and money given as follows: To son, Jacob; to Aaron, Jacob and James Mattison, sons of my son Joseph, deceased; to son, Aaron; to daughter, Catherine, the wife of Samuel Ker; to daughter, Rachel, the wife of Joseph Hankinson; to daughter, Mary, the wife of William Hugan; and to daughter, Martha, the wife of William Norcross. Executors—son, Jacob, my son-in-law, Samuel Ker, and my friend, John Henderson. Witnesses—James Harbert, Daniel Ketcham, Michael Henderson. Proved May 3, 1762.

1762, May 1. Inventory, £736.5.6, made by James Dey, Kenneth Anderson and Jacob Wikoff. Lib. H, p. 119.

1766, Jan. 6. Maxfell, John, of Borough of Elizabeth, Essex Co.; will of. To Benjamin Miller, minister of the Gospel in the Borough of Elizabeth, at the Scotch Plains, £2 yearly, while he is a minister there. Wife, Elizabeth, the interest of what is to be sold. To my four grandchildren, the children of my daughter Abigail Ludlow, deceased, £35. Grandson, John Maxfell, son of David Maxfell, dec'd, £1 and 10 shillings. Son, William, £1. Son, John, the place I live on, which I bought of Stephen Ward, and also that I bought of Stephen Ward, Jr., and the ½ of the sawmill. Rest to be sold and divided among my daughters, Elizabeth Lambart, Sarah Clarke, Hanah Jones and Esther Sayre. Executors—my wife, Elizabeth, and my friend, Recompence Stanbery. Witnesses—James Miller, Jr., Tingley Sutton, Jemima Miller. Proved May 29, 1766. Lib. H, p. 623.

1763, June 8. Maxfield, Caleb, of Essex Co. Ward. Petition of Caleb Maxfield, an orphan, of 14 years of age, and other inhabitants of Elizabeth Town, Showing that Samuel Maxfield, of said town, deceased, did die intestate, leaving three children, viz., Rachel, Caleb and Rhoda; and the children, Rachel and Caleb, made choice of their father-in-law, Ephraim Frazee (who had married their mother), to be their Guardian, who obtained Letters accordingly; that said Ephraim Frazee, being reduced in his circumstances and about to remove into the back parts of Virginia, and his security being doubtful, makes it necessary that another Guardian be appointed; and the said Caleb hath made choice of John Darby, of Elizabeth Town, for that purpose; and the estate of the youngest of the said children, named Rhoda (now under 14) being in possession of Daniel Potter, who is become aged and infirm, and desires that said Darby be ap-

CALENDAR OF WILLS—1761-1770   279

pointed for the youngest child: Therefore we desire that John Darby, be made Guardian of said children, although the eldest child, Rachel, has not joined in the application, she living with her father-in-law, and not being willing to give any uneasiness in the family by any act of hers. Signed by Caleb Maxfield, Thomas Squire (grandfather), Daniel Potter, who was the guardian of the children; Recom Stanbery, William Darby.
1763, June 16. Guardian—John Darby. Fellowbondsman—Thomas Marsh; both of Essex Co. File No. 3269-3272 G.

1763, Feb. 20. Maxfield, David, of Borough of Elizabeth, Essex Co., yeoman; will of. My wife, Susannah, rent of ⅓ my farm. Sons, John, Samuel, Isaac and William, all my land, when they are 21. Daughter, Ruth, £100, when 18. Executors—friends, John Stites, and John Miller. Witnesses—Samuel Littell the third, Jonathan Willis, Richard Clark. Proved May 30, 1763.
1763, March 30. Inventory, £534.11.2. Lib. H, p. 259.

1763, March 11. Maxfield, Hannah, of Salem Co., widow. Int. Adm'r—Jehiel Dearwin (Darvin). Fellowbondsmen—Joseph Champneys and Richard Sparks; all of Pilesgrove, said Co., yeomen.
1763, March 2. Inventory, £95.16,3, made by John Dickinson and Erasmus Kent. Lib. 11, p. 374.

1762, May 6. Maxfield, Rachel and Caleb, of Essex Co. Wards. Rachel is aged 16, and Caleb aged 14, and are children of Samuel Maxfield, of said Co., deceased. Guardian—Ephraim Frazee, of said Co. Fellowbondsman—Thomas Griffen, of Somerset Co. (See under "Maxfield, Caleb"). Lib. H, p. 98; File No. 3149-3150 G.

1764, May 19. Maxfield, Rebecca, of Salem Co. Ward. Daughter of William Maxfield, of said Co., deceased. Rebecca is under 4 years of age.
1764, May 19. Guardian—John Maxfield, of Philadelphia. Fellowbondsman—John Lawrence, of City of Burlington. Lib. 11, p. 517.

1761, Jan. 17. Maxfield, William, of Elsinboro, Salem Co.; will of. Wife, Hannah, ⅓ my goods. Son, William, my apparel. My wife, and children, viz: Hannah Maxfield, William Maxfield, James Maxfield, Margret Maxfield, Mercy Maxfield and Rebecca Maxfield, the rest of my goods. Executors—son, William, and Grant Gibbon. Witnesses—William Goodwin, Clement Hall, Augustine Moore. Proved April 15, 1761.
1761, April 6. Inventory, £387.3.9, made by Joshua Thompson and Clement Hall. Lib. 11, p. 12.

1762, April 19. Maxwell, Esther, widow, of Burlington; will of. Daughter, Latitia Darby, widow, £150. Daughter, Sarah Evans (wife of Caleb Evans), £150. Remainder to daughter, Rebecca Maxwell. Executrix—said Rebecca Maxwell. Witnesses—John Shaw, Isaac Heulings, Jasper Smith. Proved June 30, 1762. Lib. 11, p. 205.
1762, June 30. Inventory, £564.17.5, made by Isaac Heulings and Jasper Smith.

1766, May 16. Maxwell, James, of Greenwich, Sussex Co. Int. Adm'r—John Maxwell, of Greenwich, yeoman. Fellowbondsman—Nathaniel Pettit, Esq., of Newton, said Co. Witness—Ayres Pettit.
1766, May 12. Inventory, £78.15.6, made by John Cowan and Alexander White.
Lib. 12, p. 434.

1761, Feb. 26. May, Christian, of Burlington Co. Int. Adm'r—William Cubberley. Fellowbondsman—Joseph Chambers; both of Nottingham, said Co. Witness—John Carty. Lib. 10, p. 173.
1761, Feb. 22. Inventory, £28.17.11, made by Joseph Chambers and John Cuberley.

1762, Aug. 12. Mead, John, of Pompton, Bergen Co., yeoman; will of. Wife, Mary, use of real and personal. Eldest son, John, £130 and 4 acres by the River, to build a mill. Sons, Jacob, Isaac and Yelles, £25 each. Sons, Peter, John, Jacob, Isaac and Yelles, personal. Son, Peter, rest of real. Executrix—my wife. Witnesses—Robert Hogg, Nathaniel Ford and Jacob Haulenbek. Proved May 4, 1769.
Lib. K, p. 95.

1765, May 20. Meadlis, Samuel, of Newark, Essex Co.; will of. Daughters, Sarah and Hannah Meadlis, all real and personal. Wife, Hannah, use of whole estate. To Sarah Holdridge's children. Executors—Robert Plume and Stephen Young, and my wife. Witnesses—John Plume, Sr., John Campbel, Robert Boyd. Proved Aug. 7, 1765.
Lib. H, p. 560.

1761, May 14. Meeker, Gabriel, of Essex Co. Ward. Son of Nathaniel Meeker, of said Co., deceased. Guardian—Cornelius Hetfield. Fellowbondsman—Robert Ogden, Esq.; both of said Co.
Lib. G, p. 380.

1768, March 12. Meeker, John, of Elizabeth Borough, Essex Co., cooper; will of. Wife, Phebe, ⅓ the moveables, and use of ⅔ the lands. Sons, John (not 14) and Jotham, my lands. If the child my wife is big with be a boy, then it is to have its share of land. Refers to a legacy left him by his uncle, Joseph Ogden. Daughters, Sarah Meeker, Rhoda Meeker, Phebe Meeker, Joanna Meeker, and to the child my wife goes with, the residue, when they are 18. Executors—friends, Recompence Stanberry, and James Bounnel. Witnesses—Samuel Hicks, Lawrence De Camp, Samuel Stell Coberly. Proved April 6, 1768. Lib. I, p. 228.

1763, March 3. Meeker, Jonathan, of Elizabeth Borough, Essex Co.; will of. Daughter, Martha Woodruff, the use of £30, and, at her death, to her surviving children. Daughter, Mary Ogden, £30. Daughter, Jemimah Chandler, £40. Daughter, Keziah Woodruff, £100, who is a widow with children. Daughter, Elizabeth Thompson, £5. Executors—William Harriman and John Parson. Witnesses—Nathaniel Woodruff, Jonathan Woodruff, Jr., Nathan Woodruff. Proved March 16, 1768. Lib. I, p. 231.

1765, June 18. Meeker, Mary, of Elizabeth, Essex Co.; will of, Widow of Daniel Meeker. Daughter, Mary, wife of Joseph Corey, £100. Granddaughter, Mary, wife of Joseph Conkling, £25. Granddaughters, Mary Conklen and Hannah Conklen, to each a silver

CALENDAR OF WILLS—1761-1770   281

spoon; and to my granddaughters, Mary, Hannah and Sarah Conklen, daughters of David Conklin, £15 each, when 18. If they should die, then to my granddaughters, Mary Meeker, daughter of Abraham Meeker, and Mary Conklen, daughter of Joseph Conklen. Granddaughter, Sarah Meeker, daughter of my son, Abraham Meeker, £8. Granddaughter, Rebekah Meeker, £5. Granddaughter, Susannah Meeker, daughter of Moses Meeker, £5. Son-in-law, Joseph Corey, the rest. Executor and Guardian—said Joseph Corey. Witnesses—Thomas Williams, William Seaman and David Crane. Proved March 9, 1770.
Lib. K, p. 187.

1768, April 14. Meeker, Moses, of Elizabeth Town, Essex Co. Ward. Son of Moses Meeker, of said place, dec'd. Guardian—Joseph Cory. Fellowbondsman—Stephen Crane, Esq.; both of said Co. Witnesses—Abraham Clark and John Mackay.   Lib. I, p. 302.

1770, Jan. 10. Meghee, Safety, of Bordentown, Burlington Co., cordwainer; will of. To my five children, to wit, Amy Meghee, William, Mary, Safety and Sarah Meghee, when of age, the remainder after debts are paid. Executors—friends, William Potts, of Mansfield, farmer, and Caleb Carman, of Chesterfield. Witnesses—Alexander Moore, Joseph Potts, Thomas White. Proved March 1, 1770.
1770, March 1. Inventory, £437.3.8, made by Jonathan Quicksall and Samuel Farnsworth.   Lib. 15, p. 32.

1765, Feb. 26. Meirs, Christopher, of Upper Freehold, Monmouth Co. Int. Adm'r—Joseph Meirs. Fellowbondsman—John Wetherill; both of said place.
1765, Feb. 15. Inventory, £102.9.4, made by James Lawrence and John Wetherill.   Lib. 12, p. 62.

1767, Aug. 9. Meisinger, Nicholas. Int. Adm'r—Conraad Wandemaker.   Lib. I, p. 208.

1763, Dec. 2. Meldrom, Abigail, of Kingwood, Hunterdon Co. Int. Adm'r—Dennis Woolverton. Fellowbondsman—Lazarus Adams; both of said place. Witness—John Opdyck.
1763, Nov. 28. Inventory, £102.16.10, made by Lazarus Adams and Henry Snyder.   Lib. 11, p. 447.

1759, May 7. Meldrum, George, of Kingwood, Hunterdon Co.; will of. To my brother's son, John Meldrum, my apparel, gun, sword and cane. To my niece, Margaret Meldrum, one cow. Executors—wife, Abigail, and my father-in-law. Witnesses—Joel Woolverton, Charles Woolverton, Henry Bird. Proved March 16, 1762. Letters granted to Abigail Meldrum and Dennis Woolverton.
1762, March 13. Inventory, £115.2.6, made by Joel Woolverton and Joshua Waterhouse.   Lib. 11, p. 139.

1766, Sept. 10. Melick, Godfrey, of Greenwich Twsp., Sussex Co.; will of. Wife, Margaret, all my personal estate, and, after her death, to be divided among my nine children. Plantation on which I live, and the woodland bought of William Lovet Smith, to be divided in two parts; the part, where the house stands, I give to my eldest son, Godfrey, and the other ½ to my son, Christopher. When my son, Godfrey, comes of age, the tracts are to be appraised by my wife,

Margaret, Andrew Melick, John Sharps and Hugh Hughes, and then the said sons are to pay the amount to my wife and each of my other children, William, Jacob, Henry, Andrew, John, Mary Margaret and Mary Catherine, when of age. The place upon Musconetkonk, formerly my father-in-law's, Christopher Falkenberger, to be sold on the death of my mother-in-law, and £100 devised to said Christopher and £100 devised to Mary Margaret by my father-in-law, shall be paid out of the money. Executors—my wife, Andrew Malick, John Sharp and Hugh Hughes. Witnesses—Philip Cline, Mary Catherine Cline, Margaret Sharp. Proved Nov. 17, 1766.

1766, Nov. 13. Inventory, £397.6.0, made by Christan Sharps, and Alexander White, and signed by Margret Malick, Andrew Malick and John Sharps, the Executors. Lib. 12, p. 428.

1767, Sept. 26. Melick, John, of New York City, currier and tanner; will of. Whereas there is a Lutheran Church built and a piece of ground in Hunterdon Co., in East Jersey, which ground is in possession of the said church, and belongs to me and my brother, Teunis, and whereas by deeds of partition this day executed between us of a larger tract of land I have vested the said church ground in my brother in fee, it is my desire that he convey the same for the use of said church. Son, John, £50, when he is 21. Wife, Christena, £50, and the rents of my real estate, for supporting my children, till my said son is 21; then my land is to be sold, and I give the money to my wife and all my children, Mary, John, Elizabeth, Catharine, Margaret and Sarah. Executors—my brother, Teunis Melick, of Hunterdon Co., Henry Miller, of same place, and Peter Grim, of New York City, tanner. Witnesses—Benjamin Kissam, Henry W. Van Dewater, John Middidoler, Henry Miller. Proved Oct. 15, 1767.
Lib. 13, p. 367.

1737, Oct. 30. Mellenot, Elenor, of New Barbadoes Neck, called the Polifie, in Bergen Co., widow; will of. To my five daughters, 100 acres of land at Polifly, bounded by Derick Terhoun and Gisbart Van Blarkem; also six acres of meadow, which was left me for a third by my first husband, John Christine, and made over to me by my son, John Christine. Daughters named as Elizabeth, wife of Henry Post, Mary, wife of Jacobus Post, Margaret, wife of John Berry, Ann, wife of Gisbert Van Blarkem, and Sarah, wife of Leanerd Degrave. Executors—sons-in-law, John Berry and Henry Post. Witnesses—Abraham Ackerman, Henreck Van Gesle and John McDowell. Proved May 10, 1765, and at same time Henry Post, the surviving Executor, was qualified. Lib. H, p. 580.

1765, Nov. 9. Melvan, William, of City of Perth Amboy, Middlesex Co., yeoman; will of. Real and personal to be sold. Sons, Jeams and John, that I had by my present wife, Ann, each to have £40. My sons, by my wife, Ann, viz., Thomas, Daniel, George and William, each £20, when they come of age. My daughters, by my wife, Ann, viz., Rachel, Elizabeth and Margret, to have their share, when of age. Wife, Ann, to have benefit of my estate to bring up the children. Executors—son, Jeams, and my friend, Nicholas Everson. Witnesses—Simon Loofborrow, Thomas Buckelu, Daniel Willmot. Proved July 10, 1766. Lib. H, p. 627.

1768, Aug. 29. Mercer, William, of Middlesex Co.; will of. All my lands in and about Quibble Town, to be sold. My dwelling house and mills, and the farm adjoining where I live, and the salt meadow I lately bought of Benjamin Van Veghten, with my negroes, cattle, etc., to be kept by my wife, Lucy, for her use, and that of my younger children, namely, Archibald, John, Isaac, Robert, Hellen and Gabriel. Money given to the seven children, William, Archibald, John, Isaac, Robert, Hellen and Gabriel. Son, William, is now of age. My sister, Hellen Mercer, is to live with my family. Executors—my wife and my friends, Anthony White and George Harrison. Witnesses— Richard Merrell, Sarah Voorhees, Stephen Campbell. Proved March 15, 1770. Lib. K, p. 208.

1768, March 17. Merrit, Sarah, of Springfield, Burlington Co., widow of Abraham. Int. Adm'r—Jacob Merrit, of said place. Fellowbondsman—Samuel How, of Burlington. Witness—James Talman. Lib. 13, p. 330.
1768, March 22. Inventory, £67.3.0, made by William Ridgway and Lott Ridgway.

1766, March 10. Merritt, Abraham, of Springfield, Burlington Co., yeoman; will of. Son, Caleb, £5, when 21. To Charity Gaskil, one cow, which my wife may choose for her. Daughter, Anne, £50, when 18. Wife, Rachel, profits of plantation, till boys are 21. Sons, Caleb, Levi and Abram, my plantation, when 21. Executors—my wife and my neighbor, Jacob Shinn. Witnesses—William Budd, William Fox, William Shinn, Jr., William Ridgway. Proved April 24, 1766.
1766, April 24. Inventory, £293.5.1, made by Samuel Lippincott and William Fox. Lib. 13, p. 1.

1765, March 5. Merry, Job, of Woodbridge, Middlesex Co. Int. Adm'r—Ebenezer Foster. Fellowbondsman—David Evens; both of said place. Same date, renunciation by Phebe Force, sister of Job Merry, in favor of Ebenezer Foster.
1765, March 15. Inventory, £308.9.3, of goods and rights of Job Merry, as the same came to my hands from David Crow, Executor of Joseph Merry, late of Woodbridge, as well as the residue of a legacy due to said Job from the hands of David Evans, Executor of Ebenezer Merry (father to said Job and Joseph), late of Woodbridge. Signed by Ebenezer Foster, Adm'r. Lib. H, p. 404.

1763, ———, ———. Merry, John, of Morris Co.; will of. My lands in Boston government to be for my wife. Brother, Nathaniel Miller, joint Executor. Witnesses—Isaac Ogden, Benjamin Clark. (Above will is much torn and parts missing.)
1768, April 26. Adm'x—Elizabeth Merry, the widow of John, late of Morris Co. Fellowbondsman—Nathaniel Miller, of Springfield, Essex Co. Witnesses—Abraham Ogden and John B. Scott.
Elizabeth Merry, the Adm'x, said that John Merry, her late husband, died without a will, except some small pieces of paper that was supposed to have been intended for one, from which the meaning could not be taken, and which was lodged in the Prerogative Court office.
1768, April 5. Inventory, made by Obadiah Lum and Thomas Vail. Lib. I, p. 301; File No. 240 N.

1761, April 4. Merry, Joseph, of Woodbridge, Middlesex Co.; will of. Sister, Annah Care, £5 and a horse. Sister, Phebe Forse, £25. Cousin, Icabod Tharp, £20, when 21. Cousin, David Tharp, £20, when 21. To Hanna Tappen, £15. To Rachel Cotheal, £3 and 10 shillings. To William Eddy, £5, to be in the care of his father, Gawen Eddy, till William is 21. Brother, Job Merry, the rest, when he is 22. Executors—friends, Joseph Freeman and David Crow. Witnesses—Henry Cotheal, Gawen Eddy, James Clarkson. Proved April 24, 1761.
Lib. G, p. 429.

1767, April 30. Merseroll, John, of New Brunswick, Middlesex Co.; will of. Son, John, my gun. Wife, Leanah, rest of personal and real, in order to bring up my child, Abraham. At wife's death all to go to sons, John, Jacob, Peter, Karl and Abraham, and to daughters, Leanah (wife of Adrian Van Nosbrant), and Elizabeth, and to the children of my daughter Jane, deceased, formerly the wife of James Whitelock. Executors—brother, Peter, my brother-in-law, Albert Voorhees, and my wife. Witnesses—William Nevius, Ernestus Van Harlingen, George Wetsel. Proved June 3, 1767. Lib. I, p. 128.

1760, May 20. Messeler, Johannis, of Somerset Co., farmer; will of. Wife, Catrine,, must be maintained by the children. Sons, Abraham Messeler, Cornelius and Peter, and daughters, Ealfie (Eaffie), the wife of Jacob Buyse, Harmpie, the wife of Johannis Powelse, Sarah, the wife of Jacobus Stryker, each to pay my wife £3. Real and personal to be sold and divided among my children. Executors—my sons, Abraham and Cornelius, and my friend, John Brokaw. Witnesses—John Aten, Thomas Aten, Rike Vanderbilt. Proved March 6, 1761.

1761, Feb. 24. Inventory, £847.18.6, made by Hendrick Blaw and Rike Vanderbilt. Lib. G, p. 367.

1760, March 1. Messenger, William, of Woodbridge, Middlesex Co.; will of. Son, William Messenger, 5 shillings. Enough of my real and ½ of a boat to be sold, so as to build a small house for my wife. Wife, Mary, rest of real estate, till my youngest child is 14, when all is to be sold, except my house, and the money given to my sons, William and Joseph. Daughters, Sarah, Mary, Deborah and Hannah, the rest. Executors—friends, Francis Everit and William Moore. Witnesses—William Moore, Abner Wright, George Brown. Proved Jan. 13, 1761. Lib. G, p. 342.

1761, June 20. Metseler, Peter, of Somerset Co., weaver; will of. Children, John Metseler, Antje Metseler, Simon Metseler, and Peter Metseler; each ¼ of my estate. Executors—my brother-in-law, Jacob Buyse, and my friend, John Brokaw. Witnesses—Abram Messeler, Cornelus Messeler, Hanna Messeler. Proved April 9, 1764.
Lib. H, p. 425.

1768, Sept. 9. Meyer, George, of Upper Alloways Creek, Salem Co. Int. Adm'r—Benjamin Thompson. Fellowbondsman—Thomas Thompson; both of Alloways Creek, said Co., yeomen.

1768, Aug. 5. Inventory, £52.14.3, made by Andrew Thompson and Thomas Thompson. Lib. 12, p. 524.

1765, April 19. Mickle, John, of Town and Co. of Gloucester; will of. Daughter, Elizabeth Mickle, all my real and personal; and my Executors shall pay the interest to my sister, Hannah Ladd, to maintain and educate said daughter, till she is 18; but if said Hannah die, then I desire that Sarah, the wife of William Mickle, my brother, take charge of Elizabeth, my only daughter. If my daughter die under age, then the said estate to go to my four nephews, William, James and Samuel Mickle, sons of my brother, William Mickle, and Samuel Mickle, son of my brother, Samuel Mickle, dec'd, except £200, which I give my sister, Hannah Ladd; and my lot in Northern Liberties, Philadelphia, to be divided between Hannah Hugg and Sarah Hugg, daughters of Sarah Hugg, of Gloucester Twsp., widow. Brother, William, my apparel. Executors—my cousin, David Cooper, and Robert Friend Price. Witnesses—Mary Price, Margery Price, Samuel Harrison. Proved April 27, 1765.
1765, April 27. Inventory, £1,475, made by Samuel Harrison and Thomas West. Lib. 12, p. 110.

1762, March 5. Mickle, Joseph, of Newton, Gloucester Co., yeoman. Int. Adm'r—Isaac Mickle. Fellowbondsman—Robert Friend Price; both of Newton Twsp., said Co., yeomen. Witnesses—John Ladd and Hannah Ladd. Lib. 11, p. 87.

1762, July 12. Mickle, Samuel, of Newton, Gloucester Co. Ward. Eldest son and heir-at-law of Samuel Mickle, sadler, of said place, deceased, having lands by the will of his father, makes choice of his friend, David Cooper, as Guardian. Witnesses—John Cooper.
1762, July 12. Guardian—David Cooper. Fellowbondsman—John Brown, yeoman; both of Deptford Tounship, said Co. Witness—Sarah Howell. Lib. 11, p. 126.

1768, March 19. Middagh, Dirck, of Bridgewater, Somerset Co., blacksmith; will of. My wife, Engeltje, to be maintained by my son, Dirck; and she is to have a wagon and two horses, and a driver, to attend Divine worship. Son, Dirck, all my real and personal; and my daughter, Elizabeth (now wife of Peter Biggs), to have £120. Executors—wife, Engeltje, and my son, Dirck. Witnesses—Cornelius Tunison, Jr., Lawrence Van Derveer, Jacob Noorstrand. Proved May 21, 1768.
1768, July 12. Inventory, £311.13.0, made by John Arrison and Cornelius Tunison, tertius. Lib. I, p. 357.

1766, Nov. 1. Middleton, Asa, of New Hanover Twsp., Burlington Co. Int. Adm'rs—Jonathan Middleton and Abel Middleton.
1766, Oct. 18. Inventory, £461.12.1½, made by Anthony Sykes and William Newbold. Lib. 12, p. 385.
1790, May 17. Adm'rs—John Middleton, Jr., and William Cook, both of said Co., on estate of Asa Middleton, left unadministered by Abel Middleton and Jonathan Middleton, who are also deceased. Fellowbondsman—Robert Pearson. Lib. 32, p. 94.

1770, Jan. 12. Middleton, George, of Burlington Co.; will of. Son, Nathan, land I bought of John Lovell; also four lots that I bought of William Bunting, he paying £100 to his 3 youngest sisters when they are 18. Son, Jacob, the plantation where I live; also the land

I bought of Richard Watson, when he is 21. Wife, Hannah, £200. Daughter, Elizabeth Middleton, £115. Daughter, Hannah Middleton, £100, when 18. Daughter, Rhoda Middleton, £100, when 18. Daughter, Phebe Middleton, £100, when 18. I give my three boys, John Allen, William Lippincott and Ramoth Bunting, to my son Jacob, to fill their indentures. Executors—wife, Hannah, and sons, Nathan and Jacob. Witnesses—Thomas Middleton, Joseph Borden, Jr., Mary Middleton. Proved July 28, 1770. Lib. 15, p. 48.

1770, July 25. Inventory, £1168.18.7, made by William Miller and Peter Harvey.

1766, Sept. 5. Middleton, Hudson, of Chester Twsp., Burlington Co., yeoman; will of. My son, Nathaniel, that part of my plantation which was purchased of Richard Satterthwaite from the estate of Joshua Wright, he paying to his sister, Christian, £50, when she is 18. Son, Thomas, plantation where I live, when 21, he paying to his two sisters, viz., Sarah and Rachel, £50 each. Daughter, Mary Middleton, £50. To my two youngest daughters, Sarah and Rachel, apparel, which was their mother's. Executors—my brother, John, and my brother-in-law, Nathan Haines. Witnesses—Abraham Heulings, John Cox, Samuel Sorency. Proved Jan. 23, 1768.

1768, Jan. 20. Renunciation of Nathan Haines, unless in case of death of John Middleton before the estate is settled.

1768, Jan. 19. Inventory, £541.3.5, made by Abraham Heulings, Jacob Hollinshead and John Cox. Lib. 13, p. 294.

1781, May 14. Account by John Middleton, acting Executor.

Lib. 23, p. 211.

1761, May 1. Middleton, Jane, of Evesham, Burlington Co.; will of. Daughter, Ann Albertson, £100. Daughters, Ann, Mary Matlack and Sarah Risdon, my clothing and household goods. My grandchildren, to wit, the children of William Matlack and John Risdon, the residue. Executors—my sons-in-law, William Matlack and John Risdon. Witnesses—John Cox and George Matlack. Proved June 3, 1761.

1761, June 1. Inventory, £345.9.6, made by George Matlack and John Cox.

1764, May 7. Account by Ex'rs. Lib. 10, p. 357.

1763, Oct. 11. Middleton, John, of New Hanover Twsp., Burlington Co., yeoman; will of. Son, Asa, 100 acres off south end of plantation where I live. Son, Joel, 40 acres adjoining. Sons, Jonathan and John, the rest. Daughter, Achsah, £60. Executors—brother, Abel, and my sons, Asa and Jonathan. Witnesses—George Middleton, Abigal Brittan, Samuel Kirby. Proved Feb. 25, 1765. Lib. 12, p. 73.

1765, Feb. 16. Inventory, £601.19.1, made by Joseph Steward and Anthony Sykes.

1763, Dec. 5. Middleton, John, of Deptford, Gloucester Co., laborer. Int. Adm'r—John Wilkins. Fellowbondsman—James Wood, Jr.; both of said place, yeomen. Witness—John Mickle.

1763, Dec. 12. Inventory, £43.5.4, made by Joseph Low and James Whitall. Lib. 11, p. 440.

1761, May 10. Middleton, Thomas, of Evesham, Burlington Co., yeoman; will of. Son, John, land I bought of George Matlack and that bought of William Hooton. Son, Thomas, plantation where I live. Sons, John and Thomas, my still, bottles, etc. Son, Hudson, £50. My three daughters, Martha Wilson, Deborah Armstrong and Ruth Higbee, £5 each, and goods. Executors—sons, John and Thomas. Witnesses—John Roberts, Enoch Roberts, Abram Allen. Proved June 2, 1761.
1761, May 27. Inventory, £435.2.0, made by Enoch Roberts and Abraham Allen. Lib. 10, p. 337.

1765, May 6. Middleton, William, of Greenwich, Gloucester Co., husbandman. Int. Adm'r—Aaron Middleton, of Philadelphia, waterman. Fellowbondsman—Joseph Tatem, of Deptford, Gloucester Co., cordwainer and innholder.
1765, April 7. Inventory, £78.9.4, made by Thomas Clark and Thomas Thomson.
1767, July 9. Account by Aaron Middleton, Adm'r. Includes "For board and schooling, of his son, William, £10." Lib. 12, p. 285.

1762, July 23. Mifflin, Samuel, of Township and Co. of Gloucester; will of. My saw mills and lands to be sold. Wife, Mary, £300; and as she may be pregnant, if so she is to have the profits of the meadow I bought of Abraham Chattin, to bring up said child and my son, Edward. Son, Edward, my plantation, when 21; but, if he die, then it is to descend to my brother, Daniel's, children, viz., Daniel and Sarah Mifflin. I owe to my mother, Mary Mifflin, a sum. Executors —my wife and my friend, Ebenezer Miller, Jr. Witnesses—Alexander Blackwood, John Wild, Hannah Jesup.
1762, July 30. Codicil. Wife, Mary, to have various goods. Witnesses—Anthony Sharp, Sarah Hinchman, Ruth Miller. Proved Sept. 3, 1762.
1762, Aug. 23. Inventory, £1,838.2.0, made by William Wilkins and Joseph Gibson, Jr. Lib. 11, p. 255.

1768, Feb. 17. Miles, Francis, of Penns Neck, Salem Co.; will of. Wife, Ann Miles, £250, and the plantation where I live. If my wife marry, then the plantation is to be taken by the Magistrates of Lower Penns Neck Twsp., and laid out towards education of the poor, and they may rent the same forever for that purpose. Rest of land to be sold. The debt due to me from my sister, Catherine Williams, I release to her. Rest of personal estate I give to the children of my two sisters, Catherine Williams and Sarah Sinnickson, namely, Albert Bilderback, William Bilderback, Isaac Bilderback, Luranah Bilderback and Hance Bilderback, children of my sister, Catherine Williams, and Thomas Sinnickson, Elenor Mecum, Mary Trenchard, Andrew Sinnickson, Rebecka Sinnickson, Sarah Sinnickson and John Sinnickson, children of my sister, Sarah Sinnickson. Executors— friends, Andrew Sinnickson, Sr., and William Bilderback. Witnesses —Daniel Garrison, Hester Garrison, Ann Danielson.
1768, Feb. 22. Codicil. I release to John Owen a debt due to me from him. Stones are to be placed at the head of the graves of my father, my mother, and at my own grave. Witnesses—Samuel Dick, Michael Butler. Proved May 21, 1768.
1768, March 16. Inventory, £933.10.22, made by Andrew Standly and Michael Pedrick. Lib. 13, p. 397.

1765, Feb. 5. Miller, Andrew, of Deptford Twsp., Gloucester Co.; will of. Brother, John Miller, £10, and to each of my sisters, £5. Apparel to my other brothers. Son, Andrew, rest of personal and real, when 21. Executors—my brother, Mark Miller, and David Cooper. Witnesses—Moses Ward, Sarah Whiteall. Proved July 10, 1765. Lib. 12, p. 253.

1769, Aug. 13. Miller, Hance Michael, of Upper Alloways Creek Twsp., Salem Co., yeoman; will of. Wife, Cathron Miller, plantation where I live. To my son, George Miller, and "to my grandson, Michael Miller, the plantation where they live on my son, Michael Miller, did live, that is to say, my grandson, Michael Miller, is to have 240 acres, and my son, George Miller, the remainder of the land," where he now lives, and where Simon Becklar lives. Son, Jacob, that plantation where he lives, in Cumberland Co., and contains 500 acres. Daughter, Barbary Johnson, the plantation where she lives, agreeable to a deed taken from Jarman, it being in Cumberland Co., and contains 220 acres. Executors—wife, Catherine; and my friend, Peter Johnson, and Jacob Miller. Witnesses—Daniel Stretch, Christopher Coolmann, Magdalen Julian Kuhlemann. Proved Aug. 29, 1769, by Christopher Coolmann, and Magdalen Julian, his wife.

1769, Aug. 19. Inventory, £585.15.10, made by Samuel Hannah and Peter Dufflel. Lib. 14, p. 109.

1764, Aug. 13. Miller, Johannes, of Paquanack Twsp., Morris Co.; will of. Wife, Catharine, ⅓ of the moveable estate. Son, Hendrick, the land where he lives, of 131 acres. Son, Jacob, the land where he lives, of 180 acres. Son, John, land where he lives, of 216 acres. Son, Adam, £50. Son, Fradrick, £100. My three daughters, Elizabeth, Margaret and Charlotta, £75 each. Executors—sons, Adam and Fradrick. Witnesses—Lewis Stewart, Cornelius Peer, Daniel Peer. Proved Dec. 5, 1769.

1770, March 1. Inventory, £25.4.7, made by Lewis Stewart and Adam Demont. Lib. K, p. 217.

1765, Oct. 10. Miller, Mathias, of Elizabeth Town, Essex Co., yeoman; will of. My freehold land in said Town, joining Joseph Micker, Edward Spining, Ebenezer Spining and Joseph Hinds, I devise to my daughters, Mary Ann Miller (alias Price), Phebe Miller, Susanna Miller, Jane Miller and Hannah Miller; but my wife, Ann, is to enjoy the same till such time as it is disposed of. All land to be sold, and wife to have ⅓ the money, in order to educate my younger children, viz., Susanna Miller, Jane Miller and Hannah Miller. Executors—wife, Ann, Captain Jonathan Hampton and Captain Elias Dayton. Witnesses—Isaac Schelleney, Andrew Miller, Robert Picken. Proved Feb. 28, 1766. Lib. I, p. 196.

1769, Jan. 13. Miller, Michael, of Alloways Creek Twsp., Salem Co., yeoman; will of. To my son, Michael, my interest in the plantation where I reside, with the concurrance of my father, if he see fit to confirm the same. My saw mill in Greenwich Twsp., Gloucester Co., to be sold or rented, and the money divided among my other children. My wife to have her share. Executors—my brother, George Miller, and my friend, Jacob Frees. Witnesses—George Jacob Weiss, Magdalina Weissen, William Pullen. Proved Jan. 30, 1769.

CALENDAR OF WILLS—1761-1770

1769, Jan. 25. Inventory, £570.6.11, made by John Jarman and Joseph Sneathen.
1782, Aug. 8. Account by Jacob Freese.
Lib. 13, p. 501; Lib. 23, p. 411.

1769, Dec. 27. Miller, Phebe, of Essex Co. Ward. Daughter of Mathias Miller, of said place, deceased. Guardian—Thomas Woodruff. Lib. K, p. 143.

1759, Dec. 7. Miller, Richard, of Elizabeth Town, Essex Co., yeoman; will of. Son, Matthias, land in said Town, joining Joseph Meeker, Ebenezar Spining, Edward Spining and Joseph Hinds. To Isaac Skellenger, Samuel Scudder, John Briant and Benjamin Miller, my lands on north side of road, to be divided between the daughters, and Benjamin Miller, and my son, Andrew Miller, if he returns back in six years. Grandson, David Ross, land that joins to Aaron Miller. Great-grandson, Richard Miller, son of Richard Miller, deceased, 5 acres of meadow. Great-grandson, John Hendricks Miller, £5. To Isaac Skellenger, Samuel Scudder, John Briant and Joanna Miller, a salt marsh. To Benjamin Miller, Rachel Skellenger, Phebe Scudder, Mary Briant and Joanna Miller, my moveable estate. Executors—Samuel Scudder, and David Ross. Witnesses—Mathias Hetfield, John Burrows, Andrew Miller. Proved June 5, 1761. Lib. G, p. 440.

1770, Jan. 20. Miller, Richard, of Essex Co. Ward. Son of Richard Miller, of said place, deceased. Guardian—Cornelius Miller.
Lib. K, p. 143.

1761, Sept. 29. Miller, Richard and John Hendricks, of Elizabeth Town, Essex Co. Wards. The said wards are children of Richard Miller, Jr., of said place, deceased. Guardians—Elijah Davis and Sarah Davis, both of said town. Fellowbondsman—Lewis Mulford, of said Co. Lib. H, p. 34.

1770, Aug. 11. Miller, Sarah, of Burlington Co. Ward. Daughter of William Miller. Guardian—Amos Middleton, of Upper Freehold, Monmouth Co. Fellowbondsman—Abel Middleton, of Chesterfield, Burlington Co. Witnesses—Gabriel Allen and George Tudor.
Lib. 14, p. 436.

1766, Oct. 15. Miller, Thomas, of New Hanover, Burlington Co. Int. Adm'rs—Elizabeth Miller and Martha Miller, daughters of said Thomas. Fellowbondsman—William Miller, of Nottingham, said Co., yeoman. Lib. 12, p. 384.
1766, Oct. 9. Inventory, £612.19.7, made by William Miller and James Lawrie.

1762, June 16. Miller, William, of Newton, Sussex Co., collier. Int. Adm'r—John Hackett, yeoman. Fellowbondsman—Benjamin Cooper, yeoman, of said Co. Witness—John English.
1762, June 15. Inventory, £200.10.5, made by John English and John Burns.
1762, June 17. Renunciation by Charity Miller, widow of William Miller. Witness—Benjamin Cooper. Lib. 11, p. 286.

1768, Sept. 14. Miller, William, of Morristown, Morris Co., yeoman; will of. Wife, Magra, 17 acres in Somerset Co., joining Abraham Southard and Elisha Ayers, while she lives. Son, William, plantation where he lives, it being at a place called The Cove, in York Government, of 153 acres. Son, Henry, the plantation he lives on, of 150 acres, it also being at The Cove. Son, John, plantation he lives on, of 150 acres, it also being at The Cove. Son, Garret, plantation he lives on, of 150 acres, it being at The Cove. My daughter, Sarah, 50 acres at The Cove. Daughter, "Lishaferver," the sum of £100. Daughters, Elizabeth and Katrien, the plantation I live on, with the 70 acres that joins it; but my wife is to live on the place as long as she lives. Executrix—my wife, Magra. Witnesses—Amariah Sutton, Blackert Whitneck, Paultus Miller. Proved Sept. 21, 1768.

1768, Sept. 20. Inventory, £357.0.6, made by Amariah Sutton and Edward Lewis, signed by Catherine Miller, as Executrix. Lib. I, p. 348.

1765, Oct. 13. Miller, William, of Nottingham Twsp, Burlington Co.; will of. Wife, Elizabeth, £150, and house and lot. Daughter, Sarah Miller, the said house at her mother's death; also 66 acres I bought of Isaac Heulings. My housekeeper, Ann Thomas, the place that I live in. To Joseph Wood, £10. To Benjamin Titus, £6. To Rebecca Dingwell, £10. To Martha Readford, a bowl. To Gisberd Hendrickson, clothing. To Amos Miller, plantation where I live, after seven years. My daughter-in-law, Ann Miller, land where she lives. Executor—Gysbert Hendrickson. Witnesses—George Davies, Samuel Titus, Andrew Titus. Proved Aug. 8, 1770.

1770, Aug. 13. Inventory, £1,316.14.6¾, made by Thomas Thorn and John Thorn. Lib. 15, p. 52.

1772, Nov. 4. Account of Gysbert Hendrickson, the Executor.
Lib. 14, p. 503.

1770, Nov. 26. Milles, William, of Burlington Co.; will of. Son, Francis Milles, £1 and 10 shillings. Son, William, rest of my personal estate. Executor—son, William. Witnesses—John Bowker, Aaron Bowker, Jemima Bowker. Proved Dec. 22, 1770. Lib. 15, p. 82.

1759, Feb. 4. Mills, Richard, of Hopewell, Cumberland Co.; will of. Wife, Lydia, the use of lands, and moveable estate while she lives. Son, Richard, the lands after her death; but he is to pay to Benony Mills, my daughter, Mary's, son, £10 when Benony is 21. Eldest daughter, Sarah Robbins, 5 shillings, and my daughter, Paciance Sayre, a like sum. My daughters, Bethiah Mathews, Lydia Yapp and Mary Mills, rest of moveable estate, after my wife's death. Executor—friend, Maskell Ewing. Witnesses—Moses Platts, Aaron Ayars, Ethan Sayer. Proved Aug. 15, 1767.

1767, Aug. 15. Renunciation by Maskell Ewing. Witnesses—Thomas Ewing and Moses Platts.

1767, Aug. 15. Adm'r—Richard Mills, with the will annexed. Fellowbondsman—Moses Platts; both of Hopewell, Cumberland Co.

1767, Oct. 19. Inventory, £33.14.3, made by Aaron Moore and Richard Cayford. Lib. 13, p. 159.

1762, April 22. Misner, Richard, of Newton, Sussex Co. Int. Adm'r—Adam Misner, Fellowbondsman—Henry Misner; both of Hardwick, said Co., yeomen.

1762, April 20. Renunciation by Elizabeth Misner, the widow of Richard. Witness—Simon Horn.
1762, April 20. Inventory, £31.16.0, made by Moses Thomkens and Jacob Mitzger.
1763, May 5. Account by Adm'r. Lib. 11, p. 290.

1770, July 12. Mizener, Nicholas, of Hardwick, Sussex Co.; will of. Wife, Margaret, her ⅓. Son, Coonrod, ⅔ of my real estate. My daughter, Rosanna Calshear, ⅓ my estate. Executors—my brother, Adam Misener, and my son, Coonrod. Witnesses—Daniel Landon, Jacob Metzer. Proved Aug. 21, 1770.
1770, Aug. 10. Inventory, £73.15.0, made by Daniel Landon and Jacob Metzgar.
1770, Aug. 27. Inventory, £28.1.2, made by John Wortman and Cornelius Lane, of goods in Somerset Co. Lib. 15, p. 77.

1762, Aug. 20. Moelick, Johannis, of Somerset Co.; will of. Witness—Robert Allen. Proved Jan. 10, 1764.
(This will is very much torn, and much of it is missing. Not recorded. See "Story of an Old Farm," p. 304). File No. 620 B.

1752, Feb. 14. Molenar, Ari, of Somerset Co., gentleman; will of. Forty foot square, in my orchard, is to be laid out for a burying place, and I order a stone to be placed, on which is to be my age and day of death. To my nephew, Ari Legrange, son of Jacobus Legrange, of Albany, New York, £100. To Ari Molenear Legrange, son of my nephew, Christian Legrange, £100. Wife, Antie, the rest. Names "my nephew, Barnardus Legrange." Executrix—my wife. Witnesses—Courtland Skinner, John Broughton, George Brasier. Proved July 18, 1761. Lib. H, p. 5.

1757, Dec. 22. Molenier, Antye, of Somerset Co.; will of. Brother, Isaac Legrange, of Albany Co., £100. Brother, Jacobus Legrange, of same Co., £100. Niece, Anatie Legrange, the wife of Jelis Legrange, £50. Niece, Deborah Tunison, the wife of Phillip Tunison, £50. To Catlyntie Legrange, the widow of my late nephew, Christian Legrange, £50. The rest of my estate, which was left to me by my husband, Ari Molenaer, I give to my nephew, Barnardus Legrange. Executor—said Barnardus. Witnesses—John Beekman, Francis Brasier, George Hagawout. Proved July 22, 1761. Lib. H, p. 6.

1764, Sept. 8. Molleson, Henry, of Piscataway, Middlesex Co.; will of. Wife, Catharine, £200 and many goods; and rest of goods to be sold, and money to the two children of my sister, Ann Macferson, namely, Reuben Macferson and Sarah Macferson; and to the three daughters of my sister, Ruth Runyon, namely, Mary Runyon, Anne Runyon and Rachel Runyon, when they are of age. My two lots of land, which I bought of Elisha Whitehead, I give to my brother, Gilbert Molleson. My 32-acre lot that I bought of John Leforge, and my 7-acre lot, that I bought of Gilbert Mollison, I give to my brother, Benjamin Molleson. My wife can use the said lots. To my father, John Molleson, my apparel. To the Baptist Church of Piscataway, £5. To sister, Sarah Molleson, £10. To John Ury Bright, £5. To Sarah Drake, who I brought up, £5. Executors—my friends, Reuben Fitz Randolph and Joseph Fitz Randolph. Witnesses—Samuel Dayton, Reune Runyon, Jr., Reune Runyon. Proved Oct. 1, 1764.
1764, Sept. 27. Inventory, made by Reune Runyon and David Fitz Randolph. Lib. H, p. 456.

1764, May 1. Moneal, Frans Anton (Francis Anthony Monteal; also, Francis Anton Monckel; also, Francis Santon Monckel) of Kingwood, Hunterdon Co., practitioner; will of. To John Clarkson, £400. To Robert Emley, £200. To Mary Emley, Rebecca Emley and Ann Emley, £50 each. To Caterine Farnsworth, £50. To John Stocdon, £25. To Robeson Rockhill and Acsah Rockhill, children of John Rockhill, £50 each. Rest to John Clarkson and Robert Emley. My Executors are to call for and receive, or in case of refusal to pay, to sue for, £1,500, from 1758, which is due from William Leford, Esq., at Charen Cross, London. To Capt. Henry Robison, £200. Executors —friends, John Clarkson and Robert Emley. Witnesses—Henry Coate, John Stockton, William Rea. Proved July 25, 1764.
Lib. 12, p. 12.

1762, Aug. 28. Montgomerie, Robert, Esq., of Upper Freehold, Monmouth Co.; will of. To grandson, Robert Montgomerie, plantation on north side of Shrewsbury road, and a lot south of the road, when he is 21; but his mother, Esther Montgomerie, is to have the use of the same till he is of age, for the bringing up of her children. Grandsons, John and William Montgomerie, rest of land on south of Shrewsbury road; their mother to use the same till they are of age. To grandson, James Montgomerie, after the death of his aunt, Ann Pangburn, my plantation at Millstone. Grandson, Joseph Montgomerie, land in Cumberland Co., and the meadow in Gloucester Co., when 21. Grandson, Robert Montgomerie, rest of land in West Jersey. Two oldest daughters, Mary Debo and Elizabeth Hepburn, £450 each. Daughters, Ann Pangburn, her life rent, in plantation at Millstone. Daughter, Jane English, £450. To Esther Montgomerie, my son's widow, the use of the plantation where Michael Kelly now lives, while a widow. To granddaughter, Rebecca, £150; and to her sister, Sarah Montgomerie, £150. Executors—James Deboe, James Hepburn, Robert English and my grandson, Robert Montgomerie. Witnesses—John Liming, Richard Cox, Stephen Pangburn. Proved Oct. 1, 1766.
Lib. 12, p. 440.

1764, Oct. 24. Montgomery, Mary, of Monmouth Co., widow. Int. Adm'r—Alexander Montgomery. Fellowbondsman—Robert Montgomerie; both of Upper Freehold, said Co.
1764, Oct. 11. Inventory, £232.4.0, made by Moses Robins and John Wetherill.
1765, Oct. 3. Account by Alexander Montgomerie, Administrator of estate of his mother, Mary Montgomery. Includes "Paid her son, Robert Montgomery."
Lib. 12, p. 31.

1764, May 3. Moone, Anne, of Somerset Co.; will of. Widow of Doctor Jacob Moone. "Being old." Eldest son, Jacob Moone, a negro. Son, Martin Moone, a bed and negro. Daughter, Anne Griggs, silver ware. To Abigal Larrison a table. To my children, Jacob, Martin and Anne Griggs, rest of goods. The £150 in the hands of Daniel Griggs is to remain there till the death of his wife, and then I give to each of Daniel Griggs' two children £25, and to Anne, the daughter of my son, Jacob Moone, £25; and to my sons, Jacob and Martin, £50. Executors—son, Jacob Moone, and friend, Hendrick Cruser. Witnesses—Gilbert Barton, Stephen Warne, Joseph Carson. Proved Aug. 6, 1764.
Lib. 12, p. 22.

CALENDAR OF WILLS—1761-1770   293

1765, Dec. 27. Moore, Augustine, of Morristown, Morris Co.; will of. Brother, John Moore, my apparel; and to John's son, Augustine, £10. My sister, Sarah's, son, Augustine Moore Tooker, £10. My sister, Mary's, son, Augustine Williams, £10. My sister, Elizabeth's, son, Augustine Moore, £10. My wife, Mary, rest of personal and real. Executrix—my wife. Witnesses—Timothy Johnes, Samuel Tuthill, Thomas Budd. Proved Nov. 30, 1767. Lib. I, p. 193.

1763, Sept. 23. Moore, Bostian, of Newton, Sussex Co. Int. Adm'r—John Woolverton. Fellowbondsman—Amos Pettit; both of said Co., yeomen.
1763, Sept. 23. Inventory, £11.14.7, made by Nathaniel Pettit and Amos Pettit. Lib. 11, p. 476.

1767, Nov. 24. Moore, Daniel, of Deerfield, Cumberland Co.; will of. Wife, Rachel, ⅓ my moveable estate and use of my plantation, to bring up my two youngest sons. Daughter, Rachel Moore, £3. Son, Daniel, plantation where my buildings are, when 21; but, if he die, then to my two youngest sons, Jonathan and David. Daughter, Amey Moore, £35, when 18; but, if she die, then to Rachel Moore, Jonathan Moore and David Moore. Sons, Jonathan and David, the land in Russels Neck. Executor—son, John. Witnesses—Daniel Robinson, Daniel Clark, Abraham Bowen. Proved Feb. 24, 1768.
1768, March 15. Inventory, £357.7.0, made by Elnathan Davis, surveyor, and Daniel Clark.
1779, Feb. 27. Account by Executor. Lib. 13, p. 411; Lib. 22, p. 67.

1768, Aug. 11. Moore, Daniel, of Cumberland Co. Ward. Son of Daniel Moore, of Dearfield, said Co., deceased. Guardian—John Moore. Fellowbondsman—Aaron Moore; both of Deerfield, yeomen.
Lib. 13, p. 441.

1754, March 19. Moore, John, of New York City, cooper; will of. To my father, William Moore, an equal part of my estate; to my brothers, George and Christopher, an equal part; and to my sisters, Jane and Nancy, an equal part, both real and personal, and to be sent to them to Ireland, near Newry, at a place called Drummullough. Executors—James McCartney, mariner, and Hugh Gaine, printer. Witnesses—Alexander Stewart, Henry Agnew, Robert Hull. Proved July 28, 1764. Lib. H, p. 358.

1768, Feb. 10. Moore, John, of Hopewell, Hunterdon Co., yeoman; will of. To my wife, Love, £20 and all the goods she brought to me at the time of marriage. Son, Nathaniel, £50, having paid toward the purchase of the plantation where he lives. Son, Theophilus, 40 acres, to be run off from the north side of the plantation, on which I dwell, and he is to pay to Joanna Temple, the wife of John Temple, £20, when she is 21. Son, John, the new shop. Son, Amos, that part of my plantation on the north side of Jacobs Run, except the 40 acres above mentioned, and he is to pay to Sarah, daughter of Benjamin Temple, £25, when she is 21; and he must pay to his two youngest brothers, Samuel and Joseph, £40 each, when they are 21. My son, Amos, is to allow his sister, Elizabeth, the use of the back room, while single. Son, William, that part of plantation on south side of Jacobs Run. Daughter, Sarah, a negro girl, named Flora. To daughter, Elizabeth, one named Dinah. Daughters, Kezia, Sarah and Elizabeth, the rest of moveable estate, deducting from Kezia the amount she has had. Executors—my brother, Samuel Moore, and my son, John. Witnesses—John Carpenter, Joseph Moore, John Guild. Proved Sept. 19, 1768.

1768, Sept. 15. Inventory, £284.19.7, made by John Welling and Timothy Smith. Lib. 13, p. 445.

1766, July 10. Moore, Samuel, of Bergen Co. A citation was issued to Michael Moore and Samuel Moore, both of said Co., which states, upon the complaint of Catharine Smith, John Lee and Christopher Benson, Executors and Guardians of the children of John Smith, late of New York City, who was a legatee of John Smith, late of Bergen Co., that Michael and Samuel had in their possession the will of Samuel Moore, which they neglect to prove, which you are now cited to appear and prove.

1766, July 15. Samuel Moore and Michael Moore, appeared and offered to prove the will, without witnesses, "which kind of proof not being customary, it was declined, and they took back the said will." Lib. H, p. 625.

1763, April 20. Moore, Thomas, of Northampton, Burlington Co.; will of. Wife, Meriam, £50. Son, Samuel, £200, when 21. Rest to son, Samuel, and my five daughters, viz., Rebecca, Hannah, Catharine, Miriam and Sarah. Sons, Job and Thomas, £200, and also my plantation. Executors—wife, Miriam, and my son, Job. Witnesses—Benjamin Moore, Francis Venicomb, Isaac Evens. Proved June 16, 1767.
Lib. 13, p. 82.

1767, June 12. Inventory, £1,453.15.6, made by Francis Venicomb and Hezekiah Jones.

1764, April 7. Moran, Henry, of Gloucester Twsp. and Co.; will of. Wife, Mary, my house and 10 acres, and use of rest of real and personal. Executrix—my wife. Witnesses—William Clark, Jr., Joel Clark, Constantine Chew. Proved Nov. 14, 1765. Lib. 15, p. 241.

1770, Nov. 2. Morfet, Thomas, of Somerset Co. Int. Adm'r—Hugh Gaston, of Bedminster Twsp., said Co. Witness—Bowes Reed.
Lib. K, p. 251.

1760, Feb. 15. Morford, Jarrett, of Shrewsbury Twsp., Monmouth Co., yeoman; will of. Wife, Rebeckah, all real and personal estate while my widow. Son, Thomas, to have the upper part of my plantation, and son, George, the lower part. Executors—wife, Rebecca, and my brother, Job Throckmorton. Witnesses—George Taylor, Nathaniel Taylor, William Price. Proved Sept. 5, 1761.

1761, July 3. Inventory, £495.14.9, made by Martin Vandyk and Samuel Scott. Lib. H, p. 229.

1764, March 16. Morford, John, of Shrewsbury, Monmouth Co. Int. Adm'rs—Garret Morford and David Knott. Fellowbondsman—Philip Cooper; all of said place, yeomen.

1764, March 14. Renunciation by Margaret Morford, widow of said John, in favor of her son, Garret Morford, and David Knott. Witnesses—Margaret Emmons and Samuel Romine.

1764, May 1. Inventory, £149.8.4, made by John Williams, Daniel Seabrook and John Hance.

1765, March 16. Account filed by David Knott. Lib. H, p. 350.

1765, Aug. 16. Morford, Joseph, of Freehold Twsp., Monmouth Co.; will of. All my lands and moveable estate, except what my father-in-law, William Vancurk, did give to my wife, Sarah, to be sold, and of the money I give ¼ to my wife, Sarah, and the other ¾ to my three children, Lidia, William and (name not given in will), when the boy is 21, and the girls 18. Executors—John Forman and John Vancurck. Witnesses—Peter Schenck, Richard Hults, James Robinson. Proved Aug. 21, 1765.
1765, Sept. 2. Inventory, £391.7.3, made by Thomas Leonard, William Wikoff and Michael Henderson. Lib. H, p. 543.

1767, March 5. Morford, William, Lydia and Hannah, all of Monmouth Co. Wards. Children of Joseph Morford, of said Co. Guardian—Nathaniel Scudder, of Lower Freehold, said Co., doctor of physic. Fellowbondsman—William Vankirk, Sr., of same place, yeoman.
1767, Feb. 12. Letter from Elias Boudinot, stating that he has read the will of Joseph Morford, wherein legacies are left to Sarah Morford; also a release from Sarah to the Executors of said Joseph, intended to release her dower, but she is entitled to every legacy, notwithstanding.
1767, March 2. Renunciation, by Sarah Morford, the widow; in favor of Doctor Nathaniel Scudder.
1767, March 2. John Vankirk, an Executor, states that he is satisfied with the choice of Nathaniel Scudder. Lib. 12, p. 479.

1767, April 4. Morgan, Daniel, of South Amboy, Middlesex Co.; will of. My lands and moveable estate to be sold, except what is bequeathed to my wife, Jane, which is some of the goods, and £100. Son, John, to have the residue, when 21; but, if he die, then his part is to go to all my brothers' and sisters' children, except £20 that I give to my brother, William Morgan's, son, Daniel. Executors—my wife and my brother, James Morgan. Witnesses—Samuel Ker, John Ker, Lewis Forman. Proved April 27, 1767.
1767, April 30. Release by Jane Morgan, widow of Daniel Morgan, in which she accepts the legacies stated in the will as given to her, but gives up all right of dower to the lands. Witnesses—Lewis Forman and William Morgan. Lib. I, p. 114.

1763, March 27. Morgan, Isaac, of Pilesgrove Twsp., Salem Co., yeoman; will of. Brothers, William Morgan and Joseph Morgan. Sisters, Mary and Dorrothy. My estate to be given to the above, after debts are paid. Executors—friends, Samuel Bassett and John Richman. Witnesses—William Morgan, John Duell, Thomas Davis. Proved May 23, 1763.
1763, May 23. Inventory, £502.0.7, made by John Richman and John Loyd. Lib. 11, p. 391.

1768, Nov. 5. Morgan, Joseph, of Alloways Creek, Salem Co.; will of. Brother, William Morgan, all my estate; but, if he die and leave no issue, then to my two sisters, Mary Test and Dorothy Morgan. Executors—friends, William Craig and Samuel Bassett. Witnesses—John Gray, Edward Dunlap, Joseph Vanmeter. Proved Nov. 18, 1768.
1768, Nov. 14. Inventory, £82.8.3, made by Jacob Paullin and Samuel Ray. Money is due from the estate of Isaac Morgan, dec'd.
Lib. 12, p. 537.

1768, Dec. 10. Morgan, Morris, of Burlington Co. Int. Adm'r—Zachariah Rossell. Fellowbondsman—William Calvert; both of Mount Holly, said Co., shopkeepers. Witness—Daniel Jones, Jr.
Lib. 12, p. 524.

1761, Jan. 21. Morgan, Samuel, of Pilesgrove Twsp., Salem Co., blacksmith; will of. Wife, Margaret, third of moveable estate. Son, Samuel, my home plantation where I live, of 150 acres. Son, William, the grist mill and house, and 120 acres to be taken off the land where the mill stands. Son, Joseph, the land where Charles Ryley lives, when 21. Rest of moveable estate to all my daughters. Thomas Cowperthwaite is to have a deed for the land I sold him. Executors—son, William, and my friend, Samuel Lippincott. Witnesses—John Hampton, Isaac Morgan, Jacob Richman. Proved Feb. 6, 1761.

1761, Feb. 2. Inventory, £1,575.1.0, made by Elisha Bassett and Joseph Champneys.

1765, Feb. 25. Account, by Adm'rs. Includes: "Paid Margaret Morgan, the widow, due to her as Adm'x of the estate of Mark Dickinson, deceased, £200." Lib. 10, p. 527.

1761, May 16. Morison, Mathew, of Allaways Creek Precinct, Salem Co., yeoman; will of. Youngest son, George Morrison, 50 acres and four of swamp; also ½ of 50 acres I bought of Charles Fogg, lying between Fishing Creek and Hope Creek, near the Delaware. Son, Mathew Morrison, rest of my plantation and marsh on which I live. Daughters, Mary, Anne, Elizabeth, Judith and Margrit, my moveable estate, as they are 18. The goods that Mary received shall be deducted. My two sons, and Margret, to have schooling. Executors—son, Matthew, and friend, William Craig. Witnesses—Joseph Fogg, Samuel Fogg, John Holme. Proved June 23, 1761.

1761, June 18. Inventory, £347.5.2, made by John Holme and William Oakford.

1765, June 17. Account by William Craig, Executor. Lib. 11, p. 3.

1764, Jan. 12. Morrell, Samuel, of Middlesex Co.; will of. Lands to be sold and wife, Phebe, to have one-third. Son, Samuel, 10 shillings. One-third to son, John, and daughter, Ieavsha Morrell, and the other one-third to the other children, Thomas, Dannel and Mary Morrell, and the part which my wife has, after her death, to go to Amos Morrell, Phebe Morrell and Hannah Morrell. Executor—son, John. Witnesses—Peregrine Van Emburgh, Jr., Samuel Smith, Nathan Smith. Proved Dec. 16, 1765.

1765, Dec. 20. Inventory, £122.9.6, made by Thomas Palmer and Robert Morison, "of the goods in Cheesequakes." Lib. H, p. 583.

1767, Nov. 19. Morrin, Cornelius, of New Barbadoes Neck, Bergen Co.; will of. Son-in-law, John Wilson, house and lot in New York City on Guster Street. Son, Paul, house and lot in said City. Wife, Alice, 12 pence. Executor—son-in-law, John Wilson. Witnesses—William Stuart, Edward Simpson and Francis Corbines. Proved Jan. 23, 1768. Lib. I, p. 262.

1766, Feb. 14. Morris, Jacob, of Shrewsbury Twsp., Monmouth Co.; will of. Wife, Elizabeth, use of my estate till son, Jacob, comes of age. The child that my wife is now pregnant with to have its share. Executors—friends, William Crawford and James Grover. Witnesses

—Levi Hart, William Anderson, Benjamin Morris. Proved April 14, 1766.
1766, April 14. Renunciation by James Grover and William Crawford. Witness—John Patterson.
1767, Sept. 23. Adm'x—Elizabeth Morris. Fellowbondsman—William Vanskiak; both of Monmouth Co. Witnesses—Samuel Leonard and Sarah Huse. Lib. I, p. 176; File No. 3209 M.

1769, Jan. 16. Morris, James, of Monmouth Co.; will of. It is my will that my lands and family be kept together till my sons arrive to man's estate—Amos Morris and Joel White Morris. Wife to have £200. When land is sold the money to be divided between my two sons and my two daughters. Executors—my father-in-law, Amos White, and Edward Patterson Cook, of Shrewsbury, yeomen. Witnesses—James Rice, Anthony Smith, Christopher Garretson. Proved March 18, 1769.
1769, March 17. Inventory, £389.4.6, made by Robert Lippincott and Samuel Heulitt. Lib. K, p. 74.

1762, Feb. 24. Morris, John, of Borough of Elizabeth, Essex Co., yeoman; will of. Plantation where I live to be sold and the money to be given to wife, Elizabeth, ⅓, son, Nathaniel, ⅓, daughter, Elizabeth, ½ of the other third, and daughter, Mary, the other ½. Executors—my wife and my friend, John Moores. Witnesses—Samuel Pangburn, Stephen Burrowes, Edward Frazee. Proved March 20, 1762. Lib. H, p. 91.

1767, Feb. 13. Morris, John, of Woodbridge, Middlesex Co.; will of. Son, Benjamin, apparel. Grandson, John Morris, son of Benjamin, ½ of the money due on a bill from Asa Morris. Grandson, Joseph Morris, son of Joseph Morris, deceased, the other ½ of said bill. Grandson, Lewis Morris, son of Lewis Morris, deceased, 20 dollars when he is 21. Granddaughter, Katherine Morris, daughter of Thomas Morris, looking glass. Granddaughter, Mary Morris, daughter of said Thomas, a platter. Son, Thomas, the rest of my estate. Executor—friend, John Moores. Witnesses—Robert Moores, John Daton, William Moores. Proved May 28, 1770. Lib. K, p. 210.

1769, March 29. Morris, John, Sr., of Squancum, in Shrewsbury Twsp., Monmouth Co. Int. Adm'r—John Morris, Jr. Fellowbondsman—Elazerus Brewer; both of said place. Witnesses—George Poole and Mary Bainbridge.
1769, March 9. Inventory, £19.5.7, made by David Johnston and George Packer. Lib. K, p. 77.

1763, March 14. Morris, Joseph, of Shrewsbury, Monmouth Co.; will of. Wife, Joanna, all real and personal, to support her and my children while my widow; after which it is to be divided between children, John Morris, Mary Morris and Joseph Morris. Whatever may be left to me by my father, Richard Morris, to be deemed as part of my estate. If my wife and children all die, then my estate is to go to my brother, Benjamin Morris. Executors—my wife, my brother, Benjamin Morris, and my brother-in-law, William Hulit. Witnesses—Philip Lewis, Elizabeth Bonham, Josiah Holmes. Proved April 2, 1763.
1763, April 4. Inventory, £77.3.0, made by Josiah Holmes and John Gamage. Lib. H, p. 235.

1762, May 10. Morris, Richard, of Middletown, Monmouth Co.; will of. Wife, Mary, £50. Son, William, 10 shillings. Daughters, Phebe, Anny, Rebekah and Catherine, £50 to each, when 18. Sons, Jacob, Richard, Lewis, Robert and George, £50 each, when 21. My daughters, Sarah Burdge, Mary Burdge and Margaret Morford, £20 each. Son, James, £50, and he is to give bond for the keeping of my son, Henry. My wife to be maintained by my son, Benjamin, who is also to maintain my nine children, to wit, Richard, Lewis, Robert, George, Anny, Phebe, Rebecca, Lidiah and Catharine. To son, Benjamin, land where I live and the land on south side of Mill Brook. Son, John, a piece of fresh meadow. The rest of my estate to my nine sons, William, Job, James, Joseph, Jacob, Richard, Lewis, Robert and George. Executors—son-in-law, Joseph Burdge, of Freehold, and my friend, William Crawford, of Middletown. Witnesses—Benjamin Tharp, David Morris, John Taylor. Proved May 3, 1763.
1763, May 2. Inventory, £1,566.9.1, made by Benjamin Tharp, John Smock, Jr., and Richard Crawford, Jr. Lib. H, p. 237.

1757, Sept. 24. Morris, Robert Hunter, of Tinton, Monmouth Co.; will of. "I intend to take a voyage to Great Britain." To my friends, David Ogden and Richard Morris, my real estate, which may be sold, in order to bring up my children. My niece, Anne Morris, that lives with me, £500. My nephew, John Morris, an officer in Lasscelles Regiment, £500. My shares in the Copper Mines at Rocky Hill to be deemed a part of my personal estate until my son, Robert Morris, who lately lived with Richard Salter, and now lives with Mr. Dove, a school master, at Gloucester, in West Jersey, shall be of age, when my son shall take said shares and retain ½ of the profits, and the other ½ he is to give to my said niece, Anne Morris, and nephew, John Morris, and to my daughter, Mary Morris, who now lives with Rev. Samuel Cooke. Son, Robert, to have my shares of Propriety, when he is 21, except a third, which I give to Richard Morris. If my share of the land above the Highlands remains after debts are paid, I give same to Thomas Lawrence, of Philadelphia. My part of the land near the Mohock River, devised to my brother and myself by my father's will, to be conveyed to my nephews, Lewis and Richard Morris. Rest to my son and daughter, Robert and Mary Morris. To Sarah Robinson, £200, as I am grateful, for her care to my mother. To Elizabeth Stogdell, £300. Executors—friend, David Ogden, and my nephew, Richard Morris. Witnesses—Anthony Dennis, Thomas Liming, Hannah Leming. Proved Feb. 24, 1764. Lib. H, p. 361.

1766, May 2. Morris, Samuel, of Somerset Co. Int. Adm'r—Richard Cutter, principal creditor. Fellowbondsman—Richard Hughes; both of Middlesex Co. Witness—John Mackay. Lib. H, p. 632.

1761, Dec. 24. Morris, William, of Middlesex Co. Int. Adm'x—Susannah Morris, widow of William. Fellowbondsman—Joseph Thorn; both of said place. Lib. H, p. 62.

1766, June 20. Morris, William, Jr., of Philadelphia. Int. Adm'rs—Samuel Preston Moore and Joseph Morris. Fellowbondsman—George Anthony Morris. Lib. 12, p. 421.

1761, Jan. 23. Morrison, Isaac, of Somerset Co. Ward, aged 16 years. Son of John Morrison, of said Co., deceased. Guardian—William Hamilton, of Baskingridge, said Co. Fellowbondsman—John Hill, of Elizabeth Town, Essex Co. Lib. G, p. 344.

1767, June 26. Morrison, James, of Sussex Co. Int. Adm'r—Isaac Morrison. Fellowbondsman—Thomas Anderson; both of New Jersey. Witness—William Parks. Lib. 13, p. 248.

1762, Dec. 31. Morrison, John, of Somerset Co. Ward, aged 14. Son of John Morrison, of said Co., deceased. Guardian—David Morrison. Fellowbondsman—James Morrison; both of said Co.
Lib. H, p. 207.

1761, Oct. 30. Morton, Elianor, Rebeckah and Elizabeth, of Chester Co., Pennsylvania, daughter of Andrew Morton of said place, deceased. They petition (severally) that they have lands devised to them in New Jersey by will of their uncle, John Morton, and make choice of John Knowles, of Chester Co. aforesaid as Guardian. Same day John Knowles appointed. Fellowbondsmen—Thomas Bright and Thomas Thompson, both of Gloucester Co., yeomen. Lib. 11, pp. 89, 90.

1759, Nov. 17. Moss, Richard, of Alloways Creek, Salem Co.; will of. Wife, Rebecca Moss, the plantation where I live during her life. Son, Abraham, said place; but, if he does not reach 21, then I give the place to my son, Isaac. Daughters, Sarah and Rebecca Moss, £50 each. Executors—wife, Rebecca, and son, Abraham. Witnesses—Page Perry, Henry Stubbines, Thomas Rice. Proved Feb. 18, 1761.
1760, Feb. 28. Inventory, £302.12.0, made by William Hancock and Henry Stubbins. Lib. 10, p. 498.

1770, Aug. 11. Mott, Ebenezer, of Northampton, Burlington Co., yeoman; will of. To my son, Ebenezer, £5. My house, land and personal estate to be for the use of my wife, and, at her death, the household goods to go to my six daughters, Sarah Downs, Barsheba Jones, Martha Fenimore, Abigal Rodes, Ruth Barnes and Huldah Mott. Son, John, rest of personal, as well as all land at death of my wife. Executrix—wife, Sarah. Witnesses—John Woolman, Isaac Powell, Job Coverley. Proved Dec. 3, 1770. Lib. 14, p. 347.

1769, May 15. Mount, George, of Lower Freehold, Monmouth Co.; will of. Wife, Sarah, £50 and moveable estate. Land to be sold and the proceeds to be given to my children, John, Francis, Thomas, Nanny Wetherill and Rebecca Gaa. Executors—sons, Francis Mount and John Wetherill. Witnesses—John Wetherill, Jr., Lewis Bastedo, Joseph Braiden. Proved April 2, 1770.
1770, March 28. Inventory, £41.3.3, made by Samuel Parent and Michael Johnston.
1774, Feb. 22. Account by Executors. Lib. 14, p. 244; Lib. 15, p. 515.

1764, June 22. Mount, Joseph, of Somerset Co. Int. Adm'x—Frances Mount, widow of said Joseph. Fellowbondsman—Samuel Brunson; both of said Co.
1764, June 13. Inventory, £518.13.8, made by Jeremiah Field and William Williamson.
1764, June 22. Letter filed, stating that the brother of Frances Mount is good security, as he has purchased a good farm.
Lib. H, p. 349.

1764, July 4. Mount, Simon and Mathias, of Somerset Co. Wards, aged 18 and 15 years. Children of Joseph Mount, of said Co. Their mother died "a long time ago," and father "was lately drowned," and they desire that their uncles, Nicholas Van Wickle, George Anderson and Jacob Suidam, may be made their Guardians.

1764, July 4. Guardians—Nicholas Van Wickle, of Middlesex Co., and Jacob Suidam, of Somerset Co. Fellowbondsman—James Dey, of Middlesex Co. Lib. H, p. 508.

1763, Feb. 19. Mount, William, of New Hanover, Burlington Co., innholder. Int. Adm'rs—Sarah Mount and Charles Collins. Fellowbondsman—Amos Wright; all of said Co.

1763, Feb. 17. Inventory, £57.4.7, made by Amos Wright and Joseph Arney.

1765, March 8. Account by Adm'rs. Lib. 11, 262.

1767, April 12. Muchmore, Ebenezer, of Piscataway, Middlesex Co.; will of. All my personal and real estate to be sold, except my trusty servant, William Hoy. Wife, Lucy, to have the profit of the money, to bring up my children till they are of full age; but she is to have £50 in her own right. Son, Daniel, 100 acres, which I bought of William Mercer, if it should not be sold. Son, Daniel, to have a gun, which I had with my wife. Daughters, Rebeckah, Catherine and Martha Muchmore, to have their share of the money, when they are of full age. My servant, William Hoy, is to have his freedom. Executors—my wife and friends, Micajah Dunn and Joseph Fitz Randolph. Witnesses—Nathan Wright, Philip Drake, Daniel Barto. Proved June 25, 1767.

1767, June 15. Inventory, £420.7.3, made by John Hepburn and John Dunn. Lib. I, p. 131.

1763, Aug. 13. Muirheid, John, of Middlesex Co. Int. Adm'rs—George Muirheid and Joseph Skelton. Fellowbondsmen—Thomas Story and Samuel Bayles; all of said Co.

1763, Aug. 11. Renunciation by Sarah Muirheid, the widow, in favor of Joseph Skelton and George Muirheid. Witnesses—Thomas Story and Samuel Bayles.

1763, July 27. Inventory, £388.7.0, made by Thomas Story, Samuel Bayles and Charles Barclay.

1765, Sept. 15. Account by both Adm'rs. Lib. H, p. 271.

1767, Aug. 29. Muisinger, Nicholas, of Bergen Co. Int. Adm'r—Conrad Wannemaker. Fellowbondsman—John Cornelius Banta; both of said Co. Witness—Stephen Voorhees.

1767, Aug. 28. Renunciation by Conrad Mysinger (the son), in favor of said Wannemaker. File No. 756 B.

1761, March 17. Mulford, Daniel, of Hopewell, Cumberland Co. Ward. Son of Aaron Mulford. Daniel makes petition and states that he had personal estate, lately fallen to him by the death of a brother, and he makes choice of John Miller to be his Guardian, till 21.

1761, March 17. Guardian—John Miller. Fellowbondsman—John Reeves; both of Hopewell, said Co. File No. 252 F.

1770, March 3. Mulford, Daniel, of Cape May Co.; pilot. Int. Adm'rs—Ruth Mulford (the widow) and Silas Swain. Fellowbondsman—James Swain; all of said Co. Witnesses—Henry Hand and Daniel Swain.
1770, Feb. 24. Inventory, £117.1.5, made by John Eldredge and Henry Hand.
1772, Jan. 21. Account by Ruth Stites (late Ruth Mulford) and Silas Swain, the Adm'rs. Lib. 15, pp. 70, 488.

1769, Jan. 26. Mulford, John, of Stow Creek, Cumberland Co. Int. Adm'rs—Eunice Mulford, Aaron Cresse and Jonathan Bowen, Jr., all of said place.
1769, Jan. 23. Inventory, £146.17.6, made by John Barracliff and Ananias Sayre, Jr.
1770, April 29. Account by all Adm'rs. Includes: "For keeping two young children, the eldest under 6 years of age, £10."
Lib. 13, p. 497; Lib. 15, p. 12.

1763, May 27. Mulford, Stephen, of Hopewell, Cumberland Co.; will of. Son, Stephen, all my interest in Tindals Island. Son, Isaac, my plantation on east side of old road, where I live, and he to pay to my son, Silas, £30, when 21, and £5 to my grandson, Thomas Mulford, when 21. My wife to have use of said place till John Mulford's time is out in it. Son, Nathaniel, rest of plantation that I bought of Job Shepard and Joseph Shepard, dec'd, after my wife's decease. Sons, Ephraim and Henry, my lands in Salem Co. that I bought of Elizabeth Dare. Daughter, Sarah, £20. Daughter, Filathea, also £20. Daughter, Rachel, £20. Wife, Hannah, the use of land I give to son, Nathaniel. Executrix—my wife. Witnesses—John Shepherd, Eunice Creesey, Ephraim Shepard. Proved Aug. 20, 1763.
1763, Aug. 19. Inventory, £229.9.9, made by Jacob Mulford and Ephraim Shepard. Lib. 11, p. 448.

1761, Feb. 28. Mulford, William, of Hopewell Twsp., Cumberland Co. Int. Adm'r—Benjamin Mulford. Fellowbondsmen—Job Shepherd and Peleg Bowen; all of said Hopewell.
1762, Jan. 26. Inventory, £56.7.3, made by Hugh Strathem and John Shepherd. Legacy due from his father's estate, in hands of John Miller; another due from estate of his sister, Mary Mulford, in hands of Benjamin Mulford; and one in hands of Rachel Mulford, Executrix of Moses Mulford. Lib. 10, p. 179.

1768, July 27. Mullady, Samuel, of Hunterdon Co. Int. Adm'rs—Charity Mullady and Alexander Biles. Fellowbondsman—Stephen Burrows; all of Hopewell, said Co.
1768, Oct. 25. Inventory, £114.5.0, of goods of Samuel Mullady, of Hopewell, tanner; made by Samuel Moore and Henry Woolsey.
Lib. 13, p. 438.

1760, Sept. 5. Mullen, Edward, of Northampton, Burlington Co., carpenter; will of. Woodland at the fork of Ancokus to be sold, and it is the same which I bought of Edward Tonkin and Henry Cooper as Ex'rs of Thomas Atkinson. The house and land my father gave me to be leased till the rents pay for it. Wife, Mary, the goods that I had with her, and the use of house and land where I live, and meadow adjoining Joseph Mullen and Joseph Farrington, while my widow. To the child yet unborn my house and land where I dwell, and also the said meadow, when 21, and also the residue after my wife's death or marriage, but, if the child do not live till 21, then the land to be sold and money paid to my wife and all my brothers and sisters, to wit, John Mullen, Joseph Mullen, Mary, wife of Joseph Burr, Meriby, wife of Daniel Wills, Elizabeth Mullen and Martha Mullin. Executors—father-in-law, John Monrow, and my wife, Mary. Witnesses—John Budd, William West, Daniel Jones, Jr. Proved July 29, 1766.

1765, Dec. 26. Inventory, £141.12.0, made by Zachariah Rossell and John Clark. Lib. 13, p. 30.

1765, April 29. Mullica, Erick, of Greenwich Twsp., Gloucester Co., yeoman; will of. Wife, Ann Catheren, ⅓ of my real and personal, after it be sold, and £50 more to bring up my children. Son, John Mullica, £30, when 21. Daughters, Rebecca and Sarah Mullica. Executor—friend, Thomas Denny. Witnesses—Mary Matson, Abraham Matson, John Wiksell. Proved July 27, 1765.

1765, May 28. Inventory, £173.13.10, made by Jacob Spicer and John Lock.

1766, Sept. 30. Account by Adm'r. Lib. 12, p. 166.

1761, Feb. 23. Mullicar, Jonas, of Greenwich Twsp., Gloucester Co. Int. Adm'r—Erick Mullicar. Fellowbondsman—Samuel Carman, yeoman; both of said place.

1761, Feb. 18. Inventory, £7.5.0, made by John Pinyard, Jr., and Joseph Carman. Lib. 10, p. 290.

1766, July 2. Mullicka, John, of Greenwich, Gloucester Co., yeoman; will of. Daughter, Cathrine MacCall, ⅓ of the plantation where I live; and, after her death, it shall be to my daughter, Sarah Mullacka. Daughter, Sarah Mullacka, the other two-thirds of said plantation. Daughter—Magdelena Parks, £10. Granddaughter, Hannah Carman, £10. Executors—daughters, Catherine MacCall and Sarah Mullica, and my friend, William Guest. Witnesses—Ezenezer Cook, Burroughs Abit, Elizabeth Cook. Proved March 31, 1767.

1767, March 28. Renunciation by Cathrine McCall. Signed by "Robert McCall," and wife, "Cathrine McCall." Witness—Mathew Gill.

1767, March 30. Inventory, £26.2.6, made by Ebenezer Cook and William Guest, Jr. Lib. 13, p. 130.

1765, Dec. 18. Mullin, William, of Trenton, Hunterdon Co.; will of. The house and land in possession of Joseph Reed, merchant; the tavern house and land; the plantation in possession of Jonathan Reed, and the lands left me by my father, John Mullin, or that fell to me as heir-at-law to my father, are all to be sold, and £600 are to be put to interest during the life of my mother, Elizabeth Stevenson, late Elizabeth Mullin, and the interest paid to her every year. The rest of money arising from the said sales I give to my sisters, Rebecca Reading, the wife of George Reading, Esq.; Sarah Biles, the widow of Thomas Biles, Elizabeth Mullin and Mary Mullin. Names Samuel Reading, son of George and Rebecca. Executor—Samuel Tucker, Esq. Witnesses—John Ely, Ralph Norton, Samuel John Wells. Proved March 21, 1766.

1772, Oct. 28. Account by Executor. Includes "Rents from lands, £120.2.3. Sales of lands, £2,000 (there being no chattles)."

Lib. 12, p. 411; Lib. 14, p. 503.

CALENDAR OF WILLS—1761-1770   303

1763, Dec. 1. Mulock, James, of Newton, Gloucester Co., "doctor of phisick." Int. Adm'x—Priscilla Mulock, widow. Fellowbondsman—Samuel Clement, Jr.; both of said place. Witness—John Hinchman.
Lib. 11, p. 441.

1770, July 30. Murdock, Andrew, of Salem Co. Int. Adm'r—John Shee, of Philadelphia, merchant. Fellowbondsman—Joseph Burroughs, of Town of Salem. Lib. 15, p. 74.

1754, Oct. 1. Murfin, Sarah, of Nottingham, Burlington Co., widow; will of. Grandson, John Murfin Williams, my red chest that was my son, Joseph's. Granddaughter, Ann Murfin, black trunk. Granddaughter, Sarah Large, and her sister, Mary Large, wheel, bed and other things. Son, William, and his son, John, ½ of the rest, and his daughter, Ann Murfin; the other ½ to my other grandchildren, Thomas, William and John, the children of my son, Robert Murfin, deceased. Executor—my son, William Murfin. Witnesses—Preserve Brown, Mary Brown, Joseph Scholey. Proved June 9, 1763.
1762, Aug. 14. Inventory, £86.6.2, made by William Bunting and John Abbott. Lib. 11, p. 320.

1761, April 18. Murphy, Timothy, of Penns Neck, Salem Co. Int. Adm'x—Mary Murphy, of said place, widow. Fellowbondsman—Edward Dougherty.
1761, April 14. Inventory, £474.15.2, made by Andrew Sinnickson and Francis Miles. Lib. 10, p. 436.

1769, June 12. Murray, Leonard, of City of Burlington. Int. Adm'r—Joseph Fenimore, of Wellingborough Twsp., Burlington Co. Fellowbondsman—Ephraim Phillips, of Burlington.
1769, Aug. 5. Inventory, £36.11.1, made by Daniel Ellis and William Borradaill. Lib. 14, p. 64.
1770, Oct. 19. Account of Adm'r. Lib. 15, p. 65.

1769, July 26. Murrell, Joseph, of Northampton, Burlington Co., carpenter; will of. Lot on New Street, and ½ my meadow, to be sold. Wife, Ann, all except my tools and gun, and use of house and land where I live, and ½ my meadow till my youngest daughter, Margaret, is 18. Son, William, my tools, when 21. Daughters, Mary Murrell and Margaret Murrell, £20 each. Son, William, to have the land. Executors—wife, Ann, and friend, Joseph Mullin. Witnesses—John Burr, Thomas Paxson, Thomas Shinn. Proved Nov. 28, 1769.
1769, Nov. 27. Inventory, £104.1.3, made by Daniel Jones, Jr., and Aaron Smith. Lib. 14, p. 136.

1766, Nov. 4. Murry, Robert, of Gloucester Co. Ward. Only son of Francis Murry, of said place, ferryman. He makes choice of friend, Benjamin Rambo, as his Guardian.
1766, Nov. 4. Guardian—Benjamin Rambo, shop joyner. Fellowbondsman—John Sparks, yeoman; both of Deptford, said Co.
Lib. 12, p. 383.

1764, June 16. Myres, Simon, of Pilesgrove, Salem Co., yeoman. Int. Adm'r—George Gouger. Fellowbondsmen—Burgin Ayars and Michael Rosz; all of said place, yeomen.
1763, Aug. 30. Inventory, £42.3.5, made by Burgin Ayars and James Ayars. Lib. 12, p. 72.

1761, May 31. Nailor, John, of Gloucester Co.; will of. Personal property to be sold, and the money put to interest, and all to be paid to my daughter, Elizabeth, when she is 18. Executor—John Wilkins, and he is to be the Guardian of my child. Witnesses—William Wood, Henry Treadway. Proved June 5, 1761.

1761, June 4. Inventory, £64.8.5, made by William Wood and Henry Treadway. Lib. 11, p. 101.

1761, Jan. 14. Neilson, Samuel, of New Brunswick, Middlesex Co.; will of. Wife, Mary, use of small house and lot in Kingston, that Nany Neilson now lives in, till my son, Samuel, is of age, when I give the same to him, and he is to pay my son, James, £5. Daughter, Mary Neilson, a cow. Son, James, one acre, where the gate is. Sons, Samuel, James and John, my books. Executors—Joseph Read, merchant, of New York; Phillip Kerney, attorney, of Perth Amboy; John Lyal, at New Brunswick, and Daniel Bayley. Witnesses—Thomas Combs, Jonathan Rolfe, Cornelius Hulls, John Disbrow. Proved Aug. 17, 1761.

1761, July 17. Renunciation by John Lyle, in favor of the widow.

1761, July 29. Renunciation by Joseph Reade and Philip Kearny.

1761, Aug. 17. Adm'x—Mary Neilson, widow of Samuel. Fellowbondsman—Whitehead Leonard, both of said Co. Three of the executors renounced, and Daniel Bayley, the other, removed to Maryland, and intends to remain there.

1761, Aug. 20. Inventory, made by Andrew Smyth and Peter Low. Lib. H, p. 25.

1762, Aug. 12. Neilson, Samuel, of Middlesex Co. Ward, aged 17 years. Son of Samuel Neilson, of said Co. Guardian—James Leonard, of Kingstown. Fellowbondsman—Christopher Hoogland, both of said Co. Lib. H, p. 172.

1765, May 8. Neitzert, John William. Certificate: The bearer hereof, John William Neitzert, was legitimately begotten of Christian parents, named Herbert Neitzert and Eve, who did formerly live here and were members of our congregation, in 1742, July 15, and baptised the 22 instant, and, when he attained the age of maturity, was taught the fundamentals of our Evangelical Reformed Religion, and admitted to the Sacrament. Now, the said Neitzart, intends to take a voyage to America, to fetch an heritage left behind by his father's brother, named Peter Neitzert, merchant, upon Rariton, for himself and his only co-heiress, Elizabeth, daughter of John Anthony Neitzert, deceased; and he is impowered by said heiress to have the foregoing granted to him; to which this Certificate is granted.

ANNA ELIZABETH NEITZERT.

The foregoing was written by a Minister of the County of Wild Runckel, named Daniel Miller. Lib. H, p. 595.

1761, Sept. 21. Nelson, Abraham, of Pilesgrove, Salem Co., yeoman; will of. Son, Jacob Nelson, farm where I live, that joins Oldmans Creek; also the marsh I bought of Benjamin Howell, in Penns Neck. Moveable estate to be sold, and my wife, Elenor, to have the profits from the money. Forty-two and a-half acres of land in Quhockin, to be sold, and my wife to have the profits of that money. Son, John, my apparel. Son, Abraham, 5 shillings. Daughter, Susanah, a like amount. Daughter, Elenor, £15. Daughter, Sarah, a

CALENDAR OF WILLS—1761-1770   305

like amount. Executors—son, Jacob, and John Mayhew. Witnesses—
Elizabeth Harding, Samuel Linch, Jr., Hance Blumer. Proved March
1, 1762.
1762, Feb. 12. Inventory, £324.12.5, made by Matthew Gill and
Robert Patterson. Lib. 11, p. 32.

1768, June 25. Nelson, Daniel, of Salem Co. Int. Adm'r—Anthony
Nelson. Fellowbondsmen—John Elwell and Benjamin Weathering-
ton; all of Piles Grove, said Co. Lib. 12, p. 524.

1762, June 2. Nevill, Samuel, Esq., of City of Perth Amboy, Middlesex Co.; will of. Wife, Mary Nevill, all my real and personal; and
she is to maintain my sister, Martha Morris. Executrix—my said
wife. Witnesses—R. L. Hooper, James Hooper, Philip Kearny.
1763, Sept. 1. Codicil. I also appoint my brother-in-law, Thomas
Walker, as Executor. Witnesses—Az. Dunham, Henry Cuyler, James
Hooper. Proved Oct. 31, 1764.
1764, Oct. 31. Renunciation by Mary Nevill, the widow. Witnesses—Joseph Vickers and John Heath. Lib. H, p. 467.

1761, Feb. 21. Nevius, Johannis, of Somerset Co., yeoman; will of.
Wife, Jannetie, the goods she brought from her father. Rest of real
and personal to be sold. Son, Marteynus, to have a double portion,
and the rest to be given to my wife, and 2 daughters, Willemtie and
Femmetie. Executors—my brothers, Peter and Martinus Nevius.
Witnesses—Joris Bergen, Cornelius Van Houtin, Abraham Lott.
Proved May 11, 1761.
1761, April 9. Inventory, £249.13.9, made by John Shippey and
Jacobus Van Arsdalen. Lib. G, p. 433.

1761, Aug. 6. Nevius, Martin, of Sowerland, Somerset Co., yeoman;
will of. Eldest son, Peter Nevius, £50. Daughters, Willemtye, Maria
and Leah, who are not married, £40 as an outset. Son, Martynes, my
plantation, for which he is to pay £850. Residue to be divided between daughter, Janetye; daughter, Willemtye; son, Lucus; my
grandchildren (the children of my son, Johanes, deceased), named
Willemtye, Fammetye and Martynes; my son, Martynes; daughter,
Maria, and daughter, Leah. Executors—sons, Peter, Lucus and
Martynes. Witnesses—Joseph Coernel, Peter Schenk, Peter Stryker.
Proved Aug. 16, 1766. Lib. I, p. 2.

1767, Jan. 22. Nevius, Pieter, of Blawenburgh, Somerset Co.; will
of. My wife to have my estate, while my widow. Personal estate
to all children. Son, Peter Nevius, £5. Son, James, lands where
I live. The lands in Hunterdon Co. to be sold. Son, Tobias, £200.
To the children of my daughter, Jenney, £200. Daughter, Joanna,
£200. Grandchild, Peter Voorheas, son of my daughter, Sarah, £200.
To 6 children of my daughter, Jenny, £33. Names grandson, Jacob
Corshow, and Mary Corshow. Executor—son, James. Witnesses—
Peter Van Voorhees, Henry Harrison, Henry Crusee. Proved Nov.
24, 1768. Lib. K, p. 7.

1769, Dec. 29. Newbold, John, of Chesterfield Twsp., Burlington
Co. Int. Adm'x—Mary Newbold, of same place. Fellowbondsman—
Samuel Coles, of Gloucester Co. Lib. 14, p. 124.
1770, Feb. 20. Inventory, £1,349.5.2½, made by William Wood and
Caleb Newbold.

20

1763, June 8. Newbold, Michael, of Chesterfield, Burlington Co., yeoman; will of. Son, John, £5 (I gave him already). Son, Cleayton, the farm I bought of William French, where he now lives; also the farm that I purchased of Thomas Staples, Sr., and Thomas Staples, Jr., in Springfield Twsp., and £500. Son, Joseph, plantation where I live and the other farm adjoining to it, and £200. Daughter, Ann Newbold, that lot in Kensington, Northern Liberties, Philadelphia, on Hanover St. Daughter, Rebecca Newbold, the next lot to it. Daughter, Mary Newbold, the next lot to it. Grandchildren, Rachel, Martha, Ann and Charlotte Newbold, the next lot. My daughter, Susannah Newbold, the lot in Northern Liberties that I bought of Mary Fairman, and lot in Chesterfield I bought of John Horner, and cedar swamp on Ancocus Creek. Daughters, Ann, Rebecca, Mary and Susannah Newbold, land in Bethlehem, Hunterdon Co. Wife, Ester, interest of £500. Executors—sons, John Cleayton and Joseph. My cousin, Michael Newbold, son of William and Susannah Newbold, to have £25 when 21. Witnesses—Caleb Newbold, Anthony Taylor, Henry Burr, Jr., John Robinson. Proved Aug. 12, 1763. Lib. 11, p. 381.

1763, Aug. 9. Inventory, £6,350.18.8, made by Samuel Emley, Jacob Lawrence and Anthony Sykes.

1762, April 22. Newell, Johannes, of Hunterdon Co., yeoman; will of. Daughter, Altia, wife of William Housel, £50. Granddaughter, Gertry, daughter of William Van Nest, that married my daughter, Margaret, £50, when 18. The land whereon my son, Hendrick, lived, and now in tenure of Henry Worly, I give to my granddaughter, Gertry, the daughter of my said son, Hendrick. Son, Peter, my homestead, except ⅓ of the profits I give to my wife, Gertry. Executor—son, Peter. Witnesses—Jacob Demott, Henry Worley, Edward Wilmot. Proved June 1, 1762.

1762, May 24. Inventory, £362.5.2, made by Edward Wilmot and David McKinney. Lib. 11, p. 339.

1764, Feb. 18. Newell, Mary, of Perth Amboy, Middlesex Co., widow. Int. Adm'r—Doctor James Newell, of Upper Freehold, Monmouth Co. (nearest relation). Fellowbondsman—William Burnet, of Perth Amboy.

1764, Feb. 18. Inventory, £25.1.6, made by James Brooks and Thomas Skinner, Jr. Lib. H, p. 330

1761, May 25. Newman, John, of Monmouth Co. Int. Adm'r—John Everingham. Fellowbondsman—Guysbert Guysbertson; both of said Co.

1761, May 22. Renunciation by Jane Hall, the mother of John Newman, in favor of John Everingham. Witnesses—James Killpatrick and John Bennet. Lib. G, p. 381.

1768, Feb. 20. Newman, John, of Shark River, Shrewsbury Twsp., Monmouth Co.; will of. To son, Joseph Newman, £3 and the land where he lives. Daughter, Catherine Croxon, £1. Son, Emanevel, 10 shillings. Son, David, £20. Daughter, Mary Dunigan, 40 shillings. To children of my son, Thomas, £20 (I have already paid Thomas). Son, Samuel, £1 and 10 shillings. My wife, Deliverance, is to have her living out of my estate. Son, John, the rest. Executors—my wife and my son, John. Witnesses—William Bruver, William Worton. Proved May 2, 1768.

1768, May 23. Inventory, £58.12.0, made by William Allgor and Benjamin Jackson. Lib. I, p. 243.

1761, Feb. 28. Newton, Caleb, of Cape May Co. Int. Adm'r—John Newton. Fellowbondsman—Christopher Foster; both of said Co. Witnesses—Ebenezer Johnson and Mehetabel Godfrey.
1761, Feb. 24. Inventory, £334.5.8, made by Christopher Foster and Ebenezer Johnson. Lib. 10, p. 162.

1760, Oct. 1. Nicholls, Robert, of Stow Creek, Cumberland Co., school master; will of. Friend, Samuel Davis, Sr., all my goods. Executor—said Samuel Davis. Witnesses—Solomon Hall, John Bereman, Theosallo Lennox. Proved June 24, 1761.
1761, June 17. Inventory, £17.1.0, made by Jonathan Davis and Silas Parvin. Lib. 11, p. 167.

1764, May 28. Nichols, Humphry, of Newark, Essex Co.; will of. Sons, Robert and Moses, about 23 acres at the Great Swamp, in the Great Neck of Newark, being the west part of a tract I bought of the Executors of Josiah Ogden. Daughter, Sarah Nicholls, £15. Rest of personal and real to my sons, Robert, Moses, Lewis and Isaac, and to my daughters, Sarah and Abigail Nicholls. Executors—sons, Robert, Moses and Lewis. Witnesses—John Crane, David Ogden, Isaac Ogden. Proved July 7, 1764. Lib. H, p. 443.

1761, June 20. Nicholson, Abel, of Waterford, Gloucester Co., yeoman; will of. Brother, Joseph, £5. My wife, Rebecah, live stock and furniture; and, as she is pregnant, I give her £25 yearly, while the child is a minor. Plantation to be rented and personal estate to be sold, and wife given £200. Rest to my brother-in-law, Daniel Hillman's son, James, and my brother, Joseph, Nicholson's son, Mark. My child to have the land when it is 21. Executors—my wife, and my father-in-law, Aaron Aaronson. Witnesses—James Johnson, Samuel Parr, Samuel Spicer. Proved Aug. 15, 1761.
1761, July 2. Inventory, £325.4.0, made by Henry Wood and John Shivers.
1768, July 20. Account by Isaac Burroughs, Executor, in conjunction with Rebecca Burroughs, late Rebecca Nicholson, deceased, who was surviving Executor of Abel Nicholson.
Lib. 11, p. 99; File 768 H.

1768, July 13. Nicholson, Abel, of Gloucester Co. Ward. Son of Abel Nicholson, of said Co. Petition of Joseph Nicholson, of said Co., uncle of said Abel, the son, stating that Abel, Jr., is under 14, and prays that he may be appointed Guardian of said minor. Signed by Joseph Nicholson.
Petition (no date) of sundry persons, relations and friends, of Abel Nicholson, an infant under 14, stating that the infant, by the will of his late father, Abel Nicholson, is entitled to a tract of land in said Co., to the value of £30 or more, and we are informed that Letters of Guardianship have been granted to Joseph Nicholson, uncle and next of kin to said infant; and Joseph, being the person to whom the inheritance will descend, in case of the death of said infant, is not qualified, by law to be Guardian, and for these and other reasons, we pray that the Letters may be vacated and set aside, and that Samuel Burroughs may be appointed till the infant is 14. Signed by Samuel Burrough, Sr., Joseph Burrough, Thomas Thorne, Isaac Burrough, Jr., Samuel Burrough, Jr., Rebecca Aaronson (grandmother to the child), Kezia Parr (an aunt), John Burrough, Jr., Isaac Burrough, Sr. (Vacated on a hearing before the Governor.)

1768, July 25. Guardian—Samuel Burrough, of Gloucester Co. Fellowbondsman—Joseph Burrough, of said Co. Whereas, Abel Nicholson at the time of his death, left a son named Abel, an infant under 14, and made his wife Guardian of said infant, who hath since departed this life, and whereas sundry persons, pray that Samuel Burrough may be appointed Guardian till said infant is 14; therefore he is appointed to that service.

1775, Nov. 28. Account by Samuel Burrough, the Guardian. "Cash paid a lawyer, against the claim of Isaac Burrough, in behalf of his wife, deceased, £1.2.4." "Cash paid a doctor for curing of Nicholson's hare lip, and settling his pallate, £10."

1775, Nov. 29. Petition of Abel Nicholson, of Waterford, Gloucester Co.; stating "that being under the care of my cousin, Samuel Burrough, this six years past, and now being of the age of fourteen years, do hereby nominate and appoint my said cousin" to act as Guardian, till I am 21 years. Witnesses—John Gallagher and William Black.

1775, Nov. 29. Guardian—Samuel Burrough. Fellowbondsman—Joseph Burrough, both of Gloucester Co.
   Lib. 13, p. 437; Lib. 15, p. 546; Lib. 15, p. 547; File 969 H.

1765, June 4. Nieukirk, Abraham, of Pilesgrove, Salem Co., yeoman; will of. Son, Isaac Nieukirk, 200 acres of my plantation where I live, and ½ the cedar swamp next to John Mayhew. Son, Jacob, 100 acres now under lease to Henry Hoveour, and ½ my swamp. Wife, Sarah, the rent of the place where Henry Hoveour lives. My wife to have the chest of drawers that came from Penn'a., till my daughter, Anna, comes to age. Daughters, Elizabeth, Rebecca and Mary, moveables. I desire that my sister-in-law, Magdalen Dollisen, would divide the clothing in the chest between my 3 daughters. Daughter, Anna, to have her part of the moveable estate. The 120 acres of land, now in possession of Allen Dunlap, to be sold. Executors—my brother, Mathew Nieukirk, and Jacob Richman. Witnesses—Elizabeth Rose, William McMongill, Jeremiah Garrison. Proved June 24, 1765.

1765, June 20. Inventory, £418.1.2, made by Jacob Elwell and Jacob Dubois.

1784, May 5. Account by Mathew Nieukirk, surviving Executor.
   Lib. 12, p. 227; Lib. 26, p. 224.

1768, Feb. 29. Nightingale, Sarah, alias Sarah Leddel, of Somerset Co. Ward. One of the children of William Leddel of said Co.; who makes choice of Dr. Moses Bloomfield, of Woodbridge, as her Guardian till 21. Signed, "Sarah Leddel."

1768, Feb. 29. Guardian—Moses Bloomfield. Fellowbondsman—John Moores; both of Middlesex Co.   Lib. I, p. 302.

1769, Feb. 2. Nipe, Jonathan. Int. Adm'r—Isaac Quigley.
   Lib. 14, p. 124.

1763, Oct. 8. Nitser, Peter, of Roxbury, Morris Co. Int. Adm'r—Hermon Cline, of Hunterdon Co. Fellowbondsmen—John Stine and Roelof Roelofson; both of Morris Co.

1763, Oct. 14. Inventory, £1,033.1.1, of goods of Peter Neitzert, shopkeeper; made by Roelof Roelofson and William Schuiler.

1766, March 14. Account filed by Adm'r.

1766, Oct. 29. Account filed by Adm'r.   Lib. H, p. 291.

1766, July 28. Nixon, Jeremiah, Sr., of Fairfield Twsp., Cumberland Co., yeoman; will of. Wife, Seabornfoy, her lawful dower, and use of dwelling house. Sons, Vavasus and Jeremiah, the plantation where I dwell. Sons, Reuben and William, the land I bought of Ebenezer Miller, and land I bought of Dickeson Shephard. Daughters, Judith Buck and Candace Fithian, £5 each. Daughter, Ruth, £20. Daughter, Susannah, £20. Executors—sons, Vavasus and Jeremiah. Witnesses—Carll Shaw, Joseph Norbury, Bathsheba Millar. Proved Nov. 21, 1766.
 1766, Sept. 2. Inventory, £209.10.8, made by Joseph Daten and Joseph Ogden.
 1768, Feb. 1. Account by both Executors.
Lib. 12, p. 323; Lib. 13, p. 324.

1763, April 14. Noblit (Noblelight), Joseph, of Alloways Creek, Salem Co., carpenter. Int. Adm'x—Latitia Noblit, widow. Fellowbondsman—William Oakford, yeoman; both of said place.
 1763, April 1. Inventory, £182.19.6, made by John Holme and William Oakford.
Lib. 11, p. 374.

1765, Jan. 10. Nochber, Leonard, of Morris Co.; will of. Wife, Margreata, all my estate; and, after her death, my son, Leonard, to have my lands; but if he die leaving no heir, then the lands to be sold, and money given to my grandchildren. To children of my oldest daughter, Anna Margreata, late wife of Henry Shankle, £200. To the children of my daughter, Anna Martha Trimmer, the wife of Mathias Trimmer, £200. To the children of my daughter, Mary Elizabeth Welsh, the wife of William Welsh, £200. Executors—son, Leonard, and Roelof Roelofson. Witnesses—Jacob Graa (Gray), Johan Andrew Hansell, Elizabeth Roelofson. Proved 1765. Lib. 12, p. 453.

1767, Dec. 19. Noe, Elias, of Middlesex Co.; will of. Brother, Marsh Noe, all my estate, except £5 to my brother, Daniel Noe, and £5 to my sister, Susannah Noe. Witnesses—Elias Marsh, Benjamin Marsh. Proved Jan. 22, 1768.
Lib. I, p. 202.

1769, Nov. 15. Norbury, Joseph, of Cumberland Co.; school master; will of. At present of said Co., but formerly of the Parish of St. Clements, in Liberty of Westminster, County of Middlesex, in England, taylor, son of Joseph Norbury of Little Share Lane, in said Parish, born in 1722, christened and registered in the Register Book of said Parish, which Kingdom I left in 1753. My plantation in New England Town to be sold. Children, Joseph, Heath and Mary, to have my money, when they come of age. My sons, Joseph and Heath, to be disposed of, as my Executors think best, till they are 14, then I wish them to be put to apprenticeship in Philadelphia to trades. My daughter, Mary, I leave to the discretion of her mother. Wife, Lida, the rest of my estate. Executors—Doctor Samuel Ward and my wife, Lydia. Witnesses—Abel Shepherd, William Fithian, Joseph Fithian. Proved Dec. 6, 1769.
 1769, Nov. 23. Inventory, £74.6.8, made by Abel Shepherd and Joseph Fithian.
Lib. 14, p. 162.

1766, May 2. Norcross, Joseph, of Hampton, Hanover Township, Burlington Co., shopkeeper; will of. Daughter, Rachel Norcross, £5, when 18. Real and personal estate to be sold and the money given to wife, Judith, and son, William, when he is 21. Executors—John Goldy, Sr., and Samuel Jones. Witnesses—Joshua Norcross, Thomas Platt, James Reynolds. Proved June 3, 1766.

1766, May 30. Renunciation by Samuel Jones and John Goldy.

1766, June 3. Adm'x—Judith Norcross, the widow, of Northampton Twsp. Fellowbondsmen—Thomas Budd and Marmaduke Fort; both of Burlington Co., yeomen.

1766, May 28. Inventory, £217.7.4, made by Thomas Budd and James Dobbin.

1767, May 20. Account by Judith Norcross, the Administratrix with will annexed. File No. 8031 C.

1762, May 29. Norris, John, of Borough of Elizabeth, Essex Co.; will of. Half of the land that I bought of John Oliver to be sold. Wife, Abigail, the use of all my estate till my sons are 21. My son, Henry, my homestead, that is bounded by land of John Lee, Samuel Oliver and Benjamin Brookfield, when he is 21. Sons, James and William, land on northeast of road. Son, Philip, the other ½ of the land I bought of John Oliver. Moveables to daughters, Sarah, Johannah, Abigail and Margreet. Executors—John Marsh and Samuel Shotwell. Witnesses—Phillip Porter, Abraham Lee, Joseph Morss, Jr. Proved July 22, 1762. Lib. H, p. 169.

1763, Feb. 9. North, Daniel, of Hopewell, Hunterdon Co. Int. Adm'r—Timothy Smith, of said place. Fellowbondsman—Theophilus Severns, of Trenton, said Co. Witness—Joseph Warrell.

1763, Feb. 23. Inventory, £150.9.2, made by Seth Field and George Corwin. Lib. 11, p. 338.

1758, Aug. 31. Norton, Mary, of Cape May Co., spinstress; will of. Brother, Isaac Reevs, my Bible, and to his wife, Mercy, a suit. To Mrs. Phebe Young a suit. To Lydia Smith, the wife of Carman Smith, rest of apparel. To Nathaniel Ogden, son of David Ogden, Esq., £5. One-third of residue to Martha Smith, daughter of Carman Smith, and ⅔ to Mary Hoskins, daughter of the said Lydia Smith, and, if either of the daughters of Lydia Smith die, then to the survivor. Executors—Carman Smith and Lewis Cresse. Witnesses—Jonadab Jenkins, Joseph Hildreth, James Hildreth, Nathaniel Jenkins. Proved Sept. 26, 1766.

1766, Sept. 22. Inventory, £60.16.5½, made by Benjamin Stites and Joshua Hildreth. Lib. 12, p. 336.

1763, June 2. Nutt, Levi, of Springfield, Burlington Co., yeoman. Int. Adm'x—Ann Nutt. Fellowbondsman—William Lovett Smith; both of said place. Lib. 11, p. 314.

1763, July 28. Inventory, £814.3.6, made by Thomas Pryor, Jr., and William Elton.

1764, Dec. 12. Account by Ann Nutt.

1761, Aug. 17. Nuttman, John, of Elizabeth Town, Essex Co. Ward, aged 14 years, son of Isaac Nuttman, of said place. Guardian—Samuel Nuttman. Fellowbondsman—Isaac Lyon; both of Newark, said Co. Witness—John Smyth. Lib. H, p. 12.

1760, Oct. 10. Ogborne, Samuel, of Middletown, Monmouth Co.; will of. Daughter-in-law, Mary Ogborne, widow of my son John,

CALENDAR OF WILLS—1761-1770

use of part of the house. Daughter, Elizabeth Ogborne, use of part of the house, while single. Grandsons, Samuel and William Ogborne, my farm; and Samuel is to pay to his 4 sisters, viz., Mary Ogborne, Sarah Ogborne, Hannah Ogborne and Ann Ogborne, £15 to each; and William is to pay to his 5 sisters, viz., Elizabeth, wife of William Applegate, Mary Ogborne, Sarah Ogborne, Hannah Ogborne and Ann Ogborne, £12 to each. Daughter, Elizabeth, to have £60, to make her equal with my daughters, Mary and Abigail. Daughter, Sarah, wife of Obadiah Holmes, £63. Rest of goods to daughters, Mary, Sarah, Abigal and Elizabeth. Executors—friend James Mott, and my sons-in-law, Obadiah Holmes and Edward Taylor, Sr., all of Middletown. Witnesses—George Taylor, Nathaniel Tilton, John Taylor. Proved Aug. 4, 1768. Lib. K, p. 22.

1765, Feb. 16. Ogden, David, of Fairfield Twsp., Cumberland Co., yeoman; will of. Wife, Sarah, £50, and use of the plantation, till son, Norton, is 21. Son, Norton, all my land which I hold by deed of gift of my father, David Ogden, deceased. Daughter, Mary Ogden, £8, when 18. Daughter, Sarah Ogden, £5, when 18. Executors —father-in-law, Thomas Harris, and my wife, Sarah. Witnesses— Daniel Lummus, Nathan Lawrance, Joseph Norbury.

1767, April 2. Codicil. The marsh on Jones' Island, which my father gave to Jonathan Learance and Abigail Learance, to be sold. Witnesses—Joseph Ogden, Theophilus Elmer, Eleazar Smith. Proved April 21, 1767.

1767, April 16. Inventory, £127.7.11, made by John Bower and Joseph Daten. Lib. 12, p. 479.

1765, July 1. Ogden, David, of Roxbury, Morris Co.; will of. Real and personal estate to be sold. Son, Gilbard, £45. Daughter, Elizabeth, £30. Daughter, Nancee Salmon, £30. Daughter, Mary, £30. Granddaughter, Nancee Ogden, my bed. Grandson, David Ogden, my cane. Son, Gabriel, my gun. Son, David, 7 shillings. Son, John, £25. My daughter, Abigail, £15. Sons, Joseph, Amos, Nathan and Gabriel, the rest. Executors—son, Amos; and kinsman, Daniel Budd. Witnesses—Constant King, George King, Josiah Crane. Proved June 12, 1767. Lib. I, p. 156.

1761, April 22. Ogden, Joseph, of Borough of Elizabeth, Essex Co., cordwainer; will of. Wife, Esther, ⅓ of personal and use of my real estate. To First Presbyterian Church of Elizabeth Town, £100. My brother, Daniel Ogden, ½ of the rest of moveables. To children of my sister, Johannah, deceased, the other ½, viz., John Meeker, Joanna Baldwin (the wife of Nathan Baldwin), Rebecca Squire (the wife of David Squire), Mary Potter (the wife of Amos Potter), Hannah Hicks (the wife of Samuel Hicks), Phebe Meeker (the wife of Stephen Meeker), and Unis Alling (daughter of John Alling), share and share alike. Executors—friends, Samuel Woodruff, Robert Ogden and William Herriman. Witnesses—Abner Woodruff, Thomas Tyson, Daniel Dayton. Proved May 30, 1761. Lib. H, p. 63.

1768, Sept. 15. Ogden, Joseph, of Morris Co., doctor; will of. Wife, Grais, £50. Oldest son, Gabral, £5, besides what I gave him by deed. Daughters, Elesabeth, Mary and Eme, £30 each. Son, Justus Swazey Ogden, lot near the Raraton Landing, being part of a lot formerly belonging to Peter Bodine. Rest of land to be sold and the money to be given to my 5 sons, Garabrant, Joseph, Stephen, Ames and Benjamin. Executors—Andrew Miller, Jr., and David Estill. Witnesses—Ebenezer Titus, Daniel McKinney. Proved Nov. 21, 1769.

1768, Nov. 21. Renunciation, made by David Estill and Andrew Millar, Jr. Witness—Abraham Ogden.

1768, Nov. 27. Adm'r—Gabriel Ogden, of Somerset Co. Fellowbondsman—Jonathan Stiles, of Morris Co.

Lib. K, p. 15; Lib. I, p. 364.

1762, July 15. Ogden, Josiah, Esq., of Newark, Essex Co.; will of. All real and personal estate to be sold. Wife, Mary, £250. The interest of £400 to be paid to my daughter, Catherine Longworth, and, at her death, the £400 to be divided among her children. Son, David, ¼ part of the money from said sale, and a like amount to son Jacob. Grandchildren, the children of my daughter Catherine, also ¼ part; the names of whom are David, Caleb, Abigail, James, Jacob and Catherine. Grandsons, John Ogden and Henry Ogden, sons of my son Josiah, deceased, ⅙ part of residue. Granddaughters, Sarah Banks and Catherine Banks (daughters of my daughter Mary Banks, deceased), and my grandson, Josiah Ogden Banks (son of James Banks, Jr.), ⅛ part of re idue, when they are 21. The money that shall be due to me from the estate of my deceased son-in-law, David Ogden, Jr., is to be taken from the money given to children of my daughter, Catherine Longworth. Executors—sons, David and Jacob, and my son-in-law, Isaac Longworth. Witnesses—Isaac Myer, Joseph Hedden, Jr., Jabez Harrison.

1762, Sept. 13. Codicil. To grandchildren, viz., Josiah Banks, Jacob Banks, David Banks and Joseph Banks, £15 each, when 21. To Trinity Church, at Newark, my silver cup, for the use of said church. Witnesses—Isaac Myer, Thomas Pool, Abraham Ogden. Proved May 20, 1763. Lib. H, p. 372.

1769, Nov. 14. Ogden, Justus Swayze, of Roxbury Twsp., Morris Co. Ward. Son of Joseph Ogden, of said place, deceased; makes choice of Caleb Swayze as his Guardian.

1769, Nov. 14. Guardian—Caleb Swayze, of said place. Fellowbondsman—John Carnes, of Mendham Twsp., said Co. Lib. K, p. 223.

1763, March 14. Ogden, Mary, of Fairfield Twsp., Cumberland Co.; will of. Son, Eleazar Smith, the grain and swine. Daughter, Marthar Elmer, long cloak. Daughter, Rebecca Smith, my saddle. Daughter, Sarah Smith, £4. Daughter, Abigail Smith, £4. To all my daughters, Mary Banks, Esther Mayhise, Martha Elmer, Rebecca Smith, Elizabeth Smith, Sarah Smith and Abigail Smith, the remainder. Executors—Theodorus Elmer and my son, Eleazar Smith. Witnesses—Joseph Bateman, Theophilas Elmer, Rebecca Smith. Proved April 9, 1763.

1763, April 8. Inventory, £110.12.3, made by Theophilus Elmer and Joseph Bateman. Lib. 11, p. 401.

1767, June 5. Ogden, Moses, of Borough of Elizabeth, Essex Co.; will of. Sons (all under 19), John Couzens, Barne, Moses, Aaron and David, all my lands. Makes mention of brothers, Robert and David. Wife, Mary, £100. To my daughters, Frances, Anne and Mary Couzens, rest of personal estate, when 18. My brother, David, and my wife, to be Guardians of children, but, in case of the death

of my brother, then I devise my kinsman, Oliver Spencer, to act. Executors—my kinsman, Robert Ogden, Jr., my son, John Couzens, and my wife, while she remains my widow. If both Robert Ogden, Jr., and John Couzens Ogden should die, then my will is that the said David Ogden and my kinsman, Timothy Edwards, be Executors. Witnesses—William Halstead, Stephen Wheeler, Uzal Woodruff.
1768, Oct. 10. Codicil. Wife, Mary, is pregnant, and the child is to be provided for. Witnesses—David Meeker, Uzal Woodruff, Stephen Wheeler. Proved Dec. 26, 1768. Lib. K, p. 40.

1767, April 6. Ogden, Nathaniel, of Fairfield, Cumberland Co., yeoman; will of. Son, Jeremiah, all my land, and he is to pay to my daughter, Phebe, £25, when she is 21. Personal estate to be sold and money given to the said children when they are 21, but, if they die before that time, then both real and personal is to go to my brothers and sisters. Executors—my uncle, Joseph Ogden, Esq., and my brother, Jason Ogden. Witnesses—Abigail Ray, Tamer Seeley, Joseph Norbury. Proved April 21, 1767.
1767, April 20. Inventory, £214.3.3, made by Theophilus Elmer and Ephraim Harris.
1774, Nov. 25. Account by Jason Ogden, surviving Executor.
Lib. 13, p. 162; Lib. 15, p. 497.

1764, March 20. Ogden, Stephen, of Somerset Co. Int. Adm'x— Elizabeth Ogden, widow of said Stephen. Fellowbondsman—Elipielet Whitaker; both of said Co.
1764, April 17. Inventory, made by John Lyon and John Collyer.
Lib. H, p. 333.

1761, Feb. 18. Ogden, Thomas, of Elizabeth Town, Essex Co. Int. Adm'r—John Clawson, bricklayer. Fellowbondsman—John Black, ship carpenter; both of said place. Witness—Elizabeth Hetfield.
Lib. G, p. 371.

1768, Jan. 22. Ogden, Thomas, Jr., of Fairfield, Cumberland Co. Int. Adm'x—Abigail Ogden, widow. Fellowbondsman—Joseph Ogden, Esq.; both of said place.
1768, Jan. 19. Inventory, £179.13.0, made by Joseph Ogden and Ephraim Harris. Lib. 13, p. 325.

1765, Oct. 12. Oggburn, Mary, of Middletown, Monmouth Co. Int. Adm'r—William Applegate, "a relation of Mary." Fellowbondsman— Edward Taylor; both of said place, yeomen. Witness—David Hance.
1765, Oct. 15. Inventory made by Joseph Golden and Richard Crawford. Lib. I, p. 5.

1768, March 7. Olbers, Nicholas, of Upper Allaways Creek Precint, Salem Co. Int. Adm'r—Richard Wistar, of Philadelphia, merchant.
1768, March 5. Inventory, £18.16.0, made by George Dickinson and Benjamin Thompson. Lib. 13, p. 334.

1760, April 23. Oldden, Mary, of Middlesex Co.; will of. Sister, Susannah Stokes, £20. "Cozen," Bershebay Olden, £5. Brother, John Olden, sheets and pillow cases. Brother, Joseph Olden, 20 yards of linen. Brother, David Oldden, 20 yards. "Cozen," Samuel Olden, £5. To Joseph Olden, son of Joseph, £2. To Ann Oldden, daughter of

James Olden, £2. To Carthine Olden, daughter of said James, £2. To Amey Olden, daughter of Joseph Olden, £2. To the child of Joseph Olden, not yet born, spoons. Amey Olden, daughter of Joseph, mentioned. The rest of my estate I give to my brothers and sisters, and my "cozen," Bershebay Olden, Susannah, John, James, Joseph, David, Thomas and Benjamin. Executor—brother, Thomas Olden. Witnesses—John Clark, Ursulla Worth, Ebenezer Scott. Proved Sept. 28, 1763. Lib. H, p. 308.

1770, Oct. 28. Olden, Thomas, of Piscataway, Middlesex Co.; will of. To the Presbyterian Church at Bound Brook, in Bridgwater, £60. Daniel Blackford, of Bridgwater, is indebted to me, which sum I give to his children. Residue to the children of my brothers and sisters. Executors—Daniel Blackford and Jeremiah Field. Witnesses—Michael Field, Elias Golden, Elias V. Court. Proved Nov. 21, 1770.
1770, Nov. 2. Inventory, £1466.8.0, made by Michael Field and Elias Van Court. Lib. K, p. 253.

1764, May 10. Olden, William, of Piscataway, Middlesex Co., yeoman; will of. Wife, Abegal, £100, and the use of my real. Granddaughter, Abigail Hutchens, 10 acres of my home place, opposite the houses of Joseph and John Ross; also 2 acres of meadow; but, if she die, then to be the right of her sister, Anne Hutchens. My grandson, William Degrote, the rest of my home place and other real, except that in a lease given to John Hutchens, and he is to pay £50 to his sister, Elizabeth, and £50 to his sister, Sophia, and £50 to his brother, John Degrote. To the children of daughter Elizabeth, money to each. Goods are to be sold and money given to daughters, the wife of John Degrote and the wife of John Hutchens. The land which my wife, Abigail, bought of Benjamin Bond, is to be to her. Executors—Reune Runyon, Leffart Sebring and Jeremiah Field. Witnesses—Thomas Oldden, John Ross, Jr., Brice Riky. Proved Oct. 30, 1764.
1764, Oct. 26. Inventory, £343.7.2, made by Peter Williamson and William Wortman. Lib. H, p. 465.

1763, Feb. 22. Olge, Jeremiah, of Cumberland Co. Int. Adm'r—Robert Peters. Fellowbondsman—Nebecunezer Riggin; both of Morris River, said Co. Witnesses—Ezekiel Bennett and David Reeve.
1763, Feb. 5. Inventory, £38.9.9, made by Joseph Lord and Peter Massy.
1763, Dec. 27. Account by Adm'r. Lib. 11, p. 410.

1766, Feb. 27. Oliver, David, of Elizabeth Borough, Essex Co., yeoman; will of. Son, David, the northwest ½ of my plantation, which binds lands of Ephraim Terrill. Sons, Samuel and Ichobad, the southeast ½; also a tract in Raway that I bought of John Marsh and Samuel Shotwell, as Ex'rs of John Norris. Sons, David, Samuel and Ichobad, my salt meadows. Wife, Zerviah, my negro wench, Phebe, and, at my wife's death, she is to be sold, with her issue, and the money given to my daughters, Jemima Ward, Sarah Oliver and Zerviah Oliver. My half part of land above the mountain to be sold, and is the same which I have in partnership with Ephraim Terrill, and the money to be given to my said three daughters. Wife to have use of lands till sons are of age. Mother-in-law, Elizabeth Oliver, £7 yearly. Executors—my brother, John Oliver, and my

friend, John Wood. Witnesses—David Terrill, Josiah Terrill, Abraham Clark. Proved June 3, 1766.
1768, Aug. 11. Inventory, £400.4.0, made by Amos Morss and Benjamin Shotwell. Lib. I, p. 36.

1761, Dec. 16. Opdyck, Elizabeth, of Maidenhead, Hunterdon Co. Int. Adm'r—John Opdyck, of Amwell, said Co. Fellowbondsman—Joseph Inslee, Jr., of said Maidenhead.
1761, Dec. 15. Inventory, £50.12.6, made by James French and Cornelius Slacht. Lib. 11, p. 133.

1764, June 9. Orgill, John, of Essex Co. Int. Adm'r—William Harrison, of Barns Island, New York, yeoman. Fellowbondsman—Ephraim Frazee, of Elizabeth Town, Essex Co., yeoman. (The said Adm'r was one of the creditors, and gave bond at the instance of St. George Talbert, the largest creditor). Witnesses—Samuel Ogden and Robert Ogden. On the back of the bond was written: "The letter of Adm'n on this bond was never granted, owing to the discovery of a great fraud in the pretended creditor, St. George Talbott." Dated June 28, 1764. Signed, "John Smyth."
"This bond was received into the office the 28 June, 1764. John Smyth." File Nos. 3391-3392 G.

1770, March 5. Osbern, Cooper, of Essex Co. Ward. Son of Nathaniel Osbern, of said place, deceased. Guardian—Thomas Woodruff, Esq. Lib. K, p. 185.

1770, Jan. 16. Osbern, Timothy, of Newark Twsp., Essex Co. Int. Adm'rs—James Osbern and Moses Osbern. Lib. K, p. 156.

1764, Aug. 8. Osborn, Anne, of Shrewsbury, Monmouth Co.; will of. Daughter, Rebaco Swane, a platter. Daughter, Catrin, "bedde," and she is to have schooling. Executor—Samuel Longstreet. Witnesses—Andrew Allen, Faith Tilton, Thomas Bell. Proved Oct. 9, 1764.
[No date]. Inventory of the estate of Anne Osborn, widow, made by Thomas Bell and Samuel Osborn. Lib. H, p. 495.

1759, Nov. 18. Osborn, James, of Shrewsbury, Monmouth Co.; will of. Wife, Anne, half of my plantation, and half the acre lots on south side of Squan River, and half my right down the beach. Son, John, other half of the above. Daughter, Rebecca Swain, £50. Daughter, Kathrine Osburn, £55. Executors—Richard Longstreet and my brother, Samuel Osborn. Witnesses—Thomas Bell, Remembrance Lippincott, Mary Wilkens. Proved April 18, 1761.
[No date.] Inventory, made by John Denman and Thomas Bell.
Lib. G, p. 381.

1760, May 8. Osborn, Joseph, of Borough of Elizabeth, Essex Co.; will of. Son, James, the place I live on, joining lan'd I sold to Henry Pirson, lying for 50 acres; also my land in the Great Swamp by the Long Hill, in Morris Co. Sons, Thomas, Enos and Jesse, the other ½ part of my 50 acres in the said Swamp. Daughters, Sarah, Abirgal and Desier, my moveable estate. Executors—friend, Caleb Brown, and Amos Day. Witnesses—John Ogden, William Parsel, John Nester. Proved March 5, 1761.
1761, March 9. Inventory, £17.13.5, made by William Broadwell and Silvanus Totten. Lib. H, p. 16.

1765, Sept. 20. Osborne, Richard, of Cape May Co.; will of. Brother, Nathan Osborne, all of my land, only my wife's part during her life; and then all that land to Philip Godfrey's eldest son, Philip, and said Philip Godfrey, Jr., is to pay to his brother, Nathan Godfrey, £50. Brother, Nathan, ½ the moveable estate, and my sister, Ruth Godfrey, the other ½. To Daniel Smith, Jr., the son of Jeremiah Smith, £20, but, if Daniel die before he comes of age, then it is to go to Jesey Smith, also a son of Jeremiah, and, if Jesey die, then to his brother, James Smith. Executors—brother-in-law, Philip Godfree, and cousin, David Smith. Witnesses—John Willets, John Nickelson. Proved Nov. 2, 1765.
1765, Dec. 12. Inventory, £408.3.10, made by John Willets and Levi Billings.
1767, April 22. Account of Philip Godfrey, the Executor.
Lib. 12, p. 347.

1761, Sept. 27. Osler, Samuel, of Gloucester Co.; will of. Wife, Patience, all moveable estate, and my plantation while my widow. Son, Samuel, the plantation, and, when he comes to 21, he is to pay to my son, Thomas, £30, and to each of my daughters, Barsheba, Mary and Hannah, £10. Executors—my wife and Joseph Osler. Witnesses —John Stocker, Joseph Osler. Proved Nov. 16, 1761.
1761, Nov. 10. Inventory, £138.16.10, made by Samuel Burrough, Sr., and Henry Wood. Lib. 11, p. 102.

1751, Feb. 15. Outwater, Thomas, of Monaykie, in Precinct of New Barbadoes, Bergen Co., yeoman; will of. My wife to have a negro wench and no more. Children of my son, Frans, deceased, Thomas, Catharine, Yonete and Mary, 1/9 of my estate; my son, John, 1/9; my son, Jacob, 1/9; my son, Peter, 1/9; my son, Thomas, deceased, his children (Catherine, Thomas, Mary, Jacobus and Anetie) 1/9; my grandson, Thomas Romyn, 1/9; the children of "Dater" Elisabeth, 1/9; the children of "Dater," Yueke, (namely, Roelef, Geret and Dericke) 1/9; my "dater," Ann, 1/9, and my daughter, Trintie, 1/9. My land at Moneyky is layed out in 8 lots (being where I live), and son, Jacob, to have Nos. 1 and 4, 5 and 7; my grandchildren, the children of my son, Thomas, dec'd, (viz., Catherine, Thomas, Mary, Jacobus and Annatie), lots 2, 3, 6 and 8. Wife, Jannetie, the goods mentioned in a writing dated 1747-'8, Feb. 10. Executors—son, John, Johanes Slot and Claas Romyn. Witnesses—Henry Earl, Abraham Allen and Poulus Vanderbeck. Proved March 23, 1763. Lib. H, p. 557.

1767, April 9. Overfield, Peter, of Kingwood Twsp., Hunterdon Co. Int. Adm'r—Peter Overfield. Fellowbondsmen—Isaac Leet and Joshua Waterhouse; all of said place.
1767, April 8. Inventory, £784.16.5, made by Isaac Leet and Joshua Waterhouse. Lib. 13, p. 208.

1761, March 2. Owen, John, of Elizabeth Borough, Essex Co., weaver; will of. Son, Daniel, 25 acres joining John Meeker. Son, Jedediah, my homestead place, and 10 acres joining Thomas Squier. Wife, Sarah, £5. Daughters, Mary, Rebekah, Hannah and Sarah, rest of personal estate. Executors—my wife and friend, John Meeker. Witnesses—John Clark, Samuel Hicks, Jacob Winans. Proved March 16, 1761.
1761, March 9. Inventory, made by James Bonnel and Samuel Hicks. Lib. G, p. 399.

CALENDAR OF WILLS—1761-1770 317

1764, Oct. 22. Pack, Benjamin, of Rahway, Middlesex Co. Int. Adm'r—Jacob Pack, the only son. Fellowbondsman—Samuel Jaquess, Jr.; both of said Co. Lib. H, p. 372.

1762, Aug. 10. Pack, Isaac, of Woodbridge, Middlesex Co. Int. Adm'r—John Moores. Fellowbondsman—Joseph Moore; both of said place. (Mary Pack, the widow, renounced in favor of John Moores.) Witness—Samuel Jones. Lib. H, p. 167.

1764, March 16. Pack, Zachariah, of Woodbridge, Middlesex Co., weaver; will of. Wife, Ruth, a horse and saddle. Brother, Jacob Pack, my apparel. Friend, Jonathan Coddington, a hat. Wife, Ruth, use of all my estate to bring up my children, till the youngest is 21; and then all real and personal to be sold and money given to my children, viz., William, Isaac, Hannah Pack, and my wife. Executors—friends, Jonathan Bishop and Jonathan Brooks. Witnesses—Ephraim Cutter, David Jaques, Joseph Moore. Proved April 12, 1764. Lib. H, p. 429.

1766, Feb. 1. Page, Joseph, of Fairfield, Cumberland Co.; will of. Son, Jonathan, northwest part of my plantation. Son, David, rest of said farm. The other plantation, below Dividing Creek, to be sold, and money divided among my grandchildren, Daniel Page, Ambrose Page and John Page, when they are 21, but Mary Page, my son's widow, is to enjoy the place till it is sold. Daughters, Martha and Hannah, the remainder. Executor—son, David. Witnesses—William Paullin, William Paullin, Jr., David Shepherd. Proved June 12, 1767.
1767, June 9. Inventory, £214.15.11, made by David Shepherd and William Newcomb. Lib. 12, p. 484.

1759, Sept. 13. Page, William, of New Windsor Twsp., Middlesex Co., yeoman; will of. Son, Benjamin, the land this side of Mire Run, at his death, to his son, William, and William is to pay to his brother, Thomas, and his oldest sister, £5 each. My granddaughter, Mary Arey, a bed, when she is 18. Granddaughter, Rodey Arey, pans. Land on north side of Muddy Brook, where Isaac Arey lives, to be sold, and money to be given to Isaac Arey's children, when they come of age. Executor—William Cubberley. Witnesses—John Taylor, Thomas Walton, Kezia Cubberly.
1760, Sept. 8. Codicil. Cousin, Elizabeth Page, £5. Proved April 6, 1765.
1765, April 2. Inventory, £171.15.6, made by John Abbott and Isaiah Robins. Lib. 12, p. 133.

1769, May 8. Pagett, John, of Salem Co., farmer; will of. Daughter, Prudence Hall, 5 shillings. Wife, Rebecca, all my lands and moveable estate. Executrix—my wife. Witnesses—Nathaniel Hancock, Benjamin Corliss, Edward Bradway. Proved May 13, 1769.
Lib. 13, p. 542.

1762, March 25. Pain, Isaac, of Mendham, Morris Co., yeoman; will of. Wife, Abigail, household goods, etc. Sons, Isaac and John, £50 each. Daughters, Deborah, Sarah, Mary and Ruth, £10 each, when they are 18. Executors—my wife and Samuel Roberts. Witnesses—Henry Clark, William Hulburd, Alexander Aikman. Proved April 15, 1762.

1762, April 3. Inventory, made by Robert Adams and Henry Clark. Includes house and 122 acres of land, £114. Lib. H, p. 364.

1764, March 15. **Palmer, Nathaniel,** of Chester Town, in Kent Co., (Del.), merchant. Int. Adm'r—Daniel Ellis. Fellowbondsman—Samuel Allinson; both of Burlington. Witness—Joseph Read.
Lib. 11, p. 537.

1762, March 6. **Pancoast, Caleb,** late of Philadelphia, but now of Burlington Co., bricklayer; will of. Wife, Hannah, a bed. Rest of personal and real to be sold. Wife and my daughter, Ann, to have ½ when Ann is 18. Son, William, the other ½, when 21. Executors —brothers, David Pancoast and William Andrews. Witnesses—Henry Delatush, Aaron Pancoast, Hannah Lippincott. Proved March 11, 1762. Lib. 11, p. 194.

1762, Nov. 1 **Pancoast, Joseph,** of Mansfield Twsp., Burlington Co., yeoman; will of. Wife, Thomasin, the profit of my farm. Daughter, Mary Folkes, £30. Daughter, Thomasin Wright's 3 daughters, £30. Daughter, Anna Bacon's 2 children, viz., Daniel and Mary, £20 between them, Elizabeth being heretofore considered. Daughter, Elizabeth Curtis' 2 children, viz., Thomas and Grace, £30. Daughter, Susannah Willkins' 3 sons, £30. Daughter Pheby's children, £23. Grandson, John Pancoast (son of my son John), and Joshua and Joseph Wright (sons of my daughter Thomasin Wright), 10 shillings each. To the Mansfield meeting, £5. Son John's 2 daughters, viz., Thomasin and Hannah, £3 each; and to Mary Butler's 3 children, £3. Son Thomas' 4 daughters, £5 each. Son Benjamin's 3 daughters, £5 each. Grandson, Thomas Pancoast (son of my son, Thomas), my lands in the mountains, lying on a ranch of Delaware river, called Pawlins Cut. Grandson, Joseph (son of my son Benjamin), farm where I live, when 21. To my 3 daughters, £50 each. To grandson, Thomas, and my grandson, Joseph (son of my son Benjamin), and my grandson, Joseph (son of my son John), my swamp on Wading river. Executors—kinsman, Thomas Scattergood, and my son-in-law, Thomas Folkes, and my grandson, Thomas Pancoast. Witnesses—Thomas Newbold, Samuel Rockhill, John Curtis. Proved Oct. 27, 1766.

1766, Jan. 18. Codicil. My granddaughter, Hannah Young, is dead, and I give ½ of her share to my granddaughter, Thomasin Shourds, and the other half to my granddaughter Mary Butler's children. Witnesses—John Curtis, Samuel Rockhill, Ruth Southward. Proved Oct. 27, 1766.

1766, Nov. 3. Inventory, £701.6.0, made by Henry Delatush and John Imlay. Lib. 13, p. 18.

1769, Sept. 9. Account of Thomas Foulke, Thomas Scattergood and Thomas Pancoast, the Executors. Lib. 14, p. 74.

1764, Sept. 10. **Pancoast, Meribah,** of Chesterfield, Burlington Co., widow. Int. Adm'r—Samuel Allen, of Nottingham Twsp. Fellowbondsman—Mahlon Thorn, of Mansfield; both of said Co.
Lib. 12, p. 16.

1764, Aug. 25. Inventory, £60.16.0, made by Abraham Brown and Samuel Farnsworth.

1763, April 10. **Pancoast, William,** of Mansfield, Burlington Co.; will of. Real estate to be sold. Wife, £140, and the negro girl she

brought. She is to have her thirds. Rest to my 5 children and 2 grandchildren, viz., son, Edward, 1/7; son, David, 1/7; son, Aaron, 2/7; daughter, Sarah, 1/7; daughter, Mary, 1/7, and 1/7 to my son Caleb's 2 children, William and Ann, when of age. Executors—sons, Edward and David. Witnesses—Caleb Scattergood, Jonathan Scattergood, Joseph Biddle, Jr. Proved Sept. 3, 1763.
1763, Sept. 3. Inventory, £459.12.0, made by Benjamin Gibbs and George Folwell. Lib. 11, p. 397.

1767, Nov. 18. Parcel, Nicholas, of Elizabeth Town, Essex Co. Int. Adm'rs—Rachel Parcel and Thomas Parcel. Fellowbondsman— Timothy Whitehead, Jr.; all of said town. Witnesses—Lewis Morris and Robert Ogden. Lib. I, p. 208.

1764, March 2. Park, William, of Hopewell, Hunterdon Co. Int. Adm'x—Sarah Park, widow of William Park. Fellowbondsmen— John Hart and Joab Houghton; all of said place.
1764, Feb. 16. Inventory, £204.7.6, made by David Stout and Joab Houghton. Lib. 11, p. 526.

1764, March 13. Parke, Thomas, of Greenwich, in Cohansey, Cumberland Co., shoemaker; will of. Daughters, Sarah Isley, Martha Wolston, Prudence and Anna Parke, 5 shillings each. Son, Annanias Parke, £5, to be paid to him when my 2 children come of age, viz., Rachel and Rebecca. Son, Annanias, 1,000 acres, which was bought of Benjamin Firman, in Philadelphia, and which was formerly the property of Anna Salter, dec'd. Daughter, Miriam Parke, 5 shillings. Wife, Sarah, my daughter, Rachel, and youngest daughter, Rebecca, the rest of my personal and real estate, when the children are of age. Executors—my wife and my friend, Thomas Ewing. Witnesses— Jacob Noble, James Talbott, Jeremiah Bishop. Proved Feb. 2, 1767.
1766, Dec. 24. Inventory, £178.19.3, made by William Carll and Jeremiah Bishop. Includes "Purse and armor, valued at £23.15.0." Lib. 13, p. 149.

1770, Feb. 17. Parker, Jacob, of Monmouth Co. Int. Adm'r— Thomas Morford, Jr. Fellowbondsman—Miln Parker; both of Shrewsbury, said Co. Witness—William Taylor. Lib. K, p. 232.

1761, March 18. Parker, James and Jannet, of Somerset Co. Wards. Children of John Parker, of said Co., and aged 19 years and 15 years, respectively. Guardian—John Roy, of said Co. Lib. G, p. 369.

1761, April 13. Parker, John, of Cumberland Co. Int. Adm'r— Samuel Hannah.
1761, March. Inventory, £19.13.7, made by Frederick Hofman and Philip Grace. Lib. 10, p. 176.
1763, Aug. 24. Account by Adm'r.

1764, March 2. Parker, John, of Perth Amboy, Middlesex Co. Int. Adm'r—James Parker, brother of said John. Fellowbondsman—John Smyth; both of said place. Lib. H, p. 331.

1768, June 6. Parker, John, of Elizabeth, Essex Co., weaver; will of. I have agreed to sell the house and land where I live to Moses Seayre for £100, which I desire my Executors to collect and give a deed for. Grandson, James Mills, 5 shillings. Wife, Sarah, the rest of my estate for her support, and to bring up my children. Executors—my son-in-law, John Mills, and my friend, Joseph Bird. Witnesses—William Dennison, Joshua Tucker and Joseph Shotwell. Proved July 9, 1768.

1769, April 18. Inventory, £137.8.6, made by John Marsh and Robert Fitz Randolph. Lib. I, p. 309.

1766, Feb. 25. Parker, Nathaniel, of Shrewsbury, Monmouth Co., yeoman; will of. Wife, Hannah, use of my lands; but if any must be sold to pay debts, it is to be the 15 acres that is next to North River, and 3 acres of salt meadow that lies at the Great Meadow, and that which lies next to Thomas Borden. Eldest son, Jacob, 32 acres, to be taken off the north end of my plantation where I live. Youngest son, Miln, the rest of the plantation, and ½ of the salt meadow at the Great Meadow; and the other ½ to son Jacob. Daughters, Mary and Elizabeth, the two best beds in the house, and son, Miln, to pay each at the day of their marriage, £20. Executrix—my wife, Overseers—Richard Lawrence and George Allen. Witnesses—Joshua Parker, Thomas White, Anthony Dennis. Proved Aug. 18, 1767.

1767, Aug. 4. Inventory, £269.12.6, made by Richard Borden, Mauritz Dehart and John Hartshorne. Lib. I, p. 152.

1770, Feb. 15. Parker, Peter, of Evesham Twsp., Burlington Co., yeoman; will of. Advanced in age. Wife, Amey, to be provided for and to have the personal estate to better enable her to provide for my youngest daughter, I having provided for my other children heretofore. Executor—my wife. Witnesses—Joshua Bispham, John Cox. Proved June 21, 1770.

1770, June 16. Inventory, £132.16.4, made by John Cox and Joshua Bispham. Lib. 14, p. 219.

1761, Feb. 5. Parker, Thomas, of Twsp. and Co. of Gloucester. Int. Adm'r—John Parker. Fellowbondsman—Samuel Lukemanear; both of said Co.

1761, Feb. 9. Inventory, £178.6.11, made by William Hampton and William Davis. Lib. 10, p. 172.

1762, Dec. 12. Parr, Samuel, of Waterford, Gloucester Co., yeoman; will of. Wife, Kezia, the goods she had when I married her. Son, Aaron Aaronson Parr, my lands in said place, when 21, and, if my son die in minority, then Parr Willard, my sister's son, shall enjoy the lands, and he is to pay my wife £20 yearly. Ten pounds to be put to interest, to repair the graveyard on my plantation, wherein my late father, Samuel Parr, is interred. If any of the lands in Pennsylvania be recovered, it is to be sold. Executors—my wife and my father-in-law, Aaron Aaronson. Witnesses—Ann Davis, John Caffrey, Samuel Burrough, Thomas Willard. Proved Feb. 23, 1763.

1763, Feb. 9. Inventory, £357.16.10, made by Henry Wood and John Shivers. Lib. 11, p. 314.

1768, Feb. 3. Parr, William, of Burlington Co. Int. Adm'r—Peter Parr, late of Warrington, in Great Britain, now of Chester, in Gloucester Co., N. J. Fellowbondsman—John Wallace, of said Chester. Witnesses—Robert Burchan and Henry Casey. Lib. 13, p. 330.

CALENDAR OF WILLS—1761-1770 321

1767, Feb. 21. Parrit, Thomas, of Newark, Essex Co., innholder. Int. Adm'x—Mary Parrit, widow of said Thomas. Fellowbondsmen —William Parrit and Caleb Ball; all of said place. Lib. I, p. 301.

1765, May 3. Parsons, William, Sr., of Elizabeth Borough, Essex Co.; will of. Wife, Deborah, my moveable estate, except what I give to my son, William; and, after wife's death, said moveables to be sold and money divided between my daughters, Mary Robinson, Jean Meaker and Cloe Parson. My only son, William, all my lands. Daughter, Cloe Parson, £30 when of age or married. Executors— wife, Deborah, my son, William, and my friend, Capt. Benjamin Bonnel. Witnesses—Jonathan Elmer, Jonathan J. Dayton, John Clark. Proved Nov. 11, 1765. Lib. I, p. 41.

1758, Feb. 6. Parvin, Josiah, of Hopewell Twsp., Cumberland Co., yeoman; will of. Wife, Susanna, ½ my moveable estate. Five shillings to each of my married daughters. My two unmarried daughters, Lydia and Phebe, the rest of moveable estate, when 18. Son, Josiah, all my lands. Wife to have use of land. Executors—John Miller and Jonathan Holmes, Esq., both of said Co. Witnesses— Abraham Reeves, Joseph Peck and Lydia Parvin. Proved Aug. 26, 1761. Lib. 11, p. 160.

1762, Sept. 8. Parvin, Matthew, of Fairfield, Cumberland Co., yeoman; will of. Son, Thomas, 100 acres on east side of Cohansey Creek. To son, Theophilus, plantation where I live, of 158 acres. Wife, Sarah, to have her dower. Executors—sons, Thomas and Theophilus. Witnesses—Thomas Whitecar, Joseph Norbury, Ebenezer Bower. Proved May 31, 1769.
1769, May 30. Inventory, £121.9.8, made by Thomas Harris and Joseph Ogden. Lib. 14, p. 15.

1769, July 31. Patten, Henry, of Salem Co., laborer. Int. Adm'r— Samuel Linch, of Upper Penns Neck. Fellowbondsmen—Joseph Burroughs and Bateman Lloyd, both of Town of Salem; all of said Co.
Lib. 14, p. 113.

1769, March 14. Patterson, James, of Freehold, Monmouth Co. Int. Adm'r—Peter Schenck, Jr. Fellowbondsman—Peter Patterson; both of said place.
1769, March 14. Renunciation by Catharine Patterson, widow of said James, and Peter Patterson, brother of said James. Witness— James Kelly. Lib. K, p. 70.

1763, July 6. Patterson, Joseph, of Penns Neck, Salem Co. Int. Adm'r—Andrew Standly, of said place, yeoman. Fellowbondsmen— William Pritchett, of said place, yeoman, and Samuel Baker, of said place, cordwainer.
1763, July 5. Inventory, £50.4.9, made by Samuel Baker and William Pritchett.
1768, May 31. Account by Adm'r. Lib. 11, p. 453; Lib. 13, p. 410.

1763, April 15. Patterson, Robert, of Penns Neck, Salem Co., shopkeeper. Int. Adm'x—Magdalene Patterson, widow, of said place. Fellowbondsmen—John Richman, of Pilesgrove, and Michael Richman, of same place.
1763, April 12. Inventory, £3,550.19.9, made by Mathew Gill and Joseph Shinn. Lib. 11, p. 373.

21

1762, March 31. Paul, Nathan, of Greenwich, Gloucester Co.; will of. To William Finlaw, the horse I bought of him. My wife, Elizabeth, rest of personal and real, till the child she is pregnant with comes to 21 years of age. Executrix—my wife. Witnesses—Samuel Paul, Sr., Ansell Long, William Finley. Proved April 16, 1762.

1762, April 15. Inventory, £250.15.0, made by Andrew Long and Ansell Long. Lib. 11, p. 127.

1767, Jan. 12. Paxton, James, of Trenton, Hunterdon Co. Ward. Son of Joseph Paxton of said place. Makes choice of Charles Coxe, of Philadelphia, merchant, as his Guardian.

1767, Jan. 12. Guardian—Charles Coxe. Fellowbondsman—John Lawrence, of City of Burlington. Witness—John Shaw.
File No. 710 J.

1764, Oct. 12. Peairs, Lewis, of Amwell, Hunterdon Co. Int. Adm'r—Andrew Peairs (Pearse), of said place. Fellowbondsman—Samuel Baker, of Hopewell, said Co. Lib. 12, p. 127.

1769, May 31. Pearson, Abel, late of Philadelphia. Int. Adm'x—Mary Pearson, widow of said Abel Pearson. Fellowbondsman—Daniel Ellis, of Burlington. Lib. 14, p. 64.

1769, June 6. Inventory, £1,237.11.11, made by John Lippincott and David Kinsey.

1769, Sept. 1. Account by Mary Pearson.

1761, Feb. 15. Pearson, James, of Willingborough, Burlington Co.; will of. Son, Able, land I bought of Thomas Rodman and Daniel Ellis. Rest of estate to son, Able, my daughter, Rebecca Fenimore, and my daughter, Sarah Pearson. Executor—son, Able. Witnesses—Samuel How, Joseph Hollinshead, Daniel Ellis. Proved March 27, 1761. Lib. 10, p. 327.

1761, March 28. Inventory, £555.18.0, made by Daniel Ellis and James Collum.

1761, Sept. 10. Pearson, John, of Burlington Co. Ward. Guardian—Isaac Pearson, John Pearson being son of Thomas Pearson, of Nottingham, in said Co. Lib. 11, p. 204.

1765, Sept. 30. Pearson, Joseph, of Burlington; will of. Son, Thomas, land I bought of Obediah Ireton, and land I bought of Ebenezer Wright and Patrick Reynolds, and that bought of Jonathan Wright, Jr., except the grist mill and 2 acres. Rest of estate to be sold and the proceeds given as follows: to son, James, ⅛; son, Josephus, ⅛, and interest of other ⅛ to my daughter, Rebeckkah Cook and, after her death, to her children. Executors—sons, James, Thomas and Josephus. Witnesses—Abraham Scott, Joseph Pancoast, William Smith, Thomas Wire. Proved Oct. 10, 1765.

1765, Oct. 10. Renunciation by Thomas Pearson. Lib. 12, p. 196.

1765, Oct. 10. Inventory, £399.8.8, made by George Deacon and John Antram.

1769, Feb. 3. Peck, Joseph, of Dearfield, Cumberland Co.; will of. Wife, Elizabeth, ⅓ of personal, and use of plantation while my widow. Daughter, Elizabeth Leek, £5. Daughters, Abigail Peck and Rachel Peck, rest of personal. Son, Constant, ½ of my cleared lands

in three fields that join the plantation of son, Constant; also ½ of my 10-acre meadow, and 10 acres that join Samuel Leek and Daniel Clark; also ½ of my cedar swamp in Salem Co. Son, Joseph, rest of lands, when 21. Daughters, Rachel and Abigail, £20 each. Son, John, to have a good education, and son, Joseph, to pay for it; he is to be sent to college. Rev. Enoch Green to be Guardian of my son, John. Executors—sons, Constant and Joseph. Witnesses—John Leake, Daniel Clark, Azariah Moore. Proved March 13, 1769.
1769, March 10. Inventory, £388.11.7, made by Azariah Moore and John Moore. Lib. 14, p. 1.

1768, May 14. Pecker, Richard, of Amwell Twsp., Hunterdon Co.; will of. Wife, Anne Ghart, use of personal and real, while my widow, and, after that, to my children, namely, son, Christian, son, Peter, and daughter Cathrine. Executors—my wife, Anne Ghart, and Francis Posson. Witnesses—Richard Heath, Andrew Heath, Richard Rounsavell, Jr. Proved Nov. 4, 1768.
1768, Oct. 15. Inventory, £51.1.6, made by Richard Heath and Richard Rounsavell, Jr. Lib. 13, p. 483.

1760, July 21. Peer, John, of Hanover, Morris Co.; will of. To my wife the house and lands where I live, and, after her death, I give my lands to my 4 sons, Abraham, Daniel, Cornelius and David. Son, Tunis, £27. Son, John, £30. Son, Samuel, £20. Daughter, Catharine, £30. Daughter, Jean, £30. Executors—sons, Daniel and Cornelius Peer. Witnesses—Lewis Stewart, John Parlaman. Proved April 21, 1763.
1763, April 27. Inventory, £267.5.1, made by George Bowlby and John Parlaman. Lib. H, p. 387.

1765, Feb. 3. Peirson, Azel, of Stow Creek, Cumberland Co.; will of. Wife, Mary, £20, and all she brought with her, and she may use provisions that are in the house for the use of her and son. Daughter, Ruth, the bed that she has. Son, Azel, clothing. Son, George, plantation where I live. Daughter, Marce. a bed. Son, Zablun, £5, and clothing, when 21. Daughter, Amey, a bed and chest of drawers. Daughter, Abigail, a bed, when 18. Son, Rubin, £5, when 21. Executors—sons, Azel and George. Witnesses—Michael Hashel, Thomas Sparks, David Long. Proved April 8, 1765.
1765, April 8. Inventory, £249.12.1, made by Daniel Stretch and Philip Souther. Lib. 12, p. 162.

1765, March 11. Peirson, Samuel, of Borough of Elizabeth, Essex Co.; will of. Wife, Phebe, £100, and if my wife, Phebe, should have a child, then my estate to be to it, but, if she do not have a child, then I give to my brother, Abraham Peirson, £50. Rest of real and personal to my brothers and sisters, viz., David Peirson, William Peirson, Zeruiah Miller and Sarah Meeker. Executors—my father-in-law, Caleb Brown, and my friend, Josiah Crane. Witnesses—Amos Day, Joel Brown, Asher Brown. Proved April 13, 1765.
Lib. H, p. 524.

1766, Aug. 8. Peirson, William, of Amwell Twsp., Hunterdon Co., blacksmith; will of. There have been some lots of land purchased, and buildings erected thereon, and a smith's trade carried on by myself and my brother, Lemuel, but the deeds and accounts are in my name; therefore I give to brother, Lemuel, the one southerly half of said lots, and one northerly half of said lots to my son, Ely Peirson; but my son Ely's share to be under the care of his mother, Ann Peirson, till he is 21, if she remains my widow. To my mother, Elizabeth Peirson, £20. Wife, Ann, the goods she brought to me at our marriage. Executors—brother, Lemuel, and my friend, Thomas Reading. Witnesses—Alexander Fleming, Joseph Reading, Jacob Servoss. Proved May 18, 1767.

1766, Nov. 8. Inventory, £119.3.11, made by George Reading and Henry Booz. Lib. 13, p. 200.

[No date]. **Pennington, Josiah,** of Penns Neck, Salem Co., farmer; will of. Son, Joseph Pennington, 10 acres of upland and 4 of marsh. Son, John, rest of my land. My two grandchildren, William Pennington and Mary Pennington, 20 shillings each. Executors—sons, Joseph and John. Witnesses—John Marshall, William Pritchet, Rebecca Richmond. Proved Sept. 30, 1761.

1761, Sept. 25. Inventory, £266.8.3, made by Andrew Sinnickson and John Marshall. Lib. 11, p. 25.

1761, Jan. 30. Pennington, Thomas, of Penns Neck, Salem Co. Int. Adm'r—Josiah Pennington. Fellowbondsmen—Andrew Sinnickson and Jeremiah Baker; all of Lower Penns Neck Twsp., yeomen. Witness—Philip Alexander.

1761, Jan. 26. Inventory, £185.5.3, made by Andrew Sinnickson and John Marshall.

1762, Jan. 27. Adm'r de bonis non—John Pennington. Fellowbondsmen—Andrew Standly and Peter Bilderback; all of Penns Neck, yeomen.

"Whereas, Thomas Pennington of Penns Neck died intestate, and letters were granted to Josiah Pennington, who is also deceased; Therefore the said John Pennington is now appointed Adm'r."

Lib. 10, p. 441; Lib. 11, p. 185.

1763, Jan. 10. Penton, Isaac, of Greenwich, Cumberland Co. Int. Adm'rs—Elizabeth Penton and Thomas Ewing, both of said place. Witnesses—David Shepherd and Josiah Fithian.

1762, Dec. 30. Inventory, £154.14.6, made by David Shepherd and Josiah Fithian. Lib. 11, p. 305.

1763, Dec. 30. Penton, Job, of Alloways Creek, Salem Co., blacksmith. Int. Adm'x—Elizabeth Penton, widow, of said place. Fellowbondsmen—Samuel Fogg, of said place, wheelwright, and Patrick Moore, of Mannington, said Co., yeoman.

1763, Nov. 25. Inventory, £119.10.7, made by Samuel Fogg and Patrick Moore. Lib. 11, p. 487.

1769, Dec. 26. Peppinger, John, of Redding Township, Hunterdon Co. Int. Adm'r—William Peppinger. Fellowbondsman—Sidney Berry; both of said place.

1770, Jan. 27. Inventory, £132.15.3, made by Aaron Lane and John Forrester, on estate of John Peppinger, late of Tewksbury.

Lib. 14, p. 122.

1763, Dec. 28. Perce, Joseph, of Deptford Twsp., Gloucester Co., cordwinder; will of. Wife, Jane, all my land and goods. Executrix —my wife. Witnesses—James Thomson, John Peirce, Andrew Hudson. Proved March 2, 1764.

1764, March 2. Renunciation of Jane Perce, the widow. Adm'r— John Sparks. Fellowbondsman—John Perce; both of said place. Witness—Sarah Howell. Lib. 11, p. 518.

1768, Oct. 10. Perine, Henry, Jr., of Middlesex Co. Ward. Son of Mathew Perine, of said Co., deceased. Makes choice of Henry Perine, Sr., as his Guardian.

1768, Oct. 10. Guardian—Henry Perine, Sr., of Monmouth Co. Fellowbondsman—John Johnston, of Perth Amboy, Middlesex Co.
Lib. I, p. 336.

1764, April 7. Perkins, Abraham, of Willingborough, Burlington Co.; will of. Son, Joseph, the farm where I live, except 14 acres joining my cousin, Jacob Perkins, on the Delaware River; also the marsh on the Point of Rancocas Creek, and ½ my cedar swamp that I purchased of Vincent Leeds. Son, John, the farm I purchased of Henry Dill, and the 14 acres joining my cousin, Jacob; also the marsh I purchased of Wright Perkins on the Point and ½ the swamp I purchased of Vincent Leeds. Daughter, Anne Perkins, £30. The rest of my estate I give to my two daughters. Executors—son, Joseph, and my son-in-law, Abraham Hewlings. Witnesses—Richard Fenimore, Joseph Hollinshead and Seth Lucas, Jr. Proved April 25, 1764.

1764, April 24. Inventory, £273.8.9, made by Jacob Perkins and Richard Fenimore. Lib. 11, p. 500.

1762, Oct. 18. Perkins, David, of Middlesex Co. Int. Adm'r— Samuel Barron. Fellowbondsman—William Stone; both of Woodbridge, said Co.

1762, Oct. 16. Hannah Perkins, the widow, renounced in favor of her brother, Samuel Barrow. Lib. H, p. 191.

1767, March 13. Person, Abraham, of Elizabeth Borough, Essex Co., cooper; will of. All real and personal to be sold. My sister, Zurviah, all my estate. Executors—Samuel Headley and Lewis Miller. Witnesses—Isaac Headly, Rebecca Headley, Moses Gardner. Proved April 10, 1767. Lib. I, p. 149.

1764, March 26. Peters, Abraham, of Windsor Twsp., Middlesex Co. Ward. Son of Godfrey Peters, of said place, deceased. Makes choice of Richard Carnes as his Guardian.

1764, March 26. Guardian—Richard Carnes. Fellowbondsman— Henry Peters; both of said place. Witnesses—Joseph Read and Samuel Allinson. File No. 4149 L.

1767, Feb. 23. Peters, David, of Chesterfield Twsp., Burlington Co. Int. Adm'r—Henry Peters, of Amwell, Hunterdon Co., weaver. Fellowbondsman—Lawrence Minor, of Burlington Co., yeoman. Witness—Robert Burchan. Lib. 13, p. 101.

1767, Feb. 21. Inventory, £57.0.10, made by Joseph Richards and Robert Pearson.

1767, Feb. 23. Renunciation of Phebe Peters, the widow, in favor of her brother-in-law, Henry Peters.

1763, June 5. Peters, John, of Amwell, Hunterdon Co. Int. Adm'r Richard Reading. Fellowbondsman—John Horn; both of said place.
Lib. 12, p. 9.

1766, Oct. 17. Peters, Mathias, of Gloucester Co.; will of. After my debts are paid, I leave the rest to my two brothers. Witnesses —John Gill, George Allen. Proved Oct. 23, 1766.
1766, Oct. 30. Inventory, £84.0.10, made by James Wood, Joseph Cooper and Bowyer Brooke. "The Inventory of Mathias Peter Swimer we made at the request of his brothers, Peter Peter Swimer and Adam Peter Swimer." File No. 917 H.

1770, Sept. 7, Peterson, Dare, of Fairfield Twsp., Cumberland Co. Int. Adm'r—John Peterson, of said place, yeoman. Fellowbondsman —Abraham Jones, Esq., of Morris River, said Co. Witness—Maskell Ewing. Lib. 15, p. 73.

1760, Nov. 27. Peterson, Lucas, of Penns Neck, Salem Co., yeoman; will of. All personal and real estate to be sold and what is left after debts are paid to go to my sons, John and Peter, when of age. John is to be put out as an apprentice to a carpenter, and Peter to a mason, and to be bound out by Henry Zanes, or my brother-in-law, James Nixon. Executors—William Beetle and Cornelius Corneliusson. Witnesses—Robert Howard, Cornelius Casperson, Rebecca Casperson. Proved June 27, 1761.
1760, Dec. 19. Inventory, £23.6.2, made by Thomas Carney and Robert Howard. Lib. 11, p. 21.

1760, Nov. 18. Peterson, Peter, of Penns Neck, Salem Co., yeoman; will of. My Executor is to give a deed of conveyance for the plantation where I live to Elias Meredith, according to the bond I gave him when I sold him my plantation. Wife, Magdalane Peterson, ⅓ of my moveable estate. Son, Peter, £25. Rest of moveable estate to my five daughters, Prudence, Mary, Sarah, Rebecca and Rachel Peterson, when they are 18. Executor—friend, Henry Jeanes. Witnesses—Lucas Peterson, Jane Courtney, Samuel Whitehorne. Proved Feb. 3, 1761.
1760, Dec. 4. Inventory, £252.10.0, made by Thomas Carney and Samuel Whitehorne.
1766, Feb. 6. Account by Executor. "Paid Jane Courtney, for keeping Rachel, one of the children, £11.18.4. Paid Gabriel Danielson, for keeping Peter, another child, £4.10.0. Paid Albert Bilderback, a balance due from estate, to said Bilderback's wife, Sarah, to whom the deceased was Guardian, £91.10.2." Lib. 10, p. 495.

1766, June 23. Peterson, Peter, of Lower Penns Neck, Salem Co., carpenter. Int. Adm'x—Anne Peterson, widow. Fellowbondsman— Andrew Sinnickson, Esq.; both of said place.
1766, Feb. 3. Inventory, £108.19.4, made by Francis Miles and William Mecum. Lib. 12, p. 317.

1767, Aug. 15. Pettit, Jonathan, of Kingwood Twsp., Hunterdon Co., yeoman; will of. Wife, Mary, £100, and use of all real and personal, and, after her death, all to be sold and divided among my children, as follows: son, John, 1/9; daughter, Susanna Combs, 1/9; son, Jonas, 1/9; daughter, Mary Greensworth, 1/9; daughter, Hannah Fouks, 1/9;

son, Aaron, 1/9; son, Nathaniel, 1/9; daughter, Sarah Pettit, 1/9; daughter, Rachel Pettit, 1/9. Executors—my wife, Mary, and my son-in-law, Thomas Combs, of Kingwood Twsp. Witnesses—James Warford, George Warne, James Ruckman, Jacob Irbul. Proved Oct. 1, 1768. Mary Pettit was sworn as Executrix, same date.
1768, Sept. 26. Inventory, £253.13.9, made by James Worford and George Warne.
1785, June 28. Thomas Combs was sworn as Executor.
1791, May 6. Account by Aaron Pettit, acting Executor of Mary Pettit, who was Executrix of Jonathan Pettit. "Cash paid to Rachel Pettit, widow of Jonas Pettit, for signing deed to convey lands sold to the Testator in his life time by the said Jonas Pettit, £3."
Lib. 13, p. 458.

1768, Oct. 20. Pettit, Jonathan, of Easton, Northampton Co., Penna., yeoman; will of. My wife, Deborah, and my sons, Nathaniel, Jonathan, Isaac, Andrew, John, and William, and my daughters, Dinah and Elizabeth, shall share equally in my real and personal estate; except that Nathaniel and Dinah, shall have £20 less each than the rest. My real estate is not to be sold till my youngest child, William, is 21. Executors—wife, Deborah, my brother, Nathaniel Pettit, and my brother-in-law, William Robins. Witnesses—William Ledlie, John Godfrey Enax, Robert Fraill. Proved Feb. 4, 1769.
1769, Feb. 4. Renunciation by William Robins.
1768, Nov. 15. Inventory, £166.19.1, made by Tunis Young and George Geasser. Lib. 13, p. 543.

1763, Oct. 11. Petty, Israel, Jr., of Fairfield, Cumberland Co., yeoman; will of. After my debts are paid, the rest to Elias Petty, Charles Howel and Ebenezar Seeley (son of Enos Seeley). Executor—my brother, Elias Petty. Witnesses—Enos Seeley, Charles Howell, Tamer Seeley. Proved Oct. 28, 1763.
1763, Nov. 3. Inventory, £95.14.10, made by Joseph Westcot and John Whitecar. Lib. 11, p. 495.

1765, Feb. 9. Petty, Israel, of Fairfield Twsp., Cumberland Co., yeoman; will of. Son, Elias, my plantation. Granddaughter, Hannah Petty, £100, at age of 18. Son-in-law, Charles Howel, £20. To Rev. William Ramsey, of this place, £5. My wife to have her dower. Remainder to my son, Elias, my daughter, Naomi Seely, and her three children, viz., David Seely, Ebenezar Seely and Ruth Seely. Executor—son, Elias. Witnesses—Stephen Peirson, Tamer Seeley, Joseph Norbury. Proved June 3, 1767.
1767, June 2. Inventory, £253.15.7, made by Joseph Ogden and David Wescote.
1772, Jan. 17. Account by Executor. Lib. 12, p. 482; Lib. 14, p. 421.

1712, Aug. 23. Petty, John, of Burlington; will of. To John Gosling and Thomas Bryon, all real and personal, and they to pay my debts, and the rest is to maintain my father, William Petty, and my mother, Jane Petty. Executors—said John Gosling and Thomas Bryon. Witnesses—Samuel Furnis, Isaac De Cow, Richard Wright. Proved March 13, 1765, by Joseph De Cow, son and heir of Isaac De Cow, one of the witnesses, aged 60 years, and James Hancock, of Burlington, nephew of John Petty, the testator, aged 74 years, who knew the writing of the witnesses, and said that Richard Wright and Isaac De Cow died within 18 years. Lib. 12, p. 63.

1769, March 2. Pew, William, Jr., of Morris Co. Int. Adm'r—Joseph King. Fellowbondsman—Frederick King; both of said Co.
1769, Feb. 15. Renunciation by Margaret Pew, the widow; William Pew, the father; and Samuel Pew and Thomas Pew, brothers of said William Pew, Jr., in favor of Joseph King. Witness—William Pew.
Lib. K, p. 142.

1768, Oct. 8. Phares, William, of Hanover, Burlington Co. Int. Adm'rs—Mary Phares and John Lawrie. Fellowbondsman—Ralph Allen; all of said place. Lib. 13, p. 476.
1768, Sept. 15. Inventory, £640.10.0, made by John Wetherill and Joseph Steward.
1783, March 24. Account by Adm'rs. Lib. 24, p. 218.

1760, Dec. 8. Phillips, Matthew, of Essex Co.; will of. Wife, Ledia, all real and personal, and, after her death, to be to my children. Son, Robert, 5 shillings, and, after death of wife, 1/9 to him. Sons, Richard, David, Thomas, Mathew, Feady, Jesse, each 1/9; and to daughters, Sarah Phillips and Mary Phillips, each 1/9. Executors—my wife and Peter Degarmo. Witnesses—Thomas Gould, Alexander Peterson, Peter Tice. Proved Feb. 24, 1761. Lib. G, p. 394.

1762, Dec. 13. Phillips, Philip and Mary, of Hunterdon Co. Wards. Son and daughter of Joseph Phillips, late of Maidenhead, said Co., deceased. They make choice of their brother, Joseph Phillips, as their Guardian. Witnesses—Alexander Chambers and Rebeckah Phillips.
1762, Dec. 7. Guardian—Joseph Phillips, yeoman. Fellowbondsman—Joseph Scudder, yeoman; both of said Co. Lib. 11, p. 249.

1761, May 29. Phillips, Theophilus, of Maidenhead, Hunterdon Co., yeoman; will of. Wife, Abigail, all the estate I had with her; also many goods, meat and grain; also one and a quarter acres of land. Son, Richard, £25, and son, John, a like amount. Son, William, £75. Daughter, Francis Bainbridge, £50. Son, William, all my lands, below the road. Legacies to son Joseph's youngest children, viz., Elizabeth, Hezekiah, Mary and Joseph. Grandson, Theophilus Moore, £10. Granddaughter, Keziah Moore, £5. Granddaughter, Elizabeth Moore, £10. Grandson, Theophilus Phillips, son of Joseph, deceased, the lands above the road, when he is 20 years old, and he is to pay to his two sisters, Elizabeth Phillips and Mary Phillips, £15 each. Executors—sons, John and William. Witnesses—Ralph Hunt, John Bainbridge, Abner Phillips. Proved Feb. 18, 1762.
1762, Feb. 16. Inventory, £513.9.11, made by Abner Phillips and Ralph Hunt. Lib. 11, p. 360.

1768, Feb. 17. Philpot, Earick, of Penns Neck, Salem Co. Ward. Son of John Philpot, of said place, yeoman. Makes choice of Andrew Sinnickson as his Guardian.
1769, Jan. 12. Guardian—Andrew Sinnickson. Fellowbondsman—William Mecum; both of said place. Lib. 13, p. 493.

1761, July 22. Philpot, John, of Lower Penns Neck, Salem Co. Int. Inventory, £276.4.1, made by Andrew Sinnickson and John Marshall. Ann Philpott sworn as Adm'x. File No. 1286½ Q.
1763, April 2. Adm'rs—Andrew Sinnickson and Hance Lambson. Fellowbondsman—Francis Miles; all of said place. Lib. 11, p. 374.

1767, April 16. Philpot, Joseph, of Penns Neck, Salem Co.; will of. My personal estate I give to my wife, my youngest son, Joseph, and my daughter, Mary Philpot. Son, Samuel, to be put to a trade. Executors—wife, Margaret, and my brother, Francis Philpot. Witnesses—Sinnick Sinnickson, Cathrine Philpot, Francis Miles. Proved Feb. 4, 1768.

1767, June 11. Inventory, £231.16.2, made by Andrew Sinnickson and Francis Miles. Lib. 13, p. 389.

1765, Dec. 2. Pickel, Baltheser, of Hunterdon Co.; will of. Son, Baltheser Pickel, John Stein, Ruloph Rulophs, a silver plate and cup, to be delivered by them to the German Protestant Lutheran Church at New Germantown, in Hunterdon Co. I order my Executors to transfer to Balteser Pickel, John Stein and Ruloph Rulophs, all the bonds I have of some of the members of said church, except the obligation I paid on the demand of George Remer and Jacob Dest, which I give to our minister, Paul Bryzelius, so as to make up a legacy of £1,000, and the interest thereof is to teach two poor children to read at the German school of said congregation. Executors—Rev. Paul Bryzelius and my sons, Balteser and Henry Pickel, Philip Wise, John Mohlich, Jacob Klein and Valentine Reinhard. Witnesses—Ananias Randall, Weinland Vandeventer, Jacob Neff. Proved April 19, 1766.

1765, Dec. 31. Inventory, £4,688.2.5, made by Samuel Wyckof and Winand Van de Vender. Lib. 13, p. 236.

1766, April 19. Pickel, Henry, of Readingtown, Hunterdon Co. Int. Adm'rs—Baltes (Baltheser) Pickel and John Melich, both of said place. Fellowbondsman—Philip Weiss (Wise) of Roxbury, Morris Co.

1765, Dec. 31. Inventory, £663.3.3, made by Waland Van De Vander and Samuel Wyckof. Lib. 13, p. 207.

1767, April 7. Pidcock, William, of Evesham, Burlington Co. Int. Adm'x—Rosannah Pidcock (the widow). Fellowbondsman—David Stratton; both of same Evesham.

1766, Dec. 9. Inventory, £51.13.4, made by David Stratton and Daniel Stratton. File No. 8049 C.

1762, May 29. Pierce, Thomas, of Windsor, Middlesex Co. Ward. Guardians—Joseph Skelton and Joseph Oldden; both of said Co. It was represented by the Overseers of Poor of New Windsor Twsp., that Thomas Pierce, of New Windsor, aged upwards of 21 years, is an idiot, and not able to take care of his effects, and may become a charge on the Township, but at present can work, and the Overseers wish Guardians to be appointed, which is now approved of. Also dated Oct. 11, 1762. Lib. H, p. 190.

1768, Nov. 22. Pierson, John, of Hanover, Morris Co., clerk; will of. Children—Abraham, Anne, Elizabeth, John, Wyllys. The house where John lives to be in his share, and at the death of John and his wife, or her marriage, to be sold, and divided among his children. My granddaughter, Ruth, the only child of my daughter Abigail Grave, deceased, £10. My daughters, Margaret and Hannah, each to have £50 less than Abraham, Ann and Elizabeth; and the reason is that I have spent money on the estate at Jamaica, that belongs to Margaret and Hannah. A tombstone is to be erected at my grave. Executors—my friends, Joseph Tuttle, Samuel Kitchel and John Kitchel. Witnesses—John Dixon, Samuel Alleson, Susannah Williams. Proved Sept. 2, 1770. Lib. K, p. 282.

1768, Nov. 15. Pierson, Joseph, of Newark, Essex Co. Int. Adm'r —Bethuel Pierson, heir-at-law. Fellowbondsman—Daniel Riggs; both of same place. Witness—Mathias M. Dermott.

1759, Oct. Inventory, made by Samuel Crowell and Ebenezer Hedden. Testis—Joseph Ball.

1768, Nov. 30. Inventory filed. Lib. I, p. 363.

1768, June 22. Pierson, Moses, of Morris Co., gentleman; will of. My wife to have ½ the household goods and the other ½ to my daughter, Elizabeth. I give my brother, Daniel Person, my coals. Executors—brother, Elijah Person and Soloman Munson. Witnesses —Aaron Pierson, David Cory. Proved July 11, 1768. Lib. I, p. 296.

1760, Nov. 5. Pike, James, of Woodbridge, Middlesex Co.; will of. Son, Zebulon Pike, the land that lies by William Pike's. Son, James, the land that joins Jonathan Harned. Son, Robert, two lots on Strawberry Hill, and the lot that was formerly John Reaves'. Moveable estate to be sold and money divided among my sons and two daughters. I desire that my father give to my son, Zebulon, his home place, after his decease. Executors—friends, David Herriot and William Pike. Witnesses—Jonathan Inslee, James Moores, Joseph Coe.

1761, June 1. Renunciation by Zebulon Pike and Janet Pike, who refuse to undertake their son, James Pike's, business, and recommend George Brown as a suitable person.

1761, June 17. Jonathan Inslee and James Moore, two of the witnesses, declared that James Pike was not in his senses when he signed his will.

1761, June 17. Adm'r—George Brown. Fellowbondsman—George Herriot; both of Woodbridge. Lib. G, p. 443; File No. 3731 L.

1769, Feb. 6. Pike, Jennet, of Woodbridge, Middlesex Co.; will of, being widow of Zebulon Pike, of said place, shopkeeper. Grandson, James Pike, my large Bible. Grandson, Robert, a book, which is to be left in the care of my sister, Ursilla Herriot, till he is 18. Grandsons, James Pike and Robert Pike, all my lands over the road that I bought, and that was my son, John Pike's, by virtue of a judgment (by) consent, in favor of my son, James Pike's, estate, to George Brown, Adm'r. Rest of real and personal to be sold, and proceeds given to my grandchildren. Executors—George Herriot and George Brown. Witnesses—David Herriot, Jonathan Inslee, Alfoard Herriot. Proved Feb. 28, 1769. Lib. K, p. 183.

1761, March 24. Pike, John, of Woodbridge, Middlesex Co. Int. Adm'r—James Pike. Fellowbondsman—George Herriot; both of said Woodbridge. Hannah Pike, the widow of John Pike, has desired that James Pike might administer.

1762, Oct. 29. Whereas John Pike died intestate, and on 24th of March, 1761, letters of administration were granted to James Pike, of Woodbridge, who is also deceased, and on the 7th of Aug., 1761,

CALENDAR OF WILLS—1761-1770   331

letters were granted to Zebulon Pike of said place, who is also deceased, and it is now desired that the estate of said John Pike that is not yet administered by the said James or Zebulon Pike may be so done by Jannet Pike, of Woodbridge, mother of said John Pike; therefore she is appointed Adm'x of the estate of said John Pike, with George Brown, of Woodbridge, on her bond.
1761, March 31. Inventory made by Thomas Gach and George Herriot. Lib. G, p. 369; Lib. H, p. 198.

1766, Oct. 13. Pike, Nathaniel, of Middlesex Co. Int. Adm'x—Sarah Pike, the widow of said Nathaniel. Fellowbondsman—Rezia Runyon; both of said Co. Witness—John Terrill. Lib. I, p. 6.

1761, Jan. 6. Pike, Thomas, of Woodbridge, Middlesex Co. Int. Adm'r—William Pike, eldest brother of said Thomas. Fellowbondsman—Nathaniel Pike; both of said place.
1761, Jan. 5. Renunciation by Elizabeth Pike, the widow, in favor of William Pike. Lib. G, p. 341.

1761, June 6. Pike, Zebulon, of Woodbridge, Middlesex Co.; will of. Wife, Janet Pike, to have a good maintainance. Grandson, Joseph Pike, £15. Grandson, Zebulon Pike, £15. Daughter-in-law, Hannah, the widow of my son John, deceased, £20, to bring up her two youngest children. Grandson, Robert, son of James Pike, deceased, £15 towards his bring up. Real to be sold. Rest to grandchildren, except Joseph and Zebulon. Executors—wife, Janet, and my friend, George Brown. Witnesses—George Herriot, David Herriot, John Waterhouse. Proved March 15, 1762.
1762, March 22. Inventory made by Thomas Gach and George Herriot. Lib. H, p. 88.

1768, March 7. Pilgrim, Frederick, of Upper Alloways Creek Precinct, Salem Co. Int. Adm'r—Richard Wistar, of Philadelphia, merchant.
1768, March 5. Inventory, £19.15.3, made by George Dickinson and Benjamin Thompson. Lib. 13, p. 334.

1769, June 16. Pinyard, John, of Greenwich, Gloucester Co. Ward. Son of John Pinyard, of said place, yeoman, deceased. Makes choice of his mother, Martha Pinyard, as his Guardian.
1769, June 16. Guardian—Martha Pinyard, widow. Fellowbondsman—Jacob Spicer, yeoman; both of said place. Lib. 14, p. 21.

1768, Feb. 19. Pinyard, John, Jr., of Greenwich, Gloucester Co. Int. Adm'x—Martha Pinyard, widow. Fellowbondsman—John Pinyard, yeoman; both of said place. Witness—James Hinchman.
1768, Jan. 19. Inventory, £170.6.4, made by James Hinchman and Jacob Spicer. Lib. 13, p. 437.

1767, Jan. 13. Pitman, Ann, of Hanover Twsp., Burlington Co. Int. Adm'r—Uriah Pitman. Fellowbondsman—Oliver Gallop; both of same place. Witness—William Heulings. Lib. 13, p. 101.
1764, Dec. 18. Inventory, £29.9.6, made by Oliver Gallup and Jonathan Fox.

1767, March 28. Pitman, John, of Salem Co. Int. Adm'x—Elizabeth Pitman, widow. Fellowbondsmen—Peter Boon and John Dalbo, yeomen; all of Upper Penns Neck, said Co.
 1767, Feb. 21. Inventory, £215.19.1, made by Peter Boon and Henry Peterson (Smith). The said John Pitman, before his death, was Guardian of Sarah, Christopher, Christiana and Nicholas Lynmyer.
Lib. 13, p. 189.

1768, Aug. 12. Platt, Thomas, of New Hanover, Burlington Co. Int. Adm'r—Thomas Platt. Fellowbondsman—Isaac Ivins; both of Burlington Co.
 1768, Aug. 1. Inventory, £273.13.6, made by William Harris, Jr., and Isaac Ivins. Lib. 13, p. 436.

1765, Feb. 7. Platz, Jean Paul, of Greenwich, Sussex Co., tanner; will of. Wife, Susan Plats, ⅓ the goods, 2 cows and half the hogs, and the money I owe her son, and now my stepson, which by name is called John Caspor Sim. Remainder to my sons, Adam and Philip Platz. Executors—James Anderson, Frederick Swartz and Daniel Shearer. Witnesses—Bernard Michael Hansike, D. V. M., Henry Vollert, Robert O'Neale. Proved May 20, 1765.
 1765, Feb. 22. Inventory, £60.13.6, made by Peter Morgan and Martin Dorsheimer. Lib. 12, p. 247.

1763, June 10. Plum, Mary, of Newark, Essex Co.; will of. Daughter, Elizabeth Lum, £45. Sons, William Cooper and Caleb Cooper; daughter, Martha Burnet and my said daughter, Elizabeth, and daughter, Mary Plum, the rest of my estate. Executors—Timothy Whitehead, Esq., and my son-in-law, David Burnet. Witnesses—Samuel Meadlis, Jonathan Sergeant. Proved June 1, 1764.
Lib. H, p. 554.

1769, Oct. 3. Plume, Robert, of Essex Co. Int. Adm'x—Deborah Plume, widow of said Robert. Lib. K, p. 143.

1762, Dec. 6. Pointsett, John, of New Hanover, Burlington Co. Int. Adm'r—Peter Pintset. Fellowbondsman—Samuel Rogers; both of said place. Lib. 11, p. 240.
 1762, Dec. 4. Renunciation of Susanna Pinset, in favor of Peter Poincett.
 1762, Dec. 4. Inventory, £15.9.8, made by Jonathan Branson and Samuel Rogers.

1767, March 28. Polack, Charles, of Sussex Co., chapman. Int. Adm'r—Richard Moore, of Philadelphia, merchant. Fellowbondsmen—John Moore, of Hardwick, Sussex Co., hatter, and Nathaniel Pettit, Esq., of Newton, Sussex Co. Witnesses—Gershom Mott and Michael Van Court.
 1767, March 28. Inventory, £101.18.8, made by Hezekiah Dunn and Gershom Mott. Lib. 12, p. 466.

1764, Feb. 22. Polgreen, Elizabeth, of City and County of Burlington, widow; will of. Son, James, of the Island of Barbados, the house and lot where I live, and, after death of James, to my son Thomas Bickley. To Elizabeth Snowden, £10 and clothing, for her

kindness to me. Daughter, Katharine, wife of John Miller, of the
Island of Barbadoes, and, in case of her death, to her children ⅛ of
the sales of my estate. Grandchildren, Joseph, Thomas Polgreen
and Abraham Hewlings, Jr., children of my daughter, Susanna, deceased, the late wife of Abraham Hewlings, of this city, ⅛ of the
sales. Son, Thomas, the other part. Executor—son, Thomas Bickley.
Witnesses—Mary Tong, Abraham Hewlings and Thomas Gardiner.
Proved Sept. 16, 1768. Lib. 13, p. 431.

1765, Feb. 11. Polhemius, Abraham, of Somerset Co., yeoman; will
of. My wife to have the interest of £200 and the goods she had
when I married her. Son, Daniel, £100. Son, John Polhemius, a set-out, as my other children. Children, Daniel, Neiltie, Albert, Tiney
and John Polhemus, the rest. Son, John, to be bound out to a trade.
Executors—brother, Hendrick Polhemus, my son, Daniel, and Henry
Crusee. Witnesses—Henry Harrison, Peter Monfort, Henry Monfort.
Proved March 18, 1765.
1765, March 13. Inventory made by Henry Harrison and David
Snowden. Lib. 12, p. 80.

1767, Feb. 7. Polhemius, Hendrik, of Somerset Co.; will of. Wife
to have the goods she brought, and to be maintained out of the farm.
Son, Daniel, the farm I live on. Eldest daughter, Eleanor, £25.
Daughter, Anna, £25. Daughter, Margret, £25. Daughter, Dorothy,
£25. Two daughters, who are not married, shall have £50. Farm over
the river to be sold. Executors—son, Daniel Polhemous; Daniel
Prince (my brother-in-law), and Johannas Voorhees (my son-in-law).
Witnesses—Johannes Stryker, Nicklaes Amerman, Thomas Davis.
Proved Jan. 17, 1769. Lib. K, p. 25.

1769, Aug. 20. Polhemus, Albert, of Freehold, Monmouth Co., yeoman; will of. Wife, Alkey, all that her father gave to her. Son,
Daniel, ½ of my real and personal. Daughter, Mary, the other half.
Executors—my brothers, John and Tobias Polhemus, and my two
brothers-in-law, Chrineyonce Van Mater and Daniel Hendrickson.
Witnesses—Samuel Holmes, Jr., Asher Holmes, John Holmes (son of
S. H.). Proved Sept. 26, 1769.
1769, Sept. 15. Inventory, £237.9.4, made by Benjamin Van Mater
and Joseph Van Mater.
1769, Sept. 25. Inventory, £61.8.0, made by Benjamin Van Mater
and Joseph Van Mater, of the goods of the late widow of Albert
Polhemus. Lib. K, p. 125.

1763, Sept. 21. Polhemus, Daniel, of Middletown, Monmouth Co.,
yeoman; will of. Wife, Margaret, £20, and use of farm where I live.
Son, John, my farm in Shrewsbury, and ⅓ of my salt meadow, he
paying in 10 years after my death, £300 to my daughter, Elenor, wife
of Peter Covenhoven. Son, Albert, farm in Freehold, and ⅓ my
salt meadow, he paying £300 to my daughter, Annauchy. Son, Tobias,
the farm where I live, and ⅓ of my salt meadow, he paying £300
to my daughter, Mary. Rest of my estate to my six children, John,
Albert, Tobias, Elenor, Annauchy and Mary. Executors—sons, John
and Tobias. Witnesses—Cyrenius Vanmater, Chrineyonce Vanmater,
Richard Lawrence. Proved Dec. 2, 1763.
1763, Dec. 3. Inventory, £566.15.0, made by Benjamin Vanmater,
Joseph Van Mater and Cyrenius Vanmater. Lib. H, p. 394.

1768, Nov. 28. Pond, John, of Gloucester Co. Int. Adm'x—Hannah Pond, of Newton, said Co. Fellowbondsman—Benjamin Graisbury, of said place.
    1768, Nov. 9. Inventory, £240.10.7, made by Benjamin Graisbury and West Patient Kimble. Lib. 12, p. 525.

1763, Oct. 10. Pope, Joseph, of Mansfield Twsp., Burlington Co.; will of. Wife, Mary, £130. Sons, Nathaniel and John, not yet 21. To son, John, £180. Son, Nathaniel, £180, and a cedar swamp. Son, Joseph, plantation where I live. Executors—wife, Mary, and Samuel Black. Witnesses—Caleb Scattergood, Jonathan Scattergood, Janet Scattergood. Proved Feb. 23, 1767.
    1767, Jan. 8. Inventory, £1,544.5.2, made by Benjamin Gibbs and William Potts. Lib. 13, p. 54.
    1769, Sept. 21. Account by Exr's. Lib. 14, p. 79.

1765, June 10. Post, Garret, of Saddle River, Bergen Co., yeoman; will of. Wife, Elizabeth, all real and personal, and, if any land remain, then to be to the use of my son, Arie Post. Daughter, Elizabeth, £25. Daughter, Annatje, £25. Executor—friend, Adryaen A. Post. Witnesses—Harmanus Van Bossum, Philip Van Bossum and David Marinus. Proved Oct. 15, 1765. Lib. H, p. 577.

1765, Oct. 26. Post, Jacobus, of Ackqueghenonck, Essex Co., husbandman; will of. Son, Frans, my right in land in the mountain, to the westward of Weesel, being in his possession, and is part of No. 4 as laid out; and I also give him No. 13. Son, Jacobus, a lot as was surveyed by Hassel Peterse, 25 Oct., 1765, which is ½ of my lands in Ackqueghenonck Patent. Son, Johannes, the other ½ of said lands. Daughter, Leena, £140. Executors—son, Jacobus, and Hassel Peterse. Witnesses—Jacob Van Winkel, Henderick Gerritse, Barent Cool. Proved Oct. 19, 1768. Lib. I, p. 359.

1764, Sept. 1. Post, Teunis, of Bridgewater, Somerset Co.; will of. Son, Peter, farm where I live, and he shall take care of his sister, Elizabeth. Wife, Hannah, £15 yearly. Children, Hannah Cock, Kathrine Post and Peter Post, goods after my wife's death. Executors—my wife, Samuel Cock and Peter Post. Witnesses—Matthew Ten Eick, Peter Ten Eick, Jacob Ten Eick, Peter Dumont. Proved Nov. 29, 1764.
    1764, Nov. 26. Inventory, £796.4.8, made by Mathew Ten Eick, Jacob Ten Eick and Peter Sutphin. Lib. H, p. 476.

1760, Oct. 13. Potter, David, of Bound Brook, Somerset Co., physician; will of. My mother, the widow Phebe Potter, £25 and the use of what I give my brother, Joseph Potter, till he is 21. Brothers, Nathaniel and Noadiah, £25 each. Sister, Phebe Potter, goods. To my brothers the lands given to me in the will of my father, Noadiah Potter, Esq. Executors—brothers, Nathaniel and Noadiah. Witnesses—Isaac Livermore, Robert Headly, Isaac Man. Proved Jan. 19, 1761.
    1760, Dec. 20. At Springfield, Borough of Elizabeth. Renunciation by Nathaniel Potter. Lib. H, p. 168.

CALENDAR OF WILLS—1761-1770 335

1768, July 28. Potter, Ephraim, of Barnagat, Monmouth Co. Int. Adm'r—Thomas Potter, Jr. Fellowbondsman—John Williams; both of said Co.
1768, July 28. Renunciation by Sarah Potter, widow of said Ephraim. Witnesses—John Holmes and Isaac Wilcockson.
Lib. I, p. 336.

1770, Jan. 29. Potter, Joseph, of Hanover, Morris Co.; will of. Wife, Mary, my personal estate and the use of the real, in order to help her bring up my children till my daughter, Phebe, is 18, paying to daughters, Abigail, Sarah and Joanna, what is reasonable, after they are 18. Daughter, Elizabeth, 15 and ¾ acres of my plantation. Daughters, Abigail, Sarah, Joanna and Phebe, rest of real estate, but they are to pay to my grandson, John Wood, £50, when he is 21. Grandson, John Wood, son of my daughter, Mary, deceased, £50. Executors—my wife, and my friend, Abraham Pierson, Jr., who are to collect the money due from Benoni Thomas, Joseph Lacey and Samuel Frost, which is due on their lands. Witnesses—Aaron Burnet, Ezekiel Cheever, Mary Benjamin. Proved April 14, 1770.
1770, April 14. Inventory, £1,377.12.10, made by John Rose and Joseph Lasey. Lib. K, p. 212.

1768, July 18. Potter, Noadiah, of Elizabeth Town, Essex Co., yeoman; will of. Wife, Joannah, all moveable estate. Sons, David and William, 7 acres and house. Daughters—Phebe Potter and Betsy Potter, £20 each. Executors—my wife, Robert Ogden and John Potter. Witnesses—Thomas Dean, Samuel Headley, Thomas Ball. Proved Sept. 5, 1768. Lib. K, p. 36.

1765, Oct. 31. Potter, William, of Shrewsbury Twsp., Monmouth Co., yeoman; will of. To Ann, once the wife of John Soper, £5, yearly, for 6 years, and no more, as she has been very wicked to me and destructive to my interest. Daughter, Susannah Dickeson, and her husband, John, 5 shillings, and no more, for good reasons known to me. Son, Samuel Potter, £10, and he is to pay for the benefit of my daughter, Ann Cowperthwaite, the wife of John, £27, and to his 4 children, £109, and to my grandson, William Potter Brock, £200 when 18, and to the two daughters of my daughter, Mary Brock, £54; and then he is to have all my lands. Rest to my daughter, Mary Brock. Executrix—said Mary Brock. Witnesses—William Stevenson, Joseph Arney, Jr., Joseph Arney. Proved Nov. 25, 1766.
1766, Nov. 10. Inventory, £322 10.3, made by Amos Wright and Oliver Gallap. Lib. 12, p. 446.

1761, June 27. Potts, Nathaniel, of Mansfield, Burlington Co. Int. Adm'rs—Susannah Potts and William Potts. Fellowbondsman—John Folwell; all of same place. Lib. 10, p. 222.
1761, June 26. Inventory, £408.9.10, made by Benjamin Talman and John Folwell.

1766, Oct. 2. Poulse, Johannes, of Achquecknonk, Essex Co., yeoman; will of. Wife, Gurtruy, all the things she brought with her when we were married, and £100, one-half then to be paid to her by my grandson, Hendrick Gerritse, the son of my daughter Catrina, deceased, and the other ½ to be paid by my grandchildren, the children of my daughter, Antje, deceased. To grandson, Hendrick Gerritse, land at Weasel, being between the land of Hendrick Gerritse and Richard Broadberry. The rest of lands I give to my grandchildren, Lawrence Ackkerman and Catrina Ackkerman. My stepson, Barent Spier, shall hold my lands and personal estate for 12 years after my death. Executors—my wife and my stepson, Barnet Spier. Witnesses —David Marinus, Jacob J. Van Houten, Petrus Poulisse. Proved Jan. 27, 1767. Lib. I, p. 183.

1764, Aug. 6. Powel, Richard, of Fairfield Twsp., Cumberland Co., yeoman; will of. Wife, Elizabeth, use of all my lands. Sons, Reuben and Richard Powell, my lands on Jones Island. Son, John, 50 acres in the Fork. Daughters, Elizabeth Powel and Abigail Powel, my personal estate, when 18. Executor—my wife. Witnesses—James Diament, Bersheba Miller, Enos Seeley. Proved Oct. 3, 1764.

1764, Sept. 24. Inventory, £295.4.8, made by James Diament and Ephraim Harris. Lib. 12, p. 47.

1762, Nov. 9. Powell, Christopher, of Northampton, Burlington Co., yeoman; will of. Wife, Sarah, £7 yearly; also livestock and household goods. My brother, John Powell, part of my plantation. Brother, Jacob, land. Brother, Joseph, rest of plantation. Cousin, Virgin Gaskill, the daughter of Joseph Gaskill, £10, when 18. Sister, Sarah Powell, £10. Cousin, Hannah Powell, daughter of my brother, John Powell, £6, when 18. Executors—my wife, Sarah, and my brother, Joseph. Witnesses—Isaac Powell, Jane Gaskill, John Burr, Jr. Proved Jan. 3, 1763.

1763, Jan. 6. Inventory, £304.19.6, made by Thomas Budd and Samuel Lippincott. Lib. 11, p. 247.

1770, June 7.. Powell, Elizabeth, of City of Burlington. Int. Adm'r John Richardson. Fellowbondsman—Daniel Ellis; both of Burlington Co. Lib. 15, p. 2.

1770, June 9. Inventory, £20.1.4, made by Isaac Heulings and Joseph Richardson.

1770, Aug. 31. Account by Adm'r. Lib. 15, p. 48.

1766, June 23. Powell, Isaac, of Somerset Co. Int. Adm'x—Margaret Powell, widow of Isaac. Fellowbondsman—James Powell; both of said Co.

1766, June 9. Inventory, £492.7.9, made by James Powell, Isaiah Younglove and Joseph Coulter. Lib. H, p. 620.

1763, Nov. 4. Powell, Jacob, of Northampton, Burlington Co., yeoman; will of. Wife, Mary, the bed she brought with her. Mentions brothers, John and Joseph. Son, Samuel, a part of my plantation, when 21. My son, Jacob, the rest of land. Wife, rest of personal. Executors—my wife and my brother, Joseph. Witnesses—James Budd, David Ewan. Proved Nov. 22, 1763.

1763, Nov. 21. Inventory, £120.7.4, made by James Budd and Absalom Ewan. Lib. 11, p. 425.

1765, April 12. Powell, John, of Mannington, Salem Co., taylor. Int. Adm'rs—Ann Powell, of said place, widow, and John Dickeson, of Alloways Creek, said Co. Fellowbondsmen—Elisha Bassett, Jr., and John Johnson, both of Mannington; yeomen.

1765, March 27. Inventory, £139.16.9, made by John Roberts and Elisha Bassett, Jr. Lib. 12, p. 175.

CALENDAR OF WILLS—1761-1770   337

1755, Sept. 24. Pownall, Mary, of Chester, Burlington Co., widow; will of. My sister, Ruth Atkinson, is deceased, and I give to her daughters, viz., Rebekah Say and Ruth Bispham, and to my sister, Rebeckah Potts, ½ of estate between them. Sister, Elizabeth Janney, is deceased, and I give to her two daughters, Rebekah Poolly and Elizabeth Stakehouse, the rest. Executors—Thomas Say, of Philadelphia, merchant, and Joshua Bispham, of Chester Twsp. in said Co. Witnesses—Earl Shinn, Samuel Atkinson, John Cox. Proved May 10, 1763.
1763, April 25. Inventory, £967.11.6, made by Samuel Atkinson, Jr., and John Cox.   Lib. 11, p. 334.

1758, June 30. Praal, Aaron, of Somerset Co.; will of. Wife, Mary, £90, to be paid to her by my two sons, William George and Hendrick Praal. Wife to have use of other estate while my widow. To my son, Peter, my daughter, Mary, who married Henry Paynter, Elizabeth, widow of John Bruse, and Antje, married to ———, of Pennsylvania, £10 each. Daughter, Hansey, married to Folkert Buys, a negro. My other estate I give to sons, William George and Hendrick Praal, and daughter, Hansey. Executors—sons, William George Praal and Hendrick Praal. Witnesses—William Ouke, John Ouke. Proved May 17, 1766.
1766, May 5. Inventory, £455.7.5, made by Jacobus Messelar and Jonathan Smith.   Lib. I, p. 113.

1766, May 24. Prall, Henry, of Somerset Co.; will of. My mother, Mary Prall, the use of real and personal, during her life. Brother, Peter, and sisters, Mary Painter, Elizabeth Brees and Ann Whytey, £10 each. Brother, William George Prall, and sister, Handershe Buys. Executors—William George Prall and my brother-in-law, Fulkert Buys. Witnesses—Isaac Brokaw, Jacobus Stryker, Hendrick Fisher. Proved April 23, 1767.
1766, Oct. 3. Inventory, £151.10.7, made by Hendrick Fisher and Jacobus Messelar.   Lib. I, p. 112

1760, Sept. 20. Prall, Mary, of Amwell, Hunterdon Co., widow; will of. To three of my blood children, Elizabeth Prall, Benjamin Prall and Jemime Prall, all my personal estate, which I have of the estate of my husband, Aaron Prall, dec'd. If the said Benjamin Prall receive of his brother, James Prall, from the estate of their father the sum equal to one-third and half-third of my estate, then Benjamin shall return his part of my estate to his sisters, Elizabeth and Jemime Prall. Executor—Joseph Higgens. Witnesses—Edward Prall, James Fulkerson. Proved Nov. 9, 1761.
1761, Nov. 9. Inventory, £262.10.6, made by John Stout and Edward Prall.   Lib. 11, p. 137.

1761, May 12. Prall, Peter, of Amwell Township, Hunterdon Co.; will of. Eldest son, Peter, ten shillings. Wife, Sarah, bed, etc. Sons, Peter and Abraham, the land I purchased of my brother, John Prall. Son, Aaron, the tract where he lives. Son, John, tract where he lives. To my youngest son, Isaac, the homestead where I live, and he is to provide for his mother. Daughters, Mary, Sarah and Catherine, £50 each. The shares of Mary and Sarah, to be kept in the hands of my Executors during their married state with their pres-

22

ent husbands; and, if Mary and Sarah should die, then their share to become the right of each own's daughters named Sarah. Executors—sons, Abraham and John. Witnesses—John Reading, Thomas Reading, Jacob Mattison. Proved July 7, 1761.

1761, June 20. Inventory, £668.17.0, made by Thomas Atkinson and Jacob Mattison. Lib. 11, p. 38.

1761, Sept. 22. Predmore, John, of New Brunswick, Middlesex Co.; will of. My real and personal to be sold. Wife, Ruth, £100. My only child, Mary, the wife of Doctor Stites, £50. Nephew, John Predmore, the son of my brother, Benjamin Predmore, £50. My kinswoman, Phebe Munteer, £20. My brothers and sisters to have the rest after wife's death. Executors—wife, Ruth, and my brother, Daniel Predmore, and my wife's brother, Samuel Bayles. Witnesses—Stephen Warne, Stephen Warne, Jr., Benjamin Lukes. Proved March 18, 1763.

1763, March 17. Inventory, £104.3.10, made by John Story and John Dunan.

1764, Dec. 24. Citation to Ruth Patten (late Ruth Predmore), Daniel Predmore and Samuel Bayles, Executors of John Predmore. Whereas Hezekiah Stites and Mary Stites, his wife (late Mary Predmore, only child and one of the legatees), have made complaint that the Executors have neglected to file an account of the administration, you are now cited to exhibit it, etc.

1766, July 28. Citation. John Predmore, nephew and one of the legatees, made the same complaint, and parties are cited to exhibit an account. Lib. H, p. 223; Lib. H, p. 376; Lib. H, p. 631.

1762, Feb. 17. Price, Edward, of Allentown, Monmouth Co. Int. Adm'r—Isaac Price. Fellowbondsman—Peter Bruere; both of said place. Witness—Mary Severns. Lib. 11, p. 135.

1768, Jan. 20. Price, Isaac, of Allentown, Monmouth Co.; will of. Sister, Elinor Bruere, £150. The interest of £100 to be paid to my sister, Ann Saunders, yearly, and after her death the said £100 to be divided among my sister's, Mary Imlay's, children. The interest of £150 to my sister, Mary Imlay. Sister, Sarah Burson, £150. Real estate to be sold. Executors—my friend, Nathan Robins, and brother, Peter Bruere. Witnesses—John Robins, Moses Robins. Proved March 23, 1768.

1768, March 9. Inventory, £1,242.17.7, made by John Robins and Moses Robins.

1771, July 30. Account by Executors.

Lib. 13, p. 406; Lib. 14, p. 408.

1763, April 6. Price, John, of Willinborough Twsp., Burlington Co. Int. Adm'r—Jacob Perkins, of said place. Fellowbondsman—Isaac Heulings, of Burlington. Lib. 11, p. 301.

1763, April 18. Inventory, £81.19.1, made by William Heulings and Seth Lucas.

1764, June 26. Account by Adm'r.

1769, Jan. 13. Price, Richard, of Gloucester Twsp., and Co.; will of. Wife, Rebecca, all my estate during her life, and, after her death, to my children. Son, Jacob, to be bound to a trade, and son, Ellis, to be put to anything that suits him best. Executors—Jacob Jenning and my wife. Witnesses—Josiah Hillman, William Miller, Jacob Matlock. Proved Nov. 24, 1770.

1770, Nov. 16. Inventory, £185.16.7, made by John Hinchman and Richard Weekes.
1771, Oct. 10. Account by Rebecca Price.
Lib. 15, p. 83; Lib. 14, p. 408.

1762, Nov. 15. Price, Samuel, of Borough of Elizabeth, Essex Co.; will of. My eldest brother, Isaac Price, 6 shillings. I give ¼ of my estate to George Amory, an orphan child, son of George Amory, deceased. To Mary Ann Rich, daughter of George Rich, dec'd, one other ¼. To Philip Hyat, son of Catharine Blackledge, otherwise Hyat or Wilment, one other ¼. To Matthias Townly, son of James Townly, deceased, one other ¼. Executors—Robert Ogden, Jr., son of Robert Ogden, Esq., and Matthias Ogden, son of Samuel Ogden. Witnesses—John Foster, Mary Thomas, Thomas Tobin. Proved Dec. 29, 1762. Lib. H, p. 522.

1766, Aug. 26. Prickitt, Josiah, of Northampton, Burlington Co.; will of. Wife, Sarah, the rest of my estate, after debts are paid; but, as my wife is now very sick, if she die, then same to be divided between my father, Jacob Prickitt, and John Cowperthwaite. Executor—father, Jacob Prickitt, but, if he be dead, then my friend, William Rogers. Witnesses—Isaac Evans, Bathsheba Evens, Atlantica Stokes. Proved Oct. 31, 1766.
1766, Oct. 28. Inventory, £449.0.10, made by Isaac Evans and Jacob Evens. Lib. 13, p. 27.

1769, May 29. Prior, John, of Essex Co. Ward. Son of Andrew Prior, of said place, deceased. Guardian—William Parsons, of said Co. Lib. K, p. 93.

1762, July 31. Pritty, John, of Hardwick, Sussex Co. Int. Adm'rs —Rebecca Pritty, widow, and Edward Oatley. Fellowbondsman— Francis Glover, of Hardwick, yeoman.
1762, July 29. Inventory, £22.7.6, made by Francis Glover and Thomas Lundy.
1766, Dec. 13. Account by both Adm'rs. Lib. 11, p. 290.

1760, Feb. 21. Provoost, David, of New Barbadoes, Bergen Co.; will of. Eldest son, William, £10. Wife, Geertruyd, goods. Son, David Rynders, goods. Daughter, Catharine, goods. Daughter, Affie, goods. Real estate to be sold and the proceeds divided among my wife and the said children. If any children die under age, then it is to go to the rest. Daughters, Effie and Catharine, my linen. Executors—wife, Geertruyd, my sons, William and David Rynders, and my daughters, Catharine and Effie. Witnesses—Abraham Westervelt, Nicasie Kip and Sarah Gutridge. Proved March 15, 1765. Lib. H, p. 570.

1768, Jan. 20. Pryer, Andrew, of Elizabeth Borough, Essex Co.; will of. Wife, Lydia, ⅓ my moveable estate, and the apparel, which were her mother's, and the use of my lands, till my sons are 14. Sons, John, Simon and Moses, my lands. If the child my wife is pregnant with be a boy, then it is to have its share of land. Daughter, Sarah, curtains and the apparel that was her mother's. Daughters, Sarah and Jane, rest of moveables. Executors—friends, Amos Potter, Esq., and Alexander Simson. Witnesses—Jonathan Elmer, Jabish Rogers, Stephen Ball. Proved Feb. 23, 1768.
Lib. I, p. 304.

1760, Jan. 28. Pulling, John, of Great Egg Harbor, Gloucester Co., cordwainer; will of. Daughter, Elizabeth Pulling, £1. Wife, Deborah, the rest. Executrix—my wife. Witnesses—Daniel Leeds, Rebecca Leeds, Benjamin Hofmin. Proved Feb. 11, 1764.

1764, Aug. 24. Renunciation by Deborah Pullin, widow of John Pullin, in favor of her brother, Nehemiah Leeds.

1764, Sept. 14. Adm'r—Nehemiah Leeds. Fellowbondsman—Peter Risley; both of said Co., yeomen.

1764, Jan. 9. Inventory, £90.6.8, made by Daniel Leeds and Francis Smith. Lib. 12, p. 25.

1769, April 11. Quick, Francis, of Kingwood, Hunterdon Co. Int. Adm'rs—Hannah Quick and Abraham Bonnel. Fellowbondsman—Johan Bartholomew; all of said Co. Witness—Philip Crandin.

1769, April 3. Inventory, £369.8.0, made by Philip Grandin and Nehemiah Dunham.

1773, Nov. 25. Account by both Adm'rs.
Lib. 13, p. 532; Lib. 14, p. 540.

1768, Oct. 22. Quick, Peter, of Sowerland, Somerset Co., yeoman; will of. Wife, Maria, use of farm till son, Peter, is 21. Son, Teunis, farm where he lives, that I bought of Cornelius Van Arsdalen; also 50 acres of woodland along line of Hendrick Harder. Son, Jochem, the farm where he lives, that I bought of Peter Dumont. Son, Jacobus, farm where he lives, that I bought of Robert Lettes Hooper and Philip Kearney. Son, Peter, farm I live on, that I bought of Hendrick Hoogeland and John Jewel. Daughters, Vrowtye, Geertye and Neeltye, £500 each. Executors—sons, Teunis, Jochem and Jacobus, and my cousin, Abraham Quick. Witnesses—Gerret Van Aersdalen, Jacobus Van Nuys, Peter Stryker. Proved Feb. 23, 1769.
Lib. K, p. 65.

1761, May 26. Quick, Thomas, of Greenwich, Sussex Co., weaver. Int. Adm'x—Rachel Quick, widow. Fellowbondsman—Jonathan Pettit, Esq.; both of said Co. Witness—Samuel Tucker, Jr.

1761, May 1. Inventory, £56.1.3, made by William Lander and John Anderson. Lib. 10, p. 465.

1768, May 16. Quicksall, Sarah, of Chester Twsp., Burlington Co.; will of. Son, Thomas Quicksall, sheet and blanket. Son, Daniel Quicksall, 5 shillings. Son, William Quicksall, 5 shillings. Granddaughter, Mary Taylor, case of drawers. Daughter, Sarah Taylor, residue. Executors—son-in-law, John Taylor, and my daughter, Sarah Taylor, his wife. Witnesses—Sarah Scholey, Samuel Stevenson, Richard Brown. Proved July 13, 1768.

1768, July 9. Inventory, £52.2.6, made by Edward Wheatcraft.
Lib. 13, p. 422.

1767, Aug. 12. Quimby, Ephraim, of Amwell, Hunterdon Co.; will of. Sons, Daniel, Samuel and Ephraim Quimby, and my wife Elizabeth, and my daughters, Pheby, Elizabeth, Marcy, Sarah, and Filenah Quimby, all my lands. Executors—my wife and Isaiah Quimby. Witnesses—William Rettinghousen, Peter Rettinghousen, Adam Hall, Jr. Proved Sept. 25, 1767.

1767, Sept. 23. Inventory, £418.12.0, made by John Mullinner and William Rettinghousen. Lib. 14, p. 90.

1765, June 3. Randolph, Jeremiah, of Borough of Elizabeth, Essex Co.; will of. Wife, Ruth, such part of my moveable estate as she chooses. A part of my plantation, joining to James Manning, may be sold to pay debts, if it should be needed. Wife to have the use of all lands till my son, Benjamin, comes to 21. The plantation over the mountains to be sold, and my wife to have £100 of the money. Son, Jeremiah, £60. Son, Benjamin, £60. Daughter, Mary, the wife of Daniel Lambert, £20. Daughter, Unus, the wife of Daniel Lyon, £25. Daughter, Sarah, Randolph, £30. Daughter, Martha Randolph, £30. Daughters, Rachel and Elizabeth Randolph, £30 each. Sons, Jeremiah and Benjamin, my salt meadow. Executors—Benjamin Dunn, Jr., of Piscataway, and my wife. Witnesses—Elizabeth Sutton, Henry Davis, Soviah Parker. Proved Oct. 9, 1765. Lib. H, p. 638.

1761, March 12. Raper, Abigail, of Burlington, shopkeeper; will of. Sisters, Mary (the wife of John Hoskins) and Sarah (the wife of Daniel Smith, Jr.), all my goods. Nephew, Joshua Raper Smith, house and lot where I live, when 21, and, if he die before 21, then to my sister, Sarah Smith. My niece, Sarah Hoskins, £20, when 21. Nephew, Raper Hoskins, £20, when 21. Niece, Ruth Hoskins, £20, when 21. Nephew, Joseph Hoskins, £20, when 21. Niece, Lydia Hoskins, £20, when 21. Cousin, Mary Barker, £10, when 21. Executors—brother-in-laws, John Hoskins and Daniel Smith, Jr. Witnesses—Edward Cathrall, Martha Barker, Elizabeth Barker. Proved Oct. 28, 1763. Lib. 11, p. 417.

1768, April 16. Ray, James, of Fairfield, Cumberland Co. Int. Adm'rs—Abigail Ray, widow, and Silas Newcomb, both of said place. Witness—Thomas Harris.
1768, March 31. Inventory, £431.17.4¾, made by Thomas Harris and Daniel Elmer.
1769, May 2. Account by both Adm'rs. Lib. 13, p. 420.

1770, Nov. 14. Ray, William, of Alexandria, Hunterdon Co. Int. Adm'r—George Ray. Fellowbondsman—Alexander Rea; both of Kingwood Twsp., said Co.
1770, Nov. 12. Inventory, £72.15.0, made by Samuel Everett and Ralph Johnson. Lib. 15, p. 99.

1769, Oct. 31. Raymond, Seth, of Essex Co. Ward. Son of Peter Raymond, of said place, deceased. Guardian—Timothy Day.
Lib. K, p. 130.

1769, Feb. 8. Read, Alice, of Burlington Co.; will of; being the wife of Charles Read, Esq., of New Jersey, and daughter of Jacob Thibou, late of the Island of Antigua, and Dorothy, his wife, who, after the decease of Jacob Thibou, married Francis Delap of said Island, by articles of marriage of the Honorable Thomas Jarvis, of said Island. At or about the time of his marriage with Rachel Thibou, sister of me, the said Alice Read [was] intitled to money, and am by virtue of the will of my mother, Dorothy Delap, intitled to money which was bequeathed to me by the will of said Dorothy Delap, made during the life of Francis Delap, and dated about Nov. 1, 1757, and proved and recorded in the Registry of Wills in Antigua, which was made during the coverture of the said Dorothy

[and] reserved to her by one Indenture Tripartite, entered into between Francis Delap, of one part, James Doig and Nisbett Darby, of 2nd part, and Dorothy Thibou, of 3rd part, and dated July 1, 1745; and one other Indenture between Francis Delap and his wife, Dorothy, of one part, and James Doig and Nisbett Darby, of other part, dated Feb. 10, 1747; and another Indenture between the last recited parties, dated March 12, 1750; and by the will of Dorothy Delap, after reciting the Indentures, she bequeaths to Francis Delap and James Doig all her estate in trust, and the share given to Alice, the wife of Charles Read, shall not be paid in the life of said Charles, either to him or Alice, but, notwithstanding the coverture, the same shall be disposed of as said Alice shall direct by writing, and to go as she directs after her death; but if the said Charles Read dies before his wife, Alice, then it shall be paid into her hands; and Dorothy, the mother of Alice is long since dead, and the sums due to Alice Read, by virtue of the marriage articles and by the will of Dorothy Delap, is now in the hands of William Livingston, of Island of Antigua; and therefore I bequeath £700 of the same to my cousins, James Pemberton and John Pemberton, of Philadelphia, merchants, and my friend, Samuel Allinson, of Burlington, in trust, to receive what I give to my son, Jacob, and my grandson, Charles Read, and such part as is necessary is to be sent to Philadelphia in the produce of Antigua, there to be sold, and out of the proceeds I give to Jacob Read the interest of £500, and, if he dies without issue after his father, the principal is to be paid to my grandchildren, reckoning what he·will have at my decease of the money which was settled on me by the marriage articles of Thomas Jarvis, as part of the £500. Grandson, Charles Read, to have £200 in trust, and he is to be put to school. The rest of money I give to my husband, Charles Read, and my son, Charles. Witnesses—Jonathan Odell, Anne De Cow, John Lawrence. Proved Nov. 15, 1769, by Rev. Jonathan Odell, minister of St. Mary's Church in Burlington, and John Lawrence, Mayor of said City. Lib. 14, p. 82.

1765, Aug. 28. Read, Samuel, of Somerset Co. Int. Adm'rs—Peter Perrine and William Thompson; both of said Co.
1765, Aug. 29. Inventory, made by Daniel Perrine and Hendrick Probasco.
1770, April 6. Account by Peter Perrine. "Paid the lawyers, when I was cited before the Governor, when Robert Read wanted to get possession of the estate, £8.3.0. Paid Jean Read, Elizabeth Read and Robert Read, for their accounts. Paid James Anderson, the Adm'r of the estate of the widow of said Samuel Read, and was received out of the estate, £62.10.4." Lib. H, p. 521.

1763, Jan. 22. Read, Thomas, of Hopewell, Cumberland Co.; will of. Wife, Susannah, all the law gives her. Sons, Thomas and Israel, 10 shillings each. Remainder to my children, Experience Miller, Patience Sayre, Rachel Miller and Mary Freman. All my estate to be sold. Executors—son-in-laws, Annanias Sayre and John Miller. Witnesses—Samuel Clark, Josiah Harris, Ruth Harris. Proved at Stow Creek, May 13, 1763.
1763, March 18. Inventory, £524.1.5, made by John Reeves and William Shute. Lib. 11, p. 404.

CALENDAR OF WILLS—1761-1770   343

1767, Sept. 20. Reade, John, of Twixbar, Hunterdon Co.; will of. Wife, Mary, ⅓ the whole estate, and the rest to my sons and daughters when the rest are of age. Executors—friends, Philip Schuiler, Jacob Schuiler and Roelof Roelofson. Witnesses—David Jones, Matthias Backer. Proved Oct. 17, 1767.
1767, Oct. 10. Inventory, £166.17.10, made by Hendrick Hoffman and John Rose.   Lib. 13, p. 270.

1768, Oct. 31. Reading, Daniel, of Amwell, Hunterdon Co. Int. Adm'rs—John Gregg and Gershom Lee. Fellowbondsman—Jasper Smith; all of said place. Witness—John Porter.
1768, Oct. 29. Inventory, £172.12.6, made by John Gregg and Gershom Lee, Adm'rs, and William Norcross and Ludwig Smith, appraisers.
1772, Oct. 26. Account by Adm'rs.
                              Lib. 12, p. 524; Lib. 15, p. 518.

1767, Oct. 1. Reading, John, of Amwell Township, Hunterdon Co., yeoman; will of. Have already conveyed land by deeds to several of my sons and daughters. Have conveyed to my eldest son, John, in his lifetime, the farm where he did then dwell, in Amwell; and he died, and did appoint his wife, Isabel Reading, his brothers, Joseph and Thomas Reading, his Executors, and ordered them to sell said farm; and now I give to his Executors several tracts in Morris and Sussex Counties, viz., the northeast part of a tract near Zuckasuning Plains, in Morris Co., which is part of 538 acres, besides 56 acres of pine right land, on northwest thereof; also ½ of a tract on the road leading from Greenwich to Hardwick, in Sussex Co., of 303 acres; also 1/6 part of three pieces in Oxford Twsp., Sussex Co., containing in the whole 702 acres, and taken up by me, and suitable for an iron works; also ¼ of 1,000 acres, being the northwest part of 12,050 acres, at Newtown, Sussex Co.; all of which the said Executors may sell and pay debts, and divide what money is left to widow, Isabel Reading, and to all surviving children, except sons, John and Charles. To my son, George, 1/6 part of said lands in Sussex Co.; also 60 acres in Amwell, lying in the rear of the homesteads of his brothers, Daniel and Thomas; also 7 acres opposite the Dutch Church in Amwell, which was purchased from Ruloff Skank; as well as other lands. Son, Daniel, 1/6 of the above said 3 tracts, and ½ of two tracts in Newtown. Son, Joseph, also has his share of said lands, as also son Richard. Son, Thomas, has his 1/6 part, and also ⅛ part of a Propriety, formerly grandfather Reading's. To son-in-law, Charles Beatty, and Ann, his wife, 200 acres near the heads of Merritt's Brook, on Scott's Mountain, Oxford Twsp., Sussex Co., and other lands. To my wife, Mary, £55, and part of the personal estate, and £20 yearly. To my grandson, John Reading, eldest son of my late son John, a silver tankard. Headstones to be at my grave and that of my wife and son, Samuel. To the Presbyterian Church of Amwell Twsp., £10. Mentions a son-in-law, by name of Mills. Executors—sons, Daniel, Joseph and Thomas. Witnesses—William Peters, Thomas Lowrey, Jacob Mattison.
1767, Oct. 29. Codicil. Farm in Amwell and Reading Townships, Hunterdon Co., now in the possession of my son, Daniel, of 390 acres, to be held in trust by my Executors, and the profits to be received by my son, Daniel, and Euphenia, his wife, till his young-

est child is 12 years of age; and then the farm shall be for the use of John Read Reading and Daniel Reading, the two eldest sons of my son Daniel. Son, Thomas, and his wife, Rebecca, to have the profits of a farm of 400 acres to bring up his children, which farm is to go to the use of his two oldest sons, Joseph and Thomas. Son, Joseph, and his wife, Amey, provided for in like manner, who have eldest sons, William and John. Son, George, 1/5 of a tract in Sussex Co., which was taken up and surveyed to John Reading, the elder, by a warrant, dated 10 of March 1714/15 (Lib. A, fol. 160), which is to be held in trust for the benefit of his sons, John Mullen Reading and George Reading, Jr. Proved Jan. 27, 1768.

1767, Nov. 20. Inventory, £736.0.6, made by John Gregg and Gershom Lee. Lib. 13, p. 338.

1766, Nov. 15. Reading, John, Jr., of Amwell, Hunterdon Co., yeoman; will of. As it pleased my father, by several deeds, to give to me several tracts in various parts of New Jersey, and he hath given expectation of granting some more of his real estate before the time of his death to some of my surviving children, therefore I recommend the management thereof to my Executors. The farm whereon I live is, by deed from my father, given to my two eldest sons, viz., John and Charles, yet I give the profits thereof to my wife, Isabella, till my youngest children come to the age of 12 years. To sons, John and Charles, a lot of land in Amwell (near the east end of the Great Swamp), of 125 acres. To sons, Montgomery and Alexander, a tract on the northwest side of the Paquaess River, of 190 acres, and the meadow joining the northwest side of said tract of 172 acres, and 19 acres of woodland; it is bounded southeast by brother Thomas' land, northwest by Augustin Reid's, northeast by father's land (but designed for brother George), and southwest by land of John Beaumont. Legacies are given to children, Rebecca, Montgomerie, Alexander and Mary, when they come of age. Executors—my wife, and my brothers, Joseph and Thomas Reading. Witnesses—Hugh Hunter, Henry Baillie, Thomas Bess. Proved March 21, 1767.

1767, March 4. Inventory, £478.6.6, made by Thomas Atkinson and John Sharp. Lib. 13, p. 232.

1769, March 21. Rederick, Andreas, of Reading Twsp., Hunterdon Co., yeoman; will of. To my grandchildren, Hendrick Yagar, Anna Maria (wife of Anthony Fordtooff), and to Elizabeth, the wife of James White, all children of my daughter Catherine, wife of Peter Yagar, £80 to each. The 3 children of my daughter, Eleanor, late the wife of Christian Harsel, to wit, Anthony, Christean, wife of John Smith, and Hannah, wife of William Shaver, £80 each. The rest of my estate I give to my daughter, Catherine Yagar, the wife of Peter Yagar. Executors—my friend, Jacob Vanderbilt, Edward Wilmot, and my son-in-law, Peter Yagar. Witnesses—Marten Wyckoff, Samuel Mannon, Daniel Hunt. Proved April 7, 1770.

1770, April 6. Inventory, £1,062.11.0½, made by Marten Wyckoff and Mordecai McKinney. Lib. 14, p. 226.

1759, Nov. 7. Redford, John, of Monmouth Co.; will of. Grandson, Redford Ashfield, 5 shillings. Wife, Lydia, house and land where I live, and rest of my estate, having no doubt but that she will bequeath it to our daughter, Elizabeth Ashfield. Executrix—my wife. Witnesses—Josiah Parker, Margaret Parker, Richard Lawrence. Proved Aug. 15, 1764. Lib. H, p. 542.

CALENDAR OF WILLS—1761-1770　　　345

1762, Jan. 30. Redman, Thomas, of Newton, Gloucester Co., merchant; will of. My wife, Marcy, £350. Daughter, Mary Redman, goods. Son, Thomas, house and lot where I live, in Haddonfield, and the land I bought of John Hillman, Jr., of 12 acres in Newton, and he to pay to my daughter, Mary Redman, £20. Son, John, plantation which I bought of Mary Smith and Josiah Smith, in Newton, of 171 acres. Executors—eldest son, Thomas, my son, John, and my daughter, Mary Redman. Witnesses—William Griscom, Richard Gibbs, Richard Weekes.
1766, Sept. 12. Codicil. Wife, Marcy, house in Haddonfield which I lately bought, and daughter, Mary Redman, is to have a home there while she is single. Sons, Thomas and John, the cedar swamp, which I bought of John Eastlack, on a branch of the Great Egg Harbor River. Witnesses—William Griscom, Joseph Roberts, Samuel Clement. Proved Oct. 28, 1766.
1766, Nov. 29. Inventory, £5,087.4.10, made by David Branson and John Gill.　　Lib. 12, p. 363.

1768, Nov. 1. Redstreak, John, of Lower Penns Neck, Salem Co.; will of. Wife, Isable Redstreak, use of all real and personal while my widow, in order to bring up my children. Daughters, Martha Redstreak and Isable Redstreak, £100 each, when they are 18. Son, Francis, the plantation where I live, when he is 21. My wife is now pregnant, and, if it be a boy, it is to be called John, and he shall have that plantation whereon Alexander Hill now lives. Executors—friend, Alexander Hill, my wife, Isabella, Trustee and my friend, Andrew Standly. Witnesses—John Dunlap, Aaron Dunlap, William Stretch. Proved Dec. 15, 1768.
1768, Dec. 2. Inventory, £243.16.9, made by William Robinson and Jacob Townsend.　　Lib. 14, p. 98.

1765, Sept. 11. Reed, Anna, of Millstone, Somerset Co., widow of Samuel Reed. Int. Adm'r—James Anderson, Attorney-at-law, of Sussex Co., by the desire of Anna Reed, before her death. Fellowbondsman—Daniel Perrine, of Millstone.　　Lib. H, p. 530.

1761, April 11. Reed, Benjamin, of Trenton, Hunterdon Co. Int. Adm'x—Jemima Reed. Fellowbondsmen—Obadiah Howell and Isaac Green, all of said place. Witnesses—Evan Reynolds, John Hendrickson and Benjamin Holden.　　Lib. 10, p. 460.

1768, Jan. 28. Reed, Giles, of Amwell, Hunterdon Co. Int. Adm'rs—Mary Reed, widow of said Giles, and Samuel Corwine, both of said place. Witness—Richard Reed.
1768, Jan. 21. Inventory, £248.18.6, made by Richard Reed and George Corwine.
1770, June 1. Account by both Adm'rs. Lib. 13, p. 312; Lib. 15, p. 42.

1766, Sept. 9. Reed, Henry, of Fairfax Twsp., Cumberland Co.; will of. Land in Piney Neck to be sold. Sister, Mary Page, 50 acres at Gravelly Run. My brother, Daniel Reed, a gun. Wife, Phebe, rest of personal estate and plantation where I live, during life. If my wife prove with child, then I give it my lands; but, if not, then I give my brother's, James Reed's, son James, 100 acres; and my brother, Daniel, the place where I live; and my brother, Isaiah, the salt meadow. Executors—my wife and David Page. Witnesses—

Joseph Ludlam, Silvanus Townsend, Jr., Abigail Ludlam. Proved Oct. 13, 1766.
1766, Nov. 22. Inventory, £340.5.6, made by David Shepherd and William Nucome.
1769, March 25. Account by Phebe Reed.
Lib. 12, p. 329; Lib. 13, p. 495.

1760, Dec. 22. Reed, John, of Upper Freehold, Monmouth Co., yeoman; will of. My executors to have the care of my children and bring them up to trades, and they are to have all my estate. Executors—my brother, Joshua Reed, and John Clauson. Witnesses—Richard Reed, James Vaughan, William Lawrence. Proved Jan. 21, 1761.
1761, Jan. Renunciation by Joshua Reed and John Closson. Witnesses—Obadiah Howell and Stephen Howell.
1761, Jan. 21. Adm'r—Richard Reed. Fellowbondsman—Joseph Robins; both of Upper Freehold, farmers. Witness—Samuel Phillips.
1761, Jan. 17. Inventory, £57.6.0, made by Edward Taylor and John Combs.
Lib. 10, p. 423.

1762, Sept. 24. Reed, John, Sr., of Freehold, Monmouth Co., yeoman; will of. Wife, Anna, my personal estate, and, after her death, to be divided between my three daughters and my two granddaughters, daughters of my daughter Anna, late of Lamberton, deceased, viz., Margaret and Catherine. The names of the three daughters are, Elizabeth, Isabella and Jane. Son, John, the land I live on and ½ a meadow, which I bought of Charles Gordon; and I give him the other ½ of the meadow, but he is to pay to his sisters and his two nieces, viz., Anna's two daughters, and to his brother James, £5. Son, James, that land in Cranberry, Middlesex Co., that I bought of Robert Burnet, a Proprietor, and now in possession of my son, John Reed, but paying to my daughter, Elizabeth, £40, and to my daughter, Isabella, £40, and to my granddaughters, Margaret and Catherine Bartley, £40, and to my daughter, Jane, £40. To grandson, John Combs, £10, and grandsons, John and Aaron Reed (sons of James), £14. Executors—sons, John and James, and my son-in-law, Jonathan Combs. Witnesses—Peter Bowne, Zebulon Baird, Thomas Bullman.
1766, Dec. 1. Codicil. To my three daughters, Elizabeth, Isabella and Jane; and my granddaughter, Catharine Barckley, various goods. Grandson, Robert Combs, £10. Witnesses—Peter Bowne, Zebulon Baird, Thomas Bullman. Proved Oct. 27, 1770. Lib. K, p. 274.

1767, May 30. Reed, Jonathan, of Egg Harbor, Gloucester Co., yeoman. Int. Adm'rs—Dinah Reed and Joseph Ingersoll. Fellowbondsman—Benjamin Ingersoll, yeoman; all of said place. Witness—Samuel Risley.
1767, March 9. Inventory, £174.8.8, made by Edward Doughty and Edmund Cordeary.
Lib. 13, p. 133.

1761, Feb. 18. Reed, Sarah, of Monmouth Co. Int. Adm'r—Andrew Reed, brother of said Sarah. Fellowbondsman—William McKnight; both of said Co.
1760, Sept. 1. Inventory, £3.6.1, made by William Craig and Samuel Ker.
1761, June 8. Inventory, £3.15.0, made by David Clayton and Thomas Tomson.
Lib. G, p. 360.

1759, May 23. Reed, William, of Trenton, Hunterdon Co., yeoman; will of. Son, John, 5 shillings; he has already had £60. Sons, Joshua and William, my plantation where I live in Trenton, of 180 acres, excepting thereout 7 acres. Son, Richard, £30, when 21. Daughter, Elizabeth Smith, 5 shillings. Son, Jesse, 4 acres out of my plantation. Son, Joseph, 4 acres. Wife, Elizabeth, ⅓ my plantation, while my widow. Executors—wife, Elizabeth, my kinsman, David Howell, and my sons, Joshua and William. Witnesses—William Welling, Joseph Yard, Ralph Jones. Proved June 5, 1762.
1762, June 4. Inventory, £80.5.6, made by Joseph Jones and William Welling. Lib. 11, p. 353.

1760, Nov. 25. Reed, William, of Dividing Creek, Cumberland Co., farmer; will of. Wife, Dinah, ½ of my farm and ⅓ of my moveable estate. Daughters, Dinah Reed and Mary Reed, the other ⅔ of the moveable estate. Sons, Henry and Daniel, my homestead plantation, and a tract in Pine Neck. Sons, William and James, the lands west of John's. Son, Iselas, 5 shillings. Daughter, Margaret, a "heffer." Daughter, Prissillah, a cow. Executors—son, Henry, and my wife, Dinah. Witnesses—Stephen Clark, Henry Shaw, John Bragg. Proved April 18, 1761. (No Inventory made). Lib. 10, p. 200.

1762, Dec. 28. Reed, William, late a Soldier in the American Troops. Int. Adm'r—Lambart Barns. Fellowbondsman—Levi Murrel, both of City of Burlington. Lib. 11, p. 241.

1760, Dec. 30. Reeder, Isaac, of Trenton, Hunterdon Co., yeoman; will of. To John Yard, son of my former wife, Elizabeth, £2. To Sarah, daughter of my former wife, Elizabeth, 20 shillings. My granddaughter, Franche, my negro girl Flora. Son, John, rest of personal and real. Executor—son, John. Witnesses—Thomas Houghton, George Green, George McNish. Proved March 26, 1763.
Lib. 11, p. 363.

1758, May 9. Reeve, Jonathan, Jr., of Northampton, Burlington Co., laborer; will of. To Jonathan Patterson, the son of Thomas Patterson, of said place, £15, when 21. My brother, Barzillai Reeve, and his 3 children, to wit, John Reeve, Elizabeth Reeve and Samuel Reeve, rest of real and personal. Executor—friend, John Mullin, of Northampton, carpenter. Witnesses—Martha Burr, John Burr, Jr. Proved Jan. 29, 1763. Lib. 11, p. 444.
1766, July 26. Renunciation of John Mullen.
1766, July 28. Adm'r—Micajah Reeve. Fellowbondsman—Thomas Cooper; both of said place. Lib. 12, p. 386.
1766, Nov. 12. Inventory, £82.5.9, made by William Ridgway and Solomon Southwick.
1772, June 22. Account of Micajah Reeve, Adm'r with will annexed. Lib. 14, p. 504.

1760, Dec. 31. Reeve, Joseph, of Cumberland Co.; will of. Wife, Milysent, the profit of my plantation, till son, Samuel, is 21; then he to have ⅓ thereof. Son, Samuel, the said plantation where I live, lying between Mark Reeve and John Reeve. Son, Joseph, my other lands, when 21. Daughter, Martha, £100, when 18. Executors—my wife and Mark Reeve. Witnesses—Samuel Ayers, Hannah Reeve, John Barracliff. Proved June 7, 1763. Lib. 11, p. 454.

1767, Aug. 28. Reeve, Joseph, of Northampton, Burlington Co., yeoman; will of; being the son of William Reeve and very sick. Wife, Jane, my moveable estate and use of my marsh as long as she shall dwell on the plantation where I live (being my father's plantation), and I give her the rent of the house and land hereafter devised to my son, Henry, till he is 21. Eldest son, John, the marsh I bought of Walter Reeve, after my wife shall leave the place of my father. Son, Abraham, £5, when 21. Son, Henry, house and land in Willingborough, which I bought of William Ferrell, and he is to pay to my son, Abraham, £10. Sons, Joseph and Abraham, to be put to trades. Son, Joseph, that land joining Nathaniel Hains, which I bought of Walter Reeve. Executors—wife, Jane, and my son, John. Witnesses—Samuel Roneyans, Isaac Hillier and John Burr, Jr. Proved Sept. 26, 1767.

1767, Sept. 26. Inventory, £201.6.9, made by John Fort and George Elkinton.

1772, July 1. Account made by Jane Reeve, acting Executor.

File No. 4233 C; Lib. 14, p. 501.

1761, May 18. Reeves, Abraham, of Hopewell Twsp., Cumberland Co., yeoman; will of. My wife, Damaris, to have ½ my moveable estate, and ⅓ my homestead, same to return to my son Thomas after her decease. Son, John, ½ my marsh, below Thomas Brown's; also 50 acres of upland, for which he has a deed. To son, Thomas, ⅔ my homestead, and the rest after my wife's death; also the other ½ of said marsh. Son, Abraham, £20. To my daughter, Lydia Garrison, 20 shillings. Daughter, Sarah Moore, £3. Daughter, Abigail Miller, £3. Daughter, Hannah McGallird, £10. Son, Stephen, £10. Children are Abraham, Sarah, Abigail, Hannah and Stephen. Executors—wife, and my son, Thomas. Witnesses—Nicholas Johnson, Noah Miller, Abijah Holmes. Proved June 9, 1761.

1761, June 4. Inventory, £395.17.1, made by Samuel Fithian and John Miller.

1762, June 24. Account by both Executors. Lib. 11, p. 150.

1765, Aug. 7. Reeves, Allen, of Great Egg Harbor Twsp., Gloucester Co. Int. Adm'r—Thomas Clark. Fellowbondsman—Andrew Blackman; both of said place. Elizabeth Reeves, widow of Allen Reeves, renounced in favor of her friend, Thomas Clark, in presence of Elijah Clark. Lib. 12, p. 154.

1762, Feb. 9. Reeves, Elizabeth, of Alloways Creek, Salem Co. Ward. Only daughter of Joshua Reeves, of said place, deceased. Has lands, which fell to her from her father; and she now makes choice of Ezekiel Bennett as her Guardian, till 21.

1762, Feb. 9. Guardian—Ezekiel Bennett. Fellowbondsman—John Bereman; both of Stow Creek, Cumberland Co. Witnesses—Thomas Ware and Phebe Ewing. Lib. 11, p. 164.

1768, May 2. Reeves, Walter, of Burlington Co. Int. Adm'x— Tabitha Reeves. Fellowbondsman—Samuel Garwood; both of said Co. Witness—Samuel Bard.

1768, May 2. Inventory, £51.3.6, made by Nathaniel Haines and William Rogers, Jr. Lib. 13, p. 433.

CALENDAR OF WILLS—1761-1770

1763, Aug. 10. Reeves, William, of Springfield, Burlington Co. Int. Adm'x—Sarah Reeves. Fellowbondsman—John Fenimore; both of same place. Witness—John Reid. Lib. 11, p. 413, 424.
1763, Aug. 18. Inventory, £211.7.0, made by John Fenimore and Nathaniel Haines.

1769, March 7. Reid, Andrew, of Monmouth Co. Int. Adm'r— Henry Perine, principal creditor. Fellowbondsman—David Brooks; both of said Co. Lib. K, p. 68.

1761, Dec. 31. Reid, William, of Great Egg Harbor, Gloucester Co., cooper; will of. Wife, Abigail, ⅓ the profits of my plantation where I live. Son, John, 200 acres where he lives, between Robert Smith and Edward Higgbe. Son, William, part of cedar swamp, on Badcock's Creek; also £200. Son, Jonathan, the plantation where I dwell, and the ½ of 100 acres of meadow. Son, Obediah, the land between Elias Steelman and my son, Jonathan; and ½ of the 100 acres. Daughter, Mary Reid, 2 negroes and some household goods. Executor—son, Jonathan. Witnesses—Edward Doughty, Edward Doughty, Jr., Millisent Doughty. Proved March 21, 1766.
1767, May 21. Whereas William Reid made his will and appointed his son, Jonathan, as Executor, who also died and left goods unadministered, Obadiah Reid and William Reid, sons of said William, deceased, in order to take care of said goods, pray that administration may be granted to them, with will annexed, which was allowed, and Henry Paxson, of Mount Holly, in Burlington Co., became bondsman.
1766, Jan. 23. Inventory, £664.17.3, made by Edward Doughty and Edmund Cordeary.
1767, May 26. Inventory, £648.14.3, made by Edward Doughty and Edmund Cordeary.
1775, Jan. 13. Account by the Adm'rs with will annexed. Legacies were paid to Benjamin Brush, Obadiah Reid, Dinah Reid, Samuel Disorency.
Lib. 12, p. 291; Lib. 12, p. 299; Lib. 15, p. 537.

1760, June 17. Reiley, Dennis, of Kingwood Twsp., Hunterdon Co., yeoman; will of. Wife, ⅓ my moveable estate, and ⅓ the income of my land. Son, Robert Ryley, 50 acres, to be off the east side of my plantation. Sons, James, Dennis, Abraham and John, the rest of the plantation, being 150 acres, and they are to pay to my wife, Sarah, her share yearly. Daughters, Mary Price, Alice Ryley and Grace Ryley, ⅚ of my moveable estate. Executors—my sons, Dennis and Abraham. Witnesses—Henry Slack, Jane Slack, Uriah Bonham. Proved May 10, 1769.
1769, May 10. Inventory, £62.10.0, made by William Allen and Thomas Hankerson. Lib. 14, p. 177.

1770, Jan. 4. Reinolds, William, of Newton, Sussex Co. Int. Adm'r David Lindsay. Fellowbondsman—David Frazer; both of said place.
1770, Jan. 5. Inventory, £16.3.3, made by Amos Pettit and Elijah Allen.
1771, Aug. 22. Account by Adm'r of the estate of "William Reynolds." Lib. 14, p. 414; Lib. 15, p. 2.

1770, Nov. 12. Reinsmith, Henry, of Alexandria Twsp., Hunterdon Co. Int. Adm'r—William Morckel. Fellowbondsman—Abraham Young; both of said place.

1770, Nov. 10. Inventory, £170.6.5¾, made by Abraham Young and Samuel Everitt.

1772, May 7. Account by "William Morckell." Paid Herbert Hiner, John Leonard, Matthias Smith and William Morckel, to each £44.14.10.
Lib. 14, p. 502; Lib. 15, p. 99.

1769, April 21. Remer, George, of Hunterdon Co. Int. Adm'r—Stephen Johnes, of Maidenhead, Hunterdon Co. Fellowbondsman—Jonathan Baldwin, of Princeton, Middlesex Co. Witness—Samuel Furman.
Lib. 13, p. 498.

1766, Nov. 3. Reminton, John, of Hopewell, Cumberland Co.; will of. Grandson, John Reminton, £15, watch and clothing. Granddaughter, Sarah Anderson, the furniture that is in her possession, and her husband's. Grandchildren, Moses, Thomas and Clement and Mary Remington and William Ewing and Remington Ewing, the rest of my estate. Executor—grandson, John Remington. Witnesses—Job Ireland, David Smith, James Talbott. Proved Nov. 23, 1766.

1766, Nov. 22. Inventory, £122.0.6½, made by Enoch Shepherd and Ephraim Shepherd.
Lib. 12, p. 319.

1762, Dec. 17. Rennells, William, of Kingwood, Hunterdon Co. Int. Adm'r—John Opdyck. Fellowbondsman—Robert Campbell; both of Amwell, said Co. Witness—Isaac Yard.

1762, Dec. 14. Inventory, £12.11.0, made by Robert Campbell and Roger Park. (Testator died Sept. 19, 1762).

1765, Sept. 10. Account by Adm'r. One pair of buckles sold belonging to "Robert Reynolds," and was delivered him, valued at £2.6.0.
Lib. 11, p. 338.

1761, Dec. 9. Reves, Josiah, of Gloucester Co. Ward. Guardian—Biddle Reves, of said Co. Fellowbondsman—Thomas Bispham, of Burlington Co. Said Josiah Reves, son of Biddle Reeve, by his petition prayed that the above named Biddle Reeve be appointed his Guardian.
Lib. 11, p. 127.

1766, Nov. 6. Reyerse, Dirk (will is signed, Deerick Verrinkeisn), of Wagraw, Bergen Co., yeoman; will of. Wife, Leana, all real and personal, while my widow, except one lot of land in New York. Son, John Reyerse, 20 shillings, he being eldest son; also the west ½ of homestead lot; also lot in New York City, No. 22. Son, Franses, ½ of homestead, and ½ of lot in New York, No. 25. Daughter, Jean Reyerse, £80. Daughter, Geertie, £80. Sons, John and Francis, not yet 21 yrs. Executors—George Fr. Reyerse and John Fr. Ryerse, and my friend, Cornelius Gerrit. Witnesses—Cornelius Westervelt, George I. Ryerson and Hassel Ryerson. Proved Jan. 23, 1767.
Lib. I, p. 88.

1767, March 3. Inventory, £318, made by Cornelius Westervelt and Hendrick Garrison.

1763, Dec. 6. Reyerse, Luke, of Pequanek, Bergen Co., yeoman; will of. Eldest son, Luke, 10 shillings. Son, George, farm where I live, on east side of Peequanek River, which I had by will from

CALENDAR OF WILLS—1761-1770   351

my father; also 240 acres in Bergen Co., except 16 acres, subject to portions for 3 daughters, amounting to £100, viz., Mary Brown, Ann Reyerse and Elizabeth Reyerse. To Johanna Vanderhoff 8 acres of land, but, if she marry, then to her three sons, Samuel, Joseph and John. Daughters of said Johannas Vanderhoff, viz., Fietie, Elizabeth and Sarah, money from sale of land. To Johanna Vanderhoff, for the use of her six children, Samuel, Joseph, John, Fitie, Elizabeth and Sarah, money from sale of land in Morris Co. Executors—cousins, Marten Frances Reyerse, and Jacobus Bargo, and my son, George. Witnesses—Caleb Worden, Roelef Yacobes, Thomas Jones. Proved March 17, 1764. Lib. H, p. 413.
1764, Feb. 20. Inventory, £425.7.6, made by Thomas Jones and Hendrick Brown.

1766, June 23. Reynolds, Gilbert, of Greenwich Twsp., Gloucester Co.; will of. Plantation I live on to be sold, and all my right in Pennsylvania also to be sold. Wife, Mary, £50, to bring up my two daughters, Rahab and Sarah. Rest of moveables to my four children, viz., Valentine, William, Anne and Rachel. Executors—wife, Mary, and John Reynolds. Witnesses—Nathan Boys, Jr., Mary Cook, Rachel Mattson. Proved March 9, 1768.
1768, March 3. Inventory, £36.7.0, made by Nathan Boys and William Watson. Lib. 12, p. 503.

1769, Feb. 4. Reynolds, Michael, of Middlesex Co., merchant; will of. Wife, Grace, goods and a negro woman. Oldest son, John, my plate. Rest of personal and real to be sold, and proceeds to my wife and my children, John, James, Michael, Francis, Ann, Mary and Elizabeth, when children are of age. My eldest daughter, Francis, I left in Ireland. Executors—my wife and son, John. Witnesses—William Ayers, Charles Rhodes, Hezekiah Stites. Proved Jan. 16, 1770.
Lib. K, p. 169.

1760, July 26. Rhe, David, of Freehold, Monmouth Co.; will of. Wife, Ann, £50. I have provided for my sons, Robert and John. Son, Jonathan, the plantation where he lives, which I bought of William Kerr. Daughter, Anna Rhea, a negro. Son, David, a negro. My homestead is to be valued, and my son, David, may take it at that valuation, but, if he refuse, then son, Robert, may take it, but, if he decline, then son, Jonathan, may take it, and, if he decline, then son, John, can have it; and, if they all decline, then it is to be sold, and £100 given to son Robert, £100 to son Jonathan, and the rest to be divided among my daughters, Elenor, Jannet and Anna. Son, David, £1,000. Daughter, Jannet, £100. Daughter, Anna, £200. Executors—sons, Robert and John; and my friend, Rev. William Tennent. Witnesses—Samuel McConkey, James Gordon, William Hamton. Proved June 23, 1761. Lib. G, p. 458.

1752, April 1. Rhe, Jannet, of Freehold, Monmouth Co.; will of; being widow of Robert Rhe. To friend, William Tennent, £5. Son, David Rhe, a great Bible. Granddaughter, Jannet Rhe, some clothing. Granddaughter, Margret Gordon, wife of John Yeetmare, bed, etc. Granddaughter, Anne Van Skyack, bed, etc. Granddaughter, Isable Van Skyck (daughter of John), a gown. Son-in-law, James English, sheep. To granddaughter, Elizabeth English, a pot. Executors—son, David Rhe, and my son-in-law, James English. Witnesses—Robert English, blacksmith, James Cole, James English, Jr., David English. Proved Aug. 14, 1761.

1761, Jan. 29. Inventory, £164.0.10, made by Joseph Ker and Robert McGallird. Lib. H, p. 27.

1767, May 21. Rhea, Jonathan, of Freehold, Monmouth Co., yeoman; will of. My wife, Lidia, £100 and the furniture. Son, David, £120. Son, Aaron, £100. Son, John, £100. To daughter, Easter, £70. It is supposed that my wife is now with child, and, if it be a son, it is to have £100, and, if a daughter, £70. When son, David, is 21, my plantation to be sold. Executors—my brothers, Robert and John Rhea. Witnesses—Dirck Sutfin, Jacob Van Arsdalen. Proved June 24, 1767. Lib. I, p. 134.

1763, Sept. 30. Ribel, George, of Tewksbury Twsp., Hunterdon Co.; will of. Eldest son, Antony, 30 shillings. To Marlena Schryner, daughter of John Schryner, £15, when she is 18. My land mentioned in a deed, dated Sept. 1, 1760, of 400 acres, to be divided into 3 parts, and given to my sons, Antony Rubel, John George Rubel and William Ribel. Wife, Anne Eve, rest of moveable estate. Executors—sons, Anthony and John George Rubel. Witnesses—William Schuiler, Johannes Counce, Johannes Dennis. Proved Nov. 15, 1763.

1763, Oct. 22. Inventory, £208.2.8, made by William Servis and Johannes Hagar. Lib. 11, p. 535.

1766, Aug. 7. Rich, Mary Ann, of Essex Co. Ward. Daughter of George Rich, of said Co., deceased. Guardian—Caleb Halstead, yeoman. Fellowbondsman—Josiah Wynants, yeoman; both of Elizabeth Town, said Co. Lib. 12, p. 455.

1755, Oct. 15. Richards, James, of Hunterdon Co.; will of. Son, James, a horse and my bed. Son, William, the bed which he uses. Daughter, Mary, the bed she uses. Daughter, Martha, £5. Daughter, Ann, the geese. My lands to said sons. Executors—sons, James and William. To my son, Ananias Brooks, the loom which I lent to him. Witnesses—Jacob Reeder, John Dean. Proved Jan. 27, 1762.
Lib. 11, p. 364.

1769, Dec. 15. Richards, Joseph, of Springfield, Burlington Co. Int. Adm'r—William Ridgway. Fellowbondsman—Joseph Imlay; both of said Co. Witnesses—John Ridgway and William Taylor.

1769, Dec. 12. Inventory, £92.18.6, made by Cornelius Morford and John Ridgway. Lib. 14, p. 133.

1770, Oct. 4. Account of Adm'r.

1770, June 15. Richards, Stephen, of Morris Co. Int. Adm'r—Charles Richards. Fellowbondsman—Samuel Cozort; both of said Co.
Lib. K, p. 223.

1758, March 10. Richman, John, of Pilesgrove Twsp., Salem Co., yeoman; will of. My wife, Sarah Richman, the rent of the home place, while she is my widow, and then to be sold. If the moveables and what is coming of Isaac Vanmeter's estate is not enough to pay the debts, then my brother, Jacob Richman, is to take the rent of the place, and of the grist mill, to do it. Son, Isaac, 2 parts of the home place, to be divided when my son, Abraham, is 20. Son, Abraham, my grist mill and saw mill, and a third of the home place.

Son, Benjamin, the place that is in Quihawking, of 200 acres, when he is 21. My daughter, Rebecca Richman, a colt and cow. Mentions "my daughters." Executors—friends, Jacob Richman and Abraham Newcark. Witnesses—Robert Patterson, James Bond, Joseph Paullin. Proved May 6, 1768.

1768, Feb. 15. Renunciation by Jacob Richman. Witnesses—Harmon Richman and Matthias Richman.

1768, May 6. Adm'r with will annexed—Isaac Richman. Fellowbondsmen—Joseph Paullin and Jacob Paullin, all of Pilesgrove, yeomen.

1768, Feb. 24. Inventory, £815.7.7, made by Elisha Bassett and Joseph Paullin. Lib. 13, p. 393.

1761, Jan. 1. Richmond, John, of Penns Neck, Salem Co., yeoman; will of. To be buried by my ancestors. Wife, Rebecca Richmond, ⅓ my real and personal. Son, Daniel, my lands, he paying my son, William, £50. Daughter, Ann, 2 cows. Executors—my wife and son, Daniel. Witnesses—Sinnick Sinnickson, Joseph Britnell, John Rudeus, John Marshall. Proved Feb. 7, 1761.

1761, Feb. 3. Inventory, £173.19.4, made by John Marshall and John Phillpott. Lib. 10, p. 496.

1760, March 6. Ricketts, William, of Elizabeth Town, Essex Co.; will of. Sons, William, John, Jacob and James, my plantation and sugar works on the Island of Jamaica, West Indies, and my slaves and other lands on said island. Wife, Elizabeth, my farm in Elizabeth Town, where I now dwell. Daughter, Mary, £1,000. Daughter, Jane Tongrelow, £1,000. Both of said daughters are to have a handsome outset. There remains a bond in the hands of John Lawrence, of New York City, and another in the hands of John Kelly, both of which were given for the proper debt of my brother-in-law, Philip Van Horne, and which I order to be paid. To my father-in-law, John Emott, and to George Emott, each a suit of mourning. My body is to be carried to New York and buried in my father's family vault, and my child, interred in Elizabeth Town, is to be put in the same decent mahogany coffin with me, and none to attend my funeral here to the Point but my relations and particular acquaintance, and none but my relations and wife's to attend my interment at New York, except the pall bearers. I desire that Col. John Schuyler and Col. Peter Schuyler, be two of my pallbearers here. To my wife I give 30 acres of land, which I bought of Peter Vanpelt. Executors—wife, Elizabeth; my kinsman, William Walton, of New York City, merchant; the Rev. Chandler, Rector of St. Johns Church in Elizabeth Town; my kinsman, William Walton, of Staten Island; and James Emott, attorney-at-law for my estate, except in Jamaica, for which I make my kinsman, Jacob Johnson, sole Executor. Witnesses—John Chetwood, Margery Vance, George Emott.

1760, June 28. Codicil. To my godson, William Van Cortlandt, a silver mug. To my godson, Charles Hicks, a silver mug. To my godson, William Williamson, a silver mug. To godson, Cyrus DeHart, a silver mug. My godson, William Chandler, a silver mug. Godson, William Man, a silver mug, and £20. Witnesses—John Keyt, Ichabod Dean, George Emott.

1760, Sept. 3. Codicil. I also appoint William Chetwood, Esq., to be one of my Executors. Witnesses—Anthony W. Waters, Phillip V. Cortlandt, John Jones. Proved Feb. 3, 1761. Lib. H, p. 106.

23

1767, Feb. 23. Rider, James, of Deptford, Gloucester Co., laborer. Int. Adm'r—John Rambo, innholder. Fellowbondsman—Benjamin Rambo, joyner; both of said place. Witnesses—Sarah Howell and John Ladd.
Lib. 13, p. 132.

1769, Sept. 26. Ridgway, Allen, of Burlington Co. Ward. Son of Joseph Ridgway. Guardian—David Ridgway, of said Co. Fellowbondsman—John Ridgway.
Lib. 14, p. 124.

1766, Dec. 1. Ridgway, Henry, of Springfield, Burlington Co. Ward. Son of Joseph Ridgway of same place, yeoman. Guardian—Joseph Ridgway, of said place. Fellowbondsman—Thomas Butcher, of Northampton Twsp., said Co., yeoman. Witness—Robert Burchan.
Lib. 12, p. 386.

1761, Feb. 10. Ridgway, Job, of Springfield, Burlington Co.; will of. Sons, John and William, my tracts where I dwell, John to have the west part. I also give them the swamp which my son, Solomon, and I bought of John Monrow. Daughter, £4 yearly during her widowhood (that is to Mary). Sons, Solomon and Job, the land which I had from my brother-in-law, William Butcher, and they are to pay £4 yearly to their sister, Mary, during her widowhood. Rest of moveable estate to my daughters, Mary Butcher and Merriam Moore, the wife of Thomas Moore. Executors—son, John, and my daughter, Mary. Witnesses—Jacob Ridgway, John Fenimore, Joseph Ridgway, Jr. Proved March 6, 1761.

1761, June 2. Inventory, £174.10.6, made by Edward Tonkin and John Fenimore.
Lib. 10, p. 344.

1760, Feb. 16. Ridgway, Joseph, of Springfield, Burlington Co., yeoman; will of. Son, Joseph, my 3 tracts on south side of Barker's Creek in the Great Swamp, except 10 acres. I also give him ½ of that 100 acres which I bought of John Bowlby, and the table which was his mother's; and he is to pay to my daughter, Hannah Ridgway, £50, when she is 18. Son, David, land in Springfield that I bought of John Butcher, and the 10 acres in the Great Swamp, and he is to pay to my daughter, Sarah, £50, when she is 18. Son, Henry, plantation in said Twsp. which I bought of George Harbert, and he is to pay to my daughter, Rebecca Ridgway, £50, when she is 18. Son, Allen, land where I dwell, and he is to pay to my daughter, Jane Ridgway, £50, when she is 21. Son, Henry, ½ of that said 100 acres. Daughters, Sarah, Rebecca and Jane, £30 each, when they are 18. Daughter, Hannah, a negro. Daughters, Abigail, Catharine and Mary, £50 each, when 18. Daughters, Abigail, Hannah, Sarah, Catharine, Mary, Rebecca and Jane, rest of moveable estate. Executors—brothers-in-law, David Budd and Samuel Allen. Witnesses—William Ridgway, Josiah Haines, John Burr, Jr.

1761, Feb. 26. Codicil. My daughter, Abigail, now wife of Josiah Haines, has received her portion, and the goods she has had shall be deemed a part of my estate. Instead of David Budd and Samuel Allen, I appoint my sons, Joseph and David, as my Executors. Witnesses—Benjamin Jones, Richard Ridgway, John Fenimore. Proved March 21, 1761.

1761, March 18. Inventory, £718.18.7, made by Edward Tonkin and John Fenimore.
Lib. 10, p. 157.

1769, Dec. 19. Riggin, John, of Morris River, Cumberland Co. Int. Adm'r—John Daniels, of said place, yeoman. Fellowbondsman—Silas Newcomb, Esq., of Fairfield, said Co.
1769, Dec. 28. Inventory, £89.10.3, made by Silas Newcomb and Thomas Daniels.
1771, June 22. Account by the Adm'r.   Lib. 14, p. 406; Lib. 15, p. 4.

1766, Oct. 4. Righart, Peter, of Greenwich Twsp., Sussex Co.; will of. My brothers and sisters to have my estate, and, if they do not come, then £10 to be given to the poor, and the rest laid out towards building a meeting-house. Executors—Valentine Metts and Matthias Shipman. Witnesses—Frederick Mutchler, Hannah Mats. Proved Nov. 5, 1766.
1769, Feb. 14. Account by both Executors.
Lib. 12, p. 427; Lib. 13, p. 494.

1768, Nov. 4. Rightmire, Daniel, of Somerset Co. Int. Adm'rs—John Rightmirer, eldest brother of said Daniel, and George Rowland. Fellowbondsman—Jacobus Rechtmeyer; all of said Co. Witnesses—Oliver Barnet and William Redford Crawford.
1768, Nov. 14. Inventory, £52.0.5, made by John Sebring and Robert Bolmer.
1769, Jan. 10. Account, made by both Adm'rs.   Lib. I, p. 363.

1767, Nov. 8. Riling, Valentine, of Alloways Creek, Salem Co., cordwainer; will of. Wife, Margaret, all real and personal estate. Executrix—my wife. Trustee—my neighbor, Jacob Freas, Jr. Witnesses—Herman Witscher, George Meyer, William McKasson. Proved Dec. 7, 1767.
1767, Dec. 3. Inventory, £128.6.6, made by Matthias Plaininger and William Craig.   Lib. 13, p. 409.

1760, Sept. 13. Rinearson, Tunes, of Somerset Co.; will of. To my friends, Jacob Fontine and Jaremy Stillwill, all my personal and real estate. Executors—the said Jacob Fontine and Jeremy Stillwell. Witnesses—John Probasco, Jacobus Stryker, Mary Covert. Proved April 29, 1761.   Lib. G, p. 432.

1768, Feb. 13. Ringo, Cornelius, of Maidenhead, Hunterdon Co.; will of. Wife, Frances, all of my estate, after debts are paid. Executrix—my wife, Frances. Witnesses—Mary Severns, Francis Costigin. Proved April 18, 1768.   Lib. 12, p. 512.

1759, Nov. 19. Risley, Peter, of Great Egg Harbor, Gloucester Co., farmer; will of. Son, Peter, ½ of my plantation, the northern part. Son, Richard, the other half, and also 7 acres of meadow that lay close to Absecon Bridge. To my wife and six daughters, my moveable estate. Executors—my wife, Ann, and my son, Richard. Witnesses—Richard Risley, Jr., Mary Risley, Thomas Risley.
1762, Oct. 28. Codicil. Daughters, Ann Risley, Marget Risley, Sarah Risley, Elizabeth Risley, Zibiah Risley, Zesiah Resley and Leah Resley, the moveables, when they are 21. Witnesses—Richard Risley, Thomas Risley. Proved by Richard Risley, Jr., one of the witnesses to the will; but Mary Risley, who was the wife of Richard Risley, Jr., and Thomas Risley, who was an uncle of said Rich-

ard, have been dead upwards of 2 years. Signed by Richard Risley, Jr., Jan. 15, 1767. (The above codicil was never proved, as both of the witnesses were deceased.)
1766, Nov. 6. Renunciation by Richard Risley, the 3rd. Witness—Richard Risley, "Sauer" (Senior).
1765, Nov. 4. Inventory, £80.7.6, made by John Ingersul and John Covenover, Sr.
1767, Aug. 5. Account by Ann Risley. Lib. 13, p. 105.

1767, Jan. 15. Risley, Richard, of Great Egg Harbor, Gloucester Co.; will of. Wife, Rebecca, all my personal estate, and the dowry in my land. Eldest son, Richard, 120 acres of my plantation. Youngest son, Morris, rest of plantation. Son, Thomas, the land I had from my uncle, Thomas Risley. Granddaughter, Rebecca Risley, a "hefer." My daughter, Rebecca, to have 3 cows. Executors—sons, Richard and Thomas. Witnesses—Jonathan Reynolds, Noah Smith, John Covenover, Jr. Proved Feb. 20, 1767.
1767, June 1. Inventory, £115.16.10, made by John Ingersul and Richard Gant. Lib. 13, p. 121.

1764, Sept. 14. Risley, Thomas, of Great Egg Harbor, Gloucester Co. Int. Adm'r—Peter Risley. Fellowbondsman—Nehemiah Leeds; both of said place.
1764, Aug. 7. Inventory, £41.2.6, made by Richard Risley, Jr., and Nehemiah Leeds, Sr.
1767, Jan. 15. Account by Anne Risley, who was Executrix of Peter Risley, who was Adm'r of Thomas Risley, both of whom are deceased. Lib. 12, p. 20.

1761, Aug. 27. Rittinghousen, William, of Amwell, Hunterdon Co.; will of. Son, William, the land where he lives. Son, Peter Rittinghousen, the land where he lives, with the saw mill. Son, Isaac, 5 shillings. Son, Lot, the plantation where I live, and he is to allow my widow, Cathrine, to live in the house and provide for her. Son, Moses, plantation on which he lives. To my daughter, Priscilla's, heir, called and known by the name of William Search, 20 shillings. To my widow, Catherine, and my daughters, Susannah, Anne and Hannah, my personal estate. Executors—sons, William and Peter. Witnesses—Edward Prall, Malakiah Bonham, Lot Rittinghousen. Proved April 13, 1767.
1767, March 13. Inventory, £323.5.2, made by John Opdycke and George Wilson.
1771, May 2. Account by William and Peter Rettinghousen, the Executors. "Paid William Search, £1."
 Lib. 13, p. 205; Lib. 14, p. 407.

1770, Dec. 17. Rivetts, Tunis, of Shrewsbury, Monmouth Co. Int. Adm'r—John Williams. Fellowbondsman—Thomas Leonard; both of Freehold, said Co. Witness—Joseph Leonard. Lib. K, p. 257.

1764, June 21. Roberson, John, of Cape May Co. Int. Adm'r—Daniel Mulford. Fellowbondsman—George Norton; both of said Co. Witnesses—Elizabeth Frasher and Ledosha Robens.
1764, June 22. Inventory, £210.6.10¼, made by Daniel Crowell and Elijah Hughes. Lib. 12, p. 333.

1763, April 12. Roberson, Mary, of Parish of Westfield, Borough of Elizabeth, Essex Co.; will of. To my granddaughter, Elizabeth Roberson (that I brought up), £5, when she is 18. Daughter, Mary, wife of Daniel Ross, Jr., £10. Son, John Roberson, £5. Son, William Roberson, Jr., £10, when 21. Son, Samuel Roberson, a bond I have against him of £8, and I forgive him of all other debts. Executor—William Miller, but, if he die, then I appoint Daniel Ross, Jr. Witnesses—Jonas Baldwin, John Johnson, Ebenezer Price. Proved Jan. 11, 1768.
1768, Jan. 23. Inventory, £79.6.10, made by Thomas Woodruff and William Miller. Lib. I, p. 213.

1770, Oct. 17. Roberts, John, of Chester Twsp., Burlington Co. Int. Adm'rs—Joshua Roberts and Enoch Roberts, both of said Twsp. Fellowbondsman—Joshua Bispham, of Evesham Twsp., said Co. Witness—John Cox. Lib. 15, p. 71.
1770, Oct. 13. Renunciation of Esther Roberts, widow of said John Roberts.
1770, Oct. 12. Inventory, £846.6.7, made by John Cox, William Higbee, Joshua Bispham.

1763, June 21. Roberts, Thomas, of Monmouth Co. Int. Adm'r— John Walling, principal creditor. Fellowbondsman—Thomas Walling; both of said Co. The widow, Ann Roberts, had made request that her brother, John Walling, might administer.
1763, June 24. Inventory, £273.1.1, made by James Mott and Joseph Dorsett. Lib. H, p. 247.

1762, April 7. Roberts, William, of Mannington Precinct, Salem Co., yeoman; will of. Brother, John Roberts, the part of the plantation I live on, and contains 300 acres, with 40 of woodland. Brother, Jonathan Roberts, the rest, and contains 500 acres. Sister, Elizabeth Elliott, £20. To Mary Harris, daughter of my sister, Ruth, £20. To William and Charles Phillpott, sons of my sister Margery, £20, when 21. Executors—my brothers, John Roberts and Jonathan Roberts. Witnesses—Bartholomew Wyatt, Jr., Henry Miller, William Carpenter. Proved Sept. 25, 1762.
1763, Dec. 10. Inventory, £475.13.10, made by Abel Harris and Bartholomew Wyatt, Jr. Lib. 11, p. 275.

1762, Nov. 25. Robeson, Edward, of Oxford Twsp., Sussex Co., blacksmith; will of. I have this day given a quit claim to John Lowry of the plantation that lays on the west side of the Delaware River, on the banks thereof, above the forks, which contains 250 acres, and is the same I had from James Quick; and Lowrey is to pay to my wife, Eleanor, £6 yearly as long as she lives. Daughter, Mary, now wife of Cornelius Albertson, the plantation where I live, on the east side of the Delaware, of 200 acres; but if she die without heirs, then it is to go to the children of, my daughter Sarah, now the wife of John Lowrey, and they are to pay to my wife £8 yearly. Executors—my wife, Eleanor, and my two sons-in-law, John Lowrey and Cornelius Albertson. Witnesses—Peter LaBarr, Sr., Peter LaBarr, Jr., Richard Shackleton. Proved Jan. 17, 1765.
1764, June 25. Inventory, £382.12.9, made by Edward Hunt and Richard Shackleton. Lib. 12, p. 241.

1761, March 26. Robeson, Maurice, of Orange Co., New York, ironmonger; will of. My real and personal estate in this Province and in New Jersey to be sold; that is to say, ironworks in the Highlands, plantation in Jersey, at Green's "Poun," my land called the White Rocks, and the tract where Samson Howell lives; and the money to be given as follows: To wife, Ann, 1/6 part, and to my 5 children, Elizabeth, Mary, John, Acsha and David, the other five-sixths parts. If my wife be now with child, and it be a boy, it is to be named Maurice, and have its share. The children are to be educated. The family may have enough furniture for their use. Executors—wife, Ann, and my brother, Jonathan Robeson, of White Marsh, in Pennsylvania, and my brother-in-law, Dr. John Rockhill, of New Jersey. Witnesses—William Millington, Charles Bessonet, Jonathan Robeson, Mary Robeson. Proved Dec. 31, 1761.

1762, Jan. 5. Inventory, £200.18.6, of the goods of Maurice Robeson, "late of Sussex Co., N. J.," made by John Green and Richard Shackleton.

1785, Oct. Term. John Rockhill, surviving. Executor, is cited to file an account.

1786, June 24. Account by John Rockhill, and there remains £1,603.7.6, to be disposed of, agreeably to the will.   Lib. 10, p. 537.

1762, Sept. 4. Robeson, William, of Amwell, Hunterdon Co. Int. Adm'rs—Sarah Robeson, widow, of said place. Fellowbondsmen—Joseph Robeson, of Pennsylvania, and Robert Spencer, of Trenton. Witness—Mary Severns.   Lib. 11, p. 236.

1765, Sept. 1. Robet [Roberts], Isaac, of Hunterdon Co.; will of. Wife, Mary Roberts, household goods, apparel, hogs, and the things in the lot I rent from Mark Ellis, and also in the lot I have from Robert Lettis Hooper; also ½ the money in the hands of George Tucker. Daughter, Mary Roberts, the other ½ of said money, and she is to have schooling till she is 12 years of age. Executor—friend, Robert Lettis Hooper. Witnesses—James Hooper, George Akinsyelar, Godfry Wimer, Christopher Rider. Proved Oct. 14, 1765.
     Lib. 12, p. 245.

1763, Feb. 21. Robins, Daniel, of Amwell, Hunterdon Co. Int. Adm'x—Frances Robins, widow. Fellowbondsman—Thomas Atkinson, merchant; both of said place. Witness—Samuel Hornor.

1763, Feb. 25. Inventory, £1,099.19.6, made by John Mullinner and John Emley.

1764, Sept. 14. Account by John Peirce and Frances, his wife, late Frances Robins.   Lib. 11, p. 339.

1763, Nov. 28. Robins, Elisha, Jr., of Newton, Sussex Co., yeoman. Int. Adm'r—Elisha Robins. Fellowbondsman—Ephraim Darby; both of said place.

1763, Nov. 28. Inventory, £78.4.11, made by John Loder and William Tharp.   Lib. 12, p. 5.

1762, July 5. Robins, Elizabeth, of New Hanover Twsp., Burlington Co., widow; will of. Grandsons, Arney Biddle and Joseph Arney, each 5 shillings. Son, Joseph Arney, £25. Daughter-in-law, Elizabeth Arney, and her son, Samuel Hall Arney, £50. Daughter, Sarah Wardal's, 3 children £70 amongst them. John owes me £10 and that

CALENDAR OF WILLS—1761-1770   359

is a part of his share. Daughter, Mary Lippincott, £70, if she please to accept it. Granddaughter, Lydia Howell's, two daughters, Rebecca and Elizabeth, £30 each, when 18. My granddaughter, Mary Shinn, the wife of Restore Shinn, the residue. Executor—my son-in-law, Restore Shinn. Witnesses—George Shinn, Jonathan Sleeper, Joseph Goldy. Proved April 6, 1765.
1765, April 6. Inventory, £10.12.6, made by Joseph Goldy and Marmaduke Fort. Lib. 12, p. 83.

1762, May 26. Robins, John, of Cumberland Co. Int. Adm'r—Matthew Parvin, of Dearfield. Fellowbondsman—Silas Parvin, of Hopewell; both of said Co., yeoman. Witnesses—Jonathan Lorance and Thomas Reeves. Lib. 11, p. 239.

1768, March 30. Robinson, Henry, of Freehold, Monmouth Co.; will of. Wife, Anne, the lands that I got with her. My daughter, Charity, negro wench, named Catharine, which my father gave to me. My brother, Joseph, my watch. My apparel to the child that my wife is pregnant with, if it be a boy. Executors—my wife, my father, James Robinson; and my friend, Nathaniel Scudder. Witnesses—John Campbell, William Cole, Peter Schenck. Proved June 16, 1768. Lib. I, p. 285.

1770, June 9. Robinson, Joseph, of Freehold, Monmouth Co.; will of. Son, James, a watch. Daughter, Mary, a watch. Wife, Eunice, rest. Executors—my wife and my friend, Doctor John Lawrence. Witnesses—William Covenhoven, Peter Schenck. Proved July 7, 1770.
Lib. K, p. 227.

1770, April 6. Robinson, Sarah, of Monmouth Co. Int. Adm'r—Robert Hartshorne, of the estate, which was left unadministered on by Thomas Robinson. Fellowbondsman—John Taylor; both of said Co. Witness—William Taylor.
1770, Sept. 6. Inventory, £225.7.5, made by the Adm'r. Balance of the legacy which was bequeathed by the late Chief Justice Morris, and also of her account with said Robert Hunter Morris, and his Executors, settled with said Executors.
1771, July 25. Account by Adm'r. "Paid Rachel, widow of Thomas Robinson, £110.9.0." Lib. K, p. 190.

1765, Aug. 18. Robords, John, of Newark, Essex Co.; will of. Wife, Sarah, use of whole estate, until my son, William, is 14 years of age; then she to have use of house and garden, and she to be paid 30 shillings yearly for each of my sons. When wife is done with moveables, they are to go to my daughters. My sons, Jesse, Ichabod, Joseph and William, to keep for her a cow. Sons, Samuel and Amos Robords, 20 shillings each. I desire to comply with my father's will, and they are to pay mother Robords her dues, and keep her cow. Sons, Jesse, Ichabod, Joseph and William, all that land lying along Elizabeth River, and the land I bought of Daniel Roberts, lying behind Hugh Roberts; also a salt meadow that I bought of Daniel Riggs, lying below Wheeler's Creek; also my purchase right over the mountain. Daughters, Phebe, Hannah and Sarah, £25 each, the day they come to 18. Children are young. If wife be with child, it is to have its share. Executors—my wife,

Sarah, and my friends, Samuel Camp and Jonathan Day. Witnesses —Daniel Riggs, Jedidiah Tichenor, Jane Tichenor.
1765, Aug. 20. Codicil. My son, Samuel, is to be an Executor with the others. Proved April 1, 1766. Lib. I, p. 178.

1763, Dec. 6 Rockerfeller, Pieter, Sr., of Amwell Twsp., Hunterdon Co., yeoman; will of. Son, William Rockafelt, my plantation in said Twsp., which was purchased of William Burlis, Samuel Green and Justis Gonce, bounded by Ezcal Rose, James Abits, Peter Fisher and Noah Hixson, and contains 275 acres. Son, Peter, £10. Daughter, Mary Gaber, moveables. Daughter, Ann Runk, moveables. Daughter, Elizabeth Johnson, moveables. My daughter, Else Snuke, has departed this life and left children, William, Ann, John and Peter, and they are to have goods. Daughter, Cristane, has married a man that uses her ill, that she cannot live with, and my Executors are to keep her's in their hands and give it to said Cristane, and, at her death, what is left given to her children. Executors—son, Peter, and Philip Peters. Witnesses—William Abit, John Garrison. Proved Aug. 16, 1766.
1766, Aug. 11. Inventory, £730.10.5, made by Jacob Snyder and William Abit.
1771, Dec. 23. Account by Executors. Paid, legatees, as follows: Peter Rockafellar, Mary Caver, Ann Runk, Elizabeth Johnson, the children of Alice Snook, and Christian Miller.
Lib. 12, p. 418; Lib. 14, p. 405.

1770, Nov. 13. Rockhill, John, of Burlington Co. Int. Adm'r—Edward Rockhill, of Chesterfield Twsp. Fellowbondsman—John Folwell of Mansfield Twsp.; both of said Co. Witness—Ezra Black.
1770, Nov. 13. Inventory, £47.2.0, made by Ezra Black and John Folwell. Lib. 15, p. 71.

1760, Sept. 13. Rockhill, Robert, of Mansfield Twsp., Burlington Co., yeoman; will of. Daughter, Marcy Curtis, now wife of John Curtis, £5; and to each of her 5 children, which she had by the said John, £10 each, when of full age. Daughter, Hannah Rockhill, £100, and the goods she calls hers. Daughter, Edith Shreve, now the wife of Abraham Shreve, £80. Granddaughter, Elizabeth Shreve, the daughter of said Abraham and Edith, my bed. Grandson, Robert Shreve, son of Abraham and Edith, £5, when of full age. Son, Joseph, all my lands. Executor—son, Joseph. Witnesses—John Rockhill, John Newbold, Isaac De Cow. Proved Jan. 26, 1761.
Lib. 10, p. 155.

1764, Jan. 23. Rodgers, John, of Burlington; will of. Advanced in years. Grandson, John Rodgers, son of Samuel Rodgers, land where I live, when he is 21; and he is to pay to his brother, Samuel Rodgers, £200. My loving daughter-in-law, Elizabeth, now the wife of William Lyndon, land on York Street, till my grandson, Samuel Rodgers, is 21. To Martha, the wife of John Jones, and Hetteble Staples, daughters of my late daughter Mary Staples, £15 each. To Elizabeth, the wife of William Lyndon, negros. Of the residue I give to son, Thomas, ⅓, and to Elizabeth, the wife of William Lyndon, and her three daughters, Elizabeth, Martha and Ann, ⅓, and to the children of my daughter, Martha, now wife of Robert Hosier, ⅓. Executors—son-in-law, William Lyndon, and my friend, John

Antrum. Witnesses—Zachariah Antram, Thomas Oakly, William Heulings. Proved March 26, 1767.
1767, March 7. Inventory, £243.17.4½, made by William Heulings and Zachariah Antram. Lib. 13, p. 57.
1769, June 12. Account by Executors.

1757, Oct. 21. Rodman, Mary, of Burlington; will of. Advanced in years. Son, Samuel Rodman, negroes. Daughters, Anna Rodman and Elizabeth Rodman, the residue. Executors—sons, Scammon Rodman and Samuel Rodman. Witnesses—William Heulings, William Heulings, Jr., John Walling. Proved Oct. 6, 1761.
1761, Oct. 16. Renunciation of Scamon Rodman.
1761, Oct. 16. Adm'x—Elizabeth Rodman, of Burlington, gentlewoman. Fellowbondsman—Scamon Rodman, of same place, gent.
Lib. 10, p. 419; File No. 7163 C.

1760, June 28. Rodman, Samuel, of Burlington; will of. My brother, William, my land in Bucks Co., Pennsylvania, now in possession of Daniel Juddawn and Alexander Harvey; and he is to pay £10 yearly to my brother, John, for 10 years. My brother, Scamon, all my real and personal at Block Island in Rhode Island; also the place where I live; and he is to pay £300 to my brother, William Lister, and Anna, his wife, and £300 to my sister, Elizabeth Rodman, and £100 to my brother, Thomas. To my brother, Thomas Rodman, the plantation which my father bought of Samuel Bayard and lately occupied by Matthias Meek. Executor—brother, Scamon. Witnesses—Daniel Smith, Edward Cathrell, Richard Smith. Proved Oct. 5, 1761.
Lib. 10, p. 417.

1761, Nov. 1. Rodman, Scamon, of Burlington; will of. Brother, Thomas, place where I live. Brother, William, my riding horse. Sister, Anna Lister, land in possession of Benjamin Snodgrass; also the farm where Thomas West lately lived, and now occupied by James Snograss, situated in Warwick Twsp., Bucks Co., Pa. Sister, Elizabeth Rodman, plantation where John Divin lives, and farm now in tenure of John Lawhead. Brother, John, plantations in Warwick, one in possession of Hugh Shaw, and the other in possession of Samuel Shanny. Brother, William, all real and personal estate on Block Island, in Newport Co., Rhode Island, and the land I bought of Godfrey Mallbone and wife, James Honyman and wife and Mary Wickham, by several deeds, and being in Sussex Co., when he is 28. Executor—brother, William. Witnesses—Thomas Pryor, Jr., Robert Smith, Jr., Samuel Allinson.
1761, Dec. 29. Codicil. To Joseph Rodman, son of my brother, John, the place where Hugh Shaw lives, and, if he leave no issue, then to his sister, Margaret Rodman. To Samuel Rodman, son of my brother, John, the place where Samuel Shanny lives, but, if he die, then to his sister, Sarah Rodman. Witnesses—Daniel Smith, Jr., Thomas Pryor, Jr., Samuel Allinson. Proved Feb. 8, 1762.
Lib. 11, p. 219.

1764, Dec. 15. Rogers, John, of Burlington Co.; will of. Brother, William Biddle, watch. Sister, Sarah Biddle, £30. Cousin, Elizabeth Eayre, daughter of John and Rebekah Eayre, £30, when 18. Cousin, Cathrine Eare, daughter of John and Rebekah Eayre, £30. Brother, Isaac Rogers, rest. Executor—brother, Isaac. Witnesses—William Fox, Mary Fox, Ann Antram. Proved Oct. 18, 1765. Lib. 12, p. 187.

1766, May 23. Rogers, John, of Kingwood, Hunterdon Co. Int. Adm'r—Alexander Rogers, of said place. Fellowbondsman—Samuel Fleming, of Amwell, said Co. Lib. 14, p. 92.

1761, May 14. Rogers, Nathaniel, of Morris Co.; will of. Wife, Jemima, ⅓ my place during her life time, and ⅓ the moveables. Son, Jabesh, £7. Son, John, all my lands. To each of my sons, Nathaniel, Benjamin, Simeon, Henry, Amos and David, £10, when of age. Daughters—Phebe, Sarah, Elizabeth and Agnas, each £8. Executors—my wife and William Parrot. Witnesses—Jonathan Elmer, William Johnston, Lewis Winans. Proved May 27, 1761.
Lib. H, p. 19.

1762, Dec. 29. Rogers, Samuel, of Newton, Sussex Co., yeoman. Int. Adm'r—Samuel Rogers. Fellowbondsman—Constant Hart; both of said place, yeomen.
1762, Dec. 28. Renunciation by Margaret Rogers, the widow, in favor of her son, Samuel Rogers. Witness—Isaac Hull.
1762, Oct. 16. Inventory, £21.11.3, made by Hezekiah Smith and Constant Hart. Lib. 11, p. 288.

1761, March 9. Rogers, Thomas, of Hunterdon Co.; will of. Son, Alexander Rogers, the part of the plantation over the river, in Lebanon Twsp., joining James Martin, and commonly called "The Island." Second son, Samuel, the rest of said plantation. Son, Alexander, all real and personal estate in Kingwood Township. Third son, John, £200. Fourth son, William, £200. Daughter, Ruth Rogers, £100. Executors—sons, Alexander and Samuel. Witnesses—Samuel Johnson, James Martin, Jr., Nathaniel Foster. Proved May 23, 1766.
Lib. 14, p. 88.

1762, July 26. Rogers, Thomas, of Kingwood, Hunterdon Co. Int. Adm'r—Alexander Rogers. Fellowbondsman—Samuel Rogers; both of said place. Witnesses—Mary Severns and James Martin.
1762, Sept. 11. Inventory, £278, made by James Martin and John Miller. Lib. 11, p. 337.

1768, April 2. Rolfe, Joseph, of Elsinboro, Salem Co., yeoman; will of. Sister, Elizabeth Rolfe, the plantation where Jacob Evens lives; also the land laying by John Ambler, when she is 18; but, if she die, then I give it to Archable Rolfe, when 21; but, if he also die under age, then I give it to Aaron Bradway's 3 sons, Aaron, Edward and Thomas, when 21. To Aaron Bradway the rest of above plantation, for taking care of my sister, Elizabeth Rolfe. Executor —my father-in-law, Aaron Bradway. Witnesses—Hill Smith, Ann Simmons, Richard Smith, Jr. Proved Dec. 17, 1770. Lib. 15, p. 236.

1762, Nov. 30. Rolph, Benjamin, of Middlesex Co. Int. Adm'r— Moses Rolph, of Suffolk Co., New York. Fellowbondsman—George Brown, of Middlesex Co.
1762, Nov. 29. Renunciation by Sarah Rolph, widow of Benjamin, in favor of Moses Rolph. Witness—Joseph DeCamp. Lib. H, p. 203.

1766, Dec. 9. Rolph, Moses, Jr., of Woodbridge, Middlesex Co.; will of. To John Thomas DeCamp, the son of Joseph DeCamp, £30. To my aunt, the widow Sarah Rolph, the remainder. I am concerned with

Joseph Stringham, Daniel Marsh and Samuel Moore in the sloop called the "Success," and the share of the cargo belonging to me to be sold. Executors—my friend, Joseph DeCamp, and my aunt, the widow Sarah Rolph. Witnesses—Jonathan Bishop, Samuel Burwell, Benjamin Moores, John Wright. Proved Dec. 22, 1766.
Lib. I, p. 15; Lib. I, p. 69.

1753, Oct. 13. Romyn, Jan, of Bergen Co., yeoman; will of. Son, Claas, 10 shillings. Of my personal and real estate, to son, John, 1/7 part; to son, Roelif, 1/7; to son, David, 1/7; to son, Isaac, 1/7; to daughter, Rachel Van Giesen, wife of Joris Van Giesen, 1/7; to daughter, Christina Vrelant, wife of Abraham Vrelant, 1/7, and to grandchildren, children of my daughter, Anganitie Stegg, deceased, late wife of Isaac Stegg, by name John, Isaac and Thomas Stegg, 1/7, when they are 21. Executors—sons, John and Roeliff. Witnesses—Abraham N. Gouverneur, David Provoost, Jacob Roome. Proved June 23, 1763. Lib. H, p. 350.

1769, April 4. Roosevelt, Nicholas, of New York City; will of. Son, Nicholas Roosevelt, silver tankard and English Bible. Wife, Elizabeth, old negro wench Grace. My wife and my daughter, Sarah, are to have support, and my son, Nicholas, and daughter, Elizabeth, to have support and education. If my daughter, Catherine Kirby, become a widow, before the division of my estate, then she is to have support. Then my real and personal I give to my wife, Elizabeth, and children, Catherine Kirby, Sarah Roosevelt, Nicholas Roosevelt and Elizabeth Roosevelt, when Nicholas is 21. Mentions husband of Catherine Kirby, but does not give name. Executors—Abraham Duryee, Isaac Roosevelt and John Thurman, Jr., all of New York City, merchants. Witnesses—Samuel Farmer, Samuel Bayard, Rudolphus Ritzama.
1769, April 16. Codicil. Daughter, Catharine Kirby, £100. Witnesses—Daniel Dunscomb, John Thurman, Jr., Cornelius Roosevelt. Proved June 1, 1769. Lib. K, p. 100.

1761, April 9. Rope, Michael, of Greenwich, Sussex Co., yeoman. Int. Adm'rs—Magdalena Rope and Michael Rope. Fellowbondsman—Peter Melick; all of said Co. Witness—Isaac Hull.
1760, Dec. 10. Inventory, £150.2.0, made by Godfree Melick and John Sharp.
1762, Sept. 18. Account by both Adm'rs. Lib. 10, p. 464.

1761, Feb. 2. Rosbrugh, William, of Sussex Co.; will of. To my brother, John Rosebrough, £10. The rest to my wife, Jane, and my 3 children. Executors—my wife, and my brother, John Rosbrugh. Witnesses—Robert Breden, Thomas Shields, Thomas Little. Proved March 27, 1761.
1761, Feb. 6. Inventory, £407.4.6, made by Thomas Shields and Thomas Likens. Lib. 10, p. 481.

1762, Jan. 14. Rose, Christopher, of Hunterdon Co. Int. Adm'r—Richard Laning. Fellowbondsman—Stephen Rose; both of Trenton, said Co. File No. 578 J.

1768, May 26. Rose, Ezekiel, of Amwell Twsp., Hunterdon Co., yeoman; will of. Well advanced in years. Eldest son, Ezekiel, the plantation in Hopewell, joining lands of John Phillips, Jonathan Smith and others, he paying to his mother the ⅓ of the profits of the place. Son, Jonathan, the plantation I live on, joining lands of William Rokefelt, Jonathan Borross and others, when he is 21, he paying to his mother ⅓ the profits. Son, Charles, £200, when he is 21. Daughter, Sarah Phillips, 20 shillings. Daughter, Hannah Woolverton, 20 shillings. Daughter, Jean Quick, same amount. Daughter, Rachel Rose, various goods. Daughter, Jarusia Rose, also goods. Wife, Mary, is well provided for. Executors—Andrew Smith, Jr., John Fidler and my son, Ezekiel. Witnesses—Andrew Smith, Sr., Timothy Fidler, William Rockfaller. Proved Aug. 9, 1768.

1768, Aug. 2. Inventory, £528.1.11, made by William Rockfaller and Nicholas Stillwell.

1773, June 14. Account by John Fidler and Ezekiel Rose.

Lib. 13, p. 454; Lib. 14, p. 514.

1762, Jan. 16. Rose, Samuel, of Little Egg Harbor, Burlington Co. Int. Adm'x—Anna Rose, widow, of same place. Fellowbondsmen—Joseph Price, of Hopewell, and George Tucker, of Trenton; both in Hunterdon Co. Witness—Isaac Yard.

1762, Feb. 3. Inventory, £363.4.0, made by Joseph Parker and Jeremiah Baker. Lib. 11, p. 133.

1768, April 19. Account by Anna Price, late Anna Rose, on estate of Samuel Rose, as Administratrix

1768, Oct. 15. Rosekrons, James, of Wantage, Sussex Co., husbandman; will of. Wife, Katharine, the best bed. Son, Daniel, daughters, Lenah, Blandenah and Kerche, each five shillings; and the rest I give to my wife and my other children, John, Hezekiah, Aulidaw (daughter), and Solomon; the last one being under age. Land has been sold to Johanes Drake, for which he is to have title. Executors—wife, Katharine, and son, John. Witnesses—Jacob Middaw, Deborah Middaw, John Herring. Proved Feb. 20, 1769.

1769, Jan. 2. Inventory, £422.3.0, made by George Cimber and Samuel Melker. Lib. 13, p. 550.

1756, April 19. Rosell, Zahariah, of Northampton, Burlington Co., yeoman; will of. Wife, Mary Rossell, one cow, and use of land I bought of John Hilliard, while my widow. Daughter, Mary Rossell, household goods. Grandson, Hezekiah Rossell, son of Joseph Rossell, dec'd, 20 shillings. Son, Zacheriah Rossell, the said farm. To sons, Zebulon, James and Barzillai, 20 shillings each. Daughter, Mary Rossell, £3, when 18. Grandson, William Rossell, £5, when 21. Executors—wife, Mary, and son, Zacheriah. Witnesses—Edward Andrews, Sarah Woolman, John Woolman. Proved March 26, 1761.

Lib. 10, p. 328.

1768, Sept. 1. Ross, George, of Springfield, Borough of Elizabeth, Essex Co.; will of. Daughter, Susanna, £10, and what I have on my book against her. Son, William, £120, and the account against him. Daughter, Joanna, £50, and the account against her. Daughter, Abigail, 5 shillings. Wife, Joanna, and daughters, Sarah and Nancy, the rest of my moveable estate. Son, Jehiel, the new house, for services done by him since he was 21; also 15 acres on which the house stands, which land I bought of Timothy Whitehead; also 9 acres on the mountains, which I purchased of Abraham Lacey; also ½ of my tanyard. Son, Matthias, £20, for service he has done since 21. I also give him 33 acres of land, lying between Joseph Wade and Joshua Horton, which I bought of Joseph Wade and John Tucker. Son, George, the rest of lands. Executors—my wife, and my son, Matthias. Witnesses—Joseph Marsh, Ezekiel Cheever, Mary Pierson. Proved Oct. 17, 1768. Lib. K, p. 46.

1765, Oct. 29. Ross, Jacob, of Elizabeth Town, Essex Co., printer; will of. I order my board, lodging, washing and nursing to be paid for to Mary Baldwin. Real and personal estate to be sold, except my clothing. My oldest brothers, John, David and Andrew, one shilling each. To William Baldwin my wearing apparel. My sisters, Sarah, Mary, Elizabeth, Phebe and Joanna, rest of my estate. Executors—friends, Andrew Ross and Mary Baldwin. Witnesses—Saly Baldwin, Benjamin Winans, John Chetwood. Proved Oct. 25, 1766.

1766, Oct. 23. Inventory, £82.4.4, made by George Badgley and Nathaniel Higgins. Lib. I, p. 144.

1764, Nov. 6. Ross, John, of Woodbridge, Middlesex Co.; will of. Son, James, my apparel. My personal and real estate and my right in the boat called "Huming Bird," to be sold. Wife, Ursilla, £20. Daughter, Mary, £30. The rest of money to my wife and daughters, Mary and Jane. Executors—my son, James Ross, of Piscataway; John Ross, son of my brother, John Ross, deceased, and David Crow. Witnesses—Janes Drake, Lewis Stelle, Joseph Davis. Proved Nov. 28, 1764.

1764, Nov. 30. Inventory, £1.206.8.9, made by Jeremiah Manning and Robert Martin. Lib. H, p. 471.

1768, Nov. 15. Ross, Marcy, of Lower Precinct, Cape May Co., widow; will of. Daughter, Priscilla Reyney, the house and land where she lives, she paying to her brother, Jeremiah Eldredge, £26. Daughters, Priscilla Reyney and Sarah Ewings, my apparel. Son, Jeremiah Eldredge, residue, but, if he die before 21, then his share to my children, Aaron Eldredge, Jacob Eldredge, Priscilla Reyney and Sarah Ewings. Executors—sons, Aaron Eldredge and Jeremiah Eldredge. Witnesses—Christopher Foster, Francis Taylor, Abishai Stiles. Proved July 26, 1769.

1769, July 25. Inventory, £273.0.4, made by Christopher Foster and Richard Stiles. Lib. 14, p. 194.

1766, Dec. 24. Ross, Thomas, of Elizabeth Borough, Essex Co.; will of. Wife, Sarah, use of real, that is not ordered sold. My homestead to be divided into two equal parts, and the part that joins Mathias Crane to be sold. The land lying in Elizabeth Town, which I bought of Ephraim Terrill, to be sold. Rest of my homestead to my daughter, Phebe. I am bound to pay debts for my son, David. Executors—my wife and my friend, Stephen Parsell. Witnesses—Humphere Spining, Ichabod Crane, John Chandler. Proved Feb. 4, 1767. Lib. I, p. 197.

1761, June 25. Ross, William, of Cape May Co. Int. Adm'x—Margaret Ross. Fellowbondsman—James Hedges; both of said Co. Witnesses—John Eldredge and Christopher Foster.

1761, May 25. Inventory, £51.1.7, made by James Hedges and John Eldredge. Lib. 11, p. 71.

1761, Dec. 28. Rouse, John, of Hopewell, Hunterdon Co. Int. Adm'r —John Opdyck. Fellowbondsman—Samuel Furman; both of Amwell, said Co. Witness—Joseph Warrell.

1761, Dec. 26. Inventory, £61.11.4, of goods of John Rouse and Deborah Rouse, his widow, both of Amwell Twsp., said Co., made by Samuel Furman, Jr., and John Peters.

1765, Sept. 10. Account by Adm'r of goods of John Rouse, of Amwell. Lib. 11, p. 133.

1766, July 30. Rowland, James, of Salem Co., mariner. Int. Adm'r—Jonathan Roberts. Fellowbondsmen—Andrew Peterson and William Philpot, Jr.; all of Manington, said Co. Lib. 12, p. 316.

1760, April 10. Rowland, Jonathan, of Woodbridge, Middlesex Co.; will of. Sons, James and Jacob, my lands. Elder son, Jonathan, £150. Son, John, £100, but, if he die before the end of two years, then the same to be given to his children, son Marvin, and three daughters. Son, Samuel, £40. Wife, Mary, ⅓ the household goods. Daughter, Deborah, £20. Granddaughter, Phebe Pearson, 20 shillings. Executors—sons, Jonathan and James. Witnesses—Richard Carman, Samuel Herriot, Richard Carman, Jr. Proved March 28, 1761.

1761, March 29. Inventory by [names not given]. Lib. G, p. 408.

1767, Nov. 30. Royal, William, of Upper Alloways Creek Twsp., Salem Co. Int. Adm'x—Hannah Royal, of said place, widow. Fellowbondsmen—Jonathan Stratton, of Deerfield, yeoman, and John Woodruff, of Hopewell, Cumberland Co., yeoman.

1767, Dec. 7. Inventory, £104.1.7, made by Joseph Van Meter and James Crommey. Lib. 13, p. 333.

1763, Sept. 30. Rubel, George, of Tewksbury Twsp., Hunterdon Co., yeoman; will of. Eldest son, Anthony, 30 shillings. To Marlena Schryner, daughter of John Schryner, £15, when 18. The 400 acres of land to my three sons, Anthony, John George and William. Wife, Anne Eve, the moveable estate. Executors—sons, Anthony and John George. Witnesses—John Counce, John Denis, William Schuller. Proved Nov. 15, 1763. Lib. 11, p. 535.

1767, Feb. 24. Ruddarow, John, of Chester Twsp., Burlington Co., yeoman; will of. Son, Joseph, 125 acres on west branch of Pensawking Creek, and is to pay my daughter, Susannah, £15. Son, Samuel, 125 acres on said creek, and is to pay to my grandson, Joshua Ruddarow, £5, when 21. Daughter, Grace, the wife of John Wilson, 5 shillings. Daughter, Mary, the wife of Samuel Thomas, 5 shillings. Daughter, Hannah, the wife of Francis Wilson, £10. Daughter, Sarah, the wife of William Vanhorn, £10. Daughter, Elizabeth, the wife of James Wilson, £10. Daughter, Ruth, the wife of Darious Vaneman, £10. Daughter, Susannah Ruddarow, £15 and furniture. My daughter, Hannah, ½ my pewter. Executor—my son, William, who is to have rest of estate. Witnesses—Ephraim Stiles, Mercy Stiles, Enoch Roberts. Proved June 13, 1769.

1769, June 10. Inventory, £30.18.0, made by Enoch Roberts and Ephraim Stiles. Lib. 14, p. 76.

CALENDAR OF WILLS—1761-1770   367

1762, Dec 8. Rue, John and Mathias, of Monmouth Co. Wards. Children of William Rue, of said Co., deceased. John is aged 18 years and Mathias 16. Guardian—James Abraham, Jr. Fellowbondsman—James Abraham, Sr., both of Middlesex Co. "We, the under subscribers, do choose James Abraham, Jr., for a Guardian to act instead of mother, deceased." Signed by Ellen Rue, Ann Rue (these are of age), John Rue and Mathias Rue.   Lib. H, p. 204.

1765, May 20. Rue, Joseph, of Southward of Perth Amboy, Middlesex Co.; will of. My plantation, lying along Manalopan, known by the name of Grape Vine Neck, to be sold. The plantation which I purchased of William Perine I have conveyed to my son, John Rue. Wife, Sarah, shall enjoy the rest of my estate. The 200 acres where I live, which was conveyed to me by my father, John Rue, she is to enjoy. What is left, after my wife's death, I give to my children, Matthew, William, Joseph, Abigail (now Abigail Perine), Ann Rue and Mary Rue. My part of the mine at Somerset, known as Leonard's Mine, I give to my three sons. Executors—wife, Sarah, and my friends, William Laird, Sr., and Matthew Rue, blacksmith. Witnesses—James Rue, James Bradshaw, Bryan Gollohar. Proved June 5, 1765.
1765, June 6. Inventory, £366.17.8, made by James Dey and John Lloyd.
1768, March 24. Account by Executors. "Paid Margaret Rue, daughter of Mathew Rue, deceased."   Lib. H, p. 534.

1766, June 28. Rue, Mathew and Rachel, of Monmouth Co. Wards. Children of William Rue, of said Co. Guardian—William Perrine, of Upper Freehold, said Co. Fellowbondsman—John Rue, of said Co.
     Lib. H, p. 620.

1757, May 27. Rue, William, of Freehold, Monmouth Co., carpenter; will of. Wife, Elizabeth Rue, all my estate, while my widow. Sons, John, Mathias and Mathew, all my lands. Daughters, Elizabeth Rue, Eleanor Rue, Anne Rue, Rachel Rue and Mary Rue, moveable estate, after their mother's death. Executors—my wife and brother, Joseph Rue. Witnesses—John Truax, Joseph Newton, James Abraham, Jr. Proved Oct. 4, 1761.   Lib. H, p. 37.

1761, Nov. 27. Rumsey, Charles, of Pilesgrove Twsp., Salem Co., weaver; will of. Wife, Susannah, my plantation till my son, Daniel, is 21, when I give it to him; said place contains 75 acres. My wife is to be at cost of bringing up my three youngest children, which are hereafter named, till they are 18. To my wife and to my daughters, Prudence, Hannah, Rebecca, Mary, and to my sons, Robert and Benjamin, and daughters, Grace and Elizabeth, my moveable estate, when they are of age. Executor—my friend, Jacob Davis. Witnesses—Samuel Moore, John Gray, Jacob Barber. Proved Feb. 6, 1762.
1761, Dec. 8. Inventory, £99.15.2, made by Elisha Bassett and Samuel Lippincott.
1764, Jan. 20. Account by Executor. Legacies were paid to Prudence Rumsey, Hannah Rumsey and Rebecca Rumsey.
     Lib. 11, p. 30.

1769, Nov. 13. Rumsey, Daniel, of Gloucester Co. Ward. Who is heir-at-law of Sarah Millar, his aunt, of said Co., widow, deceased. Said ward makes choice of William Hugg and John Sparks as his Guardians, till he is 21. Witness—Joseph Hugg.

1769, Nov. 13. Guardians—William Hugg, of said Co., and John Sparks, of Deptford, said Co. Fellowbondsman—Arthur Hamilton, of said Co., yeoman. Witnesses—John Ladd and Joseph Ladd.
Lib. 14, p. 125.

1770, Jan. 23. Runyon, Thomas, of Kingwood, Hunterdon Co., taylor; will of. Son, Absolem, my apparel. Two youngest daughters, Catherine Runyon and Rachel Runyon, household goods. Real estate to be sold. Children, Absolem, Rosanna (wife of Francis Peirce), Elizabeth (wife of Thomas Jewel), Sarah (wife of Adam Conrod), Catherine Runyon and Rachel Runyon. Executor—son, Absalom. Witnesses—Daniel Cahill, William Morrison, Charles Hoff. Proved March 31, 1770.

1770, March 12. Inventory, £48.11.4, made by John Mullinner and Daniel Cahill.

1771, June 5. Account by Executor. 150 acres of land sold for £225.
Lib. 14, p. 256; Lib. 14, p. 406.

1761, June 29. Rusco, Nathaniel, of Elizabeth Town, Essex Co. Int. Adm'x—Sarah Rusco, the widow, of New York City. Fellowbondsman—Joseph Woodruff, Jr., of Elizabeth Town, merchant. Witness—John Blanchard.
Lib. H, p. 14.

1769, Sept. 21. Russ, Martin, of Bergen Co. Int. Adm'x—Margaret Russ, of Ramapogh, Saddle River Precinct, said Co. Bondsman—John Russ, of same place. Witnesses—Jacob Horman and Lawrence Vanbuskirck.

1769, Oct. 13. Inventory, £169.16.5¼, made by Henry Brickman and Harmanus Wanamaker.
File No. 858-862 B.

1762, April 17. Russell, Charles, of Hardwick, Sussex Co. Int. Adm'r—George Silverthorn. Fellowbondsmen—Thomas Newman and Abram Giles; all of said Co., yeomen.

1762, April 16. Renunciation by Sarah Russel, in favor of George Silverthorn. Witnesses—Thomas Newman and Abraham "Goyls."

1762, April 16. Inventory, £9.16.7, made by Thomas Newman and Abraham Giles.
Lib. 11, p. 290

1761, July 14. Russell, James, of Shrewsbury, Monmouth Co.; will of. To each daughter, £10. Rest to my sons and they are to provide for their mother. Executors—my wife, Abigal, and her brother, Josiah Halstead, and Josiah Holmes. Witnesses—James Simpson, Timothy Halstead, Josiah Holmes. Proved Aug. 4, 1761.
Lib. H, p. 113.

1767, April 7. Rust, Albert, of Fairfield, Cumberland Co., yeoman; will of. Friend, Anthony Roree, all real and personal after debts are paid. Executors—said Anthony Roree. Witnesses—Rebecca Bateman, Amos Bateman, Joseph Norbury. Proved April 21, 1767.

1767, April 13. Inventory, £22.8.6, made by Joseph Ogden and Ephraim Harris.
Lib. 13, p. 167.

1762, Nov. 29. Rutan, Daniel, of Morris Co. Ward, aged 15 years, and one of the children of Peter Ratan, of said Co., deceased. Guardian—Thomas Baker, of Essex Co. Fellowbondsman—William Calwall, of Morris Co. Lib. H, p. 203; File No. 177 N.

1761, Feb. 23. Rutan, John, of Morristown, Morris Co.; will of. Wife, Sarah, use of my plantation for 13 years, and then she is to have ⅓ of the same. Daughter, Sarah, £10, at her marriage. At the end of 13 years my daughters, Rachel, Elizabeth and Mary, to have £10 each. When the plantation is sold the money to be divided between my daughters, Sarah, Rachel, Elizabeth and Mary. Son, John, £30, when 21. Son, John, to have my plantation in Hempshire Co., in Virginia. Executors—wife, Sarah, and my friend, Elias Soullud. Witnesses—James Calwall, William Broadwell, Zacheriah Vansickel. Proved April 3, 1761.
1761, March 30. Inventory, made by John Carl and Abraham Rutan. Lib. G, p. 414.

1762, Sept. 4. Rutan, John and Peter, of Morris Co. Petition of Kennedy Vance, Mica Howell, John Maxfell, Jr., William Baker, James Calwall, Thomas Cushman and Jonathan Littell, praying that Thomas Baker may be appointed Guardian of John Rutan and Peter Rutan.
1762, Nov. 15. It is ordered that the above request be granted and that their eldest brother, Daniel, also have a Guardian appointed.
File No. 177 N.

1767, Aug. 24. Rutherford, Samuel, of Trenton, Hunterdon Co.; will of. Wife, Mary, all real and personal estate. Son, Samuel, Ensign of the 15th Regiment, £200, and all my military arms and musical instruments. Executors—Elijah Bond, of Nottingham, in Burlington Co., and my wife, Mary. Witnesses—David Pinkerton, Isaac Smith, Richard Cox. Proved Oct. 24, 1767. Lib. 13, p. 271.

1767, Nov. 12. Ryker, Elizabeth, of Newton, Sussex Co. Int. Adm'r—Alpheus Gustin. Fellowbondsman—Francis Price; both of said place. Witness—Thomas Biggs.
1767, Nov. 10. Inventory, £7.2.7, made by John Dewitt and Francis Price.
1770, Jan. 15. Account by Adm'r. Lib. 13, p. 279; Lib. 15, p. 16.

1760, Sept. 13. Rynearson, Tunis, of Somerset Co.; will of. My friends, Jacob Fontine and Jaremy Stilwill, all my real and personal estate. Executors—said Jacob Fontine and Jaremy Stilwell. Witnesses—John Probasco, Jacobus Stryker, Mary Covert. Proved April 29, 1761. Lib. G, p. 432.

1765, June 23. Ryner, James, of Burlington, baker; will of. To the poor of this city 10 shillings' worth of bread, after my funeral is over. As gratitude for the friendship and trouble she has been at for me, I give the interest of £5 to Ann Price, the wife of Ralph Price. To James Cullum, £5. Rest to be used for bread for the poor. Executor—William Skeeles. Witnesses—James Craft, Daniel Bacon, Mary Peacock. Proved July 8, 1765.
1765, July 8. Inventory, £47.14.0, made by Thomas Rodman and Daniel Bacon. Lib. 12, p. 122; File No. 7857 C.

1767, Oct. 26. St. Clair, John, now of Elizabeth Town, Essex Co., Baronet, Deputy Quartermaster General, to his Majesty's Forces in America; will of. Wife, Elizabeth, commonly called Lady St. Clair, 1,714 pounds and five shillings, to make up 4,286 Spanish milled dollars, which is equal to £1,000, and my plate, goods, etc. Son, John St. Clair, all my real estate and £2,571 (is not yet 10 years of age). If my wife and son both die before he is 21, then my estate to go, ⅓ to Maria Gage, daughter of Major General Thomas Gage; ⅓ to Elizabeth Elliott, daughter of Andrew Elliott, Esq., Collector of his Majesty's customs for the Port of New York, and the other ⅓ to Lauchland McClean, Deputy Secretary of State. My wife, Col. Richard Maitland and Andrew Elliott, Esq., to be Guardians of my son, John, till 21. Executors—my wife and Andrew Elliott. Witnesses—Daniel Cox, John Crawford, Elias Boudinot. Proved Nov. 30, 1767.
Lib. I, p. 208.

1768, March 9. Salmon, Abner F., of Essex Co. Ward. One of the sons and legatee of Stephen Salmon, of said Co., dec'd. Guardian—Samuel Meeker, Jr. Fellowbondsman—Abner Frost; both of said Co. Witness—John Mackay. File Nos. 3771-3774 G.

1764, Jan. 9. Salnave, Sarah, of Elizabeth Town, Essex Co.; will of. Grandson, Gabriel Meeker, 5 shillings. Granddaughter, Mary Salnave, the daughter of my son, Peter Salnave, deceased, 5 shillings. Daughter, Magdalen Salnave, 5 shillings. Daughter, Sarah Tobin, also 5 shillings. Daughters, Anne and Elizabeth Salnave, rest of real and personal. Executors—my brother, Cornelius Hetfield, and my daughter, Anne Salnave. Witnesses—George Ross, Samuel Smith, Jacob Croes. Proved Feb. 3, 1764. Lib. H, p. 401.

1767, Aug. 10. Saltar, Anne, of Trenton, Hunterdon Co., widow; will of. Daughter, Mary Cherry, house and lot where I live. Son, John Rockhill, 50 acres which he now has. Daughter, Ann Roberson, £350. Grandddaughter, Anne Godly, bed and chairs. I have given directions to Achsah Lambert to distribute my other goods. Executor—friend, Achsah Lambert. Witnesses—Elizabeth Clayton, John Barnes, Joseph Warrell. Proved Aug. 31, 1767. Lib. 13, p. 245.

1762, Jan. 11. Saltar, Richard, of Burlington Co.; will of. Wife to have £100, and all the goods that were hers before my marriage with her. I have given to my three sons, Joseph, John and Lawrence, the plantation on which I live; and they are to do justice to their sister, Elizabeth Saltar, and my grandson, Richard Saltar, son of my son Elisha Saltar, in manner and proportion as my brother-in-law, Elisha Lawrence, and my nephew, Thomas Salter, shall order. Executors—sons, Joseph, John and Lawrence. Witnesses—Isaac Quigley, Thomas Quigley, Jemima Quigley. Proved Nov. 17, 1762.

1765, March 6. Joseph Saltar and John Saltar, sworn as Executors.
1762, Nov. 1. Inventory, £1,268.1.10, made by Thomas Watson and John Abbott.
1768, Sept. 3. Account by both Executors. Lands sold in Sussex by vendue, for £21.6.0. Lib. 12, p. 115; Lib. 12, p. 522.

1770, Oct. 24. Sampson, Hazadiah, of Egg Harbor, Gloucester Co., wheelwright. Int. Adm'r—Gideon Scull, of Great Egg Harbor. Fellowbondsman—Samuel Risley, of said place.
1770, May 9. Inventory, £52.15.3, made by William Risley and William Bise. Lib. 15, p. 73.

CALENDAR OF WILLS—1761-1770 371

1763, July 20. Sanderlin, George, of Penns Neck, Salem Co., weaver. Int. Adm'x—Mary Sanderlin, of Upper Penns Neck, widow. Fellowbondsmen—Isaac Howell, of said place, yeoman, and John McManus, of Philadelphia, laborer. Lib. 11, p. 455.

1767, March 24. Sanford, John, of Newark, Essex Co. Int. Adm'x —Hannah Sanford, the widow. Fellowbondsmen—Isaac Myers and Isaac Ogden; all of said place. Lib. I, p. 108.

1761, Feb. 24. Saucuil, Eve, of Fairfield, Cumberland Co., widow; will of. To my son, Jonadab, my daughter, Leah, my daughter, Rachel, my daughter, Eve, my son, Jonathan, my daughter, Elizabeth, my son, Lansalet Saucuil, 5 shillings each. Rest of estate to my daughters, Experience and Patience Saucuil, when 18. Executor —William Paullin. Witnesses—Jonadab Shepherd, Jr., Temperance Shepherd, David Shepherd, Jr. Proved Aug. 18, 1761.
1761, Aug. 14. Inventory, £36.9.4, made by Jonadab Shepherd and David Shepherd. Lib. 11, p. 166.

1765, Oct 25. Sayers, David, of Fairfield Twsp., Cumberland Co., husbandman; will of. Wife, Liddia, ½ the profits of my plantation and ½ my moveable estate. Daughter, Ruth Sayers, lands where I live, when 18. Cousin, James Sayers, son of James Sayers, the said land in case Ruth dies; he paying to my cousin, Anias Sayers, son of Daniel Sayers, £30. Executors—my wife, my brother, Thomas, and my friend, Philip Shephard. Witnesses—James Davis, David Ryley, Johannah Davis. Proved April 25, 1767.
1767, April 24. Inventory, £458.11.8, made by Joseph Ogden and David Wescote.
1769, Oct. 26. Account by Executors.
Lib. 13, p. 152; Lib. 14, p. 126.

1763, Jan. 29. Sayre, Daniel, of Borough of Elizabeth, Essex Co., yeoman; will of. Wife, Phebe, use of ⅓ my farm, except that part which I gave to my son, Daniel. Son, Daniel, a small plantation, which I bought of John Sayre, of 35 acres. Sons, John and Abraham, rest of my homestead, and they are to provide for my daughter, Phebe, during her life. To my five daughters, who are married, viz., Hannah Smith, Sarah Terel, Abigail Bruckfeald, Mary Higgins and Elizabeth Smith, £10 each. Granddaughters, Jemima and Mary Higans, £10 each, when 18. My small plantation on the mountain, which I bought of Joshua Morehous, to be sold. Executors—sons, Daniel Sayre and Jacob Bruckfeald, and my friend, John Stites. Witnesses—Job Mulford, Margaret Stites, Jr., James Hindes. Proved May 30, 1763.
1764, June 6. Inventory, £116.19.5, made by Thomas Thompson and Job Mulford.
1766, Jan. 6. Account by Executors. Lib. H, p. 256.

1765, Feb. 14. Sayre, Ebenezer, of Morris Co. Int. Adm'x—Mary Sayre, his widow.
1765, Feb. 12. Inventory, made by Jeremiah Genung and Ephraim Price. Lib. H, p. 423.

1762, March 2. Sayre, Ethan, of Cumberland Co. Int. Adm'r—Timothy Brooks. Fellowbondsman—John Miller; both of said Co. Witnesses—Jacob Mulford and Seth Brooks, Jr.
1762, Feb. 23. Inventory, £75.17.3, made by Jacob Mulford and John Miller.   Lib. 11, p. 149.

1765, Dec. 12. Sayre, John, of Elizabeth Borough, Essex Co.; will of. Estate to be sold, and ⅓ of proceeds to my wife, Esther. Cousin, Daniel Owens, £10. Cousin, Jedidiah Owens, £10. Each of my sister Sarah's daughters, £5, viz., Mary, Rebecca, Hannah and Sary Owens. To each of my brothers, £5, viz., David, Benjamin and Jedidiah Sayers. My brother David's son, John Sayres, £10. The rest of my estate to the children of my brothers, David and Benjamin. Executors—Mathias Hatfield, cordwainer, and David Sayre, blacksmith. Witnesses—William Sarry, David Sayre. Proved July 4, 1767.
1767, July 6. Inventory, made by David Miller and Henry De Money.   Lib. I, p. 139.

1762, Oct. 15. Sayre, Jonathan, of Elizabeth Borough, Essex Co.; will of. Plantation where I live and the goods to be sold, and the money used to bring up my children that cannot maintain themselves. Wife, Jane, ⅓ the remainder, and the rest to my children, Ezra, Moses, Sarah, Abner, Corneleous, Abigal, Cathrine, Fredrick, Franky, Hannah, Isaac and Lidea. Executors—son, Ezra, and my friends, Jacob Shotwell and Benjamin Shotwell. Witnesses—Thomas Latham, John Hindes, Mary Clerk. Proved Nov. 1, 1762.
1764, April 13. Inventory, £656.13.10, filed by Ex'rs. Lib. H, p. 198.

1770, June 2. Schamp, George, of Somerset Co. Ward. Son of Clause Schamp, of said Co., deceased. He makes choice of Harman Lane as his Guardian. (See Schomp).
1770, June 2. Guardian—Harman Lane. Fellowbondsman—John Mehelm; both of Hunterdon Co. Witness—William Paterson.
   Lib. 15, p. 1.

1761, May 21. Schanck, Garret (son of Cort), of Monmouth Co.; will of. Wife, Nelle, use of real and personal. Son, John, £20, when 21. If my wife is pregnant, that child is to have equal with the other children, Mary, Cort, Peter, Sarah, Anna, Garrit and Nelle. Executors—my brother, Peter Schanck; Aurt Sutphen and John Van d'Vear. Witnesses—Koert Schanck, Derick Van Cleeve, William Clark. Proved June 26, 1761.
1761, June 26. Inventory, £570.5.5, made by Gerrit Wyckoff and Peter Bowne.   Lib. G, p. 460.

1769, Jan. 21. Schanck, Peter, Jr., of Freehold, Monmouth Co. Int. Adm'r—Peter Schanck, farmer, father of said Peter. Fellowbondsman—Daniel Covenhoven, son of Roelif; both of said Co.
   Lib. I, p. 364.

1769, Nov. 13. Schellenx, Isaac, of Elizabeth Borough, Essex Co.; will of. I, Isaac Scanlang, desire my wife, Rachel, to pay my debts. To my kinsmen, Matthias Ogden, son of Samuel Ogden, and William Hushson, son of Samuel Hushson, in Morris Town, the house and land where I live, and my wife to have the use of the whole, and at her death to be to them. Executors—Matthias Ogden and William Hushson. Witnesses—John Borrows, Cornelius Miller, John Ogden. Proved Jan. 4, 1770. Letters to Matthias Ogden and William Hudson, as Executors.   Lib. K, p. 166.

1745, Oct. 9. Schenck, Garret. Inventory, £195.16.3, made by Elias Covenhoven, Rulof Covenhoven and Edward Taylor. Filed March 21, 1769.   File No. 4641 L. (See N. J. Archives, Vol. 30, p. 417).

1766, Aug. 23. Schenck, Hendrick, of Freehold Twsp., Monmouth Co.; will of. Lands hereafter stated to be sold, viz., part of my plantation as here stated, land and bog in the pines, called Boel's Bogg; meadow near John Clark's; woodland on east side of Causeway near Reedy Bridge; land at Conaskunk, and salt meadow at Cheesequakes. Son, Roeleff, rest of lands. Wife, Catharine, to have ½ the profits of my lands, in order to bring up my children. Roeleff, when 21, shall have the other ½ of profits, and he is to pay my wife £20 a year; and he is to pay to each child, as it becomes 21, £160. Executors—my uncle, John Schenck, of Middletown, Daniel Holmes and Obadiah Herbert, of Freehold. Witnesses—John Tice, William Tice, Cornelius Covenhoven. Proved Sept. 12, 1766.

1767, March 3. Inventory, made by John Tice, Isaac Vandorn and Samuel Holmes.   Lib. I, p. 105.

1764, Oct. 10. Schenck, Jemimah, of Freehold, Monmouth Co. Int. Adm'r—Rolef Schenck, the eldest son, of said place. Fellowbondsman—Benjamin Van Cleef, of said Co.   Lib. H, p. 370.

1765, April 10. Schenck, Roelef, of Freehold, Monmouth Co., yeoman; will of. Grandson, Roelef Schenck, my lot at the Point. Grandsons, Roelef Schenck and Cornelias Schenck, the plantation I bought of Peter Voorhees. Daughter, Nelly Covenhoven, 100 acres of the south side of my home plantation. My son, Hendrick, a part of my plantation, and he is to pay to my granddaughter, Geesye Schenck, £280; to my six grandchildren, children of my daughter, Catherine Covenhoven, namely, Symon Dehart, Geesye Dehart, Jacob Covenhoven, Roelof Covenhoven, Mary Covenhoven and John Covenhoven, £280; to my three grandchildren, children of daughter, Sary Van Matre, £280; to my daughter, Nelley Covenhoven, £280. My bogg, by the widow Schenck's, I give to son, Hendrick, and grandsons, Roelef Schenck and Cornelius Schenck; a lot of salt meadow to three grandchildren, children of my son, John. Executors—son, Hendrick, and my sons-in-law, Garret and Peter Covenhoven. Witnesses—John Tice, Cornelius Covenhoven, William Tice. Proved March 3, 1766.

1766, Feb. 12. Inventory, made by Daniel Holmes, Isaac Vandorn and John Longstreet. In said Inventory mention is made of 14 negros.   Lib. I, p. 93.

1762, Sept. 18. Schenck, Roelef, Jr., of Freehold, Monmouth Co., brewer; will of. Wife, Anelty, ½ my place in Monmouth Co. Son, Garrit, is to pay to my daughter, Mary's, two children, £100; then he may have all the lands that I have in Hunterdon Co. Son, Jacob, is to pay to my daughter, Nelly, £100, and pay to my son, Rolif, £100. Son, William, to pay, as I have ordered him, to my daughter, Caty,

£100. My youngest son, John, all my lands in Monmouth Co., and he is to pay to my daughter, Anne, £40, and to daughter Margret's 5 children, £100. Daughter, Agnes, £50. Son, Rolif, £200. Executors —sons, John and Jacob, and my son-in-law, John Tise. Witnesses—John Bray, Jacob Vandorn, Isaac Vandorn.
1766, March 28. Codicil. Witnesses—Ann Vandorn, Catharine Kallam, Isaac Vandorn. Proved Sept. 5, 1768. Lib. I, p. 344.

1766, Dec. 11. Schenk, Hendrick, of Millstone, Somerset Co., merchant; will of. My brother, Peter Schenk, is to have all my estate sold. Son, Johanes, £20. Rest to my wife and my children, born and unborn, when they are of age. Executor—my brother, Peter, of Millstone, merchant. Witnesses—John Brokaw, Peter Perrine, Cornelius Lott. Proved Feb. 23, 1767. Lib. I, p. 103.

1761, April 9. Scholey, William, of Greenwich Twsp., Sussex Co., yeoman; will of. Wife to have ⅓ the moveable estate and living off the plantation. Oldest son to have £10 more than the others. They may keep the plantation in their hands till my brother Robert's son comes of age. Should there be anything coming from brother Joseph's estate, my three daughters are to have a third. Son, John, the plantation that lays on the Marvel Hill, whereon Joshua Wege now lives. Executors—Alexander White and my son, John. Witnesses—David Hays, Joseph Hixson, Margaret White. Proved May 5, 1761.
1761, April 16. Inventory, £143.0.3, made by David Hays and Joseph Hixson.
1764, May 17. Account by both Executors. Lib. 11, p. 57.

1770, June 2. Schomp, Peter, of Hunterdon Co. Ward. Son of George Schamp, of said Co., deceased. He asks for Harman Lane to be his Guardian, as he has real and personal estate that requires care. (See Schamp).
1770, June 2. Guardian—Harman Lane. Fellowbondsman—John Mehelm; both of said Co. Witness—William Paterson. Lib. 15, p. 1.

1767, April 20. Schooley, James, of Newton, Sussex Co. Int. Adm'r —Samuel Schooley, of said place. Fellowbondsman—Josiah Dyer, of Hardwick, said Co. Witness—John Pettit.
1767, April 20. Renunciation by Margaret Schooley, widow of James. Witnesses—Benjamin Schooley and Josiah Dyer, Jr.
1767, April 13. Inventory, £86.16.2, made by Jacob Lundy, Samuel Lundy and Benjamin Schooley.
1769, April 12. Account by Adm'r. Money was paid to Avis Schooley, William Schooley and Asa Schooley.
Lib. 12, p. 466; Lib. 13, p. 533.

1764, April 25. Schoonhoven, Henry, Jr., of Walpack, Sussex Co.; will of. Wife, Rachel, house, lot and bonds. Son, Nicholas, £50 and the said house and land. Eldest daughter, Catherina Schoonhoven, £100. Daughter, Mary Schoonoven, £100. My wife to have the goods she had of her father. Executors—my wife and Allan Nixon. Witnesses—John Schoonoven, Peter Vandermark. Proved Aug. 24, 1764.
1764, Aug. 17. Inventory, £272.15.0, made by Peter Vandermark and John Depue. Lib. 12, p. 233.

1759, Jan. 2. Schoonhoven, Nicholas, of Walpack, Sussex Co., yeoman; will of. Wife, Pattenella, use of all real and personal while my widow. To my third son, Peter, £15. To my eldest son, Henericus, the house and lot for which I gave him a deed. Rest of my estate to sons, Henericus, James, Benjamin, Ezekiel, Joseph and my two daughters, Sarrah and Mary. If my wife, Peternela, should marry, then I give her £40. Executors—sons, Henricus and James. Witnesses—James Russell, Nicoles Brink, Joseph Chestnor. Proved Sept. 28, 1764.
1761, Oct. 6. Codicil. Son, James, to have the upper lot that formerly belonged to Derrick Kermer. Witnesses—Johannis Cornelius Westbrook, Joseph Chestnor. Proved Sept. 28, 1764.
1764, Sept. 25. Inventory, £303.5.7, made by Nicoles Brink and Johannis Cornelius Westbrook.
1770, April 21. Joseph Chestnor, being sworn, said that he was sent for to write the above will, which he did.
Lib. 12, p. 235; Lib. 14, p. 153.

1761, May 20. Schuyler, Adoniah, of New York City; will of. Wife, Geertruy, the use of my goods and slaves. My real estate in New York and New Jersey to be sold. After debts are paid, all to be given to my wife, Geertruy, and my children, Ranslaer Schuyler, Mary Schuyler, Swan Schuyler, John Schuyler, Peter Schuyler, Adoniah Schuyler and Phillip Schuyler. Executors—wife, Geertruy, and my brothers, John and Peter, and David Johnston, of New York City. Witnesses—James Still, James Melrose, David Ogden. Proved May 28, 1762. Lib. H, p. 180.

1761, March 21. Schuyler, Peter; will of. Wife, Mary, £1,500. Sister, Cornelia De Peyster, £100. Daughter, Catherine Schuyler, the residue. Executors—my daughter and my brother John. Witnesses—William Smith, Jr., Samuel Jones, George Clinton. Proved May 28, 1762, and Catherine Schuyler was sworn same date.
1768, Jan. 21. John Schuyler, surviving Executor, was sworn.
Lib. H, p. 178.

1760, April 29. Schuyler, Phillip, of Pompton, Bergen Co.; will of. Wife, Hester, use of real and personal. Son, Arent, small lot joining the back of his land. Son, Phillip, tract formerly known as Cutlosses plantation, where he lives, and a tract on the Plains, the two containing 333 acres; and he is to pay to my daughter, Johannah Kingsland, £100. Son, Isaac, lot No. 3, of 300 acres, and he is to pay to my daughter, Elizabeth Vanderlinda, £100. Son, Peter, lot No. 1, and he to pay to my daughter, Hester Dye, £100. Son, Casparus, my homestead of 200 acres, and a tract in tenure of Michael Hearty; and he to pay to my daughter, Ann Board, £100. Executors—my wife, Hester, and my sons, Arent, Phillip, Isaac, Peter and Casparus. Witnesses—Uzal Ogden, Gerrit Thibou and John Ogden, 3d. Proved Jan. 27, 1764. Lib. H, p. 397.

1763, Sept. 6. Scoggin, Hannah, of Alloways Creek, Salem Co. Ward. Daughter of Jonah Scoggin, of said place, deceased. Has land which descended to her on the death of her father, and now makes choice of Robert Johnson as her Guardian till 21.
1763, Sept. 6. Guardian—Robert Johnson. Fellowbondsman—Grant Gibbon; both of Salem. Lib. 11, p. 448.

1763, Sept. 7. Scoggin, Sarah, of Alloways Creek, Salem Co. Ward. Daughter of Jonah Scoggin, of said place. She has lands which descended to her on the death of her father, and now makes choice of Robert Johnson, as her Guardian, till 21.
1763, Sept. 7. Guardian—Robert Johnson. Fellowbondsman—Grant Gibbon; both of Salem. Lib. 11, p. 453.

1761, Feb. 6. Scqley, Joseph, of Windsor Township, Middlesex Co., yeoman; will of. Wife, Mary, the household goods. Lands to be sold and money to go to my wife. Executors—my friends, John Ely and John Chamberlin. Witnesses—Jacob Reticor, Benjamin Chambers, John Mecarrell. Proved March 3, 1761. Lib. 10, p. 565.

1727, May 14. Scot, Alexander, of Elizabeth Town, Essex Co.; will of. Moveable estate to be sold and the money to be converted to the use of my wife, Hannah; and she is to have the use of my lands till my son, Samuel, is 21; but if he die before he is of age, then it is to be sold and the money divided amongst my children, that is, my sons, Samuel, John and James, and the child my wife is big with. Executors—John Shotwell and Joseph Shotwell, eldest son of said John Shotwell. Witnesses—Erasmus Allton, John Willis, John Chanders. Proved Oct. 12, 1764.
1764, Oct. 10. Renunciation of Joseph Shotwell, in which he states that John Shotwell is deceased; the said John having been appointed Executor. Witness—Anthony Badgley.
1764, Oct. 12. Renunciation of Benjamin Scott, son of Alexander Scott, deceased, and desires letters be granted to Thomas Woodruff, of Elizabeth Town. Witness—John Smyth.
1764, Oct. 12. Adm'r—Thomas Woodruff; at the request of Benjamin Scott, eldest son of Alexander Scott. Fellowbondsman—Thomas Willis, of Essex Co. Witness—John Smyth.
1765, ——, ——. Account by Adm'r. Lib. H, p. 462.

1761, Nov. 30. Scott, William, of Shrewsbury, Monmouth Co.; will of. Daughter, Susannah, a bed. Rest of personal and real to be sold and money given to my 8 children, viz., Richard, John, George, Job, Ralph, Warner, Susannah, Hannah and Sarah, when of age. My eldest son, Richard, is entitled to lands, as heir to his mother. Executors—brother, Samuel Scott, and Richard Lawrence. Witnesses—George Allen, James Lafetra, Jr., Edmond Lafetra. Proved Aug. 9, 1762.
1762, Aug. 9. Inventory, £123.14.0, made by George Allen and Edmond Lafetra. Lib. H, p. 176.

1769, April 5. Scudder, John and Ann, of Essex Co. Wards. Infants of John Scudder, of said place, deceased. Guardian—James Fitzrandolph, of Middlesex Co. Lib. K, p. 76.

1763, June 18. Scudder, Richard, of Essex Co. Ward. Son of Thomas Scudder, of said Co., deceased. Guardian—David Miller. Fellowbondsman—Abraham Clark, Jr.; both of Borough of Elizabeth.
1763, June 8. Petition of Abraham Clark, Jr., and Richard Scudder, stating that Thomas Scudder, of Elizabeth Town, deceased, by his will made David Edgar and Abraham Clark Guardians of his children, and the said Edgar refused to act as such, so that the said Clark had charge of the children, and Richard (one of the children) having lands some distance from Clark, and Clark refusing to act, the

said Richard, now being 18, makes choice of David Miller of said Borough as his Guardian.

1766, May 14. Richard Scudder, yeoman, states that "I have settled all accounts with David Miller, my late Guardian." Witness—Jeremiah Oliver. Lib. H, p. 247.

1760, Dec. 29. Scudder, Thomas, of Borough of Elizabeth, Essex Co.; will of. Son, David, land on Robinson's branch, and along land which I bought of Richard Skinner, together with the grist mill, pond, dam and stream. Son, James, the land bounded by Peter Tranbles, with the sawmill, pond, dam and stream. Son, Richard, land along Samuel Marsh. Son, Thomas, land on east side of Robinson's Branch, whereon my son, John, formerly lived, and is along land I sold to Samuel Miller, the third. Son, Elias, tract of land which is bounded by Lambert Decamp and Henry Jaquesh. Wife, Sarah, ½ of the lands devised to son Thomas, during her life; also £135. To sons, David and Thomas, salt meadow, lying in Raway meadows, which I bought of John Crane. To sons, Richard and Elias, salt meadow, lying in Raway meadows, which I purchased of Nathaniel Hubble. Son, James, salt meadow, in the Raway meadows, which I bought of Caleb Dill; and James is to pay to my granddaughter, Anne Scudder, and my grandson, John Scudder (children of my son John, deceased) £35 each, when they are of age. Daughter, Sarah, £100. Several tracts of land are to be sold. If any of my sons should die under age, without issue, then his lands are to be sold. Executors—my friends, David Edgar and Abraham Clark, Jr. Witnesses—David Miller, John Lee, Benjamin Skinner, John Debourepose. Proved Jan. 15, 1761.

1761, Jan. 20. Inventory, £1,451.16.7, made by Abraham Clark and Joseph Hindes. Lib. G, p. 347.

1759, March 7. Scull, Abel, of Greenwich, Gloucester Co., yeoman; will of. My son, Abel, is to pay to my daughters, Mary Doughty and Sarah Hawkins, £10 each; and to his brother, Joseph, £50. Son, Abel, to have the plantation where I live, and, if he does not pay the above, then son, Joseph, and my brother-in-law, Edward Tomkin, to sell enough of the cedar swamp to pay the same. Son, John, the cedar swamp at Egg Harbor, that I bought of Evy Ballenger. Son, Joseph, the plantation at Springfield, Burlington Co. Wife, Martha, and my two daughters, Rachel and Naomy, the moveable estate. (Rachel and Naomy are under 18). Executors—sons, Abel and Joseph, and my brother, Edward Tomkins. Witnesses—Alexander Randall, Susannah Lock, John Rambo. Proved Dec. 11, 1762.

1762, Nov. 26. Inventory, £514.13.4, made by William Guest and Mathew Gill.

1764, May 18. Account by Edward Tonkin. "Cash paid Caleb Bickham, one of the legatees." Lib. 11, p. 242.

1763, Feb. 8. Scull, Abel, Jr., of Greenwich, Gloucester Co., yeoman. Int. Adm'r—Samuel Shivers, yeoman. Fellowbondsman—Benjamin Lodge, yeoman; both of the said place. Witness—Sarah Howell.

1763, Feb. 1. Renunciation of Martha Scull, the widow; who states that Abel died without leaving any children, and she desires her father, Samuel Shivers, to act as Adm'r. Witnesses—Joseph Tonkin, Benjamin Lodge.

1763, Dec. 31. Inventory, £640.16.6, made by Benjamin Lodge and Joseph Tonkin. Lib. 11, p. 286.

1764, Jan. 26. Scull, Daniel, of Twsp. and Co. of Gloucester; will of. Wife, Rachel, all my land in said Co. Daughter, Jemiay, 3 cattle, etc. Daughter, Hannah, a bed. Daughter, Jeane, a bed. Daughter, Judey, a table. Sons, John and David, 5 shillings each. Son, Phillop, 3 cattle. Executrix—my wife. Witnesses—Elisha Smith, John Bond. Proved Feb. 16, 1764.
1764, Feb. 10. Inventory, £243.1.11, made by Thomas Bate and Joseph Hillman. Lib. 11, p. 479.

1761, June 4. Scull, Hezekiah, of Cape May Co. Int. Adm'r—John Scull. Fellowbondsman—Jacob Spicer; both of said Co. Witnesses—Henry Young and Phebe Young.
1761, June 25. Inventory, £473.17.3, made by James Godfrey and Silvanus Townsend. Lib. 10, p. 417.

1764, Feb. 10. Scull, Peter, of Great Egg Harbor, Gloucester Co.; will of. Wife, Susannah, ½ of my land. She is to bring up my children, Samuel, Susanna, John, Nicolis, Hezeciah and Jeams. Son, Peter, the other part of my land. Daughter, Mary, 10 shillings. Daughter, Cathrine, a "heffer." Son, Samuel, a horse. Executors—my wife and son, Peter. Witnesses—Francis Few, Jean Cooks, David Sayrs. Proved March 22, 1764.
1764, March 8. Inventory, £76.0.6, made by Elisha Smith and David Sayrs. Lib. 11, p. 484.

1768, Oct. 28. Searing, Samuel, of Morristown, Morris Co.; will of. Wife, Younas, what the law gives her and no more. Daughters, Ann, Theordoshe and Margrit, £10 each, whey they are 18. Sons, Samuel, Joshua and Soloman, rest of my personal and real estate. Executors—wife, Younas, and my brother, Josiah Broadwell. Witnesses—Seth Crowell, Jr., Mary Gerner, Edward Crowell. Proved Nov. 17, 1768. Probate to Eunice Searing, same date. Lib. K, p. 11.

1765, Feb. 14. Sears, Ebenezer, of Hanover, Morris Co. Int. Adm'x—Mary Sears, the widow. Fellowbondsman—David Burnet; both of said place. Lib. H, p. 423.

1763, Nov. 19. Sebering, Daniel, of Reading Twsp., Hunterdon Co.; will of. Wife, Catherine, house and 5 acres, and furniture; also the wench I bought of Peter Bodine, and £25 yearly. To Daniel McKenney, £50. The rest of estate to my nephews, Daniel Belew, Peter Belew, Mordicai McKenney and Peter Bodine. My son-in-law, Peter Bodine, and my nephew, Isaac Belew, apparel. Executors—my wife, Thomas Atkinson, Sr., and Mordica McKenney. Witnesses—Jacob Mattison, William Hunt, Hannah Hunt, Jr. Proved Jan. 31, 1764.
1764, Jan. 28. Inventory, £350.10.0½, made by Pieter Middogh and Gerret Van Vlit. Lib. 11, p. 532.

1763, May 11. Seeley, Job, of Fairfield, Cumberland Co. Int. Adm'r—Joseph Ogden, Esq. Fellowbondsman—Ephraim Harris, of said place. Witness—Elizabeth Mulford.
1763, April 29. Inventory, £85.17.11, made by David Westcoat and Ephraim Harris. Lib. 11, p. 291.

CALENDAR OF WILLS—1761-1770 379

1762, Jan. 6. Seely, David, of Mannington, Salem Co., bricklayer. Int. Adm'x—Magdalin Seely, widow. Fellowbondsmen—Elisha Bassett, Jr., and Richard Hackett, yeomen; all of said place.
1761, Dec. 23. Inventory, £123.12.5, made by Elisha Bassett, Jr., and Richard Hackett.
1765, March 8. Account by Adm'x. Lib. 11, p. 37.

1767, Sept. 30. Seely, Henry, of Deerfield, Cumberland Co.; will of. Wife, ⅓ my moveable estate and use of ⅓ my lands. Daughters, Elizabeth Shute and Sarah Conklin, 10 shillings each. Grandson, Joel Moore, 10 shillings. Daughters, Hannah Bateman and Rode Nickles, 10 shillings each. Son, Henry, my lands. Son, John, £100. Daughter, Abigail Seely, £25, when 18. Son, John, to be put to trade till 21. Executors—friends, Daniel Clark and Samuel Ogden. Witnesses—Jonathan Stratton, Fithian Stratton, Aaron Stratton. Proved Feb. 24, 1768.
1768, Feb. 3. Inventory, £250.0.2, made by Fithian Stratton and Ezekiel Foster. Lib. 13, p. 416.

1768, Sept. 17. Servey, Uri, of Hopewell Twsp., Hunterdon Co. Int. Adm'r—Samuel Stout, Jr., of same place. Fellowbondsman—Johannes Servey (Service) of Amwell, said Co. Witness—Timothy Brush.
1768, Sept. 14. Inventory, £136.1.6, made by Abraham Stout and Timothy Brush.
1770, Jan. 15. Account. Lib. 13, p. 441; Lib. 15, p. 14.

1766, Sept. 11. Seward, Isaac, of Morris Co.; will of. Wife, Phebe, £20, and use of my land till my son, Daniel, is 21; then to be divided among my sons, Samuel, Daniel and Abraham. Mentions daughters, without giving names. Executrix—wife, Phebe. Witnesses—Ebenezar Blachly, Nathan Cooper, Jr., John Seward. Proved Dec. 5, 1769.
1769, Dec. 5. Adm'r with will annexed—John Seward, eldest brother; Phebe, the wife, being deceased. Lib. K, p. 222; File No. 149 S.

1770, April 18. Seward, Samuel, of Morris Co. Ward. Son of Isaac Seward of said Co., yeoman; deceased. Had lands left to him by his father, and makes choice of Nathan Cooper, Jr., as his Guardian till he is 21.
1770, April 18. Guardian—Nathan Cooper, Jr. Fellowbondsman—Nathan Cooper; both of Roxbury Twsp., said Co., yeomen. Witness—Richard Kemble. Lib. K, p. 223.

1769, June 22. Shankel, Henry, of Roxbury Twsp., Morris Co.; will of. Wife, Mary Elizabeth, ⅓ of my real and personal, for 14 years, to bring up my small children; and, after that time, the lands to be sold. Oldest son, Anthony, 5 shillings above his share. Sons, John Peter, Leonard, Henry and Adam, £10 each. My four youngest daughters, Margrit, Mary Elizabeth, Catrin and Anna Mary, £8 each. What remains to be divided among all my children. Executors—friends, Leonard Nochber and Morice Crator, Jr. Witnesses—Anthony Woldorf, Adam Lorantz, Roelof Roelofson. Proved June 28, 1770.
1770, June 21. Inventory, £209.5.6, made by Leonard Nighbour and Morris Crater, Jr., Executors, and John Waldorf and Roelof Roelofson, appraisers. Lib. 14, p. 233.

1764, May 30. Shapher, Micheal, of Lebanon, Hunterdon Co.; will of. To wife, some goods, besides her dower. Daughters, Margrit, Elizabeth and Pations, the rest, when they come of age. Executor—my friend, Roelof Roelofson. Witnesses—Anthony Garlick, Fanny Fox, Christian Trackseller. Proved Aug. 21, 1764.
1764, Aug. 8. Inventory, £71.11.2, made by James Beaty and Andrew Palmer.
1766, Oct. 3. Account by Executor. Lib. 12, p. 239.

1767, Dec. 25. Sharp, Hannah, of Evesham Twsp., Burlington Co. Int. Adm'r—Isaac Sharp, of said place. Fellowbondsman—Lambert Barnes, of City of Burlington.
1768, Jan. 6. Inventory, £91.12.2½, made by Thomas Shinn and Joseph Willcox. "To cash due by Jacob Prickitt, Adm'r of Samuel Sharp, late dec'd, £4.0.0." File No. 8247 C; Lib. 13, p. 277.

1767, Oct. 3. Sharp, Samuel, of Evesham, Burlington Co., yeoman. Int. Adm'rs—Rosanna Sharp (widow of Samuel) and Jacob Prickitt, of Evesham. Fellowbondsmen—Thomas Shinn and Joseph Willcox, of same place, yeomen.
1767, Oct. 2. Inventory, £255.1.7, made by Thomas Shinn and Joseph Willcox.
1769, Jan. 9. Inventory, £15.7.2, which could not be comprised in first inventory. Lib. 13, p. 105.

1768, Jan. 4. Sharp, William, Jr., of Evesham. Ward. Petition of Benjamin Haines, of said place, uncle on the mother's side and Guardian in socage to William Sharp and Mary Sharp, children of William Sharp of Evesham, and Mary his wife, both deceased; petitioner prays to be made Guardian; and was appointed, with Daniel Ellis, Esq., of Burlington, on his bond. File No. 8425 C.

1767, June 27. Sharpenstine, John Peter, Jr., of Roxbury Twsp., Morris Co. Ward. Son of John Peter Sharpenstine, of said place. Guardian—Samuel Grandine, Esq. Lib. 12, p. 478.

1770, June 31. Sharps, John, of Greenwich Twsp., Sussex Co., yeoman; will of. To my wife, £100. Oldest son, Peter Sharps, a horse, over his share. Son, John, a horse. My plantation, and the one at Marvel Hill, to be valued. Children to have schooling. Executors—my wife, Mathias Shipman and my son, Peter. Witnesses—Robert Martin, Alexander White, Christian Sharps. Proved Aug. 8, 1770.
1770, June 12. Inventory, £865.0.6, made by Alexander White and Christian Sharps.
1774, Jan. 10. Account by Mathias Shipman and Peter Sharps, Executors. Lib. 14, p. 342; Lib. 15, p. 496.

1764, April 23. Shephard, Beelby, of Alloways Creek Precinct, Salem Co., tailor. Int. Adm'x—Lydia Shephard, of said place, widow. Fellowbondsman—Samuel Fitz Patrick, of said place, yeoman.
1764, March 27. Inventory, £147.15.0, made by James Young and James Sims. Lib. 12, p. 73.

1759, Dec. 19. Shepherd, Deborah, of Middletown, Monmouth Co.; will of. Widow of the late Thomas Shepherd, of said place. To the heirs of my eldest son, Joseph Shepherd, deceased, 10 shillings. Son, Thomas Shepherd, all my lands, he paying the legacies. To Thomas Shepherd, the son of my son, Ebenezer, dec'd, £200, when he is 21. To Sarah Shepherd, sister of my said grandson, Thomas Shepherd, £100, when 18, or at marriage. Daughters, Sarah Stillwell, Rebecca Cox, Deborah Burrows, Hannah Stelle and Mary Jonston, my moveable estate. Executors—son, Thomas Shepherd, and my friend, James Grover (son of James). Witnesses—Cyrenius Vanmater, Josiah Holmes, Chrineyonce Van Mater. Proved Nov. 12, 1768.
1769, Jan. 4. Renunciation by James Grover. Witness—Hugh Patten. Lib. K, p. 30.

1769, Oct. 29. Shepherd, Dicason, of Fairfield, Cumberland Co., yeoman; will of. Son, Peter, the south side of my land, where Silas Bradford lives, he paying to my son, Ansell, £20, when 21. Son, Dicason, rest of lands, he paying to my son, Ansell, £10. Daughters, Priscilla, Eloner, Sarah, Prudence, Pleasant and Hannah, and wife Eloner, to enjoy the lands. Executor—my wife. Witnesses—Jonadab Shepherd, Jonathan Socwell, David Shepherd. Proved Dec. 6, 1769.
1769, Nov. 13. Inventory, £110.1.3, made by David Shepherd and Jonadab Shepherd. Lib. 14, p. 275.

1769, June 29. Shepherd, Enoch, of Hopewell, Cumberland Co., yeoman; will of. Wife, Martha, ⅓ the rents of my farm and ⅓ the moveables. Friend, David Shepherd, Jr., a suit. Daughter, Lucy Smith, the salt marsh that I bought of Hezekiah Lore. Son, Furman, my home plantation, when 21. Daughter, Dorcas Shepherd, £15, when 18. Daughters, Lucy Smith, Elizabeth Robinson, Dorothy Brooks, Rachel Bacon and Dorcas Shepherd, rest of personal estate. Stones to be placed at my grave. Son, Furman, is to be in the care of Ephraim Shephard and David Shephard, Jr. Executors—Ephraim Shephard, David Shephard, Jr., and my son, Furman. Witnesses—Elijah Bowen, Jr., Elnathan Shepherd, David Jenkins. Proved July 27, 1769.
1769, July 26. Inventory, £164.9.3, made by Jacob Mulford and Jonathan Ayars.
1771, June 29. Account by Ephraim Shepherd.
Lib. 14, pp. 113, 406.

1769, Dec. 14. Shepherd, John, of Stow Creek Twsp., Cumberland Co. Int. Adm'x—Hannah Shepherd, of said place, widow. Fellowbondsman—Nathan Bacon, of Hopewell, said Co., yeoman.
1769, Dec. 13. Inventory, £80.4.6, made by Ananias Sayre, Jr., and Job Butcher. Lib. 15, p. 5.

1765, Feb. 9. Shepherd, Jonadab, of Fairfield, Cumberland Co.; will of. Wife, Phebe, £15, and benefit of ⅓ the plantation where son, Jonadab, lives. Sons, Jonadab and Nathaniel, plantation where Jonadab lives. Son, Read Shepherd, my swamp at Buckshutam. Marsh, called Winter Pasture, to my sons, Jonadab, Nathan, Read, Nathaniel and Silvanus. Son, Nathan, £20. Daughters, Temperance,

Rhuma and Marah, £1 each. My son-in-law, David Shepherd, to pay my daughters, Eve and Annah, £6 each. Executors—son-in-law, David Shepherd, my brother-in-law, William Paulin, and my "cozen," Able Shepherd. Witnesses—Thomas Shepherd, Jonathan Ryley, David Smith. Proved April 9, 1765.

1765, March 30. Inventory, £127.1.2, made by William Newcomb and Thomas Shepherd.

1768, Feb. 5. Account by Abel Shepherd and William Paullin, Executors. "Cash paid Cornelios Asten, a legacy—£1.0.0."

Lib. 12, p. 160; Lib. 15, p. 9.

1767, Aug. 26. Shepherd, Samuel, of Fairfield, Cumberland Co., yeoman; will of. Brother, Abraham, all my estate, except walnut drawers to cousin, Martha Brooks. Executors—Abraham Smith, Sr., and Joseph Shepherd, Jr. Witnesses—Phillip Ayars, Lovicy Shepherd. Proved March 22, 1768.

1768, March 22. Inventory, £23.7.0, made by John Jones and Phillip Ayars.

1769, July 24. Account by both Executors.

Lib. 13, p. 329; Lib. 14, p. 121.

1768, March 14. Shepperd, Abraham, of Cumberland Co. Ward. Son of Samuel Shepperd, of said place, deceased. He makes choice of his brother-in-law, Bostun Shull, to be his Guardian. Witnesses—Joseph Bateman and Jacob Shull.

1768, March 14. Guardian—Bostun Shull. Fellowbondsman—John Jarman; both of Salem Co. Lib. 13, p. 325.

1764, Aug. 31. Sherrington, Thomas, of Salem Co. Int. Adm'r—John Budd. Fellowbondsmen—Joseph Burroughs, Esq., and Edward Test, gentleman, all of said Co. Lib. 12, p. 73.

1768, Dec. 19. Sherwin, Grace, of Burlington Co. Ward. Daughter and legatee of William Sherwin, of said Co., yeoman, deceased. She makes choice of James Hinchman as her Guardian.

1768, Dec. 19. Guardian—James Hinchman, yeoman. Fellowbondsman—John Sparks, yeoman; both of Deptford, Gloucester Co. Witness—Samuel Mickle. Lib. 13, p. 477.

1764, Sept. 18. Shields, Robert, of Bethlehem Twsp., Hunterdon Co.; will of. Wife, Jane, £100. Sister, Jane Cowan, £50. To Robert Clifford, son of Charles Clifford, £15. To Robert Gordon, £10. To Archibald Shields, son of William, £20. To Thomas Shields the amount of what he ows me on bond to his children. Brother, John Shields, £10. To Margaret Young, £10; and to Joseph McCafferty, £10, when of age. Rest to wife, Jane. Executors—my wife, John Cowen and Francis McShane. Witnesses—Archibald Stewart, Thomas Little, Thomas Flemen. Proved Nov. 23, 1764.

1764, Sept. 24. Inventory, £463.9.9, made by Thomas Lake and Nehemiah Dunham. Lib. 12, p. 131.

1763, April 19. Shinn, Jairus, of Greenwich, Gloucester Co., husbandman. Int. Adm'r—Jacob Spicer, yeoman. Fellowbondsman—Azariah Shinn, carpenter; both of said place. Witnesses—Sarah Howell and John Ladd. Lib. 11, p. 313.

CALENDAR OF WILLS—1761-1770

1763, April 19. Shinn, Jairns, of Greenwich, Gloucester Co., husbandman. Int. Adm'r—Jacob Spicer, yeoman, of said place. Fellowbondsman—Azariah Shinn, carpenter. Witness—Sarah Howell.
Lib. 11, p. 314.

1766, June 17. Shinn, John, of New Hanover, Burlington Co., yeoman. Int. Adm'x—Mary Shinn, the widow, of said place. Fellowbondsman—John Goldy, of said place, yeoman. Witness—Gabriel Blond.
1766, May 20. Inventory, £46.10.8, made by James Dobbin and John Goldy.
Lib. 12, p. 291.

1767, May 19. Shinn, William, Jr., of Springfield, Burlington Co.; will of. Sons, Joseph, Eli and Aaron, my plantation. Daughters, Mary and Lydia, £50 each, when 18. My said plantation is under a lease for 9 years, and my wife is to have the rent, and is to bring up the children. Executors—wife, Sarah, and my friend, William Smith. Witnesses—Josiah White, Henry Paxson, John Fenimore. Proved June 1, 1767.
1767, May 29. Inventory, £595.2.9, made by Jonathan Hough and Thomas Gaskill.
Lib. 13, p. 79.
1768, Aug. 1. Account by Sarah Shinn, acting Ex'trx.
Lib. 13, p. 435.

1763, July 8. Shipman, Benjamin, of Hanover, Morris Co. Int. Adm'r—Jacob Ford, of said Co. Fellowbondsman—Samuel Jaques, of Middlesex Co.
1763, March 28. Renunciation by Charity Shipman, his widow; in favor of Jacob Ford, the principal creditor. Witness—Samuel Nuttman.
Lib. H, p. 259.

1761, Sept. 9. Shipman, Jacob, of Tewksbury Twsp., Hunterdon Co., yeoman; will of. Wife, Mary, use of all personal and real estate while my widow, and afterwards the plantation to descend to my youngest son, Jacob, in case he can hold the same by the deed obtained by me from Stephen Crane, Thomas Clark and John Crane, dated Oct. 4, 1754, and contains 216 acres; and he is to pay £25 to Matthias Shipman, £25 to Anne, the wife of John Stine, £25 to Gertrude Wyckof, the wife of Samuel, £25 to Elizabeth Kinny, the wife of Peter, £25 to Lena Cole, the wife of Ezekiel, £25 to Jannetje, the wife of Jacob Commins, and £25 to Margaret Teeble, the wife of George Teeble. I give £7 to the Lutheran Church; £20 to Casper Hendershet, the son of Michael Hendershet; £20 to Mary Helford, the daughter of Christopher Helford, and £1 to Matthias Shipman; the rest to my children, Matthias, Jacob, Anne Stine, Gertrude Wyckof, Elizabeth Kinny, Lena Cole, Jannetje Commins and Margaret Teeble. Executor—son, Matthias. Witnesses—William Schuiler, Nicholas Shipman, Elizabeth Murchland.
1761, Sept. 12. Codicil. Witnesses—William Schuiler, Elizabeth Marchland, Aaron Lane. Proved Oct. 16, 1761.
1761, Oct. 14. Inventory, £341.5.11, made by Aaron Lane, William Pippenger and William Schuiler.
Lib. 11, p. 40.

1762, Jan. 6. Shipman, Nathan, of Elizabeth Town, Essex Co. Int. Adm'x—Phebe Shipman. Fellowbondsman—Samuel Little, farmer; both of said town. Witness—Edward Thomas.
Lib. H, p. 119.

1768, April 19. Shivers, Josiah, of Waterford, Gloucester Co., yeoman; will of. Wife, Ann, use of my plantation, situate between John Shivers and Isaac Horner, where I now live, during her life. Daughters, Latitia, Hope and Ann Shivers, household goods. Son, John, plantation I bought of Robert Friend Price, as Sheriff, that formerly belonged to Charles Day, except 8 acres of meadow, and 20 of woodland; and he is to pay to my daughter, Abigail Weaver, £50, and to my daughters, Letitia, Hope and Ann Shivers, £50. Son, Josiah, all my plantation where I live, and the 8 acres of meadow and 20 of woodland; and he is to pay £10 to my grandson, Shivers Paul, when 21, and £10 to my grandson, Josiah Paul, when 21, and £5 to my granddaughter, Mary Paul, when she is 25. Sons, John and Josiah, my cedar swamp. Executors—friend, Josiah Stokes, and my son, John. Witnesses—Griffith Morgan, Samuel Kenard, Richard Weekes. Proved May 24, 1768.

1768, May 6. Inventory, £612.19.1, made by Henry Wood and John Barton. Lib. 13, p. 375.

1753, Feb. 5. Shoort, Adolph, of Romopuck, Bergen Co., yeoman; will of. Eldest son, Jost, the cow which I lent him. Wife, Margaret, use of real estate while my widow, and at her decease to my three youngest sons, William, Hendrick and Johanes; and they are to pay to my eldest son, Jost, £20. Daughter, Magdelena, £25. If son, Hendrick, and daughter, Janetie, should marry as the other children have, they are to have an outset. Executors—my eldest daughter and my friend, Johanes Brower. Witnesses—Theodore Valleau, Daniel Brower, Maria Brower. Proved April 28, 1761.

1761, April 28. Probate granted to eldest daughter, Magdalen Shoort, and Johanes Brower. Lib. G, p. 430.

1759, Jan. 10. Shotwell, John, of Borough of Elizabeth, Essex Co.; will of. Wife, Mary, £200, and sons, Abraham and Samuel, are to each pay her £5 yearly, and son, Benjamin, is to keep her a horse. Son, Benjamin, the land below the road. Son, Samuel, the land north of the road. Son, John, the rest of land which I bought of Caleb Jeffers and Daniel Potter, and that I took upon the right of Symon Rouse, near the mountain. Son, Abraham, rest of plantation which I bought of John Morris, Justus Morris and William Allton, except what I sold to Daniel Marsh. The above sons have already had lands deeded to them. Daughter, Mary Marsh, 100 acres laid out in my grandfather's right in the last division. Son, Jacob, £200. Son, Joseph, £400. Son, Joseph, my right in the unsurveyed land in Elizabeth Town. Executors—my sons, Joseph and Benjamin. Witnesses—Benjamin Jenkins, Charles Howel, David Brant. Proved June 26, 1762.

1762, June 30. Inventory, £1,773.8.9, made by Solomon Hunt and Cowperthwait Copeland. Lib. H, p. 156.

1766, June 3. Shoulder, Hans Erick, of Greenwich, Gloucester Co.; will of. My plantation and that tract of land I bought of Mathew Gill, to be sold, and the money to be given to my wife, Magdalan, while she is my widow, and, when she shall cease to be my widow, then to be divided between my wife and my two children, Jacob and Susannah, when they are of full age. Executors—my wife and Mathew Gill. Witnesses—Richard Haslam, Sarah Starr, William Guest, Sr. Proved Aug. 9, 1766.

1766, Aug. 6. Inventory, £52.9.4, made by William Guest and James Mathews. Lib. 12, p. 373.

CALENDAR OF WILLS—1761-1770   385

1763, May 2. Shourds, Joseph, of Little Egg Harbor, Burlington Co. Int. Adm'rs—Daniel Shourds and Kezia Shourds. Fellowbondsman—Job Mathis; all of said place. Witness—Robert Norris.
Lib. 11, p. 305.
1763, April 8. Inventory, £487.5.8, made by James Bellanger and John Leek.
1764, June 20. Account by Adm'rs.

1768, Sept. 29. Shourds, Samuel, of Little Egg Harbor, Burlington Co.; will of. Wife, Elizabeth, ⅓ my moveable estate, except my clock for Stephen, and desk for Solomon (my sons), and the rest to be sold to support my sons. Sons, Stephen and Solomon, my lands, when 21. Executors—Daniel Shourds and Jonathan Pettit. Witnesses—Joseph Gaunt, John Gaunt, John Moore. Proved Oct. 27, 1768.
1768, Oct. 8. Inventory, £73.7.1, made by John Gaunt and Joseph Lippincott.   Lib. 13, p. 460.
1771, May 15. Account by Daniel Shourds, as Ex'r.   Lib. 15, p. 101.

1766, Dec. 8. Shute, Ann, of Greenwich, Gloucester Co., widow. Int. Adm'r—Samuel Shute, of Chester, Burlington Co., tailor. Fellowbondsman—Joseph Shute, of said Greenwich, yeoman.
1766, Dec. 22. Inventory, £95.8.6½, of Ann, widow of William Shute; made by William Guest and Mathew Gill.   Lib. 12, p. 380.

1765, Feb. 1. Shute, William, of Greenwich, Gloucester Co., yeoman; will of. Wife, Anne, ⅓ my real and personal. Grandson, George Shute, 10 shillings, when he is 21. Son, Samuel, £20. Son, John, £20. Son, Joseph, £10. Son, Isaac, £10. Daughter, Dianna Eselick, 5 shillings. Daughter, Anne, £10 and bed. Sons, Henry and Thomas, plantation where I live, except the right of their mother. Daughters, Hannah Chew and Edith Anderson, 5 shillings each. Executors—my son, Joseph, and my wife, Anne. Witnesses—Magdelen Gill, John Gill, Mathew Gill. Proved Oct. 11, 1766.
1766, Oct. 8. Inventory, £341.1½, made by William Guest and Mathew Gill.
1767, Nov. 5. Account by Joseph Shute, surviving Executor.
Lib. 13, p. 108.

1766, Aug. 19. Sickles, Zachariah, of Elizabeth, Essex Co. Int. Adm'x—Sarah Sickles, the widow. Fellowbondsman—John Vreeland; both of Elizabeth Town. Witness—Cornelius Miller.   Lib. H, p. 642.

1765, June 7. Siddens, William, of Gloucester Co. Ward. Son of Henry Siddons, of said place. He makes choice of Elijah Weed, of Philadelphia, cordwainer, as his Guardian.
1765, June 7. Guardian—Elijah Weed, of Philadelphia. Fellowbondsman—Samuel Smith, of Burlington, hatter.   Lib. 12, p. 114.

1763, Feb. 5. Silver, David, of Nottingham Twsp., Burlington Co., laborer; will of. Wife, Mary, £10, and various goods. Rest to be sold. Children to be educated. Son, William, to be put to a trade, when 14. Children are Lucy, Margaret, William, Lydia. Executors —wife, Mary, and William Cubberly. Witnesses—John Taylor, Timothy Abbott. Proved April 11, 1763.   Lib. 11, p. 347.
1763, April 8. Inventory, £109.16.9, made by William Murfin and Timothy Abbott.

25

1769, Jan. 21. Simkins, Mary, of Cape May Co. Ward. Daughter of William Simkins. Guardian—Nathaniel Hand. Fellowbondsman—Joshua Hildreth; both of said co., gentlemen. Witness—Zeruiah Hughes. Lib. 13, p. 495.

1766, March 12. Simkins, William, of Cape May Co. Int. Adm'rs —John Conner and Hannah Simkins. Fellowbondsmen—Christopher Foster and Richard Stites; all of said Co. Witnesses—John Shaw and Jer. Leaming.
1766, March 7. Inventory, £214.17.1, made by Christopher Foster and Richard Stites. Lib. 12, p. 357.

1759, Aug. 2. Simons, John, of Northampton Twsp., Burlington Co., yeoman; will of. Eldest son, Thomas, £20. Daughter, Hannah, £20, and a lot of land where my house stands of about 3 acres. Daughter, Sarah, £20. Son, Richard, £20. Grandson, Isaiah Peters, books. Sons, John and William, the rest. Executors—son, John, and son, William. Witnesses—Samuel King, Samuel Jones, John Goldy. Proved Oct. 18, 1765.
1765, Oct. 17. Inventory, £5.4.6, made by Samuel King and John Goldy. Lib. 12, p. 189.

1766, July 28. Simons, William, of Evesham, Burlington Co., yeoman. Int. Adm'x—Joanna Simons, the widow. Fellowbondsman—Joseph Stokes of the same place, yeoman. Lib. 12,. p. 295.
1766, July 29. Inventory, £176.4.4, made by Thomas Shinn and Joseph Burr, Jr.

1768, April 15. Simpson, Alexander, of Elizabeth Borough, Essex Co., yeoman; will of. Daughters, Mary and Elizabeth, all my household goods, and Mary is to have £5 cash. Daughter, Phebe, £5. Daughter, Anne, £20, when 18. Sons, Simeon, Abraham and Stephen, my lands. Executors—friend, Benjamin Bonnel, and my son, Simeon. Witnesses—John Clark, Samuel Ross, Jeremiah Clark. Proved May 4, 1768. Lib. I, p. 308.

1765, Aug. 22. Simpson, Eleanor, of Trenton, Hunterdon Co.; will of. Son, James Simpson, 5 shillings. Granddaughter, Susannah Robison, apparel, household goods, etc., when she is 18; but all to be left in care of Elizabeth Tucker, the wife of Samuel Tucker; and if said granddaughter die before 18, then all to be given to my granddaughter, Sarah Simson, daughter of James Simson. Executor—John Ely. If Elizabeth Tucker declines to take charge of the goods, then I desire Maccy Norton to do so instead. Witnesses—Aaron Forman, John Mounteer. Proved Oct. 14, 1765.
1768, April 23. Account by Sarah Ely, Executrix of John Ely, who was sole Executor of Eleanor Simson.
Lib. 12, p. 255; Lib. 13, p. 333.

1768, June 1. Sims, Abner, of Mannington, Salem Co., carpenter; will of. Son, Joshua Sims, that part of my lands lying on the south side of the Branch, the run to be the line up to the old bridge, from thence to land of John Sims; also land joining on Abel Smith; also a lot of woodland on the west end of Samuel Sims. To my eldest son, Lewis Sims, rest of my lands. Lands are to be rented out, to school my sons. Wife, Elizabeth, ½ my goods. Executors—my wife

CALENDAR OF WILLS—1761-1770   387

and my son, Lewis. Witnesses—Daniel Smith, John Sims, Edward Keasbey.
1769, March 23. Codicil. Witnesses—John Sims, James Wright, Edward Keasbey. Proved March 10, 1770.
1769, Nov. 3. Inventory, £345.8.9, made by Daniel Smith and James Smith. Lib. 14, p. 209.

1764, Aug. 30. Simson, James, of Somerset Co. Int. Adm'x—Margaret Simson, the widow of said James. Fellowbondsman—Robert Hewit, of Morris Co.
1763, Oct. 22. Inventory, £196.2.6, made by John Roy and Brice Riky. Lib. H, p. 353.

1766, July 16. Simson, Samuel, of Hardwick, Morris Co. Int. Adm'x—Catharine Simson. Fellowbondsman—Daniel Landon; both of Hardwick, Sussex Co.
1766, July 2. Inventory, £52.16.1, made by Daniel Landon and John Bulkly.
1767, June 4. Account by Catharine Simson. Lib. 12, p. 433.

[No date]. Sinnick, Andrew, of Pilesgrove, Salem Co., farmer; will of. Wife, Elizabeth, my plantation while my widow. After death, or marriage of said wife, I give said plantation of 150 acres to William Tuft and his wife, Elizabeth. Granddaughters, Gartre and Mary Besley, £80 each, when they come 21. Grandson, John Besley, £25, when 21. I give my wife ⅓ of rest of personal estate, and the rest to my granddaughters, Elizabeth Tuf, Garther Beasley and Mary Besley. Executors—grandson, William Tuft, and my wife, Elizabeth. Witnesses—John Firth, Henry Woodnutt, Thomas Rice. Proved Dec. 27, 1764.
1764, Feb. 18. Inventory, £156.1.10, made by Mounce Keen and Robert Clark. Lib. 12, p. 130.

1762, Aug. 16. Sip, Arie, of Achquecknonk, Essex Co., yeoman; will of. Son, Helmich Sip, 200 acres on which he lives, which were bought of Christoffel Stynmetz. Son, John, 150 acres on which I live, and the lots of 14 acres that joins the highway. Son, Helmich, my land in the Commons of Achquecknonk. To my daughters, Annatje Post and Jannitje van Houten, £110 each. Executors—my two sons. Witnesses—David Marinus, Benjamin Dubois, Anna Marinus. Proved Aug. 5, 1766. Lib. I, p. 64.

1760, April 19. Sip, Eida, of Town of Bergen, in Bergen Co., yeoman; will of. Eldest son, John, 20 shillings. Son, Cornelious, my homestead where I live. Son, Gerrit, my orchard over the street. Sons, Cornelious and Gerrit, land in Bergen, and land in Essex Co., and 3 horses, as each of my daughters had when married. Daughter, Annatje, the wife of Leveyius Winne, ¼ of other land in Bergen Co., and daughter, Harrijantje, wife of Eyde Marcelious, ¼ part, and daughter, Jannetje, wife of Helmigle Vrelandt, ¼ part, and to the child of my daughter Cattealyntje, deceased, late wife of Close Vrelandt, when of age, ¼ part. To sons, Johannes, Cornelious and Gerrit, and daughters, Annatje, Harrejantje and Jannetje, and the child of my daughter, Cattealyntje, deceased, rest of personal estate. Executors—sons, Cornelious and Gerrit, and my son-in-law,

Leveyius Winne. Witnesses—David Abiel, Pieter Van Burthuysen, Hendrick Van Winkle.

1761, March 7. Codicil. Grandson, Magheil Vrelandt, son of my daughter, Cattealynte, deceased, a negro that is in possession of his father, Class Vrelandt. Witnesses—David Abiel, Pieter Van Burtlaayse, Abraham Pryer. Proved April 12, 1762. Lib. H, p. 138.

1765, Oct. 18. Skeeles, William, of City and Co. of Burlington; will of. I desire a tombstone at the head of my grave, with the inscription as I shall leave a copy of. My brother, Thomas Skeeles, and his wife, both living at St. Ives, in Huntingtonshire, £20. My brother-in-law, Samuel Prat, and his wife, Elizabeth, living at St. Ives, £20. To my kinsman, Samuel Jackson Pratt, son of the said Samuel and Elizabeth, £100. The rest of my personal estate to my brother, Thomas Skeeles, in trust for his children, to be paid them when 21, or the day of their marriage. Brother, Thomas Skeeles, ⅓ of my real estate. Sister, Elizabeth Pratt, wife of Samuel Pratt, Esq., ⅓ my real estate. Godson, William Skeeles, son of said Thomas Skeeles, ⅓ of my real, when 21. To Ann Price, wife of Ralp Price, shoemaker of this city, £20. To my housekeeper, £5. To Ralph Price, one suit of apparel. Money to be sent to my devisees living in England. Executors—friends, Thomas Rodman, Esq., Daniel Ellis, Esq., and Daniel Smith, Jr., all of Burlington. Witnesses—Levi Murril, Ephraim Phillips and Samuel Scattergood. Proved Feb. 2, 1768.

1768, Jan. 29. Inventory, £812.2.4, made by William Smith and Samuel How. Lib. 13, p. 300.

1760, July 8. Skinner, Elizabeth, of Perth Amboy, Middlesex Co., widow; will of. I have by deed, conveyed to my children, to wit, Courtland Skinner, William Skinner, Stephen Skinner, John Skinner and Gertruy de Skinner, all my land and interest in the manor of Courtland, in New York, which I confirm. To Elizabeth Skinner, daughter of Courtland, my son, £50. Daughter, Gertruyd Skinner, my house and lot in Amboy, which I bought of Reverend Cook. Executors—my daughter, Gertruyd, and my son, Courtland. Witnesses Alexander Campbell, Jonathan Deare, John Smyth. Proved June 2, 1763. Lib. H, p. 345.

1761, Dec. 24. Skinner, Richard, Jr., and Sarah. Wards. Petition of Richard Skinner, Richard Skinner, Jr., and Sarah Skinner, states that William Britton, formerly of Woodbridge, deceased, died intestate, leaving one son and one daughter, the said Sarah Skinner; that the said son of said Britton has since deceased, whereby the said Sarah hath become the sole heir to all the estate of her said father, both personal and real; that the said Sarah hath married the said Richard Skinner, Jr., both of whom are under age, and the said Britton has left a very valuable estate, and it is necessary that some person should take charge thereof, and the said Richard Skinner, the elder, father to said Richard Skinner, Jr., being old and infirm, therefore the petitioners desire that Abraham Clark, Jr., may be made Guardian of the estate of Richard Skinner, Jr., and Sarah his wife, till they come of age.

1761, Dec. 24. Abraham Clark, Jr., of Elizabeth Town, appointed Guardian of Richard Skinner, Jr., and Sarah Skinner. Fellowbondsman—Robert Ogden, of said town. Lib. H, p. 62.

1762, Aug. 2. Skinner, William, of Perth Amboy, Middlesex Co., minister. Int. Adm'rs—Courtland Skinner and Stephen Skinner, two of the sons of said William. Fellowbondsman—Andrew Smyth; all of said place. Witness—John Smyth. Lib. H, p. 165.

1766, Jan. 16. Slater, William, of Kingwood Twsp., Hunterdon Co., yeoman; will of. Wife, Jean, all moveable estate, and ½ the income of the plantation where I dwell, till my youngest son, Peter, comes of age, when plantation is to be divided between my eldest son, Samuel, and my youngest son, Peter. My son, Thomas, and my daughter, Mary, £100 each. Executors—my son, Samuel, and Francis McShane. Witnesses—Lazarus Adams, Henry Heite. Proved June 6, 1767.

1767, May 25. Inventory, £402.8.0, made by Daniel Leake and John Taylor. Lib. 13, p. 197.

1764, Aug. 8. Slengerlandt, Samuel, of Hanover, Morris Co.; will of. Wife, Marritje, use of all real and personal estate for her support and education of my daughter, Lea. Daughter, Lea, after wife's death or marriage, all my estate; but, if she die, then £10 is to be given to my brother, Niclaes Slengerlandt, son of Peter Slengerlandt; and the rest to my wife; but, if she have no heirs, then to my brother, Niclaes, and my sister, Elizabeth Ryerse. Executors—my wife and brother, Niclaes, and Nathaniel Ford. Witnesses—David Marinus, Dirk Francisco, Peter Roome. Proved Nov. 6, 1764. Lib. H, p. 553.

1764, Dec. 15. Sloan, Andrew, of Newtown Twsp., Gloucester Co., cordwainer; will of. Children, Jacob, Joseph, Hannah, Rachel and David, all estate, after debts are paid. Daughters, Hannah and Rachel, to have their mother's clothes. All my children to have their shares when they are men and women. Executor—my friend, John Branson. Witnesses—Robert Sloan, David Branson, Thomas Redman, Jr. Proved Jan. 15, 1765.

1765, Jan. 5. Inventory, £219.2.6, made by David Branson and John Mickle, Jr.

1772, Aug. 11. Account by John Branson, the Executor.

Lib. 12, p. 49; Lib. 14, p. 435.

1763, June 14. Sloan, James, of Newton, Gloucester Co., yeoman. Int. Adm'x—Mary Sloan. Lib. 11, p. 409.

1768, March 28. Sloan, James, of Gloucester Co. Ward. Son of James Sloan, of said Co. He makes choice of John Hinchman, Esq., as his Guardian.

1768, March 28. Guardian—John Hinchman, of said Co. Fellowbondsman—Abraham Hewlings, of City of Burlington.

Lib. 13, p. 330.

1768, Aug. 21. Small, John, of Evesham, Burlington Co., yeoman; will of. Wife, Ruth, use of my lands to bring up my younger children. Son, William, use of house and 6 acres, where he lives. Son, John, 6 acres joining William's. Son, Robert, also 6 acres. Daughter, Ruth Small, £5. Daughter, Mary, the wife of Thomas Archer, 20 shillings. My sons, Israel and Jonas, rest of lands. Executors—

wife, Ruth, and my friend, Edward Darnel, and my son, Israel. Witnesses—Samuel Borton, William Borton, John Burr, Jr. Proved Feb. 27, 1769. Renunciation of Israel Small in favor of his mother and Edward Darling. Lib. 13, p. 510.

1769, Feb. 25. Inventory, £93.15.0, made by Samuel Garwood and Abraham Borton.

1762, July 27. Smalley, Jonathan, of Piscataway, Middlesex Co.; will of. Son, Andrew Smalley, my lands and salt meadows; and he is to pay to my son, John, £210, and to son, Jonathan, £260, and to my daughter, Hannah Fitz Randolph, £25, and to my daughter, Martha Clawson, £25. My grandson, Jonas Smalley, eldest son of my eldest son, Isaac, deceased, £10. To John Smalley, son of my son, Isaac, 5 shillings. Granddaughter, Ann Smalley, daughter of my son, Isaac, 5 shillings. Granddaughters, Mary Ruth and Elizabeth Ruth, each £5; Grandchildren, David Shreave, Sarah Shreave, Elizabeth Shreave and Mary Shreave, each £5, when they come of age. Executors—my son-in-law, Cornelius Clawson, and my friend, Azariah Dunham. Witnesses—Lucas Voorhees, Henry Moore, John Dennis. Proved April 27, 1763. Lib. H, p. 285.

1761, May 31. Smalley, Joshua, of Piscataway, Middlesex Co.; will of. I am in my 63rd year. Wife, Margaret, a bed and cow. Twenty-one acres of land, where my son, Joshua, deceased, did live, to be sold; also 3 acres of salt marsh in the Raritan Meadows, that I bought of my brother, Isaac Smalley. Son, Isaac, to give his mother support. Son, Isaac, rest of lands, and he is to pay my son, John, £20. Daughter, Margaret Smalley, £30. Isaac is to pay to his sisters, Anna Davis, Catron Thornton, Prudence Runyon and Mary Cox, £3 each. Grandson, Jacob F. Randolph, and my granddaughter, Mary Smalley, £15 each, when of age. Executors—friend, Isaac Stelle, Fitz Randolph Drake, and my son, Isaac. Witnesses—John Hardy, William Thomson, Jonathan Hall. Proved Jan. 5, 1764. Lib. H, p. 482.

1770, Jan. 20. Smiley, Robert, of Tewksbury, Hunterdon Co. Int. Adm'r—John Smiley. Fellowbondsmen—John Bender and Daniel Handly; all of said Co.

1770, Jan. 27. Inventory, £226.19.11, made by John Mehelm and John Wurts. Lib. 15, p. 3.

1760, May 24. Smith, Abijah, of Shrewsbury, Monmouth Co., yeoman; will of. To my four children all my money, if my wife does not wish it to bring up the children. Sons, John and Jesse, the land. Wife, Mary, the moveable estate. Executors—my wife, Amos White and Benjamin Woolley, Jr. Witnesses—Joel White, Joshua Boude, Esebel Maccoy. Proved July 1, 1760, and March 3, 1761.

1760, July 2. Inventory, made by James Woolley and Jacob Brewer.

1765, June 19. Amos White and Benjamin Woolley, two of the Executors, are cited to appear, upon the complaint of William Wardell and Mary, his wife (late Mary Smith), that Amos and Benjamin have the will in their possession and refuse to have it registered; therefore they are cited to bring the will on July 6th next.

Lib. H, p. 476; Lib. H, p. 497.

CALENDAR OF WILLS—1761-1770   391

1770, Oct. 25. Smith, Abraham, of Fairfield, Cumberland Co., yeoman; will of. Wife to have all the household goods and farming utensils that she brought with her. Son, Nathaniel, the land I bought of John Shepard and that I bought of Charles Dennes. Son, Elias, £10. Son, Abraham, homestead where I formerly lived. Daughter, Sarah Mulford, warming pan. Son, Elias, land where Joab Sely formerly lived. Son, David, rest of land. Executor—son, Abraham. Witnesses—Mark Reeve, Philip Shepard, John Jones. Proved Dec. 13, 1770.
1770, Dec. 1. Inventory, £155.8.8, made by Daniel Dixson and Mark Reeve.   Lib. 14, p. 323.

1763, Nov. 2. Smith, Andrew, of Hopewell Twsp., Hunterdon Co., yeoman; will of. Eldest son, Andrew, £5. Son, Jonathan, £5. Son, George, £5. Daughter, Ann Titus, £5. Grandson, Jonathan Smith, land whereon his father, Charles, lived, of 60 acres, when he is 21; but, if he die, then my granddaughter, Rachel North, shall have said land. Granddaughter, Rachel North, £20. Son, Timothy, rest of my land. Executor—son, Timothy. Witnesses—Felix Lott, John Corwine, Thomas Wilson. Proved April 24, 1767.   Lib. 13, p. 220.

1763, March 15. Smith, Anne, late of Colony of New York, now of New Brunswick, Middlesex Co., widow; will of. Eldest son, Jacob Carl, £10. Granddaughter, Anne, the daughter of my son, Thomas Smith, my gold ring, when she is 18. My son, Thomas Smith, has wife, Jamima. Rest of personal and real to son, Thomas Smith. Executors—son, Jacob Carl, son, Thomas Smith, and Nehemiah Smith. Witnesses—Samuel Bayles, Joseph Warne, Phebe Woolsey. Proved April 27, 1763.
1763, May 16. Inventory, £332.16.0, filed by Cornelius Arven and Charles McClean.   Lib. H, p. 231.

1767, June 3. Smith, Benjamin, of Hanover, Morris Co.; will of. Wife, Hannah, ⅓ of the moveable estate, and ⅓ the rents of my real, as long as she lives. The rest of the rents are to be used to bring up my children. What is not used to go to my four sons, Caleb, Hyram, Benjamin and Richard, when the oldest is 21. The child that is yet unborn is to have its share. My daughter, Elizabeth, £50, when 18. Executors—my wife, Samuel Smith and Aaron Dod. Witnesses—Ebenezer Cobb, Isaac Sergeant, John Cobb. Proved July 27, 1767.   Lib. I, p. 188.

1762, Oct. 7. Smith, Caleb, of Newark, Essex Co., minister of Gospel; will of. Wife, Rebecca, all which she brought to me; also ⅓ of my land, bought of Robert Ogden, that is what it shall sell for. Daughter, Anna, the books that were her mother's. Daughter, Elizabeth, those books that were written by her grandfather, Dickinson. Daughter, Jane, books. To these my three daughters I give the apparel and goods that were their mother's, and the silver that was in the house before my second marriage. Son, Apollos, £100. Children, Anna, Elizabeth, Jane and Apollos, rest of my estate, when of age. My daughter, Anna, is to be put to the care of my sister, Martha, the wife of Caleb Smith, of Smith Town. Daughter, Elizabeth, to be put to the care of my sister, Sarah, the wife of Rev. James Sproutt, of Guilford, New England. Daughter, Jane, to be put to the care of my sister-in-law, Abigail Sergeant, the wife of Jonathan Sergeant, of Maiden Head. Will speaks of church members, Joseph Riggs and Bethuel Peirson. Executors—my brother, Thomas Cooper, of Southampton, and my brother-in-law, Jonathan Sergeant, Esq., of Maiden Head. Witnesses—Alexander Mitchel, John Keeny, Isaac Cundeet. Proved Nov. 13, 1762.

1762, Nov. 15. Inventory, £1579.3.1, made by Bethuel Peirson and Joseph Riggs. Lib. H, p. 334.

1760, Dec. 7. Smith, Carman, of Cape May Co., yeoman; will of. Daughter, Martha Smith, all my lands. Wife, Lydia, use of lands. daughter, Mary, 5 shillings. Executors—my wife and my brother, John Smith. Witnesses—Nathaniel Jenkins, Thomas Stites, Nathan Stites. Proved May 6, 1761.

1761, June 4. Inventory, £122.8.10, made by Joshua Hildreth and James Cresse. Lib. 10, p. 222.

1762, Nov. 15. Smith, Casper, of Deptford Township, Gloucester Co., wheelwright. Int. Adm'x—Abigail Smith, widow. Fellowbondsman—John Down, yeoman; both of said place. Witness—Sarah Howell.

1757, Nov. 29. Inventory, £47.2.6, made by Isaac Albertson and Samuel Harrison, Jr. Lib. 11, p. 264.

1760, Oct. 14. Smith, Christeen, of Amwell Twsp., Hunterdon Co.; will of. Eldest son, John, 20 shillings. Son, Lowdawick, £12, and to son, Matthias, a like amount. Son, Abraham, £10. Son, Jacob, my lands. My daughter, Christien Smith, bed, Bible, sheep, etc. Executor—son, Jacob. Witnesses—Joseph Hill, Daniel Robins, Mark Blair. Proved Jan. 5, 1761.

1761, Jan. 3. Inventory, £217.14.6, made by Joseph Hill and Mathias Smith. Lib. 10, p. 561.

1766, May 6. Smith, Daniel, of Gloucester Co.; will of. Wife, Sarah, all my lands, swamps, beaches and marshes, and all moveable estate. Executrix—my wife. Witnesses—Elizabeth Osborne, Mary Dannally. Proved April 12, 1768. Lib. 13, p. 331.

1768, Nov. 24. Smith, Daniel, of Burlington, merchant; will of. Granddaughter, Mary Litefoot, £100, and goods enough for a room. Granddaughter, Sarah, Litefoot, £50. Daughter, Sarah Pemberton, the residue. Executors—daughter, Sarah Pemberton, and my nephew, Daniel Smith. Witnesses—John Carty, Joseph Ferguson, Jr., William Smith. Proved March 28, 1769.

1769, April 4. Inventory, £1,126.1.8½, made by William Smith and John Hoskins. File No. 8593 C; Lib. 14, p. 29.

1769, Jan. 16. Smith, Daniel, of Gloucester Co. Ward. Son of Richard Smith, of said Co. He makes choice of Philip Cresse as his Guardian.

1769, Jan. 16. Guardian—Philip Cresse. Fellowbondsman—Nathan Hand; both of Cape May Co., gentlemen. Witnesses—Jacob Hughes, Jr., and Elijah Hughes. Lib. 13, p. 495.

1766, Oct. 1. Smith, Ezekiel, of Stony Brook, Middlesex Co. Int. Adm'rs—John Robins, of Monmouth Co., and John Hill, of Bucks Co., Pa. Fellowbondsman—Ezekiel Smith, of Hunterdon Co.
1766, Sept. 30. Inventory, £933.14.11, made by Edmund Bainbridge and Joseph Olden. Lib. 12, p. 456.

1764, March 8. Smith, George, of Shrewsbury, Monmouth Co., yeoman; will of. To granddaughter, Margaret Hartshorne, £25. Grandson, Thomas Hartshorne, £25. My daughter, Elizabeth Fisher, £100. To Stephen Edwards, £5. Son, James, my lands. Executors—friend, Webley Edwards, and my son, James. Witnesses—Stephen Woolley, Thomas Cooper, Margaret Tallman. Proved June 6, 1766.
1766, June 6. Renunciation by Webley Edwards. Lib. H, p. 625.

1762, Aug. 30. Smith, Hannah, of Newton, Gloucester Co., widow of Richard Smith; will of. Daughter-in-law, Experience Smith, together with my own daughters, viz., Rachil, Judith and Hannah Smith, to them share and share alike. My daughters are not 18. Executors—my brother, John Summers, of Great Egg Harbor, and my brother-in-law, Daniel Smith, of Cape May. Witnesses—Peter Breach, Richard Weekes. Proved Oct. 9, 1762.
1762, Oct. 9. Inventory, £302.6.9, made by Jeremiah Smith and Isaac Mickle. Lib. 11, p. 263.

1765, May 15. Smith, Hannah, of Windsor, Middlesex Co., widow. Int. Adm'r—John Robins, of Freehold, Monmouth Co. Fellowbondsman—Joseph Reckless, of Chesterfield, Burlington Co.
Lib. 12, p. 113.

1764, May 29. Smith, Hendrick, of Mine Brook, Somerset Co.; will of. Wife, Anna Cathrein Smith, to have her support on my plantation, at the expense of my son, John George Smith; and he is to have said place, he paying the mortgage on the said 317 acres; but I reserve 70 acres at the upper end, which I conveyed some years ago to Hendrick Smith and Peter Smith, my grandsons, which were the sons of Peter Smith, deceased. Daughter, Anna Ursal Smith, £10. Daughter, Mary Smith, £15. Daughter, Cathrien Smith, £10. Daughter, Margaret Smith, £10. Grandchildren, the children of my daughter, Elizabeth Smith, deceased, viz., Andrew Hamler, Mary Hamler, Eve Hamler, Jacob Hamler, Peter Hamler, Nicholas Hamler and Elizabeth Hamler, £10. The mortgage on my place is held by Alexander Linn. Executors—son, John George Smith, Alexander Linn, Leonard Straight, and my wife. Witnesses—William Linn, Aaron Malick, Robert Allan, Jr. Proved Oct. 14, 1766.
1766, July 28. Inventory, £156.6.10, made by William Linn and Aaron Melick. Lib. I, p. 23.

[No date]. Smith, Henry, of Roxbury Twsp., Morris Co.; will of. Wife, Hanner, to have all lands and moveables, to enable her to bring up my young children. Executrix—wife, Hanah. Witnesses—Ladey Darland, Charety Suten, Searey Anderson.
Codicil. (No date). To son, Henry, 5 shillings, when he comes of age. Witnesses—William Dorland, Michel Abel, Searey Anderson. Proved March 20, 1765.
1765, Jan. 2. Inventory, £86.11.8, made by Edward Wilmot and William Dorland. Lib. 12, p. 138.

1762, Jan. 13. Smith, Jacob, of Upper Freehold, Monmouth Co. Int. Adm'x—Elizabeth Smith, his widow. Fellowbondsman—John Coward; both of said place.
 1761, Dec. 13. Inventory, £62.7.0, made by John Coward and Richard James.
 1763, July 6. Account by Elizabeth Smith.   Lib. 10, p. 434.

1762, Nov. 15. Smith, Jasper, of Deptford Twsp., Gloucester Co., wheelwright. Int. Adm'x—Abigail Smith.   Lib. 11, p. 264.

1769, Nov. 29. Smith, Jasper, of Maidenhead Twsp., Hunterdon Co., freeholder; will of. Oldest son, John, plantation where he lives. The plantation where my second son, Jasper, was dwelling upon, when he died, I give to his oldest son, Waters Smith. Third son, Thomas, plantation where he lives. Fourth son, Samuel, 20 shillings. My grandson, John Smith, my son Samuel's 4th son, 100 acres, taken from my own plantation, where I live, and to be on the east side of the road that leads from Trenton to Princeton; and my said grandson, John Smith, is to maintain his mother, Elizabeth Smith, his father's wife; he is also to have a meadow of 4 acres, called the Widow Anderson's lot. My son, John's second son, Jasper, 2 acres of meadow, joining the Widow Hunt's lot. My youngest son, Joshua, the rest of plantation where I live; and he is to pay to my son, Ralph (his brother), £100. Moveable estate to my sons, Samuel, Ralph and Joshua. Executors—my son, Ralph, and my grandson, Waters Smith. Witnesses—Daniel Peirson, Benjamin Vancleave, William Ball.
 1770, April 9. Renunciation by Waters Smith. Witnesses—Israel Smith and Jean Smith.
 1770, April 7. Renunciation by Ralph Smith. Witnesses—John Biles and Samuel Smith.
 1770, June 15. Adm'r—Joshua Smith, with will annexed. Fellowbondsmen—Christopher Howell, Jr., and Benjamin Vanclease. Witness—Abram Cottnam.
 1770, March 29. Inventory, £154.11.0, made by Daniel Hunt and Benjamin Vancleave.
 1772, March 23. Account by Joshua Smith, Adm'r with will annexed.   Lib. 14, pp. 279, 420.

1762, Oct. 24. Smith, Jeremiah, of Turkeyhoe, Gloucester Co.; will of. Wife, Abigail, £100, and negro girl called Tab, and use of plantation, mill, etc., till my sons, Jeremiah and William, are 20, when they shall have the same; and, if Jeremiah die, then his share shall fall to his brother, James. If William die, then his share to fall to his brother, Jesse. Rest to my children, Rebecca Smith, Abigal Smith, James Smith and Jesse Smith, and the child that is yet not born. Executors—my brothers, Jonathan Smith and Daniel Smith, and, if either die, then my cousin, Thomas Smith, Sr., of Cape May, is to be Executor. Witnesses—John Van Gelder, William McGlaughlin, Silas Youngs. Proved May 4, 1763.
 1763, May 4. Inventory, £577.10.2½, made by John Goldin and Joseph Savage.
 1764, Nov. 14. Account by Executors.   Lib. 11, p. 332.

1767, March 26. Smith, Jeremiah, of Alloways Creek Precinct, Salem Co., gentleman; will of. Brother, Samuel Smith, farm where I live. To Phebe Smith, the wife of my brother, Job Smith, all my late wife Susannah's apparel, except one gown, which I give to Elizabeth Smith, wife of John Smith. Cousin, Charles Hamilton, £5. Cousin, John Hamilton, £5. My apprentice girl, Elizabeth Fister, 40 shillings, when she is 18. Executor—brother, Samuel Smith. Witnesses—Nehemiah Hogbin, David Wood, John Holme. Proved April 15, 1767.

1767, April 11. Inventory, £243.3.1, made by John Holme and William Oakford. Lib. 13, p. 183.

1759, Sept. 20. Smith, John, of Freehold, Monmouth Co., yeoman; will of. To wife, Bardina, 6 acres of land on north side of highway, and the land on south side, to be sold. After wife's death, what remains, to be divided among my children, Joseph, Samuel, John (except my son Mathew one shilling), daughter, Margaret, and the daughter of my son, Thomas, viz., Margaret. Executors—friend, Richard Francis, of Middletown Point, and John Van Brockell, of Freehold. Witnesses—John Tice, Garret Schanck, Garret Covenhoven. Proved March 2, 1761.

1803, March 10. Whereas, John Smith, by will of Sept. 20, 1759, appointed Richard Francis and John Van Brockell as his Executors, and they took the execution of said will, and have since died, therefore William Bennet is appointed Adm'r. Fellowbondsmen—James Morris and William H. Bennet, all of said Co.

Lib. G, p. 365; Lib. 40, p. 253.

1762, June 30. Smith, John, of New Windsor Twsp., Middlesex Co. Int. Adm'x—Hannah Smith, relict of said John. Fellowbondsman—Gilbert Barton; both of said place. Witness—Samuel Allinson.

1762, June 26. Inventory, £146.17.8, made by John Robins and Joseph Lawrence. Lib. 11, p. 226.

1765, April 16. Smith, John, of Hackinsack, Bergen Co. Citation to Samuel Moore, Sr., of said Co., Ex'r of said John Smith. Whereas Catherine Smith, John Lee and Christopher Benson, of New York City, which said Catherine is Executrix, and said John Lee is Executor and Guardians in will of John Smith, late of said City, dec'd, who was one of the legatees of said John Smith, of Bergen Co., dec'd, have complained that you, as Executor of John Smith, of Bergen Co., have neglected to file an Inventory, you are cited to do so, etc.

Lib. H, p. 419.

1767, Oct. 27. Citation to Executors of Samuel Moore, dec'd, late surviving Ex'r of John Smith, dec'd, at request of Ex'rs and Guardians of John Smith, of New York, who was son and legatee of John Smith, late of Bergen Co. You are cited to file an Inventory and account. Lib. I, p. 152. (See also Lib. H, p. 625.)

1769, Nov. 14. Smith, John, of Maidenhead, Hunterdon Co.; will of. Wife, Rachel, £40, when land is sold. Children, Joanthan, Philip, Enoch, Sarah and Isaiah, rest of estate, when they are of age. Niece, Sarah Hunt, £5. Executors—my wife and my friends, Philip Palmer and Nathan Hunt. Witnesses—William McCoy, Philip Palmer, Jr., Azariah Hunt. Proved Dec. 20, 1769.

1769, Dec. 7. Inventory, £169.3.6, made by Azariah Hunt and Nathan Moore. Lib. 14, p. 127.

1769, Jan. 16. Smith, John George, of Somerset Co. Int. Adm'rs —Mary Smith, the widow, and Jonathan Whitaker. Fellowbondsman —John Barkley; all of said place. Lib. K, p. 118.

1762, Feb. 18. Smith, Jonathan, of Alloways Creek, Salem Co., yeoman. Int. Adm'rs—James Smith and Samuel Smith, yeomen. Fellowbondsmen—Richard Hackett and Thomas Cowperthwaite, yeomen; all of said place. Lib. 11, p. 38.

1765, Oct. 25. Smith, Jonathan, of Cape May Co.; will of. Wife, Abigail, ½ my moveable estate, and use of plantation till my son, Thomas, is 21. Daughters, Sarah Smith and Hannah Smith, and my three youngest sons, Jonathan, Carmon and Jeremiah, the other ½ of my moveable estate. Son, Thomas, my land, and he to pay to my son, Constantine, £100, when 21. My brother, Daniel, a suit of clothes. Executors—my wife, my brother, Daniel, and my son, Thomas. Witnesses—Joshua Smith, Thomas Richardson, Abigail Hewit, John Bliss. Proved April 19, 1766.
1766, May 2. Inventory, £554.16.5½, made by Thomas Smith and Joseph Savage.
1767, Sept. 17. Account by Daniel Smith and Abigail Smith, surviving Executors. Lib. 12, p. 349.

1769, March 17. Smith, Jonathan, of Cumberland Co. Int. Adm'r —David Smith. Fellowbondsman—John Bateman; both of Fairfield, said Co., yeomen.
1769, March 7. Inventory, £66.8.4, made by John Bateman and Benjamin Chard. Lib. 13, p. 531.

1769, Aug. 14. Smith, Jonathan, of Upper Freehold, Monmouth Co. Ward. Son of John Smith, of said place. He makes choice of Gilbert Barton as his Guardian.
1769, Aug. 14. Guardian—Gilbert Barton, of said place. Fellowbondsman—Daniel Griggs, of Perth Amboy. Lib. 15, p. 1.

1770, Dec. 20. Smith, Joseph, of Bristol Twsp., Bucks Co., Pa. Int. Adm'x—Hannah Smith, of Bucks Co., Pa. Fellowbondsmen—Walter Vansciver, Jr., and John Hayes; both of Burlington. Witness—Colin Campbell.
1770, Dec. 13. Inventory, £799.15.9, made by John Brown and William Bidgood. (Contains many names of Bucks Co. people, but no important information). Lib. 15, p. 72.

1761, Aug. 1. Smith, Mary, of Burlington; will of. Aunt, Anne Carlile, the personal estate that was devised to me by my father, Thomas Smith, or my mother, Rebecca Smith, as also the ⅛ part of the residue devised by my grandfather, Sollomon Smith, to my said father. Executor—said Anne Carlile. Witnesses—Elizabeth Hughes, Esther Heulings, William Heulings. Proved Feb. 11, 1763.
File No. 7561 C; Lib. 11, p. 270.

1766, Sept. 14. Smith, Mathias, of Greenwich Twsp., Sussex Co.; will of. Son, John Adam Smith, 150 acres of that land lately purchased of Hollinshead, and he must keep my wife (his mother) during her life. Sons, Peter and Hendrick, rest of my real and the per-

CALENDAR OF WILLS—1761-1770   397

sonal. Executor—son, John Adam Smith. Witnesses—George Lies, P. Joh. Patteson. Proved Oct. 14, 1766.
1766, Oct. 3. Inventory, £355.5.4, made by Henry Winter and Alexander White.   Lib. 12, p. 423.

1763, Jan. 17. Smith, Moses, of Monmouth Co. Int. Adm'r—Joseph Smith, of Hunterdon Co., who is a brother-in-law of said Moses Smith. Fellowbondsman—Zebulon Baird, of Monmouth Co.
1763, Jan. 17. We, who are sisters of Moses Smith, deceased, desire that letters be granted to Joseph Smith, who married our sister, Dorothy. Signed by Anna Baird, Eleanor Clark and Deborah Smith.
1763, March 14. Inventory made by Peter Bowne and Andrew Baird.   Lib. H, p. 214.

1763, May 7. Smith, Peter, of Alloways Creek Precinct, Salem Co., yeoman; will of. Son, John Smith, 10 acres which I bought of David Allen. Son, Peter, 7 acres east of the grist mill. Eldest son, William, rest of land. Daughters, Elizabeth, Sarah, Maryan and Bethsheba, £5 each, when of age. My wife to have her ⅓. Executor—son, William. Witnesses—Thomas Test, Thomas Sayre, Jeremiah Robins. Proved May 27, 1763.
1763, May 20. Inventory, £163.13.9, made by Thomas Sayre and Thomas Test.   Lib. 11, p. 387.

1769, Nov. 21. Smith, Pilee, of Mannington Twsp., Salem Co., yeoman; will of. To wife, Hannah, use of my plantation till my son, Samuel, is 21, to bring up my children. Sons, Samuel and John, my said plantation. Son, Samuel, to have the land in Pilesgrove. Wife, Hannah, and my daughters, Hannah Smith, Elizabeth Smith, Mary Smith, Martha Smith and Rebecca Smith, my moveable estate. Executors—wife, Hannah, and my friend, Bartholomew Weyat, Jr. Witnesses—John Gray, Mary Sharp, John Holme. Proved March 20, 1770.
1769, Dec. 26. Inventory, £911.12.10, made by John Dickeson and Daniel Huddy.
1776, April 20. Account by Elisha Allen, late the husband of Hannah Smith, deceased, who was the Executrix of Pilee Smith, late of Salem.   Lib. 14, p. 291; Lib. 16, p. 485.

1763, Feb. 12. Smith, Richard, of Hanover, Morris Co.; will of. Wife, Sarah, ⅓ the goods. Daughter, Rachel Person, rest of goods; but to my granddaughter, Elizabeth Cobb, I give £10; also grandson, Thomas Cobb, £10, when 21. To my wife I give £10, it being now in the hands of Frances More. Sons, Samuel and Benjamin, £10, and my land. Executors—sons, Samuel and Benjamin. Witnesses—Francis Moore, Robart Jinkens, William Howard. Proved July 1, 1763.   Lib. H, p. 390.

1750, Aug. 20. Smith, Robert, of Great Egg Harbor, Gloucester Co., yeoman; will of. Wife, Ann, all the goods she had when I married her, and ⅓ my personal estate. Son, Robert, part of the land where I live (courses given). Son, Daniel, part of said land (courses are given). Daughter, Christian Cordeary, a negro girl. Granddaughter, Deborah Cordeary, a cupboard, that formerly belonged to her Aunt Deborah. Son-in-law, John Squire, one shilling. To six of my children, namely, John Smith, Sarah Addoms, Silvanus Smith, Eve Smith, Robert Smith and Daniel Smith, all the rest. Executors

—my two youngest sons, Robert and Daniel Smith. Witnesses—Daniel Leeds, Sarah Leeds, Japhet Leeds. Proved June 11, 1765.
1765, May 7. Inventory, £73.7.2, made by Nicholas Sooy and Nehemiah Leeds. Lib. 12, p. 158.

1761, Feb. 25. Smith, Seth, of Pilesgrove, Salem Co.; will of. Wife, Sarah, personal estate, but she is to make title by deed to my son, Abel, for 100 acres near Salem, belonging to her. Abel is to pay to my daughter, Nansey, when she is 18, £100. Son, Sollomon, the part of the place where I live that was formerly Gabriel Peterson's, of 263 acres; he paying to his sister, Margaret Hill, £40, and to his sister, Rachel Smith, £100, when she is 18. Son, Eaton Smith, the 100 acres that join his brother, Solomon, which I bought of Andrew Trauberg. Executrix—my wife, Sarah. Witnesses—Isaac Sharp, Larance Holsten, Margaret Holsten. Proved June 6, 1761.
1761, May 5. Inventory, 524.10.0, made by Joseph Champneys and Obadiah Loyd. Lib. 11, p. 16.

1766, Nov. 12. Smith, Shobal, of Woodbridge, Middlesex Co., yeoman; will of. Son, William, the land I bought of John Townsend, that is not disposed of; also a Freehold right, that formerly belonged to John Taylor; also ½ part of a meadow that I bought of Matthias Dehart. Daughter, Prudence Jackson, 35 acres that join on the east side of land of her husband, William Jackson, bought of me, where he dwells. Grandson, John Smith Shotwell, £20. The plantation where I live, the 40 acres given to me by my father, and the 70 acres which I bought of Reuben Bun, and one Freehold right which formerly belonged to my father, to be sold. Daughter, Mary Dunham, the widow of Jonathan Dunham, house and land, and ½ of the meadow that I bought of Docter Dehart, that joins on the south side to land I bought of Francis Walker. Daughters, Sarah Merriot, of Bristol, Frances Kirkbride, of Makefield, and Margret Thorne, of Woodbridge, £300 each. Daughters, Elizabeth Pound and Sarah Vail, £130 each. Grandson, Samuel Smith, £300. Executors—son, William, and my brother-in-law, Jacob Fitz Randolph. Witnesses—Miriam Latham, Thomas Latham, Joseph Shotwell. Proved June 10, 1768.
Lib. I, p. 272.

1761, April 26. Smith, Thomas, of Upper Freehold, Monmouth Co., yeoman; will of, being old. The land I live on, of 262 acres, to be sold; also the lot near Burdintown, of 27 and ¾ acres. Son, Jacob, land on the creek. To Joseph Smith and Rebecca Smith, children of my son, Abraham, deceased, each £20. Rest of my estate to my 6 children, John, Thomas, Content Smith, Jacob Smith, Mercy Smith and Mary Smith. I am on bonds for my sons, Content and Jacob, which, if my estate pay, is to be taken out of their share. Executors—my brothers, Joseph Smith and William Smith. Witnesses—Mary Parent, John Parent, John Lawrence.
1761, June 26. Codicil. Witnesses—William Stevenson, Elisha Lawrence, John Lawrence. Proved June 24, 1762. Lib. 11, p. 176.

1767, June 5. Smith, Thomas, of Cape May Co. Int. Adm'r—Daniel Smith. Fellowbondsman—Shamgar Hand; both of said Co. Witness—John Cresse.
1767, June 5. Inventory, £81.2.3, made by John Cresse and Shamgar Hand. Lib. 13, p. 147
1767, Sept. 17. Account by Adm'r.

CALENDAR OF WILLS—1761-1770   399

1762, May 15. Smith, Toddy, of Middlesex Co. Int. Late a soldier in the New Jersey Regiment. Adm'r—Axford Burt, of Woodbridge, said Co. Fellowbondsman—Robert Sproull, of Perth Amboy, said Co. Lib. H, p. 103.

1761, May 10. Smith, Uriah, of Cape May Co.; will of. Son, Joseph, the plantation I live on, when he is 21. Wife, Mary, use of my lands and what she brought to me at marriage. Joseph may be put to a trade when 14. My daughters, Neome and Experience, rest of moveable estate. Executors—my wife and friend, Elihu Smith. Witnesses—Jonathan Smith, Shamgar Hand, Richard Osborne. Proved May 17, 1764.
1764, April 28. Inventory, £305.10.6, made by John Shaw and Lewis Cresse. Lib. 12, p. 331.

1759, Nov. 15.—Smock, Catrina, of Middletown, Monmouth Co.; will of, being old. To my two daughters, Anne and Marrite, all the estate that my husband, Johannes Smock, devised to me. Daughter, Anne Tunison, to have ½ the money, live stock and negros; and my youngest daughter, Marritie Vanderveer, the other half, and all what is money worth belonging to me. Executor—Cornelius Vanderveer. Witnesses—Coonrod Ten Eick and Elbert Williamson. Proved April 16, 1764. Lib. H, p. 430.

1763, Oct. 11. Smyth, Andrew, of Perth Amboy, Middlesex Co. Int. Adm'r—John Smyth, eldest and only brother, of said place.
Lib. H, p. 540.

1769, July 14. Smyth, Benjamin, of Knowlton, Sussex Co., gentleman; will of. Oldest son, Benjamin, 10 shillings with what he had. Son, Dolvus, the land where he lives, according to the lines that Benjamin Depue run for him, he paying £20 to my son, Henry. Sons, Abraham and John, the land they live on, they paying £15 to my son, Henry. Son, Joseph, rest of real. Daughter, Catherene, £25, and £25 besides for keeping house, equal to her sister, Nancy. Joseph is to keep my wife, Dority, during her life. Executors—my son, Joseph, and Thomas Anderson, attorney-at-law. Witnesses—Daniel Moore, Elizabeth Rush, Samuel Kennedy, Jr. Proved Aug. 7, 1769.
1769, Aug. 25. Inventory, £149.16.9, made by Daniel Moore and Isaiah Ball. Lib. 14, p. 158.

1763, Jan. 30. Snook, Catharine, of Amwell Twsp., Hunterdon Co.; will of. Widow of William Snook. All the lands that I hold, by virtue of my late husband's will, I give to my son, Phillip Snook, and he is to pay the several legacies. Eldest son, John Snook, £36, for the use of his children. My son, William Snook, £36 for use of children. My son, George Snook, £36 for the use of his children, if he shall have any. Daughter, Catharine, the wife of Rodolfe Stineman, £36 for the use of her children. Daughter, Elizabeth Plulpher, the wife of William Phulpher, £36 for use of children. To Christian, the wife of Jacob Kitchain, £36 to her children. To Ann, the wife of Henry Wambock, £36 for use of her children. To Mary, the wife of Benjamin Abet, for use of her children, £36. Daughter, Catharine, a black gown. To my two sons, George and Philip, 2

cows, etc. Granddaughter, Christian Stineman, a "heffer." To Henry Wambock a chain. Rest of moveable estate to be sold and divided among my 9 children, before named. Executors—sons, George and Philip. Witnesses—Richard Reid, George Corwine, John Hart. Proved June 3, 1769.
1769, May 22. Inventory, £184.19.1, made by Timothy Brush and Samuel Corwine.
1770, Aug. 1. Account by Executors   Lib. 14, p. 196; Lib. 15, p. 28.

1763, June 25. Snook, William, of Newton, Sussex Co., yeoman. Int. Adm'rs—Phillip Snook and John Snook. Fellowbondsman—Phillip Wiker; all of said place, yeomen.
1763, June 9. Inventory, £73.10.4, made by Hugh Hagerty and Stephen Hagerty.
1765, Oct. 31. Account by both Adm'rs.   Lib. 11, p. 456

1763, July 14. Snowden, James, of Deptford Township, Gloucester Co.; will of. My daughter, Hannah Snowden, my tracts of land in and near Woodbury, except plantation where I live; but, if she dies before 18, then my wife to have the profits of same, and, at her death, to be divided between my two sisters, Ledia Fletcher and Ruth Lord. Plantation to be sold. Wife the remainder. Executors—wife and Constantine Wilkins. Witnesses—James Miller, Mary Sloan, Constantine Wilkins. Proved Aug. 1, 1763.
1763, Aug. 1. Inventory, £363.4.7½, made by William Wilkins and John Wilkins.   Lib. 11, p. 441.

1761, April 28. Snowden, John, of Deptford Twsp., Gloucester Co., yeoman; will of. Son, William, my plantation on north side of Horshoo Creek, he paying £20 to my son, James, and £20 to my granddaughter, Hannah Lord. Son, James, my house and lot, where Thomas Enoch lives. Daughter, Lidia Fletcher, house and lot, joining Edward Richardson's in Woodbury, and, after her death, to her two sons, William and James Fletcher. Daughter, Ruth Lord, land in Woodbury. Granddaughter, Sarah Fletcher, house and lot which I bought of Mary Holloway in Woodbury, when she is 18. Executors—sons, William and James. Witnesses—Catherine Burk, William Wood, Mary Small. Proved Jan. 27, 1762.
1761, Sept. 3. Inventory, £45.15.6, made by James Whitall and William Wood. Account was filed by William Snowden, acting Executor.
1762, Jan. 22. Receipt given by William Fletcher for the legacy devised to Ledia Fletcher.   Lib. 11, p. 95.

1763, June 4. Snowden, William, of Hunterdon Co. Int. Adm'r—William Snowden, of Nottingham, Burlington Co. Fellowbondsman—William Welling, of Trenton, Hunterdon Co.
1763, Aug. 29. Inventory, £5.15.0, made by Josiah Furman and William Reed.   Lib. 12, p. 7.

1765, May 20. Snyder, Hendrick, of Middletown, Monmouth Co. Int. Adm'x—Mary Snyder, the widow. Fellowbondsman—William Covenhoven; both of said Co.
1764, Nov. 5. Inventory, £78.3.1, made by John Bowne and Stephen Vanbrackel.   Lib. H, p. 424.

1769, Dec. 18. Sockwell, Eve, of Fairfield, Cumberland Co. Account made by William Paullin, sole Executor. (No will on file.) "Paid Jonadab Socwell, Elizabeth Sockwell, Jonathan Sockwell, each a legacy of 5 shillings. Lancet Sockwell, also a legatee, an infant. Lib. 15, p. 10.

1758, April 30. Somers, James, Sr., of Great Egg Harbor, Gloucester Co., yeoman; will of. Son, John, a tract on Great Egg Harbor River, of 450 acres, whereon he now lives, but he shall return ⅓ of the rent thereof to Abigail Somers, his mother. One acre to the people commonly called Quakers, whereon the meeting house stands. Son, James, Jr., the homestead, where I live, of 449 acres, with the grist mill, dam and one acre purchased of Return Badcock; but he shall return ⅓ the rent thereof to his mother, Abigail Somers. Son, Isaac, land on the southwest side of Peter Covenover's, of 250 acres; and he shall return ⅓ the rent thereof to his mother, Abigail. Son, John, land lying on the Beach, of 100 acres, known by the name of Great Hammock, at the east end of the beach. Son, James, a tract at the beach. Son, Isaac, a tract at the beach. Son, James, the rest of the west end of the beach; I also give him Lone Tree Island, of 70 acres; also 5 acres of swamp below the Cedar Swamp bridge. Wife, Abigail, ½ my moveable estate, and, what is left after her decease, to be divided among my 7 daughters. To my daughters, Sarah Steelman, Hannah Smith, Judith Swain, Abigail Smith, Rebekah Badcock, Mary Somers and Rachel Somers, ½ my moveable estate; and my daughter, Mary Somers, to be made equal with the rest of them. Executors—my wife, Abigail, and my son, James. Witnesses—Joseph Mapes, James Robison, Mathew Dennis. Proved April 15, 1761.

1761, April 10. Inventory, £416.0.1, made by Joseph Mapes and James Robison. Lib. 10, p. 376.

1768, May 5. Somers, John, of Penns Neck, Salem Co., yeoman; will of. Wife, Rachel, my moveable estate and use of plantation for 7 years, and she is to bring up the children till they are of age. Sons, Jacob and John, my plantation. Daughters, Hannah Somers and Rachel Somers, use of my house and plantation till my son, Jacob, is 21. A child that is yet unborn is provided for. Hannah and Rachel to have £50 each, when 21. Executors—my wife, Rachel, and my brother, Jacob Somers. Witnesses—Isaac Somers, John Sparks, Margaret Sparks. Proved May 30, 1768.

1768, May 28. Inventory, £395.0.4, made by Isaac Somers and Thomas Pedrick. Lib. 13, p. 401.

1761, April 28. Somers, Judith, of Great Egg Harbor, Gloucester Co.; will of. Eldest son, John Somers, £10. Son, Richard Somers, £10. Daughter, Sarah Somers, £30. Daughter, Elizabeth Somers, £10. Daughter, Judith Risley, now wife of Samuel Risley, £20. Daughter, Hannah Somers, £23. Son, James Somers, £10. Son, Joseph Somers, £30. Son, Edmund Somers, £30. Daughter, Sarah Somers, bedding. The rest to Judith Somers, the daughter of my son, John Somers. Executor—daughter, Sarah Somers. Witnesses—Richard Dole, Gideon Scull, Judith Scull. Proved Sept. 7, 1761.

1761, Sept. 5. Inventory, £228.7.3½, made by Joseph Mapes and Gideon Scull. Lib. 11, p. 110.

1752, April 18. Somers, Richard, of Great Egg Harbor, Gloucester Co.; will of. Wife, Judith, £200, and use of ½ the plantation where I live, that is to say, the half of the thousand acres which my father left me. Son, John, ½ the plantation where I live, with the Islands, flats and waters adjoining the same (according to drafts and surveys about 120 acres); also ½ the right that is in the Islands below the house, between that and the east end of the beach, which is about 200 acres more; also 20 acres of marsh at Tookhow Marsh. Son, Richard, all the land that joins James Steelman; also the right that I took up below it, by three surveys, on the north side of the channel of Great Egg Harbor Inlet, containing 426 acres; also ½ my right on Peck's Beach; and he is to pay his younger brother, Edmund Somers, £34, when 21. Son, James, the land at Grederes Neck, which was taken up by five surveys; also 13 acres at Cedar Hammock; also 200 acres in Tookahow Meadows; also all of Garits Island, of 138 acres; and he is to pay £34 to his brother, Edmund. Son, Joseph, the land that I bought of John Price, 21 Dec., 1749, on South River, in two surveys, and one on Miere Run with my old cedar swamp, and the 67 acres of other land, with other lands; and he is to pay to his brother, Edmund, £30. Rest of moveable estate to my four daughters, Sarah, Judith, Elizabeth and Hannah. Executors—wife, Judith, and my son, John. Witnesses—Isaiah Scull, Fredrick Steelman, Recompence Scull, David Covenover. Proved April 15, 1761.

1761, April 2. Inventory, £479.10.10, made by Joseph Mapes and Fredreck Steelman. Lib. 10, p. 379.

1761, Sept. 18. Somers, Samuel, of Great Egg Harbor, Gloucester Co.; will of. Wife, Mary, my stock on the plantation and the household goods. Eldest son, John, plantation where he lives, 10 acres of meadow being excepted. Son, Isaac, plantation I lately bought of William Jarret, 10 acres of meadow and 4 of upland being excepted; also ⅔ of the sawmill. Son, Jacob, plantation where I live, and all my right in Peck's Beach, and ⅓ the sawmill. Wife, Mary, is to have £15 yearly. Daughter, Millesent Doughty, £50. Son-in-law, James Somers, 5 shillings. Granddaughter, Martha Somers, £200. Executors—sons, John and Isaac. Witnesses—David Lee, Hannah Price, Gideon Scull. Proved May 24, 1768.

1768, May 24. Inventory, £253.11.7, made by Thomas Pedrick and Moses Hoffman. Lib. 13, p. 403.

1770, Jan. 3. Sooper, Obadiah, of Woodbridge, Middlesex Co.; will of. Son, Daniel, 4 acres off the southeast corner of my plantation, where I live, and one acre of salt meadow off the south end of the lot which I bought of Timothy Bloomfield, deceased. Daughter, Catharine, wife of James Faurot, £5. Grandson, William Soper, son of my son, Joseph, £5, when 21. Grandson, Obadiah Soper, son of my son, Benjamin, £20, when 21. Son, Benjamin, rest of real and personal estate. Executors—my son, Benjamin, of Woodbridge Twsp., and my friend, David Crow, of same town. Witnesses—Samuel Martin, Edward Griffith, John Ross. Proved Oct. 18, 1770.

Lib. K, p. 245.

1769, March 3. Southard, Caleb, Jr., of Dover Twsp., Monmouth Co.; will of. My estate to be sold, and called in, after being put to interest, when wanted, to bring up my 2 children, Ame and Job;

and if any be left when they come of age, to be divided between them; and, if they die, then to be paid to my wife, Elizabeth. Executor—father-in-law, David Woodmansee. Witnesses—Gabriel Woodmansee, John Grant, Francis Latts. Proved April 25, 1769.

1769, April 12. Inventory, £124.18.0, made by John Holmes and Gabriel Woodmansee. Lib. K, p. 91.

1769, March 16. Souther, Phillip, of Hopewell Twsp., Cumberland Co., yeoman; will of. Wife, Christena, what the law allows her out of the profits of my land. Son, Peter, ⅓ of my plantation, and he is to pay to Phillip £6, and to John £6. Son, Siman, plantation I purchased of Silas Ireland, of 100 acres. Son, Phillip, ⅓ my home plantation. Son, John, the rest of plantation, 105 acres. Daughter, Mary, £40, the day of her marriage, to make her equal with her sister, Susey, who has had her share. Executors—son, Peter, and my son-in-law, George Miller. Witnesses—Michael Hoshel, Adam Fix, Jacob Richman. Proved March 9, 1770.

1770, March 7. Inventory, £549.14.5, made by Joseph Sneathan and Samuel Hannah.

1773, March 6. Account by both Executors. Lib. 14, pp. 261, 513.

1760, May 19. Southwick, Maham, of Twsp. and Co. of Gloucester; will of. Wife, Grace, £10. Daughter, Rachel, my furniture. Daughter, Pricilla, £5. Daughter, Rebecka, £5. Daughter, Sarah, 5 shillings. Sons, Samuel and William, the rest of my goods. Executor—my friend, Joseph Harrison. Witnesses—Hugh Creighton, Ephraim Stiles, Alexander Ferguson. Proved Jan. 29, 1765.

1760, May 19. Power of attorney given by the above Maham Southwick to his friend, Joseph Harrison, to collect all monies for the proper use thereof.

1765, Feb. 4. Inventory, £65.17.5, made by Robert Taylor and Robert Sparks.

1765, Feb. 9. Whereas Maham Southwick made a will and appointed Joseph Harrison as his Executor, who is also deceased, therefore John Myers, of New Hanover Twsp., Burlington Co., yeoman, is appointed Adm'r, with will annexed, and Robert Taylor, of Springfield Twsp., said Co., goes on his bond. Lib. 12, p. 41.

1768, May 3. Soverhill, Matthias, of Newark, Essex Co. Int. Adm'r —John Dod, Jr. (at the special request of Abigail Soverhill, the widow). Fellowbondsman—Daniel Dod; all of said place. Witness —Lewis Ogden. Lib. I, p. 301.

1770, May 3. Speer, Hendrick, Sr., of Bergen Co. Int. Adm'r— Hendrick Speer. Bondsman—William Campbell; both of said Co. Witnesses—Jacob Roome, John Zabrisky. File No. 903 B.

1762, May 6. Spicer, Jacob, of Cape May Co.; will of. Personal estate to be sold to pay debts, and, if needed, the 250 acres which I bought of Robert and Sarah Ewing, except 10 acres reserved, and the 200 acres I bought of Christiana Peterson (now Grover), and the plantation I bought of Gabriel Powell (and many others). Son, Jacob, I desire to be educated. Wife, Deborah, by marriage settlement I agreed to give £100. Daughter, Sarah Leaming, a wood lot. Daughter, Silvia Spicer, a bed. Daughter, Judith Spicer, a bed.

Whereas, at the death of Christopher Leaming, I married his widow, and I administered, but as yet no settlement has been made, which I order my Executors to do; and his son, Christopher Leaming, made me his Guardian; also Thomas Spicer, Sr., made me one of his Executors; also Lydia Hand made me Executor to her will, and gave her personal estate to her daughter, Experience Hand, who did marry John Robertson, to whom I gave the proceeds of Lydia's estate, and Experience has since died. I appoint John Townsend and Aaron Leaming, Esq., the appraisers of my personal estate, and, if either die, then James Whilden and Providence Ludlam to assist. Daughter, Silvia Spicer, ½ of Two Mile Beach. Daughter, Judith Spicer, also to have land. Daughter, Sarah Leaming, land. Daughter, Judith Spicer, is to dwell with her mother-in-law, so long as she is my widow. I desire my wife, children-in-law and own children, to live in union with each other. Executors—Abel James, Jacob Spicer, Sr., of Gloucester Co., my wife, Deborah, my son-in-law, Christopher Leaming, his wife, Sarah Leaming, Silvia Spicer and Judith Spicer. Overseers—Daniel Lawrence, Nicholas Stillwell and John Eldredge. Witnesses—Ebenezer Johnson, Henry Hand, Henry Stiles, Christopher Church. Proved Oct. 9, 1765.

Lib. 12, p. 256.

1769, Sept. 23. Spicer, Jacob, medius, of Gloucester Co. Int. Adm'r—Samuel Spicer. Fellowbondsman—George Brownig; both of said Co.

1769, Sept. 21. Inventory, £195.8.6, made by Henry Wood and George Brownig.

1772, Dec. 8. Account by Samuel Spicer, as Adm'r. Includes "To cash paid to my daughter's husband, £50."

Lib. 14, p. 80; Lib. 14, p. 501.

1742, April 8. Spier, Barendt, of Bergen Co., gent.; will of. Wife, Cattelemtie, use of personal and real during her life; then to be sold and all my children to have share alike, but my son, Hendrick, is to have £10 for his birthright over the others, viz., Benjamin, Hannes, Abraham and Alberties Spier, and my daughters, Jeeseye Spier, Annatye Toers, Helena Newkerck and Seytye Spier. Witnesses—Samuel Beeckman, Jacob G. Van Waagenen, Laurens Van Boskerck. Proved Aug. 21, 1762. Lib. H, p. 274.

1763, Oct. 31. Adm'r—Benjamin Spier, of said Co., son of said Barendt, who made a will but appointed no Executor. Lib. H, p. 333.

1768, Oct. 26. Spier, Barent, of Bergen Co. Int. Adm'x—Ame Spier, the widow. Bondsman—John Berdan; both of said Co. Witness—John Mackay.

1768, Oct. 17. Inventory, £10.12.6, which were left in hands of widow at this time, and appraised by Cornelus Doremus and Thomas Dey.

1766, Nov. 17. A public vandue made, at which Amy Spear bought a pair of "britches." Lib. I, p. 353.

1769, Dec. 28. Springer, William, of Borough of Elizabeth, Essex Co., weaver; will of. A tract of land, of 4 acres, joining lands of Henry Frazee and David Hetfield, which I bought of Timothy Craig; and another lot of 2 acres, joining John Oliver, Jr., and Daniel Terrill,

CALENDAR OF WILLS—1761-1770 405

which I bought of Philip Porter, to be sold. Wife, Sarah, all the moveable estate, and the income of my land where I live, and, after her death, to the Presbyterian Church in Elizabeth Town, Raway. Executors—my wife and my friend, Abraham Clark. Witnesses—Samuel Olliver, Jonathan Olliver, Jr., Henry Norris. Proved May 14, 1770. Lib. K, p. 236.

1765, May 14. Sprong, Garret, of Little Egg Harbor, Burlington Co. Int. Adm'x—Sarah Sprong, widow, of said place. Fellowbondsmen—Job Mathis, of same place, yeoman, and Richard Westcott, of Great Egg Harbor, in Gloucester Co. Lib. 12, p. 112.
 1765, Feb. 28. Inventory, £26.9.3, made by Stephen Cramer and Job Mathis.

1767, Jan. 17. Sproull, Robert, of Perth Amboy, Middlesex Co. Int. Adm'x—Elizabeth Sproull, widow of Robert. Fellowbondsman—John Johnston; both of said place. Lib. I, p. 48.

1770, May 5. Stalcop, Andrew, of Lower Penns Neck, Salem Co. Int. Adm'x—Isabella Redstrake, widow. Fellowbondsmen—Jacob Townsend and Alexander Hill; all of said place.
 1770, April 23. Inventory, £35.3.3, made by Alexander Hill and Jacob Townsend. Lib. 15, p. 7.

1762, March 29. Stanbury, Nathan, of Woodbridge Twsp., Middlesex Co.; will of. Moveable estate to be sold. Wife, Prudence, £20. Son, Josiah, £20. Son, Robert, £20. Son, David, £20. Son, Recompence, £20. Son, Joshua, £20. Son, Annijah, £20. Son, Nathan, £30. Daughter, Pheby, £20. Daughter, Polly, £20. Wife to have the use of lands to bring up the younger children till my daughter, Polly, is 14, and then the lands to be sold. Executors—my brother, Recompence, and my son, Josiah. Witnesses—John Neefus, Anna Neefus, Joseph De Camp. Proved April 21, 1762.
 1762, April 15. Inventory, £137.9.11, made by William Smith and Jonathan Brooks. Lib. H, p. 114.

1766, Feb. 12. Stapel, Caspar Michel, of Amwell Twsp., Hunterdon Co., doctor of Divinity and physick; will of. My executors are to send to my brother-in-law, John Peter Franks, of City of Rostock, in Germany, Secretary to the Duke of Macklenburg Swerin, the sum of 72 ducketts; out of which I request my brother-in-law to pay 50 German dollars to the Commissary Fleur; and for his trouble I give him 20 dollars, and the remainder I give to my two sons, which I left behind me in Germany, namely, John Casper and John Andries, who were born of my wife, who I also left behind me; and, if either die before 21, then his share to the survivor. To Catharine, the wife of John Housilt, of Amwell, £10. To the youngest son, now living, of Peter Huffman, late of Amwell, deceased, £6 when he is 21. To friend, Peter Mires, who formerly lived with me, my large High Dutch Bible, and also £6, but, if he die, then to his wife. To each of my kind friends and neighbors, Gearlough Loop, Joseph Bast and Hones Godderd, £4. To a poor man in Amwell Twsp., named Mathias Becker, and his son, who is a "criple," £6. Executors—friends, Peter Mires and John Young. Witnesses—Philip Young, George Anthony, George Reading. Proved April 2, 1766.

1766, March 5. Codicil. Legacy to apprentice, Phillip Bemer. Witness to codicil—Phillip Bemer.
1766, March 26. Inventory, £349.9.11, made by George Andreas Vierselius and Richard Rounsavell, Jr.
1769, Oct. 27. Account by John Young and Peter Myers, the Executors.   Lib. 12, p. 413; Lib. 14, p. 126.

1767, Aug. 26. Stark, Enos, of Morristown, Morris Co., yeoman; will of. All my lands in this and Sussex Co. to be sold, if my Executors think best. Wife, Hannah, all the personal and real she had when I married her, and £45 beside. Remainder to my children, Abraham, Isaac and Jacob; and my Executors are to consider the child that my wife is now pregnant with. Executors—Aaron Stark and Capt. John Brookfield. Witnesses—Job Brookfield, Uzal Tomkins, James Gillispie. Proved Sept. 18, 1767.   Lib. I, p. 159.

1765, Jan. 29. Stark, Jonathan, of Hardwick, Sussex Co., wheelwright. Int. Adm'rs—Sarah Stark (widow) and James Stark. Fellowbondsman—Joseph Lacock; all of said place.
1765, Jan. 3. Inventory, £121.4.10, made by John Laforge and Samson Dildine.   Lib. 12, p. 232.

1768, May 4. Starndall, John, of Middlesex Co. Int. Adm'r—Richard Cursan, principal creditor, of New York City. Fellowbondsman—Cortland Skinner, of City of Perth Amboy, Middlesex Co.
Lib. I, p. 301.

1764, July 14. Statesir, John, of Shrewsbury, Monmouth Co. Int. Adm'r—Edmund Williams. Fellowbondsman—Stephen Tallman, Jr., yeoman; both of said place. Witnesses—John Longstreet, Jr., and Timothy Russell.
1764, July 12. Renunciation by Mary Statesir, the widow of said John, in favor of Edmund Williams, principal creditor. Witnesses—Amos Tilton and Miriam Tilton.   Lib. H, p. 375.

1760, Sept. 18. Statham, Jonathan, of Greenwich Twsp., Cumberland Co., yeoman; will of. Wife, Deliverence, ⅓ the profits of my land. Son, Phillip, the land that was my uncle Zebulon Statham's, except 20 acres of woodland. Son, Aaron, the land I bought of John Dare and Christiana, his wife, called Lummis Place. Sons, Isaac and Amos, the home place and the said 20 acres. Daughters, Hannah Sayer and Sarah Statham, £50 each. (Sarah is not yet 18.) My sister, Catherine Lester, 5 shillings. Executors—my wife and my son, Phillip. Witnesses—Ephram Gilman, Sarah Carle, Maskell Ewing. Proved March 7, 1763.
1763, Feb. 26. Inventory, £524.4.9, made by Thomas Ewing and Maskell Ewing.   Lib. 11, p. 292.

1770, April 23. Stathem, Deliverance, of Greenwich Twsp., Cumberland Co., widow; will of. Son, Philip Stathem, £5. Son, Isaac Stathem, 5 shillings. Son, Aaron Stathem, a desk that was his father's. Son, Amos Stathem, £9. Daughter, Hannah Sayre's children, £10. Daughter, Sarah Bowen, residue. Executrix—daughter, Sarah. Witnesses—James Ewing, Rebecca Finley, Cathrine Lastar. Proved May 3, 1770.
1770, May 3. Inventory, £240.9.7, made by Thomas Ewing and William Carll.   Lib. 14, p. 249.

1764, April 6. Steelman, Charles, of Morris River Twsp., Cumberland Co. Int. Adm'r—Jonas Hoffman. Fellowbondsman—Hezekiah Lore; both of said place, yeomen. Witness—Thomas Ewing.
1764, April 6. Inventory, £52.16.0, made by Hezekiah Lore and Frederick Hoffman. Lib. 12, p. 5.

1762, Dec. 10. Steelman, Deborah, of Gloucester Co. Ward. Guardian—Japhet Leeds, of Great Egg Harbor, said Co. Deborah is daughter of Peter Steelman, late of Great Egg Harbor, she being under 14, and said Japhet being her uncle, on her mother's side. Fellowbondsmen—Noah Smith and Jesse Smith, yeomen; both of said place. Lib. 11, p. 279.

1763, March 23. Steelman, Elias, of Great Egg Harbor, Gloucester Co., yeoman. Int. Adm'x—Esther Steelman, widow. Fellowbondsman—William Reid, yeoman; both of said place. Witness—Robert Friend Price.
1763, March 23. Inventory, £64.10.0, made by Daniel Leeds and William Reid. Lib. 11, p. 313.

1762, Dec. 10. Steelman, Hannah, of Great Egg Harbor, Gloucester Co. Int. Adm'r—Jachet Leeds. Fellowbondsmen—Noah Smith and Jesse Smith, yeomen; all of said place. Lib. 11, p. 241.

1761, Nov. 4. Steelman, Hans, of Greenwich, Gloucester Co., yeoman; will of. Wife, Sarah, profit of plantation where I live, during the minority of my son, John, to bring up my young children. Son, John, when 21, the said plantation. Land I lately bought of Henry Hendrickson to be sold. Remainder to my daughters. Executors—wife and my brother, James. Witnesses—William Harrison, Charles Steelman, Alexander Randall. Proved Dec. 15, 1761.
1761, Nov. 21. Inventory, £104.10.2, made by Thomas Clark and Charles Steelman. Lib. 11, p. 112.

1762, Dec. 10. Steelman, Isaac, of Gloucester Co. Ward. Guardian—Japhet Leeds, of Great Egg Harbor, said Co. Isaac Steelman is son and heir of Peter Steelman, late of Great Egg Harbor, he being under 14, and the said Japhet being his uncle on the mother's side. Fellowbondsmen—Noah Smith and Jesse Smith, yeomen; both of said place. Lib. 11. p. 280.

1767, May 19. Steelman, James, Jr., of Egg Harbor, Gloucester Co. Int. Adm'r—Andrew Steelman, of Great Egg Harbor, said Co. Fellowbondsman—John Lawrence, of City of Burlington. Witness—Robert Burchan. Lib. 13, p. 103.

1762, Jan. 7. Steelman, John, of Great Egg Harbor, Gloucester Co., yeoman; will of. Son, John, ⅛ of my lands, and he to pay to my daughter, Catherine, £3, to my daughter, Susannah, £2, and to my daughters, Jemima and Easter, £15. Son, Jeremiah, ⅛ my lands, joining the land of Edward Doughtey, and he to pay to my daughter, Rachel, £7. Son, Zephaniah, ⅛ my land, joining Amos Ireland, and he to pay to my daughter, Rachel, £3, and to daughter, Mary, one shilling, and to daughter, Rabackka, one shilling. To my daughter Rachel's son, John, I give one "heffer" and 3 sheep. The bond from

Ezekiel Wix I give to my sons, John, Jeremiah and Zephaniah. Executor—son, Zephaniah. Witnesses—Amos Ireland, James Ireland, Edmond Ireland. Proved March 19, 1762.

1762, Feb. 11. Inventory, £195.7.6, made by Richard Risley and John Covenover. Lib. 11, p. 87.

1762, Dec. 10. Steelman, Susannah, of Gloucester Co. Ward. Guardian—Japhet Leeds, of Great Egg Harbor, said Co., to be Guardian of Susannah Steelman, daughter of Peter Steelman, late of Great Egg Harbor, she being under 14, and the said Japhet being her uncle, on the mother's side. Fellowbondsmen—Noah Smith and Jesse Smith, yeomen; both of said place. Lib. 11, p. 280.

1763, May 14. Stephens, Henry, of Deptford, Gloucester Co., wool comber; will of. Daughter, Elizabeth Britton, a bond of £20 that I have against her husband, John Britton. Cousin, Sarah Saunders, daughter of my late brother, Isaac, £20. Cousin, Thomas Egiton, Jr., £5. To the 4 youngest children of my brother, Isaac, viz., John, Isaac, Rachel and James, £5 each, when 21. Cousin, Isaac Saunders, £100, when 21. Cousin, Elizabeth Saunders, daughter of John Saunders, £20, when 18. Executor—said John Saunders. Witnesses—Sarah Hopkins, John Estaugh Hopkins, Bartholomew Alder. Proved Dec. 26, 1763. Letters to John Sanders, as Executor, same date.

1763, Dec. 26. Inventory, £420.5.4, made by James Whitall and John Estaugh Hopkins. Lib. 11, p. 477.

1763, May 11. Stevens, Benjamin, of Maidenhead, Hunterdon Co.; will of. Son, Richard, 5 shillings. Daughter, Catharine Stevens, land in Trenton, where John Reckey now lives; and she is to pay £100 to her sister, Elizabeth Stevens. Daughter, Martha Stevens, land that joins Ralph Smith, Ephraim Bonam and William Morris. Daughter, Sarah Stevens, £20 and wench, Febe. Daughter, Anney, the lot that John Yard has possession of. Son, John, the land left to me by my brother, John Stevens, deceased, and he is to pay to the Elders of Cranbury, £100. Son, Benjamin, the plantation where I live, but my wife, Sarah, is to have ⅓ the profits of said place. Executors—wife, Sarah, and my son, Benjamin. Witnesses—Ralph Smith, Benjamin Van Cleave, Thomas Stevens. Proved June 6, 1763.

1763, June 6. Inventory, £1,025.14.1, made by John Anderson and John Vancleave. Lib. 11, p. 326.

1760, Dec. 28. Stevens, John, of Monmouth Co.; will of. To my beloved Catherine Stevens, £550. I order my Executors to take care of father and Jonathan, and, at father's death, they are to run off at the west end of my lands 250 acres, which I give to my brother, Benjamin, and, at his death, to his son John. My brother, Thomas, is to pay to my cousin, John Henderson, and one year after £50 more to the three daughters of my sister Anne. To brother, Thomas Stevens, the rest of my real and personal estate, provided he take care of Jonathan till death. Executors—brother, Benjamin Stevens, and Thomas Stevens. Witnesses—Charles McClean, Thomas Little, James Mackland. Proved Feb. 10, 1761. Lib. 10, p. 318.

1766, May 27. Stevens, Richard, of Upper Freehold, Monmouth Co. Int. Adm'r—Michael Henderson, the principal creditor. Fellowbondsman—William Carlile; both of said Co.

1766, April 21. Renunciation by Elizabeth Stevens, widow of Richard, in favor of Michael Henderson, who is her eldest brother and principal creditor of her husband. Witnesses—John Henderson and Ann Henderson.
1767, May 27. Bill of sale and account filed by Adm'r.
Lib. H, p. 602.

1765, Oct. 25. Stevenson, Edward, of Amwell Hunterdon Co., yeoman; will of. Wife, Mary, ¼ of my real and personal. Son, Ellithon, ¼ of real and personal. Son, John, another ¼. Son, Charles, another ¼. Executors—wife, Mary, my brother, Cornell Stevenson, and my father-in-law, Nicolas Stilwill. Witnesses—John Stevenson, Augustin Stevenson, Ann Riche. Proved June 18, 1766.
1765, Nov. 27. Inventory, made by Jacob Reeder and John Akers.
Lib. 12, p. 386.

1760, Feb. 9. Stevenson, William, of Amwell, Hunterdon Co.; will of. Being now going to take the smallpox. Sister, Phebe, my black mare. Brother, Augustine, my apparel. Sisters, Mary and Sarah, my young mares. Brothers, Thomas and Cornelius, £50 each. To my father, my lands during his life, and afterwards to my brothers and sisters. Executors—my father, and my brother, Edward. Witnesses —William Pettit, Jr., John Fidler, Jonathan Milbourn. Proved May 27, 1764. Probate to William Stevenson, father, and Edward Stevenson.
Lib. 12, p. 60.

1767, Aug. 26. Stevenson, William, of Amwell, Hunterdon Co., yeoman; will of. Wife, Hannah, use of my plantation while my widow; also many goods. To eldest son, Robert, £5; second son, Edward, £3; and third son, John, a like amount. To fourth son, Thomas, fifth son, Augustin, and sixth son, Cornelius, £3 each. Daughters, Phebe and Mary, £50 each. Daughter, Susanna, wife of William Kennedey, £40. Daughter, Sarah, wife of John Stilwell, £30. Daughters, Deborah, Charity, Susanna, Phebe, Mary and Sarah, the rest of my moveable estate. After the death of my wife the plantation to be sold, and my son, Cornelius, to have £150; my grandson, William Stevenson, son of my son Edward, £60; and my grandson, William Stevenson, son of my son John, £50. Executors—wife, Hannah, and my sons, Robert, Edward and Thomas. Witnesses—John Christopher, Nicolas Drake, Josiah Ellis. Proved April 12, 1768.
1768, April 26. Inventory, £760.19.11, made by John Akers and Andrew Muirheid.
1769, May 8. Account by Thomas Stevenson, acting Executor.
1780, Oct. 30. Robert Stevenson was sworn as one of the Executors of his father, William Stevenson, to the performance of all things.
Lib. 12, p. 504; Lib. 13, p. 534.

1762, March 31. Steward, Robert, of Mendham Twsp., Morris Co., yeoman; will of. Wife, Jane, to have a comfortable support on my land. Son, William, all my real. To daughter, Margret Stuard, £100. Executors—my wife and son, William. Witnesses—John Logan, James McVicker, Brice Ricky. Proved May 28, 1762. Lib. H, p. 127.

1763, June 15. Stibbins, Hezekiah, of Essex Co. Ward. Son of Ebenezer Stibbins, of said Co. Guardian—William Barnet. Fellowbondsman—Elias Woodruff; both of said Co. Lib. H, p. 246.

1768, July 11. Stiles, Ephraim, of Pequannack Twsp., Morris Co.; will of. Wife, Anna, all real and personal till my two sons, Levi and Ephraim, are of age, when I give to them all lands. To my son, Moses Halsey, £20. Daughter, Anna, £20. My wife is pregnant, and I give to that child £20. Daughter, Elizabeth, is to be maintained out of the estate. Executors—John Stiles and Jonathan Stiles and my wife. Witnesses—Lewis Stewart, Ebenezer Haywood, Jacob Minton. Proved Aug. 22, 1768. Lib. I, p. 326.

1770, Nov. 12. Stile, Pontius, of Nottingham, Burlington Co. Int. Adm'r—Benjamin Biles. Fellowbondsman—Stacy Potts; both of Trenton. Lib. 15, p. 71.

1765, Oct. 29. Stillwell, Elijah, of Cape May Co. Int. Adm'rs—Richard Stites and Aaron Eldredge, gentlemen. Fellowbondsman—Isaac Newton, gentleman; all of said Co. Witnesses—Job Young and Jacob Hughes.
1764, June 22. Inventory, £66.2.10, made by Jacob Hughes and Isaac Newton. Lib. 12, p. 358.

1768, May 30. Stillwell, Elizabeth, of Hunterdon Co. Int. Adm'r—John Stillwell. Fellowbondsman—Edward Wilmot.
1768, May 20. Inventory, £46.17.0, made by Edward Wilmot and Peter Brunner. Lib. 13, p. 440.

1763, Nov. 22. Stillwell, William, of Allentown, Monmouth Co., tailor. Int. Adm'x—Catherine Stillwell, widow, of Freehold. Fellowbondsman—William Montgomerie; both of said Co.
1764, March 1. Inventory, £41.4.6, made by Catherine Stillwell, his widow; and David Knott, Elazarus Brewer and Jarratt Morford.
Lib. 11, p. 425.

1766, Oct. 3. Stilwell, Daniel, of Mendham, Morris Co. Int. Adm'r—Benjamin Lindslay, brother of said Daniel Stilwell. Fellowbondsman—Stephen Beach; both of said Co. Lib. I, p. 7.

1770, June 2. Stites, Eli, of Cape May Co. Int. Adm'x—Temperance Stites. Fellowbondsman—Thomas Matthews; both of said Co. Witnesses—Joshua Hildreth and Zeruiah Hughes.
1770, May 26. Inventory, £44.15.10, made by Joshua Hildreth and Thomas Mathews. Lib. 14, p. 399.

1764, Jan. 22. Stites, Isaiah, of Cape May Co.; will of. Wife, Elizabeth, use of ⅓ my lands while widow, and ⅓ my moveable estate. Son, Esaiah, ½ that tract in Middle Precint, which formerly belonged to my father. Son, Henry, the west ½ of said tract. Sons, John and Israel, land that I live on. My daughters, Sarah Stites and Hannah Stites, rest of moveable estate. Executors—my son, Isaiah Stites, my wife, and my daughter, Sarah Stites. Witnesses—John Goldin, Joseph Badcock, Daniel Gerretson. Proved May 21, 1768.
1768, May 23. Inventory, £235.10.3, made by Nicholas Stillwill and Leuben Ludlam. Lib. 13, p. 442.

1768, Oct. 26. Stites, John, of Cape May Co. Ward. Son of Isaiah Stites. Guardian—Isaiah Stites. Fellowbondsman—Joseph Ludlam; both of said Co. Witnesses—Jonathan Jenkins, Joshua Hildreth, James Townsend. Lib. 12, p. 523.

1765, Oct. 30. Stits (Stites), Elijah, of Elizabeth Borough, Essex Co., yeoman; will of. Wife, Mary, ⅓ of my goods and use of ⅓ the farm where I live. My two daughters, who are married, viz., Rebecca Scodder and Rachel Hand, all the goods that they have. Daughter, Nancey, £10. My six daughters, Nancey, Mary, Hannah, Providence, Chloe and Asenah, the rest of moveable estate. The 30 acres on the northwest side of the road may be sold. Sons, Elijah and Abner, that part of my farm on the southeast of the road, of 70 acres. Executor—my brother, John Stites, who is to be Guardian of my children. Witnesses—John Whitehead, Margaret Stits. Proved Nov. 9, 1767. Lib. I, p. 173.

1755, Feb. 10. Stockton, Daniel, of Wellingboro, Burlington Co.; will of. Daughters, Ann, Carma, Elizabeth Jons and Abygal Gaskill, 20 shillings each. Sons, John, Daniel, Richard, Abraham and William, rest of estate when the youngest is of age. Wife, Hannah, the income of real till youngest son is of age. Executors—sons, John and Daniel, and my wife. Witnesses—Benjamin Borden and Joseph Welch. Proved March 22, 1763.

1763, March 21. Inventory, £166.10.0, made by James Hammell and Thomas Buzby. Lib. 11, p. 280.

1763, Aug. 9. Stockton, David, of Springfield, Burlington Co., yeoman; will of. Wife, Ruth, £12 yearly, to be paid by my son, David, till my son, Benjamin, is of age, and then David and Benjamin each to pay one-half. Son, David, the plantation I bought of my brother, Daniel. Son, Benjamin, homestead where I dwell, when 21. Son, David, to pay to my 5 daughters, Mary, Sarah, Hannah, Ruth and Abigail, £50 each. Executor—son, David. Witnesses—Samuel Gaunt, John Robinson, Joshua Shreve. Proved Nov. 26, 1763.

1763, Nov. 23. Inventory, £673.4.3, made by Solomon Ridgway, Job Lippincott and Joseph Lamb. Lib. 11, p. 437.

1772, Feb. 14. Account made by Executor. Lib. 14, p. 408.

1763, Nov. 19. Stockton, John, of Wellingboro Twsp., Burlington Co.; will of. Wife, Hannah, use of house and 16 acres, which was bought of my father's plantation. The 65 acres I bought of my brother, Daniel, and the cedar swamp bought of Revel Elton, to be sold. Son, John, my dwelling and the land belonging thereto, when 21, and he is to pay to my son, Samuel, £10. Daughters, Hannah Stockton, Rhoda Stockton and Sarah Stockton, 30 shillings each, when they are 18. Executors—brother, Daniel, and my neighbor, Samuel Newton. Witnesses—Jonah Woolman, Joseph Eayre, Asher Woolman. Proved Dec. 9, 1763. Lib. 11, p. 442.

1763, Nov. 9. Inventory, £126.18.7½, made by Thomas Buzby and Joseph Buzby.

1768, April 1. Stockton, Joseph, of Somerset Co., farmer; will of. Wife, Elizabeth, firewood, which is to be cut by my son, John. Eldest son, Daniel, 5 shillings. Son, John, 130 acres where I live, and 20 acres of woodland, and he is to pay to my wife £100. Wife, Elizabeth, rest of my home tract, or 300-acre tract. If my wife dies without a will, then her estate is to go to my daughters, Amey Stockton, Elizabeth Nicholson, Mary Anderson and Sarah Stockton. Executors—my wife, and my son, Daniel Stockton. Witnesses—Thomas Stockton, Christopher Doughty, Samuel Stockton. Proved April 11, 1770. Lib. 14, p. 235.

1767, Jan. 3. Stockton, Samuel, of Somerset Co. Int. Adm'x—Amy Stockton. Fellowbondsmen—Samuel Stockton (son of Joseph) and Philip Phillips; first two of said Co., and Phillips of Hunterdon Co. Witness—John Stockton.

1767, Jan. 3. Inventory, £3, made by Joseph Hornor and Joseph Olden.

1768, March 8. Account by Amy Stockton.

Lib. 12, p. 479; Lib. 13, p. 319.

1769, May 12. Stone, Jeremiah, of Middlesex Co. Ward. Son of Joshua Stone, of said Co., deceased, and makes choice of David Flin, of said Co., cooper, as his Guardian.

1769, May 12. Guardian—David Flin. Fellowbondsman—Moses Bishop, of said Co.

1772, Aug. 17. The above Letters were revoked, upon the petition of said Jeremiah Stone, and other Letters of Guardianship are now granted to his grandfather, Benjamin Tharp.

Lib. K, p. 89; Lib. K, p. 441.

1762, Oct. 25. Stone, William, of Waterford, Gloucester Co. Int. Adm'r—John Stone, yeoman. Fellowbondsman—Samuel Parr, yeoman; both of said place. Witnesses—Jasper Smith and Samuel Allinson.

1762, Oct. 21. Inventory, £178.15.2, made by Henry Wood and Samuel Parr.

Lib. 11, p. 240.

1770, Jan. 20. Stoothoff, Jaques, of Somerset Co. Int. Adm'r—Jaques Voorheese, of said Co. Fellowbondsman—William Williamson, of Middlesex Co. Witness—Thomas Andrews.

1770, Jan. 19. Renunciation by Catolina Stoothoff, the widow.

1770, Jan. 23. Inventory, £1,258, made by Abraham Voorhees, Sr., Petrus Nevius and Abraham Voorhees, Jr.

Lib. K, p. 143.

1767, Aug. 27. Stout, Benjamin, of Amwell Twsp., Hunterdon Co.; will of. Eldest son, Joseph, £5. Wife, Ruth, £20 yearly, to be paid by my son, Benjamin; and she is otherwise provided for. Rest of moveables to be sold and the money to be given to wife, and sons, Joseph and Benjamin, and my daughters, Elizabeth, Sarah, Ruth, Mary, Rachel, Ann and Johannah. Daughters, Rachel, Ann and Johannah, to have an outset, as the older sisters had. Son, Benjamin, my plantation. Grandson, John, son of my son Joseph, a small tract of land in Kingwood, when he is 21. Rest of land in Kingwood to be sold and money given to my 7 daughters, Elizabeth, Sarah, Ruth, Mary, Rachel, Ann and Johannah. Son, Benjamin, land I bought of William Anderson, in Amwell Twsp. Executors—my nephew, John Jewell, and my friend, Gershom Lee. Witnesses—Joseph Hudnut, Jacob Mattison, Peter Latourrette. Proved Sept. 19, 1767.

1767, Sept. 14. Inventory, £947.15.7, made by Thomas Atkinson and James Clark. The one-third part of Martin Tagan's estate, consisting of wearing apparel, bonds, bills, and notes, as appears by an Inventory appraised by James Stout and Peter Peterson, taken the 16th day of Sept., 1767, with addition of £10 more than the other legatees amounted to £144.9.8. (See, for explanation, under Tagen, Michael, whose Executor was Benjamin Stout).

1769, March 14. Account made by Executors.

Lib. 13, p. 191; Lib. 13, p. 493.

1764, Sept. 19. Stout, David, of Lancaster Borough, Pennsylvania. Int. Adm'x—Margaret Stout, relict of David Stout. Fellowbondsman—Peter Worrall, of Burlington, gent. Witness—George Craig.
Lib. 12, p. 20.

1763, June 9. Stout, Freegift, of Amwell Twsp., Hunterdon Co., yeoman; will of. Wife, Mary, household goods, etc., and son, Isaac, to pay to her £10 yearly. In the lifetime of my son, Jodiah, I gave him a deed for his portion, which land is in Windsor Twsp., Middlesex Co., and I give to my granddaughter, Rebecca Stout, the eldest surviving daughter of said Jodiah, the sum of £40 shillings. Son, Freegift Stout, farm in Amwell Twsp., which I bought of James Oliphant; also 76 acres out of my homestead where I live, and also 8 acres of meadow. Son, James, land in Amwell, which he now has, and which I bought of Valentine End. Son, Joshua, tract of land in Hopewell Twsp., which I purchased of Josiah Furman. Son, Obadiah, the tract which I lately bought of Jonathan Stout, being in Rocksbury Twsp., Morris Co., at a place called Schooleys Mountain. Son, Isaac, the plantation where I live, except the 84 acres laid off to my son Freegift, and 30 acres which I sold to Hannis Case. Names daughter, Mary Chamberlain, wife of Richard Chamberlain. Moveable estate to Sarah Oliphant, wife of Ephraim Oliphant, of Kingwood Twsp.; Rebecca Taylor, wife of Edward Taylor, and Rachel Rounsavell, wife of Richard Rounsavell, Jr., both of Amwell Twsp. (Mary Chamberlain having 20 acres of land). Executors—sons, Freegift and James. Witnesses—Joseph Higgins, John Stout, John Manners.

1766, May 18. Codicil. By my last will I gave to my son, Obadiah, a tract of land which I bought of Jonathan Stout, in Rocksburg Twsp., Morris Co., but, instead of the land I give him £150. Granddaughter, Ann Stout, daughter of my son, Jodiah Stout, 40 shillings, when she is 18. The said land in Rocksburg to be sold, and the money given to my four daughters—Mary, wife of Richard Chamberlain; Sarah, wife of Ephraim Oliphant; Rebecca, wife of Edward Taylor, and Rachel, wife of Richard Rounsavell, Jr. Witnesses—Joseph Higgins, John Stout, John Manners.

1768, July 10. Codicil. My daughter, Sarah, wife of Ephraim Oliphant, is deceased, so her legacy is to be divided between her surviving children, when they come of age. Witnesses—Peter Vandyck, Peter Vandyck, Jr., Benjamin Stout. Proved Aug. 2, 1769.

1769, Aug. 2. Inventory, £208.19.8, made by Peter Vandicke and Joseph Moore.

1772, Jan. 23. Account by Executors.
Lib. 14, p. 64; Lib. 14, p. 68; Lib. 14, p. 420.

1760, Dec. 27. Stout, John, of Somerset Co., yeoman; will of. Wife, Catharine, all the profits of my estate, while my widow, except what I give to daughter, Ruth. Daughter, Ruth, £25 and use of 2 rooms, till she marry. Moveables to my 3 daughters, Mary, Ruth and Rachel. To two eldest sons, Richard and Daniel, all my lands. Son, Jehu, £25 yearly, till he has gone through the college. Son, Jehu, the house and lot where Samuel Bowne lives. To my daughter, Rebeckah's, two oldest children, each a cow. Executors—my wife, Catrin, and Thomas Leonard. Witnesses—Timothy Merrell, Samuel Bowne, Patience Bowne. Proved Aug. 31, 1761. Lib. 11, p. 59.

1763, Dec. 2. Stout, Jonathan, of Hopewell Twsp., Hunterdon Co.; will of. Wife, Elizabeth, lot of one acre in Sommerset, but, if she marry, then it shall be the property of my daughter, Ruth. Son, Joseph, ⅕ of the money from the sale of 40 acres in lower end of Amwell. Son, Wilson, ⅕ of said money. Son, Daniel, ½ of said money. Said sons not yet 21. Daughter, Ruth, £100, when 18. Wife, rest of personal. Executors—my wife, Wilson Hunt and Gisbert Lane. Witnesses—Joseph Stout, Isaac Eaton, Ruth Stockton. Proved Nov. 3, 1766, by Isaac Eaton; Joseph Stout, one of the witnesses, being dead. Lib. 13, p. 222.

1764, March 29. Stout, Joseph, of Hopewell Twsp., Hunterdon Co.; will of. "Being old." Grandson, Joseph Stout, the oldest son of my son, Jonathan Stout, deceased, 294 acres of the place whereon I live, bounded by David Stout on the south, Benjamin Stout on the west, and Benjamin Stout, Samuel Stout, Benjamin Merell on the north. Grandson, Wilson Stout, son of my son Jonathan, deceased, my land in Twsp. of Oxford, in Sussex Co., whereon Henry Bogard now lives, of 500 acres. Grandson, Daniel Stout, son of Jonathan foresaid, 200 acres, which is part of my tract in Oxford Twsp., and is north of land given to Wilson Stout, and is the rest. I also give to said Daniel Stout 150 acres in Hopewell, which is part of land where I live. Grandson, St. Leger Cod Stout, land to the west of him, of 120 acres. Grandsons, Joseph Stout, Wilson Stout and Daniel Stout, land south of land hereafter given to my grandsons, Richard Stout and Daniel Stout, sons of John Stout. Grandsons, Richard Stout and Daniel Stout, sons of my son John, deceased, 50 acres in Amwell. Grandson, Joseph Stout, son of my son Joseph, land north of Paulins Kiln, of 132 acres. Granddaughter, Ruth Stout, daughter of my son Jonathan, negro girl Peg. Son, Joseph, £50. Daughter-in-law, Elizabeth Stout, a mare. My wench, Kate, formerly belonging to my mother-in-law Horner, shall be free after the death of my wife, and to be property of Weynam, a mulatoo man, formerly belonging to Mr. Horner abovesaid, as his wife. My wife, Ruth, all my furniture, and a joint use with my daughter-in-law, Elizabeth Stout, widow of Jonathan Stout, to ½ the personal estate, to bring up my 4 grandchildren, the children of my son Jonathan, till they are 21. Executors—my wife, and friends, John Berien and Reuben Armitage. Witnesses—Isaac Eaton, Jonas Wood, James Hunt. Proved Nov. 3, 1766.

1767, March 26. The executors of "Col. Stout" decline to act, and we desire that David Stout and John Hart may be appointed Administrators. Signed, Ruth Stout and Elizabeth Stout.

1767, March 26. Adm'rs with will annexed—John Hart and David Stout, of Hopewell. Fellowbondsmen—Wilson Hunt, of Maidenhead, and Noah Hunt, of Hopewell.

1767, April 14. Inventory, £713.3.10, made by David Stout and John Hart, Adm'rs, and by William Bryant and Samuel Stout, Jr., Appraisers.

1779, May 8. Account made by Adm'rs.

Lib. 13, p. 227; Lib. 22, p. 66.

[No date]. Petition of David Stout and John Hart, stating, that 26 of March, 1767, they obtained Letters of Administration on the estate of Joseph Stout, of Hunterdon Co., with the will annexed, and in said will lands were left to 3 grandsons, viz., Joseph, Wilson and

Daniel Stout, and one granddaughter, Ruth Stout, and all being under 14 years of age, prayer is that Wilson Hunt, the grandfather, may be made their Guardian.

1768, May 17. Guardian—Wilson Hunt. Fellowbondsmen—Abram Hunt and Azariah Hunt, all of Hunterdon Co. Witness—William Taylor.

1780, May 9. Account of Wilson Hunt, Guardian of Joseph, Wilson, Daniel and Ruth Stout, children of Jonathan Stout, of Hunterdon Co., and Devisees of Joseph Stout.

1782, Oct. 18. Account of Wilson Hunt, deceased, late Guardian of Joseph, Wilson, Daniel and Ruth Stout, children of Jonathan Stout, exhibited by Abram Hunt, John P. Hunt and Peter Gordon, Executors of Wilson Hunt. Lib. 13, p. 439; Lib. 23, p. 218; Lib. 24, p. 350.

1769, July 6. Stout, Joseph, of Hopewell Twsp., Hunterdon Co., yeoman; will of. My daughter, Martha, the wife of James Bennet, of Twsp. of Kingwood, £37, to be paid her by my sons, Job, Jacob, Abner, Noah, Reader, Joseph and Benjamin. Sons, Job, Jacob and Abner, all my lands in Kingwood Twsp., of 319 acres, as by deed executed by Charles and Langhorn Biles. Son, Noah, plantation in Kingwood, of 98 acres, which I bought of James Bennet, the 5th of July, 1769. To sons, Reader, Joseph and Benjamin, rest of estate. Executors—sons, Reader, Joseph and Benjamin. Witnesses—Hannah Kinney, Richard Rounsavell, Jr., Eden Burrowes. Proved June 1, 1770.

1770, May 30. Inventory, £217.19.0, made by Timothy Titus and Timothy Smith. Lib. 14, p. 246.

1768, Feb. 8. Stout, Ruth, of Hopewell, Hunterdon Co.; will of. Widow of Colonel Joseph Stout. To Ann Worth, my granddaughter, and the daughter of William Worth, a bed. To my granddaughter, Ruth Worth, the daughter of William Worth, a bed, etc. My eldest daughter, Rachel Stockton, formerly the wife of Samuel Stockton, late of Stony Brook, in Somerset Co., the rest of estate. Executrix —my daughter, Rachel Stockton. Witnesses—Joseph Olden, Obadiah Pettit. Proved Aug. 10, 1768.

1768, Aug. 2. Inventory, £115.2.6, made by Joseph Olden and Joseph Mershon. Lib. 12, p. 509.

1767, March 6. Stout, St. Leger Cod, of Amwell, Hunterdon Co. Int. Adm'x—Susannah Stout. Fellowbondsman—Hezekiah Stout; both of said Co.

1767, Feb. 18. Inventory, £179.6.6, made by David Stout and John Hart.

1770, May 16. Account by George Nicholson, Jr., representative of Susannah Nicholson, Adm'x of St. Leger Cod Stout. Three years' rent of plantation, £24. For 3 years and 3 months maintainance of 8 children, £97.10.0. Lib. 13, p. 207; Lib. 15, p. 67.

1768, Aug 22. Stoutenburgh, John, of Essex Co. Int. Adm'r— Tobias Stoutenburgh, of New York City, baker. Fellowbondsman— Lourens L. van Boskerk, of Hackensack, Bergen Co. Witnesses— John Zabrowisky and John Zabriski, Jr. Lib. I, p. 336.

1764, Jan. 14. Stratton, David, of Stow Creek, Cumberland Co. Int. Adm'x—Elizabeth Stratton. Fellowbondsman—Daniel Stretch, of Hopewell, said Co., yeoman. Witnesses—Hugh Dunn and Maskell Ewing.
1764, Jan. 10. Inventory, £83.16.5, made by Daniel Stretch and Samuel Carll. "Cash due from his son Isaac, £12.8.0."
1764, July 1. Account made by Adm'x. Lib. 11, p. 495.

1762, May 3. Stratton, John, of Cumberland Co. Ward. Son of Benjamin Stratton, of Fairfield, said Co. Guardian—Joseph Daten. Fellowbondsman—David Datten; both of said Fairfield. Witness—Ambrose Whitacar. Lib. 11, p. 239.

1766, Jan. 22. Stretch, Joseph, of Alloways Creek Precinct, Salem Co.; will of. Wife, Elizabeth, ⅓ my moveable estate, and that house my son Joshua has moved from, with the field wherein the house stands, and £5 yearly from the rent of that place where my son Joseph lives, while my widow. Eldest son, Joseph, plantation where he lives, and 40 acres that I purchased of Richard and Edward Smith; and he is to pay to my son, Nathan, £50, and to my sons, Samuel and Aaron, £25 each. Son, Joshua, the land I bought of Aaron Bradway, except the house and lot devised to my wife; he paying £25 to my son, Jonathan. Daughter, Mary, £5. Daughters, Rebecca and Elizabeth, £30 each. Rest of moveable estate to my sons, Samuel, Jonathan, Nathan and Aaron. Executors—sons, Samuel and Jonathan. Witnesses—Joseph Ware, Elijah Ware, Thomas Sayre. Proved Feb. 9, 1767.
1767, Feb. 6. Inventory, £339.3.4, made by John Stewart and Thomas Sayre. Lib. 13, p. 169.

1767, April 26. Stretch, Joseph, Jr., of Alloways Creek, Salem Co.; will of. Brother, Nathan Stretch, all my plantation, except 25 acres, provided that he give to my 2 children £300; that is, £150 to my eldest daughter, Jaley, and the like sum to my youngest daughter, Martha; and he to pay my wife the interest of £300. Brother, Joshua, 25 acres above mentioned. Of that 40 acres of Woodland, I give 30 to Nathan, and 10 to Jonathan. If my 2 daughters die, then the £300 is to be given to my five brothers, Samuel, Jonathan, Joshua, Nathan and Aaron. My mother, according to my father's will, must have her third. Executors—brothers, Joshua and Nathan. Witnesses—John Ware, Peter Stretch, Thomas Bent. Proved June 29, 1767.
1767, June 29. Inventory, £204.6.5, made by Richard Moore and John Stewart. Lib. 13, p. 179.

1761, April 7. Stryker, Peter, of Millstone, Somerset Co., cordwainer; will of. Wife, Mary, to stay on the premises with my children, until my son, Barent, comes of age; then my real and personal shall be sold. Son, Barent, £5. To my wife, son Barent, son Peter, daughter Elizabeth Stryker, and my daughter, Rachel Stryker, each 1/5 of my estate. Executors—my wife, Mary, and my brothers, Barent Stryker and Hendrick Stryker. Witnesses—Allebartus Cornell, Jaques Voorheese, Chrystofel Hogeland. Proved June 15, 1761.
1761, June 8. Inventory, made by Christofel Hogelant, William Baird, Joseph Coernel. Lib. G, p. 443.

CALDENDAR OF WILLS—1761-1770   417

1760, March 10. Stubbines, Henry, of Elsinboro, Salem Co., yeoman; will of. Wife, Mary, my plantation during her life, provided she pay to my sister, Hannah Vicary, £5 a year. In case she is not able to get a living, I give the said plantation to Henry Firth, son of John Firth, of Salem, he paying the said Hannah as aforesaid; but if Henry die before 21, then to John Firth, son of said John Firth; but if he die, then to Henry Daniel, son of William Daniel, by his wife Rebecca. Personal estate to my wife, Mary, and my brother, John Firth. Executors—my wife, Mary, and my brother, John Firth. Witnesses—James Hudson, Thomas Johnson, Joshua Thompson. Proved Aug. 19, 1761.
1761, July 24. Inventory, £766.3.3, made by Joshua Thompson and John Stewart. Lib. 11, p. 18.

1763, March 1. Stubbins, Mary, of Salem Town, Salem Co., widow; will of. To my near relation, Rebecca Daniel, wife of William, £30. Nephew, Thomas Baker, £5, when he is 21. Cousins, Naomy Ballenger, Sarah Test and Deborah Dunn, £5 each. Sister, Sarah Elliot, £5. Friend, Mary Thompson, widow, £6. Sister-in-law, Elizabeth Windor, £3. Niece, Prudence Owen, remainder. Executors—nephew, Lewis Owen, and Prudence, his wife. Witnesses—Thomas Goodwin, John Dickie, Robert Wilson. Proved April 7, 1764.
1764, April 3. Inventory, £120.2.8, made by Robert Wilson and Thomas Goodwin. Lib. 12, p. 93.

1767, July 7. Stuyversant, Peter, of Bergen Co., carpenter; will of. Sons, Casparus, Peter and Johannes, and daughters, Jane Sickles, Sarah Post and Catherine Stuyversant, personal estate. Son, Peter, all my real estate. Executors—my brothers-in-law, Casparus Prior, of New York City, and Abraham Prior, of Bergen Co. Witnesses—John Stephens, Jr., Jacobus Van Sice, John Nath. Hutchins. Proved Sept. 29, 1770. Lib. K, p. 305.

1763, Feb. 16. Style, John, of Newark, Essex Co.; will of. Two tracts at Canoe Brook, and a piece of meadow at Black State, to be sold. Wife, Sarah, use of real and personal, until my children come of age. Daughter, Mary, £5, and a bed. Sons, William and Isaac, my lands. Executors—friends, Daniel Peirson, Thomas Longworth and Nathaniel Farrand. Witnesses—Humphry Nichols, Isaac Crane, John Cochrem. Proved March 22, 1763. Lib. H, p. 357.

1768, April 9. Sullivan, Matthias, of Mannington Precinct, Salem Co., yeoman; will of. Wife, Ann Sullivan, the profits of my plantation till my son, John, is of age. Son, John, said plantation. Daughter, Mary, bed and drawers. Son, Matthias, £11 and a negro. Daughter, Martha, a bed. Executrix—my wife. Witnesses—John Ormond, Bartholomew Wyatt, Jr. Proved June 1, 1768.
1768, May 13. Inventory, £664.13.6, made by Richard Hackett and John Roberts. Lib. 13, p. 383.

1765, June 13. Supplee, Bartholemew, of Greenwich Twsp., Gloucester Co. Int. Adm'r—Isabel Supplee, the widow. Fellowbondsman—Thomas Clark, yeoman; both of said place.
1765, June 11. Inventory, £66.17.6, made by Thomas Clark and Jeffery Clark, Jr.

1768, May 5. Account by Isabel Supplee, the Adm'x. "Allowed for nursing, doctoring, etc., of a cripple child, for 12 months, £38."
Lib. 12, p. 285; Lib. 13, p. 335.

1769, Sept. 27. Sutton, Benjamin, of New Windsor, Middlesex Co. Int. Adm'rs—Esther Sutton and Joseph South. Fellowbondsman—John Height; all of said place.
1769, Sept. 28. Inventory, £74.12.10, made by John Height and Andrew Davison. Lib. 15, p. 8.

1761, Feb. 23. Sutton, Jane, of Burlington Co. Ward. Daughter of Daniel Sutton. Guardian—Arent Schuyler, of Burlington, yeoman.
File No. 7177 C.

1758, Aug. 25. Sutton, John, of Somerset Co.; will of. Wife, Mary, ⅓ of the moveable estate and ⅓ the income of the land. Daughters, Elizabeth, Anne, Lois and Mary, £70 each. To sons, Jeremiah, Abner and Philip, my land. Executors—my brother, David Sutton, my wife and son, Jeremiah. Witnesses—Joseph Pound, John Pound, Adoniiah Pound. Proved Jan. 22, 1761.
1761, Jan. 15. Inventory, £252.1.0, made by William Worth and Nathaniel Ayers. Lib. G, p. 356.

1754, Oct. 23. Sutton, Joseph, of Piscataway, Middlesex Co., yeoman; will of. Wife, Priscilla, use of personal and all of real, except 19 acres. Eldest son, Henry, after the death of my father, Thomas Sutton, the said 19 acres, which lies on highway between Piscataway and New Brunswick, and which joins Moses Fitz Randolph. Youngest son, Jacob, the place where I live; also the lot I bought of William Robert and Edward Potter; also that lot which was my father, Thomas Sutton's, homestead, with 3 acres of salt meadow, at Roundabout, after the decease of my father. After the death of my wife, the personal estate is to be given to my 2 daughters, and granddaughter, Priscilla Foster. (The said daughters are named Sarah and Priscilla.) If my said granddaughter dies before she comes of age, then her share is to go to her sister, Johannah Foster. Executors—sons, Henry Sutton, of Woodbridge, and Jacob Sutton, of Piscataway, and my friend, Isaac Ferrit. Witnesses—William Potter, Ebenezer Collins, Josiah Davis. Proved April 21, 1762.
1762, April 24. Inventory, made by William Potter and James Walker. Lib. H, p. 93.

1762, Dec. 11. Sutton, Julius, of Middletown, Monmouth Co. Int. Adm'r—Isaac Vandorn, of Freehold, the principal creditor. Fellowbondsman—Jacob Vandorn, Jr.; both of said Co. Lib. H, p. 204.

1768, March 8. Sutton, Richard, of Monmouth Co. Int. Adm'x—Elizabeth Sutton, widow of Richard. Fellowbondsmen—John Anderson and Amos Sutton; both of said Co. Witness—Richard Sutton.
1768, March 14. Inventory, £69.1.2, made by John Hamton, Aaron Decamp, Benajah Ayres. Lib. I, p. 301.

1766, March 30. Sutton, Robert, of Burlington Co.; will of. My house and lot in Burlington, and my meadow, to be sold, and the money divided among my 5 children, Robert, Daniel, James and John Sutton, and daughter, Deborah Bird. Witnesses—Ann Price, Christopher Flower, Gabriel Blond. Proved June 25, 1766.

1766, June 25. Whereas Robert Sutton made his will and appointed no Executor, therefore James Sutton, of Burlington, mariner, is made Adm'r with will annexed, and John Carty of same place, taylor, goes on his bond.

1766, June 24. Inventory, £88.15.6, made by Joseph Hollinshead and John Carty. File No. 8083 C.; Lib. 13, p. 25.

1764, March 20. Swaim, Abigail, of Borough of Elizabeth, Essex Co.; will of. "Being the widow of Antoney Swaim." Daughters, Abigail Sanford and Marey Swaim, £25 each. Sons, John, Cornelius, Antoney and Jacob Swaim, the rest of my estate. My son, John, is under age, and his father died without a will; therefore he is heir to all land of his father's, and, if he conveys to his 3 brothers the homestead of 25 acres, and a grist mill and sawmill, which was his father's, then he shall have his equal part; otherwise his part shall be divided among his brothers. Executors—my friends, Samuel Broks and Samuel Miller; and they are to be Guardians of my children. Witnesses—Philip Denman, Abigail Foretice, John Stites. Proved April 30, 1764.

1764, April 23. Inventory, £306.14.10, made by Samuel Meeker and Joseph Halsey. Lib. H, p. 432.

1766, May 20. Swain, Lemuel, of Cape May Co. Int. Adm'x— Elizabeth Swain. Fellowbondsman—Robert Parson, of said Co. Witnesses—James Whilldin and David Tounsend.

1766, April 4. Inventory, £137.0.5, made by Robert Parson and James Whilldin. Lib. 12, p. 357.

1766, Oct. 10. Swarths, Baltis, of Bridgwater Twsp., Somerset Co.; will of. "Being overseer on farm of Cornelius Low, Sr., of Raritan Landing." To my brother, Fredrick Swarths, and to the children of my cousin, Hans Jurry Swarths (eldest son of my brother, Hans Jurry Swarths, deceased), the residue. Executors—friends, William Welch and Leonard Nipper, both of Hunterdon Co. Witnesses—Jacob Noorstrand, Hugh Blackhall, Garrit Carritson, Cornelius Vanclef. Proved Dec. 2, 1766.

1766, Nov. 19. Inventory, £63.12.10, made by Leonard Nighbour and William Welch, Executors, and John Baptist Dumont, Garrit Garritson and John Vroom, Appraisers.

1768, April 19. Account by both Executors. Lib. I, p. 68.

1761, July 7. Sweasey, John, of Roxbury, Morris Co. Int. Adm'rs —Jabish Mapes Sweasey and William Larrison; both of said Co. Renunciation by Peggy Sweazey, widow of John Sweasey, in favor of William Larrason and her son-in-law, Mapes Sweasey. Witnesses —Aaron Gillet and Joseph Luse.

1761, June 16. Inventory, £383.5.0, made by Walter Brown and Jacob Drake. Lib. G, p. 444.

1761, Oct. 30. Sweetman, Michael, of Freehold, Monmouth Co., yeoman; will of. Wife, Mary, is well provided for. Sons, Michael, Thomas and Henderson Sweetman, all my lands. Daughter, Catharine Sweetman, £50; daughter, Margaret Sweetman, £50, and daughter, Anne Sweetman, £50, when she is 21; also to daughter, Mary Sweetman, £50, when she comes of age; and to granddaughter, Jane Brannan, £50, when she is 21. Executors—my wife, Mary, and my sons, Michael, Thomas and Henderson. Witnesses—Michael Johnston, Euphen Johnston, John Henderson, John Johnston, Jr. Proved Oct. 21, 1767. Lib. I, p. 164.

1762, March 6. Swik, John, of Tewksbury, Hunterdon Co., farmer; will of. Wife, Chatrine, ⅓ my estate. The other ⅔ to my three children, John, Mary and Teunis, when they come of age. Brother, Peter Swik, a house. Executors—my wife and my brothers, Tuenis and Martin. Witnesses—John Read, Samuel Thomson and John Montange. Proved Oct. 26, 1765. Lib. 12, p. 391.

1762, July 31. Swine, Cornelius, of Middlesex Co. Int. Adm'rs—Daniel Swine and Absalom Hankins. Fellowbondsmen—Abel Hankins and Robert Karson; all of said Co.
1762, July 31. Inventory, £152.10.9, made by Abel Hankins and Martin Hoogland. Lib. 11, p. 337.

1761, June 20. Swisher, Jacob, of Oxford, Sussex Co., yeoman. Int. Adm'rs—Margaret Swisher and Lawrence Swisher. Fellowbondsmen—Christion Minear and Johannis Vanetta; all of said Co. Witness—Robert Peterson.
1761, June 18. Inventory, £198.1.9, made by Jonathan Pettit and John Vanetor.
1763, June 29. Account by Margaret Lydia, late Margaret Swisher; and Lawrence Swisher, the Adm'rs. Lib. 10, p. 464.

1767, May 9. Tagan, Martin, of Hunterdon Co.; will of. I give all my estate to Benjamin Stout, his son, Benjamin Stout, and his son, Joseph Stout. Executor—said Benjamin Stout. Witnesses—Charles Hoff, James Johnston, Martha Osmun. Proved June 8, 1767.
1767, Sept. 16. Inventory, £413.9.¾, made by James Stout and Peter Peterson.
1769, March 14. Account made by Gershom Lee and John Jewell, Executors of Benjamin Stout, of Amwell, and thereby Executors of the state of Martin Tagin, in the place of said Benjamin Stout, deceased, who was Executor of said Martin Tagin. (See, further, under Stout, Benjamin.) Lib. 13, p. 194.

1765, May 11. Talbot, St. George, of Town and Port of Dover, in Great Britain, but now of New York City in America; will of. I was born 25th of July, 1662, and am in good health. To Mrs. Rachel Gould, my housekeeper, an annuity. To each child of my brother, Thomas Talbot; and of my 2 sisters, Catherine Talbot (alias Garrison) and Arabella Talbot (alias Harrison), to each £5. Much money given to various churches, under the trust of various persons. Executors—the Rev. Jeremiah Leaming, John Livingston, of New York City, and Mrs. Rachel Gould. Witnesses—David Frazee, Jacob Deyckman, Jr., Edward Stevenson. Proved May 16, 1768.
Lib. I, p. 235.

1766, April 10. Talman, James, of Twsp. and Co. of Gloucester. Ward. Son of James Talman, of said place, deceased, who makes choice of John Hinchman as his Guardian.
1766, Aug. 7. Guardian—John Hinchman, Esq., of said place. Fellowbondsman—William Heulings, Esq., of Burlington. Lib. 12, p. 383.

1764, Sept. 26. Tappon, Abraham, of Hanover, Morris Co., yeoman; will of. Wife, Sarah, some household goods, stock and the use of the house where I live, and 20 acres. My daughters, Sarah, Mary, Cecil and Margaret, 20 shillings to each. Daughter, Hannah Bloodgood, £15. Daughter, Isabel, £25. To son, Benjamin, 10 acres, to be taken off of the woodlot east of the land given to Asher, by deed. Son, Asher, 5 acres of the woodlot that joins to that given to him by deed. Son, Moses, 40 acres, joining Asher's land. Sons, Jacob and John, my homestead, of 20 acres. Sons, Isaac, Abraham and William, £7 each. Executors—wife, Sarah; son-in-law, George Cooper, and my sons, Moses and Asher. Witnesses—William Dixon, Benjamin Searing, Martha Dixon. Proved Nov. 7, 1766. Lib. I, p. 57.

1770, Nov. 23. Taylor, Abigail, of Monmouth Co. Int. Adm'r—Edward Taylor, Jr., of Middletown, husband of said Abigail Taylor, late Abigail Ogborne. Fellowbondsmen—John Van Cleaf and John Williams, both of said Co. Witness—James Kelly. Lib. K, p. 256.

1763, Dec. 30. Taylor, Frances, of Perth Amboy, Middlesex Co.; will of. I am to be buried at Topenemus Church in Freehold, and have a stone at the head of my grave. Daughter, Catherine, goods. John Smyth to be paid £12, so much being due from my son-in-law, William Smith, Jr., to the estate of Andrew Smyth, deceased, brother of said John. My wedding ring I give to my daughter, Elizabeth Williams. Rest of my estate to my daughters, Catherine and Elizabeth. Executors—my son-in-law, James Williams, and my daughters, Catharine and Elizabeth. Witnesses—John Smyth, John Thomson, William Clark.
1764, Sept. 13. Codicil. Daughter-in-law, the wife of my son Hugh, a gold ring. Witnesses—John Smyth, John Mackay, John Thomson. Proved Aug. 26, 1769. Lib. K, p. 127.

1761, Jan. 12. Taylor, John, of Middlesex Co.; will of. Brother, Joseph Taylor, 10 shillings. Wife, Mary, rest of real and personal. Executors—William Hankinson, Sr., and Mary Taylor. Witnesses—John Feavel, Cornelius Wyckoff, James Hankinson. Proved Feb. 26, 1761.
1761, Jan. 24. Inventory, £268.8.6, made by John Feavel and James Hankinson. Lib. 10, p. 557.

1766, Oct. 1. Taylor, John, of Evesham, Burlington Co. Int. Adm'r —William Hartly, of Mount Holly in said Co., waterman. Fellowbondsman—John Clark, of same place, yeoman. Witness—Joseph Imlay. Lib. 12, p. 384.
1766, Nov. 1. Inventory, £41.16.6, made by Zachariah Rossell and John Clark.

1766, Nov. 10. Taylor, Joseph, of Upper Freehold Twsp., Monmouth Co.; will of. The 60 acres of the lower end of the place to be sold. Son, Joseph, the place I live on, and 10 acres of woodland off the other place. Son, John, £250, when of age. My cedar swamp, to sons Joseph and William. Wife to have the moveable estate till my daughter, Lydia, comes of age, and then to be sold and divided between my wife and my daughters, Elizabeth, Catherine and Lydia. Executors—wife, Elizabeth, and friends, William Tapscott and Thomas Farr. Witnesses—James Adams, Abigal Adams, Thomas Cox, Jr. Proved Dec. 17, 1766.

1766, Nov. 28. Inventory, £809.16.7, made by Peter Covenhoven and Joseph Cox. Lib. 12, p. 451.

1770, Aug. 8. Taylor, Joseph, of Essex Co. Int. Adm'rs—Samuel Pierson and David Cundit. Lib. K, p. 245.

1764, Oct. 4. Taylor, Lydia, of Cape May Co., spinster; will of. Sons, George Taylor and John Taylor, my back land, lying at the head of my plantation where I live, of 140 acres. Son, Daniel Taylor, my land at Prince Morrises River, in Cumberland Co., of about 300 acres. Grandson, William Taylor, 100 acres in Middle Precinct. Should Lydia Skellinks outlive her husband, Cornelius Skellinks, then Daniel Taylor is to give his sister, Lydia Skellinks, moveable estate, and, if Lydia should choose not to live with her husband, then she can have it. To daughter, Lydia, my apparel. Executors—George Taylor and Daniel Taylor. Witnesses—Henry Hand, Joshua Shaw, Jr., Jonathan Leaming. Proved Nov. 20, 1766. Lib. 13, p. 472.

1767, March 20. Taylor, Samuel, of Chesterfield, Burlington Co. Int. Adm'x—Ann Taylor, the widow of said Samuel. Fellowbondsman—John Taylor, of Nottingham, in said Co. Lib. 13, p. 102.

1767, Feb. 14. Inventory, £77.19.8, made by Benjamin Field and Joseph English.

1767, Aug. 3. Taylor, William, of Freehold, Monmouth Co.; will of. Wife, Hannah, is provided for. Son, Edward, £600. Son, William, plantation where I live. Personal estate to be sold and the money applied to the use of my 5 surviving daughters, and also for the use of my 2 deceased daughters' children. My daughter, Martha Shepherd, wife of John Shepherd, to have £40 less. Executors—friend, John Williams, brother-in-law, James Grover, and John Taylor. Witnesses—William Hankinson, John Clayton, David Taylor, Joseph Dyer. Proved Oct. 12, 1767. Lib. I, p. 203.

1763, April 22. Teed, Andrew, of Essex Co.; will of. Son, James, £60. Daughter, Phebe, £20. Son, Samuel, £10. Children of my daughter, Joanna, £20. Son, Andrew, that land on Long Island and £10. Daughter, Anna, £20. Son, Solemon, £5, and the "talers traid." My wife the remainder. Witnesses—Henary Pasel, Rebecaker Connet. Proved May 16, 1763.

1763, May 16. Adm'x—Rachel Teed, the widow of Andrew Teed, with will annexed. Fellowbondsman—Elijah Hedden, of said Co. Witness—William Butler. Lib. H, p. 419.

CALENDAR OF WILLS—1761-1770   423

1769, April 4. Teed, Samuel, of Antuxet; will of. Wife, Elizabeth, to pay to granddaughter, Sarah Teed, £5, when she is of age. Daughter, Esther Blissard¡ 5 shillings. Wife rest of personal and real. Executrix—wife. Witnesses—Jonathan Ryley, Silas Bradford, Sarah Ryley. Proved May 18, 1769.
1769, April 2. Inventory, £40.7.6, made by Jonathan Lore and Jonathan Ryley.   Lib. 14, p. 19.

1770, March 20. Teel, Cornelius, of Middlesex Co.; will of. Wife, Lenah, £20 and ⅓ my real and personal. Rest of my estate to my 4 daughters, Eve, Kathurine, Lena and Barbara. Executors—wife Lenah, Christian Harvel and John Brown. Witnesses—Wilhelmus Stoothof, Johannis Stoothof, Ruloff Voorhees. Proved July 28, 1770.
                                                Lib. K, p. 285.

1769, March 2. Teireberger, George. Account by Japheth Byram and Peter Corselius, the Executors. Amount of inventory was £57.3.10. Legacies paid to Philip Nightingale, in part of wife's legacy; to Philip Hoffman, in part of wife's legacy; to John Terreberger as legacy; and to Philip Nightingale and his wife, for her legacy. (See will under George Duseberry).   Lib. 13, p. 533.

1763, Feb. 5 Temout, Frederick, of Pequannock, Morris Co., yeoman; will of. Wife, Charlotte, use of my real and personal while my widow. Sons, Adam and Coonrod, my plantation where I dwell, of 600 acres, and also land by Rockaway River, of 50 acres, and all other lands, except 4 lots at New Foundland. When son, Coonrod, shall get married, he is to have a setout, equal to his brother and sisters. Daughters, Elizabeth and Catharine, 4 lots at New Foundland. Executors—my two sons, Adam and Coonrod. Witnesses—John Van Winkle, Frederick Miller, Ezekiel Cheever. Proved Sept. 8, 1766.   .   Lib. I, p. 56.

1768, Sept. 10. Ten Eyck, Anderis, of Somerset Co.; will of. Wife, Ariontie, given various goods, and £20 yearly, to be paid by sons Matthew, Andrew, John and Abraham. Son, Matthew, the plantation where he lives, on Raritan River. Son, Andrew, plantation where he lives at Raritan Landing, in Middlesex Co. Son, John, plantation where he lives, on east side of South Branch of Raritan River. Son, Abraham, plantation where I live. Son, Peter, the land on Hollands Brook, which is the mill lot. Daughter, Neltie, £430. Daughter, Jane, £430. Daughter, Mary, who has 4 children by her former husband, Jaques Vander Beek, £430. Executors—sons, Mathew, John and Abraham, and my cousin, Jacob Ten Eyck. Witnesses—Abraham Van Nest, Hendrick Van Sted, Richard Forster. Proved Aug. 5, 1769.
1769, Sept. 5. Inventory, £845.10.8, made by John Vroom, Peter Dumont and John Van Neste, Jr.   Lib. K, p. 121.

1763, Oct. 20. Tennent, Gilbert, of Philadelphia, clerk; will of. Son, Gilbert, £300 and my library, when of age. All the rest of my real and personal estate I give to my wife, Sarah, and my children, Gilbert, Cornelia and Elizabeth, when they are of age, but, if they should all die, then to William, the son of my brother, William Tennent, of Freehold, in New Jersey; but if he die, then to John and

Gilbert, the sons of my brother, William, aforesaid, that is, the one-half thereof, and the other half to James and Gilbert, the sons of my brother, Charles, of Whitely Creek, in Pennsylvania. It is advisable that the real be sold as soon as possible. Executors—wife, Sarah, and my Rev'd brother, William Tennent, of Lower Freehold. Overseers—my friends, Rev. Samuel Finley, President of College of New Jersey, the Worshipful John Lyal, Esq., of New Brunswick, and the Rev'd William Tennent, Jr., of Freehold. Witnesses—John Williams, William Falconer, John George. Proved Oct. 23, 1764. (The above will was proved at Philadelphia).

1764, Oct. 23. Letters were granted in Pennsylvania to Sarah Tennent and William Tennent, as Executors.

1767, Nov. 19. William Tennent, Executor, was sworn at Burlington.

1777, June 11. Sarah Cheesman, formerly wife of Rev. Gilbert Tennent, of Philadelphia, was sworn and said the copy is a true copy of the will. Signed before Charles Pettit, Surrogate.

File No. 8265-8277 C; Lib. 13, p. 289.

1770, March 5. Tennent, Gilbert, of Middletown, Monmouth Co., Doctor of physick; will of. Wife and child, which I now have, and, in case my wife is now pregnant, then both of my children with my wife to be maintained out of the estate, as long as she is my widow; and, if my child or children should marry, what remains in the hands of my widow shall be divided between them. Executrix—wife, Catharine. Witnesses—William Tennent, Thomas Henderson. Proved March 14, 1770, by Doctor Thomas Henderson and William Tennent, Sr.

1770, March 13. Renunciation by Catherine Tennent, the widow, on estate of Doctor Gilbert Tennent, late of Mount Pleasant. Witnesses—Thomas Henderson and Henry Waddell.

1770, March 14. Adm'r—William Tennent, Jr., brother of said Gilbert, with will annexed.

1770, March 15. Inventory, £302.0.4, made by Samuel Forman and Thomas Henderson.

1773, Oct. 6. Inventory, £216.0.11, of the book accounts, made by same appraisers.

1773, Oct. 14. Account filed by the Adm'r. Lib. K, p. 189.

1766, Sept. 8. Terheun, Derck, of Bergen Co.; will of. Wife, Betty, to be supported. Sons, Albert and Nickasie, lands I bought of John Christeen and Isaac Kingsland. Sons, Jacob and John, lands I bought of Reynier Van Gesen, Jores Van Gesen and Class Romine. Daughters, Gertye and Leya, an outset when they are married, equal to the other daughters. Daughters, Annatye, Weyntye, Betye and Gertye, £400. Executors—sons, Albert, Nickasie, Jacob and John. Witnesses—Henry Barr, John Romine, Guilliam Bertholf. Proved Nov. 5, 1766. Lib. I, p. 60.

1739, April 2. Terrill, Ephraim, Sr., of Elizabeth Town, Essex Co., blacksmith; will of. Eldest son, Ephraim, 10 shillings. Son, Isaac, rest of real and personal estate. Executor—son, Isaac. Witnesses—John Terrill, Daniel Terrill, Mary Doty. Proved June 17, 1761.

Lib. G, p. 451.

1761, Aug. 4. Terrill, John, of Elizabeth Borough, Essex Co., yeoman; will of. Eldest son, Thomas, 10 shillings. Son, Amos, my homestead. Son, Jacob, land that joins Daniel Terrill and Joseph Clark. Two youngest sons, Jacob and Amos, my salt meadow. Daughters, Jemima (wife of James Miller), Mary (wife of Jacob Hampton), and Sarah Terrill, personal estate. Executors—my son-in-law, James Miller, and Jacob Terrill. Witnesses—Daniel Terrill, David Olliver, John Wood. Proved Jan. 12, 1764. Lib. H, p. 325.

1764, Sept. 25. Terrill, Samuel, of Borough of Elizabeth, Essex Co., weaver; will of. The land I bought of Henry Bonnel, which formerly belonger to Benjamin Wade, to be sold. Wife, Mary, use of my lands, while widow. My lands to my sons, when they come of age. Nathaniel, my son, shall take care of my brother, Lemuel Terrill, and also of my 2 youngest sons, Amos and John, to see that they have trades. To each of my daughters, £15. Executors—wife, Mary, and my friends, Amos Day and William Brant. Witnesses—John Riggs, Daniel Baker, Jonathan Lambert. Proved Jan. 1, 1765.
1765, Jan. 7. Inventory made by John Riggs and Henry Bonnel.
Lib. H, p. 488.

1770, Dec. 19. Terry, Richard, of Cumberland Co.; will of. Wife to have ⅓ my moveable estate. Son, Ephraim, 10 shillings. Son, Nathan, 5 shillings. Daughter, Rebekah, 5 shillings, and a table that is in her Granney's care, and to have it after Granney's death. Son, Daniel, 5 shillings. To Jeremiah and Ashbery, my land, of 121 acres, lying near Cranbury Ponds, near Morris River, and joins to Richard Lore and Jacob Garrison, and my son, Jeremiah, to have the east end. Daughters, Laurea, Sarah and Letcher, the rest of estate. Executors—my wife, Elizabeth, and my son, Ashbury. Witnesses—William Pepper, Jean Pepper. Proved Dec. 24, 1770.
1770, Dec. 24. Inventory, £91.5.8, made by David Shepherd and William Pepper. Lib. 15, p. 205.

1762, Feb. 1. Test, Francis, of Alloways Creek Twsp., Salem Co., weaver; will of. Wife, Elizabeth, use of my lands and moveable estate. Son, Benjamin, £15. Son, Francis, £15. Son, Abner, £15. Daughter, Rachel Hilmon, £10. Daughter, Elizabeth Haines, £5. Daughter, Ruth Test, £10. Daughter, Laticia Test, £10. Son, Thomas, house and lands on north side of Coopers Creek, where I live, after my wife's death; he paying son, Benjamin, £15; son, Francis, £15; son, Abner, £15; daughter, Elizabeth, £5. Executors—my wife and son, Francis. Witnesses—Peter Smith, William Smith, Philip Dennis. Proved Aug. 23, 1762. Lib. 11, p. 249.

1765, March 26. Thackery, Jacob, of Salem Co. Int. Adm'r—Thomas Thackra. Fellowbondsman—Daniel Garrison; both of Lower Penns Neck, said Co., yeomen. Lib. 12, p. 177.

1761, Dec. 4. Thackray, Joseph, of Newton, Gloucester Co., yeoman; will of. Wife, Mary, ⅓ of my goods and ⅓ of a mortgage which I have on John Erwin's plantation; also the use of ⅓ my real estate; and she is to have the care of my 2 youngest children. Son, Benjamin, 5 shillings. Daughter, Elizabeth Thackery, £5. The rest of personal estate to son, John, and my daughter, Mary Thackery, when they are of age. Son, Stephen, plantation where I live, and he

to pay to my son, Joseph, £8 yearly. Executors—son, Stephen, and my wife, Mary. Witnesses—James Sloan, Benjamin Graisbury, Richard Weekes. Proved Dec. 30, 1761.
1761, Dec. 16. Inventory, £697.7.5, made by Isaac Mickle and Ezekiel Linzey. Lib. 11, p. 106.

1767, Aug. 4. Thackray, Stephen, of Newton Township, Gloucester Co.; will of. Son, James, the improved part of the plantation where I live. Son, Joseph, 50 acres unimproved land, to be surveyed off from the head of my land, bounding on John Burrough's and Isaac Cooper's land. Youngest son, Thomas, 50 acres, which is to join my son, Joseph, and Job Haines. Wife, Elizabeth, to have the profits from all real and personal to bring up my children till they are 21. Executors—my wife, and my friend, James Cooper. Sons, Joseph and Thomas, to be put to trades. Witnesses—Benjamin Thackray, John Burrough, Jr., John Gruffyth. Proved Sept. 23, 1767.
1767, Sept. 19. Inventory, £281.12.8, made by Isaac Mickle and Job Haines. Lib. 13, p. 133.

1759, Feb. 10. Tharp, Job, of Woodbridge, Middlesex Co.; will of. All moveables and real to be sold, except a piece of salt marsh. To wife, Sarah, £1. Son, Joseph Tharp, £100. Sons, Icabod, David and Paul, £100 each. Daughters, Mary Tharp and Annah Tharp, £1 each. Son, Ruben, £1. Daughter, Jennet Tharp, £1. Remainder to my wife. Executors—friends, Jacob Fitz Randolph and David Evans. Witnesses—William Coats, Jeremiah Randolph, James Clarkson, Jr. Proved Dec. 5, 1761. Lib. H, p. 48.

1762, Nov. 6. Tharp, Peter and Elizabeth, both of Morris Co. Int. Adm'r—Samuel Day, of said Co., principal creditor.
1763, Aug. 15. Inventory made by Ebenezer Lindsly and Abraham Casterline. Lib. H, p. 271.

1767, Sept. 23. Thomas, Elias, of Morris River, Cumberland Co. Int. Adm'r—Lemuel Edwards. Fellowbondsman—David Vaneman; both of said place.
1767, Sept. 15. Inventory, £11.0.0, made by David Vanneman and Cornelius Clark. Lib. 13, p. 441.

1761, June 22. Thomas, Jonathan, of Upper Freehold, Monmouth Co.; will of. To wife, Elizabeth Thomas, £100, exclusive of the legacy left to her by her father, William Beakes, dec'd; also £10 yearly. Daughter-in-law, Priscilla Bloodgood, a negro girl. Daughter, Sarah Thomas, a negro, and the silverware, when 18. To my cousin, Jonathan Thomas Kirk, £10. Rest of real and personal to be sold. A deed is to be given to John Harris for my part of Success Sawmill. My daughter, Sarah, to be well educated by her mother, if said mother does not marry. Rest of estate to daughter, Sarah, when 18. Executors—wife, Elizabeth, and friends, James Lawrence, Edward Tonkin and Joseph Arney. Witnesses—John Wetherill, John Wetherill, Jr., Christopher Neirs. Proved July 23, 1761.
1761, July 21. Inventory, £682.11.0, made by William Lawrie and John Wetherill. Lib. 10, p. 294.

CALENDAR OF WILLS—1761-1770   427

1763, March 21. Thompson, Benjamin, of Pilesgrove Twsp., Salem Co.; will of. Wife, Abigail, £100, as by an Indenture before our marriage. Son, Benjamin, land where he lives. My youngest sons, Newcomb Thompson and Butler Thompson, plantation where I live. Daughter, Anna Whitaker, £15. Daughter, Marey Thompson, £30. Daughter, Patience Davis, £15. Daughter, Percilla Thompson, £40. Executors—sons, Benjamin Thompson and Lewis Whitacar. Witnesses—Elijah Davis, James White, Daniel Clark. Proved April 8, 1763.
    1763, April 7. Inventory, £611.12.8, made by Jeremiah Foster and Henry Seely.   Lib. 11, p. 393.

1764, Dec. 12. Thompson, James, of Town of Salem, Salem Co., sadler. Int. Adm'r—Aaron Thompson, yeoman. Fellowbondsmen—William Robinson, cordwainer, and Moses Hill, cooper; all of Lower Penns Neck, said Co.
    1764, Dec. 11. Inventory, £63.4.7, made by William Robinson and Moses Hill.   Lib. 12, p. 72.

1767, Oct. 21. Thompson, John, of Mannington, Salem Co. Int. Adm'x—Mary Thompson, widow, of said place. Fellowbondsmen—William Carpenter, of said place, and Thomas Thompson, of Lower Penns Neck, said Co., yeomen.
    1767, Oct. 20. Inventory, £176.7.3, made by William Harvey and Nathaniel Hall.   Lib. 13, p. 278.

1762, Feb. 4.—Thompson, Mary, of Essex Co. Int. Adm'r—Thomas Thompson, the eldest son of said Mary. Fellowbondsman—Thomas Baker; both of said Co.
    1762, March 29. Inventory, £102.11.8, made by Nathaniel Taylor and William Maxfield. "Due to me, Thomas Thompson, on account of the estate of my father, Aaron Thompson, which did remain in the hands of my mother, Mary Thompson, at time of her death, £6.12.3. Due to Sarah Thompson, £6.12.3. Due to Elizabeth Thompson, £6.12.3."   Lib. H, p. 76.

1765, May 20. Thompson, Moses, of Borough of Elizabeth, Essex Co.; will of. Wife, Abigail, £50. Sons, Moses and Benjamin, my lands. Children, Moses Thompson, Benjamin Thompson, and Elizabeth (wife of Paul Day), and my grandsons, John Mery and Benjamin Mery, my moveable estate. Executors—son, Moses Thompson, and son-in-law, Paul Day. Witnesses—Aaron Faitout, Edward Ross, Timothy Whitehead. Proved Aug. 12, 1765.   Lib. H, p. 521.

1763, Dec. 4. Thompson, Samuel, of Borough of Elizabeth, Essex Co.; will of. My plantation, on which I live, may be sold. Wife, Susanah, ⅓ of the money, and the other ⅔ to be paid to my 3 sons and my daughters. Executors—my wife, Susanah, my son, Hezekiah, and my friend, Capt. Enos Baldwin. Witnesses—Timothy Whitehead, Rachel Sturges, Henry Bonnel. Proved Dec. 20, 1763.
    1763, Dec. 22. Inventory made by Joseph Wade and Job Mulford.   Lib. H, p. 327.

1765, Feb. 8. Thompson, William, of Amwell, Hunterdon Co. Int. Adm'x—Catharine Thompson, widow of said William. Fellowbondsman—Henry Gulick; both of said place.
    1765, Feb. 7. Inventory made by Abraham Prall and William Schank.

1767, Oct. 17. Account by Abraham Terhuncy and Catharine, his wife, late Catharine Thompson, who was Adm'x of William Thompson, of Amwell. Lib. 12, p. 127; Lib. 13, p. 328.

1761, Jan. 29. Thomson, Alexander, of Piscataway, Middlesex Co.; will of. Wife, Margrit, use of place, except what is to be sold. Son, Alexander, my plantation, except what is to be sold. Son, James, £40, when 21. Daughter, Sarah, £25. Daughter, Rachel, £25. Executors—uncle, James Thomson, my beloved Joseph Ayers, and my friend, Joseph Fitz Randolph. Witnesses—Jacob Laing, John Macknight Crow, Andrew Herriott. Proved Feb. 18, 1761.
1761, Feb. 16. Inventory made by Samuel Kelly and Daniel Drake.
Lib. G, p. 363.

1761, June 3. Thomson, Alexander, of City of Perth Amboy, Middlesex Co.; will of. Wife, Barsheba, house and ½ that lot by Edward Higgins, that I bought of Nicholas Britin. Son, William, the large house. Eldest daughter, Elizabeth Turner, the house that Alexander Walker formerly lived in. Second daughter, Elenar Carhart, lot lying by Jeane Lyal. Daughter, Mary Carman, house back of the one I gave to son William. Daughter, Sincha Lyal, house south of the one I gave to William. Daughter, Susannah, house I gave to my wife, after wife's death. Grandson, Alexander Turner, ½ the lot by Edward Higgins. Grandson, John Webb, £50. To Barsheba Turner, daughter of Richard Turner, £30. The wood lot that I bought of Obadiah Ayres, to be sold. Executors—my wife, my son, William, and my son, James Carman. Witnesses—Thomas Kinnan, John Thompson, David Herriot. Proved June 9, 1763. Lib. H, p. 251.

1766, Jan. 12. Thomson, Benjamin, of Millstone, Somerset Co.; gentleman; will of. Wife, Mary, my household goods, and £35 annually, and the house and lot now in possession of William Millan, and ½ the profits of my farm, till my grandson, Benjamin Thomson, is 21. My daughter-in-law, Margaret Thomson, widow of my son William, deceased, ½ the profits of the farm, till Benjamin is 21. To my said grandson, Benjamin, my farm; and he shall pay to my grandchildren, George Thomson, Elizabeth Thomson and John Thomson, his brothers and sister, £100 each, when they are 21. Executor —my friend, Peter Schenk. Witnesses—William Millan, James Leslie, James Anderson. Proved March 21, 1768. Lib. I, p. 220.

1760, Nov. 27. Thomson, James, of Piscataway, Middlesex Co.; will of. Wife, Charity, use of my plantation till it is sold, for the support of such of my grandchildren as may be in her care. Real estate to be sold, and my wife to have the interest of ½ the money, and the other ½ to be the property of my daughter, Rachel Dunn. After my wife's death the rest of my estate to be divided into 16 parts. To my daughter, Rachel Dunn, 3 parts. To grandson, Thomson Stelle, 3 parts. To grandson, Lewis Stelle, 3 parts. To grandson, Alexander Dunn, 2 parts. To grandson, James Thomson, 2 parts. To granddaughter, Experience Dunn, 1 part. To granddaughter, Charity Stelle, 1 part. To granddaughter, Phebe Stelle, 1 part. Executors—wife, Charity, my daughter, Rachel, my son-in-law, Benjamin Dunn, and my friend, Reune Runyon. Witnesses—Isaac Stelle, Rachel Randolph, Azariah Dunham. Proved Sept. 19, 1763.
Lib. H, p. 277.

CALENDAR OF WILLS—1761-1770   429

1769, May 24. Thomson, John, of Pilesgrove, Salem Co.; will of. My wife, Mary Thompson, and my cousin, James Dunlap, are to sell my lands, and the money is to be divided between my wife and my 2 children. Executors—my said wife and my said cousin. Witnesses —William Guest, Nathaniel Thompson, Frances Thomson. Proved March 7, 1770.
1769, June 19. Inventory, £183.4.4, made by William Guest, Sr., and John Creag, Sr.   Lib. 14, p. 217.

1764, July 19. Thomson, William, of Perth Amboy, Middlesex Co., victualler; will of. Son, William Thompson, all my ready money, and all livestock, and the rest of my personal estate. Executor— son, William. Witnesses—James Reed, Goodson Cart, Thomas Fox. Proved July 2, 1767.   Lib. I, p. 133.

1765, Sept. 14. Thomson, William, of Somerset Co., attorney-at-law; will of. Wife, Margaret, interest in all estate, while my widow, to bring up my children. Executors—my wife, my father, Benjamin Thomson, my brother-in-law, Edmund Leslie, and my friend, Peter Schank. Witnesses—James Leslie, Hugh Thomson, William Millan. Proved Oct. 2, 1765.   Lib. H, p. 551; Lib. H, p. 556.

1765, March 26. Thorn, Abraham, of Woodbridge, Middlesex Co.; will of. Son, Isaac, ½ of a lot of land I bought of Isaac Thorn, which is located along land I bought of Jacob Thorn and Mary Alston; also ½ the lot I bought of Jacob Thorn; and Isaac is to pay to my son, Abraham, £100, and to my daughter, Hannah Thorn, £27, and to my daughter, Elizabeth, £27, and to my daughter, Ann, £27. Sons, John and Benjamin, rest of my lands. Wife, Ann, moveable estate. Executors—my wife and my kinsman, Abraham Shotwell, of Elizabeth. Witnesses—Benjamin Shotwell, Jacob Laing, Mary Edger. Proved May 9, 1765.   Lib. H, p. 575.

1766, Nov. 19. Thorn, Katharina, of Chesterfield, Burlington Co.; will of. Widow of John Thorn. To grandchild, Humphrey Thorn, my silver "tancard," if he settles on land, but if he follows the sea, my son, Joseph Thorn, shall have it. Daughters, Catharine, Hannah, Sarah and Mary, my clothing. Sons, Samuel and Benjamin, 1 shilling each. Son, Joseph, the rest. Executor—son, Joseph Thorn. Witnesses—John Thorn, Stacy Fenton, Thomas Thorn. Proved Nov. 29, 1766.
1766, Dec. 6. Inventory, £25.3.6, made by John Lawrence and Jacob Lawrence.   Lib. 13, p. 15.

1766, June 14. Thorn, Zacheus, of Twsp. and Co. of Gloucester, yeoman. Int. Adm'r—Isaac Albertson, of Newton, said Co., yeoman. Fellowbondsman—Robert Friend Price, Esq., of Twsp. and Co. of Gloucester. Witnesses—Sarah Howell and John Ladd.
        Lib. 12, p. 380.

1766, June 14. Thorne, John, of Gloucester Twsp. and Co. Ward. Brother and heir of Zacheus Thorne, of said place, yeoman, deceased. John makes choice of his friend as his Guardian, viz., Isaac Albertson.
1766, June 14. Guardian—Isaac Albertson, of Newton, said Co., yeoman. Fellowbondsman—Robert Friend Price, Esq., of Gloucester Twsp. Witness—Sarah Howell.   Lib. 12, p. 382.

1768, June 2. Thorne, John, of Haddonfield, Gloucester Co., yeoman; will of. To the lawful heir of my deceased son, Thomas Thorne (if any there be), 5 shillings. To my wife, £25. Son-in-law, John Glover, land in Gloucester town, where he lives, of 262 and ½ acres, purchased of John Redden, 2 of June, 1704, and said John Glover is to pay to my daughter, Sarah Thorne, £150. Daughter, Sarah Thorne, a tract in Newton Twsp. purchased of Thomas Breach, of 18 acres. To Susannah Dukemaneer, £3. Executors—daughter, Sarah Thorne, and said John Glover. Witnesses—Joseph Roberts, Joseph Lippincott, Benjamin Hartley. Proved Sept. 1, 1769.
Lib. 14, p. 192.

1765, Aug. 15. Thorne, Thomas, of Chesterfield, Burlington Co. Int. Adm'r—John Imlay, of Bordentown, merchant. Fellowbondsman—John Lawrence, of Burlington, attorney-at-law. Lib. 12, p. 154.
    1765, Aug. 15. Renunciation of Mary Thorn, widow of Thomas Thorne. Witnesses—William Imlay, Jr., and Humphrey Thorn.
File No. 7875 C.
    1765, Aug. 24. Inventory, £545.18.8, made by William Imlay and John Taylor. File Nos. 8095-8098 C.
    1766, Sept. 15. Account by John Imlay, the Adm'r. (Paid Mary Thorn for signing release, 5.0. Paid Catharine Thorn, £200. Sold farm of 220 acres, £840.) File Nos. 7869-7872 C.

1766, June 2. Thorp, Israel, of Woodbridge, Middlesex Co. Account by Thomas Thorp, of estate of Mary Thorp, who was widow and sole executrix of Israel Thorp. To boarding and clothing Israel Thorp, son of said Israel, 12 years, £120; schooling said Israel, 4 years, £4; boarding the other son, Thomas, 4 years and one-half, £45; to necessaries for Israel after he was bound and apprentice, and ran away from his master, £7.8.3.
File No. 4371 L. (See Lib. C, p. 68.)

1762, Feb. 23. Thorp, Joseph, of Woodbridge, Middlesex Co. Ward. Aged 20 years, and one of the children of Job Thorp, of Woodbridge, deceased. Guardian—Richard Wright. Fellowbondsman—David Wright; both of said place. Lib. H, p. 77.

1763, Jan. 7. Thorp, Morris, of City of Perth Amboy, Middlesex Co.; will of. To son, John, 5 shillings. Rest of estate to be given equally to son, John, son, Morris, daughter, Sarah Patterson, daughter, Abigail Thorp, and daughter, Mary Thorp. Executors—sons, John and Morris, and daughters, Sarah and Abigail and Mary, when they come of age. Witnesses—William Burnet, Isaac Bunnell, William Kinnan. Proved Jan. 9, 1765. Lib. H, p. 480.

1765, Jan. 14. Throckmorton, Job, of Freehold, Monmouth Co., yeoman; will of. To wife, Mary, use of my real estate. Children, Sarah, Jemima, Mary, Anne, Susannah, Hannah, and son Job, each to have their share of my estate, when of age. Executors—brother-in-law, Joseph Morford; Thomas Leonard and James Hankinson. Witnesses—George Rhe, Catherine Rhe, Mary Leonard. Proved Feb. 11, 1765. Lib. H, p. 568.

1763, Feb. 13. Throckmorton, Thomas, of Roxbury, Morris Co.; will of. Moveable estate to be sold, except what my Executors think best to keep for my son, Thomas, till he comes to the age of 5 years old, which will be in 1768, and which is ½ of the moveable estate that belongs between my brother, Daniel, and myself. Wife, Merium, all the goods she brought to me when I married her; also ⅓ the money after sale of lands and moveable estate. Son, Thomas, the rest, when he is 21; but, if he do not live, then to my brothers and sisters, and my wife, namely, John, William, Daniel, Job and Lewis Throckmorton, Mary Foster, Rebecca Throckmorton. Executors—my wife, Hartshorn Fitz Randolph and Job Throckmorton. Witnesses—Benjamin Hart, John Throckmorton. Proved May 3, 1763.
Lib. 11, p. 470.

1763, March 7. Inventory, £945.5.7½, made by Hercules Young and Benjamin Heart. File No. 86 S.

1770, Feb. 21. Tice, William, of Freehold, Monmouth Co.; will of. Real and personal to be sold and the proceeds to be divided among my wife, Elizabeth, and my children, when they are 21. Executors—friends, John Tice, John Burrowes and Garret Wall. Witnesses—Benjamin Van Cleaf, Jr., Daniel Covenhoven, Roelef Schanck. Proved May 22, 1770. Lib. K, p. 204.

1765, Feb. 26. Tietsoort, William, of Raritan Landing, Middlesex Co., shop keeper; will of. Real and personal to be sold. Wife, Mary, a bed, and she is to live with my son-in-law, George Doremus, and Margaret his wife, my daughter. To daughter, Margaret, £100, but her husband, George Doremus, to give the interest thereof to my wife. Son, John, rest of my estate. Executors—son, John, son-in-law, George Doremus, and Francis Brasier, of Raritan Landing. Witnesses—Henry Beekman, Josias Goldsmith, William Horn. Proved May 5, 1765. Lib. H, p. 501.

1770, March 5. Tilley, Robert, of Essex Co. Int. Adm'r—Anthony Willmot, principal creditor. Lib. K, p. 190.

1764, Nov. 19. Tillinghast, Charles, of New York City. Int. Adm'r—William Wiley, of said City. Fellowbondsman—James Banks, of Newark, Essex Co. Lib. H, p. 422.

1758, April 19. Tillton, Peter, of Middletown, Monmouth Co.; will of. Daughter, Abigail Potter, £50. Son, Daniel, £100. Daughter, Lydia Tilton, £50. Daughter, Hannah Tillton, £50. Son, Amos, my land. Executor—son, Amos. Witnesses—George Allen, Joseph Allen, Richard Lawrence. Proved March 28, 1761.

1761, March 31. Inventory, £720.11.11, made by John Tillton and Robert Tillton. Lib. G, p. 406.

1758, July 7. Tillton, Samuel, of Middletown Twsp., Monmouth Co.; will of. Wife, Elizabeth, a bond that is due from John Willet, and she is to be maintained out of my estate. Son, Peter, all my lands. Son, Samuel, 5 shillings. Moveable estate to be sold after wife's death and money given to sons, Nathaniel, Peter, Thomas and John, and my daughters, Susannah and Rebeckah Tillton. Witnesses—Thomas Stillwell, Edward Burowes, Jeremiah Stillwell. Proved Aug. 3, 1764.

1764, Aug. 9. Adm'r—Peter Tillton, principal legatee; with will annexed. Fellowbondsman—John Chasey; both of said Co. Renunciation was made by Elizabeth Tilton, the widow; in favor of Samuel's son, Peter Tilton. Witnesses—John Chasey, David Eldridge and Samuel Coleman. Lib. H, p. 421.

1765, Aug. 5. Tilsilver, George, of Cumberland Co. Ward. Son of Michael Tilsilver, of Stow Creek, said Co., yeoman, deceased. Guardian—John Sowder, of Hopewell, yeoman. Fellowbondsman—Abraham Rose, of Dearfield, yeoman; both of said Co. Witness—Daniel Clark. Lib. 12, p. 170.

1765, Aug. 5. Tilsilver, Jacob, of Cumberland Co. Ward. Son of Michael Tilsilver, of Stow Creek, said Co., yeoman, deceased. Guardian—John Sowder, of Hopewell, yeoman. Fellowbondsman—Abraham Rose, of Dearfield, yeoman; both of said Co. Witness—Daniel Clark. (See Dilshaver). Lib. 12, p. 170.

1761, Dec. 21. Tilton, Abraham, of Nottingham, Burlington Co.; will of. Wife, Elizabeth, ⅓ of my moveable estate, and the other ⅔ to my 5 children, Patience, Sarah, Hannah, Lucey and Abraham, when they are of age. Daughters, Patience Tilton and Sarah Tilton, the land I bought of Samuel Stevenson, but son Abraham may have it when of age, if he pay them £400. My daughter, Hannah, the land I bought of Nathan Allen, lying in Monmouth Co. To my daughter Lucey, the land I bought of Mahlon Wright. Son, Abraham, rest of lands. Witnesses—Amos Middleton, Joseph Killey, John Bruce. Proved Jan. 5, 1762.
 1762, Jan. 2. Inventory, £747.15.2, made by William Lawrie, Thomas Miller, Thomas Folkes. Lib. 11, p. 217.
 1762, Jan. 5. Elizabeth Tilton appointed Adm'x with will annexed, as Abraham Tilton neglected to name Executors. Fellowbondsman—Joseph Thorn, of Burlington. Witness—Gabriel Blond.

1767, June 24. Tilton, Abraham, of Nottingham, Burlington Co. Ward. Son of Abraham Tilton, of said place, who died intestate, leaving real estate, and the widow married a 2nd husband, who makes waste of the timber. Guardian—Joseph Thorn. Fellowbondsmen—Thomas Thorne and Thomas Folkes, all of Chesterfield, said Co., yeomen. File No. 8279 C.

1765, Oct. 8. Tilton, Amos, of Middletown, Monmouth Co.; will of. My farm to be sold. I bought 2 tracts of land from my brother, Daniel Tilton, which I now give to him. To my sister, Abigail, the wife of Joseph Potter, a looking glass. To sister, Lydia Tilton, a bed and books. Sister, Hannah Tilton, bed and books. To Daniel, son of Joseph and Abigail Potter, silver buckles. To Lydia, daughter of said Joseph and Abigail, silver buttons. To Rhoda, daughter of my brother, Daniel, teaspoons, marked A. T. To Lydia, daughter of my said brother, a bed. To friend, Benjamin Walcot, books. The money that Peter Weaver owes me may remain in his hands for 4 years. Nathan Tilton, my kinsman, may have my covered wagon, if he pay £15 for it. I direct that in case Ebenezer Allen should now take the smallpox, that he may have £5. Executors—kinsmen, Elihu Williams and Edmund Williams. Witnesses—Richard Lawrence, Obadiah Tilton, Margaret Foard. Proved Oct. 17, 1765.

CALENDAR OF WILLS—1761-1770   433

1765, Oct. 30.   Inventory, £839.3.2, made by Richard Lawrence and
Joseph Potter.   Lib. H, p. 566.

1762, Oct. 11. Tilton, Robert, of Middletown, Monmouth Co.; will of. The farm where I live and one-half the farm at Shrewsbury to be sold. Wife, Meriam, £100, enough goods to furnish a room, 5 cows and a horse, etc. Son, Obadiah, ½ of my farm, if not sold. Son, David, the other half. Son, Jedediah, £300, and he is to have schooling. Daughter, Deborah, wife of Anthony Woodard, £30. Daughter, Dinah, £90. Daughter, Merian, wife of Edmond Williams, £50. Executors—my son, Obadiah, and kinsman, Amos Tilton, both of Middletown. Witnesses—Nathan Tilton, John Tilton, Jr., John Tillton. Proved Nov. 1, 1762.
1762, Oct. 23. Inventory, £636.2.4, made by John Tillton and John Tilton, Jr.   Lib. H, p. 204.

1764, Feb. 27. Tilton, Sylvester, of Monmouth Co. Int. Adm'r—Joseph Potter, of Shrewsbury, the principal creditor. Fellowbondsman—John Williams, of Freehold; both of said Co.
1764, Feb. 11. Renunciation by Hannah Tilton, the widow, in favor of Joseph Potter. Witness—John Williams.   Lib. H, p. 353.

1766, Oct. 13. Timier, George, of Alexandria Twsp., Hunterdon Co.; will of. Wife, Margaret, ⅓ of real and personal. To the Dutch Meeting-house, £5. To Court Winegardener, the money that he owes me. Friend, Abraham Young, my books. To Carricat Firsbough, the rest of my effects. Executors—Peter Dilts and Abraham Young. Witnesses—John Holmes, Abraham Young, Howell Beam. Proved Nov. 1, 1766.
1766, Oct. 31. Inventory, made by John Dilts and William Wagenor.   Lib. 12, p. 404.

1769, Sept. 1. Tindall, Joseph, of Trenton, Hunterdon Co.; will of. Wife, Mary, ½ my plantation while she lives, and ½ the livestock. Son, Joseph, my lands, and he is to pay to my daughter, Elizabeth, £25. Daughters, Issable and Sarah, £25 each. If my son, Joseph, should die, then his widow to live on the land. Executors—son, Joseph, and my son-in-law, John Phillips. Witnesses—Samuel Hart, Ralph Jones, Daniel Laning. Proved Oct. 7, 1769.
1769, Sept. 30. Inventory, made by Stephen Laning and Samuel Hart.   Lib. 14, p. 199.

1766, July 28. Tingley, Ebenezer, of Borough of Elizabeth, Somerset (?) Co.; will of. Son, Ebenezer, 5 shillings. Wife, Elizabeth, various goods. Son, Nathaniel, land bought of Stephen Crane, of 80 acres. Son, Samuel, homestead. Son, Ebenezer, the east ⅓ of the land that I bought of Benjamin Sutton; Samuel the middle third, and my son, Joseph, the west third. My 5 daughters to have £7 each. Daughter, Dorcas, £2. Grandson, Ebenezer Bebout, £10. Executors—Ebenezer (my son), and Henry Davis. Witnesses—Samuel Dunn, Jonathan Dunn, Francis Dunn. Proved Oct. 3, 1766.   Lib. I, p. 26.

1769, March 2. Tireberger, George. Account by Japhet Byram and Peter Corselius, executors. Balance remaining in their hands, £9.9.8.
                                                       Lib. 13, p. 533.

1761, Jan. 21. Titus, John, of Hopewell, Hunterdon Co., yeoman; will of. Son, Samuel, plantation where I live, except what I will give to my youngest son, Benjamin; but Samuel is to pay to his brothers, John, Phillip, Joseph and Andrew, £10 each. Sons, John, Phillip, Joseph and Andrew, £20 each. Moveables given to daughters. To son, Thomas, 5 shillings. Son, Benjamin, part of the plantation. Executors—my sons, John, Phillip and Samuel. Witnesses—Timothy Titus, Moore Scott, John Guild. Proved March 3, 1761.
1761, Feb. 23. Inventory, £121.0.10, made by Timothy Smith and Timothy Titus. Lib. 11, p. 1.

1762, Sept. 9. Titus, Rebeckah, of Hopewell, Hunterdon Co.; will of. Widow of John Titus. My daughters, Rebeckah, Mary and Susannah, £5.6.8 each. Son, Thomas, a mare. Son, Benjamin, rest of stock. Executors—Andrew Titus and Benjamin Titus. Witnesses —Cornelius Slacht, Matthes Baker. Proved Nov. 1, 1762.
Lib. 11, p. 349.

1769, Oct. 14. Titus, Thomas, of Hunterdon Co. Int. Adm'r— Samuel Titus. Fellowbondsmen—Joseph Tindall and Jonathan Burroughs; all of said Co. Witness—John Barnes.
1769, Oct. 17. Inventory, made by Joseph Titus and John Van Campen. Lib. 14, p. 123.

1761, Jan. 2. Tomkins, Ichabod, of Morristown, Morris Co.; will of. Wife, Hannah, ½ of the moveable estate, and use of my real to support the children. Son, Uzel, my lands. Sons, Isaac, Robert and Nathan, £100 each, when 21. Daughters, Salome, Phebe and Huldah, £50, when 18. My wife being pregnant, that child is to have a share. Executors—Capt. John Brookfield and Gabriel Ogden, both of said town. Witnesses—Robert Goble, Jonas Goble, Amos Crane. Proved March 5, 1761.
1761, March 19. Inventory, made by Amos Crane. Lib. H, p. 17.

1765, April 26. Tomkins, Joel, of Newark, Essex Co. Int. Adm'rs —Aaron Tomkins and Joseph Tomkins, brothers of said Joel. Fellowbondsman—Benjamin Freeman; all of Newark. Lib. H, p. 541.

1764, Dec. 22. Tomkins, Mercy, of Newark, Essex Co. Int. Adm'r —Joseph Tomkins, son of said Mercy. Fellowbondsman—Aaron Tomkins; both of Newark. Witness—Lewis Ogden. Lib. H, p. 422.

1760, March 12. Tomlinson, John, of Twsp. and Co. of Gloucester, laborer; will of. My brother, Ephraim Tomlinson, my clothing and gun; and to Letisia Shivers, out of regard I have for her, the rest of my estate. Executor—Richard Thorne. Witnesses—Thomas Smith, Robert Friend Price. Proved Jan. 29, 1761.
1760, Nov. 25. Inventory, £37.5.3, made by Robert Friend Price and Samuel Clement, Jr.
1765, March 8. Account by Executor. Lib. 10, p. 387.

1767, Dec. 11. Toms, Charles, of Middlesex Co. Int. Adm'r— Michael Toms, the only son. Fellowbondsman—Henry Martin; both of said Co.
1767, Dec. 10. Renunciation by Hannah Toms, widow of Charles

Toms, late of Woodbridge, in favor of her son, Michael Toms. Witnesses—Ephraim Cutter and Jacob Pack.
1768, Jan. 4. Inventory, £27.5.2, made by Ephraim Cutter and Thomas Bloomfield. Lib. I, p. 208.

1768, April 1. Tonkin, Edward, of Springfield Twsp., Burlington Co.; will of. Son, Samuel, my plantation in Greenwich, Gloucester Co., which I purchased of James Hinchman, but, if he die, it is to be sold and the money given to my daughter-in-law, Elizabeth, wife of said son Samuel, and all the rest of my children, share and share alike. Son, John, my farm where I live. Son, Edward, the rest of land in Springfield and Mansfield; also the house where William West lives, when son is 21. Son, Israel, £1,000 when 21; also the house and lot I bought of Micajah Wills and Joseph Mullen, and the lot I bought of John Fenimore, and a lot in Burlington I bought of Edward Brooks, after his mother's death, if she chooses to live there. Son-in-law, David Clayton, £562. Son-in-law, Robert Taylor, £500. Daughter, Mary Tonkin, £500, at day of marriage. Daughter, Martha Tonkin, £500 at day of marriage. My wife, Mary, £500, and the use of the house in Burlington. To my sister-in-law, Jane Cole, £60. To St. Mary's Church in Burlington, £20, to repair the church. Residue of my estate equally between my wife, my sons, Samuel, John, Edward and Israel, and my daughters, Bathsheba, Susanna, Mary and Martha. Executors—sons, John and Edward, and I request my cousin, Daniel Ellis, to assist them. Witnesses—Samuel Rockhill, John Ridgway, Samuel Treat. Proved May 20, 1768.
Lib. 13, p. 371.
1768, April 19. Inventory, £5,749.3.18½, made by Thomas Budd and Caleb Newbold. File 8453 C.
1774, Jan. 4. Account of John Tonkin and Edward Tonkin, Ex'rs of Edward Tonkin. Lib. 14, p. 539.
1821, Oct. 30. Petition to the Legislative Council and General Assembly, made by Bathsheba Clayton, Martha Talman and Mary Carpenter (wife of Thomas Carpenter), stating that Edward Tonkin made will and left to his son, Samuel, a plantation in Greenwich and if he died it was to be sold, and money be paid to daughter-in-law, Elizabeth, wife of said Samuel, and the rest of his children, and if any children die, their share to go to the others; and he made his sons, John and Edward, Executors. Now, Samuel died on the 24th of February, 1821, without issue, and his wife, Elizabeth, died before him, and both Executors also died in the lifetime of Samuel. Therefore we, being now the only children, and the Executors being both dead, no sale can be made of the plantation, and we pray for the appointment of Trustee to make sale and divide the money according to law. Signed by Bathsheba Clayton, Thomas Carpenter, Mary Carpenter, Martha Talman.

[No date]. Tonkin, Joseph, of Deptford Twsp., Gloucester Co.; will of. If my wife, Kezia, be delivered of a child alive, then I give it all real and personal, except £500 I give to my wife. Executors—my father, Edward Tonkin and my wife. Witnesses—Caleb Bickham, Martha Scull, Ann Russell. Proved Aug. 2, 1765.
1765, July 29. Inventory, £1,146.8.10, made by Jacob Spicer and Thomas Denny. Lib. 12, p. 358.

1769, June 20. Tooker, Charles, of Elizabeth Borough, Essex Co.; will of. Son, Charles, the southeast part of my homestead; also ½ of my salt meadow; also ½ of Lot No. 102, on Stony Hill, in Somerset Co., and a small woodlot, which I bought of Ebenezer Sayre. Son, Abraham, the northwest part of my homestead, and ½ the salt meadow, and ½ of No. 102. Sons, Charles and Abraham, ½ the land I bought of Joseph Mase, and the other ½ I give to my daughters, Hannah Clawson, Elizabeth Clark and Mary Tooker, which land is at Turkey, on the Second Mountain. Daughter, Mary, is not married. To my granddaughter, Sarah Spinning, £15, when 18; also the clothing that was worn by her mother in her lifetime, as well as other things that she had. Wife, Elizabeth, the rest. Executors—my wife and son, Charles. Witnesses—Isaac Winans, Joseph Morse, Jr., Abraham Wyans. Proved Aug. 21, 1769.
1769, Aug. 26. Inventory, made by Benjamin Winans and Samuel Wood. Lib. K, p. 118.

1764, May 7. Tossey, Joseph, of Pilesgrove, Salem Co.; will of. Daughter, Hannah Tossey, £10. Daughter, Sarah Tossey, £10. Daughter, Margareta Tossey, £50. Daughter, Rebecca Tossey, £50. Executor—Captain Jacob Dubois. Witnesses—John Cregg, John Gray, Samuel Craig. Proved Sept. 1, 1765.
1765, Feb. 9. Inventory, £189.1.11, made by John Creag and Jacob Elwell. Lib. 12, p. 180.

1761, Dec. 14. Totten, Jasper, of Morristown, Morris Co. Int. Adm'rs—Lewis Winans and Richard French, both of said Co., principal creditors. Fellowbondsman—Silvanas Totten, of said Co.
1761, Dec. 10. Renunciation by Patience Totten, widow of said Jesper. Witnesses—Jonathan Elmer and Peter Fleming.
1761, Dec. 18. Inventory made by Jacob Bedell and William Parsens.
1763, Oct. 18. Three accounts filed by the Adm'rs, wherein they pay to Joseph Totten, James Totten, Samuel Totten, Salvanas Totten, Sarah Totten, Aaron French, John Totten, Salvenus Oakley, and others. Lib. H, p. 74.

1762, March 25. Totten, John, of Morris Co. Ward. Aged 18 years, and one of the children of Jasper Totten, of said Co., dec'd; makes choice of James Totten, of said Co., as his Guardian; and said James was appointed. Fellowbondsman—John Winans, of Essex Co. Lib. H, p. 78.

1769, Oct. 13. Totten, Peter, of Sowerland, Somerset Co. Int. Adm'x—Mary Totten, widow of said Peter. Fellowbondsman—Zachariah Van Voorhes; both of said Co.
1769, Oct. 16. Inventory, £282.16.10, made by Isaac Van Nuys, Jr., Roelef Terhune and Joseph Arrowsmith. Lib. K, p. 125.

1765, Oct. 15. Townley, Matthias, of Elizabeth Town, Essex Co. Ward. Son of James Townley, of said place, deceased; makes choice of Jeremiah Garthwait as his Guardian.
1765, Oct. 15. Guardian—Jeremiah Garthwait. Fellowbondsman —William Garthwait; both of said place. Lib. 12, p. 186.

CALENDAR OF WILLS—1761-1770 437

1767, Dec. 23. Toy, Daniel, of Mount Holly, Burlington Co., cordwainer; will of. My wife, Sarah, all estate after debts are paid, to educate my 5 children, viz., Elizabeth, Fradrick, Mary, John and Daniel Toy. Executors—my wife, and friend, John Clerk, is to assist her. Witnesses—Thomas Brian, Joseph Butterworth, John Woolman. Proved Jan. 30, 1768.
1768, Jan. 20. Inventory, £175.15.11, made by Joseph Butterworth and Joseph Mullen. File No. 8461 C; Lib. 13, p. 299.

1763, April 9. Toy, Elias, of Chester, Burlington Co. Int. Adm'x —Elizabeth Toy. Fellowbondsman—Henry Wood, of Gloucester Co. Witness—Joseph Morgan.
1763, Feb. 5. Inventory, £811.19.10, made by Samuel Stokes and Joseph Morgan. Lib. 11, p. 301.
1779, Account by Elizabeth Atkinson (late Elizabeth Toy), Adm'x of Elias Toy, of Chester Twsp.

1770, March 23. Toy, Margaret, of Chester, Burlington Co., spinster; will of. Cousin, Esaah Toy, 10 shillings. Cousin, John Toy, £5. My relation, Sarah Overturf, 50 shillings, when 18. To Richard Toy, son of James, 50 shillings when 21. My brother, James Toy, rest. Executors—brother, James Toy, and my friend, Thomas Vennibal. Witnesses—Joseph Morgan and James Lecony. Proved May 21, 1770.
1770, May 15. Inventory, £56.13.1, made by James Leconeny and Joseph Morgan. File No. 8825 C; Lib. 15, p. 30.

1761, April 22. Tracy, Daniel, of Alloways Creek Precinct, Salem Co. Int. Adm'x—Mary Tracy, of said place, widow. Fellowbondsman—Joseph Stretch, of said place, yeoman.
1761, April 7. Inventory, £44.16.6, made by Nathaniel Chamless and Joseph Stretch. Lib. 10, p. 436.

1762, July 3. Treadaway, Kezia, of Gloucester Co. Ward. Whereas John Treadaway, of Deptford Twsp., said Co., yeoman, died intestate, and left only one child, named, Kezia, of about 10 years; and whereas Sarah Treadaway, mother of said infant, being since deceased also, so that the Guardianship rests on me, Joshua Mills, of New Hanover Township, in Burlington Co., sawyer; I renounce, and leave it unto Joshua Lord and John Wilkins, of Deptford Twsp.
1762, July 5. Guardians—Joshua Lord and John Wilkins, both of Deptford Township, Gloucester Co., yeomen, who are to be Guardians of said Kezia; Sarah Treadaway, the mother, became Guardian, but she soon departed this life, and the Guardianship fell to Joshua Mills, uncle by the mother's side, and he renounced; therefore the above Guardians were appointed. Witness—Sarah Howell.
Lib. 11, p. 126.

1766, May 27. Treadaway, Keziah, of Deptford Twsp., Gloucester Co. Ward. Only daughter of John Treadway, of said place, yeoman, deceased, who makes choice of her friend, John Wilkins, as her Guardian.
1766, May 27. Guardian—John Wilkins. Fellowbondsman—William Wilkins, yeoman; both of said place. Witnesses—John Estaugh Hopkins and John Ladd. Lib. 12, p. 383.

1767, Oct. 15. Tresneau, Peter, of Middletown, Monmouth Co.; will of. My estate in Albany and Orange County, and in West Chester Co., in New York; also my right in the mines, lands and houses, in Twsp. of Simsberry, and my right to lands in Stratford, now in possession of David Lewis of Stratford and Simsberry, both being in Connecticut; also my right in Co. of Monmouth and Middlesex, in East Jersey, shall stand in the hands of my Executors, Agness Tresneau and John Morin Scott, of New York City. All my personal estate to remain between my widow and children, for their use, till my youngest child is of age, and then to be divided among them, but my wife is to have 1/5. Executors—said Agness Tresneau and John Morin Scott. Witnesses—Hones Vanpelt, David Watson, John Burrowes. Proved Feb. 7, 1770. Lib. K, p. 161.

1770, Nov. 1. Trimmer, Anthony, Jr., of Morris Co. Ward. Son of Anthony Trimmer, of said Co., yeoman, deceased; he has personal estate, given to him by the will of his father, and now makes choice of his friend, Thomas Fearclo, as his Guardian, till he is 21.
1770, Nov. 1. Guardian—Thomas Fearclo. Fellowbondsman—David Brown, both of said Co. Witnesses—Richard Kemble and Robert Tuite Kemble. Lib. K, p. 257.

1760, Oct. 21. Troth, Elizabeth, of Evesham, Burlington Co., widow; will of. Advanced age. To my infant granddaughter, Mary Haines, daughter of Amos Haines, dec'd, all my land in Evesham, when 21; and the profits thereof I give to my daughter, Rebeckah Haines, till she is that age, to bring up the said child; and, if she die before 21, then my daughter, Rebeckah, to have it; but, if my daughter die, then to my granddaughter, Elizabeth Cooper. Daughter, Jane Garwood, £10. My granddaughter, Jane Prickitt, £10. My granddaughter, Sarah Bishop, £10. My granddaughter, Rebeckah Garwood, £10. The rest of my grandchildren, one shilling each. My daughter, Rebeckah Haines, the remainder. Executor—friend, Isaac Evens. Witnesses—Abraham Leeds, Jacob Evens, William Troth. Proved June 22, 1761. Lib. 10, p. 215.
1761, June 19. Inventory, £544.11.6, made by Abraham Leeds and Jacob Evens.
1762, Oct. 30. Account by Executor.

1768, May 21. Troup, Robert, of Hanover, Morris Co., gentleman; will of. Children, John, Robert, Elizabeth and Eleanor, all my estate in New York and New Jersey. Elizabeth has had some goods. Executors—son, John Troup, Jr., and my son-in-law, Benjamin Johnson, and John Tuttle, of Hanover. Witnesses—William Broadwell, Jonathan Wilkison, William Diron. Proved Jan. 19, 1769.
Lib. K, p. 63.

1766, Sept. 17. Trout, John, of Monmouth Co., yeoman; will of. Wife, Mary, various goods. Daughter, Margaret, £50, and her husband is to have no part of it; and if she dies without issue, her 2 sisters, Elizabeth and Catherine, are to have it. Daughter, Elizabeth, £50. Daughter, Catherine Morris, £50. Sons, Peter, John and Jacob, rest of personal estate, and money from sale of my land. Executors—Elisha Lawrence, John Anderson, Esq., and my son, Peter. Witnesses—William Lawrence, William Morris, Thomas Fenton. Proved April 4, 1768.

1768, April 4. Renunciation by Peter Trout and John Anderson. Witnesses—Peter Schenck and Henry Waddell. Lib. I, p. 226.

1768, Nov. 9. Trowbridge, David, of Morris Twsp., Morris Co., farmer; will of. My lands and goods to be divided among my 8 children, with this reserve, that my wife, over her equal proportion, is to have her choice of one cow, and any one jade (horse) belonging to the estate, and she is to have the possession of my estate, as long as ¦she is my widow. Son, Shubal Trowbridge, has built and improved on 11 acres, and he is to have a deed for the same land. Executrix—my wife, Lydia. Witnesses—James Smyth, William Locy, John Losee. Proved Dec. 9, 1768. Lib. K, p. 58.

1770, March 19. Tucker, George, of Trenton, Hunterdon Co. Int. Adm'rs—Catherine Tucker, William Tucker and Stacy Potts; all of Trenton. Fellowbondsman—Hezekiah Howell, of said place.
1790, Aug. 20. Account by Stacy Potts, surviving Adm'r of George Tucker and Marcy Tucker, Ellet Howell and Joseph Brittain, Executors of William Tucker, who was likewise Adm'r of George Tucker. Goods were retained by Catherine Tucker, the widow of said George Tucker. Lib. 15, p. 7.

1767, Feb. 15. Tufford, Philip, of Roxbury, Morris Co.; will of. To grandson, Jurrey Staffey Tufford, and to my 2 sons, George and Adam, each 5 shillings. Wife, Catrena, rest of my estate, and, after her death, to go to my daughter, Mary Magdilen. Executors—my wife and Stuffey Derburger. Witnesses—Roelof Roelofson, Elizabeth Roelofson, Lawrance Roelofson. Proved Feb. 1, 1769.
1769, Jan. 18. Inventory, £67.7.6, made by Roelof Roelofson and John Tackerd. Lib. 14, p. 170.

1767, Feb. 13. Tuft, James, of Alloways Creek Neck, Salem Co., yeoman; will of. To son, Robert, and daughter, Jane, all of my estate, and they are to keep my son, James, as I have done, and to let him teach a school. Executor—my friend, Alexander Hill. Witnesses—Thomas Bent, Thomas Halsted, Henry Spence. Proved March 25, 1767.
1767, March 25. Inventory, £187.19.0, made by Richard Smith and William Abbott. Lib. 13, p. 171.

1770, Jan. 18. Tuft, Robert, of Lower Penns Neck, Salem Co., yeoman; will of. To eldest son, William Tuft, the part of my plantation that I bought of Daniel Taylor and his wife, Rebecca, when my son is 21. To the child my wife now goes with, the ground which I own in Salem. Son, John Tuft, the part of my plantation, which I got with my wife. To my wife all real and personal, to bring up the said children, till they are of age. Executor—my brother, Brathwait Tuft. Witnesses—Robert Kennedy, William Stretch, Giles Lambson. Proved Feb. 9, 1770.
1770, Feb. 6. Inventory, £398.2.6, made by Allen Congelton and Giles Lambson.
1774, ———, ———. Account by Braithwaite Tuft.
Lib. 15, p. 515; Lib. 16, p. 34.

1762, Feb. 18. Tuft, William, of Salem Co.; will of. Son, William Tuft, the house and lot where I live. Son, Broffet, 2 rods of land, off of the land I gave to my son, William. Moveable estate to be divided among my 3 children, Robard Tuft, Jane Griffen and Broffet Tuft. Executors—sons, William and Broffet. Witnesses—James Tuft, Balster Heil, Erasmus Kent. Proved April 17, 1762. Probate to William Tuft and Brathwait Tuft.
1762, Feb. 24. Inventory, £1,052.11.4, made by Erasmus Kent and Henry Woodnutt. Lib. 11, p. 182.

1765, Feb. 12. Tuly, Jonathan, of Mansfield Twsp., Burlington Co., yeoman; will of. Son, Thomas, a part of my plantation, which was left to me by my father, when he is 21. Son, John, a tract I bought of Joseph Kemble. Son, Joseph, the house that I live in, with the land on north side of the York road. My sons, Thomas, John and Joseph, to pay to their sister, Mary, £50. Wife, Martha, to have a small house built for her, and 6 acres. Executors—my father-in-law, Thomas Bowlby, and my wife, Martha. Witnesses—Henry Scott, Leah Ellis, John Watkinson. Proved June 9, 1768.
1768, June 9. Inventory, £367.9.0, made by Henry Scott and Abraham Scott, and sworn to by Thomas Bowlby and Martha Archer (late Martha Tuly), the Ex'rs. Lib. 13, p. 426.
1771, Nov. 11. Account by Thomas Bowlby and Martha Archer, late Martha Tuly. Lib. 14, p. 409.

1765, Sept. 18. Turner, Richard, of Perth Amboy, Middlesex Co. Int. Adm'r—William Burnet, principal creditor. Fellowbondsman—Robert King; both of said place.
1765, Sept. 16. Renunciation, by Margaret Turner, the widow. Witness—Alexander Henry. Lib. H, p. 530.

1762, Oct. 21. Tussey, Stephen, of Penns Neck, Salem Co. Int. Adm'r—John Tussey, of Cecil Co., Maryland. Fellowbondsmen—Peter Boon, of Penns Neck, and Solomon Alman, of Mannington, Salem Co., yeomen.
1762, Oct. 22. Inventory, £26.9.11, made by Peter Boon and Solomon Alman. Lib. 11, p. 278.

1762, Dec. 20. Tuttle, Abraham, of Morris Co. Int. Adm'r—Jonathan Stiles, brother-in-law, and one of the largest creditors, of said Co., yeoman. Fellowbondsman—Benjamin Brush, of Great Egg Harbor, Gloucester Co. Witness—Sarah Thomas. Lib. H, p. 271.

1768, Aug. 12. Tuttle, Ebenezer, of Hanover, Morris Co. Ward. Son of Samuel Tuttle, of said place, deceased, having real and personal estate, which needs care, makes choice of Thomas Milledge as his Guardian, till he is 21, being at the present time 17 years old.
1768, Aug. 12. Guardian—Thomas Millidge. Fellowbondsman—Enoch Beach; both of said place. Lib. I, p. 336.

1751, May 21. Tuttle, Samuel, of Hanover Twsp., Morris Co.; will of. Wife, Rachel, household goods and one cow; also the rents of my homestead, till my son, Ebenezer, is 21, when he is to have all my lands; but, if he die, then the lands to be divided among all my brothers, viz., John, Joseph, David, Moses and James, and my wife, Rachel. Executors—friends, John Tuttle and David Hitchell. Wit-

CALENDAR OF WILLS—1761-1770   441

nesses—Amos Williams, Thomas Dickson, Thomas Bates. Proved Jan. 6, 1762. Lib. H, p. 144.

1770, Feb. 27. Tweedy, Nathaniel, of Burlington Co. Int. Adm'r— William Richards, of Philadelphia, merchant. Fellowbondsman—John Cox, of said city, merchant. Witness—Esther Cox. Lib. 15, p. 3.

1762, Jan. 26, Twentyman, Joseph, of Penns Neck, Salem Co., yeoman; will of. My goods, and the tract of 116 acres to be sold, and, after debts are paid, what remains I give to my wife, Mary Twentyman, now living in Dundron, County of Cumberland, in England. Executor—Joseph Saul, of Philadelphia, chairmaker. Witnesses—Henry Sevel, Charity Savel, Thomas Pedrick. Proved April 6, 1762.
1762, April 6. Inventory, £9.3.0, made by Thomas Pedrick and Henry Sevel. Lib. 11, p. 184.

1765, March 13. Tyler, Sarah, of Alloways Creek, Salem Co. Ward. Daughter of William Tyler, of said place, yeoman, deceased, having land devised to her by her father, makes choice of John Dickeson, as her Guardian.
1765, March 13. Guardian—John Dickeson, of said place. Fellowbondsmen—Thomas Kelly, of said place, and William Abbott, of Elsinboro, said Co. Lib. 12, p. 178.

1763, March 4. Tyte, Thomas, of Monmouth Co.; will of. Wife, Grace, a warrantee to a lot, in town of Jamaica, Long Island, of 50 feet square; and a warrantee to a lot of land in Monmouth Co., of 30 acres, about 2 miles from the Court House, and all the rest of my estate. Executrix—my wife. Witnesses—Daniel Grandin, Joseph Vanmater, Jr., Samuel Throckmorton, Jr. Proved April 9, 1764.
Lib. H, p. 426.

1763, Dec. 19. Urian, Fredrick, of Greenwich Twsp., Gloucester Co., yeoman; will of. Wife, Sarah, all my personal estate, to bring up my 5 children. Executors—my wife, and my brother-in-law, Joseph Addams. Witnesses—Thomas Denny, Isaac Shute, Thomas Roberts. Proved May 26, 1764.
1764, Jan. 11. Inventory, £192.15.2½, made by Thomas Denny and Thomas Roberts. Lib. 11, p. 521.

1768, Feb. 22. Urnison, Giles, of Penns Neck, Salem Co. Ward. Son of Lawrence Urnison, of said place, yeoman; who makes choice of William Mecum, yeoman, as his Guardian till he is 21.
1769, Jan. 12. Guardian—William Mecum, of Penns Neck, Salem Co. Fellowbondsman—Andrew Sinnickson, Esq., of said place.
Lib. 13, p. 493.

1770, April 4. Vail, Isaac, of Bernards Twsp., Somerset Co.; will of. Wife, Rachel, £100. Rest of personal and real to be sold and given to my children, Samuel, James, Sarah Vail and Margaret Vail. Executors—my father-in-law, James Compton, and my brother, Daniel Vail. Witnesses—John Vail, William Cross, James Boylan. Proved April 20, 1770.
1770, April 24. Inventory, £171, made by Jeremiah Sutton and Nathaniel Ayers. Lib. K, p. 214.

1766, Feb. 28. Valentine, Elizabeth, of Borough of Elizabeth, Essex Co.; will of. Brother, Ichabod Valentine, ½ of my real and personal, and the other ½ to Roda Valentine, Sarah Pettit, Barthomew Pettit and Hanah Littell; but Ichabod is to keep their share in his hands till they are of age. Executor—my brother, Ichabod. Witnesses—Recom. Stanbery, Benjamin Stites, Jr., Jedidiah Swan. Proved May 29, 1766.
1766, March 26. Inventory, £6.9.9, made by Abraham Hampton and Recompence Stanbery. Lib. H, p. 614.

1766, March 7. Valentine, Hannah, of Borough of Elizabeth, Essex Co.; will of. Son, Ichabod Valentine, my land. To grandchildren, Rhoda Valentine, Sarah Petit and Barthewmew Petit moveable estate. Executors—son, Ichabod Valentine, and my friend, Jedidiah Swan. Witnesses—David Clark, Thomas Cushman, Jr., Jedidiah Swan. Proved May 29, 1766. Lib. H, p. 616.

1764, July 6. Valentine, Richard, of Borough of Elizabeth, Essex Co., yeoman; will of. To sons, Jonas and Ephraim, my homestead of 100 acres. Son, Obidiah, land he lives on, on north side of Stony Hill. Wife, Phebe, my said 3 sons, and my 5 daughters, Phebe, Mary, Rachel, Sarah and Elizabeth, my moveable estate. Executors—my wife and 3 sons. Witnesses—Samuel Johnson, Lydia Johnson, William Willcock. Proved March 25, 1766. Lib. H, p. 597.

1761, Jan. 22. Vallantine, Ichabod, of Borough of Elizabeth, Essex Co.; will of. Wife, Hannah, ⅓ my land and moveable, forever; and to son, Ichabod, ⅓, and daughter, Elizabeth Valantine, ⅓. Executors—said children. Witnesses—Isaac Stanbery, Recom. Stanbery, Jedidiah Swan. Proved May 29, 1766.
1766, March 26. Inventory, £88.16.3, made by Abraham Hampton, Esq., and Recompence Stanbery; and by James Miller as clerk. (The testator died Feb. 23). Lib. H, p. 618.

1761, Nov. 27. Van Aken, Isaac, of Montague Twsp., Sussex Co., yeoman. Int. Adm'r—Abraham Isaac Van Aken. Fellowbondsman—William Ennes; both of said Co., yeomen.
1761, Nov. 7. Inventory, £434.8.0, made by Jacob Westbrook and William Ennes.
1761, Nov. 21. Renunciation by Abraham Van Kampen and Rachel Van Campen, in favor of Abraham Isaac Van Aken. Lib. 11, p. 286.

1762, Sept. 2. Van Allen, Andrew, of Saddle River Precinct, Bergen Co., yeoman; will of. To John Van Allen, son of my brother, Garret Van Allen, deceased, £15. Wife, Eleanor, all real and personal, and, at her death, to daughter Catharine Van Allen. Executors—my wife, Isaac Bohart, of Bergen Co., and John Parsil, of New Hamstead in New York. Witnesses—Robert Hogg, Jacob Mead, Jacob Garreson. Proved April 18, 1763. Lib. H, p. 386.

1769, June 26. Van Allen, Dirik, of Somerset Co. Int. Adm'x—Catharine Johannah Vah Allen. Fellowbondsman—Dirk Van Veghten; both of said Co. Witness—Ryck Van der Bilt. Adm'x sworn at New Brunswick.
1769, Aug. 8. Inventory, £1268.11.10, of estate of Dirck Van Allen, of New Brunswick, made by James Hude and John Voorhees.

1787, March 20. Adm'r—Peter Dumont. Fellowbondsman—Ephraim Loree; both of Somerset Co. The said Dumont is Adm'r of all left unadministered by Catharine Johannah Van Allen, who is also dead. Above Adm'r was sworn at Millstone.
Lib. K, p. 112; Lib. 29, p. 440; File No. 4655 L.

1767, Sept. 3. Van Alstyne, Mathew, of New York City, merchant; will of. Wife, Sarah, use of the house and lot where I live, and income of rest of real and personal, to support such of my children as shall remain unmarried. Son, Abraham Van Alstyne, being my eldest son, £5. Son, Mathew, £500, which will be equal to what I gave Abraham. To each of my daughters, Sarah, Helena and Catherine, £400, which is equal to what I advanced to my daughter, Mary, as an outset. Land to be sold. Wife, Sarah, £400. Rest of money to my wife, Sarah, daughter, Mary, and her husband, son Abraham, daughters Sarah, Helena and Catherine, son Mathew. Executors—wife, Sarah, and my daughters, Sarah and Helena, and son Abraham. Witnesses—Jeronemus Alstyne, John Wylley, John McKesson. Proved April 15, 1769. Lib. K, p. 85.

1760, April 14. Van Blarkom, Gisbert, of Bergen Co.; will of. Son, John, 20 shillings as birthright. Wife, Antie, real and personal while widow. Son, Hendrick, ½ of my plantation where I live on Saddle River, and he is to pay £40 to Lena Perdon, and £40 to Antie Vreland. Son, Jacobus, ½ the land with the house, and he to pay £40 to his sister, Lena Perdon, and £40 to his sister, Antie Vreland. I gave to son John a deed for his land, and a deed to son Antone for his, and also to son William. Executors—my wife and Jacob Perdon. Witnesses—Pieter Kip, Jacobus Hynsman, Reinier V. Giese. Proved March 3, 1764. Lib. H, p. 408.

1762, May 24. Van Boskerck, Andries, of Bergen Co., yeoman; will of. Wife, Margaret, two of my slaves, and as much of my goods as she thinks fit; also the profits of my real, and, after her death, said real to be sold, as also the rest of personal estate, and the money therefrom to be divided as follows. To daughter, Geertie, 1/6 part, and 1/6 part to 4 children of said daughter, Geertie, and 1/6 part to daughter, Tryntie, and 1/6 part to the 3 children of said daughter, Tryntie, and 1/6 part to Barent Van Horne and my 5 grandchildren, the children of my late daughter, Rachel, and 1/6 part to the said Barent Van Horne and my said last grandchildren. Executors—my wife, and my friends, Helmach Vreeland, Esq., and William Duglass, Esq., of Richmond Co., N. Y. Witnesses—Silas Bedell, Joseph Bedell, Jr., Dirck Marlatt. Proved Dec. 23, 1762. Lib. H, p. 208.

1765, Sept. 14. Van Buskirk, Jacobus, of Bergen township and Co., yeoman; will of. Eldest son, Peter, a part of my homestead joining land of my brother, Andries, deceased, and a piece of salt meadow joining Kill Van Kull. Son, John, the north side of plantation, that joins York Bay. Wife, Margaret, the profit of said land while my widow; also the use of the moveable estate. Executors—my wife and said sons, Peter and John. Witnesses—Daniel Smith, Deborah Smith, Abraham Clark, Jr. Proved Feb. 18, 1767. Lib. I, p. 99.

1766, Oct. 26. Van Campen, Abraham, Esq., of Walpack Twsp., Sussex Co.; will of. I have already made deeds of gift. Son, John, 30 acres of land adjacent to Buttermilk Falls, in Lower Smithfield Twsp., Northampton Co., Penn'a. Son, Benjamin, a tract I bought of the heirs of Moses Dupui, on which his dwelling stands, in said Lower Smithfield, of 100 acres. Daughter, Maria, the wife of John Dupui, £400. To daughter, Catherine, the wife of Benjamin Dupui, £400. To daughter, Susanna, the wife of Thomas Romine, £400. Sons, Abraham and Moses, cows, horses, etc. Wife, Rachel, £12 yearly. Executors—sons, John and Abraham. Witnesses—Daniel de Pue, Morgan De Sha, Robert Severs.

1766, Oct. 26. Codicil. Witnesses—same as in will. Proved May 25, 1767.

1767, May 25. Inventory, £1296.12.0, made by Johannis Cornelius Westbrook and Christian Kress. Lib. 12, p. 458.

1765, Oct. 28. Vance, Patrick, of Middlesex Co. Int. Adm'r—William Vance. Fellowbondsman—David Gosling; both of said Co.

1765, Oct. 28. Renunciation by Elizabeth Vance, widow of Patrick, in favor of her son, William.

1765, Dec. 10. Inventory, £523.17.1, made by Robert Montgomerie and Samuel Forman. Lib. H, p. 641.

1765, Sept. 1. Van Cleve, Richard, of Freehold Twsp., Monmouth Co., yeoman; will of. Wife, Elizabeth, all real and personal, while she is my widow. Sons, Benjamin and John, my whole estate, but they are to pay £400 to their 4 sisters, Elizabeth, Hendiracha, Eleanor and Mary. Executors—friend, John Vanbrakle, of Freehold, carpenter, and sons, Benjamin and John. Witnesses—John Clark, Gershom Bullman, Thomas Bullman. Proved April 18, 1766.

Lib. H, p. 599.

1724, Oct. 5. Vandelinda, Peter, of Hackinsack, Bergen Co., yeoman; will of. Wife, Geesche, real and personal during her life, and, after her death, the real to son Roulef, he paying £400 to his 4 sisters, Susannah Vandilinda, Uselche Vandelinda, Janneche Vandelinda, and Vjche Vandelinda. Executors—friends, Hendrick Vandelinda and Caspares Westerfelt. Witnesses—Richard Edsall, Jan Zabrowsky, Roelef Westerfelt. Proved Sept. 29, 1766. Lib. I, p. 48.

1766, Sept. 9. Adm'r, Johannes Terhune, of Bergen Co., with will annexed, Hendrick Vandelinda being deceased, and the other Executor, Carpares Westervelt, having removed from the Province without acting.

1767, July 29. Inventory, £2.10.0, "which is yet unadministered by the Executors," made by Jan Boogert and Pieter Boogaert.

1761, June 5. Vanderbeak, Paulus, of New Barbadoes, Bergen Co.; will of. Son, Conradus, £1 as his birthright, and I give him my land at Weremis, which I bought of Thomas Van Boskirk, and, after his death, to his 3 sons, Paulus, Urian and Abraham, and my said 3 grandsons are to pay to their sister, Cornelia, enough to make her share equal. Son, Isaac, land which I bought of John Berdan and Nicholas Johnse Romyn, and, after his death, to his sons, Barent and Isaac. His other son, Paulus, has been provided for. The said Barent and Isaac shall pay to the other children of my son, Isaac (except Paulus), enough to make their part equal. Personal estate to be

CALENDAR OF WILLS—1761-1770 445

sold, except a silver tea pot to my granddaughter, Jane, the daughter of my daughter, Eltje Kipp. Money to be paid to the children of deceased son Jacob. Executors—son, Isaac, friend, Peter Zabriske, grandson, Abraham Kipp. Witnesses—Jacob Zabrishei, John Demaree, D. Isaac Browne. Proved April 3, 1762. Lib. H, p. 150.
1762, March 30. Inventory, £213.10.0, made by Hendrick Van Giesen and Jacob Titsort.

1766, April 9. Vanderbeck, Paulus, of Pequannock, Morris Co.; will of. To John Deboog, son of my daughter, Marytje, deceased, land where he lives, and also the land as his father, Garret Deboog, in his lifetime did possess. Daughter, Elizabeth, my house lot where I live; but the east end of my dwelling is to belong to my stepdaughter, Debora Berry, during her life. Rest of my lands to my daughters, Catlyntje and Elizabeth. Step-daughter, Debora Berry, the room in the east end of my house, and £300. Executors—Reverend David Marinus and Peter Rome, Jr. Witnesses—Marthe Berry, Paulus Berry, Samuel Roome. Proved Aug. 19, 1766. Lib. I, p. 62.

1762, Jan. 16. Vander Beek, Jaques, upon the South "Brence," Somerset Co.; will of. To wife, Mary, the goods she brought with her; and then the real and rest of personal to be sold. Wife, Mary, to have £50. Son, Andrew, £50. Rest to my wife, eldest daughter, Adriana, Doritia, Mary and son Andrew. Executors—wife, Mary, brother-in-law, Hendrick Middelswart, and brother-in-law, Abraham Ten Eyck. Witnesses—John Stryker, Denyse Stryker, Barnardus Ver Bryck. Proved Oct. 27, 1762. Lib. H, p. 195.

1764, Sept. 10. Vanderbelt, Denice, of Somerset Co. Int. Adm'x—Sarah Vanderbelt, widow of Denice. Fellowbondsman—Cornelius Rappeyle; both of said Co. Lib. H, p. 367.

1742, July 16. Vanderhoof, Cornelius, of Hackinsack, Bergen Co., yeoman; will of. Elizabeth, my wife, all real and personal, while widow. Eldest son, Johanis, to assist my wife on the plantation where I live. Son, Lourence, lands as per my deed to him, after death of wife, he paying £200 to my children, viz., son, Johanis, daughter, Geertie Earle, son, Lourence, my daughter, Dorety Bomgaert, my daughter, Catherin Vanderhooff, son, Jacob, son, Cornelius, daughter, Mally Vanderhoof, son, Egburt, and daughter, Jannetie Vanderhoof. Executors—wife, Elizabeth, and friends, Jacobus Blinckerhoof and Jacob Oldwatter. Witnesses—David Demarest, David Lockerman, William Earle. Proved May 28, 1765.
Lib. H, p. 512.

1761, Aug. 5. Vanderipe, Mattis, of New Brunswick, Middlesex Co.; will of. Real and personal to be sold and money put to interest, and money due to be given to my wife, Jane, to bring up my younger children, namely, Sarey, William and Elizabeth. To oldest children, Jane and Letey, to have a share. Executors—my wife and Andrew McDowell. Witnesses—David Gano, James Patten, Michael Snatterly. Proved Sept. 10, 1761.
1761, Sept. 16. Inventory, £28.2.2, made by George Hance and David Gano, of the personal estate of Mathias Vanderipe.
1762, Account made by Jeane Barclay, formerly widow and Executrix of Mathias Vanderipe. Lib. H, p. 41.

1769, Nov. 8. Vander Pool, John, of Essex Co. Int. Adm'x—Apphia Vander Pool, widow of said John. Lib. K, p. 143.

1766, Sept. 18. Van Derripe, Mathias, of Freehold Twsp., Monmouth Co.; will of. Sons, John and Mathias, the plantation I live on. To son, Richard, £5. Daughter, Ann Boyce, £50. Daughter, Mary Campbell, one heifer. Daughter, Jane Van Derripe, £60. John and Mathias are to provide for my wife, Mary. Executors—son, John, daughter, Jane, and my son-in-law, Adam Boyce. Witnesses—Benjamin Clark, Benjamin Kallam, O. Herbert. Proved Nov. 6, 1766.
1771, Dec. 21. Account filed by Adam Boice, one of the Executors. (The account of the inventory as filed, was £33.6.0). Lib. I, p. 19.

1768, Nov. 12. Van Derveer, Joseph, of Sowerland, Somerset Co.; will of. Wife, Catrina, bed, etc. Son, Jacob, £40. Wife, one-third of rest. To my children, Jacob and Femetye, each ⅓ of my estate. Children are to stay with their mother till they are of age. My wife is to have the furniture she brought. Executors—my "father, Jacob Vanderveer, Johanes Vanderveer, brother, Grades Beekman, and my brother, John Vanderveer." Witnesses—Peter Staats, John Van Nuys, Peter Doty. Proved March 3, 1769.
1769, Feb. 27. Inventory made by Jacob Vander Veer, Gerodus Beekman and John Vanderveer, the Executors, and by Joseph Arrismith and Abraham Staats, the appraisers. Lib. K, p. 181.

1760, Dec. 26. Vandevier, Henry, of Penns Neck, Salem Co.; will of. Daughter, Mary Vandevier, my lands and moveables. I desire that John Beetle and Christiana, his wife, may take care of Mary till she is 21. Executors—said John and Christiana Beetle. Witnesses—William Runard, William Beetle, William Hutson. Proved Jan. 4, 1762.
1761, Jan. 7. Inventory, £26.16.6, made by Thomas Crawford and Samuel Whitehorne. Lib. 11, p. 181.

1765, March 29. Vandorn, Rachel, (late Rachel Longstreet) of Monmouth Co. Int. Adm'r—William Vandorn, her husband. Fellowbondsman—John Vandorn, of Morris Co. Lib. H, p. 419.

1728, Dec. 20. Van Dyck, Carl, of Shrewsbury, Monmouth Co., yeoman; will of. To wife, Elizabeth, the profits of my farm, and sons, John and Thomas, to provide her fire wood. **Eldest son, John, the** west ½ of my plantation, which joins Francis Borden. Son, Thomas, the other ½, which joins Isaac Horne. To my sons the island called the Great Meadow Island. To the children of my son Aart, late of the Island of Bermuda, deceased, £60. My daughter, Gertye Romine, £50. To daughter, Annica Van Wey, £50. Executors—sons, John and Thomas. Witnesses—Jacob Dennis, Benjamin Wollcott, Nathaniel Parker. Proved Sept. 17, 1764. Lib. H, p. 455.

1763, March 16. Van Dyck, Hendryck, of Western Precinct, Somerset Co., yeoman; will of. Wife, Margaret Van Dike, tables, etc. Eldest son, Domenecus, £3. My children, not of age, to be bound out. Estate to be sold and interest to wife, while my widow, and then to be divided among my sons and daughters. Executors— my wife, my son-in-law, Abraham Du Boy, and my friend, Peter

Schenk. Witnesses—Garret Van Arsdalen, Joris Bergen. Proved May 26, 1763.
1763, May 17. Inventory, £127.5.6, made by Philip Van Arsdalen, Garret Van Arsdalen and Albert Voorhees. Lib. H, p. 260.

1757, April 12. Van Dyck, John, of Corporation of New Brunswick, Middlesex Co., yeoman; will of. Eldest son, John, the farm in Somerset Co., where he lives, which I bought of Gershom Wiggins, of about 230 acres. Son, Ruloef, the farm where he lives in Somerset Co., of 230 acres, which I bought of widow Thomsin Hollinshead and Francis Hollinshead, and partly of Thomas Leonard, Esq. Son, Matthias, the farm where he lives at Maples Town, in Middlesex Co., which I bought of Thomas South, of 200 acres; also £50 to be paid him by my son, Isaac. Son, Simon, farm where he lives, near Fresh Pond, in Middlesex Co., of 300 acres, which I bought of Andrew Johnston, Esq. Son, Isaac, the farm where he lives, at Maples Town, of 264 acres, which I bought of Benjamin Pridmore, and partly of Frederick Dolhagen. Son, Jacob, that land near Rocky Hill, in Somerset Co., which I bought of John Harrison, of 150 acres; also tract near same place, of 50 acres, which I bought of Thomas Yates, Esq.; also 35 acres adjoining it, that I bought of Thomas Soden. To my 3 daughters, Tuentje (wife of Johannes Emans), Catharine (wife of Gerrardus Beekman) and Ann (wife of Albert Voorhees), £250 to each. Wife, Ann, my homestead farm, where I live, of 600 acres, which I bought partly of John Moss, and partly of Benjamin Harrison; and 80 acres of woodland, which I bought of Samuel Drake; also rest of real and personal estate; and, after her death, all to be sold, and the money I give to my children, John, Ruloef, Mathias, Simon, Isaac, Jacob, Tuentje, Catharine and Ann. Executors—wife, Ann, and sons, John, Ruloef, Mathias, Simon, Isaac and Jacob. Witnesses—Jacob Bergen, Peter Berrien, John Berrien. Proved Jan. 25, 1765. Lib. H, p. 484.

———. **Vandyke, Jacobus;** will of. (Not in English). Wife, Annate Van Dyck. Executrix—said wife. Witnesses—John Kingsland, Ann Kingsland, Jacob Kidmy. Proved Feb. 19, 1761.
1761, Feb. 25. Inventory, £71.8.0, made by John Kingsland and Thomas Cadmus, Jr., appraisers, and Hanah Van Diyke, the Executrix. Lib. G, p. 377.

1761, Aug. 7. Vaneman, Lawrence, of Upper Penns Neck, Salem Co., weaver. Int. Adm'x—Hannah Vaneman, widow. Fellowbondsmen—Robert Howard and William Reynolds, cordwainers; all of said place.
1759, May 28. Inventory, £37.18.3, made by William Ronald and Robert Howard. Lib. 10, p. 435.

1762, July 26. Van Emburgh, Gideon, of Hackinsack, Bergen Co. Int. Adm'r—Abraham Van Emburgh, of New Barbadoes Neck, said Co., brother of said Gideon. Fellowbondsman—Thomas Griffith, of Second River.
1762, Nov. 5. Account of goods sold at vendue, by Isaac Kingsland; totals sum of £16.4.3.
[No date]. Inventory of meat, clothing, "slay," etc., made by Abraham Van Emburgh, of £13.11.1. Lib. H, p. 185.

1760, May 3. Van Emburgh, Guisbert, of New Barbadoes, Bergen Co.; will of. Wife, Ann, to remain in the house in which I live at New Barbadoes Neck, and have use of lands for 7 years, to maintain my children. Son, Abraham, ½ my land where I live, that is next to Col. John Schuyler. My 3 sons, Guisbert, Simeon and Jacob, the other ½. Executors—my said sons. Witnesses—John Schuyler, Abraham Pier, Samuel Brown.

1760, May 3. Codicil. All my land which I have at Hackinsack to be sold, and the money applied for the use of my three children, Elizabeth, John and Adoniah. Witnesses—John Schuyler, Abraham Peir, Samuel Brown. Proved July 26, 1762. Lib. H, p. 275.

1761, April 20. Inventory, £134.6.6, made by Abraham Van Ripe and Garrabrant Garrabrants.

1761, June 9. Van Eydersteyn, Casparus Taudus, of Bergen Co. Int. Adm'r—Tadeus Van Eydersteyn, heir-at-law, of said Co. Fellowbondsman—John Vreeland, of Acquacknung, Essex Co. Witness—Lewis Ogden.

1757, June 8. Inventory, £91.17.6, made by Isaac Kingsland and John Vreland, as appraisers, and Tadeus Van Eydersteyn, as Adm'r.
Lib. H, p. 14.

1764, June 16. Van Giesen, Hendrick, of Essex Co., farmer; will of. Wife, Hendrica, my real and personal estate. Executrix—said wife. Witnesses—Dirk Joralemon, Henry King, John Joudinot. Proved May 18, 1765. Lib. H, p. 526.

1768, Feb. 9. Van Giesen, Hendrica, widow of Hendrick Van Giesen, of Essex Co.; will of. Nephew, Fransose Van Winckle, £50. Niece, Anoiche, the wife of Hendrick Van Blarracham, £50. My house and land, where I live, to be appraised. Rest of real and personal to go to my brothers and sisters, Nicholas and Fransose Van Dykes, and the widow Bradbury and Van Winkle, share and share alike. Executors—brothers, Nicholas and Fransose Van Dykes. Witnesses—Mary Burnet, Mary Wane, William Burnet. Proved Feb. 16, 1768. Lib. I, p. 260.

1767, July 15. Van Giesen, Renier, of Totawag, in Bergen Co., yeoman; will of. Wife, Catrintie, use of all estate while widow. Brother, Derck, what she leaves. Executors—wife, Catrintee, my brother, Dirck, and John Roelef Vanhouton, all of Bergen Co. Witnesses—George Reyerse, Gerrebrant Vanhouten and Hellemigh. Proved Oct. 26, 1768. Lib. K, p. 4.

1764, Aug. 23. Van Gorden, Hendrick, of Sussex Co. Int. Adm'x—Leonora Van Gorden. Fellowbondsmen—Hezekiah Dunn and Amos Pettit; all of said Co. Lib. 12, p. 233.

1759, Nov. 26. Vanhist, Ranier, of Supana, in Penns Neck, Salem Co., Gent.; will of. I wish to be decently buried by the side of my ancestors. Wife, Mary Vanhist, my plantation I live on, while my widow; after wife's death or marriage, plantation is to be for Syntha Cash. Grandson, Ranier Vanhist, £25. Granddaughter, Gartrud Vanhist, £25. My wife and my 2 daughters, Syntha Cash and Bar-

bary Sinclar, to have my slaves. Executors—my wife, and my sons-in-law, Thomas Cash and Joseph Sinckler. Overseers—Joshua Thompson, Edward Caseby and Andrew Sinnickson. Witnesses—John Hill, Daniel Lambson, John Marshall.
1763, April 25. Codicil. Daughter, Barbary Sinkler, to have £150 more as a legacy. Witnesses—John Van Culin, Andrew Sinnickson, William Robinson. Proved May 9, 1763.
1763, May 18. Inventory, £1080.5.10, made by Edward Keasbey, Joshua Thompson and Andrew Sinnickson. Lib. 11, p. 390.

1763, Feb. 19. Van Horn, Cornelius, of New York City; will of. Eldest brother, Abraham Van Horn, of New Jersey, tanner and shoemaker all my real and personal. Executors—my friend, William McKim, of New York, innkeeper; Abraham Van Horn and John Jones, also of said City. Witnesses—James Lent, Mary Watson, Andrew Anderson. Proved March 2, 1763. Lib. H, p. 226.

1733, May 26. Van Horn, Derrick Barent, of Saddle River, Hackinsack Township, Bergen Co., yeoman; will of. Eldest son, Barent, a lot of land on the Great Pond. Son, Garret, £21.13.4. Third son, John, £21.13.4. Eldest daughter, Gertje, £21.13.4. Second daughter, Leah, the like sum. Third daughter, Nelsie, like sum. To the said children my land at Wagrawe in Bergen Co. My wife, Elizabeth. Executors—my brothers, Gerret Gerretse and John Gerretse. Witnesses—William Santfordt Van Emburgh, John Nefeus, William Howard. Proved Aug. 27, 1768.
1768, Aug. 27. Adm'rs—Barent Van Horn and John Van Horn, as Executors named in will are deceased. Lib. I, p. 332.
1768, Nov. 7. Inventory, £262.10.0, made by Dierck Van Giesen and Hassel Peterse.

1768, Feb. 19. Van Horne, Cornelius, of Somerset Co., gentleman; will of. Wife, Elizabeth, use of all estate. Son, Philip, one half of the farm where I live, which contains 1,102 acres. Son, John, the other half. Rest of lands to said sons. Philip has children, Cornelius, William, Philip, John, Mary, Elizabeth, Cornelia and Violetta. Son John has children, Hannah, Elizabeth and Catharine. Executrix—my said wife. Witnesses—Isaac Brokaw, Coonrod Ten Eick, Jr., Andrew Kirkpatrick. Proved May 23, 1770.
1771, Sept. 9. List of goods made; below which was the statement that Elizabeth Van Horne had lately become blind. Lib. K, p. 381.

1760, Oct. 29. Van Horne, James, of Middlesex Co.; will of. Eldest son, John, ½ of my personal and real, and and a lot of negros; also ½ of his late mother's things, when he is 21. Son, James, the other ½, when he is 21. My body to be buried in the vault, on Smith's hill, near my late wife, Margaret, deceased. Executors—my nephews, James McEvers and William Cockeroft, both of New York City, merchants, and my friend, John Berrien, of Rockey Hill. Witnesses—James Cebra, Catherine Cebra, Catharina Van Horne. Proved April 20, 1761.
1761, May 18. Inventory, £136.17.9, made at Rocky Hill, by Jacob Beryer and Henry Crusee.
1761, March 16. Inventory, £1449.7.0, made at Dover Farm, by J. Burrowes and Lewis Forman. Lib. G, p. 371.

29

1769, May 16. Van Houten, Dirck, of Achquechnonk, Essex Co., yeoman; will of. Son, Gerrebrand, that land joining Dirrick Van Gieson and Passaic River; also ½ of the land on which he and my son, Helmich, now dwell. Son, Helmich, ½ of the land where Gerrebrand and Helmich live. Son, Jacob, the ½ of the land in the Patent, in Bergen Co. Grandson, Dirk Van Houten, son of Jacob, the last lot. To my 3 sons my right in the brew house and brew kettle, on the farm of my brother, Jacob. To my 4 children, to wit., Gerrebrand Van Houten, Helmich Van Houten, Marritje Thomasse and Jannitje Sip, all the mines and minerals on my lands. To my 2 daughters, £100 each. Executors—sons, Gerrebrand and Helmich. Witnesses—David Marinus, Derick Vreland, Derick Van Ripen. Proved Dec. 16, 1769.   Lib. K, p. 154.

1762, June 16. Van Houten, Roelef, of Bergen Co., yeoman; will of. Wife, Fytje, use of real and personal while my widow, and, at her death, my lands to my sons, Robert, Johannes and Cornelus. Personal estate to all my children, viz., Helmogh, Eachje (now wife of Jacob Spier), Robert, Johannes, Cornelus, Geertruy (now wife of Manes Van Wagenen), Catelyntie (now wife of Frans Post). Witnesses—George Vreland, Teunis Dey, Dierck Van Giesen.
1769, July 6. Codicil. Executors—sons Robert, Johannis and Cornelus. Witnesses—Dierck Van Giesen, Theunis Dey, John Vanwincle. Proved Dec. 1, 1770.   Lib. K, p. 294.

1753, Sept. 7. Van Iman, Garret, of Gloucester Co.; will of. Being the son of John. Wife, Christian, my moveable estate, and use of real while my widow; after which the land is to be to my 4 daughters. Executors—brother-in-law, Thomas Denny, and William Mickle, Esq. Witnesses—Alexander Randall, William Williams, Garret Vaneman. Proved June 9, 1761.
1761, July 24. Inventory, £140.4.6, of goods of "Garret Vaneman," of Greenwich Township, made by John Bright and John Irwen.
   Lib. 11, p. 90.

1758, March 4. Vaniman, Jacob, of Penns Neck, Salem Co., yeoman; will of. I wish to be buried by the side of my ancestors. To my son-in-law, Sinnick Sinnickson, all my lands. My personal estate I give to my wife, Ann, and son-in-law, Sinnick Sinnickson. Executors—my said wife and said son in law, and my friend, Andrew Sinnickson. Witnesses—John Marshall, George Howell, Rebecca Richmond, Catherine Bilderback. Proved March 17, 1763.
1763, March 11. Inventory, £135.0.7, made by Francis Miles and Peter Bilderback.   Lib. 11, p. 395.

1770, June 29. Vankirk, John, of Freehold, Monmouth Co., yeoman; will of. Son, John, £30. Son, Peter, that land I bought of John Sutphin. Son, Mathias, the land I bought of John Morehead, in Cranbury. Son, James, the other lands, except 25 acres which I will leave to my daughter, Anna. Daughter, Anna, 25 acres, where she lives, and £150. Son, Peter, £25. Daughter, Alice, £200. Grandsons, John and Stephen House, £200, when 21. My children are John, Peter, Mathias, James, Stephen, Anna, Alice and Sarah. Daughter, Sarah, £200. Son, Stephen, £30. Executors—son, James; and my brothers-in-law, John Van Brackle and Stephen Van Brackle. Witnesses—Arthur Honce, David House, Thomas Bullman. Proved July 10, 1770.
   Lib. K, p. 223.

CALENDAR OF WILLS—1761-1770   451

1758, March 7. Van Mater, John, of Middletown, Monmouth Co., yeoman; will of. Wife, Eitie, all my estate, and, after her decease, to my son, Chrineyonce Vanmater, £100 and Bible. Son, Richard, £100. Sons, Chrineyonce Van Mater, Richard Van Mater, and Guisbert Van Mater, and my daughters, Yonnechy Sutfan, Nelly Vanlevy, Eitie Sutfan, Mary Van Mater, Caty Van Mater, Anne Van Hater and Charity Van Mater, all my moveable estate, except my negro James, to be for my son, Guisbert. Son, Guisbert, all my lands, and he is to maintain my son John, as long as he shall live. Executors—sons, Chrineyonce, Richard and Guisbert. Witnesses—Benjamin Lefferts, Peter Lefferts, John Polhemus. Proved April 1, 1761.
1761, April 25. Inventory made by, Benjamin Van Mater, Cyrenius Van Mater and Joseph Van Mater.   Lib. G, p. 413.

1766, Sept. 21. Van Matre, Chryne, of Middletown Twsp., Monmouth Co.; will of. Wife, Mary, my bed and 2 cows. Son, John, £5 and Bible. Rest to be sold and divided between my wife, Mary, and my 6 children, to wit., John, Anne, Gysbert, Isaac, Ida and Nelly. Executors—my brother, Gysbert Van Matre, and brother-in-law, Isaac Sutphen. Witnesses—Auris Vanderbelt, O. Herbert, Gideon Crawford. Proved Oct. 17, 1766.
1766, Oct. 18. Inventory, £504.16.7, made by, Aurus Vanderbelt, Jr., Thomas Hunn and Lewis Forman.   Lib. I, p. 21.

1770, April 1. Van Middlesworth, John, of Somerset Co., yeoman; will of. Wife, Maritje, a negro man. My Goddaughter, Famitje Brokaw, daughter of Brogun Brokaw, £100. Granddaughter, Sarah Veghte, daughter of my late son-in-law, Hendrick Veghte, deceased, £400. Wife, Maritje, rest of real and personal. Granddaughter, Jacamintje, daughter of my said son-in-law Hendrick Veghte, and now wife of Peter Wikoff, 300 acres of my farm, after my wife's death. Granddaughter, Sarah Veghte, 350 acres of said farm. The rest of the farm and Robinson's Island, I give to my grandson, Rynier Veghte, son of my son-in-law, Hendrick Veghte, deceased. Rest of my estate to my 3 grandchildren, the said Rynier, Jacamintje and Sarah. Executors—wife, Maritje, and my friends, Hendrick Van Middlesworth, Jacob Van Noordstrand and Peter Dumont (son of Abraham). Witnesses—Abraham Dumon, Bergon Brokaw, Barnard Lagrange. Proved April 18, 1770.   Lib. K, p. 193.

1763, June 4. Vannatta, Ann, of Oxford Twsp., Sussex Co., widow; will of. Son, Benjamin Vannatta, all the money that may be due on bond that was given by my children for my support, which bond is in the hands of John Reading, one of the Council. Daughter, Hannah Robart, my apparel. Executors—son, Benjamin, and John Vannest. Witnesses—William Harding, John Vannatta, Jr., Jonas Abbitt. Proved March 24, 1764.
1764, March 24. Renunciation by John Vannest.   Lib. 12, p. 1.

1753, Jan. 5. Vanneman, Garret, of Pilesgrove, Salem Co., yeoman; will of. Wife, Mary, the ½ of my plantation, where I live. Son, John, the other half; also 6½ acres I bought of Andrew Peterson; also 200 acres I bought of Penn. Son, Andrew, the plantation where he lives, of 100 acres, which I bought of Thomas Procter, and the other part I bought of Penn. My son, John, is to pay my daughter, Mary, £15, and daughter, Sara, £15, and daughter, Rebecca, £15, and daughter, Regeena, £15, when they are of age. Daughters, Elizabeth, Mary, Sarah, Rebecca and Regeena, to have goods. Executors—sons, John and Andrew. Witnesses—Nathaniel Parr, Samuel Linch, Jr., Andrew Vanneman. Proved March 23, 1761.

1761, Jan. 12. Inventory, £337.14.9, made by Samuel Linch and John Helm. Lib. 11, p. 6.

1765, March 8. Vanneman, Isaac, of Salem Co. Ward. Son of John Vanneman, of said Co., deceased; having lands devised to him by his father, makes choice of Jonas Keen as his Guardian, till he is 21.

1765, March 8. Guardian—Jonas Keen. Fellowbondsmen—Andrew Vennaman and Peter Keen; all of Pilesgrove, said Co. Lib. 12, p. 232.

1761, May 26. Vanneman, Israel, of Penns Neck, Salem Co., yeoman; will of. To Daniel Vanneman the land I purchased of William Sumrill, of 50 acres, joining to land where I live. To Peter Vanneman, my brother-in-law, ½ my moveable estate; and the other ½ to my said brother-in-law, Daniel Vanneman. Executor—John Vanneman. Witnesses—Thomas Allen, James Thomas, Robert Howard. Proved March 19, 1762.

1762, March 19. Adm'r—Thomas Allen, of Pilesgrove, Salem Co., with will annexed, the executor having died before probate. Fellowbondsman—William Beetle, of Penns Neck, said Co., yeoman.

1761, Aug. 1. Inventory, £39.18.0, made by Samuel Linch and Samuel Linch, Jr. Lib. 11, p. 191.

1762, Jan. 4. Vanneman, John, of Pilesgrove, Salem Co., yeoman; will of. Wife, Mary, ⅓ of the moveable estate. Son, Isaac, the place where I live, and 6½ acres of marsh on Salem Creek, and a meadow on Twopenny Run. Son, Garret, the rest of 200 acres on Twopenny Run and 12 acres that I bought of William Peters and Thomas Harris. Son, John, 62 acres that I bought of Peters and Harris, when he is 21. Daughters, Cristian, Rebecca, Sarah, Joannah and Mary, rest of moveable estate, when they come of age. Executors—my wife, and my brother, Andrew Vanneman. Witnesses—Jeremiah Lounsberry, Joseph Wood, Samuel Linch, Jr. Proved June 16, 1762.

1762, April 19. Inventory, £216.14.3, made by Samuel Linch and Robert Clark. Lib. 11, p. 185.

1761, Oct. 20. Vanneman, Joseph, of Gloucester Co. Ward. Son of Garret Vanneman of said Co. Guardian—Hugh Hollinshead, of Chester Twsp., Burlington Co., yeoman, who is uncle to said Joseph Vanneman. Fellowbondsman—Joseph Hackney, of said Chester, yeoman. Witness—Samuel Allinson. File No. 7077C.

1770, Dec. 29. Vanneman, Joseph, of Gloucester Co. Ward. Son of Garret Vanneman of said Co. Guardian—Hugh Hollinshead. Fellowbondsman—Jacob Hollinshead; both of Burlington Co. Witness —James Williams.

1770, Dec. 28. Account of Hugh Hollinshead, Adm'r of Hugh Hollinshead, who was Guardian of Joseph Vanneman, son of Garret Vanneman. Lib. 15, pp. 63, 68.

1765, Jan. 4. Vanneman, William, of Salem Co. Int. Adm'r—John Yournson, Jr. Fellowbondsmen—John Yournson, Sr., and Francis Philpot; all of Penns Neck, said Co., yeomen.

1763, March 5. Inventory, £28.16.5, made by John Hickman and John Bilderback. Lib. 12, p. 176.

1770, June 19. Van Nest, Peter, of Somerset Co., weaver; will of. Sister, Susanna Van Nest, one-half of my real and personal, and the other half I give to my two brothers, Jeronimus Van Nest and Van Vanders Van Nest. Brother, John Van Nest, £25. Executors —said brothers, Jeronimus Van Nest and Van Vandres Van Nest. Witnesses—Dirck Middagh, Margret Middagh, George Fisher. Proved Oct. 19, 1770. Lib. K, p. 249.

1753, Nov. 13. Vanneste, Pieter, of Somerset Co., farmer; will of. Wife, Mardeleantie, £20 yearly. To the children of my son, Jacob, deceased, and to son, Peter, the lands which join the west side of the North Branch of Raritan River. Son, John, is to have a plantation bought for him. Moveables to be divided amongst Jacob's children, and Peter, John, Margaret and Elizabeth. To daughter, Margaret, wife of France Cossaart, £70. Executors—Francis Cossaart, my son-in-law; and Peter, my son. Witnesses—Aurie Lane, Jacob Demott, John Brokaw. Proved July 9, 1768.
1768, Feb. 26. Inventory, £806.4.12, made by Cornelius Cosine and Aurie Lane. Lib. I, p. 298.

1731, Sept. 30. Van Newkerk, Catrina Mattheuse, widow, of Bergen Co.; will of. Son, Peter Mattheuse Van Newkerk, a cow as his birthright; also a small plantation where he lives. Son, Gerrit Mattheuse Van Newkerk, £37. Son, Paulus Mattheuse Van Newkerk, 2 acres where he lives. Son, Cornelius, the plantation where he lives. Daughter, Yannetje Mattheuse Van Newkerk, £25. Witnesses—John Loots, Sr., Robert Livesey, Johannes Loots, Jr. Proved May 7, 1764.
Lib. H, p. 474.

1766, Jan. 9. Van Nortwick, Fulcart, of Piscataway Twsp., Middlesex Co.; will of. To my wife the use of all personal and real, to bring up my small children, while she is my widow, and after that my estate to be sold. My eldest son, Simeon, £100, and the rest to my other children. Executors—friends, John Field and John Snock. Witnesses—Charles Fontine, Christeyoan Van Noortwick, Elias V. Court. Proved Aug. 12, 1766.
1766, April 17. Inventory, £99.0.6, made by Jeremiah Field and Charles Sodam. Lib. I, p. 1.

1763, Dec. 17. Van Orden, Andries, of Schralenburgh, Bergen Co., yeoman; will of. Wife, Antje, use of whole estate while my widow. Son, John, 3 acres joining the two which I deeded to him, as his birthright; also ½ of the land which is over by Johannes Westervelt. Son, Andries, the other half. Son, David, land along line of Samuel Demarest. Son, Jacobus, land over by David Van Orden. Son, Petrus, an equal share of land with the others. Daughter, Rachel, £10 after her husband's, Siba Banta's, decease. Also Jannetie, Elizabeth and Wybreek Van Ordens to have land. Executors —sons, David Van Orden and Andries Van Orden. Witnesses—Johannes Westervelt, David Demaree, William Christie. Proved April 5, 1768. Lib. I, p. 251.
1768, April 7. Inventory, £14.8.0, made by David Demaree and William Christie.

1766, July 30. Van Pelt, Alexander, of Somerset Co. Int. Adm'x—Jane Van Pelt, widow of Alexander. Fellowbondsman—Martin Van Nortwick; both of said Co.
1766, Aug. 4. Inventory, made by Zebulon Stout and Roelof Van Dike.
1767, June 9. Account by Jane Van Pelt.
Lib. H, p. 632; Lib. I, p. 131.

1763, Oct. 11. Van Pelt, Hendrick, of New Brunswick, Middlesex Co. Int. Adm'rs—Sarah Van Pelt, the widow, and Thomas Newton. Fellowbondsman—John Vanpelt; all of said Co.
1763, Sept. 24. Inventory, £93.19.6, made by Jonathan Combs and Simon Van Dike.
1764, Oct. 31. Sale by vendue. Goods were sold to John Vanpelt, Jr., Aurt Vanpelt, Tunis Vanpelt, and others. Lib. H, p. 293.

1770, Aug. 17. Van Ripe, Abraham, of Second River, Essex Co., carpenter; will of. My moveables to be sold and the money put to interest for the use of my 2 daughters, Rachel and Altie. Executors —friends, William Dow and Peter Cadmus. Witnesses—Ary King, Abraham Winne, Sarah Kingsland. Proved Sept. 24, 1770.
Lib. K, p. 270.

1761, Feb. 17. Van Ripen, Garrit Thomassen, of Essex Co.; will of. Grandson, John Van Winkel, £2. My daughter, Marite, the wife of Henry Van Winkle, £10; also ½ of a tract of land, called Stone House land, the north side; also a lot lying between Derck Vreland and Seal Post, called No. 12; also ⅛ the rest of my land. Daughter, Jannitie, the wife of John Van Winkel, the south side of said Stone House land; also lot called No. 3; also ⅛ of the rest of lands. Daughter, Lea, the wife of Peter Jacobusse, my homestead where I live; also ⅓ of rest of lands. Executors—Jacob Van Ripen, Jr., and Peter Degarmo. Witnesses—Isaac Powelsen, George Walls, Thomas Sigler. Proved Nov. 23, 1761. Lib. H, p. 68.

1767, Sept. 19. Van Rypen, Johannes, of Achqueghenonck, Essex Co.; will of. Wife, Marregriety, all real and personal, while my widow. Son, Cornelus, 5 shillings. After wife's death, all the estate to be divided between all my sons, Cornelus, Jurrie, John and Garret. Executors—brother-in-law, Garret Van Rypen, and my friend, Hassel Peterse. Witnesses—George Vreland, Hendrick Post, Samuel Mc-Nik. Proved Sept. 28, 1767. Lib. I, p. 190.

1762, Nov. 29. Van Sickle, Elizabeth, of Morris Co. Ward. Aged 6 years and one of the children of Abraham Van Sickle, of said Co., deceased. Guardian—Thomas Baker, of Essex Co. Fellowbondsman—William Calwall, of Morris Co. Lib. H, p. 203; File No. 177N.

1770, April 12. Van Sickle, Elizabeth, of Morris Co. Ward. Daughter of Abraham Van Sickle, of said Co., deceased; who makes choice of Cornelius Ludlow as her Guardian.
1770, April 12. Guardian—Cornelius Ludlow. Fellowbondsman—Abraham Rutan; both of Morris Township. Witness—Abraham Burgean. Lib. K, p. 191.

CALENDAR OF WILLS—1761-1770 455

1769, Aug. 1. Vanstee, Hendrick, of Somerset Co., farmer; will of. Son, Henry Vanstee, 300 acres on my plantation. Daughter, Wyntie Vanstee, 100 acres of my plantation. To Jane Vanstee, so-called, daughter of Jane Vroom, a cow. Susannah Hendrickson to be part of her life maintained out of my estate, and the other part by those who receive part of John Hendrickson's estate. Wife, Ruth Van Stay, £100. Executors—friends Edward Bunn, Abraham Van Nest, Jacob Van Oastrander. Witnesses—Abraham Ten Eick, Henry V:Middleswaert, John Goldstrap, Sr. Proved Oct. 19, 1769.
Lib. K, p. 129.

1764, Feb. 1. Vantine, Abraham, of Somerset Co. Inventory, £396.13.1, made by Gerret Voorhees and Winen Rappelia, and signed by Elizabuth Funtine. File, No. 313R. (See Lib. H, p. 324).

1763, June 3. Van Tuyl, Walter, of Montague, Sussex Co., gentleman. Int. Adm'r—Bryant Hammel. Fellowbondsman—Abraham Van Acken; both of said Co., yeomen. Witness—William Hyndman. Lib. 11, p. 457.

1757, Feb. 1. Van Voorhees, Jan, of Peramus, Bergen Co.; will of. Wife, Elizabeth, to command all while my widow. Oldest son, Albert, the great Bible. Sons, Albert and Adam, each to have ½ my farm where I live. Daughter, Rachel, to have an outfit, as the rest had. Daughters, Lena Ackerman, Eliz. Post, Margreat Larou and Rachel Van Voorhis to have their share of moveables. Executrix—wife, Elizabeth and my son, Albert; and son-in-law, Peter Post, to assist her. Witnesses—Cumrat Van Allman, Isack Vanblercum, William Cairns. Proved Sept. 23, 1767. Lib. I, p. 270.
1766, Nov. 24. Inventory, £93.0.9, made by Roelef Westervelt and James Christie.
1767, Sept. 23. Peter Post (son-in-law) was made Adm'r, with will annexed. Bondsman—Gerret Ackerman and Adrian P. Post.

1763, July 18. Van Wagene, Peter Garretse, of Bergen Co.; will of. Wife, Antye, personal and real while my widow. Son, Hassell, £7 as birthright. Son, John, to have an outset as sons Hassel and Garret had. Daughter, Luja, an outset the same as my other daughters had. Daughter, Nesye, a wench. Daughter, Leutye, a wench. After wife's death, moveables to be divided among my children, Hassel, Garret, John, Peter, Elizabeth, Nesye, Vroutye, Leya, Lenaw. Executors—friend, Jacobus F. Post, and Garret Y. Van Rype. Witnesses—John Berdan, John D. Berdan, Guilliam Bertholf.
1766, Aug. 18. Codicil. Witnesses—Geese Drems, John D. Berdan, Guilliam Bertholf. Proved Oct. 21, 1766. Lib. I, p. 80.

1769, July 17. Van Wagennig, Gerrit, of Achquechnonk, Essex Co.; will of. Wife, Sarah, a good support, to be found by my sons, Hermanis and John. Wife to have all goods that belonged to her before marriage. Son, Hermanis, land where he lives. Son, John, land which I live on. Daughters, Annatje, Helena and Catrina, £100 each. To the children of my daughter, Jennike, £100, the said Jennike being deceased. Executors—son, Hermanis, and my son-in-law, Joris E. Vreland. Witnesses—David Marinus, George Thompson, Archbald Thompson. Proved Aug. 1, 1770. Lib. K, p. 228.

1768, Sept. 17. Van Waggener, Cornelius, of Bergen Co. Int. Adm'r—John Van Waggener, the eldest son, of said Co. Fellowbondsman—John Bartram, of said Co.
1768, Sept. 13. Catrina Van Waggener, the widow, renounced.
1768, Oct. 17. Inventory, £924.5.0, made by Ed. Meseler and Robert Secels. Lib. I, p. 336.

1751, June 3. Van Winckel, Daniel, of Bergen Co.; will of. Wife, Johnitie, real and personal during life. Youngest daughter, Autice Van Winckel, the farm that I now possess, she paying at the end of 10 years £100 to heirs of my daughter, Margaret Vanriper, and £100 to heirs of my daughter, Jonnitie Didricks, and £100 to heirs of daughter, Alltie Vanriper. The above Margaret and Alltie have husbands living. Daughter, Sophia Vanwinckel, the farm in Bergen Twsp., now in possession of Cornelius Vanriper, she paying to my daughter, Rachel Sickells, £50. Daughter, Mattye Vanwinckel, £100. My moveables to my daughter, Margaret Vanriper, heirs of Jonnetye Dedricks, heirs of Alltie Vanriper, Alchie Van Winckel, Sophia Vanwinckel, Mattye Van Winckel, and Rachel Sickells. Executors—Zacharias Sickellse and Michel Freeland. Witnesses—Coarnelis Bouskerk, Jorus Cadmus, Frederick Cadmus. Proved Feb. 2, 1764.
Lib. H, p. 399.

1764, Nov. 8. Van Winckel, Gideon, of Essex Co.; will of. Daughters, Anatie, Maritie, Ariantie, Lydia and Rachel, all my real estate. If Maritie die without issue, then her share is to go to the others. Executors—my daughter, Anatie, my son-in-law, Casparus Van Winkle, my daughter, Lydia, my son-in-law Samuel Stivers, my daughter, Rachael, my son-in-law, Jedediah Dean, and my daughter, Ariantie. Witnesses—Samuel V. Cortlandt, Philip Van Cortlandt, Abraham Ogden. Proved Dec. 28, 1764.
1764, Dec. 17. Inventory, £308.5.5, made by William Dow and Peter Cadmus. Lib. H, p. 478.

1766, Dec. 29. Van Winkel, Henderik, of town of Bergen, yeoman; will of. Wife, Catherina Van Winckel, real and personal during life; and, after her death, £50 to son, Henderick, and the rest to sons, Jacob, Daniel, Henderick and Joseph. Son, Jacob, my house and 40 acres. Executors—sons, Jacob, Daniel, Henderick and Joseph. Witnesses—Robert Sickels, Hartman Sickels, Zacharias Sickels. Proved April 20, 1769. Lib. K, p.108.

1758, Jan. 6. Van Winkel, Johannis Walings, of New Barbadoes Neck, Bergen Co., yeoman; will of. Wife, Hillegond, use of real and personal. Son, Waling Van Winkel, my brew house. Daughter, Catrina, wife of Pieter H. Pieterse, £150. Daughter, Annatje, wife of Johannis Sip, £150. Executors—son, Waling, and my son-in-law, Pieter H. Pieterse. Witnesses—David Marinus, Johannis J. Van Winkle, Cornelus Vanvorst. Proved Oct. 19, 1769. Lib. K, p. 135.

1762, May 10. Van Winkel, Marynis, of Acquacknung, Essex Co.; will of. My personal estate to my wife, Gettie Van Winkle, my daughters, Rachel Van Wagane, Margaret Vreelandt, Annatie Garretse, Janatie Vreelandt and Katrintie Van Winkle. My lands to wife and daughters, Rachel Van Wagane, Margaret Vreelandt, Annatie Garretse, Janatie Vreeland and Katrintie Van Winkle. Executors—sons-in-law, Hendrick Garretse and Michael Vreelandt. Witnesses—Elizabeth Ogden, Uzal Ogden, Jr., Lewis Ogden. Proved Sept. 28, 1767. Lib. I, p. 253.

1767, Oct. 2. Vaughan, William, of Upper Freehold, Monmouth Co.; will of. Wife, Massey, real and personal while my widow, in order to support her family. My estate to be given equally among my children, except my daughters, and they are to have £30 less, and those that are married to be "reduct" £12 out of their portions. Executors—my friends, Thomas Morphet, Thomas Farr and Peter Sexton, and my wife, Masey. Witnesses—William Mount, Ezekiel Mount, James Mooney. Proved Oct. 28, 1767. Probate granted to Thomas Farr and Mercy Vaughn.
1767, Oct. 16. Inventory, £311.6.8, made by David Stout and Ezekiel Mount. Lib. 13, p. 261.

1763, Jan. 22. Veal, Joseph, of Paramus, Bergen Co.; will of. Wife, Sarah, use of real and personal while my widow. Daughter, Jemime, to have an outset as my other children who are married. Son, Thomas, £20. After death of my wife the estate to be divided among son, Thomas, daughter, Elizabeth, daughter, Abegal, daughter, Sarah, and daughter, Jerneyme. Executors—my wife and son-in-law, Christeyaun Dedricks. Proved Oct. 25, 1768. Lib. K, p. 1.

1767, Sept. 14. Veghte, Hendrick, of Sowerland, Somerset Co., yeoman; will of. Wife, Nelly, to have use of all real and personal while my widow. Son, Reynier, plantation I live on. Daughters, Jackemeintje and Sarah, all my bonds. Children under 21. Executors—brother-in-law, Abraham Quick, son-in-law, Peter Wyckoff, and my friend, Abraham Staats. Witnesses—Joris Bergen, John Staats, Abraham Van Buren. Proved Nov. 3, 1767. Lib. I, p. 171.

1764, April 19. Voorhees, Hendryck, of Freehold, Monmouth Co., yeoman; will of. Wife, Sarah, £50, and to be maintained. Grandson, Hendrick, son of my son John, £5. Sons, Anidrew, and Peter, to each £100. Son, William, 50 acres, which are bounded by Peter Schenck and John Crage, Jr., for which he is to give £250. Rest of my estate to daughter, Geertye, daughter, Willimpy, daughter, Catherine, son, Andrew, son, Peter, son, William, son, Hendrick, daughter, Jean, son, Rulef, son, Albert, and son, Garret. Executors—son, Peter, my son-in-law, David Williamson, and my friend, Dirck Sutphen, son of Dirick. Witnesses—Abiel Akin, Peter Schenck, Ephraim Buck. Proved Feb. 1, 1766.
1766, Feb. 5. Inventory, £1344.6.4, made by John Longstreet, Richard Pitinger and Tunis Vanderveer, Jr.
1772, Nov. 30. Account filed by Derrick Sutphen, surviving Executor. Lib. H, p. 592.

1769, Sept. 19. Voorhees, Johannes, of New Brunswick, Middlesex Co.; will of. My father, Peter Voorhees, in his lifetime, had a plantation in New Brunswick on Larencis Brook; also a small lot of Salt meadow at mouth of South River; and my father died without a will, whereby I, the eldest son, am heir to said premises, which I order to be sold. To wife, Catlina, and my 5 children, and my brothers and sisters, being 13 in number, I give the rest of my estate. Executors

—uncles, Johannes Ryder and Garret Voorhees, and my brother-in-law, Jeremiah Vanderbilt. Witnesses—John Schuurman, John Woglum, John Whitlock. Proved Nov. 2, 1769. Lib. K, p. 133.

1763, Sept. 27. Voorhies, John, of Monmouth Co. Int. Adm'r—John Van Der Veer. Fellowbondsman—Peter Voorhees; both of said Co.

1763, Sept. 24. Renunciation by Nelley Voorhees, the widow of said John, in favor of her brother, John Vanderveer. Signed at Upper Freehold by Nelley Voorhees. Lib. H, p. 289.

1758, Aug. 18. Vorhis, Lammetie, of Somerset Co.; will of. Granddaughter, Idah Van Lewe, wife of Denys Van Lewe, and my grandson, Jacob Wycof, all my estate. Executors—said Jacob Wycof, and Denys Van Lewe. Witnesses—John Van Voorhees, Willemsn, Jabesh Ashmore. Proved May 1, 1764.

1764, May 14. Inventory, made by Jacob Wycoff, Denice Van Lewe, Barnardus Gerretsen and Stoffal Probasco. Lib. H, p. 434.

1769, March 30. Vreeland, George, of Essex Co. Int. Adm'rs—Michael Vreeland, brother of said George, and Hessel Peterse.
Lib. K, p. 89.

1770, Oct. 29. Vreeland, John, of Borough of Elizabeth, Essex Co. Int. Adm'r—Enoch Vrelandt, the father of said John. Fellowbondsman—William Deulea; both of said place. Lib. K, p. 251.

1762, March 19. Vreeland, Machiel Hartmanse, of Gemoenepa, in Bergen Co., yeoman; will of. Son, Hartman, £12, as my eldest son. Wife, Elizabeth, use of my estate while my widow. Son, Hartman, my right that I purchased from Claes Romyn, at a place called Weesel, where he now lives. Son, Garret, my right I purchased of Jacob Symonse Van Winckle, also lying in Weesel, and he may will to one of his brother's or sister's children, and none other. Son, Claas, land on south side of Regpokes Island, and, if he die before my grandchild, Machiel Vreeland, son of Claas, then it shall go to said Machiel. My daughter, Beletje Vreelandt, two lots of land. Daughter, Marritje Vreelandt, 2 other lots. Executors—my wife and my son, Hartman, and my sister's son, Robbert Sickels. Witnesses—Hendrick Blinkerhof, John Van Horne. Proved Feb. 4, 1768.
Lib. I, p. 266.

1761, May 29. Vrelandt, Simon, of Bergen Co.; will of. Wife, Rachel, real and personal while single. The child yet to be born is provided for. Speaks of brothers and sisters, viz., Enoch, John, Abraham, Leya and Annaty. Executors—my wife, Rachel, and my brother, Enogh. Witnesses—Albert Terheun, Michel Van Wincle, Guilliam Bertholf. Proved Feb. 9, 1765. Lib. H, p. 492.

1765, Feb. 12. Inventory, £177.17.4, made by Albert Terheun and John Berry.

1756, Oct. 16. Vroom, Henderck, of Bridgewater Twsp., Somerset Co.; will of. Son, Hendreck, £5. Son, Hendreck, lives on one of my plantations, and my son, George, now deceased, did live on another in Middlesex Co., and my son, Peter, now lives on one. Eldest daughter, Sarah, £70. Second daughter, Marratia, £75. Third daugh-

CALENDAR OF WILLS—1761-1770   459

ter, Brachtra, £75. There remains a balance due me on land my son-in-law, Peter Dumont, bought of me. Grandson, Henderick Vroom, son of George Vroom, deceased, £33, and to his brother, Peter Vroom, £33, when 21. Granddaughter, Janatia, daughter of George Vroom, £33. Granddaughter, Janatia, daughter to my youngest daughter, Janatia, £33. Wife, Dority, to be maintained out of my 3 real estates; and she is to have all she brought with her. Executors —my three sons, Hendrick, John and Peter, who are to have my lands. Witnesses—Cornelius Van Kaempen, Aurie Lane, Gisbert Lane. Proved July 3, 1769.

1769, June 2. Inventory, £112.14.9, made by William Lane and John Ten Eick.   Lib. K, p. 114.

1766, Aug. 31. Vroom, Peter, of Somerset Co., yeoman; will of. Wife, Jenetie, to have the money that was due to her from the estate of George Vroom. Son, Peter, gray mare. Rest of estate to my wife and children. Executors—brothers, Hendrick and John Vroom, my wife, Jenetie, and Peter Dumont, Sr. Witnesses—Joris Bergen, John Van Neste, Andres Ten Eick, Jr. Proved Sept. 22, 1768.

Lib. I, p. 343.

1768, April 18. Waddington, William, of Salem Co. Int. Adm'rs— Samuel Hancock and William Bradway, both of Alloways Creek, said Co. Fellowbondsmen—Nathaniel Hancock, of said place, and Thomas Goodwin, of Town of Salem. 'Whereas, William Waddington, by will made Elizabeth his wife, sole Executrix, and she died after probate intestate; therefore the above Adm'rs are now appointed.'

Lib. 13, p. 410.

1760, Jan. 7. Wade, Robert, of Elizabeth Borough, Essex Co., yeoman; will of. Wife, Sarah, use of ⅛ my land. Granddaughter, Sarah Cherry, £20. Granddaughter, Sarah Brown, £5, when 18. Son, Daniel, plantation where I live and the swamp on the other side of the way, joining land of John Wade, Jotham Clark and Benjamin Wade, which is 18 acres. Sons, Henry and Daniel, two lots of salt meadow, of 15 acres; also one joining to the Oyster Creek, of 6 acres. Son, Benjamin, salt meadow that joins Bound Creek, of 7 acres. My son, Daniel, and my daughter, Patiensce, wife of Josiah Woodruff, moveable estate. Executors—friend, Timothy Whitehead, and my son, Daniel. Witnesses—Andrew Whitehead, Timothy Whitehead, Jr., Elias Whitehead. Proved Aug. 18, 1766.

1766, Aug. 21. Inventory, £53.0.7, made by Nathaniel Ball and Amos Day.   Lib. I, p. 43.

1770, May 18. Wadlin, Anthony, of Northampton Twsp., Burlington Co. Int. Adm'r—Zachariah Prickett, of said Twsp., yeoman. Fellowbondsman—Thomas Shinn, of Mount Holly.   Lib. 15, p. 47

1770, Oct. 15. Waggoner, Harman, of Fairfield, Cumberland Co. Int. Adm'r—Thomas Whitecur. Fellowbondsmen—David Husted and Samuel Bennett; all of said place.

1770, Oct. 9. Inventory, £82.14.7, made by David Huested and Samuel Bennett.   Lib. 15, p. 68.

1764, June 13. Waldron, Frans, of Somerset Co.; will of. Eldest son, Samuel Waldron, £3 after my wife's decease. Wife, Catline, the profits of my real and personal estate, while she is my widow. Son, Samuel, the east ½ of my farm where I live, and it is to include Samuel's house. Son, Jerome, the other half of said place. Son, John, the farm I lately purchased of John Hazlet, on Muskenekung Hill. Son, William, £100. Children, Nelthe, Neiche, Samuel, Jerome, Johanis and William, each to have money. Executors—wife, Catline, son, Samuel Waldron, and Jerome Waldron. Witnesses—John Vannest, Susannah Hawkins, Jacob Mattison. Proved June 11, 1765.

1765, April 16. Inventory, £390.5.1, made by Derck Marlatt and Rem Lupardus. Lib. H, p. 508.

1758, Oct. 20. Wales, John, of Essex Co., joyner; will of. Wife, Hana Wales, ½ of the personal. To Mary Carter, a bed. To David Wales, £5. To George Wales, £15. My son James Wales all my fast estate. Executors—John Condet, Benjamin Johnson and James Wales. Witnesses—William Ennis, Richard Ennis. Proved Jan. 5, 1770. Lib. K, p. 195.

1761, Aug. 15. Walker, William, of Woodbridge, Middlesex Co., yeoman; will of. All lands and moveables to be sold. Daughter, Sarah, £60, when 18. Sons, John, and Samuel, the residue. Executors—John Moors, Joseph Shotwell, Jr. Witnesses—Daniel Shotwell, Jonathan Beesly, James Kealley. Proved April 20, 1762.
Lib. H, p. 90.

1766, Nov. 9. Wallace, Benjamin, of Pilesgrove, Salem Co.; will of. Wife, Martha, her right in land and goods, while my widow. My daughter, Rebekah Wallace, bed, etc. Son, John, the land where I live. Daughter, Elizabeth Wallace, 2 cows. To my younger children, Mary, Jane and Martha Wallace, other goods. Son, James, a pair of bullocks. Youngest son, Thomas, £15 when 21. Executors—my wife and son, John. Witnesses—Thomas Kelly, Thomas Carney, John Walker. Proved Dec. 22, 1766.

1766, Dec. 10. Inventory, £243.4.1, made by John Dickeson and Thomas Carney. Lib. 13, p. 185.

1767, Feb. 4. Wallace, Hope and Mary, both of Burlington Co. Wards. Children of Thomas Wallace, both under 14. John Wallace and Joshua Lippincott make petition, in which they state that Thomas Wallace appointed them, together with Hope, his wife, as his Executors, but the petitioners have not meddled with the estate, and by their consent the widow hath taken possession of the same, but has again married, and the estate of the children may be in danger; and now they pray that Isaac Evans and Micajah Wills may be appointed their Guardians.

1767, Feb. 4. Guardians—Isaac Evans and Micajah Wills, both of Evesham, said Co., yeomen. Fellowbondsmen—Joshua Lippincott, of said place, yeoman, and John Wallace, of Waterford, Gloucester Co., yeoman. File 952 H.

1767, Oct. 9. Wallin, John, of Burlington. Int. Adm'r—Isaac Heulings. Fellowbondsman—Abraham Hewlings; both of said city.

1767, Oct. 7. Renunciation of Hope Wallin (the widow) in favor of Isaac Hewlings. Lib. 13, p. 105.

1767, May 26. Walling, Gershom, of Middletown, Monmouth Co. Int. Adm'rs—Thomas Craven, of Somerset Co., and Thomas Bullman, of Monmouth Co.; both sons-in-law. Fellowbondsman—John Wall, of Monmouth Co.
1767, May 10. Inventory, £79.7.5, made by John Walling and Joel Beddel. (Account was filed by Thomas Craven; without date).
Lib. I, p. 109.

1769, Feb. 8. Walling, Jonathan, of Greenwich Twsp., Cumberland Co., yeoman; will of. Sons, Ladus, and Jonathan, the plantation where I live; and Jonathan is to have the part with the buildings, and Ladus is to have 30 acres more than Jonathan. To my daughter, Cynthus, £100. Daughter, Mary, £100, when she is 18. My wife is to have her dower. Executrix—my wife, Mary. Witnesses—Thomas Ewing, Sarah Woodruff, Joseph Norbury. Proved March 18, 1769.
1769, March 15. Inventory, £317.5.6, made by Thomas Ewing and Enos Woodruff.
Lib. 14, p. 4.

1763, Oct. 20. Walling, Sarah, of Greenwich, Cumberland Co. Int. Adm'r—Jonathan Walling. Fellowbondsman—Enos Woodruff; both of said Greenwich, yeomen. Witness—Thomas Ewing.
1763, Oct. 18. Inventory, £99.16.9, made by Thomas Ewing and Enos Woodruff.
1764, Oct. 23. Account by Adm'r.
Lib. 11, p. 475.

[No date]. Walling, Thomas, of Cumberland Co., shopkeeper; will of. Brother, Jonathan Walling, and sister, Mary, each 5 shillings. To the child my wife goes with, £50. Wife, Sarah, rest of estate. Executor—wife, Sarah. (Will not signed and has no witnesses). Proved Oct. 10, 1761, by Jonathan Walling, brother to testator, and by Thomas Ewing, a near neighbor, who said they knew his writing.
1761, June 30. Inventory, £322.19.3, made by Theophilus Elmer and James Ray.
Lib. 11, p. 156.

1767, May 15. Wallis, William, of Woolwich, Gloucester Co.; will of. Daughter, Susanah, £10. Daughter, Margaret, £10. Daughter, Bettey, £10. Son, William, remainder, when he is 21. Executor—friend, David Davis. Witnesses—Peter Louderbach, Francis Chattin, Isaac Richman. Proved Dec. 6, 1768.
1769, April 3. Inventory, £428.11.9, made by Isaac Barber and John Hoffman.
Lib. 13, p. 482.

1766, June 21. Walters, Thomas, of Maidenhead, Hunterdon Co.; will of. Wife, Percilah, all my real and personal estate. Executors—my said wife and Henry Woolsey, of Pennington. Witnesses—Abner Phillips, John Bainbridge. Proved Feb. 16, 1767.
1767, Feb. 16. Inventory, £216.12.5, made by Ralph Hunt and Azariah Hunt.
Lib. 13, p. 218.

1770, Oct. 19. Walton, John, Jr., of Morristown, Morris Co. Int. Adm'rs—Elizabeth Walton and Ezekiel Goble; both of said place.
Lib. K, p. 256.

1768, July 20. Walton, Mary, of New York City; will of. Widow of William Walton, of said City, merchant. To my grandson, William Walton, land and buildings on Duke St., New York City, and possessed by Philip John Livingston. To my grandchildren, Mary Morris, Magdalene Johnston and Catherine Thompson, my apparel, plate and household goods. Daughter, Cornelia Walton, wife of my late son, William Walton, £50. Of the rest of my estate I give ⅛ part to my grandson, William Walton, and ⅛ part to my grandson, Jacob Walton, and ⅛ part to my grandson, Thomas, and ⅛ part to my grandson, Gerrard, and ⅛ part to my grandson, Abraham, and ⅛ part to my granddaughter, Mary Morris, and ⅛ part to my granddaughter, Magdalene Johnston, and ⅛ part I direct my executors to put at interest and pay the interest to my granddaughter, Catharine Thompson, and, at her death, the principal to be paid to her children. As James Thompson, the husband of Catharine, has received large sums, it is now understood that the above legacies to Catharine and her children are upon the conditions that James or Catharine, or both, shall release and discharge the estate of my son, William, and discharge my grandson, William, and also the representatives of my son, Jacob, dec'd, from all demands, which James and his wife may have. Whereas Lewis Morris, husband of my granddaughter, Mary Morris, is indebted to me for £274 lent him in 1755, and also for other sums, I now order same to be deducted from the share of Mary Morris. Executors—grandsons, William Walton and Jacob Walton. Witnesses—Robert Waddell, Robert Cocks, Benjamin Jones. Proved Sept. 13, 1768.

1768, Aug. 25. Codicil. Witnesses—James Wilmot, James Beekman, Robert Waddell. Proved Sept. 13, 1768. Lib. I, p. 337.

1768, June 8. Walton, William, Esq., of New York City; will of. Wife, Cornelia, house and lot where I live, except the water lot in rear. Wife is also given several servants, wine and family stores; also £700 yearly. Nephew, Jacob Walton, land on Water St., which is bounded by my brother, Jacob, deceased; also the right to purchase from the City ground under the water in East River, fronting 2 lots of my late father, William Walton. Nephew, Thomas Walton, £1,000. Nephew, Gerard Walton, £1,000. Niece, Mary, the wife of Lewis Morris, Esq., £500. Niece, Magdelane, the wife of David Johnston, £500. My niece, Catherine, the wife of James Thompson, on his decease, £5,000. Nephew, William Walton, £500. Nephew, Jacob Walton, £7,000. Friend, Charles Hicks, of Mount Misery, in Flushing, £5. After death of my wife I give my nephew, William Walton, the house where I live, and, after his death, to my grandnephew William Walton, his son; and, if he die, then to my nephew, Jacob Walton; and, if he die, then to my grandnephew William Walton, son of Jacob. Grandnephew, James Delancey Walton, son of my nephew, William Walton, household goods. Executors—my nephews, William Walton and Jacob Walton. Witnesses—James Roosevelt, Jr., Thomas Shreve, Whitehead Hicks. Proved July 25, 1768. Lib. I, p. 288.

1763, July 3. Wamback, George William, of Amwell Twsp., Hunterdon Co., yeoman; will of. My 212 acres in said Twsp., that I purchased of William Scouley and Jacob Burcham, I give to my 3 children, Henry, Elizabeth and Mary Wamback. Wife, Margret, £100. Son, Antoney, is not capable of providing for himself, therefore the others are to keep him for life. Executors—Jacob Snyder, Christian Wart and John Young. Witnesses—George Servis, John Garrison, John Yoager. Proved Aug. 15, 1763.

1763, July 28. Inventory, £277.12.0, made by Jonathan Smith and Richard Reed.
1764, June 14. Inventory, £44.19.1, made by Richard Reed and Jonathan Smith. "Goods found since the other Inventory was taken."
1766, June 16. Account by Executors. Lib. 11, p. 405

1765, April 26. Wanemake, Peter, of Ramapo, Bergen Co. Int. Adm'r—Henry Wanemake, eldest son of said Peter, of said place. Fellowbondsman—Jacob Stort, of said place. Lib. H, p. 541.

1767, March 5. Wanshaer, John, of Aquahennok, Essex Co.; will of. Son, John, silver tankard marked "I. W. H.," and my "bighouse Byble." Rest of real and personal to my wife, while my widow. Residue to son, John, and my daughter, Susanna. Executors—my wife, son, John, and Henry Winkoop. Witnesses—Michael Vreeland, Christoffel Van Rypen, Nicholas Vreeland. Proved Sept. 20, 1768.
1768, Sept. 22. Inventory, £1123.15.6, made by Michael Vreeland and Thomas Griffith; with Henry Wynkoop, Executor. Lib. I, p. 350.

1764, May 4. Ward, Benjamin, of Chester Twsp., Burlington Co.; will of. Twenty-five acres of the upper end of my land to be sold. Son, Jesenbery, the rest of plantation, when 21, paying to my two daughters, Ann Ward and Mary Ward, £10 each, and, if he die before 21, then my wife, Martha, and the said daughters shall have the land. Wife, Martha, my moveable estate. Executors—my wife and my friend, Thomas Hackney. Witnesses—Samuel Stokes, Joseph Hackney, Joseph Stokes, Jr. Proved Jan. 26, 1765. Lib. 12, p. 52.

1764, Sept. 9. Ward, David, of Newark, Essex Co.; will of. Being aged and infirm. Daughter, Phebe Chandler, £250, and my household goods, and, after her death, to her daughter's. Son, Moses, my home lot, where I live. Son, Ezekiel, the money that my land sold for, at Bear Swamp, which is 90 acres. Son, David, to pay Moses ½ of the money that the land at Bear Swamp and a meadow sold for, "which was sold to purchase my said son, David's, plantation in Morris Co.," and David and Moses to have the rest of lands. Executors—son, David, and son-in-law, Nathaniel Chandler. Witnesses—Daniel Matthuves, Phinehas Baldwin, Robert Boyd. Proved Feb. 18, 1768. (Inventory £2.1.8). Lib. I, p. 264.

1770, Dec. 5. Ward, Elias, of Newark, Essex Co. Int. Adm'rs— Mary Ward and Matthias Ward. Lib. K, p. 321.

1762, Nov. 1. Ward, Michael, of Middlesex Co. Int. Adm'r—Benjamin Ward, the eldest son. Fellowbondsman—Frederick Buckelow; both of said Co.
1763, March 3. List of goods as were sold to John Ward, William Ward, Mary Ward, Benjamin Ward. Lib. H, p. 197.

1764, July 25. Ward, Samuel, of Newark, Essex Co. Ward. Son of Josiah Ward, of said place. Guardian—Joseph Heddin.
Lib. 12, p. 11.

1761, Dec. 29. Ward, Stephen, of Morristown, Morris Co. Int. Adm'rs—William Lloyd and Elizabeth, his wife. Fellowbondsman— Abraham Tuttle; all of said place.
1762, March 14. Inventory, £45.0.9, made by the Adm'rs, who re-

tained 1/5 part; and the rest was delivered to Samuel Tuthill for Jonathan Stiles, for the use of the other 4 heirs. Lib. H, p. 119.

1768, Oct. 6. Wardell, Joseph, Sr., of Shrewsbury, Monmouth Co., yeoman; will of. Eldest son, John, 50 acres where he lives. Son, Joseph, house and land that I bought of John Miln; also the tract I bought of John Shepherd, and ½ the salt meadow in Ltttle Silver Neck. Son, William, land on west side of road, that goes to Oyster Shell Point. Wife, Margaret, use of ½ my land. Son, William, and daughters, Elizabeth, Margaret, Meribah, Phebe and Lydia Wardell, rest of lands. Executors—sons, Joseph and John. Witnesses—Jacob Dennis, Jr., Benjamin Dennis, Jacob Dennis. Proved Dec. 6, 1769.
Lib. K, p. 146.

1761, Aug. 19. Wardell, Mary, of Shrewsbury, Monmouth Co., widow; will of. Son, Stephen, 5 shillings. Eldest daughter, Esther, my bed, and great Bible. Daughter, Sarah, cupboard. Rest to my daughters, Esther, Sarah and Catherine. Executors—my friends and neighbors, Thomas Burden, Jr., and Webley Edwards. Witnesses—Jeremiah Bonham, David Allen, George White. Proved March 24, 1762.

1762, March 24. Renunciation by Webley Edwards. Witness—Asher West. Lib. H, p. 184.

1766, April 28. Ware, Elisha, of Alloways Creek Twsp., Salem Co. Ward. Son of Solomon Ware, of said place, yeoman, deceased, having lands devised to him by his father, makes choice of Joshua Stretch as his Guardian.

1766, April 28. Guardian—Joshua Stretch. Fellowbondsman—John Ware, both of said place, yeomen. Lib. 12, p. 318.

1762, July 31. Ware, Sarah, of Alloways Creek Precinct, Salem Co., widow; will of. My son, Solomon Ware, one-half my estate, and the other half to my daughter, Sarah Ware. If either of them die under age, then to the 2 next youngest. Executor—Joshua Stretch. Witnesses—Nathan Stretch, Esther Hays, Samuel Stretch. Proved Dec. 27, 1765.

1765, Dec. 24. Inventory, £581.5.9, made by Thomas Sayre and James Evans. Lib. 12, p. 297.

1762, Dec. 25. Ware, Susanah, of Greenwich, Gloucester Co., wife of Alexander Ware; will of. Whereas Jacob Atwood, of Manington Township, in Salem Co., carpenter, by will dated 28 July, 1742, did give to me, his niece, Susannah Lord, alias Ware, a plantation in Manington, which I order to be sold, and, after payment of a mortgage made to my son, Abraham Lord, I give as follows, viz., to husband, Alexander Ware, and my children, Abraham, James and Joshua Lord, Mary, Hannah, Alexander, Susannah, William, John, Sarah and Faithful Ware, the money, to be equally divided amongst my children and husband; same to be paid to the sons when 21, and to the daughters when 18. Executors—my friends, Mathew Gill and William Guest, who are to sell the said lands.

1762, Dec. 25. Alexander Ware gives full consent to the above will. Witnesses—Gabriel Strang, Daniel Strang, Frederick Hoffman. Proved April 6, 1763.

Memorandum (no date). "That Executors in the annexed will, have never been qualified, the reason being that the heir-at-law made them a title for the land in the said will mentioned. Lib. 13, p. 520.

1769, May 24. Ware, Thomas, of Stow Creek, Cumberland Co., cordwainer; will of. Plantation where I live, which I bought of Leonard Gibbon, to be sold. My wife, ⅓ my moveable estate, and money from said sale, after debts are paid, and use of house and lot where Isaac Sutton lives. Son, Jacob, said house and lot, after his mother's death, when he is 21. Son, Thomas, the house and lot where my father, Jacob Ware, now lives, after the death of my father and his wife. Son, Isaac, £30 when 21. Son, Enoch, £30 when 21. Daughters, Priscilla, Amme, Hannah and Lydia, rest of moveable estate, when they are 18. Executors—friends, Thomas Ewing and Samuel Ewing. Witnesses—Samuel Ward, Thomas Waithman, Richard Ware. Proved July 1, 1769.
    1769, June 15. Inventory, £135.12.5, made by William Fithian and Jonathan Bowen.
    1771, June 24. Account by Samuel Ewing, surviving Executor.
                                                                                      Lib. 14, pp. 117, 406.

1761, June 9. Watford, John, of Kingwood, Hunterdon Co., yeoman; will of. Wife, Elizabeth, my moveable estate, and, at her death to my daughters, Abigail Warne, Elizabeth Colvin, Rachel Quimby, Jane Allen and Ann Fox. Son, James, my lands, and he is to provide for my wife. Son, Joseph, £20. Son, John, £20. Executor—son, James. Witnesses—Isaac Leet, Malakiah Bonham, Absalem Bonham. Proved Jan. 3, 1770.
    1769, Dec. 23. Inventory, £82.8.0, made by James Stout and Malakiah Bonham.   Lib. 15, p. 18.

1759, May 24. Warne, Thomas, of Monmouth Co.; will of. Real and personal to be sold, after debts are paid; the rest to be divided between my children, Thomas, Richard, Samuel, Benjamin, George, Hannah and Euphemia; the rest of my children being as well or better already provided for. Executors—brother-in-law, Richard Franses, and my brother, Samuel Warne. Witnesses—Thomas Warne, Jr., Hannah Warne, Robert Savage. Proved Nov. 13, 1761.
                                                                                                     Lib. H, p. 47.

1760, May 22. Warrick, Jacob, of Newton Twsp., Gloucester Co.; will of. Real and personal to be sold for the benefit of my children. I desire my children to learn to read and write. Executors—David Branson and Joseph Bullock. Witnesses—Elizabeth Culling, Mary White, James Sloan. Proved Feb. 9, 1762.
    1762, Jan. 27. Inventory, £495.3.11½, made by John Hinchman and Robert Friend Price.   Lib. 11, p. 92.

1765, April 30. Warrick, Samuel, Jr., of Chester Twsp., Burlington Co., laborer; will of. Brothers, Jacob, John and David Warrick, all my estate when they are 21. Executor—friend, Thomas Cummings, of Newton Twsp., in Gloucester Co. Witnesses—David Branson, Moses Branson. Proved June 4, 1765.
    1765, May 17. Inventory, £172.19.8, made by William Griscom and Thomas Redman, Jr.   Lib. 12, p. 113.

1765, Aug. 20. Warrington, Henry, of Chester, Burlington Co., yeoman; will of. Son, Thomas, plantation on Pensawkin Creek, of 210 acres, which I bought of Samuel Parr. Son, Joseph, plantation where

I dwell, of 245 acres; also 104 acres which I bought of Abraham Heulings, dec'd. Son, Thomas, is to take care of his sister, Ruth's, legacy. To my 6 daughters the personal estate. Executors—son, Thomas, and my friend, Joshua Roberts. Witnesses—Joshua Bispham, Sarah Bispham, Samuel Atkinson.

1768, Feb. 8. Codicil. Witnesses—John Cox, Joseph Lippincott, John Lippincott. Proved July 28, 1769.

1769, July 26. Renunciation by Joshua Roberts.

1769, July 25. Inventory, £556.13.10, made by Enoch Roberts and John Lippincott. Lib. 14, p. 23.

1763, May 7. Washborne, Zenus, of Morris Co. Int. Adm'r—Jephthah Byram, of Newton. Fellowbondsman—Isaac Harlow, of Hardyston; both of Sussex Co., yeomen. Witness—William Hyndman. Lib. 11, p. 455.

1762, March 5. Washburn, Ebenezer, of Monmouth Co. Int. Adm'r—Jonathan Washburn, son of said Ebenezer. Fellowbondsman—Jonathan Herbert; both of said Co., yeomen. Witnesses—James Throckmorton and Timothy Halstead.

1762, Feb. 26. Renunciation by Patience Washburn, the widow, in favor of her son, Jonathan Washburn. Witness—William Bowne.

1762, Feb. 25. Inventory, £33.8.0, made at Middletown, by Nathaniel Leonard and William Bowne. Lib. H, p. 77.

1766, Oct. 30. Waterhouse, John, of Perth Amboy, Middlesex Co., doctor. Int. Adm'rs—Sophia Waterhouse, his widow, and Alexander Watson. Fellowbondsman—Jonathan Deare; all of said place. Witness—Robert Wallace. Lib. I, p. 6.

1764, Nov. 8. Waters, Henry, of Alloways Creek Precinct, Salem Co., yeoman; will of. Wife, Elenor, ⅓ my moveable estate, and ⅓ my land, during her life. Son, Henry, my land. Daughter, Elenor, 40 shillings yearly; but if she recovers, as other people, then Henry may be released from paying it. Son, Daniel, £25. Rest of moveable estate to my other children, Hannah, and the one yet not born, and the said Elenor. Executrix—my wife. Witnesses—John Finlaw, Mary Paiten, Thomas Sayre. Proved Oct. 9, 1766.

1766, Oct. 7. Inventory, £110.3.9, made by Thomas Sayre and John Finlaw. Lib. 12, p. 310.

1760, Jan. 2. Waters, Jonathan, of Hopewell, Hunterdon Co.; will of. All my goods to my son, William, and my daughter, Elizabeth. Executors—son, William, and Andrew Muirheid. Witnesses—Robert Akers, John Davison, Stephen Jones. Proved Sept. 27, 1762.

1762, Sept. 27. Inventory, £46.10.9, made by Stephen Burrows and Jeremiah Woolsey. Lib. 11, p. 357.

1765, May 21. Waters, Jonathan, of Amwell, Hunterdon Co. Ward. Son of William Waters, of Hopewell, said Co., deceased; making choice of Stephen Jones, of Amwell, as his Guardian.

1765, May 21. Guardian—Stephen Jones. Fellowbondsman—John Seaverns; both of Amwell, said Co. Lib. 12, p. 114.

CALENDAR OF WILLS—1761-1770   467

1766, June 21. Waters, Thomas, of Maidenhead, Hunterdon Co.; will of. Wife, Priscilla, all real and personal estate. Executors— my wife and Henry Woolsey, of Pennington, said Co. Witnesses— Abner Phillips, John Bainbridge. Proved Feb. 16, 1767.
Lib. 13, p. 218.

1762, May 6. Waters, William, of Hopewell, Hunterdon Co.; will of. My aged father is to have a comfortable maintainance out of his and my estate. Real and personal to be sold. Daughters, Sarah Wilson and Deborah Woolsey, and my granddaughter, Letitia Burrows, £5 to each. Daughters, Kezia and Elizabeth, to each $30. Sons, William and Jonathan, the residue, allowing William £25 more than Jonathan. Letitia Burrows is to be paid when she arrives to age of 18. Executors—son, William, and my brother-in-law, Andrew Muirhead. Witnesses—Dennis Titus, David Adair, John Guild. Proved June 21, 1762.
1762, June 21. Inventory, £180.11.6, made by Jeremiah Woolsey and Stephen Burrows.   Lib. 11, p. 367.

1769, Dec. 2. Waters, William, of Pilesgrove, Salem Co. Int. Adm'x—Rebecca Waters, widow. Fellowbondsmen—Daniel Bassett and Peter Keen, yeomen; all of said place.
1769, Nov. 25. Inventory, £208.0.6, made by Daniel Bassett and Peter Keen.   Lib. 14, p. 113.

1768, Oct. 29. Waterworth, William. Int. Adm'r—John Lawrence, Esq., of Burlington. Fellowbondsman—Joseph Wharton, Jr., of Philadelphia, merchant. Witness—Robert Burchan.   Lib. 12, p. 525.

1765, Oct. 26. Watkins, Benjamin, of Hanover Twsp., Burlington Co. Int. Adm'r—Solomon Watkins, of said place.
1764, Oct. 18. Inventory, £36.2.8, made by Joseph Lamb and Thomas Kirby.   Lib. 12, p. 284.

1763, May 20. Watkins, David, of Borough of Elizabeth, Essex Co.; will of. Wife, Zerviah, use of real and personal, while my widow. To Zarviah Bond 10 acres, to be taken off the land I bought of Nathan Stanbery, which is to take in the house that Nathan formerly lived in, and is to be bound by land of Amos Morss and William Oliver; also my 4-acre lot, except a small square at the top of the hill, and is to join Mephibosheth Marsh, and is to be for a public burying-ground, where I am to be "buryed." My sisters, Mary Brandbury and Johannah Ball, after my wife's death, to have my farm and saltmeadows, and the rest of land I bought of Nathan Stanbury and John Wood. Executors—friends, Amos Morss and Capt. Ephraim Terrill. Witnesses—Daniel Trembtes, Jr., Comfort Marsh, Joseph Morss, Jr. Proved Aug. 3, 1763.   Lib. H, p. 268.

1756, Sept. 28. Watson, John, of Perth Amboy, Middlesex Co., merchant; will of. Niece, Sophia Watson, daughter of my brother, Alexander Watson, £500. Niece, Sophia Watson, daughter of my brother, William Watson, £1,000. To the 2 sons of my sister, Elizabeth, £100 each. To Robert Wallace, £50. Nieces, Elonaer and Christian, daughters of my sister, Christian, £100 each. Brother, William Watson, £20 a year. My sister, Christian Watson, £20 a year. Nephew, Alexander Watson, rest of personal and real. Executor—nephew, Alexander Watson. Witnesses—William Skinner, Robert King, Gertrude Skinner. Proved Aug. 31, 1768. Lib. I, p. 322.

1761, March 13. Watson, Peter, of Freehold, Monmouth Co.; will of. To brother, Garven Watson, £10. To sister, Euphema, the wife of Joseph Ker, £100. To sister, Ann, the wife of Walter Ker, £100. To the Presbyterian Church of Freehold, £100. Rest of personal and real to my wife, Mary. Executors—my wife and John Anderson. To my sister-in-law, Margaret Ker, £100. Witnesses—Ann Forman, Thomas Edwards, Robert Cumming. Proved April 3, 1761.
Lib. G, p. 416.

1761, March 27. Watson, William, of Nottingham, Burlington Co.; will of. To the 4 sons of my brother, John Watson, the land I have up at Passiak in the mountains. To the 2 daughters of my brother, John, table, chest of drawers, etc. Rest to my brother, John. Executor—brother, John. Witnesses—Jane Coleman, William Bunting, William Willgus. Proved June 28, 1762.
1762, April 17. Inventory, £344.8.7, made by William Bunting and Joseph DeCow.
1765, Sept. 8. Account by Executor. Lib. 11, p. 213.

1767, Sept. 5. Weatherby, Henry, of Deptford Twsp., Gloucester Co.; will of. To my wife all personal and real estate, and she is to be my Executrix. Witnesses—Reuben Jennings, Isaac Ballinger, Johannes Usback. Proved Nov. 2, 1767.
1767, Oct. 24. Inventory, £182.6.6, made by Samuel Paul and Isaac Ballinger. Lib. 13, p. 256.

1740, Sept. 13. Webb, John, of City of Perth Amboy, Middlesex Co., merchant; will of. Wife, Jane, my house and wharf, where I live, and the lot of 4 acres which I bought of Guisbert Lane, during her life. Son, Abraham, the house and lot which I bought of Mathias Iseltine, and now occupied by Mrs. Hill, when he comes of age. Son, Isaac (after his mother's death), the said house and wharf. Son, William, £25; and a like amount to son, John. Son, William, my lot on High Street of ½ acre; also my right to the house and lot which was mortgaged by Samuel Pray to Gabriel Stelle, who assigned the mortgage to me. Rest to my 4 sons, Abraham, Isaac, William and John. Executrix—wife, Jane. Witnesses—Philip Kearny, Samuel Lewis, James Mallown, George Webb. Proved Jan. 14, 1765. Lib. H, p. 586.

1763, Aug. 20. Webster, John, of Piscataway, Middlesex Co., yeoman; will of. Son, John, land, when 21. Sons, Thomas and Robert, rest of land. Daughter, Sarah Webster, £300. My seat in meetinghouse at Bound Brook to all my children. Executors—friends, Reune Runyon and Jeremiah Field, of Piscataway, and Jonathan Smith, of Somerset Co. Witnesses—David Leforge, Samuel Whitehead, Cornelius Bice. Proved Sept. 28, 1763. Lib. H, p. 301.

1763, Oct. 11. Webster, Joseph, of Bethlehem, Hunterdon Co.; will of. Sons, Joseph, Abraham and William, £30 each. Wife, Elizabeth, £30. Rest of personal estate to my daughters, Elizabeth Tomer, May Webster, Hannah, Sarah, Rachel, Deborah, Susanah and Martha.

Executors—John Webster, Hugh Webster, and Joseph Webster, my son. Witnesses—Robert Rea, Hannah Webster, Samuel Everitt. Proved Feb. 18, 1769, by Hannah Laing, late Hannah Webster.
1769, Feb. 8. Renunciations made by John Webster and Hugh Webster, in the stations of Executors of the estate of Joseph Webster, late of Newtown, Sussex Co. Witness—John Laing.
1769, Feb. 18. Inventory, £113.9.10, made by John Laing and Samuel Lundy, Jr.   Lib. 13, p. 546.

1770, Sept. 27. Welding, Ann, of Burlington Co. Ward. Daughter of John Welding, of Bordentown, in said Co. Guardian—Marmaduke Watson, of Chesterfield, in said Co. Fellowbondsman—James Sterling, Esq., of Burlington. Witness—James Williams.
Lib. 15, p. 68.

1761, June 20. Weller, Philip, of Greenwich Twsp., Sussex Co.; will of. Eldest son, Philip, all my lands. Second son, John, £250. Son, Jacob, £250. To my second daughter, Mary, £15. Daughter, Cateron, £15. Daughter, Elener, £15. Daughter, Sarah, £15. My son, Philip, is to maintain my wife, Elizabeth. Executor—son, Philip. Witnesses—James Hogeland, Mushael Hart, John Johnson. Proved July 3, 1761.
1761, July 18. Inventory, £316.18.3, made by Vallentine Sholts and Jonathan Pettit.   Lib. 10, p. 469.

1761, July 29. Wentzell, William, of Alloway Creek, Salem Co.; will of. My right in a tract of land I bought of Christian Nassel and John Shute to be sold. Wife, Mary Wentzell, a bed. Rest of personal estate to be divided between my wife and 6 sons, Philip, Theodorius, Charles, William, Daniel and Adam, when sons are of age. Executors—my wife, and son, Philip. Witnesses—Dennis O'Harrow, Mary O'Harrow, Johann Adam Foster. Proved Sept. 12, 1761. (The above William Wentzell, the testator, is sometimes called Johann William Wentzell).
1761, Sept. 8. Inventory, £321.10.0, made by William Oakford and John Holme.
1779, April 2. Account by Philip Wentzell, surviving Executor.
Lib. 11, p. 28; Lib. 22, p. 68.

1766, April 1. West, Bartholomew, of Shrewsbury, Monmouth Co., yeoman; will of. Wife, Ruth, use of my plantation. Daughter, Sarah, now wife of John Wardell, £12. Daughter, Margrate, now wife of Philip Edwards, £10. Son-in-law, John Dennis, 10 shillings. Son, Joseph, gun and mare. Son, Daniel, gun, clock, etc. Sons, Joseph and Daniel, my lands, after wife's death. Rest of personal to my wife, Ruth, and her 3 children, Joseph, Daniel and Margreat. Executors—my wife and sons, Joseph and Daniel. Witnesses—Job Cook, James Wardell, Joseph Wardell. Proved July 4, 1770.
1770, June 26. Inventory, £220.10.6, made by Job Cook and Jacob Wardell.   Lib. K, p. 226.

1762, May 17. West, Joseph, of Shrewsbury, Monmouth Co., cooper. Int. Adm'r—Daniel Wainright, yeoman. Fellowbondsman—Stephen West, yeoman; both of said place. Witnesses—Thomas Leonard and Nathaniel Scudder.
1762, May 15. Renunciation by Audria West, the widow, in favor

of her brother-in-law, Daniel Wainright. Witnesses—David Knott and George Brown.

1762, June 1. Inventory, £90.4.10, made by Peter Knott and David Knott. Lib. H, p. 207.

1768, Nov. 29. West, Richard, of Deptford, Gloucester Co., yeoman; will of. My wife, £15 a year. My brother, John West, a horse. Mother, Rachel West, a colt. My brother, Thomas West, a horse. Sister, Elizabeth, a heiffer. Son, Edmond, rest of personal and real; and he is to have 7 years' schooling; and my friend, Thomas Clark, is to be his Guardian. Executors—brothers, Thomas and John. Witnesses—Thomas Clark, Jonathan Paul, Ann Hammon. Proved Jan. 17, 1769.

1768, Dec. 10. Inventory, £134.5.4, made by Thomas Clark and John Jesup. Lib. 14, p. 52.

1770, April 15. West, Thomas, of Deptford Twsp., Gloucester Co., yeoman; will of. Wife, Deborah, beds, spoons, etc. Son, Charles, silver tankard. Son, Joseph, silver watch. Rest of my personal estate and cedar swamp to be sold, and the money divided between my wife and 3 children, Charles, Joseph and Mary; said children not yet 21. Plantation where I live to my wife, and at her marriage or death to son, Charles, he paying to my daughter, Mary, £100. Son, Joseph, land in Northern Liberties, Philadelphia. Mentions brother, Charles, and also brother, James, as deceased. Daughter, Mary, land that lies between 2 lots of my brother, Charles. To Jehu Airs, of Kensington, a lot located there, in order to perform a contract. My son, Joseph, to be given £70, which will arise by devise of will of my father. Executors—my wife, Deborah, my brother, Charles, my brother-in-law, Joseph Warner, of Philadelphia, and friend, Robert Friend Price. Witnesses—Samuel Ladd, Samuel Mickle, Samuel Blackwood. Proved May 10, 1770.

1770, May 10. Inventory, £506.16.0, made by Samuel Ladd and Joseph Gibson, Jr. Lib. 14, p. 221.

1764, Oct. 30. West, Vincent, of Evesham Twsp., Burlington Co., millwright. Int. Adm'r—John West, of Philadelphia. Fellowbondsmen—Jacob Prickitt and Francis Austin, both of Evesham, yeomen.

1764, Oct. 29. Inventory, £232.7.10, made by Jacob Prickit and Francis Austin. Lib. 12, p. 29.

1764, Jan. 10. Westbrook, Benjamin, of Sandyston, Sussex Co., blacksmith. Int. Adm'rs—Cornelius Westbrook and Cattriena Westbrook. Fellowbondsman—Hendrick Cortrecht.

1764, Jan. 3. Inventory, £534,13.9, made by Hendrick Cortrecht and Abraham Westbrook. Lib. 12, p. 4.

1769, Jan. 21. Westbrook, Johannas, of Sussex Co.; will of. To my wife, for the term of her life, £10, and her bread, yearly. Son, Abraham, £5. Son, Derick, my dwelling and grist mill, and plantation. Moveables to grandchildren. Daughter, Maria, a piece of linen. Executors—my wife and sons Derick, and Abraham. Witnesses—Gilbert Smith, Hendrick Kuykendall, Frederick Hayn. Proved Feb. 28, 1769.

1769, Feb. 27. Inventory, £482.1.6, made by Hendrick Kuykendal and Frederick Hayn. Lib. 13, p. 548.

1766, Dec. 22. Westcote, Joel, of Cumberland Co. Ward. Son of Henry Westcoat, of Fairfield, said Co., who, by will, left goods to said son. Guardian—Amos Westcote. Fellowbondsman—Nathan Lawrence; both of said Fairfield, yeomen. Lib. 12, p. 328.

1760, Sept. 9. Westveal, Jurryan, of Montague Twsp., Sussex Co., yeoman; will of. My son, Petrus Westveal, a horse, as his birthright, when he is 21, if he lives to come back from his captivity among the Indians. Children, Petrus Westveal, Joseph Westveal and Sarah Westveal; and my brother Petrus Westvael's son, Abraham, all my real and personal. My wife to remain in possession of my estate while she is my widow. Executors—my wife, Catharine, and my cousins, Abraham Cornelisse Van Aken and Jacobus Van Aken. Witnesses—Cornelis Van Aken, Cornelis Westvael, William Ennes. Proved Oct. 12, 1761.
1761, April 10. Inventory, £156.0.9, made by Abraham Van Aken and Johannis Kool. Lib. 11, p. 294.

1760, July 5. Wetherby, Edmund, Esq., of Mannington Precinct, Salem Co.; will of. Wife, Martha, a bed and saddle, over what the law allows her. Brother, Henry Wetherby, £10. My son, Edmund, law books and apparel. Daughter, Sarah Elliot, given personal goods. To Charles Elliot and my daughter, Sarah Elliot, the house and 8 acres where I live, and, after their deaths, to my grandson, Samuel Ashton, when of age. To son, Edmund, the plantation in Lower Penns Neck Twsp., where he lives; also 50 acres on Mill Creek. Executors—son, Edmund, and my friend, Edward Keasbey. Witnesses—Abigel Holaday, Dorothy Pledger, Alexander Miller. Proved Dec. 27, 1766.
1766, Nov. 14. Inventory, £1,904.5.8, made by Preston Carpenter and Jedidiah Allen. Lib. 12, p. 312.

1767, Oct. 22. Wetherby, Martha, of Mannington, Salem Co., widow. Int. Adm'r—Edmund Wetherby. Fellowbondsmen—Jonathan Woodnut and Whitten Cripps, yeomen; all of said place.
1767, Nov. 4. Inventory, £42.16.0, made by Charles Ellet and Daniel Wetherby. Lib. 13, p. 278.

1761, May 12. Wetherby, Mary, of Salem, Salem Co., widow; will of. Granddaughter, Mary Marshall, my house and lot in Salem; but, if she die under age, then to her brother, William Marshall. The personal estate to be divided into 2 parts, and the use of ½ I give to my daughter, Elizabeth O'Harow, to be disposed of as follows, viz., £5 to each of her 2 children, Mathew and Margaret O'Harow, when they are of age, and the rest to William Marshall, her son, when he is of age; but, if he die before he comes of age, then to Mary. The other half I give to my daughter, Isabel Moore, for life, and then to be divided between her 3 children, William, Joshua and John Moore. Executors—my friend, George Trenchard, and my granddaughter, Mary Marshall. Witnesses—Thomas Rice, Samuel Vance, Mary Wiggins. Proved Aug. 1, 1763.
1763, July 5. Inventory, £51.12.10, made by Henry Miller and Dennis O'Harrow. Lib. 11, p. 452.

1765, Jan. 10. Wetherill, Thomas, of Mannington, Salem Co. Int. Adm'x—Ann Wetherill, widow. Fellowbondsmen—Matthias Sullivan and John Kidd, yeomen; all of said place.

1765, Jan. 10. Inventory, £270.8.1, made by Elisha Bassett and Matthias Sullivan.
1766, June 28. Account by Adm'x.
Lib. 12, p. 177; File No. 1180 Q; File No. 1321 Q.

1761, Jan. 16. Wetherill, William, of Middlesex Co. Int. Adm'x—Martha Wetherill, the widow. Fellowbondsman—Samuel Cheesman; both of New Brunswick, said Co. Lib. G, p. 344.

1762, May 3. Wheaten, Elizabeth, of Newark, Essex Co.; will of. My friend, David Johnson, Jr., my house I live in. My cattle may be sold. My friend, Thomas Camfield, my negro. My friend, Hannah Lyon, widow, apparel. Executors—friends, David Johnson, Jr., and Thomas Canfield. Witnesses—Uzal Johnson, Abraham Lyon, David Johnson, Jr. Proved June 18, 1765. Lib. H, p. 555.

1761, June 12. Wheaten, Isaac, of Hopewell Twsp., Cumberland Co., yeoman; will of. Wife, Hannah, the ⅓ of moveable estate and use of plantation till my son, Isaac, is 21. Son, John, my lands on Stow Creek, and my lands in New England in township of Swansey. Son, Isaac, my plantation. Three youngest sons, Bagley, Reuben and Charles, £50 each. Daughters, Hephzibah, Sarah and Hannah, rest when 18. Executors—wife, Hannah, and my brother-in-law, Enos Woodruff. Witnesses—Nathan Bacon, Walter Ewing, John McGalliard. Proved March 22, 1762.
1762, Feb. 16. Inventory, £296.2.5, made by Charles Davis and Obediah Robins. Lib. 11, p. 157.

1760, Dec. 13. Wheaten, Noah, of Hopewell, Cumberland Co., yeoman; will of. My wife, Elizabeth, ⅓ of real and personal during life. Son, Jonathan, 10 acres at upper end. Son, Robert, rest of land where I live, and rest of moveables, and he to pay to my son, Henry, £50, when 21. Daughter, Sarah Reed, ten shillings. Daughter, Mary Wheaton, a bed. Daughter, Martha Wheaton, a bed. Executors—my wife, Elizabeth, my son, Jonathan, and my son, Robert. Witnesses—Samuel Harris, Jr., Jacob Harris, Ephraim Shepard. Proved Jan. 31, 1761.
1760, Dec. 30. Inventory, £274.3.10, made by David Jenkins and Samuel Harris, Jr. Lib. 10, p. 197.

1754, Feb. 28. Wheeler, Nathaniel, of Newark, Essex Co.; will of. Wife, Jemima, £100, and £20 yearly. Son, David, ½ of my Indian right at Paseppeny. Son, Nathaniel, my house and lot where I live, and the lot in the Neck, and the one over the hill. Daughter, Sarah Ross, 1,000 acres of my Indian purchase, which is in partnership with Garretbrant Garretbrant. Daughter, Johanna Foster, 500 acres in the Indian right. Executors—son, Nathaniel, and John Ross. Witnesses—Joseph Camp, Ebenezer Camfield, Israel Canfield. Proved March 28, 1761. Lib. G, p. 405.

1762, Feb. 2. Wheeler, Samuel, of Newark, Essex Co.; will of. Wife, Sarah, the rents of my lands while my widow. Daughter, Mary Ogden, the land on east side of road that goes out to widow Jane Smith, which binds on land which I sold to Josiah Quimby, and land I formerly gave to Samuel Ogden; also all the things that were my first wife's. To daughter, Sarah Lindsly, and daughter, Sarah Wheeler, and my granddaughter, the child of my son, Samuel, de-

ceased, the rest of my lands. Executors—friends, Amos Harrison, Esq., and David Harrison. Witnesses—John Dod, Jr., David Dod, Rebeca Ward. Proved May 12, 1762.
1762, May 20. Inventory, £263.7.0, made by Isaac Cundeet and Eleazar Lamson. Lib. H, p. 137.

1753, Feb. 19. Wheten, Joseph, of Greenwich, Cumberland Co., cordwainer; will of. Wife, Mary, all my personal estate, except what is given to my daughter, Prisilla. Wife the use of all estate till said daughter is 8 years old. Daughter, Priscilla Wheten, my plantation. Names sisters, Elizabeth Dun and Rachel Hudson. Executor—friend, Charles Davis, Esq. Witnesses—Thomas Ewing, John Williams, Samuel Fithian. Proved Feb. 12, 1767.
1767, Feb. Renunciation by Charles Davis. Witnesses—Gabriel Davis and Jonathan Potts.
1767, Feb. 12. Adm'x—Mary Wheten, widow. Fellowbondsman—Isaac Fithian, both of said Greenwich. Witness—Samuel Fithian.
1767, April 2. Inventory, £465.6.9, made by Samuel Fithian and Obadiah Robins. Lib. 13, p. 147.

1762, Feb. 13. Whillden, David, of Cape May Co., yeoman; will of. A head and foot stone to be bought for the graves of my mother, Mary Whillden, sister Lois Mills (both dead), and myself. Brother, James Whillden, Esq., my wearing apparel. Of the rest of my moveable estate I give ¾ thereof to said James Whillden, my sister, Hannah Eldredge, and sister, Rachel Mills; and the other ¼ to Ellis Hughes, Judith Hughes and Mary Hughes (the legal representatives of my sister, Mary Hughes, deceased). My right in Five Mile Beach, which I bought of James Swaine, I order to be sold. To Matthew Whillden, son of my brother, James, cedar swamp. To Seth Whillden, the 2nd son of my brother, the use of my homestead till said Matthew Whillden is 21; then it shall belong to Mathew. Executors —said James Whillden and Ezekiel Eldredge. Witnesses—William Flower, John Hughes, Mary Edwards, Jacob Spicer. Proved May 13, 1762.
1762, May 14. Inventory, £482.3.5, made by John Eldredge and Richard Stites. File 237 E.

1763, Aug. 12. Whitaker, Jonathan, of Bernards Town. Somerset Co., yeoman; will of. To wife, Elizabeth, one-half the profits of the place where I live, and, after her death, the place is to be sold and money given to children, Jonathan, Eliphelet, Nathaniel and Elizabeth, the wife of Stephen Ogden. Executors—friends, John Roy and Edward Lewis. Witnesses—Platt Bayles, Mary Robertson, Brice Rikey. Proved Oct. 14, 1763. Lib. H, p. 311.

1770, Dec. 12. White, Amos, of Deal, Shrewsbury Twsp., Monmouth Co.; will of. I have given a deed to my eldest son, Joel, for the farm where he lives; and I give him the west ½ of that neck of land, lying to the west of the land formerly belonging to John Drummond. Son, Amos, is to have the east half; also the farm I live on, and 4 acres of salt meadow. Daughter, Leah Morris, £200. Rest of moveable estate to my 4 daughters, Rachel, Leah, Deborah and Mary; but Rachel being dead, I give her share to her 3 children, John, Mary and Rachel. Executors—friends, John Tucker and Samuel Tucker, of said Township. Witnesses—Thomas Shearman, Lewis Smith. Proved Dec. 29, 1770. Lib. K, p. 290.

1761, March 26. White, Andrew, of Middletown, Monmouth Co.; will of. My land to be sold, and ⅓ of the money I give to my wife, Esther. Son, Amos, my walking staff, that was my father's. Son, Zephaniah, my silver knee buckles. Daughter, Anne, pewter platter, plates, etc. Son, Garrison, silver shoe buckles. The use of the rest is to educate my son, Andrew, till he is 14 years, and then the whole is to be divided among all my children, Amos, Zephaniah, Anne, Garrison and Andrew. Executors—my friends, Esek Hartshorne and John Herbert. Witnesses—Jonathan Stout, William Applegate, Robert Hartshorne. Proved April 17, 1761.

1761, April 18. Inventory, £19.17.6, made by, William Applegate and Edward Andrews. Lib. H, p. 175.

1764, Sept. 22. White, George, of Shrewsbury, Monmouth Co., yeoman; will of. Children—John, Thomas, Robert, Benjamin, William, Joseph and Sarah, all my lands, when they are of age. Executors—friends, Joseph Jackson and Benjamin Wolcott. Witnesses—Peter White, Thomas Hulitt, John West. Proved June 29, 1768.
Lib. I, p. 287.

1761, Dec. 1. White, James, of Cumberland Co. Int. Adm'rs—Rebecca White and Thomas Joslin. Fellowbondsmen—John Dare and Mark Riley; all of Deerfield, Cumberland Co. Witnesses—Isaac Stathem and Ephraim Shaw.

1761, Nov. 27. Inventory, £93.0.1, made by John Dare and Mark Ryley.

1763, Dec. 23. Account by both Adm'rs. Lib. 11, p. 156.

1763, March 4. White, Jeremiah, of City of Perth Amboy, Middlesex Co., yeoman; will of. Daughter, Sarah Crips, wife of William Crips, £10 and my household goods. Son, Benjamin White, equal share with the rest of children, viz., Nancy, Phebe, Richard and Samuel, which will be 1/6 part. To Jeremiah White, son of John White, deceased, £10. I have a lot in Perth Amboy as being the only surviving heir of John White, of Perth Amboy, and I order the said land to be sold. Executors—William Crips and Sarah, his wife, and my daughter, Nancy. Witnesses—Gedion Bornum, Robert Sproull. Proved March 22, 1763. Lib. H, p. 224.

1767, Aug. 19. White, John, of Salem Co. Int. Adm'r—Jonathan White. Fellowbondsmen—Daniel Bassett and Robert Clark, yeomen; all of Pilesgrove, said Co.

1767, Aug. 1. Inventory, £137.18.6, made by Daniel Bassett and Robert Clark. Lib. 13, p. 190.

1769, Oct. 28. White, Robert, of Monmouth Co. Int. Adm'r—Thomas Borden. Fellowbondsman—Isaac Vandyke; both of Shrewsbury, said Co. Witnesses—John Brinley and Jacob Hance.

1769, Oct. 30. Inventory, made by Josiah Parker and William Pintard. Lib. K, p. 142.

1766, May 28. White, Stephen, of Morris River, Cumberland Co. Int. Adm'r—William Dalles, Jr. Fellowbondsman—Silas Newcomb, Esq.; both of Fairfield, said Co.

1766, May 6. Inventory, £23.3.7, made by William Doulas and Silas Newcomb. Lib. 12, p. 326.

CALENDAR OF WILLS—1761-1770 475

1768, March 21. Whitehead, Leonard, of Middlesex Co. Int. Adm'rs —Elijah Dunham and Richard Carnes, two of the creditors. Fellowbondsman—Isaac Bonnell; all of said Co. Witness—Lawrence Taylor. Lib. I, p. 301.

1758, Nov. 13. Whitson, Thomas, of Am'well, Hunterdon Co., yeoman; will of. Wife, Elizabeth, the house I live in. Eldest son, John, £3. My oldest daughter, Elizabeth Burthshell, £3. Daughter, Martha Canbe, £15. Daughter, Deborah Prall, £10. Daughter, Anna Whitson, £100, when 18. Son, Thomas, ½ my lands. Son, Henry, the other half, and this house and farm. Executors—my wife, John Corwine, and my son, Thomas. Witnesses—Hugh Hughs, George Sarvis, Johannis Sarvis. Proved March 5, 1761.
1761, Feb. 25. Inventory, £260.14.3, made by Richard Reed and Johannis Servis.
1771, April 22. Account by Elizabeth Whitson and Thomas Whitson, two of the Executors. "Paid John Whitson, £3." Lib. 10, p. 549.

1763, Oct. 13. Whittaker, Elizabeth, of Bernards Town, Somerset Co.; will of. Widow of Jonathan Whittaker. To son, Jonathan, 5 shillings. Daughter, Elizabeth Ogden, apparel. Rest to children, Jonathan, Elizabeth, and Eliphelet. Executors—son, Eliphelet Whittaker, and Stephen Ogden. Witnesses—John Roy, John Collyer, John Lyon. Proved March 20, 1764. Lib. H, p. 416.

1768, Aug. 25. Whittall, William, of Salem Co. Ward. Aged 18 years and son of John Whittal, of said Co., who says Erasmus Fetters, by will, left him a house, lot and tanyard in town of Salem, and that he has been advised by counsel that he has a right to choose a Guardian, to take charge of his estate, notwithstanding his father is the natural Guardian of his person; therefore he makes choice of Robert Wilson, to be his Guardian, till he is 21.
1768, Aug. 30. Guardian—Robert Wilson, shopkeeper. Fellowbondsman—Thomas Goodwin, yeoman; both of Salem. Lib. 13, p. 411.

1768, Oct. 7. Wickes, Jonas, of Huntington, on Long Island. Int. Adm'x—Hannah Wickes, widow, of said place. Fellowbondsmen—Benjamin Abit and Abdon Abit, yeomen; both of Pilesgrove, Salem Co.
1769, June 12. Inventory, £6.19.5, made by Samuel Mead and Burroughs Abit. Lib. 13, p. 476.

1755, Dec. 9. Wiggins, James, of Salem, Salem Co., yeoman; will of. I give to that child with which my wife is now pregnant, £50, when it is of age. Wife, Hannah, rest of personal estate. Executors—my wife and Aaron Bradway. Witnesses—John Sedden, Joseph Zane, Josiah Kay. Proved Aug. 28, 1761.
1761, Aug. 21. Inventory, £338.3.10, made by Grant Gibbon and John Firth. Lib. 11, p. 29.

1770, Nov. 20. Wiggins, James, of Salem Co. Ward. Aged 11 years. Son of James Wiggins, of said place, deceased. Whereas Hannah, the mother of said child has married Nathaniel Thompson, and they desire that Edward Keasby may be appointed Guardian, etc.
1770, Nov. 28. Guardian—Edward Keasbey, of Salem Co. Fellowbondsman—Samuel Allinson, of Burlington. Lib. 15, p. 67.

1764, Jan. 19. Wildey, John, of Deptford Twsp., Gloucester Co. Int. Adm'x—Grace Wildey, widow. Fellowbondsman—Joseph Low, yeoman; both of said place. Witness—Nixon Chattin.
1764. Jan. 14. Inventory, £30.2.4, made by John Wilkins and Nixon Chattin. Lib. 11, p. 476.

1760, Aug. 8. Wilkins, Amos, of Evesham, Burlington Co., yeoman; will of. Wife, Sarah, ½ my moveable estate, and use of 2 rooms on plantation I bought of Enoch Haines, and other priviledges while my widow. Son, John, when 21, 200 acres, being part of 300 where I live. Son, Benjamin, when 21, the other 100 acres, and to be on the east end; also 2 lots in Pennsylvania, one on Patties Island of 5 acres, and the other in Kensington of 1 acre. Son, Amos, when 21 plantation I bought of Enoch Haines, of 190 acres. Son, Caleb, £100, when 21, and when he is 14 he is to be put to a trade. Son, Joshua, £100, and also to be put to a trade. Son, Samuel, £100, and to be put to a trade. Executors—my son, John, and my friend, Noah Haines. Witnesses—Hugh Sharp, Joshua Stratton, Richard Parke. Proved April 2, 1761.
1761, March 25. Inventory, £653.4.2, made by Jacob Prickit and James Cattell.
1774, Jan. 15. Account by both Ex'rs.
1774, Jan. 15. Account of Thomas Wilkins, surviving Ex'r of William Wilkins, late of Evesham, and of Noah Haines and John Wilkins, Executors of Amos Wilkins, who was the Executor of William Wilkin's estate, of so much of the estate of William Wilkins, as came to the hands of said Executors. Lib. 10, p. 330; Lib. 15, p. 520.

1760, Oct. 18. Wilkins, Thomas, of Greenwich Twsp., Gloucester Co., yeoman; will of. Sons, Thomas and Constantine Wilkins, all my land in said Twsp., and land in Deptford Twsp., fronting on Great Manto Creek, they paying £20 yearly to their mother (my wife Joanna). My two youngest daughters, Asuba and Amy Wilkins, the land joining David Cooper's plantation. To my 3 daughters, Adelicia Snowden, Asuba, and Amy Wilkins, my lots at Woodbury. Executors—sons, Thomas and Constantine. Witnesses—William Wood, Abigail Chew, Robert Jamson. Proved Jan. 8, 1762.
1761, Dec. 31. Inventory, £653.9.3, made by William Wilkins and William Wood. Lib. 11, p. 93.

1763, Aug. 1. Wilkins, Thomas, of Greenwich Twsp., Gloucester Co., yeoman. Int. Adm'r—Constantine Wilkins, of said place, yeoman. Fellowbondsman—William Wilkins, of Deptford Twsp., said Co., yeoman. Witness—James Miller.
1763, July 3. Inventory, £443.4.5, made by William Wilkins, and Joseph Tonkin. Lib. 11, p. 440.

1767, Sept. 24. Wilkinson, Crowell, of Hanover, Morris Co. Int. Adm'r—Jacob Ford, principal creditor. Fellowbondsman—Jacob Ford, Jr.; both of said place. Witness—Chloe Bridge.
1767, June 22. Renunciation by Martha Wilkinson, the widow. Witness—John Johnson. (The said Crowell Wilkinson died April 25, 1767). Lib. I, p. 208; File No. 229 N.

1763, Aug. 23. Wilkison, John, of Woodbridge, Middlesex Co. Ward. Son of James Wilkison, and makes choice of Isaac Tappen as his Guardian.

CALENDAR OF WILLS—1761-1770   477

1764, Feb. 21. Guardian Isaac Tappen, of Woodbridge, said Co. Fellowbondsman—Isaac Freeman, of said Co.   Lib. H, p. 331.

1761, May 11. Wilkinson, Joseph, of Gloucester Co., yeoman; will of. Wife, Hannah, all lands and moveable estate. Executrix—wife, Hannah. Witnesses—Ansell Long, Adam Sharp, Philip Skualboker. Proved June 5, 1761.
1761, June 4. Inventory, £352.12.11, made by Samuel Paul, Sr., and Ansell Long.   Lib. 11, p. 103.

1748, July 24. Wilkinson, Nathaniel, of Springfield, Burlington Co., yeoman; will of. Daughter, Mary, the house and 20 acres where I dwell, when she is 18; also £100. Son and heir, Richard, who is left in England, 5 shillings. My wife, Rachel, all the rest. Executor—my wife. Witnesses—Daniel Harker, Enoch Fenton, John Fenimore. Proved April 16, 1764.   Lib. 11, p. 494.

1760, April 3. Willard, Benjamin, of Waterford, Gloucester Co., yeoman; will of. Son, James, my plantation, where I live, when he is 21. Wife, Rebecah, all personal estate, and to support my child in his minority; she to have use of land, till he is 21. If my son die under 21, without issue, then the land, after wife's death, to go to my cousin, Jacob Spicer. Executrix—my wife. Witnesses—Thomas Willard, Joseph Morgan. Proved Aug. 8, 1761.
1761, July 20. Inventory, £149.14.2, made by Henry Wood and Joseph Morgan.
1761, Nov. 16. Renunciation of Thomas Willard, of Gloucester Co., yeoman, who says that he is a brother of Benjamin Willard, deceased, and has a right to administer, but now surrenders the same to his uncle, Thomas Willard.
1761, Nov. 27. Whereas Benjamin Willard, of Waterford, deceased, made will and appointed his wife, Rebecca, as Executrix, and she did prove the will, and hath since died intestate, leaving part of the same unadministered; now Thomas Willard is made administrator of all left unadministered by Rebecca Willard, with the will annexed. Fellowbondsman—Joseph Morgan, of Waterford.
1761, Nov. 21. Inventory, £136.0.9, of the goods of Benjamin Willard and Rebecca Willard, his wife; made by Joseph Morgan and Henry Wood.
1765, Oct. 31. Adm'rs—Joseph Morgan and Henry Wood, both of Waterford Township. Fellowbondsman—John Shaw, of City of Burlington. The said Joseph Morgan and Henry Wood are to administer the goods of Benjamin Willard, left unadministered by Thomas Willard, who was Adm'r with the will annexed of Benjamin Willard, late of Waterford Twsp., deceased.
1774, Feb. 16. Account by Joseph Morgan and Henry Wood, Adm's de bonis non of Benjamin Willard. Paid Sarah Willard, legacy, £25.18.0. Paid Walter Burk, for keeping Rebecca Willard, £15.
1774, May 16. A further account by the Adm'rs, which was overlooked. Mentions Joseph Armstrong, Bartholomew Eggman, etc.
     Lib. 10, p. 442; Lib. 11, p. 104; Lib. 12, p. 284; Lib. 15, p. 515.

1761, Nov. 11. Willard, Rebecca, of Gloucester Co., widow. Int. Adm'x—Rebecca Walker. Fellowbondsmen—Elias Toy and James Toy; all of Burlington Co.   Lib. 11, p. 224.

1763, March 18. Willard, Thomas, of Waterford, Gloucester Co., yeoman; will of. Wife, Mary, all moveable estate. Son, Parr Willard, my lands, but if he die before 21, then the lands to go to the child that my wife is big with. Daughters—Rebeccah and Hannah Willard, £20, when 18. Executors—my wife and Joseph Morgan. Witnesses—John Cobb, Isaac Fish, Walter Burk. Proved April 9, 1763.
1763, April 4. Inventory, £136.14.11, made by Henry Wood and Joseph Morgan.
1768, Feb. 23. Account made by Mary Willard. Lib. 11, p. 300.

1763, April 20. Willard, Thomas, of Waterford, Gloucester Co., shipwright; will of. My brother, Richard Willard, my apparel. The remainder to my 2 brother's children, namely, Isaac Willard's children and Richard's children, and to my 2 cousin's children, namely, Thomas Willard's children and Benjamin Willard's children, when they are 21. Executors—friends, Joseph Morgan and Henry Wood. Witnesses—Griffith Morgan, Ann Burk, Walter Burk. Proved June 11, 1763.
1763, June 4. Inventory, £403.5.4¾, made by John Shivers and Joshua Roberts.
1774, Feb. 17. Account by Henry Wood and Joseph Morgan.
Lib. 11, p. 327; Lib. 15, p. 515.

1763, June 8. Willcock, Peter, of Elizabeth Borough, Essex Co., yeoman; will of. Wife, Phebe, 30 acres of my home plantation, to join son William's land. Son, Peter, 5 shillings, as he has had his portion by deed of gift. Son, William, 80 acres, bounded by James Badgley and Richard Vallentine, and ½ the land laid out and drawn in right of John Meeker, dec'd. Son, John, rest of home lot, and 30 acres which I gave to my wife, after her death. Son, Stephen, land where he lives, in Elizabeth Town, which I bought of William Jones, dec'd, and 6 acres lying by Brackets Brook. Daughter, Sarah, wife of Joseph Allen, Jr., £25. Executors—wife, Phebe, and my sons, William, John and Stephen. Witnesses—Anthony Badgley, Jr., Robert Badgley, Ebenezer Price. Proved June 22, 1768. Lib. I, p. 281.

1764, Feb. 24. Willcock, Peter, Jr., of Borough of Elizabeth, Essex Co., yeoman; will of. Sons, David and Noah, my plantation, and it is to be divided by a line running from my brother John's grist mill. Eldest daughter, Bette Willcock, £70. My second daughter, Phebe Willcock, £60. Third daughter, Hannah Willcock, £50, when 18. My 3 youngest daughters, Sabra, Joanah and Mary, £50 each, when 18. To Baptist Church on Scotch Plains, £20. Wife, Elizabeth, £30. Executors—wife, Elizabeth, and Joseph Allen. Witnesses—Uriah Daniells, Benjamin Gray, William Willcock. Proved March 6, 1764.
Lib. H, p. 411.

1770, March 28. Willcock, Stephen, of Borough of Elizabeth, Essex Co. Int. Adm'rs—Martha Willcock and William Willcock. Fellowbondsman—John Megie; all of said place. Witnesses—Mary Ogden and Robert Ogden. Lib. K, p. 190.

1759, Nov. 29. Willets, Richard, of Newton Twsp., Gloucester Co.; will of. Wife, Patience, £50. Mentions sons and daughters, as being yet young, but does not name them. Executrix—my wife. Over-

seers—Isaac Andrews and Joseph Butcher. Witnesses—Thomas Redman, Thomas Redman, Jr., John Gill. Proved March 6, 1761.
1760, Dec. 9. Inventory, £397.4.11, made by John Shivers and John Gill. Lib. 10, p. 395.

1764, June 12. Willets, Sarah, of Alloways Creek Twsp., Salem Co., widow; will of. Being the widow of Richard Willets. Grandson, Amos Bunten, all my real and personal estate. Executors—said grandson, and my brother, John Willets of Cape May. Witnesses—John Hillman, Thomas Sayre, Reubin Sayre. Proved April 11, 1767.
1767, April 9. Inventory, £195.5.6, made by John Hillman and Thomas Sayre. Lib. 13, p. 174.

1762, Oct. 4. Willett, Samuel, of Monmouth Co. Int. Adm'r—William Willett, eldest son of said Samuel. Fellowbondsman—Phinehas Skinner; both of Hunterdon Co. Lib. H, p. 189.

1762, May 22. Willett, Thomas, of Middletown, Monmouth Co.; will of. Wife, Abigail, negros, silverware, etc. Daughter, Mary Willett, negro girl. Son, Gilbert, a negro. Sons, Benjamin, Thomas and John, each a negro. The land where I live, lately purchased of Samuel Hunt, to be sold, and the money given to my wife and children, Gilbert, Benjamin, Thomas, John, Mary Willett, Isaac, James, Anne Willett, Euphame Willett and William. Executors—my wife, son Gilbert, and my brothers-in-law, John Stevenson and Thomas Hicks. Witnesses—James Stevenson, Edward Stevenson, Richard Stillwell. Proved Sept. 13, 1764.
1764, Nov. 16. Inventory, £1560.19.0, made by Richard Crawford, Jr., Samuel Hunt and Edward Stevenson. Lib. H, p. 604.

1763, March 28. Williams, Benjamin, and others. Wards. Children of Ebenezer Williams. Petition of Moses Miller and Sarah, his wife, John Doobs, Benjamin Williams and Sarah Williams, and other inhabitants of Borough of Elizabeth, stating that Ebenezer Williams, of said Borough, deceased, by his will appointed his wife, Sarah, and the said John Dobs, his Executors, but appointed no Guardian to his children, to whom he gave personal and real estate, and his widow, having since married the said Moses Miller, and the children, Benjamin and Sarah, having arrived at the age of 14 years, and the other children, viz., Mindwell, Enoch, Ebenezer and Margant, being under that age; and Moses Miller, and his wife, and the said John Doobs, and the said Benjamin and Sarah Williams, makes choice of John Stites of said Borough, as a suitable person for Guardian. Signed by Moses Miller, Sarah Miller, Sarah Williams, Benjamin Williams, Benjamin Marsh, Thomas Williams, Jonathan Williams, Abraham Clark, Jr., Samuell Woodruff, Robert Ogden and John Doobs.
1763, June 16. John Stites and Jonathan Williams, both of Essex Co., go on bond, wherein John Stites is appointed Guardian of Benjamin, Sarah, Mindwell, Enoch, Ebenezer and Margant Williams.
Lib. H, p. 258.

1770, Jan. 21. Williams, Daniel, of Shrewsbury, Monmouth Co., yeoman; will of. Wife, Ann, some household goods, which are to be given to my son, George, after her death. Son, John, the land 1 bought of John Brinley, which is in Shrewsbury, near Steven Wolley's. Grandson, Daniel Worthley, £30, and his father, Richard, is to pay him £25, which was lent to him by me. Son, George, my mortgages. A good title to be made to the mill, for the support of son, George; and he is to be put to a trade. Executor—my friends, Webley Edwards, and Peleg Slocum. Witnesses—Job Cook, Noah Taber, David Hance. Proved March 27, 1770.

1770, March 7. Inventory, made by John Brinley and James West.
Lib. K, p. 196.

1768, Nov. 29. Williams, David, of Borough of Elizabeth, Essex Co.; will of. Brother, Samuel Ogden, moveables. Sister, Rebecka, a bed. Executor—Timothy Woodruff. Witnesses—Seth Woodruff, Nathaniel Meeker, David Meeker, Jr. Proved Dec. 20, 1768.
Lib. K, p. 50.

1766, Dec. 30. Williams, Gershom, of Newark, Essex Co. Int. Adm'rs—Daniel Cundict and Joseph Baldwin, at request of Martha Williams, the widow, she having renounced. Fellowbondsman—John Nisbit; all of Newark.

1767, Jan. 15. Inventory, £60.17.6, made by Isaac Cundet and John Dod Jr.
Lib. I, p. 208.

1769, Dec. 29. Williams, James, of Middlesex Co. Int. Adm'r—John Lewis Johnston. Fellowbondsman—John Smyth; both of City of Perth Amboy.

1770, Jan. 6. Inventory, £19.19.5, of goods, sold at public vendue. (Cow sold to Elizabeth Williams. Wood sled sold to George Williams).
Lib. K, p. 142.

1768, Oct. 10. Williams, John, of Shrewsbury, Monmouth Co.; will of. Wife, Elizabeth, use of the land where I live. Sons, James and Daniel, the place where I live, that lies on the east side of Deal road; and the land on Goose Neck, and a salt meadow which I bought of William Cook, when they are 21. Son, George, the south part of the land that I bought of the Executors of Jedediah Allen; also my fulling mill. Son, John, the land where I dwell. Sons, Obadiah and Joseph, north part of the tract I bought of Jedidah Allen. Daughters, Elizabeth, Joannah, Hannah and Mary, £60 each, at marriage or when 21. Executors—wife, Elizabeth, my brother, Ezekiah Williams, and my sons, James and Daniel. I give my brother, Hezekiah, power to make title to Joseph Potter for ½ the grist mill and land near John Woodmansee. Witnesses—Sarah Tole, Stephen Wardell, Joseph Potter. Proved Nov. 8, 1768.

1768, Nov. 18. Inventory, made by Richard Lawrence, Benjamin Wolcott and Edmund Williams.
Lib. K, p. 27.

1763, Jan. 25. Williams, Joseph, of Squan, Monmouth Co., cooper; will of. I sailed from Sandy Hook, in the "Charlotte," commanded by James Oman, but being taken by the French, and carried into Cape Francis, and being very sick. To friend, Thomas Stymest, all estate, who is to demand from Abraham Emmens, son of Jacob Emmans, now living on the lands that did belong to me, my chest in which I left my papers; also to demand of Capt. Van Cleef, brother of Benjamin Van Cleef, a bond of £100. Executors—said Thomas Stymest. Witnesses—William Lyell, Robert Lerycraft, William Smith. Proved Oct. 11, 1766.
File No. 2983 M.

CALENDAR OF WILLS—1761-1770   481

1770, Feb. 15. Williams, Samuel, of Cheapside, Newark Twsp., Essex Co.; will of. My brothers, Joseph and John Williams, ½ of my lands. To Nicholas Squier, my sister Anibel's son, £50, when he is of age. Mother, Sarah Dixon, and sisters, Anabel Squire, and Mary Dixon, are provided for. To sister, Annabel Squire, ¼ of my lands. My sister, Mary Dixon, ¼ of my lands, she paying to my mother, Sarah Dixon, £50. My brother-in-law, John Dixon, £50. Names brother, Benjamin Williams. Executors—John Campfield, of Hanover, Ellis Cook, Jr., and Zophar Squire. Witnesses—Daniel Young, Daniel Dixon, Jane Dixon. Proved May 8, 1770.
1770, May 10. Inventory, £40.3.0, made by William Reeve and Matthew Moores. Lib. K, p. 220.

1757, Sept. 18. Williams, Thomas, of Trenton, Hunterdon Co.; will of. Wife, Katherine, all lands and goods, and what remains after her death I give to her grandson, Nathan Wright, and, if he die, then to his brother, William Wright. Executrix—my wife. Witnesses—John Rickey, James Dougherty, William Ball. Proved June 29, 1765. Lib. 12, p. 205.

1766, July 2. Williamson, Cornelius and Jemima, of Monmouth Co. Wards. Cornelius is aged 18, and Jemima 16. Children of Arthur Williamson. Guardian—Jacob Ten Eyck. Fellowbondsmen—Peter Ten Eyck and Peter Post; all of Somerset Co. Lib. H, p. 620.

1767, April 30. Williamson, Cornelius, of Amwell, Hunterdon Co. Int. Adm'rs—Jehokim Griggs and Abraham Williamson. Fellowbondsman—Jacob Sutphen; all of said place.
1767, April 30. Renunciation by Elizabeth Williamson and Gesberd Gulick, in favor of Jehokim Griggs and Abraham Williamson.
1767, Oct. 5. Inventory, £394.18.0, made by John Platt and Jacob Sutphen.
1768, Aug. 9. Account by, Joachim Griggs and Abraham Williamson, the Administrators. (Paid Elizabeth Williamson, the widow, £6. Paid Bartholomew Williamson, 4 shillings and 10 pence).
Lib. 13, p. 200.

1766, Jan. 31. Williamson, David, of Freehold, Monmouth Co., farmer; will of. Eldest son, Aurt, £5. Wife, Geertye, bed and use of real estate, to maintain my children. Son, Hendrick, ½ of my 4 tracts in Freehold. Son, William, other ½. Daughter, Anne Williamson, £200, when 21. Daughter, Sarah Williamson, £200. Executors—brother, William Williamson, and brothers-in-law, John Covenhoven and Peter Voorhees. Witnesses—Art Sutphen, John Hanson, Jr., Isaac Voorhees. Proved May 21, 1766.
1766, May 21. Inventory, £463.15.3, made by Samuel Leonard, Art Sutphen and Peter Holsart. Lib. I, p. 45.

1761, Aug. 10. Williamson, Jacobus, of Middlesex Co. Int. Adm'rs —Peter Perrine, of Somerset Co., and William Williamson, Jr., of Middlesex Co.
1761, Aug. 7. Renunciation by William Williamson and Garret Williamson, who are brothers of said Jacobus. Witnesses—Samuel Gerretson, and Isaac Broocks.
1761, Aug. 7. Inventory of estate of Jacobus Williamson, of Six-Mile-Run, Middlesex Co., made by Cornelius Dehart and Samuel Garretson. Lib. H, p. 1.

1769, July 29. Williamson, John, of Amwell, Hunterdon Co.; will of. Wife, Mary, use of ⅓ my farm where I live, till son, John, shall marry, after which she is provided for. Son, Wilhelmus, 200 acres where he lives, joining lands of Johannes Fox and Thomas Lake. Son, Abraham, rest of plantation. Where Wilhelmus lives. Son, John, part of the homestead. Son, Jacob, 120 acres that I lately bought of the estate of James Prall. Daughters, Catharine Whitenack, Anne Housel and Rebecca Williamson, moveables. Executors—friend, William Schenck, and my son, Abraham. Witnesses—Aaron Vandoren, Joseph Hogeland, John Lequear. Proved Sept. 26, 1769.
    1769, Aug. 26. Inventory, £1,173.1.3, made by Lewis Chamberlin and Jacob Mattison.
    1774, Oct. 22. Account by Executors.
    Lib. 14, p. 164; Lib. 15, p. 499.

1766, April 19. Willits, David, of Sussex Co. Int. Adm'rs—Solomon Willits and Solomon Willits, Jr. Fellowbondsman—Isaac Pettit.
    1766, April 19. Inventory, £27.8.6, made by Elisha Cooke and Edward Oatley.
    Lib. 12, p. 434.

1770, Jan. 19. Willits, Solomon, of Hardwick Twsp., Sussex Co.; will of. Son, Solomon, 10 shillings. Son, Jonathan, £4. Son, Joseph's 2 daughters, £8 each, to remain in the care of my brother, Joseph Willits, till they are 18. Son-in-law, Andrew Collins, rest of estate. Executors—Joseph Willits and Andrew Collins. Witnesses—James Bell, Samuel Lundy, Nathaniel Hazen. Proved March 7, 1770.
    1770, March 1. Inventory, £98.13.0, made by Nathaniel Hazen and Thomas Lundy.
    Lib. 14, p. 239.

1767, June 30. Willover, Peter, of Mansfield Woodhouse Twsp., Sussex Co., farmer; will of. Wife, Margrit, ⅓ of the profits of plantation, while she lives. Son, Peter Willeaver, ½ of the place where I live, and ½ the land on the hill on the over side of Muskenekin Creek; and the other ½ to my son, Jacob Willever. Son, John, £40. Son, David, £34. Son, Samuel, £34. Son, Henry, £34. Son, Abram, £34. Daughter, Margrit, the wife of John Peatey, £34. Daughter, Mary, the wife of Peter Winter, £34. Executors—my friend, Fredrick Eveland, and my son, Peter Willever. Witnesses—Robert Laning, Joseph Parke, Christian Cummins. Proved Nov. 19, 1767.
    1767, Oct. 30. Inventory, £42.11.6, made by Joseph Parke and Christian Cummins.
    Lib. 13, p. 325.

1764, April 8. Wills, Daniel, of Burlington Co., carpenter; will of. Wife, Meribah furniture in the lodging room, use of said room, cellar and east end of house, etc. Rest of personal and real to be sold, and proceeds to be given to wife and 5 children, viz., Jacob, James, Samuel, Mary and Bulah. My 3 sons to be put out to farmers, till they are 14. Executors—brother-in-law, Joseph Mullen, and my cousin, Micajah Wills. Witnesses—John Wills, Joseph Goldy, Lawrence Webster. Proved Oct. 23, 1764.
    1764, Oct. 15. Inventory, £285.18.9, made by Joseph Burr, Jr., and Thomas Eayre.
    Lib. 12, p. 27.

1761, June 19. Wills, John, of Willingborough, Burlington Co. Int. Adm'r—Aaron Wills, yeoman. Fellowbondsman—Jonathan Wills; both of same place.
    1761, June 20. Inventory, £30.1.3, made by Asher Woolman and Samuel Kemble.
    Lib. 10, p. 207.

CALENDAR OF WILLS—1761-1770   483

1766, Aug. 21. Willson, David, Sr., of Roxbury, Morris Co. Int. Adm'r—David Willson, eldest son of said David, of said place. Fellowbondsman—Samuel Day, of Morristown, Morris Co., yeoman. Witness—Joseph Cory.
    1766, Aug. 19. Renunciation by Deborah Willson, the widow, in favor of David Willson, the eldest son. Witness—Samuel Parkhurst.
    1766, Aug. 22. Inventory, made by Andrew Miller and Samuel Parkhurst. Lib. H, p. 642.

1750, June 19. Willson, Hendrick, of Somerset Co., farmer; will of. Wife, Annatje, one-third of my moveable estate, and she and the children that live with her on the plantation to have the profits thereof, till my son, Peterus, is 21; and then the place is is to be divided among my 4 sons, and one daughter. Oldest son is named Mindert. Other sons, John and Hendrick. Daughter, Annatje Willson. Executors—my wife, Annatje, my cousin, John Brokaw, and my friend, Peter Stryker. Witnesses—Isaac Brocaw, Burgon Brocaw, Wilhelmes Speeder. Proved Jan. 23, 1764.
    1763, Dec. 12. Inventory, £407.15.2, made by Peter Perrine and Cornelius Van Lewe. (An account was filed by the Executors, with no date). Lib. H, p. 395.

1765, June 19. Willson, James, of Gloucester Co. Int. Adm'x—Mary Willson, widow of James Wilson. Fellowbondsman—Henry Davis; both of Great Egg Harbor, said Co.
    1765, June 19. Inventory, £240.12.0, made by Henry Davis and Robert Morss. Lib. 12, p. 126.

1761, May 30. Willson, John, of Hardwick, Sussex Co.; will of. Wife, Margaret, ⅓ of the personal estate and the profits of the land, while my widow. Son, Mordecai, all my lands. To my 3 daughters the other ⅔ of my personal estate. Executors—my wife, Margaret, and Samuel Lundy. Witnesses—Robert Willson, Gabriel Willson, Jonathan Willson. Proved March 16, 1761.
    1761, March 13. Inventory, £255.9.2, made by Samuel Willson, Peter Schmuck, and Gabriel Willson.
    1771, Nov. 27. Account by Samuel Lundy, surviving Executor.
Lib. 10, p. 480; Lib. 14, p. 409.

1760, Dec. 9. Willson, Joseph, of Newark Twsp., Essex Co.; will of. Wife, Elizabeth, £10, and she to have the whole care of my real and personal, in order to bring up my children. My father, Joseph Wilson, died without a will, and I being legal heir, bargained with my mother to quit all claim to his estate for £25, which was made in the presence of Joseph Camp and Israel Crane, and now I allow this to be paid, and my brother, Zebulon, also will quit his claim. Executors—my wife, Samuel Huntingdon and Thomas Eagles. Witnesses—Robert Jenkins, Alexander McWhorter, Griffith Jenkins. Proved Feb. 25, 1761.
    1761, Feb. 9. Inventory, £85.18.0, made by Daniel Pierson and Thomas Bows. Lib. G, p. 395.

1762, Sept. 25. Willson, Lambert, of Middletown Twsp., Monmouth Co., yeoman; will of. Wife, Ann, goods, live stock and farming utensils; also use of the plantation, till my two sons, Andrew and James, are 21, when they are to have said farm, paying to their sister, Martha, £25 when she is of age. Nephew, Joseph Wilson, a cow. Executors—my wife, and my brother, James Willson. Witnesses—Joseph Willson, John Wall, Daniel McDaniel. Proved Aug. 20, 1768. Lib. K, p. 16.

1766, March 18. Willson, Margant, of Hardwick, Sussex Co.; will of. I give my son all the rents of the lands, with his father's apparel, which I have kept. My apparel I give to my two daughters, who are not 18. Executors—Gabriel Willson and Samuel Lundy. Witnesses—Joseph Brown, Ann Lundy, Jonathan Willson. Proved Dec. 19, 1766.

1766, May 6. Inventory, £38.11.0, made by Robert Willson, Samuel Willson and Ebenezer Willson. Lib. 12, p, 425.

1759, April 25. Willson, Sarah, of Deptford Twsp., Gloucester Co., widow; will of. Son, John Willson, my negro girl, Abigail, and he is to pay £30 to my daughter, Susannah's 3 children, viz., to Sarah £10, to Joseph £10, and to Benjamin Moffatt, £10. Son, John, my lot near Woodbury, of one and ¼ acres. Son, Thomas, bed and yarn. To granddaughter, Sarah Maffatt, linen, etc. My daughter, Susannah Maffatt, gowns. Granddaughter, Sarah Maffatt, saddle. Executor—son, John Willson. Witnesses—John Jefferis, Deborah Fish, James Cooper. Proved July 30, 1766.

1766, April 16. Inventory, £155.11.5, made by John Wilkins, Jr., and Joseph Low.

1770, June 25. Account by John Wilson, Executor. (The children of James Maffet received £30). Lib. 12, p. 374; Lib. 15, p. 15.

1769, Feb. 7. Wilson, Deborah, of Monmouth Co. Ward. Daughter of Peter Wilson, of Freehold, said Co., deceased; who makes choice of Joshua Anderson as her Guardian.

1769, Feb. 7. Guardian—Joshua Anderson. Fellowbondsmen—John Van Mater and Daniel Grandin; all of Freehold Twsp., said Co.

1771, July 8. Account by Guardian. (Rent of plantation, in Freehold Twsp., 13 years, at £26.10 pr. year, £344.10. Rent of pew 12 years, at 14/8, £5.7.4). Lib. I, p. 364; Lib. 15, p. 103.

1757, Dec. 24. Winans, William, of Bridgewater Twsp., Somerset Co.; will of. Being of old age. Wife, Elizabeth, use of ⅓ the land. Daughters, three in number, to have £20 each. Son, William, ½ my lands. Son, Philip, other ½. Executors—my wife, son William, and friend Thomas Scudder, of Elizabeth. Witnesses—Philip Cox, Peter Cox, Elias V. Court. Proved Jan. 17, 1761.

1760, Dec. 22. Inventory, £220.9.9, made by Peter Williamson and Jacob Cosad. Lib. G, p. 357.

1762, Nov. 30. Winans, William, of Elizabeth Town, Essex Co.; will of. To Doctor Ichabod Burnet, £5. Son-in-law, Josiah Winans, £5. Grandson-in-law, Edward Thomas, £5. Great-grandson, Robison Thomas, youngest son of Edward Thomas, £10. Granddaughters, Mary Thomas, Ann Winans, and Elizabeth Winans, rest of moveable estate. Son-in-law, Josiah Winans, use of the house and land where he lives, which I bought of his father, John Winans, deceased, also meadow that I bought of Nathaniel Ross, during his life. Grand-son-in-law, Edward Thomas, use of the land which I bought of John Hinds and John Codrington, during his life. Granddaughter, Mary Thomas, wife of Edward Thomas, the land I bought of John Hinds and John Codrington, which is to be entailed from generation to generation; also my 9 and one-half acres of pasture; which lands are entailed and never to be sold. Grandson, William Winans, the house and 18 acres where I live, which I bought of William Winans, Jr.; also the house and 14 acres which I bought of my brother, John Winans, deceased; also 6 acres of meadow, which I bought of Nathaniel Ross; all to be for generation to generation, forever. Grandson, John Winans, 100 acres on the low lands, which bind Richard Beach; also 10 acres of meadow, which I bought of Henry Norris. Executors—sons-in-law, Josiah Winans and Ephraim Terril, and my grandson in law, Edward Thomas. Witnesses—Samuel Hetfield, Elias Winanes, James Wynants. Proved March 26, 1763.

1763, March 28. Inventory, £161.8.2, made by Josiah Wyants and Edward Thomas. Lib. H, p. 252.

1768, March 8. Winds, Ebenezer, of Hanover Twsp., Morris Co. Ward. Son of Isaiah Winds, of said place, deceased, and makes choice of Benjamin Halsey as his Guardian.

1768, March 8. Guardian—Benjamin Hallsey. Fellowbondsman—Samuel Day; both of said Co. Lib. I, p. 302.

1767, Aug. 23. Wirtz, Conrad, of Roxbury, Morris Co.; will of. Mother, Anna Wirtz, £10. Wife, Anna, ⅓ of my personal estate, and rest to my children. Executors—friend, George Woldorf, and brother, John Wirtz. Witnesses—John Woldorf, Peter Wirtz, Maurice Wirtz. Proved Oct. 17, 1767. Lib. 13, p. 274.

1769, Oct. 14. Witzel, Jacob, of Upper Penns Neck, Salem Co., yeoman. Int. Adm'r—Francis Waggoner, yeoman. Fellowbondsmen—Jacob Slye, cordwainer, and Adam Clark, yeoman; all of said place.

1769, Sept. 15. Inventory, £27.18.5, made by Robert Howard and Jacob Slye. Lib. 14, p. 112.

1758, May 15. Wood, David, of Morristown, Morris Co., farmer; will of. To Thomas Wood and Bethier Wood, my father and mother, the use of my house and land during their lives, and then to be sold. Brother, Jonathan Wood, £10. Brother, Jeremiah Wood, £8. Sister, Susanna Wood, £15. Sister, Phebe Freeman, £4. Executor—my brother, Jonathan Wood. Witnesses—Reuben Holloway, Stephen Freeman. Proved June 9, 1761.

1761, June 8. Inventory, made by Reuben Halloway and Elijah Pierson. Lib. H, p. 20.

1760, Nov. 28. Wood, James, of Deptford Twsp., Gloucester Co., yeoman; will of. Son, John, plantation where I live, except 2 acres that I will devise to my son, Samuel. John is to pay to my daughter, Ann Wood, £40. Son, James, my house and 3 acres of the south end of my lots in Woodbury, and ½ my land on Woodbury Creek, joining lands of Henry Wood, and ⅓ my lands in the woods. Son, Jonathan, the rest of my land in Woodbury, and ½ my land on Woodbury Creek, and ⅓ the land in the woods. Son, Samuel, 2 acres on the northwest side of Kings Road, near Rooty Hill, and ⅓ my land in the woods; and also the legacy left his mother by Margret Gerrard, his grandmother. My daughter, Ann Wood, bed and 6 spoons. Wife, Rebecca, £100, and use of house and lot in Woodbury before devised to son James, till he is 21. Executors—my wife and son, John. Witnesses—William Wilkins, Elizabeth Hamton, James Cooper. Proved Jan. 26, 1765.

1765, Jan. 8. Inventory, £276.17.0, made by John Brown and Joshua Lord. Lib. 12, p. 50.

1762, July 24. Wood, Jehu, of Gloucester Co. Ward. Petition of said Jehu, eldest son and heir of Jeremiah Wood, of Deptsford in said Co., yeoman, deceased, stating that he is out of wardship of his late Guardian, William Wood, by his decease, and, having lands by descent from his father, now makes choice of his friend, Joseph Low, of Deptford Twsp., as his Guardian, till he is 21.

1762, July 24. Guardian—Joseph Low, yeoman. Fellowbondsman—James Hinchman, yeoman; both of Deptford Twsp. Witness—Samuel Mickle. Lib. 11, p. 126.

1766, June 6. Wood, Joseph, Sr., of Chesterfield Twsp., Burlington Co. Int. Adm'r—Thomas Wood, yeoman. Fellowbondsman—Marmaduke Watson, yeoman; both of same place. Witnesses—Anne Curtis.

1766, May 5. Inventory, £56.14.1, made by William Murfin and Marmaduke Watson. Lib. 12, p. 291.

1769, Jan. 28. Wood, Martha, of Bordentown, Burlington Co.; will of. To Obadiah Eldridge, son of Obadiah, £10, when 21, but, if he die, then to go to my sister Mary's son, Thomas Moore, but, if he die, to his sister, Martha Moore. To sister, Mary's son, Thomas Moore, £10. To Duck Creek Monthly Meeting in Kent Co., Delaware, 50 shillings. To sister Mary's daughter, Martha Moore, rest. Executor—niece, Martha Moore aforesaid. Witnesses—Thomas Watson, Edward Wheatcraft, John Biggins. Proved April 10, 1770.

1770, April 7. Inventory, £14.15.0, made by Samuel Farnsworth and Jonathan Wright. Lib. 15, p. 24.

1762, April 30. Wood, William, of Woodbury Creek, Gloucester Co., yeoman; will of. Wife, Rachel, 10 acres along the creek. Son, William, plantation where I live; also the land I bought of Henry Tredaway and wife, when he is 21, and he shall pay his mother £15 yearly. The lands on Mantoes Creek to be sold, and the moneys given to my four daughters, when they are 21, or married, viz., Rachel Wood, Sarah Wood, Letitia Wood and Anna Wood. My brother, Francis Wood, £5 yearly for 5 years. My sister Letitia's son, Constantine Jefferies, £5 yearly for 2 years. To my nephew, Elizabeth Smith, £5 yearly for 4 years. Cousin, Mary Small, £5, when 24. My lad, Jacob Hews, to have £5 and a suit of clothes, if he will be bound apprentice; and the other lad, Jervas Hews, to have a suit of clothes. Executors—my wife, and my friend, Ebenezer Miller, Jr. If my wife should marry or die, then I also appoint David Cooper, Joshua Lord and James Cooper. Witnesses—George Ward, Jeffery Chew, Samuel Mifflin. Proved May 26, 1762.

1762, May 19. Inventory, £1,351.12.9, made by John Wilkins and James Whitall. Lib. 11, p. 129.

1767, Nov. 2. Woodeth, John, of Gloucester Co. Int. Inventory, £35.7.0, made by John Reynolds and Isaiah Davenport.

1767, April 14. Account of Peter Kyer (Kier) as Adm'r. "To burying, nursing, and other funeral charges of his wife, £12."

1768, Feb. 4. Account of Adm'r. File 971 H.

CALENDAR OF WILLS—1761-1770   487

1767, June 8. Woodhouse, John, of Evesham, Burlington Co. Int. Adm'r—Peter Kier. Fellowbondsman—Isaiah Davenport; both of Woolwich in Gloucester Co. Witness—William Down. Lib. 13, p. 104.

1768, June 22. Woodruff, John, of Westfield, Elizabeth Borough, Essex Co., yeoman; will of. Wife, ⅓ my moveable estate, and use of ⅓ my lands. Son, John, £5. Son, Moses, £5. Son, Cornelius, my house and land, where I live. Executors—sons, John and Cornelius. Witnesses—Nathaniel Baker, Henry Baker, Ichabod Ross. Proved Sept. 14, 1768.   Lib. I, p. 341.

1769, Feb. 8. Woodruff, Joseph, Jr., of Borough of Elizabeth, Essex Co., merchant; will of. To wife, Rebeckah, £500, provided she release her dower. Son, Hunloke, rest of estate, real and personal. If my son die under age, then all is to be sold, and there is to be paid to my brother, Benjamin, Woodruff, and my sister, Elizabeth Treat, £500 each, and my nephew, Samuel, the son of said Benjamin, £100, and to Mary Woodruff, daughter of said Benjamin, £50, and to my wife, Rebeckah, £200. My friends, William Peartree Smith and Elias Boudinot to be Guardians of my son Hunloke, till 21. Executors—my uncle, Isaac Woodruff, Esq., William Peartree Smith and Elias Boudinot. Witnesses—James Caldwell, David Ogden, Puah Woodruff. Proved Feb. 18, 1769.
1769, Feb. 22. Inventory, £1,687.9.4, made by William Harraman and George Price.   Lib. K, p. 89.

1768, Aug. 15. Woodruff, Samuel, of Borough of Elizabeth, Essex Co. Int. Adm'rs—Elizabeth Woodruff, widow of said Samuel; Benjamin Woodruff, Esq., minister of the Gospel, Joseph Woodruff, merchant, and Isaac Woodruff, Esq.; all of said place. Witnesses—William Harriman and Hannah Barnet.
1768, Aug. 18. Inventory, £3,662.8.4, made by William Harriman, and Timothy Edwards.   Lib. I, p. 364; File Nos. 3799-3824 G.

1769, Dec. 27. Woodruff, Stephen, of Essex Co. Ward. Son of Stephen Woodruff, of said place, deceased. Guardian—Daniel Pierson.   Lib. K, p. 143.

1766, Nov. 14. Woodruff, Timothy, of Borough of Elizabeth, Essex Co.; will of. Wife, ⅓ my personal estate, and use of ⅓ the real. Daughters, Katherine and Sarah, ⅔ of the rest of personal estate, and the other ⅓ to the children of my daughter, Mary, dec'd. Sons, Jacob, Timothy, Nathaniel, Enos, Moses, Nathan, Mathias and Thomas, all real estate. Executors—sons, Timothy and Nathan. Witnesses—David Woodruff, William Woodruff, Abraham Woodruff, Jr. Proved Dec. 29, 1766.   Lib. I, p. 140.

1767, March 14. Woodward, Elizabeth, of Upper Freehold, Monmouth Co. Renunciation by Thomas Farr, of said place, who was appointed Executor by the will of said Elizabeth Woodward, which was dated Feb. 25, 1767. The said Thomas Farr requests that Thomas Woodward, Jr., may be allowed to act in his place. Signed by Thomas Farr. Witnesses—James Lawrence and John Lawrence.
                                                              File No. 3393 M.

1761, March 19. Woodward, Joseph, of Monmouth Co. Int. Adm'rs —Hannah Woodward, of said Co., and Joseph Reckless, of Burlington Co. Fellowbondsman—Abraham Hewlings, of Burlington Co.
Lib. 10, p. 174.

1762, March 31. Woodward, Samuel, of Chesterfield, Burlington Co., inn holder; will of. Son, Anthony £100. Daughters, Rhoda Woodward and Sarah Woodward, £80 each. To Sarah Peak, my present housekeeper, £10. The remainder to my 3 children, when of age. Daughter, Sarah, to have hers when 18. Executors—brother, Anthony Woodward, and my friend, Abel Middleton. Witnesses—Thomas Duglass, Jacob Lawrence, Thomas Woodward, Jr. Proved April 24, 1762.
1762, April 10. Inventory, £507.10.10, made by Jacob Lawrence and Thomas Duglass. Lib. 11, p. 207.

1767, April 17. Woolf, John Martin, of Hopewell, Cumberland Co., yeoman; will of. Wife, Mary Elizabeth, all my bonds, bills, etc. Executrix—said wife. Witnesses—Jonathan Fithian, Jr., Jonathan Fithian, Sr., Adam Raisur. Proved April 22, 1767.
1767, April 22. Inventory, £57.16.3, made by Jonathan Fithian and Adam Rasar. Lib. 13, p. 153.

1761, March 10. Woolley, William, Sr., of Shrewsbury, Monmouth Co., yeoman; will of. To my only son, James, all my lands and $100. Grandson, William Woolley, my cane. Granddaughter, Patience Woolley, £5. Daughter, Amey Allen, £50. Daughter, Mary, now wife of James Corlies, £10. Granddaughter, Elizabeth, now wife of Jacob Hance, £40. Granddaughter, Margaret, now wife of Michale Price, £30. To the other 4 children of my daughter, Mary, viz., William, Mary, James and George, £7 each. Daughter Mary, to have the interest of £200, as long as she remain the wife of James Corlies; but, if he die, then the £200 to be paid to her, and, if she die, before her husband, then the £200 to be paid to her 6 children. Daughter, Margret, wife of Josiah Parker, £300. Granddaughter, Elizabeth Parker, £5. Executors—friends, Job Cook and Richard Lawrence (merchant). Witnesses—Vincent White, Joseph Allen, Philip Lewis. Proved March 22, 1769.
1769, March 7. Inventory, £1,734.16.7, made by Benjamin Woolley, Jr., and Josiah Parker. Lib. K, p. 72.

1761, Feb. 1. Woolsey, George, of Hopewell, Hunterdon Co., yeoman; will of. Son, Jeremiah, all my real and personal estate, he paying to my other children and grandchildren the money hereafter mentioned. Son, Henry, £43. Son, Daniel, £43. Son, Joseph, £43. To children of my daughter, Jemima, namely, Jerusha, Noah, Hannah, and Elizabeth, £43, when they are of age. Sons, Danial and Joseph, apparel. Executor—son, Jeremiah. Witnesses—John Guild, Stephen Burrows, Josiah Ellis. Proved March 11, 1762.
Lib. 11, p. 145.

1769, Sept. 5. Woolsey, Henry, of Pennington, Hunterdon Co. Int. Adm'x—Martha Woolsey. Fellowbondsmen—Jeremiah Woolsey and Azariah Hunt; all of said Co. Witness—William Chambers.
1769, Sept. 2. Inventory, £537.17.6, made by John Hart and Azariah Hunt.

CALENDAR OF WILLS—1761-1770   489

1773, Jan. 13. Account by Robert Combs and Martha Combs (late Martha Woolsey), which Martha was Adm'x of Henry Woolsey, of Pennington.
1788, April 7. Account by Robert Combs, and Martha, his wife, late Martha Woolsey, she being Adm'x of Henry Woolsey.
1789, Feb. 4. Exceptions filed by Philip Van Cleve and Martha his wife (daughter of Henry Woolsey) to account filed by Robert Combs and Martha his wife.
1790, May Term.   Account allowed.   Lib. 14, p. 80; Lib. 14, p. 515.

1769, March 16. Woolson, Hance, of Cape May Co. Int. Adm'r—Abraham Woolson. Fellowbondsman—Isaac Newton, Sr.; both of said Co. Witness—John Eldredge.
1769, March 14. Inventory, £100.6.4, made by John Eldredge and Isaac Newton.   Lib. 13, p. 532.

1753, Nov. 29. Woolston, Samuel, Sr., of Northampton, Burlington Co., yeoman; will of. Son, Samuel, 20 shillings. Son-in-law, George Briggs, 20 shillings. Son-in-law James Allen, 20 shillings. Daughter, Margaret Doty, £20. Wife, Susannah, rest of personal, she dividing with my daughter, Susannah. Son, William, all my lands, he paying £15 yearly to his mother and sister, Susannah. Executor—son, William. Witnesses—Nathan Watson, Thomas Atkinson, Thomas Lawrence. Proved June 20, 1761.
1761, June 13. Inventory, £78.5.6, made by James Dobbin and Thomas Budd.   Lib. 10, p. 210.

1761, May 7. Woolverton, Charles, of Amwell Twsp., Hunterdon Co.; will of. Wife, Margaret, £10 yearly. Son, Morris, the plantation he lives on, of 168 acres. Son, John, land that the grist mill stands on, of 70 acres, joining the Delaware. Executors—Sons, Morris and John. Witnesses—Evans Godown, Richard Reading, Richard Green. Proved Oct. 30, 1765.   Lib. 12, p. 250.

1763, Dec. 2. Woolverton, Charles, of Kingwood, Hunterdon Co. Int. Adm'r—Dennis Woolverton. Fellowbondsman—Lazarus Adams; both of said place. Witness—John Opdyck.
1763, Nov. 28. Inventory, £702.0.7, made by John Opdyck and Henry Snyder. (The above Charles Woolverton died 7th of Oct. last).
1767, April 23. Account by Adm'r.   Lib. 11, p. 447.

1770, Oct. 14. Woolverton, Morris, of Amwell Twsp., Hunterdon Co., yeoman; will of. Wife, Mary, 1/7 of the money arising from the sale of my whole estate. Rest of the money to be put to interest, and children to be kept, till they are of age, and then each child to receive its share, namely, John, Margaret Woolverton, Mary Woolverton, Abigail Woolverton and Zurviah Woolverton. Executors—brother, John, and friend, Richard Green. Witnesses—Isaac Woolverton, Uriah Bonham, Anchor Bonham. Proved Nov. 26, 1770.
1770, Nov. 23. Inventory, £272.0.10, made by William Hoogland and Uriah Bonham.
1792, Oct. 22. Account by John Lambert and Samuel Wilson, surviving Executors of John Woolverton, who was Executor of Morris Woolverton. (A debt was due from Charles Woolverton, son of Dennis).   Lib. 15, p.86.

1768, March 9. Woortman, Benjamin, of Morris Co. Int. Adm'r—Peter Woortman, second brother of said Benjamin. Fellowbondsman—Joseph Montanye; both of said Co. Witness—Joseph Wortman.

1769, July 4. Inventory, £32.3.10, made by Edward Demund and Joseph Montayne. (Money was received from John Workman, the son of Dirick Dirick, on the account of Benjamin Workman; from Joseph Workman, and from Peter Workman. Benjamin Workman deceased at Peter Workman's, laying sick 6 weeks and 5 days).
Lib. I, p. 301.

1766, April 25. Worthington, John, of Alloways Creek, Salem Co. Ward. Son of Ephraim Worthington, of said place, yeoman, deceased; having lands devised to him by his father, makes choice of Daniel Clark as his Guardian.

1766, April 25. Guradian—Daniel Clark, of Deerfield Twsp., Cumberland Co., yeoman. Fellowbondsmen—Michael Hoshell and George Peirson, both of Stow Creek Twsp., yeomen. Lib. 12, p. 318.

1765, March 1. Wortman, William, of Piscataway Twsp., Middlesex Co., yeoman; will of. To wife, Margaret Wortman, use of my plantation where I dwell, in order to bring up my children. Son, Andrew, £500. To my 2 daughters, Anne Mary and Margaret, £100 to each, when 21. To my son, David, and William Hallemus, farm where I live. Executors—my wife and my friends, John Roy, of Baskenridge, and Michael Field, of Piscataway. Witnesses—Benjamin Field, Ryneer Van Nest, Jr., Elias V. Court. Proved April 18, 1765.

1765, April 19. Inventory, £820.8.7, made by John Miller and Benjamin Field. Lib. H, p. 537.

1766, July ⸺. Wrath, William, of Tinicum Island. Int. Adm'r—Aaron Musgrove, of Philadelphia, merchant. Fellowbondsman—Robert Friend Price, Esq., of Gloucester Co.

1766, July 7. Renunciation of Rebecca Wrath, widow of said William. Witnesses—John Morton and William Worrall. Lib. 12, p. 381.

1758, April 19. Wright, Joseph, of Penns Neck, Salem Co.; will of. Son, Joseph Wright, £200 when 21, and, if he die, it is to be given to sons, Thomas and James. Son, James, the land I bought of Margaret Vanniman. Son, Thomas, plantation where I live. Daughters, Sarah Wright, Mary Wright, Hannah Wright, Rebecca Wright and Eleanor Wright, rest of moveable estate. Executors—wife, Edith, and son, Thomas. Witnesses—Lennard Nix, Elizabeth Philpot, Andrew Sinnickson.

1760, Dec. 18. Codicil. Youngest son, Joseph, £100 more. Daughters, Sarah and Mary to have £16 less. Witnesses—Same as in will. Proved Feb. 14, 1761.

1761, Feb. 13. Inventory, £419.16 5, made by Andrew Sinnickson and Francis Miles. Lib. 10, p. 492.

1761, Oct. 5. Wright, Mary, of Sussex Co. Ward. Aged 14 years, and daughter of John Wright, of said place. Guardian—Richard Wright, of Woodbridge, Middlesex Co. Fellowbondsman—David Wright, of Middlesex Co. Lib. H, p. 35.

CALENDAR OF WILLS—1761-1770 491

1762, Nov. 28. Wright, Samuel, of New Hanover Twsp., Burlington Co., tanner; will of. My wife, Rebeckah, £250, and the goods she brought, and ½ the profits of plantation where I dwell, and of the plantation that is rented to Jonathan Brown. My grandson, Samuel Wright Hartshorn, plantation which was given me by my father, Joshua Wright, and also that land which I bought of William Kirby and Ann Kirby, which remains unsold; also the plantation I bought of David Starkey. To daughter, Rachel Scholly, during her widowhood, the above 2 tracts of land; also £50 and ½ the profits of plantation where Jonathan Brown lives. Granddaughter, Frances Schooley, £50. Granddaughter, Pheby Hartshorn, £50, and also the land I bought of Abraham Brown, on Crosswicks Creek where Abraham Estwood now dwells. To my granddaughters, Eleanor Hartshorn, Mary Tantum, Francis Schooley and Sarah Emley, the 2 tracts in the mountain which I bought of Joseph Biddle and the Curtises, being called 1,200 acres. Residue to my wife Rebecca, my daughter, Rachel Schooley, and my grandchildren, Eleanor Hartshorn, Mary Tantum, Samuel Wright Hartshorn, Phebe Hartshorn and Sarah Emley. To Anne Lovett, £5, and to Elizabeth Cleavinger 40 shillings. Executors—wife, Rebecca, my daughter, Rachel Schooley, and my grandson, Samuel Wright Hartshorn. Witnesses—Amos Wright, Thomas Folkes, Michael Burrows. Proved Jan. 4, 1763.

1762, Dec. 28. Inventory, £2,195.1.1, made by Samuel Emley and Amos Wright. Lib. 11, p. 245.

1761, May 22. Wright, Thomas, of Burlington Co. Int. Adm'r—Henry Delatush. Fellowbondsman—Gilbert Smith; both of said Co. Witnesses—S. Blackwood, Gabriel Blond, Samuel Allinson.

1761, May 12. Inventory, £23.17.0, made by Thomas Shreve and Gilbert Smith. Lib. 10, p. 176.

1762, Feb. 24. Wright, Thomas, of New Hanover, Burlington Co., yeoman; will of. Son, Ezekiel, a part of my plantation, and he is to pay to his 4 sisters, Sarah Norris, Margaret Bullock, Elizabeth Bullock and Jemima Thorn, £20 each. Son, Amos, the rest of my lands, and he is to pay to his sister, Lydia French, £20, and to his sister, Deborah Foxe's children, William, Jonathan, George, Elemuel and Sarah Fox, £4 each when 21. Daughter, Sarah Fox, my spice box. Residue to daughters, Sarah Norris, Lydia French, Margaret Bullock, Elizabeth Bullock, Jemima Thorn, and the 5 children of my daughter, Deborah Fox, viz., William, Jonathan, George, Elemuel and Sarah Fox. Executors—sons, Amos and Ezekiel, and my son-in-law, John Bullock. Witnesses—Alexander Kimmings, Joseph Kirby, William Harris, Jr. Proved April 15, 1769.

1769, April 12. Inventory, £242.9.9, made by Alexander Kimmings and Joseph Kirby. Lib. 14, p. 46.

1763, Nov. 8. Wright, William, of Roxbury, Morris Co., yeoman. Int. Adm'r—Robert Wright, of said Co., yeoman. Fellowbondsman—Robert Braden, of Hardwick, Sussex Co., yeoman. Witness—John Todd.

1763, Oct. 29. Inventory, £45.15.0, made by John Todd and Robert Breden.

1766, July 29. Account by Adm'r. Lib. 11, p. 538.

1761, Nov. 27. Wyckof, Cornelius, of Reading Township, Hunterdon Co., yeoman; will of. Daughter, Sara, the widow of William Poling, and Cornelius Poling, her eldest son, all my real and personal. Executor—my cousin, Nicolas Wyckof. Witnesses—Andries Shock, Cornelius Wyckoff, Nicolas Wyckoff. Proved April 12, 1762.
1762, Jan. 28. Inventory, £32.9.0, made by Peter Middagh and Loimens Lou. Lib. 11, p. 345.

1765, Sept. 1. Wyckof, Gerrit, of Freehold Twsp., Monmouth Co., yeoman; will of. Son, Garrit, £5, he being my eldest son. Daughter, Catharine, my Dutch Bible. Sons, Garrit, Samuel, Peter, and Oukey, my apparel. Children, Garrit, Samuel, Peter, Oukey, Catharine, Eyda and Alice Wicoff, rest of estate. Executors—my sons, Garret, Samuel and Peter. Witnesses—James Reed, David Vanderveer, Thomas Bullman. Proved Nov. 7, 1770. Lib. K, p. 251.

1759, July 14. Wyckof, Symon, of Somerset Co., yeoman; will of. Eldest son, John, a silver tankard. Daughter, Annatie Wyckof, now wife of Folkert Van Oestrand, £30 and a negro woman. Daughter, Majeka Wyckof, now the wife of Jacob Bennet, £30 and a negro woman. Daughter, Margrat, now the wife of Johannes Van Cleave, £30 and a negro woman. Daughter, Gertie, now the wife of Cornelius Van Horne, £30 and a negro woman. Daughter, Sarah, now the wife of Adrian Hegeman, Jr., £30 and a negro woman. Grandchildren, John Adders; Simon Adders; Gertie Adders, now wife of John Manley; and Maria Adders, £30. Real to be sold, and residue divided among son John Wyckof; Cornelius Wyckof; daughter, Annatie, wife to Folkert van Oestrand; Majeka, wife of Jacob Bennet; Margrat, wife to Johannes Van Cleave; Gertie, wife to Cornelius Van Horne; Sarah, wife to Adrian Hegeman Jr.; and my 4 grandchildren, John Adders; Simon Adders; Gertie Adders; and Maria Adders. Wife, Gertie, given an annuity. Executors—son Cornelius, and sons in law, Folkert Van Oestrand and Cornelius Van Horne. Witnesses—James Vannuis, Wicoff Van Norstrand, Aaron Van Nord Strand. Proved Aug. 15, 1765.
1765, March 25. Codicil. Witnesses—Simon Vliet, Simon Addes.
Lib. H, p. 515.

1762, June 22. Yamans, Edward, of Essex Co. Ward. Aged 15 years, son of Edward Yamans, of said Co., deceased. Guardian—Thomas Woodruff. Fellowbondsman—Samuel Yamans; both of said Co. Lib. H, p. 133.

1765, Jan. 1. Yard, Ann, of Trenton, Hunterdon Co.; will of. Daughter, Mary Ann Yard, the goods and furniture that my husband, Joseph Yard, left me. Son, Jethro Yard, various goods. When 21. Sons, Joseph Yard and Archebel William Yard, and my daughter, Mary Ann Yard, and my grandson, Firman Yard, the rest of my estate. Executors—friend, Alexander Chambers, and my daughter, Mary Ann Yard. Witnesses—Benjamin Yard, Hannah Howell. Elizabeth Pearson. Proved Feb. 23, 1765. Lib. 12, p. 104.

1760, Dec. 4. Yard, Jethro, of Trenton, Hunterdon Co., carpenter; will of. Sister, Elizabeth Justice, £20. Nephews, Benjamin Mershon, Daniel Yard and Elijah Yard, £5 each. Nieces, Mary Ann Yard, Mary

CALENDAR OF WILLS—1761-1770   493

Justice and Achsah Yard, £5 each. Nephew, John Justice, £5, when 21. Nephew, William Justice, my tools. Nephew, Jethro Yard, lot on south side of Second St., Trenton, joining Benjamin Yard, when he is 21. Niece, Mary Yard, daughter of Benjamin Yard, £5. To the Presbyterian Church of Trenton, £7. Sister-in-law, Ann Yard, £5. Brothers, Joseph, John and Benjamin, 3 lots on the Maidenhead road, being part of a tract called the 100-acre tract, late belonging to my father, William Yard, deceased; the said lots contain 22 acres. Rest of lands to be sold. Executors—brothers, Joseph and Benjamin. Witnesses—John Guild, Samuel Tucker, Jr., George Bright. Proved Feb. 16, 1761.   Lib. 10, p. 581.

1763, Aug. 11. Yard, John, of Trenton, Hunterdon Co. Int. Adm'x—Hannah Yard, widow. Fellowbondsmen—Benjamin Yard and Lott Dunbar; all of said place. Witnesses—Isaac Yard and William Yard.
1763, Aug. 13. Inventory, £122.18.11, made by Joseph DeCow and James Cumine.   Lib. 11, p. 409.

1763, Nov. 30. Yard, Joseph, of Trenton, Hunterdon Co., yeoman; will of. Wife, Anne, £100 and furniture. Grandson, Furman Yard, £50, when 21. Son, Joseph, £75. Son, Archibald William Yard, £75. Son, Jethro Yard, £75, when 21. Daughter, Mary Ann Yard, £100. To Elijah Yard and Mary Yard, children of my brother, William Yard, deceased, £30 each, when they are 21. My sister, Elizabeth Justice, wife of Mounce Justice, £6. Rest of my real and personal to my wife and 4 children. Real to be sold. Executors—wife, Ann Yard, and brother Benjamin Yard. Witnesses—Wilson Hunt, Abram Hunt, Joseph Warrell.
1763, Dec. 9. Codicil. The house and lot in Philadelphia is intailed to my son, Joseph. I appoint friend, Jonathan Sergant, to be an Executor, with the others. Witnesses—Edmond Beakes, Thomas Yard, William Justice. Proved Jan. 26, 1764.   Lib. 11, p. 481.

1762, July 17. Young, Henry, of Cape May Co.; will of. To be buried as near my first wife, Abigail, as possible. Son, Stephen, lands northeast of Line Creek; and to son, Job, the land southwest of said line, and plantation where I live. Granddaughter Mehetibel Godfrey, £30, but, if she die before she should be married, then to my 5 children. To my children, Stephen Young, and my daughters, Tabitha Tounsend, Abigail Smith and Elizabeth Mackey, and my son, Job, the personal estate. Executors—sons, Stephen and Job. Witnesses—Silvanus Tounsend, Joseph Corson, John Tounsend. Proved June 2, 1767.
1767, April 24. Inventory, £1,106.6.9¾, made by John Tounsend and John Mackey.   Lib. 12, p. 488.

1761, Sept. 1. Young, Phebe, of Cape May Co.; will of. My brother, Jeremiah Ludlam, £60. My sister, Abigail Scull, £20. My sister, Elizabeth Cresse, a suit of apparel, from top to toe. To Phebe Ludlam, my brother's Joseph's, daughter, £5. To Phebe Ludlam, my brother's Isaac's, daughter, £10. To Norton Ludlam my watch. To Lu.l-lam Hand my gold buttons. To my "nephews," Elizabeth Cresse, £10, to Rubin Ludlam, £10, to Jeams Hildreth, £10, to Joseph Hildreth, £5, to David Hildreth, £5, and to Danial Hildreth £5; and the remainder

I give as follows: ⅓ part to my brother, Joseph's 6 children, viz., Joseph Ludlam, Phebe Ludlam, Thomas Ludlam, Aletheir Ludlam, Hester Ludlam and Henry Ludlam; and to my sister, Abigail Scull's 4 daughters, and one granddaughter ⅓, viz., Catherine Droman, Abigail Ludlam, Elizabeth Bacor, Phebe Scull and Temperance Richardson; and to my brother, Jeremiah's, daughter, Deborah Hand, ⅓. Executors—my brother, Jeremiah Ludlam, and my friend, Cornelius Hand. Witnesses—Benjamin Stites, Rhoda Stites, Martha Ludlam. Proved Aug. 26, 1766.

1766, Aug. 25. Inventory, £598.11.1, made by John Shaw and John Smith.

1768, June 13. Account by Jeremiah Ludlam, the surviving Executor. Lib. 12, p. 341; Lib. 13, p. 408.

1769, Feb. 18. Young, Thomas, of Pequanack, Morris Co., yeoman; will of. Wife, Thankfull, a bed. Rest of personal estate to be sold. Son, Arthor, 30 acres off the upper end of my home lot. Wife, Thankfull, to have the home lot, in order to bring up my children. After decease of wife, land to be sold, and money to be given to sons, Thomas, Morgain, Daniel and David. To daughters, Margaret, Elizabeth, Phebe, Thankfull, Mary and Hannah, the money from sale of personal estate. Executors—my friends, James Brotherton and Thomas Carrel. Witnesses—Daniel Carol, Morgin Young, Nathan Simcock. Proved March 6, 1769. Lib. K, p. 157.

1765, Oct. 30. Zaboroski, Jan, Sr., of Hackensack, Bergen Co.; will of. Eldest son, Albert, £10 as birthright; also 200 acres of that farm where he lives; also 70 acres on north side of the farm I bought of John Dirjie. Sons, Claes, Jan and Peter, my lands on Passkek River. Son, Jacob, woodland I bought of Hendrick Kip. Son, Joost, out of my farm where I live, as many acres as my son, Christian, hath of his brother, Joost, out of the lot I bought of Hans Banta. My youngest son, Christian, part of farm where I live. Daughter, Chrystyntje, £300. Daughter, Machtel, £300. Daughter, Rachel, 200 acres at Messanekes. The meadows at Old Hackensack to be sold to the highest bidder among my 7 sons, and the money divided to them, viz., Albert, Claes, Jan, Jacob, Peter, Joost and Christian. Executors —sons, Albert, Jacob and Peter. Witnesses—Johannes Terhune, Derrik Banta, Albert Terheunen.

1765, Oct. 30. Codicil. Executors same as above. Witnesses— same as above. Proved Jan. 21, 1766. Lib. I, p. 84.

1761, May 19. Zabriski, Andreas, of Bergen Co. Ward, aged near 15, and son of Albert Zabriski, of said Co. Guardian—Johannis Bougart. Bondsman—Samuel Provoost; both of said Co. Witness— John Smyth. Lib. G, p. 380.

1764, March 17. Zabriski, Casparus, of Bergen Co., yeoman; will of. Wife, Cathrine Zabriskie, alias Vanwagen, by an agreement, is to have possession of the house where she lives, and the merchant shop with the goods, and £50 to bring up her children, she being contented therewith, and we agreeing to part from each other, and having a writing of divorce. My son, Joost, watch. Rest of real and moveable estate to my children, Joost Zabriskie, Christena Zabriskie and Sarah Z. Zabriskie. (Said Joost not yet of age). Executors

—Johannis Demerest, Albert Zabriske and Stephen Baldwin. Witnesses—William Cairns, Jan Zabreski, Cornelus Bogert. Proved Sept. 13, 1764. Lib. H, p. 474.

1764, Sept. 12. Inventory, £175.16.0, made by Aert Cuyper and Isaac Boogert.

1768, Dec. 19. Zane, Robert, Jr., of Woolwick, Gloucester Co. Int. Adm'rs—Mary Zane, widow, and Nathan Zane. Fellowbondsman—William Zane; all of said place.

1768, Dec. 5. Inventory, £361.8.8, made by Thomas Denny and William Zane. Lib. 13, p. 478.

INDEXES

I. INDEX OF NAMES OF PERSONS
II. INDEX OF PLACE-NAMES

Index of Names of Persons

NOTE.—The names of testators, intestate persons, or wards, printed in heavy type in the preceding text, are not repeated in this Index, as a rule.

Where surnames in common use to-day, or at least with well-known spellings, are unusually or curiously used in the text, the current modern spelling is substituted in this Index, to facilitate reference. An exception is where proper spelling is uncertain. To a lesser extent the same rule has been applied to Christian names.

A

Aalse, Jurrie, 5
  Maragrietje, 5
Abbet (Abit, Abott, etc.), Abdon, 475
  Benjamin, 5, 399, 475
  Burroughs, 6, 302, 475
  Catherine, 5, 6
  Hannah, 6
  James, 5, 6, 360
  Job, 6
  John, 146, 265, 303, 317, 370
  Jonas, 451
  Joseph, 6
  Mary, 100, 399
  Rebecca, 6
  Timothy, 265, 385
  William, 5, 6, 255, 360, 439, 431
Abiel, David, 388
Able, Daniel, 193
  Michael, 393
Aborn, Jonathan, 34
Abraham, Abraham, 7, 260
  Abraham, Jr., 7
  Ann, 6
  Charles, 7
  Elizabeth, 6
  George, 6, 7
  Hannah, 6
  James, 6, 7, 224, 367
  James, Jr., 70, 109, 367
  Jeanne, 6
  John, 6, 7
  Margaret, 6
  Mary, 6
  Phœbe, 6
  Sarah, 6
Acken, John, 34
  Joseph, 107, 150, 193
Acker, John, 257
Ackerman, Abraham, 7, 8, 282
  Abraham A., 8
  Abraham L., 7, 8
  Albert, 8, 29
  Altje, 7, 8
  Antje, 203
  Catherine, 336
  Cornelius, 8
  David, 7, 29, 113, 240
  Elizabeth, 7, 89
  Gerret, 7, 8, 455
  Hendrick, 7
  Hendrickje, 7
  Jacobus, 8
  Jannetie, 7, 8
  John, 7, 8
  Lawrence, 7, 46, 336
  Lena, 7, 8, 455
  Margaret, 7
  Maria, 113
  Neltje, 8
  Nicholas, 113
  Peter, 7, 8
  Rachel, 7
  Staltie, 8
  Thellitie, 8
  William, 8
Ackland, Elizabeth, 8
Ackley (see Akeley)
Acon, Joseph, 98
  Rebecca, 98
Acritt, Isaac, 8
  James, 8
  John, 8
  Joseph, 8
  Mary, 8
Actell, Henry, 265
Acton, Benjamin, 170
  John, 170
  Joseph, 171
  Sarah, 170
Adair, David, 467
Adams, Abigail, 422
  Benjamin, 9
  Catherine, 9, 10
  Daniel, 104
  David, 9
  Deborah, 10
  Eleanor, 9
  Elijah, 9
  Eve, 10
  Ezra, 10
  Hannah, 10
  Isaac, 119
  James, 9, 422
  Jane, 10
  Job, 9
  John, 9, 10
  Jonas, 9
  Joseph, 10, 224, 441
  Joseph, Jr., 9
  Lazarus, 49, 142, 281, 389, 489
  Lydia, 9
  Mary, 10
  Matthew, 267

Rebecca, 10
Robert, 10, 65, 74, 154, 318
Sarah, 9, 10, 397
Seth, 9
Silvanus, 10
Thomas, 30, 63
Uriah, 10, 137
William, 9, 241, 266
Addis, Gertrude, 492
  John, 10, 492
  Maria, 492
  Mary, 10
  Simon, 492
  Thomas, 134
Agner, Frances, 247
Agnew, Henry, 293
Aike, Tunis, 49
Aikman, Alexander, 258, 317
Akeley, Ezekiel, 164
Akers, John, 409
  Robert, 466
Akin, Abel, 457
  (see Atkin)
Akinsyelar, George, 358
Albach, William, 167
Albertson, Aaron, 11, 86
  Ann, 286
  Cornelius, 357
  Elizabeth, 10
  Ephraim, 11
  Isaac, 10, 109, 392, 429
  Jacob, 193
  Josiah, 11, 192, 227, 271
  Mary, 357
  Nathan, 26
  Patience, 10
  Rebecca, 10
  William, 11
Alder, Bartholomew, 408
Alexander, Ann, 124
  Catherine, 11, 123
  David, 123
  George, 80
  James, 249
  Philip, 324
  Sarah, 231
Alford, Benjamin, 11
  Joanna, 11
  John, 11, 35
  Margaret, 11
Alkinton, Frances, 13
  Saboelah, 13
Allback, Anna, 12
  Elizabeth, 12
  John W., 12
  Philip, 12
Allegar, Benjamin, 84, 114, 127
  William, 306
Allan, Elizabeth, 12
  Hannah, 12
  John, 12
  Joseph, 12
  Margaret, 12
  Rachel, 12
  Robert, 12
  Sophia, 12
  William, 12
Allen, Abigail, 13
  Abraham, 86, 137, 193, 252, 277, 287, 316
  Amy, 488
  Andrew, 315
  Anna, 130
  Benjamin, 13, 75

Caleb, 227
Catherine, 12, 14
Christian, 13
Daniel, 13
David, 13, 169, 464
Deborah, 13
Dorothy, 13
Ebenezer, 13, 432
Elijah, 349
Elisha, 397
Ephraim, 13
Gabriel, 94, 289
George, 13, 86, 200, 223, 320, 326, 376, 431
Hance, 13
Hannah, 13
Henry, 12, 58
Isaac, 120
James, 13, 489
Jane, 465
Jechamiah, 246
Jedediah, 471, 480
Jeremiah, 14
Johanna, 13
John, 13, 14, 19, 65, 139, 213, 286
John, Jr., 125
Jonathan, 97
Joseph, 151, 125, 215, 431, 478, 488
Joseph, Jr., 227, 478
Joseph, 3rd, 219
Ledona, 14
Lydia, 13
Margaret, 13
Mary, 13, 14
Mercy, 12
Nathan, 432
Patience, 13
Ralph, 14, 328
Rebecca, 13
Richard, 14
Robert, 13, 291
Robert, Jr., 393
Samuel, 12, 13, 69, 130, 170, 318, 354
Sarah, 13, 478
Seth, 173
Thomas, 14, 452
William, 14, 349
William J., 13
Aller, Adam, 238
  Ann, 203, 238
  Peter, 203
Allerton, Jacob, 121
  Thomas, 183
Alling, Abigail, 14
  Benjamin, 9
  Daniel, 14
  Eunice, 311
  John, 311
  Joseph, 14
  Matthias, 14
Allinson, Eleanor, 14
  Elizabeth, 14
  Jacob, 14
  Mary, 14
  Peter, 14, 225
  Samuel, 14, 17, 20, 26, 28, 46, 61, 70, 92, 102, 134, 139, 147, 200, 254, 259, 269, 318, 325, 330, 342, 361, 395, 412, 452, 475, 491
  Thomas, 14
Allison, Anna, 15
  Burgiss, 14

INDEX OF NAMES OF PERSONS 501

John, 14
Joseph, 14
Richard, 51
Ruth, 14, 51
Allman, Catharine, 161
Jane, 15
Solomon, 239, 440
Allton, Erasmus, 376
William, 384
Alrich, Lydia, 174
Rebecca, 174
Samuel, 174
Vesser, 174
William, 174
Alston, Jonathan, 126
Mary, 429
Alstyne, Jeronemus, 443
Amack, Helena, 240
Amble, Peter, 9
Ambler, John, 156, 362
Thomas, 171
Amerman, Isaac, 146
Nicholas, 333
Amory, George, 339
Anderson, Abraham, 110
Amos, 17
Andrew, 95, 449, 17, 60, 95, 449
Bartholomew, 16
Benjamin, 15
Catherine, 15
Cornelius, 15, 138, 200
Edith, 385
Elijah, 15
Ephraim, 259
George, 300
Hannah, 16
Isaac, 16, 75, 76
James, 16, 87, 332, 342, 345, 428
John, 15, 81, 82, 137, 273, 340, 408, 418, 438, 439, 468
Joseph, 15
Joshua, 15, 484
Kenneth, 15, 278
Margaret, 16
Martha, 16
Mary, 15, 16, 55, 76, 83, 411
Nathaniel, 221
Pamela, 17
Penelope, 17
Priscilla, 16
Rachel, 15
Reuben, 17
Sarah, 16, 350, 393
Simon, 16
Theodosia, 53, 115
Thomas, 15, 16, 55, 83, 299, 399, 412
Timothy, 16
William, 297, 412
Andress, Nathaniel, 16
Timothy, 16
Andrews, Alice, 17
Ann, 17
Benajah, 17
Benjamin, 17
Edward, 17, 33, 61, 364, 474
Elizabeth, 16, 17, 18, 137
Esther, 17
Isaac, 17, 136, 137, 224, 227, 479
Jacob, 17, 20
Jeremiah, 18
John, 179, 189
Joseph, 17
Mary, 17, 18

Nathaniel, 16
Nehemiah, 204
Peter, 17, 18, 149
Prudence, 17
Sarah, 17, 18
Thomas, 16, 122, 150
William, 318
Androvet, Catherine, 18
Eleanor, 18
Leah, 18
Mary, 18
Peter, 18
Rebecca, 18
Angell, James, 62
Angelo, Deborah, 186
Annin, William, 165
Anthony, George, 405
Antill, Anne, 18
Edward, 18, 255
Henry, 258
Isabella, 18
John, 18
Lewis, 18, 268
Mary, 18
Sarah, 18
Antram, Ann, 361
David, 18
Isaac, 18
John, 55, 68, 139, 229, 322, 361
Joseph, 231
Margaret, 238
Priscilla, 169
Sarah, 231
Zachariah, 18, 361
Applegate (Appleget), Anthony, 19
Benjamin, 19
Catherine, 19
Catteam, 19
Ebenezer, 19
Elizabeth, 311
Ezekiel, 19
Gabriel, 19
George, 41
John, 201
Josiah, 155
Rachel, 19
Sarah, 19
Sylvester, 19
William, 86, 311, 313, 474
Appleman, Abraham, 210
John, 73, 74
Appleton, Cornelius, 146
Josiah, 19, 38, 146
Josiah, Jr., 19
Apthorp, Mary, 267
Archer, Joseph, 171
Martha, 440
Mary, 171, 389
Sarah, 171
Thomas, 389
Arey, Abner, 236
Isaac, 236, 317
Mary, 317
Rhoda, 317
Armitage, James, 243
Reuben, 78, 120, 121, 138, 414
Armstrong, Catherine, 33
Deborah, 287
Hugh, 34
Joseph, 125, 477
Nathan, 86, 117
Nathaniel, 265
Robert, 33, 58

502   NEW JERSEY COLONIAL DOCUMENTS

Arney, Elizabeth, 358
  Joseph, 139, 300, 335, 358, 426
  Joseph, Jr., 335
  Samuel H., 358
Arnold, Boyley, 123
  Henry, 20
  John, 20, 241, 226
  Sarah, 19, 20
Aronson, Aaron, 20, 307, 320
  Mary, 111
  Rebecca, 20, 307
Arrison, Agnes, 48
  John, 285
Arrowsmith, Antje, 19
  Benjamin, 19
  Edmund, 19
  John, 19
  Joseph, 19, 436, 446
  Mary, 19
  Nicholas, 19
  Thomas, 19
Arven, Cornelius, 391
Arvey, Cate, 163
Ashfield, Catherine, 20
  Elizabeth, 20, 344
  Euphemia, 20
  Helena, 20
  Lewis M., 20
  Lydia, 20
  Mary, 20
  Patience, 182
  Redford, 20, 344
  Richard, 182
  Vincent P., 18, 20
Ashmore, Jabesh, 458
Ashton, James, 221
  Samuel, 471
  Robert, 167
Asson, Pinset, 20, 61
Asten, Cornelius, 382
Aten (Auten), John, 284
  Mary, 247
  Thomas, 284
Atkin, Thomas, 93
  (see Akin)
Atkinson, Aaron, 21
  Adin, 21
  Elizabeth, 437
  Hannah, 20, 21
  Hope, 246
  James, 21
  John, 44
  Jonathan, 21
  Michael, 21
  Moses, 21
  Ruth, 337
  Samuel, 21, 60, 78, 337, 466
  Samuel, Jr., 337
  Sarah, 159
  Susannah, 21
  Thomas, 56, 132, 165, 187, 213, 301, 338, 344, 358, 378, 412, 489
  William, 21
  (see Hatkinson)
Atwood, Jacob, 464
  Phebe, 222
Austin, Ann, 22
  Caleb, 21
  Esther, 21
  Francis, 21, 22, 158, 210, 470
  Hannah, 22
  Jacob, 21
  Patience, 21
  Seth, 21
  Susannah, 21
  Tamer, 22
Auten (see Aten)
Axford, Abraham, 22
  Charles, 22
  Charles, Jr., 271
  James, 22
  John, 22
  Jonathan, 22
  Samuel, 22
Axtell, William, 266
Ayers (Ayres, Ayars), Aaron, 290
  Azariah, 22
  Benajah, 418
  Burgon, 22, 303
  Caleb, 22
  David, 74, 266
  Elijah, 22
  Elisha, 151, 290
  Elizabeth, 22, 266
  Esther, 23
  Frazee, 153
  Hannah, 23
  Hester, 22
  Isaac, 38
  Isaac, Jr., 22
  James, 275, 303
  Jane, 22
  Jehu, 470
  John, 64, 249, 258
  Jonathan, 32, 38, 58, 107, 165, 381
  Joseph, 22, 153, 214, 428
  Levi, 100
  Lydia, 22
  Martin, 23
  Micajah, 22
  Michael, 21, 91
  Moses, 21, 91, 95
  Nathan, 22
  Nathaniel, 95, 165, 225, 418, 441
  Obadiah, 152, 428
  Phebe, 22, 153
  Philip, 382
  Reuben, 92, 153
  Ruth, 22
  Samuel, 275, 347
  Stephen, 195
  Surrage, 22
  Susanna, 22
  Thomas, 482
  William, 351
Ayston, Benonia, 95

B

Babbit, Isaac, 70, 198
Babcock, Thomas, 132
  (see Badcock)
Backer, Matthias, 343
Backes, Mr., 62
Backlar, Simon, 288
Bacon, Abel, 23
  Anna, 318
  Daniel, 31, 318, 369
  Deborah, 23
  Elizabeth, 23
  Esther, 23
  Hannah, 23
  Jacob, 24
  Jeremiah, 24
  Jesse, 23
  John, 265
  Joseph, 23
  Lydia, 23

INDEX OF NAMES OF PERSONS 503

Margaret, 23
Mark, 50
Mary, 318
Nathan, 24, 381, 472
Nathaniel, 23
Prudence, 23
Rachel, 23, 24, 381
Richard, 23
Sarah, 23
Shepherd, 23
Tabitha, 24
Thomas, 214
Uriah, 57
William, 24
Bacor, Elizabeth, 494
Badcock, Catherine, 198, 199
  Joseph, 410
  Rebecca, 401
  Return, 214, 401
  William, 199
Badger, Cecil, 236
  Mary, 236
Badgley, Anthony, 376
  Anthony, Jr., 478
  George, 365
  James, 98, 478
  Robert, 478
Bagley, John, 5
Bail, John, 149
Bailey (Baley, etc.), Daniel, 21
  Deborah, 21
  Elias, 118, 183
  Esther, 27
  Hannah, 24
  Henry, 344
  John, 24, 27, 75
  Joseph, 24
  Mary, 27, 183
  Nancy, 27
  Nathaniel, 24
  Phebe, 27
  Samuel, 27
  Squire, 27
  Thaddeus, 27
  Thomas, 27
Bainbridge, Abigail, 24, 25
  Absalom, 24
  Edmund, 24, 25, 393
  Francis, 328
  Hannah, 25
  John, 24, 25, 210, 328, 461, 467
  Mary, 25, 297
  Peter, 24
  Rebecca, 25
  Sarah, 24, 25
  Theophilus, 25
  William, 25, 27
Baird, Andrew, 397
  Anna, 397
  Elizabeth, 25
  John, 25
  Margaret, 25
  Richard, 25
  Sarah, 71
  William, 25, 166, 41*f*
  Zebulon, 346, 397
Baker, Agnes, 25
  Daniel, 425
  Ephraim, 219
  Ephraim, Jr., 219
  Hannah, 26
  Henry, 487
  Jacob, 60
  Jeremiah, 9, 324, 36*(*

  John, 26
  Matthias, 434
  Nathaniel, 487
  Rachel, 26
  Samuel, 168, 272, 321, 322
  Susannah, 26
  Thomas, 26, 369, 417, 427, 454
  William, 369
Baldwin, Anne, 240
  Benjamin, 163
  Caleb, 27
  Cornelius, 26
  Dorcas, 26
  Ebenezer, 26, 27
  Eleazer, 28
  Elias, 26
  Elijah, 26
  Elizabeth, 26, 27
  Capt. Enos, 427
  Eunice, 27, 118
  Hannah, 26, 27
  Isaac, 26, 27
  Jemima, 27
  Jesse, 27
  Joanna, 311
  Joel, 27
  Jonas, 217, 235, 357
  Jonathan, 26, 205, 350
  Joseph, 480
  Luther, 26
  Mary, 27, 365
  Moses, 49, 65, 186, 229
  Nathan, 311
  Nehemiah, 26, 27, 35, 98, 235
  Phebe, 26, 27, 49
  Phinehas, 28, 463
  Samuel, 27, 183
  Sarah, 27, 365
  Stephen, 27, 495
  William, 365
  Zaccheus, 26
Ball, Abigail, 28
  Benjamin, 262
  Betty, 28
  Caleb, 321
  Daniel, 222
  Ephraim, 28
  Isaiah, 27, 399
  Jemima, 28
  Johannah, 467
  John, 28
  Joseph, 13, 221, 330
  Lucy, 28
  Mary, 28
  Moses, 28
  Nathaniel, 459
  Samuel, 28, 87
  Sarah, 28
  Stephen, 339
  Thomas, 335
  William, 28, 394, 481
  Zopher, 27
Ballinger, Amariah, 86
  Charity, 28
  Enoch, 28
  Eve, 377
  Isaac, 144, 203, 468
  James, 385
  Joshua, 28, 85, 238
  Martha, 28
  Naomi, 28, 417
  Samuel, 86
  Thomas, 28
  Zaccheus, 28

Bamforth, William, 67
Bancraft (Bancroft), Abigail, 28
  David, 28, 29
  Elizabeth, 101
  Ephraim, 29, 172
  Johanna, 29
  John, 29
  Margaret, 29
  Phebe, 29
  Samuel, 29
Bane, John, 153
Baner, Isaac, 156
Banks, Ann, 136
  Catherine, 222, 312
  David, 312
  Jacob, 312
  Jacob J., 222
  James, 431
  James, Jr., 312
  Joseph, 312
  Josiah O., 312
  Mary, 126, 312
  Sarah, 312
Banta, Albert H., 257
  Catalintje, 113
  David, 29, 256
  Derrick, 29, 494
  Hendrick, 29, 261
  Jacob, 8, 126, 256
  Jacob D., 261
  John, 29, 494
  John C, 300
  John H., 256, 257
  Lena, 8, 29
  Paulus, 256
  Rachel, 453
  Sibe, 113, 257, 453
  Wiert, 29, 256
Barber, Alida, 221
  Hannah, 123, 196
  Isaac, 30, 107, 121, 208, 461
  Jacob, 367
  Jane, 30
  John, 196, 221, 239
  Magdelena, 221
  Rebecca, 30
  Samuel, 221
  Thomas, 121, 123
Barberie, Andrew, 30
  Catherine, 30
  Frances, 30
  Gertrude, 30, 223
  John, 30, 223
  Lambert, 30
  Oliver, 30
  Peter, 30
  Susanna, 30
Barclay (Barkley), Charles, 300
  Elizabeth, 45
  Jeane, 445
  John, 12, 396
  Margaret, 45
  Robert, 45, 63, 266
  Samuel, 62, 63, 95
  Walter, 63
Bard, Dr. John, 30
  Mary, 30
  Peter, 30, 71, 131
  Samuel, 30, 40, 44, 348
  Sarah, 30
Bardan, Eva, 30
  Hendrick, 30
  Isaac, 30
  John, 30, 141
  Sarah, 30
Bargo, Jacobus, 351
Barkalow, Aeltie, 31
  Arthur, 31
  Daniel, 32
  Derrick, 31, 240
  Farrington, 32
  Jane, 264
Barker, Elizabeth, 341
  Hannah, 32
  Isaac, 31
  John, 31, 32
  Martha, 341
  Mary, 31, 341
  Richard, 31
  Ruth, 31
  Samuel, 31
  Wade, 31
  William, 31, 140
Barkley (see Barclay)
Barnes (Barns), David, 32
  Gershom, 16, 270
  Hannah, 235
  John, 105, 170, 235, 370, 434
  John, Jr., 36
  Jonathan, 32
  Lambert, 347, 380
  Phebe, 32
  Priscilla, 32
  Ruth, 299
  Samuel, 32, 235
  Sarah, 235
  Thomas, 164, 271
  William, 235
Barnet, Hannah, 487
  Oliver, 355
  William, 37, 210, 409
  Dr. William, 80
Barr, Henry, 424
  Joseph, 149
Barracliff, John, 301, 347
Barret (Barratt), Caleb, 32
  Elijah, 214
  Enoch, 32
  James, 32
  Moses, 37
  Rachel, 32
  William, 46, 116, 230
Barrick, Peter, 117
Barron, Samuel, 76, 152, 325
Barrow, Samuel, 325
Bartenheart, John, 181
Bartholomew, Elizabeth, 33
  John, 32, 33, 254, 340
Bartlett, Nathan, 226
Bartley, Catherine, 346
  Margaret, 346
Barton, Gilbert, 292, 395, 398
  Joseph, 110, 113, 114
  John, 75, 384
  Thomas, 132
Bartow, Daniel, 45, 238, 300
  Eunice, 33, 104
  John, 74
  Thomas, 223
Bartram (Bartrom), Agnes, 33
  Ann, 33
  Antony, 33
  John, 456
  Joseph, 33, 47, 250
Bartron, James, 60
  John, 33, 40
  (see Bertron)

INDEX OF NAMES OF PERSONS 505

Bassett, Abigail, 33, 107
  Ann, 33
  Daniel, 33, 121, 197, 208, 261, 467, 474
  Eleanor, 33
  Elisha, 107, 123, 197, 266, 296, 353, 367, 472
  Elisha, Jr., 94, 190, 336, 379
  Elizabeth, 208
  John, 135
  Mary, 33, 252
  Phebe, 33
  Rachel, 33
  Samuel, 295
  Susannah, 33
  William, 106
Bast, Joseph, 405
Bastedo, Anne, 34
  Catherine, 33
  George, 34
  Hannah, 34
  Lewis, 299
  Thomas, 34
  William, 34
Bastelowe, Lydia, 80
Bastick, John, 34
Bate, Thomas, 193, 199, 228, 276, 378
  William, 200
Bateman, Amos, 368
  Daniel, 115
  Hannah, 379
  John, 34, 177, 396
  Joseph, 312, 382
  Moses, 184
  Nehemiah, 34
  Rebecca, 368
  Thomas, 34
Bates, Aaron, 35
  Abigail, 34
  Catherine, 35
  Daniel, 35
  David, 34
  Elizabeth, 35
  Eunice, 35
  Hannah, 35
  John, 35
  Joseph, 35
  Joshua, 35
  Mary, 35
  Rachel, 35
  Rebecca, 35
  Rhoda, 35
  Sarah, 35, 85
  Thomas, 441
  William, 34, 277
Batten, Abner, 35
  Ann, 35
  Deborah, 35, 195
  Edward, 35
  Elinor, 195
  Francis, 35
  John, 35
  Richard, 35
  Sarah, 35
  Thomas, 35
Bayard, Catherine, 267
  Samuel, 361, 363
  William, 135
Bayles, Platt, 473
  Samuel, 300, 338
Baylis, George, 235
Baynton, Benjamin, 35
  Benjamin, Jr., 35

  Esther, 35
  John, 35, 36
  Mary, 35
  Peter, 36
Beach, Abner, 36
  Deborah, 36
  Elias, 36
  Elisha, 36
  Enoch, 28, 440
  Eunice, 36
  Ezekiel, 258
  Isaac, 36
  Joseph, 36, 70
  Josiah, 206
  Mary, 36
  Matthias, 36
  Nathaniel, 36
  Rachel, 36
  Richard, 485
  Samuel, 36
  Sarah, 36
  Stephen, 35, 410
  Zophar, 222
Beakes, Abraham, 36
  Anne, 36
  David, 36
  Edmund, 36, 41, 108, 248, 271, 493
  Edmund, Jr., 36
  Hannah, 132
  Lydia, 41
  Nathan, 131, 132
  Ruth, 41
  Samuel, 36
  Stacy, 41
  Stephen, 36
  William, 36, 426
Beam, Abram, 33
  Conrad, 33, 250
  Howell, 433
  Joost, 33, 250
Bean, Samuel, 6
Beasley, Gertrude, 387
  John, 100, 387
  Jonathan, 460
  Mary, 387
Beatty (Beaty), Alexander, 36
  Ann, 343
  Charles, 343
  George, 37, 106
  Esther, 36
  Isabel, 36
  James, 36, 380
  Jane, 36
  Mary, 36
  Robert, 37
  Samuel, 36
Beaumont, John, 344
Beavers, Joseph, 96, 139
Bebout, Ebenezer, 262, 433
Beck, John, 37
Becker, Matthias, 405
Bedell, Absalom, 37
  Agnes, 37
  Benjamin, 37, 38
  Esther, 96
  Hannah, 37
  Jacob, 37, 110, 436
  John, 27
  Joel, 461
  Joseph, 37, 443
  Martha, 37
  Michael, 37
  Silas, 443

Bedent, Abigail, 37
Bedford, Elias, 98
  Stephen, 27
Bedlow, Mary, 38
Bee, Ann, 38
  Asa, 38
  Elizabeth, 38
  Ephraim, 38
  Sophia, 38
Beekman, Anne, 38
  Catherine, 447
  Elizabeth, 38
  Gerardus, 446, 447
  Henry, 38, 55, 247, 431
  James, 462
  John, 38, 291
  Martin, 38
  Samuel, 38, 404
Beers, Jabesh, 65, 258
Beetle, Christiana, 446
  John, 446
  William, 259, 326, 452
Belanger, James, 276
Belew, Daniel, 378
  Isaac, 378
  Peter, 378
Bell, Elizabeth, 38
  Jabesh, 93, 121, 228
  James, 482
  Martha, 139
  Thomas, 256, 315
Bellis, Catherine, 39
  Cristine, 38
  Han W., 39
  Peter, 38, 39
  Philip, 38
  William, 38, 39
Bellosfelt, William, 205
Belsire, Robert, 142
Belton, Jonathan, 136
Bemer, George, 267
  Philip, 406
Bender, John, 390
  John G., 137
Benjamin, Mary, 335
Benner, Christian, 230
Benners, Maudlin, 39
Bennet, Aaron, 166
  Abiah, 39
  Abner, 191
  Adrian, 25, 167
  Barbary, 167
  Daniel, 60, 71, 187
  Ezekiel, 314, 348
  Gertrude, 39
  Jacob, 492
  Jane, 166
  John, 169, 306
  Joseph, 39
  Lois, 115
  Ludwick, 232
  Majeka, 492
  Margaret, 167
  Martha, 143
  Mary, 39, 74
  Rachel, 39, 40
  Richard, 39
  Samuel, 459
  William, 39, 395
Benson (Bensen), Christopher, 294, 395
  Elizabeth, 40
  Eva, 40
  Jannetje, 40

John, 40, 112, 113, 261
  Marytje, 40
Bent, Thomas, 83, 416, 439
Benthall, Elizabeth, 182
  Mary, 182
  Priscilla, 182
  Walter, 182
Berdan, Berck, 188
  John, 404, 444, 455
  John D., 455
Bereman, John, 34, 307, 348
Berg, William, 195
Bergen, Elsie, 40
  Gertrude, 40
  Hendrick, 40
  Jacob, 40, 124, 447
  Jacob, Jr., 201
  Joris, 201, 305, 447, 457, 459
Berger, Jacob, 229, 449
Berkinshea, Esther, 148
  Thomas, 148
Berrien, Margaret, 125
  John, 42, 162, 247, 248, 414, 447, 449
  Peter, 124, 447
Berry, Abraham, 40
  Deborah, 445
  John, 40, 282, 458
  Margaret, 282
  Martha, 445
  Mary, 40
  Paulus, 445
  Phillip, 40
  Samuel, 40
  Sidney, 324
  Thomas, 99, 254
  William, 40
Bertholf, Rev. Guilliam, 7, 8, 31, 153, 264, 424, 455, 458
  Jannetie, 216
  John, 242
Bertron, Abraham, 104
  (see Bartron)
Bescherer, John, 74
Bess, Thomas, 344
Besson, Francis, 195
Bessonet, Charles, 358
Best, James, 117
  William, 117
Betts, Benjamin, 214
  Ephraim, 63, 64
  Sarah, 238
Bevens, Hannah, 40
Bevin, Ann, 51
  Elizabeth, 40
Beyer, Catherine, 195
Bicker, Henry, 169
Bickerdike, Esther, 41
  Hannah, 41
  Mary, 41
Bickham, Caleb, 204, 377, 435
Bickley, Samuel, 56
  Thomas, 332, 333
Biddle, Arney, 358
  Joseph, 491
  Joseph, Jr., 319
  Sarah, 361
  Thomas, 134, 173
  William, 361
Bidgood, William, 396
Bigger (Biggers), Ann, 41, 42
  Elizabeth, 41
  James, 41, 42, 254
  John, 42

INDEX OF NAMES OF PERSONS 507

Joseph, 41, 42
Martha, 41
Robert, 41
Biggins, John, 486
Biggs, Elizabeth, 385
  George, 187
  Thomas, 369
  William, 42
Bilderback, Albert, 287, 326
  Catherine, 450
  Hance, 287
  Isaac, 287
  John, 453
  Lurana, 287
  Peter, 324, 450
  Sarah, 326
  William, 287
Biles, Alexander, 301
  Benjamin, 42, 131, 410
  Charles, 415
  Elizabeth, 131
  John, 132, 394
  Langhorn, 415
  Sarah, 302
  Thomas, 42, 302
  William, Jr., 42
Billings, Levi, 316
  William, Jr., 99
Billington, Samuel, 118
Billop (Billopp), Catherine, 42
  Christopher, 42
  Elizabeth, 42
  Jasper, 42
  Mary, 42
  Sarah, 42, 247, 248
  Thomas, 42, 247
Bills, Daniel, 42
  Elizabeth, 42
  Gersham, 214, 227, 256
  Margaret, 42
  Nathaniel, 42
  Rachel, 42
  Rebecca, 42
  Sarah, 42
  Sylvester, 42
  Solvanes, 42
  Thomas, 42
Binge, Elizabeth, 43
  Hannah, 43
  Jacob, 43
  William, 43
Bird, Deborah, 419
  Henry, 281
  John, 43
  Joseph, 150, 243, 320
Birdsall (see Burdsall)
Birkham, Dinah, 43
Bishop, Abigail, 140
  Anne, 43
  Benjamin, 43
  David, 44
  Jeremiah, 319
  Jonathan, 60, 130, 217, 317, 363
  John, 43, 44
  Joseph, 44
  Joshua, 44
  Moses, 273, 412
  Rebecca, 43
  Robert, 22, 55, 61, 158
  Ruth, 43
  Sarah, 43, 158, 438
  Thomas, 34, 43
  William, 43, 44, 131, 186, 188

Bispham, Benjamin, 44
  Elizabeth, 44
  Hinchman, 44
  Joshua, 51, 320, 337, 357, 466
  Ruth, 337
  Sarah, 44, 466
  Thomas, 44, 350
Bissett, Andrew, 224
  Nancy, 224
Bivan, Elizabeth, 242
Bivins, Joseph, 38
Black, Achsah, 44
  Amy, 243
  Ann, 44
  Edward, 44
  Ezra, 44, 360
  Garret, 46
  John, 44, 313
  Mary, 44
  Samuel, 44, 159, 179, 334
  Sarah, 46
  Ursilla, 62
  William, 44, 308
Blackford, Benjamin, 44
  Daniel, 314
  Desia, 45
  Francis, 247
  John, 44, 270
  Mary, 44
  Nathaniel, 44
  Sophia, 45
Blackhall, Hugh, 419
Blackhorn, Catharine, 150
Blackledge, Ann, 45
  Benjamin, 45
  Catherine, 45, 339
  Elena, 45
  Jacob, 45
  Willempe, 45
  Zachariah, 45
Blackman, Andrew, 348
Blackwood, Abigail, 77, 81
  Alexander, 287
  Joseph, 77
  Margaret, 45
  Mary, 77
  Samuel, 35, 45, 77, 102, 174, 216, 470, 491
Blaine, Benjamin, 45
  Elizabeth, 45
  Farley, 45
  Hannah, 114
  James, 45
  John, 45
  Margaret, 45, 46
  Mary, 45
  Thomas, 45
Blair, Jannetje, 46
  Mark, 39, 392
  Mary, 41, 94
  Samuel, 101, 141
Blake, Elizabeth, 46
Blakey, Joshua, 41
  Lydia, 41
  William, 41
Blanchard, John, 76, 98, 368
Blatchly, Ebenezer, 379
  Miller, 204
Blauw, Hendrick, 284
  Mary, 46
Blewer, Samuel, 122
Bliss, George, 246
  John, 396
  Thomas, 154

Blinkerhoff, Clasie, 46
  George, 112
  Eegje, 46
  Hartman, 46, 126
  Hendrick, 46, 456
  Jacobus, 112, 445
  (see Brinkerhoff)
Blizard, Esther, 423
  Naomi, 37
  Rebecka, 37
Blond, Alexander, 46
  Gabriel, 13, 200, 383, 419, 432, 491
  James A., 46
  Mary A., 46
  Philipa, 46
Bloodgood, Abigail, 72
  Abraham, 47
  Francis, 47
  Hannah, 421
  John, 47
  Judah, 47
  Martha, 47
  Mary, 47, 189
  Moses, 103
  Priscilla, 426
  William, 47, 189
Bloomfield, Andrew, 103, 207
  Benjamin, 47, 152
  Ezekiel, 47
  Jonathan, 47, 186
  Joseph, 47
  Moses, 47, 126
  Dr. Moses, 245, 308
  Thomas, 103, 435
  Thomas, Jr., 103
  Timothy, 402
  William, 47
Blumer, Hance, 305
Blumlain, Johan C., 181
Board, Ann, 375
  David, 47, 142
  James, 33, 47, 142
  Joseph, 47
  Martha, 47
Boazorth, Andrew, 97
Bobet, Elizabeth, 198
Bodine, Abraham, 260
  Catrine, 47, 48
  Cornelius, 47, 171
  Elizabeth, 48
  Gysbert, 48
  Isaac, 48
  Jane, 47
  John, 47, 48, 117
  Judith, 47
  Mary, 47, 48, 260
  Peter, 311, 378
  Sarah, 47, 48
Bogert (Bogart), Cornelius, 495
  Henry, 414
  Isaac, 112, 442, 495
  Jacob, 48
  Jan, 444
  Johannis, 40, 494
  Peter, 444
  Mrs., 187
Boggs, James, 11, 18, 268
  Mary, 18
  Samuel, 81
Boice (Boyce, Buys), Abraham, 54
  Adam, 446
  Ann, 446
  Cornelius, 48, 468

  Dennis V., 48
  Effie, 284
  Elias, 35, 54
  Folkert, 337
  Handershe, 337
  Hannah, 35
  Jacob, 18, 45, 247, 284
  John, 48, 77, 337
  Leonard, 48
  Lydia, 48
  Martha, 54
  Nathan, 54, 77, 351
  Robert, 54
  Susannah, 54
  William, 370
Bolmer, Abraham, 48
  Alabartes, 48
  Ann, 48
  Elizabeth, 48
  Jane, 48
  Magdalen, 48
  Robert, 48, 335
  Rosanna, 48
Bomgaert, Dorothea, 445
Bond, Benjamin, 314
  Elijah, 369
  James, 116, 266, 353
  John, 378
  Joseph, 121
  Nathaniel, 48
  Robert, 48
  Zerviah, 467
Bonham, Absalom, 178, 465
  Anchor, 489
  Anna, 49
  Catherine, 49
  Elizabeth, 297
  Ephraim, 408
  Hezekiah, 194
  Jeremiah, 125, 464
  Joseph, 15
  Malakiah, 138, 178, 356, 465
  Uriah, 178, 349, 489
  Zerujah, 49
Bonin, John, 5
Bonnel, Abraham, 49, 235, 340
  Benjamin, 386
  Capt. Benjamin, 321
  Frederick, 194
  Henry, 425, 427
  Isaac, 49, 475
  Jacob, 49
  James, 316
  John, 49
  Joseph, 49
  Joseph, Jr., 49
  Kezia, 49
  Mary, 49
  Nathaniel, 98
  Phebe, 49
  Sarah, 49
  Synesey, 49
  Thomas, 68, 85
  Dr. Wats, 49
  (see Bunnel)
Bonney, James, 50
Boof, Barbara M., 50
Boon, Christiana, 227
  Peter, 332, 440
Boosy, Abraham, 50
Booz, Henry, 324
Borden, Benjamin, 50, 411
  Elizabeth, 51
  Francis, 446

INDEX OF NAMES OF PERSONS 509

Hannah, 51
James, 160
James, Jr., 54
John, 40
Jonathan, 50, 51
Joseph, 51, 61
Joseph, Jr., 51, 224, 286
Martha, 51
Richard, 51, 54, 168, 320
Rynier, 234
Samuel, 51
Thomas, Jr., 50, 90, 149, 320, 474
Bornum, Gideon, 474
Borradaill, Arthur, 51
  John, 51
  Ruth, 51
  Sarah, 51
  William, 51, 303
Borton, Abigail, 52
  Abraham, 52, 390, 126
  Benjamin, 52
  Caleb, 52
  Hannah, 52
  Jane, 52
  Job, 52
  John, 52
  Joshua, 52
  Josiah, 52
  Mary, 52
  Phebe, 52
  Samuel, 52, 390
  Sarah, 52
  William, 52, 390
Boshcerer, Abraham, 266
Boude, Joshua, 390
Boudinot, Elias, 295, 370, 487
Boughanan, Mary, 265
Boulsbey, Samuel, 31
  Thomas, 31
Boulton, Edward, 134
Bouser, William, 67
Bouttenhouse, Saphira, 52
Bowell, Thomas, 182
Bowen, Abraham, 293
  Dan, 58, 157, 255
  Elijah, 75
  Elijah, Jr., 255, 381
  Enoch, 32
  Grace, 114
  Jonathan, 465
  Jonathan, Jr., 143, 249, 301
  Mark, 164
  Peleg, 301
  Sarah, 406
  Seth, 23, 32, 61, 83
Bower, David, 52, 53
  Ebenezer, 52, 321
  Edmond, 180, 231
  Eli, 52
  Hannah, 52
  John, 52, 53, 311
  Priscilla, 53
  Tamsen, 52
Bowker, Aaron, 290
  Jemima, 290
  John, 290
Bowlby, George, 323
  John, 354
  Jordan, 31
  Martha, 31
  Thomas, 440
Bowman, John, 53, 207
Bowne, Andrew, 53, 248
  Andrew, Jr., 55

Ann, 53
Catharine, 53
Deliverance, 199
Frederick, 53
Gershom, 53
Helena, 53
James, 53
John, 53, 118, 264, 400
Mary A., 53
Matilda, 53
Obadiah, 53
Patience, 413
Peter, 199, 346, 372, 397
Philip, 53
Samuel, 53, 90, 248, 413
William, 53, 56, 248, 466
Bows, Thomas, 483
Boyce (see Boice)
Boyd, Eunice, 14
  Martha, 209
  Robert, 124, 280, 463
  William, 120, 220
Boylan, Aaron, 12, 165, 225
  James, 441
Boyle, Charles, 141
  Margaret, 204
Brackney, John, 54
  Joseph, 54
  Matthias, 54, 225
Bradbury, Elizabeth, 54
Braddock, Barzilla, 54
  Daniel, 54
  John, 54
  Rehoboam, 54
  Reuben, 54
  Robert, 54
Braden, Joseph, 299
  Robert, 491
Bradford, Silas, 381, 423
Bradick, Sarah, 11
Bradshaw, James, 116, 367
  Paul, 139
Bradway, Aaron, 362, 416, 475
  Edward, 55, 317, 362
  Jonathan, 54, 269
  Nathan, 54, 55
  Sarah, 55
  Susannah, 54, 55
  Thomas, 362
  William, 54, 76, 459
Bragg, John, 157, 162, 258, 347
Brain, Samuel, 128
Brakel, John, 56
Braman, Benjamin, 60
Brandbury, Mary, 467
Brannin, Andrew, 53
  Elizabeth, 55
  Jane, 420
  Joem, 55
  John, 54
Branson, David, 90, 164, 173, 231, 345, 389, 465
  Jane, 114
  John, 164, 389
  Jonathan, 332
  Moses, 465
  Samuel, 114
Brant, David, 384
  Mary, 76
  William, 425
Brasier, Francis, 38, 55, 291, 431
  George, 291
Brasonton, John, 271

510   NEW JERSEY COLONIAL DOCUMENTS

Brass, Henry, 55
  Luke, 55
Bray, Daniel, 46, 247
  Elizabeth, 55, 56
  James, 55, 56
  John, 55, 56, 142, 374
  John, Jr., 95
  Samuel, 55, 56
  Susannah, 56
Brayman, Elizabeth, 56
  Ezekiel, 56
  Isaac, 56
  Samuel, 56
  Sarah, 56
Brazeil, Jane, 56
Breach, Peter, 173, 393
  Thomas, 430
Brearley, David, 236
  David, Jr., 131
  John, 210
Brede, William, 234
Breden, Robert, 363
Breese, Elizabeth, 337
  John, 249
  Rebecca, 141
  Samuel, 141
Brewer, Aaron, 93
  Adam, 56
  Deborah, 56
  Elazarus, 55, 297, 410
  Elizabeth, 56
  George, 56
  Hannah, 56
  Hendrick, 264
  Jacob, 390
  Magdalene, 56
  Margaret, 56
  Mary, 56
  Rachel, 56
  William, 56, 130, 170, 214, 256
Brewster, Anne, 57
  Benjamin, 57
  Daniel, 57, 58
  Ebenezer, 57
  Francis, 85
  Gilbert, 57
  Hannah, 57
  Joseph, 57
  Rebecca, 57
  Ruth, 57
  Samuel, 57
Brian, Abraham, 57
  Mary, 57, 77, 169
  Rebecca, 57
  Thomas, 57, 109, 437
  (see Bryan)
Briant, John, 289
  Martha, 57
  Mary, 289
  Uriah, 57
  William, 57
  (see Bryant)
Brick, Elizabeth, 58
  Ephraim, 58
  Hannah, 58
  John, 58, 77
  Joseph, 58
  Joshua, 58
  Rachel, 58
  Sarah, 58
  William, 58
Brickman, Henry, 368
Bridge, Chloe, 58, 156, 476
Brierly, Louldae, 67

Briggs, Abel, 59
  Ann, 59
  David, 58, 59
  Elizabeth, 59
  George, 20, 21, 59, 191, 489
  Hannah, 59
  Job, 44, 59
  John, 44, 58
  Levi, 59
  Margaret, 15
  Mary, 59
  Rachel, 59
  Rebecca, 59
  Sarah, 59, 245
Bright, Amy, 59
  Elizabeth, 59
  George, 493
  James, 59, 60
  Jeremiah, 12
  John, 56, 450
  John U., 291
  Mary, 59
  Thomas, 299
Brink, Alida, 60
  Anne, 60
  Catherine, 60
  Eve, 60
  Franzintie, 60
  Hendrika, 60
  James, 60
  Janatie, 60
  John, 60
  Nicholas, 60, 375
  Rachel, 60
  Sarah, 60
  Thomas, 60
Brinkerhoff, Calasa, 126
  Cornelius, 234
  Elizabeth, 234
  Hartman, 126
  (see Blinkerhoff)
Brinkinshire, Richard, 211
Brinley, Hannah, 68
  John, 174, 474, 480
Britnell, Joseph, 353
Britton (Britain, etc.), Abigail, 286
  Benjamin, Jr., 201
  Catherine, 51
  Daniel, 60
  Elizabeth, 408
  John, 60, 408
  Joseph, 439
  Keziah, 60
  Martha, 201
  Nicholas, 428
  Nicholas, Jr., 201
  Phebe T., 60
  Sarah, 201
  William, 388
Broach, Adam, 210
Broadberry, Richard, 336
Broadwell, Henry, 254
  Josiah, 14, 378
  Mary, 207
  William, 28, 87, 315, 369, 438
Brock, Burbridge, 59, 60, 66, 67, 139
  Frances, 60
  John, 60, 232
  Martha, 60
  Mary, 335
  Mercy, 60
  Millicent, 60
  Oddy, 60
  Thomas, 60

INDEX OF NAMES OF PERSONS 511

Uriah, 60
William P., 335
Brockholls, Mary, 61
Brodenbach, Johannes, 167
Brokaw, Brogun, 451, 483
  Isaac, 19, 337, 449, 483
  John, 284, 374, 453, 483
  Phebe, 451
Brook, Ambrose, 241
  Canoe, 417
Brooke, Bowyer, 326
Brookfield, Benjamin, 14, 310
  Job, 406
  John, 82
  Capt. John, 406, 434
Brooks, Abigail, 61
  Ananias, 352
  Burrhus, 53
  David, 349
  Dorothy, 381
  Edward, 435
  Henry, 263
  Isaac, 481
  James, 17, 306
  Jonathan, 317, 405
  Lucy, 53
  Martha, 382
  Mary, 106
  Samuel, 419
  Seth, Jr., 372
  Thomas, 52
  Timothy, 372
Broome, John, 246
Brotherton, James, 494
Broughton, John, 291
Brower, Daniel, 384
  David, 112
  Elizabeth, 164
  Jacob, 112
  Jan, 112
  Johannes, 384
  Maria, 384
Brown (Browne), Aaron, 63, 64
  Abigail, 63, 64
  Abraham, 64, 318, 491
  Agnes, 62
  Alice, 63
  Andrew, 114, 169, 198
  Anne, 61, 62, 64
  Asa, 64
  Asher, 98, 323
  Bathniphleath, 64
  Bathsheba, 65
  Benjamin, 64
  Benoni, 63, 64
  Caleb, 49, 61, 63, 64, 219, 315, 323
  Catherine, 62
  Clark, 62
  Clayton, 64
  D. Isaac, 445
  David, 63, 65, 71, 438
  Daniel, 27, 62, 64
  Daniel I., 46
  Eleazer, 62, 63
  Elijah, 258
  Elizabeth, 51, 58, 61, 62, 64, 65
  Enoch, 65
  Eunice, 27, 64
  Ezekiel, 63
  George, 62, 82, 103, 138, 151, 234, 275, 284, 330, 331, 362, 470
  Greer, 71
  Hannah, 63
  Hendrick, 226, 351
  Henry, 64
  Hermione, 62
  Hope, 62
  Isaac, 248
  Isaiah, 63, 64
  Jacob, 58
  James, 38, 62, 63, 64, 76, 218
  James N., 62
  Jane, 47, 65
  Job, 62
  Joel, 54, 63, 323
  John, 19, 62, 64, 65, 71, 167, 198, 212, 285, 396, 423
  John, Jr., 198
  Jonathan, 63, 65, 491
  Joseph, 51, 61, 62, 64, 160, 484
  Leah, 63
  Lyndon, 230
  Mabel, 64
  Margaret, 62
  Martha, 63, 165
  Mary, 61, 63, 64, 65, 84, 303, 351
  Moses, 65, 251
  Phebe, 62, 63, 64
  Preserve, 303
  Prudence, 64
  Rebecca, 51
  Richard, 340
  Robert, 62, 224, 259
  Rynear, 226
  Safety, 90
  Samuel, 61, 63, 448
  Sarah, 61, 63, 459
  Sibel, 65
  Solomon, 62, 147
  Stephen, 63, 64
  Temperance, 64
  Thomas, 27, 62, 64, 87, 235, 348
  Turah, 64
  Walter, 419
  William, 64
  Zebedee, 65
  Zebulon, 63, 65
Brownig, George, 404
Browning, Joseph, 277
  Sarah, 277
Bruce, John, 432
Bruckfeald, Abigail, 371
Bruen, David, 68
  Elijah, 264
  Obadiah, 26, 63, 65, 235
  Timothy, Jr., 222
Bruere, Eleanor, 338
  Peter, 338
Bruff, James, 211
Bruger, John, 74
Bruin, Edward, 252
Brunner, Peter, 410
Brunson, Samuel, 299
Bruse, Elizabeth, 337
  John, 337
Brush, Benjamin, 8, 184, 349, 440
  Timothy, 276, 379, 400
Bruver, William, 306
Bryan, Martha, 54
  Thomas, 327
  (see Brian)
Bryant, Elizabeth, 65, 66
  Joshua, 65
  William, 66, 120, 414
  (see Briant)
Brynberry, Peter, 66, 218
Bryzelius, Paul, 329

512 NEW JERSEY COLONIAL DOCUMENTS

Buchanan (see Boughanan)
Buck, Enos, 220
  Ephraim, 457
  Jeremiah, 143
  John, 217
  Judith, 66, 309
  Lemuel, 66
  Lydia, 66
  Phebe, 143
  Sarah, 29
  Swain, 66
  Theody, 66
Buckalew, Frederick, 463
  Martha, 129
  Obadiah, 129
  Thomas, 282
Budd, Daniel, 66, 86, 311
  David, 67, 354
  Deborah, 66
  Eli, 67
  Elizabeth, 67
  George, 67
  Hannah, 66
  Henry, 66
  James, 158, 336
  John, 66, 148, 153, 206, 302, 382
  Dr. John, 73
  Joseph, 66, 67, 217
  Jonathan, 67
  Levi, 67
  Lydia, 66
  Margaret, 66
  Mary, 66, 67, 85
  Rachel, 67
  Rebecca, 67
  Samuel, 67
  Sarah, 59, 66
  Stacy, 161
  Susannah, 67, 85
  Theodocia, 66
  Thomas, 59, 66, 67, 109, 191, 233, 241, 246, 293, 310, 336, 435, 489
  William, 66, 79, 283
Buddock, Thomas, 45
Buffin, John, 230
  John, Jr., 157
  Mary, 158
  Michael, 64
  Rachel, 157, 158
Bulky, John, 387
Bull, Sarah, 81
Bullman, Gershom, 444
  Thomas, 346, 444, 450, 461, 492
Bullock, Elizabeth, 491
  George, 69, 181
  John, 61, 181, 491
  Joseph, 69, 181, 465
  Margaret, 491
  Thomas, 46
Bullus, John, 67
  Mary, 31
  Samuel, 31, 67
Bunadaill, Arthur, 276
Bunn, Edward, 455
  Mary, 27
  Miles, 152
  Reuben, 398
Bunnell, Isaac, 430
  James, 280
  Stephen, 45
  (see Bonnel)
Bunting, Aaron, 151
  Amos, 479
  Israel, 151

  Joshua, 151, 154, 269
  Phineas, 119
  Ramoth, 286
  Timothy, 51
  William, 285, 303, 468
Burcham (Burchan), Jacob, 462
  John, Jr., 67
  Robert, 48, 161, 73, 206, 276, 320, 325, 354, 407, 467
Burden, Jonathan, 64
  Rebecca, 231
  Richard, 131
  Thomas, Jr., 464
Burdett, Stephen, 78
  Stephen, Jr., 78
Burdge, David, 67
  Joseph, 250, 298
  Mary, 298
  Patience, 67
  Sarah, 298
  Uriah, 67
Burdsall, Deliverance, 67
  Elizabeth, 67, 475 (?)
  Jacob, 6
  Joseph, 67
  Mary, 67
  Phebe, 67
  Richard, 67
  Sarah, 67
  Stephen, 67
Burgean, Abraham, 454
  John, 42
Burger, Gilbert, 246
Burges, Elizabeth, 121
Burgie, Thomas, 244
Burk, Ann, 478
  Catherine, 400
  John, 105
  Walter, 197, 477, 478
Burlis, William, 360
Burn, Elizabeth, 230
Burnet, Aaron, 335
  Abigail, 68
  Alexander, 124
  Daniel, 68, 87, 124
  David, 332, 378
  Hannah, 68
  Henry, 28
  Dr. Ichabod, 68, 484
  Jacob, 98
  James, 237
  John, 56
  Martha, 332
  Mary, 68, 448
  Matthias, 237
  Rhoda, 68
  Robert, 346
  Thomas, 124
  William, 26, 27, 68, 220, 306, 430, 440, 448
Burns, John, 289
  Richard, 70
Burr, Jane, 68
  John, 126, 139, 191, 303
  John, Jr., 43, 100, 126, 191, 229, 336, 347, 348, 354, 390
  Henry, 68, 125, 126
  Henry, Jr., 306
  Jane, 68
  Joseph, 68, 246, 302
  Joseph, Jr., 43, 386, 482
  Martha, 347
  Mary, 302
  Rebecca, 68

INDEX OF NAMES OF PERSONS 513

Robert, 68
Sarah, 125
William, 68
Burroughs (Burrough), Isaac, 68, 307, 308
  Isaac, Jr., 307
  Jacob, 11
  John, 426
  John, Jr., 228, 307, 426
  Jonathan, 434
  Joseph, 20, 153, 200, 220, 303, 307, 308, 321, 382
  Rebecca, 307
  Samuel, 20, 68, 307, 308, 316, 320
  Samuel, Jr., 307
Burrowes, Charity, 68
  Deborah, 381
  Eden, 68, 415
  Edward, 68, 431
  Foster, 27, 69
  Hannah, 68, 69
  John, 68, 154, 200, 253, 289, 373, 431, 438, 449
  Jonathan, 364
  Letitia, 467
  Mercy, 68, 69
  Michael, 61, 491
  Rachel, 68
  Rebecca, 25, 68
  Stephen, 15, 68, 297, 301, 466, 467, 488
  Thomas, 68
Burson, Sarah, 338
Burt, Axford, 399
Burthshell, Elizabeth, 475
Burtis, Ann, 69
  Elizabeth, 69
  Susannah, 69
  William, 69
Burton, Alpheus, 227
  Brittah, 227
Burwell, Agnes, 69
  Catherine, 258
  John, 69
  Joseph, 69
  Samuel, 363
Bush, David, Jr., 107
Butcher, Aaron, 69
  Ann, 227
  Esther, 227
  Job, 69, 381
  John, 354
  Joseph, 479
  Mary, 354
  Thomas, 21, 128, 354
  William, 354
Butler, Amos, 69
  Elizabeth, 69
  Esther, 233
  Evan, 58
  James, 233
  John, 69
  John, Jr., 15, 28
  Lydia, 69
  Mary, 69, 318
  Michael, 161
  Priscilla, 69
  Rachel, 69
  Thomas, 45
  William, 422
Butter, Daniel, 102
Butterworth, Isaac, 94, 190
  Joseph, 161, 437

Buzby, John, 70, 170
  Joseph, 70, 411
  Priscilla, 70
  Samuel, 70
  Sarah, 70
  Thomas, 70, 411
Buzzard, Timothy, 195
Byram, Abigail, 70
  Anna, 70
  Ebenezer, 70
  Edward, 70
  Huldah, 70
  Japheth, 124, 158, 184, 423, 433
  Jephthah, 26, 70, 466
  Joseph, 70
  Mary, 70
  Napthali, 70
  Phebe, 70
  Mr., 36
Byvanck, Evert, 234

C

Cadmus, Abraham, 70
  Dirk, 70
  Frederick, 456
  Geertje, 55
  Isaac, 70
  John, 70
  John A., 188
  Joris, 456
  Maragrietje, 70
  Marritje, 70
  Peter, 83, 454, 456
  Thomas, Jr., 447
Caffrey, John, 320
Cahill, Daniel, 80, 144, 268, 368
Cain (see Cane)
Caldwell, James, 369, 487
  Joseph, 93
  William, 37, 369, 454
Calshear, Rosanna, 291
Calvert, William, 40, 125, 296
Calvin, Philip, 41
  (see Colvin)
Cameron (Camron), Abraham, 71
  Allan, 122
  George, 71
  John, 71
  Mary, 71
  Rebecca, 71
Cammegaar, Geesje, 256, 257
  Tryntje, 257, 266
Camp, Ezekiel, 232
  Job, 163
  Joseph, 472, 483
  Samuel, 186, 360
  Sarah, 71, 222
  (see DeCamp)
Campbell, Alexander, 160, 223, 388
  Archibald, 62, 71
  Colin, 66, 396
  David, 71
  Dugald, 275
  Elizabeth, 112
  Hope, 62
  Jesse, 71
  John, 80, 93, 100, 280, 359
  Margaret, 71
  Mary, 66, 71, 446
  Neill, 275
  Othaniel, 60
  Robert, 350

33

Stephen, 263, 283
Thomas, 85
William, 112, 113, 247, 403
Campfield, Ebenezer, 42
  Jabez, 147, 235
  John, 91, 481
  Thomas, 472
Campion, Francis, 103, 184
  John, 71
  Sarah, 71
Canbe, Martha, 475
Cane, Charity, 85
  Mary A., 209
  Walter, 185, 209
Canfield, Israel, 472
Caperson, Cornelius, 326
  Rebecca, 326
Carhart, Eleanor, 428
Carkuff (see Kerkuff)
Carlle (Carl), Catherine, 72
  Jacob, 72, 263
  John, 52, 71, 216, 244, 245, 263, 369
  Jonas, 71
  Joseph, 71
  Mary, 71
  Rebecca, 71
  Samuel, 72, 221, 416
  Sarah, 118, 406
  Uriah, 71
  William, 118, 224, 319, 406
Carlyle (Carlisle), Anne, 396
  David, 62, 63
  Robert, 160
  William, 408
Carman, Abigail, 72
  Caleb, 281
  Hannah, 302
  Isabel, 72
  James, 428
  John, 265
  Joseph, 302
  Kezia, 72
  Mary, 72, 428
  Phineas, 72
  Richard, 72, 366
  Richard, Jr., 72, 366
  Samuel, 72, 302
  Stephen, 72
  Stephen, Jr., 146
Carmichael, Daniel, 109
Carne (Carnes), Christopher, 92
  Cornelia, 8
  Don, 8
  John, 86, 312
  Richard, 325, 475
  William, 8, 29, 485, 495
  Zophar, 166
  (see Cairns)
Carney, Thomas, 326, 460
Carpenter, Abigail, 209, 212
  Benjamin, 272
  James, 23
  John, 68, 294
  Mary, 212, 435
  Preston, 171, 471
  Samuel, 201
  Thomas, 435
  William, 212, 357, 427
Carr, Capt. James, 62
Carroll, Daniel, 205, 494
  Thomas, 494

Carson, Joseph, 292
  William, 257
  (see Karson)
Cart, Goodson, 429
Carter, Abraham, 73
  Anna, 73
  Barnabas, 91
  Comfort, 73
  Daniel, 73
  David, 73
  Experience, 73
  Fisher, 191
  George, 73
  Hannah, 73
  James, 147
  Jeremiah, 73, 216
  Joanna, 73
  John, 73, 191
  Jonathan, 73
  Kezia, 73
  Mary, 460
  Nehemiah, 73
  Nicholas, 73
  Reuben, 73
  Samuel, 73
  Sarah, 191
  Susanna, 73
  Thomas, 73
  William, 191
  William, Jr., 191
Carty, John, 43, 174, 280, 392, 419
  William, 119
Cary, Anna, 284
  Daniel, 70
  Eleazer, 184
  John, 26, 123, 184
Case, Abigail, 73
  Adam, 227
  Catherine, 227
  Charity, 227
  Christian, 227
  Elizabeth, 227
  Frank, 227
  Hannah, 73
  Henry, 227
  Jacob, 205
  Johannis, 236, 413
  John, 237
  Joseph, 73
  Kezia, 73
  Margaret, 227
  Mary, 227
  Peter, 227
  Philip, 227
  William, 73
  (see Kase)
Casey, Henry, 320
Cash, Synthia, 448
  Thomas, 449
Cashow, Joshua, 241
  (see Corshow)
Cass (see Gass)
Cassert (see Kessart)
Casterline, Abraham, 109, 426
Castner, Anne, 73
  Conrad, 73
  Daniel, 73
  Kathrine, 73
  Jacob, 73
  John, 73
  John, Jr., 267
  Margaret, 73

INDEX OF NAMES OF PERSONS 515

Michael, 73
Peter, 73
Ursula, 73
Catchion, Huldah, 135
Cathrall, Edward, 140, 341, 361
Catt, George, 228
  Lutes, 228
  Michael, 228
  Ursilla, 228
  (see Kattz)
Cattell, James, 18, 28, 52, 138, 212, 238, 476
  Jonas, 168
  Sarah, 73
  William, 116
Catterling, Benjamin, 74
  Francis, 74
  Isaac, 74
  Jacob, 74
  James, 74
  Joseph, 74
  Martha, 74
  Mary, 74
  Phebe, 74
  Susannah, 74
Caver, Mary, 360
Caydle, Joseph, 45
Cayford, Richard, 195, 290
Cebra, James, 449
  Catherine, 449
Chamberlain, James, 74
  Jane, 74
  John, 376
  Lewis, 235, 482
  Mary, 413
  Thomas, 74
  Richard, 413
  Samuel, 74
Chambers, Alexander, 38, 108, 328, 492
  Ann, 74
  Benjamin, 376
  David, 74
  Eleanor, 74
  Elizabeth, 74
  John, 9, 38, 73, 74, 164
  Joseph, 146, 265, 280
  Lydia, 74
  Martha, 74
  Mary, 74
  Robert, 74, 201
  William, 73, 488
Chamless (Chamlis), Christian, 156
  James, 75
  Joseph, 156
  Nathaniel, 437
  Sarah, 75
  Susanna, 75
Champion, Deborah, 75
  John, 75, 137
  Joseph, 75, 163
  Nathaniel, 75
Champneys, Joseph, 279, 296, 398
Chanders, John, 376
Chandler, Abigail, 75, 76
  Asahel, 75
  Benjamin, 75
  Dorothy, 75
  Elizabeth, 75
  George, 75
  Jemima, 280
  John, 75, 76, 190, 365
  Joseph, 75, 76

Josiah, 76
Leady, 75
Marian, 76
Mary, 76
Nathaniel, 463
Phebe, 76, 463
Pontias, 75
Rebecca, 75
Stephen, 100
Susanna, 76
Thomas, 75
Thomas B., 211, 217
William, 353
Rev., 353
Chapman, Ann, 25
  John, 215
  Martha, 180
  Philip, 44, 267
  William, 61
Chard, Benjamin, 396
Chasey, John, 432
Chattin, Abraham, 76, 287
  Francis, 76, 461
  James, 76
  John, 76
  Josiah, 76
  Nixon, 65, 76, 234, 476
  Phebe, 76
Cheesman, Benjamin, 35
  Deborah, 77
  Ephraim, 193, 252
  Isabel, 252
  Margaret, 77
  Naomi, 77
  Peter, 77
  Richard, 252
  Richard, Jr., 252
  Samuel, 472
  Sarah, 77, 424
  Thomas, 77
  Uriah, 252
  William, 77, 132
Cheever, Ezekial, 12, 13, 27, 73, 87, 237, 335, 365, 423
Cherry, Mary, 370
  Sarah, 459
Chester, Amy, 77
  Catherine, 77
  Samuel, 77
Chesterman, Hannah, 77
Chestnor, Joseph, 60, 117, 375
Chetwood, John, 76, 111, 353, 365
  William, 353
Chew, Abigail, 476
  Constantine, 294
  Elizabeth, 77
  Hannah, 385
  Jeffery, 486
  Jonathan, 71
Chidester, Samuel, 78
Childs, Hannah, 105
  Henry, 105
  Isaac, 104
  James, 61, 92, 232
Christine, John, 282, 424
Christopher, Anne, 78
  Barnet, 78
  Catherine, 78
  Daniel, 78
  Elizabeth, 78
  Jesse, 78
  John, 78, 409
Christy, Daniel, 78
  David, 78

Jacomyn, 78
James, 455
John, 78
Magdalin, 78
Mary, 78
Sarah, 78
William, 78, 453
Church, Alice, 78
Christopher, 78, 404
Deborah, 78
Edward, 145
Joseph, 78
Martha, 78
Nathan, 29
Cimbel, John, 156
Cimber, George, 364
Clap, John, 78
Rebecca, 78
Tacy, 78
William, 78
Clark (Clarke), Aaron, 80
Abraham, 79, 80, 92, 189, 281, 315, 405
Abraham, Jr., 43, 60, 103, 151, 243, 376, 377, 388, 443, 479
Adam, 79, 485
Benjamin, 73, 79, 283, 446
Benjamin, 3rd, 223
Charles, 177, 217
Cornelius, 84, 426
Daniel, 73, 79, 117, 157, 177, 178, 207, 216, 293, 323, 379, 427, 432, 490
David, 147, 442
Edward, 206
Eleanor, 397
Elijah, 348
Elizabeth, 79, 80, 436
Hananiah, 79
Henry, 56, 317, 318
Isaac, 37, 105
Jacob, 219
James, 45, 96, 138, 250, 412
James, Jr., 80, 236
Jeffery, 187
Jeffery, Jr., 417
Jeremiah, 386
Joel, 109, 294
John, 14, 30, 131, 185, 215, 217, 225, 302, 314, 316, 321, 373, 386, 421, 437, 444
John P., 151
Joseph, 425
Jotham, 459
Lutitia, 92
Mary, 34, 79, 372
Matthias, 37
Moses, 147
Richard, 160, 189, 279
Robert, 228, 250, 265, 387, 452, 474
Samuel, 57, 79, 177, 342
Sarah, 79, 189, 206, 223, 278
Stephen, 37, 76, 347
Thomas, 38, 43, 56, 60, 80, 90, 187, 212, 249, 287, 348, 383, 407, 417, 470
William, 55, 80, 193, 372, 421
William, Jr., 294
Clarkson, Elizabeth, 61
Gerardus, 170
James, 62, 92, 100, 105, 135, 284
James, Jr., 426
John, 292

Clawson, Anne, 80
Brant, 80
Cornelius, 390
Elizabeth, 80
Hannah, 80, 436
John, 80, 193, 194, 313, 346
Jonathan, 76
Josiah, 80
Martha, 390
Mary, 80
Richard, 80
Sarah, 80
William, 80, 262
Clay, Charles, 101
Clayton, Bathsheba, 435
David, 346, 436
Elizabeth, 370
John, 306, 422
Joseph, 51, 69, 306
Pernal, 5
William, 41, 42
Clement, Abel, 81
Abigail, 180
Beulah, 137, 180
Jacob, 61, 75, 81, 85, 109, 148, 202
James, 85
Joseph, 81
Rachel, 81
Rebecca, 81, 180
Ruth, 81
Thomas, 81
Samuel, 5, 11, 20, 44, 68, 70, 81, 137, 192, 199, 202, 345
Samuel, Jr., 22, 61, 137, 180, 228, 303, 434
Clevenger, Elizabeth, 491
John, 204
Mary, 204
Mercy, 81
William, 20, 81
Cleverly, Thomas, 186
Clickener, Peter, 158
Clifford, Robert, 382
Cline, Hermon, 99, 308
Philip, 282
Mary C., 282
(see Kline)
Clinton, George, 375
Clopper, Catherine, 246
Elizabeth, 246
Peter, 246
Clothier, Mary, 14
Clough, John, 67
Clover, Catherine, 81, 82
Peter, 81, 82
Coalman, Mary, 206
Coate, Henry, 80, 292
John, 213
Thomas, 232, 233
William, 271, 428
Coats, Lindsay, 36
Cobb, Calop, 82
Ebenezer, 391
Elizabeth, 397
John, 36, 82, 88, 121, 391
Joshua, 82
Paul, 82
Priscilla, 82
Theodoa, 82
Thomas, 397
William, 82
Coberly, James S., 150
Samuel S., 280
(see Cubberly)

INDEX OF NAMES OF PERSONS 517

Cocever, Abraham, 45
Cochran, John, 180, 255, 417
  Dr. John, 248
  Mary, 18
  Richard, 18, 268
Cock (Cocks), Catherine, 82
  Edward, 82
  George, 260
  Hannah, 334
  Henry, 82
  Humphrey, 45
  Jacob, 82
  John, 82
  Joseph, 221
  Mary, 82
  Robert, 462
  Samuel, 334
  (see Cox; Koch)
Cockcroft, William, 449
Coddington, Abigail, 82
  Enoch, 82
  John, 62, 82
  Jonathan, 317
  Keziah, 82
  Phebe, 82
  Sarah, 82
  Thomas, 96
Codrington, John, 484, 485
Coe, Benjamin, 221
  Joseph, 82, 330
Coejeman (Coeman), Annatie, 83
  Aryantje, 83
  Hendrick, 83
  John, 83
  Lea, 83
  Margrietje, 83
  Marytie, 83
  Samuel S., 145
Coffer, Jacob, 235
Coffin, Cynde, 83
  Mary, 83
  Rane, 83
  Sarah, 83
  Thomas, 83
Coffyson, John, 64
Cogswell, Daniel, 58
Cohoon, Catren, 83
  Elizabeth, 83
  Esther, 83
  Jannet, 83
  Margaret, 83
  Martha, 83
  Mary, 83
  Walter, 83
Coke, Ann, 92
  George, 92
Colavel, William, 267
Cole, Ariantje, 83
  Benjamin, 83, 84
  Cathrynje, 84
  David, 83, 84
  Ezekiel, 83, 84, 187, 383
  Gertrude, 83
  Isaiah, 83, 84
  Jacob, 84
  James, 352
  Jane, 435
  John, 84, 114, 230, 272
  Josias, 84
  Lena, 187, 383
  Lenora, 84
  Margretje, 84
  Mary, 48
  Mercy, 230
  Michael, 187
  Samuel, 84, 85
  Sarah, 83, 84
  Simon, 48
  Sophia, 84
  Thomas, 84
  Tunis, 84
  William, 116, 135, 359
  (see Coles)
Coleman, Abraham, 46
  Christopher, 288
  Dorothy, 84
  Elizabeth, 86
  Israel, 84
  Jacob, 84
  Jane, 468
  Jared, 84
  Joel, 84
  Joshua, 84
  Lydia, 84
  Magdalen J., 288
  Margaret, 46
  Mary, 156
  Mehitable, 86
  Penelope, 86
  Rebecca, 84
  Samuel, 84, 432
  Sarah, 84, 86
  Susanna, 86
  Timothy, 84
Coles, Beersheba, 84
  Grace, 84
  Hannah, 84, 85
  Kindle, 84, 85
  Martha, 84
  Mary, 84
  Samuel, 84, 305
  Samuel, Jr., 18, 85
  Thomas, 84
  William, 110
  (see Cole)
Colhoun, John, 90
Collard, Elijah, 156, 184
  Rachel, 156
  Richard, 156
Collier (see Colyer)
Collins, Andrew, 482
  Charles, 300
  Ebenezer, 418
  Edward, 85
  Elizabeth, 85, 86
  Francis, 86
  Henry, 86
  Jane, 164
  Job, 85, 86
  John, 85, 86
  Joseph, 85, 136, 208
  Joshua, 85
  Lydia, 86
  Mary, 86
  Patience, 86
  Priscilla, 85
  Richard, 85, 128
  Samuel, 208, 211
Collum, James, 322
Colson, George, 32, 33
  William, 33
Colter, Joseph, 95
Colvin, Elizabeth, 465
  (see Calvin)
Colyer, John, 109, 234, 244, 313, 475
Combs, Dennis, 146
  John, 6, 7, 8, 70, 124, 346

John, Jr., 6
Jonathan, 25, 346, 454
Martin, 489
Mary, 6
Robert, 346, 489
Sarah, 6
Susannah, 326
Thomas, 304, 327
Comins, Jannetje, 383
Robert, 273
(see Cumine)
Compton, Daniel, 275
James, 441
Jane, 86
Matthias, 86
William, 86, 110
Conarroe, Andrew, 52
Darling, 18, 92, 168
Thomas, 18, 158
Conave, Johannis, 124
Condict, Daniel, 480
Ebenezer, 86, 251
Elizabeth P., 109
Isaac, 480
Joseph, 87, 109
Nathaniel, 87
Peter, 87
Phebe, 86, 87
Silas, 87, 109, 135
(see Cundict)
Condit, John, 460
Conger, Abigail, 87
Anna, 135
Benjamin, 87
Daniel, 87
David, 87, 241, 422
Elizabeth, 87, 272
Enoch, 87
Eunice, 180
Experience, 87
Gershom, 165
James, 87, 165
Jane, 271
John, 87
Jonas, 87
Joseph, 87
Lydia, 87
Mary, 87, 165
Moses, 82
Phebe, 87
Sarah, 87
Stephen, 87
Thomas, 87
Zenus, 87
Zipporah, 87
Congleton, Allen, 11, 119, 272, 439
Conkling (Conklin), Abigail, 86
David, 281
Hannah, 280, 281
Joseph, 280, 281
Mary, 280, 281
Sarah, 281, 379
William, 113
Stephen, 156, 186
Conner, John, 386
Connet, Rebecca, 422
Conover, David, 402
John, 408
John, Jr., 356
Peter, 401
(see Couwenhoven)
Conrod, Adam, 368
Sarah, 368
Conrow, Patience, 21

Conroy, Peter, 148
Cons, Mary, 87
Constant, Johannes, 87
Conyngham, Redmond, 155
Coofman, Barnard, 58
Cook (Cooke), Adam, 171
Asa, 70, 273
Ebenezer, 302
Edward P., 13, 75, 297
Elisha, 482
Elizabeth, 302
Ellis, Jr., 481
George, 58
Hannah, 88
Jacob, 88
Jean, 378
Job, 13, 75, 88, 113, 165, 240, 480, 469, 488
John, 478
Joseph, 88, 165
Lydia, 75, 88
Margaret, 88
Mary, 351
Phebe, 88
Rebecca, 322
Samuel, 248
Rev. Samuel, 298, 388
Sarah, 165
Stephen, 13
Thomas, 15
William, 88, 90, 285, 480
Cool, Barent, 334
Catharine, 88
Christopher, 88
Crest, 88
Elizabeth, 88
Eve, 88
Isaiah, 84
Mary, 88
Paul, 88
Paul, Jr., 88
Peter, 88
Phillip, 88
Simon, 88
William, 88
(see Kuhl)
Cooley, Jonathan, 156
Coon, Abraham, 88
Benjamin, 88
Catherine, 88
James, 259
Michael, 88
Moses, 88
John, 88
Thomas, 88
Cooper, Abigail, 229
Arent, 261
Barbery, 89
Benjamin, 90, 120, 248, 289
Caleb, 332
Daniel, 52
Daniel, Jr., 71
David, 90, 137, 285, 288, 476, 486
Elizabeth, 89, 438
Ezekiel, 90
Gennot, 232
George, 421
Hannah, 89
Helen, 90
Henry, 301
Isaac, 90, 426
James, 89, 137, 160, 218, 426, 484, 486

INDEX OF NAMES OF PERSONS

John, 89, 265, 285
Joseph, 89, 90, 326
Lydia, 90
Marmaduke, 89, 90
Mary, 251
Moses, 86
Nathan, Jr., 379
Philip, 89, 294
Robert, 148, 234
Samuel, 90
Thomas, 170, 347, 392, 393
William, 89, 90, 104, 136, 332
Copland, Cowperthwaite, 27, 173, 384
Coppothite, Hannah, 21
John, 21
Corbet, Joseph, 119
Corbines, Francis, 296
Corcelius, Peter, 124, 158, 423, 433
Cordeary, Christian, 397
Deborah, 119, 397
Edmund, 214, 346, 349
Elizabeth, 224
Isaac, 224
Coriell, David, 247
Corlies, Abigail, 90
Benjamin, 90, 317
Britten, 90
Elizabeth, 90
George, 90, 488
Jacob, 90, 488
John, 50
Joseph, 90
Mary, 488
Sarah, 90
Timothy, 88
William, 488
Corne, Peter, 232
Cornell, Adrian, 90
Allebartus, 416
Cornelius, 90, 91, 326
Gerribragh, 90
Gertje, 91
Helena, 90
Jacobus, 90
Jannetje, 91
Johanna, 90
Joseph, 305, 416
Margaret, 91
Matje, 91
Peter, 90
Peterneletje, 91
Puness, 210
Roeloff, 90
Sarah, 91
William, 91, 154
Corshow, Jacob, 305
Mary, 305
(see Cashow)
Corson (Corssen), Abner, 91, 99, 127
Benjamin, 91
Darius, 91
David, 209
Elizabeth, 91
Florandor, 257
Hester, 93
Isaac, 91
Jacob, 91
James, 91
Jesse, 91
John, 91
Joseph, 91, 183, 493
Levy, 91

Peter, 91
Rachel, 91
Rem, 91
Richard, 91
Vantuyle, 91
William, 91
Cortrecht, Henry, 470
Henry W., 60
John, 60
Corwin (Corwine), Benjamin, 86
George, 6, 310, 345, 400
John, 391, 475
Samuel, 6, 210, 276, 345, 400
Cory, Abner, 92
Abraham, 86, 91
Daniel, 91, 92
David, 91, 92, 330
Ebenezer, 91, 92
Elnathan, 37, 92
Hannah, 92
Jacob, 92
James, 91, 92
Jeremish, 91, 92
Job, 92
John, 36, 92, 193, 263
Joseph, 91, 92, 164, 280, 281, 483
Martha, 92
Mary, 91, 92
Phebe, 92
Rachel, 92
Sarah, 91, 92
Thomas, 91, 92
Cosad, Jacob, 484
Cosart, Anthony, 88
Francis, 165, 453
Jacob, 88
Margaret, 453
Samuel, 352
Cosine, Cornelius, 453
Coss (see Gass)
Costigin, Francis, 208, 355
Cotheal, Alexander, 92
Charlotte, 92
Elizabeth, 92
Henry, 92, 284
Isaac, 92, 152
Rachel, 92, 284
Sarah, 92
William, 92, 100
Cottnam, Abraham, 120, 268, 394
George, 120
Wanell, 120
Coulter, Joseph, 336
Counce, Johannes, 352, 366
Counting, Ann S., 94
Courtlandt (see Van Courtlandt)
Courtney, Jane, 326
Couwenhoven (Covenhoven, Abraham, 99
Anna, 93
Catherine, 373
Cornelius, 93, 373
Cristian, 93
Daniel, 264, 372, 431
David, 93
Dominicus, 93, 167
Eleanor, 333
Elias, 373
Garret, 395
Gilbert, 93
Hermanus, 93
Jacoba, 93
James, 183
Jannetie, 93

John, 93, 356, 373, 481
Mary, 93, 373
Matthias, 93
Nellie, 373
Peter, 10, 25, 93, 154, 333, 422
Roelof, 372, 373
Sarah, 93, 183
William, 93, 133, 134, 135, 268, 359, 400
Williampe, 93
Couzens, Anne, 312
Frances, 312
John, 312, 313
Mary, 312
(see Cozens)
Coverley, Job, 299
Covert, Mary, 355, 369
Sarah, 93
Coving, Mary, 157
Cowan, Jane, 382
John, 14, 253, 280, 382
Coward, John, 188, 394
Cowell, Christian, 93, 195
David, 94
Ebenezer, 94
Joseph, 94
Samuel, 94
(see Cowl)
Cowens, Michael, 94
Cowgill, George, 94
Isaac, 94, 180
Isaac, Jr., 102
Jemima, 94
John, 94
Lydia, 94
Margaret, 66
Rachel, 94
Cowl, Conrad, 93
John, 93
Mortice, 93, 94
Sophia, 94
(see Cowell)
Cowman, John, 55
Cowperthwaite, Ann, 335
Hugh, 94
John, 94, 276, 335, 339
Mark, 94
Samuel, 94
Thomas, 94, 296, 396
William, 94
Cox (Coxe), Benjamin, 95
Catrine, 95
Charles, 155, 322
Daniel, 37, 370
Deborah, 95
Dorcas, 95
Elizabeth, 95
Esther, 441
Jacob, 95
John, 48, 51, 54, 77, 85, 93, 95, 160, 167, 169, 189, 197, 211, 212, 276, 286, 320, 337, 357, 441, 466
Joseph, 201, 263, 422
Marcy, 95, 254
Mary, 95, 390
Moses, 141
Peter, 484
Phebe, 95
Philip, 207, 484
Phinehas, 95
Rebecca, 84, 95, 381
Richard, 95, 229, 292, 369
Samuel, 95

Sarah, 95
Thomas, 19, 95, 422
William, 95
(see Cock; Koch)
Cozens, Benjamin, 95
Daniel, 96
Elijah, 95
Elizabeth, 95
Hannah, 96
Jacob, 95
Joshua, 95
Samuel, 95
(see Couzens)
Cozier, Sarah, 96
Craddock, John, 252
Sarah, 193
Craft, James, 369
Craig, Andrew, 79, 95, 97, 194, 211
Daniel, 96, 97
Elizabeth, 136
George, 413
Hannah, 96
James, 96, 97
John, 96, 124, 429, 436
John, Jr., 457
Joseph, 96
Lydia, 96
Margaret, 116
Mary, 96, 124
Moses, 208
Nancy, 96
Phebe, 96
Samuel, 62, 436
Sarah, 96
Susannah, 96, 97
Thomas, 96, 267
Timothy, 404
William, 96, 116, 295, 296, 346, 355
Cramer, Andrew, 226
Ann, 97
Caleb, 224
Hannah, 49
Levi, 226
Phebe, 97
Sarah, 97
Seymour, 97
Stephen, 405
Crandel, Levi, 162, 163, 262
Rebecca, 97, 98
Crandin, Philip, 340
Crane, Abigail, 97
Affia, 97
Amos, 434
Benjamin, 98, 264
Caleb, 76, 193
Christopher, 96
David, 97, 281
Elihu, 89
Elizabeth, 98
Esther, 98
Ezekiel, 97
Hannah, 98
Ichabod, 365
Isaac, 97, 226, 417
Israel, 98, 483
Jacob, 97
James, 97
John, 26, 91, 97, 98, 180, 193, 307, 377, 383
John, Jr., 96
Joseph, 97
Josiah, 64, 97, 98, 180, 311, 323
Martha, 97

INDEX OF NAMES OF PERSONS 521

Mary, 97, 98
Mary A., 209
Matthias, 365
Samuel, 98, 217, 226
Sarah, 98
Stephen, 66, 97, 98, 207, 281, 383, 433
Crater, Maurice, Jr., 379
Craven, Gershom, 270
John, 123
Thomas, 195, 461
Crawford, Andrew, 249
Ann, 98
Eleazer, 101
George, 98
Gideon, 451
Henry, 22
John, 370
Joshua, 98
Phebe, 98
Redford, 99
Richard, 56, 93, 98, 199, 313
Richard, Jr., 298, 479
Thomas, 446
William, 77, 98, 199, 296, 297, 298
William R., 99, 208, 355
Crawley, David, 190
Creger, Ann, 99
Christina, 99
Elizabeth, 99
Jacob, 99
John, 99
Peter, 99
William, 99
Creighton, Hugh, 61, 403
Cresse, Aaron, 143, 301
Amos, 99
Anthony, 99, 127
Christian, 444
Claes, 46
Daniel, 172, 236
David, 99
Elizabeth, 99, 262, 493
Ellit, 76, 80, 210
Esther, 99
Eunice, 301
Garret, 46
Hannah, 99, 163
Jacob, 370
James, 176, 366, 392
John, 99, 162, 191, 398
Jonathan, 99
Lewis, 99, 127, 147, 152, 163, 174, 175, 177, 190, 240, 278, 310, 399
Mary, 99
Nathan, 99
Philip, 99, 149, 392
Robert, 99
Cripps, Benjamin, 100
Grace, 100
Hannah, 100
Martha, 100
Mary, 100
Samuel, 99
Sarah, 474
Whitten, 228, 268, 471
William, 474
Crispin, Mary, 140
Rachel, 54
Sarah, 140
Crissy, William, 210
Crommey, James, 366

Crooke, William, 145, 270
Crooks, Richard, 253
Crosby, John, 100
Crosley, Henry, 86, 200
Crosman, Michael, 156
Cross, Mary, 63
William, 63, 441
Crow, Abraham, 100
David, 92, 100, 135, 283, 284, 365, 402
Elizabeth, 100
James, 100
John, 100
John Mac K., 428
Martha, 100
Samuel, 100
Sarah, 100
Thomas, 100
Crowell, Edward, 62, 378
Daniel, 14, 43, 175, 208, 356
David, 101
Hannah, 175
Jacob, 127
Joseph, 10, 100
John, 110, 111, 191
Josiah, 101
Lowes, 101
Matthew, 101
Phebe, 101
Rachel, 127
Ruth, 101
Seale, 101
Seth, Jr., 378
Thomas, 101, 256
Crower, Samuel, 126
Croxon, Catherine, 306
Crozier, Sarah, 101
Crummey, Elizabeth, 100
Crusen, Henry, 25, 305, 333, 449
Nicholas, 162
(see Kroesen)
Cruser, Hendrick, 292
Cryster, Leonard, 254
Cubberly, John, 101
Kezia, 317
Mary, 101
Thomas, 101
William, 101, 280, 317, 385
(see Coberly)
Cubert, Peter, 80
Cudlip, Mary, 45
Culin, Andrew, 187
Culley, Hannah, 101
Culling, Elizabeth, 465
Cullum, James, 369
Cumine (Cummin), James, 101, 119, 493
Jane, 101
Joseph, 101
Samuel, 101
William, 101
Cumming, Ann, 101
Catherine, 101
James, 65
John, 101
Lawrence, 101
Margaret, 101
Robert, 468
Thomas, 137, 465
Cummins, Christian, 482
Jacob, 383
Cundict, Daniel, 118
Eunice, 101, 102
Isaac, 102, 392, 473

Timothy, 102
(see Condict)
Curlis, John, 56
  Mary, 56
  William, 170
Curry, Samuel, 26
Cursan, Richard, 406
Curtis, Anne, 102, 158, 486
  Barnabus, 73
  Clem, 102
  David, 102
  David, Jr., 42
  Elizabeth, 102, 318
  Grace, 318
  John, 89, 102, 318, 360
  Jonathan, 102
  Joseph, 89, 94, 158, 173
  Marcy, 102, 360
  Mary, 102
  Meribah, 102
  Peter, 102
  Rachel, 102
  Rebecca, 102
  Robert, 102
  Sarah, 102
  Thomas, 102, 180, 318
Cushman, Thomas, 369
  Thomas, Jr., 442
Cutland, Zacharias, 267
Cutler, Eleanor, 102
  Agnes, 103
  Ann, 103
  Campion, 103
  Charity, 103
  Christian, 62
  Ebenezer, 60
  Ephraim, 103, 317, 433
  Esther, 62
  Eunice, 146
  Joanna, 103
  John, 103
  Joseph, 103
  Mary, 103
  Mercy, 103
  Richard, 103, 298
  Samuel, 103
  Susannah, 103
  Thomas, 102
  William, 103
Cuyler, Barend R., 103
  Henry, 103, 305
Cuyper, Aert, 495

D

Dains, Thomas, 179
Dair, Robert, Jr., 79
Dalbo, Alice, 104
  Andrew, 104
  Charles, 104, 195
  Eals, 104
  Gabriel, 104
  John, 332
  Jonas, 104
  Peter, 104
  Samuel, 104
  Susannah, 104
  William, 104, 206
Dalglish, Nathaniel, 98
Dalles, William, 161, 176, 206, 258, 474
  William, Jr., 206, 474
Daniel, Edmond, 104
  Henry, 417
  James, 104
  Joel, 104
  John, 104, 238
  Joseph, 104
  Rebecca, 104, 417
  Sarah, 104
  Thomas, 104
  William, 104, 417
Daniels, Benajah, 105, 104, 144
  Clement, 162
  Deborah, 162
  Ebenezer, 273
  Johanna, 104
  John, 150, 355
  Jonathan, 104
  Mary, 104
  Mercy, 156
  Thankful, 104
  Thomas, 257, 355
  Uriah, 478
  William, 104
Danielson, Ann, 287
  Gabriel, 87, 326
Dannally, Mary, 392
Darby, Ephraim, 16, 19, 21, 91, 123, 209, 358
  John, 50, 278, 279
  Rev. John, 209
  Letitia, 279
  Nisbett, 342
  William, 105, 279
Dare, Abiel, 105
  Benjamin, 105
  Benoni, 105
  Christiana, 406
  Clemens, 105
  Eleanor, 105
  Elizabeth, 105, 301
  Elkanah, 105
  James, 105
  John, 406, 474
  Rachel, 105
  Reuben, 23, 105
  William, 105
  (see Dair)
Darling, Edward, 390
  Elizabeth, 94, 135
  George, 152
Darnel, Edward, 52, 390
  Lewis, 97
Darompel, James, 221
Dates, Adam, 227
Davenport, Ann, 106
  Catherine, 106
  Cornelius, 106
  Elizabeth, 106
  Isaiah, 26, 106, 486, 487
  Jacob, 106
  Jacobus, 84
  John, 106
  Mary, 106
  Nathaniel, 106
  Peter, 106
David, Benjamin, 243
  Charles, 472
  Elijah, 289
  Elnathan, 108, 293
  Gabriel, 11
Davies, George, 290
  James, 109
Davis, Abigail, 106, 219
  Abraham, 108
  Amon, 106
  Ann, 108, 109, 390, 320

INDEX OF NAMES OF PERSONS 523

Arthur, 106
Benjamin, 263
Bradway, 106, 157
Charles, 23, 114, 473
David, 107, 197, 208, 461
Deborah, 106
Dorcas, 100
Dorothy, 197
Edith, 107
Elijah, 97, 427
Elisha, 33
Elizabeth, 33, 107, 109
Ellen, 106
Elnathan, 22, 107
Esther, 107
Gabriel, 109, 192, 473
George, 94
Hannah, 106
Henry, 107, 219, 270, 341, 433, 483
Howell, 108, 109
Hugh, 131
Isaac, 33
Jacob, 33, 107, 116, 123, 367
James, 38, 57, 148, 371
James, Jr., 178
Jarman, 107
Johanna, 371
John, 33, 107, 108, 162, 193, 218
Jonathan, 22, 47, 307
Joseph, 106, 108, 121, 123, 365
Josiah, 418
Keziah, 107
Malachi, 9
Mary, 106
Moses, 133, 134
Naomi, 107
Owen, 108, 125
Patience, 427
Rachel, 106, 178
Samuel, 67, 107, 216, 222, 307
Rev. Samuel, 108
Sarah, 106, 108, 289
Susannah, 107
Thomas, 33, 42, 216, 295, 333
Uriah, 106
William, 108, 109, 320
Zachariah, 107
Davison, Amasiah, 201
  Andrew, 418
  Anne, 109
  Catherine, 109
  George, 109
  James, 109
  Jemima, 109
  John, 109, 129, 201, 466
  Margaret, 109
  Mary, 109
  Peter, 109
  Providence, 109
  Rozanah, 109
  Sarah, 109
  Susannah, 109
  William, 109, 122, 201
Dawson, Lydia, 195
Day, Abraham, 109
  Amos, 49, 315, 323, 425, 459
  Charles, 22, 265, 364
  David, 109
  Elizabeth, 427
  Ezekiel, 109
  Jared, 109
  Jeduthun, 109
  Jehiel, 109
  Jemima, 164
  John, 78
  Jonathan, 360
  Joseph, 58
  Leticia, 109
  Paul, 251, 427
  Phebe, 109
  Robert, 109
  Samuel, 36, 109, 426, 483, 485
  Timothy, 341
Dayton (Daton), Anne, 105, 106
  Daniel, 311
  David, 106, 416
  Eli, 105
  Capt. Elias, 288
  Ephraim, 106, 142
  Hannah, 106
  Henry, 105
  John, 297
  Jonah, 105, 221
  Jonathan J., 27, 321
  Joseph, 32, 53, 105, 106, 179, 243, 260, 263, 309, 311, 416
  Joseph, Jr., 106
  Leonard, 105
  Mary, 105
  Phebe, 105
  Prudence, 105
  Ruth, 106
  Samuel, 291
  William, 7
  Zerviah, 105
Deacon, Ann, 68
  George, 68, 322
  Hannah, 130
  John, Jr., 131
Dean, Ichabod, 353
  Jacob, 110
  James, 110
  Jedediah, 456
  John, 110, 352
  Keziah, 37
  Stephen, 110
  Thomas, 335
Deare, Jonathan, 162, 258, 388, 466
Dearwin, Jehiel, 279
Deats, John, 88
  William, 236
Debo (Deboogh), Deborah, 110
  Garret, 445
  James, 110, 292
  John, 110, 445
  Mary, 110, 292
  Marytje, 445
  Robert, 263
  William, 110
Debois, Jacob, 100
  Margaret, 100
  (see Dubois)
Debourepose, John, 377
DeCamp, Aaron, 418
  John, 110
  John T., 362
  Joseph, 5, 60, 194, 362, 363, 405
  Lambert, 377
  Lawrence, 110, 280
  Susannah, 110
  (see Camp)
Decker, Andreas, 110
  Casparus F., 110
  Christopher, 110
  Dievertie, 110
  Elinor, 111
  Elizabeth, 110

524 NEW JERSEY COLONIAL DOCUMENTS

Esther, 75
Gretie, 110
Hannah, 110
Jacob, 110
Johannis, 110
Lydia, 110
Peter, 110, 111
Phillipus, 110
Sarah, 110
DeCou (DeCow), Anne, 268, 342
Eber, 111
Hannah, 18, 111, 158
Isaac, 65, 111, 158, 168, 327, 360
John, 111
Joseph, 131, 327, 468, 493
Dedricks, Christian, 457
Jannitie, 456
Deeds, Adam, 236
Degarmo, Matthias, 244
Peter, 156, 328, 454
Degrave, Leonard, 282
Sarah, 282
De Groot, Elizabeth, 314
John, 314
Sophia, 314
William, 314
DeHart, Abigail A. C., 111
Balthas, 111
Catharine, 111
Cornelius, 169, 481
Cyrus, 111, 353
Geesje, 373
Jacob, 98, 111
Johanna M., 111
John, 98, 111
Dr. Matthias, 111, 398
Maurice, 50, 111, 320
Samuel, 111
Simon, 373
William, 111
Dekay, Hillah, 20
Jane, 19
Delamater, Abraham, 167, 272
Isaac, 249
Sarah, 272
Delany, Martin, 141
Delap, Dorothy, 341
Francis, 341, 342
Delatush, Eleanor, 111
Elizabeth, 111, 157, 158
Hannah, 111
Henry, 111, 230, 318, 491
Henry, Jr., 111
John, 111, 157
Rebecca, 111
Dell, Framton, 155
Richard, 258
Demarest, Annatie, 112
Catalyntje, 113
Catrina, 112
Christian, 112
Cornelius, 112, 113
David, 78, 112, 113, 261, 445, 453
David J., 78
David S., 112
Daniel, 112, 113
Elizabeth, 112
Gerret, 112
Gertrude, 112
Guilliam, 112
Jacob, 112, 113
Jacobus, 78, 112
Johannis, 46, 112, 113, 257, 445, 495

Joost, 112
Leah, 112
Lydia, 112
Maatie, 112
Madalena, 112
Maria, 112, 113
Nicholas, 112
Peter, 112, 113
Rachel, 112
Rebecca, 112
Samuel, 112, 113, 453
Sarah, 112
Simon, 112
Tryntje, 112
Vroutie, 113
Demond, Adam, 288
Edward, 490
(see Dumont)
DeMoney, Henry, 372
Demott, Isaac, 104, 114
Jacob, 306, 453
Matthias M., 330
Dempsey, Mark, 233
Denman, John, 98, 315
Philip, 419
Denn, Elizabeth, 74, 83
Dennelsbeck, Frederick, 113
John, 113
Dennis, Anthony, 89, 113, 150, 214, 298, 320
Benjamin, 89, 150, 174, 464
Charles, 391
Dorothy, 229
Elizabeth, 114, 115
Gideon, 120
Jacob, 12, 173, 446, 464
Jacob, Jr., 214, 464
John, 113, 155, 270, 352, 366, 390, 469
Jonathan, 113
Joseph, 113
Lucy, 113
Matthew, 401
Nathaniel, 113
Philip, 28, 114, 425
Prudence, 23, 113
Rachel, 113
Robert, 88, 160
Samuel, 199
Sarah, 23, 113
Zilpha, 113
Dennison, Arthur, 114
Jane, 114
Mary, 114
William, 320
Denny, John, 114, 134, 187
Miles, 114
Priscilla, 114
Sarah, 114
Thomas, 77, 114, 120, 134, 178, 195, 207, 227, 254, 302, 435, 441, 450, 495
De Normandie, John, 30
Denton, Anthony, 114
John, 114
Margaret, 160
Sarah, 114
William, 114
De Peyster, Cornelia, 375
Depue, Benjamin, 399, 444
Catherine, 444
Daniel, 444
John, 114, 374, 444
Maria, 444

INDEX OF NAMES OF PERSONS 525

Moses, 444
Rachel, 114
Derburger, Stuffey, 439
Derby, William, 105
Derickson, John, 114
Derick, 490
De Riemer, Abraham, 221
Jacob, 146
Dermott (see De Mott)
Derry, John, 64
De Sha, Morgan, 444
Dest, Jacob, 329
Deulea, William, 458
Devoe, David, 91
Devooer, Anne, 114
Catherine, 114
Daniel, 114
Elizabeth, 114
Henry, 114
James, 114
John, 114
Leah, 114
Margaret, 114
Rachel, 114
Sarah, 114
Dewees, Cornelius, 198
DeWitt, John, 369
Luke, 114
Dey, Ann, 115
James, 278, 300, 367
Jane, 115
Mary, 115
Thomas, 404
Tunis, 115, 450
Diament, Dorcas, 115
Elizabeth, 115
Hedges, 115
James, 115, 336
Jonathan, 115
Lois, 115
Nathaniel, 115
Rhoda, 115
Diatz, William, 236
Dibble (see Teeple)
Dick, Samuel, 287
Dickeson (Dickason), Abigail, 116
Ann, 116
James, 116
John, 115, 116, 335, 336, 397, 441, 460
Judith, 116
Margaret, 116
Mark, 115
Mary, 116
Susannah, 335
William, 115, 116
Dickerson, Joshua, 228
Peter, 82
Dickie, John, 417
Dickinson, George, 116, 313, 331
Hannah, 67
Jacob, 116
Jane, 116
John, 9, 67, 279
Joseph, 116
Mark, 116, 296
Sarah, 116
Dickson, Thomas, 441
(see Dixon)
Dikers, Esther, 76
Dildine, Ann, 117
Catherine, 117
Daniel, 116, 117
Elizabeth, 117

Eve, 117
Henry, 116, 117
Herman, 117
Rachel, 117
Samson, 91, 117, 406
Sarah, 117
Uriah, 117
Yanakico, 117
Dilkes, Aaron, 269
John, 269
Dill, Caleb, 377
Henry, 325
Dilshaver, John, 117, 178
(see Tilsilver)
Dilts, Christian, 195
Harman, 117
Henry, 117
John, 117, 433
Mary, 117, 195
Peter, 117, 195, 433
Peter, Jr., 117
Philip, 195, 203
Dingman, Adam, 117
Andries, 117
Eve, 117
Jacob, 117
Jacobus, 117
Mary, 117
Marytie, 117
Peter, 117
Samuel, 117
Dingwell, Rebecca, 290
Dirjie, John, 494
Dirkinderin, Jane, 35
Diron, William, 438
Disborough, Charity, 69
Mercy, 69
Rachel, 69
Disbrow, John, 304
Disorency, Samuel, 349
Disosway, Cornelius, 118
Ditchfield, John, 129
Divin, John, 361
Dixon, Daniel, 391, 481
Jane, 481
John, 330, 481
Martha, 421
Mary, 481
Sarah, 481
William, 97, 421
Dobbin, James, 13, 59, 191, 310, 383, 489
Dodd (Dod), Aaron, 391
Abel, 118
Adonijah, 118
Amos, 118
Caleb, 118
Daniel, 118
Elizabeth, 118
Isaac, 118
James, 118
Jemima, 118
John, 102
John, Jr., 118, 403, 473, 480
Joseph, 118
Mary, 180
Matthew, 118
Nekoda, 118
Robert, 120
Sarah, 118
Thaddeus, 87
Thomas, 118
Doig, James, 342
Dole, Richard, 401

Dolhagen, Frederick, 447
Dollas, William, 258, 474
  (see Dalles)
Dollisen, Magdalen, 308
Donaldson, Elizabeth, 227
Donham, Amos, 237
  David, 152
  Catharine, 71
  Ephraim, 156
  Mary, 152, 153
  (see Dunham)
Donnington, John, 76
Doobs, John, 82, 96, 479
Doremus, Cornelius, 404
  George, 431
  Margaret, 431
Dorland, Altie, 201
  Ladey, 393
  William, 393
Dorsett, Andrew, 118
  Ann, 118
  Catherine, 118
  Elizabeth, 118
  James, 118
  John, 126
  Joseph, 24, 118, 126, 357
  Mary, 118
  Samuel, 118
Dorsheimer, Martin, 332
Doty, Anthony, 118
  Elizabeth, 118, 262
  George, 118
  Isaac, 207
  Jacob, 118
  John, 118, 119
  Margaret, 489
  Mary, 424
  Nathaniel, Jr., 118
  Peter, 446
  Sarah, 118, 119
  William, 249
  (see Doughty)
Doud, Aaron, 119, 149
Dougherty, Catherine, 119
  Edward, 303
  Elizabeth, 119
  James, 119, 481
  Rebecca, 119
Doughty, Abner, 119
  Christopher, 172, 411
  Edward, 119, 346, 349, 407
  Edward, Jr., 119, 238, 349
  George, 262
  John, 86, 119
  Jonathan, 119
  Margaret, 119
  Mary, 377
  Millicent, 349, 402
  Robert, 119
  Thomas, 119
  (see Doty)
Douglas, Elisabeth, 119
  George, 275
  Samuel, 98
  Thomas, 119, 488
  William, 154, 166, 443
Dove, John, 92
  Mr., 298
Dow, Adrian, 235
  William, 83, 226, 235, 454, 456
Dowd, Ann, 120
  Cornelius, 119, 120
  Hannah, 119

Down, John, 392
  Robert, 216
  William, 487
Downs, Sarah, 299
Downy, Ann, 120
  Elizabeth, 120
  John, 120
Dragstrum, Elizabeth, 120
Drake, Abraham, 120
  Catherine, 121
  Daniel, 15, 17, 33, 121, 138, 247, 428
  Edward, 107, 120
  Elisha, 120
  Elizabeth, 121
  Embly, 121
  Ephraim, 95, 121
  Fitz Randolph, 390
  Francis, 121
  Hannah, 120
  Henry, 121
  Jacob, 120, 419
  James, 121, 365
  Jeremiah, 123
  John, 120, 121, 364
  Joseph, 121
  Nathan, 121
  Nathaniel, 120
  Nathaniel, Jr., 121
  Nicholas, 121, 409
  Patience, 121
  Philip, 300
  Randolph, 18, 48
  Rebecca, 120
  Reuben, 121
  Samuel, 121, 247, 447
  Sarah, 291
  Thomas, 121
  William, 120
  Zachariah, 120
Draper, Edward, 107, 123
Drems, Geesje, 455
Driller, Mary, 121
Driver, John, 58
Droman, Catherine, 494
Drum, John, 15
Drummond, Abigail, 236
  Gawen, 236
  John, 473
  Robert, Jr., 33
Drvedt, Lucas, 31
Du Bois, Abraham, 182, 201, 446
  Benjamin, 122, 387
  Cornelius, 122
  David, 122, 123
  Jacob, 122, 182, 308
  Capt. Jacob, 436
  John, 122
  Josiah, 122
  Lurany, 122
  Mary, 122
  Peter, 122
  Solomon, 122
  (see Debois)
Duckworth, John, 117
Dudley, Francis, 28, 276
  Susannah, 168
Duell, John, 295
Duemineer, Samuel, 57
Duffield, Peter, 288
Duffle, Elizabeth, 46
Dukemaneer, Susannah, 430
Dumont, Abraham, 451
  Hannah, 122

INDEX OF NAMES OF PERSONS 527

Isaac, 40
John B., 38, 419
Mary, 38
Peter, 48, 240, 334, 340, 423, 443, 451, 459
(see Demond)
Dunbar, Lott, 493
Duncan, Thomas, 19
Dunham, Azariah, 49, 208, 263, 274, 305, 390, 428
Daniel, 71, 76, 123, 274
Elijah, 118, 475
Francis, 16, 75, 76
Hezekiah, 121
Jonathan, 123, 194, 274, 398
Mary, 152, 398
Nehemiah, 123, 340, 382
Samuel, 274, 275
(see Donham)
Dunigan, Mary, 306
Dunlap, Aaron, 345
Allen, 308
Edward, 295
James, 123, 429
Jane, 123
John, 163, 345
Dunn, Abigail, 72
Alexander, 428
Ann, 80
Benjamin, 72, 107, 123, 341, 428
Catherine, 123
Deborah, 417
Edith, 107
Elizabeth, 123, 473
Experience, 428
Francis, 433
Hezekiah, 19, 22, 72, 107, 123, 332, 416, 448
Jephtha, 123
Jeremiah, 49, 72, 123, 275
John, 57, 300
Jonathan, 433
Margaret, 72, 275
Micajah, 72, 300, 275
Phinehas, 121
Rachel, 123, 428
Reuben, 123
Samuel, 433
Sarah, 72, 123, 207, 274
William, 209
Dunnan, John, 338
Dunscomb, Daniel, 363
Dunterfield, William, 31
Durand, Samuel, 27
Durham, John, 154
Durie, Annatje, 263
Cornelius, 263
Durney, John, 144
Duryee, Abraham, 363
Dusenbury, Catherine, 124
George, 423
John, 124
Dusosways, Israel, 18
Duyckinck, Evert, 239, 260
Dyckman, Jacob, Jr., 420
Dye, Andrew, 124
Anne, 124
Benjamin, 124
David, 124
Hester, 375
James, 124
John, 124
Mercy, 124
Rachel, 124

Sarah, 124
Vinson, 124
Dyer, Joseph, 422
Josiah, 374
Josiah, Jr., 374

E

Eacritt, Isaac, 124
James, 124
John, 124
Joseph, 124
Mary, 124
(see Acritt)
Eagles, Alexander, 124
Margaret, 124
Mary, 124
Thomas, 124, 483
William, 124
Earle (Earl), Anttebee, 126
Eliakim, 107
Elizabeth, 126
Esther, 171
Gertrude, 445
Henry, 316
Henry, Jr., 147
John, 7, 181
Morris, 7, 8
Silvester, 261
William, 445
Eastlack (Eastlake), Ann, 124
Francis, 60
Hannah, 124, 231
John, 173, 345
Reuben, 11
Eastwood, Abraham, 491
John, 243
Eaton, Abigail, 230
Isaac, 120, 208, 414
Rev. Isaac, 194
Jabesh, 230
Joanna, 125
John, 125
Joseph, 270
Lucy, 125
Sarah, 125
Thomas, 125
Eayre, Asa, 125
Catherine, 361
Elizabeth, 361
Grace, 125
Habakkuk, 125, 126
Hannah, 125, 126
Hosea, 126
John, 125, 126, 197, 361
Joseph, 125, 411
Katura, 126
Levi, 126
Mary, 125, 126
Rebecca, 126, 361
Richard, 125, 126
Sarah, 125, 126
Thomas, 125, 126
Thomas, Jr., 126
Eckeson, Jan, 112
Mary, 112
Thomas, 112
Eddy, Gawen, 92, 284
James, 155
Sarah, 92
William, 284
Edgar, Alexander, 146
David, 50, 62, 126, 376, 377
James, 126

Jannet, 126
Mary, 126, 429
Sarah, 126
Thomas, 126
William, 82, 126, 245
Edgerton, Thomas, 136
Edgman, Elizabeth, 229
William, 229
Edgment, Thomas, 167
Edmiston, David, 161
Edmon, Thomas, 59
Edmonds (Edmunds), Arthur, 70
Downes, 145, 176, 220
Experience, 176
John, 137
Mary, 177
Edsall, Anne, 126
Catharine, 126
Hannah, 126
John, 126
Richard, 444
Samuel, 126
Edwards, Brandriff, 127
Daniel, 127
Elizabeth, 127
Ephraim, 244, 278
Esther, 278
James, 244, 278
Jane, 278
John, 127
Joseph, 127
Lemuel, 426
Margaret, 469
Mary, 127, 473
Philip, 469
Stephen, 393
Thomas, 468
Timothy, 224, 313, 487
Webley, 113, 393, 464, 480
Egberts (Egbert), Barbara, 127
Catharine, 127
Femmetje, 127
Francyntje, 127
Jacobus, 127
Maria, 127
Nicholas, 84, 187
Susanna, 127
Thomas, 127
Egborson, Christian, 127
Lawrence, 127
Ege, Adam, 194
Elizabeth, 194
Eggman, Bartholomew, 477
Deborah, 127
Egiton, Thomas, 408
Eglington, John, 128
Egmond, Bartholomew, 249
Christopher, 249
Eick, Philip, 12
Elbertson, Isaac, 263
Eldredge (Eldridge), Aaron, 29, 149, 175, 365, 410
Abigail, 21, 128
Aner, 219
Daniel, 128
David, 128, 432
Eli, 28, 128, 175, 219
Elihu, 128
Elisha, 101
Esther, 128
Ezekiel, 101, 128, 271, 473
Glory, 128
Hannah, 156, 252, 473
Jabez, 128, 225, 265

Jacob, 365
James, 149
Jeremiah, 365
Job, 128
John, 29, 101, 127, 128, 145, 149, 175, 176, 209, 242, 243, 264, 278, 301, 365, 404, 473, 489
John, Jr., 101
Levi, 66, 174
Mary, 101, 128
Noah, 128
Obadiah, 128, 486
Reuben, 128
Samuel, 145, 272
Sarah, 128
Solomon, 192
Elkinton, George, 192, 348
Ellett, Charles, 128, 240, 268, 471
Elliot, Andrew, 370
Elizabeth, 357, 370
Sarah, 417, 471
Ellis, Aaron, 129
Barzillai, 129
Daniel, 21, 28, 30, 43, 68, 71, 84, 141, 185, 200, 212, 225, 303, 318, 322, 336, 380, 388, 435, 218
Elizabeth, 129
Job, 129, 191
John, 129
Jonathan, 129
Joseph, 48, 70, 77, 181, 193
Josiah, 15, 25, 27, 68, 197, 409, 488
Kezia, 70
Leah, 129, 63, 65, 440
Mark, 358
Martha, 25
Peter, 65, 129, 158
Sarah, 129
Simeon, 181
Simon, Jr., 68
Thomas, 181
Ellison, Amos, 130
Ann, 134
Elizabeth, 130
Hannah, 130
James, 129, 134
Jane, 129
John, 129
Joseph, 129
Lewis, 130
Margaret, 129, 130
Martha, 129
Mary, 129, 130
Rebekah, 130
Samuel, 129
Sarah, 129
Seth, 129
Seth, Jr., 129
Thomas, 47, 129, 130, 214, 226
Thomas, Jr., 135
Elmer, Abigail, 130
Daniel, 130, 341
Deborah, 130
Ebenezer, 130
Jonathan, 37, 92, 130, 224, 262, 312, 321, 339, 362, 436
Theodorus, 52, 312
Theophilus, 52, 105, 106, 115, 224, 260, 311, 313, 461
Timothy, 130
Victorina, 130
Violetta, 130
Elsellow, Christian, 59

INDEX OF NAMES OF PERSONS 529

Elston, John, 130, 173
  Samuel, Jr., 173
  Spencer, 130
Elton, Ann, 131
  Elizabeth, 66, 131
  Hannah, 51, 131
  Revell, 100, 131, 411
  Robert, 131
  Thomas, 131
  William, 310
Elwell, Ananias, 272
  David, 106
  Isaac, 157, 177, 218
  Jacob, 106, 107, 122, 123, 182, 308, 436
  Joel, 106
  John, 218, 305
  Mary, 218
  Samuel, 122, 161
Ely, Elizabeth, 131
  Frances, 131
  George, 131
  Isaac, 131
  Jemima, 131
  John, 131, 200, 302, 376, 386
  Mary, 131
  Rebecca, 131
  Sarah, 131, 386
  Stephen, 131
  Thomas, 131
  William, 248
Embley, John, 239
  Robert, 15
Emerson, John, 67
Emley, Ann, 132, 292
  John, 132, 168, 204, 226, 241, 358
  Mary, 132, 242, 292
  Peter, 134
  Rebecca, 132, 292
  Robert, 132, 233, 242, 292
  Samuel, 204, 251, 306
  Sarah, 132, 491
  Thomas, 88
  William, 132
Emmons (Emans), Abraham, 480
  Henry, 132
  Isaac, 132
  Jacob, 480
  John, 114, 230, 447
  Margaret, 294
  Nicholas, 117, 187
  Rebecca, 132
  Tuentje, 447
Emott, George, 111, 353
  James, 19
  John, 353
Enax, John G., 327
End, Valentine, 413
Endicott, Abraham, 133, 134
  Abraham, 133, 134
  Anne, 133
  Catherine, 133
  David, 116, 134, 267, 352
  Elizabeth, 116, 129, 133, 351
  Esther, 64
  Jacob, 133
  James, 116, 133, 134, 135, 267, 268, 351, 352
  James, Jr., 352
  Jane, 133, 134, 292
  John, 116, 133, 212, 289
  Jonathan, 116, 133, 267, 268
  Joseph, 102, 112, 129, 133, 146, 158, 422
  Margaret, 64, 116, 133
  Mary, 133, 134
  Moses, 134
  Robert, 133, 134, 135, 292, 352
  Ruth, 132
  Samuel, 134
  Sarah, 133
  Thomas, 133, 134
  William, 133, 134
Enliston, Ann, 182
  Theodore, 182
Ennis, Francis, 182
  Richard, 460
  William, 60, 84, 110, 442, 460, 471
Enoch, Mary, 85
  Thomas, 400
Ent, Susannah, 134
Enyard, Alche, 135
  Benjamin, 135
  David, 135
  Elsie, 135
  John, 135
  Mary, 135
  Silas, 135
Erick, Casper, 237
Erickson, John, 135
  Martha, 135
  Susannah, 135
Ernest (Earnest), Anna M., 135
  Anthony, 135
  Daniel, 21, 22
  John, 135
  Matthew, 135
  Sarah, 135
Erwin (Ervin), John, 65, 425
  Martha, 14
  Sarah, 47
Eseld, Christian, 59
Eselick, Diana, 385
Eskill, Davis, 135
  Elizabeth, 135
  Hannah, 135
  John, 135
  Mary, 135
  Noah, 135
Estaugh, David, 136, 228
  Elizabeth, 202, 203
  Grace, 136, 227
  Hannah, 136
  James, 136
  John, 136
  Joseph, 136
Estill, David, 135, 312
  John, 184
  William, 135
Evans (Evens), Aaron, 137
  Abigail, 211
  Bathsheba, 339
  Caleb, 279
  David, 103, 146, 152, 184, 230, 236, 283, 426
  Deborah, 137
  Elizabeth, 137
  Enoch, 137
  Esther, 137
  Grace, 70
  Hannah, 137
  Isaac, 21, 28, 52, 137, 169, 170, 238, 294, 339, 438, 460
  Jacob, 137, 211, 362, 438
  James, 464
  Joseph, 137
  Joshua, 35, 227

34

Lewis, 230
Margaret, 206
Mary, 137
Nathan, 137
Priscilla, 85
Rachel, 138
Rebecca, 137
Reuben, 72, 152
Samuel, 170
Sarah, 137, 279
Susannah, 137
Syllania, 137
William, 70, 137, 170, 238
Eveland, Catherine, 137
Frederick, 137, 482
Frederick, Jr., 137
John, 137
Magdelane, 137
Margreta, 137
Mary, 137
Peter, 137
Everingham, John, 159, 306
Mary, 138
Everitt, Abel, 138
Benjamin, 138
Elizabeth, 138
Francis, 275, 284
Hannah, 138
John, 138, 248
Joseph, 138
Mary, 138
Moses, 138
Phebe, 138
Samuel, 96, 194, 341, 350, 469
Sarah, 138
Everson, Nicholas, 6, 214, 258, 282
Ewan, Absalom, 138, 336
David, 138, 158, 336
Levi, 138
Rachel, 138
Thamer, 158
Ewing, Abigail, 22, 34, 143, 145, 150
James, 143, 179, 195, 249, 406
John, 23
Joshua, 179
Mary, 145
Maskell, 23, 32, 50, 57, 85, 117, 143, 179, 290, 326, 406, 416
Phebe, 23, 32, 34, 348
Remington, 350
Robert, 403
Samuel, 465
Sarah, 365, 403
Thomas, 50, 57, 163, 290, 319, 324, 406, 407, 461, 465, 473
Thomas, Jr., 143, 179
Walter, 472
William, 350
Exeene, Daniel, 270
Eyre, Ann, 139
Benjamin G., 139
Emanuel, 139
George, 139
Jehu, 139
John, 139
Martha, 139
Mary, 139
Samuel, 139
Sarah, 139
(see Eayre)

F

Faber, Hendrick, 250
Fagan, Ann, 139
Fairchild, Jesse, 171
Matthew, 153
Zechariah, 221
Fairman, Mary, 306
Faitout, Aaron, 427
Falconbury, Margaret, 139
Falconer, William, 424
Falkenberger, Christopher, 282
Fallon, Laughlen, 18
Fancher, Amy, 140
Benjamin, 139
David, 139
Martha, 140
Richard, 139
William, 139
Farley, Caleb, 197, 221, 239
Gertrude, 221
Thomas, 45
Farmer, Jasper, 155
Samuel, 363
Farnsworth, Amariah, 140
Catherine, 292
Daniel, 209
Nathaniel, 140
Samuel, 28, 102, 140, 167, 281, 318, 486
Farquhar, John, 269
Farr, Thomas, 422, 457, 487
Farrand, Margaret, 140
Nathaniel, 28, 180, 417
Farrill, Mary, 140
Farrington, Joseph, 61, 301
Mary, 247
Samuel, 61
Faurot, Catherine, 402
David, 237
James, 402
Henry, 237
Fawcet, John, 140
Lydia, 140
Nathan, 140
Walter, 140
Feagins, Alice, 180
Fearclo, Thomas, 438
Feavel, John, 166, 421
Fenell, Sebina, 141
Fenimore, Ann, 216
John, 21, 61, 129, 169, 232, 349, 364, 383, 435, 477
John, Jr., 129
Joseph, 303
Martha, 299
Peter, 39
Priscilla, 232
Rebecca, 322
Richard, 198, 325
Thomas, 21, 57
Sarah, 232
William, 60
Fenton, Elizabeth, 21, 141
Enoch, 477
Martha, 141, 201
Mary, 141
Robert, 229, 245
Samuel, 141
Sarah, 141
Stacy, 41, 141, 429
Thomas, 141, 438
William, 141

Ferebe, George, 106
Ferguson (Forgeson), Alexander, 403
  Alexander, 403
  Dinah, 121
  Jacomiah, 65
  Jeremiah, 65
  John, 156, 225
  Joseph, Jr., 392
  Martha, 141
  Susannah, 147
Ferrell, William, 348
Ferrit, Isaac, 275, 418
Fetters, Erasmus, 475
Feurt, Bartholomew, 132
  Francis, 166
  Thomas, 229
Few, Francis, 378
Fiddis, John, 69
Fidler, John, 239, 364, 409
  Timothy, 364
Field, Benjamin, 141, 422, 490
  Elijah, 111
  Jeremiah, 299, 314, 453, 468
  John, 453
  Michael, 16, 46, 314, 490
  Nathaniel, 185
  Seth, 310
Filer, Hannah, 32
Finlaw, John, 466
  William, 322
Finley, Ann, 141
  Ebenezer, 141
  Edward, 141
  James, 75
  John, 141
  Joseph, 141
  Rebecca, 406
  Samuel, 20, 101, 141
  Rev. Samuel, 424
  Susannah, 141
  William, 322
Finn, Elizabeth, 141
Firsbough, Carricat, 433
Firth, Henry, 417
  John, 255, 387, 417, 475
Fish, Deborah, 484
  Casper, 141
  Isaac, 249, 478
  John, 141, 142
Fisher, Abigail, 136, 137
  Ann, 94, 142
  Avis, 252
  Charles, 73
  Conrad, 142
  David, 158
  Elizabeth, 142, 393, 395
  George, 453
  Hannah, 150
  Henry, 39, 201, 259, 337
  Hendrick, Jr., 16
  Isaac, 142
  Jacob, 142
  John, 73, 126, 142
  Leah, 142
  Margaret, 94, 142
  Mary, 142
  Michael, 10, 73, 274
  Peter, 142, 360
  Philip, 142
  Richard, 94
Fislar, Jacob, 106
Fitch, Anna, 142
  Charity, 142
  James, 142
  Rachel, 142
  William, 142
Fithian, Aaron, 143
  Ann, 143
  Candace, 309
  David, 142
  Deborah, 130
  Ephraim, 105, 143
  Humphrey, 85
  Isaac, 473
  Jonathan, 142, 143, 488
  Jonathan, Jr., 488
  Joseph, 309
  Josiah, 143, 324
  Judith, 143
  Lot, 130, 142, 143
  Phebe, 85
  Samuel, 61, 64, 143, 159, 348, 473
  Temperance, 143
  William, 69, 143, 309, 465
Fitzpatrick, Grace, 143
  Lydia, 143
  Mary, 143
  Samuel, 143, 380
  Sarah, 143
Fitz Randolph, Benjamin, 185
  Catherine, 27, 144
  David, 291
  Edward, 27
  Elizabeth, 27, 144, 185
  Hartshorne, 215, 431
  Eseck, 27
  George, 17
  Grace, 144
  Hannah, 390
  Jacob, 82, 144, 390, 398, 426
  James, 376
  Joseph, 185, 274, 291, 300, 428
  Malachi, 49
  Margaret, 27
  Mary, 185
  Moses, 418
  Nathaniel, 19, 27, 103, 118, 146, 185, 230
  Reuben, 185, 291
  Robert, 27, 320
  Sarah, 49
  Thomas, 27
  Zedekiah, 49
  (see Randolph)
Fix, Adam, 403
Flanavan, Roger, 154
Flanagan (Flaningam, etc.),
  George, 34, 57, 72, 73, 189, 274
  Isaac, 189
  Samuel, 34
Flemen, Andrew, 41, 42
  Mary, 41
  Tely, 41
  Thomas, 41, 382
  William, 41
Fleming, Alexander, 324
  Ham, 189
  Josas, 189
  Peter, 92, 436
  Samuel, 362
  Thomas, 253
Fletcher, James, 400
  Lydia, 400
  Sarah, 400
  William, 144, 400
Flin, David, 412

Flomerfelt, Cornelius, 142
  Mary, 144
Flower (Flowers), Christopher, 419
  Judith, 145
  Mary, 145
  Silvitha, 145
  William, 145, 473
Fogg, Charles, 6, 75, 76, 145, 296
  Joseph, 232, 296
  Mary, 145
  Samuel, 145, 296, 324
Folke, Thomas, 111
Folkenberg, Christopher, 131
Folkersen (Fulkerse), Anne, 154
  Dirck, 48, 145, 154
  Elizabeth, 145
  Folkert, 145
  James, 337
  Joseph, 145
  Kezia, 154
  Mary, 154
  Philip, 145, 154
Folwell, Elizabeth, 146
  George, 129, 134, 158, 319
  Hope, 146
  John, 146, 173, 335, 360
  Joseph, 63, 146
  Lydia, 215
  Nathan, 18
  William, 65, 129
Fontine, Agnes, 146
  Charles, 146, 453
  Elizabeth, 146, 455
  Jacob, 146, 355, 369
  Lena, 146
  Lydia, 48
  Renyer, 146
  Sarah, 146
  (see Fountain)
Force, Charity, 152
  Isaac, 147
  Mary, 152
  Phebe, 283
  Rachael, 147, 152, 153
  Thomas P., 130
Ford (Foord), Anne, 146
  Chilion, 147
  David, 147
  Elizabeth, 146
  Eunice, 13
  Grace, 35
  Jacob, 147, 153, 383, 476
  Jacob, Jr., 13, 74, 147, 229, 476
  James, 146
  John, 146, 231
  Jonathan, 13
  Lydia, 146
  Mahlon, 147
  Margaret, 146, 432
  Mary, 146
  Nathan, 147
  Nathaniel, 280, 389
  Rebecka, 146
  Samuel, 97, 146, 183
  Sarah, 146
  William, 146
Fordtooff, Anna M., 344
  Anthony, 344
Foretice, Abigail, 419
Forman, Aaron, 148, 386
  Andrew, 148
  Ann, 468
  David, 148
  Elizabeth, 57
  Ezekiel, 148
  George, 148
  John, 147, 295
  Jonathan, 147
  Joseph, 148
  Lewis, 118, 147, 148, 242, 295, 449, 451
  Lydia, 148
  Margaret, 147
  Mary, 148
  Newel, 172
  Peter, 31, 147, 148
  Phebe, 148, 284
  Priscilla, 148
  Rebecca, 148
  Robert, 148
  Samuel, 53, 147, 148, 159, 424, 444
  Samuel, Jr., 167
  Thomas, 148
  (see Furman)
Forrester, John, 142, 324
Forster, Richard, 423
Fort, Edith, 148
  Joanna, 148
  John, 271, 348
  Marmaduke, 310, 359
  Rodger, 148
Foster, Amariah, 59
  Amy, 149
  Ann, 149
  Benjamin, 270
  Constantine, 177
  Christopher, 145, 166, 215, 307, 365, 386
  Ebenezer, 283
  Elizabeth, 149, 156, 215
  Ezekiel, 106, 216, 379
  Hannah, 149
  Jeremiah, 106, 427
  Johanna, 418, 472
  John, 339
  John A., 469
  Jonathan, 149
  Joseph, 35, 73, 94
  Lydia, 163
  Mathias, 163
  Mary, 149, 254, 431
  Nathaniel, 66, 101, 149, 362
  Priscilla, 418
  Rebecca, 149
  Robert, 39
  Salathiel, 149
  Samuel, 149, 244
  William, 52, 137, 149, 170
  (see Forster)
Foulk (Foulkes), Anna D., 146
  Barbary, 146
  Hannah, 326
  Hendrick, 146
  Judah, 218
  Mary, 318
  Philip, 146
  Thomas, 102, 112, 182, 318, 429, 432, 491
Fountain, Abram, 150
  Charles, 150
  Ephra, 150
  Eve, 150
  Isaac, 150
  Jacob, 150
  Samuel, 150
  Sophira, 150
  (see Fontine)

INDEX OF NAMES OF PERSONS 533

Fouracres, Elizabeth, 54
  John, 54
Fowler, Alice, 180
  Benjamin, 172
  John, 190
  Josiah, 35, 54
Fox, Anne, 150, 465
  Deborah, 491
  Elemuel, 491
  Fanny, 380
  George, 491
  Johannes, 482
  Jonathan, 331, 491
  Mary, 240, 361
  Peter, 203
  Sarah, 491
  William, 283, 361, 491
Fraill, Robert, 327
Francis, Richard, 395
Francisco, Dirck, 389
  Peter, 171
  Rachel, 216
Franklin, Mary, 164
Franks, John P., 405
Franses, Richard, 465
Frasher, Elizabeth, 356
Frazee, Abraham, 150
  Benjamin, 151
  David, 151, 420
  Edward, 297
  Eliphalet, 103, 151
  Elisha, 244
  Ephraim, 151, 245, 278, 279, 315
  Gershom, 150
  Henry, 60, 404
  Isaac, 108, 150
  Isaac, Jr., 150
  Jonathan, 76, 100, 151
  Joseph, 151
  Mary, 108
  Moses, 150
  Samuel, 150, 151
  Sarah, 151
  Stephen, 151
  Susannah, 107, 108
  Timothy, 105, 150
Frazer, David, 60, 123, 268, 349
  Hannah, 151
  Mary, 151
  Thomas, 151
  William, 151
Freame, John, 182
  Priscilla, 182
Freas (Fries), George, 217
  Jacob, 217, 240, 288
  Jacob, Jr., 355
  John, 38
Freek, William, 51
Freeman, Alexander, 152
  Benjamin, 152, 153, 434
  Charity, 152, 153
  Edmund, 178
  Elizabeth, 152
  Grace, 151
  Henry, 152
  Isaac, 152, 153, 477
  Isaac, Jr., 151
  James, 152, 153
  John, 152
  Jonathan, 152, 153
  Joseph, 126, 151, 152, 153, 284
  Margaret, 92
  Martha, 152
  Mary, 152, 342
  Phebe, 485
  Samuel, 63, 152
  Sarah, 118, 152, 153
  Stephen, 485
  William, 151
French, Aaron, 436
  Abigail, 142
  Catherine, 137
  Charles, 165
  Edward, 189
  Elizabeth, 169
  Esther, 277
  Hannah, 169
  Henry, 142, 153
  James, 315
  Jonathan, 277
  Lydia, 491
  Philip, 208
  Richard, 436
  Susannah, 61
  William, 233, 306
Fresneau, Agness, 153
Frost, Abner, 370
  Alice, 154
  James, 79
  Samuel, 172, 335
Fry, Richard, 89
Fryer, Cornelius, 110
Fulper, Elizabeth, 399
  William, 399
Furman, Benjamin, 319
  Isaac, 186
  Jonathan, 65, 195, 235
  Josiah, 400, 413
  Josiah, Jr., 205
  Moore, 94, 131, 132, 138, 229, 275
  Samuel, 239, 350, 366
  Samuel, Jr., 366
  Thomas, 154
  (see Forman)
Furnis, Milton, 154
  Samuel, 327
  Wilton, 154

G

Gaa, Rebecca, 299
Gaber, Mary, 360
Gach, Anne, 155
  Elizabeth, 155
  Esther, 155
  John, 154
  Martha, 155
  Mary, 155
  Philip, 154
  Sarah, 155
  Thomas, 154, 230, 331
Gage, Maria, 370
  Thomas, 370
Gaggers, Hannah, 157
Gaine, Hugh, 293
Gallagher, John, 308
Gallahan, Anna, 155
Gallop, Oliver, 331, 335
Galloway, Joseph, 243
Gamage, John, 174, 297
Gamble, John, 155
Gammon, Mary, 212
Gano, Catherine, 155
  Daniel, 120, 194
  David, 10, 155, 445
  Elizabeth, 155
  John, 194

Mary, 155
Rachel, 155
Sarah, 194
William, 197, 239
Gant, Ann, 136
Richard, 356
Gard, Phebe, 212
Gardner (Gardiner), Ephraim, 155
Hannah, 156
Hendrick, 187
Isabel, 156
Job, 155
Joseph, 155
Margaret, 155
Thomas, 333
Garlick, Anthony, 380
Garner, William, 139
Drusilla, 58
Garon, Elizabeth, 156
Garrabrants, Abraham, 156
Catharine, 156
Garrabrant, 156, 448, 472
Maritie, 156
Peter, 156
Rykje, 156
Trintie, 156
Garrel, John, 6
Garretson (Gerritson), Anna, 159
Annatie, 456, 457
Barnardus, 458
Catherine, 335
Christopher, 297
Daniel, 156, 410
Eyda, 159
George, 34
Gerret, 216, 419, 449
Hendrick, 334, 335, 336, 457
John, 159, 449
Martha, 156
Mary, 159
Rem, 91, 159
Samuel, 159, 481
Garrison, Abraham, 156, 157
Alpheus, 157
Ann, 31
Benjamin, 79, 117, 167, 177, 219
Bennet, 157
Catharine, 157
Christian, 156
Damaris, 157
Daniel, 156, 221, 287, 425
David, 157, 178
Elizabeth, 156
Esther, 128, 157
Eunice, 157
Frederick, 113, 178
Garret, 156, 157
Hendrick, 159, 287, 350
Isaac, 156, 157, 178
Jacob, 425, 442
Jemima, 157, 178
Jeremiah, 157, 308
John, 113, 157, 178, 230, 236, 360, 462
John, Jr., 237
Joseph, 156, 157, 178
Levi, 156
Lydia, 157, 348
Marcy, 156
Margaret, 159
Nancy, 157
Peter, 159
Phebe, 157
Prudence, 157
Rachel, 167

Rem, 156
Reuben, 157
Rumey, 157
Samuel, 156, 157, 178
Sarah, 157, 163
Stephen, 157
Silas, 157
Susannah, 197
William, 144, 157, 221
Garthwaite, Henry, 253
James, 111
Jeremiah, 436
William, 436
Garwood, Alice, 63
Charity, 85
Elizabeth, 157
Hannah, 204
Jacob, 157, 158
James, 204
Jane, 158, 438
John, 86
Joseph, 34, 134, 158
Lydia, 158
Mary, 136, 158
Rachel, 157
Rebecca, 158, 438
Samuel, 63, 157, 348, 390
Susannah, 85, 86
Thomas, 85, 86
Gary, John, 220
Gaskill, Aaron, 158, 271
Abigail, 411
Ann, 191
Charity, 283
Edward, 21
Jacob, 158
Jane, 336
Jonathan, 158
Joseph, 158, 336
Joshua, 158
Josiah, 158
Mary, 158
Samuel, 95, 158
Stephen, 271
Sybila, 85
Thomas, 383
Virgin, 336
Gass, Barbary, 158
Cattern, 158
George, 158
Peter, 158
Gaston, Hugh, 294
James, 158
John, 246
Gauger, Casper, 51
George, 22
Gaunt, Ananiah, 17
Hannah, 44
John, 17, 97, 385
Joseph, 385
Samuel, 44, 411
Sarah, 44
Geasser, George, 327
Genung, Jeremiah, 68, 371
George John, 424
Thomas, 68, 73, 86, 91
William, 337
Gerner, Mary, 378
Gerrit, Cornelius, 350
Gethings, Thomas, 102
Ghart, Anne, 323
Gibbon (Gibbons), Grant, 171, 244, 279, 375, 376, 475
John, 159
Leonard, 58, 465

INDEX OF NAMES OF PERSONS 535

Martha, 159
Mary, 159
Mason, 159
Nicholas, 58
Rebecca, 159
Gibbs, Barbara M., 50
  Benjamin, 18, 159, 319, 334
  Edward, 102, 192
  Elizabeth, 159
  Francis, 159
  Joseph, 111
  Mary, 159
  Richard, 159, 208, 345
Giberson, Esther, 159
  Elizabeth, 159, 201
  Elydia, 159
  Guisbert, 159, 201
  Hannah, 159
  Helenor, 159
  John, 159, 201
  Mary, 159
  Meribah, 159
Gibson, Joseph, 169, 267
  Joseph, Jr., 287, 470
  Sarah, 257
Giddes, Asher, 160
  Jeremiah, 160
  John, 160
  Prudence, 160
  Rachel, 160
Giesen, Reynier V., 7, 234
Giffin, George, 160
  Francis, 57
Gifford, Ananiah, Jr., 12
  Catherine, 160
  Hannah, 160
  James, 160
  John, 67
  Josiah, 160
  Mary, 18
Gilbert, Josiah, 206
Gilbertson, Gibert, 201
Gilchrist, Marion, 62
Gildersleeve, John, 147
Giles, Abram, 368
Gill, Hannah, 160
  James, 90
  John, 22, 23, 61, 102, 136, 137, 173, 192, 202, 228, 271, 326, 345, 385, 479
  Magdalen, 385
  Mary, 160
  Matthew, 77, 114, 227, 254, 261, 302, 305, 321, 377, 384, 385, 464
  Thomas, 160
  Zillah, 35
Gillam, Isaac, 127
Gillet, Aaron, 419
Gilliland, David, 160
  Elinor, 160
  Elizabeth, 160
  James, 160
  John, 160
  Matthew, 160
Gillispie, James, 406
Gilljohnson, Catherine, 161
  Errick, 161
  Isabella, 161
  John, 87, 239
  Margaret, 161
  Martin, 161
  Rebecca, 161
  William, 161

Gilman, Ephraim, 406
  Rachel, 161
Githens, John, 68
Givin, Joseph, 251
Glan, Gabriel, 161
Glass, Henry, 252
Glassling, Job, 82
Glasspell, James, 58
Glover, Charles, 162
  Deborah, 162
  Francis, 339
  John, 162, 430
  Martha, 162
  Uriah, 162
Goble, Abigail, 87
  Benjamin, 87
  Elizabeth, 87
  Ephraim, 35
  Ezekial, 461
  Jacob, 251
  Jonas, 27, 434
  Lydia, 87
  Martha, 87
  Robert, 186, 434
  Sarah, 87
  Simeon, 87
Gobrecht, Christopher, 195
Godbeer, William, 151
Godderd, Johannes, 264, 405
Godfrey, Andrew, 163
  Anne, 183
  James, 91, 176, 183, 277, 378
  Mehitable, 307, 493
  Nathan, 316
  Philip, 128, 316
  Philip, Jr., 316
  Ruth, 316
Godhart, Johannes, 254
Godly, Achsah, 162
  Ann, 162, 370
  Edward, 162
  John, 162
  Joseph, 162
  Mary, 162
  Rebecca, 162
  William, 162
Godown, Evans, 489
Goelet, Elizabeth, 162, 247, 248
  Francis, 42, 248
  Hendrick, 126
  John, 248
Goff, Asenath, 162
  David, 162
  Hannah, 162, 163
  John, 162
  Joseph J., 162
  Margaret, 99, 163
  Mary, 162, 163
  Nathan, 162
  Phebe, 162
  Priscilla, 163
  Rachel, 162
  Rhoda, 163
  Silas, 131, 163, 175
  Thomas, 162
  William, 99, 131, 162, 163, 190
Goforth, William, 109
Golden (Goldin), Ariantje, 240
  Catherine, 163
  Elias, 314
  Hannah, 163
  Jacob, 185
  James, 163
  Jean, 163

John, 164, 394, 410
Joseph, 93, 164, 264, 318
Judith, 163
Phebe, 156
Rachel, 163
Rebecca, 163
Samuel, 163, 164
Golder, Abigail, 164
Sarah, 164
Goldsmith, Joseph, 163
Josias, 431
John, Sr., 455
Goldy, John, 59, 66, 109, 233, 241, 246, 310, 383, 386
Joseph, 59, 66, 67, 108, 109, 265, 369, 482
Gollohar, Bryan, 116, 135, 267, 367
Gomez, Deborah, 163
Esther, 163
Matthias, 163
Gonce, Justis, 360
Gonsales, Emanuel, 60
Gontryman, Conrod, 158
Goodin, Samuel, 92
Goodwin, Thomas, 6, 17, 32, 225, 417, 469, 475
William, 68, 137, 279
Gordon, Andrew, 166
Charles, 346
David, 163, 167, 189
Grace, 201
James, 351
Jonathan R., 135
Joseph, 42
Margaret, 351
Peter, 415
Robert, 132, 382
Thomas, 238
Gosling, David, 7, 223, 248, 260, 444
John, 240, 327
Gouger, George, 303
Gould, Abigail, 164
John, 163, 164
Joseph, 164
Rachel, 420
Samuel, 163, 164
Sarah, 164
Stephen, 164
Thomas, 164, 328
Gouverneur, Abraham N., 363
Experience, 222
Grace, Isaac, 105
Philip, 82, 319
Graff (Groff), Christopher, 23, 195
Henry, 137, 336
Ladena, 84, 178
Sarah, 76
Graham, James, 9, 164, 208
John, 164
Mary, 164
Sarah, 164
William, 164
Graisbury, Benjamin, 164, 334, 426
James, 164
Joseph, 164
Mary, 164
Grammong, Ichabod, 264
Grandin, Abigail, 252
Daniel, 441, 484
John, 132, 252
Samuel, 179, 380
Grant, Christian, 165
David, 165
Eleanor, 165

George, 165
John, 165, 214, 403
Margaret, 165
Martha, 165
Mary, 165
Grasbury, Elizabeth, 100
James, 100
Nancy, 100
Grave (Graves), Abigail, 329
Ruth, 329
Thomas, 107
Gray, Ann, 165
Arthur, 165
Benjamin, 478
Elizabeth, 165
Isaac, 165
Jacob, 309
James, 72
John, 105, 122, 250, 295, 367, 397, 436
Mary, 165
Patrick, 116, 261
Susannah, 165
William, 37
Gregg, John, 88, 344
Green, Benjamin, 23
Charity, 165
Elizabeth, 165
Enoch, 194
Rev. Enoch, 323
Eve, 165, 166
George, 347
Henry, 113, 165
Isaac, 150, 345
Jacob, 236
James, 165
Jean, 165
John, 39, 121, 129, 165, 201, 343, 358
Lydia, 166
Martha, 110
Mary, 165
Rachel, 165
Rebecca, 165
Richard, 134, 235, 489
Samuel, 132, 181, 360
Sarah, 165
William, 165
Greensworth, Mary, 326
Gridges, Thomas, 51
Griffin (Griffing), Ebenezer, 166
Edward, 247
Francis, 166
Gabriel, 166
Jane, 186, 440
Jasper, 166, 228
John, 166
Lydia, 228
Robard, 166
Sarah, 166
Thomas, 279
William, 140, 166, 228
Zadok, 166
Griffith, Abraham, 68
Benjamin, 247
Edward, 402
John, 11, 181, 228, 275, 426
Rachel, 275
Sarah, 275
Thomas, 447, 463
Griggs, Ann, 167, 292
Barrent, 166
Benjamin, 166
Catherine, 166

INDEX OF NAMES OF PERSONS 537

Daniel, 166, 292, 396
Eleanor, 166
Jane, 166
Joachim, 166, 481
John, 160, 162, 166, 248
Margaret, 166
Martha, 166
Martin, 292
Mary, 166
Reuben, 166
Samuel, 166
Grim, Peter, 282
Grimes, John, 143, 188
Grinaway, Abigail, 34
Griscom, William, 81, 345, 465
Groom, Elizabeth, 167
  Moses, 167
  Peter, 167
  Samuel, 34
  Sarah, 167
  Thomas, 167
Grover, James, 38, 296, 297, 381, 422
  Joseph, 188
Grummon, Ichabod, 264
Guest, Esther, 23
  Henry, 208
  William, 35, 227, 228, 250, 302, 377, 384, 385, 429, 454
  William, Jr., 302
Guild, John, 69, 294, 434, 467, 488, 493
Guinnell, Thomas, 227
Guisbertson, Elizabeth, 167
  Esther, 167
  Guisbert, 167, 306
  Hannah, 167
  Helena, 167
  John, 167
  Lydia, 167
  Mary, 167
  Meribah, 167
  William, 167
Gulick, Gerbert, 481
  Henry, 427
  Joachim, 34, 132, 229
  John, 142
  Peter, 25
  Samuel, 34
Gustin, Alpheus, 369
Guthrey, Robert, 138
Guthridge, Sarah, 339

H

Hackenburger, Anna E., 167
  Catharine, 167
  Christopher, 167
  Elizabeth, 167
  Elsie, 167
  Eve A., 167
  Harman, 167
  Henry, 167
  John, 167
  Joost, 167
  Margaret, 167
  Mary, 167
  Peter, 167
  (see Hockenbury)
Hackett, Elizabeth, 168
  John, 72, 237, 289
  Richard, 230, 379, 396, 417
Hackney, Agnes, 169
  Grace, 170

Joseph, 168, 452, 463
Joshua, 168
Thomas, 168, 463
William, 168
Haddon, Christopher, 110
  John, 136
  William, 80
Haff, Abraham, 168
  Cornelius, 168
  John, 168
  Lawrence, Jr., 168
  Martha, 168
  Peter, 168
  Richard, 168
  (see Hoff, Huff)
Hagar, Johannes, 352
  Lawrence, 169
Hagawout, George, 291
Haggerty, Hugh, 113, 400
  Patrick, 113
  Stephen, 400
Haines, Abigail, 229
  Abram, 169, 170
  Amos, 192, 199, 438
  Ann, 170
  Benjamin, 22, 52, 170, 212, 380
  Catherine, 170
  Charity, 170
  Elizabeth, 169, 425
  Enoch, 212, 476
  Ephraim, 85, 170
  Ezekiel, 246
  Grace, 169
  Hannah, 169, 170
  Henry, 63, 64
  Hope, 85
  Hugh, 169
  Isaac, 125, 170
  Isaiah, 169
  Jemima, 169
  Job, 160, 426
  John, 68, 70
  Joseph, 32, 169, 170
  Joshua, 170
  Josiah, 140, 170, 229, 354
  Margaret, 238
  Mary, 170, 436
  Moses, 169, 232
  Nathan, 165, 285
  Nathaniel, 348, 349
  Noah, 168, 170, 197, 476
  Rebecka, 63, 64, 170, 438
  Richard, 170
  Sarah, 169
  Silas, 212
  Simeon, 169, 170
  Solomon, 125, 126
  Thomas, 125, 169, 170
  Thomas, Jr., 238
Hall, Abel, 171
  Abner, 171
  Adam, Jr., 340
  Ann, 171
  Burgiss, 15
  Catherine, 24, 171
  Clement, 171, 200, 268, 279
  Edward, 82, 171
  Elizabeth, 170
  Francis, 24
  George, 171
  Jane, 306
  John, 171
  Jonathan, 390
  Joseph, 171

Margaret, 171
Morris, 171
Naomi, 171
Nathaniel, 116, 171, 427
Prudence, 105, 171, 317
Rachel, 94
Richard, 171
Sarah, 24, 171
Solomon, 307
William, 170
Hallemus, William, 490
Halloway (see Holloway)
Halsey, Benjamin, 13, 183, 186, 258, 485
Daniel, 193, 194
Ezra, 265
Joel, 88
Joseph, 194, 419
Moses, 410
Sarah, 80
Silas, 27, 80
Halstead (Halsted), Caleb, 189, 352
Josiah, 226, 368
Thomas, 439
Timothy, 368, 466
William, 313
Halter, Catharine, 172
Francis, 145
Margaret, 172
Mary A., 172
Peter, 172
Halton, James, 134
Hamersley, John, 231
Hamilton, Anna, 46, 172
Archibald, 141
Arthur, 368
Charles, 46, 395
John, 172, 395
Judith, 116
Sarah, 172
William, 299
Hamler, Andrew, 393
Elizabeth, 393
Eve, 393
Jacob, 393
Mary, 393
Nicholas, 393
Peter, 393
Hammell, Bryant, 455
Catherine, 173
Deborah, 173
Elizabeth, 173
James, 173, 411
John, 173
Laban, 173
Mary, 173
Rachel, 173
William, 173
Hammitt, Ann, 193
Samuel, 173
Hammon, Ann, 470
Hampton (Hamton), Abner, 173
Abraham, 173, 442
Andrew, 80, 173
Anna, 173
Elizabeth, 486
Jacob, 172, 173, 425
John, 87, 184, 192, 245, 296, 418
Jonathan, 80, 96
Mary, 173, 425
Sarah, 173
William, 192, 320, 351
Hance, Catherine, 174
David, 313, 480

Elizabeth, 488
George, 445
Isaac, 214
Jacob, 173, 174, 474, 488
John, 31, 173, 294
Mary, 173
Rachel, 174
Timothy, 173, 174
Waples, 174
(see Honce)
Hancock, Daniel, 231
Edward, 9
Grace, 102
James, 327
Lydia, 174
Nathaniel, 317, 459
Rachel, 55
Rebecca, 174
Samuel, 75, 459
Sarah, 75
William, 231, 299
William, Jr., 68
Hand, Abigail, 174, 175, 176
Abraham, 176
Absalom, 175
Ann, 176, 177
Cornelius, 176, 494
Daniel, 242
David, 174, 176
Deborah, 175, 176, 494
Eli, 175
Elihu, 183
Elijah, 174, 175
Elisha, 177
Elizabeth, 175
Ellis, 175
Esther, 149, 174
Experience, 404
Gideon, 174
Henry, 66, 127, 145, 175, 177, 220, 242, 243, 264, 301, 404, 422
Isaiah, 177
Jacob, 128
James, 175
Jane, 176, 177
Japheth, 183
Jemima, 99, 175
Jesse, 99, 174, 175, 176, 262
Johanna, 175
John, 175
Jonathan, 176, 177
Judah, 175
Judith, 176
Ludlam, 493
Lydia, 175, 404
Martha, 176
Mary, 177, 220
Nathan, 176, 392
Nathaniel, 176, 190, 386
Patience, 177
Rachel, 411
Rhoda, 177
Sarah, 127, 177
Shamgar, 99, 174, 177, 398, 399
Silas, 101, 175
Stephen, 176
Susannah, 175
Thomas, 176, 177, 242
Timothy, 145
William, 176
Handly, Daniel, 390
Hankerson, Joseph, 104
Peter, 131

INDEX OF NAMES OF PERSONS 539

Thomas, 349
(see Hankinson)
Hankins, Abel, 420
  Absalom, 420
  Rachel, 201
Hankinson, James, 421, 430
  Joseph, 278
  Rachel, 278
  Susannah, 9
  William, 9, 109, 421, 422
  (see Hankerson)
Hann (Hayn), Elizabeth, 203
  Frederick, 470
  Peter, 203
Hanna (Hannah), Abigail, 177, 178
  James, 39, 121, 177, 178
  John, 33, 253, 267, 273
  Rev. John, 9, 164, 266
  Lida, 177
  Lydia, 178
  Mary, 164, 177, 178, 266
  Miriam, 177
  Preston, 177
  Samuel, 79, 106, 117, 177, 195, 288, 319, 403
  Sarah, 177
  Silas, 177
Hansell, Johan A., 309
Hansike, Bernard M., 332
Hanson, John, 481
Harbart, Amy, 243
  George, 354
Harcourt, Rachel, 178
Harder, Hendrick, 340
Hardin, Anna, 178
  Catherine, 178
  Samuel, 178
Harding, Elizabeth, 305
  William, 451
Hardy, Elizabeth, 182
  John, 390
Harker, Ahimaaz, 179
  Daniel, 16, 91, 179, 477
  Deborah, 179
  Ezekiel, 132
  James, 178
  Jemina, 179
  John, 34
  Joseph B., 34
  Mary, 34, 178
  Massa, 179
  Rachel, 140, 179
  Samuel, 259
Harlow, Isaac, 466
Harned, John, 154
  Jonathan, 154, 330
Harpell, Christian, 179
Harriman, William, 280, 487
Harrington, Joseph, 148
Harris, Abel, 14, 55, 204, 357
  Abigail, 53
  Daniel, 179
  Ephraim, 115, 130, 143, 224, 263, 313, 336, 368, 378
  Hannah, 179
  Isaac, 33, 105, 180
  Dr. Isaac, 33
  Jacob, 16, 472
  James, 32
  Jeremiah, 52, 179
  John, 123, 426
  Jonathan, 179
  Josiah, 342
  Mary, 179, 357

  Nathaniel, 43
  Rachel, 179
  Ruth, 342
  Samuel, 21, 32, 102, 198
  Samuel, Jr., 179, 472
  Sarah, 105, 128
  Stephen, 139
  Susannah, 179
  Thomas, 53, 130, 263, 311, 321, 341, 360, 452
  William, Jr., 332, 491
Harrison, Abigail, 180, 181
  Amos, 118, 473
  Anna, 180, 181
  Benjamin, 447
  David, 473
  Demaras, 180
  Gannatta, 268
  George, 250, 283
  Hannah, 181
  Henry, 305, 333
  Isaac, 181
  Jabez, 180, 217, 226, 312
  Jared, 102
  John, 447
  Jonas, 180
  Joseph, 10, 102, 403
  Lydia, 102
  Mary, 81, 180, 181
  Priscilla, 181
  Rachel, 181
  Rebecca, 81, 180, 181
  Samuel, 68, 101, 180, 181, 285
  Samuel, Jr., 392
  Sarah, 180, 181
  Stephen, 181
  Tacey, 181
  William, 11, 181, 208, 315, 407
  William, Jr., 11, 180
Harshall (Harsel), Anthony, 181, 344
  Christian, 344
  Christine, 181
  Eleanor, 344
  Elizabeth, 181
  Michael, 323
  Susanna, 181
Hart, Amy, 182
  Ann, 182
  Benjamin, 431
  Cattrin, 19
  Chamless, 75
  Constant, 362
  Daniel, 138
  Elizabeth, 182
  Hannah, 75
  John, 15, 17, 75, 182, 185, 194, 208, 220, 266, 319, 400, 414, 488
  Jonathan, 182
  Levy, 19, 297
  Michael, 469
  Nehemiah, 182
  Noah, 239
  Penelope, 17
  Peter, 209
  Ralph, 17
  Samuel, 182, 433
  Zebulon, 182
Hartley, Benjamin, 199, 430
  William, 421
Hartshorn (Hartshorne), Eleanor, 491
  Eseck, 90
  Francis, 90

540   NEW JERSEY COLONIAL DOCUMENTS

Hugh, 182
Isaac, 265, 474
John, 50, 320
Margaret, 182, 393
Phebe, 491
Richard, 53, 90
Robert, 183, 359, 474
Samuel W., 491
Thomas, 90, 182, 393
Harvel, Christian, 423
Harvey, Alexander, 361
  Peter, 65, 158, 173, 211, 286
  William, 116, 170, 190, 204, 222, 427
Haselton, Ann, 185
  James, 185
  Mary, 185
  Mercy, 185
  William, 185
Haslam, Richard, 384
Hathaway, Abigail, 183
  Benjamin, 79, 183
  Benoni, 87, 109, 183
  Clark, 183
  Clemens, 183
  Eleazar, 97, 183
  Elizabeth, 183
  Gershom, 183
  Job, 183
  John, 109, 183
  Jonathan, 183
  Joseph, 183
  Kezia, 183
  Rebecca, 183
  Thankful, 183
Hathorn, Catherine, 183
  Hugh, 176, 183
  James, 91
Hatkinson, Elizabeth, 43, 44
  John, 43, 44, 271
  (see Atkinson)
Hatton, Jabesh, 166
  John, 206
Haulenbeck, Jacob, 280
Havens, Abigail, 184
  Darling, 184
  Experience, 184
  George, 184, 275
  Hannah, 184
  Isaac, 184
  Joseph, 184
  Mary, 184
  Moses, 102
  Sarah, 184
  William, 184
Haviland, Martha, 184
Hawkins, Elizabeth, 184
  John, 249
  Sarah, 377
  Susannah, 460
Hawks, Samson, 99
Hawly, Benjamin, 272
Haws, Olive, 94
Hay, Andrew, 122
Hayden, Elizabeth, 274
Haydock, James, 153, 173
Hayes, Henry, 262
  James, 108
  John, 396
  Joseph, Jr., 264
  Samuel, 264
  Susannah, 27
Hays, David, 16, 44, 83, 374
  Esther, 464

Jacob, 133, 134
Phebe, 32
Sarah, 150
Thomas, 16
(see Heays)
Hayton, Jabez, 93
Hayward, Anna, 206
  Ebenezer, 206
Haywood, Charity, 185
  Ebenezer, 410
  George, 185
  John, 185
  Martha, 185
  Thomas, 185
  William, 185
  Zipporah, 185
Hazen, Nathaniel, 482
Hazlet, John, 460
Headly, Robert, 334
  Samuel, 325, 335
Heard, Nathaniel, 47, 273, 274
  Samuel, 79
  Susannah, 185
Heath, Andrew, 323
  David, 185, 203
  John, 305
  Richard, 323
Heaton, Benjamin, 185
  Daniel, Jr., 220
  Ephraim, 157
  Gideon, 258
  Jabez, 93
  Jabesh, Jr., 220
  Levi, 162
  Samuel, 162
  Thomas, 157
Heays, Margaret, 185
  Mary, 185
  William, 185
  (see Hayes)
Hectar, Margaret, 186
Hedden, Ebenezer, 100, 330
  Edward, 186
  Eleazar, 186
  Elijah, 186, 422
  Fietje, 186
  Jonas, 186
  Joseph, 221, 463
  Joseph, Jr., 312
  Keziah, 186
  Mary, 186
  Nehemiah, 186
  Phebe, 186
  Ruth, 186
Hedger, Benjamin, 186
  John, 186
  Joseph, 186
  Margaret, 186
  Phebe, 119
  Samuel, 186
  Sarah, 186
  Stevenson, 186
  Thomas, 186
  Uriah, Jr., 119
Hedges, David, 186
  James, 101, 186, 365
  Mary, 186
  Zeruiah, 99, 186
Hegeman (Hageman), Adrian, 169, 492
  Barnt, 201
  Benjamin, 169
  Cathrine, 169
  Cornelius, 20, 200

INDEX OF NAMES OF PERSONS 541

Darling, 144
Geertje, 169
Hendrick, 169
Jacobus, 169
John, 169
Joseph, 169
Mary, 169
Michael, 145
Sarah, 492
Simon, 169
Height, John, 418
Heil, Balster, 440
Heire, John, Jr., 93
Heite, Henry, 389
Helford, Christopher, 383
Mary, 383
Hellings, Robert, 213
Helme, Benjamin, 74
John, 104, 228, 251, 452
Hemmery, Peter, 142
Hemsted, Jeremiah, 48
Hendershot, Casper, 383
Jeremiah, 30
Michael, 383
Henderson, Ann, 240, 409
John, 148, 240, 278, 408, 409, 420
Michael, 278, 295, 408, 409
Thomas, 424
Hendricks, Abigail, 96
Catherine, 187
Conrad, 242
Isaac, 96, 97
Isaac, Jr., 98
Jacob, 96
Lena, 187
Lydia, 96
Mary, 187
Hendrickson, Catharine, 187
Conrod, 236
Daniel, 93, 198, 333
David, 187
Elizabeth, 187
Guisbert, 290
Henry, 407
John, 93, 134, 345, 455
Jonas, 187
Mercy, 236
Modelen, 187
Okenus, 187
Susannah, 455
William, 200
Hennion, Abraham, 188
David, 188
Elizabeth, 188
John, 188
Peter, 188
Henry, Alexander, 188, 440
Arthur, 186, 188
Daniel, 164, 186, 187, 188
David, 44, 186, 187, 188
Elizabeth, 140, 229
Esther, 187
Jane, 186, 188
John, 44, 62, 63, 140, 186, 187, 188, 229, 230
Margaret, 187
Mary, 230
Michael, 186, 187, 188
Nathaniel, 187, 188
Sarah, 44, 164, 187, 188
William, 186, 188, 229
Hepard, Thomas, 90
Hepburn, Elizabeth, 292
James, 292
John, 45, 300

Herbert, Elizabeth, 188
James, 278
John, 47, 474
Jonathan, 466
Mary, 200
Obadiah, 47, 129, 373, 446, 461
Richard, 118
Heritage, Benjamin, 160, 189, 277
Daniel, 189
Hannah, 189
Joseph, 189
Joshua, 189
Judah, 189
Keziah, 189, 276
Samuel, 189
Sarah, 189
Herpel, Christian, 189
Herriman, Job, 235
William, 311
Herring, Isaac, 142
John, 156, 354
Herriot, Alfred, 330
Andrew, 428
David, 146, 152, 185, 330, 331, 428
Ephraim, 84
George, 47, 330, 331
Mary, 160, 189
Samuel, 366
Ursilla, 330
Hertlings, Abraham, 46
Hesom, Thomas, 60
Hetfield (Hatfield), Cornelius, 280, 370
Andrew, 98, 189
Dameras, 153
David, 243, 404
Elizabeth, 111, 313
Isaac, 189
Jacob, Jr., 189
Mary, 98
Matthias, 189, 217, 289, 372
Matthias, Jr., 193
Moses, 189
Phebe, 189
Samuel, 189, 485
Sarah, 189
William, 60
Heulings (Hewlings), Abraham, 57, 60, 71, 174, 225, 228, 252, 286, 325, 333, 389, 460, 466, 488
Abraham, Jr., 333
Agnes, 28
Esther, 396
Isaac, 43, 71, 228, 279, 290, 336, 338, 460
Israel, 197
Joseph, 137
Samuel, 137
Susannah, 333
William, 71, 79, 100, 182, 331, 338, 361, 396, 421
William, Jr., 361
(see Hullings)
Heulitt, Samuel, 297
Heurtin, Joshua, 190
Susannah, 190
Hewes (Hews), Daniel, 201
Jacob, 486
Jervis, 486
John, 190
Martha, 190
Samuel, 207
Hewit, Abigail, 396
Benajah, 190
Daniel, 176

Elijah, 190
Hannah, 190
Henry, 190
Lydia, 190
Moses, 190
Nathaniel, 258
Phebe, 190
Robert, 387
Shamgar, 190
Thomas, 190
Zeruel, 190
Heyer, Abraham, 169
Jacob, 50
Hickman, John, 96, 131, 218, 453
Hicks, Charles, 353, 462
Hannah, 14, 311
Hugh, 259, 272
Samuel, 280, 311, 316
Thomas, 479
Whitehead, 462
William, 244
Hide, Capt. Richard, 62
Hider, John, 45
Higbe (Higbee), Edward, 349
Jemima, 150
Joseph, 24
Ruth, 287
William, 198, 357
Higgins, Edward, 57, 123, 428
Eliakim, 111, 194
Jemima, 371
Jonathan, 178, 210
Joseph, 196, 239, 337, 413
Joshua, 198
Mary, 371
Nathaniel, 14, 368
Hildebrand, Elinor, 190
Isaac, 190
Hildidge, Elizabeth, 37
Hildreth, Aaron, 191
Aaron, 191
Daniel, 128, 163, 191, 493
David, 493
Elizabeth, 191
James, 191, 310, 493
Jonathan, 99, 190, 191, 310, 493
Joseph, 99, 177, 190, 191, 218, 310, 386, 392, 410
Joshua, Jr., 128
Lydia, 191
Phebe, 191
Priscilla, 191
Zibiah, 191
Zillah, 191
Hill, Alexander, 345, 405, 439
Anne, 191
Archabald, 194
Elizabeth, 270
James, 13, 38
John, 265, 270, 299, 393, 449
Joseph, 270, 392
Margaret, 398
Marvel, 380
Moses, 191, 266, 296, 427
Rebecca, 270
Robert, 191
Samuel, 270
Sarah, 191
William, 230
Mrs., 468
Hilliard (Hillyard), Abraham, 193
John, 364
Joseph, 193

Hillier, Abraham, 192
Elizabeth, 191
Isaac, 191, 192, 348
Jacob, 191, 192
John, 60, 191, 192, 197
Joseph, 192
Mary, 191
Samuel, 191, 192
Sarah, 191
Hillman, Abigail, 192
Daniel, 192, 193, 507
Drusilla, 192, 252
Elizabeth, 192
Hannah, 192
James, 192, 307
Joab, 192, 193, 277
Joel, 109
John, 75, 132, 192, 269, 479
John, Jr., 345
Joseph, 192, 193, 378
Josiah, 192, 193, 338
Leticia, 193
Mary, 192, 277
Priscilla, 193
Samuel, 192, 193
Sarah, 192
Rachel, 425
Hinchman, James, 58, 76, 144, 204, 282, 331, 435, 486
John, 44, 81, 85, 180, 192, 193, 271, 303, 339, 389, 421, 465
Joseph, 58
Sarah, 287
William, 85
Hinds, Elizabeth, 193
James, 148, 216, 371
John, 107, 193, 235, 372, 484, 485
Joseph, 288, 289, 377
Levi, 274
Lydia, 194
Mary, 194
Rebecca, 194
Richard, 197
Samuel, 193
Sarah, 194
Stephen, 194
William, 193, 194
Hiner, Herbert, 194, 350
John, 194
Hinksman, Nehemiah, 262
Robert, 262
Hinsman, Jacobus, 443
Hitchell, David, 440
Hixson, Joseph, 374
Noah, 360
Hoagland (Hogeland), Abigail, 194, 196
Abraham, 196
Amos, 196
Annatie, 145
Arianche, 196
Christopher, 196, 201, 304, 416
Christopher, Jr., 201
Cornelius, 196
Daniel, 196
Dirck, 145, 196
Derrick, Jr., 194
Dinah, 201
Elinor, 196
George, 196
Henry, 196, 340
Ida, 196, 201
Jacob, 200, 201

INDEX OF NAMES OF PERSONS 543

Jacobe, 196
James, 196, 469
Jane, 196
John, 196, 197, 201
Joseph, 196, 482
Lena, 201
Margaret, 201
Maria, 201
Martin, 82, 196, 420
Mary, 196, 201
Ouke, 196
Phebe, 196
Rhoda, 196
Sarah, 196
Siche, 196
Susanna, 200
William, 117, 196, 489
Hobbs, Elizabeth, 194
Hockenbury, John, 124
  (see Hackenburger)
Hodge, Martha, 235
Hodges, Rachel, 24
Hodshon, William, 247
Hoff, Abraham, 19
  Angelica, 194
  Ann, 220
  Bergon, 19
  Charles, 140, 144, 194, 195, 368, 420
  Charles, Jr., 14
  Cornelius, 138, 194, 195, 220
  Gabriel, 140, 194
  James, 194
  Johanna, 195
  John, 43
  Neltje, 19
  Patience, 195
  Peter, 194
  (see Haff, Huff, Hough)
Hoffman, Anna M., 195
  Benjamin, 245, 340
  Elizabeth, 114, 195
  Frederick, 319, 407, 464
  Gertrude, 195
  Henry, 195, 343
  Jeremiah, 195
  John, 195, 216, 461
  Jonas, 84, 407
  Mary, 195, 220
  Moses, 114, 195, 402
  Peter, 210, 405
  Philip, 21, 95, 225, 423
  Thomas, 195
  William, 195
Hogate, Samuel, 24
Hogbin, Mary, 196
  Nehemiah, 196, 395
Hogg, John, 225
  Robert, 188, 280, 442
Holaday, Abigail, 471
Holcomb, Eleanor, 197
  Elijah, 197
  Elizabeth, 197
  George, 197
  Jacob, 197
  John, 197
  Phebe, 197
  Richard, 197
  Samuel, 197
  Thomas, 197
Holden, Benjamin, 345
Holdridge, Sarah, 280
Hollings, Abraham, 197
  Lawrence, 197
  Michael, 197
  (see Heulings)
Hollinshead, Anna, 198
  Benjamin, 197
  Francis, 447
  Hugh, 198, 452
  Jacob, 129, 169, 170, 198, 286, 452
  Jerusha, 197
  John, 197, 198
  Joseph, 129, 149, 198, 233, 322, 325, 419
  Rynier, 198
  Susannah, 198
  Thomasin, 447
Hollister, Timothy, 84
Holloway, Ann, 198
  Avis, 198
  Benjamin, 198
  David, 198
  Elijah, 198
  Elizabeth, 198
  Elkanah, 198
  George, 198
  James, 198
  Joseph, 198
  Judith, 198
  Mary, 198, 400
  Nehemiah, 198
  Patience, 198
  Rebecca, 198
  Reuben, 485
  Samuel, 198
  Sarah, 227
Holman, Catherine, 198
  Daniel, 198
  Elizal, 201
  Francis, 199
  Jean, 198
  Mary, 198
  Robert, 198
Holme, Benjamin, 64, 199
  Esther, 199
  Johanna, 199
  John, 115, 116, 145, 172, 196, 199, 296, 309, 395, 469
  Lydia, 199
  Phebe, 199
Holmes, Abijah, 64, 348
  Asher, 199, 333
  Daniel, 199, 200, 373
  Deliverance, 199
  Elizabeth, 182
  Esther, 140
  Hannah, 184
  James, 268
  John, 333, 335, 397, 403, 433
  Jonathan, 6, 74, 143, 199, 321
  Josiah, 38, 125, 215, 226, 297, 368, 381
  Margaret, 134
  Mary, 14, 199
  Nathaniel, 123
  Obadiah, 199, 311
  Obadiah, Jr., 199, 200
  Philip, 199, 200
  Samuel, 56, 199, 373
  Samuel, Jr., 333
  Sarah, 200, 311
  Thomas, 200
Holsart, Peter, 481
Holsten, Lawrence, 259, 398
  Margaret, 398

Holton, John, 260
  John, Jr., 274
Holtz, August F., 228
Homan, Peter, 187
  William, 254
Honce, Arthur, 450
  (see Hance)
Honeyman, James, 361
Honnold, Barbara, 200
Honywell, Bathsheba, 200
  Elizabeth, 200
  John, 200, 266
  Margaret, 200
  Martha, 200
  Mary, 200
  Rachel, 200
Hooghteling, Petrus, 110
Hoole, Benjamin, 67
Hooper, Isabella, 201
  James, 305, 358
  Robert L., 201, 305, 340, 358
Hooton, Benjamin, 13
  Thomas, 178
  Rachel, 275
  William, 287
Hoovy, Thomas, 251
Hopewell, Benjamin, 212
  Mary, 66, 215
Hopkins, Ann, 136, 137, 202
  Ebenezer, 11, 136, 137, 201, 202, 203
  Elizabeth E., 136, 137
  Ephraim, 166
  Estaugh, 408
  Haddon, 136, 203
  Hannah, 202
  Hezekiah, 202
  John, 241
  John E., 136, 137, 202, 203, 408, 437
  Jonathan, 200
  Mary, 136, 137
  Sarah, 135, 136, 137, 201, 202, 241, 408
  William, 241
  William, Jr., 140
Hoppaugh, Ann, 203
  Elizabeth, 203
  John, 195, 203
  Lena, 203
  Mary, 203
  Peter, 203
Hoppe, Albert, 203
  Garret, 203
  Hendrick, 203
  Hendrickje, 203
  John, 7, 203
  Marytie, 203
  William, 8
Hopper, Catherine, 204
  Elizabeth, 55, 204
  Isaac, 203, 204
  John, 204
  Joshua, 203
  Mary, 204
Hopple, Mary, 204
Hoppock (see Hoppaugh)
Horman, Jacob, 368
Horn (Horne), Andrew, 204
  Charity, 204
  Crose, 199
  Isaac, 446
  James, 20
  John, 204, 326

Samuel, 204
Simon, 291
William, 204, 247, 431
Hornbeek, Jacobus, 110
Horner, Amy, 205
  Ann, 35
  Content, 204
  Hannah, 204
  Isaac, 5, 20, 204, 384
  John, 204, 205, 306
  Joseph, 205, 412
  Joshua, 204
  Mary, 204, 205
  Samuel, 205, 358
  Sarah, 205
  William, 204
Horsfull, Hannah, 205
  Martha, 205
  Mary, 205
  Richard, 205
  Ruth, 205
  Sarah, 205
Horton, Catherine, 187
  Joshua, 365
  Paul, 187
Hosier, Martha, 360
  Robert, 360
Hoskins, Esther, 41
  John, 14, 341, 392
  Joseph, 341
  Lydia, 341
  Mary, 310, 341
  Raper, 341
  Ruth, 341
  Sarah, 341
Hough, Charity, 204
  Christian, 205
  Jonathan, 56, 271, 383
  (see Hoff)
Houghton, Joab, 319
  John, 15
  Sarah, 15
  Thomas, 347
House, David, 450
  John, 450
  Stephen, 450
Housel (Houshell), Altia, 306
  Anne, 482
  Elizabeth, 205
  Matthias, 205
  Martin, 205
  Mary, 205
  Michael, 403, 490
  Nellie, 205
  Peter, 117, 205, 264
  William, 205, 306
Housilt, Catherine, 405
  John, 405
Hoveour, Henry, 308
How, Mary, 51
  Micajah, 119, 206
  Samuel, 206, 283, 322, 388
Howard, James, 80
  Joseph, 274
  Mary, 79
  Prudence, 274
  Robert, 14, 51, 79, 259, 326, 447, 452, 485
  Robert, Jr., 206
  William, 397, 449
Howell, Abigail, 206, 207
  Ann, 207
  Arthur, 94, 206
  Benjamin, 36, 304

Bethia, 206
Caleb, 206
Charles, 327, 384
Christopher, Jr., 394
D., 117
Daniel, 207
David, 347
Elizabeth, 359
Ellet, 439
Eunice, 213
George, 450
Hannah, 206, 492
Henry, 206
Hezekiah, 207, 439
Isaac, 371
John, 206, 207
Jonathan, 207
Josiah, 194
Lydia, 359
Mary, 206, 207
Micah, 207, 369
Obadiah, 132, 150, 196, 206, 345, 346
Phebe, 207
Rebecca, 207, 359
Rednap, 65, 133
Richard, 206
Samson, 358
Samuel, 206
Sarah, 10, 11, 26, 45, 72, 77, 144, 178, 190, 206, 232, 285, 325, 354, 377, 382, 383, 392, 429, 437
Sibbah, 207
Silas, 206
Stephen, 68, 346
Sylvanus, 63, 206
William, 207
Howke, Ann, 207
Daniel, 207
Jacob, 207
Howton, Elsie, 208
Hoy, William, 300
Hubbell, Abijah, 207
Asa, 207
Elizabeth, 207
Esther, 207
Ezekiel, 207
Lois, 207
Mary, 207
Nathaniel, 60, 207, 377
Susannah, 207
Hubbs, Lucy, 136
Hublar, John, 195
Huckings, Barbara, 196
Mary, 196, 197
Mercy, 197
Patience, 196
Rebecca, 196
Samuel, 196
Huddy, Daniel, 397
Hude, Ann, 45, 208
Catherine, 207
Helena, 208
James, 15, 207, 208, 260, 442
James, Jr., 45
Margaret, 208
Mary, 207, 208
Robert, 208
Susannah, 208
Hudnut, Joseph, 412
Naomi, 208
Hudson, Andrew, 325
Hannah, 178
Isaac, 208

James, 417
Jedediah, 178
Rachel, 473
Samuel, 36, 70
William, 36
Huff, Catherine, 208
Jane, 134
(see Haff, Hoff)
Hugan, Mary, 278
William, 278
Hugg, Ann, 181
Elizabeth, 85, 208
Hannah, 285
Joseph, 77, 368
Mary, 86
Samuel, 85, 86, 180
Sarah, 285
William, 172, 180, 193, 368
Huggens, Barbara, 208
Elizabeth, 208
Hannah, 208
Mary, 208
Patience, 208
Rebecca, 208
Samuel, 208
Thomas, 208
Hughes, Aaron, 186
Archibald, 214
Constantine, 177
Elijah, 29, 208, 209, 242, 356, 392
Elizabeth, 196, 396
Ellis, 101, 473
Hannah, 208, 209
Hugh, 282, 475
Humphrey, 238
Jacob, 243, 392, 410
James, 197
Jedediah, 209
John, 473
Judith, 473
Martha, 209
Mary, 242, 473
Mercy, 175
Richard, 298
Sarah, 209
Zeruiah, 145, 175, 176, 177, 214, 386, 410
(see Hewes)
Huie, Robert, 251
Hulberd, William, 65, 317
Hulit (Hulitt), Joseph, 252
Thomas, 474
William, 173, 297
Hull, Daniel, 209, 210
David, 209
Elizabeth, 270
Gershom, 209
Isaac, 209, 272, 362, 363
Jacob, 209
Jane, 238
John, 209
Joseph, 123
Margaret, 209
Martha, 162
Mary, 201
Meshack, 123
Moses, 209
Phebe, 209
Rebecca, 162
Robert, 269, 293
Samuel, 209
Sarah, 209
Stille, 209
Winifred, 238

Hullings, Israel, 210
  Lawrence, 210
  (see Heulings)
Hults, Cornelius, 304
  Sarah, 224
  Richard, 295
Hummer, Adam, 210
  Elsie, 210
  Eve, 210
  Herbert, 210
  Jacob, 142, 210
  Tunis, 210
Humphris, Joshua, 85
Hunloke, Mary, 210
Hunn, Thomas, 118, 148, 451
Hunsinger, George, 161
Hunt, Abraham, 24, 138, 415, 493
  Azariah, 15, 121, 142, 160, 164, 395, 415, 461, 488
  Bartholomew, 58
  Daniel, 344, 394
  Edward, 211, 357
  Elijah, 138
  Elizabeth, 211
  Esther, 211
  Hannah, 211, 378
  Hope, 211
  Isabella, 50
  James, 78, 414
  James B., 50
  John, 50, 131, 178, 208, 210, 211
  John P., 415
  Joseph, 211, 232
  Joshua, 131, 211
  Mansfield, 232
  Martha, 34, 211, 212
  Mary, 270
  Mercy, 209, 232
  Nathan, 395
  Nathaniel, 211, 241
  Noah, 142, 210, 414
  Patience, 210
  Ralph, 132, 164, 210, 328, 461
  Robert, 211
  Samuel, 50, 185, 210, 211, 229, 479
  Sarah, 131, 395
  Solomon, 384
  Stephen, 208
  Thomas, 178
  William, 6, 50, 211, 378
  Wilson, 229, 414, 415, 493
Hunter, Amy, 242
  Rev. Andrew, 242
  Hugh, 165, 344
  Thomas, 37
Huntin, Susannah, 212
Huntington, John, 35, 212
  Samuel, 16, 212, 220, 483
  Samuel, Jr., 212
  Simon, Jr., 212
  Thankful, 212
Huse, Sarah, 297
Hushson, Samuel, 372
  William, 372, 373
Husman, John, 53
Husted, David, 459
  David, Jr., 53
Huston, Agnes, 212
  James, 244
Hutchens (Hutchins), Abigail, 314
  Anne, 314
  John, 57, 79, 314

  John N., 417
  William, 201
Hutchinson, Elizabeth, 81
  John, 24
  Jonathan, 101
  Mary, 24
  Richard, Jr., 196
  Robert, 133
  Thomas, 24
  William, Jr., 196
Hutson, James, 190
  Mary, 190
  William, 446
Hutton, Barsheba, 54
  Joseph, 349
Huykendal, Hendrick, 111
Hyatt, Bartholomew, 172
  Philip, 339
Hyer, Jacob, 244
Hyland, William, 181
Hyndman, William, 26, 149, 455
Hyndshaw, James, 209

I

Imlay, Elizabeth, 133, 243
  Gilbert, 213
  Isabel, 213
  John, 213, 318, 430
  Joseph, 99, 111, 352, 421
  Mary, 338
  Peggy, 213
  Peter, 114, 212, 213
  Robert, 213
  William, 28, 51, 205
  William, Jr., 430
Inger, Barbara, 245
Ingersoll, Benjamin, 96, 213, 346
  Daniel, 213
  Ebenezer, 213
  John, 119, 213, 356
  Joseph, 213, 346
Ingram, Archibald, 11
  Benjamin, 145, 222, 264
Innes, James, 226
Inslee, Ann, 213
  Elizabeth, 213
  Jonathan, 330
  Joseph, 152, 213
  Joseph, Jr., 315
  Margaret, 213
  Samuel, 155
  Sarah, 213
  Thomas, 239
Irbul, Jacob, 327
Ireland, Amos, 119, 214, 238, 407, 408
  Ananias, 214
  Daniel, 213
  Edmond, 408
  Jacob, 214
  James, 213, 408
  Job, 350
  John, 214
  Jonathan, 213
  Joseph, 214
  Mary, 213
  Phebe, 213
  Rebecca, 213, 214
  Reuben, 213
  Rhoda, 213
  Ruth, 213
  Silas, 403
  Thomas, 213, 214

Ireton, Obadiah, 322
  William, 170
Irons, Ellen, 214
  James, 12
Irwin, Daniel, 122
  John, 450
  Thomas, 71, 265
Iseltine, Matthias, 468
  Robert, 89, 258
Isley, Sarah, 319
Iszard, Gabriel, 214
  James, 214
  Michael, 214
  Sarah, 214
Ivins, Anne, 158
  Isaac, 81, 215, 332
  Isaac, Jr., 20
  Joseph, 138, 215
  Moses, 89, 215
  Samuel, 215
  Solomon, 215
  William, 215
Iynner, Samuel, 144

J

Jackson, Athaliah, 215
  Benjamin, 42, 183, 184, 236, 306
  Deborah, 215
  George, 62
  Hannah, 42
  John, 177
  Joseph, 13, 215, 474
  William, Jr., 184
  Lydia, 215
  Margaret, 215
  Mary, 215
  Nathan, 215
  Prudence, 398
  Stephen, 215
  Susannah, 67
  William, 165, 215, 398
  William, Jr., 42, 130, 183
Jacoaks, Thomas, 216
Jacobus (Jacobse), Aaltje, 216
  Adriantje, 216
  Derrick, 216
  Egje, 216
  Fytje, 216
  Garret, 216
  Helena, 216
  Hendrick, 216
  Jacobus, 216
  Jannetje, 216
  Joanna, 216
  Johannis, 216
  John, 216
  Leah, 454
  Peter, 216, 454
  Roelof, 351
  Simon, 216
Jagard, Anne, 216
  James, 216
  Samuel, 216
  Thomas, 216
  William, 216
Jagger, John, 216
James, Abel, 404
  David, 207
  Elizabeth, 216
  Hannah, 110
  Richard, 394
  Robert, 268
  Thomas, 77, 104, 181, 186
  Whitall, 286

Jamson, Robert, 476
Jane, Grace, 217
Janney, Elizabeth, 337
  Thomas, 217
Jaquat, Hance, 131
  Joseph, 131
Jaques, Annibell, 62
  David, 234, 317
  Enos, 217
  Hannah, 217
  Henry, 217, 377
  Richard, 86
  Dr. Richard, 258
  Rhoda, 217
  Samuel, 101, 130, 217, 271, 273, 383
  Samuel, Jr., 217, 317
  Sarah, 217
Jarman, Azariah, 217
  Daniel, 217
  Elizabeth, 217
  Ezekiel, 217
  John, 79, 289, 382
  Jonathan, 217
  Malachi, 217
  Mary, 217
  Reuben, 31, 32, 79
  Sarah, 217
Jarret, William, 402
Jarvis, Thomas, 341, 342
Jatt, John, 217
Jay, John, 74
  Peter, 74
Jeanes, Henry, 326
Jefferis, Alice, 218
  Asa, 218
  Barzilliah, 218
  Caleb, 384
  Constantine, 218, 486
  Francis, 218
  John, 218, 484
  Joshua, 218
  Mary, 218
Jeffery, Caleb, 194
  John, 151
  Lewis, 165
  Mercy, 12
  Richard, 165
  Thomas, 12
Jenkins, Ann, 161
  Ansis, 218
  Benjamin, 384
  David, 381, 472
  Deborah, 218
  Elizabeth, 101
  Ephraim, 218
  Esther, 218
  Griffith, 483
  Hannah, 218
  Jonadab, 218, 310
  Jonathan, 175, 218, 410
  Mary, 218
  Nathaniel, 149, 176, 190, 218, 310, 392
  Nicholas, 218
  Rhoda, 218
  Robert, 397, 483
  Treviss, 218
Jennings, Agnes, 219
  Dennis, 218, 219
  Isaac, 219
  Isaiah, 25
  Jacob, 193, 338
  Joseph, 219

Margaret, 25
Mary, 218
Reuben, 468
Jessup, Daniel, 219
　Hannah, 287
　Isaac, 219
　John, 219, 277, 470
　Mary, 219
　Sarah, 219
Jewell, Cornelius, 219
　Elihu, 219
　Elizabeth, 219, 368
　George, 219
　James, 219
　John, 17, 196, 201, 219, 340, 412, 420
　Mary, 219
　Moses, 219
　Rachel, 26, 229
　Samuel, 219
　Thomas, 368
　William, 229
Job, George, 124
　John, 201
Johnes, Stephen, 350
　Timothy, 153, 183, 206, 230, 251, 293
Johnson, Abigail, 180, 220
　Abraham, 15
　Amos, 277
　Amy, 220
　Andrew, 220
　Anna, 219, 221
　Barbara, 288
　Benjamin, 19, 123, 180, 219, 221, 222, 275, 277, 438, 460
　Catherine, 66, 221, 223
　Christian, 220
　Cornelius, 219, 220
　Daniel, 180, 219, 220
　David, 42, 219, 222
　David, Jr., 472
　Ebenezer, 175, 307, 404
　Elinor, 220
　Eliphalet, 98, 180, 220, 221, 222
　Elizabeth, 140, 219, 221, 223, 360
　Eunice L., 180
　Eve, 220
　George, 223
　Gideon, 220, 222
　Hannah, 15, 220, 221
　Henry, 220, 221
　Isaac, 230
　Jabez, 222
　Jacob, 353
　Jacobus, 219
　James, 222, 307
　Jean, 221
　Jemimah, 221
　Jerusha, 220
　Johanna, 219, 221
　John, 43, 164, 169, 220, 221, 336, 357, 469, 476
　Jonathan, 222
　Joseph, 219, 220, 221
　Jotham, 222
　Judith, 220
　Lewis, 217, 220
　Lydia, 220
　Maria, 221
　Mary, 219, 220, 222, 224, 230
　Mary L., 220
　Matthew, 221
　Matthias, 224
　Naomi, 220
　Nathaniel, 63, 221, 222, 264
　Nicholas, 179, 214, 348
　Patience, 220
　Penelope, 277
　Peter, 288
　Phebe, 220, 221, 230
　Rachel, 219
　Ralph, 341
　Rebecca, 219
　Richard, 220
　Robert, 200, 220, 222, 244, 375, 376
　Rutt, 220
　Samuel, 221, 362, 442
　Sarah, 92, 219, 221, 222, 223
　Stephen, 222
　Susannah, 221, 223
　Thomas, 190, 222, 417
　Timothy, 221, 222
　Uzal, 180, 472
　Uzal, Jr., 180
　William, 135, 221
　Winifred, 219
　Zaccheus, 220
　Zacherias, 220
Johnston, Andrew, 122, 447
　Catherine, 223
　Daniel, 224
　David, 12, 151, 170, 223, 224, 297, 375
　Elizabeth, 223
　Euphen, 420
　Gertrude, 223
　Hannah, 224
　Hendrick, 223
　James, 150, 420
　John, 122, 200, 223, 325, 375
　John, Jr., 30, 420
　John L., 480
　Joseph, 224
　Lewis, 267
　Lydia, 442
　Magdalene, 462
　Mary, 223, 224, 381
　Michael, 224, 268, 299, 420
　Peter, 375
　Robert, 258
　Sarah, 223
　Simon, 208
　Stephen, 30, 223
　Susannah, 30
　William, 224, 362
Joline, Matthias, 224
Jolly, Charles, 224
　Deborah, 77
　Elizabeth, 224
　George, 224
　James, 51
　John, 224
　Parthenia, 77
　Rebecca, 66
　William, 70
Jones, Abigail, 224
　Abraham, 82, 257, 326
　Alice, 225
　Barsheba, 299
　Benjamin, 142, 144, 168, 195, 354, 462
　Caleb, 224, 245, 251
　Catherine, 224
　Coneactia, 168
　Cornelius, 225
　Daniel, 148, 204, 215

INDEX OF NAMES OF PERSONS 549

Daniel, Jr., 26, 30, 39, 128, 131, 158, 215, 296, 302, 303
David, 226, 343
Edward, 224
Elijah, 150
Elizabeth, 411
Grace, 226
Hannah, 224, 226, 278
Henry, 77, 95, 251
Hezekiah, 126, 294
Hope, 251
Isaac, 97, 224, 226
James, 224
Jeremiah, 77
John, 211, 226, 253, 353, 360, 382, 391, 449
Jonathan, 164
Joseph, 107, 225, 347
Martha, 121, 226, 360
Mary, 164, 224, 225
Naomi, 77
Owen, 17
Phebe, 226
Rachel, 225
Ralph, 150, 347, 433
Rebecca, 226
Samuel, 59, 145, 310, 317, 375, 386
Sarah, 215, 226, 247, 251
Stephen, 466
Susannah, 225
Tabitha, 224
Tamer, 252
Thomas, 216, 225, 351
William, 77, 149, 188, 200, 224, 478
Joralemon, Derrick, 233, 448
  Henry, 226
  Jacobus, 226
  John, 72
  Richard, 226
  Tunis, 233
Jorden, Zachariah, 228
Joslin, Thomas, 34, 474
Joudinot, John, 448
Jouet, Abigail, 189
Journey, Ann, 226
  Audery, 226, 227
  Catherine, 226
  Elizabeth, 226, 227
  James, 226, 227
  John, 226, 227
  Joseph, 226
Journson (see Yournson)
Juddawn, Daniel, 361
Justeson, Isaac, 120, 227
Justice, Andrew, 227
  Elizabeth, 492, 493
  Isaac, 120
  John, 493
  Mary, 493
  Mounce, 493
  Peter, 227
  Rebecca, 227
  Susannah, 227
  William, 493

K

Kaighin, Elizabeth, 136
  Hannah, 77, 144
  James, 136, 227
  John, 136
  Joseph, 136, 227

Kallam, Benjamin, 446
  Catherine, 374
Kam, Simon, 35
Karson, Robert, 420
Kase, Tunis, 40
  (see Case)
Katz, Martin, 51
  (see Catt)
Kay, Ann, 228
  Francis, 228
  Isaac, 22, 208, 228, 199
  Joseph, 17
  Josiah, 228, 475
  Mary, 140
  Rebecca, 228
  William, 140
Kayford (see Cayford)
Kearney, James, 53
  Michael, 20
  Philip, 201, 207, 304, 305, 340, 468
  Ravaud, 30
  Thomas, 53
Kearns, William, 171
Keasbey, Bradway, 55
  Edward, 104, 123, 387, 449, 471, 475
Keating, Ann, 228
Keen, James, 65
  John, 106, 145, 392
  Jonas, 452
  Mounce, 94, 387
  Mounce, Jr., 230, 266
  Peter, 30, 33, 452, 467
  Seeley, 266
Kelly (Kelley), James, 82, 321, 421, 460
  James, Jr., 126
  James Y., 33
  John, 22, 74, 353
  Joseph, 432
  Mary, 228
  Michael, 292
  Patrick, 100
  Samuel, 153, 428
  Thomas, 441, 460
Kelsey, Daniel, 6
  Robert, 255
  Sarah, 228
  Thomas, 64
  William, 228
Kemble (Kembell), Christian, 229
  George, 26, 180
  Joseph, 440
  Mary, 229
  Peter, 74, 156
  Philip, 229
  Richard, 379, 438
  Robert T., 438
  Samuel, 16, 26, 85, 229, 255, 482
  Vespasian, 229
  William, 229
  (see Kimble)
Kempel, Philip, 263, 264
Kenard, Samuel, 384
Kendall, Ann, 17
  Benjamin, 17
Kennedy, Robert, 439
  Samuel, Jr., 399
  Susannah, 409
  William, 409
Kenney, Daniel, 212
  Elizabeth, 229
  Kertitie, 229

Simon, 229
Thomas, 92, 229
Kent, Abigail, 230
  Charity, 230
  David, 230
  Elizabeth, 230
  Ephraim, 172
  Erasmus, 232, 279, 440
  Mercy, 230
  Phebe, 230
  Phineas, 230
Kenton, Mary, 245
Ker (Kerr), Ann, 468
  Cathern, 129, 278
  Euphema, 468
  John, 295
  Joseph, 116, 133, 268, 352, 468
  Margaret, 468
  Samuel, 129, 148, 278, 295, 346
  Walter, 468
  William, 62, 63, 351
Kerkuff, Catherine, 230
  John, 230
  (see Carkuff)
Kerlin, John, 230
  Joseph, 230
  Mary, 230
  Susannah, 230
Kermer, Derrick, 375
Kern (Kerns), Christopher, 87
  Thomas, 201
Kessart, Catherine, 229
  Williampe, 229
  (see Cassart)
Kester, Rebecca, 241
  Samuel, 132, 242
Ketcham, Daniel, 278
Key, William, 54
Keyt, James, 230
  John, 353
Kidd, John, 471
  Joseph, 230
Kidmy, Jacob, 447
Kier, Peter, 486, 487
Kiger, Adam, 39
Kikendal, Lar, 38
Kille (Killey), Abraham, 50
  David, 231
  John, 16
  Joseph, 146
  Samuel, 231
Kilpatrick, David, 267
  James, 165, 306
Kimble, George, 114
  Joseph, 231
  Rachel, 26
  Thomas, 26
  West P., 334
  (see Kemble)
Kimmings, Alexander, 491
Kimpson, Mary, 231
  Samuel, 232
  Solomon, 231
  Susannah, 231
Kindal, Phebe, 171
  Rachel, 171
  Reese, 33
King, Abigail, 232
  Alexander, 113
  Ann, 232
  Ary, 454
  Benajah, 158
  Capt., 211
  Constant, 73, 162, 311
  David, 232
  Frederick, 147, 162, 328
  George, 233, 271, 311
  Hannah, 233
  Henry, 226, 448
  James, 63
  Jane, 233
  Jeremiah, 142, 232, 233
  John, 9, 63, 266
  Joseph, 162, 213, 232, 328
  Justus, 73
  Martha, 232
  Mary, 232, 233
  Nathan, 233
  Rachel, 232
  Robert, 158, 160, 440, 468
  Samuel, 232, 386
  Theodocia, 59, 233
  William, 232, 235
Kingsland, Aaron, 234
  Abraham, 234
  Ann, 447
  Charles, 234
  Elizabeth, 233
  Henry, 226
  Hester, 233
  Isaac, 233, 234, 424, 447, 448
  Johannah, 375
  John, 233, 447
  Joseph, 226
  Mary, 233, 234
  Nathaniel, 233
  Nedemia, 233
  Richard, 233
  Sarah, 233, 454
Kinnan, Mehitable, 265
  Ruth, 234
  Thomas, 234, 428
  William, 430
Kinney, Elizabeth, 383
  Hannah, 415
  Peter, 83, 383
  Thomas, 13, 74
Kinsey, Annabel, 234
  David, 322
  Job, 232, 234
  Jonathan, 62
  Thomas, 232, 234
Kint, David, 71
Kip (Kipp), Abraham, 445
  Elizabeth, 234
  Eltje, 445
  Geesje, 234
  Hendrick, 40, 234, 239, 494
  Isaac, 234
  Jane, 445
  Nicasie, 339
  Peter, 234, 443
Kirby, Ann, 180, 491
  Benjamin, 180
  Catherine, 363
  John, 189
  Joseph, 491
  Richard, 259
  Samuel, 286
  Stephen, 181
  Thomas, 189, 467
  William, 491
Kirk, Adam, 190
  Jonathan T., 426

INDEX OF NAMES OF PERSONS 551

Kirkbride, Frances, 398
Kirkpatrick, Andrew, 449
  Margaret, 17, 33, 211, 215
  William, 17, 211
  Rev. William, 235
Kissam, Benjamin, 282
Kitchel, Abraham, 34
  John, 330
  Joseph, 34, 35, 97, 121, 206, 230
  Moses, 34, 35
Kitchin, Ann, 235
  Benjamin, 235
  Christian, 399
  Elizabeth, 235
  Hannah, 235
  Jacob, 399
  Mary, 230
  Mercy, 235
  Samuel, 94
  Sarah, 235
  Thomas, 235
Kitt, Robert, 116
Klein (Kline), Jacob, 329
Kleinehoff, Hannah, 235
  John, 235
  Peter, 235
  Sarah, 235
Kline, Harman, 142
  Hermanus, Sr., 142
  (see Cline)
Knap, Elizabeth, 236
  James, 235
  Jonathan, 235
  Samuel, 264
  Thomas, 235
Knight, Hannah, 236
  Henry, 26
  Joseph, 189
  Mary, 245
Knoffe, Johannis, 158
Knott, Abigail, 236
  Catherine, 236
  David, 74, 87, 89, 236, 294, 410, 470
  Jane, 236
  Mercy, 236
  Peter, 470
  Rachel, 236
  Rebecca, 236
  Samuel, 236
Knowles, John, 299
Koch, Barnard, 236
  Catherine, 236
  Margaret, 236
  Maria, 236
  (see Cock)
Kool, Johannis, 471
Kotts, Conrad, 108
Kough, Christine, 236, 237
  Jacob, 242
Kroesen, Derrick, 159
  Jan, 39
  (see Cruesen)
Kuhl, Crist, 88
  Paul, 88
  (see Cool)
Kuns, Anne M., 87
  John, 87
Kuykendal, Catherine, 237
  Hendrick, 237, 470
  Solomon, 237
Kuyper, Catherine, 237
  Elizabeth, 237
  Gertrude, 237
  Henry, 237
  Jannetie, 237
  Marretie, 237
Kyer, Peter, 486, 487

L

LaBar, Peter, 357
  Peter, Jr., 357
Lacey, Abraham, 237, 365
  David, 237
  Hannah, 237
  Joseph, 172, 237, 335, 406
  Mary, 237
  Prudence, 237
  Rebecca, 237
  Sarah, 237
Ladd, Hannah, 54, 141, 144, 172, 173, 202, 203, 250, 269, 285
  John, 10, 120, 141, 144, 172, 173, 178, 190, 193, 202, 203, 250, 285, 354, 368, 382, 429, 437
  Joseph, 368
  Samuel, 203, 470
Lafetra, Edmond, 13, 376
  James, 13
  James, Jr., 376
Lafevre, John, 220
Lafoliot, Isaac, 120
Laforge, John, 406
Laing, Abraham, 237
  Elizabeth, 238
  Hannah, 469
  Isaac, 237
  Jacob, 237, 238, 428, 429
  John, 238, 469
  Joseph, 237
  Mary, 75, 237, 238
  Samuel, 237
  Sarah, 238
  Susannah, 238
Lains, Martha, 37
Laird, Alexander, 268
  Moses, 159, 167
  William, 15, 101, 268, 367
Lake, Daniel, 49, 138
  Ellen, 238
  Garret, 33, 238
  Jane, 238
  John, 138, 238
  Thomas, 33, 94, 144, 382, 482
Lamb, Ann, 238
  Joseph, 67, 238, 411, 467
  Lydia, 238
  Sarah, 238
Lamberson, Cornelius, 129, 238
  Sarah, 129, 238
  Simon, 238
Lambert, Achsah, 370
  Anna, 239
  Christine, 240
  Daniel, 239, 341
  Elizabeth, 278
  Gershom, 239
  Jeremiah, 239
  John, 120, 238, 425, 489
  Joseph, 238
  Mary, 239, 341
  Sarah, 238, 239
  Mrs., 189
Lambson (Lamson), Ann, 161
  Daniel, 449
  Eleazar, 473
  Giles, 11, 439

Hance, 15, 272, 328
Joseph, 11
Matthias, 15
William, 11
Lancaster, Job, 68
Mary, 271
Lander, Henry, 239
John, 239
William, Sr., 239, 340
Landon, Daniel, 291, 387
William, 123
Lane, Aaron, 25, 48, 56, 239, 240, 324, 383, 453, 459
Areantje, 240
Cornelius, 93, 113, 165, 240, 291
Elizabeth, 100, 240
Gesie L., 240
Guisbert, 93, 239, 414, 459, 468
Hannah, 239, 240
Harman, 48, 117, 372, 374
Helena, 240
Hendrick, 247, 272
Jane, 239, 240
John, 139
Lucretia, 239
Mary, 239
Martha, 37
Matthias, 240
Rebecca, 239
Susannah, 237
William, 48, 240, 459
Langbog, Paul, 240
Langdale, John, 81
Langevelt, Christine, 240
Langley, Mary, 240
Ruth, 255
Sarah, 240
Langstaff, Charlotte, 241
Elizabeth, 240
George, 240, 241
Henry, 241, 275
Henry, Jr., 275
James, 128
Laban, 34
Martha, 241
Mary, 241
Priscilla, 241
Sarah, 241
Susannah, 240
Laning, Daniel, 132, 206, 433
John, 11, 110
Richard, 39, 110, 121, 206, 363
Robert, 162, 482
Stephen, 65, 433
Larew, Abraham, 185, 239, 241
David, 241
Margaret, 241, 455
Moses, 241
(see Laroe)
Large, Jacob, 132, 241, 242
Mary, 303
Robert, 241, 242
Robert, Jr., 242
Samuel, 132, 141, 186
Sarah, 303
Laroe, Jacobus, 242
Lambartus, 242
Mary, 242
Waybrough, 242
(see Larew)
Larrison, Abigail, 292
William, 419
Lashells, Anne, 242

Latham, Thomas, 153, 232, 272, 372, 398
William, 398
Latourette, Peter, 412
Latts, Francis, 403
Laughton, Benjamin, 29
Launder, William, 15
Lavenner, John, 21
Lawhead, John, 361
Lawrence, Abigail, 243, 311
Alice, 183
Ann, 243
Benjamin, 242, 243
Catherine, 243
Daniel, 243, 404
Rev. Daniel, 242
Deborah, 242, 243
Elisha, 133, 370, 398, 438
Elizabeth, 10, 247
George, 30, 227
Hannah, 51, 243
Jacob, 119, 122, 151, 243, 306, 429, 488
James, 31, 102, 256, 281, 426, 487
John, 30, 42, 79, 110, 216, 223, 243, 247, 279, 322, 328, 342, 353, 359, 407, 429, 430, 467, 487, 498
Jonathan, 311, 359
Joseph, 12, 395
Nancy, 242, 243
Nathan, 311, 471
Rachel, 243
Richard, 13, 174, 183, 236, 246, 252, 320, 333, 344, 376, 431, 432, 433, 480, 488
Samuel, 243
Sarah, 242
Susannah, 242, 243
Thomas, 243, 298, 489
William, 56, 167, 243, 346, 438
(see Lorance)
Lawrie, James, 289
Thomas, 133
William, 36, 88, 231, 251, 426, 432
Lay, Joana, 148
Layton, Andrew, 249, 250
Ann, 250
Catherine, 250
Hannah, 250
Hester, 250
John, 248, 250
Peter, 52, 71, 244, 245
Safety, 249, 250
Samuel, 250
Thomas, 250
William, 249, 250
Leake, Daniel, 389
Leaming, Aaron, 244, 277, 278, 404
Christopher, 404
Elizabeth, 244
Hannah, 298
Jeremiah, 244, 386
Rev. Jeremiah, 420
John, 292
Jonathan, 176, 220, 277, 422
Mary, 277
Sarah, 403, 404
Thomas, 298
Leans, Rebecca, 228
le Boyteul, Paul, 188
Lecony, James, 437

INDEX OF NAMES OF PERSONS 553

Leddel, Elizabeth, 245
  Esther, 245
  Joseph, 245
  Mary M., 244, 245
  Sarah, 244, 308
  William, 308
  (see Littell)
Ledlie, William, 327
Ledson, Robert, 170
Lee, Abel, 238
  Abraham, 245, 310
  Catherine, 116
  David, 402
  Elizabeth, 116
  Gersham, 88, 165, 187, 210, 343, 344, 412, 420
  John, 150, 294, 310, 377, 395
  Mary, 119
  Mary A., 116
  Michael, 105
  Robert, 103, 245
  Sarah, 116
  William, 245
Leeds, Abraham, 28, 238, 245, 438
  Anne, 224, 238, 245, 246
  Daniel, 340, 398, 407
  Dorcas, 245
  Felix, 245
  Hannah, 224
  Isaiah, 246
  Japhet, 9, 10, 224, 245, 398, 407, 408
  Jemima, 246
  John, 245
  Joseph, 246
  Josiah, 224
  Laban, 245
  Marcy, 246
  Mary, 245
  Nehemiah, 9, 10, 222, 245, 340, 356, 398
  Philo, 246
  Rachel, 245
  Rebecca, 245, 340
  Robert, 245
  Samuel, 246
  Sarah, 224, 246, 398
  Susannah, 245
  Titan, 245, 246
  Vincent, 21, 59, 325
Leek, Elizabeth, 322
  John, 29, 97, 222, 323, 385
  Nathan, 79, 106
  Samuel, 106, 269, 323
Leet, Isaac, 49, 142, 316, 465
Leferty, Bryan, 225, 257
  Margaret, 225
  Mary, 246
Lefetra, James, 56
  Mary, 56
Lefferson, Aurie, 246
  Benjamin, 246
  John, 246
  Leffert, 31, 246
  Mary, 246
  Peter, 246
Lefferts, Benjamin, 246, 451
  Dirck, 246
  Elizabeth, 246
  John, 246
  Mary, 246
  Peter, 451
  Sarah, 246

Lefler, Peter, 205
Leford, William, 292
Leforge, David, 247, 468
  Jacob, 247
  John, 247, 291
  Nathaniel, 247
  Nelly, 247
  Rachel, 247
  Sarah, 247
Legat, Rebea, 201
Legg, Elizabeth, 247
  Elsie, 247
  Henry, 247
  Phebe, 247
  Sarah, 247
Legrange (LaGrange), Anatie, 291
  Ari, 291
  Ari M., 291
  Barnabus, 46
  Bernardus, 91, 239, 240, 291, 451
  Catherine, 291
  Christian, 291
  Isaac, 291
  Jacobus, 291
  Jelis, 291
Leigh, Joseph, 196, 241
Lemmon, John, 201
Lennox, James, 33
  Theosallo, 307
Lent, James, 449
Leonard, Abigail, 251
  Anne, 163
  Deliverance, 248
  Eupham A., 248
  James, 205, 304
  John, 69, 88, 99, 163, 174, 176, 248, 350
  Joseph, 125, 248, 356
  Mary, 430
  Nathaniel, 86, 466
  Paul, 248
  Samuel, 247, 248, 297, 481
  Capt. Samuel, 247
  Sarah, 248
  Susannah, 248
  Thomas, 148, 223, 295, 356, 413, 430, 447, 469
  Whitehead, 304
Leport, Nancy, 265
Lerycraft, Robert, 480
Leslie, Edmund, 15, 429
  George, 248
  James, 428, 429
  William, 62
Lester, Catherine, 406
Letts, Catherine, 248
Leuquear, Elizabeth, 55
  Hannah, 55
  John, 482
  Rebecca, 165
Lewis, Ann, 249
  Benjamin, 63, 64, 154
  David, 153, 438
  Edward, 234, 245, 249, 290, 473
  Elizabeth, 186
  Hendrick, 83
  Jacob, 109, 235
  John, 235, 249
  Mary, 83, 235, 249
  Philip, 183, 297, 488
  Rachel, 249
  Samuel, 468

Sarah, 249
Squire, 38
Zephaniah, 249
Liddon, Henry, 250
  Samuel, 250
Liens, Abraham, 250
  Anthony, 250
  Catherine, 250
  Conrad, Jr., 250
  Daniel, 250
  Henry, 250
  John, 250
  Magdalen, 250
  Margaret, 250
  Peter, 250
  Rachel, 250
Lies, George, 397
Lightfoot, Mary, 392
  Sarah, 392
Likens, John, 149
  Thomas, 37, 363
Lile, John, Jr., 155
Limcox, William, 45
Limmier, Andrew, 14
Linch, Elizabeth, 250
  Hannah, 250
  Magdalen, 250
  Mary, 250
  Rebecca, 250
  Samuel, 104, 195, 228, 321
  Samuel, Jr., 228, 259, 305, 452
  Sarah, 250
Lincoln (see Linken)
Lindal, Elizabeth, 131
  William, 131
Lindon, John, 212
Lindsay, David, 349
  Ezekiel, 426
Lindsley, Benjamin, 183, 251, 410
  Agur, 251
  Charity, 251
  Daniel, 230
  Ebenezer, 426
  Elizabeth, 251
  Ephraim, 251
  Hannah, 251
  Jabes, 251
  John, 186, 251
  Junia, 251
  Kezia, 251
  Mary, 251
  Nehemiah, 251
  Rachel, 251
  Sarah, 251, 472
  Stephen, 251
Line, William, 107, 219, 238
  Daniel, 251
  Hannah, 251
  Tabitha, 251
  Thomas, 251
Linn, Alexander, 267, 393
  David, 40
  Henry, 28
  William, 393
Linnenberger, Nicholas, 167
Lipper, Thomas, 232
Lippincott, Abigail, 252
  Bathsheba, 277
  Caleb, 252, 277
  Daniel, 85, 137, 252
  Darius, 252
  David, 108
  Esther, 18, 231
  Ezekiel, 252, 277

Freedom, 52
Hannah, 252, 318
Increase, 252
James, 149, 252
Job, 57, 252, 411
John, 51, 160, 276, 322, 466
John, Jr., 125, 223
Jonathan, 251
Joseph, 18, 139, 158, 385, 430, 466
Joshua, 137, 155, 193, 252, 460
Judiah, 252
Lamuel, 33
Lydia, 252
Margaret, 252
Mary, 125, 139, 252, 359
Nathaniel, 277
Phebe, 252
Rachel, 136, 137
Rebecca, 155, 236, 251
Remembrance, 236, 256, 315
Restore, 95
Rhoda, 251
Robert, 87, 252, 297
Samuel, 107, 236, 252, 277, 283, 296, 336, 367
Sarah, 252
Solomon, 96, 251, 252
Thomas, 252
Wilbur, 252
William, 236, 286
William, Jr., 93
Lishman, Henry, 271
Lisk, Peter, 187
Lister, Ann, 361
  William, 271, 361
Littell, Andrew, 96
  Catherine, 42, 96
  David, 96
  Elizabeth, 96
  Hannah, 442
  Isaac, 150
  Jane, 42
  Jonathan, 369
  Lydia, 96
  Moses, 150, 206
  Samuel, 3rd, 279
  Thomas, 140
  (see Leddel)
Little, Amy, 254
  Andrew, 253
  Christopher, 253
  Elizabeth, 254
  Esther, 253
  James, 253
  Jane, 42, 253, 254
  John, 60, 75, 200, 253
  Jonathan, 253
  Joseph, 253, 254
  Martha, 253
  Mary, 253
  Moses, 151
  Nathaniel, 96
  Robert, 42
  Samuel, 383
  Sarah, 253
  Thomas, 42, 363, 382, 408
  William, 253, 254
Liven, Richard, 245
Livermore, Isaac, 334
Livesey, Robert, 8, 40, 112, 249, 257, 261, 453
Livingston, Harry B., 61
  John, 74, 420

INDEX OF NAMES OF PERSONS 555

Philip J., 462
Susannah, 61
William, 61, 342
Lloyd (Loyd), Bateman, 141, 261, 321
  Elizabeth, 261, 463
  Elizabeth, Jr., 266
  Ephraim, 58
  Fullaky, 266
  Hannah, 261
  John, 30, 199, 216, 261, 295, 367
  Mary, 160, 260, 261
  Nicodemus, 261
  Obadiah, 250, 261, 265, 398
  Thomas, 56, 199
  Thomas, Jr., 98
  William, 463
  Wood, 261
Lock, Andrew, 89, 254
  Charles, 187, 254
  Francis, 144
  Israel, 228
  Jester, 187
  John, 302
  Jussta, 257
  Peter, 254
  Sarah, 254
  Susannah, 377
Locker, Ann, 253
  John, 253
  John Y., 253
  Phebe, 253
  Robert L., 253
Lockerman, David, 445
Lockhart, Mary, 254
Loder, John, 358
Lodge, Benjamin, 89, 95, 142, 198, 377
  John, 274
  Patience, 274
  Rebecca, 13
Logan, John, 409
  Stanfel, 150
  Thomas, 254
London, James, 204
Long, Abraham, 255
  Andrew, 60, 204, 255, 322
  Ansell, 204, 255, 322, 477
  Constantine, 254
  David, 58, 104, 105, 161, 254, 255, 323
  Jonathan, 254
  Lucy, 255
  Moses, 89
  Peter, 255
  Prudence, 255
  Uriah, 254
  William, 89
Longacre, Israel, 227
Longbog, Paul, 217
Longfield, Catherine, 255
  Cornelius, 255
  Mary, 255
  Thomas, 50, 255
Longstreet, Alice, 256
  Anne, 256
  Aaron, 256
  Catherine, 256
  Christopher, 188
  Derick, 256
  Garret, 130, 214
  John, 373, 457
  John, Jr., 163, 406
  Mary, 256
  Moica, 256
  Rachel, 446
  Richard, 315
  Samuel, 236, 256, 315
Longworth, Abigail, 312
  Caleb, 312
  Catherine, 312
  David, 312
  Isaac, 256, 312
  Jacob, 312
  James, 312
  Thomas, 54, 98, 417
Loofborrow, Kezia, 72
Loomis (see Lummis)
Loop, Gearlough, 405
Loots, Johannes, Jr., 453
  John, 257, 453
  Paulus, 256
  Rachel, 257
Loper, James, 164
  James, Jr., 164
Lorance, Abigail, 257
  Adam, 379
  Jonathan, 130
Lord, Abraham, 464
  Absalom, 257
  Constantine, 277
  Elizabeth, 257
  Eunice, 257
  George, 257
  Hannah, 257, 400
  Isaac, 65
  James, 464
  Joseph, 163, 314
  Joshua, 96, 160, 212, 216, 437, 464, 486
  Mary, 257
  Nathan, 144, 234
  Nathaniel, 257
  Phinehas, 257
  Ruth, 400
  Sarah, 257
  Susannah, 464
Lore (Loree), Anne, 37
  David, 257, 258
  Deborah, 257
  Dollis, 258
  Elizabeth, 257, 258
  Ephraim, 443
  Hannah, 257, 258
  Hezekiah, 82, 258, 381, 407
  Ichabod, 257
  Joanna, 258
  Job, 65, 147
  Jonathan, 206, 257, 258, 423
  Lewis, 258
  Mary, 258
  Phebe, 258
  Rebecca, 257, 258
  Richard, 150, 206, 425
  Sarah, 257, 258
  Seth, 258
  Sybil, 258
Loring, John, 11
  Elizabeth, 11
Lorton, William, 47, 248
Losey, Cornelius, 258
  Elizabeth, 258
  James P., 258
  Jane, 258
  John, 258, 439
  Philip, 258
  Timothy, 258
  William, 439

556 NEW JERSEY COLONIAL DOCUMENTS

Lott, Abram, 258, 305
  Abraham, Jr., 145
  Catherine, 258, 259
  Charles, 258
  Cornelius, 374
  Daniel, 258
  Felix, 391
  George, 258
  Gershom, 258
  Henry, 197, 258
  Levi, 258, 270
  Mary, 258
  Peter, 155, 156, 234, 258
  Phebe, 197
  Richard, 232, 258, 259
  Ruth, 258
  William P., 263
Louderbach, Peter, 461
Loung, Elizabeth, 11
Lounsbury, Ann, 259
  Hannah, 259
  Jeremiah, 259, 452
  John, 259
  Mary, 259
  Phebe, 259
  Samuel, 259
  Sarah, 259
Louzada, Abigail, 259
  Benjamin, 259
  Blume, 259
  Hannah, 7, 260
  Jacob, 7, 260
  Moses, 7, 259, 260
Lovce, John, 27
Loveberry, Jacob, 247
Loveless, John, 94
Lovell, John, 140, 259, 285
Lovett, Anne, 491
  Joseph, 89
Low, Abraham, 82, 259
  Albert, 82
  Antje, 260
  Catherine, 260
  Charity, 260
  Cornelius, 82, 259, 260, 272, 419
  Cornelius, Jr., 117
  Derick, 259, 260
  Elizabeth, 260
  Gerret, 259
  Guisbert, 260
  Henry, 260
  Isaac, 260
  James, 260
  Joannah, 260
  John, 140, 260
  Joseph, 286, 476, 484, 486
  Judick, 259, 260
  Loimens, 492
  Maria M., 260
  Marytje, 260
  Nicholas, 260
  Peter, 304
  Robert, 143, 179
  Susannah, 259
  William, 82
  Wynea, 260
  Yanaca, 260
Lowrey, Barney, 45
  John, 267, 268, 357
  Sarah, 357
  Thomas, 168, 188, 229, 343
Loyd (see Lloyd)
Lozier, Abraham, 261
  Anthony, 261
  Antje, 261
  Benjamin, 261
  Derick, 40, 261
  Elizabeth, 261
  Hester, 261
  Hillebrant, 261
  Jacob, 261
  Jacobus, 261
  Jannetje, 261
  John, 261
  Lea, 261
  Lucas, 261
  Margaret, 261
  Mary, 261
  Nicholas, 261
  Peter, 261
  Rachel, 261
  Trintje, 261
Lucar, Catherine, 160
Lucas, Benjamin, 338
  Christopher, 8, 249
  Seth, 338
  Seth, Jr., 325
Ludlam (Ludlum), Abigail, 346, 494
  Abraham, 262
  Alethea, 494
  Ann, 262
  Anthony, 262
  Cornelius, 262
  Deborah, 261
  Elizabeth, 261, 262
  Gilbert, 65
  Hester, 494
  Isaac, 262
  Jacob, 263
  Jeremiah, 31, 37, 175, 177, 262, 277, 493, 494
  Joseph, 262, 346, 410, 494
  Maline, 262
  Martha, 494
  Mary, 67, 261, 262
  Matthias, 262
  Norton, 493
  Obadiah, 263
  Phebe, 493, 494
  Providence, 128, 262, 404
  Reuben, 28, 214, 410, 493
  Samuel, 261
  Sarah, 263
  Susannah, 262
  Temperance, 261, 262
  Thomas, 214, 494
  Wilky, 262
Ludlow, Abigail, 278
  Cary, 20
  Cornelius, 262, 454
  Daniel, 262
  Deborah, 262
  Elizabeth, 118, 262
  George, 103
  Jeremiah, 118, 262
  John, 262
  Mary, 20
  Samuel, 262
  Temperance, 262
  Wilky, 262
  William, 103
  William W., 103
Lufburrow, Kezia, 256
  Simon, 282
Luff, Gabriel, 229
Luke, Elizabeth, 263
  William, 263

INDEX OF NAMES OF PERSONS 557

Lukemanear, John, 199
  Samuel, 320
  Thomas, 199
Lum, Elizabeth, 332
  John, 23
  Matthew, 183, 230
  Obadiah, 283
Lummis (Lummus), Catherine, 263
  Daniel, 263, 311
  David, 106
  Ebenezer, 263
  Edward, 106
  Hannah, 263
  Henry, 106
  Jonathan, 263
  Joseph, 263
  Judith, 263
  Sarah, 263
  Tomson, 263
Lundy, Ann, 484
  Jacob, 374
  Samuel, 16, 185, 209, 374, 482, 483, 484
  Samuel, Jr., 469
  Thomas, 86, 339
Lupardus, Antje, 263
  Christianus, 263
  Lammetje, 263
  Lem, 263
  Rem, 460
  William, 263
Lupp, Christian, 205, 229, 263
  Elizabeth, 263
  Jacob, 263
  John, 263
  Maria, 263, 264
  Mary, 263
  Peter, 263, 264
Lupton, Benjamin, 43
  Marcy, 264
Luse, Joseph, 419
  Shubel, 228
Lutes (see Loots)
Luvis, Ananias, 62
Luyster, Cornelius, 93, 264
  Peter, 264
  Sarah, 264
Lyal (Lyell), Jeane, 428
  John, 304, 424
Lycan, Jacob, 264
  John, 304, 424
  Mary, 220
  Sincha, 428
  Thomas, 72
  William, 480
Lydecker, Abraham, 249
  Catherine, 249
  Cornelia, 249
  Cornelius, 249, 261
  Elizabeth, 249
  Gerrit, 249
  Margaret, 249
  Mary, 249
  Rachel, 249
  Sam B., 249
Lyle, John, 114, 155, 188
  John, Jr., 114, 188
Lynch (see Linch)
Lyndon, Ann, 360
  Elizabeth, 360
  Martha, 360
  William, 360

Lynmyer, Christiana, 332
  Christopher, 332
  Nicholas, 332
  Sarah, 332
Lynott, Edmund, 249
Lyon, Abigail, 264
  Abraham, 264, 341, 472
  Daniel, 341
  Eliphalet, 264
  Eunice, 341
  Hannah, 264, 472
  Isaac, 54, 98, 310
  Jane, 264
  Johannah, 223
  John, 54, 264, 313, 475
  Jonathan, 264
  Josiah, 221, 222
  Mattaniah, 264
  Peter, 223, 264

M

McAdams, Hugh, 9
McBride, Alexander, 269
McCafferty, Joseph, 382
MacCall, Catherine, 302
  Robert, 302
McCannon, Patrick, 65
McCarguin, Phillip, 249
McCarroll, John, 376
  William, 191
McCartney, James, 293
McCarty, Deborah, 16
McLaughlin, Elizabeth, 268
  William, 257, 394
McClean, Charles, 391, 408
  Lauchland, 370
  Peter, 160
  Samuel, 265
MacCleese, Catherine, 265
  Cornelius, 265
  John, 265
McClenahan, John, 15
McClong, William, 50
McClutch, Amy, 128, 265
  Hugh, 265
McCollister, John, 265
McCollum, Elizabeth, 266
  Ephraim, 266
  Jacob, 266
  John, 266
  Margaret, 266
  Thomas, 266
McConkey, Samuel, 351
McConnell, Elizabeth, 201
  John, 199
  Robert, 135
McCormick, John, 160
MacCorpin, Joseph, 266
  Humphrey, 266
McCouny, Malcolm, 215
McCoy, Gawen, 234
  Isabel, 390
  William, 164, 395
McCrea, Catherine, 266
  Creighton, 266
  Gilbert, 266
  James, 266
  Rev. James, 164
  Jane, 266
  John, 266
  Philip, 266
  Robert, 266

Samuel, 266
Stephen, 164, 266
William, 266
McCreery, Andrew, 266
McCullough, David, 101
James, 101
McCully, James, 269
Joseph, 185
McDaniel, Daniel, 484
William, 135
McDermott, Matthias, 46
McDonald, Richard, 147
McDowell, Andrew, 114, 155, 445
Benjamin, 267
Elizabeth, 267
Ephraim, 267
John, 9, 267, 282
Matthew, 266, 267
Peggy, 267
Peter, 267
McElhage, James, 39, 215, 269
McEowen, Alexander, 9, 267
Ann, 267
Daniel, 267
George, 267
Hugh, 267
Mary, 164, 267
William, 267
McEvers, Charles, 267
James, 267, 449
McFarland, Anne, 267
Elizabeth, 267
James, 267
Mary, 267
William, 267
McFerran, Isabel, 267
Margaret, 267
Susannah, 267
McGalliard, Hannah, 348
John, 472
Robert, 116, 134, 267, 268, 352
McGee, Safety, 15
(see Megie, Meghee)
McGill, Neill, 101
McGrachy, Neal, 57
McGraw, Cathrine, 268
McKean, Isabelle, 268
Robert, 268
Thomas, 268
William, 268
McKesson, John, 246, 443
William, 172, 355
McKim, William, 449
McKinley, James, 126
McKinney, Abraham, 187
Daniel, 312, 378
David, 306
Mordecai, 181, 344, 378
McKnight, James, 135
Jane, 135
Sarah, 268
William, 346
McManus, John, 371
McMonagle (McMonigill), Esther, 50
William, 50, 100, 308
McMurtrie, Abram, 268
John, 268
Robert, 15
Thomas, 269
McNik, Samuel, 454
McNish, George, 347
McPherson, Ann, 291
John, 226

Reuben, 291
Samuel, 274
Sarah, 291
Thomas, 80, 211
McQuarlin, James, 96
McQuean, Elizabeth, 269
John, 269
William, 269
McShane, Francis, 9, 42, 254, 382, 389
McSurley, Felix, 269
McVickar (McVicker), Archibald, 144
James, 273, 409
McWhorter, Alexander, 483
Mary, 101
Mackey (Mackay), Elizabeth, 493
John, 5, 12, 29, 80, 98, 110, 122, 163, 264, 269, 281, 298, 370, 404, 421, 493
Joseph, 270
Mary, 269, 270
Prudence, 269, 270
Richard, 270
Mackland, James, 408
Macklucke, John, 10
Mackon, William, 31
Madock, Hannah, 148
Maffett (see Moffat)
Mahurin, Stephen, 40
Maid, Andrew, 6
Maine (Maines), Hannah, 127
Samuel, 45, 171
Maitland, Col. Richard 370
Major, Richard, 200
Mallbone, Godfrey, 361
Mallown, James, 468
Man, David, 189
Isaac, 334
Samuel, 45
William, 64, 353
Manley, Gertrude, 169, 492
John, 169, 492
Manlove, Christopher, 80, 111
Manners, John, 270, 413
Joseph, 270
Rebecca, 270
Manning, Benjamin, 166, 270
Christian, 270
Enoch, 270
Ephraim, 172
Gershom, 270
Isaac, 270
James, 236, 247, 270, 275, 341
James, Jr., 247
Jeremiah, 270, 365
Joseph, 184, 270
John, 270
Margaret, 270
Mary, 270
Nathaniel, 263, 268, 270
Rachel, 27, 270
Sarah, 270
Thomas, 270
William, 123, 270
Mannon, Samuel, 344
Mapes, Joseph, 17, 213, 401, 402
William, 213
Marain, David, 84
Marcelis, Eden, 271
Elizabeth, 271
Eyde, 387
Hannah, 271
Harrijantje, 387

INDEX OF NAMES OF PERSONS 559

Mary, 271
Rachel, 271
Margerum, Henry, 220
Marinus, Anna, 387
  David, 5, 33, 70, 144, 159, 216, 334, 336, 387, 389, 450, 455, 456
  Rev. David, 445
Mariott, Abraham, 271
  Isaac, 271
  Jacob, 271
  Joseph, 140
  Sarah, 271, 398
Maris, Alice, 233
Marlatt, Derrick, 211, 443, 460
  John, 117
Marple, David, 275
  George, 192
  Mary, 275
Marsh, Abraham, 79
  Benjamin, 60, 79, 80, 272, 309, 479
  Charles, 69
  Comfort, 271, 272, 467
  Cornelius, 271, 272
  Daniel, 101, 194, 363, 384
  Elias, 271, 309
  Elizabeth, 271
  Esther, 271
  Jacob, 271, 272
  Jane, 271
  Jehial, 271
  John, 101, 310, 314, 320
  Jonathan, Jr., 98
  Joseph, 232, 271, 365
  Mary, 98, 271, 284
  Mephibosheth, 271, 272
  Mordecai, 185
  Noah, 263
  Richard, 271
  Samuel, 377
  Stephen, 271
  Susannah, 20
  Suviah, 271
  Thomas, 279
  Thomas E., 57
  William, 98
  Zeruiah, 272
Marshall, Catherine, 272
  Charles, 272
  Elizabeth, 272
  Francis, 178, 272
  George, 21, 274
  John, 324, 328, 353, 449, 450
  Joseph, 272
  Mary, 272, 471
  Rachel, 272
  Randall, 216
  William, 471
Marss, Jacob, 108
Martin, Alexander, 273
  Anne, 273, 274
  Azariah, 273, 274
  Benjamin, 49, 274, 275
  Catherine, 274
  Elijah, 273
  Elizabeth, 273, 274
  Ephraim, 184, 209
  Esther, 274
  Gideon, 273
  Henry, 434
  Hope, 275
  Hugh, 275
  Jacob, 273
  Jacob, Jr., 274
  James, 37, 49, 81, 237, 273, 274, 362
  James, Jr., 273, 274, 382
  Jane, 273, 274
  Jean, 273
  Jemima, 273
  John, 273, 274, 275
  John, Jr., 275
  Jonathan, 274
  Joseph, 275
  Joshua, 275
  Katherina, 275
  Kezia, 72
  Margaret, 275
  Martha, 273, 274
  Mary, 273, 274
  Moses, 270, 275
  Moses, Jr., 275
  Mulford, 275
  Nathaniel, 275
  Peter, 273, 274
  Peter, Jr., 49
  Phinehas, 273
  Rachel, 273, 274, 275
  Rhoda, 273
  Richard, 71
  Robert, 273, 365, 380
  Runyon, 275
  Ruth, 263, 274
  Samuel, 152, 273, 275, 402
  Sarah, 273, 274
  Thomas, 273, 275
  Valentine, 271
  William, 273, 274, 275
Mase, Joseph, 436
Maskell, Daniel, 31, 248, 249
  Thomas, 32, 57, 105, 143, 248, 249
Mason, James, 230
  John, 68, 143, 171
  William, 262
Massy, Peter, 314
Masters, Mary, 243
  William, 275
Mathis, Hannah, 18, 276
  Henry, 276
  James, 131
  Job, 276, 385, 405
  William, 276
Matlack, Abigail, 84
  Bathsheba, 277
  Benjamin, 84, 277
  Elizabeth, 168, 276
  Ephraim, 277
  Esther, 277
  George, 189, 276, 286, 287
  Isaac, 22
  Jacob, 133, 277, 338
  Jeremiah, 276
  John, 199, 276
  Joseph, 84
  Josiah, 276
  Lydia, 277
  Mary, 168, 276, 277, 286
  Rebecca, 84, 168, 276
  Sarah, 277
  Susannah, 168, 276
  Thomas, 276
  William, 276, 286
Mats, Hannah, 355
Matson, Abraham, 302
  Elizabeth, 277
  Hepsebath, 277
  Mary, 277, 302

Matthias, 173
Rachel, 351
Sarah, 277
William, 114, 277
Matthews, Bathia, 278, 290
  Daniel, 463
  Elijah, 277
  Elishaba, 278
  Elizabeth, 278
  Isaac, 175, 277, 278
  James, 384
  John, 277, 278
  Lydia, 278
  Martha, 278
  Mary, 277
  Richard, 136, 277, 278
  Samuel, 277, 278
  Thomas, 278, 410
  Col. Vincent, 74
  William, 209
Mattison, Aaron, 278
  Aaron, Jr., 187
  Catherine, 278
  Elizabeth, 278
  Jacob, 81, 82, 88, 165, 166, 187, 188, 229, 230, 235, 278, 338, 343, 378, 412, 460, 482
  James 278
  Martha, 278
  Mary, 278
  Rachel, 278
  Sarah, 165
Maxel, Hannah, 276
  John, 276
Maxfell, David, 278
  Elizabeth, 278
  John, 278
  John, Jr., 369
  William, 226, 228
Maxfield, Caleb, 278, 279
  Hannah, 279
  Isaac, 279
  James, 279
  John, 279
  Margaret, 279
  Mercy, 279
  Rachel, 278, 279
  Rebecca, 279
  Rhoda, 278
  Ruth, 279
  Samuel, 278, 279
  Susannah, 279
  William, 279, 427
Maxwell, James, 46
  John, 166, 280
  Thomas, 265
Mayer, Johan G., 73
Mayhew, John, 22, 122, 124, 157, 305, 308
Mayhise, Esther, 312
Mead, Isaac, 280
  Jacob, 280, 442
  John, 280
  Mary, 280
  Peter, 280
  Samuel, 201, 475
  Yelles, 280
Meadlis, Samuel, 332
  Hannah, 280
  Sarah, 280
Mecum, Eleanor, 287
  Jean, 161
  John, 11, 66, 123
  William, 326, 328, 441

Meek, Matthias, 361
Meeker, Abraham, 281
  Daniel, 280
  David, 313
  David, Jr., 480
  Gabriel, 370
  Isaac, 264
  Jean, 321
  Joanna, 280
  John, 280, 311, 316, 478
  Jonathan, 219
  Joseph, 288, 289
  Jotham, 280
  Mary, 281
  Moses, 281
  Nathaniel, 280, 480
  Phebe, 44, 280, 311
  Rebecca, 281
  Rhoda, 280
  Samuel, 96, 156, 419
  Samuel, Jr., 370
  Sarah, 280, 281, 323
  Stephen, 14, 311
  Susannah, 281
  Temperance, 64
Meeks, William, 105
Meghee, Amy, 281
  James, 51
  Mary, 281
  Safty, 51, 281
  Sarah, 281
  William, 281
Megie, John, 478
  (see McGee)
Mehelm, John, 160, 266, 372, 374, 390
Meirs, Joseph, 281
Meldrum, Abigail, 281
  John, 281
  Margaret, 281
Melick, Aaron, 393
  Andrew, 282
  Catherine, 282
  Christine, 282
  Christopher, 281
  Crastful, 139
  Elizabeth, 282
  Godfrey, 139, 261, 363
  Henry, 282
  Jacob, 282
  John, 282, 329
  Margaret, 139, 281, 282
  Mary, 282
  Mary C., 282
  Mary M., 282
  Peter, 363
  Sarah, 282
  Tunis, 282
  William, 282
Melker, Samuel, 364
Mellenot, Ann, 282
  Elizabeth, 282
  Margaret, 282
  Mary, 282
  Sarah, 282
Mellin, George, 218
Melrose, James, 375
Melvan, Ann, 282
  Daniel, 282
  Elizabeth, 282
  George, 282
  James, 282
  John, 282
  Margaret, 282

INDEX OF NAMES OF PERSONS

Rachel, 282
Thomas, 282
William, 282
Menish, Samuel, 144
Mercer, Archibald, 283
  Gabriel, 283
  Helen, 283
  Isaac, 283
  John, 283
  Lucy, 283
  Robert, 283
  William, 208, 300
  Dr. William, 80
Meredith, Elias, 326
Merrol (Merrell), Ann, 88
  Benjamin, 414
  Jean, 88
  Mary, 88
  Philip, 88
  Richard, 49, 283
  Timothy, 413
Merritt, Abram, 283
  Anne, 283
  Caleb, 283
  Isaac, 271
  Jacob, 169, 241, 283
  Levi, 283
  Rachel, 283
  Sarah, 271
  Thomasin, 169,241
Merry, Benjamin, 427
  Elizabeth, 283
  Job, 283, 284
  John, 283, 427
Mershon, Benjamin, 492
  Henry, 69
  Houghton, 201
  Joseph, 415
  Mercy, 69
Meshat, James B., 38
Messenger, Deborah, 284
  Hannah, 284
  Joseph, 284
  Mary, 284
  Sarah, 284
  William, 284
Messler, Abraham, 237, 284
  Antje, 284
  Carl, 284
  Catherine, 284
  Cornelius, 284
  Edward, 456
  Effie, 284
  Elizabeth, 284
  Hannah, 284
  Harmpie, 284
  Jacob, 284
  Jacobus, 19, 337
  Jane, 284
  John, 284
  Lena, 284
  Peter, 284
  Sarah, 284
  Simon, 284
Mets, John, 48
  Valentine, 355
Metzer, Jacob, 291
Meyer (see Myer)
Mickle, Elizabeth, 212, 277, 285
  Isaac, 11, 70, 125, 170, 227, 231, 285, 393, 426
  James, 285
  John, 180, 192, 286
  John, Jr., 389

Samuel, 136, 160, 227, 254, 285, 382, 470, 486
Sarah, 285
William, 137, 285, 450
Middagh, Deborah, 364
  Dirck, 285, 453
  Elizabeth, 285
  Engeltje, 285
  Isaac, 55
  Jacob, 364
  Margaret, 453
  Peter, 378, 492
  Tunis, 259, 260
Middelswart, Hendrick, 445
Middleton, Aaron, 287
  Abel, 51, 122, 221, 243, 285, 286, 289, 488
  Achsah, 286
  Amos, 231, 243, 289, 432
  Asa, 285, 286
  Christian, 286
  Elizabeth, 286
  George, 119, 171, 231, 286
  Hannah, 286
  Hudson, 287
  Jacob, 285, 286
  Joel, 286
  John, 56, 286, 287
  John, Jr., 285
  Jonathan, 285, 286
  Mary, 286
  Nathan, 285, 286
  Nathaniel, 286
  Patience, 231
  Phebe, 286
  Rachel, 286
  Rhoda, 286
  Samuel, 231
  Sarah, 286
  Thomas, 171, 286, 287
  William, 287
Mifflin, Daniel, 287
  Edward, 287
  Mary, 287
  Samuel, 45, 486
  Sarah, 287
Milbourn, Jonathan, 409
Miledolar, John, 282
Miles, Ann, 287
  Daniel, 127
  Francis, 66, 127, 303, 326, 328, 329, 450, 490
Millan, William, 428, 429
Miller, Aaron, 289
  Abigail, 348
  Alexander, 471
  Amos, 173, 288, 290
  Andrew, 288, 289, 483
  Andrew, Jr., 312
  Ann, 288, 290
  Bathsheba, 309, 336
  Benjamin, 194, 278, 289
  Catherine, 288, 290, 333
  Charity, 289
  Charlotte, 288
  Christian, 360
  Cornelius, 289, 385
  Daniel, 304
  David, 107, 372, 276, 377
  Ebenezer, 114 ,309, 486
  Ebenezer, Jr., 287
  Elizabeth, 288, 289, 290
  Experience, 342
  Frederick, 288, 423

Garret, 290
George, 288, 403
Hannah, 288
Henry, 282, 283, 290, 357, 471
Jacob, 288
James, 33, 176, 234, 400, 425, 442, 476, 490
James, Jr., 278
Jane, 288
Jemima, 278, 425
Jeremiah, 106
Joanna, 289
John, 9, 16, 157, 179, 219, 279, 288, 290, 300, 301, 321, 333, 342, 348, 362, 372
John H., 289
Josiah, 50, 68, 73
Lewis, 325
Margaret, 288, 290
Mark, 288
Martha, 289
Mary, 234
Mary A., 288
Matthias, 39, 45, 289
Michael, 113, 288
Moses, 479
Nathaniel, 283
Noah, 64, 348
Patience, 106
Paul, 40, 290
Phebe, 288
Rachel, 342
Richard, 289
Richard, Jr., 289
Ruth, 287
Samuel, 419
Samuel, Jr., 193, 263
Samuel, 3d, 377
Sarah, 290, 368, 479
Susannah, 288
Theophilus, 73
Thomas, 36, 141, 205, 432
William, 9, 108, 119, 141, 206, 243, 269, 286, 289, 290, 338, 357
Zeruiah, 323
Millidge, Thomas, 189, 229, 440
Millington, William, 358
Mills, Benony, 290
  Ephraim, 255
  Francis, 290
  Jacob, 192
  James, 320
  Jedediah, 87
  John, 320
  Jonathan, 145
  Joshua, 437
  Lois, 473
  Lydia, 290
  Mary, 290
  Nathan, 193
  Rachel, 473
  Richard, 290
  Samuel, 258
  Seley, 58
  William, 290
Miln, John, 464
Minear, Christion, 420
Minor, Lawrence, 325
Minthorn, Richard, 251
Minton, Jacob, 410
Mires, Isaac, 24
  Peter, 405
  (see Myers)

Misner, Adam, 290, 291
  Conrad, 291
  Elizabeth, 291
  Henry, 290
  Jacob, 291
  Margaret, 291
  Richard, 291
Mitchell, Alexander, 392
  George, 111
  John, 69, 138
  John, Jr., 153
  Joseph, 123
  Nathaniel, 215, 258
  Rachel, 240
Moffat, Benjamin, 484
  John, 57
  Rachel, 274
  Sarah, 274, 484
  Susannah, 484
Molenar (see Mulliner)
Molleson, Benjamin, 291
  Catherine, 291
  Gilbert, 291
  John, 291
  Sarah, 291
Monfort, Henry, 333
  Peter, 333
  Theodorus, 166
Monroe, John, 302, 354
  Mary, 302
Montanye, Abraham, 78
  John, 420
  Joseph, 490
Montgomerie, Alexander, 205, 292
  Esther, 292
  James, 292
  John, 292
  Joseph, 292
  J. V., 213
  Rebecca, 292
  Robert, 136, 205, 292, 444
  Sarah, 292
  William, 292, 410
Monton, Audery, 48
Moon (Moone), Elenor, 155
  Dr. Jacob, 292
  Martin, 292
Mooney, James, 457
Moore (More), Aaron, 290, 293
  Alexander, 281
  Amos, 293
  Amy, 293
  Ann, 116, 140, 292
  Augustine, 73, 229, 279, 293
  Azariah, 323
  Benjamin, 52, 69, 86, 125, 294, 363
  Catherine, 294
  Christopher, 293
  Daniel, 134, 164, 293, 399
  David, 293
  Edward, 5
  Enoch, 5, 143, 208
  Elizabeth, 49, 293, 294
  Frances, 397
  George, 293
  Gersham, 68
  Hannah, 294
  Henry, 82, 390
  Isabel, 471
  Jacob, 42
  James, 330
  Jane, 293

INDEX OF NAMES OF PERSONS 563

Job, 294
Joel, 379
John, 86, 126, 151, 207, 221, 293, 294, 297, 308, 323, 332, 385, 460, 471
Jonathan, 293
Joseph, 227, 274, 275, 294, 317, 413, 471
Kezia, 293
Lambert, 74
Love, 293
Martha, 486
Mary, 293, 486
Matthew, 481
Mercy, 71
Michael, 294
Miriam, 294, 354
Nancy, 293
Nathan, 78, 395
Nathaniel, 293
Patrick, 324
Peter, 134
Rachel, 293
Rebecca, 294
Richard, 75, 123, 332, 416
Robert, 297
Samuel, 54, 294, 296, 301, 363, 367, 395
Sarah, 293, 294, 348
Theophilus, 293, 328
Thomas, 43, 78, 100, 271, 274, 294, 354, 486
William, 152, 221, 232, 284, 293, 297, 471
Moores, Agnes, 62
Daniel, 185
John, 185, 317
Matthew, 152, 185
Moran, Mary, 294
Morckel, William, 350
Morehead, John, 450
Morehouse, Joshua, 371
Stephen, 251
Morford, Cornelius, 128, 352
Garret, 294
George, 294, 296
Jarratt, 410
John, 36
Joseph, 223, 295, 430
Lydia, 295
Margaret, 294, 298
Rebecca, 294
Sarah, 295
Thomas, 19, 294
Thomas, Jr., 319
William, 36, 295
Morgan, Anna, 47
Daniel, 47, 85, 156, 295
Dorothy, 295
Griffith, 202, 384, 478
Isaac, 295, 296
James, 47, 129, 295
Jane, 295
John, 295
Joseph, 90, 108, 192, 295, 296, 437, 477, 478
Margaret, 296
Peter, 332
Rachel, 107
Samuel, 296
Susannah, 106
William, 47, 129, 295, 296
Morphet, Thomas, 457

Morrell, Amos, 296
Daniel, 129, 296
Elizabeth, 220
Hannah, 296
Ieavsha, 296
John, 296
Jonathan, 163
Lasyor, 242
Mary, 296
Phebe, 296
Samuel, 296
Thomas, 296
Morrin, Alice, 296
Paul, 296
Morris, Amos, 297
Anne, 298
Asa, 265, 297
Benjamin, 98, 297, 298
Catherine, 297, 298, 438
David, 298
Elizabeth, 130, 296, 297
George, 298
George A., 298
Hannah, 128
Henry, 298
Isaac, 135
Jacob, 296, 298
James, 89, 298, 395
Joanna, 297
Job, 298
Joel W., 297
John, 250, 297, 298, 384
John, Jr., 56, 297
Joseph, 297, 298
Justus, 384
Leah, 473
Lewis, 297, 298, 319, 462
Lovel, 219
Lydia, 298
Margaret, 199
Martha, 305
Mary, 61, 297, 298, 462
Moses, 72
Nathaniel, 297
Phebe, 236, 298
Rebecca, 298
Richard, 297, 298
Robert, 130, 248, 298
Robert H., 223, 359
Roger, 61
Susannah, 298
Thomas, 297
William, 298, 408, 438
Zephaniah, 86
Morrison, Anne, 296
David, 299
Elizabeth, 296
Isaac, 299
James, 244
John, 298, 299
Judith, 296
Margaret, 296
Mary, 296
Matthew, 145, 296
Robert, 296
William, 368
Morrow, James, 212
Thomas, 266
Morse, Amos, 243, 272, 315, 467
Joseph, 436
Joseph, Jr., 310, 467
Robert, 9, 483
Morton, Andrew, 299
John, 299, 490

Thomas, 276
William, 87, 130, 214, 227, 256
Moseley, Thomas, 74
Moss, Abraham, 299
  Isaac, 17, 299
  John, 447
  Rebecca, 299
  Richard, 136
  Sarah, 299
Mott, Ebenezer, 299
  Elizabeth, 132
  Gershom, 110, 263, 332
  Hulda, 299
  James, 56, 199, 200, 311, 357
  James, Jr., 19, 200
  John, 110, 299
  Martha, 65
  Mary, 199
  Sarah, 299
  Solomon, 132, 242
Mount, Ezekiel, 457
  Frances, 299
  Francis, 110, 299
  John, 299
  Joseph, 300
  Mary, 20
  Rebecca, 75
  Sarah, 299, 300
  Thomas, 299, 201
  William, 75, 201, 457
Mounteer, John, 386
  Phebe, 338
Mowry, Bernard, 92
Muchmore, Catherine, 300
  Daniel, 300
  Lucy, 300
  Martha, 300
  Rebecca, 300
Muckelrath, Samuel, 254
Muirhead (Muirheid), Andrew, 69, 409, 466, 467
  George, 300
  Sarah, 300
  William, 197
Muisinger, Conrad, 300
Mulford, Aaron, 300
  Benjamin, 301
  Daniel, 66, 356
  Elizabeth, 32, 378
  Ephraim, 301
  Eunice, 301
  Ezekiel, 127
  Filathea, 301
  Hannah, 85, 255, 301
  Henry, 301
  Isaac, 6, 83, 301
  Jacob, 82, 143, 301, 372, 381
  Job, 50, 371, 427
  John, 159, 301
  Jonathan, 110, 207
  Lewis, 289
  Mary, 127, 301
  Moses, 301
  Nathaniel, 301
  Rachel, 301
  Ruth, 301
  Sarah, 301, 391
  Silas, 301
  Stephen, 32, 301
  Thomas, 301
Mullady, Charity, 301
  Samuel, 15
Mullen, Edward, 148
  Elizabeth, 302

John, 66, 302, 347
Joseph, 100, 126, 301, 302, 303, 435, 437, 482
Martha, 302
Mary, 301, 302
Meriby, 302
Mullica, Ann C., 302
  Erick, 302
  John, 302
  Rebecca, 302
  Sarah, 302
Mulliner (Molenaer), Antie, 291
  John, 132, 232, 270, 340, 358, 368
Mulock, James, 26, 137
  Priscilla, 303
Munson, Solomon, 82, 330
Munteer, Phebe, 338
Murchland, Elizabeth, 383
Murdock, Amy, 123
  Andrew, 123, 228
  Hester, 123
  John, 123
Murfin, Ann, 303
  John, 229, 303
  Joseph, 303
  Robert, 303
  Thomas, 303
  William, 229, 303, 385, 486
Murphy, Esther, 148
  James, 10
  John, 245
  Margaret, 14
  Mary, 303
Murrell, Ann, 303
  Levi, 139, 147, 347, 388
  Margaret, 303
  Mary, 303
  William, 303
Murry, Francis, 303
Musgrove, Aaron, 490
  Elizabeth, 154
Mutchler, Frederick, 355
Myers (Myer), Boston, 240
  Elizabeth, 241
  George, 355
  Isaac, 312, 371
  John, 242, 403
  Peter, 406
  William, 132, 226, 241, 242
  (see Mires)

N

Nailor, Elizabeth, 304
  Esther, 21
Nassel, Christian, 469
Natar, Mary, 212
Nawley, Sarah, 167
Neall, Tamson, 43
Neefus, Anna, 405
  John, 405
Neeley, John, 50
  Joseph, 50
  William, 50
Neff, Jacob, 329
Neighbor (see Nochber)
Neilson, James, 255, 304
  Mary, 304
  Nan, 304
  Samuel, 224, 304
  William, 260
Neirs, Christopher, 426
Neitzert, Ann E., 304
  Elizabeth, 304

INDEX OF NAMES OF PERSONS 565

Eve, 304
Herbert, 304
John A., 304
John W., 304
Peter, 304, 308
Nelson, Abraham, 304
  Anthony, 305
  Eleanor, 304
  Jacob, 304, 305
  John, 122, 250, 304
  Sarah, 304
  Susannah, 304
Nephew, James, 93
Nester, John, 315
Nevens, Margaret, 124
Nevill, John, 70
  Mary, 305
Nevius, David, 229
  Femmetie, 305
  Jacobus, 91
  James, 305
  Jannetie, 305
  Joanna, 305
  John, 305, 449
  Lena, 305
  Lucus, 91, 305
  Maria, 305
  Martinus, 305
  Peter, 93, 305, 412
  Sarah, 305
  Tobias, 305
  William, 284, 305
Newbold, Ann, 306
  Caleb, 99, 305, 306, 435
  Charlotte, 306
  Clayton, 205, 306
  Esther, 306
  John, 111, 170, 306, 360
  Martha, 306
  Mary, 305, 306
  Michael, 198, 306
  Rachel, 306
  Rebecca, 306
  Susannah, 306
  Thomas, 318
  William, 285, 306
Newby, John, 89
Newcomb, Silas, 34, 106, 341, 355, 474
  William, 255, 258, 317, 346, 382
Newell, Altia, 306
  Hendrick, 306
  Hugh, 269
  James, 170
  Dr. James, 306
  Margaret, 133, 306
  Peter, 181, 270, 306
  Robert, 133
Newham, Roger, 45
Newkirk, Abraham, 353
  Anna, 308
  Catherine, 237
  Elizabeth, 308
  Gerrit, 237
  Helena, 404
  Henry, 237
  Isaac, 308
  Jacob, 308
  Jannetie, 237
  Mary, 308
  Mathew, 122, 237, 308
  Rebecca, 308
  Sarah, 308
  (see Van Newkirk)

Newman, Deliverance, 306
  Emanuel, 306
  James, 149
  John, 306
  Joseph, 306
  Samuel, 306
  Thomas, 306, 368
Newton, George, 145
  Isaac, 29, 220, 410, 489
  John, 29, 307
  Joseph, 15, 109, 367
  Samuel, 100, 411
  Thomas, 454
Nicholas, Richard, 243
Nichols, Abigail, 307
  Humphrey, 417
  Isaac, 307
  Lewis, 26, 307
  Moses, 307
  Rhoda, 379
  Richard, 74
  Robert, 307
  Sarah, 307
  Thomas, 221
Nicholson, Abel, 307, 308
  Abel, Jr., 307
  Elizabeth, 411
  George, Jr., 415
  John, 316
  Joseph, 307
  Mark, 307
  Mary, 42
  Rebecca, 520, 68, 192, 307
  Richard, 42
  Samuel, 190
  Susannah, 415
Nightingale, Esther, 244, 245
  Philip, 423
  Thomas, 25, 269, 272
Nipper, Leonard, 419
Nisbit, John, 480
Nix, Leonard, 490
Nixon, Allen, 117, 374
  James, 326
  Jeremiah, 115, 309
  Jeremiah, Jr., 115
  Rebecca, 183
  Reuben, 309
  Ruth, 309
  Seabornfoy(?), 309
  Susannah, 309
  Vavasus, 309
  William, 183, 309
Noble, Jacob, 164, 319
  Lydia, 89, 164
  Samuel, 89, 90
Noblit, Letitia, 309
Nochber, Anna M., 309
  Leonard, 309, 379, 419
  Marguerite, 309
Noe, Daniel, 309
  John, 82
  Marsh, 309
  Susannah, 309
Noles, Elizabeth, 232
Noorstrand, Jacob, 285, 419
  (see Van Noorstrand)
Norbury, Heath, 309
  Joseph, 53, 69, 176, 309, 311, 313, 321, 327, 368, 461
  Lydia, 309
  Mary, 309
Norcross, John, 68
  Joshua, 59, 66, 139, 265, 310

Judith, 310
Martha, 278
Rachel, 309
William, 278, 310, 343
Nordike, Hannah, 54
Norris, Abigail, 310
  Henry, 310, 406, 485
  James, 310
  Johanna, 310
  John, 314
  Margaret, 310
  Philip, 310
  Robert, 276, 385
  Sarah, 310, 491
  Thomas, 17, 255, 265
  William, 310
North, Rachel, 391
  Thomas, 56, 57
Norton, George, 174, 176, 356
  Maccy, 386
  Mary, 162
  Ralph, 302
  Selah, 92
Nortwick, Rachel, 135
Norwood, Andrew, 127, 208
Nowlan, Thomas, 213
Nutt, Ann, 215, 310
  William, 41, 180
Nuttman, Isaac, 310
  Samuel, 310, 383
  Sarah, 52

O

Oakford, Aaron, 70, 170, 182
  Samuel, 143
  William, 75, 116, 145, 155, 172, 196, 296, 309, 395, 469
Oakley, Abraham, 191
  Silvanus, 436
  Thomas, 361
Oatley, Edward, 339, 482
Odell, Jonathan, 30, 342
  Rev. Jonathan, 342
Ogborne, Abigail, 311, 421
  Ann, 311
  Caleb, 43
  Elizabeth, 311
  Hannah, 311
  John, 310
  Mary, 310, 311
  Samuel, 311
  Sarah, 311
  William, 311
Ogden, Aaron, 312
  Abigail, 311, 313
  Abraham, 171, 283, 312, 456
  Amos, 311, 312
  Barnet, 312
  Benjamin, 312
  David, 13, 27, 180, 257, 260, 298, 307, 310, 311, 312, 313, 375, 487
  David, Jr., 312
  Elizabeth, 311, 313, 457, 475
  Emma, 311
  Esther, 311
  Eunice, 212
  Ezekiel, 14
  Gabriel, 222, 311, 312, 434
  Garabrant, 312
  Gilbert, 311
  Grais, 311
  Henry, 312
  Isaac, 283, 307, 371
  Isaac, Jr., 206
  Jacob, 221, 312
  Jason, 313
  Jeremiah, 313
  John, 14, 16, 23, 37, 64, 219, 222, 311, 312, 315
  John, Jr., 14
  John C., 313
  John, 3rd, 375
  Joseph, 52, 105, 224, 257, 280, 309, 311, 312, 313, 321, 327, 368, 371, 378
  Josiah, 307, 312
  Justus S., 311
  Lewis, 88, 141, 217, 225, 256, 264, 403, 434, 448, 457
  Mary, 207, 226, 280, 311, 312, 313, 372, 378
  Matthias, 339, 372, 373
  Moses, 312
  Nancy, 311
  Nathan, 311
  Nathaniel, 257, 310
  Norton, 311
  Phebe, 313
  Robert, 14, 37, 43, 55, 108, 151, 226, 280, 311, 312, 315, 319, 335, 339, 388 391, 478, 479
  Robert, Jr., 108, 224, 313, 339
  Ruth, 224
  Samuel, 178, 219, 315, 339, 372, 379, 472, 480
  Sarah, 37, 311
  Stephen, 64, 312, 473, 475
  Uzal, 256, 375
  Uzal, Jr., 222, 457
Ogilvie, William, 247
Ogletree, Sarah, 110
O'Harra (O'Harrowe), Dennis, 469, 471
  Elizabeth, 471
  George, 25
  James, 25
  Margaret, 471
  Mary, 469
  Matthew, 471
Okeson, Samuel, 34
Olden, Abigail, 314
  Amy, 314
  Ann, 313
  Barsheba, 313, 314
  Benjamin, 203, 314
  Catherine, 314
  David, 313, 314
  James, 314
  John, 313, 314
  Joseph, 93, 172, 313, 314, 329, 393, 412, 415
  Samuel, 313
  Susannah, 314
  Thomas, 314
Oldis, Hendrick, 240
Oldwater, Jacob, 445
Oliphant, David, 85, 197
  Ephraim, 413
  James, 413
  Sarah, 413
Oliver, David, 314, 425
  Elizabeth, 314
  Ichabod, 314
  Jeremiah, 377
  John, 141, 310, 314
  John, Jr., 404

INDEX OF NAMES OF PERSONS 567

Jonathan, Jr., 405
Samuel, 87, 310, 314, 406
Sarah, 314
William, 233, 467
Zerviah, 314
O'Neale (O'Neill), Robert, 332
Constantine, 140
Opdyck, Catherine, 134
  John, 117, 134, 241, 281, 315, 350, 356, 366, 489
  Samuel, 134
  (see Updike)
Ormond, John, 417
Osborn (Osborne), Abigail, 315
  Anne, 256, 315
  Catherine, 315
  Desire, 315
  Elizabeth, 392
  Enos, 315
  Hannah, 74
  James, 315
  Jane, 239
  Jesse, 224, 315
  John, 92, 315
  Jonathan, 74
  Joseph, 172
  Moses, 315
  Nathan, 316
  Nathaniel, 315
  Richard, 399
  Samuel, 12, 130, 214, 239, 256, 315
  Sarah, 315
  Thomas, 37, 207, 315
  (see Ozban)
Osler, Barsheba, 316
  Hannah, 316
  Joseph, 316
  Mary, 316
  Patience, 316
  Samuel, 316
  Thomas, 316
Osmun, Joseph, 9
  Martha, 420
  Ziba, 132
Ouke (Oake), John, 337
  William, 50, 120, 127, 146, 169, 263, 337
Outwater, Anatie, 316
  Catherine, 316
  Elizabeth, 316
  Frans, 316
  Jacob, 316
  Jannetie, 316
  John, 316, 445
  Mary, 316
  Peter, 316
  Thomas, 316
  Trintie, 316
  Yueke, 316
Overfield, Peter, 316
Overturf, Sarah, 437
Owen (Owens), Daniel, 316, 372
  Hannah, 316, 372
  Jedediah, 316, 372
  John, 287
  Lewis, 17, 417
  Mary, 316, 372
  Prudence, 417
  Rebecca, 316, 372
  Sarah, 316, 372
Owman, James, 267, 480
Oxford, Charles, 164
Ozban, Jeremiah, 168

P

Pack, Hannah, 317
  Isaac, 317
  Jacob, 317, 435
  Mary, 317
  Ruth, 317
  William, 317
Packer, George, 297
Page, Ambrose, 317
  Daniel, 317
  David, 317, 345
  Elizabeth, 317
  Hannah, 317
  John, 317
  Jonathan, 317
  Joseph, 78
  Martha, 317
  Mary, 317, 345
  Thomas, 317
  William, 198, 317
Pagett, John, 39, 40
  Rebecca, 317
Pailaman, John, 106
Pain, Abigail, 317
  Deborah, 317
  Isaac, 317
  John, 50, 144, 317
  Mary, 317
  Ruth, 317
  Sarah, 317
Paiten, Mary, 466
Palmer, Andrew, 380
  Gershom, 138
  Margaret, 168
  Philip, 217, 395
  Philip, Jr., 395
  Thomas, 296
Pamely, Hial, 107
Pancoast, Aaron, 318, 319
  Adin, 102
  Ann, 89, 318, 319
  Benjamin, 318
  Caleb, 319
  David, 318, 319
  Edward, 59, 66, 319
  Elizabeth, 169
  Hannah, 318
  John, 318
  Joseph, 322
  Mary, 319
  Sarah, 319
  Shadlock, 21
  Thomasin, 89, 318
  William, 318, 319
Pangborn (Pangburn), Ann, 185, 292
  Samuel, 297
  Stephen, 134, 213, 292
Parcell (Parsel), Abraham, 82
  John, 18, 146, 442
  Mary, 18
  Rachel, 319
  Stephen, 365
  William, 315
Parent, David, 251
  Elizabeth, 180
  John, 398
  Mary, 251, 398
  Robert, 133
  Samuel, 133, 167, 299
Park, Anna, 319
  Ananias, 319
  John, 161, 239

Joseph, 482
Miriam, 319
Prudence, 319
Rachel, 319
Rebecca, 319
Richard, 476
Roger, 350
Sarah, 319
(see Parks)
Parker, Amy, 320
David, 151
Elisha, 220
Elizabeth, 17, 56, 320, 488
George, 237
Hannah, 320
Jacob, 320
James, 103, 155, 240, 319
John, 40, 319, 320
Joseph, 17, 18, 174, 228, 364
Joseph, Jr., 18
Joshua, 320
Josiah, 344, 474, 488
Margaret, 344, 488
Mary, 31, 151, 320
Miln, 252, 319, 320
Nathaniel, 446
Peter, 18
Samuel, 96
Samuel F., 155
Sarah, 320
Sophia, 341
Parkhurst, Samuel, 483
Parkinson, Thos., 13, 21, 22, 54, 158
Parks, Margaut, 20
Magdelena, 302
William, 299
(see Park)
Parlaman, John, 323
Parmley (see Pamely)
Parr, Aaron A., 320
Kezia, 5, 20, 307, 320
Nathaniel, 452
Peter, 320
Samuel, 307, 320, 412
Parrot, John, 68
Mary, 229, 321
Samuel, 36
William, 110, 207, 225, 321, 362
Parry, Joseph, 265
Parsonate, Mary, 101
Parsons (Parson), Chloe, 321
Deborah, 321
John, 37, 280
Robert, 177, 186, 419
Sarah, 186
William, 225, 321, 339, 436
Parvin, Josiah, 321
Lydia, 321
Matthew, 359
Phebe, 321
Sarah, 321
Silas, 204, 307, 359
Susannah, 321
Theophilus, 321
Thomas, 321
Pasel, Henry, 422
Passon, Francis, 41
Paterson (Patterson), Andrew, 74, 267
Catherine, 321
Elizabeth, 74
John, 297
Jonathan, 347

Magdalene, 141, 321
P. Joh., 397
Peter, 321
Richard, 265
Robert, 305, 353
Sarah, 430
Thomas, 347
William, 372, 374
Patrick, Hannah, 144
John, Jr., 144
Rebecca, 144
Patten, Hugh, 381
James, 445
Ruth, 338
Paul, David, 60
Elizabeth, 322
John, 193
Jonathan, 470
Josiah, 384
Mary, 384
Samuel, 322, 468, 477
Shivers, 384
Paullin, Henry, 22
Jacob, 122, 295, 353
Joseph, 255, 353
William, 37, 317, 371, 382, 401
William, Jr., 184, 317
Paxson, Henry, 30, 57, 66, 99, 100, 131, 349, 383
Thomas, 303
William, 233, 242
Paxton, Joseph, 322
William, 242
Payne, George, 184
Paynter, Henry, 337
Mary, 337
Peace, Joseph, 57
Peacock, Mary, 369
Peak, Sarah, 488
Pearsall, John, 33, 247
Phebe, 247
Pearson (see Pierson)
Peart, Samuel, 57
Peatey, John, 482
Margaret, 482
Peck, Abigail, 57, 322, 323
Constant, 219, 322, 323
Elizabeth, 322
John, 323
Joseph, 219, 321, 323
Rachel, 322, 323
Pecker, Catherine, 323
Christian, 323
Peter, 323
Peckwell, Henry, 267
Pedrick, James, 277
Martha, 227
Michael, 127, 227, 287
Rebecca, 140
Robert, 227
Thomas, 23, 140, 195, 401, 402, 441
Peek, Joseph, 177
Peer, Abraham, 323
Catherine, 323
Cornelius, 288, 323
Daniel, 288, 323
David, 323
Jean, 323
John, 323
Samuel, 323
Tunis, 323
Pegg, Joseph, 233
Pelton, Phillip, 247

Pemberton, James, 342
  John, 342
  Sarah, 392
Penier, Margaret, 244
  Peter, 267
Pen, Abigail, 140
Penn, William, 270
Pennington, John, 272, 324
  Joseph, 324
  Josiah, 324
  Margaret, 161
  Mary, 324
  William, 324
Penton, Abner, 232
  Elizabeth, 324
  Isaac, 145
Pepper, Jean, 425
  William, 157, 425
Peppinger (see Pittinger)
Perdon, Jacob, 443
  Lean, 443
Perkins, Ann, 62, 325
  Hannah, 325
  Jacob, 325, 338
  John, 325
  Joseph, 325
  Lucy, 62
  Mary, 39, 62
  Wright, 325
Perrine (Perine), Abigail, 367
  Daniel, 107, 342, 345
  Henry, 325, 349
  James, 201
  John, 6, 224
  Matthew, 325
  Peter, 7, 15, 342, 374, 481, 483
  William, 367
Perry, Page, 76, 299
Person, Affia, 97
  Daniel, 330
  Elijah, 330
  Elizabeth, 212
  Rachel, 397
  Rhoda, 97
  Zurviah, 325
  (see Pierson)
Peters, Catherine, 456
  Godfrey, 325
  Hassel, 449, 454, 458
  Henry, 325
  Isaiah, 59, 386
  John, 366
  Peter H., 456
  Phebe, 325
  Philip, 94, 360
  Rachel, 201
  Robert, 97, 314
  William, 343, 452
Peterson, Aaron, 157
  Alexander, 328
  Andrew, 53, 188, 366, 451
  Anne, 161, 326
  Anne, Jr., 161
  Christiana, 403
  Cornelius, 40
  Gabriel, 398
  Hassel, 334
  Henry, 239, 332
  John, 326
  Lucas, 326
  Magdelan, 326
  Mary, 128, 326
  Peter, 40, 166, 326, 412, 420
  Prudence, 326
  Rachel, 326
  Rebecca, 326
  Robert, 420
  Sarah, 326
  William, 204
Pettit, Aaron, 327
  Adam, 111, 158
  Amos, 19, 110, 120, 212, 293, 349, 448
  Andrew, 327
  Ann, 120, 186
  Ayres, 280
  Bartholomew, 442
  Benjamin, 91
  Charles, 120, 202, 424
  Deborah, 327
  Dinah, 327
  Elizabeth, 120, 327
  Hannah, 137
  Isaac, 327, 482
  John, 184, 185, 326, 327, 374
  Jonas, 326, 327
  Jonathan, 15, 16, 97, 327, 340, 385, 420, 469
  Mary, 326, 327
  Nathaniel, 19, 212, 272, 280, 293, 327, 332
  Obadiah, 186, 415
  Rachel, 327
  Sarah, 327, 442
  William, 327
  William, Jr., 409
Petty, Elias, 327
  Hannah, 178, 327
  Jane, 327
  William, 327
Pew, Abigail, 179
  John, 216
  Margaret, 328
  Samuel, 328
  Thomas, 328
  William, 328
Phares, Mary, 328
  William, 179
Pharo, Gervas, 67
Phillips (Philipse), Abigail, 328
  Abner, 328, 461, 467
  David, 328
  Elizabeth, 328
  Ephraim, 303, 388
  Feady, 328
  Col. Frederick, 61, 74
  Henry B., 61
  Hezekiah, 328
  Jesse, 328
  Johanna, 61
  John, 28, 65, 210, 244, 262, 328, 364, 433
  Joseph, 65, 120, 210, 328
  Joseph, Jr., 120
  Lydia, 328
  Mary, 328
  Matthew, 328
  Philip, 61, 412
  Rebecca, 328
  Richard, 328
  Robert, 328
  Samuel, 346
  Sarah, 328, 364
  Theophilus, 328
  Thomas, 244, 328
  William, 328
Philpot, Ann, 161, 328
  Catherine, 329

Charles, 357
Elizabeth, 490
Francis, 55, 161, 329, 452
John, 239, 328, 353
Joseph, 87, 329
Margaret, 329
Mary, 329
Samuel, 329
William, 55, 357
William, Jr., 53, 55, 366
Phineas, John, 205
Pickel, Baltheser, 329
  Conrod, 81, 82
  Henry, 329
Picken, Robert, 288
Pidcock, Rosannah, 329
Pidgeon, William, 65
Pier, Abraham, 448
Pierce (Perce), Andrew, 235, 322
  Elsie, 181
  Frances, 358
  Francis, 368
  Jane, 325
  John, 325, 358
  Joseph, 216, 256
  Levi, 216
  Mary, 165
  Rachel, 118
  Rosanna, 368
  Thomas, 181, 329
  William, 42, 62, 165
Pierson (Pearson, Peirson),
  Aaron, 330
  Abel, 322
  Abigail, 323
  Abraham, 323, 329
  Abraham, Jr., 335
  Amy, 323
  Ann, 324, 329
  Azel, 22, 79, 323
  Bethuel, 63, 183, 330, 392
  Daniel, 96, 394, 417, 483, 487
  David, 243, 323
  Elijah, 485
  Elizabeth, 324, 329, 330, 492
  Ely, 324
  Esther, 79
  George, 79, 255, 323, 490
  Hannah, 130, 329, 330
  Henry, 130, 315
  Isaac, 322
  James, 173, 322
  John, 118, 322, 329
  Josephus, 322
  Lemuel, 324
  Lucy, 264
  Marce, 323
  Margaret, 329, 330
  Mary, 322, 323, 365
  Phebe, 323, 366
  Reuben, 323
  Robert, 285, 325
  Ruth, 323
  Samuel, 422
  Sarah, 322
  Stephen, 327
  Theophilus, 222
  Timothy, 65
  William, 108, 323
  Wyllys, 40, 329
  Zebulon, 323
  (see Person)
Pike, Elizabeth, 331
  Hannah, 330, 331
  James, 112, 330, 331
  Janet, 330, 331
  John, 330, 331
  Joseph, 331
  Nathaniel, 331
  Robert, 330, 331
  Sarah, 331
  Thomas, 126, 152
  William, 330, 331
  Zebulon, 330, 331
Pimm, Hannah, 193
  Joseph, 193
  Lydia, 193
Pine, Lazarus, 252
Pinkerton, David, 369
  Henry, 195
Pintard, William, 474
Pinyard, John, 277, 331
  John, Jr., 302
  Martha, 277, 331
Piper, Daniel, 83
Piser, John, 169
Pitman, Elizabeth, 332
  Isaac, 109
  John, 251
  Uriah, 331
Pitney, Charity, 206
  James, 230
  Mary, 258
Pittinger, Mary, 259
  Richard, 457
  William, 324, 383
Plaininger, Matthias, 355
Platt (Platts, Platz), Adam, 332
  David, 157
  Mary, 67
  Moses, 290
  Philip, 332
  Susan, 332
  Thomas, 67, 310, 332
Playton, George, 94
Playtor, Elizabeth, 41
  George, 41
  Watson, 41
Pledger, Dorothy, 471
Plum, Mary, 332
Plume, Deborah, 332
  John, Sr., 280
  Robert, 280
Plumer, James, 183
  Joseph, 183
  Sarah, 183
Poag, John, 218
Poinsett, Peter, 332
  Susannah, 332
Polgreen, Catherine, 333
  James, 332
  Joseph, 333
  Susannah, 333
  Thomas, 35, 333
Polhemus, Albert, 246, 333
  Alkey, 333
  Anna, 333
  Annatje, 333
  Cornelius, 138
  Daniel, 333
  Dorothy, 333
  Eleanor, 333
  Hendrick, 333
  John, 114, 213, 333, 457

INDEX OF NAMES OF PERSONS 571

Margaret, 333
Mary, 333
Neiltie, 333
Tiney, 333
Tobias, 246, 269, 333
Poling, Cornelius, 492
Samuel, 9
William, 492
Pollard, Margaret, 11
Pond, Hannah, 334
Poog (Poock), Adam, 195
John, 161
Pool, George, 297
Robert, 223
Thomas, 312
William, 223
Poolly, Rebecca, 337
Pope, John, 44, 334
Joseph, 44, 334
Mary, 44, 334
Nathaniel, 44, 344
Porter, Andrew, 164
John, 343
Philip, 310, 405
Richard, 25
William, 25
Posson, Francis, 323
Post, Adrian A., 334
Adrian P., 455
Annatje, 334, 387
Arie, 334
Catherine, 334, 450
Cornelius, 70
Elizabeth, 61, 282, 334, 455
Francis, 156, 334, 450
Gerret, 159
Hannah, 334
Henry, 282, 454
Jacobus, 282, 334
Jacobus F., 455
Johannes, 334
Lena, 334
Martinus, 61
Mary, 282
Peter, 334, 455, 481
Sarah, 417
Potter, Abigail, 335, 431, 432
Amos, 14, 49, 311, 339
Ann, 335
Betsy, 335
Daniel, 49, 207, 278, 279, 384, 432
David, 335
Edward, 418
Elizabeth, 335
Guly (Julia?), 231
Joanna, 335
John, 97, 335
Joseph, 12, 49, 90, 215, 252, 334, 432, 433, 480
Mary, 311, 335
Nathaniel, 49, 334
Noadiah, 49, 254, 334
Phebe, 49, 334, 335
Reuben, 223
Rhoda, 432
Samuel, 49, 226, 335
Sarah, 23, 49, 335
Stephen, 28
Thomas, 74
Thomas, Jr., 335
Potts, Amy, 44, 51
Ann, 51
Jonathan, 473

Joseph, 281
Rebecca, 337
Stacy, 41, 271, 410, 439
Susannah, 335
Thomas, 134
William, 28, 51, 173, 204, 281, 334, 335
Poulson (Poulise), Gertrude, 335
Peter, 33, 336
Poulis, Jr., 159
(see Powelson)
Pound, Adoniah, 418
Benjamin, 238
Elizabeth, 398
John, 418
Joseph, 418
Powell, Abigail, 336
Ann, 336
Daniel, 194
Elizabeth, 336
Elkanah, 115
Gabriel, 403
Hannah, 336
Howell, 206
Isaac, 299, 336
Jacob, 158, 336
James, 336
John, 105, 336
Joseph, 194, 336
Margaret, 336
Mary, 336
Reuben, 336
Richard, 336
Robert, 125, 126
Samuel, 336
Sarah, 336
Powelson (Powelse), Harmpie, 284
Isaac, 454
Johannis, 284
(see Poulson)
Powers, Dinah, 110
Powner, Elizabeth, 131
Prall, Aaron, 337
Abraham, 337, 338, 427
Antje, 337
Benjamin, 337
Catherine, 337
Deborah, 475
Edward, 337, 356
Elizabeth, 337
Hansey, 337
Hendrick, 337
James, 337, 482
Jemima, 337
John, 337, 338
Mary, 337
Peter, 205, 337
Sarah, 337
William G., 337
Pratt, Elizabeth, 388
Samuel, 388
Samuel J., 388
Pray, Samuel, 468
Predmore, Benjamin, 338
Daniel, 338
John, 338
Mary, 338
Ruth, 338
Pressmill, Robert, 62
Preston, Hannah, 53
Isaac, 53, 177
Levi, 53

Samuel, 236
Sarah, 260
William, 70
Price, Ann, 148, 241, 369, 388, 419
  Daniel, 51
  Ebenezer, 262, 357, 478
  Edith, 148
  Elizabeth, 241
  Ellis, 338
  Ephraim, 371
  Francis, 369
  George, 487
  Hannah, 148, 402
  Isaac, 133, 338, 339
  Jacob, 338
  Johannah, 229
  John, 402
  Capt. John, 43
  Joseph, 200, 364
  Margaret, 488
  Margery, 285
  Mary, 285, 349
  Michael, 488
  Moses, 48
  Philip, 106
  Ralph, 369, 388
  Rebecca, 338, 339
  Richard, 133
  Robert F., 102, 285, 384, 407, 429, 434, 465, 470, 490
  Thomas, 111
  Thompson, 242
  William, 294
Prickitt (Prickett), Jacob, 21, 54, 138, 339, 380, 470, 476
  Jacob, Jr., 13
  Jane, 158, 438
  Josiah, 28
  Richard, 13
  Sarah, 339
  William, 321, 324
  Zachariah, 459
Pridmore, Benjamin, 447
Primrose, Henry, 79, 230
  John, 87, 249
Prince, Daniel, 333
Pritt, Rebecca, 241, 242, 339
Probasco, Hendrick, 342
  John, 355, 369
  Stoffel, 458
Prockler, Sarah, 123
Procter, John, 127
  Thomas, 451
Prosser, William, 192
Provoost, Affie, 339
  Catherine, 339
  David, 129, 363
  Gertrude, 339
  Samuel, 494
  William, 7, 337
Pruden Boice, 27
  Joseph, 74
Pryer (Prior), Abraham, 388, 417
  Andrew, 339
  Casparus, 417
  Jane, 339
  John, 339
  Lydia, 339
  Moses, 339
  Sarah, 339
  Simon, 339
  Thomas, 361
  Thomas, Jr., 200, 310, 361
Puckins, Andrew, 96

Pullen (Pulling), Deborah, 340
  Elizabeth, 340
  Jonathan, 101
  Tabitha, 189
  William, 288
Pyatt, John, 481
Pyfrow, William, 172

Q

Quackinbush, Nicholas, 135
  Reynier, 112
Quick, Abraham, 340, 457
  Cornelius, 132
  Geertje, 340
  Hannah, 340
  Jacobus, 340, 357
  Jean, 364
  Joachim, 340
  Maria, 340
  Neeltje, 340
  Peter, 155, 340
  Rachel, 340
  Tunis, 340
  Vrowtje, 340
Quicksall, Daniel, 340
  Jonathan, 281
  Thomas, 340
  William, 141, 340
Quigley, Isaac, 236, 308, 370
  Jemima, 370
  Robert, 38
  Thomas, 370
Quimby, Daniel, 340
  Elizabeth, 340
  Ephraim, 340
  Filenah, 340
  Isaiah, 340
  Josiah, 472
  Marcy, 340
  Phebe, 340
  Rachel, 465
  Samuel, 340
  Sarah, 340

R

Rabbit, Isaac, 36
Radley, Elizabeth, 80, 125
  Henry, 80
  Ichabod, 80
  John, 80
  William, 80
Raisur, Adam, 488
Rake, Johannes, 205
Rambo, Benjamin, 303, 354
  Elizabeth, 141
  John, 141, 142, 198, 354, 377
Ramsey, William, 52, 130
  Rev. William, 242, 327
Randall, Alexander, 56, 65, 187, 255, 377, 407, 450
  Ananias, 329
  Samuel, 237
  Silas, 255
Randolph, Benjamin, 341
  Elizabeth, 341
  Eunice, 341
  Jeremiah, 341, 426
  Joseph, 247
  Joseph F., 238
  Martha, 341
  Mary, 341

INDEX OF NAMES OF PERSONS 573

Nathaniel, 43
Paul, 270
Rachel, 341, 428
Rebecca, 43
Ruth, 341
Samuel, 43
Sarah, 49, 341
 (see Fitz Randolph)
Rappelje, Cornelius, 445
 Derick, 146
 Jeromus, 272
 Winen, 455
Rarick, Conrod, 12
Rasor, George, 158
Ratun, Peter, 369
Rawlison, John, 50
Ray, Abigail, 130, 313, 341
 George, 341
 James, 130, 257, 461
 Samuel, 295
 William, 79
 (see Rea)
Raymond, Peter, 341
Rea, Alexander, 37, 341
 John, 115
 Margaret, 115
 Robert, 469
 William, 37, 292
 (see Ray, Rhe)
Read, Alice, 342
 Charles, 44, 155, 341, 342
 Elizabeth, 342
 Israel, 342
 Jacob, 342
 Jean, 342
 John, 8, 16, 62, 124, 167, 168, 266, 420
 Joseph, 21, 34, 42, 46, 61, 138, 164, 182, 184, 233, 265, 276, 304, 318, 325
 Samuel, 8, 124, 342
 Susannah, 342
 Thankful, 266
 Thomas, 342
 William, 222
 (see Reed, Reid)
Reade, Mary, 343
Readford, Martha, 290
Reading, Alexander, 344
 Amy, 344
 Charles, 343, 344
 Daniel, 181, 343, 344
 Euphemia, 343
 George, 40, 41, 83, 84, 137, 155, 168, 213, 240, 260, 302, 324, 343, 344, 405
 George, Jr., 344
 Isabel, 343, 344
 John, 168, 338, 343, 344, 451
 John M., 344
 John R., 344
 Joseph, 324, 343, 344
 Mary, 343, 344
 Montgomery, 344
 Rebecca, 302, 344
 Richard, 326, 343, 489
 Samuel, 302, 343
 Thomas, 129, 168, 181, 272, 324, 338, 343, 344
 William, 344
Reckless, Anne, 57
 Elizabeth, 180
 Joseph, 179, 393, 488

Redden, John, 430
Redford, Lydia, 344
Redman, Hannah, 136
 John, 345
 Marcy, 345
 Mary, 345
 Thomas, 102, 136, 345, 389, 479
 Thomas, Jr., 81, 465, 479
Redstreak, Francis, 345
 Isabel, 345, 405
 John, 253
 Martha, 345
Reed, Aaron, 346
 Andrew, 131, 346
 Anna, 345, 346
 Bowes, 30, 88, 103, 248, 294
 Daniel, 345, 347
 Dinah, 346, 347
 Elizabeth, 178, 346, 347
 George, 93
 Henry, 347
 Isabella, 346
 Isaiah, 345, 347
 James, 345, 346, 347, 429, 492
 Jane, 346
 Jemima, 178, 345
 Jesse, 347
 John, 200, 346, 347
 Jonathan, 302
 Joseph, 302, 347
 Joseph, Jr., 24, 168
 Joshua, 346, 347
 Margaret, 347
 Mary, 345, 347
 Phebe, 345, 346
 Priscilla, 347
 Richard, 6, 201, 345, 346, 347, 463, 475
 Samuel, 345
 Sarah, 472
 William, 347, 400
 (see Read, Reid)
Reeder, Elizabeth, 347
 Jacob, 352, 409
 John, 347
 Joseph, 91, 138
 Rachel, 91
Reeve (Reeves), Abigail, 145
 Abraham, 321, 348
 Barzillai, 347
 Biddle, 350
 Damaris, 348
 David, 314
 Elizabeth, 29, 66, 347, 348
 Hannah, 347
 Henry, 348
 Isaac, 310
 Jane, 348
 John, 300, 330, 342, 347, 348
 Joseph, 347, 348
 Joshua, 348
 Josiah, 350
 Mark, 114, 347, 391
 Martha, 347
 Mercy, 310
 Micajah, 347
 Millicent, 347
 Samuel, 148, 347
 Sarah, 349
 Stephen, 348
 Tabitha, 348
 Thomas, 348, 359
 Walter, 348
 William, 348, 481

Reid, Abigail, 349
  Augustin, 12, 53, 344
  Dinah, 349
  George, 55
  John, 349
  Jonathan, 349
  Mary, 53, 349
  Obediah, 349
  Richard, 400
  Samuel, 53
  William, 349, 407
  (see Read, Reed)
Reily (Riley), Abraham, 349
  Alice, 349
  Charles, 296
  David, 371
  Dennis, 349
  Grace, 349
  James, 349
  John, 349
  Jonathan, 382, 423
  Mark, 474
  Robert, 349
  Sarah, 349, 423
Reinhard, Valentine, 329
Remer, George, 329
Remington, Clement, 350
  John, 350
  Mary, 350
  Moses, 255, 350
  Thomas, 350
Resler, Hontel, 41
Reticor, Jacob, 376
Reyney, Priscilla, 365
Reynolds, Anne, 351
  Autis, 66
  Broughton, 28
  Catherine, 54, 66
  Elizabeth, 351
  Evan, 88, 345
  Francis, 351
  Grace, 351
  James, 230, 310, 351
  John, 187, 254, 351, 486
  Jonathan, 356
  Mary, 351
  Michael, 351
  Patrick, 322
  Rachel, 351
  Rahab, 351
  Samuel, 225
  Sarah, 351
  Thomas, 59, 139, 185
  Valentine, 351
  William, 134, 351, 447
Rhe (Rhea), Aaron, 352
  Ann, 351
  Catherine, 430
  David, 351, 352
  Eleanor, 351
  Esther, 352
  George, 147, 250, 430
  Jannet, 351
  John, 351, 352
  Jonathan, 351
  Lydia, 352
  Robert, 31, 148, 351
  (see Rey, Ray)
Rhodes, Abigail, 299
  Charles, 351
Ribel (Ribble), Anne E., 352
  Anthony, 352
  John G., 352
  William, 352

Rice, James, 89, 297
  Thomas, 198, 299, 387, 471
Rich, George, 339, 352
  Mary A., 339
Richard (Richards), Ann, 352
  Charles, 352
  James, 352
  John, 37
  Joseph, 94, 325
  Martha, 352
  Mary, 352
  Moses, 256
  Thomas, 230
  William, 352, 441
Richardson, Edward, 400
  Jacob, 172, 244
  Jane, 61
  John, 185, 336
  John, Jr., 138
  Joseph, 336
  Temperance, 494
  Thomas, 40, 396
Riche, Ann, 409
Richman, Abraham, 352
  Benjamin, 353
  Harmon, 353
  Isaac, 352, 353, 461
  Jacob, 8, 22, 24, 32, 113, 124, 157, 178, 277, 296, 308, 352, 353, 403
  John, 116, 265, 295, 321
  Matthias, 353
  Michael, 321
  Rebecca, 353
  Sarah, 352
Richmond, Ann, 353
  Daniel, 353
  Rebecca, 324, 353, 450
  William, 353
Ricketts, Elizabeth, 353
  Jacob, 353
  James, 353
  John, 353
  Mary, 353
  William, 353
Rickey, Brice, 151, 154, 251, 254, 273, 314, 387, 409, 473
  Gideon, 269
  John, 132, 408, 481
Rider (Ryder), Christopher, 358
  Johannes, 458
  John, 150, 458
Ridgway, Abigail, 354
  Allen, 354
  Catherine, 354
  David, 232, 354
  Hannah, 21, 354
  Henry, 354
  Jacob, 354
  Jane, 68, 354
  Job, 65, 185, 354
  John, 170, 352, 354, 435
  Joseph, 232, 354
  Joseph, Jr., 354
  Lot, 128, 271, 283
  Martha, 191
  Mary, 68, 354
  Rebecca, 245, 354
  Richard, 354
  Sarah, 354
  Solomon, 68, 230, 354, 411
  Timothy, 67
  William, 169, 283, 347, 352, 354
Riggin, Nebuchadnessar, 97, 268, 314

INDEX OF NAMES OF PERSONS 575

Riggs, Abigail, 64
  Daniel, 330, 359, 360
  John, 425
  Joseph, 16, 27, 63, 235, 392
  Joseph, Jr., 100
  Reuben, 121
  Thomas, 234
Right, Catherine, 183
  George, 183
  Margaret, 183
  Rebecca, 183
Rightmyer, Jacobus, 355
  John, 355
Riley (see Reily)
Riling, Margaret, 355
Ringo, Cornelius, 205, 210
  Frances, 355
  John, 205, 210
Risdon, John, 211, 286
  Sarah, 286
Risler, Johantiel, 40
Risley, Ann, 355, 356
  Elizabeth, 355
  Judith, 213, 401
  Leah, 355
  Margaret, 119, 355
  Mary, 355
  Morris, 356
  Peter, 340, 355, 356
  Rebecca, 119, 356
  Richard, 119, 355, 356, 408
  Richard, Jr., 355, 356
  Richard, 3rd, 356
  Samuel, 213, 346, 370, 401
  Sarah, 355
  Thomas, 355, 356
  William, 370
  Zesiah, 355
  Zibiah, 355
Risnar, Poltis, 23
Rittenhouse (Rittinghousen), Anne, 356
  Catherine, 356
  Hannah, 356
  Isaac, 356
  Lot, 356
  Moses, 178, 356
  Peter, 340, 356
  Priscilla, 356
  Susannah, 356
  William, 340, 356
Ritticer, Johannes, 201
Ritzama, Rudolphus, 363
Road, Andrew, 39
Robart, Hannah, 451
Roberdeau, Daniel, 141
Roberson, Ann, 266, 370
  Elizabeth, 357
  Michael, 256
  John, 357
  Samuel, 357
  William, 266
  William, Jr., 357
Roberts, Ann, 357
  Bradford, 89
  Edward, 240
  Enoch, 28, 85, 86, 198, 211, 276, 287, 357, 366, 466
  Esther, 357
  Daniel, 359
  Hannah, 242
  Hugh, 221
  John, 137, 212, 276, 287, 336, 357, 417
  Jonathan, 53, 357, 366
  Joseph, 137, 276, 345, 430
  Joshua, 264, 276, 357, 466, 478
  Mary, 358
  Rachel, 85
  Ruth, 357
  Samuel, 183, 317
  Thomas, 54, 77, 441
  William, 179, 204, 449
Robertson, Experience, 404
  John, 106, 404
  Mary, 473
  Sarah, 106
Robeson, Acsha, 358
  Ann, 358
  David, 358
  Eleanor, 357
  Elizabeth, 358
  Capt. Henry, 292
  John, 358
  Jonathan, 358
  Joseph, 358
  Mary, 357, 358
  Maurice, 358
  Sarah, 76, 357, 358
Robins (Robbins), Aaron, 57
  Ann, 235
  Daniel, 41, 209, 235, 392
  Elisha, 358
  Ellen, 6
  Frances, 358
  Isaac, 41
  Isaiah, 69, 317
  Jeremiah, 107, 397
  John, 37, 119, 161, 235, 338, 358, 393, 395
  Jonathan, 131, 239
  Joseph, 110, 346
  Ledosah, 356
  Mary, 37
  Moses, 205, 292, 338
  Nathan, 69, 338
  Obadiah, 23, 64, 235, 472, 473
  Rachel, 24
  Richard, 88
  Sarah, 107, 235, 290
  Vincent, 235
  William, 131, 162, 235, 327, 418
Robinson, Anne, 359
  Beverly, 61
  Beverly, Jr., 61
  Charity, 359
  Daniel, 293
  Elizabeth, 381
  Eunice, 359
  Hannah, 98
  James, 50, 133, 148, 295, 401
  John, 111, 215, 306, 411
  Joseph, 359
  Mary, 321, 359
  Rachel, 359
  Robert, 144
  Sarah, 61, 298, 386
  Thomas, 207
  William, 51, 214, 253, 345, 427
Robords, Amos, 359
  Hannah, 359
  Ichabod, 359
  Jesse, 359
  Joseph, 359
  Phebe, 359
  Samuel, 359, 360
  Sarah, 359, 360
  William, 359

Rockefeller, Modlean, 93
  Peter, 195, 203, 210, 360
  William, 94, 360, 364
Rockhill, Acsah, 292
  David, 111
  Edward, 44, 146, 360
  Elizabeth, 44
  Hannah, 360
  John, 292, 360, 370
  Dr. John, 358
  Joseph, 102, 179, 360
  Robeson, 292
  Samuel, 318, 435
Rodenbach, Herbert, 167
Rodes (see Rhodes)
Rodgers, John, 360
  Margaret, 186
  Samuel, 360
  Thomas, 360
  Vesti, 21
  (see Rogers)
Rodman, Anna, 361
  Elizabeth, 361
  Isaac (?) P., 84
  John, 361
  Joseph, 361
  Margaret, 361
  Samuel, 361
  Sarah, 361
  Scammon, 361
  Thomas, 71, 322, 361, 369, 388
Roelofson, Elizabeth, 309, 439
  Lawrence, 439
  Roelof, 92, 308, 309, 329, 343, 379, 380, 439
Roenbaug, Johannes, 99
Roff, John, 365
  (see Rolfe)
Rogers, Agnes, 362
  Alexander, 362
  Amos, 362
  Benjamin, 170, 362
  David, 362
  Elizabeth, 362
  Henry, 362
  Isaac, 95, 189, 361
  Jabish, 339, 362
  Jecamiah, 86
  Jemima, 362
  Job, 59
  John, 362
  Joseph, 180
  Margaret, 362
  Michael, 205
  Nathaniel, 362
  Phebe, 362
  Ruth, 362
  Samuel, 108, 273, 332, 362
  Sarah, 362
  Simeon, 362
  William, 125, 212, 273, 339, 362
  William, Jr., 348
  (see Rodgers)
Rolfe (Rolph), Archibald), 362
  Elizabeth, 362
  John, 263
  Jonathan, 258, 259, 304
  Moses, 362
  Samuel, 249
  Sarah, 234, 274, 362, 363
  (see Roff)
Rollin, George, 150

Romeyn (Romine, Romaine), Barent, 444
  Claas, 316, 363, 424, 458
  Claes D., 234
  David, 363
  Gertje, 446
  Isaac, 19, 363, 444
  John, 363, 424
  Mary, 148
  Nicholas J., 444
  Peter, 10
  Roelof, 363
  Samuel, 227, 294
  Susannah, 444
  Thomas, 316, 444
Ronald, William, 447
Roneyans, Samuel, 348
Roome, Jacob, 363, 403
  Peter, 389
  Peter, Jr., 445
  Samuel, 445
Roosevelt, Cornelius, 363
  Elizabeth, 363
  Isaac, 363
  Jacobus, 246
  James, Jr., 462
  Nicholas, 363
  Sarah, 363
Rope, Magdalena, 363
  Michael, 363
Roree, Anthony, 368
Rosbrough, Jane, 363
  John, 363
Rose, Abraham, 219, 432
  Anna, 364
  Charles, 364
  Elizabeth, 308
  Ezekiel, 360, 364
  Hannah, 65
  Jarusia, 364
  John, 25, 335, 343
  Mary, 364
  Rachel, 364
  Stephen, 207, 363
  William, 82, 238
Rosekrans, Blandina, 364
  Aulidaw, 364
  Catherine, 364
  Daniel, 364
  Harmen, 75
  Hezekiah, 364
  John, 364
  Kerche, 364
  Lena, 364
  Solomon, 364
Ross, Abigail, 364
  Alexander, 66, 215, 269
  Andrew, 230, 365
  Daniel, Jr., 97, 357
  David, 289, 365
  Edward, 427
  Elizabeth, 25, 66, 108, 215
  George, 55, 365, 370
  Henry, 151
  Ichabod, 487
  James, 365
  Jane, 365
  Jehiel, 364
  Joanna, 364
  John, 25, 45, 226, 314, 402, 472
  John, Jr., 314
  Joseph, 314

Margaret, 365
Mary, 357, 365
Matthias, 365
Michael, 303
Nancy, 364
Nathaniel, 484, 485
Phebe, 365
Samuel, 386
Sarah, 364, 365, 472
Susannah, 364
Thomas, 76
Ursilla, 365
William, 76, 364
Rossell, Barzillai, 364
  Hezekiah, 364
  James, 266, 364
  Joseph, 364
  William, 364
  Zachariah, 30, 40, 139, 185, 296, 302, 364, 421
  Zebulon, 364
  (see Rozell)
Roth, Andrew, 172
Rounsavell, Rachel, 413
  Richard, 238
  Richard, Jr., 94, 203, 235, 323, 406, 413, 415
Rousby, Gesie L., 240
  William, 240
Rouse, Deborah, 366
  Elizabeth, 107
  Simon, 384
  Thomas, 102
Rowland, Deborah, 366
  George, 355
  Jacob, 366
  James, 72, 135, 252, 366
  John, 366
  Jonathan, 366
  Marvin, 366
  Mary, 366
  Samuel, 366
Roy, John, 64, 88, 151, 165, 172, 207, 266, 267, 319, 387, 473, 475, 490
Royal, Hannah, 366
Rozell, George, 132
  John, 132
  Thomas, 39
  (see Rossell)
Rubel, Anne E., 366
  Anthony, 366
  John G., 366
  William, 366
Rubert, John, 187
Ruckman, James, 327
  Thomas, 67
Ruddarow, Joseph, 366
  Joshua, 366
  Samuel, 366
  Susannah, 366
Ruddock, William, 46
Rudeus, John, 353
Rue, Abigail, 367
  Ann, 367
  Eleanor, 367
  Elizabeth, 367
  Ellen, 367
  James, 367
  John, 367
  Joseph, 367
  Margaret, 367
  Mary, 367
  Mathias, 367

Mathew, 134, 367
Rachel, 367
Sarah, 367
William, 109, 134, 367
Ruelofsen (see Roelofson)
Ruff, John, 368
Rumford, Mary, 35
Rumsey, Benjamin, 367
  Daniel, 367
  Elizabeth, 367
  Grace, 367
  Hannah, 367
  Mary, 367
  Prudence, 367
  Rebecca, 367
  Robert, 367
  Susannah, 367
Runard, William, 446
Runk, Ann, 360
Runkle, Abram, 142
Runnels, Joseph, 200
Runyon, Absolom, 368
  Anne, 291
  Benjamin, 247
  Catherine, 368
  Elias, 71
  Elizabeth, 152, 153, 368
  Ephraim, 121
  Mary, 291
  Peter, 247
  Prudence, 390
  Rachel, 121, 152, 153, 291, 368
  Reuben, 150
  Reune, 48, 247, 291, 314, 428, 468
  Reune, Jr., 291
  Rezia, 100, 331
  Richard, 109, 263
  Rosanna, 368
  Ruth, 291
  Sarah, 368
  Thomas, 92
  (see Roneyans)
Rusco, Sarah, 368
Rush, Anthony, 38
  Elizabeth, 266, 399
  Margaret, 368
  William, 27, 266
Russell, Abigail, 368
  Ann, 435
  James, 375
  Robert, 54
  Sarah, 368
  Timothy, 406
  William, 106, 214
  Zachariah, 225
Russeler, John T., 195
Rutan, Abraham, 37, 110, 369, 454
  Alice, 250
  Elizabeth, 369
  John, 369
  Mary, 369
  Peter, 369
  Rachel, 369
  Sarah, 369
Rutherford, Adam, 33
  Mary, 369
  Rachel, 178
  Samuel, 369
Ryder (see Rider)
Ryerson (Ryerse), Ann, 351
  Elizabeth, 351, 389
  Francis, 350
  Gertrude, 350
  George, 216, 350, 448

George F., 350
George I., 350
Hassel, 350
Jean, 350
John, 350
John F., 350
Lena, 350
Luke, 350
Martin F., 351
Ryker, Sarah, 164
Rynders, David, 339
Rynor, Andrew, 9

S

Sacket, James, 20
Saint Clair, Elizabeth, 370
  John, 370
Sale, Daniel, 80
  Elizabeth, 80
Salmon, Stephen, 370
  William, 204
Salnave, Anne, 370
  Elizabeth, 370
  Magdalen, 370
  Mary, 370
  Peter, 370
Salter (Saltar), Anna, 319
  Elias, 370
  Elizabeth, 370
  John, 370
  Joseph, 370
  Lawrence, 370
  Richard, 298, 370
Sanderlin, Mary, 371
Sanford, Abigail, 419
  Hannah, 371
Sarish, Stephen, 126
Sarry, William, 372
Satterthwaite, Mary, 111
  Richard, 286
  Samuel, Jr., 111
Saucuil, Elizabeth, 371
  Eve, 371
  Experience, 371
  Jonadab, 371
  Jonathan, 371
  Lancelot, 371
  Leah, 371
  Patience, 371
  Rachel, 371
Saul, Joseph, 441
Saunders, Ann, 338
  Isaac, 408
  John, 408
  Sarah, 408
  William, 45
Savage, Jane, 116
  Joseph, 150, 162, 163, 257, 394, 396
  Mary, 76
  Mary A., 116
  Robert, 465
Saxton, Daniel, 251
  (see Sexton)
Say, Thomas, 337
Sayre (Sayres), Abigail, 372
  Abner, 372
  Abraham, 371
  Ananias, 23, 105, 342, 371
  Ananias, Jr., 159, 301, 381
  Benjamin, 372
  Catherine, 372

  Cornelius, 194, 372
  Daniel, 245, 371
  David, 153, 245, 263, 274, 372, 378
  Ebenezer, 173, 193, 436
  Esther, 278, 372
  Ethan, 290
  Ezekiel, 226
  Ezra, 193, 372
  Frank, 372
  Frederick, 372
  Hannah, 372, 406
  Isaac, 372
  Jabez H., 180
  James, 371
  Jane, 372
  Jedediah, 372
  John, 371, 372
  Jonathan, 180
  Lydia, 180, 263, 371, 372
  Mary, 24, 371
  Moses, 319, 372
  Patience, 290, 342
  Phebe, 371
  Reuben, 479
  Ruth, 371
  Sarah, 372
  Thomas, 10, 40, 69, 75, 100, 104, 143, 144, 255, 397, 416, 464, 466, 479
Scanlang, Isaac, 372
  Rachel, 372
Scattergood, Caleb, 319, 334
  Janet, 334
  Jonathan, 319, 334
  Samuel, 388
  Thomas, 14, 318
Schandler, Andrew, 25
Schelleney, Isaac, 288
Schellenger, Cornelius, 175
Schenck (Schanck), Agnes, 374
  Anelty, 373
  Anna, 372, 374
  Catherine, 199, 373
  Cornelius, 373
  Garret, 372, 373, 395
  Geestje, 373
  Hendrick, 373
  Jacob, 93, 373
  Johannes, 374
  John, 372, 373, 374
  Koert, 372
  Margaret, 374
  Mary, 93, 372, 373
  Nellie, 372, 373
  Peter, 39, 91, 200, 295, 305, 359, 372, 374, 428, 429, 446, 457
  Peter, Jr., 321
  Roelof, 343, 373, 374, 431
  Sarah, 372
  William, 373, 427, 482
Schomp (Schamp), Claus, 372
  George, 374
  John, 196
Schooley, Asa, 374
  Avis, 374
  Benjamin, 374
  Frances, 491
  John, 111, 374
  Joseph, 69, 201, 303
  Margaret, 374
  Mary, 201, 376
  Michael, 71
  Rachel, 491

INDEX OF NAMES OF PERSONS 579

Robert, 374
Samuel, 374
Sarah, 340
William, 374, 462
Schoonhoven, Benjamin, 375
  Catherine, 374
  Ezekiel, 375
  Henricus, 375
  James, 375
  John, 374
  Joseph, 375
  Mary, 374, 375
  Nicholas, 374
  Peter, 375
  Petronella, 375
  Rachel, 374
  Sarah, 375
Schryner, John, 41, 352, 366
  Marlena, 352, 366
Schunamon, Harman, 10
Schureman, John, 127, 146, 155, 488
Schuyler (Schuiler), Arent, 12, 63, 133, 185, 375, 418
  Adoniah, 375
  Casparus, 61, 375
  Castina, 61
  Catherine, 375
  Gertrude, 375
  Hester, 375
  Isaac, 375
  Jacob, 87, 343
  John, 375
  Col. John, 353, 448
  Mary, 185, 375
  Peter, 375
  Col. Peter, 353
  Philip, 87, 142, 343, 375
  Rensselaer, 375
  Swan, 375
  William, 235, 308, 352, 366, 383
Scobey, Alexander, 6
Scott, Abraham, 322, 440
  Amy, 38
  Benjamin, 376
  David, 134
  Ebenezer, 314
  George, 376
  Hannah, 376
  Henry, 440
  James, 376
  Job, 376
  John, 104, 274, 376
  John B., 283
  John M., 153, 438
  Jonathan, 274
  Moore, 434
  Ralph, 376
  Richard, 376
  Samuel, 13, 38, 294, 376
  Sarah, 376
  Susannah, 119, 376
  Warner, 376
Scroggin, Ann, 143
  Jonah, 143, 375, 376
Scudder, Ann, 377
  Caleb, 150
  David, 207, 377
  Elias, 377
  Enoch, 28
  James, 377
  John, 107, 108, 193, 376, 377
  Joseph, 328
  Nathaniel, 295, 359, 469
  Dr. Nathaniel, 101, 295
  Phebe, 289
  Rebecca, 411
  Richard, 377
  Samuel, 39, 289
  Sarah, 107, 108, 377
  Thomas, 103, 376, 377, 484
Scull, Abel, 377
  Abigail, 262, 493, 494
  Catherine, 378
  David, 378
  Gideon, 214, 370, 401
  Hannah, 378
  Hezekiah, 378
  Isaiah, 402
  Jacob, 382
  James, 328
  Jean, 378
  Jemima, 378
  John, 262, 377, 378
  Joseph, 377
  Judith, 378, 401
  Martha, 377, 435
  Mary, 378
  Naomi, 377
  Nicholas, 378
  Peter, 378
  Phebe, 494
  Philip, 75, 378
  Rachel, 377, 378
  Recompence, 402
  Samuel, 378
  Susannah, 378
  William, 13
Seabrook, Daniel, 236, 294
Seaman, William, 281
Search, William, 356
Searing, Ann, 262, 378
  Benjamin, 421
  Eunice, 378
  John, 50, 262
  Joshua, 378
  Margaret, 378
  Samuel, 378
  Soloman, 378
  Theodosia, 378
Searle, George, 187
Sears, Ephraim, 113
  Jacob, 102
  Mary, 378
Sebring, Catherine, 378
  Cornelius, 154
  John, 355
  John, Jr., 179
  Leffart, 314
Sedden, John, 475
Seed, William, 60
Seeley (Seely), Abigail, 379
  David, 266, 327
  Ebenezer, 327
  Enos, 32, 178, 327, 336
  Henry, 106, 379, 427
  Joab, 391
  John, 379
  Magdalin, 379
  Naomi, 327
  Ruth, 327
  Tamer, 313, 327
Sergeant, Abigail, 392
  Isaac, 36, 391
  Jonathan, 265, 332, 392, 493
  Margaret, 267
  Rachel, 247, 248
  Samuel, 42, 162
  Sarah, 201

Servey, Johannes, 379
Servis, George, 462, 475
　Jacob, 324
　Johannis, 475
　William, 352
Sevel, Charity, 441
　Henry, 441
Severns, John, 466
　Mary, 108, 178, 210, 229, 355, 358, 362
　Theophilus, 108, 210, 229, 275, 310, 338
Severs, Robert, 444
Seward, Abraham, 379
　Daniel, 379
　Isaac, 379
　John, 379
　Obadiah, 162
　Phebe, 379
　Samuel, 379
Sewell, Richard, 243
Sexton, Peter, 457
　Sarah, 251
　(see Saxton)
Shackleton, Richard, 162, 357, 358
Shackley, Mary, 211
　Peter, 211
　Sarah, 211
　William H., 211
Shafer (Shapher), Elizabeth, 380
　Margaret, 380
　Patience, 380
　Susanna, 181
　William, 181
　(see Shaver)
Shankel, Adam, 379
　Anna M., 309, 379
　Anthony, 379
　Catherine, 379
　Henry, 309, 379
　John P., 379
　Leonard, 379
　Margaret, 379
　Mary E., 379
Shanny, Samuel, 361
Shanow, Lawrence, 70
Sharp, Adam, 26, 38, 56, 224, 477
　Allan, 35
　Ann, 38, 215
　Anthony, 257, 287
　Christian, 139, 282, 380
　Henry, 121
　Hugh, 476
　Isaac, 171, 380, 398
　John, 83, 139, 181, 195, 267, 282, 344, 363, 380
　Margaret, 282
　Mary, 136, 170, 257, 380, 397
　Peter, 380
　Rosanna, 380
　Samuel, 81
　Stogdel, 56
　William, 380
Sharpenstine, Christian, 131
　George, 117
　John P., 380
Shaver, Hannah, 344
　William, 344
　(see Shafer)
Shaw, Ananias, 258
　Carl, 309
　David, 115
　Edmond, 78
　Ephraim, 474

Henry, 347
Hezekiah, 268
John, 34, 43, 57, 99, 131, 147, 149, 163, 174, 175, 176, 190, 244, 264, 279, 361, 386, 399, 477, 494
Joshua, 147, 186, 244
Joshua, Jr., 422
Mary, 115
Nathan, 190, 244
Richard, 244, 278
Samuel, 276
William, 43
Shay, Rebecca, 337
Shearer, Daniel, 332
Shearman, Josias, 184
　Mary, 16
　Thomas, 473
Shee, John, 303
Sheldon, Millicent, 60
　Samuel, 60
Shepherd (Sheppard), Abel, 255, 309, 382
　Abraham, 382
　Anna, 382
　Ansel, 381
　David, 23, 37, 78, 143, 161, 176, 184, 258, 317, 324, 346, 381, 382, 425
　David, Jr., 371, 381
　Dickson, 309, 381
　Dorcas, 381
　Ebenezer, 381
　Eleanor, 381
　Enoch, 350
　Ephraim, 83, 105, 301, 350, 381, 472
　Eve, 382
　Furman, 381
　Hannah, 381
　John, 22, 114, 269, 301, 391, 422, 464
　Job, 301
　Jonadab, Jr., 37, 371, 381
　Jonathan, 219
　Joseph, 301, 381
　Joseph, Jr., 382
　Lovica, 382
　Lydia, 380
　Marah, 382
　Mark, 105, 114
　Martha, 176, 381, 422
　Nathaniel, 381
　Peter, 381
　Phebe, 381
　Philip, 371, 391
　Pleasant, 381
　Priscilla, 381
　Prudence, 381
　Reed, 381
　Rhuma, 382
　Samuel, 37, 382
　Sarah, 184, 381
　Silvanus, 381
　Temperance, 371, 381
　Thomas, 381, 382
Sheridan, John J., 275
Sherman (see Shearman)
Sherred, John, 142, 168, 242
　Robert, 13
Sherron, Roger, 9, 76
Sherry, Samuel, 100
Sherwin, William, 382
Shields, Archibald, 382
　Jane, 382

INDEX OF NAMES OF PERSONS

John, 382
Thomas, 363, 382
William, 382
Shimer, Abraham, 110
Shinn, Aaron, 383
  Abigail, 78
  Aquila, 57
  Azariah, 72, 382, 383
  Earl, 337
  Eli, 383
  Francis, 21, 79
  George, 359
  Jacob, 283
  Job, 78
  Joseph, 67, 261, 321, 383
  Lydia, 383
  Mary, 359, 383
  Restore, 359
  Samuel, 21
  Sarah, 383
  Solomon, 66
  Thomas, 21, 55, 66, 158, 184, 303, 380, 386, 459
  William, 78
  William, Jr., 283
Shipley, Martin, 121
Shipman, Charity, 383
  Jacob, 383
  John, 49
  Mary, 383
  Matthias, 355, 380, 383
  Nicholas, 383
  Phebe, 383
Shippey, Ishmael, 247
  John, 305
Shivers, Ann, 384
  Hope, 384
  John, 109, 197, 307, 320, 384, 478, 479
  John, Jr., 5, 20
  Josiah, 75, 89, 197, 384
  Letitia, 384, 434
  Samuel, 24, 72, 377
Shock, Andries, 492
Shoemaker, Amos, 171
  Benjamin, 171
  Isaac, 171
  Jacob, 171
  Mabel, 171
  Mary, 171
  Susannah, 171
Sholts, Valentine, 469
Short (Shoort), Abraham, 83
  Hendrick, 384
  Janetie, 384
  Johannes, 384
  Joost, 384
  Magdelena, 384
  Margaret, 384
  Rebecca, 19
  William, 384
Shotwell, Abraham, 232, 384, 429
  Benjamin, 315, 372, 384, 429
  Daniel, 460
  Jacob, 72, 272, 372, 384
  John, 376, 384
  John S., 398
  Joseph, 27, 151, 153, 232, 272, 320, 376, 384, 398
  Joseph, Jr., 151, 460
  Lydia, 274
  Mary, 384
  Samuel, 5, 233, 310, 314, 384
  Thomas, 155

Shoulder, Jacob, 384
  Magdalin, 384
  Susannah, 384
Shourds, Daniel, 17, 276, 385
  Elizabeth, 385
  Kezia, 17, 385
  Samuel, 94, 167
  Solomon, 385
  Stephen, 385
  Thomasin, 318
Shreve (Shreeve), Abraham, 360
  Caleb, 89, 102, 215
  David, 390
  Edith, 360
  Elizabeth, 171, 360, 390
  Grace, 102
  Joshua, 411
  Mary, 390
  Robert, 360
  Sarah, 390
  Thomas, 462, 491
  William, 89, 215
Shull, Boston, 382
Shumway, Nehemiah, 199
Shurts, Abraham, 83
Shute, Ann, 385
  Barnaby, 80
  Elizabeth, 379
  George, 385
  Henry, 385
  Isaac, 385, 441
  John, 385, 469
  Joseph, 35, 243, 385
  Mary Ann, 80
  Rebecca, 51
  Samuel, 51, 385
  Thomas, 385
  William, 342
Sickles (Sickels), Abram, 46
  Eegje, 46
  Elizabeth, 237
  Hartman, 456
  Jane, 417
  John, 172
  Rachel, 456
  Robert, 456, 458
  Sarah, 385
  William, 172, 237, 246
  Zacharias, 456
Siddons, Henry, 385
Sidle, Andrew, 200
Sigler, Thomas, 454
Silver, Aaron, 140, 170
  Anna, 140
  Lucy, 385
  Lydia, 385
  Margaret, 385
  Mary, 385
  Samuel, 195
  William, 385
Silverthorn, George, 368
  Susannah, 178
  Thomas, 149
Simcock, John, 233
  Nathan, 494
Simmons (Simons), Ann, 362
  Hannah, 386
  Joanna, 386
  John, 386
  Peter, 33
  Richard, 386
  Sarah, 386
  Thomas, 386
  William, 386

Simonson, Cornelius, 166
  Jan, 167
Simonton, Ephraim, 267
  Mary, 267
Simpkins (Simkins), Daniel, 159
  Hannah, 386
  John, 58
  Mary, 29
  William, 172, 386
Simpson (Simson), Abraham, 386
  Alexander, 339
  Ann, 181, 386
  Catherine, 387
  Edward, 296
  Eleanor, 386
  Elizabeth, 386
  Henry, 265
  James, 58, 162, 368, 386
  Margaret, 387
  Mary, 386
  Phebe, 386
  Samson, 259
  Sarah, 386
  Simeon, 386
  Stephen, 386
Sims, Elizabeth, 386
  James, 143, 380
  John, 386, 387
  John C., 332
  Joshua, 386
  Lewis, 386, 387
  Samuel, 16, 123, 198, 386
Sinclair, Elizabeth, 253
  Barbara, 449
  Joseph, 253, 449
Singer, Robert, 131, 229
Sinnickson, Andrew, 15, 161, 287, 303, 324, 326, 328, 329, 441, 449, 450, 490
  Elizabeth, 387
  John, 287
  Rebecca, 287
  Sarah, 287
  Sinnick, 161, 239, 329, 353, 450
  Thomas, 287
Sip, Annatje, 456
  Cornelius, 387
  Gerret, 387
  Helmich, 387
  Jannetje, 450
  John, 387, 456
Skeeles, William, 147, 369, 388
  Thomas, 388
Skellenger, Isaac, 289
  Rachel, 289
Skellinks, Cornelius, 422
  Lydia, 422
Skelton, Joseph, 93, 167, 300, 329
Skillman, Anna, 123
  John, 123
Skinner, Anne, 152
  Benjamin, 377
  Courtlandt, 248, 267, 291, 388, 389, 406
  Elizabeth, 388
  Gertrude, 388, 468
  John, 122, 388
  Jonathan, 206
  Nathaniel, 162
  Phinehas, 479
  Richard, 377
  Stephen, 223, 248, 267, 388, 389
  Thomas, 220, 223
  Thomas, Jr., 82, 220, 256, 306
  William, 388, 468
  Rev. William, 189
Skualboker, Philip, 477
Skyort, Martha, 5
Slacht (Slack), Cornelius, 315, 434
  Henry, 349
  Jane, 349
Slater, Jean, 389
  Mary, 389
  Peter, 389
  Samuel, 389
  Thomas, 389
Sleeper, Hannah, 85
  Jonathan, 359
Slengerlandt, Lea, 389
  Marritje, 389
  Nicholas, 389
  Peter, 389
Slit, Easter, 124
Sloan, David, 389
  Hannah, 389
  Henry, 267
  Jacob, 389
  James, 389, 426, 465
  John, 267
  Joseph, 389
  Mary, 389, 400
  Rachel, 389
  Robert, 389
Slocum, Peleg, 480
Slot, Johannes, 316
  Mary, 47
Sly, Catherine C., 228
  Christiana, 228
  Jacob, 51, 485
Small, Israel, 389, 390
  John, 389
  Jonas, 389
  Mary, 389, 400, 486
  Robert, 389
  Ruth, 389, 390
  William, 389
Smalley, Andrew, 274, 390
  Ann, 390
  Elisha, 218
  Elizabeth, 56
  Isaac, 390
  John, 56, 274, 390
  Jonas, 390
  Jonathan, 275, 390
  Joshua, 390
  Margaret, 390
  Mary, 390
  Prudence, 56
  Samuel, 55, 56
  Samuel S., 56
  Surviah, 56
  William, 55
Smallwood, Margaret, 77, 252
Smart, Margaret, 251
Smiley, John, 390
Smith, Aaron, 39, 303
  Abel, 386, 398
  Abigail, 312, 392, 394, 396, 401, 493
  Abraham, 54, 382, 391, 392, 398
  Andrew, 68, 206, 389, 391
  Andrew, Jr., 364
  Ann, 210, 391, 397
  Anna C., 393
  Anna U., 393
  Anthony, 297
  Apollos, 391
  Bardina, 395

INDEX OF NAMES OF PERSONS 583

Bethsheba, 397
Benjamin, 391, 397
Caleb, 391
Carmen, 262, 310, 396
Catharine, 94, 294, 393, 395
Charles, 391
Christian, 344
Christine, 392
Christopher, 222
Clark, 23, 75
Constant, 208
Constantine, 396
Content, 398
Daniel, 102, 149, 190, 218, 245, 361, 387, 392, 393, 394, 396, 397, 398, 443
Daniel, Jr., 232, 316, 341, 361, 388
David, 316, 350, 382, 391, 396
Deborah, 397, 443
Dorothy, 397
Eaton, 398
Edward, 416
Eleazer, 311, 312
Elias, 391
Elihu, 162, 191, 399
Elisha, 378
Elizabeth, 312, 347, 371, 391, 394, 395, 397, 486
Eve, 224, 245, 397
Experience, 393, 399
Ezekiel, 217, 393
Francis, 340
George, 113, 391, 470, 491
Hannah, 371, 391, 393, 395, 396, 397, 401
Henry, 87, 393, 396
Hezekiah, 114, 362
Hill, 362
Hiram, 391
Huldah, 87
Isaac, 369
Isaiah, 395
Israel, 394
Jabez, 48
Jacamiah, 49
Jacob, 174, 392, 398
Jacob C., 391
James, 7, 62, 210, 316, 387, 393, 394, 396
Jane, 391, 472
Jasper, 94, 155, 279, 343, 394, 412
Jemima, 391
Jeremiah, 316, 393, 394, 396
Jesse, 245, 316, 394, 407, 408
Job, 395
Jean, 394
John, 12, 14, 15, 45, 50, 99, 101, 133, 140, 149, 151, 152, 162, 172, 181, 197, 201, 206, 218, 236, 294, 344, 390, 392, 394, 395, 396, 397, 494
John A., 396, 397
John G., 393
Jonathan, 68, 149, 194, 337, 364, 391, 394, 395, 396, 399, 463, 468
Joseph, 101, 151, 157, 171, 210, 229, 244, 395, 397, 398, 399
Joshua, 394, 396
Joshua R., 341
Josiah, 345
Judith, 393
J., 117

Lewis, 473
Lucy, 381
Ludwig, 343, 392
Lydia, 262, 310, 392
Margaret, 393, 395
Marion, 397
Martha, 99, 310, 391, 392, 397
Mary, 163, 171, 218, 239, 345, 390, 392, 393, 396, 398, 399
Matthew, 395
Matthias, 392, 350
Mercy, 398
Moses, 163
Nancy, 398
Naomi, 399
Nathan, 53
Nathaniel, 296, 391
Nehemiah, 391
Noah, 213, 356, 407, 408
Obadiah, 49
Peter, 268, 393, 396, 425
Phebe, 218, 395
Rachel, 114, 393, 395, 398
Ralph, 87, 394, 408
Rebecca, 75, 76, 245, 312, 391, 394, 396, 397, 398
Richard, 197, 361, 391, 392, 393, 416, 439
Richard, Jr., 362
Robert, 120, 349, 397, 398
Robert, Jr., 361
Samuel, 34, 140, 167, 296, 370, 385, 391, 394, 395, 396, 397, 398
Sarah, 94, 106, 152, 210, 312, 341, 392, 395, 396, 397, 398
Silvanus, 397
Solomon, 259, 396, 398
Susannah, 395
Tallman, 51, 269
Thomas, 6, 99, 152, 175, 176, 190, 191, 219, 230, 391, 394, 396, 398, 434
Timothy, 15, 239, 258, 294, 310, 391, 415, 434
Walter, 147
Waters, 394
William, 126, 139, 147, 170, 210, 215, 228, 230, 251, 322, 383, 388, 392, 394, 397, 398, 405, 425, 480
William, Jr., 375, 421
William L., 271, 281, 310
William P., 43, 65, 66, 487
Zebulon, 97
(see Smyth)
Smock, Anne, 399
Charles, 55
Johannes, 399
John, Jr., 264, 298
Leah, 146
Maritje, 399
Smyth, Abraham, 399
Andrew, 99, 220, 304, 421
Benjamin, 399
Catherine, 399
Dolvus, 399
Dorothy, 399
Eupham, 220
Henry, 399
James, 439
John, 30, 43, 68, 103, 130, 151, 152, 220, 245, 248, 310, 315, 319, 376, 388, 389, 399, 421, 480, 494
Laurence, 220
Margaret, 220

Nancy, 399
(see Smith)
Snatterly, Mary, 150
  Michael, 445
Sneathen, Joseph, 178, 217, 289, 403
Snedeker, Isaac, 160
  Elizabeth, 236
Snell, Samuel, 214
Snier, Peter, 106
Sniter, Jacob P., 203
Snodgrass, Benjamin, 361
  James, 361
Snook, Alice, 360
  George, 399, 400
  John, 399, 400, 453
  Philip, 399, 400
  William, 399
  (see Snuke)
Snowden, Adelicia, 476
  David, 333
  Elizabeth, 332
  Hannah, 400
  James, 400
  John, 76
  William, 144, 400
Snuke, Ann, 360
  Elsie, 360
  John, 124, 158, 360
  Peter, 360
  William, 264, 360
  (see Snook)
Snyder, Anna E., 195
  Henry, 281, 489
  Jacob, 360, 462
  Mary, 400
  (see Sneider)
Sockwell, Elizabeth, 401
  Jonadab, 401
  Jonathan, 184, 381, 401
  Lancet, 401
Soden, Thomas, 447
Solegard, Mary, 74
Solomon, Jonas, 19
Somers, Abigail, 401
  Edmund, 401, 402
  Elizabeth, 401, 402
  Hannah, 401, 402
  Isaac, 401, 402
  Jacob, 401, 402
  James, 213, 402
  James, Jr., 401
  John, 401, 402
  Joseph, 401, 402
  Judith, 402
  Martha, 402
  Mary, 401, 402
  Rachel, 401
  Richard, 401, 402
  Sarah, 401, 402
  (see Summers)
Sooy, Nicholas, 9, 10, 398
Soper, Benjamin, 402
  Catherine, 402
  Daniel, 402
  John, 335
  Joseph, 18, 402
  Obadiah, 402
  William, 402
Sorency, Samuel, 286
Soullard, Elias, 369
  John, 161
South, Daniel, 34, 198, 201
  Edmund, 209

Johanna, 209
Joseph, 201, 418
Thomas, 447
Southard, Abraham, 290
  Amy, 402
  Elizabeth, 403
  Isaac, 258
  Job, 402
  Ruth, 318
Souther, Christina, 403
  John, 94, 403, 432
  Mary, 403
  Peter, 403
  Philip, 172, 323, 403
  Simon, 403
  Susan, 403
Southwick, Grace, 403
  Maham, 192
  Priscilla, 403
  Rachel, 403
  Rebecca, 403
  Samuel, 403
  Sarah, 403
  Solomon, 347
  William, 403
Soverill, Abigail, 403
Space, George, 139
  Peter, 124
Spader, John, 117, 144
Sparks, Henry, 119, 272
  John, 193, 216, 232, 272, 303, 325, 368, 382, 401
  Margaret, 104, 401
  Richard, 39, 272, 279
  Robert, 217, 403
  Thomas, 124, 178, 272, 323
Speeder, John, 117
  Wilhelmus, 483
Speer, Hendrick, 403
Spence, Henry, 439
Spencer, Joanna, 125
  Oliver, 121, 313
  Robert, 358
Spicer, Deborah, 403
  Jacob, 6, 13, 24, 35, 71, 72, 90, 155, 156, 176, 250, 262, 302, 331, 378, 382, 383, 403, 404, 435, 473, 477
  Judith, 403, 404
  Silvia, 403, 404
  Thomas, Sr., 404
  Samuel, 85, 192, 227, 307, 404
Spier, Abraham, 404
  Albertis, 404
  Amy, 404
  Barent, 336
  Benjamin, 404
  Catalintje, 404
  Echje, 450
  Geape, 83
  Hendrick, 404
  Jacob, 450
  Jessie, 404
  Johannes, 404
  Lea, 83
  Sytje, 404
Spinning, Benjamin, 76
  Ebenezer, 76, 253, 288, 289
  Edward, 288, 289
  Humphrey, 365
  Sarah, 436
Springer, Sarah, 405
Sprong, Sarah, 405

INDEX OF NAMES OF PERSONS 585

Sproull, Elizabeth, 405
  Robert, 7, 214, 223, 260, 399, 474
Sproutt, Rev. James, 391
  Sarah, 391
Squier (Squire), Abigail, 97
  Anabel, 481
  David, 311
  John, 397
  Jonathan, 97
  Nicholas, 481
  Rebecca, 311
  Thomas, 279, 316
  Zophar, 481
Staats, Abraham, 446, 457
  John, 457
  Peter, 446
Stackhouse, Elizabeth, 337
  Mary, 229
Stacy, Robert, 134
Stage, Antie, 78
Stanbury, Annijah, 405
  David, 405
  Isaac, 442
  Joshua, 405
  Josiah, 259, 405
  Margaret, 226
  Nathan, 405, 467
  Phebe, 405
  Polly, 405
  Prudence, 405
  Recompence, 105, 110, 278, 279, 280, 405, 442
  Robert, 405
Standley, Andrew, 119, 161, 321, 324, 345
  Valentine, 243
Stanten, Daniel, 136
Stapleford, Elizabeth, 35
Stapler, Hannah, 215
  Stephen, 215
Staples, Ahitophel, 360
  John A., 405
  John C., 405
  Mary, 360
  Thomas, Sr., 306
  Thomas, Jr., 306
Stark, Aaron, 166, 204, 406
  Abraham, 406
  Hannah, 406
  Isaac, 406
  Jacob, 406
  James, 406
  Sarah, 406
Starkey, David, 491
Starr, Eunice, 257
  John, 257
  Sarah, 384
Statesir, Mary, 406
Statham, Aaron, 406
  Amos, 406
  Deliverence, 406
  Hugh, 85
  Isaac, 406, 474
  Philip, 406
  Sarah, 406
  Zebulon, 406
Stebbins, Ebenezer, 409
Steelman, Andrew, 407
  Catherine, 407
  Charles, 407
  Deborah, 407
  Elias, 349
  Esther, 407
  Frederick, 402
  Isaac, 407
  James, 402
  Jemima, 407
  Jeremiah, 407, 408
  John, 119, 407, 408
  Mary, 407
  Peter, 407, 408
  Rachel, 407
  Rebecca, 407
  Sarah, 401, 407
  Susannah, 407, 408
  Zephaniah, 407, 408
Stegg, Angenitje, 363
  Isaac, 363
  John, 363
  Thomas, 363
Stein, John, 329
  (see Stine)
Stelle, Benjamin, 121
  Charity, 428
  Gabriel, 468
  Hannah, 381
  Isaac, 275, 390, 428
  Lewis, 365, 428
  Phebe, 428
  Thomas G., 20
  Thomson, 428
Stephens, Andrew, 252
  Isaac, 408
  James, 408
  John, 192, 408
  John, Jr., 417
  Mary, 136
  Rachel, 408
  Robert, 136
  (see Stevens)
Stephenson, Aaron, 219
  Jinnens(?), 231
  Joseph, 231
  Sarah, 219
  (see Stevenson)
Stevens, Annie, 408
  Benjamin, 408
  Catherine, 408
  Elizabeth, 408, 409
  Henry, 242
  John, 157, 223, 408
  Margaret, 145
  Martha, 408
  Richard, 155, 408, 409
  Sarah, 408
  Thomas, 408
  (see Stephens)
Stevenson, Augustine, 409
  Charity, 409
  Charles, 409
  Cornelius, 409
  Cornell, 154, 409
  Cornwall, 186
  Daniel, 24
  Deborah, 409
  Edward, 409, 420, 479
  Elithon, 409
  Elizabeth, 302
  Elizabeth, Jr., 242
  Hannah, 409
  James, 479
  Jane, 168
  John, 209, 233, 409, 479
  Martha, 51
  Mary, 186, 409
  Phebe, 409
  Rebecca, 168
  Robert, 409

Samuel, 241, 340, 432
Sarah, 409
Susannah, 409
Thomas, 241, 409
William, 129, 335, 398
 (see Stephenson)
Steward, Jane, 409
 John, 26, 180, 213
 Joseph, 61, 171, 286, 328
 Josiah, 180
 Margaret, 409
 Susannah, 180
 William, 180, 409
 (see Stuard)
Stewart, Alexander, 293
 Archibald, 168, 382
 Charles, 72, 168, 273
 John, 10, 55, 76, 190, 416, 417
 Lewis, 288, 323, 410
 William, 266, 273, 296
Stiles, Abishai, 365
 Anna, 410
 Bartholomew, 35
 David, 217
 Edward, 44
 Elizabeth, 410
 Ephraim, 366, 403, 410
 Henry, 404
 Isaac, 417
 John, 107, 410
 Jonathan, 87, 206, 312, 410, 440, 464
 Levi, 410
 Martha, 44
 Mercy, 366
 Richard, 29, 365
 Robert, 264
 William, 230, 417
Still, James, 375
Stillwell, Catherine, 410
 Elizabeth, 29
 Jeremiah, 355, 369, 431
 John, 138, 409, 410
 Nicholas, 147, 364, 404, 409, 410
 Richard, 93, 479
 Sarah, 381, 409
 Thomas, 431
Stine, Anne, 383
 John, 308, 383
 (see Stein)
Stineman, Catherine, 399
 Christian, 400
 Rodolfe, 399
Stinson, Archibald, 269
 James, 269
Stires, John, 187
 Mary, 187
Stirling, James, 30, 469
 Lord, 64, 184
Stites, Abner, 411
 Asenath, 411
 Benjamin, 78, 163, 175, 176, 190, 310, 494
 Benjamin, Jr., 442
 Chloe, 411
 Elijah, 150, 411
 Elizabeth, 149, 410
 Hannah, 218, 410, 411
 Henry, 410
 Hezekiah, 262, 338, 351
 Israel, 410
 John, 96, 98, 253, 279, 371, 410, 411, 419, 479
 Jonathan, 218

Margaret, 371, 411
Mary, 338, 411
Nancy, 411
Nathan, 176, 392
Providence, 411
Rhoda, 494
Richard, 175, 208, 386, 410, 473
Ruth, 301
Sarah, 410
Temperance, 410
Thomas, 218, 392
Dr., 338
Stivers, Samuel 456
Stockton, Abigail, 411
 Abraham, 411
 Amy, 241, 411, 412
 Ann, 411
 Benjamin, 411
 Carma, 411
 Daniel, 411
 David, 39, 411
 Elizabeth, 411
 Hannah, 411
 Job, 205
 John, 242, 292, 316, 411, 412
 Mary, 411
 Philip, 15
 Rachel, 415
 Rhoda, 411
 Richard, 39, 101, 108, 141, 411
 Robert, 205
 Ruth, 411, 414
 Samuel, 411, 412, 415
 Sarah, 411
 Thomas, 411
 William, 36, 411
Stoddard, Margant, 11
 Sampson, 11
Stogdell, Elizabeth, 248, 298
Stokes, Atlantica, 339
 Elizabeth, 202
 Joseph, 13, 386
 Joseph, Jr., 198, 463
 Joshua, 35, 85, 86, 202, 276, 277
 Josiah, 384
 Samuel, 160, 276, 437, 463
 Susannah, 313
Stoll, John, 188
Stone, Jeremiah, 412
 John, 89, 90, 127, 412
 Joshua, 412
 Mary, 230
 Rebecca, 230
 William, 62, 152, 325
Stonebanks, Thomas, 116
Stoothof, Catolina, 412
 Johannis, 423
 Wilhelmus, 423
Stort, Jacob, 463
Story, John, 338
 Thomas, 300
Stout, Abner, 415
 Anne, 270, 412
 Anthony, 270
 Benjamin, 185, 272, 379, 412, 413, 414, 415, 420
 Catherine, 413
 Charity, 68
 Daniel, 413, 414, 415
 David, 266, 270, 319, 414, 415, 457
 Capt. David, 194
 Elizabeth, 270, 412, 414
 Freegift, 413
 Freegift, Jr., 236

INDEX OF NAMES OF PERSONS 587

Hezekiah, 415
Isaac, 413
Jacob, 121, 415
James, 219, 413, 415, 420, 465
Jediah, 413
Jehu, 413
Job, 415
Johanna, 412
John, 69, 337, 412, 413
Jonathan, 413, 414, 415, 474
Joseph, 144, 412, 414, 415, 420
Col. Joseph, 415
Joshua, 413
Lydia, 270
Margaret, 413
Martha, 415
Mary, 412, 413
Nehemiah, 194
Noah, 415
Obadiah, 413
Rachel, 412, 413
Reader, 415
Rebecca, 413
Richard, 413
Ruth, 412, 413, 414, 415
St. Leger C., 414, 415
Samuel, 266, 414
Samuel, Jr., 194, 379, 414
Sarah, 412
Susannah, 415
Theodosia, 144
Wilson, 414, 415
Stoutenburgh, Jacobus, 237
Tobias, 415
Straight, Leonard, 393
Strang, Daniel, 464
Gabriel, 464
Laurance, 77
Strathem, Hugh, 301
Stratton, Aaron, 379
Benjamin, 416
Daniel, 54, 158, 329
David, 329
Elizabeth, 416
Fithian, 105, 156, 379
Isaac, 54, 221
Jonathan, 105, 366, 379
Joshua, 476
Levi, 52, 143
Street, Elizabeth, 85
Strempfel, Christopher, 195
Stretch, Aaron, 416
Daniel, 122, 255, 288, 323, 416
Elizabeth, 416
Jaley, 416
John, 55
Jonathan, 55, 416
Joseph, 416, 437
Joshua, 137, 416, 464
Martha, 416
Mary, 416
Nathan, 416, 464
Peter, 416
Rebecca, 416
Samuel, 55, 416, 464
William, 15, 119, 127, 345, 439
Stringham, Joseph, 363
Stroble, Tetrick, 12
Strong, Abraham, 236
Thomas, 194
Stryker, Barent, 416
Denyse, 445
Elizabeth, 416
Hendrick, 416

Jacobus, 284, 337, 355, 369
Johannes, 201, 333
John, 91, 445
Mary, 416
Peter, 91, 305, 340, 416, 483
Rachel, 416
Sarah, 284
Stubbines (Stubbins), Henry, 6, 190, 299
Mary, 417
Stuard, David, Jr., 105
John, 105
(see Steward)
Sturgis, Ebenezer, 218
Mary, 218
Nathaniel, 27
Rachel, 427
Stutte, Anthony, 39
Stuyvesant, Casparus, 417
Catherine, 417
Johannes, 417
Peter, 417
Style, Mary, 417
Sarah, 417
Stynmetz, Christoffel, 237, 387
Thomas, 480
Subbery, Peter, 195
Sullivan, Ann, 417
John, 417
Martha, 417
Mary, 417
Matthias, 417, 471, 472
Summerill, Sarah, 259
William, 79, 452
Summers, Isaac, 23
John, 393
Mary, 21
(see Somers)
Supplee, Isabel, 417, 418
Sutherland, Susanna, 47
Sutphen (Sutphin), Arthur, 93, 372, 457
Catherine, 238
Derick, 352, 457
Derick, Jr., 240
Eitie, 451
Eleanor, 166
Isaac, 240, 451
Jacob, 481
John, 114, 166, 450
Peter, 95, 334
Sutton, Abner, 418
Amariah, 290
Amos, 207, 418
Anne, 418
Benjamin, 433
Charity, 393
Daniel, 249, 419
David, 48, 76, 418
Rev. David, 270
Elizabeth, 341, 416, 418
Esther, 418
Henry, 418
Isaac, 465
Jacob, 418
James, 419
Jeremiah, 418, 441
John, 196, 274, 419
Jonathan, 109
Lois, 418
Mary, 418
Oswell, 23
Peter, 123
Philip, 418

588 NEW JERSEY COLONIAL DOCUMENTS

Priscilla, 418
Richard, 418
Robert, 419
Thomas, 6, 108, 209, 239, 278, 418
Yonnechy, 451
Zachariah, 249
Suydam (Sedam), Antje, 19
  Charles, 453
  Cornelius, 19
  Hendrick, 48
  Jacob, 300
  Mary, 146
  Peter, 169
  Sarah, 264
Swackhamer, Samuel, 237
Swain, Abraham, 211
  Anthony, 419
  Benjamin, 146
  Daniel, 145, 176, 177, 201, 301
  Elizabeth, 419
  James, 301, 473
  Judith, 401
  Rebecca, 315
  Richard, 175
  Silas, 301
  Zebulon, 128
Swallow, Jacob, 235
Swan, Jedediah, 442
Swart, Cornelius, 264
Swarths, Hans J., 419
Swartz, Frederick, 332, 419
Swayze, Amos, 83
  Caleb, 86, 312
  Israel, 16
  Jabish M., 419
  Margaret, 419
  Richard, 73
Sweeten, William, 77
Sweetman, Anne, 420
  Catherine, 420
  Henderson, 419
  Margaret, 420
  Mary, 419, 420
  Michael, 268, 419
  Thomas, 419
Swick (Swik), Catherine, 420
  John, 420
  Martin, 420
  Mary, 420
  Peter, 420
  Tunis, 420
Swimer, Adam P., 326
  Matthias P., 326
  Peter P., 326
Swine, Daniel, 420
Swing, Sarah, 115
  Lawrence, 420
  Margaret, 420
Sykes, Anthony, 285, 286, 306

T

Taber, Noah, 480
Tackerd, John, 439
Tagan, Martin, 412
Tagart, Jacob, 261
Talbert, St. George, 315
Talbot, Arabella, 420
  Catherine, 420
  James, 319, 350
  Thomas, 420
Talmage, Thomas, 64
Talman (Tallman), Benjamin, 335
  Gideon, 165

James, 11, 84, 193, 283, 421
Joseph, 146
Margaret, 393
Martha, 435
Peter, 134, 173, 223, 254
Stephen, Jr., 406
Tanner, John, 22
Tantum, John, 31
  Joseph, 182
  Mary, 491
Tappen (Tappon), Abraham, 129, 229, 230, 421
  Asher, 421
  Benjamin, 421
  Cecil, 421
  Hannah, 284
  Isaac, 72, 103, 476, 477
  Isabel, 421
  Jacob, 421
  John, 421
  Leah, 18
  Margaret, 421
  Mary, 18, 421
  Moses, 421
  Sarah, 421
  William, 421
Tapscott, William, 422
Tate, Andrew, 140
Tatem, Joseph, 45, 272, 287
Taylor, Aaron, 215
  Abigail, 421
  Ann, 422
  Anthony, 179, 306
  Catherine, 421, 422
  Daniel, 87, 422, 439
  David, 232
  Edward, 311, 313, 346, 373, 413, 422
  Edward, Jr., 421
  Elizabeth, 422
  Frances, 29
  Francis, 183, 191, 365
  Frederick, 139
  George, 147, 294, 311, 422
  Hannah, 154, 422
  Henry, 59
  Jane, 70
  John, 24, 51, 94, 126, 147, 154, 185, 200, 246, 298, 311, 317, 340, 359, 385, 389, 398, 422, 430
  Joseph, 421, 422
  Lawrence, 475
  Lucy, 205
  Lydia, 244, 422
  Marcy, 147
  Martha, 73
  Mary, 145, 340, 421
  Nathaniel, 294, 427
  Rachel, 51
  Rebecca, 413, 439
  Robert, 403, 435
  Samuel, 170
  Sarah, 340
  William, 18, 24, 221, 319, 352, 359, 415, 422
Teach, Adam, 137
Teats, Jacobus, 236
Teed, Andrew, 422
  Ann, 422
  Elizabeth, 423
  James, 422
  Phebe, 422
  Rachel, 422

INDEX OF NAMES OF PERSONS 589

Samuel, 422
Sarah, 423
Solomon, 422
Teel, Barbara, 423
  Catherine, 423
  Eve, 423
  Lena, 423
Teeple, George, 383
  Lucas, 73, 74
  Margaret, 383
Temout, Adam, 423
  Catherine, 423
  Charlotte, 423
  Conrad, 423
  Elizabeth, 423
Temple, Benjamin, 293
  Joanna, 293
  John, 293
  Sarah, 293
Tenbrook, John, 95
Ten Eyck, Abraham, 48, 423, 445, 455
  Andrew, 45, 239, 423
  Andres, Jr., 459
  Anthony, 135
  Ariantie, 423
  Conrod, 399, 449
  Koenraet, Jr., 40
  Elsie, 40
  Jacob, 334, 423, 481
  Jane, 423
  John, 122, 423, 459
  Mary, 423
  Matthew, 334, 423
  Neltie, 423
  Peter, 200, 334, 423, 481
Tennent, Catherine, 424
  Charles, 424
  Cornelia, 423
  Elizabeth, 423
  Gilbert, 423, 424
  James, 424
  John, 423
  Sarah, 423, 424
  William, 423, 424
  Rev. William, 101, 351
  Rev. William, Jr., 424
Terhune, Abraham, 428
  Albert, 114, 153, 424, 458, 494
  Anatje, 424
  Betty, 424
  Catherine, 234, 428
  Derick, 282
  Gerret, 91
  Gertje, 424
  Jacob, 424
  Johannes, 424, 444, 494
  Leya, 424
  Nicholas, 424
  Roelof, 436
  Stephen, 91
  Wyntje, 424
Terreberger, John, 423
  George, 124
Terrill, Abraham, 60, 97
  Amos, 97, 425
  Anne, 223
  Daniel, 404, 424, 425
  David, 315
  Ephraim, 43, 60, 97, 232, 314, 365, 424, 485
  Capt. Ephraim, 467
  Isaac, 424
  Jacob, 425
  John, 72, 79, 151, 331, 424
  Josiah, 97, 315
  Keziah, 97
  Lemuel, 425
  Mary, 425
  Nathaniel, 425
  Sarah, 371, 425
  Thomas, 95, 425
  William, 46, 223
Terry, Asbury, 425
  Ephraim, 425
  Hannah, 98
  Jeremiah, 425
  John, 162, 215
  Laura, 425
  Letcher, 425
  Nathan, 425
  Rebecca, 425
  Sarah, 425
  William, 98
Test, Abner, 425
  Benjamin, 107, 425
  Edward, 153, 382
  Elizabeth, 425
  Francis, 143, 425
  John, 155
  Letitia, 425
  Mary, 295
  Ruth, 425
  Sarah, 417
  Susannah, 75
  Thomas, 172, 397, 425
Thackery, Benjamin, 68, 102, 170, 425, 426
  Elizabeth, 425, 426
  James, 426
  John, 425
  Joseph, 164, 426
  Mary, 425, 426
  Stephen, 164, 425
  Thomas, 119, 161, 425, 426
Tharp, Anna, 426
  Benjamin, 298, 412
  David, 284, 426
  Grace, 243
  Ichabod, 284, 426
  Jannet, 426
  Joseph, 426
  Lois, 104
  Mary, 426
  Paul, 426
  Reuben, 426
  Sarah, 243, 426
  William, 358
Thatcher, Amos, 235
  Bartholomew, 209, 272
  Joseph, 209
  Margaret, 209
  Samuel, 249
Thibou, Dorothy, 341, 342
  Gerret, 375
  Jacob, 341
  Rachel, 341
Thomas, Abel, 128, 140
  Ann, 290
  Benjamin, 21, 61
  Benoni, 335
  Cornelius, 57
  David, 51
  Edward, 28, 383, 484, 485
  Elizabeth, 36, 426
  James, 452
  Mary, 339, 366, 450, 484
  Nathaniel, 246

Rebecca, 246
Robison, 484
Samuel, 366
Sarah, 225, 426, 440
Thomas, 101
Thompson, Aaron, 427
　Abigail, 427
　Andrew, 284
　Archibald, 455
　Benjamin, 172, 194, 284, 313, 331, 427
　Butler, 427
　Catherine, 427, 428, 462
　David, 36, 70
　Dorothea, 268
　Elizabeth, 280, 427
　Eunice, 64
　George, 455
　Hezekiah, 427
　James, 462
　John, 6, 111, 116, 167, 268, 428
　Jonathan, 111, 194
　Joseph, 172
　Joshua, 6, 279, 417, 449
　Marcy, 427
　Mary, 6, 116, 417, 427, 429
　Moses, 427
　Nathaniel, 429, 475
　Newcomb, 427
　Percilla, 427
　Samuel, 49, 228
　Sarah, 427
　Susannah, 427
　Thomas, 75, 76, 253, 284, 299, 371, 427
　William, 19, 70, 342, 428, 429
Thomson, Abigail, 143
　Alexander, 237, 428
　Barsheba, 428
　Benjamin, 428, 429
　Charity, 428
　Elizabeth, 428
　Frances, 429
　George, 428
　Hugh, 429
　James, 141, 236, 325, 428
　John, 30, 122, 198, 256, 274, 421, 428
　Margaret, 428, 429
　Mary, 428
　Rachel, 428
　Samuel, 420
　Sarah, 428
　Susannah, 428
　Thomas, 287
　William, 232, 390, 428
　(see Tomson)
Thorn, Abigail, 77, 430
　Abraham, 429
　Ann, 429
　Benjamin, 429
　Catherine, 429
　Elizabeth, 429
　Hannah, 429
　Henry, 89
　Humphrey, 429, 430
　Isaac, 429
　Jacob, 429
　Jemima, 491
　John, 19, 77, 204, 205, 215, 290, 429, 430
　Joseph, 41, 298, 429, 432
　Mahlon, 318
　Margaret, 398

Mary, 136, 137, 429, 430
Morris, 430
Richard, 434
Samuel, 429
Sarah, 429, 430
Thomas, 69, 231, 290, 307, 429, 430, 432
William, 156
Zaccheus, 429
Thornell, Anna, 152
　Benjamin, 152, 184, 275
　Jean, 135
　Robert, 135
Thornton, Catherine, 390
Thorp, Benjamin, 56
　Israel, 430
　Job, 430
　Norris, 248
　Thomas, 430
Throckmorton, Anne, 430
　Daniel, 431
　Hannah, 430
　James, 30, 466
　Jemima, 430
　Job, 294, 430, 431
　John, 166, 199, 431
　Joseph, 199
　Lewis, 431
　Mary, 430
　Miriam, 431
　Rebecca, 431
　Samuel, Jr., 441
　Sarah, 199, 430
　Susannah, 430
　Thomas, 120, 431
　William, 204, 431
Thurman, John, Jr., 363
Tice, Dedrick, 33
　Elizabeth, 431
　Jacob, 199
　John, 373, 374, 393, 431
　Peter, 328
　Rebecca H., 199
　William, 373
Tichenor, Jane, 360
　Jedidiah, 360
　Jonathan, 221
Tidd, Jacob, 188
Tieple (see Teeple)
Tietsoort, Jacob, 445
　John, 431
　Mary, 431
　William, 247
　(see Titsworth)
Tillinghast, Elizabeth, 62
　Joseph, 62
　Nicholas, 62
Tilman, Nicholas, 240
Tilshaver, Michael, 117
Tilsilver, John, 117
　Michael, 432
Tilton, Abraham, 432
　Amos, 406, 431, 433
　Daniel, 231, 431, 432
　David, 433
　Dinah, 433
　Elizabeth, 231, 431, 432
　Faith, 315
　Hannah, 19, 431, 432, 433
　Jedediah, 433
　John, 19, 431
　John, Jr., 433
　Lucy, 432

INDEX OF NAMES OF PERSONS 591

Lydia, 231, 431, 432
Miriam, 406, 433
Nathan, 19, 252, 432, 433
Nathaniel, 311, 431
Obadiah, 432, 433
Patience, 432
Peter, 19, 214, 431, 432
Rebecca, 19, 431
Rhoda, 231
Robert, 431
Samuel, 431
Sarah, 432
Solomon, 19
Susannah, 431
Thomas, 42, 431
William, 231
Timler, Margaret, 433
Tindall, Elizabeth, 433
  Isabel, 433
  John, 263
  Joseph, 433, 434
  Mary, 120, 433
  Sarah, 433
  Thomas, 120, 167
Tingley, Christian, 270
  Dorcas, 433
  Ebenezer, 433
  Elizabeth, 433
  Joseph, 270, 433
  Nathaniel, 258, 433
  Samuel, 433
Titsworth, Jacob, 247
  (see Tietsoort)
Titus, Andrew, 290, 434
  Ann, 391
  Benjamin, 290, 434
  Dennis, 467
  Ebenezer, 312
  John, 194, 239, 434
  Joseph, 434
  Mary, 434
  Philip, 253, 434
  Rebecca, 434
  Samuel, 290, 434
  Susannah, 434
  Thomas, 434
  Timothy, 239, 415, 434
Tobin, Sarah, 370
  Thomas, 339
Todd, John, 30, 62, 63, 491
  Joseph, 267
  Martha, 267
Toers, Anatje, 404
Tole, Richard, 252
  Sarah, 125, 480
Tomb, Hugh, 172
Tomer, Elizabeth, 468
Tomkins (Tompkins), Aaron, 434
  Edward, 377
  Hannah, 434
  Huldah, 434
  Isaac, 434
  Joseph, 434
  Michael, 221
  Moses, 78, 291
  Nathan, 434
  Phebe, 434
  Robert, 434
  Salome, 434
  Usel, 406, 434
Tomlins, Matthew, Jr., 58
Tomlinson, Ephraim, 434
  Isaac, 193, 252

Toms, Charles, 434
  Hannah, 434
  Michael, 434, 435
Tomson, Agnes, 25
  Anna, 178
  Elizabeth, 267
  George, 178
  John, 25, 80, 124
  Phebe, 178
  Sarah, 236
  Thomas, 346
  (see Thomson, Thompson)
Tong, Mary, 333
Tongrelow, Jane, 353
Tonkin, Bathsheba, 435
  Edward, 149, 301, 354, 426, 435
  Elizabeth, 435
  Israel, 435
  John, 435
  Joseph, 377, 476
  Kezia, 435
  Martha, 435
  Mary, 85, 435
  Samuel, 435
  Susannah, 435
Tooker, Abraham, 436
  Augustine M., 293
  Charles, 436
  Joseph, 92
  Mary, 436
Tossey, Hannah, 436
  Margaret, 436
  Rebecca, 436
  Sarah, 436
Totten, James, 436
  Jasper, 436
  John, 436
  Joseph, 436
  Mary, 436
  Patience, 436
  Rachel, 207
  Samuel, 436
  Sarah, 436
  Silvanus, 315, 436
Tousen, Frances, 164
  Ruth, 164
Towers, William, 186
Townley, James, 339, 436
  Matthias, 339
  Richard, 49
Townsend, Daniel, 91
  David, 419
  Jacob, 253, 345, 405
  James, 410
  John, 147, 277, 398, 404, 493
  Silvanus, 28, 174, 262, 378, 493
  Silvanus, Jr., 174, 346
  Tabitha, 149, 493
Toy, Daniel, 437
  Elias, 437, 477
  Elizabeth, 437
  Esau, 437
  Frederick, 437
  James, 437, 477
  John, 437
  Mary, 437
  Richard, 437
  Sarah, 437
Trackseller, Christian, 380
Tracy, Mary, 437
Trafford, Mrs., 20
Tranbles, Peter, 377
Trauberg, Andrew, 398

Treadway, Henry, 304, 486
  John, 437
  Kezia, 437
  Sarah, 437
Treadwell, Sarah, 30
Treat, Elizabeth, 487
  Samuel, 435
Trembles, Daniel, Jr., 467
Trenchard, Carter, 157
  George, 23, 471
  Mary, 287
Tresneau, Agnes, 438
Trimmer, Andrew, 205
  Anna M., 309
  Anthony, 438
  George, 235
  Mary, 205
  Matthias, 309
Tropt, Margaret, 201
Troth, Elizabeth, 137
  William, 438
Trotter, John, 140
Troup, Eleanor, 438
  Elizabeth, 438
  John, 438
  John, Jr., 438
  Robert, 438
  Thomas, 183
Trout, Elizabeth, 438
  George, 210
  Jacob, 438
  John, 438
  Margaret, 438
  Mary, 438
  Peter, 201, 438, 439
Trowbridge, Edmund, 11
  Lydia, 439
  Shubal, 439
Truax, John, 109, 367
Truesdal, Stephen, 186
Tucker, Catherine, 439
  Elizabeth, 386
  George, 358, 364, 439
  John, 365, 473
  Joshua, 320
  Mary, 439
  Ralph, 183
  Samuel, 168, 302, 386, 473
  Samuel, Jr., 94, 340, 493
  Sarah, 108
  William, 164, 439
Tudor, George, 289
Tufford, Adam, 439
  Catherine, 439
  George, 439
  Jeremiah S., 439
  Mary M., 439
Tuft, Brathwait, 439
  Broffet, 440
  James, 439, 440
  Jane, 439
  John, 439
  Robert, 439, 440
  William, 268, 387, 439, 440
Tullis, John, 182
Tully, John, 440
  Joseph, 440
  Martha, 63, 440
  Mary, 440
  Thomas, 440
Tunison, Anne, 399
  Cornelius, 145, 285
  Cornelius, Jr., 285
  Deborah, 291

  Phillip, 291
  Rebecca, 145
Turner, Alexander, 428
  Barsheba, 428
  Elizabeth, 428
  Hannah, 168
  Jemima, 179
  John, 67
  Margaret, 440
  Richard, 428
Tussey, John, 440
Tuthill, Samuel, 147, 293, 464
Tuttle, Abraham, 463
  David, 248, 440
  Deacon, 222
  Ebenezer, 440
  James, 440
  John, 206, 438, 440
  Joseph, 330, 440
  Joseph, Jr., 87
  Col. Joseph, 222
  Moses, 147, 440
  Rachel, 440
  Samuel, 440
Twentyman, Mary, 441
Tyler, Benjamin, 23, 50, 104
  Philip, 75, 100
  Samuel, 127
  William, 441
Tyng, Eleazer, 11
  James, 11
  John A., 11
  Jonathan, 11
Tyson, Thomas, 235, 311
Tyte, Grace, 441

U

Updike, Edith, 167
  William, 167
  (see Opdyck)
Urian, Hance, 187, 254
  Sarah, 441
Urmston, Hannah, 88, 266
  Lawrence, 441
  Thomas, 88
Usback, Johannes, 468

V

Vail, Daniel, 441
  James, 441
  John, 100, 441
  Joseph, 107
  Margaret, 441
  Rachel, 441
  Samuel, 441
  Sarah, 398, 441
  Thomas, 283
Valentine, Elizabeth, 442
  Ephraim, 442
  Hannah, 442
  Ichabod, 442
  Jonah, 37, 442
  Mary, 442
  Obadiah, 37, 442
  Phebe, 442
  Rachel, 442
  Rhoda, 442
  Richard, 478
  Sarah, 442
Valleau, Theodore, 113, 384
Van Aken, Abraham, 50, 455
  Abraham C., 471

INDEX OF NAMES OF PERSONS 593

Abraham I., 442
Cornelius, 471
Jacobus, 471
Van Allen, Catherine, 442
  Catherine J., 442, 443
  Eleanor, 442
  Garret, 442
  John, 442
Van Allman, Conrad, 455
Van Alstyne, Abraham, 443
  Catherine, 443
  Helena, 443
  Mathew, 443
  Sarah, 443
Van Arsdalen, Cornelius, 340
  Gerret, 340, 447
  Hendrick, 146
  Isaac, 146
  Jacobus, 305, 352
  Philip, 447
Vanatta, Benjamin, 451
  John, 108, 420
  John, Jr., 451
Van Blarcom, Alice, 7
  Ann, 282, 443, 448
  Anthony, 443
  Guisbert, 282
  Hendrick, 443, 448
  Isaac, 455
  Jacobus, 443
  John, 443
  William, 443
Van Bomel, Christofel, 115
  Gerrit, 115
Van Bossum, Harmanus, 334
  Philip, 334
Van Brackle, Alice, 199
  James, 183
  John, 58, 182, 395, 444, 450
  Obadiah, 53
  Samuel, 182
  Stephen, 400, 450
Van Brunt, Nicholas, 20
Van Buren, Abraham, 457
  John, 127, 132, 146
Van Burthuysen, Peter, 388
Van Buskirk, Abraham, 203
  Andrew, 112, 445
  Cornelius, 261, 456
  John, 443
  Lawrance, 112, 368, 404
  Lawrence L., 415
  Margaret, 443
  Peter, 443
  Thomas, 444
Van Campen (Van Kampen), Abraham, 117, 442, 444
  Benjamin, 444
  Cornelius, 459
  Isaac, 84
  John, 434, 444
  Moses, 444
  Rachel, 442, 444
Vance, Elizabeth, 444
  Kennedy, 37, 153, 369
  Margery, 353
  Patrick, 235
  Samuel, 471
  William, 444
Van Cleve (Van Cleef), Benjamin, 373, 394, 408, 444, 480
  Benjamin, Jr., 431

Capt., 480
Cornelius, 419
Derrick, 372
Eleanor, 444
Elizabeth, 444
Hendrica, 444
Jane, 240
John, 148, 408, 421, 444, 492
Margaret, 492
Martha, 489
Mary, 444
Philip, 489
Van Court, Elias, 16, 81, 154, 259, 274, 314, 453, 484, 490
  Michael, 332
Van Courtlandt, Augustus, 74
  Frederick, 74
  Jacobus, 74
  James, 74
  Philip, 353, 456
  Samuel, 456
  William, 353
Van Culin, John, 9, 449
Van Dalson, Gertrude, 237
  John, 237
Van Dam, Rip, 182
Vandehovar, Cornelius, 236
Vandelinda, Elizabeth, 375
  Geesje, 444
  Hendrick, 444
  Jannetje, 444
  Marretje, 237
  Roelof, 237
  Susannah, 444
  Uselche, 444
  Viche, 444
Vanderbeek (Vanderbeck), Abraham, 444
  Adriana, 445
  Andrew, 445
  Catalyntje, 445
  Conradus, 444
  Doritia, 445
  Elizabeth, 445
  Isaac, 31, 444, 445
  Jacob, 445
  Jaques, 423
  Martha, 166
  Mary, 423, 445
  Paulus, 31, 316, 444
  Rem, 166
  Urion, 444
Vanderbilt, Auris, 451
  Aurus, Jr., 451
  Jacob, 344
  Jeremiah, 458
  Ryck, 284, 442
  Sarah, 445
Vanderhoof, Catherine, 445
  Cornelius, 445
  Egbert, 445
  Elizabeth, 351, 445
  Fietje, 351
  Jacob, 445
  Jannetje, 445
  Joanna, 351
  John, 351, 448
  Joseph, 351
  Lawrence, 445
  Mally, 445
  Samuel, 351
  Sarah, 351

Vandermark, Peter, 374
Vanderripe, Elizabeth, 445
  Jane, 445, 446
  John, 446
  Letey, 445
  Mary, 446
  Mathias, 446
  Richard, 446
  Sarah, 445
  William, 445
Vanderpool, Apphia, 446
Vanderveer, Catherine, 446
  Cornelius, 399
  David, 492
  Femmetje, 446
  Jacob, 446
  Jacobus, 208
  John, 39, 208, 372, 446, 458
  Lawrence, 285
  Mary, 399, 446
  Tunis, Jr., 457
Vandeventer, Mary, 246
  Peter, 260
  Weinland, 329
Van Dewater, Henry W., 282
Vandolah, Peter, 221
Van Doren (Van Dorn), Aaron, 482
  Abraham, 154
  Ann, 374
  Eleanor, 147, 148
  Isaac, 56, 373, 374, 418
  Jacob, 374
  Jacob, Jr., 418
  John, 446
  William, 48, 446
Vanduyn, William, 154
Van Dyck (Van Dyke), Aart, 446
  Ann, 447
  Deborah, 243
  Dominicus, 446
  Elizabeth, 446
  Francis, 54, 448
  Gerretje, 40
  Hannah, 447
  Isaac, 447, 474
  Jacob, 132, 447
  John, 25, 32, 446, 447
  John, Jr., 40
  Margaret, 446
  Martin, 294
  Matthias, 447
  Nicholas, 448
  Peter, 236, 413
  Peter, Jr., 413
  Rachel, 236
  Roelof, 447, 454
  Simon, 25, 91, 447, 454
  Thomas, 127, 446
Van Emburgh, Abraham, 447, 448
  Adoniah, 448
  Ann, 448
  Elizabeth, 448
  Guisbert, 448
  Jacob, 448
  John, 448
  Peregrine, Jr., 296
  Simeon, 448
  William S., 449
Van Etten, Anthony, 55
Van Eydersteyn, Thadeus, 448
Van Fleet, Thomas, 260
Van Gelder, John, 394

Van Giesen, Catherine, 448
  Dirck, 449, 450
  Hendrick, 54, 282, 445, 448
  Joris, 363, 424
  Rachel 363
  Reynier, 29, 46, 424, 443
Van Gorden, Leonora, 448
Van Harlingen, Ernestus, 284
Vanhauman, Mary, 110
Van Hengelen, Cornelius, 39
Vanhist, Gertrude, 448
  Mary, 448
  Rynier, 9, 448
Vanhook, Samuel, 44
  William, 258
Van Horn (Van Horne), Abraham, 449
  Ann, 61
  Barent, 443, 449
  Catherine, 449
  Cornelia, 449
  Cornelius, 449, 492
  David, 61
  Elizabeth, 449
  Garret, 449
  Geertje, 449, 492
  Hannah, 449
  James, 449
  John, 70, 449, 458
  Leah, 449
  Margaret, 449
  Mary, 449
  Nelsie, 449
  Philip, 449, 353
  Sarah, 366
  Violetta, 449
  William, 366
Van Houten, Cornelius, 305, 450
  Dirck, 450
  Fytje, 450
  Garrebrant, 448, 450
  Helmig, 46, 450
  Hester, 216
  Jacob, 450
  Jacob J., 336
  Jannetje, 387
  Johannes, 450
  John R., 448
  Marritje, 46
  Robert, 450
Van Kampen (see Van Campen)
Van Kirk, Alice, 450
  Anna, 450
  Henry, 155
  James, 450
  John, 295, 450
  Matthias, 450
  Peter, 450
  Sarah, 450
  Stephen, 450
  William, 295
Van Leer, George, 104, 106
  Samuel, 106
Van Levy, Nelly, 451
Van Liew (Van Lewe), Cornelius, 483
  Dennis, 458
  Ida, 458
Van Mater (Van Meter), Abigail, 246
  Anne, 451
  Benjamin, 333, 451
  Catherine, 451

Charity, 451
Chrineyonce, 19, 246, 330, 381, 451
Cornelius, 246
Cyrenius, 185, 246, 333, 381, 451
Eitie, 451
Elizabeth, 240
Guisbert, 246, 451
Ida, 451
Isaac, 451, 352
Jacob, 246
John, 451, 454
Joseph, 295, 333, 366, 451
Joseph, Jr., 441
Mary, 53, 451
Nelly, 451
Richard, 451
Sarah, 373
Van Middlesworth, Hendrick, 451, 455
John, 145
Marritje, 451
Vanneman, Andrew, 120, 451, 452
Ann, 450
Christian, 450, 452
Daniel, 452
Darius, 90, 366
David, 426
Elizabeth, 452
Garret, 90, 450, 452
Hannah, 447
Isaac, 452
Joannah, 452
John, 451, 452
Joseph, 244
Margaret, 490
Mary, 451, 452
Peter, 452
Rebecca, 451, 452
Regina, 452
Ruth, 366
Sarah, 451, 452
Van Nest (Van Neste), Abraham, 145, 423, 455
Elizabeth, 453
Gertrude, 306
Hendrick, 216
Isaac, 84, 216
Jacob, 453
Jeronimus, 453
John, 47, 48, 201, 260, 451, 453, 459, 460
John, Jr., 423
Joris, 145
Judick, 260
Mardeleantie, 453
Margaret, 306
Peter, 47, 48, 145, 453
Ryneir, 48
Ryneir, Jr., 490
Sarah, 48
Susannah, 453
Van Vanders, 453
William, 306
Van Newkirk, Cornelius, 453
Gerrit M., 453
Jannetje M., 453
Paulus M., 453
Peter M., 453
(see Newkirk)
Van Norden, Tobias, 81
(see Van Orden)
Van Norstrand, Aaron, 492
Adrian, 284

Folkert, 492
Jacob, 48, 56, 145, 451
Lena, 284
Wyckoff, 492
(see Noorstrand)
Van Norte, Catherine, 160
Thomas, 160
Van Nortwick, Christian, 453
Folkertje, 145
John, 155
Martin, 454
Simeon, 453
Simon, 145
William, 145
Vannoy, Cornelius, 220
Van Nuys (Van Nuis), Isaac, Jr., 436
James, 340, 492
John, 446
Van Orden, Andries, 453
Antje, 453
David, 78, 453
Elizabeth, 453
Jacobus, 453
Jacomyn, 78
Jannetie, 453
John, 453
Leah, 78
Peter, 453
Rachel, 453
Wybreek, 453
(see Van Norden)
Van Ostrander, Jacob, 455
Vanover, Henry, 201
Van Pelt, Arthur, 454
Jane, 454
Johannes, 154, 438, 454
John, Jr., 454
Peter, 353
Sarah, 454
Tunis, 454
Van Ripe (Van Rype), Abraham, 83, 448
Altje, 454
Dirck, 5
Garret, 5
Garret Y., 455
Hendrick, 83
Jacob, 216
Johannis, 5
Margrietje, 83
Rachel, 454
Van Ripen, Christoffel, 463
Cornelius, 454
Derrick, 450
Garret, 454
Jacob, Jr., 454
Jeremiah, 454
John, 454
Margaret, 454
Vanriper, Altje, 456
Cornelius, 456
Margaret, 456
Van Sciver, Walter, Jr., 396
Van Sice, Jacobus, 417
Van Sickle (Van Syckel), Aaron, 239
Abraham, 454
Gysbert, 10
John, Jr., 117
Mary, 10, 239
Steintie, 117
Zacheriah, 369

Van Sklack, Anne, 351
  Isabel, 351
  John, 351
  William, 297
Van Sted, Hendrick, 423
Van Stee, Henry, 455
  Jane, 455
  Ruth, 455
  Wyntje, 455
Van Tuyl, Abraham, 43, 88, 160
  Isaac, 48, 55
  John, 54, 78, 120, 220
  Mary, 48
Van Veghten, Benjamin, 238, 283
  Dirck, 442
  Dirck, Jr., 146
  John, 5
  (see Veghte)
Van Vliet, Gerret, 378
Van Voorhees, Adam, 455
  Albert, 455
  Alice, 7
  Anatje, 234
  Elizabeth, 455
  Jacob, 237
  Jacobus, 8, 48
  John, 458
  Peter, 305
  Rachel, 455
  Zachariah, 436
  (see Voorhees)
Van Vorst, Cornelius, 456
  Gerret, 40
Van Wagenen, Antje, 455, 456
  Catherine, 455
  Elizabeth, 455
  Garret, 188, 455
  Gertrude, 450
  Hassell, 455
  Helena, 455
  Hermanus, 455
  Jacob G., 404
  John, 455, 456
  Lenaw, 455
  Leya, 455
  Manes, 450
  Nesje, 455
  Peter, 455
  Rachel, 456
  Sarah, 455
  Vroutje, 455
Van Wey, Annica, 446
Van Wickle, Nicholas, 300
Van Winkle, Anne, 263, 456
  Ariantie, 456
  Autice, 456
  Casparus, 83, 455
  Catherine, 456, 457
  Daniel, 456
  Francis, 448
  Gertrude, 456
  Henry, 454, 456
  Hillegond, 456
  Jacob, 334, 456
  Jacob S., 458
  Jannetie, 454
  Johannis J., 456
  John, 423, 450, 454, 456
  Joseph, 456
  Lydia, 456
  Maritje, 454, 456
  Michael, 153, 458
  Rachel, 456

  Sophia, 456
  Walling, 456
Van Wyck, Theodorus, 135
Van Zeyl, Evert, 233
Varck, Jane, 115
  John, 115
Vaughan, James, 201, 346
  Capt. Joseph, 201
  Mercy, 457
  Thomas, 123
Veal, Abigail, 457
  Elizabeth, 457
  Jemima, 457
  Sarah, 457
  Thomas, 457
Veghte, Hendrick, 451
  Jacamintje, 451, 457
  Nelly, 457
  Nicholas, 166
  Rynier, 451, 457
  Sarah, 451, 457
  (see Van Veghten)
Venable, Esther, 51
Venicomb, Ann, 59
  Francis, 271, 294
Verselius, George A., 406
  Mary, 51
  Thomas, 437
Ver Bryck, Barnardus, 445
  John, 260
Vert, Hendrence, 197
Vicary, Hannah, 417
Vickers, Joseph, 120, 305
Vliet, Simon, 492
  (see Van Vliet, Van Fleet)
Voght, Christopher, 81, 82
Valtin, 16
Vollert, Henry, 332
Voorhees, Abraham, Sr., 412
  Abraham, Jr., 412
  Albert, 284, 447, 457
  Andrew, 457
  Ann, 447
  Catherine, 457
  Cornelius, 196
  Crikes, 91
  Garret, 146, 164, 208, 455, 457, 458
  Gertrude, 457
  Hendrick, 20, 93, 457
  Isaac, 481
  Jaques, 39, 412, 416
  Jean, 457
  John, 333, 442, 457
  Koert, 196
  Lucas, 10, 25, 91, 229, 390
  Nelly, 458
  Peter, 93, 305, 373, 457, 458, 481
  Ruloff, 423, 457
  Sarah, 283, 457
  Stephen, 300
  William, 457
  Willimpy, 457
Voto, Paul I., 44
Vreeland, Abraham, 153, 363, 458
  Antje, 153, 443, 458
  Beletje, 458
  Catalynje, 387
  Christina, 363
  Claes, 46
  Close, 387
  Derrick, 450, 454
  Elizabeth, 458

INDEX OF NAMES OF PERSONS 597

Enoch, 153, 458
Garret, 46, 458
George, 40, 450
Hartman, 458
Helmach, 387, 443
Jannetje, 387, 456, 457, 459
John, 153, 385, 443, 458
Joris E., 455
Leya, 153, 458
Margaret, 456, 458
Michael, 72, 159, 216, 457, 456, 458, 463
Rachel, 153, 458
Sarah, 11
Vroom, Brachia, 459
Dorothy, 459
George, 458, 459
Hendrick, 458, 459
Jane, 455, 459
John, 122, 240, 419, 423
Maretje, 458
Peter, 240, 458, 459
Sarah, 458

W

Waddell, Henry, 163, 424, 439
Robert, 462
Waddington, Elizabeth, 459
William, 459
Waddis, William, 45
Wade, Benjamin, 425, 459
Daniel, 23, 459
Joseph, 365, 427
Mary, 49
Nehemiah, 50, 55
Robert, 55
Sarah, 459
Wagoner, Francis, 485
William, 433
Wainwright, Daniel, 150, 469, 470
Vincent, 265
Waithman, Thomas, 465
Wakefield, Mrs. 11
Walcot (Wolcott), Benjamin, 90, 173, 252, 432, 446, 474, 480
Josiah, 96
Waldorf, Anthony, 92, 379
George, 485
John, 92
Margaret, 92
Martin, 92
Waldron, Catherine, 169, 459, 460
Jerome, 460
John, 460
Leffert, 91
Nelthe, 460
Samuel, 169, 459, 460
William, 460
Wales, David, 460
George, 460
Hannah, 460
James, 460
Walker, Alexander, 428
Francis, 152, 398
George, 148
James, 418
John, 460
Rebecca, 477
Robert, 145, 155
Samuel, 460
Sarah, 460
Thomas, 305

Thomas S., 89
William, 155
Wall, Garret, 431
George, 454
John, 86, 183, 461, 484
Wallace, Elizabeth, 460
Hope, 251, 460
James, 460
Jane, 460
John, 108, 127, 320, 460
Martha, 460
Mary, 251, 460
Philip, 211
Rebecca, 251, 460
Robert, 466, 467
Thomas, 251, 460
William, 54, 160
(see Wallis)
Wallen, Elizabeth, 54
Hope, 480
Walling, Cynthus, 461
Hope, 460
John, 24, 183, 195, 357, 361, 461
Jonathan, 24, 461
Ladus, 461
Mary, 461
Sarah, 461
Thomas, 357
Wallis, Betty, 461
Margaret, 461
Susannah, 461
William, 461
(see Wallace)
Walter, Samuel, 49
Walters, Perchiah, 461
Walton, Cornelia, 462
Elizabeth, 461
Gerard, 462
Jacob, 462
James D., 462
John, Jr., 13
Richard, 51
William, 215, 246, 317, 353, 461, 462
Wambock, Ann, 399
Anthony, 462
Elizabeth, 462
Henry, 399, 400, 462
Margaret, 462
Mary, 462
Wamsly, Christopher, 207
Wane, Mary, 448
Wanamaker, Conrad, 281, 300
Harmanus, 368
Henry, 463
Wanshaer, John, 463
Susannah, 463
Ware, Alexander, 261
Ward, Ann, 463
Benjamin, 463
David, 12, 58, 463
Ebenezer, 207
Elihu, 63
Ezekiel, 463
George, 486
Habakkuk, 76
Israel, 12, 58
James, 141
Jehu, 76
Jesenbery, 463
John, 463
Joseph, 76
Joshua, 76

Josiah, 222, 314, 463
Martha, 222, 453
Mary, 463
Matthias, 463
Moses, 288, 463
Rebecca, 473
Samuel, 465
Dr. Samuel, 159
Stephen, 68, 278
Stephen, Jr., 278
Susannah, 101
William, 463
Wardell, Catherine, 464
Ebenezer, 240
Elizabeth, 464
Esther, 464
Henry, 20
Jacob, 469
James, 469
John, 20, 464, 469
Joseph, 464, 469
Lydia, 464
Margaret, 464
Mary, 390
Meribah, 464
Phebe, 464
Sarah, 358, 464, 469
Stephen, 125, 464, 480
William, 390, 464
Ware, Alexander, 464
Amy, 465
Elijah, 416
Elnathan, 24, 143
Enoch, 465
Faithful, 464
Hannah, 464, 465
Isaac, 465
Jacob, 109, 465
Job, 76
John, 23, 83, 464
Joseph, 416
Lydia, 465
Mary, 464
Priscilla, 465
Richard, 465
Sarah, 464
Solomon, 464
Susannah, 464
Thomas, 348, 465
William, 464
Warford, Elizabeth, 465
James, 138, 327, 465
John, 465
Joseph, 465
Warne, Abigail, 465
Benjamin, 465
Euphemia, 465
George, 327, 465
Hannah, 465
Joshua, 47, 129
Richard, 465
Samuel, 129, 465
Stephen, 124, 196, 292, 338
Stephen, Jr., 124, 338
Thomas, 47, 465
Thomas, Jr., 465
Warner, Andrew, 182
Ann, 164
George, 16, 76
Godfried, 206
John, 182, 231
Joseph, 470
Simon, 116
Warrell, Joseph, 310, 366, 370, 493

Warrick, David, 465
Jacob, 465
John, 465
Warrington, Joseph, 169, 465
Ruth, 466
Thomas, 465, 466
Wart, Christian, 462
Washburn, Ebenezer, 90
Jeremiah, 10
Jonathan, 466
Patience, 466
Waterhouse, John, 258, 331
Joshua, 281, 316
Sophia, 466
Waters, Anthony W., 353
Daniel, 466
Elenor, 466
Elizabeth, 466, 467
Hannah, 466
Henry, 466
Jonathan, 467
Kezia, 467
Priscilla, 467
Rebecca, 467
William, 466, 467
Watkins, Solomon, 467
Zerviah, 467
Watkinson, John, 41, 63, 64, 440
Watson, Aaron, 94, 231, 232
Abraham, 200
Alexander, 248, 466, 467, 468
Christian, 467
David, 154, 438
Garven, 468
Isaac, 57
John, 138, 216, 468
Marmaduke, 41, 102, 469, 486
Mary, 449, 468
Nathan, 489
Richard, 286
Sarah, 132
Sophia, 467
Thomas, 51, 370, 486
William, 351, 467
Watts, John, 51
Wauters, Auriantje, 226
Weaver Abigail, 384
Peter, 432
Webb, Abraham, 468
George, 468
Isaac, 468
Jane, 468
John, 428, 468
William, 468
Webster, Abraham, 468
Deborah, 468
Hannah, 468, 469
Hugh, 469
John, 18, 48, 238, 468, 469
Joseph, 468, 469
Lawrence, 17, 61, 125, 482
Martha, 468
May, 468
Rachel, 468
Robert, 468
Samuel, 241
Sarah, 468
Susannah, 468
Thomas, 17, 468
William, 468
Weed, Elijah, 385
Weeks, Richard, 90, 125, 231, 339, 345, 384, 393, 426
Wege, Joshua, 374

INDEX OF NAMES OF PERSONS 599

Weiss, George J., 288
Weissen, Magdalina, 288
Welding, John, 469
Welldon, Anne, 41
  Hannah, 41
Weller, Catherine, 469
  Eleanor, 469
  Elizabeth, 469
  Jacob, 469
  Johannis, 110, 469
  Lydia, 110
  Mary, 469
  Philip, 469
  Sarah, 469
Welling, John, 294
  William, 347, 400
Wells, Mary, 181
  Samuel J., 131, 302
Welsh, John, 25, 160
  Joseph, 411
  Mary E., 309
  Michael, 149
  Valentine, 199
  William, 309, 419
Wendell, Mary, 126
Wentzell, Adam, 469
  Daniel, 469
  Charles, 469
  Mary, 469
  Philip, 172, 469
  Theodorus, 469
  William, 469
Wessells, Lawrence, 115
West, Asher, 75, 464
  Audria, 469
  Charles, 89, 90, 470
  Daniel, 469
  Deborah, 470
  Edmond, 470
  Hannah, 89
  Israel, 13
  James, 470, 480
  John, 18, 256, 470, 474
  Joseph, 183, 469, 470
  Keziah, 19
  Martha, 170
  Mary, 89, 238, 470
  Rachel, 470
  Ruth, 469
  Stephen, 469
  Thomas, 13, 285, 361, 470
  William, 302, 435
Westbrook, Abraham, 470
  Catherine, 470
  Cornelius, 470
  Derrick, 470
  Jacob, 442
  John, 60, 117, 137
  John C., 375, 444
  Maria, 470
Westcote (Westcot, Westcoat), Amos, 471
  Catherine, 257
  David, 105, 115, 130, 143, 327, 371, 378
  Ebenezer, 32
  Elizabeth, 143
  Henry, 471
  John, 53
  Joseph, 130, 327
  Richard, 249, 405
  Samuel, 52
Westervelt, Abraham, 339
  Andries, 257
  Benjamin, 112, 261
  Casparus, 257, 444
  Cornelius, 350
  Jacob, 257
  Jacob A., 256
  Johannes, 78, 453
  Roelef, 8, 444, 455
  Tryntje, 8
Westfall, Jacob, 237
Weston, Abraham, 471
  Catherine, 471
  Cornelius, 110, 471
  Gretie, 110
  Jacob, 84
  Joseph, 471
  Peter, 471
  Samuel, 151
  Sarah, 471
Wetherby, Daniel, 128
  Edmund, 128, 471
  Henry, 471
  Martha, 471
Wetherill, Ann, 471
  Christopher, 140
  George, 34
  John, 36, 133, 281, 292, 299, 328, 426
  John, Jr., 160, 299, 426
  Martha, 472
  Nancy, 299
  Samuel 140
  Thomas, 140
Wetherington, Benjamin, 305
  David, 122
  Hannah, 122
  John, 122
  Rachel, 122
  Sarah, 123
Wetsel, George, 284
Wharton, John, 75
  Joseph, Jr., 467
  Rebecca, 75
Wheatcraft, Edward, 340, 486
  Samuel, 141
Wheaten, Bagley, 472
  Charles, 472
  Daniel, 85
  Elizabeth, 472
  Hannah, 472
  Henry, 472
  Hephzibah, 472
  Isaac, 472
  John, 69, 255, 472
  Jonathan, 472
  Martha, 472
  Mary, 472, 473
  Priscilla, 473
  Reuben, 472
  Robert, 472
  Sarah, 472
  William, 62
Wheeler, Ann, 35, 36
  Caleb, 28
  David, 472
  Jemima, 472
  Nathaniel, 472
  Capt. Nathaniel, 222
  Sarah, 472
  Stephen, 313
Whilldin, Elinor, 242, 243
  James, 66, 177, 186, 242, 243, 404, 419, 473
  Mary, 473

Matthew, 473
Seth, 29, 473
Whitaker, Ambrose, 115, 416
　Anna, 427
　Christian, 143
　Eliphalet, 266, 313, 473, 475
　Elizabeth, 473
　John, 327
　Jonathan, 396, 473, 475
　Lewis, 427
　Lydia, 178
　Nathaniel, 473
　Ruth, 115
　Thomas, 321, 459
Whitall, James, 137, 144, 202, 203, 218, 234, 400, 408, 486
　John, 475
　Sarah, 288
White, Alexander, 16, 44, 83, 139, 166, 280, 282, 374, 380, 396
　Amos, 215, 297, 390, 473, 474
　Andrew, 474
　Ann, 74, 102, 474
　Anthony, 208, 255, 283
　Benjamin, 474
　Charity, 152, 165
　Deborah, 182, 214, 475
　Elizabeth, 16, 344
　Esther, 474
　Eve, 74
　Frances, 182
　Garrison, 474
　George, 116, 464
　Hannah, 214
　Hulda, 197
　James, 344, 427
　Jeremiah, 474
　Joel, 390, 473
　John, 132, 474
　Joseph, 474
　Josiah, 383
　Margaret, 83, 182, 374
　Mary, 465, 473
　Nancy, 474
　Peter, 474
　Phebe, 474
　Philip, 63
　Rachel, 165, 214, 473
　Rebecca, 474
　Renes, 208
　Richard, 182, 474
　Robert, 182, 474
　Samuel, 474
　Sarah, 474
　Thomas, 75, 88, 165, 214, 216, 281, 320, 474
　Thomas, Jr., 88
　Vincent, 165, 488
　William, 111, 171, 474
　Zephaniah, 474
Whitehead, Andrew, 66, 459
　Elias, 459
　Elisha, 291
　Elizabeth, 242
　John, 411
　Samuel, 265, 468
　Timothy, 49, 332, 365, 427, 469
　Timothy, Jr., 98, 319, 459
Whitehorne, Samuel, 218, 326, 446
Whitenack, Blackert, 290
　Catherine, 482
Whitlock, James, 284
　Jane, 284
　John, 150, 458

Whitson, Anna, 475
　Elizabeth, 475
　Henry, 6, 475
　John, 475
　Thomas, 475
　Thomas, Jr., 6
Whittemore, Jonas, 163
Whytey, Ann, 337
Wickes, Hannah, 475
Wickham, Mary, 361
Wickward, Rachel, 70
Wiggins, Gershom, 447
　Hannah, 475
　James, 475
　Mary, 471
　Thomas, 244
Wigmore, Jacob, 126
Wigton, John, 101
Wiker, Philip, 400
Wiksell, John, 302
Wiley (see Wylley)
Wilcox (Willcock), David, 478
　Elizabeth, 478
　Isaac, 335
　Joanna, 478
　Joseph, 54, 276, 380
　Mary, 478
　Noah, 478
　Peter, 478
　Phebe, 478
　Sabra, 478
　Stephen, 478
　William, 119, 442, 478
Wild, John, 287
Wildey, Grace, 476
Wiley, William, 431
Wilkie, George, 192
　William 201
Wilkins, Amos, 476
　Amy, 476
　Asuba, 476
　Benjamin, 476
　Caleb, 476
　Constantine, 192, 400, 476
　Isaac, 166
　John, 234, 286, 304, 400, 437, 476, 486
　John, Jr., 484
　Joshua, 476
　Mary, 256, 315
　Samuel, 476
　Sarah, 476
　Susannah, 318
　Thomas, 140, 149, 216, 475
　Thomas, Jr., 140
　William, 96, 257, 287, 400, 437, 486
Wilkinson, Edward, 152
　Edward, Jr., 217
　Hannah, 477
　James, 476
　John, 254
　Jonathan, 438
　Martha, 476
　Mary, 477
　Nathaniel, 61, 232
　Rachel, 477
　Richard, 477
Willard, Benjamin, 478
　Hannah, 478
　Isaac, 478
　James, 477
　Mary, 478
　Parr, 320, 478

INDEX OF NAMES OF PERSONS 601

Rebecca, 477, 478
Richard, 478
Sarah, 477
Thomas, 320, 477, 478
Willet (Willets), Abigail, 479
  Abraham, 62
  Anne, 479
  Benjamin, 479
  Eupham, 479
  Gilbert, 479
  Isaac, 479
  James, 479
  John, 156, 163, 183, 316, 479
  Jonathan, 482
  Joseph, 61, 482
  Mary, 479
  Micaiah, 226
  Patience, 478
  Richard, 479
  Solomon, 482
  Solomon, Jr., 86, 482
  Thomas, 479
  Thomas, Jr., 86
  William, 479
Willever, Jacob, 137
  Peter, 482
  Samuel, 482
Willgus, William, 468
Williams, Amos, 441
  Ann, 479
  Augustine, 293
  Benjamin, 193, 194, 479, 481
  Benjamin, Jr., 118
  Catherine, 287, 481
  Daniel, 13, 167, 480
  Ebenezer, 193, 479
  Edmund, 231, 406, 432, 433, 480
  Edward, 90, 167
  Elihu, 252, 432
  Elinor, 201
  Elizabeth, 101, 108, 421, 480
  Enoch, 479
  Ezekiel, 480
  George, 25, 479, 480
  Hannah, 480
  James, 66, 89, 421, 469, 480
  Joanna, 480
  John, 118, 226, 294, 335, 356, 421, 424, 433, 473, 479, 480, 481
  John M., 303
  Jonathan, 479
  Joseph, 480, 481
  Margaret, 479
  Martha, 480
  Mary, 480
  Meriam, 433
  Mindwell, 479
  Mrs., 11
  Obadiah, 480
  Samuel, 95
  Sarah, 479
  Susannah, 330
  Tatum, 34, 193
  Thomas, 281, 479
  William, 450
Williamson, Abraham, 235, 481, 482
  Ann, 229, 481
  Arthur, 481
  Bartholomew, 481
  Cornelius, 39, 205, 481
  David, 457
  Elbert, 399
  Elizabeth, 481

Garret, 210, 481
Geertje, 481
Hendrick, 481
Jacob, 482
Jemima, 481
John, 482
Mary, 482
Matthias, 211
Patience, 209
Peter, 95, 165, 314, 484
Rebecca, 482
Sarah, 481
William, 31, 209, 241, 299, 353, 412, 481, 482
William, Jr., 481
Willis, Amos, 74
  John, 376
  Jonathan, 279
  Joseph, 207
  Samuel, 135
  Thomas, 136, 376
  William, 172
Wilmot, Anthony, 217, 431
  Daniel, 282
  Edward, 40, 83, 104, 114, 117, 187, 188, 306, 344, 393, 410
  James, 462
  Martilla, 224
  Peter, 224
Willover, Abram, 482
  David, 482
  Henry, 482
  Jacob, 482
  John, 482
  Margaret, 482
Wills, Aaron, 50, 191, 482
  Beulah, 482
  Daniel, 191, 302
  Jacob, 482
  James, 259, 482
  John, 126, 482
  Jonathan, 482
  Mary, 482
  Meribah, 302, 482
  Micaiah, 85, 137, 252, 435, 460, 482
  Samuel, 482
Wilson (Willson), Abraham, 211, 212
  Andrew, 10, 483
  Ann, 483
  Annetje, 483
  Catherine, 236
  David, 483
  Deborah, 483
  Ebenezer, 484
  Elizabeth, 366, 483
  Francis, 366
  Gabriel, 201, 483, 484
  George, 356
  Grace, 366
  Hannah, 366
  Hendrick, 483
  Isabel, 275
  James, 236, 242, 366, 483, 484
  John, 296, 366, 483, 484
  John, Jr., 241
  Jonathan, 483, 484
  Joseph, 264, 414, 483
  Joshua, 275
  Lawrence, 12, 251
  Margaret, 275, 483
  Martha, 287, 484
  Mary, 483

Mindert, 483
Mordecai, 483
Peter, 483, 484
Rebecca, 156
Robert, 32, 184, 275, 417, 475, 483, 484
Samuel, 185, 483, 484, 489
Sarah, 467
Thomas, 391, 484
William, 63, 64, 146
Zebulon, 483
Wimer, Godfrey, 358
Winans (Wynans), Benjamin, 365, 436
  Elias, 193, 194, 485
  Elizabeth, 484
  Isaac, 251, 436
  Jacob, 150, 316
  James, 485
  John, 207, 436, 485
  Josiah, 484, 485
  Lewis, 362, 436
  Philip, 484
  William 80, 95, 253, 484, 485
  William, Jr., 485
Windor, Elizabeth, 417
Winds, Isaiah, 485
Winegardener, Court, 433
Winkoop, Annetie, 237
  Henry, 463
  Nicholas, 237
Winne, Abraham, 454
  Annatje, 387
  Leveyius, 387, 388
Winslow, Rev. Edward, 11
  Hannah, 11
  John, 11
  Joshua, 11
  Margaret A., 11
  Mary, 11
  Sarah, 11
  Thomas A., 11
Winter, Henry, 397
  Mary, 482
  Peter, 482
  Sarah, 212
Wire, Thomas, 322
Wirtz, Anna, 485
  John, 485
  Maurice, 485
  Peter, 485
  (see Wurts)
Wise, Philip 329
Wiser, Jacob, 120
Witscher, Herman, 355
Wistar, Richard, 172, 313, 331
Wix, Ezekiel, 408
Woglom, Elinor, 18
  John, 458
Wolfenden, Thomas, 100
Wolcott (see Walcot)
Wollin, Gersham, 167
Wood, Ann, 485
  Anna, 486
  Bethier, 485
  David, 395
  Edward, 100
  Francis, 486
  Henry, 20, 85, 90, 109, 192, 307, 316, 320, 384, 404, 412, 437, 477, 478, 485
  James, 326, 485, 486
  James, Jr., 286
  Jechonias, 30, 121, 195, 217, 261
  Jehu, 486
  Jeremiah, 485, 486
  John, 233, 251, 315, 336, 425, 467, 485, 486
  Jonas, 414
  Jonathan, 471, 485
  Joseph, 147, 251, 290, 452
  Letitia, 486
  Rachel, 486
  Rebecca, 485
  Richard, 149
  Samuel, 31, 43, 189, 262, 436, 485
  Sarah, 486
  Susannah, 262, 485
  Thomas, 213, 485
  William, 17, 185, 204, 205, 232, 234, 304, 305, 400, 476, 485, 486
Woodcock, Elizabeth, 67
  Richard, 67
Woodmansee, David, 403
  Gabriel, 214, 403
  John, 480
Woodnutt, Henry, 387, 440
  Jonathan, 268
Woodruff, Abner, 311
  Abraham, Jr., 487
  Benjamin, 487
  Catherine, 487
  Charles, 222
  Cornelius, 487
  David, 487
  Elias, 14, 37, 224, 409
  Elijah, 98
  Elihu, 253
  Elizabeth, 487
  Enos, 461, 472, 487
  Huploke, 210, 487
  Isaac, 14, 27, 487
  Isaac, Jr., 210
  Jacob, 487
  John, 366
  Jonathan, 193
  Jonathan, Jr., 263, 280
  Joseph, 487
  Joseph, Jr., 66, 210, 368
  Josiah, 459
  Keziah, 280
  Martha, 280
  Mary, 263, 487
  Mathias, 487
  Moses, 487
  Nathan, 80, 280, 487
  Nathaniel, 280, 487
  Patience, 459
  Pearsons, 194
  Puah, 487
  Rebecca, 487
  Samuel, 23, 43, 108, 149, 311, 479, 487
  Samuel, 4th, 23
  Sarah, 98, 461, 487
  Seth, 194, 480
  Stephen, 98, 487
  Thomas, 206, 289, 315, 357, 376, 480, 487, 492
  Uzal, 127, 194, 313
  William, 487
Woodrow, Henry, 193
Woods, Johannah, 104
  John, 247
  Mary, 63
Woodward, Anthony, 433, 488
  Anthony, Jr., 12
  Deborah, 433

INDEX OF NAMES OF PERSONS 603

Hannah, 57, 488
Jesse, 36
John, 224
Rhoda, 488
Sarah, 488
Thomas, Jr., 487, 488
Thomas L., 69
William, 133
Wooff, Christopher, 117
Woolf, Mary E., 488
Wooling, William, 198
Woolley, Benjamin, Jr., 390
  James, 231, 390, 488
  Patience, 488
  Steven, 13, 36, 113, 393, 480
  William, 488
Woolman, Abner, 20, 64, 171
  Asher, 5, 20, 191, 192, 411, 482
  John, 21, 52, 100, 128, 140, 158, 169, 215, 241, 299, 364, 437
  John A., 5, 20
  Jonah, 50, 411
  Mary, 5, 20, 146
  Samuel, 5, 20
  Sarah, 5, 20, 21, 52, 128, 364
  Uriah, 192
Woolsey, Benjamin, Jr., 488
  Daniel, 488
  Deborah, 467
  Henry, 301, 461, 467, 488, 489
  Jeremiah, 68, 466, 467, 488
  Joseph, 488
  Martha, 488, 489
Woolson, Abraham, 220, 222, 489
  Hance, 156, 175, 222
  Rachel, 156
Woolston, Charity, 128
  Martha, 319
  Milentus, 128
  Samuel, 489
  Susannah, 489
  William, 13, 489
Woolverton, Abigail, 489
  Charles, 281
  Dennis, 281, 489
  Hannah, 364
  Isaac, 489
  Joel, 281
  John, 139, 293, 489
  Margaret, 489
  Mary, 489
  Morris, 489
  Zurviah, 489
Woolwever, Wilhelm, 139
Worden, Caleb, 351
Worly, Henry, 306
Worrall, Peter, 413
  Philip, 490
Worth, Ann, 415
  Elinor, 152
  Giles, 217
  James, 80
  Joseph, 210
  Ruth, 415
  Ursula, 314
  William, 415, 418
Worthington, Ephraim, 490
  Thomas, 55
Worthley, Daniel, 480
  Lydia, 183
  Richard, 480
Wortman, Andrew, 490
  Anne M., 490
  David, 490

John, 291, 490
Joseph, 490
Margaret, 490
Peter, 490
Worton, William, 306, 314
Wrath, Rebecca, 490
Wright, Abner, 44, 284
  Amos, 44, 81, 204, 300, 335, 491
  Ann, 44
  Catherine, 41
  Deborah, 135
  David, 69, 131, 430, 490
  Ebenezer, 322
  Edith, 490
  Eleanor, 490
  Elizabeth, 44
  Ezekiel, 178, 491
  Hannah, 41, 490
  James, 387, 490
  John, 101, 363, 490
  Jonathan, 486
  Jonathan, Jr., 322
  Joseph, 71, 318, 490
  Joshua, 95, 286, 318, 491
  Mahlon, 131, 432
  Mary, 71, 490
  Nathan, 41, 173, 300, 481
  Rebekah, 41, 173, 490, 491
  Richard, 154, 327, 430, 490
  Robert, 491
  Samuel, 21, 56, 182, 490
  Thomas, 44, 490
  Thomasin, 318
  William, 218, 481
Wurts, John, 390
  (see Wirtz)
Wyans, Abraham, 436
Wyatt, Bartholomew, Jr., 357, 397, 417
Wyckoff (Wikoff), Alice, 492
  Altie, 246
  Annatie, 492
  Aukes, 246
  Catherine, 227, 492
  Cornelius, 165, 421, 492
  Eyda, 492
  Garret, 246, 372, 492
  Gertrude, 383
  Jacamintje, 451
  Jacob, 15, 278, 458
  John, 492
  Majeka, 492
  Martin, 344
  Nicholas, 492
  Oukey, 492
  Peter, 56, 91, 99, 159, 227, 256, 451, 457, 492
  Samuel, 329, 383, 492
  Sarah, 492
  William, 93, 295
Wylley, John, 443
Wynants, Josiah, 189, 352

Y

Yager (Yaeger), Catherine, 344
  Hendrick, 344
  John, 93, 462
  Peter, 344
  Philip, 236
Yamans, Edward, 492
  Samuel, 107, 108, 492
Yapp, Lidia, 290

Yard, Achsah, 493
  Ann, 493
  Archibald W., 120, 492, 493
  Benjamin, 19, 38, 94, 108, 493
  Benjamin, Jr., 185
  Daniel, 492
  Elijah, 492, 493
  Firman, 492, 493
  Hannah, 493
  Isaac, 350, 364, 493
  Jethro, 492, 493
  John, 347, 408, 493
  Joseph, 94, 120, 347, 492, 493
  Mary, 493
  Mary A., 492, 493
  Sarah, 120, 347
  Thomas, 493
  William, 493
Yardley, Thomas, 213, 447
  Andrew, 210
Yeandall, Sarah, 266
Yeark, Gertrude, 229
Yeetmare, John, 351
  Margaret, 351
Yorks, Agnes, 146
  Peter, 146
Young, Abigail, 493
  Abraham, 194, 350, 433
  Andres, 83, 166
  Arthur, 494
  Daniel, 481, 494
  David, 494
  Elizabeth, 494
  Hannah, 318, 494
  Henry, 147, 175, 176, 209, 262, 378
  Hercules, 431
  James, 143, 258, 380
  Job, 213, 410, 493
  John, 39, 137, 166, 405, 406, 462
  Kerlach, 88
  Lena, 203
  Margaret, 382, 494
  Marjery, 149
  Mary, 149, 209, 251, 494
  Morgan, 254, 494
  Nathan, 150, 214
  Peter, 203, 210, 236
  Peter, Jr., 270
  Phebe, 209, 213, 262, 310, 378, 494
  Philip, 405
  Silas, 394
  Stephen, 280, 493
  Thankful, 494
  Thomas, 494
  Tunis, 327
  Walter, 83
  William, 227, 236
Younger, Marget, 140
Younglove, Isaiah, 73, 336
Yournson, John, Sr., 452
  John, Jr., 452

Z

Zabriskie, Albert, 113, 494, 495
  Catherine, 494
  Christian, 494
  Christine, 494
  Claes, 494
  Jacob, 7, 29, 31, 445, 494
  Jan, 444, 494, 495
  John, 78, 264, 403, 415
  John, Jr., 415
  Joost, 494
  Machtel, 494
  Peter, 234, 257, 445, 494
  Rachel, 494
  Sarah Z., 494
  Tryntie, 203
Zane, Henry, 326
  Joseph, 475
  Mary, 68, 76, 495
  Nathan, 495
  Nicholas, 238
  William, 495
Zelley, John, 128
  Silvanus, 170
Zimmerman, Christian, 216

Index of Place-Names

NOTE.—This Index has the modern spelling as a rule. Where towns and townships have the same name it is not always certain which is intended. Names of counties in New Jersey are omitted.

A

Absecon bridge, 355
  beach, 119
  creek, 119
Acquackanonk township, 5, 54, 72, 144, 156, 159, 164, 334, 335, 387, 448, 450, 454, 455, 456, 463
Albany (N. Y.), 246, 291
Albany county (N. Y.), 153, 291, 438
Alexandria township, 98, 142, 194, 341, 350, 433
Allentown, 119, 167, 338, 410
Alloways township, 9, 16, 38, 39, 58, 75, 76, 100, 104, 107, 115, 116, 143, 145, 155, 172, 186, 196, 208, 217, 284, 288, 295, 296, 299, 309, 324, 348, 355, 375, 376, 380, 395, 396, 397, 416, 425, 437, 441, 459, 464, 466, 469, 479, 490
  Neck, 9, 83, 439
Amboy, 155, 199 (see Perth Amboy)
Ambrose brook, 241
Amwell township, 5, 6, 32, 39, 40, 56, 88, 93, 117, 129, 134, 137, 144, 154, 162, 165, 166, 178, 195, 196, 197, 203, 205, 209, 210, 221, 227, 230, 233, 235, 236, 238, 239, 240, 241, 249, 263, 266, 270, 272, 276, 315, 322, 323, 326, 337, 340, 343, 344, 345, 356, 358, 360, 364, 366, 379, 392, 399, 405, 409, 412, 413, 414, 415, 420, 427, 462, 466, 475, 481, 482, 499
Ancokus creek, 125, 306 (see Rancokus creek)
Antigua island, 341, 342
Antuxet, 423
Arneystown, 71
Assanpink creek, 167
Attercliff (Eng.), 67

B

Badcock creek, 349
Barbadoes, 332, 333
Barker creek, 354
Barlbrough (Eng.), 31
Barnegat, 198, 335
Barns island (N. Y.), 315
Baskingridge, 63, 299
Bear swamp, 115, 463
Beaver creek, 227
  dam, 113
Bedminster township, 12, 164, 266, 267, 294
Bergen, 46, 387
Bermuda island, 446
Bernards township, 63, 74, 122, 151, 165, 207, 234, 244, 249, 266, 441, 473, 475
Bethlehem township, 9, 14, 33, 41, 42, 135, 138, 140, 144, 200, 239, 240, 249, 254, 268, 306, 382, 468
Black Horse, 111
Blawenburgh, 305
Block Island (R. I.), 361
Bloomingdale, 171
Boel's bog, 373
Bordentown, 15, 51, 140, 141, 154, 167, 231, 281, 398, 430, 469, 486
Boston (Mass.), 11, 46
Bound Brook, 16, 314, 334, 468
Bound creek, 459
Bridgeton, 26, 39, 100, 149
Bridgewater township, 16, 48, 73, 95, 145, 259, 269, 285, 314, 334, 419, 458, 484
Bristol township (Pa.), 396
Broad Neck, 177
Brooklyn (N. Y.), 263
Bucks county (Pa.), 51, 68, 213, 217, 267, 275, 361, 393, 396
Buckshutem, 105
  marsh, 381
Burlington, 12, 14, 18, 21, 28, 30, 35, 42, 43, 46, 65, 71, 84, 102, 103, 129, 139, 140, 141, 147, 182, 185, 197, 200, 206, 216, 218, 223, 225, 228, 229, 233, 254, 265, 279, 283, 303, 318, 322, 327, 332, 336, 338, 341, 342, 347, 360, 361, 369, 380, 385, 388, 389, 392, 396, 407, 418, 419, 421, 430, 432, 435, 460, 467, 469, 475, 477
Buttermilk falls, 444

C

Cambridge (Mass.), 11
Canaskunk, 118, 373
Canoe brook, 417
Canterbury (Eng.), 46
Cape May, 479
Cecil county (Md.), 440
Cedar brook, 246
  creek, 130
  hammock, 402
  swamp, 401
Charlestown (Mass.), 11
Charlotte Enburgh, 171
Cheescocks (N. Y.), 74
Cheesequakes, 373
  meadow, 129

Chelmsford, 11
Chester, 60, 160, 385
Chester (Del.), 318
Chester county (Pa.), 101, 225, 299
Chester township, 54, 92, 95, 189, 197, 198, 211, 252, 276, 289, 320, 337, 340, 357, 364, 366, 437, 452, 463, 465
Chesterfield township, 41, 44, 51, 57, 61, 71, 94, 111, 119, 122, 141, 151, 170, 179, 198, 204, 243, 269, 281, 289, 305, 306, 318, 325, 360, 393, 422, 429, 430, 432, 469, 486, 488
Chestnut island, 128
Clemnel creek, 90
Cohansey, 107, 230, 272
  creek, 321
Colestown, 211
Coopers creek, 90, 192, 425
Courtland (N. Y.), 388
Craines Neck, 152
Cranbury, 201, 219, 346, 450
  brook, 19
  Ponds, 425
Crosswicks, 51, 243
  creek, 204, 491
Cumberland county (Eng.), 164, 444

D

Darby county (Eng.), 31
Dead river, 270
Deal, 473
Deerfield township, 39, 79, 106, 145, 156, 157, 161, 164, 177, 195, 216, 219, 221, 293, 322, 359, 366, 379, 432, 474, 490
Delaware river, 318, 325, 357, 489
  bay, 145
Deptford township, 35, 45, 73, 76, 95, 144, 160, 172, 173, 181, 189, 190, 192, 202, 203, 212, 216, 218, 232, 234, 257, 269, 272, 277, 285, 286, 287, 288, 354, 369, 392, 394, 400, 408, 435, 437, 468, 470, 476, 484, 485, 486
Dismal, 270, 273
Dividing creek, 214, 258, 317, 347
Dover (Eng.), 420
Dover township, 402
Drummullough (Ire.), 293
Dundron (Eng.), 441
Dunstable, 11
Dutchess county (N. Y.), 19

E

Easthampton, 194
Easton (Pa.), 327
East river, 462
Eayrestown, 126
Egg Harbor township, 96, 214, 249, 346, 370, 377, 407
Elizabeth (Town, Borough), 14, 23, 27, 28, 37, 43, 45, 49, 50, 55, 60, 64, 65, 79, 80, 89, 91, 92, 96, 97, 98, 101, 103, 107, 108, 111, 118, 127, 140, 150, 151, 171, 173, 189, 193, 194, 210, 211, 217, 218, 219, 223, 224, 226, 230, 232, 235, 242, 253, 254, 262, 263, 271, 274, 278, 279, 280, 281, 288, 289, 297, 299, 310, 311, 312, 314, 315, 316, 319, 321, 323, 325, 334, 335, 339, 341, 353, 357, 364, 365, 368, 370, 371, 372, 376, 377, 383, 384, 385, 386, 388, 404, 405, 411, 419, 424, 425, 427, 433, 436, 441, 442, 458, 459, 467, 478, 480, 484, 487
  river, 65
Elsinboro township, 6, 137, 170, 174, 190, 200, 255, 279, 362, 417
Enfield (Eng.), 182
Evesham township, 21, 22, 28, 52, 54, 61, 85, 125, 137, 149, 158, 165, 169, 184, 197, 210, 211, 212, 238, 251, 276, 286, 287, 320, 329, 357, 380, 386, 389, 421, 438, 470, 476, 487

F

Fairfield township, 32, 34, 37, 52, 53, 78, 105, 106, 115, 130, 142, 143, 150, 157, 161, 176, 179, 184, 206, 224, 243, 255, 257, 260, 263, 309, 311, 312, 313, 317, 321, 326, 327, 336, 341, 345, 355, 368, 371, 378, 381, 382, 391, 396, 401, 416, 459, 471, 474
Fishing creek, 101, 175, 296
Five-Mile beach, 99, 175, 278, 473
Flatbush (L. I.), 263
Flushing (L. I.), 462
Flying Point, 130
Forsters Neck, 223
Fortascue island, 257
Frederick county (Va.), 67
Freehold township, 6, 15, 36, 93, 101, 109, 116, 133, 134, 135, 147, 163, 199, 201, 223, 226, 240, 267, 268, 278, 295, 298, 321, 333, 346, 351, 352, 356, 359, 367, 372, 373, 393, 395, 410, 418, 419, 421, 422, 423, 424, 430, 431, 433, 444, 446, 450, 457, 468, 481, 484, 492
Freetown (N. E.), 148
Freshkill, 18
Fresh pond, 447

G

Garits island, 402
Gemonepa, 46, 458
Georgia, 125
Gerrish's landing, 131
Gloucester township, 10, 11, 34, 48, 70, 77, 81, 132, 133, 172, 180, 192, 193, 225, 252, 271, 285, 287, 294, 320, 338, 378, 421, 429, 430, 434
Goshen (N. Y.), 84, 246
Gravelly run, 345
Great Mantoes creek, 35, 476
Great Egg Harbor, 8, 9, 10, 17, 49, 75, 119, 213, 222, 223, 237, 245, 249, 264, 340, 348, 349, 355, 356, 370, 378, 393, 397, 401, 402, 405, 407, 408, 440, 483
  river, 81, 180
Great Meadow, 132, 320
  island, 446

INDEX OF PLACE-NAMES 607

Great pond, 251, 270, 444
Great swamp, 71, 118, 132, 177, 219, 307, 315, 344, 354
Grederes Neck, 402
Greenwich township, 6, 13, 15, 16, 23, 24, 26, 32, 55, 38, 44, 56, 57, 59, 65, 69, 71, 72, 77, 83, 85, 89, 95, 104, 105, 106, 108, 113, 128, 131, 134, 139, 140, 141, 143, 144, 145, 165, 173, 178, 179, 181, 186, 187, 188, 190, 198, 204, 207, 208, 227, 229, 248, 250, 254, 255, 267, 269, 274, 280, 281, 287, 288, 302, 319, 322, 324, 331, 332, 340, 343, 351, 355, 363, 374, 377, 380, 382, 383, 384, 385, 396, 406, 407, 417, 435, 441, 461, 464, 469, 473, 476
Guilford (N. E.), 391

H

Hackensack, 40, 112, 113, 249, 257, 261, 395, 415, 444, 445, 447, 448, 449, 494
river, 233
Haddonfield, 22, 61, 75, 135, 136, 192, 202, 208, 227, 345, 430
Haines Neck, 127
Hampton, 309
Hanover township, 13, 28, 34, 35, 36, 61, 68, 73, 78, 86, 87, 88, 121, 153, 180, 221, 229, 309, 323, 328, 329, 331, 335, 378, 383, 389, 391, 397, 421, 438, 440, 467, 476, 485
Hardwick township, 30, 86, 91, 117, 120, 185, 225, 290, 291, 322, 339, 343, 368, 374, 387, 406, 482, 483, 484, 491
Hardyston township, 184, 265, 272, 466
Hempshire county (Va.), 369
Hempstead (L. I.), 129
Highlands, 358
Hill Neck, 58
Hohokus, 203
Hollands brook, 423
Hope creek, 296
Hopewell township, 14, 15, 17, 25, 27, 32, 42, 43, 61, 64, 68, 72, 78, 79, 107, 120, 121, 122, 138, 154, 179, 185, 194, 195, 208, 210, 214, 217, 220, 229, 239, 255, 266, 270, 276, 290, 293, 300, 301, 310, 319, 321, 322, 342, 348, 350, 359, 364, 366, 379, 381, 391, 403, 413, 414, 415, 416, 432, 434, 466, 467, 472, 488
Hornsey (Eng.), 45
Horse Hill, 97
Horseneck, 164
Huntington (L. I.), 475
Huntingtonshire (Eng.), 388

I

Indian Neck, 217
Ireland, 228, 244

J

Jacobs creek, 25
Jamaica (L. I.), 441
Jamaica (W. I.), 353
Jones' island, 115, 130, 311, 336

K

Kensington, 306, 476
Kent county (Del), 486
Kettle creek, 173, 252
Kill Van Kull, 443
Kings road, 29
Kingston, 205, 304
Kingwood township, 47, 49, 80, 81, 132, 140, 142, 144, 168, 178, 203, 211, 213, 219, 226, 232, 233, 238, 241, 242, 253, 270, 281, 292, 316, 326, 327, 340, 341, 349, 350, 362, 368, 389, 412, 413, 415, 465, 489
Kitts island, 11
Knowlton township, 27, 266, 399

L

Lamberton, 346
Lancaster (Pa.), 413
Lawrence brook, 457
Lebanon township, 36, 81, 87, 99, 116, 142, 149, 167, 171, 207, 237, 270, 273, 275, 362, 380
Line creek, 493
Little Egg Harbor township, 17, 18, 97, 222, 276, 364, 385, 405
Little Silver Neck, 464
London (Eng.), 45, 182
Londonderry (Ire.), 155
Long Hill, 315
Long Island (N. Y.), 194, 207, 422
Long Neck, 18
Lower Alloways Creek, 9, 23
Lower Freehold township, 295, 299
Lower Makefield (Pa.), 213
Lower Penns Neck township, 15, 87, 131, 161, 324, 326, 328, 345, 405, 427, 439, 471
Lower Smithfield township (Pa.), 444
Ludlam's beach, 262

M

Macachkemeek, 84
Maidenhead, 24, 43, 132, 138, 164, 210, 315, 328, 350, 355, 392, 394, 395, 408, 414, 461, 467, 493
Manalopan, 367
Manasquan, 12, 102, 170
Manington township, 39, 46, 53, 94, 116, 128, 141, 169, 170, 171, 190, 204, 212, 222, 230, 232, 268, 336, 357, 366, 379, 386, 397, 417, 427, 440, 464, 471
Mannahockin, 184, 185
Mansfield township, 51, 63, 64, 69, 102, 111, 129, 133, 134, 146, 157, 159, 171, 173, 179, 180, 215, 223, 230, 254, 281, 318, 334, 335, 360, 435, 440
Mansfield Woodhouse, 145, 149, 162, 168, 482
Mantua creek, 13, 56, 95, 486
Maplestown, 447
Marcus Hook (Pa.), 225
Marineck township (N. Y.), 47
Marvel Hill, 374
Maryland, 148, 174
Matawan, 53
Matcheponix, 223

Maurice ("Morris") River township, 82, 84, 97, 150, 162, 163, 177, 195, 214, 216, 257, 268, 314, 326, 355, 407, 425, 426, 474
Mendham township, 26, 36, 65, 70, 118, 135, 183, 198, 258, 273, 312, 317, 409, 410
Merritt brook, 343
Middlesex county (Eng.), 182, 309, 458
Middlesex county (Mass.), 11
Middletown, 17, 19, 53, 55, 86, 90, 93, 98, 118, 129, 148, 153, 182, 185, 199, 246, 248, 264, 265, 298, 310, 311, 313, 333, 381, 399, 400, 418, 421, 424, 431, 432, 433, 438, 451, 461, 474, 479, 483
Middletown Point, 56, 395
Miere run, 402
Mill Brook swamp, 222
Mill creek, 198, 471
Millstone, 91, 292, 345, 374, 416, 438, 443
Mine brook, 393
Mine mountain, 87
Monachie, 316
Montague township, 55, 60, 110, 237, 442, 455, 471
Moorestown, 48, 77, 189, 211
Morris township, 439, 454
Morristown, 12, 27, 37, 74, 79, 86, 87, 97, 109, 147, 156, 172, 183, 186, 206, 212, 230, 237, 251, 265, 276, 290, 293, 369, 372, 378, 406, 434, 436, 463, 483, 485
Mount Holly, 13, 71, 99, 161, 184, 191, 215, 225, 229, 238, 249, 265, 271, 296, 421, 437, 459
Mount Pleasant, 424
Mount Misery, 462
Musconetkong, 282, 460
   creek, 482

N

Nantuxet Neck, 257
Newark, 16, 26, 27, 28, 62, 63, 65, 98, 100, 101, 118, 124, 140, 141, 180, 190, 206, 207, 212, 217, 221, 222, 225, 235, 256, 264, 280, 307, 310, 312, 315, 321, 330, 332, 359, 371, 391, 403, 417, 431, 434, 463, 472, 480, 483
New Barbadoes township, 7, 30, 40, 233, 316, 339, 444, 448
   Neck, 233, 282, 296, 447, 448, 456
New Britain, 119
New Brunswick, 10, 25, 45, 50, 103, 114, 120, 127, 150, 155, 160, 188, 207, 208, 248, 255, 260, 284, 304, 338, 391, 418, 424, 442, 445, 447, 454, 457, 472
Newcastle county (Del.), 94, 268
New Foundland, 106, 423
New Germantown, 160, 329
New Haddonfield 136
New Hampstead (N. Y.), 442
New Hanover township, 20, 21, 56, 59, 66, 67, 108, 181, 182, 204, 233, 285, 286, 289, 300, 332, 358, 383, 403, 437, 491
New Pilesgrove, 22

Newport, (R. I.), 62, 361
Newry (Ire.), 293
Newton, 19, 21, 26, 89, 90, 114, 119, 120, 123, 124, 136, 137, 139, 209, 212, 225, 268, 272, 275, 280, 289, 290, 293, 303, 343, 349, 358, 362, 369, 374, 389, 393, 400, 425, 466
   township, 11, 70, 81, 102, 135, 147, 164, 170, 173, 201, 202, 203, 227, 231, 285, 334, 345, 389, 426, 429, 430, 465, 478, 481
New Windsor township, 80, 217, 236, 317, 329, 395, 418
New York City, 7, 19, 45, 74, 103, 115, 135, 144, 153, 155, 163, 182, 194, 196, 201, 211, 233, 234, 237, 240, 246, 247, 260, 267, 282, 293, 294, 296, 304, 350, 353, 363, 368, 370, 375, 391, 395, 406, 415, 417, 420, 431, 438, 443, 449, 461, 462
Norreshonck (N. Y.), 237
Northampton county (Pa.), 60, 117, 444
Northampton township, 13, 18, 21, 26, 39, 43, 44, 57, 58, 59, 60, 66, 68, 71, 99, 100, 125, 126, 131, 139, 148, 158, 170, 191, 197, 229, 233, 245, 265, 269, 294, 299, 301, 303, 310, 336, 339, 347, 348, 354, 364, 386, 459, 489
North Branch, 47
North river, 320
Norwich (Conn.), 62
Nottingham township, 19, 41, 69, 132, 146, 231, 265, 269, 280, 289, 290, 303, 318, 332, 369, 385, 400, 410, 422, 432, 468
Nottingham (Pa.), 101
Nummies, 177

O

Old Bridge Neck, 183
Oldmans creek, 24, 195, 304
Orange county (N. Y.), 74, 163, 358, 438
Otter creek, 62
Oxford township, 200, 268, 343, 357, 414, 420, 451
Oyster creek, 459

P

Papiack Neck, 62
Paquaess river, 344
Paramus, 7, 8, 29, 240, 455, 457
Parsippany, 472
Passaic, 468
   river, 91, 450, 494
Patties island, 476
Pawlins cut, 318
Paulins Kiln, 38, 414
Peckmans river, 216
Peck's beach, 402
Pemberpog, 46
Pennington, 467, 488
Pensawkin creek, 465
Penns Neck, 9, 11, 14, 30, 55, 58, 66, 93, 116, 119, 123, 128, 131, 161, 174, 195, 201, 204, 218, 227, 228, 239, 250, 251, 253, 272, 287,

INDEX OF PLACE-NAMES 609

303, 304, 321, 324, 326, 328, 329, 353, 371, 401, 440, 441, 446, 448, 450, 452, 490
Perth Amboy, 7, 30, 42, 47, 62, 68, 72, 103, 122, 124, 129, 156, 162, 201, 214, 223, 247, 248, 256, 258, 260, 267, 268, 274, 282, 304, 305, 306, 319, 367, 388, 389, 396, 399, 405, 406, 421, 428, 429, 430, 440, 466, 467, 468, 474, 480. (See Amboy).
Pequannock township, 13, 35, 215, 216, 288, 350, 410, 423, 445, 494
Philadelphia, 17, 34, 35, 42, 44, 90, 92, 101, 132, 136, 155, 172, 181, 182, 197, 207, 215, 216, 218, 227, 243, 277, 279, 285, 287, 298, 303, 306, 309, 313, 318, 319, 322, 331, 332, 337, 342, 371, 385, 423, 424, 441, 467, 490, 493
Phillipsburg, 16
Piles creek, 193
Pilesgrove, 8, 22, 24, 30, 33, 79, 100, 105, 106, 107, 113, 116, 121, 122, 123, 124, 141, 157, 170, 178, 182, 195, 196, 208, 216, 221, 228, 250, 259, 260, 266, 279, 295, 296, 303, 304, 305, 308, 321, 352, 353, 367, 387, 398, 427, 429, 436, 451, 452, 460, 467, 474, 475
Piney Neck, 345, 347
Piscataway, 18, 44, 48, 49, 121, 123, 179, 194, 237, 241, 246, 247, 263, 270, 273, 274, 275, 291, 300, 314, 341, 390, 418, 428, 453, 468
township, 55, 80, 490
Pittsgrove, 122
Pohateung creek, 17
Polifly, 282
Pompton, 61, 280, 375
Popopow creek, 187
Portsmouth (R. I.), 148
Preakness, 188
Princeton, 88, 108, 141, 205, 265, 350, 394
Providence (R. I.), 62

Q

Queen Anne county (Md.), 148
Quhockin, 304, 353
Quibbletown, 283

R

Raccoon creek, 35
Rahway, 317, 405
meadows, 96, 97, 377
river, 97
Ramapo, 242, 384, 463
Rancokus, 301
creek, 325 (see Ancokus creek)
Raritan, 38, 47, 145, 259
landing, 46, 55, 311, 419, 423, 431
meadows, 152, 154, 390
river, 423, 453
Ratcliffe (Eng.), 45
Reading (Readington) township, 25, 40, 83, 95, 104, 114, 186, 187, 188, 230, 259, 260, 324, 329, 343, 344, 378, 492
Readington, 33, 84, 181
Recklesstown, 57

Red Root, 243
Reedy bridge, 373
Regpokes island, 458
Richland (Pa.), 68
Richmond county (S. I.), 18, 443
Rindageamak, 113
Robinson's island, 451
Rockaway, 254
river, 423
Rocky Hill, 298, 447, 485
Rooty hill, 485
Rostock (Ger.), 405
Roundabout, 152, 418
Roxbury township, 12, 64, 73, 78, 86, 92, 93, 120, 121, 139, 147, 149, 154, 162, 166, 169, 179, 204, 220, 228, 230, 308, 311, 312, 329, 379, 380, 393, 413, 419, 431, 439, 483, 485, 491
Roxiticus, 274
Rumson, 173, 174
Russels Neck, 293

S

Saddle River township, 8, 142, 234, 250, 334, 368, 442, 449
Salem, 17, 32, 55, 75, 123, 141, 153, 169, 170, 171, 200, 206, 225, 244, 255, 268, 303, 321, 375, 376, 398, 417, 427, 459, 471, 475
Salem creek, 452
Sandy Hook, 480
Sandyston, 470
Schooleys mountain, 413
Schralenburgh, 78, 453
Schuylkill river, 243
Scotch Plains, 194, 278, 478
Scotland, 220
Scotts hill, 165, 343
Second river, 83, 226, 235, 447, 454
Sepack's Neck, 8
Shark river, 236, 256, 306
Sheffield (Eng.), 67
Shrewsbury, 13, 14, 18, 20, 38, 42, 50, 74, 75, 87, 89, 90, 113, 125, 130, 150, 160, 165, 170, 173, 174, 183, 200, 214, 215, 226, 231, 236, 240, 249, 252, 294, 296, 306, 315, 319, 320, 333, 356, 368, 376, 390, 393, 406, 433, 446, 464, 469, 474, 479, 480, 488
township, 12, 51, 56, 94, 97, 102, 335, 473
Simsberry township (Conn.), 153, 438
Six-Mile Run, 481
Slotterdam, 70, 188
Smithtown, 391
Smoats meadow, 216
Sourland, 166, 201, 305, 340, 436, 446, 457
South Amboy, 19, 129, 224, 295
township, 47, 232
Southampton township, 392
South river, 402, 452
Springfield, 18, 39, 128, 183, 310, 334, 352, 364, 383, 477
township (Burlington co.), 20, 21, 154, 169, 232, 240, 271, 306, 349, 354, 377, 403, 411, 435
Staten Island (N. Y.), 18, 71, 118, 129, 353

39

Stony brook, 393, 415
Stafford township, 226
Stratford (Conn.), 11, 153, 438
Strawberry hill, 154
Stow Creek township, 22, 23, 31, 34, 50, 58, 69, 72, 79, 83, 105, 107, 117, 122, 161, 269, 301, 307, 323, 348, 381, 416, 432, 436, 465, 470, 472
Suffolk county (N. Y.), 163, 362
Sunken marsh, 18, 62
Supana, 448
Squan, 214, 480
Squancum, 56, 252, 297
Squan river, 151, 315
Swansey township (N. E.), 472

T

Teaneck, 256, 257
Tenafly, 256
Tewksbury township, 25, 62, 87, 104, 324, 343, 352, 366, 383, 390, 420
Thompson creek, 97
Timber Creek, 81, 187, 216
Tindals island, 301
Tinicum island, 490
Tinton, 298
Totawa, 448
Transbee's Point, 97
Trenton, 19, 38, 41, 65, 73, 94, 101, 108, 110, 119, 120, 131, 150, 164, 168, 206, 207, 210, 217, 229, 248, 268, 271, 275, 302, 310, 322, 345, 347, 368, 363, 364, 369, 370, 386, 394, 400, 408, 410, 433, 439, 481, 492, 493
Tuckahoe, 394
Turkey, 14, 97, 436
Two Mile beach, 404
  creek, 221, 222
Twopenny run, 452

U

Upper Alloways Creek township, 116, 284, 288, 313, 331, 366
Upper Freehold township, 31, 36, 69, 88, 95, 110, 133, 181, 188, 189, 199, 205, 212, 231, 251, 281, 289, 292, 306, 346, 367, 394, 396, 398, 408, 422, 426, 457, 487
Upper Penns Neck township, 14, 22, 51, 79, 104, 195, 206, 251, 259, 321, 332, 427, 485
Upper Smithfield (Pa.), 60, 117

V

Virginia, 220, 278

W

Wading river, 31, 318
Wagrawe, 449
Walpack township, 60, 84, 114, 117, 156, 374, 375, 444
Waltham Cross (Eng.), 182
Wantage township, 10, 110, 111, 114, 147, 156, 184, 364
Wapping (Eng.), 45
Wards landing, 216
Warrington (Eng.), 320
Waterbury (Conn.), 244
Waterford township, 5, 20, 22, 75, 77, 84, 86, 109, 124, 127, 173, 191, 192, 193, 197, 199, 208, 210, 228, 249, 276, 307, 308, 320, 384, 412, 460, 477, 478
Warwick township (Pa.), 361
Weasel, 336, 458
Westchester county (N. Y.), 47, 153, 438
Westfield township, 92, 108, 262, 357, 487
Whale pond, 13, 165
Wheelers creek, 359
Whippaning river, 183
Whitely creek (Pa.), 424
White Marsh, 105
White Marsh (Pa.), 358
Wimbeamis, 33
Willingborough township, 50, 100, 303, 322, 325, 338, 411, 482
Windsor township, 101, 167, 172, 196, 200, 201, 209, 263, 274, 325, 329, 376, 393, 413
Wolf Harbor, 222
Woodbridge, 18, 27, 47, 50, 62, 71, 72, 82, 92, 100, 103, 104, 118, 126, 130, 135, 138, 144, 146, 151, 152, 153, 155, 184, 185, 230, 234, 236, 245, 273, 274, 275, 283, 284, 297, 317, 325, 330, 331, 362, 365, 366, 388, 398, 399, 402, 418, 426, 429, 430, 435, 460, 476, 477, 490
  township, 47, 72, 76, 152, 154, 189, 402, 405
Woodbury, 76, 400, 476, 485
  creek, 216, 234, 485, 486
Woodstown, 216
Woolwich township, 54, 104, 114, 120, 155, 180, 461, 487, 495

Y

York bay, 443
York county (Eng.), 67

Z

Zuckasuning Plains, 343